P. Huter

THE TRAVELER'S READING GUIDE

Ready-Made Reading Lists
for the Armchair Traveler

Revised, Expanded Edition

MAGGY SIMONY, EDITOR

Facts On File Publications
New York, New York ● Oxford, England

For Bill and for Seth

"Bibliography is for books what Ariadne's thread was for Theseus in the labyrinths, and what the compass is to sea travel."
—Georg Schneider, *Theory and History of Bibliography.*

The Traveler's Reading Guide
Revised, Expanded Edition
Copyright © 1987 by Freelance Publications

Library of Congress Cataloging-in-Publication Data

The Traveler's reading guide.

   Bibliography: p.
   Includes index.
   1. Travel—Bibliography. I. Simony, Maggy, 1920- .
Z6004.T6T73 1987   016.9104   86-8963
[G151]
ISBN O-8160-1244-X

Jacket & text design by Levavi & Levavi
Composition by Facts On File Publications/Maxwell Photographics

Printed in the United States of America

10 9 8 7 6 5 4 3 2 1

ACKNOWLEDGMENTS

My thanks to Joan Casale (Watkins), Bob Watkins and Frances Koltun. If I hadn't come across their two books at the library, I'd never have thought to begin this book in the first place.

I'd never have finished it if I hadn't been able to use libraries all over the country and thus combine work with pleasant times visiting children and grandchildren, holidays on the Maine coast, shopping, lunch meetings with friends. When I began I lived on Long Island and relied on the libraries in Bayport, Sayville, Patchogue, East Islip, and West Islip, now that I live in New Hampshire I use the libraries in Meredith and Concord, the Plymouth State College Library, and occasionally the library in Laconia. I've used extensively, also, the Coronado and San Diego libraries in California while visiting my daughter there, and the West Dade Regional and Miami Main Branch libraries in Florida, where another daughter lives. To all of the above libraries, and many other libraries used occasionally, my gratitude for their existence.

I'm fortunate in having family and friends who, while I suspect they have wondered what on earth I was doing all these years on this rather odd project, and don't necessarily understand that bibliography can be an enjoyable enterprise, nevertheless restrained themselves from comment, and provided positive help and companionship along the way.

Reading complaints about publishers in the "My Say" column of *Publishers Weekly* over the years, I was a bit paranoid in anticipation of working with an editor of an established publishing house after the years of answering only to myself as an independent publisher. Thus far the editorial hassle I anticipated hasn't really happened, and for that I'm appreciative.

Finally, thanks to my parents, who somehow gave me the lifelong gift of enjoying books and the libraries that house them.

The Georg Schneider quotation was reprinted by permission from *Theory and History of Bibliography*, by Georg Schneider, translated by Ralph Shaw (Metuchen, N.J.: Scarecrow Press, 1962), copyright © 1962 by Ralph Shaw.

CONTENTS

ACKNOWLEDGMENTS iii

PREFACE ix

NOTES xi

   I. Africa 1

        Central Africa 7
        Eastern Africa 9
        Indian Ocean Islands 16
        Northern Africa 18
            Algeria 20
            Morocco 21
            Tunisia 24
        Southern Africa 25
        Western Africa 33

  II. The Middle East 39

        Egypt 44
        Israel 52
        Saudi Arabia and the Arabian Peninsula 63
        Turkey 67

III. Asia 72

    Burma 76
    China 78
    Hong Kong and Macau 92
    India and the Himalayan Mountain Kingdoms 96
    Indonesia 111
    Japan 114
    Malaysia and Singapore 126
    Pakistan 130
    The Philippines 131
    South Korea 133
    Sri Lanka (including the Maldives) 135
    Taiwan 137
    Thailand 138
    Tibet (including Ladakh) 141

IV. The Pacific and Oceania 145

    Australia 155
    New Zealand 163

V. Europe (includes the Mediterranean) 168

    Austria 178
    Belgium and Luxembourg 185
    Bulgaria 189
    Czechoslovakia 190
    Denmark (including Scandinavia) 194
    England (including Great Britain) 198
    Finland 242
    France 245
    Germany 266
    Greece (including Cyprus) 279
    Hungary 288
    Iceland 291
    Ireland 294
    Italy 306
    The Netherlands 330
    Norway (including Lapland) 334
    Poland 338
    Portugal 342
    Rumania 346
    Scotland 347
    Soviet Union 358
    Spain 373
    Sweden 383
    Switzerland (including Liechtenstein) 386
    Wales 392
    Yugoslavia 396

VI. Latin America 400

    The Caribbean 402
        The Bahamas 422
        Bermuda 424
    Central America 426
        Mexico 430
    South America 443
        Antarctica 446
        Argentina 449
        Bolivia 453
        Brazil 454
        Chile 459
        Colombia 460
        Ecuador 462
        The Guianas 463
        Paraguay 465
        Peru 466
        Uruguay 469
        Venezuela 469

VII. North America 472

    The Arctic and Greenland 472
    Canada 475
        Alberta 482
        Atlantic Canada and Labrador 483
        British Columbia 488
        Manitoba 490
        Ontario 491
        Quebec 495
        Saskatchewan 498
        The Yukon and the Northwest Territories 499
    United States (including North America) 501
        The East 520
        The South 529
        The Midwest 534
        The West 539
        Alabama 548
        Alaska 550
        Arizona 556
        Arkansas 561
        California 563
        Colorado 593
        Connecticut 598
        Delaware 602
        The District of Columbia 603
        Florida 610
        Georgia 617

Hawaii 622
Idaho 627
Illinois 628
Indiana 634
Iowa 637
Kansas 639
Kentucky 641
Louisiana 644
Maine 650
Maryland 657
Massachusetts 661
Michigan 673
Minnesota 677
Mississippi 679
Missouri 682
Montana 685
Nebraska 688
Nevada 690
New Hampshire 693
New Jersey 696
New Mexico 698
New York 703
North Carolina 736
North Dakota 740
Ohio 741
Oklahoma 744
Oregon 746
Pennsylvania 748
Rhode Island 754
South Carolina 756
South Dakota 760
Tennessee 761
Texas 765
Utah 773
Vermont 777
Virginia 781
Washington 786
West Virginia 789
Wisconsin 791
Wyoming 793

APPENDIX 1   Key to Source Codes and Series Guides 796
APPENDIX 2   Editorial and Research Notes 798
APPENDIX 3   England (Novels and Mysteries) 801
INDEX 805

PREFACE

My interest in armchair travel as a theme for library-browsing and reading goes back so many years I can't remember when it started. I do know it was largely due to my father's influence.

After one adventurous spurt when Seth (my father) emigrated from Stockholm to Brooklyn at age seventeen, he could never afford to travel more than a few hundred miles from home. But he *was* an ardent armchair traveler. A trip to Maine led to Kenneth Roberts' novels. His characteristic parting comment to me (leaving by car to move to California in 1948) was "Be sure now to stop at a library before you leave Reno to read about the Donner party." And he was right—crossing the mountains into northern California for the first time having just read the Donner story was a far more memorable experience with the heartbreak of those earlier travelers vividly in mind.

For me, then, using the local library both before I go on a trip and after I get back, to re-enjoy and enhance the experience, is an integral part of travel planning and something I've just always done.

The catalyst for moving from that avocational interest to compiling this book occurred some fifteen years ago when I happened upon two books in the library, within five minutes of each other, both of which made a persuasive case for pre-travel reading as part of planning for travel. One of them—*World Travel Planner*—even gave suggestions for readers on how to go about using the library to compile a reading list for travel. I'd not seen this kind of advice before in a travel book.

I didn't need convincing—that day at the library I was putting together a reading list for a trip to Hungary and Austria with my husband—but it struck me that ready-made reading lists for travelers would be a great idea for a reference book. And I thought also that one day (if no one beat me to it) I'd like to attempt the job myself. This reading guide for travelers, many years later and with many false starts and sidetracks along the way, is the end result.

With such a huge project, I found it necessary to have the end user—the armchair traveler—always in mind to keep me on target over the months and years I worked on it. I never had any difficulty in conjuring up an armchair traveler for the foreign countries. That traveler is a composite beginning with me, and reflecting also the kind of books my husband and a few friends would enjoy. It includes also a writer looking for ideas for a travel article or a setting for a book, an imaginary corporate wife about to accompany her husband to some foreign country on business and intellectually curious enough to want to make the most of that experience, and even a deceased, unconventional Aunt Eva in the family who always traveled alone.

For America, however, my composite armchair traveler didn't seem to provide the editorial mind-set I needed. Fortunately two readers out there eventually solved that problem. First, a nice note came from the director of the Washington Center of Meridian House International, indicating that my self-published volume on North America was useful in the work this organization does—cultural orientation of foreign visitors, businessmen, members of government delegations, who often are here for lengthy periods, or take up residence. Since these people represent their countries and businesses here, I assume they read English well. With this audience in mind I could think of America as an exotic place.

Then I received an order for that same book, along with a book review clipped out of a magazine, which I finally tracked down to *Trailer Life*. The clipping included used a term I had never heard before—"full timing"—to indicate those retirees who live and travel year-round by motor home. Here's a quote from that book review:

"One of the best things about full-timing is that you can loll down the yellow brick road timelessly, taking all the days needed to savor the sights . . . immerse yourself in the moods and ambiences of each new area. Now I've discovered *Traveler's Reading Guides*, which are a boon to full-timers who love to read . . . an invaluable reference that can't quite be duplicated by the card index or Reader's Guide because fiction is included. During one six-month period we lost ourselves in the Civil War, visiting battlegrounds and museums by day, and at night reading Civil War history or good novels set during the period. It resulted in a deeper and more memorable travel experience . . . "

Here was the American populist counterpart to the leisure-class, nineteenth-century travelers taking the "grand tour"! Thereafter *all* retirees (in motor homes or not) who love to read and travel and have the time to do it well, became the second half of my composite armchair traveler for America.

Traveler's Reading Guide was originally self-published as a three-volume paperback series. Moving on to this single-volume version, published by Facts On File, is gratifying. My hope is that it will be updated regularly and come to be a standard item in the travel/reference collections of libraries.

I hope I'll continue to receive letters and suggestions from librarians, travelers, and armchair travelers. Comments are always welcome whether negative or positive.

Maggy Simony
Box 1385, Meredith, NH 03253

NOTES

"In travel, as in most other things, what we understand best we enjoy the most. When you visit a country, you should know at least those facts about its religion, history, arts, and politics that are dearest to its people."
—Frances L. Koltun, *Complete Book for the Intelligent Woman Traveler*

Armchair travel—described by Longfellow as "travels by the fireside . . . while journeying with another's feet"—is that delicious mix of reading and daydreaming about far-off places seen, or to be seen. This fantasy travel can be an end in itself and almost as good as the real thing.

When armchair travel is part of getting ready for actual travel, it is one of the best things you can do to make the most of the experience with what you have to spend in time and money. Pre- and post-travel reading can turn an ordinary tourist into a perceptive, observant traveler, and a routine group tour into a memorable travel experience.

Traveler's Reading Guide is intended to make it easier for armchair travelers, writers, teachers, travel professionals, and the librarians who counsel them, to locate interesting background books, place-set novels and mysteries, travel memoirs, special guides, travel articles for the destination of choice.

The format and text is deliberately less formal than many reference-type books to invite browsing for an intriguing title, a favorite author, a book that jogs the memory.

Background reading includes history, culture, commentary by perceptive observers, travel memoirs, guides. Reading from this area will enable you to indeed "know at least those facts about religion, history, arts, and politics that are dearest to its people" for the destination you're planning to visit. This kind of background reading can add a whole new dimension to your travel experience.

Novels, family sagas and mysteries offer sense of place, ambience, people in ordinary and extraordinary lives—a painless way to learn the history of a country.

Travel articles end each country's reading list because they provide information on current "in" places; itinerary ideas, special slants and approaches to travel, enjoyable trivia, new travel writing. These sections include major travel publications and the Sunday travel section of the *New York Times*, which is available on microfilm in many libraries. It also includes a selection of general consumer magazines that feature travel articles.

How to Use Traveler's Reading Guide

This may be obvious, but is worth a mention. Always scan the larger geographical area titles that include the smaller geographical entity (England in general before its subheads, the Caribbean before Puerto Rico, South America before Brazil, Middle East before Egypt, the United States and the West before Arizona, and so on). Note also that asterisked entries for some countries pertain to more than one country (Denmark includes entries for Scandinavia in general, England includes books on Great Britain and therefore possibly pertaining also to Scotland, Wales, and so on).

I recommend that you run your finger down and scan all titles of nonfiction under the "Background Reading" sections, and all authors under the "Novels" sections, as the best way to begin compiling a personal reading list. Ideally, books you read will lead to further exploration into books not within the editorial guidelines for the *Reading Guide*. Histories just naturally lead to biographies of individuals who are especially intriguing. Books such as *Africa Explored* by Hibbert, *A Person from England* by MacLean, *Discovering America* by Savage, invite the reader to seek out the orginal writings of early explorer/travelers.

For articles, take time at the library to look over those magazines that are not familiar to you to find out if the slant and type of article suits your travel and reading tastes. Some of the articles listed have lengthy subtitles that make clear the contents of that article. Others, notably those from *Gourmet*, simply use the place name for a title and don't begin to reflect the evocative content of the article itself. It is worthwhile therefore to get to know magazines you don't ordinarily read.

Read the Preface and look over the Appendices, to understand how this book was compiled, the editorial guidelines used, and to be aware of sources and resources at the library you may wish to explore in going beyond the books and articles listed herein.

A Final Note

Despite the fact that research throughout was planned to be consistent, and the entire book was compiled by a single individual, the resultant reading lists for the countries and states vary greatly in length. Some regions simply do not elicit the kind of response from authors as others.

The State of Texas commissioned James Michener to write one of his big novels combining history and family saga. State and national tourism departments might do well to follow Texas' lead and encourage the writing of good novels and mysteries that provide history, ambience and local color for the potential traveler. Has a study ever been done of the effect on tourism of *The Third Man* for Vienna, of *The Thorn Birds* for Australia? I suspect it has been considerable.

I. AFRICA

Series Guidebooks (See Appendix 1)

Fielding: AFRICA SOUTH OF THE SAHARA
Fodor: ANIMAL PARKS
Lonely Planet: AFRICA ON A SHOESTRING

Background Reading

See also books on Islam under "Middle East," for Islam in Africa.

Allen, Charles and Fry, Helen, eds.   TALES FROM THE DARK
                                          CONTINENT
   Based on a BBC series. This is oral history—candid, funny recollections of British men and women who served in colonial Africa up until the coming of independence—with a superb introduction that provides a historical perspective. (BRD) St. Martin, 1980.

Baker, Carroll   TO AFRICA WITH LOVE: A TRUE ROMANTIC
                     ADVENTURE
   The film star's story of a romantic, adventurous trip to Africa in 1971. (PW) Fine, 1986.

Chinweizu   THE WEST AND THE REST OF US
   Historical perspectives of the conversion of Africa into a Western satellite. The book has been called the best general introduction to Africa. (BRD) Random, 1975.

Davidson, Basil   LET FREEDOM COME
   A readable overview of the development of nationalism in Africa—1890-1970—that combines personalities and anecdotes, as well as European and African perspectives, and African responses. Atl Monthly Pr, 1978.

Dinesen, Isak   ISAK DINESEN'S AFRICA: IMAGES OF THE WILD CONTINENT FROM THE WRITER'S LIFE AND WORDS
A splendid work combining excerpts from the author's writings with photographs by various nature photographers. (BL) Sierra Club, 1985.

Heminway, John   NO MAN'S LAND: THE LAST OF WHITE AFRICA
By the filmmaker, who has been in love with the continent for thirty years—a series of candid and admiring portraits of diverse characters: a hunter-turned-sculptor, a flying woman doctor, a game warden, the Sultan of M'Simbati, a diamond prospector, and more. (TL) HarBraceJ, 1983.

Hone, Joseph   AFRICA OF THE HEART: A PERSONAL JOURNEY
Journey by a BBC correspondent down the Congo; begun as a travelogue, transformed into a "beleaguered journey." (Publisher) Morrow, 1986.

Kaplan, Marion   FOCUS AFRICA
For the reader who likes politics, travel and adventure, by a journalist who lived there over twenty years covering newsworthy events. (LJ) Doubleday, 1982.

Lamb, David   THE AFRICANS
Written with humor and sympathy, by the *Los Angeles Times* correspondent for Africa—a combination of travelogue and news analysis, personal anecdotes, portraits of individual nations. (PW) Random, 1983.

Marnham, Patrick   FANTASTIC INVASION
An iconoclastic view of the consequences of northern hemisphere "medicine" (drought relief, wildlife preservation, religion, etc.) on a southern hemisphere continent. (PW) HarBraceJ, 1980.

Moorehead, Alan   THE BLUE NILE; THE WHITE NILE
The Nile River is a vehicle for recounting history and expeditions. *The Blue Nile* covers the early period from 1798, *The White Nile* 1856-1900, but each can be read separately. (BRD) Har-Row, 1972, 1980.

Naipaul, Shiva   NORTH OF SOUTH
A travelogue/essay of the author's travels in Kenya, Tanzania and Zambia, reported via a collection of encounters and related with a novelist's vivid descriptions and characterizations. (BRD) Penguin, 1980.

Newby, Eric   ON THE SHORES OF THE MEDITERRANEAN
See under Europe/Mediterranean Background Reading.

Scholefield, Alan   THE DARK KINDGOMS
A South African novelist's story of the impact of white civilization on three great African monarchs in Congo, Dahomey and Basutoland, and the differing reactions to white pressure. Morrow, 1975.

Ungar, Sanford J.   AFRICA: THE PEOPLE AND POLITICS OF AN EMERGING CONTINENT
Introduces the general reader to the complexity, fascination and tragedy of Africa. Liberia, Nigeria, Kenya and South Africa are examined in depth with a summary of the situation today in many other countries. (PW) S&S, 1985.

Van der Post, Laurens   VENTURE TO THE INTERIOR
An insightful book of travel and adventure, about a trip from London to Nyasaland in 1951, that catches the spirit of the continent. (BRD) Greenwood, 1973 (first published 1951).

Van der Post, Laurens   FIRST CATCH YOUR ELAND
A travelogue that looks at food as an expression of the various cultures of the continent. The author is also editor of the Time-Life cookbook for Africa. (BRD) Morrow, 1978.

AFRICAN CULTURE & COMMENTARY

Bebey, Francis   AFRICAN MUSIC: A PEOPLE'S ART
An overview of the place of music in African life. Independent Pub Group, 1975.

Davidson, Basil   THE AFRICAN GENIUS
In a unique synthesis, a general religious and social history makes African society intelligible to the lay reader. (BRD) Little, 1970.

Gordon, Rene   AFRICA, A CONTINENT REVEALED
A photojournalist's north to south journey revealing intimate glimpses of many varied traditional societies. St. Martin, 1981.

Harris, Joseph E., ed.   AFRICA AND AFRICANS AS SEEN BY CLASSICAL WRITERS
Howard U Pr, 1977.

Hastings, Adrian   A HISTORY OF AFRICAN CHRISTIANITY
Scholarly but readable book, by a priest, and based on extensive African experience. Cambridge U Pr, 1980.

Jefferson, Louise E.   THE DECORATIVE ARTS OF AFRICA
Viking, 1973.

Mphahlele, Ezekiel   THE AFRICAN IMAGE
A discussion of the African personality by a leading literary critic. Praeger, 1974.

Murray, Jocelyn, ed.   CULTURAL ATLAS OF AFRICA
A panoramic view of Africa—text, photos, maps and articles by specialists explore the continent's cultural and ethnic diversity; includes information that brings each country up-to-date as to politics and economics. Facts On File, 1981.

Nketia, Joseph   THE MUSIC OF AFRICA
Musical heritage of the continent. Norton, 1974.

Riefenstahl, Leni   VANISHING AFRICA
A travelogue by the noted German photographer who has traveled in Africa since 1956. Crown, 1982.

Shostak, Margorie   NISA: THE LIFE AND WORDS OF A KUNG WOMAN
A remarkable, outrageous story, told in her own words, of birth, marriage, life's events, from hundreds of taped conversations. Harvard U Pr, 1981.

Turnbull, Colin   THE LONELY AFRICAN
Sketches of Africa, from powerful chiefs to the dispossessed city dwellers, centering on the importance and meaning of the tribe. (BRD) S&S, 1968.

Watson, Lyall   LIGHTNING BIRD: ONE MAN'S JOURNEY INTO AFRICA'S PAST
The story of Adrian Boshier, who spent twenty years in the African bush and eventually became a spirit-diviner who was instrumental in the revival of a nearly dead culture. (BRD) S&S, 1983.

EXPLORERS AND EXPLORATIONS

Hall, Richard   LOVERS ON THE NILE
The African journeys of a unique couple, Lord Baker and the wife he purchased at a Turkish slave auction. (BRD) Random, 1980.

Hammond, Dorothy and Jablow, Alta   THE AFRICA THAT NEVER WAS: FOUR CENTURIES OF BRITISH WRITING ABOUT AFRICA
A critique of fiction and nonfiction that unveils myths masquerading as reality. (BRD) Irvington, 1978.

Hibbert, Christopher   AFRICA EXPLORED: EUROPEANS IN THE DARK CONTINENT, 1769-1889
Enthralling exploits of well-known (Mungo Park, Speke, Livingston and Stanley) and not so well-known (Nachtigall, Rebmann) early travelers to Africa; based on diaries, letters and books of and by them. Norton, 1982.

Severin, Timothy   THE AFRICAN ADVENTURE; FOUR HUNDRED YEARS OF EXPLORATION IN THE DANGEROUS CONTINENT
A fascinating account of the history of African explorers of all kinds —missionaries, sportsmen, the military and so on. Dutton, 1973.

ANIMALS IN AFRICA

Grzimek, Bernhard and Michael   AMONG ANIMALS OF AFRICA
The author's experiences returning zoo animals to Africa—anecdotes and in-

formation on various familiar species, and some of the less well-known. Stein & Day, 1971. Also *Serengeti Shall Not Die*, an early (1960) and eloquent plea for preservation of animals and the National Park, and for exclusion of people from the area.

Schaller, George B.   GOLDEN SHADOWS, FLYING HOOVES
This is a personal, popular account for the general reader, of experiences observing a pride of lions and other large predators. Knopf, 1973. By a leading zoologist and author of a scholarly report, *Serengeti; a Kingdom of Predators*.

GUIDEBOOKS

See also guidebooks under separate areas of Africa.

Allen, Philip M. and Segal, Aaron   THE TRAVELER'S AFRICA
An encyclopedic guide that provides extensive information on every country and major area of the continent and outlying islands. Hopkinson & Blake, 1973.

Blumenthal, Susan   BRIGHT CONTINENT: A SHOESTRING GUIDE TO SUB-SAHARAN AFRICA
Doubleday, 1974.

Capstick, Peter H.   SAFARI—THE LAST ADVENTURE: HOW YOU CAN SHARE IN IT
How to self-plan a safari: when to go, what you need to take along, how to select the right one and book it, chapters on hunting big game, etc. St. Martin, 1984.

Carim, Enver, ed.   AFRICA GUIDE
World Almanac, 1983.

Taylor, Jane and Leah,   AFRICA EXOTICA
"Written for both African explorers and armchair travelers" and providing seven innovative itineraries based on seven books: *Lost Cities of Africa, Livingstone, The White Nile, Lunatic Express, Flame Trees of Thika, Out of Africa, The Africans*. Also provides a review of the contemporary scene and complete, practical travel information for planning your trip. (Publisher) Morrow, 1987. Also *African Safaris* (1986), which provides 50 do-it-yourself safaris for various budgets and interests, from wildlife and spelunking to motorcycling and art collecting.

HISTORY

Davidson, Basil   AFRICA IN HISTORY
An absorbing introduction to Africa's past. (BRD) Macmillan, 1974 (rev. ed. first published 1969).

Dubois, W.E.B.   THE WORLD AND AFRICA
By the celebrated American black scholar—history that suggests new and illuminating perspectives. (BRD) Intl Pub Co, 1965 (first published 1947).

Fage, J.D.   A HISTORY OF AFRICA
An outstanding one-volume narrative history. (BRD) Knopf, 1978. Also *An Atlas of African History* (1978).

July, Robert W.   A HISTORY OF THE AFRICAN PEOPLE
Third edition of this history organized by regions. (BRD) Scribner, 1985.

Oliver, Roland and Fage, J.D.   A SHORT HISTORY OF AFRICA
History dealt with chronologically and regionally. (BRD) NYU, 1962.

Novels

Gordimer, Nadine   LIVINGSTONE'S COMPANIONS
Short stories about Africa and the complex lives of the people, black and white, who inhabit it. Ms. Gordimer is a leading novelist of African life; most of her titles are listed under "South Africa/Novels." (FC) Viking, 1970.

Gordimer, Nadine   A GUEST OF HONOR
The machinations of African politics when the former administrator of a British colony returns to a mythical, composite African colony to help build it into a new nation. Viking, 1970.

Harrison, William   BURTON AND SPEKE
Based on the lives of the nineteenth-century explorer Richard Burton and his contemporary, John Speke, and their nightmarish explorations in Africa, this novel takes us on a tour of nineteenth-century manners and morals. (FC) St. Martin, 1982.

Lessing, Doris   AFRICAN STORIES
S&S, 1965.

Montserrat, Nicholas   THE TRIBE THAT LOST ITS HEAD
This novel and its sequel concern neo-colonialism on a fictional African island—new tyrannies, intertribal hatreds. Sloane, 1956. *Richer Than All His Tribe* is the sequel.

Updike, John   THE COUP
An imaginary state (a former French colony in upper Africa) is the setting for the narration of its dictator's present and former life. Knopf, 1978.

Waugh, Evelyn   BLACK MISCHIEF
A satirical tale of an Oxford-educated black, with a grandiose one-year plan to found a new civilization on an island off the coast of Africa. FS&G, 1932.

TRAVEL ARTICLES

ESQUIRE
1985 Oct "Thirty-one Romantic Vacations." Includes places in Kenya and Morocco. Neal Karlen and Wendy Lowe, p. 54

ESSENCE
1985 Dec "Travels with Lorraine." Travels with an African-American heritage
      studies program in Kenya, Tanzania, Zambia. Elaine C. Ray, p. 26

HARPER'S
1985 May "Africa Brought Home." *Heart of Darkness* and its journey downriver.
      Edward Hoagland, p. 71

NATIONAL GEOGRAPHIC
1984 Nov "Africa Adorned." Angela Fisher, p. 600

N.Y. TIMES SUNDAY TRAVEL SECTION (X)
1984 Oct 7 (Part 2, "Sophisticated Traveler") "Congo on My Mind." A voyage up
      the river in the spirit of Joseph Conrad—Zaire River from Kinshasa to
      Kisangani. Alberto Moravia, p. 34
      Dec 30 "Paddling Down the Zambezi." A stretch of river offers hippos and
      good fishing. Alan Cowell, p. 9

CENTRAL AFRICA

Series Guidebooks (See Appendix 1)

U.S. Government: Cameroon: Area Handbook; Background Notes;
                   Post Report
                   Central African Republic: Background Notes;
                   Post Report
                   Chad: Area Handbook; Background Notes; Post Report
                   Congo: Area Handbook; Background Notes;
                   Post Report
                   Equatorial Guinea: Background Notes
                   Gabon: Background Notes
                   Sudan: Country Study; Background Notes; Post Report
                   Zaire: Background Notes

Background Reading

Forbath, Peter   THE RIVER CONGO
A popular account of the river's history. (BRD) Dutton, 1979.

Gide, André   TRAVELS IN THE CONGO
Travel notebook by a distinguished French man of letters. (BRD) Knopf, 1929.

Hoagland, Edward   AFRICAN CALLIOPE: A JOURNEY TO THE SUDAN
Travels in the Sudan in 1977, from the equator to the Sahara—people, small
towns, the capital of Khartoum told with astonishing vividness. Random, 1981.

Kenny, Lona B.   MBOKA: THE WAY OF LIFE IN A CONGO VILLAGE
An evocative portrait by the wife of a tropical-disease specialist. (BRD) Crown, 1972.

**Shoumatoff, Alex   IN SOUTHERN LIGHT: TREKKING THROUGH ZAIRE
                        AND THE AMAZON**
A journey to the land of the pygmies and to a nature preserve on Zaire's border with Uganda; and a trek to Rio Nhamunda in northwest Brazil. Extraordinarily colorful. (PW) S&S, 1986.

Turnbull, Colin M.   THE FOREST PEOPLE
Anthropology of the pygmies, by an anthropologist who makes it a pleasure for the lay reader. (BRD) S&S, 1961. See also *The Lonely African* under "Africa."

Worrall, Nick   SUDAN
An account of a 10,000-mile trip through Sudan—largest, most varied country in Africa. Quartet, 1981.

GUIDEBOOKS

**Casimati, Nina   EASTERN AND CENTRAL AFRICA:
                        A TRAVEL HANDBOOK**
Int Pub Svc, 1979.

TRAVELLER'S GUIDE TO CENTRAL AND SOUTH AFRICA
Watts, 1982.

HISTORY

Needham, D.E.   FROM IRON AGE TO INDEPENDENCE: A HISTORY
Longman, 1984.

Wilson, Derek   HISTORY OF SOUTH AND CENTRAL AFRICA
Cambridge U Pr, 1975.

Novels

Brain, Robert   KOLONIALAGENT (Cameroon)
Diary of a German, seeking to acquire slaves and art for German museums, who becomes a virtual prisoner of the natives—a symbolic tale of colonial exploitation set at the end of the 1800s. (BRD) Har-Row, 1977.

Conrad, Joseph   HEART OF DARKNESS
The classic novel of the Congo. Penguin, 1976 (first published 1902).

Crichton, Michael   CONGO
Adventure story involving a Houston-based expedition searching for a lost city in the Congo and its treasure of diamonds. A science story with a charming talking gorilla. (FC) Knopf, 1980.

Forester, C.S.   THE AFRICAN QUEEN
Basis for the marvelous Hepburn/Bogart movie—a missionary's sister joins up with the owner of a dilapidated boat and devises a plan to blow up a German warship in World War I. Little, 1935.

Forester, C.S.   THE SKY AND THE FOREST
A Central African tribe builds an empire that falls to European exploitation by the Belgians. Little, 1948.

Gary, Romain   THE ROOTS OF HEAVEN
Philosophical novel of a Frenchman's efforts to save the elephants in French Equatorial Africa. S&S, 1958.

Haggard, H. Rider   FIVE ADVENTURE NOVELS
Nineteenth-century period pieces, including *King Solomon's Mines*. Dover, 1951 (first published 1885-1889).

Theroux, Paul   THE JUNGLE LOVERS (Malawi)
A Massachusetts insurance salesman comes to a small central African country during a revolution; dark comedy mixed with serious themes of race prejudice and colonialism. (BRD) HM, 1971.

Tyler, W.T.   THE ANTS OF GOD
A woman missionary, an American girl drifter, and a pilot are protagonists in this story of the Sudan and the influence of Africa on their lives. (FC) Dial, 1981.

Tyler, W.T.   ROGUE'S MARCH
An espionage/adventure story involving a CIA agent who sets out to investigate a coup in the Congo that results in the execution of the president. Har-Row, 1982.

TRAVEL ARTICLES

N.Y. TIMES SUNDAY TRAVEL SECTION (X)
1985 Aug 11 (Zaire) "A glimpse of Eden on safari." Mountain gorillas survive as symbols of a lost world. James M. McIlvaine, p. 37

EASTERN AFRICA

Series Guidebooks (See Appendix 1)

Berlitz: Kenya
Fodor: Kenya
Insight: Kenya

U.S. Government:	Burundi - Area Handbook; Background Notes; Post Report
	Djibouti: Background Notes
	Ethiopia: Background Notes; Country Study; Post Report
	Horn of Africa: Pocket Guide (Djibouti, Ethiopia, Kenya, Somalia, Sudan)
	Kenya: Background Notes; Country Study; Post Report
	Rwanda: Background Notes; Country Study
	Somalia: Background Notes; Country Study; Post Report
	Tanzania: Background Notes; Country Study
	Uganda: Area Handbook; Background Notes

Background Reading

Adamson, Joy   BORN FREE (Kenya)
This, along with *Living Free* (1961) and *Elsa* (1960), is a widely popular book about lions reared by the author and returned to the wilds. Also *The Peoples of Kenya* (1966), an account of her travels in Kenya to paint and photograph tribal people. (BRD) Pantheon, 1960.

Dinesen, Isak   OUT OF AFRICA (Kenya)
Experiences and observations of the author's early days on an African farm until eight years later when the farm was sold. Random, 1972 (first published 1938).

Edberg, Rolf   THE DREAM OF KILIMANJARO
A book that extols the intuitive knowledge of Africans, and what Europeans and Americans can learn from them, by a prominent Swedish writer. Pantheon, 1979.

Farrant, Leda   THE LEGENDARY GROGAN
The story of Kenya's controversial pioneer. Hamish Hamilton, 1981.

Hanley, Gerald   WARRIORS AND STRANGERS
Amalgam of autobiography, history, and travelogue of the author's early experiences in the deserts of Somalia and Kenya, and his return years later. Har-Row, 1972.

Hemingway, Ernest   GREEN HILLS OF AFRICA
Account of a hunting expedition in the 1930s. Hudson River Ed (first published 1935).

Hillaby, John   JOURNEY TO THE JADE SEA (Kenya)
By the English naturalist-writer, a charming, gentle account of a journey to Lake Rudolf, in his attempt to escape the boredom of civilization. (BRD) Granada, 1982 (first published 1965).

Huxley, Elspeth   FLAME TREES OF THIKA (Kenya)
A vibrant childhood memoir about growing up on a coffee plantation. (BRD) Pyramid, 1973. Also about Kenya, by this author: *The Mottled Lizard* (1982), *On the Edge of the Rift: Memories of Kenya* (1962), *The Sorcerer's Apprentice: A Journey Through East Africa* (1948).

Jackman, Brian   THE MARSH LIONS: THE STORY OF AN AFRICAN PRIDE
Well-written and entertaining account of the wildlife in Kenya's vast Masai Mara, from 1978 through 1981. (BRD) Godine, 1983.

Kapuscinski, Ryszard   THE EMPEROR: DOWNFALL OF AN AUTOCRAT (Ethiopia)
An illuminating account of the last months of Haile Selassie. (LJ) HarBraceJ, 1983.

Laurence, Margaret   NEW WIND IN A DRY LAND (Somalia)
Somaliland through the keen eyes of the wife of a British civil engineer. (BRD) Knopf, 1964.

Leslie-Melville, Betty and Jock   ELEPHANTS HAVE THE RIGHT OF WAY
Doubleday, 1973. Also, *There's a Rhino in the Rose Bed, Mother*—two entertaining books by a couple who run camera safaris and have hosted many celebrities.

Markham, Beryl   WEST WITH THE NIGHT
Eloquent memoir of an adventurous life in British East Africa of the early 1900s, when the author hunted wild animals, bred racehorses, flew primitive airplanes. North Point, 1983 (first published 1942).

Matthiessen, Peter   SAND RIVERS (Tanzania)
Account of an extraordinary safari into the Selous Game Preserve. Viking, 1981.

Matthiessen, Peter   THE TREE WHERE MAN WAS BORN, THE AFRICAN EXPERIENCE
A contemporary classic; impressions of African experiences (1960-70) in Sudan, Tanzania, to Lake Rudolf—Masai herdsmen, Serengeti. (BRD) Dutton, 1983 (first published 1972).

Murphy, Dervla   IN ETHIOPIA WITH A MULE
By the leading Irish travel writer; three months in the highlands—"enthusiastically recommended" for armchair travelers. (BRD) Transatlantic, 1970.

Nesbitt, Ludovico M.   HELL HOLE OF CREATION (Ethiopia)
A landscape of an infernal land—the Danakil country, with temperatures of 150 degrees or more. (BRD) Knopf, 1934.

Norden, Hermann   WHITE AND BLACK IN EAST AFRICA
A vivid travelogue by an experienced traveler who had not been in East Africa before. (BRD) AMS, 1980 (first published 1924).

Reader, John   KILIMANJARO
The story of Reader's long, exhausting climb to the summit and descent. (LJ) Universe, 1982.

Saitoti, Tepilit Ole   MAASAI
Records the customs and traditions of the Masai tribe in spectacular photos and text. Abrams, 1980.

Slater, Mariam   AFRICAN ODYSSEY: AN ANTHROPOLOGICAL ADVENTURE
Lively, irreverent chronicle of life in a Bantu tribe in Tanzania, based on 1962-63 travels of the author; for the general reader or as an introduction to anthropology. (BRD) Anchor, 1976.

Tetley, Brian   WILLIAM HOLDEN'S JOURNEY THROUGH KENYA
An introduction to Kenya, and a superior travelogue—game reserves, ranches and resorts, Lake Turkana, Great Rift Valley, coral beaches, native peoples, crafts, bits of local lore, history, geology. Chatto Bodley, 1983.

Waugh, Evelyn   THEY WERE STILL DANCING and TOURIST IN AFRICA
The first, written in the early 1930s, is the author's impressions of travel in Africa and Arabia. The second is the diary of a two-month trip in East Africa in 1960. (BRD) Greenwood, 1977 (first published 1931 and 1960, respectively).

ANIMALS IN EAST AFRICA

Moss, Cynthia   PORTRAITS IN THE WILD: ANIMAL BEHAVIOR IN EAST AFRICA
Published under the auspices of the African Wildlife Leadership Foundation in Kenya. U of Chicago Pr, 1982.

Ziesler, Gunter   SAFARI: THE EAST AFRICAN DIARIES OF A WILDLIFE PHOTOGRAPHER
Text and photos evoke the private lives of wild beasts. (BL) Facts On File, 1984.

GUIDEBOOKS

Casimati, Nina   GUIDE TO EAST AFRICA: KENYA, TANZANIA, THE SEYCHELLES & MAURITIUS
Background history, geography, culture; treks and safaris; practical tourist information, cuisine and more. Hippocrene, 1984.

Cox, Thornton, ed.   THORNTON COX'S GUIDE TO KENYA AND NORTHERN TANZANIA
A guide for planning a safari along with practical information on hotels and transportation, plus a list of wildlife parks and preserves. Hippocrene, 1984.

Engstrom, Barbie   ENGSTROM'S GUIDE TO SAFARIS IN KENYA AND TANZANIA
A combination of personal travelogue and practical information. Kurios, 1985.

Magary, Alan and Kerstin   EAST AFRICA: A TRAVEL GUIDE
Thoroughly covers Kenya, Tanzania, Ethiopia, Zambia, Malawi. (LJ) Har-Row, 1975.

Tomkinson, Michael   KENYA: A HOLIDAY GUIDE
Natural and cultural uniqueness, as well as practical information. (LJ) Scribner, 1977.

TRAVELLER'S GUIDE TO EAST AFRICA AND THE INDIAN OCEAN
Watts, 1981.

Yogerst, Joe   EAST AFRICA WITH MALAWI AND ZAMBIA
Bradt, 1984.

HISTORY

Ingham, Kenneth   A HISTORY OF EAST AFRICA
Praeger, 1962.

Marsh, Zoe and Kingsnorth, G.W.   A HISTORY OF EAST AFRICA
Cambridge U Pr, 1972.

Oldhiambo, E.S. and others   A HISTORY OF EAST AFRICA
Longman, 1978.

Novels

Bagley, Desmond   WINDFALL
An American private eye is called on to deal with a massive swindle of the heirs to a South African fortune—action, murder, Soviet SAM rockets, conspiracies, with a climax at an animal migration laboratory in Kenya. Summit Bks, 1982.

Boyd, William   AN ICE-CREAM WAR
Comic novel involving the conflict between Germany and Great Britain for East Africa in World War I, and which also traces the lives of two English brothers. Morrow, 1983.

Caputo, Philip   HORN OF AFRICA (Ethiopia)
Three men accept a proposal to turn a savage people in the Ethiopian desert into a modern army—exploration of evil and morality. HR&W, 1980.

Gellhorn, Martha   THE WEATHER IN AFRICA (Kenya)
Two novellas and a short story explore relationships between whites and blacks in post-colonial Kenya; set in a luxury hotel and brimming with the attitudes, atmosphere and landscape of Africa. Dodd, 1980.

Halkin, John   KENYA
Adventure and romance in an authentic novel of turn-of-the-century Kenya and building of a railroad from Mombasa to Uganda by a Scottish engineer. Beaufort, 1986.

Hanley, Gerald   GILLIGAN'S LAST ELEPHANT
Psychological warfare between two men on a big-game hunt through the East African landscape. World, 1962.

Hanley, Gerald   DRINKERS OF DARKNESS
A Christmas party and a strike are focuses for this novel of the newly-emerging Africa and down-at-the-heels men and women to whom it once represented escape. Macmillan, 1955.

Hanley, Gerald   CONSUL AT SUNSET
Story of English officialdom in an African outpost when the British are taking over the region from the Italians. Macmillan, 1951.

Hemingway, Ernest   SNOWS OF KILIMANJARO, AND OTHER STORIES
Scribner, 1982 (*Snows* first published 1938).

Innes, Hammond   THE BIG FOOTPRINTS
The narrator of a TV documentary on elephant herds in Africa becomes involved in the conflict over preservation of the animals. Knopf, 1977.

Kaye, M. M.   DEATH IN KENYA
Revised version of a novel published in 1958. Eerie happenings culminate in the murder of Alice (wife of the heir to a cattle farm in the Rift Valley) and others. St. Martin, 1983.

Kessel, Joseph   THE LION (Kenya)
The adoption of a lion cub by the daughter of a game warden, and the repercussions caused by her intense love for animals. Knopf, 1959.

Naipaul, V.S.   A BEND IN THE RIVER
A brilliant political novel set in an African country after one post-independence revolution and on the eve of another. Knopf, 1979.

Ngugi Wa Thiong'o   PETALS OF BLOOD (Kenya)
An anti-imperialist novel set in rural Kenya involving a triple murder and the intertwined lives of four suspects. Dutton, 1978.

Rhodes, Richard   THE LAST SAFARI

A professional hunter, after his Masai wife is murdered, many years later meets a young American tourist and allows himself to care again. Doubleday, 1980.

Ruark, Robert   SOMETHING OF VALUE (Kenya)

The lives of two boys—one white and English, the other a native black—portrays life in Kenya and the beginning of the Mau-Mau movement. Doubleday, 1955.

Smith, Wilbur   CRY WOLF (Ethiopia)

Adventures of a Briton and a Texan who sell arms at high profit to Ethiopia in 1935, as the Italians invade. Doubleday, 1977.

Stevenson, William   THE GHOSTS OF AFRICA

An adventure epic of one of the sideshows of World War I—the battle against the British for German East Africa, involving native troops led by Col. Lettow-Vorbeck and allied with troops led by an American black revolutionary. HarBraceJ, 1980.

Theroux, Paul   GIRLS AT PLAY

The stresses of life in the tropics on a group of schoolteachers that concludes with an orgy of gore. HM, 1969.

Wibberley, Leonard   MEETING WITH A GREAT BEAST

The effect on an English writer's philosophy of his experience in Africa and his relationship with the white hunter, a guide, and the great beast. Morrow, 1971.

Wibberley, Leonard   THE LAST STAND OF FATHER FELIX

An American journalist's involvement in the machinations of two African political leaders. Morrow, 1974.

TRAVEL ARTICLES

ESQUIRE

1985 Oct "The Day the Earth Spit Warthogs." An African odyssey worth almost any risk. Selous Game Reserve, largest in the world. Tom Robbins, p. 125

ESSENCE

1985 Mar "Kenya Welcomes Woman Power." Elaine C. Ray, p. 47

NATIONAL GEOGRAPHIC

1985 Sep (Ethiopia) "Eritrea: Region in Rebellion." Marxists fight Marxists. Anthony Suau, p. 384

N.Y. TIMES SUNDAY TRAVEL SECTION (X)

1985 Apr 7 "Just an Old-Fashioned Safari." In Kenya, two ways to view the wildlife with a little panache. Michael Korda, p. 9

Oct 6 ("Sophisticated Traveler") "Treks for the Sophisticated Traveler." The Improbability of Kilimanjaro. Michael Korda, p. 8

Nov 10 "Kenya's Island of Peace." Lamu, just south of the Equator, provides a deserted beach, fish galore and tea at 4. Gregory Jaynes, p. 9
1984 Mar 18 "New Perspective on African Wildlife." From a balloon basket, observe a game park in Kenya. Michael T. Kaufman, p. 24
Nov 11 "Kenya's Windy Retreat by the Sea." Pyke Johnson, Jr., p. 18
Dec 16 "What's Doing in Nairobi." Sheila Rule, p. 10

TRAVEL & LEISURE
1985 Sep "In Peaceful Pursuit of Wildlife on Safari in Tanzania." A glorious profusion of animals in the green hills of East Africa. p. 94
1984 May "Face-to-face with the Mighty Gorilla." A peaceful encounter in the high country of Rwanda. Mike Bryan, p. 160
Dec "The Giraffe Manor in Kenya." A haven for animal lovers on the outskirts of Nairobi. Bern Keating, p. 158

VOGUE
1985 Nov (Kenya) "The Norfolk—Nairobi's Oldest Hotel." Edward Zuckerman, p. 322

WORLD PRESS REVIEW
1984 Sep "Conquering Kilimanjaro." Emily Murphy (*Irish Times*, Dublin), p. 62

INDIAN OCEAN ISLANDS

See also "Eastern Africa," for overlapping background reading, guidebooks, history.

Series Guidebooks (See Appendix 1)

U.S. Government:	Comoros Islands: Background Notes
	Indian Ocean Territories: Country Study (Five Island Countries)
	Madagascar: Background Notes
	Mauritius: Background Notes; Post Report
	Seychelles: Background Notes; Post Report

Background Reading

Attenborough, David   JOURNEY TO THE PAST
Encounters with rare and dangerous animals and fascinating tribal peoples in Madagascar, New Guinea and Australia. Salem Hse, 1983 (first published 1970).

Durrell, Gerald   ARK ON THE MOVE
A lively mix of adventure, discomfort and humor in an account of the author's preparation for a TV series on animal reserve operations. (PW) Coward, 1983. Also *Golden Bats and Pink Pigeons* (1978) about a trip to Mauritius to gather rare animals and birds.

Heyerdahl, Thor   THE TIGRIS EXPEDITION: IN SEARCH OF OUR BEGINNINGS
See under "Middle East."

Islands of the World Series   THE SEYCHELLES
Part of a series that emphasizes history, past and present cultures, and geography, geology, climate, wildlife. David.

Ricciardi, Lorenzo   THE VOYAGE OF THE MIR-EL-LAH
See under "Middle East."

Severin, Tim   SINDBAD VOYAGE
See under "Middle East."

GUIDEBOOKS

Casimati, Nina   GUIDE TO EAST AFRICA: KENYA, TANZANIA, SEYCHELLES & MAURITIUS
See under "Eastern Africa."

Hildebrand, Volker   THE SEYCHELLES
Part of a new guidebook series originating in Germany. Hippocrene, 1985.

TRAVELLER'S GUIDEBOOK TO EAST AFRICA AND THE INDIAN OCEAN
Watts, 1981.

Novels

Durrell, Gerald   THE MOCKERY BIRD
Satirical story of British plans to establish a military airstrip and the potential effect on the ecology and on the mocking bird. (FC) S&S, 1982.

Fraser, George M.   FLASHMAN'S LADY
One of a series of picaresque historical novels; this time Flashman encounters a pirate and has a liaison with a queen of Madagascar. Knopf, 1978.

Kaye, M. M.   TRADE WIND
Rewritten and expanded version of a book first published in 1963. The plot concerns a young Bostonian's journey to Zanzibar in 1859 with a mission to stop the slave trade—intrigue, romance, a pirate raid, evoke the beauty and barbarity of Zanzibar in the period. (FC) St. Martin, 1981. Also *Death in Zanzibar* (1983) that continues the story of gold buried a hundred years earlier.

Waugh, Evelyn   BLACK MISCHIEF
Satirical story of an Oxford-educated black determined to found a new civilization in his native state off the coast of Africa. Little, 1975 (first published 1932).

TRAVEL ARTICLES

N.Y. TIMES SUNDAY TRAVEL SECTION (X)
1985 Mar 17 (Part 2, "Sophisticated Traveler") "So You Want to Get Away." (Ile Denis in the Seychelles.) John Vinocur, p. 89

TRAVEL/HOLIDAY
1984 Nov "More Than Seashells in the Seychelles." Waking up in Eden. Robbie Vorhaus, p. 49

NORTHERN AFRICA

Series Guidebooks (See Appendix 1)

Fodor: **North Africa**

Background Reading

Brodrick, Alan   MIRAGE OF AFRICA
Succinct account of the geography, history, governments and peoples of North Africa—Algeria, Morocco, Tunisia. (BRD) Greenwood, 1979 (first published 1953).

Clark, Eleanor   TAMRART
Thirteen days in the Sahara. Wright, 1984.

Coon, Carleton   THE SEVEN CAVES
The story of the hunt for the seven caves, beginning in Tangier and going on to Afghanistan. The author is a leading archaeologist who called this his experiment

in archaeological writing in plain English for the layman. Greenwood/Gambit, 1981.

Crewe, Quentin   IN SEARCH OF THE SAHARA
Beautiful account of a two-year motor trip crisscrossing the Sahara, by the author (confined to a wheelchair) and a companion. Macmillan, 1984.

DeCombray, Richard   CARAVANSARY: ALONE IN MOSLEM PLACES
Travel experiences in the Middle East and North Africa, with a sharp Western eye. (BL) Doubleday, 1978.

MacKendrick, Paul L.   THE NORTH AFRICAN STONES SPEAK
A fascinating review of ancient history through the scrutiny of archaeological sites—for travelers who enjoy an archaeological theme. (BRD) U of North Carolina Pr, 1980.

Moorhouse, Geoffrey   THE FEARFUL VOID
A harrowing tale of crossing the Sahara alone, from the Atlantic Ocean to the Nile, on camelback. Lippincott, 1973.

Newby, Eric   ON THE SHORES OF THE MEDITERRANEAN
See under "Europe/Mediterranean" Background Reading.

Porch, Douglas   THE CONQUEST OF THE SAHARA
The French conquest of the Berbers in Central Sahara, which the author lays to France's intense pre-World War I nationalism and a desire to wield influence over the region. Knopf, 1984.

Ross, Michael   CROSS THE GREAT DESERT
An account of René Caillie's remarkable explorations in 1828, crossing the Sahara and returning to tell about it. Gordon & Cremonesi, 1977.

Swift, Jeremy   SAHARA
Part of the World's Wild Places Series. Time-Life, 1975.

Trench, Richard   FORBIDDEN SANDS: A SEARCH IN THE SAHARA
Insightful account by an English journalist who traveled from Algeria to Timbuktu, to report on working conditions in the salt mines. Academy Chi Ltd, 1980.

Vaczek, Louis C. and Buckland, Gail   TRAVELERS IN ANCIENT LANDS
See under "Middle East."

Woodin, Ann   IN THE CIRCLE OF THE SUN
This is a sensitive account of a year's sabbatical, traveling through the Sahara-Sindian deserts, by an author who (then) lived near Tucson where her husband was director of a desert museum. The book has been compared to the writings of Anne Lindbergh. (BRD) Macmillan, 1971.

GUIDEBOOKS

Glen, Simon and Jan   SAHARA HANDBOOK
Includes Egypt, Niger and Mali. Bradt, 1984.

TRAVELLER'S GUIDE TO NORTH AFRICA
Watts, 1981.

Novels

Bagley, Desmond   FLYAWAY
A thriller involving a timid clerk's search in the Sahara for his father. Doubleday, 1979.

Bryher   THE COIN OF CARTHAGE
Carthage and ancient Rome during the Second Punic War and how the common people were cruelly dislocated by the endless warfare. (FC) HarBraceJ, 1963.

Camus, Albert   EXILE AND THE KINGDOM
Short stories, four of which are set in North Africa. Knopf, 1958.

Maybury, Anne   THE MIDNIGHT DANCERS
Modern gothic set in North Africa; a young stained-glass artist, accompanying her TV commentator husband, is commissioned to design a window. Random, 1973.

Mewshaw, Michael   LAND WITHOUT SHADOW
The contrast between the First World and Third World when members of an American film company, on location in North Africa, happen upon a refugee camp. Doubleday, 1979.

Wren, Percival C.   BEAU GESTE
Adventure, mystery, and thrills in the highly romantic novel of life in the French Foreign Legion. Lippincott, 1927.

ALGERIA

Series Guidebooks (See Appendix 1)

Nagel: Algeria
U.S. Government: Algeria: Background Notes; Country Study; Post Report

Background Reading

Eberhardt, Isabelle   THE OBLIVION SEEKERS
And other writings, translated by novelist Paul Bowles. Story of Isabelle Eberhardt, a nineteenth-century woman who left Europe for Africa, dressed as a man. City Lights, 1975.

Spencer, William   ALGIERS IN THE AGE OF THE CORSAIRS
A readable introduction to Algiers in the heyday of the corsairs—customs, politics, a history of Algiers up to the French annexation in 1830. U of Oklahoma Pr, 1976.

Talbott, John E.   THE WAR WITHOUT A NAME
A concise account of France's war with Algeria. Knopf, 1981.

Novels

Camus, Albert   THE PLAGUE
Impact of an epidemic of bubonic plague on an Algerian city. Knopf, 1977 (first published 1947).

Daudet, Alphonse   TARTARIN OF TARASCON
Adventures of a Frenchman in Algeria. Dutton, 1954 (first published 1872).

Driscoll, Peter   HERITAGE
The Algerian War of Independence (1954-1962) and its consequences for Algeria's "first family," which owns a huge wine-producing plantation. (FC) Doubleday, 1982.

TRAVEL ARTICLES

N.Y. TIMES SUNDAY TRAVEL SECTION (X)
1985 Jan 13 "Ever-present Past of the Sahara." A trekker in southern Algeria encounters prehistoric art, 1,000-year-old trees, and nomads. Peter Klebnikov, p. 22

MOROCCO

Series Guidebooks (See Appendix 1)

Berlitz: Morocco
Frommer: $-a-Day: Spain & Morocco

Let's Go: Spain, Portugal & Morocco
Michelin: Morocco
Nagel: Morocco
U.S. Government: Morocco: Background Notes; Country Study;
                           Post Report

Background Reading

Canetti, Elias   THE VOICES OF MARRAKESH
An evocation of the magic of Marrakesh and of the author's response to the city.
Continuum, 1982.

Fernea, Elizabeth   A STREET IN MARRAKESH
Life of an American woman and her family in Marrakesh while her husband
attends the university—"portrays the experience . . . with vivid detail and convincing warmth." (BRD) Doubleday, 1976.

Lewis, Wyndham   FILIBUSTERS IN BARBARY
Travel writing, "generally supercilious, unfriendly," but—"shrewd observations
and a humorous way of retelling his stories." (BRD) Haskell, 1972 (first published
1932).

Maxwell, Gavin   LORDS OF THE ATLAS
Morocco through the eyes of an adventurer, scholar and journalist. Hippocrene,
1983.

Porch, Douglas   THE CONQUEST OF MOROCCO
The period 1903-1912 "vividly evoked and shrewdly observed"—a period during which France absorbed Morocco into its empire. (TBS) Knopf, 1983.

Vaidon, Lawdom   TANGIER: A DIFFERENT WAY
A "rambling, gossipy" history of Tangier, with emphasis on post-seventh-
century and the Europeans. (LJ) Scarecrow, 1977.

Wharton, Edith   IN MOROCCO
A recent reprint of a book by the famous author—an account of her travels in
1918, courtesy of the French military mission. Hippocrene, 1984 (first published
1920).

GUIDEBOOKS

**Bythines, Peter and Leocha, Charles A.   THE WHOLE EUROPE ESCAPE
                                                  MANUAL: SPAIN, PORTUGAL,
                                                  MOROCCO**
Part of a new series of guidebooks designed to "put the fantasy and excitement
back into travel." (Publisher) World Leis Corp, 1985.

Kay, Shirley   MOROCCO
Quartet, 1981.

Kininmonth, Christopher   TRAVELLER'S GUIDE TO MOROCCO
History, architecture, culture and practical travel information. Jonathan Cape,
1981.

Novels

Bawden, Nina   A WOMAN OF MY AGE
A bored, neurotic, middle-aged wife of an English professor, on holiday in
Morocco with a group of travelers, narrates a story of past and present. Har-Row,
1967.

Bayer, William   TANGIER
A panoramic novel of Europeans, Moroccans, former Nazis, decadence. Dutton,
1978.

Bowles, Paul   THE SHELTERING SKY
Existential novel of a man, wife and a male hanger-on, a "bizarre interior journey
made in the Sahara by an American couple." (BRD) New Directions, 1949.

**Kramer, Jane   HONOR TO THE BRIDE LIKE THE PIGEON THAT
GUARDS ITS GRAIN UNDER THE CLOVE TREE**
Originally appeared in the *New Yorker*—"brief, deft, racy and funny . . . offers a
remarkable glimpse into the personal lives of Arab multitudes . . . Arab attitudes
toward justice, money and women." (BRD) FS&G, 1971.

Mrabet, Mohammed   LOVE WITH A FEW HAIRS
Story of a young Moroccan, living with an English hotelkeeper, who marries an
Arab girl—"mixture of Western sophistication and ancient beliefs . . . strict
morality and easy promiscuity." (BRD) Braziller, 1968.

TRAVEL ARTICLES

GOURMET
1985 Oct Gourmet Holidays: "Northern Morocco." Doone Beal, p. 42
       Nov Gourmet Holidays: "Southern Morocco." Doone Beal, p. 60

N.Y. TIMES SUNDAY TRAVEL SECTION (X)
1985 Jul 21 Shopper's World: "In the Fez Market, Masters of Metal." Philip D.
       Schuyler, p. 6
       Sep 15 "Finding Your Way in Fez." The Moroccan city's old quarter
       (Medina). Philip D. Schuyler, p. 9
1984 Jan 15 Fare of the Country: "Moroccan Cuisine—Tradition Triumphs." R.W.
       Apple, Jr., p. 6

Oct 17 (Part 2, "Sophisticated Traveler") "A regal resort in Marrakesh." James M. Markham, p. 126

TOWN & COUNTRY
1984 Oct "Visa-Vis: Morocco." Jennifer Kramer, p. 284

TRAVEL/HOLIDAY
1985 Jan "Offbeat Ski Resorts." Includes Morocco. Ken Castle, p. 46
      Aug "Legendary Links: A Golfer's Half Dozen." p. 44

VOGUE
1985 Mar "Journey to Fez, Morocco." Carole Bovoso, p. 423

TUNISIA

Series Guidebooks (See Appendix 1)

Berlitz: **Tunisia**
Let's Go: **Italy (Tunisia)**
U.S. Government: **Background Notes; Country Study**

Background Reading

Douglas, Norman   FOUNTAINS IN THE SAND
A travel book of the period that praises what should be praised and is "coldly critical" of qualities the author disliked—he attributes "half the evils of this country to Mohammed." (BRD) Potts, 1912.

GUIDEBOOKS

Nelson, Nina   TUNISIA
A Batsford Guide. Hastings, 1974.

Thurston, Hazel   THE TRAVELLER'S GUIDE TO TUNISIA
Jonathan Cape, 1979.

Novels

Davis, Maggie   ROMMEL'S GOLD
A novel of political intrigue involving a cache of gold, supposedly hidden in the

desert by Rommel. The author "knows her terrain well and renders its social climate with atmospheric precision." (BRD) Lippincott, 1971.

Flaubert, Gustave   SALAMMBO
Classic of archaeology and ancient Carthage. Penguin, 1977 (first published 1863).

TRAVEL ARTICLES

N.Y. TIMES SUNDAY TRAVEL SECTION (X)
1984 Aug 26 "The 'Green Land' of the Arab Tunisia World." Much conquered Tunisia now captures visitors seeking sea and sun. Drew Middleton, p. 14
"A Week-Long Taste of Tunisia." Suggestions for exploring, from bazaars to beaches. Hebe Dorsey, p. 15

TRAVEL & LEISURE
1984 Nov "Exotic Nights in Tunisia." Exploring the legendary walled city of Kairouan. Anne Bradbury, p. 60

SOUTHERN AFRICA

Series Guidebooks (See Appendix 1)

Berlitz: South Africa
U.S. Government: Angola: Background Notes; Country Study;
Botswana: Background Notes; Post Report
Lesotho: Background Notes
Malawi: Area Handbook; Background Notes; Post Report
Mozambique: Background Notes; Country Study
Namibia: Background Notes
South Africa: Country Study; Post Report
Swaziland: Post Report
Zambia: Background Notes; Country Study; Post Report
Zimbabwe: Background Notes; Country Study;

Background Reading

Abrahams, Peter   TELL FREEDOM
The author's childhood and youth in the slums of Johannesburg. (BRD) Faber & Faber, 1982 (first published 1954).

Barnard, Christiaan N.   SOUTH AFRICA: SHARP DISSECTION
The famous heart surgeon gives his view as an Afrikaner of South Africa, claiming that the world press applies double standards in evaluating human rights in various countries. Hippocrene, 1978.

Becker, Peter   THE PATHFINDERS: THE SAGA OF EXPLORATION IN SOUTHERN AFRICA
Two centuries of exploration, from the Dutch landings at Capetown in the mid-seventeenth century to David Livingstone's travels on the Zambezi River. Viking, 1985.

Breytenbach, Breyten   A SEASON IN PARADISE
The author, a major Afrikaans painter, poet, and novelist, gives an account of his visit to South Africa in 1972, when he and his wife were permitted to return from exile in Europe. Persea, 1980.

Caute, David   UNDER THE SKIN: THE DEATH OF WHITE RHODESIA
"Brilliant, atmospheric account of the last five years of Rhodesia before it became . . . Zimbabwe in 1980." (PW) Northwestern U, 1983.

Coulson, David and Clark, James   THE ROOF OF AFRICA
A journey through the mountain ranges of southern Africa . . . "terra incognita to most Americans . . . adventure and dramatic photographs . . . background in history, geology and natural resources . . . a great trip." (PW) HR&W, 1984.

Crapanzano, Vincent   WAITING: THE WHITES OF SOUTH AFRICA
"Examination of South Africa . . . [focusing] on a village north of Cape Town . . . the village's white residents speak of their past and future; attitudes and expectations . . . feelings . . . experiences in Zimbabwe . . . reactions to criticism from abroad." (PW) Random, 1985.

Eliovson, Sima   GARDEN BEAUTY OF SOUTH AFRICA
Intl Spec Bk, 1982.

Goodwin, June   CRY AMANDLA
Interviews with white and black South African women by a journalist. "Amandla" means "power," "a cry threatening to the white power structure of apartheid." (PW) Holmes & Meier, 1984.

Harrison, David   THE WHITE TRIBE OF AFRICA: SOUTH AFRICA IN PERSPECTIVE
Lively, readable account of the Afrikaner people beginning with the Great Trek. U of California, 1981.

Hull, Richard W.   SOUTHERN AFRICA
A compilation that grew out of a TV series that explored the origins and development of Southern Africa, and the evolution of African, Afrikaner and English civilizations. NYU, 1981.

Lelyveld, Joseph   MOVE YOUR SHADOW: SOUTH AFRICA BLACK AND WHITE
Profile of the country and its people from Afrikaners and white liberals to black squatters, witch doctors, security police, written by a *New York Times* correspondent. Times Bks, 1985.

Luard, Nicholas   THE LAST WILDERNESS: A JOURNEY ACROSS THE GREAT KALAHARI DESERT
An account of a 2,000-mile trip across the great Kalahari Desert (a region termed "the cradle of life") by a novelist-explorer. It is a celebration of the wild and a passionate plea that it not be destroyed, with fascinating portraits of those who live and visit there. S&S, 1981.

Magubane, Peter   MAGUBANE'S SOUTH AFRICA
A photojournalist's presentation of what it means to be a nonwhite in South Africa. Knopf, 1978.

Mallows, Wilfrid   THE MYSTERY OF THE GREAT
A narrative structured like a detective story about the Stonehenge-like archaeological ruins in Zimbabwe. Norton, 1984.

Morris, James   DESTINATIONS; PLACES
Travel essays by a leading travel writer. *Destinations* includes essays on Rhodesia and South Africa; *Places* includes one on Swaziland. Oxford U, 1980; HarBraceJ, 1973.

North, James   FREEDOM RISING
The author hitchhiked across South Africa and this account of his venture is in the words of people he met—"attitudes toward their compatriots, other races, the underground organizations, the importance of sports . . . developments in Namibia . . . changes in neighboring Zimbabwe." (PW) Macmillan, 1985.

Ransford, Oliver   LIVINGSTONE'S LAKE: THE DRAMA OF AFRICA'S INLAND SEA
The fabulous waters of Lake Nyasa and history of the surrounding Nyasaland (now Malawi). Transatlantic, 1977 (first published 1966). Also, Ransford's biography *Livingstone in Africa* (1973) and his *David Livingstone, The Dark Interior* (1978).

Robeson, Eslanda C.   AFRICAN JOURNEY
A book, written by the anthropologist wife of the black singer and political activist, Paul Robeson, about a trip with her young son to South Africa in 1935. Greenwood, 1972 (first published 1945).

Taylor, Jane and Van Der Post, Laurens   TESTAMENT TO THE BUSHMEN
Story of the "tiny Stone Age people . . . once the sole occupants of the whole of Southern Africa and whose situation is now desperate." Van Der Post provides an essay on Bushman myth and folklore. (BL) Viking, 1985.

Van Der Post, Laurens   THE HEART OF THE HUNTER
Story of the African Bushmen, and the aristocracy of spirit of this aboriginal race. HarBraceJ, 1980 (first published 1961). Also, *Lost World of the Kalahari* (1959) which continues the story of the African Bushman.

Villet, Barbara   BLOOD RIVER: THE PASSIONATE SAGA OF SOUTH
                     AFRICA'S AFRIKANERS
History from 1652 and life of the Afrikaners in their embattled land—"the text is alluring . . . a controversially sympathetic view, but not a whitewash." (BL) Everest House, 1982.

Woods, Donald   BIKO
The story behind the black South African's murder by a white liberal who was his friend. Paddington, 1978.

ANIMALS IN SOUTHERN AFRICA

Owens, Mark and Delia   CRY OF THE KALAHARI
Memoir of a couple's seven-year stint in the central Kalahari on a wildlife research project—"a thoroughly captivating account that should attract animal lovers and armchair adventurers." (BL) Houghton, 1984.

GUIDEBOOKS

Cox, Thornton   TRAVELLER'S GUIDE TO SOUTHERN AFRICA
Hippocrene, 1982.

Hildebrand, Volker   SOUTH AFRICA TRAVEL GUIDE
A new guidebook series originating in Germany. Hippocrene, 1984.

TRAVELLER'S GUIDE TO SOUTHERN AFRICA
Watts, 1984.

HISTORY

Davenport, T.R.H.   SOUTH AFRICA: A MODERN HISTORY
A one-volume compact history, from the first white settlements to the 1970s. U of Toronto, 1977.

Herbstein, Denis   WHITE MAN, WE WANT TO TALK TO YOU
A "recapitulation and explanation of the recent history of the country, for outsiders . . . lively prose . . . entertaining as well as informative." (BRD) African Pub Co, 1979.

Morris, Donald R.   WASHING OF THE SPEARS
History of the rise and fall of the Zulu nation—"readable and lively narrative." (BRD) S&S, 1969.

Were, Gideon S.   A HISTORY OF SOUTH AFRICA
History "seen through the eyes of the African rather than from the point of view of the white man." (BRD) Africana Pub, 1974.

Wilson, Derek   HISTORY OF SOUTH AND CENTRAL AFRICA
Cambridge U Pr, 1975.

Novels

All are for South Africa unless otherwise noted.

Abrahams, Peter   MINE BOY
"What happened to one country boy who sought the City of Gold" in Johannesburg. (BRD) Knopf, 1955. Also, *Wild Conquest* (1950), a historical novel of both sides of the Boer trek to the north in the 1830s and why the Africans tried to stop them; and *A Wreath for Udomo*, a political novel (published in 1956) of a "possible near-future in a hypothetical African country" where there is a successful revolution with an educated black taking over as prime minister only to rouse the hatred and antagonism of his own people.

Antunes, Antonio L.   SOUTH OF NOWHERE (Angola/South Africa)
"Poignant autobiographical novel . . . focusing on the final stages of Portuguese colonialism in Angola in the 1970s." (BRD) Random, 1983.

Barnard, Christiaan   UNWANTED
A novel by the noted heart surgeon, tells of a white and a black raised together who become, respectively, a geneticist and a heart surgeon. McKay, 1975.

Bloom, Harry   TRANSVAAL EPISODE
Reprint of a classic. Life in apartheid South Africa—"violence and tragedy and destruction" result when a washerwoman is falsely accused of stealing. (FC) Second Chance Pr, 1981.

Brink, Andre   INSTANT IN THE WIND
The history of South Africa from 1749 evoked through the relationship of a white woman and the black runaway slave who rescues her. Morrow, 1977. Also, *Chain of Voices* (1982) about an 1825 slave uprising.

Brink, Andre   LOOKING ON DARKNESS
A Cape "colored" returns to South Africa. Morrow, 1975. Also *Rumours of Rain* (1978) and *A Dry White Season* (1979), novels about Afrikaners.

Cloete, Stuart   THE TURNING WHEELS
The founding of the Orange Free State and the Transvaal by the Dutch pioneers in South Africa, based on personal diaries of the author's grandfather. Houghton, 1937. Also, *The Fiercest Heart* (1960), about the Great Trek, and *Rags of Glory* (1963), about the Boer War.

Coetzee, J.M.   LIFE AND TIMES OF MICHAEL K.
A young black man's odyssey from municipal gardener to eking out "a numbing existence on an abandoned farm . . . war . . . labor camps . . . back into Cape Town . . . about what human beings do to fellow human beings in South Africa." (FC) Viking, 1984. Also, *From the Heart of the Country* (1977), a tale of madness set in the South African veldt.

Denton, Kit   THE BREAKER
Story on which the movie *Breaker Morant* was based. An Australian officer in the Boer War is court-martialed—"an irresistible character . . . an exceptional read." (FC) St. Martin, 1981.

Ebersohn, Wessel   DIVIDE THE NIGHT
"Compelling story of hatred and misplaced priorities" as a South African psychologist treats a patient who has killed eight blacks. (FC) Pantheon, 1981. Also, *Store Up the Anger* (1981), about the cruelty of the South African racial system.

Francis, Dick   SMOKESCREEN
An English film star goes to South Africa to find out why a friend's racehorses are mysteriously collapsing—"tumultuous with thrills." (FC) Har-Row, 1973.

Fugard, Athol   TSOTSI
A black thug leads a gang in taking revenge for his ghetto life, but is ultimately transformed by a cripple and an abandoned baby. Random, 1981.

Gilman, Dorothy   MRS. POLLIFAX ON SAFARI (Zambia)
The grandmotherly CIA agent is involved this time with discovering who, on safari, is out to kill the president of Zambia. Doubleday, 1977.

Gordimer, Nadine   JULY'S PEOPLE
A leading white voice through her novels and stories of contemporary Africa, and South Africa in particular. This is a recent title (Viking, 1981); other titles include: *Conservationist* (1975), *Burger's Daughter* (1979), *The Lying Days* (1953), *Not for Publication* (1965), *Occasion for Loving* (1963). Also, *Something Out There* (1984), *A Soldier's Embrace* (1980), and *Selected Short Stories* (1976), which are collections of novellas and stories.

Gordon, Sheila   UNFINISHED BUSINESS
A contemporary novel of the evils of apartheid—a white doctor returns after a ten-year exile for treating a black. Crown, 1975.

Hardy, Ronald   RIVERS OF DARKNESS (Mozambique)
Enjoyable and informative novel of Mozambique's struggle for independence in 1973, with a cast of characters of various nationalities. Putnam Pub Group, 1979.

Head, Bessie   A QUESTION OF POWER (Botswana/South Africa)
The emotional breakdown and recovery of a daughter of mixed African/English

heritage. Pantheon, 1974. Also, *When Rain Clouds Gather* (1969) about a black South African who teaches farming techniques to village women in Botswana.

Hope, Christopher   A SEPARATE DEVELOPMENT
"Wildly funny" story of the "decline and fall into the back streets and alleys of racial classification" when genes surface in the son of white parents giving him crinkly hair and coffee-colored skin. The book was once banned in South Africa. (BRD) Scribner, 1981.

Jacobson, Dan   THE BEGINNERS
Family chronicle of a Jewish girl who moves to South Africa from Lithuania and marries a Zionist. Macmillan, 1968. Also, *The Price of Diamonds* (1957).

McClure, James   THE BLOOD OF AN ENGLISHMAN
One of a series of police detective stories in which a white police lieutenant and his Zulu sergeant, Zondi, solve the mysteries. "First-rate mysteries . . . the psychology of life today in South Africa, and the racial and sexual tensions." (FC) Harper, 1981. Series includes: *Snake* (1976), *The Steam Pig* (1972), *The Sunday Hangman* (1977).

Masterton, Graham   SOLITAIRE
The plot, set in the late nineteenth century, is about the discovery of a huge diamond in the Kimberley mine area and about life in the Colony, with its class distinctions. Morrow, 1982.

Michener, James A.   THE COVENANT
One of Michener's all-encompassing historic novels. This one traces South Africa's past from 500 years ago to contemporary events and is told from the perspective of three families—African, Afrikaans and English. Random, 1980.

Paton, Alan   AH, BUT YOUR LAND IS BEAUTIFUL
Most recent novel of another leading South African writer whose novels of social protest against apartheid "make South Africa's old wounds bleed fresh again." (BRD) Scribner, 1982. Other titles include: *Cry the Beloved Country* (1948), *Too Late the Phalarope* (1953), and *Tales from a Troubled Land* (1961) (short stories).

Roberts, Sheila   JOHANNESBURG REQUIEM
A novel with a political message, about a woman teacher's affairs with two men. Taplinger, 1980.

Rush, Norman   WHITES (Botswana)
Six stories of whites in Africa "to help." Knopf, 1986.

Schoeman, Karel   PROMISED LAND
A chilling view of South Africa, sometime in the future, as a young Afrikaner, raised in Switzerland, returns on a sentimental journey, to find the family farm deserted and an oppressed white peasant class under black majority rule. Summit Bks, 1978.

Scholefield, Alan   THE SEA CAVE
A young woman and her family move from an Edinburgh slum to Africa and she is drawn into a "mysterious world involving family secrets, puzzling business dealings, and murder." (FC) Congdon & Weed, 1984.

Scholefield, Alan   THE STONE FLOWER
A two-family saga—"the brawling boom days of Kimberley . . . the Boer War . . . the fluctuating fortunes of both greedy diamond hunters and struggling farmers." (FC) Morrow, 1982. Also, *Wild Dog Running* (1978) about emigrants from England to the Cape Colony in 1820.

Shannon, John   COURAGE (Malawi)
Attempts of a white revolutionary to overthrow the government—a "Third World thriller." (BRD) Norton, 1975.

Sithole, Ndabaningi   THE POLYGAMIST (Rhodesia)
An essentially autobiographical novel—a son returns to the Ndbele tribe as a converted Christian. Third Press, 1972.

Smith, Wilbur   THE EYE OF THE TIGER (Mozambique)
Adventure story of lost treasure off the coast of Mozambique. Doubleday, 1976.

Smith, Wilbur   THE LEOPARD HUNTS IN DARKNESS (Zimbabwe)
"A thriller of high-speed excitement" involving a former resident of Zimbabwe who is sent back by the World Bank to observe conservation of wildlife, only to find that the World Bank is a cover for the CIA. (FC) Doubleday, 1984.

Smith, Wilbur   THE ANGELS WEEP (Rhodesia)
The third volume of a family saga, set in Rhodesia (now Zimbabwe), in 1977, as the family is plagued by terrorist activity. (FC) Doubleday, 1983. Previous volumes in the saga are *Flight of the Falcon* (1982) and *Men of Men* (1983), which begin in nineteenth-century Africa—"a gripping tale of high adventure . . . historical authenticity and a profound knowledge of the land and peoples of southern Africa."

Smith, Wilbur   THE SUNBIRD (Botswana)
Two novels in one: the first is about an archaeologist's search for a lost city in Botswana—"a kaleidoscopic picture of southern Africa"; the second is historical fantasy extrapolated from scrolls found in the lost city. (FC) Doubleday, 1973.

Swindells, Madge   SUMMER HARVEST
A woman is disinherited for marrying a poor wheat farmer and sets out single-mindedly to become rich once more—"a lushly textured family saga brimming with romance, power, scandal and destruction." (FC) Doubleday, 1984.

Van Der Post, Laurens   A STORY LIKE THE WIND
A European boy questions the validity of his European point of view as he "steeps himself . . . in the intuitive wisdom" of the African. (BRD) Morrow, 1972. Sequel is *A Far-Off Place* (1974).

Van Der Post, Laurens   THE HUNTER AND THE WHALE
Suspenseful adventure story of a whale hunt, told through the eyes of an Afrikaans teenager, which "can be read as an allegory or a descriptive story of whaling in the Indian Ocean just following World War I." (BRD) Morrow, 1967.

Vorster, Gordon   THE TEXTURES OF SILENCE
Story of a man rendered deaf, mute, blind and spastic in infancy, whose condition can be treated at age fifty because of advances in medical science, told through his own voice, his mother's diary, people around him—"an unusually idyllic view of South African society." (FC) Morrow, 1984.

TRAVEL ARTICLES

HARPER'S BAZAAR
1985 Feb "A Traveling Woman's Guide to the World's Great Hotels." Includes one in Kruger National Park. Kit Snedaker, p. 48

N.Y. TIMES SUNDAY TRAVEL SECTION (X)
1985 Jan 27 "Lake Malawi Steamer Cruise." John A. Kerr, p. 22
      Mar 17 (Part 2, "Sophisticated Traveler") (Zambia) "The Bush: Africa's Cradle." Alan Cowell, p. 20
1984 Nov 11 "Exploring the Highlands of Zimbabwe." A reflection of Scotland in Africa. Alan Cowell, p. 15

WESTERN AFRICA

Series Guidebooks (See Appendix 1)

Country Orientation Series: Nigeria
U.S. Government: Benin: Background Notes; Post Report
Cape Verde Islands: Background Notes
Gambia: Post Report
Ghana: Area Handbook; Background Notes; Post Report
Guinea: Area Handbook; Background Notes; Post Report
Guinea-Bissau: Background Notes
Ivory Coast: Area Handbook; Background Notes; Post Report
Liberia: Background Notes; Country Study; Post Report
Mali: Background Notes
Mauritania: Area Handbook; Background

Notes; Post Report
Niger: Background Notes; Post Report
Nigeria: Background Notes; Country Study;
Post Report
Sao Tome & Principe: Background Notes
Senegal: Area Handbook; Background Notes;
Post Report
Sierra Leone: Area Handbook; Background
Notes; Post Report
Togo: Background Notes; Post Report
Upper Volta: Background Notes

Background Reading

Alland, Alexander, Jr.   WHEN THE SPIDER DANCED
Reminiscences of visits over a decade to the Ivory Coast native tribes—what it was like to be an outsider in a fading culture, anthropology with the general reader in mind. Doubleday, 1975.

Charters, Samuel   THE ROOTS OF THE BLUES
Travel experiences and personal reflections as the author recounts his trip to West Africa to trace blues music. Boyars, 1981.

DeVere, John   BLACK GENESIS: AFRICAN ROOTS
A photographic exploration of the Mandingo culture pitched to the audience for African lore created by Alex Haley's *Roots* and including Kunta Kinte's village. St. Martin, 1980.

Fuller, Hoyt W.   JOURNEY TO AFRICA
A journal of ideology in the form of three essays by a black American in search of his heritage in Senegal; written in the late 1950s. Third World, 1971.

Gale, John   TRAVELS WITH A SON
Travels by jeep, and autobiographical reflections, in Morocco and West Africa. Hodder & Stoughton, 1972.

Gramont, Sanche de   THE STRONG BROWN GOD: THE STORY OF THE NIGER RIVER
An account of the "scholars, egotists, traders, missionaries" who penetrated the Niger River. (LJ) Houghton, 1976.

Greene, Graham   JOURNEY WITHOUT MAPS
A journey into Sierra Leone, Liberia, French Guinea, ending on the Liberian coast, in an attempt to discover the author's spiritual home. Doubleday, 1936.

Huxley, Elspeth   FOUR GUINEAS
A journey through West Africa. Greenwood, 1974 (first published 1954).

Pern, Stephen   **THE BEACH OF MORNING: A WALK IN WEST AFRICA**
A walking tour with a Nigerian friend over some of "the world's most varied, remote, and primitive territory . . . [meeting] an extraordinary variety of human beings, both African and European." (BL) Hodder & Stoughton, 1984.

Shick, Tom W.   **BEHOLD THE PROMISED LAND**
Afro-American settlers in nineteenth-century Liberia and the effects of their former status on the country. Johns Hopkins U, 1980.

Wilson, Ellen   **THE LOYAL BLACKS**
Definitive account of the first American blacks emancipated by the American Revolution who returned to Africa to establish their own country. Putnam Pub Group, 1976.

Wright, Richard   **BLACK POWER: A RECORD OF REACTIONS IN**
                      A LAND OF PATHOS
The black American novelist's report of a trip to Africa's Gold Coast—"passionate and subjective . . . important, informative and infuriating first-hand account." (BRD) Greenwood, 1974 (first published 1954).

GUIDEBOOKS

Boone, Sylvia A.   **WEST AFRICAN TRAVELS: A GUIDE TO PEOPLE**
                        AND PLACES
A combination of "survival course and tourist guide . . . written with wit, frankness and accuracy." Covers fourteen countries from Senegal to Nigeria. "Recommended for armchair reading or adventurous travel." (LJ) Random, 1974.

TRAVELLER'S GUIDE TO WEST AFRICA
Watts, 1981.

HISTORY

Ajayi, J.F.   **A THOUSAND YEARS OF WEST AFRICAN HISTORY**
Longman, 1966.

Fage, J.D.   **HISTORY OF WEST AFRICA**
History from the eleventh century to the twentieth, and the influences of North Africa, Western Europe, and the Americans. Cambridge U Pr, 1969.

Osae, T.A. and others   **A SHORT HISTORY OF WEST AFRICA: A.D. 1000**
                            TO THE PRESENT
Hill & Wang, 1975.

Novels

Achebe, Chinua   **A MAN OF THE PEOPLE (Nigeria)**
"Eloquent, acute, convincing" novel of government corruption and politics in Nigeria of the 1960s. (BRD) 1966.

Achebe, Chinua   THINGS FALL APART (Nigeria)
A remote Nigerian village before the white man had made an impact—life and mores of an Ibo tribe. Astor-Honor, 1959. Also, *Arrow of God* (1967), set in the 1920s (the conflict of Christianity and Westernization with tribal customs) and *Girls at War* (1973) (short stories).

Armah, A.K.   THE BEAUTYFUL ONES ARE NOT YET BORN (Ghana)
A parable of corruption in pre- and post-Nkrumah years. Houghton, 1968.

Armah, A.K.   FRAGMENTS (Ghana)
A young African returns to Ghana after five years in America, and finds it "too eager to ape Western ways." (FC) Houghton, 1970.

Awoonor, Kifi   THIS EARTH, MY BROTHER (Ghana)
The dilemma of African intellectuals; story of a lawyer from his birth in a back country village to success in Accra, and eventual tragedy. Doubleday, 1971.

Bebey, Francis   THE ASHANTI DOLL (Ghana)
"Conflict between the educated elite and business elite of Accra." (BRD) Hill, 1977.

Bowen, Elenore S.   RETURN TO LAUGHTER (West Africa)
Fictionalized account of the author's experience in West Africa and "the sea-change in herself that came from living with the primitives." (BRD) Houghton, 1954.

Boyd, William   A GOOD MAN IN AFRICA (West Africa)
Comic novel of a civil servant's plan for success that turns into disaster—recreates West Africa "in full and interesting detail." (FC) Morrow, 1982.

Boyle, T. Coraghessan   WATER MUSIC
A picaresque novel based on the adventures and misadventures of Mungo Park, the Scottish explorer who attempted to chart the Niger River in the eighteenth century—"reminiscent of *Tom Jones*." (FC) Little, 1981.

Cary, Joyce   COCK JARVIS (Nigeria)
A satire of the British bureaucracy, and a nonconformist, in colonial Nigeria in the 1920s and '30s. St. Martin, 1975.

Cary, Joyce   MISTER JOHNSON (Nigeria)
Character study of an African clerk "deeply attached to all things English" who loses all. (FC) Har-Row, 1951.

Chatwin, Bruce   THE VICEROY OF OUIDAH (Benin)
"Fictionalized story of a Brazilian slave trader in Dahomey . . . barbaric and decadent." (BRD) Summit Bks, 1980.

Dickinson, Peter   TEFUGA (Nigeria)
"Amusing and elegantly structured tour de force . . . interweaves a modern story

with diary entries that recount events . . . in Northern Nigeria in the 1920s." (NYTBR) Pantheon, 1986.

Echewa, T.O.   THE LAND'S LORD (Nigeria)
A French priest deserts the army for the priesthood and his black houseboy is torn between allegiance to Christianity and his native beliefs. Hill, 1976.

Emecheta, Buchi   DOUBLE YOKE (Nigeria)
Two Nigerian young people face the choice of a traditional marriage or one that the woman seeks: "both worlds—wife, mother, and academician." (FC) Braziller, 1983. Other novels by Emecheta on the clash of modern and traditional, urban and rural, ways are *The Slave Girl* (1977), *The Bride Price* (1976), *The Joys of Motherhood* (1979), *Destination Biafra* (1982).

Forsyth, Frederick   THE DOGS OF WAR
A spellbinder in which white mercenaries engage in a mission to liquidate the ruler of a West African republic. Viking, 1974.

Greene, Graham   A BURNT-OUT CASE (West Africa)
An architect "flees the glory of the wide world" to retire to a leprosarium run by priests. (FC) Viking, 1961. Also *The Heart of the Matter* (1948), set in a coastal town—a parable of doom in which a British civil servant falls in love with a young widow, is blackmailed, and the result is tragedy.

Laurence, Margaret   THIS SIDE JORDAN (Ghana)
Set in the Gold Coast just before it became Ghana—"remarkably accurate picture of language, customs, daily life" and of race relations in an emerging nation. (BRD) St. Martin, 1960. Also *The Tomorrow-Tamer* (1964) (short stories).

Ousmane, Sembene   XALA (Senegal)
Polygamy in an urban society; a successful businessman in Dakar takes a third wife. ("Xala" is a curse placed on him by those he has exploited in his rise to success.) Hill, 1976. Also, a proletarian novel, *God's Bits of Wood* (1962).

Reeman, Douglas   BADGE OF GLORY (West Africa)
The period is 1850, when the British navy was switching from sail to steam power—the hero joins the movement to stamp out slavery in West Africa. Morrow, 1984.

Sanders, Lawrence   THE TANGENT OBJECTIVE
An American oil company representative and an Army captain plan a coup to overthrow the despot of a formerly French West African nation, and work toward a United Africa—"creates a believable nation with a language, history, culture and image all its own . . . absorbing . . . often thrilling." (BRD) Putnam Pub Group, 1978.

Thomas, Audrey   BLOWN FIGURES (Ghana)
The heroine seeks to retrace her past in London and West Africa where she aborted a child years before. Knopf, 1975.

Tutuola, Amos   THE PALM-WINE DRINKARD (Nigeria)
"An allegory . . . combining myth and legend and modern symbols" and written in "young" (pidgin) English. (BRD) Grove, 1954.

Webb, Forrest   BRANNINGTON'S LEOPARD
"Splendid evocation of the West African landscape"—an Englishman's quest to kill a leopard and avenge the death of his two dogs. (BRD) Doubleday, 1974.

Wyllie, John   SKULL STILL BONE (West Africa)
Sleuth series set in "Arkhana" in West Africa, which does for West Africa what "Keating has done for India . . . full of delightful detail on a lively background." (LJ) Doubleday, 1975. Other titles in the series include: *The Butterfly Flood* (1975), *A Pocket Full of Dead* (1978), *The Killer Breath* (1979).

TRAVEL ARTICLES

BLACK ENTERPRISE
1984 Nov "Experience Senegal." Go "home" to a land of discovery. Stephanie R. Hamilton, p. 46

ESSENCE
1985 Apr "Africa's Awesome Ivory Coast." Stephanie S. Oliver, p. 85
      "Getting to the Ivory Coast." Harriette Cole, p. 106
      Special Section—"Abidjan": "The Ivory Coast's Creme de la Creme." Audrey Edwards, p. 86; "The Island of Paradise" (Ile Boulay). Dining, sun, and fun. Curtia James, p. 88; "Village Life." Curtia James, p. 94; "In the Marketplace." Bargaining Ivorian style redefines our notion of shopping. Harriette Cole, p. 98

HOUSE & GARDEN
1985 Sep (Mali) "On the Road to Timbuktu." Exploring the strange and haunting landscape of Mali. Alison Lurie, p. 46.

NATIONAL GEOGRAPHIC
1985 Aug "Senegambia—A Now and Future Nation." Confederation. Michael and Aubine Kirtley, p. 224

N.Y. TIMES SUNDAY TRAVEL SECTION (X)
1985 May 19 (Senegal) Shopper's World: "Dakar's Markets." Strategies for buyers. Angela Dodson, p. 12
1984 Jan 15 "Journey into Mali's Land of the Dogons." A rough road into Africa "as it was." Paul Chutkow, p. 15
      Apr 1 (Senegal) "The Paris of Africa." Dakar is a stylish regional blend of French, Moslem and Christian elements. Marylin Bender, p. 19

TRAVEL & LEISURE
1984 Sep (Mali) "Mysterious Timbuktu." Fabled crossroads of the Sahara. p. 152

TRAVEL/HOLIDAY
1984 Apr (Senegal) "Africa's Gateway." Al Ristori, p. 18

II. MIDDLE EAST

Background Reading

Austin, R.W.J. and others   THE ARAB WORLD
Profiles of nineteen Arabic nations in Africa and Asia—history, geography, tourism and basic topics: Islam, Arabic art, architecture, literature, oil, the Arab-Israeli conflict. Hippocrene, 1980.

Bates, Daniel G. and Rassam, Amal   PEOPLES AND CULTURES OF THE MIDDLE EAST
P-H, 1983.

Ceram, C.W.   GODS, GRAVES AND SCHOLARS
The modern classic that provides a popular story of archaeology for travelers, the story of the nineteenth-century discoveries in Troy and other archaeological sites. Bantam, 1976 (first published 1967).

Coon, Carleton   THE SEVEN CAVES
See under "Northern Africa."

Cornell, Tim and Matthews, John   ATLAS OF THE ROMAN WORLD
"A concise, extremely well illustrated introduction to ancient Rome," which at its zenith reached through the Middle East. (CSM) Facts On File, 1984.

Dempsey, Michael and Barrett, Norman   ATLAS OF THE ARAB WORLD
Profiles of twenty-one Arab countries, in a pictorial format, with a wide range of information and comparisons of social, political, economic and ecological factors in the Arab world. Facts On File, 1983.

Duncan, Andrew   MONEY RUSH
The effects of megabucks on a once proverty-stricken country—"reads like a novel." (LJ) Doubleday, 1979.

Ferna, Elizabeth W. and Robert A.   THE ARAB WORLD:
PERSONAL ENCOUNTERS
A "largely intimate" approach to the Arab World as two Middle Eastern experts came to know it through personal contacts from the 1950s and on to 1983—the "commentary brings objective analysis to a scene heavy with hatred, civil war and painful change." (PW) Doubleday, 1985.

Fisher, Sidney   THE MIDDLE EAST
Considered one of the best surveys of the Ottoman Empire, the Middle East and Islam. Knopf, 1968.

Hazleton, Lesley   WHERE MOUNTAINS ROAR, A PERSONAL REPORT
FROM THE SINAI AND NEGEV DESERT
By an author "delightfully knowledgeable about history, biology, geology, archaeology, and other disciplines" that bear on the subject—"a remarkable book." (PW) HR&W, 1981.

Heyerdahl, Thor   THE TIGRIS EXPEDITION: IN SEARCH
OF OUR BEGINNINGS
Account of a trip from Iraq to Djibouti, in a ship constructed to ancient Sumerian specifications, to places where pre-historic traders would have done business. The aim of the book was to prove the author's theory of how trade was done in the Middle East in that period. Doubleday, 1981.

Krich, John   MUSIC IN EVERY ROOM: AROUND THE WORLD
IN A BAD MOOD
The travelogue of a "Bay Area leftist. . . . impressions that are fresh and fascinating." (BL) McGraw, 1984.

Newby, Eric   ON THE SHORES OF THE MEDITERRANEAN
See entry under "Europe/Mediterranean" Background Reading.

Ricciardi, Lorenzo   THE VOYAGE OF THE MIR-EL-LAH
A trip in a diesel-powered dhow—Arab sailing vessel—in the Arabian Gulf, to Zanzibar and the Seychelles—"numerous diversions en route. . . . the photographs are lovely and the writing is just what the armchair traveler wants." (LJ) Viking, 1981.

Sachar, Howard M.   EGYPT & ISRAEL
By an author with ties to both Israeli and Egyptian officials—"astute perceptions" in analyzing the relationship of the two countries in the twentieth century. (LJ) Marek, 1981.

Schiffer, Michael   LESSONS OF THE ROAD
Journal of a Harvard man's journey in 1974 from France to Nepal (via Italy, Greece, Turkey, Lebanon, Syria, Iraq, Iran, Afghanistan, India). "A marvelously hip book" reflecting how the area must have appeared to young Americans of the 1970s. Kenan Pr, 1980.

Severin, Tim   SINDBAD VOYAGE
A trip, via the ancient Arab sea routes and in a replica of an Arabian wood ship of the period (eighth to eleventh centuries), from the Arabian Gulf to China by way of Ceylon and Southeast Asia. This book won the Thomas Cook Award for best travel book of the year in 1982. Putnam Pub Group, 1983.

Stark, Freya   THE JOURNEY'S ECHO
"A chronological collection of purple passages and aphorisms" out of the author's travel writings, 1927-58—"the ideal bedside book" by one of the outstanding travel writers of the century. (BRD) Transatlantic, 1975 (first published 1964).

Trench, Richard   ARABIAN TRAVELLERS—THE EUROPEAN DISCOVERY OF ARABIA
Explorers who succumbed to Arabia's fascination, from the first Danes to Burton, Doughty, T.E. Lawrence, oil companies, along with stories of minor travelers in the 19th century. Salem Hse, 1986.

Vaczek, Louis and Buckland, Gail   TRAVELERS IN ANCIENT LANDS
"A portrtait of the Middle East 1839-1919"— mostly photographs, but also a "rewardingly informed discussion of the social and political history before nationalism threw up barriers." (PW) Graphic Soc, 1981.

Woodin, Ann   IN THE CIRCLE OF THE SUN
See under "Northern Africa."

ISLAM

Coon, Carleton   CARAVAN, THE STORY OF THE MIDDLE EAST
By a leading archaeologist for Americans interested in the Islamic world from Morocco to Afghanistan. HR&W, 1951.

DeCombray, Richard   CARAVANSARY: ALONE IN MOSLEM PLACES
See under "Northern Africa."

Hitti, Philip K.   CAPITAL CITIES OF ARAB ISLAM
Islamic history, beginning with the first capital cities of Mecca and Medina and proceeding to Damascus, Baghdad, Cairo, and Cordova (Spain)—each described in its days of glory. U of Minnesota, 1973. Also, *Islam: A Way of Life* (1971).

Jansen, Godfrey H.   MILITANT ISLAM
An opinionated introduction for the non-Muslim to the "demanding, enveloping nature of the Islamic faith . . . gently erudite, felicitously phrased." (BRD) Har-Row, 1980.

Lewis, Bernard, ed.   ISLAM AND THE ARAB WORLD
Published in association with American Heritage. Thirteen essays by leading experts—a survey on Islam for the general reader, major centers of Islamic history and major features of the culture. Knopf, 1976.

Lippman, Thomas W.   UNDERSTANDING ISLAM
An explanation of fundamental beliefs—the Koran, life and work of Muhammad, conditions of Islamic life today. NAL, 1982.

Minai, Naila   WOMEN IN ISLAM
Childhood, adolescence, marriage, polygamy, the single, the widowed, working women. Seaview, 1981. Also *The Hidden Face of Eve* (1980) and *Women in the Arab World* (1982) by Hawal El Saadawi.

Mortimer, Edward   FAITH AND POWER
An "excellent introduction to the maze of Moslem politics and theology by a *London Times* journalist." (BRD) Random, 1982.

Naipaul, V.S.   AMONG THE BELIEVERS
See under "Indonesia."

Pipes, Daniel   IN THE PATH OF GOD: ISLAM AND POLITICAL POWER
Historical analysis of Islamic religion and law, encounters with Western cultures, and the Islamic revival in the 1970s and 1980s. Basic Bks, 1983.

Robinson, Francis   ATLAS OF THE ISLAMIC WORLD SINCE 1500
"More encyclopedia than atlas . . . lavishly illustrated . . . depicting everything from fourteenth-century tombs to contemporary Afghan nomads at prayer"—provides a framework for understanding the last 500 years of Muslim history. (BL) Facts On File, 1982.

Savory, R.M.   INTRODUCTION TO ISLAMIC CIVILIZATION
"Unique as a collection of essays . . . reworked from scripts of adult education broadcasts . . . addresses itself to the widest possible literate audience." (BRD) Cambridge U Pr, 1976.

Sitwell, Sacheverell   ARABESQUE AND HONEYCOMB
Muslim art—"a travel book for connoisseurs." (BRD) Ayer, 1958.

Walther, Wiebke   WOMAN IN ISLAM
An account derived from historical and literary evidence of the role of women in Islamic culture. Schram, 1982.

GUIDEBOOKS

Lawless, Richard   THE MIDDLE EAST
Batsford, 1980.

TRAVELLER'S GUIDE TO THE MIDDLE EAST
Watts, 1984.

Novels

Caldwell, Taylor   DEAR AND GLORIOUS PHYSICIAN
Story of Luke, author of one of the gospels of the New Testament, and his life as a physician, with scenes in Antioch, Rome, Alexandria and Judaea. Doubleday, 1959.

Erdman, Paul E.   THE CRASH OF '79
A "slam-bang novel" of international finance and scheming through the eyes of an advisor to the Saudis. (BRD) S&S, 1976.

Irving, Clive   PROMISE THE EARTH
Historical novel of the Middle East covering the period 1916-19 with a plot involving a Russian army deserter who flees to Palestine. Har-Row, 1982.

Kalb, Marvin and Koppel, Ted   IN THE NATIONAL INTEREST
A "plausible, intelligent, overplotted scenario" by two TV journalists, in which the U.S. Secretary of State's wife is kidnapped by the Palestinians, as he is carrying on shuttle diplomacy in the Middle East. (BRD) S&S, 1977.

Quinnell, A.J.   THE MAHDI
A thriller in which a retired superspy and a CIA director plan to control the Islamic world by creating a miracle, and the Russians order the defection of a ballerina to learn the British-American secret. Morrow, 1981.

Renault, Mary   THE PERSIAN BOY
Historical novel of Alexander the Great's expeditions into Asia—"brings to life a great historical period." (FC) Pantheon, 1972.

Robbins, Harold   PIRATE
Typical Robbins saga—"islands of matchless Robbins crudity . . . dotted throughout the text"—in which the hero is born Jewish, adopted by an Arab, becomes an international tycoon, with one wife in Lebanon and a second in California. The plot includes a daughter in the Fedayeen, the skyjack of wife two and children to Syria, and rescue by the hero and his *real* father. (BRD) S&S, 1974.

Saudray, Nicolas   THE HOUSE OF THE PROPHETS
The imaginary country of Marsana is a synthesis of middle eastern countries; the protagonist of the story is a young Christian architect whose design for a harbor

mosque causes religious and political problems. Saudray is a pen name for an official in the French government who is also a novelist. This is the first of his novels published in the United States. Doubleday, 1985.

Shagan, Steve   THE DISCOVERY
An archaeologist and companion find Syrian artifacts that seemingly lead to the actual words of Moses, discoveries that are "anathema in the current political climate." The plot includes the Syrians, the CIA and a Los Angeles Police Department detective—the author has "an enviable command of the classic detective themes and credibly interpolates cuneiform studies and acquisitive neuroses." (FC) Morrow, 1984.

Uris, Leon   THE HAJ
Sequel to *Exodus*; the story of a Muslim, head man of a Palestinian village, from 1922 through 1956 when he dies in a refugee camp. Doubleday, 1984.

Whittemore, Edward   SINAI TAPESTRY
"The strange fortunes of a number of characters . . . over 100 years and several cultural genealogies." (BRD) HR&W, 1977.

TRAVEL ARTICLES

NATIONAL GEOGRAPHIC
1985 Sep "Jason's Voyage." In search of the Golden Fleece. Tim Severin, p. 407

N.Y. TIMES SUNDAY TRAVEL SECTION (X)
1985 Mar 17 (Part 2, "Sophisticated Traveler") "New Eyes in an Ancient World." Egypt, Israel, Turkey. D.M. Thomas, p. 32
1984 Nov 18 "For Visiting Women, the Welcome Varies." Judith Miller, p. 19

EGYPT

Series Guidebooks (See Appendix 1)

Baedeker: Egypt
Berlitz: Egypt; Cairo
Blue Guide: Egypt
Country Orientation
Series Update: Egypt
Fielding: Egypt & the Archaeological Sites
Fodor: Egypt

Frommer: **Dollarwise**
Let's Go: **Israel & Egypt (Jordan)**
Nagel: **Egypt**
U.S. Government: **Egypt: Background Notes;**
       Country Study; Post Report

Background Reading

Bernstein, Burton   SINAI: THE GREAT
       AND TERRIBLE WILDERNESS
A "fact-rich personal travelogue" of a two-week tour of the Sinai, "geographical land bridge between Africa and Arab/Asian continents" by the staff of the *New Yorker,* and which first appeared in that magazine—excursions to little and well-known attractions, history, historical lore. (BL) Viking, 1979.

Drury, Allen   EGYPT: THE ETERNAL SMILE
The author has written novels set in early Egypt, and this book is a travelogue and personal impressions interwoven with information on Egyptian history, culture, religion. Doubleday, 1980. See also "Novels," below.

Durrell, Lawrence   THE SPIRIT OF PLACE
Letters and essays—"descriptive, frank . . . wonderful compilation of fact and fiction" that includes Egypt. (BRD) Leetes Isle, 1984 (first published 1969).

Edwards, Amelia B.   A THOUSAND MILES UP THE NILE
This is a reprint of a travel classic. In 1873, the author departed Shepheard's Hotel in Cairo for a 1,000-mile trip up the Nile by boat, complete with servants and daily high tea. "Wonderfully vivid tale of Egypt in the long, languid days when Britain's empire was at its height and Englishwomen . . . set forth on remarkable adventures." (Publisher) J.P. Tarcher, 1983.

Elon, Amos   FLIGHT INTO EGYPT
Elon was privileged to visit Egypt just following the 1979 peace agreement. This is an account of his impressions, talks with Egyptians, description of Cairo, Alexandria, Suez. Doubleday, 1980.

Forster, E.M.   ALEXANDRIA: A HISTORY AND A GUIDE
A love song to Alexandria divided into history and guide, carefully connected by cross-references to link present and past—considered by many to be the best thing written on the city. Overlook, 1974.

Golding, William   A MOVING TARGET
A collection of writings, including two essays on Egypt—one written before he'd seen the country, the other after experiencing Egypt. FS&G, 1982. Also, *An Egyptian Journal,* the author and his wife on a sojourn down the Nile (1985).

Gornick, Vivian   IN SEARCH OF ALI MAHMOUD: AN AMERICAN WOMAN IN EGYPT
An "impressionistic report" of living in Cairo in 1971 for four months with themes of "man/woman relationships, her own Jewishness, the 1967 defeat by Israel." (LJ) Saturday Rev Pr, 1973.

Gougaud, Henri and Gouvion, Colette   EGYPT OBSERVED
Culture, history, ancient sites, Egypt old and new. Oxford U, 1979.

Hopwood, Derek   EGYPT: POLITICS AND SOCIETY, 1945-1981
An "uncluttered introduction" to Egypt—some background preliminaries on history, geography, religion, prior to 1945, before covering the rule of Nasser and Sadat and ending with a survey of present conditions and everyday Egyptian life. (LJ) Allen & Unwin, 1982.

Kazantzakis, Nikos   JOURNEYING
Travels in Italy, Egypt, Sinai, Jerusalem and Cyprus in 1926-27 by the novelist—"the quintessence of intellect, synthesized with passion." (BP) Creative Arts Bk, 1984.

Koning, Hans   A NEW YORKER IN EGYPT
Impressionistic sketch of an itinerary taken in 1975 of major cities, back roads, rural villages and avoiding the typical tourist path. HarBraceJ, 1976.

Moorehead, Alan   THE BLUE NILE; THE WHITE NILE
See entry under "Africa/Background Readings."

Morris, James   DESTINATIONS; PLACES
Travel essays by a leading travel writer—*Destinations* includes an essay on Cairo, and Alexandria is one of Morris's *Places*. Oxford U, 1980; HarBraceJ, 1973.

Ruthven, Malise   CAIRO
A "gem"—photographs and lively, informative text. (LJ) Time-Life, 1980.

Steegmuller, Francis, ed.   FLAUBERT IN EGYPT
Flaubert's travel notes and letters during a trip in 1849, with accompanying narrative by Steegmuller "providing perspective and background." (BRD) Academy Chi Ltd, 1979.

Stewart, Desmond   THE PYRAMIDS AND SPHINX
"Brilliant, concise" panorama of Egyptian history down to completion of the Aswan Dam with a selection of literary excerpts about the pyramids and the Sphinx. (LJ) Newsweek, 1979.

ANCIENT EGYPT AND ARCHAEOLOGY

Baines, John and Malek, Jaromir   ATLAS OF ANCIENT EGYPT
"The most useful one-volume atlas and illustrated guide to ancient Egypt. . . . a

journey down the Nile describing sites of archaeological or historical importance." (BL) Facts On File, 1980.

Brackman, Arnold C.   THE SEARCH FOR THE GOLD OF TUTANKHAMEN
"The story of the dogged fifteen-year quest . . . for a pharaoh's unplundered tomb" written in "intimate, novelistic" style. (LJ) Van Nostrand, 1976. Also *The Luck of Nineveh: Archaeology's Great Adventure.*

Clayton, Peter A.   THE REDISCOVERY OF ANCIENT EGYPT
"Egypt, from Alexandria to Abu Simbel, seen through the eyes of travelers . . . . makes it possible for the reader to experience something of the awe and excitement that nineteenth-century European travelers felt." (LJ) Thames & Hudson, 1983.

Evans, Humphrey   THE MYSTERY OF THE PYRAMIDS
Lay person's overview of what is known or surmised about ancient Egypt through an examination of the pyramids. Crowell, 1979.

Hoving, Thomas P.   TUTANKHAMUN, THE UNTOLD STORY
The "intrigue, secret deals and private arrangements, covert political activities, skullduggery, arrogance, lies, dashed hopes, poignance, and sorrow." (BL) S&S, 1978.

Jenkins, Nancy   THE BOAT BENEATH THE PYRAMID: KING CHEOPS' ROYAL SHIP
The "discovery, excavation and reconstitution" of the ancient wooden ship. (BRD) HR&W, 1980.

Johnson, Paul   THE CIVILIZATION OF ANCIENT EGYPT
Art, religion, social and political history for the general public library audience. Atheneum, 1978.

Ragghianti, C.L.   TREASURES OF THE EGYPTIAN MUSEUM—CAIRO
Newsweek, 1978.

Romer, John   VALLEY OF THE KINGS
Traces the excavation history of the Valley—"a lively overview of a fascinating area." (LJ) Morrow, 1981.

GUIDEBOOKS

Engstrom, Barbie   ENGSTROM'S GUIDE TO EGYPT AND A NILE CRUISE
A "travelogue and a travel guide [that] generates considerable enthusiasm for its subject." Personal experiences, practical information on planning and getting around, with appendices on Egyptian history, religion, hieroglyphics and basic conversation in Arabic. (BL) Kurios Pr, 1984.

Haag, Michael   GUIDE TO CAIRO WITH THE PYRAMIDS AND SAQQARA
"Handbook for sightseeing around Egypt's capital and the outlying areas of Giza, Memphis and Saqqara" with practical tourist information, historical, cultural and archaeological background. (BL) Hippocrene, 1985.

Haag, Michael   GUIDE TO EGYPT
Practical information sections on accommodations, restaurants, entertainment, shopping and travel, an Arabic vocabulary, an Islamic calendar, a 5,000-year chronology, etc.—a guide that also explains the significance of what is seen. Hippocrene, 1984.

More, Jasper   THE LAND OF EGYPT
Batsford, 1980.

Murnane, William J.   THE GUIDE TO ANCIENT EGYPT
A guide to the major and the less well-known historical sites of Egypt arranged by location to facilitate itinerary planning, history, architectural detail, maps. (BL) Facts On File, 1983.

Price, Polly S.   SAND IN OUR SHOES: A GUIDEBOOK TO PHARAONIC EGYPT
P.S. Price, 1979.

West, John A.   TRAVELLERS' KEY TO ANCIENT EGYPT: A GUIDE TO THE SACRED PLACES OF ANCIENT EGYPT
Pyramid theories, the Great Sphinx, temples, tombs and other sacred sites. Knopf, 1985.

HISTORY

Aldred, Cyril   THE EGYPTIANS
Revised and enlarged edition of a survey history originally published in 1961. "Chronicles the birth and development of this ancient civilization by tracing the various kingdoms and dynasties . . . and portraying the everyday life of the Egyptian people." (BL) Thames Hudson, 1984.

Diop, Cheikh Anta   THE AFRICAN ORIGIN OF CIVILIZATION
Presents the theory that upper Egypt is a Negro civilization and birthplace of most Western ideas. Lawrence Hill, 1974.

Little, Tom   MODERN EGYPT
"Consistently interesting" narrative of a complicated, fact-filled history from ancient times to the 1960s. (BRD) Praeger, 1967.

Novels

Asch, Sholem   MOSES
A historical novel "at its literary best" of Moses, the Exodus and the Promised Land. (FC) Putnam Pub Group, 1951.

Barber, Noel   SAKKARA
"Exotic locale, political intrigue, high society, romance, exile, adultery, a murder trial" make up a melodrama spanning 1919 to 1953. (FC) Macmillan, 1984.

Christie, Agatha   DEATH ON THE NILE
A newly married woman is murdered aboard a Nile steamship—a Detective Poirot mystery. Dodd, 1970 (first published 1937).

Critchfield, Richard   SHAHHAT, AN EGYPTIAN
Evocative and impressionistic account (in novel form) of the daily life of an Egyptian peasant, living within walking distance of the Valley of the Kings. Syracuse U, 1978.

Devine, Laurie   NILE
Vivid, fascinating saga of Arab and Egyptian Jewish families during the period 1945-78, and the Israeli wars—and the many contrasting classes and peoples that make up modern Egypt. S&S, 1982

Drury, Allen   A GOD AGAINST THE GODS
Egypt in the fourteenth century B.C., during the reign of Nefertiti—recreates the period as the old gods are displaced. (FC) Doubleday, 1976. *Return to Thebes* (1977) is a sequel and continues with the story of Pharaoh Akhenaten—"warmly human but logical version" of the period.

DuBois, David G.   . . . AND BID HIM SING
A group of black American expatriates in Cairo of the 1960s searching for identity and integration into an alien society. Ramparts, 1975.

Durrell, Lawrence   THE ALEXANDRIA QUARTET
Modern fiction classic, set in Alexandria. The sequence is *Balthazar, Clea, Justine, Mountolive*. Dutton, 1957-60.

Durrell, Lawrence   CONSTANCE
Part of the "Avignon" series of novels (see "France"). Novelist Blandford, and Constance's husband, Sam, are in Egypt in World War II. Blandford is crippled and Sam killed in an artillery accident. Viking, 1982.

Fast, Howard   MOSES
"Masterly fictionalization of Moses' early life, told with vividness and plausibility of a firsthand account." (BRD) Crown, 1958.

Follett, Ken   THE KEY TO REBECCA
Suspense story of German espionage in World War II Egypt—"the evocation of wartime Cairo is a marvel of concise atmospherics." (FC) Morrow, 1980. Also *Triple* (1979), in which one hundred tons of uranium are hijacked—international espionage involving Egyptians, Palestinians, a KGB colonel and a Mafia don.

France, Anatole   THAIS
Classic story of a courtesan in fourteenth century B.C. Alexandria, and the holy man who is inspired to convert her. U of Chicago, 1976 (first published 1890).

Gedge, Pauline   THE TWELFTH TRANSFORMING
Set in Egypt during the reign of Pharaoh Akhenaten—"a lustrous tale . . . told in the quiet tone of an intimate chronicle." (FC) Har-Row, 1984. Also, *Child of the Morning* (1979), about the only woman pharaoh, Hatshepsut.

**Hawkes, Jacquetta   KING OF THE TWO LANDS:
                       THE PHARAOH AKHENATEN**
Historical novel that recreates the setting and mood of the period of Nefertiti and Akhenaten. Random, 1966.

Holt, Victoria   THE CURSE OF KINGS
The heroine accompanies her archaeologist husband to Egypt where the curse of kings hangs over them. Doubleday, 1973.

Hylton, Sara   THE TALISMAN OF SET
A gothic—the daughter of an archaeologist is obsessed with ancient Egypt and believes she is a reincarnated Egyptian princess. "Mystic, romantic, and beautifully described tale of Egypt in the twentieth century and in the time of the pharaohs." (FC) St. Martin, 1984.

Mailer, Norman   ANCIENT EVENINGS
Historical novel of Egypt, 1290-1100 B.C.—"magical, sensuous, and highly politicized atmosphere [portrayed with] stunning effect." (FC) Little, 1983.

Mann, Thomas   JOSEPH AND HIS BROTHERS
The biblical story recreated by a leading contemporary writer. Knopf, 1948.

Manning, Olivia   THE DANGER TREE
Continuation of *The Balkan Trilogy* (see Rumania/Novels), as Rommel's army advances. Atheneum, 1977. Following is *The Battle Lost and Won* (1979), set in World War II Cairo and the Egyptian desert, after El Alamein.

Newby, P.H.   KITH
Egypt in 1941 is recalled 30 years later, and an affair between a young English soldier and his uncle's Egyptian wife. Little, 1977. Other novels about the British colony in Egypt in the 1950s and 60s are: *The Picnic at Sakkara* (1955), *Revolution & Roses* (1957), *Something to Answer For* (1969).

Pape, Gordon   THE SCORPION SANCTION
A suspense novel about a plot to blow up the Aswan Dam and kill the presidents of both Egypt and the United States. Viking, 1979.

Peters, Elizabeth   THE CURSE OF THE PHARAOHS
Mystery, and high comedy, of an archaeological expedition in nineteenth-century Egypt—the interactions of a bunch of interesting and flamboyant participants. Dodd, 1981.

Salisbury, Carola   AN AUTUMN IN ARABY
"A Victorian fairy tale . . . glitters with romance, excitement, color and

evocations of historic events played out in 1869"—the opening of the Suez Canal. (FC) Doubleday, 1983.

Slaughter, Frank G.   THE GALILEANS
   A fictionalized story of Mary Magdalene. Doubleday, 1953.

Waltari, Mika   THE EGYPTIAN
   A fictional recreation of Egypt, before Christ, told by a physician—"we see, feel, smell and taste . . . Egypt." (FC) Putnam Pub Group, 1949.

TRAVEL ARTICLES

ARCHITECTURAL DIGEST
1985 Nov Travel notes: "Return to Egypt." Roderick Cameron, p. 280.
1984 Mar "Architect's Travel Notes." Hugh N. Jacobsen, p. 204

HOUSE & GARDEN
1985 Mar "Mortality Tale: the Beautiful Old Islamic Mansions of Cairo." May not survive the twentieth century. Roger Porter, p. 58

NATIONAL GEOGRAPHIC
1985 May "Journey Up the Nile." River of legend. Robert Caputo, p. 577

NATIONAL GEOGRAPHIC TRAVELER
1984 Winter "Splendors in Stone." Monuments of ancient Egypt. Tor Eigeland, p. 110

N.Y. TIMES SUNDAY TRAVEL SECTION (X)
1985 Jan 27 "What's Doing in Cairo." Judith Miller, p. 10
      Feb 24 "River Life, a Close-Up View." A trip on a felucca means roughing it a bit and immersion in the past. Samuel G. Freedman, p. 14
      "Journey to Abydos and Dendera." Dena Kleiman, p. 14
      "Sailing Along the Nile." Hotel boats offer a look at ancient monuments and a timeless land. Judith Miller, p. 15
      Apr 21 "In a Corner of Cairo, a Haven for Coptic Art." Museum shows works of Egypt's Christian minority. Marylin Bender, p. 12
      Oct 6 ("Sophisticated Traveler") "In the Realm of Osiris." William Golding, p. 86
1984 Jan 22 "Cairo: the Din and the Glory." Exploring the city, ancient, vibrant, exotic (also, a "Sampling of Cairo delights"). Judith Miller, p. 14
      "A Shopper's Haunt for Centuries."   The Khan-el-Khalili is as much entertainment as bazaar. Nimet Habachy, p. 15
      "A Camel Ride to the Pyramids of Abu Sir." A three-hour desert trek from Giza. John A. West, p. 16
      Mar 4 "Learning Fast on a Cruise." Swan educational cruises of ancient Greece, Egypt, Rome. Emily Greenspan, p. 28
      May 20 "Summer Abroad: the ABCs of Going with Children. Sixteen foreign correspondents and contributors of *The Times* offer tips on touring their corners of the world—includes Egypt. p. 21

Nov18 "Ancient Lands—the Harsh Splendor of the Sinai. Terence Smith, p. 19.

TRAVEL & LEISURE
1984 Feb "Cairo's Exotic Camel Market." James Horvitz, p. 153
     Dec "The Egyptian Museum in Cairo." Richard Covington, p. 66

TRAVEL/HOLIDAY
1985 Mar "Fit for a Pharaoh." Elegance along Egypt's Nile River. Barbara H.
     Matthiess, p. 76

VOGUE
1984 Mar "Eating Well Is the Best Surprise." A food critic's Cairo discoveries.
     Mimi Sheraton, p. 358

ISRAEL

Series Guidebooks (See Appendix 1)

Baedeker: Israel; Jerusalem
Berlitz: Jerusalem
Fodor: Israel, Jordan and the Holy Land
Frommer: Israel: $-a-Day
Let's Go: Israel & Egypt (Jordan)
Lonely Planet: Israel & the Occupied Territories
Nagel: Israel
U.S. Government: Israel: Country Study; Pocket Guide; Post Report

Background Reading

Bellow, Saul   TO JERUSALEM AND BACK, A PERSONAL ACCOUNT
     Observations and reflections, some of which appeared earlier in the *New Yorker*
magazine—"evokes places, ideas, people." (BRD) Viking, 1976.

Benvenisti, Meron   JERUSALEM, THE TORN CITY
     By the deputy mayor of the city—Jerusalem as a divided city and relationships
among Arabs, Jews and other factions since the 1967 war. U of Minnesota, 1977.

**Bethell, Nicholas   THE PALESTINE TRIANGLE: THE STRUGGLE FOR
                              THE HOLY LAND, 1935-48**
     "Utterly compelling" panoramic story of events that led to the birth of Israel.
(BRD) Putnam Pub Group, 1979.

Burrows, Millar   THE DEAD SEA SCROLLS
Complete story of the Dead Sea Scrolls by "one of the world's greatest Biblical scholars . . . clearly and simply written despite its fairly complex subject." (BRD) Baker Bks, 1978 (first published 1955).

Collins, Larry and Lapierre, Dominique   JERUSALEM
Vivid recreation of 1947-48 when Arabs and Jews fought for Jerusalem. (BRD) S&S, 1980 (first published 1971).

Dimbleby, Jonathan   THE PALESTINIANS
Photoessay and reportage of the Palestinian point of view in its dispute with Israel—emotionally stated combining history with interview portraits, with the aim of redressing "our balance of perception of the Palestinians." (BRD) Horizon, 1980.

Diqs, Isaak   A BEDOUIN BOYHOOD
An "idealized pastoral idyll" evoking the author's boyhood among Bedouins near the Negev Desert—a way of life that has ended. (PW) Universe, 1983 (first published 1967).

Dudman, Helga   STREET PEOPLE
Israeli city streets are named after people and this book offers vignettes about those so honored; a blend of historical tidbits and commentary to make the street people come alive. Hippocrene, 1982.

Eban, Abba   MY COUNTRY
The birth of Israel from conception in Europe to "birth by fire" in 1948. (LJ) Random, 1972.

Gavron, Daniel   WALKING THROUGH ISRAEL
Report by an Israeli journalist on a thirty-one-day exploration through Israel on foot. The book integrates history and the description of scenic and cultural discoveries into a delightful way to become acquainted with Israel, its past and its people. Houghton, 1980.

Gilead, Zerubavel and Krook, Dorothy   GIDEON SPRING: A MAN AND HIS KIBBUTZ
The author is a poet and active in the kibbutz movement and "maintains that its ideal of an egalitarian non-acquisitive society has survived." This is his life story with poems, photos and reminiscences—"a beautifully written, moving memoir." (PW) Ticknor & Fields, 1985.

Grose, Peter   A CHANGING ISRAEL
By the managing editor of *Foreign Affairs*, a picture of an Israel in transition where "culturally the values and styles of the middle European state are being diluted by Westernization . . . and the influx of Oriental Jews" as well as the critical factor of an ever-larger Arab population within its borders. (PW) Vintage, 1985.

Halabi, Rafile   THE WEST BANK STORY
A journalistic report and critical view of Israel's policy in Gaza and the West Bank by an Israeli Druse. HarBraceJ, 1982.

Halsell, Grace   JOURNEY TO JERUSALEM
An attempt "to probe cultural and religious lives of Muslims, Christians, Jews and atheists" by involvement with them "at home, at work, at school, at play." (LJ) Macmillan, 1981.

Harkabi, Y.   THE PALESTINIAN COVENANT AND ITS MEANING
The *"raison d'etre* of the PLO"—written in the 1960s, it is the roots of the Palestinian movement and (the author believes) a straitjacket that will never allow recognition of Israel's claims. (BRD) Valentine, 1980.

Har-Shefi, Yoella   BEYOND THE GUNSIGHTS
Semifictional format describes the life of the son of an Arab village family caught between sympathy for Palestinians and a fight for equal rights as an Israeli citizen. Houghton, 1980.

McGreevy, John, ed.   CITIES
Impressions of world cities as seen through the eyes of people intimately connected with them—for Jerusalem it is Elie Wiesel's impressions. Potter, 1981.

McNeish, James   BELONGING: CONVERSATIONS IN ISRAEL
Narrative interviews with Israelis representing many different cultures including new immigrants, old-time settlers, Israeli Arabs, and Christians that capture the special mystique of Israel. HR&W, 1980.

Malka, Victor   ISRAEL OBSERVED
"Spectacular photographs and enlightening text depicting life in the area from ancient times until today"—historic landmarks, kibbutzim, villages and cities, markets, diverse immigrant populations. (LJ) Oxford U, 1979.

Meyer, Lawrence   ISRAEL NOW: PORTRAIT OF A TROUBLED LAND
"A popular journalistic account of Israel"—its contradictions and paradoxes, by a *Washington Post* reporter. (BRD) Delacorte Pr, 1982.

Moskin, J. Robert   AMONG LIONS, THE BATTLE FOR JERUSALEM
Account of the battle for the Arab-held section of the city, and history of Jerusalem since 1947—"reads like a novel." (BRD) Arbor Hse, 1982 (first published 1967).

Oz, Amos   IN THE LAND OF ISRAEL
"Candid, diverse, often passionate views of Israelis on divisions now wracking that land" based on conversations with people in all walks of life, by the Israeli novelist. (PW) HarBraceJ, 1983.

Phillips, John   A WILL TO SURVIVE
Photographs of people taken during the Arab-Israeli battle for Jerusalem in 1948 are juxtaposed with photographs taken twenty-five years later of the same people, with stories of how they had come to Israel and their lives since 1948. Dial, 1977.

Rennert, Maggie   SHELANU: AN ISRAEL JOURNEY
A journal of the author's early years in Israel, to which she emigrated in 1973 knowing no Hebrew and with no family or ethnic ties, and her transformation "from American observer to *shelanu* [one of ours]." (LJ) P-H, 1979.

Said, Edward W.   THE QUESTION OF PALESTINE
A "moving and persuasive explanation of the Palestine issue" by a professor of literature who is also a Palestinian activist. (BRD) Times Bks, 1979.

Segev, Tom   1949: THE FIRST ISRAELIS
A controversial best seller in Israel by an Israeli journalist and based on newly declassified documents, diaries and letters. The author's thesis is that Israel's problems today—relationships with Arabs, bureaucracy, the black market, discrimination—are traceable to the nation's early months. Free Pr, 1985.

Tawil, Raymonda H.   MY HOME, MY PRISON
Memoirs of personal and political turmoil of a Palestinian woman journalist. Vivid, first-hand document of the yearnings and sufferings of Palestinians in Israel and occupied Jordan." (BL) HR&W, 1980.

Thubron, Colin   JERUSALEM
Part of Great Cities of the World series. Time-Life, 1976.

Uris, Leon and Jill   JERUSALEM, SONG OF SONGS
By the novelist, with photographs by his wife. Doubleday, 1981.

Wilson, Edmund   ISRAEL AND THE DEAD SEA SCROLLS
By the distinguished literary critic—an account of the discovery of the scrolls with his interpretation of their significance for the Judeo-Christian tradition, along with views on Israel, modern Jewish literature, and a foreword by Leon Edel "to put it all in focus." (NYTBR) FS&G, 1978.

THE HOLY LAND, BIBLE AND KORAN

Chase, Mary Ellen   THE BIBLE AND THE COMMON READER
Interpretation for the general reader by a novelist, of the scriptures as literature and history—"vividly and charmingly written." (BRD) Macmillan, 1962 (first published 1952).

**Converse, Gordon, and others   COME SEE THE PLACE:
THE HOLY LAND JESUS KNEW**
"Vivid photos . . . quite literally show where Jesus walked, preached, suffered and died." Text and "beautifully relevant" passages from the Bible, selected by a biblical lecturer and Holy Land archaeologist. (PW) P-H, 1978.

Dayan, Moshe   LIVING WITH THE BIBLE
By the Israeli soldier/statesman—landscapes, childhood anecdotes, retelling of biblical stories. Morrow, 1978.

Gilbert, Martin   JERUSALEM: REBIRTH OF A CITY
The reawakening of Jerusalem in the early nineteenth century with the advent of Jewish immigration from Czarist Russia, American and European interest in the Holy Land, tourism, archaeological exploration—how these events planted seeds for present-day conflicts. Viking, 1985.

Landay, Jerry M.   DOME OF THE ROCK
Social, religious, political, artistic history of the Muslim shrine; literary excerpts, a chronology, photographs—an appealing book for the layman. Newsweek, 1972.

Magnússon, Magnus   THE ARCHAEOLOGY OF THE BIBLE
A book on archaeology for the lay reader—"fun to read and educational." (The author did a TV documentary on the subject.) (LJ) S&S, 1978.

Morton, Henry C.   IN THE STEPS OF THE MASTER
This, and *In Search of the Holyland* (1984) are travel classics first published in 1934-35, based on Morton's journey in the 1930s. *In Search of the Holyland* is a book of photographs accompanied by text from *In the Steps of the Master*—"a you-are-there ambience." (PW) Dodd, 1984.

Negev, Avraham   ARCHAEOLOGY IN THE LAND OF THE BIBLE
"Terse, to-the-point" introduction to biblical archaeology with many maps, drawings, photographs. (LJ) Schocken, 1978.

Pearlman, Moshe and Yanni, Yaacov   HISTORICAL SITES IN THE HOLY LAND
Historical and archaeological background to Israeli antiquities and restorations for travelers and armchair travelers. Judson, 1985.

Peters, F.E.   JERUSALEM
The long subtitle explains the book's contents: "The Holy City in the eyes of chroniclers, visitors, pilgrims and prophets from the days of Abraham to the beginnings of modern times"—first-hand impressions by people of all religions, over the centuries. Princeton U Pr, 1985.

Rachleff, Owen S.   EXPLORING THE BIBLE
"A lavish ecumenical presentation of the Bible as cultural history . . . people and events are discussed in a clear, informal style." Accompanying photographs range from a NASA photo of the Sinai to reproductions of paintings by da Vinci, Rembrandt, El Greco. (BRD) Abbeville, 1981.

Reader's Digest, eds.   READER'S DIGEST ATLAS OF THE BIBLE
A chronology of biblical events in terms of geography and incorporating current archaeological research—fascinating trivia and biblical lore on plants, animals, how people dressed, etc. Readers Digest Pr, 1982.

Rogerson, John   THE ATLAS OF THE BIBLE
History and transmission of biblical literature, biblical history, the Bible in art, geography of the Bible. Facts On File, 1985.

Silberman, Neil A.   DIGGING FOR GOD AND COUNTRY
"Exploitation, archaeology, and the secret struggle for the Holy Land" is the subtitle—"absorbing history" of biblical archaeology in the nineteenth and twentieth centuries through the British conquest of Jerusalem in 1917. (BL) Knopf, 1982.

GUIDEBOOKS

BAZAK GUIDE TO ISRAEL
"All-purpose guide with city and touring maps. Special interest walks in Jerusalem and 25 motor trips, plus hotels, hostels, restaurants, camping, weather, history, attractions" and more. (BP) Har-Row, 1984.

Cox, Thornton   THORNTON COX'S TRAVELLER'S GUIDE TO ISRAEL
Hippocrene, 1982.

**Finegan, Jack   DISCOVERING ISRAEL: A POPULAR GUIDE
                    TO THE HOLY LAND**
Eerdmans, 1981.

Gafni, Shlomo S.   THE GLORY OF JERUSALEM: AN EXPLORER'S GUIDE
Leads the reader on a comprehensive walking tour of the Old City and environs. Cambridge U Pr, 1982.

Isaacs, Marty   MARTY'S WALKING TOURS OF BIBLICAL JERUSALEM
Hippocrene, 1982.

Kaminker, Sarah Fox   FOOTLOOSE IN JERUSALEM
Eight guided walking tours illustrated with maps and nineteenth-century engravings. Crown, 1981.

**Littell, Franklin H.   A PILGRIM'S INTERFAITH GUIDE TO
                          THE HOLY LAND**
Hippocrene, 1982.

**Miller, J. Maxwell   INTRODUCING THE HOLY LAND, A
                       GUIDEBOOK FOR FIRST TIME VISITORS**
Introduction by a professor of biblical and Israelite history; descriptions of historical periods and geographical areas, location and modern names of biblical sites, plus five itineraries for varying lengths of time. Mercer U, 1982.

**Murphy-O'Connor, Jerome   THE HOLY LAND: AN ARCHAEOLOGICAL
                            GUIDE FROM 1700 TO EARLIEST TIMES**
An archaeological guide that includes practical advice on travel, lodging, dress, etc., along with history, site plans and hints for a self-guided tour to ninety sites. Oxford U, 1980.

Rosovsky, Nitza   JERUSALEM WALKS
By a native of Jerusalem—six walking tours "on an intimate neighborhood basis." Also includes general information on food, shopping. (BL) HR&W, 1982.

Vilnay, Zev   GUIDE TO ISRAEL
Taylor & Francis, 1982.

HISTORY

Herzog, Chaim   ARAB-ISRAELI WARS
Readable history, 1948-82, from the Israeli point of view. Random, 1982.

Johnson, Paul   CIVILIZATIONS OF THE HOLY LAND
Biblical civilizations, Byzantine and Islamic—"makes an exceedingly complex history intelligible without oversimplifying." (BRD) Atheneum, 1979.

Sachar, Howard M.   A HISTORY OF ISRAEL
A history from the rise of Zionism to our time. Knopf, 1976.

Novels

See also novels under "Egypt" and the "Middle East" by Caldwell, Fast, Slaughter and others.

Asch, Sholem   THE NAZARENE
"High level fiction of biblical background . . . extraordinary recreation of time and place." (BRD) Putnam Pub Group, 1939. Also *The Apostle* (1943), *Mary* (1949), *Moses* (1951), *The Prophet* (1955).

Blair, Leona   A WOMAN'S PLACE
Traces the lives of a New York Jewish family, and events in Israel, from the beginnings of Zionism to the 1967 War. Delacorte Pr, 1981.

Broner, E.M.   A WEAVE OF WOMEN
A feminist novel about some women in Jerusalem "who recreate traditional Jewish ritual in a feminist mold." (BRD) HR&W, 1978.

Davidson, Lionel   THE MENORAH MEN
The Dead Sea Scrolls lead an English philologist to hunt for treasure—the true menorah—"learning, wit and style beautifully integrated into a rousing chase across the Negev." (FC) Har-Row, 1966.

Davidson, Lionel   SUN CHEMIST
A mix of political history and scientific thriller—a historian accidentally comes upon evidence of a cheap and inexhaustible substitute for oil. Knopf, 1976.

Dayan, Yael   THREE WEEKS IN OCTOBER
The Yom Kippur War narrated by an Israeli husband and wife. Delacorte Pr, 1979.

Douglas, Lloyd C.   THE BIG FISHERMAN
Fictional biography of Apostle Simon Peter. Houghton, 1948. Also, *The Robe* (1942), based on the life of the Roman soldier Marcellus, in charge of Christ's crucifixion.

Fish, Robert L.   PURSUIT
Unusual plot of a Nazi who assumes the role of a refugee in Palestine at the end of World War II, his life as a solid Israeli citizen, and his son's learning of his true identity many years later. Doubleday, 1978.

Freeman, Cynthia   NO TIME FOR TEARS
A Russian-Jewish family emigrates to Palestine in 1905; part of the family resettles in the United States, supporting the establishment of Israel with money, the other half remains and fights for the new country. Arbor Hse, 1981.

Gordon, Noah   THE JERUSALEM DIAMOND
An American diamond dealer is asked to procure the Jerusalem Diamond by representatives of the Muslim, Jewish and Roman Catholic religions—it has significance to all three—and embarks on the high-risk mission. An enthralling novel that, as a dividend, gives the reader a mine of information about diamond cutting and polishing. Random, 1979.

Hareven, Shulamith   CITY OF MANY DAYS
Novel of a Sephardic Jew in Jerusalem in the early half of this century that captures a way of life no longer with us. Doubleday, 1977.

Heym, Stefan   THE KING DAVID REPORT
Novelization of events in Kings 1 and Books 1 and 2 of Samuel. Putnam Pub Group, 1973.

Kaniuk, Yaram   ROCKING HORSE
A painter deserts his family in New York for his native Israel, in search of a new identity—"serious comedy." (BRD) Har-Row, 1977.

Kemelman, Harry   MONDAY THE RABBI TOOK OFF
A rabbi is embroiled in a mystery involving a TV commentator and Arab militants, with action alternating between Massachusetts and Israel. Putnam Pub Group, 1972.

Le Carré, John   THE LITTLE DRUMMER GIRL
Spy novel by the master—this time involving the Israeli-Palestinian conflict. Knopf, 1983.

Levin, Meyer   SPELL OF TIME
"A tale of love in Jerusalem . . . novel of a 'Faustian' bargain" in which the souls of a distinguished biochemist and an American student are exchanged. (BRD) Praeger, 1974.

Levin, Meyer   THE SETTLERS
A family saga, interwoven with Israeli history, beginning in 1904. S&S, 1972. *The Harvest* (1978) continues the saga to 1948 and Israeli independence.

Martin, Malachi   KING OF KINGS
The biblical story of King David—an "epic portrayal in the cinematic style of Cecil B. De Mille." (FC) S&S, 1981.

Michener, James A.   THE SOURCE
An archaeological dig in Israel, and the varied team involved in the work, provide the focal point for a recreation of the history of Israel and the Jewish religion. Random, 1965. Also, *First Fruits* (1973), an anthology of Israeli writings edited by Michener. Random, 1965.

Oz, Amos   WHERE THE JACKALS HOWL
Short stories of Israel and its people, tensions, survival. HarBraceJ, 1981. Other titles by Oz include: *The Hill of Evil Counsel* (1978), *Elsewhere Perhaps* (1973), *Touch the Water Touch the Wind* (1974), *My Michael* (1972).

Quinnell, A.J.   THE SNAP
Based on the bombing of Iraq's nuclear reactor by Israel—a photojournalist is hired by Israel to photograph a delivery of uranium to prove its premise that the bombing was justified. Morrow, 1983.

Sachar, Howard M.   THE MAN ON THE CAMEL
An emigre, while on a working vacation in Israel, becomes involved in a treason investigation. Times Bks, 1980.

Sapir, Richard B.   THE BODY
"A lively variety of political, religious and archaeological issues" are raised when an Israeli archaeologist uncovers a tomb that seems to be that of Jesus—a "fast-paced, intelligent suspense story." (FC) Doubleday, 1983.

Schmitt, Gladys   DAVID THE KING
Biblical story of David, King of Israel—"serious, profound." (FC) Dial, 1973 (first published 1946).

Segal, Brenda L.   THE TENTH MEASURE
First-century Judaea and the Jewish rebellion against the Romans, with a plot based solidly on historical fact. St. Martin, 1980.

Shahar, David   HIS MAGESTY'S AGENT
Complex plot set during the period of World War II to 1973 and the Yom Kippur War; superior writing. HarBraceJ, 1980. Also, *The Place of Shattered Vessels* (1975) and *News from Jerusalem* (1974) (short stories).

Shaw, Robert   THE MAN IN THE GLASS BOOTH
A Jewish real estate tycoon confesses that he is actually a former Nazi, is arrested, and tried in Israel. HarBraceJ, 1967.

Singer, Isaac Bashevis   THE PENITENT
A wealthy businessman, disgusted with his life-style, goes to Israel, assumes the role of a penitent, marries a rabbi's daughter and devotes himself to prayer and study. FS&G, 1983.

Spark, Muriel   THE MANDELBAUM GATE
A novel involving a half-Jewish Catholic, her fiancé, a foreign officer, and the "piece of street between Jerusalem and Jerusalem." (FC) Knopf, 1965.

Uris, Leon   EXODUS
The history of Palestine and Zionism, from the 1940s on, with flashbacks and digressions that tell of Nazi persecutions—told from the point of view of a Christian nurse. Doubleday, 1958. See also *The Haj*, listed under "Middle East" Novels.

West, Morris L.   THE TOWER OF BABEL
Espionage, intrigue, economics and politics of Israel in 1967, told through the lives of five characters. Morrow, 1968.

Whittemore, Edward   JERUSALEM POKER
Sequel to *Sinai Tapestry*, see under "Middle East" Novels—begins in December 1921, as three men begin a twelve-year poker game in which the stakes are control of Jerusalem. HR&W, 1978.

Wiesel, Elie   A BEGGAR IN JERUSALEM
Stories of a group of people who have gathered at the West Wall following the Six-Day War—"a spiritual adventure." (BRD) Random House, 1970.

Yehoshua, A.B.   A LATE DIVORCE
Set in a nine-day period around Passover as each character in a family relates the story that "reveals their tangled relationships and secrets." (FC) Doubleday, 1984.

TRAVEL ARTICLES

BLACK ENTERPRISE
1984 Apr "Touring the Holy Land." Ben F. Carruthers, p. 70

ESQUIRE
1984 Jan "Where to Take a Dive (Scuba). Edward D. Sheffe, p. 32

GLAMOUR
1984 Dec "Israel! Israel! Israel!" p. 178

HORIZON
1985 May "Israel: Arts in an Ancient Land." From Jerusalem to Tel Aviv, the arts are an integral part of Israel's past and present . . . discovering this rich cultural heritage. Meir Ronnen, p. 33

NATIONAL GEOGRAPHIC
1985 Jul "Israel: Searching for the Center." Priit J. Vesilind, p. 2

N.Y. TIMES SUNDAY TRAVEL SECTION (X)

1985 Mar 3 "Manna from Heaven." The sagacity of a guide named Jacob wins over a dubious client in Israel. Avery Corman, p. 39

May 5 "Holy Land Hospitality." At Christian hospices, pilgrims (and sometimes others) are welcome. Susan Daar, p. 9

May 12 "Garden Where Biblical Plants Come to Life." Near Jerusalem, ancient flora thrives. Matthew Nesvisky, p. 16

Jun 16 "In the Footsteps of the Crusaders." From Jerusalem to Acre, Israel is dotted with structures where soldiers lived, fought, and prayed. Nitza Rosovsky, p. 9

Jul 28 "Ancient Armies Clash in Silence at Golan Site." Remote Gamla dig rivals Masada. Matthew Nesvisky, p. 19

Aug 11 "An Armenian Art in Jerusalem." Ceramic tiles and plaques. Susan Daar, p. 6

Aug 18 "Seeing the Jerusalem of David." Archaeological park. Abraham Rabinovich, p. 19

Oct 6 ("Sophisticated Traveler") "Holy Land: Milestones of Three Faiths." Malachi Martin, p. 83.

("Sophisticated Traveler") "Afoot in Jerusalem." Barbara Gelb, p. 100

Dec 1 "Quarrying History in Jerusalem." Zedekiah's Cave. Thomas L. Friedman, p. 19

Dec 22 "Capturing the Holiday Spirit—Christmas, New Year's or Twelfth Night." Ways to take part and ways to cope, reports from 15 *New York Times* correspondents and bureaus, includes Israel. p. 12

1984 Jan 29 "A walking Tour of Jerusalem's Past." Nitza Rosovsky, p. 9

Feb 26 "Wintering Israeli Style." Resorts and spas span three climates. Nitza Rosovsky, p. 9

Mar 4 "Europe Coming and Going." Each airport imparts first and last impressions of its own country's soul; and a guide to 13 major way stations (12 major European airports plus Ben Gurion in Tel Aviv). Paul Lewis, p. 16

May 13 Shopper's World: "Everyday Objects from Ancient Israel." Helen Gorenstein, p. 6

May 27 Fare of the Country: "Along the Street of Sweets." Natalie Mendelsohn, p. 6

Oct 7 (Part 2, "Sophisticated Traveler") "An Oasis in Jerusalem." Judith Miller, p. 129

Nov 4 Correspondent's Choice: "Stopping at a Pasha's Palace." American Colony Hotel in Jerusalem. James Feron, p. 10

Nov 18 "Ancient Lands: Holy Ground to Half the World (Jerusalem)." Abraham Rabinovich, p. 16

Dec 23 "What's Doing in Jerusalem." Thomas L. Friedman, p. 8

"Pilgrimage to Bethlehem." On Christmas Eve, history, dream and reality merge in the hallowed town on the hill. Lucinda Franks, p. 9

TRAVEL & LEISURE

1985 Jun "Jerusalem's Biblical Zoo." Claudia R. Capos, p. 156

Oct "The Other Jerusalem." The ancient city's little-known passages are eternally captivating. Kate Simon, p. 83.

1984 May "Desert Adventure in Israel." Jennifer Quale, p. 30

TRAVEL/HOLIDAY
1984 Oct "The New Jerusalem." Unearthing the secrets of the past. Abby Rand, p. 22

VOGUE
1984 Feb "Going to the Source, in Certain Places We Touch the Intangible." And no more so than in Jerusalem's old city. Barbara Goldsmith, p. 6

SAUDI ARABIA & THE ARABIAN PENINSULA

Series Guidebooks (See Appendix 1)

Berlitz:	**Saudi Arabia**
Country Orientation Update:	**Bahrain; Kuwait; Saudi Arabia; United Arab Emirates**
Nagel:	**The Gulf Emirates**
U.S. Government:	

Bahrain:	**Background Notes; Post Report**
Kuwait:	**Background Notes; Post Report**
Oman:	**Background Notes; Post Report**
Persian Gulf States:	**Country Study**
Qatar:	**Background Notes; Post Report**
Saudi Arabia:	**Country Study; Post Report**
United Arab Emirates:	**Background Notes**
Yemens:	**Area Handbook**

Background Reading

Blandford, Linda   SUPER WEALTH: THE SECRET LIVES OF THE OIL SHEIKHS
   "Chatty . . . gossipy . . . incisive . . . an inside view of places rarely seen by Westerners." Morrow, 1976.

Bullock, John   THE PERSIAN GULF UNVEILED
   "Part travelogue, part history, part prophecy"—discovery of oil, rise of the great trading families, the sheikhs desire to hold onto traditional ways. The author prophesies a "cataclysmic twenty-first century scenario" when the Soviet Union and the United States compete for the region's oil. (PW) Congdon & Weed, 1985.

Buschow, Rosemarie   THE PRINCE AND I
The author's experiences and observations, as governess to the king of Saudi Arabia's nephew—"absorbing story, well told." (BRD) Doubleday, 1981.

Cottrell, Alvin J., ed.   THE PERSIAN GULF STATES
Written by British and American experts, a general survey of social structure, literature, ideologies of the region and its 5,000-year history. Johns Hopkins U, 1980.

Freeth, Zahrra and Winstone, Victor   EXPLORERS OF ARABIA: FROM THE RENAISSANCE TO THE VICTORIAN ERA
Holmes & Meier, 1978.

Gray, Seymour, M.D.   BEYOND THE VEIL: THE ADVENTURES OF AN AMERICAN DOCTOR IN SAUDI ARABIA
A Boston physician's memoir of his years as chief medical officer in the King Feisal Hospital, filled with fascinating anecdotes and social, political, and medical observations. Har-Row, 1983.

Holden, David   THE HOUSE OF SAUD
"The rise and rule of the most powerful dynasty in the Arab world"—provides "the best and fullest journalistic account of Arabia during the past 15 years." (NYTBR) HR&W, 1981.

Lawrence, T.E.   REVOLT IN THE DESERT
Shortened version of *Seven Pillars of Wisdom*—"tapestry of memoirs, philosophy, travel writing, anthropology and fiction." (BRD) Penguin, 1976 (first published 1926).

Lucey, Robert   THE KINGDOM: ARABIA & THE HOUSE OF SAUD
Thoroughly readable pop history . . . aims to provide a feel for the place, rather than orthodox analysis . . . titillating trivia on every aspect of life. (BRD) HarBraceJ, 1982.

Mansfield, Peter   THE NEW ARABIANS
"Readable and informative introduction and history of the five peninsula countries (Saudi Arabia, Kuwait, Bahrain, Qatar and United Arab Emirates) from semi-nomadic tribes to receiving of the faith of Prophet Muhammad" to present-day petro power. (LJ) J G Ferguson, 1981.

Marechaux, Pascal   ARABIA FELIX: IMAGES OF YEMEN AND ITS PEOPLE
Poetic vignettes and photographs evoke the country called "Happy Arabia" by the ancients. Barron, 1980.

Musallam, Basim   THE ARABS
Aspects of the lives of Arabs—intellectual development, women, family, etc.—based on a TV documentary series, with the aim "to rectify incorrect

Western impressions of the Arabs. . . . a delightful glance at a fascinating subject." (LJ) Salem Hse, 1985.

Phillips, Wendell   UNKNOWN OMAN
A "readable and absorbing" book of travel, geography, history, archaeology, social customs, religion. (BRD) Intl Bk Ctr, 1972 (first published 1966).

Polk, William R. and Mares, William J.   PASSING BRAVE
Two Americans cross the great Arabian desert on camelback, in search of the last Bedouin tribes. Knopf, 1973.

Raban, Jonathan   ARABIA: A JOURNEY THROUGH THE LABYRINTH
"Quicksilver observations . . . a delicious travel book" by one impelled to visit the country because of the contemporary view of oil-rich Arabs, and found that there are the oil-rich (Bahrain, Qatar, Abu Dhabi, Dubai) and the oil-poor (North Yemen, Jordan). (BRD) S&S, 1979.

St. Albans, Suzanne   GREEN GROWS THE OIL
Travels in the United Arab Republics—"a one woman view of a closed, reserved, enigmatic society bursting out of its medieval straitjacket." (BRD) Quartet, 1978. Also *Where Time Stood Still* (1980), a portrait of Oman.

Stark, Freya   THE SOUTHERN GATES OF ARABIA
A recently reprinted travel adventure classic by an author who wanted to be the first woman to venture into Arabia along the old incense roads, and one with "rare ability to interpret and appreciate the oftentimes menacing natives and medieval Islamic traditions." She traveled with native guides, via donkey, car and foot. (Publisher) J.P. Tarcher, 1983 (first published 1936).

Thesiger, Wilfred   ARABIAN SANDS
Five years among the nomadic Arab Bedouins in 1945—"vivid insight into nomad psychology." (BRD) Penguin, 1984 (first published 1959).

Tidrick, Kathryn   HEART-BEGUILING ARABY
A "captivating analysis of the Englishmen whose writings . . . enhanced a 'powerful imperial myth'"—Burton, Palgrave, Blunt and Doughty, the great Victorian travelers. (BRD) Cambridge U Pr, 1981.

Woolfson, Marion   PROPHETS IN BABYLON: JEWS IN THE ARAB WORLD
Faber and Faber, 1980.

GUIDEBOOKS

Kilner, Peter and Wallade, Jonathan   GULF HANDBOOK: A GUIDE TO THE EIGHT PERSIAN GULF COUNTRIES
Garrett, 1978.

HISTORY

Encyclopaedia Britannica, eds.   THE ARABS
"Popularly written and . . . one of the best introductions to Arab history and Islam." (BRD) Bantam/Britannica, 1978.

Mansfield, Peter   THE ARAB WORLD
Social and political history from nomadic beginnings to individual portraits of modern Arab nations. Penguin, 1979.

Novels

Bulliet, Richard   THE GULF SCENARIO
An employee of the Harvard-MIT Strategic Research Group disappears with secret documents—Cambridge, Washington and "exotic locales in the Persian Gulf region" are settings for this spy novel. (FC) St. Martin, 1984.

Coppel, Alfred   THE APOCALYPSE BRIGADE
A political novel set in the future. The Middle East is still chaotic, the Americans indecisive, the Russians oil-hungry; militant Arabs seize an American Embassy and hostages. HR&W, 1981.

Dickinson, Peter   THE POISON ORACLE
A contemporary Arab kingdom is the setting for a mystery in which a chimpanzee—who can communicate in a fashion—is the murder witness. Pantheon, 1974.

Erdman, Paul E.   CRASH OF '79
The plot involves intrigue and high finance and a retired banker working for the Saudis who observes the events of 1979 that lead to a war in the Middle East and the crash of '79 in the West. S&S, 1976.

Harvester, Simon   TREACHEROUS ROAD
An espionage novel set in Yemen and Egypt. Walker, 1967.

Innes, Hammond   THE DOOMED OASIS
Attempts to save an oasis from extinction are the basis for a "bloody, exotic, colorful, and completely plausible" adventure story. (FC) Knopf, 1960.

Thomas, Michael M.   GREEN MONDAY
"Novel of international monetary intrigue" extending from an "oil-rich Arabian kingdom into the White House" as Arab sheikhs plot to manipulate the U.S. stock market and elect a president of their choice. (FC) Wyndham Bks, 1980.

TRAVEL ARTICLES

NATIONAL GEOGRAPHIC
1985 Oct "Frankincense Trail." Retracing the route of the camel caravans (Saudi Arabia and South Yemen). Thomas J. & Lynn Abercrombie, p. 474

N.Y. TIMES SUNDAY TRAVEL SECTION (X)
1984 Nov 18 (Bahrain) "Ancient Lands: Discovering Immortal Dilmun." Geoffrey
       Bibby, p. 14
       (Bahrain) "Eden on the Isle of Bahrain." Paul Lewis, p. 14

TRAVEL/HOLIDAY
1984 Feb (Yemen) "Adventures in 'Ancient' Arabia." Ursula Wolff, p. 24

TURKEY

Series Guidebooks (See Appendix 1)

Blue Guide: **Istanbul**
Companion Guide: **Turkey**
Fodor: **Turkey**
Frommer: **Greece & Istanbul: $-a-Day**
Let's Go: **Greece (Cyprus & Turkish Coast)**
Lonely Planet: **Turkey**
Nagel: **Turkey & Angkor (Cambodia)**
U.S. Government: **Turkey: Background Notes; Country Study;
                         Pocket Guide; Post Report**

Background Reading

Cookridge, E.H.   **THE ORIENT EXPRESS: THE LIFE AND TIMES OF THE
                       WORLD'S MOST FAMOUS TRAIN**
See under "Europe."

Fraser, Russell   THE THREE ROMES
The three Romes, in this author's concept, are Constantinople (now Istanbul),
Moscow, and Rome—cities that felt they had "received divine missions to amass
and rule empires." The book is historical commentary and anecdotes, an
"entertaining overview . . . encounters with modern inhabitants . . . the shadowy
past [implanted in] the mind of citizens today." (BL) HarBraceJ, 1985.

Glazebrook, Philip   JOURNEY TO KARS
See under "Europe."

Hetherington, Paul   BYZANTIUM: CITY OF GOLD, CITY OF FAITH
"Splendidly recreates the spirit of Byzantium"—history, religious life, Byzantine
art, and accompanied by photos that reflect the opulent art and architecture.
(PW) Salem Hse, 1984.

Lister, R.P.   A MUEZZIN FROM THE TOWER OF DARKNESS CRIES
Travels in Turkey, "part a history, part travel book . . . succinct and witty." (BRD)
HarBraceJ, 1967.

Mango, Cyril   BYZANTIUM: THE EMPIRE OF THE NEW ROME
A pathway for beginners to this era of history. Scribner, 1981.

**Meinardus, Otto   ST. JOHN OF PATMOS AND THE SEVEN CHURCHES
OF THE APOCALYPSE**
"For serious tourists [to Turkey and Greece] and Christian pilgrims"—provides
history and a religious and archaeological framework. (BRD) Caratzas, 1979.

Morris, James   DESTINATIONS
Travel essays by a leading travel writer, including an essay on Istanbul. Oxford
U, 1980.

Newby, Eric   ON THE SHORES OF THE MEDITERRANEAN
See under "Europe."

Stark, Freya   GATEWAYS AND CARAVANS: A PORTRAIT OF TURKEY
A travel classic—"a text that mingles five thousand years of history with description of Turkey today [1970] . . . an irresistible book." (BRD) Macmillan, 1971.

Thubron, Colin   ISTANBUL
Part of the Great Cities of the World Series. Time-Life, 1979.

GUIDEBOOKS

**Bean, George E.   TURKEY BEYOND THE MAENDER; and TURKEY'S
SOUTHERN SHORE**
Norton, 1980 (Both Books).

Griffith, Susan   TRAVELLER'S SURVIVAL KIT TO THE EAST
Includes Turkey. Vacation Week, 1982.

Schneider, Dux   THE TRAVELLER'S GUIDE TO TURKEY
Chatto Bodley, 1979.

HISTORY

Browning, Robert   THE BYZANTINE EMPIRE
A balanced history centered in Istanbul (Constantinople), of the 1,000-year
civilization. Scribner, 1980.

Diehl, Charles   BYZANTIUM: GREATNESS AND DECLINE
A classic translated from the French by an outstanding scholar—"more of a
brilliant essay than straight and dry political history." (BRD) Rutgers U, 1957.

Kinross, Lord   THE OTTOMAN CENTURIES: THE RISE AND FALL OF THE TURKISH EMPIRE
Readable, popular approach to history, with emphasis on sultans, court life, battles. Morrow, 1979.

Ostrogorsky, George   HISTORY OF THE BYZANTINE STATE
"Uncommonly clear, orderly and readable short history" covering 1,000 years of Byzantium. Rutgers U, 1969 (first published 1958).

Novels

Ambler, Eric   THE LIGHT OF DAY
A small-time con man involved in international intrigue in Istanbul—"a picturesque and realistic" setting. (FC) Knopf, 1963.

Bawden, Nina   GEORGE BENEATH A PAPER MOON
England, then Turkey, are settings for this comedy, love story and thriller about a travel agent, his wife and a 15-year-old girl. Har-Row, 1975.

Buchan, John   GREENMANTLE
Adventure story of the English secret service in Constantinople in World War I, and a classic. Doran, 1915

Freely, Maureen   THE LIFE OF THE PARTY
Istanbul in 1969 is the setting; the plot revolves around Americans and Turks connected with an American-founded college overlooking the Bosporus. S&S, 1985.

Garve, Andrew   THE ASCENT OF D-13
A story of international espionage and suspense involving Russian and Allied efforts to recover a secret detection device in the mountains on the Soviet-Turkish border. Har-Row, 1968.

Gilman, Dorothy   THE AMAZING MRS. POLLIFAX
Istanbul is the setting; the plot involves a widow-grandmother CIA agent who helps a double agent to escape. Doubleday, 1970.

Glazebrook, Philip   BYZANTINE HONEYMOON
Misadventures of an Englishman and his bride, in 1895—a "bizarre story of a smug parson's son who is . . . forced to face his hypocritical Victorian values." (BRD) Atheneum, 1979.

Kazan, Elia   AMERICA, AMERICA
Experiences of a Greek boy in Constantinople as he attempts to establish a rug business and secure money to go to America. Stein & Day, 1962.

Kazantzakis, Nikos   THE GREEK PASSION
The crucifixion retold in a modern setting—a Greek-inhabited Turkish town in 1920. S&S, 1953.

Kemal, Yashar   SEAGULL
A "moving account of a boy's coming of age" in a small fishing town on the Black Sea, as he seeks help in saving a seagull. (BRD) Pantheon, 1981.

Kemal, Yashar   THE UNDYING GRASS
"A tale of murder, revenge, love, hate, and compassion in modern Turkey." Kemal is a leading Turkish writer. Morrow, 1978. Other of his titles include: *Iron Earth, Copper Sky* (1979), *They Burn the Thistles* (1977), *Memed My Hawk* (1961).

McCutchan, Philip   HALFHYDE TO THE NARROWS
Adventure story of the rescue of a merchant ship seized by the Soviets. St. Martin, 1977.

Michael, Prince of Greece   SULTANA
The Prince's first novel is based on the history of a little-known country. The plot, set in the late eighteenth century, concerns a Martinique-born Creole who rises to become the sultana. Har-Row, 1983.

Oldenbourg, Zoe   THE HEIRS OF THE KINGDOM
Historical tapestry of a young French couple who join the First Crusade after hearing Peter the Hermit preach. Pantheon, 1971.

Reinhardt, Richard   THE ASHES OF SMYRNA: A NOVEL OF THE NEAR EAST
Novel of 1919-22 when Smyrna was occupied by the Greeks, and then retaken by the Turks. Har-Row, 1971.

Roditi, Edouard   THE DELIGHTS OF TURKEY
A collection of stories—Istanbul in Ottoman days, folk tales, village life, Europeans in Turkey, contemporary Istanbul. New Directions, 1979.

Settle, Mary Lee   BLOOD TIE
Set in the port city of Ceramos, with a plot involving Americans and the CIA in murder and corruption. Houghton, 1977.

Whitney, Phyllis A.   BLACK AMBER
Romantic, suspenseful novel, set in Istanbul. Appleton, 1964.

TRAVEL ARTICLES

N.Y. TIMES SUNDAY TRAVEL SECTION (X)
1985 May 5 "Music Abroad 1985: Who's Performing Where." Includes Turkey.
Vernon Kidd, p. 21

1985 Oct 13 "What's Doing in Istanbul." Henry Kamm, p. 10
      Oct 27 "Cappadocia's Lunar Landscape." The ancient region in Turkey is
      dotted with fantastic rocks and subterranean cities. Henry Kamm, p. 19
1984 Feb 19 "Journey to the Mountain of the Ark." Turkey has opened Ararat to
      visitors. Marvine Howe, p. 19
      Dec 23 "The Relics of Byzantium." Scattered around modern Istanbul,
      traces of an imperial past. Fergus M. Bordewich, p. 13

TRAVEL & LEISURE
1984 Oct Travel & Architecture: "The Brilliance of the Byzantine." In Istanbul,
      Venice, and the Greek Isles. Alexander Eliot, p. 26

III. ASIA

Series Guidebooks (See Appendix 1)

Fielding: **All-Asia Budget Guide; Far East**
Fodor: **Southeast Asia**
Lonely Planet: **South East Asia; West Asia;**
North
East Asia; **Travels with Children in Asia**

Background Reading

See also Islam, under "Middle East."

Attenborough, David **SPIRIT OF ASIA**
An overview, with photographs, based on a BBC documentary. Salem Hse, 1983.

Barzini, Luigi **PEKING TO PARIS**
Reprint of an old book by a writer usually thought of in connection with *The Italians* (see Italy). As a young man Barzini took part in a race by motorcar from Peking to Paris in 1907, a "romantic and dangerous endeavor" at that time —"a good read." (LJ) Open Court, 1973.

DeGaury, Gerald and Winstone, H.V.F. **AN ANTHOLOGY OF WRITINGS ON ASIA**
From Rudyard Kipling to Fitzroy MacLean—"strong on the romantic aspects of travel especially as seen through British eyes." (TB) Macmillan, 1982.

Fleming, Peter **NEWS FROM TARTARY**
Report of a seven-month, 3,500-mile trip, in the early 1930s, despite a civil war, from Peking to Kashmir—"honest reporting, brilliantly written." J.P. Tarcher, 1982 (first published 1936). Also by this leading travel writer, *One's Company* (1934).

Lattimore, Owen   HIGH TARTARY
Lattimore has written several of the best books on Asiatic travel and exploration; this, *Desert Road to Turkestan* and *Mongol Journeys* are all reprints. AMS (first published 1934, 1929, 1941 respectively).

Lee, Sherman E.   A HISTORY OF FAR EASTERN ART
A one-volume work of background reading on Far Eastern Art; includes archaeological discoveries. Abrams, 1982.

MacLean, Fitzroy   A PERSON FROM ENGLAND, AND
OTHER TRAVELLERS
"High adventure in the forbidden cities of Central Asia"—travel by Europeans who managed to penetrate the area in the nineteenth and early twentieth centuries—"doubly interesting because these ancient cities are almost as inaccessible now" because of Communist rule. (BRD) Har-Row, 1958.

Macready, Daphne L.   THE BECKONING LAND
Account of a journey from Hong Kong to the Himalayas (the "beckoning land") to "expose her earnest British self to the wisdom of Oriental asceticism." A combination of travel diary and autobiography in "lighthearted style." (PW) Vanguard, 1969.

Maillaret, Ella   FORBIDDEN JOURNEY
A new edition, with an introduction by Dervla Murphy, the Irish travel writer, of the journey made with Peter Fleming (see *News from Tartary*, above) from Peking to Northern India. Interesting, I would think, to compare to Fleming's account. Hippocrene, 1983.

Pardey, Lin & Larry   SERAFFYN'S ORIENTAL ADVENTURE
This book begins with the Greek Isles and continues the authors' circumnavigation of the globe. Norton, 1983. A sequel to *Mediterranean Adventure* (1981) and *Seraffyn's European Adventure* (1979).

Rawson, Philip   THE ART OF SOUTHEAST ASIA
Introduction to Southeast Asian cultures—"vivid comparative impressions of the converging and diverging elements . . . of the various . . . arts." (BRD) Smith, 1979 (first published 1967).

Ross, Nancy Wilson   THREE WAYS OF ASIAN WISDOM:
HINDUISM, BUDDHISM, ZEN
History, tenets, practices of the major Oriental religions—"popularization and compression without distortion . . . pleasant and logical." (BRD) S&S, 1978 (first published 1966).

Schiffer, Michael   LESSONS OF THE ROAD
See under "Middle East."

Severin, Timothy   THE ORIENTAL ADVENTURE: EXPLORERS
OF THE EAST
Reading it "is an adventure in itself. . . and enjoyable account of a by-gone era"

told through the explorations of diverse people from Marco Polo, scholars and merchants, to eccentrics and spies. (BRD) Little, 1976. See also *The Sindbad Voyage* listed under "Middle East."

Theroux, Paul   THE GREAT RAILWAY BAZAAR
A four-month lecture tour in 1973, via the Orient Express, Khyber Mail and Trans-Siberian Express, is the basis for these conversations and impressions of people encountered. Houghton, 1975.

**Welty, Thomas   THE ASIANS: THEIR HERITAGE
AND THEIR DESTINY**
A good overview of Asia, and introduction to the three major religions and variations thereof in the various countries. Har-Row, 1976.

MARCO POLO

Bellonci, Maria   THE TRAVELS OF MARCO POLO
A new Italian version of the classic translated into English to offer a readable, modern English version. Facts On File, 1984. Other versions of Marco Polo's travels retold in popular style include: *Marco Polo* by Richard Humble (1975), *Travels of Marco Polo* edited by Manuel Komroff (1982), *Marco Polo's Travels in Xanadu with Kublai Khan* by R.P. Lister (1977).

Hart, Henry H.   MARCO POLO, VENETIAN ADVENTURER
The explorer's life and writings and his Venetian and Asian environments. U of Ohio, 1967.

GUIDEBOOKS

Brandon, James R.   BRANDON'S GUIDE TO THE THEATRE IN ASIA
Dance, opera, festivals, plays, theatres, musical performances—along with background and historical information, practical lists and information for planning attendance at performances. U. Pr of Hawaii, 1976.

**Doll, John and Terry, George, eds.   THE ON-YOUR-OWN
GUIDE TO ASIA**
Based on experiences of volunteers working in Asia; the essentials for planning low-cost travel to ten countries. C.E. Tuttle, 1984.

Far East Economic Review Staff, eds.   ALL-ASIA GUIDE
Complete in-depth guide to Asia—twenty-seven countries including China and Mongolia. C.E. Tuttle, 1983.

Griffith, Susan   TRAVELLERS SURVIVAL KIT TO THE EAST
Introductory text and detailed information on India, Nepal, Sri Lanka, Burma as well as Turkey and some countries of the Middle East. Bradt, 1982.

Jacobs, Charles and Babette   FAR EAST TRAVEL DIGEST
Arranged alphabetically by country, from Burma to Thailand. Each segment

includes a historical survey, description of people and customs, places to see, specific, useful how-to information. Travel Digest, 1984.

Stier, Wayne   SOUTHEAST ASIA HANDBOOK
A comprehensive guide for "experience hunters" with a travel philosophy that takes budget into account. Provides extensive background notes on everything from anthropology and history to flora, fauna, religion and festivals. Practical information includes where to stay and eat, capsule vocabularies and characters of key words, maps, town plans. Covers Hong Kong and Macau, Malaysia and Singapore, Indonesia, Brunei, the Philippines. (Publisher) Moon Pbns Co, 1982.

Sunset, eds.   ORIENT
Covers China, Japan, Hong Kong and Macau, Taiwan, Korea. Sunset- Lane, 1983.

History

Fairbanks, John K. and Reischauer, Edwin O.   EAST ASIA: TRADITION AND TRANSFORMATION
"One of the best standard single treatments" of east Asia, based on East Asian courses at Harvard (includes China, Japan, Korea, Vietnam). (BL) Houghton, 1978.

Hall, D.G.E.   A HISTORY OF SOUTH-EAST ASIA
Updated edition of a "marvelous . . . prescriptive read" that covers Indonesia, Burma, Malaysia, Vietnam, Thailand. (BRD) St.Martin, 1981 (first published 1956).

Williams, Lea E.   SOUTHEAST ASIA: A HISTORY
Prehistory to the present—"a readable and concise volume . . . written in a style suited for the general reader." (BRD) Oxford U, 1978.

TRAVEL ARTICLES

CONNOISSEUR
1985 Jul "From Paris to Peking." Trans-Siberian train trip through France, Germany, Poland, Siberia, Mongolia, China. Katie Leishman, p. 35

ESQUIRE
1985 Oct "Thirty-one Romantic Vacations." Includes China and India. Neal Karlen and Wendy Lowe, p. 54
1984 Feb "Special Places—Far East Suites." Special hotels in Thailand, Philippines, Singapore, Sri Lanka, and Macau. David Butwin, p. 33
    Apr "Seven Trips to Work in Around Work." Seoul, Hong Kong, Singapore, Japan. p. 114

NATIONAL GEOGRAPHIC
1984 Dec "Life Breath of Half the World—Monsoons." Priit J. Vesiland, p. 712

N.Y. TIMES SUNDAY TRAVEL SECTION (X)
1985 Sep 22 "Beyond the Gloss of the New Asia." Barbara Crossette, p. 9
     Fare of the Country: "A Classic Soup to Honor a Guest." Bird's Nest Soup.
     Eileen Yin-Fei Lo, p. 12
     Dec 22 "Capturing the Holiday Spirit—Christmas, New Year's or Twelfth
     Night." Ways to take part and ways to cope, reports from 15 *New York
     Times* correspondents and bureaus that include China, Japan and Southeast
     Asia. p. 12
1984 May 20 "Summer Abroad: the ABCs of Going with Children." 16 foreign
     correspondents and contributors of *The Times* offer tips on touring their
     corners of the world—includes China, India, Japan. p. 21

SUNSET
1985 Oct "Needlework of the Hmong." Laos, Thailand, South China. p. 54
1984 Mar "Seasonal Guide to the Many Climates of Asia." p. 62

BURMA

Series Guidebooks (See Appendix 1)

Insight: Burma
Lonely Planet: Burma
U.S. Government: **Burma Background Notes; Country Study**

Background Reading

Bixler, Norma   BURMA, A PROFILE
  "An interesting, pleasant and informative book" for the general reader—"art,
music, and literature are well covered." (BRD) Praeger, 1971.

Bixler, Norma   BURMESE JOURNEY
  The author accompanied her husband to Rangoon in 1958-60 where he set up a
new university library. She recounts the details of setting up house, acquiring
friends, understanding a new way of life—a Burma that is no more, with the influx
later of many visitors and foreigners. Antioch Pr, 1970.

Collis, Maurice   LORDS OF THE SUNSET: A TOUR IN THE SHAN STATES
  "A particularly delightful book about [then] little-known and lovely land . . .
charming and exquisitely decorative people." (BRD) AMS, 1977 (first published
1939).

Courtauld, Caroline   **IN SEARCH OF BURMA**
"Takes the reader to remote corners of the 'authentic Orient'—a land of tranquillity and timelessness"—down the Irrawaddy River, to Mandalay, the Shwedagon Pagoda in Rangoon, Inle Lake and more. (Publisher) Salem Hse, 1985.

Edmonds, Paul   PEACOCKS AND PAGODAS
Reprint of an English travel writer's impressions of Burma in the early twenties, and its people, which the author then found to be "perhaps the happiest and most contented in the world." (BRD) AMS, 1977 (first published 1924).

Lewis, Norman   GOLDEN EARTH: TRAVELS IN BURMA
Travel to Burma in 1951 at a time of civil war—"brilliant descriptive passages that give the feel and flavor of Burma . . . brushes with bandits and Communist rebels." (BRD) Hippocrene, 1984 (first published 1952).

GUIDEBOOKS

Hildebrand, Volker   THAILAND-BURMA
One of a new guidebook series originating in Germany. Hippocrene, 1985.

**Stier, Wayne and Cavers, M.   WIDE EYES IN BURMA AND
                                  THAILAND—FINDING YOUR WAY**
A travel guide "especially suited to the young, intrepid traveler." (BP) Meru Pub, 1983.

HISTORY

Hall, D.G.E.   A HISTORY OF SOUTH-EAST ASIA
See under "Asia."

Williams, Lea E.   SOUTHEAST ASIA: A HISTORY
See under "Asia."

Novels

Bates, H.E.   THE JACARANDA TREE
The effects on British civilians, an Anglo-Burmese nurse, and other refugees fleeing before the advancing Japanese—the author "writes about Burma in a beautiful shimmering prose alive with . . . Gauguinesque color sense." (BRD) Atl Monthly Pr, 1949.

Becker, Stephen   THE BLUE-EYED SHAN
Part of a trilogy that also includes *The Chinese Bandit* and *The Last Mandarin*—adventures of an American anthropologist in the Shan states on the Chinese border, before, during and after World War II and "the clash of cultures." (FC) Random, 1982.

Law-Yone, Wendy   THE COFFIN TREE
"An odyssey . . . from the childhood of a girl born of well-to-do family in a modern Burma immersed in political turmoil, to the grown young woman forced . . . to immigrate . . . to America." (FC) Knopf, 1983.

Maugham, W. Somerset   THE GENTLEMAN IN THE PARLOUR
"Records a leisurely trip from Rangoon northward to Mandalay . . . accounts of Europeans and Englishmen he meets and what's keeping them in the Orient." (BRD) Arno, 1977 (first published 1930).

Orwell, George   BURMESE DAYS
A bitter, satirical picture of the white man's rule in Upper Burma. HarBraceJ, 1974 (first published 1934).

TRAVEL ARTICLES

NATIONAL GEOGRAPHIC
1984 Jul "Time and Again in Burma." Bryan Hodgson, p. 90

SMITHSONIAN
1984 May "An Irrawaddy Itinerary." Burmese life on the river. Alexander Frater, p. 99

TRAVEL & LEISURE
1984 Dec "An Ancient Land Emerges As a Fresh, Exotic Destination." Michael J. Weber, p. 80

CHINA

Series Guidebooks (See Appendix 1)

Berlitz: China
Fielding: People's Republic of China
Fodor: People's Republic of China; Beijing, Guangzhou & Shanghai
Lonely Planet: China; Hong Kong, Macau and Canton
Nagel: China
U.S. Government: China: Area Handbook;
                              Country Study; Post Report
                              Mongolia: Area Handbook; Background Notes

Background Reading

Bernstein, Richard   FROM THE CENTER OF THE EARTH
Subtitle: The search for the truth about China.
People, places, moods, a huge cast of characters from peasants and religious pilgrims to children and prostitutes—"tight, sharp, beautiful vignettes [reflect] an ugly daily life . . . feeling of squalid cultural decay." (BRD) Little, 1982.

Bloodworth, Dennis   THE CHINESE LOOKING GLASS
Why the Chinese think and act the way they do—"a well-researched Chautauqua on the earth's most populous nation." (BL) FS&G, 1980.

Blunden, Caroline and Elvin, Mark   CULTURAL ATLAS OF CHINA
History, society, politics, religion, philosophy, literature and the visual arts—"demonstrates that it is possible to capture the vast span of history ranging from the magnificence of ancient China to the mystery of the present China within one volume." Facts On File, 1983.

Bonavia, David   THE CHINESE
"Systematically illuminates . . . major aspects of the People's Republic. . . . A China seen sympathetically, but without rose-colored glasses"—by the chief correspondent for the *London Times* who has reported on the country since the 1960s. (NYTBR) Penguin rev. ed., 1983. Also, *China Unknown* (1985), and *Peking* (1978).

Buchanan, Keith M. and others   CHINA PAST AND PRESENT
Text and photographs, a "monumental survey of China from ancient times to the present." (Publisher) Crown, 1981.

Butterfield, Fox   CHINA—ALIVE IN THE BITTER SEA
By a *New York Times* correspondent, the "ills that have overtaken" Mao's revolution forty-four years later. "Illuminates virtually every corner of Chinese life . . . a deadly accurate portrait." (BRD) Times Bks, 1982.

Clayre, Alasdair   THE HEART OF THE DRAGON
Companion book to the PBS series on China—"History/portrait of China and its people . . . depictions of Chinese life range from religious beliefs, marriage and concubinage, food and work to changing traditions of Chinese justice, art, crime and punishment." (PW) Houghton, 1985.

Danforth, Kenneth C. and Dickinson, Mary B.   JOURNEY INTO CHINA
Personal travelogues of journeys into China by first-rate journalists and scholars with great photography. National Geog, 1982.

Fairbank, John K.   CHINABOUND: A FIFTY-YEAR MEMOIR
Memoir of a China expert who lived in Peking during the 1930s and traveled extensively throughout China. Har-Row, 1983. Also *The U.S. and China* (1983) and *China Perceived* (1979).

Frolic, B. Michael   MAO'S PEOPLE
Sixteen vignettes based on interviews of refugee students, soldiers, peasants, workers, criminals, etc., protected by anonymity—"candid, devastating and funny." (BRD) Harvard U Pr, 1980.

Garside, Roger   COMING ALIVE: CHINA AFTER MAO
Eyewitness account of the events at Democracy Wall in 1978-79—"one of the most cogent and elegant accounts of revolutionary China." (BRD) McGraw, 1981.

Han, Suyin   THE CRIPPLED TREE
Followed by *The Mortal Flower* (1966) and *My House Has Two Doors* (1980), a trilogy that is at once an autobiography of the novelist and her family, and an absorbing history of China "told with distinct personal bias." (BRD) Putnam Pub Group, 1965.

Hinton, William   SHENFAN
Sequel to *Fashen* (1966), a documentary of revolution in a Chinese village. This is an account of events when Communism came to the village of Long Bow, where the author lived as a UN agricultural expert. In *Shenfan* he writes about his return to the village in 1971—"a memorable reading experience." (PW) Random, 1983.

Hopkirk, Peter   FOREIGN DEVILS ON THE SILK ROAD
The story of the sacking by Europeans of art treasures on the historic Silk Road—"adventure and intrigue. . . .fascinating story." (BP) U of Massachusetts Pr, 1984.

Isherwood, Christopher and Auden, W.H.   JOURNEY TO A WAR
Classic travel book; a travel diary with sketches of celebrities interviewed, sonnets by Auden. The book was the result of a trip to China in 1938, and the outbreak of the Sino-Japanese war. Octagon, 1972 (first published 1939).

Juliano, Annette   TREASURES OF CHINA
"Exciting and satisfying overview. . . . the essential features of Chinese culture." (LJ) Marek, 1981.

Lai, T.C.   VISITING CHINA
"For travellers who want to get the most out of their visit . . . accounts of twenty-four places of cultural interest." (Publisher) Hippocrene, 1983.

Leys, Simon   CHINESE SHADOWS
A "highly critical assessment" of present-day China's cultural values in comparison to its traditional art and architecture. (LJ) Viking, 1977.

Mathews, Jay and Linda   ONE BILLION: A CHINA CHRONICLE
By two media bureau chiefs—"observations on the Chinese ways of work, language, sex, marriage, medicine, cuisine, arts, humor . . . negotiating one's way in a country of one billion people." (BL) Random, 1983.

Meyer, Charles   CHINA OBSERVED
Knowledgeable text on Chinese culture in its various aspects, people, sights to see. Oxford U, 1981.

Morris, Edwin T.   THE GARDENS OF CHINA
History and philosophy of Chinese gardens, settings, views. Scribner, 1983.

Morris, Jan   JOURNEYS
Essays by a leading travel essayist that includes one on China. Oxford U, 1984.

Morton, W. Scott   CHINA: ITS HISTORY AND CULTURE
"Cultural history of China set in the fabric of its political development. . . . will make China take on more meaning for the traveler [and] give him a leg up on the Great Wall of Understanding that separates the traveler from the Chinese." (LJ) McGraw, 1982.

Namioka, Lensey   CHINA: A TRAVELER'S COMPANION
"Fourteen concise, casually—sometimes amusingly—written chapters" on many aspects of China today from food and housing to sports and urban/rural livelihoods, with appendices on Chinese history, by a native Chinese (now a U.S. citizen) based on her childhood and recent return visits. (PW) Vanguard, 1985.

Paludan, Ann   THE IMPERIAL MING TOMBS
Background reading for a visit to the Tombs. Yale U Pr, 1981.

Peck, Stacey   HALLS OF JADE, WALLS OF STONE: WOMEN IN CHINA TODAY
Oral history of contemporary Chinese women "of all ages, in occupations ranging from athlete to doctor . . . to university president. . . . a unique look at the lives of women whose position in society has been radically altered in the past 35 years." (PW) Watts, 1985.

Porter, Eliot and Jonathan   ALL UNDER HEAVEN: THE CHINESE WORLD
Text and photographs together "evoke the often breathtaking beauty of the Chinese scene . . . co-existing people, land, sky and spirit." (PW) Pantheon, 1983.

Rowell, Galen   MOUNTAINS OF THE MIDDLE KINGDOM: EXPLORING THE HIGH PEAKS OF CHINA AND TIBET
Goes beyond ordinary travel-adventure, blending past journeys of explorers, travelers and mountains with his own experiences. By one of the first to visit a remote area in China closed to the West for over thirty years. Sierra Club, 1983.

Schell, Orville   TO GET RICH IS GLORIOUS; CHINA IN THE 80s
The Westernization of China and the astonishing changes it is bringing, the about-face from Maoist ideology—"a riveting firsthand report" which appeared originally in the *New Yorker*. Another book by Schell, *In the People's Republic* (1977) was a first-hand view of living and working in China, as visitor, worker and resident of a Chinese commune. As a follow-up in 1981 came *Watch Out for*

Foreign Guests, about the social encounter between Chinese and Americans and the different country the author found on this second trip. *To Get Rich Is Glorious* is the last of this "trilogy." Pantheon, 1985.

Seth, Vikram   FROM HEAVEN LAKE: TRAVEL THROUGH SINKIANG AND TIBET
By an Indian, educated in the West, who speaks Chinese. The reader joins him on his "hitchhiking, walking, slogging" trip across China to India in 1981, spending nights in Chinese inns and truck parks—"the perfect travel book . . . a wonderful companion." The book won the Thomas Cook Award for travel writing in 1984. (BRD) Chatto & Windus, 1984.

Spence, Jonathan D.   THE GATE OF HEAVENLY PEACE: THE CHINESE AND THEIR REVOLUTION, 1895-1980
The interweaving of writings of three literary figures to relate events of Chinese history, from early enthusiasms and dreams to the "time when, dazed and shocked, they surveyed a later scene." (TBL) Penguin, 1982.

Terrill, Ross   THE CHINA DIFFERENCE
Essays by fifteen experts on various topics of social and cultural life. Har-Row, 1980. Also *Flowers on an Iron Tree* (1975), which captures the distinctive character of five cities of China, and *800,000,000: The Real China* (1971)—one of the best of books by China-watchers.

Theroux, Paul   SAILING THROUGH CHINA
By a leading travel writer—a 1982 riverboat journey down the Yangtze—"river lore . . . prose pictures of the cities and villages" along with observations on China and traveling companions. (PW) Houghton, 1984.

White, Theodore H. and Jacoby, Annalee   THUNDER OUT OF CHINA
Reprint of a book written in the 1940s, by two writers who were *Time* staff correspondents at that time—"China caught in the dual grip of revolution and war." (BRD) DaCapo Pr, 1980 (first published 1946).

Zewen, Luo   THE GREAT WALL
History, photographs, diagrams, maps, construction of a wonder that is on every traveler's list. McGraw, 1981.

Zhuoyan, Yu   PALACES OF THE FORBIDDEN CITY
"A magnificent introduction to Beijing's Forbidden City . . . its architectural and engineering marvels [and] myriad beauties." (BRD) Viking, 1984.

PERSONAL MEMOIRS WITH A SPECIAL SLANT

Allen, Steve   EXPLAINING CHINA
Three visits to China by the TV personality. Crown, 1980.

Bredsdorff, Jan   TO CHINA AND BACK
The author is a Danish novelist who went to China as a teacher in 1965, and

returned again in 1976. A "sad story of the disillusionment of an innocent abroad." (BRD) Pantheon, 1980.

Chen, Jack   A YEAR IN UPPER FELICITY
"Enchanting and warmly human portrayal of everyday Chinese village life." (BRD) Macmillan, 1973.

Dimond, E. Grey, M.D.   INSIDE CHINA TODAY
Memoir of a Kansas City doctor who has lived in China for fifty years, remaining after the revolution to become medical advisor to the Red armies. Norton, 1983.

Fisher, Lois   A PEKING DIARY
"A personal account of modern China" by a journalist's wife—"a wealth of detail rarely found in tourist accounts." (BRD) St. Martin, 1979.

Fraser, John   THE CHINESE
A dance and theatre critic for the *Toronto Globe* arrives at his new post in China just as the liberalization and wall-poster era begins. Summit Bks, 1980.

Gaan, Margaret   LAST MOMENTS OF A WORLD
Interweaves "recollection of Shanghai from the 1920s to 1950" [as member of a comfortable Eurasian family] with the collapse of China following the Japanese invasion, and civil war with the Communists. (BRD) Norton, 1981.

Jenkins, Peter   ACROSS CHINA
By the author of *Walk Across America* and *Walk West* (see "United States"). This is his account of a voyage into Tibet, China, Mongolia with only a Chinese-born interpreter—"high adventure . . . fascinating new people to meet." (Publisher) Morrow, 1986.

Johnson, Emilie   MY CHINA ODYSSEY
The author was a social worker in China during World War II and this is her personal memoir of a return trip to the new China in 1978—"a wee bit quirky, and a pleasure." (TBL) Silver Fox, 1981.

Kates, George   THE YEARS THAT WERE FAT: THE LAST OF OLD CHINA
Describes "with affection and insight" the author's days in Peking in the 1930s, and the Chinese people he knew. (AS) MIT, 1967.

Miller, Arthur   SALESMAN IN BEIJING
A "log of activities and thoughts during the six-week rehearsal period" for *Death of a Salesman* when, in 1983, the author was invited to Peking (Beijing) to direct his play at the People's Art Theatre. It was a success and "reaffirmed for Miller a vision of humankind that he has shared with the world, both in the original play and now in this more recent account." (BL) Viking, 1984. Also *Chinese Encounters* (1979), a photographic essay by Miller's wife, Inge Morath, for which he has provided the text—"a remarkably candid, illuminating and deliciously idiosyncratic look."

Mosher, Stephen W.   JOURNEY TO THE FORBIDDEN CHINA
This new book follows the author's *Broken Earth* (1983), which resulted from
field research as a sinologist and anthropologist and as part of an academic exchange program with China. That book was highly controversial and resulted in a
secret investigation by Stanford University where the author was a doctoral
candidate; result of the investigation was termination of his candidacy for the
doctorate.
Mr. Mosher came to the conclusion that the paramount myth of the Chinese
revolution is the tacit acceptance that, whatever its faults, the peasantry benefitted
from the revolution, thereby contradicting many more favorable reports on rural
China. A *New York Times* review says that "some people suspect that [Mr.
Mosher's difficulties] sprang [in part] from the fact that he was simply a dogged
and resourceful researcher who earned the animosity of the Chinese authorities
by uncovering material they preferred to keep secret." Free Press, 1985. There
follows below an entry for a book by Vera Schwarcz, also a Stanford doctoral
candidate, also in China in 1979.

Power, Brian   THE FORD OF HEAVEN
A memoir of Tientsin, in northeastern China, where the author grew up as child
of British-Irish parents. Michael Gesend, 1984.

Pruitt, Ida   OLD MADAM YIN; A MEMOIR OF PEKING LIFE
Memoir of the friendship between a medical social worker and Madame Yin,
along with her upper-class Chinese family. It explores family and values, and Peking life in the 1920s. "A new classic . . . a book to delight Old China Hands and to
fascinate those who never set foot in China. A good book to take along . . . to visit
the new China." (BRD) Stanford U, 1979.

Ryga, George   BEYOND THE CRIMSON MORNING
"Reflections from a journey through contemporary China" by a Canadian
playwright and novelist who led a group of Canadian tourists on a tour of China in
1977. Much about the author's view on politics combined with lively accounts of
the various tourist sites. (BRD) Doubleday, 1979.

Schwarcz, Vera   LONG ROAD HOME: A CHINA JOURNAL
Based on journals of the author's sixteen-month stint in China as a researcher
"characterized by sensitivity, humility, and discretion." (LJ) Yale U Pr, 1984. It
begs to be read in tandem with Mosher's *Journey to the Forbidden China* and
Broken Earth, listed above, as both writers were Stanford graduate students, and
both in China in 1979.

**Scott, A.C.   ACTORS ARE MADMEN: NOTEBOOK OF A
THEATREGOER IN CHINA**
An "authority on Asian theater reminisces about his first encounters with the
Chinese. . . . unique view of the actors, actresses and audiences of the time
[1940s]" and afterwards on his more recent return trip to China—"expressly
written for the general reader." (BRD) U of Wisconsin, 1982.

Spender, Stephen and Hockney, David   CHINA
Impressions of China by a poet-critic and a painter, as they visited communes,

factories, artist and writer colonies, parks, temples, roller-skating rinks, etc. Hockney provides watercolors and drawings. Abrams, 1983.

GUIDEBOOKS

Garside, Evelyn   CHINA COMPANION
This guide won the Thomas Cook Award for best travel guidebook in 1981. "Just what one would like . . . in a 'companion': knowledgeable . . . well-organized"—a combination of useful travel tips, history, background information by a woman who lived in China as a student, and then as wife of a diplomat, and has made dozens of short and long trips to China (BRD) FS&G, 1982.

Hildebrand, Volker   CHINA
One of a new guidebook series originating in Germany. Hippocrene, 1985.

Jennings, Penny and Russell   CHINA ON YOUR OWN
Thirty-one cities and tourist sites for the independent traveler, with supplements covering the Trans-Siberian railroad, trekking, bike tours, more. Bradt, 1983

Kaplan, Frederic M. and de Keijzer, Arne J.   THE CHINA GUIDEBOOK
"A mass of facts systematically presented with accuracy, charm, and excellent readability . . . would serve tourist, businessperson, and academic visitor equally well." There are special additional contributions by experts on schools, religion, arts, handicrafts, archaeology; and a phrase book "obviates the need for a separate phrase book." (BL) Houghton, 1985.

Letson, Barbara   CHINA, SOLO: A GUIDE FOR INDEPENDENT TRAVEL IN THE PEOPLE'S REPUBLIC OF CHINA
For the traveler who wants to tackle China on his/her own; intended to supplement (not replace) standard guidebooks. Jadetree Pr, 1984.

McCawley, James D.   THE EATER'S GUIDE TO CHINESE CHARACTERS
Food and menus made intelligible, by a linguistics professor—"as useful in San Francisco as in Beijing." (BP) U of Chicago, 1984.

Schwartz, Brian   CHINA OFF THE BEATEN TRACK
Directs students and other low-budget travelers to low cost hotels and restaurants, in the growing number of cities now open to foreigners. Information on train, bus and boat travel. Includes Mongolia and Tibet. St. Martin, 1983.

HISTORY

Barber, Noel   THE FALL OF SHANGHAI
The subtitle reads: "the splendor and squalor of the Imperial City of trade, and the 1949 revolution that swept an era away." A history of a city that was almost an independent British outpost—good adventure/history for the lay reader. Coward, 1979.

Boulnois, Luce   THE SILK ROAD
An account of the silk trade from earliest times to the twentieth century, based on writings of historians, reports of travelers and adventurers, literary references. Dutton, 1966.

Eberhard, Wolfram   A HISTORY OF CHINA
Considered one of the best one-volume histories. Revised 4th edition. U of California, 1977.

Hookham, Hilda   A SHORT HISTORY OF CHINA
"Well-written, objective and scholarly" text, surveying the history of China from early times to the 1970s. (LJ) NAL, 1972.

Hsu, Immanuel C.Y.   CHINA WITHOUT MAO: THE SEARCH FOR A NEW ORDER
"A brief, highly readable political history of China since 1976 . . . clear and insightful." (LJ) Oxford U, 1982.

Li, Dun J.   THE AGELESS CHINESE: A HISTORY
A "once-over-lightly introductory course in Chinese history." (BRD) Scribner, 1978. Also *Essence of Chinese Civilization* (1967).

Salisbury, Harrison E.   CHINA: 100 YEARS OF REVOLUTION
"Simply written yet sophisticated and wise story of China in revolt during the 100 years leading up to Mao's death." (TBS) HR&W, 1983.

Smith, Bradley   CHINA: A HISTORY IN ART
Overview of the pageant of Chinese art and history—a social and political history supplemented and expanded by photographs of relevant works of art. Doubleday, 1976.

Novels

Ballard, J.G.   EMPIRE OF THE SUN
"Gritty story of a child's miraculous survival" in a prison camp following the capture of Shanghai by the Japanese. (FC) S&S, 1984.

Barr, Pat   JADE
Saga of a child of English missionaries brought up in a "formidable Chinese household . . . the Chinese 'way' . . . brushes with concubinage . . . marriage to a proper English gentleman . . . opium." (FC) St. Martin, 1982.

Barrett, William E.   THE LEFT HAND OF GOD
An American pilot assumes the role of a Catholic priest to escape from the local warlord and his duties as a priest present a moral struggle. Queens Hse, 1976 (first published 1951).

Becker, Stephen   THE LAST MANDARIN
Adventure novel of an American sent, in 1949, to track down a Japanese war criminal in Peking. Random 1979.

Bosse, Malcolm   THE WARLORDS
China in 1927—a "saga that involves the reader totally in a scene, a time and place and a group of characters." (Publisher) S&S, 1984.

Boulle, Pierre   THE EXECUTIONER
Set in pre-Communist China—a dialogue between a Chinese doctor and a Western writer when a member of a hereditary family of executioners is, himself, sentenced to death. Vanguard, 1961.

Brent, Madeleine   MOONRAKER'S BRIDE
China at the time of the Boxer Rebellion is the setting; the plot involves an inheritance and a cache of emeralds. Doubleday, 1973.

Buck, Pearl S.   THE GOOD EARTH
Part of a trilogy that won the author a Pulitzer Prize, about a Chinese peasant family's rise to wealth and power, ending with a China in revolution and a now educated, Americanized generation. It is followed by *Sons* (1932) and *A House Divided* (1935). Other titles by Buck, set in China, roughly in order of publication date are *The Mother* (1934), *Dragon Seed* (1942), *Pavilion of Women* (1946), *Peony* (1948), *Kinfolk* (1949), *Imperial Woman* (1956). Crowell-Day, 1931.

Byrne, Donn   MESSER MARCO POLO
The fictionalized story of Marco Polo "as it should have been" and his love for Kublai Khan's daughter. (FC) Bentley, 1979 (first published 1921).

Chen, Jo-Hsi   THE EXECUTION OF MAYOR YIN
One of a collection of short stories of life in China, by a Taiwan native who studied in the United States, married a Chinese physicist, lived in China during its cultural revolution (1966-73) and finally returned to the West. Indiana U, 1978.

Chen, Yuan-Tsung   THE DRAGON'S VILLAGE
Autobiographical novel of the author's early years in the People's Republic and China's harsh effort to liberate its two-hundred-million peasants from thirty centuries of feudalism. Pantheon, 1980.

Ch'ien, Shung-Shu   FORTRESS BESIEGED
Translation from the Chinese of a comedy of manners set in China in 1937-39, on the eve of the Sino-Japanese War. Indiana U, 1980.

Cordell, Alexander   THE DREAM AND THE DESTINY
Historical novel of Mao Tse-tung's 6,000-mile march to begin the new Communist China, told through the experiences of a young medical student. Doubleday, 1975.

Cronin, A.J.   THE KEYS OF THE KINGDOM
Story of a Scottish priest sent on a mission to China in the early 1900s. Little, 1941.

Eden, Dorothy   THE TIME OF THE DRAGON
Saga of a British merchant family, from nineteenth-century Peking to the twentieth-century descendants living in London. Coward, 1975.

Elegant, Robert   MANCHU
Panoramic novel of the Manchu invasion of China during the Ming dynasty, seen through the eyes of a European serving the Christian cause as a soldier—"a delightful way to learn some Chinese history." (FC) McGraw, 1980.

Elegant, Robert   MANDARIN
A "family saga cum historical epic" of two merchant families, one Western, one Chinese, who are business partners—provides a "vivid picture of China and its people." (FC) S&S, 1983.

Gaan, Margaret   LITTLE SISTER
"The effect of changing times [1925] upon one Chinese-American family in Shanghai . . . unfolds through the alternative viewpoints" of a six-year-old, her seventeen-year-old cousin, and an adopted grandson who is a member of the Communist Party. (FC) Dodd, 1983.

Gaan, Margaret   RED BARBARIAN
First in a trilogy—"a good story mingling suspense and history." The hero starts as a thirteen-year-old sent to China in the 1840s to head a British tea company; he becomes involved in the opium trade and takes a Chinese wife. (FC) Dodd, 1984.

Gilman, Dorothy   MRS. POLLIFAX ON THE CHINA STATION
Another in the series in which the intelligence agent is a grandmotherly American. This time the plot involves her assignment to free a strategically important prisoner from the Chinese interior. Doubleday, 1983.

Gulik, Robert van   JUDGE DEE MYSTERIES
A unique series of suspense stories by a Dutch Orientalist and diplomat, set in China. Judge Dee is a master detective based on an extraordinary, but real, seventh-century magistrate—"addictive . . . well-realized settings . . . detective stories with a surprisingly modern air." Titles in the series include: *The Chinese Gold Murders* (1959), *The Chinese Bell Murders* (1959), *The Haunted Monastery* (1969), *The Lacquer Screen* (1970), *Poets and Murder* (1972), *The Red Pavillion* (1968), *The Willow Pattern* (1965). Harper, Scribner.

Hall, Adam   THE PEKING TARGET
An espionage novel involving British secret agent Quiller, moving from London to Peking to Korea. Playboy Pr, 1982.

Han, Suyin   TILL MORNING COMES
The marriage of a Texan girl and a Chinese physician—"rich in fascinating detail about the day to day life in China" from 1944 to 1971. (FC) Bantam, 1982.

Han, Suyin   THE ENCHANTRESS
The exploits of a set of twins having the ability to commune with nature—"well-told tale of life and love in the 18th Century. . . masterful blending of magic and science" as the pair become embroiled in adventures in China and Thailand. (FC) Bantam, 1985.

Hersey, John   A SINGLE PEBBLE
A trip up the Yangtze River, by junk, taken in the 1940s by an American engineer and seen in retrospect. Knopf, 1956.

Hsia, Chin-yen   THE COLDEST WINTER IN PEKING
From inside China, a contemporary political novel of "the coups and turmoil following Mao's death . . . a maze of created and real events and people." (BRD) Doubleday, 1979.

Hsiao, Hung   THE FIELD OF LIFE AND DEATH
An autobiographical novel of peasant life set in rural Manchuria during the Japanese occupation. Indiana U, 1978.

Hughart, Brian   BRIDGE OF BIRDS
The subtitle is, "a novel of an ancient China that never was"—set in the seventh century. The story leads two heroes through a series of adventures and encounters with characters from Chinese mythology and history. St. Martin, 1984.

Lao, She   RICKSHAW
A country boy with ambitions to buy his own rickshaw and prosper in Peking declines morally and physically and ends up carrying banners at weddings and funerals—a translation from the Chinese and a kind of moral fable of the Evils of Individualism. U Pr of Hawaii, 1979.

Lin, Yutang   LADY WU
Biographical novel based on the history of the rise of Lady Wu from chambermaid to Empress Dowager of China. Also: *The Vermillion Gate* (1953), *Moment in Peking* (1939). Putnam Pub Group, 1965.

Lord, Bette Bao   SPRING MOON
Saga of a Mandarin Chinese family, from 1892-1972, through the eyes of daughter Spring Moon; recreates the cloistered upper-class life of the early years on to modern China—history interlaced with romance and culture. Har-Row, 1981.

McKenna, Richard   THE SAND PEBBLES
Life on a U.S. gunboat in the 1920s that becomes involved in the Chinese rebellion. Har-Row, 1962.

Malraux, André   THE CONQUERORS
The Bolshevik nationalist movement in Canton. HR&W, 1976.

Milton, Nancy D.   THE CHINA OPTION
The heroine is a Washington newspaper correspondent in Pe-

king—"knowledgeable and suspenseful conjecture" of what could happen if the United States armed China with nuclear weapons. (NYTBR) Pantheon, 1983.

Montalbano, William D.   A DEATH IN CHINA
A murder mystery; an American professor tries to find out why a colleague dies suddenly—"excellent narration and thrilling plot . . . great insight into the character of the people." (FC) Atheneum, 1984.

Simon, Roger L.   PEKING DUCK
A "zany mystery-cum-travelogue" in which a private eye joins his aunt's group tour into China and becomes involved in the disappearance of an objet d'art from a museum in Peking. (FC) S&S, 1979.

Taschdjian, Claire   THE PEKING MAN IS MISSING
Reconstruction of a true incident in 1941 when the fossils of the Peking Man were packed in China, just before the Japanese invasion, never to be found again. The author provides her own explanation of what happened to them. Har-Row, 1972.

Ts'ao, Chan   THE DREAM OF THE RED CHAMBER
Novel of the early Ching period provides a "vivid picture of the social life of the times." (BRD) Greenwood, 1975.

White, T.H.   THE MOUNTAIN ROAD
One week in 1944 in China as an American major is "caught in the Chinese blockade . . . and the Japanese push for one last victory." (BRD) Sloane, 1958.

TRAVEL ARTICLES

ARCHITECTURAL DIGEST
1984 Jun "Glimpses of Global Treasures." Great museums in China, Greece and Russia. p. 218

HOUSE & GARDEN
1985 Dec "China Still Lifes." Taking in street scenes from Beijing to Shanghai and beyond. William Gass, p. 35

MS
1985 Mar "China Trip." With a delegation of women writers. Alice Walker, p. 51

NATIONAL GEOGRAPHIC
1985 Feb "Time Catches Up with Mongolia." Thomas B. Allen, p.242
    Sep "Sichuan: Where China Changes Course." Ross Terrill, p. 280
1984 Jan "The Queen of Textiles." Silk in China. Nina Hyde, p. 3
    Mar "China's Remote Peoples." Wong How-Man, p. 283

N.Y. TIMES SUNDAY TRAVEL SECTION (X)
1985 Feb 10 "Capturing Old Echoes in the New Peking." A stroller catches glimpses of an imperial past. Harrison E. Salisbury, p. 14

1985 "Options for Today's China Hands." Changed and improved situation for visitors. Stanley Carr, p. 14

"Chongquing Transformed." In the wartime Chinese capital, rice paddies and rickshaws have yielded to bridges and trains. Theodore H. White, p. 15

"Chinese Chops: a Signature in Stone." Signature seals—"chops"— one can have made up. Christopher S. Wren, p. 16

Mar 17 (Part 2, "Sophisticated Traveler") "7 days on the Yangtze," Barbara Goldsmith, p. 86

Jun 16 "Aboard the Kowloon Local," David Bragdon, p. 25

Sep 8 "Restoring the Great Wall of China." John F. Burns, p. 12

Sep 22 "In China, You'll Never Walk Alone." Lionel Tiger, p. 33

"What's Doing in Peking." John F. Burns, p. 10

Oct 6 ("Sophisticated Traveler") "Tips For the Sophisticated Traveler." Notes from the underground, subways from Paris to Peking, by *New York Times* correspondents (includes Peking). p 18

Nov 3 "Warming Up in Shanghai." Early morning exercise sessions in a city park provide a candid snapshot of Chinese life (and opportunity for contact with Chinese people). Barbara Selvin, p. 51

Dec 1 Shopper's World: "Buying Porcelain in China." Marion Kaplan, p. 6

1984 Jan 1 "A Slow Road Through China." Joining the wrong tour can bring on an MSG headache (maddening shopping groups). A.E. Hotchner, p. 19

Mar 4 "What's Doing in Shanghai," Christopher S. Wren, p. 10

Jun 3 "Where the Chinese Garden Blooms." Suzhou, near Shanghai, boasts some of the country's finest examples. Christopher S. Wren, p. 14

Jun 3 "A Tour of Old Shanghai." Though Westernized, the city offers traditional art and opera. Michael Kammen, p. 15

Jun 3 "Confucius Taught Here." The northern Chinese town of Qufu bears many reminders of the philosopher. Fergus M. Bordewich, p. 16

Jun 10 "China on Two Wheels." Bicycle tour of China. Tukey Koffend, p. 18

Sep 16 "What's Doing in Canton." Christopher S. Wren, p. 10

Sep 16 "Where a Clay Army Comes Vividly to Life." Archaeological finds in Xian. Michael Specter, p. 16

Oct 7 (Part 2, "Sophisticated Traveler") "Echoes of Old Shanghai." Christopher S. Wren, p. 22

Nov 11 "China Observed in Tianjin." Michael Kammen, p. 20

Nov 11 "Elusive Slopes of Manchuria." Despite the frosty peaks, skiing in China demands resourcefulness. Christopher S. Wren, p. 27

Dec 2 "New Hotels Bring Change to China." A great leap forward—into the pool. Orville Schell, p. 12

SUNSET

1985 Feb "China's Countryside, the Great Wall, Yangtze River Valley . . . On a Bike." p. 74

TRAVEL & LEISURE

1985 Feb "The Mystique of Macau." Neighbor to Hong Kong, this exotic Portuguese enclave is now a stop on the road to China. Charles N. Barnard, p. 95

"Visiting China from Macau." Sherbourne E. McGrath, p. 102

1985 Apr "The World Between Hong Kong and China." Intriguing one-day tours of the New Territories. Michael J. Weber, p. 172
1984 Jan "The New Ease of Getting into China." Canton. Fred Ferretti, p. 36

TRAVEL/HOLIDAY
1985 Sep "Beijing—Venturing into the Forbidden City." William Cross, p. 46
       Nov "Guardians of the Ruler of Q in China's Terra-cotta Army." William Cross, p. 6
1984 Jan "China Independently." Leaving the groups behind. Carol Goldsmith, p. 8
       Jan "Concerning Food and Wine—Beyond China's Great Wall." Robert L. Balzer, p. 42

HONG KONG AND MACAU

See also books listed under "China."

Series Guidebooks (See Appendix 1)

Baedeker: Hong Kong
Berlitz: Hong Kong
Country Orientation Series: Update Hong Kong
Fodor: Hong Kong and Macau
Insight: Hong Kong
Lonely Planet: Hong Kong, Macau and Canton
U.S. Government: Hong Kong: Background Notes
                Macau: Background Notes

Background Reading

Elegant, Robert   HONG KONG
One of the Great Cities of the World series. Time-Life, 1977.

Han, Suyin   LOVE IS A MANY-SPLENDOURED THING
Autobiography that inspired the movie and song of the same name—a Eurasian woman doctor's love affair with an English newspaperman in Hong Kong, in 1949. Little, 1952.

Hinton, A.   FRAGRANT HARBOUR
Aimed at giving the general reader and visitor a better understanding of Hong Kong; includes a short history of Macau. Greenwood, 1977 (first published 1962).

Hughes, Richard   HONG KONG, BORROWED PLACE, BORROWED TIME
"The best kind of cram course on a piece of the world increasingly turning up on everyone's itinerary." (BRD) Praeger, 1968.

Pope-Hennessey, James   HALF-CROWN COLONY
Historical profile for the general reader/traveler written by the grandson of a Hong Kong governor—Hong Kong society, the opium trade, the Japanese invasion in 1941, etc. Little, 1970.

Rand, Christopher   HONG KONG, THE ISLAND BETWEEN
"Deftly written, leisurely" book capturing various aspects of the Hong Kong scene—some of this reprinted book originally appeared in the *New Yorker*. (BRD) AMS, 1974 (first published in 1952).

GUIDEBOOKS

Nelson, Nina   HONG KONG, MACAO AND TAIWAN
Hippocrene, 1984.

HISTORY

Cameron, Nigel   HONG KONG, THE CULTURED PEARL
A history and contemporary account of Hong Kong—"articulate, richly illustrated account for the lay reader. . . . like a cultured pearl, its luster hides its flaws." (LJ) Oxford U, 1978.

Coates, Austin   A MACAO NARRATIVE
Heinemann, 1978.

Novels

Black, Gavin   THE GOLDEN COCKATRICE
A Scottish shipping executive is the hero of this novel of international intrigue set in Macau (Portuguese colony near Hong King). Har-Row, 1975.

Clavell, James   TAIPAN
"A novel of Hong Kong . . . and the most powerful trading company in the Orient" based there. "The backgrounds . . . surge with life and the plot is neatly dovetailed with history." (BRD) Atheneum, 1966.

Clavell, James   NOBLE HOUSE
Takes place in 1963—an action-filled plot that evokes "sights, sounds, smells and history of Hong Kong . . . multi-national companies . . . narcotics and gold-smuggling." (FC) Delacorte Pr, 1981.

Cohan, Tony   OPIUM
The Lin family—romance, intrigue, violence. S&S, 1984.

Davis, John G.   YEARS OF THE HUNGRY TIGER
"The major presence is Hong Kong itself . . . a vivid feel of where modern China came from." The plot is about a superintendent of police, his romantic involvement with a Chinese girl, and their role in the cultural revolution. (BRD) Doubleday, 1975.

Driscoll, Peter   PANGOLIN
A fast-paced suspense novel involving a jobless journalist who plots the abduction of an espionage agent to demand ransom from the United States. Lippincott, 1979.

Elegant, Robert   DYNASTY
Family saga of a Eurasian commercial house in Hong Kong, from the mid-nineteenth century through revolutions in the twentieth century. McGraw, 1977.

Gilman, Dorothy   MRS. POLLIFAX AND THE HONG KONG BUDDHA
Terrorists plot to take over Hong Kong. Doubleday, 1985.

Hall, Adam   THE MANDARIN CIPHER
An espionage novel—British secret service agent Quiller brings out a defecting British engineer. Doubleday, 1975.

McLachlan, Ian   THE SEVENTH HEXAGRAM
Historical events, life in Hong Kong, political turmoil in China are the background for this story of intrigue set in Hong Kong in the 1960s. The plot involves a disillusioned British reporter, his wife, a Communist hero and a pro-Communist editor. Dial, 1976.

Marshall, William   PERFECT END
One of the series of "Yellowthread Street" mysteries set around a police station in Hong Kong—"a spooky, riveting beginning" with the murder of six policemen, builds to a "thrilling climax during the height of a typhoon." (FC) HR&W, 1983. Other mysteries in the series include: *Sci-Fi* (1981), *Skulduggery* (1980), *Thin Air* (1978).

Mason, Richard   THE WORLD OF SUZIE WONG
The love story of an English artist and a Chinese prostitute. World, 1957.

Maybury, Anne   THE JEWELED DAUGHTER
A romantic suspense novel that evokes its exotic setting and centers around the fine jewelry trade. Random, 1976.

TRAVEL ARTICLES

GOURMET

1984 Jun "The Lone Marketeer: Hong Kong." Jay Jacobs, p. 50

Dec "Hong Kong Sans Chopsticks." Fred Ferretti, p. 64

HARPER'S BAZAAR

1985 Jan "Shopping Paradise: Hong Kong." Terry Malloy, p. 24

N.Y. TIMES SUNDAY TRAVEL SECTION (X)

1985 Jan 20 "A New Inn Rises from an Old Fort." Pousada reflects Macao's past. Michael Specter, p. 6

Mar 10 "What's Doing in Hong Kong." Ian Buruma, p. 10

Oct 27 "China's Shop Window in Hong Kong." William Schwalbe, p. 14

"A Fantasy Restored." Tiger Balm Gardens has been returned to its original extravagance. Fred Ferretti, p. 14

"Hong Kong, Made to Order." Bargains . . . the best Chinese cooking in the world. Marcia Seligson, p. 15

Dec 8 "45 Minutes from Hong Kong." Peng Chau offers a taste of the past. William Schwalbe, p. 19

1984 Jan 8 "What's Doing in Hong Kong." Frank Ching, p. 10

Jan 29 Fare of the Country: "Snake Soup Can Be a Charmer." Michael E. Specter, p. 6

May 13 "New Development in Old Hong Kong." East Tsimshatsui. Fred Ferretti, p. 12

Sep 16 Fare of the Country: "Where the Shark Fin Crowns the Meal." Eileen Yin-Fei Lo, p. 6

Oct 21 Shopper's World: "Suiting Up in Hong Kong." Michael Specter, p. 12

Dec 16 "Reawakening Memories of China's Taste." Despite Hong Kong's changing face, the cuisines that made the colony famous endure. Eileen Yin-Fei Lo, p. 12

SATURDAY EVENING POST

1985 Jan/Feb "Highlights of Hong Kong." Ted Kreiter, p. 90

SUNSET

1984 Nov "No-Frills Shopping in Hong Kong." p. 84

TOWN & COUNTRY

1984 Jan "Treasure Trove of the Orient." Shopping Hong Kong. Laura Bartlett, p. 82

TRAVEL & LEISURE

1985 Feb "The Mystique of Macau." Neighbor to Hong Kong, this exotic Portuguese enclave is now a stop on the road to China. Charles N. Barnard, p. 95

"Visiting China from Macau." Sherbourne E. McGrath, p. 102

Apr "The World Between Hong Kong and China." Intriguing one-day tours of the New Territories, Michael J. Weber, p. 172

Aug "Latest from Hong Kong." Fred Ferretti, p. 33

TRAVEL/HOLIDAY
1984 Jan "Hong Kong—a Bustling City Afloat." Jose Fernandez, p. 44

VOGUE
1985 May "Hong Kong: the Most Enthralling City." Jan Morris, p. 233

INDIA AND THE HIMALAYAN MOUNTAIN KINGDOMS

Series Guidebooks (See Appendix 1)

Fodor: India, Nepal and Sri Lanka
Frommer: India: $-a-Day
Insight: India; Nepal
Lonely Planet: India; Kathmandu and the Kingdom of Nepal;
    Kashmir, Ladakh and Zanskar; Trekking in the
    Indian Himalaya; Trekking in the Nepal Himalaya
Nagel: India and Nepal
U.S. Government: Bhutan: Background Notes
    India: Background Notes; Country Study;
    Post Report
    Nepal: Area Handbook Background Notes;
    Post Report

Background Reading

Ackerley, J.R.   HINDOO HOLIDAY
   The journal of a young Englishman who accepts a position with the maharajah of a small Indian state in British India—"like reading Kipling with more than a dash of Lewis Carroll . . . exotic and charming." (BRD) Viking, 1932.

Allen, Charles, ed.   PLAIN TALES FROM THE RAJ
   Anthology of reminiscences of India under British rule from Edwardian days to

1947; childhood memories, social life, "the daily round, the rains, hill holidays" and so on. (BRD) St. Martin, 1976.

Barr, Pat   SIMLA; A HILL STATION IN BRITISH INDIA
Evocative reminiscences and photographs of life in India, 1822-1903, of the ruling class. Scribner, 1978.

**Belfrage, Sally   FLOWERS OF EMPTINESS: REFLECTIONS
ON AN ASHRAM**
"An altogether remarkable essay on gurus and disciples" in which the author "keeps her wits about her [and] remains alert to the India beyond ashram walls, but loses her two close friends to the guru . . . an intelligent contribution to the travel literature of India." (BRD) Dial, 1981.

Blaise, Clark and Bharati, Mukherjee   DAYS AND NIGHTS IN CALCUTTA
A Canadian and his Indian wife, both novelists, return to India to record separate impressions of contemporary India—"like visiting . . . with a couple of intelligent, liberal, academic friends." (BRD) Doubleday, 1977.

Bohm, Robert   NOTES ON INDIA
"Attractive and highly personal commentary on life and travel in India today . . . well worth discovering." (TBL) South End Press, 1983.

Brata, Sasthi   INDIA: LABYRINTH IN THE LOTUS LAND
For "India-watchers" on India's economic system, caste system, film industry, temples, Westernization—"engrossing tour of an 'Oriental Sphinx' whose secret he unriddles." (PW) Morrow, 1985.

Carter, Lillian   AWAY FROM HOME
Interesting because it is the letters written by President Carter's mother while she spent two years in India in the Peace Corps after she had become a "senior citizen." (BRD) S&S, 1977.

Collins, Larry and Lapierre, Dominique   FREEDOM AT MIDNIGHT
An "insightful" account of the immediate events surrounding the independence of India in 1947-48, including interviews with Lord Mountbatten, Indian leaders, and those who murdered Gandhi. (LJ) S&S, 1975.

**Crowe, Sylvia, and others   THE GARDENS OF MOGHUL INDIA:
A HISTORY AND A GUIDE**
Thames Hudson, 1977.

Fatesinghrao, Gaekwad   THE PALACES OF INDIA
The exquisite residences of the *ancien régime* that ended in 1949. Vendome, 1980

Fishlock, Trevor   GANDHI'S CHILDREN
"Vivid insights into the present-day country and its people. . . . covers almost every imaginable topic—food, sex, education, sports, religion, medicine, money"

and more—a "compelling blend of history, social criticism, travel and commentary." (BL) Universe, 1983.

Forster, E. M.   HILL OF DEVI
A series of letters to the novelist's friends while on the trip to India in 1912-13, which provided background for *A Passage to India*. HarBraceJ, 1971.

Gandhi, Indira N.   ETERNAL INDIA
Survey in text and photographs by the Indian leader of recent history and the religious and spiritual life of the country. Vendome, 1980.

Godden, Jon and Rumer   SHIVA'S PIGEONS: AN EXPERIENCE IN INDIA
The two writers who have written many novels set in India (see under "Novels," below) in collaboration with a photographer, portray India "at its best, with artistry, sensitivity and intelligence." (BRD) Viking, 1972. Also *Two Under the Indian Sun* (1966), which are joint recollections by the sisters, of five childhood years in a small Indian river village—"the sights and smells of India, 1914-20, and leisurely domestic life of Englishmen in India."

Gray, Basil   THE ARTS OF INDIA
A general survey of Indian art, focusing specifically on Buddhist, Hindu, Jain, Islamic and modern art. (AS) Rizzoli, 1977.

Hillary, Sir Edmund,   FROM THE OCEAN TO THE SKY
Travel/adventure of the famous mountain climber and a group of companions on an expedition from the mouth of the Ganges, past Calcutta, to the Himalayas—"a fascinating and sympathetic view of the country, its people, and their religious heritage." (BRD) Viking, 1979.

Hobson, Sarah   FAMILY WEB: A STORY OF INDIA
The author shared, for three months, the primitive home of a twenty-six member joint family and a life "rigidly constricted by poverty and tradition." (PW) Academy Chi Ltd, 1982.

Irving, Robert   INDIAN SUMMER
"Depicts the rich and ironic combination of persons and events that shaped the new capital [moved from Calcutta to New Delhi] in the twilight of the British Empire." (AS) Yale U Pr, 1981.

Kaul, H.K.   TRAVELLERS' INDIA: AN ANTHOLOGY
Oxford U, 1979.

Kaye, M.M., ed.   THE GOLDEN CALM
Fascinating reminiscences of a young English girl growing to womanhood in the dying Moghul empire, with illustrations by some of Delhi's best artists. Viking, 1980.

Lewis, Robin Jared   E.M. FORSTER'S PASSAGE TO INDIA
Examines his personal experiences in India and the parallels to his novel (see under "Novels," below). Columbia U Pr, 1979.

Lloyd, Sarah   AN INDIAN ATTACHMENT
An account of the author's two-year relationship with a Sikh, living with him in a village mud-brick dwelling, and in a hut on Sikh temple grounds—"disturbing yet enlightening look at . . . Indian village life with detailed background on the Sikh religion." (BL) Morrow, 1984.

Lord, John   THE MAHARAJAHS
An informal, readable, gossipy, account of the feudal princes and a review of the age of the Moghuls and the coming of the British. Random, 1971.

Maharajah of Baroda   THE PALACES OF INDIA
The historical evolution of each of the Indian states, and their palaces. Vendome, 1980.

Mehta, Gita   KARMA COLA: MARKETING THE MYSTIC EAST
She describes an India of "foreign guru seekers . . . eager for instant Nirvana. . . . It's as if Tom Wolfe has gone to India . . . reported through delightfully jaundiced eyes of an Indian woman [with] enough crazy characters, stories, and wild scenes here for several novels . . . hilarious." (BRD) S&S, 1979.

Mehta, Ved   WALKING THE INDIAN STREETS
A critique of India, combined with "the vacation adventures of a sophisticated young man" home, after graduation from Oxford, with an Indian poet classmate. (BRD) Little, 1961.

Mehta, Ved   PORTRAIT OF INDIA
"Immensely readable . . . sense of immersion in the sights, scents and sounds of India . . . people from high and low walks of life." (BRD) FS&G, 1970. Also *The New India* (1978) about the rise and fall of Indira Gandhi's new India.

Mohanti, Prafulla   MY VILLAGE, MY LIFE
The author is an architecture student who left his small village south of Calcutta, to study—"affords his reader a unique opportunity to experience the flavor and flux of life in village India." (BRD) Praeger, 1974.

Moorhouse, Geoffrey   INDIA BRITANNICA
British rule in India—"fresh, astute reconstruction of events, crisply written" with many illustrations. (BL) Har-Row, 1983. Also *Calcutta*, one of the Great Cities of the World Series by Time-Life (1972).

Moraes, Don   BOMBAY
One of the Great Cities of the World series. Time-Life, 1980.

Morris, Jan and Winchester, Simon   STONES OF EMPIRE
The buildings of the Raj. Oxford U, 1984.

Morris, Jan   DESTINATIONS; JOURNEYS; PLACES; TRAVELS
All four collections of travel essays by this leading travel writer contain essays on India: Delhi in *Destinations*; Bombay in *Journeys*; Darjeeling, Calcutta, and Kashmir in *Places*; India in *Travels*. Oxford U, 1984.

Murphy, Dervla   FULL TILT: IRELAND TO INDIA WITH BICYCLE
Reprint of the diary of a bicycle trek from Dunkirk to India via the Himalayas and Pakistan, by the Irish travel writer. Overlook, 1986 (first published 1965).

Naipaul, V.S.   INDIA: A WOUNDED CIVILIZATION
The author is a Trinidadian, of East Indian descent, who did not visit India until 1962. The book is a "mixture of history, literature and travel. . . . [why] India is trapped by its past and Hinduism." (BRD) Knopf, 1977. Also, an earlier book *An Area of Darkness* (1965), recently reissued, which tells of his "sentimental journey to the land of his forebears that ended in disenchantment." Random, 1981.

Newby, Eric   SLOWLY DOWN THE GANGES
A trip by the travel writer with his wife in 1963-64, by boat, rail, bus and bullock cart, following the Ganges from Hardwar to the Bay of Bengal—"description of the river . . . cities and villages . . . temples . . . people. . . . holy men of all varieties." (BRD) Scribner, 1967.

Panter-Downes, Mollie   OOTY PRESERVED: A VICTORIAN HILL STATION IN INDIA
Ooty in 1967, when many of its residents (only thirty European families remaining) "cannot bring themselves to live anywhere but this town in the Blue Hills of South India." (BRD) FS&G, 1967.

Rice, Edward   THE GANGES: A PERSONAL ENCOUNTER
An impressionistic tour of the river and its people, sprinkled with history. Four Winds, 1974.

Rothermund, Dietmar   INDIA
History, culture, people, geography, wildlife in text and photos. St. Martin, 1982.

Rowland, Benjamin   THE ART AND ARCHITECTURE OF INDIA
"A brief survey of the whole long history . . . of Indian art in India [and] countries influenced by" Indian art—Turkestan, Tibet, Nepal, Ceylon, Cambodia, Burma, Java. (BRD) Penguin, 1977.

Schiffer, Michael   LESSONS OF THE ROAD
See under "Middle East."

Sharma, B.N.   FESTIVALS OF INDIA
South Asia Books, 1978.

Theroux, Paul and McCurry, Steve   THE IMPERIAL WAY
A journey along the railroad lines of the old Raj, a route taken because "nothing has changed . . . for over one hundred and fifty years." Photographs with evocative description. (BL) HM, 1985.

Wiser, Charlotte V.   FOUR FAMILIES OF KARIMPUR
Chronicles three generations of four families in a north Indian village. (The

author and her husband knew the families over the past half century.) A "relaxed, readable and pleasantly personal book." (BRD) Syracuse U, 1978. Also (with William H. Wiser) *Behind Mud Walls* (1963).

GANDHI

Attenborough, Richard, ed.   THE WORDS OF GANDHI
"Conveys the simple eloquence of the man" through thematically arranged selections from his writings, compiled by the director of the movie *Gandhi*. Scribner, 1982.

Fischer, Louis   GANDHI
"Long, full, affectionate" biography by an American who knew Gandhi intimately. (BRD) Harper, 1950. Also *The Life of Mahatma Gandhi* (1983) and *The Essential Gandhi: An Anthology* (1983).

Richards, Glyn   THE PHILOSOPHY OF GANDHI
A cohesive summary of beliefs and ideas. Barnes & Noble, 1982.

Shirer, William   GANDHI, A MEMOIR
Shirer's recollections and impressions of Gandhi and India in the early 1930s when Shirer was a foreign correspondent—"compellingly insightful." (BRD) S&S, 1979.

THE MOUNTAIN KINGDOMS OF THE HIMALAYAS (NEPAL, BHUTAN, SIKKIM, ZANSKAR)

See also books on "India" above.

Background Reading

Bedi, R.   LADAKH: THE TRANS-HIMALAYAN KINGDOM
Roli Pbns, 1981.

Bishop, John M. and Hawes, Naomi   AN EVER-CHANGING PLACE
A year among snow monkeys and Sherpas in the Himalayas, living in a Nepalese village—rituals, culture, everyday routine. S&S, 1978.

Coburn, Broughton   NEPALI AAMA: PORTRAIT OF A NEPALESE HILL WOMAN
The author was a tenant of "Aama" while working as a science teacher in a Nepal village. The book is an "intimate portrait of the village . . . rich in details of family life, folk medicine, religion, agricultural and housekeeping practices." (BRD) Ross-Erikson, 1982.

Cooke, Hope   TIME CHANGE
Autobiography of the American girl who became queen of Sikkim (now annexed by India)—a unique viewpoint of this tiny country. Berkley Bks, 1982.

Downs, Hugh R.   RHYTHMS OF A HIMALAYAN VILLAGE
Text and photographs present a "glimpse into the life of a remote Sherpa village in Nepal." (LJ) Harper, 1980.

Farwell, Byron   THE GURKHAS
History of the legendary fighting men from tribes of Nepal—"traditions, customs, family structure, national character . . . the love affair of the Gurkhas with the British army." (PW) Norton, 1984.

Gibbons, Robert and Ashford, Bob   THE KINGDOMS OF THE HIMALAYAS: NEPAL, SIKKIM, & BHUTAN
Written by a guide, and a specialist in natural history who is also an expert climber. "Short history of the region . . . ethnic groups and their way of life, the natural history, national parks." (Publisher) Hippocrene, 1983.

Gurung, K. K.   HEART OF THE JUNGLE: ROYAL CHITWAN NATIONAL PARK
Andre Deutsch, 1984.

Hitchcock, John   A MOUNTAIN VILLAGE IN NEPAL
HR&W, 1980.

Matthiessen, Peter   THE SNOW LEOPARD
"Radiant and deeply moving account of an expedition to Nepal"—a combination of "anthropological and natural history writing with old-fashioned adventure, plenty of introspection." (BRD) Viking, 1978.

Murphy, Dervla   WHERE THE INDUS IS YOUNG: A WINTER IN BALTISAN
By a middle-aged, Irish, intrepid woman-traveler and writer—"beautifully responsive to environment . . . sometimes exceedingly funny." (BRD) J. Murray, 1978. Also *Waiting Land: A Spell in Nepal* (1969) about her seven months in Pokhara.

Peissel, Michel   ZANSKAR: THE HIDDEN KINGDOM
The author is a French anthropologist and adventurous traveler, who speaks Tibetan, and "Zanskar [as one reviewer said] must be one of the last places on earth about which it is possible to write a really old-fashioned traveler's adventure book . . . stunning views of the barren, lunar landscape, the monasteries . . . the shrines and people and monuments." (BL) Dutton, 1979.

Pommaret-Imaeda, Françoise   BHUTAN: A KINGDOM OF THE EASTERN HIMALAYAS
"An armchair traveler's delight"—photographs and text providing history, religions, everyday background information of life in the tiny "Land of the Dragon" in the Himalayas. (PW) Shambhala, 1985.

Schaller, George B.   STONES OF SILENCE: JOURNEYS IN THE HIMALAYA
"Human and scenic observations" of remote villages and increasingly rare animals. (BL) Viking, 1980.

Ullman, James R., ed.   KINGDOM OF ADVENTURES: EVEREST
"A gallant tribute to gallant men"—extracts from writings of men who attempted to climb Everest, put together "with understanding and skill" by a writer who has written novels about mountain climbers. (BRD) Sloane, 1947.

Unsworth, Walt   EVEREST, A MOUNTAINEERING HISTORY
Historical study of climbing expeditions to Everest from 1921 to 1978, and based on published and unpublished materials made available to the author by the British Alpine Club and Royal Geographic Society (which organizations sponsored the expeditions). "The writing style is superb . . . hard to put down." (BRD) Houghton, 1981.

GUIDEBOOKS

Casimaty, Nina, ed.   INDIA & NEPAL: A TRAVEL HANDBOOK
ILS, 1979.

Engstrom, Barbie   ENGSTROM'S GUIDE TO INDIA, NEPAL & SRI LANKA
Kurios Pr, 1985.

Hildebrand, Volker   INDIA-NEPAL
One of a new guide series originating in Germany. Hippocrene, 1985.

Leak, J.   INDIA: A PRACTICAL GUIDE
A pocket guide introducing India to travelers, and outlining its seven "touring" regions. Bradt, 1982.

Nicholson, Louise   INDIA: A GUIDE FOR THE QUALITY CONSCIOUS TRAVELER
Atl Monthly Pr, 1986.

Palmer, Paige   TRAVEL GUIDE TO NORTH INDIA
The author terms India "the bargain travel discovery of the 1980s." Pilot, 1980.

Richards, Sir J.M.   GOA
Vikas, 1982.

**Shearer, Alistair   TRAVELER'S KEY TO NORTHERN INDIA: A GUIDE
TO SACRED PLACES**
Introduction and guide to the three major religions, Hinduism, Buddhism, Islam—"unusual and intriguing . . . specific temples, palaces, shrines, traveling tips." (BL) Knopf, 1983.

**Williams, L.F. Rushbrook   A HANDBOOK FOR TRAVELLERS IN INDIA,
PAKISTAN, NEPAL, BANGLADESH
& SRI LANKA**
The twenty-second edition of this valuable guidebook—"complete beyond belief." The guidebook provides an overview of the region, information on visas, currencies, languages, best season to visit, expenses, lodging, and much more. (TA) Facts On File, 1982.

HISTORY

Barber, Noel   THE BLACK HOLE OF CALCUTTA
Reconstruction of events that led to the death of prisoners in the infamous "Black Hole," in 1756. Macmillan, 1982 (first published 1966).

Lannoy, Richard   THE SPEAKING TREE
Covers the whole range of Indian cultural history from prehistoric times to the death of Gandhi, relating India's history to its contemporary problems. Oxford U, 1974.

Watson, Francis   A CONCISE HISTORY OF INDIA
Concise and colorful history of the Indian peninsula, with many supplementary photos and maps. Scribner, 1975.

Wolpert, Stanley   A NEW HISTORY OF INDIA
A survey from earliest times to the present—intended for the general reader. Oxford U, 1982.

Novels

Alter, Stephen   SILK AND STEEL
A Eurasian and an English deserter try to drive out the British East India Company—"steeped in the history and lore of nineteenth-century India." (BRD) FS&G, 1980.

Anand, Valerie   TO A NATIVE SHORE
A young English career woman's marriage to an Indian doctor—"the struggle . . . between her loyalty to . . . Exmoor, which gave identity to her being, and [the] controlling environment of India, her husband, and his family." (FC) Scribner, 1984.

Arthur, Elizabeth   BEYOND THE MOUNTAIN (Nepal)
To escape the tragic memory of a mountain-climbing expedition in which her husband and brother died, the heroine joins a women's mountain-climbing expedition in Nepal—"a journey as the setting for a spiritual quest." (BRD) Har-Row, 1984.

Ball, John   THE EYES OF BUDDHA
An excursion to Nepal by black detective Virgil Tibbs helps solve a murder in Pasadena. Little, 1976.

Banerji, Bibhutibhushan   PATHER PANCHALI: SONG OF THE ROAD
An autobiographical novel of life in a Bengali village. Indiana U, 1969 (first published 1928).

Barrett, William E.   LADY OF THE LOTUS
Novel of a marriage that provides an understanding of the basis of Buddhism. Doubleday, 1975.

Bromfield, Louis   THE RAINS CAME
An "oldie" from which a movie was made in the 1940s—"diverse and interesting personalities . . . exotic detail" as a flood destroys years of work by an enlightened native prince. (FC) Aeonian, 1976 (first published 1937).

Cadell, Elizabeth   A LION IN THE WAY
India, through the eyes of a young British girl, in pre-World War II Calcutta. Morrow, 1982.

Cleary, Jon   THE FARAWAY DRUMS
India in 1911, as King George and Queen Mary are to be crowned emperor and empress—"vividly recreates the now-faded glory of the British Empire." (FC) Morrow, 1982.

Desai, Anita   CLEAR LIGHT OF DAY
The plot is concerned equally between the triennial visit of a younger sister and her diplomat husband to the family home near Old Delhi, and memories of the past the visit engenders. (FC) Har-Row, 1980. Also, *In Custody* (1984), "shattering and comic" novel about a college teacher who is asked to interview a famous visiting poet, and *Games At Twilight* (1980).

Desai, Anita   FIRE ON THE MOUNTAIN
The story of a girl's summer with her great-grandmother in the hill country, ending tragically with rape and murder—set in post-British India. Har-Row, 1977.

Drummond, Emma   BEYOND ALL FRONTIERS
"A historical romance for readers who like a lot of history with their love stories"—India in 1837, and the British invasion of Afghanistan. (FC) St. Martin, 1983.

Farrell, J.G.   THE SIEGE OF KRISHNAPUR
Historical novel of the Sepoy Rebellion in 1857, and an English civil servant's defense of his colonial outpost in Krishnapur. HarBraceJ, 1974.

Fitzgerald, Valerie   ZEMINDAR
Historical romance (based on the experiences of the author's grandmother) of a newly-arrived Englishwoman and an English overlord, set in India during the Sepoy Rebellion (1850s). Bantam, 1982.

Forster, E.M.   A PASSAGE TO INDIA
A modern classic reveals "gross misunderstandings, and the subtler misunderstandings" that arise among various races in India, and the reactions of two visiting Englishwomen to Chandrapore. (BRD) HarBraceJ, 1924.

Fraser, G.M.   FLASHMAN IN THE GREAT GAME
The picaresque hero is a secret agent, uncovering an Indian mutiny in 1857. Knopf, 1975.

Godden, Jon   AHMED AND THE OLD LADY
A novel/fable set in Kashmir during World War II. An eighty-year-old English widow indulges her wanderlust exploring the area with a young Indian servant and they come to know the best and worst of one another. Knopf, 1976. Also by this author: *The City and the Wave* (1954)—set in Calcutta; *The Seven Islands* (1956)—about an Indian holy man on an island in the Ganges.

Godden, Rumer   THE DARK HORSE
Tale of an exiled thoroughbred horse, its trainer, a millionaire horseowner, a shrewd nun, and an ex-jockey—set in Calcutta in the early 1930s, in which Darkie wins the Viceroy Cup. Viking, 1982.

Godden, Rumer   THE PEACOCK SPRING
The plot involves two girls sent to India to be with their diplomat father, where each becomes involved with an Indian—"vivid depiction" of the country. Viking, 1976. Other novels by Rumer Godden, noted for their evocative and sensitive rendering of Indian settings are *Black Narcissus* (1939), *Breakfast with Nikolides* (1942), *Kingfishers Catch Fire* (1953), *The River* (1946).

Han, Suyin   THE MOUNTAIN IS YOUNG
The Himalayan setting is the central force as an English wife has an affair with a native engineer. Putnam Pub Group, 1958.

Hanley, Gerald   NOBLE DESCENTS
A widowed Maharajah and a British colonial are friends and philosophize "on

ultimates" in a group of "clubby English relics . . . creating havoc as they resist the
new India." (FC) St. Martin, 1983.

Hoover, Thomas   THE MOGHUL
Based on the true story of Brian Hawksworth in the seventeenth century—"a
fascinating and skillful mixture of romance, history, and adventure." (FC)
Doubleday, 1983.

Hospital, Janette T.   THE IVORY SWING
The sabbatical year of a Canadian couple in south India—"vividly shows the
conflict between the West and the traditional ways of India" as a bereaved young
Indian widow fights for freedom, leading to tragedy. (FC) Dutton, 1983.

Jhabvala, Ruth P.   HEAT AND DUST
A woman and her granddaughter lead parallel lives—abandoning their English
husbands for marriage to Indians and life in a remote mountain village. Har-Row,
1976.

Jhabvala, Ruth P.   TRAVELERS
The effect of India on some young Anglo-Saxons looking for something in India
or themselves. Har-Row, 1973. Also, *The Householder* (1960) set in New Delhi,
and two books of short stories, *A Stronger Climate* (1969) and *How I Became a
Holy Mother* (1976).

Kaye, M.M.   DEATH IN KASHMIR
Revised version of a novel published in 1953. The intrepid heroine gets
entangled in a treacherous plot that endangers the whole free world when she
looks into a series of murders. The Kashmir setting comes exotically, enticingly
alive. (FC) St. Martin, 1984.

Kaye, M.M.   THE FAR PAVILIONS
Historical novel of an Englishman who serves as a secret agent, along with a
romantic subplot. Set in mid-Victorian India—"leisurely, panoramic . . . rich in
India." (FC) St. Martin, 1979. Also, *Shadow of the Moon* (1979).

Keating, H.R.F.   INSPECTOR GHOTE MYSTERIES
Inspector Ghote of the Bombay police is the Sherlock Holmes of a series noted
for authentic background and local color, in addition to being first-rate mysteries.
Titles include: *The Sheriff of Bombay* (1984); *The Murder of the Maharajah*
(1981); *Bats Fly Up for Inspector Ghote* (1974); *Inspector Ghote Draws a Line*
(1979); *Inspector Ghote Goes By Train* (1972); *Filmi, Filmi* (1977). Doubleday.

King, Francis   ACT OF DARKNESS
Set in colonial India in the 1930s, the story involves a dreadful murder of the
young son of an "exploitive" English father—"extraordinary tension . . . no light
interludes . . . relentless" novel of sex and death. (FC) Little, 1983.

Kipling, Rudyard   PLAIN TALES FROM THE HILLS
Short stories, first published in 1898. Doubleday, 1898.

Markandaya, Kamala   SHALIMAR
"Insights into the strange encounters of diverse cultures radically separated by a common history and language" in a plot that centers around the building of a twentieth-century resort—Shalimar—by a multinational corporation. (FC) Har-Row, 1983.

Markandaya, Kamala   THE GOLDEN HONEYCOMB
Turn-of-the-century India is the setting for this coming-of-age novel, of a maharajah's son. Crowell, 1977.

Markandaya, Kamala   TWO VIRGINS
Contemporary Indian family life—"love of land, custom and humanity pitted against India's agonizing evolution into the contemporary world." (FC) Day, 1973. Also, *A Handful of Rice* (1966), and *Nectar in a Sieve* (1955).

Masters, John   THE HIMALAYAN CONCERTO
A composer, on holiday in Kashmir, uses his search for folk music to assist Indian Intelligence investigate Chinese activities on the Himalayan border. Doubleday, 1976.

Masters, John   BHOWANI JUNCTION
An Anglo-Indian's dilemma in trying to identify with her mixed heritage; the setting is just prior to Indian independence. Viking, 1954. Two additional novels of the Savage family, preceding this one, are *Nightrunners of Bengal* (1951) and *Far, Far the Mountain Peak* (1957).

Menen, Aubrey   THE PREVALENCE OF WITCHES
A satire on life in Limbo (India), involving a Limbodian chief, a swami, English civil servants, and an American missionary. Scribner, 1948.

Mukherjee, Bharati   THE TIGER'S DAUGHTER
An Anglo-Indian returns to Calcutta after education at Vassar and marriage to an American. Houghton, 1975.

Mukherjee, Bharati   WIFE
Chronicle of an Indian girl's journey from a submissive life in Bengal to a hostile New York City environment. Houghton, 1975.

Narayan, R.K.   A TIGER FOR MALGUDI
One of a series of novels set in the small Indian town of Malgudi, written in English by a leading Indian writer, with all kinds of intriguing and delightful characters and diverse plots. Titles include: *Printer of Malgudi* (1957), *The Guide* (1958), *The Man Eater* (1961), *The Vendor* (1967), *A Horse and Two Goats* (1970), *Painter of Signs* (1976), *Malgudi Days* (1982). Viking, 1983.

Narayan, R.K.   THE RAMAYANA
A short and readable modern version of the Indian epic passed on by word of mouth through the generations. Viking, 1972.

Partington, Norman   MASTER OF BENGAL
The life and work of Robert Clive, soldier/administrator, in building the British Empire in India. St. Martin, 1975.

Peters, Ellis   DEATH TO THE LANDLORDS!
Story of wealthy landholders, set in southern India, who are victims of a terrorist group. Morrow, 1972.

Rama Rau, Santha   REMEMBER THE HOUSE
An Indian girl (the period is the last years of British occupation) tastes Western culture, but finds fulfillment in her own Indian traditions. Har-Row, 1956.

Rushdie, Salman   MIDNIGHTS CHILDREN
Story of 1,001 children born on August 15, 1947, in the first hour of Indian independence and, in particular, about the fortunes of Shiva and Saleem, switched at birth by a nursemaid and destined to be enemies. Knopf, 1981.

Scott, Paul   THE RAJ QUARTET
The story of British India from 1942-45—"racist, heroic, exploitative, doomed"—brought to life through a variety of compelling characters. The four individual titles are *The Jewel in the Crown* (1966), *The Towers of Silence* (1972), *The Day of the Scorpion* (1968), *A Division of Spoils* (1975). A postscript to the *Quartet* is *Staying On* (1977) in which "a few Raj derelicts" linger in India, with their servants, in a hill town. Morrow.

Sherman, D.R.   OLD MALI AND THE BOY
Story of a young boy growing into manhood while on a journey with the gardener. Little, 1964.

Singh, Khushwant   TRAIN TO PAKISTAN
Novel of the partition of India. Grove, 1956. Also, *Land of the Five Rivers* (1965)—stories from the Punjab.

Sivasankara, Pillai   CHEMMEEN
A small coastal village in India, in 1962, is the setting. An Indian girl breaks taboos by falling in love with a Muslim and brings disaster to the village. Har-Row, 1962.

Trollope, Joanna   MISTAKEN VIRTUES
The plain daughter of an English country parson is transformed by her new life in India. Dutton, 1980.

Weston, Christine   INDIGO
Story of four young people of French, Hindu, and British backgrounds that has been compared to *A Passage to India* for "authentic feeling for the country." (BRD) Scribner, 1943.

Wolpert, Stanley   NINE HOURS TO RAMA
The story of Gandhi told from the viewpoint of a militant Hindu, and a member of the group that assassinated Gandhi. Random, 1962.

Zelazny, Roger   LORD OF LIGHT
Set in India of the future [beyond the 1960s when the book was written], revolving around "the struggle for control of the mechanisms of reincarnation." (FC) Doubleday, 1967.

TRAVEL ARTICLES

CONNOISSEUR
1985 Sep "Royal India." An escapist's guide to the best of Rajasthan. Gita Mehta, p. 84

GOURMET
1985 Sep "Bombay." Doone Beal, p. 52
1984 Nov Gourmet Holidays: "Goa." Doone Beal, p. 42

HORIZON
1985 Nov "Museums of Rajasthan." Fabulous museums in this exotic Indian province. Jessica Harris, p. 18

HOUSE & GARDEN
1985 Oct "Garden of Gladness." Nishat Bagh, a 16th-century Mughal masterpiece in Kashmir. Elizabeth B. Moynihan, p. 140

NATIONAL GEOGRAPHIC
1985 Apr "When the Moguls Ruled." Mike Edwards, p. 463
"New Delhi: India's Mirror." Bryan Hodgson, p. 506
1984 Jun "By Rail Across India." Pakistan to Bangladesh. Paul Theroux, p. 696
Jul "The Forgotten Face of Everest" and "Conquest of the Summit." James D. Morrissey, pp. 71 and 79
Dec "Tiger! Lord of the Indian jungle." Stanley Breeden, p. 748
"The Unknown Giants." Sperm and blue whales in the Indian Ocean. Hal Whitehead, p. 774

N.Y. TIMES SUNDAY TRAVEL SECTION (X)
1985 Jan 6 "Skiing Kashmir's Slopelets." James Traub, p. 9
Jun 9 Fare of the Country: "A Cook's Notebook on Dining in Delhi." Craig Claiborne, p. 12
Aug 11 "Tenderfoot Among the Sherpas." Facing the challenge of a modest trek. Steven R. Weisman, p.9
Sep 29 "What's Doing in Delhi." Steven R. Weisman, p. 10
Oct 6 ("Sophisticated Traveler") "Detours on the Indian Road." Delhi to Gwalior. John Russell, p. 89
1984 Jan 1 Fare of the Country: "Tandoori Artistry in Delhi." James Traub, p. 6
Mar 18 (Part 2, "Sophisticated Traveler") "At Anchor in Kashmir." Renting a houseboat on Lake Dal. Richard Reeves, p. 37
Jun 3 "Journey to the Top of the World." Testing limits on a Himalayan trek. Mary Herne, p. 20

Aug 19 "Rock-Cut Temple of the Many-Faced God." Sculptures on Bombay Island. Michael Specter, p. 13

Sep 16 "Following in the Footsteps of Siva." Dance throughout India. Barry Laine, p. 35

Oct 7 (Part 2, "Sophisticated Traveler") "India's Gift—Relearning the Importance of Seizing the Day." A.M. Rosenthal, p. 30

SMITHSONIAN

1984 Jun "A Fantasy Garden by Nek Chand." Epic sculpture kingdom. Bennett Schiff, p. 126

TOWN & COUNTRY

1985 May "Vis-a-Vis: India." Jennifer Kramer, p. 234

TRAVEL & LEISURE

1985 Apr "A Taste of Kashmir." India's sensuous and savory delights. Julie Sahni, p. 120

Jun "Princely India." A stirring journey to Rajasthan by way of the Taj Mahal. Christopher Hunt, p. 96

Sep "Deep in the Heart of Tiger Country." A jungle adventure at Tiger Tops in Nepal. Kitty Mackey, p. 118

1984 Sep "Memories of Nepal." The magic of the Himalayas. Kitty Mackey, p. 76

TRAVEL/HOLIDAY

1985 Sep "Cave Temples of India." A display of ancient treasures. Elizabeth Hansen, p. 16

1984 Jan "Offbeat Ski Resorts." Includes India. Ken Castle, p.46

VOGUE

1985 Nov "On Safari in India." Schuyler Ingle, p. 314

INDONESIA

Series Guidebooks (See Appendix 1)

Country Orientation Series: Update Indonesia
Insight: Bali; Indonesia
Lonely Planet: Bali & Lombok; Indonesia
U.S. Government: Indonesia: Background Notes; Country Study; Post Report

Background Reading

Attenborough, David   THE ZOO QUEST EXPEDITIONS: TRAVELS IN GUYANA, INDONESIA & PARAGUAY
Account of three animal-collecting expeditions. Penguin, 1983.

Covarrubias, Miguel   ISLAND OF BALI
Everyday life, art and culture, through the eyes of the American muralist and his wife. Knopf, 1973 (first published 1937).

Kayam, Umar   THE SOUL OF INDONESIA: A CULTURAL JOURNEY
A "sharply detailed travelogue" and photographs show how the country's traditional arts are faring as Indonesia is industrialized. (PW) Louisiana State U Pr, 1985.

Lucas, Christopher   INDONESIA IS A HAPPENING
Highly personal travel memoir by an irreverent British journalist. Weatherhill, 1970.

Lynton, Harriet R. and Rajan, Mohmi   THE DAYS OF THE BELOVED
Hahbub Ali Pasha, one of Hyderabab's "splendid monarchs," is the focal point of this book of vignettes of those he ruled; an epilogue of contemporary Hyderabab pulls it into perspective. (LJ) U of California, 1974.

McPhee, Colin   A HOUSE IN BALI
A Montreal composer spent five years in Bali studying its native music and this is his account of daily life during this period. Captures the "charm and color of an alien way of life [with] the ability to put into words the movements of the dance, sound of the music . . . special quality of the people." (BRD) AMS, 1980 (first published 1946).

Naipaul, V.S.   AMONG THE BELIEVERS
Exploration of the life and culture of four Islamic countries (Indonesia, Malaysia, Pakistan, Iran). The author repeatedly finds in the very devotion to Islam the reason for the backwardness of these countries, and an expectation that the education and technology they need will come from alien lands. Knopf, 1981.

Pelzer, Dorothy W.   TREK ACROSS INDONESIA
A "charming travelogue of anthropological and architectural interest." (Publisher) Hippocrene, 1983.

GUIDEBOOKS

Dalton, Bill   INDONESIA HANDBOOK
A "pocket encyclopedia for the Indonesianist" that provides an enormous amount of cultural and anthropological background material, along with comprehensive information needed to travel independently in this "far flung archipelago." Updated and revised edition. Includes fold-out maps, information on

low-priced accommodations and eating places, special interest travel (caving, surfing, scuba diving, etc.), transportation through the cities, mountains, beaches and villages via bus, steamrail, horse and foot—and much more. (Publisher) Moon Pbns Co, 1986.

Greenfield, Darby   INDONESIA: A TRAVELER'S GUIDE
Volume 1—Java and Sumatra; Volume 2—Bali and East Indonesia. Oleander Pr, 1976.

Hildebrand, Volker   INDIA
One of a new series of guidebooks originating in Germany. Hippocrene, 1985.

McDermott, John W.   HOW TO GET LOST AND FOUND IN BALI
Part of a series of travel guides with a personal approach. Hippocrene, 1983.

HISTORY

See also histories of Southeast Asia under "Asia/History".

Dahm, Bernard   HISTORY OF INDONESIA IN THE 20TH CENTURY
Praeger, 1971.

Neill, Wilfred T.   TWENTIETH-CENTURY INDONESIA
"Historical play of . . . influences—Malayan, Indian, Muslim, Portuguese, British and Dutch" on the Indonesian archipelago. (LJ) Columbia U Pr, 1977.

Novels

Ambler, Eric   PASSAGE OF ARMS
An intricate suspense story, involving the shipment of arms to anti-Communists in Indonesia, Knopf, 1960.

Bogarde, Dirk   A GENTLE OCCUPATION
A Dutch outpost, just after World War II, is the setting for this novel with a varied cast of characters—British, Indian, Dutch, American. Knopf, 1980.

Dermout, Maria   THE TEN THOUSAND THINGS
A "gothic mystery set in a vivid tropic Eden . . . [of] almost exasperating in-directedness." (BRD) S&S, 1958.

Dermout, Maria   YESTERDAY
A novel based on the author's life in Java—"what it was like to be a child on a Dutch plantation in Java, fifty years ago." (BRD) S&S, 1959.

Hartog, Jan de   THE SPIRAL ROAD
Effects of life in the then Dutch East Indies, on a young and smug doctor. Har-Row, 1957.

Lofts, Norah   SCENT OF CLOVES
Story of an orphan who is raised by a sea captain and later sent to the Dutch East Indies as part of a complicated plot to marry her off to the idiot son of a wealthy planter—romance, suspense, local color. Doubleday, 1957. Also, a much earlier novel, *Silver Nutmeg* (1947), a romance with a complicated plot set on one of the Dutch islands.

Rubens, Bernice   THE PONSONBY POST
A cross between a thriller and a realistic novel in which a UN liaison officer is drawn into Indonesian politics and a guerrilla movement, by the death of two UN workers. St. Martin, 1978.

TRAVEL ARTICLES

NATIONAL GEOGRAPHIC
1985 Jun "In the Shadow of Krakatau." Return of Java's wildlife (Ujon Kulon National Park). Dieter and Mary Plage, p. 750

N.Y. TIMES SUNDAY TRAVEL SECTION (X)
1985 Sep 22 "Flickering theater of myths." Shadow puppets. Suzanne M. Charle, p. 16
1984 Mar 25 Shopper's World: "Jakarta—Indonesia's Treasure Trove." Gunilla Knutsson, p. 6
       May 20 "The Dance of Jogjakarta." The many arts (cultural primacy of this Indonesian city). Michael Specter, p. 18
       Dec 9 "Rekindling Memories of Jakarta." Bernard Kalb, p. 14
       "A Batik of Temples and Palaces." In central Java, modern ways coexist with ancient artifacts. Suzanne M. Charles, p. 15
       "Exploring an Island Nation." Suzanne M. Charles, p. 16

SUNSET
1985 May "Indonesian Adventure . . ." Rituals and culture in Tanah Toraja, p. 80

TRAVEL & LEISURE
1985 Dec "Bali: on the World's Most Exotic Cruise." Ila Stanger, p. 82

TRAVEL/HOLIDAY
1985 Apr "Reliving the Stone Age in Indonesia." Norman Lobsenz, p. 132

JAPAN

Series Guidebooks (See Appendix 1)

Baedeker: Japan; Tokyo
Country Orientation Series: Update Japan

Fisher: Japan
Fodor: Japan; Tokyo and Vicinity, Budget Japan
Lonely Planet: Japan
Nagel: Japan
U.S. Government: Japan: Background Notes; Country Study; Pocket
Guide; Post Report

Background Reading

Benedict, Ruth   THE CHRYSANTHEMUM AND THE SWORD
Examines the Japanese psyche in lay language—"the love of beauty, order and harmony vs. the neurotic obsession with domination, power, and one-upmanship." (BRD) NAL, 1967.

Buruma, Ian   BEHIND THE MASK
The subtitle reads: "on sexual demons, sacred mothers, transvestites, gangsters, drifters and other Japanese cultural heroes." Japanese beliefs that are different from those of the West, as reflected in Japanese popular culture (plays, TV, movies, etc.); written by a British journalist who lives in Japan, offers . . . an illuminating, readable study of our Far Eastern friend and foe." (BL) Pantheon, 1984.

Chiang, Yee   THE SILENT TRAVELLER IN JAPAN
An "intensely personal introduction to Japan . . . through the eyes of an observant, erudite, empathetic artist." (LJ) Norton, 1972.

**Christopher, Robert C.   THE JAPANESE MIND: THE GOLIATH
EXPLAINED**
"Modern journalism in the best sense of the word. . . . provides for the American reader a fine and thorough introduction to all things Japanese, from politics to diplomacy to everyday life." (Pub ad) Linden Pr, 1983.

Cooper, Michael, ed.   THEY CAME TO JAPAN
"An anthology of European reports on Japan, 1543-1640. . . . drama and humor, small details and the broad sweep of history" as seen from selections out of diaries, journals, letters, and books by Europeans. (BRD) U of California, 1981 (first published 1965).

**Courdy, Jean C.   THE JAPANESE: EVERYDAY LIFE IN
THE EMPIRE OF THE RISING SUN**
By a French journalist and political scholar using "his personal experiences to illuminate . . . how the Japanese have come to terms both with the technological and social changes of the post-World War II era and with the ancient traditions of their civilization. . . . intriguing look at today's Japan." (BL) Har-Row, 1984.

Dazai, Osamu   RETURN TO TSUGARU: TRAVELS OF A PURPLE TRAMP
"An often amusing and altogether enchanting account of a trip Dazai made in

1944 to his birthplace. . . . something both less and much more than [a] travel guide. . . . mix of reminiscences, stories, touristy data, literary comment and description of [and conversation with] memorable locals." Tsugaru Province is in northern Honshu. Dazai was a popular novelist in pre-World War II Japan who killed himself in 1948. (PW) Kodansha, 1985.

Dore, Ronald P.   SHINOHATA: A PORTRAIT OF A JAPANESE VILLAGE
A delightful portrait of one Japanese village with fascinating details of customs, and the changes over the postwar years. Putnam Pub Group, 1979.

Fields, George   FROM BONSAI TO LEVI'S
Subtitle: When West meets East: an insider's surprising account of how the Japanese live. Description of the Japanese as consumers, by an Australian born in Japan engaged in a Japanese market research company, "who keenly comprehends the Japanese national character. . . . edifying, even entertaining." (BL) Macmillan, 1984.

Fraser, Mary and Cortazzi, Hugh   A DIPLOMAT'S WIFE IN JAPAN
An abridged version of the original published in 1899. Letters describing turn-of-the-century Japan—"very readable. . . . with anecdotes that provide fascinating contrasts and continuities with the Japan of today." (BRD) Weatherhill, 1982.

Gibney, Frank   JAPAN: THE FRAGILE SUPERPOWER
An "excellent introduction to present day Japan. . . . a tour de force of popular interpretation." (BRD) NAL, 1980. Also *Five Gentlemen of Japan* (1953), a postwar perspective foreshadowing the changes the nation was about to go through.

Hane, Mikiso   PEASANTS, REBELS, AND OUTCASTS
The "underside" of Japan, "revealing . . . [a] somewhat shocking" picture of the life of Japanese peasants and the urban poor from 1868 to the end of World War II. (PW) Pantheon, 1982.

Hearn, Lafcadio   EXOTICS AND RETROSPECTIVES
The American writer went to Japan in 1890 and stayed the rest of his life. C.E. Tuttle, 1971 (first published 1898). Other writings that came out of that experience include: *Japan: An Attempt at Interpretation* (1905), *Glimpses of Unfamiliar Japan* (1894), *Gleanings in Buddha-Fields* (1897).

Hoover, Thomas   ZEN CULTURE
The "all-pervasive influence on the total culture of Japan. . . . described in an easy, informative way." (LJ) Random, 1978.

Kamata, Satoshi   JAPAN IN THE PASSING LANE
An "insider's shocking account of life in a Japanese auto factory." Pantheon, 1982.

Kawasaki, Ichiro   JAPAN UNMASKED
"Informal, entertaining, witty . . . chat" about the negative side of the Japanese

psyche—"sense of inferiority, passivity and conformism, corruption of politics, absence of a sense of public responsibility," and so on. Written by an "intelligent and articulate Japanese . . . capable of writing objectively and critically about his own society." (BRD) C.E. Tuttle, 1969.

MacIntyre, Michael   THE SHOGUN INHERITANCE
A coffee-table book "written to build on the BBC television series." See also the Clavell novel, under "Novels," below, and *Learning from Shogun* under "History," below. (BRD) A&W, 1982.

Morley, John D.   PICTURES FROM THE WATER TRADE: ADVENTURES OF A WESTERNER IN JAPAN
"Japan . . . approached from an entirely different angle." It is written in the third person (through a young man named Boon), yet it is nonfiction. Boon decides to look for the small particulars—clotheslines, business cards, "the minute-by-minute routine of an elderly married couple," and so on. "Mr. Morley is one of those rare travelers who manages truly to enter the heart of a foreign territory. Rarer still is his ability to take the rest of us along with him." (NYTBR) Atl Monthly Pr, 1985.

Morris, Ivan   THE WORLD OF THE SHINING PRINCE
Intended to tell of the realities underlying *Tale of the Genji* (see "Novels," below). Penguin, 1979. Also *The Pillow Book of Sei Shonagun* (1971), diary of a lady-in-waiting at court in pre-1000 A.D., edited by Morris.

Norbury, Paul, ed.   INTRODUCING JAPAN
Essays by leading Japanese and Western authors on various aspects of Japan—history, way of life, its creative world, food and drink, seen and heard. St. Martin, 1978.

Paffrath, James D.   HOW DO YOU THINK JAPAN
A visual treat (that) "caught the flavor beautifully . . . places, faces, events and facts not readily found in guidebooks or through tour bus windows." (Publisher) J.P. Pubs, 1982.

Passin, Herbert   ENCOUNTER WITH JAPAN
"The author's love affair with the country . . . nostalgia for the quality of life before transformation" into today's Japan. (NYTBR) Har-Row, 1983.

Popham, Peter   TOKYO: THE CITY AT THE END OF THE WORLD
People, physical setting, architecture, with a sociological and cultural slant—"impressions of delight, astonishment, and horror . . . in a style that brings Tokyo to life." (BL) Kodansha, 1985.

Reischauer, Edwin O.   THE JAPANESE
Written by a leading scholar of Japan, and "as a friend and longtime observer of the Japanese. . . . like a long, quiet and informal chat." (BRD) Harvard U Pr, 1977. Also *Japan: The Story of a Nation* (1981).

Smith, R.J.   KURUSU: THE PRICE OF PROGRESS
Social change as reflected in the village of Kurusu, which the author first studied in 1951 and then again in 1975. He found the quality of life radically different. Stanford U, 1978.

Statler, Oliver   JAPANESE PILGRIMAGE
The author retraces an eighth-century pilgrimage by a Buddhist monk in a two-month circular trek to shrines and temples associated with Buddhism—a "re-creation of the priest's life. . . . history of medieval Japan. . . . the devotions of today's pilgrims." (BRD) Morrow, 1981. Also *Japanese Inn* (1962), a classic on Japanese life and customs.

Sutherland, Mary and Britton, Dorothy   NATIONAL PARKS OF JAPAN
A guided tour of twenty-seven parks, ranging from subarctic to subtropic—marine parks, mountains, waterfalls, crater lakes. Kodansha, 1981.

Taylor, Jared   SHADOWS OF THE RISING SUN
A critical view of the Japanese miracle. The author lived as a missionary's son in Japan, speaks fluent Japanese, and later became involved in the financing of Japanese industry. The book contrasts Japanese and American life with the point that these contrasts make it unwise and psychologically costly for America to adopt Japanese ways—"a very good overview of Japanese culture and society." (BRD) Morrow, 1983.

Tonaha, Sen'o   THE TEA CEREMONY
Kodansha, 1983.

GUIDEBOOKS

Barr, Pat   JAPAN
Batsford, 1980.

Bisignani, J.D.   JAPAN HANDBOOK
A practical guidebook intended to dispel "the myth that Japan is too expensive for the budget-minded traveler." It also provides a "cultural and anthropological manual on every facet of Japanese life" and encourages readers to seek out rural Japan, the mountains, fishing villages, beaches, nature reserves, mountain spas. (Publisher) Moon Pbns Co, 1985.

**Brown, Jan   EXPLORING TOHOKU: A GUIDE TO
                JAPAN'S BACKCOUNTRY**
Weatherhill, 1983.

Connor, Judith and Yoshida, Mayumi   TOKYO CITY GUIDE
Basic advice for tourists but also an exploration of the contemporary city and "what may be inscrutable to Occidental eyes." (BL) Kodansha, 1985.

Cooper, Michael   EXPLORING KAMAKURA: A GUIDE FOR THE CURIOUS TRAVELLER
Temples and shrines in an area near Tokyo. Weatherhill, 1979.

DeMente, Boye   THE WHOLE JAPAN BOOK
An encyclopedia of things Japanese. Phoenix, 1983. Also, by this writer, *Exotic Japan* (1976), *Reading Your Way Around Japan* (1979), *The Tourist and the Real Japan* (1966).

Demery, Leroy W., Jr. and others   JAPAN BY RAIL
Dedicated to encouraging tourists to travel by rail in a country with a remarkable dedication to rail travel. The Map Factory, 1985.

Hildebrand, Volker   JAPAN
One of a new series of guidebooks originating in Germany. Hippocrene, 1985.

Namioka, Lensey   JAPAN, A TRAVELLER'S COMPANION
"A practical crash course in contemporary Japanese culture. . . . well written and often humorous." Lists of things to do and see, where to stay and eat, customs, how to behave, visiting an inn, a bath, a home, etc. (BL) Vanguard, 1979.

Pearce, Jean   FOOTLOOSE IN TOKYO; MORE FOOTLOOSE IN TOKYO
Intended for the independent traveler—uses twenty-nine stops on the transportation system to tell what to see at each stop, suggested walking tours, maps. Weatherhill, 1976, 1984.

Plutschow, Herbert E.   INTRODUCING KYOTO
A "superlative" guidebook to Japan's most popular tourist attraction—history, cultural history, ancient customs and crafts. (LJ) Kodansha, 1979.

Popham, Peter   INSIDER'S GUIDE TO JAPAN
Off-the-beaten-track travel tips and tours. Kodansha, 1984.

Waley, Paul   TOKYO NOW AND THEN: AN EXPLORER'S GUIDE
"Divides the city into some 40 sections. . . . history [then] places to visit and things to see" with a star rating system—"above all this is a book about people, past and present. . . . Even people who aren't likely to visit Tokyo will be taken by this book." (PW) Weatherhill, 1984.

HISTORY

Beasley, W.G.   THE MODERN HISTORY OF JAPAN
Covers the one hundred years (1865 to the 1960s) in which Japan advanced from feudalism to post-World War II and modern Japan. Praeger, 1963.

Hall, John W. and Beardsley, R.K.   TWELVE DOORS TO JAPAN
"A basic and rounded view . . . of Japanese history and culture." Based on an introductory course on Japan at the University of Michigan. (BRD) McGraw, 1965.

Morton, W. Scott   JAPAN: ITS HISTORY AND CULTURE
McGraw, 1984.

Smith, Bradley   JAPAN: A HISTORY IN ART
"Rich and diverse history of Japan" as reflected in its art. (AS) Doubleday, 1971.

Smith, Henry D. and others   LEARNING FROM SHOGUN
Written by a professor at University of California in Santa Barbara, and others, as a learning extension of the novel that has caused so many to become interested in Japan. Its twelve chapters are written by Asian experts and illustrate how a historical novelist goes about comparing Japan and the West, mixing fact, fantasy, Utopianism and symbolism to promote the value system of the author. (Author) Japan Society of N.Y. (distributor).

Toland, John   RISING SUN: THE DECLINE AND FALL OF THE JAPANESE EMPIRE, 1936-45
"Popular history in the best sense of the term—accurate, interesting, lively." (BRD) Random, 1970.

Warshaw, Steven   JAPAN EMERGES: A CONCISE HISTORY OF JAPAN
U Pr of America, 1983.

Novels

Abe, Kobo   THE WOMAN IN THE DUNES
Probably the most well-known title by a leading Japanese author—story of a man, vacationing on the seacoast, who is captured by villagers and must live in a house being engulfed by the dunes. Other titles include: *Secret Rendezvous* (1979), *The Box Man* (1974), *The Ruined Map* (1969). Knopf, 1964.

Akutagawa, Ryunosuke   RASHOMON
A collection of short stories. Liveright, 1970.

Albery, Nibuko   BALLOON TOP
The plot concerns a Japanese young lady growing up in the early sixties and her contact with Americans, "hellish" examinations, liberation from her family, as she attends a Tokyo university—"exhilarating . . . often very funny." (BRD) Pantheon, 1978.

Chand, Meira   THE BONSAI TREE
A British girl's marriage to a Japanese man, and life in Japan. Ticknor & Fields, (1983). Another novel involving a Japanese-English marriage is *The Gossamer Fly* (1980).

Chand, Meira   LAST QUADRANT
A British doctor who runs an orphanage in Kobe adopts the daughter of a prostitute who reclaims the child twenty years later—everything is resolved in the wake of a typhoon. Ticknor & Fields, 1982.

Clavell, James   SHOGUN
Meeting of the East and West in seventeenth-century Japan, through a British sea pilot and his crew and a Japanese feudal lord—"creates a world, people, customs, settings, needs and desires . . . history infused with fantasy." (BRD) Atheneum, 1975.

Coppel, Alfred   THE BURNING MOUNTAIN: A 1945 NOVEL OF THE INVASION OF JAPAN
What would have happened if the atomic bomb had failed and an American invasion launched instead—a "mix of history and fiction based on actual U.S. and Japanese contingency plans . . . excellent historical foundations [and] grasp of Japanese culture." (FC) HarBraceJ, 1983.

Duncan, Robert   DRAGONS AT THE GATE
A suspense story that involves a Tokyo-based CIA financial analyst. NAL, 1976.

Duncan, Robert L.   TEMPLE DOGS
Suspense novel of big business with a complex plot involving a computer-mad general, a multinational company, and the murder of a South Korean colonel. Morrow, 1977.

Endo, Shusaku   WONDERFUL FOOL
A French penpal appears in Japan and gets himself and his hosts in trouble because of his pacifism and naiveté—"sprightly, picaresque tale." (FC) Har-Row/ Kodansha, 1983 (first published 1959).

Endo, Shusaku   THE SAMURAI
The plight of a seventeenth-century Spanish missionary who wants to preach Catholicism—by Japan's distinguished Roman Catholic novelist. Har-Row, 1982. Other novels by this writer include: *The Sea and Poison* (1980), *Silence* (1979), *Volcano* (1980), *When I Whistle* (1979).

Gardner, Mona   MIDDLE HEAVEN
Japan before and shortly after World War II—"absorbing . . . fascinating . . . perceptive portrait of the Japanese way of life." (BRD) Doubleday, 1950.

Ibuse, Masuji   BLACK RAIN
This novel, based on factual material from diaries and personal observations, tells about a day in the life of several Japanese as radioactive rain falls following Hiroshima. Kodansha, 1969.

Kawabata, Yasunari   SNOW COUNTRY and THOUSAND CRANES
Kawabata won the Nobel Prize in literature for these novels. Knopf, 1969. Other titles by the same author include: *The Lake* (1974), *The Master of Go* (1972), *The Sound of the Mountains* (1970), *Beauty and Sadness* (1975).

Kita, Mario   THE HOUSE OF NIRE
Along with *The Fall of the House of Nire*, both published originally in one book in 1964. Saga of three generations of a Japanese family between World Wars I and II, ending when Pearl Harbor is bombed. Kodansha, 1985.

Matsubara, Hisako   SAMURAI
Novel of a marriage, set in turn-of-the-century provincial Japan, and the lives of the wife in Japan, and her husband in America as an immigrant—"lovely . . . as a Japanese flower arrangement . . . brilliant evocation of Japanese culture." (BRD) Times Bks, 1980.

Melville, James   THE NINTH NETSUKE
Detective Superintendent Otani, using his wife as a cover, registers in a notorious Kobe hotel where there's been a murder, and she provides a critical clue by finding an ivory figurine (netsuke). "The details of Japanese culture, history and daily life . . . create a very satisfying and intriguing mystery." (FC) St. Martin, 1982. Other mysteries set in Japan by Melville are: *Sayonara, Sweet Amaryllis* (1984), *The Chrysanthemum Chain* (1982) and *A Sort of Samurai* (1981).

Michener, James A.   SAYONARA
An American Air Force major falls in love with a Japanese girl. Random, 1954.

Mishima, Yukio   THE SEA OF FERTILITY
A cycle of four novels: *Spring Snow* (1972), *Runaway Horses* (1973), *The Temple of Dawn* (1973), and *The Decay of the Angel* (1974). This series begins in turn-of-the-century Tokyo and ends with modern industrial Japan—"an absolute evocation of a Japanese way of life that is completely intelligible." (FC) Knopf, 1972. Also by Mishima, *After the Banquet* (1963), *Forbidden Colors* (1968), *The Sound of the Waves* (1956), *The Temple of the Golden Pavilion* (1959).

Morris, Edita   THE FLOWERS OF HIROSHIMA
Hiroshima thirteen years after the bomb—the horrors of the nuclear age told in human terms. Viking, 1959.

Murasaki, Shikibu   THE TALE OF GENJI
Considered the greatest single work in Japanese literature, and possibly the world's first novel—a "vast chronicle of court life" of the Heian period that "centers on the career of Prince Genji and the women with whom he was associated." (FC) Knopf, 1976 (dating from tenth-eleventh centuries).

Mydans, Shelley   THE VERMILION BRIDGE
Historical novel of eighth-century Japan evokes a faraway time and place—palace intrigue, conflicts between Shintoism and Buddhism, effects of Chinese political and cultural influences. Doubleday, 1980.

Raucat, Thomas   HONORABLE PICNIC
A "comedy of manners . . . quaint, saucy, provocative" involving a family outing in the country—"speaks volumes about what [the Japanese] are, who they are and where they are." (BRD) Tuttle, 1972 (first published 1927).

Roberts, James   THE Q DOCUMENT
Suspense story of an American professor in Japan, hired to decipher the early Christian "Q" document. Morrow, 1964.

Skimin, Robert   CHIKARA!
The subtitle reads: "A sweeping novel of Japan and America from 1907 to 1983."
Three generations of a Japanese family, those in Japan and those who emigrate to
America—"personal dramas are played out against a canvas that includes the rise
of . . . militarism in Japan and anti-Japanese sentiments . . . the Tokyo earthquake . . .
the Depression, and two world wars. . . . plenty of well-researched history and
exotic details." (FC) St. Martin, 1984.

Tanizaki, Junichiro   THE MAKIOKA SISTERS
Four sisters of upper middle-class background, but insufficient money, facing a
changing Japanese society. Knopf, 1957 (first published 1949). Also, *Diary of a
Mad Old Man* (1965), *Some Prefer Nettles* (1955), *Seven Japanese Tales* (1963).

Van de Wetering, Janwillem   THE JAPANESE CORPSE
A Japanese criminal family involved in smuggling art and heroin is the basis for
this mystery solved by the Dutch detective team of De Gier and Grijpstra—"an
irresistible romp . . . a superb mystery." Houghton, 1977.

Van Lustbader, Eric   THE NINJA
The Ninja are an ancient cult of Japanese assassins whose powers verge on the
supernatural—exotic adventures. The sequel, *The Miko* (1984), involves a
Japanese-American in Tokyo to negotiate a merger who becomes involved (in his
other identity as "the Ninja") in solving a series of murders. (FC) M. Evans, 1980.

TRAVEL ARTICLES

ARCHITECTURAL DIGEST
1984 May "Designer's Travel Notes: Tokyo's Enduring Pockets of Tradition."
Annette Juliano, p. 292

BON APPETIT
1984 Feb "Japan's Inland Sea." Welcoming inns, a serene tradition and superb
seafood. Patricia Brooks, p. 104

CONNOISSEUR
1985 Apr "Tokyo: the City of Villages." Donald Richie, p. 102
"Tokyo Made Easy: A Selective Guide to the City's Pleasures." Terry Trucco,
p. 106
"Grand Resort: The Old and New Japan Meet at Karuizawa." Two hours from
Tokyo. Donald W. George, p. 116

HARPER'S BAZAAR
1984 Sep "The Traditions of Kyoto." A city of ancient temples and handicrafts.
Linda Olle, p. 34

NATIONAL GEOGRAPHIC
1984 Apr "Izu Oceanic Park." Eugenie Clark, p. 465
Jun "Hagi: Where Japan's Revolution Began." Remote castle town. N. Taylor
Gregs, p. 751
Aug "The Japan Alps." Charles McCarry, p. 238

NATIONAL GEOGRAPHIC TRAVELER
1985 Autumn "Japan's Courtly Past." Kyoto and Nara. Donald Keene, p. 126

N.Y. TIMES SUNDAY TRAVEL SECTION (X)
1985 Feb 24 Shopper's World: "Kyoto's Street of Rare Textiles." Amanda M. Stinchecum, p. 6
Mar 17 (Part 2, "Sophisticated Traveler") "A Little Kyoto in Japan's Alps." Clyde H. Haberman, p. 128
May 12 "Glimpsing Japan's Hidden Face." A visit to a ryokan, a local bar, or a hot-spring resort can provide insights. John D. Morley, p. 45
Jun 2 "Tokyo's Hot New Beverage? Coffee." One Koki shop offers 21 different blends, another roasts its beans over charcoal. Alan Davidson, p. 47
Jun 9 "Where the Sun Rises First." Hokkaido is a land of rare cranes and a dwindling number of aborigines. Sam Howe, p. 22
Jun 16 Fare of the Country: "Buckwheat Noodles." Japan's fast food. Amanda M. Stinchecum, p. 12
Jun 23 "The Quiet Heart of Kurashiki." An industrial city a few hours from Tokyo preserves a few blocks of an older, calmer Japan. Susan Chira, p. 9
"Shopper's Haunts Around the World." Includes Japan. Amanda M. Stinchecum, p. 16
Aug 18 "Old Kyoto, New Kyoto." The 16th and 21st centuries can coexist. Jay McInerney, p. 35
Sep 22 Shopper's World: "Japan's Ancient Art of Lacquerware." Alan K. Ota, p. 6
Oct 6 ("Sophisticated Traveler") "Afloat on the Inland Sea of Japan." Donald Keene, p. 40
("Sophisticated Traveler") "Ski School in Japan's Shigas." Seiji Ozawa, p. 79
Nov 3 Fare of the Country: "In Kyoto, Greetings for Each Season." Amanda M. Stinchecum, p. 9
Nov 10 "A Japanese Tribute to an Adopted Son." Matsue honors Lafcadio Hearn. Michael Shapiro, p. 22
Nov 24 "A Shrine to Japan's Crafts." Japan Folk Crafts Museum. Terry Trucco, p. 24
Dec 8 "What's Doing in Tokyo." Clyde Haberman, p. 10
Dec 15 "Two on the Aisle in Tokyo." To a theater addict, Kabuki, No and Bunraku are all hits. William Weaver, p. 9
Dec 29 Shopper's World: "It looks good enough to eat." Jared Lubarsky, p. 12
1984 Mar 4 Shopper's World: "In Tokyo, Omote." Sando is a synonym for style. Terry Trucco, p. 6
Apr 1 "Feaster's Choice in Tokyo." Jack Plimpton and Russell Marcus, p. 15
Apr 8 Shopper's World: "Furnishings Fit for a Shogun." Amanda M. Stinchecum, p. 6
Apr 29 "On Foot in Hokkaido, Japan's Frontier." Much of the north island is park land. James Sterngold, p. 9
May 6 Shopper's World: "The Japanese Gift for Wrappings. Terry Trucco, p. 12
Sep 16 "The Day the Temple Opens." Once a year Daito Kuji in Kyoto brings its treasures out to air. Amanda M. Stinchecum, p. 12

1984 Sep 16 "Yokohama: Where the West Began." Meiji era. Steve Lohr, p. 24
Oct 7 (Okinawa) "The Isles are Japanese, but with a Difference." The
Ryukyus offer a warm greeting and distinctive style. Amanda M.
Stinchecum, p. 21
Nov 4 "A Livable Metropolis . . ." Tokyo is becoming "steadily a more
agreeable place." Donald Keene, p. 14
"What's Doing in Tokyo." Clyde Haberman, p. 14
"Little Corners of Tokyo's Past." Vestiges of the old can be found amid the
pressing new. Paul Waley, p. 15
Fare of the Country: "Sampling Some of Tokyo's Finest Sake." Jared
Lubarsky, p. 16
Dec 30 Shopper's World: "The Patient Art of Making Brushes." Amanda M.
Stinchecum, p. 6

SUNSET
1985 Jan "In Tokyo, Where to Buy Crafts." p. 50
Mar "Robot Rendezvous." Preview of Japan's electronic world's fair at
Tsukuba. p. 72
Apr "Japan's Far North Island—Hokkaido." p. 62
Nov "Japanese All-under-one-roof Stores—Pickles to French Paintings." p.
52
1984 May "Rail Pass Gets You Almost Any Place in Japan." p. 92

TOWN & COUNTRY
1985 Mar "Vis-a-Vis: Japan." M.F. Kennedy, p. 212

TRAVEL & LEISURE
1985 May "The Shogun Town of Takayama." Old Japan in a magical mountain
setting. Charles N. Barnard, p. 180
Dec "The Legacy of Kanazawa." Celebrating the cultural heritage of Old
Japan. Daniel Burstein, p. 166
1984 Mar "Tokyo After Dark." Malachy Duffy, p. 38
Mar "Japan Revisited." Malachy Duffy, p. 44
Jun "Tokyo's Hotel Okura." Oasis of serenity in a fast-paced city. Calvin
Trillin, p. 28
Oct Special issue—Japan: "Glimpses of Japan." Pamela Fiori, p. 4
"A Traveler's Guide to Japan." Behind the mystique. p. 100
"An American's Introduction to Ceremonies and Subtleties." Malachy Duffy,
p. 102
"The Essence of Japan: Understanding the Concepts of Culture." Donald
Richie, p. 104
"Tokyo Untangled." Plugging into a high-voltage city. David Halberstam, p.
110
"Tokyo Neighborhoods." From graceful gardens to the glitter of Ginza. Jean
Pearce, p. 112
"Tokyo Restaurants." Where to eat and what to order—from sushi to sole
Albert. George Lang, p. 126
"Tokyo Hotels." Traditional hospitality in high-rise luxury. Terry Trucco, p.
130

1984   "The Shogun Cities." Exploring Nikko and Kamakura. Charles N. Barnard, p. 138

"Kyoto Ancient and Serene." Marian Gough, p. 141

"Beyond Tokyo and Kyoto." Great shrines, museums and sights off the beaten track. Robert C. Fisher, p. 171

"Shopping in Japan." The best buys in cameras, pearls, crafts and fashions. Judith Friedberg, p. 176

"When in Japan." An expert's guide to bowing, bathing and eating as the Japanese do. Robert C. Fisher, p. 190

"Special Pleasures of a Japanese Inn." All about staying at a ryokan. Charles N. Barnard, p. 192

"Touring Japan." Patricia Brooks, p. 200

"Japan: Books to Read Before You Go." Robert C. Fisher, p. 20

TRAVEL/HOLIDAY

1985 Jan "Offbeat Ski Resorts." Includes Japan. Ken Castle, p. 46

Feb "Japanese Hideaway." The mountain village of Takayama." Michael Garza, p. 36

May "Japan's Tsukuba Expo." Science for the people. Denise D. Meehan, p. 74

1984 Apr "Shopping Japan." Taking home the treasures of Tokyo and Kyoto. James Nicholas, p. 24

Jun "Tohoku." Festive northern Japan. Denise D. Meehan, p. 54

VOGUE

1985 Dec "In Japan: the Westin Akasaka Prince Hotel." p. 245

WORKING WOMAN

1984 Jun "A Businesswoman's Guide to Tokyo." Trisha Gorman, p. 146

MALAYSIA
and
SINGAPORE

Series Guidebooks (See Appendix 1)

Baedeker: Singapore
Berlitz: Singapore
Country Orientation Series: Update Singapore

Insight: Malaysia; Singapore
Lonely Planet: Malaysia, Singapore and Brunei
U.S. Government: Singapore: Area Handbook; Background Notes;
                                Post Report
Malaysia: Background Notes; Country Study; Post Report

Background Reading

Bird, Isabella   THE GOLDEN CHERSONESE
Letters to the author's sister while on a visit to the Malay Peninsula in 1879; new reprint. Hippocrene, 1983.

Craig, Jo Ann   CULTURE SHOCK: MALAYSIA & SINGAPORE
Part of a series; see entry under "Thailand." Hippocrene, 1982.

Morris, Jan   TRAVELS
This volume of travel essays by the noted travel writer includes one on Singapore. Oxford U, 1984.

Naipaul, V.S.   AMONG THE BELIEVERS
See under "Indonesia/Background Reading."

O'Hanlon, Redmond   INTO THE HEART OF BORNEO
An account of a hazardous journey into central Borneo—"a vastly entertaining report of . . . encounters with natives . . . discomforts of jungle life . . . as much escapade as adventure." (PW) Random, 1985.

White, Walter G.   THE SEA GYPSIES OF MALAYSIA
A "very readable" anthropological study of the nomadic sea peoples of the Malaysian archipelago and their way of life. AMS, 1981 (first published 1922).

GUIDEBOOKS

Dalton, Bill   THE SOUTH PACIFIC HANDBOOK
See under "Pacific & Oceania/Guidebooks" (includes Malaysia).

Nicol, Gladys   MALAYSIA AND SINGAPORE
Batsford, 1977.

Stier, Wayne and Cavers, Mark   TIME TRAVEL IN THE MALAY CRESCENT
For the adventurous traveler—travel tips, maps, how to get around, history, culture, people. Meru Pub, 1984.

HISTORY

See also books on history of Southeast Asia under "Asia/History."

Andayn, Leonard and Barbara   A HISTORY OF MALAYSIA
St. Martin, 1982.

Turnbull, C.M.   A HISTORY OF SINGAPORE
"From Raffles's emporium to Lee Kuan Yew's barracks state." (BRD) Oxford U, 1977.

Winstedt, Richard O.   THE MALAYS: A CULTURAL HISTORY
Three Continents, 1981 (first published 1961).

Novels

Black, Gavin   THE BITTER TEA
Action and suspense story set in Kuala Lumpur and Singapore—a Scottish shipping executive is involved in an attempted assassination. Har-Row, 1972.

Burgess, Anthony   THE LONG DAY WANES: A MALAYAN TRILOGY
Three short novels set in Malay in the period of waning British rule just before Malay's independence—"one of the most revealing narratives about the East and the West" relationship. (BRD) Norton, 1965.

Clavell, James   KING RAT
Corruption, fear, despair in a World War II prison camp in Singapore. Little, 1962.

Conrad, Joseph   LORD JIM
A classic story of a man who becomes a demigod. Knopf, 1979 (first published 1899). Also, *Almayer's Folly* (1895).

D'Alpuget, Blanche   TURTLE BEACH
"Meld of movements, cultures, and beliefs ranging from feminism to mysticism" set in an exotic Malaysia. (FC) S&S, 1984.

Farrell, J.G.   THE SINGAPORE GRIP
Singapore from 1930-42 as British merchant families lose their stronghold to the Japanese. Knopf, 1977.

Hartog, Jan de   THE TRAIL OF THE SERPENT
Based on a true incident of a dramatic attempt to escape from Borneo by a diverse group of people, following the Japanese invasion in World War II, and the moral confrontation when a decadent shipowner insists the group renounce religious beliefs as a condition for his help. Har-Row, 1983.

Maugham, W. Somerset   THE CASUARINA TREE
Short stories fashioned in typical Maugham style "out of dramatic and melodramatic situations in the lives of European exiles." (BRD) Doran, 1926.

Reeman, Douglas   THE PRIDE AND THE ANGUISH
The fall of Singapore in 1941. Putnam, 1969. See also *The Deep Silence* (1968) and *The Greatest Enemy* (1971).

Shute, Nevil   THE LEGACY
A two-part story—the heroine's experiences in Malaya during World War II as a prisoner of the Japanese and her debt of gratitude to the Australian soldier who befriends her. Morrow, 1950.

Theroux, Paul   THE CONSUL'S FILE
Tales of "how uprooted individuals connect or fail to connect with each other" and places they've ended up, set in post-colonial Malaysia. (BRD) Houghton, 1977.

Wynd, Oswald   THE BLAZING AIR
Six episodes relating the effects of the Japanese conquest of Malaya in 1941 as the people involved reexamine their lives. Ticknor & Fields, 1981.

TRAVEL ARTICLES

BON APPETIT
1985 Mar "Traveling with Taste: Malaysia." Shirley Slater, p. 34

ESQUIRE
1984 Jan (Maldives) "Where to Take a [Scuba] Dive." Edward D. Sheffe, p. 32

N.Y. TIMES SUNDAY TRAVEL SECTION (X)
1985 Mar 3 "Malaysia's Bucolic East Coast." Fishing villages and islands offer
      warm hospitality. John Pomfret, p. 19
      Apr 14 Fare of the Country: "Singapore Street Food." Barbara Crossette, p. 6
      Jun 30 Correspondent's Choice: "On Penang Island, a Legend Lives."
      Barbara Crossette, p. 6
      Oct 6 "The Greening of Kuala Lumpur." David Wigg, p. 6
1984 May 22 "Singapore Byways." Ethnic neighborhoods. John Pomfret, p. 10
      Nov 18 "What's Doing in Singapore." Barbara Crosette, p. 12
      Dec 2 Fare of the Country: "In Malaysia, Spicy Satay." Michael Specter, p. 24

TRAVEL & LEISURE
1985 Sep (Borneo) "In Search of the Wild Orangutan." Rebecca Levine, p. 135
      Nov "The Pleasures of Penang." Charles Monaghan, p. 34
1984 Sep "A Shopper's Guide to Singapore." Quality and bargains in silks, jewelry,
      cameras and crafts. Erica Kleine, p. 130

TRAVEL/HOLIDAY
1984 Nov "Concerning Food and Wine." Singapore, the Lion City, offers a pride of
      fare. Robert L. Balzer, p. 62

WORKING WOMAN
1985 May "A Businesswoman's Guide to Kuala Lumpur." Eric Goodman, p. 142

PAKISTAN

Series Guidebooks (See Appendix 1)

Lonely Planet: **Pakistan**
U.S. Government: **Pakistan: Background Notes; Country Study; Post Report**

Background Reading

Amin, Mohamed and Willets, Duncan   JOURNEY THROUGH PAKISTAN
Follows the Indus River from the mountains through valleys, plains and cities. Chatto Bodley, 1982.

Moorhouse, Geoffrey   TO THE FRONTIER
Account of a journey to Baluchistan, Lahore, the Khyber Pass and the Afghan border by a leading travel writer. "Wherever he went he observed both visiting foreigners and the local people . . . keenly, respectfully and humorously." (PW) HR&W, 1985.

Naipaul, V.S.   AMONG THE BELIEVERS
See under "Indonesia."

Reeves, Richard   A PASSAGE TO PESHAWAR
"Absorbingly describes [his] experiences during a 1983 visit to Pakistan . . . the conflicts arising from the drive toward modernization . . . and the Muslim fundamentalism . . . their recent yen for TV and video games." (PW) S&S, 1984.

Singer, André   LORDS OF THE KHYBER
The story of the North West frontier. Faber & Faber, 1984.

Theroux, Paul and McCurry, Steve   THE IMPERIAL WAY
See under "India."

Woodin, Ann   IN THE CIRCLE OF THE SUN
See under "Northern Africa/Background Reading."

GUIDEBOOKS

See under "India/Guidebooks."

Williams, L.F. Rushbrook   A HANDBOOK FOR TRAVELLERS IN INDIA, PAKISTAN, NEPAL, BANGLADESH & SRI LANKA

HISTORY

Singhal, Damodar P.   PAKISTAN
History of the nation state, created in 1947. P-H, 1972.

Novels

Mojtabai, A.G.   A STOPPING PLACE
Novel of the "explosive . . . Moslem religious zealotry and ethnic power politics," with a plot that involves the disappearance of a holy relic of the Prophet Muhammad. (FC) S&S, 1979.

Rushdie, Salman   SHAME
By a Pakistani who is a Westerner by adoption and choice; and "blessed with the gift of authenticity . . . able to portray unfamiliar places and people with such clarity and conviction, the reader knows he is in the presence of truth." The novel is a "sort of modern fairy tale . . . the link between certain bizarre happenings . . . and events in a nation that is 'not quite Pakistan' is inescapable." (Publisher) Knopf, 1983. Also, *Midnight's Children*, listed under "India."

Sidhwa, Bapsi   THE BRIDE
Set at the time of India's partition. A widower adopts a girl who cannot accept the harsh life of his ancestral tribe—"marriage, loyalty, honor, and the conflict with old ways in this well-told tale." (FC) St. Martin, 1983.

TRAVEL ARTICLES

NATIONAL GEOGRAPHIC
1985 Jun "Along Afghanistan's War-Torn Frontier." Debra Denker, p. 772
1984 Jun "By Rail Across India." Pakistan to Bangladesh. Paul Theroux, p. 696

TRAVEL/HOLIDAY
1985 Aug "Timeless Land—Pilgrimage to Pakistan." Betsy Braden, p. 38

THE PHILIPPINES

Series Guidebooks (See Appendix 1)

Insight: The Philippines
Lonely Planet: The Philippines

Nagel: The Philippines
U.S. Government: The Philippines: Background Notes; Country
Study; Pocket Guide; Post Report

Background Reading

Bain, David H.   SITTING IN DARKNESS: AMERICANS IN THE PHILIPPINES
"Unique blend of history and adventure" told through the exploits of U.S. General Funston and Philippine rebel Aguinaldo, and the volatile situation in the Philippines today. (BL) Houghton, 1984.

Chesnoff, Richard Z.   PHILIPPINES
Text and photographs describe the Philippine archipelago in all its fascinating variety. Abrams, 1980.

Hahn, Emily   THE ISLANDS
The subtitle is "America's imperial adventure in the Philippines"—by a "consummate writer [who] reminds us again of the literary origins of the historian's craft." (BRD) Coward, 1981.

Ingersoll, Joshena M.   GOLDEN YEARS IN THE PHILIPPINES
"Nostalgic look into an era and a way of life gone forever"—memoirs of an American wife during the period 1910-1940. (LJ) Pacific Bks, 1971.

Nance, John   THE GENTLE TASADAY
A journalist's story of the Stone Age people in the rain forests of the Philippines. HarBraceJ, 1977.

Prising, Robin   MANILA GOODBYE
Recollection of boyhood years in a Japanese concentration camp following their occupation of Manila. Houghton, 1975.

GUIDEBOOKS

Harper, Peter   THE PHILIPPINES HANDBOOK
Moon Pbns Ca, 1985.

HISTORY

Steinberg, David   THE PHILIPPINES, A SINGULAR AND PLURAL PLACE
Westview, 1982.

Novels

Nolledo, Wilfrido D.   BUT FOR THE LOVERS
The Philippines in World War II during the Japanese and American occupations—"personalities and events [merge] into one stunning nightmare." (BRD) Dutton, 1971.

Rizal y Alonso, José   THE SUBVERSIVE
Early political novel of anti-colonialism. Norton, 1968.

Wilson, Sloan   PACIFIC INTERLUDE
Experiences of a young lieutenant as commander of a gas supply tanker in the Pacific during World War II—"adventures from shore leave in Brisbane to war-torn Manila with plenty of sea duty in between." (FC) Arbor Hse, 1982.

TRAVEL ARTICLES

N.Y. TIMES SUNDAY TRAVEL SECTION (X)
1985 Mar 17 (Part 2, "Sophisticated Traveler") "A Passion for Basketball." Steve Lohr, p. 129
Sep 22 "An Isle for Divers—and Nondivers." Panglao Island. Steve Lohr, p.21

SOUTH KOREA

Series Guidebooks (See Appendix 1)

Fodor: Korea
Insight: South Korea
Lonely Planet: Korea & Taiwan
U.S. Government: South Korea: Background Notes; Country Study; Pocket Guide

Background Reading

Bird, Isabella L.   KOREA AND HER NEIGHBORS
C.E. Tuttle, 1984.

Kim, H. Edward   KOREA: BEYOND THE HILLS
A personal portrait by an editor of the *National Geographic*—legend, history, as well as everyday life in cities and towns, are vividly conveyed. Kodansha, 1980.

Kowalczyk, Robert   MORNING CALM: A JOURNEY THROUGH THE
KOREAN COUNTRYSIDE
Dawn Pr, 1981.

Michaud, Roland   KOREA, A JADE PARADISE
Description and travel with photographs; translated from the French. Vendome,
1981.

GUIDEBOOKS

Adams, Edward B.   KOREA GUIDE
C.E. Tuttle, 1983.

Wallis, Kathleen   LET'S LOOK AT KOREA
OMF Bks, 1977.

HISTORY

Choy, Bon-Youn   KOREA, A HISTORY
C.E. Tuttle, 1971.

Goulden, Joseph C.   KOREA: THE UNTOLD STORY OF THE WAR
"Written in breezy style, aimed at a broad audience"—based on new information released under the Freedom of Information Act. (BL) Times Bks, 1982.

Hatada, Takashi   A HISTORY OF KOREA
Stone Age to the civil war following World War II—"excellent one-volume
history." Clio, 1969

Hoyt, Edwin P.   THE BLOODY ROAD TO PANMUNJOM
Final volume of a history of the Korean War—readers looking for an easily
digestible account of the war's ebb and flow . . . will find this trio to their liking."
(PW) Stein & Day, 1985.

Yi, Ki-baek   A NEW HISTORY OF KOREA
"Spans Korean political, social, military, and cultural history to 1960." (LJ)
Harvard U Pr, 1985.

Novels

Bryan, C.D.B.   P. S. WILKINSON
Post-truce Korea is the setting for this novel of an intelligence officer who
yearns for an end to his Korean duties, only to be disappointed in his life in the
States. Har-Row, 1965.

Buck, Pearl S.   THE LIVING REED
A family saga, the history of Korea through four generations from 1881 to the
Korean War in 1952. Day, 1963.

Hall, Adam   THE PEKING TARGET
One of a series of international espionage novels featuring British secret agent Quiller. Playboy Pr, 1982.

Hooker, Richard   MASH
The beginning of the TV series on the Mobile Army Surgical Hospital unit in Korea that established Hawkeye, Trapper John, etc., in TV history. Morrow, 1968.

King, Richard E.   THE MARTYRED
The betrayal of twelve Christian ministers arrested by the Communists during the Korean War. Braziller, 1964.

Lee, Peter H.   ANTHOLOGY OF KOREAN LITERATURE
Prose and poetry from 57 B.C. to the late nineteenth century. U. Pr of Hawaii, 1982.

Shagan, Steve   THE CIRCLE
A Korean general's plan for oriental world supremacy by China, Japan and Korea—"non-stop . . . intrigue, betrayal" set in a half dozen countries. (FC) Morrow, 1982.

TRAVEL ARTICLES

N.Y. TIMES SUNDAY TRAVEL SECTION (X)
1984 Jan 22 "Korea's Fiery Kimchi." Terry Trucco, p. 6
     Sep 16 "Panmunjom: Between Two Koreas."   Tour offers glimpse of a tense border. Clyde Haberman, p. 22

TRAVEL/HOLIDAY
1984 Mar "Mount Sorak, a Korean Aerie." James Ferri, p. 6

SRI LANKA
(Including The
Maldives)

Series Guidebooks (See Appendix 1)

Berlitz: **Sri Lanka**
Fodor: **India, Nepal & Sri Lanka**

Insight: Sri Lanka
Lonely Planet: Sri Lanka
Nagel: Ceylon (Sri Lanka)
U.S. Government: Maldives: Background Notes
                    Sri Lanka (Ceylon): Background Notes;
                    Country Study

Background Reading

Morris, James   PLACES
An essay on Ceylon is included in this collection of travel essays by a leading travel writer. Oxford U, 1984.

Palmer, Nigel and Page, Tim   SRI LANKA
Photographs and "enchanting essays . . . splendidly [capture] the spirit of this Garden of Eden"—history, daily life, sacred places, wildlife reserves of exotic birds and animals, folk tales and ancient customs. (PW) Thames & Hudson, 1984.

GUIDEBOOKS

See under "India/Guidebooks."

Engstrom, Barbie   INDIA, NEPAL & SRI LANKA
Combination of personal travelogue, practical travel information, and pictures. Kurios Pr, 1980.

Hildebrand, Volker   SRI LANKA
One of a new guidebook series originating in Germany. Hippocrene, 1985.

Williams, L.F. Rushbrook, ed.   A HANDBOOK FOR TRAVELLERS IN INDIA, PAKISTAN, NEPAL, BANGLADESH AND SRI LANKA

HISTORY

De Silva, K.M.   A HISTORY OF SRI LANKA
U of California, 1981. Also, *Sri Lanka, a Survey* (1977).

Novels

DeSilva, Colin   THE WINDS OF SINHALA
Portrays Ceylon's (Sri Lanka's) heroic age in the second century B.C. when Gamini was its warrior king. Doubleday, 1982.

Holt, Victoria   THE SPRING OF THE TIGER
Turn-of-the-century Ceylon and England are settings for this romantic suspense novel. Doubleday, 1979.

Innes, Hammond   THE STRODE VENTURER
The plot concerns a high-adventure search for manganese. Knopf, 1965.

Ondaatje, Michael   RUNNING IN THE FAMILY
The author departed for the West, and recently revisited Sri Lanka and the result is a "poet's nimble, impressionistic portrait of a social milieu." (BL) Norton, 1982.

TRAVEL ARTICLES

TRAVEL & LEISURE
1985 Aug "Exploring Ancient Sri Lanka." Jay Parini, p. 102

TRAVEL HOLIDAY
1985 Apr "Sri Lanka: Second Cities of the Pacific." p. 11

TAIWAN

Series Guidebooks (See Appendix 1)

Country Orientation Series: Taiwan Update
Insight: Taiwan
Lonely Planet: Korea & Taiwan
U.S.Government: Taiwan: Background Notes; Pocket Guide

Background Reading

See also Background Reading under "China."

Criswell, Colin   TAIPANS: HONG KONG'S MERCHANT PRINCES
Oxford U, 1981.

Edmonds, I.G.   TAIWAN: THE OTHER CHINA
Bobbs, 1971.

Tomikel, John   TAIWAN JOURNAL: TEN HISTORIC DAYS
Allegheny, 1979.

Wood, Christopher   TAIWAN
Viking, 1982.

GUIDEBOOKS

Nerbonne, J. J.   TAIWAN: GUIDE TO TAIPEI AND ALL TAIWAN
Heinman, 1983.

HISTORY

Lin, Robert H.   TAIPING REVOLUTION: A FAILURE OF TWO MISSIONS
U Pr of America, 1979.

Novels

Arnold, William   CHINA GATE
The Asian underworld and how a hardworking youth can, Horatio Alger style,
rise in its hierarchy; set in Taiwan in the late 1950s—fascinating . . . gripping . . .
disquieting." (Publisher) Villard, 1983.

TRAVEL ARTICLES

N.Y. TIMES SUNDAY TRAVEL SECTION (X)
1984 Sep 16 "Echoes of China Just Off the Mainland." In Taiwan, culinary
pleasures and artistic treasures. Fox Butterfield, p. 9
Oct 28 "Taking the Train Around Taiwan." Walter Wager, p. 12

THAILAND

Series Guidebooks (See Appendix 1)

Berlitz: Thailand
Insight: Thailand
Lonely Planet: Thailand
Nagel: Thailand
U.S. Government: Thailand: Background Notes; Country Study

Background Reading

Basche, James   THAILAND: LAND OF THE FREE
Thai customs, religion, arts, architecture, history. The author lived and traveled
in Thailand extensively during the 1960s and 1970s. Taplinger, 1971.

Blackwood, Sir Robert   THAILAND
A "definitive work" by one who worked and traveled in the country for over twenty years—"beautiful color photographs and splendid descriptions." (Publisher) Hippocrene, 1983.

Blofield, John, ed.   BANGKOK
Part of the Great Cities of the World Series. Time-Life, 1979.

Cadet, J.M.   RAMAKIEN: THE THAI EPIC
Based on rubbings of the bas-reliefs in a Bangkok temple, representing the classic story of the Ramayana. Kodansha, 1970.

Cooper, Robert and Nanthapa   CULTURE SHOCK! THAILAND
"Expert analysis of culture shock with deep perception, sparkling wit and little sidelights." (BP) Hippocrene, 1983.

Landon, Margaret D.   ANNA AND THE KING OF SIAM
Story on which the musical was based, of the Welsh widow, hired by the King of Siam in 1862 to teach his many children. Harper, 1944. Also, by W.S. Bristowe, *Louis and the King of Siam* (1976). Louis was Anna's son and the book is "the truth about his fabulous life." (BRD)

Lewis, Paul and Elaine   PEOPLES OF THE GOLDEN TRIANGLE
Six culturally distinct people in Thailand, each struggling to maintain its own identity. Photos and text document their skills, houses, villages, arts and crafts. Thames Hudson, 1984.

**Toth, Marian Davies   TALES FROM THAILAND: FOLKLORE, CULTURE
                            AND HISTORY**
C.E. Tuttle, 1983.

Ward, Philip   BANGKOK: PORTRAIT OF A CITY
Oleander Pr, 1974.

GUIDEBOOKS

Duncan, William   THAILAND: A COMPLETE GUIDE
Practical information for the traveler and "attractive enough to tempt the browser" seeking background information. (LJ) C.E. Tuttle, 1976.

Hildebrand, Volker   THAILAND-BURMA
One of a new guidebook series originating in Germany. Hippocrene, 1985.

Nicol, Gladys   THAILAND
Description and travel; background information. Batsford, 1980.

**Stier, Wayne and Cavers, M.   WIDE EYES IN BURMA AND
                                THAILAND—FINDING YOUR WAY**
A travel guide "especially suited to the young, intrepid traveler." (BP) Meru Pub, 1983.

HISTORY

See also Southeast Asia histories under "Asia/Background Reading."

Jumsai, M.L.   POPULAR HISTORY OF THAILAND
Paragon, 1972.

Sharp, Lauriston   BANG CHAN
"Jargon-free social history" of the change from an agrarian life to Westernized social customs.—a rare look at a culture in transition. (BRD) Cornell U, 1978.

Wyatt, David K.   THAILAND: A SHORT HISTORY
A new, one-volume history by a Cornell professor. Yale U Pr, 1984.

Novels

Boulle, Pierre   THE BRIDGE OVER THE RIVER KWAI
The story on which the memorable movie was based. "A stirring and imaginative book . . . soaked in [Kipling] atmosphere . . . unforgettable character sketches." The plot concerns a Japanese prison camp during World War II and a "stiff-upper-lip" British officer who builds a bridge using prison labor. (FC) Vanguard Bks, 1954.

Duncan, W.R.   THE QUEEN'S MESSENGER
An espionage novel in which a British courier is kidnapped after receiving a message from "an enigmatic informer in Thailand." (FC) Delacorte Pr, 1982.

Ekert-Rotholz, Alice   RICE IN SILVER BOWLS
Evokes Bangkok in the early 1950s, and involves the complicated relationships of a German businessman's family, his half-Javanese mistress, Chinese servants, and various Oriental characters. Fromm, 1982 (first published 1954).

Hall, Adam   THE 9TH DIRECTIVE
An espionage novel set in Bangkok, with agent Quiller assigned to preventing an assassination. S&S, 1967.

Han, Suyin   THE ENCHANTRESS
See under "China/Novels."

Lewis, Norman   A SINGLE PILGRIM
An Englishman elects to take a dangerous job in Thailand (Siam then) rather than return to his unhappy marriage in London—"the painfulness of the underlying theme is offset by the charm and brilliance of the Siamese scene." (BRD) Rinehart, 1954.

Mills, James   THE TRUTH ABOUT PETER HARLEY
CIA intrigue and the drug traffic in Thailand. Dutton, 1979.

TRAVEL ARTICLES

HARPERS
1985 Jul "In Bangkok, New Wealth and Old Soldiers." William Shawcross, p. 55

MODERN MATURITY
1984 Oct-Nov "Patterns on the Water." They reflect the mosaic of Thailand. Charles N. Barnard, p. 85

N.Y. TIMES SUNDAY TRAVEL SECTION (X)
1985 Mar 17 (Part 2, "Sophisticated Traveler") "Echoes of Glory in a Thai Jungle." Han Suyin, p. 34
        May 5 Fare of the Country: "A Cornucopia of Asian Fruit." Barbara Crossette, p. 12
1984 Oct 7 "What's Doing in Bangkok." David Wigg, p. 10

TRAVEL & LEISURE
1985 Mar "An American Legend in Bangkok." Lost in the jungle, the mysterious Jim Thompson lives on through the Thai Silk Company. Erica Kleine, p. 51
1984 Nov "Special Places: Bangkok's Oriental Hotel." A raffish past and a stylish present. Charles N. Barnard, p. 120

TRAVEL/HOLIDAY
1985 Apr "Bountiful Bangkok, a Shopper's Paradise." Robin Fowler, p. 62
        Apr "On Bangkok's Waterways." Thai life revealed. Karen S. Narula, p. 58
1984 Feb "Dining in Bangkok." Chef Louis Szathmary, p. 16

WORLD PRESS REVIEW
1985 Nov "Exotic Bangkok." (*South China Morning Post*, Hong Kong.) Walter Reisender, p. 62

TIBET
(Including Ladakh)

Series Guidebooks

Lonely Planet: **Tibet; Kashmir, Ladakh & Zanskar**

Background Reading

Avedon, John F.   IN EXILE FROM THE LAND OF SNOWS
"The first full account of the Dalai Lama and Tibet since the Chinese conquest"

is the subtitle. "Fascinating" account of the history of Tibet, its loss of freedom to China, and how Tibetan culture continues in exile. (BL) Knopf, 1984.

David-Neel, Alexandra   MY JOURNEY TO LHASA
One of a series of books by a remarkable Frenchwoman, the first white woman who succeeded in entering the forbidden city, and also a practicing Buddhist and lama. Great Eastern, 1983 (first published 1927). Also *Magic and Mystery in Tibet* (1932), *Tibetan Journey* (1936).

Fleming, Peter   BAYONETS TO LHASA
Story of a British expedition to Tibet's forbidden city in 1904, with a summary of later developments that led to the Communist invasion. Greenwood, 1974 (first published 1961).

Franz, Michael   RULE BY INCARNATION
Based on interviews with the Dalai Lama, the spiritual and political leader before the Chinese takeover that forced him to flee Tibet in 1962. "Describes a way of life that will probably die out in a generation." (LJ) Westview, 1982.

Han, Suyin   LHASA, THE OPEN CITY: A JOURNEY TO TIBET
By an author frankly in favor of the "new" Tibet. It describes the progression of Tibet "from the seventh to the twentieth century in one generation" as a result of the Chinese Communist takeover—"informative, even entertaining in spots, rather more like a travelogue than a piece of journalism." (BRD) Putnam Pub Group, 1977.

Harrer, Heinrich   RETURN TO TIBET
The author wanted to spend the rest of his life in Tibet but was forced to leave when the Communists took over. This is about a brief return to the country in 1982, reintroducing some of the friends from *Seven Years in Tibet* (below)—"a book of rueful echoes." (PW) Schocken, 1985.

Harrer, Heinrich   SEVEN YEARS IN TIBET
An "exotic tale, told in quick unvarnished style [of this] strange and wonderful land" where the author spent seven years and was a friend of the Dalai Lama. (BRD) J.P Tarcher, 1982. Also *Ladakh: Gods and Mortals Behind the Himalayas* (1981).

Harvey, Andrew   A JOURNEY IN LADAKH
A travel odyssey to this remote area between Kashmir and Tibet, as well as a spiritual quest—written by an English poet and Shakespearian scholar. Houghton, 1983.

Hedin, Sven   A CONQUEST OF TIBET
Retelling of the author's trip in 1896, without official permission, often in disguise and in danger from bandits. Greenwood, 1974 (first published 1934).

Hopkirk, Peter   TRESPASSERS ON THE ROOF OF THE WORLD
An account of "an extraordinary contest that spanned a century, as travellers

from nine different countries attempted to enter . . . and be the first to penetrate Lhasa, its sacred capital." A "poignant" story of a variety of people with various motives—some never returned. It ends with the invasion by the Chinese Communists of "the world's last stronghold of mystery and romance." (BRD) J.P. Tarcher, 1983.

Jenkins, Peter   ACROSS CHINA
See under "China."

Jigmei-Ngapo Ngawang and others   TIBET
Says one reviewer: "Even the *least* intrepid armchair traveler can now traverse this almost mythical land . . . breathtaking landscape, architecture . . . a miniature of Tibetan life that has the beauty of a drop of water reflecting the seven colors of the sun." The book is a series of essays by mostly Tibetan writers on culture, traditions, religion, parts of the country not open to the West. (BRD) McGraw, 1981.

Kling, Kevin   TIBET
Low-keyed travel journal and photo-essay—"mood-stirring and artistic . . . an informed appreciation of this remote, exotic land." Hudson, 1985.

Norbu, T.J.   TIBET IS MY COUNTRY
The country's story, told by the elder brother of the Dalai Lama, "as only a native-born Tibetan could. . . . fact and fancy, truth and myth, reality and imagination subtly intertwined." (BRD) Dutton, 1960.

Pallis, Marco   PEAKS AND LAMAS
"Mountains and mountaineering. . . . intelligent comment on unfamiliar ways of life, arts, customs, Buddhism." (BRD) Woburn, 1974 (first published 1936).

Rowell, Galen   MOUNTAINS OF THE MIDDLE KINGDOM: EXPLORING THE HIGH PEAKS OF CHINA AND TIBET
See under "China/Background Reading."

Salisbury, Charlotte Y.   TIBETAN DIARY AND TRAVELS ALONG THE SILK ROUTE
A record of exceptional travel experiences made possible by the status of the author's husband, Harrison Salisbury. (BL) Walker, 1981.

Snellgrove, David L. and Richardson, Hugh E.   THE CULTURAL HISTORY OF TIBET
Great Eastern, 1980. Also, *Cultural Heritage of Ladakh* (1977).

Topping, Audrey   THE SPLENDORS OF TIBET
The author and her husband were among the first foreign travelers to Tibet in 1979 after decades of no visitors—"perceptive, sensitive and informative" book on contemporary Tibet, with many photographs. (BRD) Sino, 1980.

Wahid, Siddiq   LADAKH: BETWEEN EARTH AND SKY
Introduction to and photographs of a country open to tourism since 1974. Norton, 1981.

GUIDEBOOKS

Engstrom, Barbie   INDIA, NEPAL & SRI LANKA
See under "India/Guidebooks." The book includes Ladakh.

Schwartz, Brian   CHINA OFF THE BEATEN TRACK
See under "China/Guidebooks." The book includes Tibet.

HISTORY

Richardson, Hugh E.   TIBET AND ITS HISTORY
Revised edition of a history first published in 1962. Shambhala, 1984.

Novels

Brent, Madeleine   MERLIN'S KEEP
"Suspense, love, adventure, exotic places and people" as a girl is raised in a small Tibetan village, and then sent to a "great house" in England. (FC) G.K. Hall, 1977.

Hilton, James   LOST HORIZON
That classic story of adventure and fantasy—an airplane is forced down in Tibet, and its passengers become guests at a Tibetan lamasery—Shangri-La. Morrow, 1933.

Hyde-Chambers, Frederick R.   LAMA: A NOVEL OF TIBET
Politics, the Tibetan and Buddhist philosophies, and the invasion of Tibet by China in the late 1950s. McGraw, 1985.

TRAVEL ARTICLES

HOUSE & GARDEN
1985 May "Tibet—Color in the Barren Landscape." Inger M. Elliott, p. 198

IV. THE PACIFIC and OCEANIA

Series Guidebooks (See Appendix 1)

Fodor: Australia, New Zealand and the South Pacific
Lonely Planet: Fiji; Tahiti; Papua New Guinea; Bushwhacking in Papua New Guinea
U.S. Government: Fiji: Post Report
            Nauru: Background Notes
            Oceania: Regional Study
            Papua New Guinea: Background Notes; Post Report
            Solomon Islands: Background Notes
            Tonga: Background Notes
            Western Samoa: Background Notes

Background Reading

Ballinger, William Sanborn   LOST CITY OF STONE
   The Micronesian story of Nan Madol, the "Atlantis" of the Pacific and theories of how the mysterious city on Ponape came into existence—for travelers and armchair archaeologists. S&S, 1978.

Brower, Kenneth   A SONG FOR SATAWAL
   A magical passage to a faraway Eden—life and culture on the islands of Yap,

Satawal and Palau, concentrating on three individuals who represent past and future. Har-Row, 1983.

Brower, Kenneth   MICRONESIA: THE LAND, THE PEOPLE, AND THE SEA
Reports on scenery, customs, languages, history, marine life, ruins of the islands of Micronesia, with maps and photos to help keep your bearings. Louisiana State U Pr, 1982.

Daniken, Erich von   PATHWAYS TO THE GODS: THE STONES OF KIRIBATI
The search for ancient astronauts—"reads like a daring and exotic adventure story"—whether you believe the author's reinterpretation of history or not. (BL) Putnam Pub Gp, 1983.

Davidson, J.W.   PACIFIC ISLAND PORTRAITS
The changing way of life of the Pacific using a series of biographical sketches of men and women who lived there from the early nineteenth century to just before World War I. ISB, 1972.

Dodge, Ernest S.   ISLANDS AND EMPIRES
"Narrative account . . . of relations between European and Pacific worlds"—cultures before the Europeans arrived and effects of the West on those cultures. (BRD) U of Minnesota, 1976.

Ellison, Joseph W.   TUSITALA OF THE SOUTH SEAS
The story of Robert Louis Stevenson's life in the South Pacific ("Tusitala" means "teller of tales"). Hastings House, 1953. Also by Stevenson, reprints of *In the South Seas* (1971), *The Vailima Letters* (1896), and, with his wife, *Our Samoan Adventure* (1955).

Freeman, Derek   MARGARET MEAD AND SAMOA
The subtitle, "the making and unmaking of an anthropological myth," indicates that this is a debunking of the anthropologist's landmark book, *Coming of Age in Samoa*. It disputes her scientific methods and presents the author's description of Samoan culture at the time Mead's work was published. Harvard U Pr, 1983.

Gourguechon, Charlene   CHARLENE GOURGUECHON'S JOURNEY TO THE END OF THE WORLD
A three-year adventure in the New Hebrides by a New Yorker. Scribner, 1977.

Laracy, Hugh   MARISTS AND MELANESIANS
"A history of Catholic missions in the Solomon Islands" is the subtitle—"evangelical Western religion [encountering] rising nationalism." (BRD) U Pr of Hawaii, 1976.

Martini, Frederic   EXPLORING TROPICAL ISLES AND SEAS
An introduction for the traveler and amateur naturalist. This is a combination of natural history text on the South Pacific, Hawaiian Islands and the Caribbean, for the nonspecialist, and a travel guide. P-H, 1984.

Mead, Margaret   COMING OF AGE IN SAMOA
Cultural anthropology primarily about adolescent girls—a psychological study of primitive youth for Western civilization. Morrow, 1971.

Michener, James A. and Day, A. Grove   RASCALS IN PARADISE
"Splendid samples of the curious, colorful characters, most of them escapists, who have peopled . . . the South Pacific." (BRD) Fawcett, 1979 (first published 1957).

Michener, James A.   A RETURN TO PARADISE
Informal essays and stories telling readers what he thought about a given island, and then a fictional story reflecting what the island thought about itself. Fawcett, 1978 (first published 1951).

Moorhead, Alan   THE FATAL IMPACT
The effects of Captain Cook's first three voyages on the native culture and wildlife—"scrupulously honest, yet colorful and very much alive." (BRD) Har-Row, 1966.

Morris, James   PLACES
There's an essay on Fiji in this collection of travel essays by this leading travel writer. HarBraceJ, 1973.

Price, Willard   AMERICA'S PARADISE LOST
The Micronesian Island Trust Territory in the 1930s, when it was a Japanese mandate, and in the 1960s, when book was written. Day, 1966.

Ruben, Olaf and Shadbolt, Maurice   ISLES OF THE SOUTH PACIFIC
Natl Geog, 1980.

Siers, James   FIJI CELEBRATION
Photos lend "a nice introduction to a pretty place." (BL) St. Martin, 1985.

Trumbull, Robert   TIN ROOFS AND PALM TREES: A REPORT ON THE NEW SOUTH SEAS
Blend of "history, profiles of natives, and legends . . . political and social upheaval" by an author who first became acquainted with the South Pacific as a World War II correspondent for the *New York Times*. (LJ) U of Wash Pr, 1977.

PACIFIC VOYAGES

Buck, Peter H.   VIKINGS OF THE PACIFIC
By a scholar of Polynesian history, and descendant of a Maori mother—an account of a Stone Age people who crossed the Pacific and colonized its lands long before Columbus. U of Chicago, 1959 (first published 1938).

Chiles, Webb   THE OPEN BOAT: ACROSS THE PACIFIC
A solo trip from San Diego to the New Hebrides in an eighteen-foot yawl—visits to the Marquesas, Tahiti, Bora Bora, Pago Pago, Fiji, New Hebrides. Norton, 1982.

Christian, Glynn   FRAGILE PARADISE: THE DISCOVERY OF FLETCHER CHRISTIAN, BOUNTY MUTINEER
By a descendant of Fletcher Christian, of the *Bounty* voyage—"the definitive biography" using family records—"an exciting bit of history interestingly researched." (BL) Little, 1982.

Daws, Gavin   A DREAM OF ISLANDS
"Voyages of self-discovery in the South Seas" is the subtitle of these biographical sketches of "five restless Victorians" in search of the "frontier between civilization and savagery—only to discover themselves." The five are authors Melville and Stevenson, missionary John Williams, political adventurer Walter M. Givson, and artist Paul Gauguin. (Publisher) Norton, 1980.

Dyson, John   THE SOUTH SEAS DREAM: AN ADVENTURE IN PARADISE
Travel mainly by freighter to islands of the South Seas, fulfilling a lifelong dream—"enchantingly readable." (PW) Little, 1982.

Finlay, Iain and Sheppard, Trish   A MODERN SWISS FAMILY ROBINSON
"Across the South Pacific: island-hopping from Santiago to Sydney." Story of a 15,000-mile family trip by aircraft, boat and foot and the people and cultures they met—Easter Island, Bora Bora, Cook Islands, Samoa, Fiji, Tonga and New Caledonia. Salem Hse, 1983.

Finney, Ben R.   HOKULE'A: THE WAY TO TAHITI
Voyage by Polynesian oceangoing canoe to disprove Heyerdahl's theory of settlements in Oceania. [This author believes they came from Southeast Asia, not South America.] Dodd, 1979.

Gray, William R.   VOYAGES TO PARADISE
Exploring in the wake of Captain Cook. Nat Geog, 1981.

Heyerdahl, Thor   FATU-HIVA
Story of the author's first Pacific adventure in 1936, living off nature for a year on a Pacific island. The experience led to later expeditions (see below). NAL, 1976.

Heyerdahl, Thor   THE KON-TIKI EXPEDITION
A "log turned into literature" of the author's raft journey from Peru to Polynesia, following (by his theory) the journey taken by the Polynesians who first discovered and settled the islands. Rand, 1950. Also *Aku-Aku* (1958), which explores the one-time flourishing civilization on Easter Island.

Shapiro, Harry Lionel   THE HERITAGE OF THE BOUNTY
"The story of Pitcairn through six generations"—how the author became interested in Pitcairn, a retelling of the story of the *Bounty*, and his findings as an anthropologist "caught in the toils of the Pitcairn romance." (BRD) AMS, 1979 (first published 1936).

TAHITI

Ferdon, Edwin N.   EARLY TAHITI AS THE EXPLORERS SAW IT
A recreation of pre-missionary Tahitian life through the eyes of earliest explorers. U of Arizona, 1981.

Gauguin, Paul   NOA NOA
The French artist's account of his desertion of Europe, and civilization, in 1891, and subsequent life in Tahiti. Archer, 1976 (first published 1920). See also *Moon and Sixpence* by Somerset Maugham under "Novels," below.

Howarth, David   TAHITI: A PARADISE LOST
Charts the decline of this island paradise through journals of 18th and 19th century visitors—Captains Cook and Bligh, Darwin, Melville, Robert Louis Stevenson, etc. Viking, 1983.

Siers, James   TAHITI: ROMANCE AND REALITY
Lovely photographs and a text that reveals the tension between European and Tahitian cultures. St. Martin, 1983.

THE STONE AGE ISLAND—NEW GUINEA

Attenborough, David   JOURNEY TO THE PAST
"Encounters with rare and dangerous animals and fascinating tribal peoples" in Madagascar, New Guinea and Australia. Salem House, 1983 (first published 1970).

Griffin, James ed.   PAPUA NEW GUINEA PORTRAITS
The expatriate experience. AMP, 1979.

Harrer, Heinrich   I CAME FROM THE STONE AGE
Encounters with Stone Age tribes in New Guinea. Dutton, 1965.

MacKay, Roy   NEW GUINEA
Part of The World's Wild Places series. Time-Life, 1976.

Matthiessen, Peter   UNDER THE MOUNTAIN WALL
"A chronicle of two seasons in the Stone Age. . . . masterfully written and compelling account of a primitive people . . . in final phase of savage autonomy." (BRD) Viking, 1962.

Read, Kenneth E.   THE HIGH VALLEY
"Extraordinarily vivid insight into the life and character" of the natives of New Guinea. (BRD) Columbia U Pr, 1980 (first published 1965). Also *Return to the High Valley: Coming Full Circle* (1986), a revisit to the highlands of Papua New Guinea, and sequel to *The High Valley*—"part memoir, part field report" of the mixed blessings of Westernization. (PW)

Strather, Andrew   MAN AS ART: NEW GUINEA
An "authoritative" text and fascinating photographs "capture the mystery of a

unique people behind the startling masks of warriors and ceremonial figures."
(Publisher) Viking, 1981.

Williams, Maslyn   THE STONE AGE ISLAND
New Guinea revealed, based on intimate knowledge of the country—"reads
with the elixir and rush of a fine novel." (BRD) Doubleday, 1964.

Wilson, Forbes   THE CONQUEST OF COPPER MOUNTAIN
A "fascinating, well told story" of the exploration for copper deposits in New
Guinea and the impact on its people. (LJ) Atheneum, 1981.

GUIDEBOOKS

Carter, John, ed.   THE FIJI HANDBOOK AND TRAVEL GUIDE
Intl Pbns Serv, 1980.

Corser, Frank and Rose   TAHITI TRAVELER'S GUIDE
F & R Corser, 1981.

**Inder, Stuart, ed.   PAPUA NEW GUINEA HANDBOOK AND
TRAVEL GUIDE**
Intl Pbns Serv, 1980.

Jacobs, Charles and Babette   SOUTH PACIFIC TRAVEL DIGEST
Includes Oceania, Papua New Guinea, Australia and New Zealand. Historical
and general background as well as much practical information on each area, including how to route a trip of your own; used by travel agents as a planning guide
to this complex area of the world. Travel Digests, 1984.

McDermott, John W.   HOW TO GET LOST AND FOUND IN FIJI

HOW TO GET LOST AND FOUND IN TAHITI

**HOW TO GET LOST AND FOUND IN THE
COOK ISLANDS**
Three of a new series of guidebooks with a personal approach—"delightful
reading . . . solid information on where to go and what to see." (BP) Orafa Pub Co,
1984.

Siers, James   PAPUA NEW GUINEA; TAHITI
Two new individual guidebooks. St. Martin, 1984.

**Stanley, David   SOUTH PACIFIC HANDBOOK INCLUDING SPECIAL
GALAPAGOS SUPPLEMENT**
"Comprehensive guide to the history, geography, climate, cultures and customs
of this immense area"—as well as practical details for the independent traveler
and for those with an adventurous spirit. (Publisher) Moon Pbns Ca, 1985. Also,
Micronesia Handbook: Guide to an American Lake (1985).

Stanley, David   FINDING FIJI
"Everything you'll need to plan your trip." (BP) Moon Pbns Ca, 1985.

HISTORY

Barclay, Glen St. John   A HISTORY OF THE PACIFIC FROM THE STONE AGE TO THE PRESENT DAY
"Highly readable overview of the pre- and post-European" periods of history stressing the accomplishments of various island peoples, and the impact of European cultures. (BRD) Taplinger, 1978.

Bellwood, Peter S.   THE POLYNESIANS: PREHISTORY OF AN ISLAND PEOPLE
Prehistory (to 1800 A.D.) of peoples, culture, geography of each island group, for the general reader and for those with an interest in archaeology. Thames Hudson, 1978.

Dodd, Edward   RING OF FIRE
A multivolume history and cultural history of Polynesia: Polynesian Art; Polynesian Seafaring; The Rape of Tahiti—prehistory to 1850, when the disastrous deluge of explorers, adventurers and missionaries descended upon Tahiti. Dodd, 1983.

Spate, O.H.K.   THE SPANISH LAKE
"Superb history of early European discovery and rivalry in Oceania and Australasia." (BRD) U of Minnesota, 1979.

Novels

Cleary, Jon   A VERY PRIVATE WAR
Action-filled novel set in the Southwest Pacific theatre in 1942. An expatriate American and a New Britain planter lead a disparate group of people through the jungle to Rabaul to report enemy responses to the invasion of Guadalcanal by the U.S. Morrow, 1981.

Cleary, Jon   NORTH FROM THURSDAY (New Guinea)
Vivid descriptive and dramatic novel of the customs and countryside of New Guinea, only recently emerged from the Stone Age. State Mutual, 1981 (first published 1961).

Conrad, Joseph   VICTORY
A Swedish nobleman rescues a traveling girl musician resulting in "exciting and tragic happenings." (BRD) State Mutual, 1982 (first published 1915).

Coward, Noel   POMP AND CIRCUMSTANCE
Absurd and amusing novel of what happens on an island paradise when they

have to get ready for a visit from Queen Elizabeth and Prince Philip. Dutton, 1982 (first published 1960).

Day, Arthur Grove, ed.   BEST SOUTH SEA STORIES
Duell, 1964.

Dickinson, Peter   THE GLASS-SIDED ANT'S NEST (New Guinea)
A missionary's daughter brings New Guinea tribal people to London, which leads to murder—"extraordinary criminal yarn." (FC) Har-Row, 1968.

Godden, Rumer   A BREATH OF AIR
The effects on a Scottish earl and his daughter, living on a remote island in the Pacific, when two English airmen arrive having been forced down by bad weather. Viking, 1951.

Holt, Victoria   THE SECRET WOMAN
Romance and suspense set on an island in the South Seas. Doubleday, 1970.

Holt, Victoria   THE MASK OF THE ENCHANTRESS
Romance and adventure on a South Pacific island when a young girl's double arrives from England to make mischief; and an anthropomorphic volcano. Doubleday, 1980.

Innes, Hammond   SOLOMON'S SEAL (Solomon Islands)
An estate inventory in East Anglia leads to involvement of the estate agents in philately in the South Pacific as well as gun smuggling and a small revolution. Knopf, 1980.

Jay, G. Charlotte   BEAT NOT THE BONES (Papua New Guinea)
A mystery classic with "authentic horror and atmosphere—beautifully deft plot [and] subtle picture of the interaction of an 'advanced' and a primitive race." (BRD) Har-Row, 1952.

Jay, G. Charlotte   VOICE OF THE CRAB (Papua New Guinea)
A thriller set on Kipi Island, involving "a disparate bunch of white settlers [and] natives . . . spoiled by well-meaning meddlers." (BRD) Har-Row, 1974.

London, Jack   SOUTH SEA TALES (Solomon Islands)
Eight stories about pearl divers, missionaries, cannibals—the inevitable white man in a land whose law, says the author, is "eat or be eaten." (BRD) Macmillan, 1911.

McCullough, Colleen   AN INDECENT OBSESSION
By the author of the hugely successful *Thorn Birds* (see "Australia/Novels"), this novel takes place at the close of World War II and its plot revolves about a mental ward and its nurse, Sister Honor Langtry. Har-Row, 1981.

McCutchan, Philip   HALFHYDE ON ZANATU (Polynesia)
An "episode in the naval career of . . . [an] unconventional officer" in Queen

Victoria's navy, who is charged with securing an island colony in the Pacific against "possible incursions of the Russian Empire." (FC) St. Martin, 1982.

Maugham, W. Somerset   THE MOON AND SIXPENCE (Tahiti)
Story of a European artist who deserts his family to live in Tahiti dedicated to his art—based on the life of Gauguin. Ayer, 1977 (first published 1919).

Melville, Herman   TYPEE and OMOO
Classic novels "recording the adventures of a whaling voyage in the Pacific. . . . gives a vivid picture of a civilized man in contact with the exotic dreamlike life of the tropics." (FC) Northwestern U, 1968 (first published 1846-47).

Michener, James A.   TALES OF THE SOUTH PACIFIC
Stories of World War II in the South Pacific, some of which were the basis for the musical *South Pacific*. Fawcett, 1978 (first published 1947).

Nordhoff, Charles and Hall, James N.   THE BOUNTY TRILOGY
Based on the true story of mutiny of English sailors against Captain Bligh of the ship *Bounty* and the settlement by the mutineers of Pitcairn Island. The three individual books are *Mutiny on the Bounty* (1932), *Men Against the Sea* (1934), and *Pitcairn's Island* (1934). (*Men Against the Sea* tells of Captain Bligh and those loyal to him who sailed 3,600 miles in an open boat, following the mutiny, to reach the East Indies.) Little, 1946 (first published 1932-34).

Nordhoff, Charles and Hall, James N.   THE HURRICANE (Polynesia)
Polynesian life from the point of view of a French medical officer. The climax is a hurricane—"description of the hurricane is a masterpiece." (BRD) Little, 1936.

Saxton, Mark   THE ISLAR; TWO KINGDOMS; HAVOC IN ISLANDIA
A trilogy of novels set on a wholly created, mythical island continent in the South Pacific, taking place prior to the year 1200. Houghton, 1982. Readers should first try to read *Islandia* by Austin Wright (see below), which began it all.

Theroux, Joseph   BLACK COCONUTS, BROWN MAGIC (Samoa)
Wicklowe, a former Vietnam medic on assignment in Samoa, sorts out his early years in Samoa and the mystery of his parents' past—"engaging, darkly humorous first novel. . . . nice comic relief for the brutal central threads of Wicklowe's parental tragedy." (FC) Dial Pr, 1983.

Umba, Benjamin and others   THREE SHORT NOVELS FROM PAPUA NEW GUINEA
Longman, 1975.

West, Morris L.   THE WEST QUARTET: FOUR NOVELS OF INTRIGUE AND HIGH ADVENTURE
An omnibus edition of novels originally published separately, all of which "are fine combinations of intrigue, adventure and romance." Three are set in the South Pacific (the fourth is entered under "Australia/Novels"). *The Concubine* is "about a history professor who goes hunting for treasure . . . off the Great Barrier Reef"

and *Gallows on the Sand* is about "an Irish oil prospector down on his luck."
Kundu is set in New Guinea, and is about "the attempt of a power-crazed white
man, an ex-Nazi, to usurp the spiritual leadership of the fierce indigenous population." (FC) Morrow, 1981 (originally published 1956-58).

West, Morris L.   THE NAVIGATOR
A professor at the University of Hawaii sets out to prove the existence of an
island he had described in a scholarly paper. Morrow, 1976.

Wright, Austin   ISLANDIA
Long novel of life on an imaginary South Pacific continent called Islandia,
created by a law professor—"gentle philosophical novel . . . with [people] who
come to life." (BRD) Ayer, 1971 (first published 1942). The Saxton trilogy, listed
above, continues the story.

TRAVEL ARTICLES

BLACK ENTERPRISE
1984 Jul "Fiji: A South Pacific Encounter." Tenley-Ann Jackson, p. 79

BON APPETIT
1984 Dec "Traveling with Taste: Fiji." Shirley Slater, p. 40

NATIONAL GEOGRAPHIC
1985 Oct (Samoa) "The Two Samoas, Still Coming of Age." American and
Western Samoa. Robert Booth and Melinda Berge, p. 452
1984 Oct "The Maoris, at Home in Two Worlds." Treasures of the Tradition. Yva
Momatuik, p. 542
Dec "Life Breath of Half the World—Monsoons." Priit J. Vesilind, p. 712

N.Y. TIMES SUNDAY TRAVEL SECTION (X)
1985 Sep 22 (Western Samoa) "Exploring the Polynesian Paradox." Beauty, few
modern comforts and many subtle insights. Geoffrey Dutton, p. 19
1984 Jun 10 Fare of the Country: "Okinawa—Chinese Influence." Amanda M.
Stinchecum, p. 6
Sep 16 "Atoll-Hopping in the Pacific." How to find islands where
Westernization has made the fewest inroads. Robert Trumbull, p. 15

SUNSET
1985 Oct "Fiji's Old Capital, Levuka." p. 47
Dec "Tropical Cruising in the Southwest Pacific and Southeast Asia." p. 58
1984 Apr "Riding High Above Pago-Pago." p. 52

TRAVEL & LEISURE
1984 Feb "A Boat to Bora-Bora." The world's most beautiful airport transfer.
Harvey Chipkin, p. 108

TRAVEL/HOLIDAY
1985 Mar "Fiji's Faraway Isles." Fruit of the South Pacific. Shirley Slater and Harry
      Basch, p. 10
1984 Jan "Western Samoa." The Pacific's demure duo. David G. Knibb, p. 15
      "Bora Bora." Pleasure of Polynesia. Robert Sammons, p. 58
      Nov "Total Escape in Mauritius." An exotic perfumed paradise. Carol
      Canter, p. 46
      "Micronesia—Land of Little Islands." Harold Jackson, p. 56

AUSTRALIA

Series Guidebooks (See Appendix 1)

Fodor: Australia, New Zealand and the South Pacific; Sydney
Frommer: Australia: $-a-Day
Insight: Australia
Lonely Planet: Australia
U.S. Government: Australia: Area Handbook; Background Notes;
                    Pocket Guide

Background Reading

Abbey, Edward   SLUMGULLION STEW: AN EDWARD ABBEY READER
Anthology of essays and novel excerpts covering "thirty years and thousands of miles of desert, canyon and river rapids [by] one of America's most articulate and engaging environmentalists . . . will delight his fans (while bedeviling his foes)." The book contains material on the Australian outback. Dutton, 1984.

**Attenborough, David   JOURNEYS TO THE PAST: TRAVELS IN NEW
                        GUINEA, MADAGASCAR AND THE NORTHERN
                        TERRITORY OF AUSTRALIA**
"Encounters with rare and dangerous animals and fascinating tribal peoples." Salem Hse, 1983 (first published 1970).

Austin, Clifford   I LEFT MY HEART IN ANDAMOOKA
"An odyssey through the Australian outback"—the author's 16,000-mile tour, with his dog, of the opal fields and outback—"travels, friends, adventures." (LJ) David, 1974.

Bennett, Isobel   GREAT BARRIER REEF
"A look at life on Australia's famous reef—corals, anemones, fish, and man's effect on it." (LJ) Mereweather, 1982.

Davidson, Robyn   TRACKS
This book won the Thomas Cook Award as best travel book of the year in 1980. "Inspiring, irritating, wonderful record" of a 1,700-mile trek, alone except for her dog and four camels [!], across Australia from Alice Springs to the Indian Ocean. [Camels were introduced into Australia during railroad-building days.] (BRD) Pantheon, 1980.

DeLisle, Gordon   INTRODUCING AUSTRALIA
"Delightfully written, packed with information . . . excellent introduction and tempting invitation to visit." (LJ) Taplinger, 1972.

Flood, Josephine   ARCHAEOLOGY OF THE DREAMTIME
"Dreamtime" symbolizes creation in the aborigine tradition. "Eye-opening portrait of past (and present) aboriginal life. . . . how this culture adapted and flourished in the harsh Australian environment." (BL) U of Hawaii, 1983.

Grzimek, Bernhard   FOUR-LEGGED AUSTRALIANS: ADVENTURES WITH ANIMALS AND MAN IN AUSTRALIA
"Fascinating information on the unique animal life 'down under'" and a plea for preservation of wild animals. (BRD) Hill & Wang, 1967.

Irvine, Lucy   CASTAWAY
An account of the author's "treacherous one-year adventure on a desert island in the Torres Strait off the northernmost coast of Australia"—spent there as the result of answering a newspaper ad. (BL) Random, 1984.

Keneally, Thomas   OUTBACK
The celebrated Australian novelist writes of Australia's Northern Territory—the wide-open, magnificent part of the continent—history of its European settlement, geology, aborigine culture, life of the white population. Rand-McNally, 1984.

Luck, Peter and others   THIS FABULOUS CENTURY
The story of Australia since its birth as a nation on January 1, 1901. Circus Bks, 1979.

McGreevy, John, ed.   CITIES
Impressions of world cities as seen through the eyes of people intimately connected with them—for Sydney it is Germaine Greer. Potter, 1981.

Marshall, Catherine and Daniell, Jo   THORNBIRD COUNTRY
A diary with snippets of history and legend, recording impressions of a three-month trip through Australia. Warner, 1983.

Mikes, George   BOOMERANG: AUSTRALIA REDISCOVERED
A Hungarian-born Englishman's personal, candid, critical impressions of
Australia that "by the end of his tour [have] boomeranged into a love and admira-
tion for Australia." Transatlantic, 1970.

Moorehead, Alan   COOPER'S CREEK
Account of a Victorian expedition, a 1,500-mile walk from central Australia to
the Gulf of Carpentaria that ended disastrously. The author retraced the trip in a
Land Rover. Har-Row, 1963.

Moorehead, Alan   RUM JUNGLE
Return and rediscovery of the country this journalist had left in 1936—"urbane
. . . vivid . . . lively reportage" of travels and autobiography, some of which first
appeared in the *New Yorker*. (BRD) Scribner, 1953.

Morris, Jan   JOURNEYS
A collection of travel essays by one of the leading travel writers includes one on
Australia. Oxford U, 1984.

Porter, Peter   SYDNEY
Part of the Great Cities of the World series. Time-Life, 1980.

Sloan, Ethel B.   A KANGAROO IN THE KITCHEN
Life in Sydney by an American family sent there for a two-year business stint.
Bobbs, 1978.

Walker, Murray   MAKING DO
Memories of Australia's back country people. Penguin, 1982.

GUIDEBOOKS

Bone, Robert W.   THE MAVERICK GUIDE TO AUSTRALIA
"Practical, extremely interesting, very specific, colorful, and spritely. . . . easy to
use, easy to read." (ARBA) Pelican, 1983.

Hildebrand, Volker   AUSTRALIA-NEW ZEALAND
One of a new series of guidebooks originating in Germany. Hippocrene, 1985.

McDermott, John W.   HOW TO GET LOST AND FOUND IN AUSTRALIA
Adventures based on an eight-month trek by the author and his wife in the wilds
of Australia—"delightful reading. . . . solid information on where to go and what to
see." (BP) Hippocrene, 1983.

Mead, Robin   AUSTRALIA
Acclimatizes the prospective traveler to Australian history, culture, plant and
animal life—what to see and do, state by state. Batsford, 1983.

O'Neil, Currey   **EXPLORE AUSTRALIA: TOURING FOR LEISURE AND PLEASURE**
Salem House, 1984.

Stanley, David   **SOUTH PACIFIC HANDBOOK**
Includes Australia. See under "Pacific and Oceania."

Sunset eds.   **AUSTRALIA**
Sunset-Lane, 1980.

Werchik, Ruth and Arne   **THE GREAT BARRIER REEF—A GUIDE TO THE ISLANDS AND THE REEFS**
Wide World, 1986.

Wilson, Robert   **THE BOOK OF AUSTRALIA**
An encyclopedic guide, with maps and photographs, in gazetteer format.
Lansdowne, 1983.

HISTORY

Cameron, Roderick   **AUSTRALIA: HISTORY AND HORIZONS**
"Easy-to-read, skillful evocation" of Australian history by a traveler/writer, with emphasis on the "style and quality of life" in Australia from the late eighteenth through the nineteenth centuries. (LJ) Columbia U Pr, 1971.

Isaacs, Jennifer, ed.   **AUSTRALIAN DREAMING: 40,000 YEARS OF ABORIGINAL HISTORY**
"The first aborigine history book on the Australian continent and its people, as told by the aborigines themselves." (LJ) Lansdowne, 1980.

Ward, Russel B.   **THE HISTORY OF AUSTRALIA: THE TWENTIETH CENTURY**
"Comprehensive tracing of the evolution of Australia since the six British colonies . . . were wed into an independent country." (BRD) Oxford U, 1979. Also *The Australian Legend* (1979), a "classic study of the shaping of Australia's cultural character."

Novels

Aldridge, James   **THE UNTOUCHABLE JULI**
The character of a small Australian town in the 1930s, and its people. Little, 1976.

Anderson, Jessica   **TIRRA LIRRA BY THE RIVER**
Short, beautifully written novel of a seventy-year-old woman's return home and recollections of her life—"knowledge and feeling for the small town and Sydney

gives depth and conviction to the characters and the times." (BRD) Penguin, 1984.

Cato, Nancy   FOREFATHERS
A multifamily saga that traces families of various ethnic backgrounds from 1824. St. Martin, 1983.

Cleary, Jon   HELGA'S WEB
A vivid Australian setting as Detective-Sergeant Malone solves the murder of a German girl in the Sydney opera house. Morrow, 1970.

Cleary, Jon   THE SUNDOWNERS
One year in the life of an Australian sheep drover's family, and basis for the movie. Scribner, 1952.

Coleman, Terry   SOUTHERN CROSS
Historical novel of the nineteenth century that traces the history of New South Wales, while chronicling a parallel family history. Viking, 1979.

Dark, Eleanor   THE TIMELESS LAND
"Story of the early years of the colony at Sydney . . . varied feelings of settlers, convicts . . . government officials." (BRD)Macmillan, 1941.

Denton, Kit   THE BREAKER
The novel on which the movie *Breaker Morant* was based; the plot involves the court-martial of an Australian officer during the Boer War. St. Martin, 1981 (first published 1973).

Drewe, Robert   THE BODYSURFERS
"Spare . . . sharp" character sketches in a dozen short stories of the beaches of Australia (and California). Harper 1984.

Eden, Dorothy   THE VINES OF YARRABEE
A family chronicle of vineyard owners in New South Wales. Coward, 1969.

Ekert-Rotholz, Alice   THE SIDNEY CIRCLE
Romance and intrigue as an English girl marries an Australian architect. Fromm, 1983.

Francis, Dick   IN THE FRAME
A murder mystery involving stolen antiques, that leads an English painter on a trail from England to Sydney. Har-Row, 1977.

Franklin, Miles   MY BRILLIANT CAREER
A young Australian woman is rescued by her affluent grandmother from her dreary life in the Australian outback but, in the end, "chooses spiritual independence over physical comfort and emotional security." (FC) St. Martin, 1980 (first published 1901). *The End of My Career* is a sequel (published in 1946) in

which the author relates how she came to write *My Brilliant Career*, and the reactions of those people depicted in it.

Gaskin, Catherine   FAMILY AFFAIRS
A two-family saga of an illegitimate Irish girl, befriended by a wealthy Australian sheep-ranching family and educated above her station. Doubleday, 1980.

Grant, Maxwell   INHERIT THE SUN
An "evocation of the Australian bush"—the life of a man from birth in 1897 in the outback to the mid-1970s. (FC) Coward, 1981.

Hasluck, N.   THE BLUE GUITAR
A novel set in Perth told "at a rapid pace and with racy charm" of a man facing myriad mishaps and disasters in his thirty-fourth year—"refreshingly Australian . . . talking from the hip." (BRD) Holt, 1980.

Herbert, Xavier   POOR FELLOW MY COUNTRY
Epic novel of Australia in the '30s and '40s, that follows the life of a quarter-caste aborigine to manhood, "creating a vast panorama of time and space . . . a treasury of aboriginal folk myths, culture and humor." (LJ) St. Martin, 1980.

Holt, Victoria   THE PRIDE OF THE PEACOCK
A mystery set in Australia's opal fields, and England. Doubleday, 1976. Also, *The Shadow of the Lynx* (1971), a gothic set in the Australian gold mines of the 1880s, and England.

Irish, Lola   AND THE WILD BIRDS SING
"This vigorous historical romance limns a convincing panorama of the social order in Sydney in the 1840s . . . the Hogarthian scenes of high and low life that were its gaudy manifestations." (FC) Watts, 1984.

Keneally, Thomas   THREE CHEERS FOR THE PARACLETE
A story of conflict between older conservative Catholic clergy and young priests. Viking, 1969. Also *The Chant of Jimmy Blacksmith* (1972).

Locke, Elliott S.   WATER UNDER THE BRIDGE
The opening of the Sydney Harbor Bridge in 1932 marks the beginning of this novel that follows the intermingled lives of people who first met at a party to see the fireworks of the bridge ceremony, until forty years later, in 1973. S&S, 1977. Also, *Careful He Might Hear You* (1963), about a struggle for custody of a young boy.

McCullough, Colleen   THE THORN BIRDS
The blockbuster novel of the Cleary clan in Australia, from 1915 to 1969—an old-fashioned family saga. Har-Row, 1977.

Malouf, David   HARLAND'S HALF ACRE
An "eccentric and solitary painter . . . obsessed with restoring to his kin acreage an ancestor gambled away." (FC) Knopf, 1984.

Marshall, James V.   WALKABOUT
A brother and sister (nine and thirteen years old) are the sole survivors of a plane crash in an uninhabited area of northern Australia. They set out to walk the 1,400 miles to Adelaide and are saved by a young aborigine on a "walkabout ordeal" that is part of his tribe's rites. The children manage to "bridge across the gap of more than a hundred thousand years that lies between the cultures that have produced them." (BRD) Doubleday, 1961.

Marshall, James V.   A WALK TO THE HILLS OF THE DREAMTIME
The adventures of two Japanese-aborigine orphans, raised in a Christian mission, who are stranded in a desert and decide to make the trek to the "hills of dreamtime"—the perfect land of the aborigines—and are finally rescued by a wandering tribe. Morrow, 1970.

Noonan, Michael   MAGWITCH
Retaining the Dickensian style, this novel takes Pip from where *Great Expectations* (1861) leaves off—to Australia, where he must "trace his benefactor's rise to riches and power . . . and discover the secret of the hidden fortune before Magwitch's enemies can kill him." (FC) St. Martin, 1982.

Nordhoff, Charles and Hall, James N.   BOTANY BAY
The story of the Australian penal colony at Botany Bay and some of the English prisoners sent there. Little, 1941.

Richardson, Henry H.   FORTUNES OF RICHARD MAHONEY
The overall title of a trilogy and Australian saga of Richard Mahoney. *Australian Felix* tells of his early years in Australia as a storekeeper in Ballarat during the gold rush days. He becomes a doctor, and in *The Way Home* leaves Australia for England, but realizes he is an "Australian" and returns to build *Ultima Thule* (title of the third book) to begin his medical practice all over again. It's a series "packed with woe" but an "unforgettable picture of the development of Australia." Norton, 1929, 1930 (first published 1917).

Upfield, Arthur W.   THE WILL OF THE TRIBE
Murder story with the body found in an Australian desert meteor crater—"local color . . . personalities of family and stockmen" and ending with a "chase involving two ex-aborigines." (FC) Doubleday, 1962. Also, *Death of a Swagman* (1945) and *The Lure of the Bush* (1965).

West, Morris L.   THE NAKED COUNTRY
In *A West Quartet*; set in the Australian northwest—an "unforgettable evocation" of the country. (FC) Morrow, 1981.

White, Patrick   THE EYE OF THE STORM
The author is a leading Australian writer who won the Nobel Prize in literature in 1973. Viking, 1973. Other titles include: *The Tree of Man* (1955), *Voss* (1957), *Riders in the Chariot* (1961), *The Solid Mandala* (1966), *The Vivisector* (1970), *A Fringe of Leaves* (1977).

Wongar, B.   BABARU; THE TRACK TO BRALGU
Two books of short stories by an Australian aborigine. The stories deal with the "white man's devastation of Australian aboriginal culture . . . lethal conflict between a race that sees the earth as no more than a quarry and another and more ancient one to whom it is an extension of body, soul, and family." (FC) U of Illinois, 1982 and 1977.

TRAVEL ARTICLES

BON APPETIT
1985 Sep "Traveling with Taste: Tasmania." Shirley Slater, p. 36

ESQUIRE
1985 Oct "Thirty-one Romantic Vacations." Includes places in Polynesia. Neal Karlen and Wendy Lowe, p. 54
Apr "Seven Trips to Work in Around Work." Includes Australia. p. 114

GOURMET
1984 Oct "Adelaide." Mollie E.C. Webster, p. 46

NATIONAL GEOGRAPHIC
1985 Aug "The Land where the Murray Flows from the Mountains to Sea." Murray River in New South Wales and Victoria. Louise E. Levathes, p. 252
1984 Jan "Exploring a Sunken Realm in Australia." Hillary Hauser, p. 129

NATIONAL GEOGRAPHIC TRAVELER
1984 Summer "A View of Australia." Shirley Hazzard sizes up her native land and people, p. 148
Summer "Sydney." Glittering city down under . . . pleasures come nonstop. Mary Ann Harrell, p. 140

N.Y. TIMES SUNDAY TRAVEL SECTION (X)
1985 Mar 10 "Breaking Away from Sydney." Perpetual surf, rolling uplands, and, of course, kangaroos, await. Jane Perlez, p. 20
May 19 Fare of the Country: "Oysters, Australian Style." Jane Perlez, p. 6
Nov 24 Fare of the Country: "Small Vineyards by the Barrel in Australia." Harold C. Schonberg, p. 6
1984 Oct 7 (Part 2, "Sophisticated Traveler") "Green Wilderness."Australia's Blue Mountains, complete with koalas. Colleen McCullough, p. 90
Oct 14 "Roughing It in the Outback: Guides Help Visitors Cope." Chris West, p. 12

SATURDAY EVENING POST
1985 Sep "Australia: City Side." Melbourne and Sydney. Ted Kreiter, p. 90

TOWN & COUNTRY
1985 May "Vis-a-Vis: Down Under, Etc." p. 240

TRAVEL & LEISURE

1985 Jan "Australia's new Victorian Arts Centre." Melbourne celebrates the opening of a splendid new complex for theater, opera and art. David Reed, p. 110

Nov "Across Australia by Train." From Sydney to Perth. Richard Covington, p. 192.

"Chain Hotels with a Legendary Past." Eugene Fodor, p. 203

1984 May "A Beguiling Neighborhood in Sydney." Laurence Shames, p. 94

Jun "Dashing About Australia, Glimpses Down Under." Cuddly koalas, the Melbourne Cup and glittering Sydney harbor. Maria Shaw, p. 22

TRAVEL/HOLIDAY

1985 Jan "Offbeat Ski Resorts." Includes Australia. Ken Castle, p. 46

Jan "The Difference Down Under." Tasmania, Australia's best-kept secret. John Penisten, p. 4

Mar "Opals and Dugouts Down Under." Michele Burgess, p. 140

Oct "Melbourne: A Revealing Portrait." Australia's Rugged (not Rugby) city. Robert Bone, p. 64

1984 Aug "Homegrown Australian Holidays." The joys of a farmhouse vacation. James C. Simmons, p. 54

Oct "The Renaissance of Brisbane, Australia." Queensland's vibrant capital. David Knibb, p. 10

NEW ZEALAND

Series Guidebooks (See Appendix 1)

Berlitz: New Zealand
Fodor: Australia, New Zealand and the South Pacific
Frommer: New Zealand: $-a-Day
Insight: New Zealand
Lonely Planet: New Zealand; Tramping in New Zealand
U.S. Government: New Zealand: Background Notes; Post Report; Pocket Guide

Background Reading

Joyce, Roy and Saunders, Bill   NEW ZEALAND: THE GLORIOUS ISLANDS
Text and photographs, Rand McNally, 1984.

King, Michael   NEW ZEALAND: ITS LAND AND ITS PEOPLE
C.E. Tuttle, 1979.

Leland, Louis S., Jr.   KIWI-YANKEE DICTIONARY
Humorous introduction, in dictionary format, to New Zealand's slang and terms for various things. Pelican, 1984.

Lockley, Ronald   MEN AGAINST NATURE
The deteriorating ecology in New Zealand caused first by the Maoris and then by Europeans, as well as an excellent history of the development of New Zealand. (LJ) Transatlantic, 1971.

Marsh, Ngaio   NEW ZEALAND
Reprint of a personal interpretation of the country written for young people, by the prolific writer of mysteries who was a New Zealander. Amereon, 1976 (first published 1942). Also, her autobiography *Black Beech and Honeydew* (1965).

Metge, Joan   THE MAORIS OF NEW ZEALAND
Comprehensive book on Maori culture. Routledge, 1976.

Miller, Harold G.   NEW ZEALAND
"Informal discussion by a thoughtful, well-informed and objective New Zealander" provides an introduction and history for the general reader. (BRD) Greenwood, 1983 (first published 1950).

Pownall, Glen   UNIQUE NEW ZEALAND
Flora, fauna, Maori culture. Viking Sevenseas, 1980. Also *Maori Arts and Crafts* (1980) from the same author and publisher.

**Temple, Philip   CASTLES IN THE AIR: MEN AND MOUNTAINS
IN NEW ZEALAND**
IPS, 1973. Also *South Island of New Zealand* (1975) and *Patterns of Water: The Great Southern Lakes of New Zealand* (1974), from the same author and publisher.

GUIDEBOOKS

Bone, Robert W.   THE MAVERICK GUIDE TO NEW ZEALAND
A combination of lecture, gossip session and practical guidebook—where to go, what to see, hotels, food and shopping—"the best guide to New Zealand ever seen by this New Zealander." (LJ) Pelican, 1983.

Hildebrand, Volker   NEW ZEALAND
One of a new guidebook series originating in Germany. Hippocrene, 1985.

**McDermott, John W.   HOW TO GET LOST AND FOUND IN
NEW ZEALAND**
Guidebook by two American travelers, with a personal approach—"delightful reading . . . solid information on where to go and what to see." Hippocrene, 1983.

Pope, Diana and Jeremy   **THE MOBIL ILLUSTRATED GUIDE TO NEW ZEALAND**
For travelers and armchair travelers—covers both islands, describing places of interest both natural and human made and with many photos. Facts On File, 1983.

Stanley, David   **SOUTH PACIFIC HANDBOOK**
Includes New Zealand. See under "Pacific and Oceania."

Sunset eds.   **NEW ZEALAND**
Sunset-Lane, 1984.

HISTORY

Jackson, Keith   **NEW ZEALAND**
Walker, 1969.

Oliver, W.H. and Williams, B.R.   **THE OXFORD HISTORY OF NEW ZEALAND**
Oxford U, 1981.

Turnbull, Michael   **THE CHANGING LAND: A SHORT HISTORY OF NEW ZEALAND**
IPS, 1975.

Novels

Ashton-Warner, Sylvia   **GREENSTONE**
Maori legend, history and tradition woven into the story of an English writer's family that includes a grandchild who is daughter of a Maori princess. S&S, 1966.

Ashton-Warner, Sylvia   **SPINSTER**
A spinster schoolteacher's struggles to teach a group of seventy mostly Maori children in an outpost school—"funny . . . delightful . . . deeply poetic and strikingly apropos." (FC) S&S, 1959. Also, *Bell Call* (1964), in which an unconventional mother defies school authorities.

Ashton-Warner, Sylvia   **INCENSE TO IDOLS**
"Portrait of a lost lady . . . who invades New Zealand and the orbits of several men." (BRD) S&S, 1960.

Bagley, Desmond   **THE SNOW TIGER**
A trial, involving an avalanche induced by two brothers when an Englishman inherits management of a mine. Doubleday, 1975.

Cowley, Joy   **NEXT IN A FALLING TREE**
A woman's May-December affair as a release from the many dreary years spent caring for her invalid mother. Doubleday, 1967.

Eden, Dorothy   THE IMPORTANT FAMILY
Story of an Irish woman who accompanies a family to New Zealand in the mid-nineteenth century. Coward, 1980.

Goudge, Elizabeth   GREEN DOLPHIN STREET
Historical novel of frontier life in New Zealand in the nineteenth century. Coward, 1944.

Marsh, Ngaio   PHOTO FINISH
By the popular mystery writer—lively and amusing murder mystery of a temperamental opera singer in New Zealand. Little, 1980. Also *Colour Scheme* (1943), set in a New Zealand spa.

Shadbolt, Maurice   LOVELOCK VERSION
Unconventional novel of pioneer life in which an angel appears to Lovelock, causing him to set out on a search for the meaning in life that involves a wilderness trek, a sojourn with Maoris, and the founding of a community. St. Martin, 1981. Also *Among the Cinders* (1965), about the relationship of a sixteen-year-old boy and his half-caste Maori friend.

Shadbolt, Maurice   STRANGERS AND JOURNEYS
A two-family saga—one a pioneer farm family, the other a Communist working class family—covers forty years in the lives of the two male protagonists just after World War I, and the social and political forces of the period—"enhanced by the authentic New Zealand setting." (BRD) St. Martin, 1972.

Shadbolt, Maurice   THE NEW ZEALANDERS
Short stories reflecting a variety of backgrounds from the native Maori to the sophisticated urban. Atheneum, 1961.

TRAVEL ARTICLES

ESQUIRE
1984 Apr "Seven Trips to Work in Around Work." Including New Zealand. p. 114
     May "A Trout for All Seasons." Fishing for trout in four seasons on different continents; New Zealand is "winter." p. 33

N.Y. TIMES SUNDAY TRAVEL SECTION (X)
1984 Sep 16 "A Cozy Journey Through New Zealand." Narrow-gauge line spans 1,000 miles. Fletcher Knebel, p. 21
     Dec 30 "New Zealand's Tidy Haven." The Bay of Islands (89 of them by one count) draws urbanites to the sun and sea. Fletcher Knebel, p. 17

SUNSET
1984 Nov "New Zealand, Not the Mother Lode." Gold rush town in Queensland. p. 37

TRAVEL & LEISURE
1985 Sep "The Charm of Christchurch." Pastoral crossroads of New Zealand's South Island. Anthony Weller, p. 36
Oct "Grand Adventures: New Zealand's Milford Track—the Finest Walk in the World." Anthony Weller, p. 122

TRAVEL/HOLIDAY
1985 Jan "Offbeat Ski Resorts." Includes New Zealand. Ken Castle, p. 46
Sep "New Zealand—Remembering the Good Ole' Days." Diane P. Marshall, p. 52

WORLD PRESS REVIEW
1985 Sep "New Zealand—the Great Escape (*The Statesman*, New Delhi/Calcutta)." Jug Suraiya, p. 62

V.EUROPE

Series Guidebooks (See Appendix 1)

Baedeker: Islands of the Mediterranean
Birnbaum: Europe; Europe for Business Travelers
Fielding: Europe; Economy Europe; Europe with Children;
            Sightseeing Guide to Europe: Discover Europe off the
            Beaten Path; Motoring and Camping Europe
Fisher: Europe
Fodor: Europe; Budget Europe; Eastern Europe
Frommer: Europe: $-a-Day
Insight: Continental Europe
Let's Go: Europe
Michelin: Main Cities of Europe

Background Reading

TRAVELOGUES, HISTORICAL BACKGROUND, SPECIAL PERSPECTIVES

Apple, R.W. Jr.   APPLE'S EUROPE
An "uncommon guide" by the *New York Times* correspondent who was London bureau chief for several years—special places, unusual and important sights to see, food and meals. Atheneum, 1986.

Ardagh, John   A TALE OF FIVE CITIES
An in-depth look at five provincial European cities: Newcastle (England), Toulouse (France), Stuttgart (Germany), Bologna (Italy), Ljubljana (Yugoslavia). An interesting and fascinating approach since it is a comparison of five cities not ordinarily first on a tourist's list, and could well be the starting point for planning an unusual itinerary of one's own. Har-Row, 1980.

Bailey, Anthony ALONG THE EDGE OF THE FOREST: AN IRON
CURTAIN JOURNEY
A travelogue of a journey from the Baltic to Trieste along the iron curtain that
separates East from West—"the landscape, and the people whose lives are formed
by the border. . . . escapes . . . his own adventures with border patrols." (LJ)
Random, 1983.

Barber, Richard THE PENGUIN GUIDE TO MEDIEVAL EUROPE
"The physical evidence visible to today's traveler" (churches, castles, etc.)
provides the basis for this survey of life during the Middle Ages—"bright, easily
digestible . . . fine maps." (BL) Penguin, 1984.

Barzini, Luigi THE EUROPEANS
"Examines with great shrewdness and a delightful dry wit" why political unifica-
tion of Europe has not happened—a character analysis of Britain, Germany,
France, Italy, Holland. (BRD) S&S, 1983.

Binney, Marcus and others GREAT RAILWAY STATIONS OF EUROPE
A collaboration of the editor of *Country Life* in Britain, a photographer, and a
curator of historic industrial buildings. Forty or so stations in nine countries are
included—"anyone who has traveled abroad will find it difficult to fend off a sense
of nostalgia or wanderlust." (NYTBR) Thames Hudson, 1985.

Botting, Douglas WILDERNESS EUROPE
Part of the World's Wild Places series. Time-Life, 1976.

Braudel, Fernand THE MEDITERRANEAN
Total history—geography, historical epochs and events, inventions,
biographies, environment, war and peace, kings and peasants, languages and literature. Har-Row, 1976.

Brown, Reginald A. CASTLES: A HISTORY AND GUIDE
A "splendid introduction to European castles" along with a 60-page gazetteer
and profiles of selected castles. (BL) Blandford, 1981.

Cookridge, E.H. THE ORIENT EXPRESS: THE LIFE AND TIMES OF THE
WORLD'S MOST FAMOUS TRAIN
A fascinating account of this "unique caravansary on wheels." Written by a
wartime intelligence agent, it includes espionage, hijacking, the "wry and
ridiculous." (BRD) Har-Row, 1980.

Fermor, Patrick A TIME OF GIFTS
Travel memoir of a walk, in 1933, from the Netherlands to Istanbul by an author
(only 18) "with the head of a classicist and the heart of romantic . . . frequently
hilarious." His impressions give a unique view of Germany just before the Nazis
took over; the pre-Communist Hungarian and Rumanian countryside. (BRD) Har-
Row, 1977.

Glazebrook, Philip   JOURNEY TO KARS
This is the account of a trip by a novelist who wanted to find out why earlier middle-class Victorians left comfortable England to travel in discomfort and danger to distant lands. Therefore he, his wife and children set out from Dorset, traveling via Yugoslavia, Greece and Turkey to the border of the Soviet Union, returning via Bulgaria, Rumania and Hungary. He "succeeds in involving the reader with lands and people perhaps more satisfying to read about than to visit [and] in bringing life to the familiar sites of cathedrals, palaces, ruins, and museums. . . . the book's combination of history and humor makes it ideal for browsing." (PW) Atheneum, 1984.

Hillaby, John   A WALK THROUGH EUROPE
An account of a 1,300-mile walk through Europe—Holland, Belgium, Germany, Switzerland, Italy and France—reflecting its author's enthusiasm for nature and people. Academy Chi Ltd, 1982. See also books by Hillaby entered under "England/Background Reading."

Holmes, Richard   FOOTSTEPS: ADVENTURES OF A ROMANTIC BIOGRAPHER
A visit to the houses in which they sojourned, tracing the landscapes traveled, for Robert Louis Stevenson's *Travels With a Donkey*, Mary Wolstonecraft and Paris during the French Revolution, Percy and Mary Shelley in Italy, Gerard de Verval. Viking, 1985.

Knight, Kathryn L.   ATLANTIC CIRCLE
By an author of children's books who marries "a salty blond WASP from Maine" and takes off on a sail with him across the Atlantic, and through the locks and canals and rivers of Denmark, Netherlands and France—"thoroughly engaging and funny" and a good guide as well. (NYTBR) Norton, 1984.

Méras, Phyllis   THE MERMAIDS OF CHENONCEAUX AND 828 OTHER STORIES: AN ANECDOTAL GUIDE TO EUROPE
The premise of this browsing book is that it's not guidebook data about what you see in your travels that sticks in your mind, it's the anecdotes that "bring a place to life and fix it in memory." This is an entire book of "beguiling" anecdotes—Garson Kanin calls it an "outpouring of delight and discovery. I defy anyone to open it and not be held for hours. A treasure." A book to take along and read with breakfast before the day's itinerary. (Publisher) Congdon & Weed, 1982.

Morris, Wright   AN AMERICAN DREAMER IN EUROPE
Reprint of a book of the '30s—"recaptures his first trip to Europe during the depths of the depression . . . episodes and adventures . . . minutely detailed yet dreamlike, bizarre, compellingly readable." (PW) Penguin, 1984.

Newby, Eric   ON THE SHORES OF THE MEDITERRANEAN
Winemaking in Tuscany, a Mafia wedding, sunrise over Fez, prayer at the West Wall, Holy Week in Seville, are just some of the travel episodes. "This old-fashioned travelogue, crowded with vivid detail and interlarded with snippets of history, delights and entertains." (PW) Little, 1985.

Pardley, Lin and Larry   SERAFFYN'S ORIENTAL ADVENTURE
See under "Asia."

**Rosenthal, A.M. and Gelb, Arthur   THE SOPHISTICATED TRAVELER—
BELOVED CITIES: EUROPE**
An anthology of articles from the *New York Times* Sunday Travel Section and the biennial "Sophisticated Traveler" supplement (note also the "Travel Articles" segments of this book). Personal evocation of the sights and sounds of London, Paris, Rome and Athens by thirty writers (such as Saul Bellow, V.S. Pritchett, Shirley Hazzard, Muriel Spark, etc.) and *New York Times* correspondents. (Note also under Travel Articles [for Europe and all countries] those articles with the designation "Part 2, Sophisticated Traveler" for ongoing series). Villard, 1984.

Sherwood, Shirley   VENICE-SIMPLON ORIENT EXPRESS
The return of the world's most celebrated train—restoration and history of the train that has recently resumed service between London and Venice. Weidenfeld & Nicolson, 1984.

Snyder, Louis L.   HISTORICAL GUIDE TO WORLD WAR II
"Popular history in the best sense"—the book is arranged alphabetically with entries for countries, places, events, people. Wartime art, literature, songs, social and cultural themes—"a total picture of this time period." Ideal background reading to enhance travel in both Europe and the Pacific. (BL) Greenwood, 1982.

**Thwaite, Anthony and Beny, Roloff   ODYSSEY: MIRROR OF THE
MEDITERRANEAN**
An "evocation of 30 years of living in and journeying to the lands that border on the Mediterranean Sea." (LJ) Har-Row, 1981.

Vishniac, Roman   A VANISHED WORLD
Photographs of Jewish life in the 1930s (many no longer in existence), in Germany, Czechoslovakia and Poland just before the Nazis appeared. They "vividly document a way of life . . . several moving text pieces"; there's a foreword by Elie Wiesel. (BRD) FS&G, 1983. See also the Fermor book listed above.

Waugh, Evelyn   BACHELOR ABROAD: A MEDITERRANEAN JOURNAL
Observations and experiences of a journey around the Mediterranean in the twenties—"engaging style . . . witty [and] entertaining." (BRD) Jonathan Cape, 1930.

GUIDEBOOKS

Bermont, John   HOW TO EUROPE
"Outstandingly practical handbook of both generalized and specific in-Europe strategies directed to conventional but inexperienced travelers . . . beyond the tent and vagabonding level." (BL) Murphy & Broad, 1982.

**Braganti, Nancy L. and Devine, Elizabeth   THE TRAVELERS' GUIDE TO
EUROPEAN CUSTOMS &
MANNERS**
Subtitle: How to converse, dine, tip, drive, bargain, dress, make friends and

conduct business while in Europe. Just the book to enable visitors "to act in a socially knowledgeable and correct way"—from dressing and making a good impression to eating, hotels, holidays, conversational subjects to avoid, etc. (LJ) Meadowbrook Bks, 1984.

Bourne, Bill and Marjorie   EUROPE A LA CARTE
A country-by-country guide to picnicking in Europe on regional specialties. Volare Bks, 1984.

Bridgeman, Harriet   VISITING THE GARDENS OF EUROPE
Twelve hundred gardens open to the public—botanical, formal, romantic, cottages, great country houses, cloisters, tour parks and more. Dutton, 1979.

Bryson, William   THE PALACE UNDER THE ALPS
Subtitle: And over 200 other unusual, unspoiled, and infrequently visited spots in 16 countries. "Features an outstanding castle here, an odd but intriguing museum there, a celebration, a lake" etc. (BL) Congdon & Weed, 1985.

**Chandler, David   TRAVELER'S GUIDE TO THE BATTLEFIELDS
                     OF EUROPE**
Volume 1-Western Europe; Volume 2-Eastern & Central Europe. Chilton, 1974.

**Chesanow, Neil   EUROPE FOR ONE: A COMPLETE GUIDE FOR
                   SOLO TRAVELERS**
A how-to for planning trips, checklists, evaluating travel books and agents, information on meeting people, organizations to contact, etc. Dutton, 1982.

**Eastman, John   WHO LIVED WHERE IN EUROPE: A BIOGRAPHICAL
                  GUIDE TO HOMES AND MUSEUMS**
Arranged alphabetically—residences or work places of 300 authors, composers, artists, statesmen and others, including fees and hours if open to the public. Includes the British Isles and East Germany. Facts On File, 1985.

**Ferguson, George W.   EUROPE BY EURAIL: HOW TO TOUR EUROPE
                        BY TRAIN**
There's a separate guidebook for Great Britain listed under "England/ Guidebooks"—this one covers continental Europe. B Franklin, 1983.

**Graham, Peter   INTERNATIONAL HERALD TRIBUNE GUIDE TO
                 BUSINESS TRAVEL AND ENTERTAINMENT IN EUROPE**
The focus is on thirteen major cities: Amsterdam, Brussels, Copenhagen, Dusseldorf, Frankfurt, Geneva, London, Lyons, Milan, Munich, Paris, Stockholm and Zurich. "The selection [of cities] definitely keeps the business traveler in mind in terms of accessibility, quality, and chicness . . . useful to pleasure as well as working travelers." (BL) HR&W, 1984.

Jacobsen, Bruce and Riggs, Rollin   EUROPE: WHERE THE FUN IS
"The best nightclubs, the wildest bars, the most fun restaurants . . . low-down on

the high life in 15 major European cities . . . hottest beaches from Portugal to the Greek Islands" plus activities like "flea markets, grape-picking, hiking and sailing." (Publisher) RJ Pubns, 1984.

Kingery, Phyllis and Alan   THE LIBERATED TRAVELLER
How to see Europe intelligently, independently and inexpensively, the way Europeans do, is the subtitle. Chicago Rev Pr, 1982.

Lo Bello, Nino   EUROPEAN DETOURS: A TRAVEL GUIDE TO UNUSUAL SIGHTS
"A zany travel guide . . . remarkable and bizarre towns . . . and other curious locales . . . proves entertaining for both armchair traveler and adventurous tourist." (BRD) Hammond, 1981.

Millon, Marc and Kim   THE WINE ROADS OF EUROPE
"Tourist guide and directory to the wine regions of France, Germany, Italy, Austria, Spain and Portugal . . . describes local food and wine . . . wine festivals . . . wine courses, wine museums, restaurants, lodgings, possible itineraries . . . a first-rate book." (BL) S&S, 1984.

Oakes, George and Chapman, Alexandra   TURN RIGHT AT THE FOUNTAIN
Off-the-beaten-path walking tours in 21 cities. HR&W, 1981.

Olmstead, Gerald W.   THE MORROW GUIDE TO BACKCOUNTRY EUROPE
A guide *away* from the most popular, crowded, routine attractions—itineraries and sidetrips "with terrains that range from beaches in Greece and mountains in Switzerland to river cruises in Austria and island-hopping in the Hebrides of Scotland . . . makes all of these experiences accessible to even the less-than-intrepid traveler." (BL) Morrow, 1982.

Steves, Rick   EUROPE THROUGH THE BACK DOOR
"Vital how-to's" for travel in Europe . . . "sure to make you a seasoned traveler—on your first trip"—to the less-traveled corners of Europe. For the independent traveler and the budget-minded, told with "wit and readability." John Muir, 1984. Also *Europe in 22 Days* (1985), based on a 3,000-mile car trip but adaptable to train travel.

Sunset, eds.   EUROPE DISCOVERY TRIPS
"Sixty unique side trips outside major cities in eighteen countries." Sunset, 1980.

Yeadon, David   BACKROAD JOURNEYS OF SOUTHERN EUROPE
Nineteen chapters, each devoted to a small region; "many itineraries could be combined with a major town (Lucca and the Tuscan Hills from Florence; La Mancha from Madrid) . . . small, unplanned-for adventures . . . markets and festivals, landscape and architecture, people and animals." (NYT) Har-Row, 1981.

RELIGIOUS GUIDEBOOKS

Higgins, Paul L.   PILGRIMAGES: A GUIDE TO THE HOLY PLACES OF EUROPE FOR TODAY'S TRAVELER
"Spiritual sites of Europe north of the Alps: ancient cathedrals, abbey ruins, burial grounds. Tips on how to reach these places (many are off the beaten track) and lodging." (PW) P-H, 1984.

Krinsky, Carol H.   SYNAGOGUES OF EUROPE: ARCHITECTURE, HISTORY, MEANING
Country-by-country survey and social/architectural history. MIT Pr, 1985.

McNaspy, C.J.   A GUIDE TO CHRISTIAN EUROPE
Loyola, 1984.

Madden, Daniel M.   A RELIGIOUS GUIDE TO EUROPE
A travel guide useful for browsing and for travel direction—religion and religious landmarks on the continent and British Isles. Macmillan, 1975.

Pepper, Elizabeth   MAGICAL AND MYSTICAL SITES: EUROPE AND THE BRITISH ISLES
Delphi, Malta, Stonehenge, Granada and other sites reputed to have magical qualities. Har-Row, 1977.

Postal, Bernard   THE TRAVELER'S GUIDE TO JEWISH LANDMARKS OF EUROPE
Fleet, 1971.

ART, MUSIC, LITERATURE

Bernstein, Ken   MUSIC LOVER'S EUROPE
"For the traveler who is serious but not solemn about music . . . general tourist information with facts and lore about major festivals . . . places of historical interest." (LJ) Scribner, 1983.

Crosland, Margaret, ed.   A GUIDE TO LITERARY EUROPE
For the literary-minded traveler, linking stories, plays, authors with towns, villages, views, cafes, theatres. Includes all of Europe except the Communist countries. Chilton, 1966.

Rabin, Carol Price   MUSIC FESTIVALS IN EUROPE AND BRITAIN
Comprehensive guide to 91 music festivals in 21 countries from the British Isles to Austria. Berkshire Traveller, 1984.

Steves, Rick and Openshaw, Gene   EUROPE 101: HISTORY, ART AND CULTURE FOR THE TRAVELER
An overview of 5,000 years of European culture, history, art "written in hip jargon," with appendices covering palaces, museums, festivals, ruins. (BL) John Muir, 1985.

TRAVEL ARTICLES

BETTER HOMES & GARDENS

1985 May "Grand European Vacations." Hassle-free touring strategies. George S. Bush, p. 189

CHANGING TIMES

1985 Apr "All Aboard for Europe." See Europe by train; smart ways to swap dollars; best books for your best trip yet. p. 38

CONNOISSEUR

1985 Jul "From Paris to Peking." Trans-Siberian train trip through France, Germany, Poland, Siberia, Mongolia, China. Katie Leishman, p. 35

ESQUIRE

1985 Oct "A Biased Baedeker to the Seasons's Best." Carol and Neil Offen, p. 35 (following p. 124)

"Thirty-one Romantic Vacations." Includes France, Norway, and Switzerland. Neal Karlen and Wendy Lowe, p. 54

1984 Apr "The Danube Blues." How to conquer Eastern Europe in eleven days. Alan Furst, p. 76

Oct "Detours from Your Next Business Trip." Barbara Hey, p. 19 (following p. 160)

"31 Winter Escapes." For the active traveler "via trains, planes, boats, and feet, to sun, slopes, surf and sand"; includes Europe. Wendy Lowe, p. 26 (following p. 160)

ESSENCE

1984 Aug "Europe by Rail—Your Way!" Cheryl Everette, p. 40

50 PLUS

1984 Feb "Where Next?" Secret destinations for the sophisticated traveler (France, Greece, Italy, Spain, Switzerland). Robert S. Kane, p. 47

GLAMOUR

1985 Aug "6 Great Getaways Where Early Fall is the Best Time of All." Burgundy, France and Scotland. p. 234

HARPER'S BAZAAR

1985 Feb "A Traveling Woman's Guide to the World's Great Hotels." Includes Paris, Athens, Glasgow, San Sebastian (Spain), Milan, Trieste, Sardinia. Kit Snedaker, p. 48

HOUSE BEAUTIFUL

1985 Apr "Exploring International Country Styles (Design): Travel Guide to a Host of Old-World Countries." Inns, museums, design, fabrics, handcrafts, suggested tours, etc.—includes Austria, England, France, Ireland, Italy, Spain. Patricia Brooks, p. 131

MADEMOISELLE
1985 May "How to See the Old World in a New Way: London, Paris, Rome." Mary
A. Kellogg, p. 194
1984 Mar "On the Cheap in London, Paris and Rome." Elin Schoen, p. 210

MODERN MATURITY
1985 Oct-Nov "Watch on the Rhine." A five-day odyssey on Europe's grandest
canal (from Rotterdam to Basle). Charles N. Barnard, p. 22

NATIONAL GEOGRAPHIC
1985 Mar "When the Vikings Sailed East." Early Viking raiding and trading across
the Baltic and into Russia. Robert P. Jordan, p. 278
Sep (The Balkans) "Jason's Voyage—in Search of the Golden Fleece." Tim
Severin, p. 407

N.Y. TIMES SUNDAY TRAVEL SECTION (X)
1985 Feb 17 "Coming to Terms with a Fistful of Pounds." James Sterngold, p. 19
"In Europe It's Time to Buy." Roundup of enticing "buys" for shoppers.
Various authors, p. 14
Mar 10 "Treasures in Surprising Places . . . Europe's Great Works of Art . . .
Outside of Capital Cities and Major Museums." Paul Lewis, p. 9
Apr 7 "Promenades in Europe's Parks." From Copenhagen to Madrid, open
spaces and the way the people use them offer insights into local life. Paul
Lewis, p. 15; "Secret Gardens Open to All." William H. Adams, p. 15
Apr 28 "Abroad, Not Everything Is a Bargain." Paul Goldenberger, p. 14
"Getting Around Europe in a Banner Summer." Tactics include avoiding
busy dates and major cities. Paul Grimes, p. 14
"Strategies for Avoiding the Crowds in Europe." A dozen itineraries well off
the beaten track. R.W. Apple, Jr., p. 15
"A Choice of Special Hotels." In Britain, Ireland, France, Germany, and Italy.
Paul Lewis, p. 16
May 5 "Music Abroad, 1985: Recalling the Sounds of Summer." Festivals.
Eugenia Zukerman, p. 21; "A Critic's Guide to the Noteworthy." John
Rockwell, p. 21; "Who's Performing Where." Vernon Kidd, p. 21
May 12 "Buying Antiques Abroad." Shoppers can save up to 50% (but some
are less at home). Rita Reif, p. 21; "Getting Antiques Purchased Abroad Back
Home." Phyllis Lee Levin, p. 21
Jun 30 "Critics' Choices." Personal favorites when they're not dining at
Taillevant (in Italy, England, France). Various authors, p. 14
Aug 11 "From Zurich to Rome the Easy Way." TGV's, IC's, TEE's, all
European trains. Paul Hofmann, p. 14
"Seeing the Continent by Rail." A train buff's timetable of high-speed lines,
engineering feats and spectacular scenery. Joachim M. Hill, p. 15
Oct 13 "When Europe is Europe Again: Highlights of the Cultural Season."
Ludina Barzini, p. 15
"A Tradition of Luxury Endures." The Ritz Hotel in Paris, Madrid and
London. Sally Hassan, p. 39
Oct 27 "Connections—Cheap Flights Using London as Connection." David
Duncan, p. 22

Nov. 3 "Condominiums (for Skiing) from A to Z." Stanley Carr, p. 29

Dec 22 "Capturing the Holiday Spirit—Christmas, New Year's or Twelfth Night." Ways to take part and ways to cope, reports from 15 *New York Times* correspondents and bureaus that include England, France, Germany, Italy, Norway, Soviet Union, Spain. p. 12

1984 Feb 5 "Reliving the Romance of Steam." Wagons-lits runs. George Behrend, p. 51

Feb 12 "A Grand Tour of Grand Opera." The main events from the city of light to the city of Mozart. Harold C. Schonberg, p. 14 (also articles on the individual countries, pp. 14-15, and ticket tips and other information, p. 15) "Artists at Ease in Eight Cities." A sampling of favorite haunts. Tim Page, p. 15

Mar 4 "Europe Coming and Going." Each airport imparts first and last impressions of its own country's soul; also a guide to 13 major way stations (12 major European airports plus Ben Gurion in Tel Aviv). Paul Lewis, p. 16 "Learning Fast on a Cruise." Swan educational cruises of ancient Greece, Rome, Egypt. Emily Greenspan, p. 28

Mar 18 (Part 2, "Sophisticated Traveler") "Summer and Water." An essay on the pleasures inherent in the combination, from Ireland to Greece. Hugh Leonard, p. 32

Apr 29 "Ferry Crossing First Class." France, Northern Spain, England, Ireland. Marion Kaplan, p. 22

May 6 "Festivals Widen Appeal." Music and arts festivals with listings for individual countries, sources of information, etc. Nicholas Kenyon, p. 19

May 20 "Summer Abroad: the ABCs of Going with Children." 16 foreign correspondents and contributors of *The Times* offer tips on touring their corners of the world, p. 21; "Coping with Kids in the Air." Joan Gage, p. 23 (See separate article under "France/Travel Articles" also.)

Jul 22 "Traveler Beware." A roundup of cautions for coping with irritations and dangers abroad from 17 *Times* correspondents and contributors (Paris, Spain, Greece, Germany, Rome, Poland). p. 19

Oct 7 "What's New in Europe." A special report from *Times* bureaus . . . on what to watch for in weeks and months ahead. Starts on p. 15

Nov 11 (The Alps) "Poised at the Gateway to the Alps." From Geneva, ardent skiers can sample an array of varied terrain (in France, Switzerland, Italy). Jeremy Bernstein, p. 26 "Choice Mountains, Great and Small." Guide to contrasting ski areas with notes on rooms and meals. p. 29

Dec 2 "Reserving Top Tables." Advice and a list of top restaurants in the U.S. and Europe, and how to reserve a table. Florence Fabricant, p. 20

Dec 30 "A hidden Pageant from Medieval Life." The choir seats of many European churches conceal vivid scenes of drama and humor (sculptures, called misericords, on the undersides of choir seats). Elaine C. Block, p. 23

TOWN & COUNTRY

1984 Apr Special issue on Europe.
"The top spas of Europe." Jane W. Michael, p. 126
(See also individual articles entered under "England," "France," "Germany," "Italy.")

TRAVEL & LEISURE
1985 May "Romantic Roads: a Guide to Driving in Europe." (See also individual
      articles on driving tours under "Scotland," "Germany," "France," "Italy.")
      Stephan Wilkinson, p. 134
      Jun "Seaside Bathing in Europe." Uwe Siemon-Netto, p. 71
      Aug "Autumn in the Alps." Rambling through the fabled mountains in
      Switzerland, Italy and Austria. Monique Burns, p. 78
      Oct "You Are Where You Eat." Paris (Tour d'Argent), Venice (Harry's Bar),
      Munich (Hofbrauhaus). George Lang, p. 118
      Dec "Latest from Europe's Alpine Ski Resorts." Abby Rand, p. 49
1984 May "European Theatre Etiquette." Michael Walsh, p. 152
      Jul Travel & Architecture: "The Clarity of the Classical from Acropolis to
      Monticello." Alexander Eliot, p. 54
      Aug "A musical autumn in Europe." What's on and how to get tickets in
      major capitals. Robert L. Sammons, p. 88

TRAVEL/HOLIDAY
1985 Feb "Eurail Pass Travel." Carol MacGuineas, p. 6
      Sep "Mediterranean Spectacular." The beauty of a cruise. Tom Bross, p. 40
1984 Aug "Autumn in the Alps, a Season of Splendor." Robert Hoffman, p. 35

VOGUE
1985 Feb "A Luxurious Mediterranean Cruise." Maggie Paley, p. 276

AUSTRIA

Series Guidebooks (See Appendix 1)

Baedeker: Austria; Vienna
Berlitz: Austria—The Tyrol; Vienna
Blue Guide: Austria
Fodor: Austria; Vienna
Frommer: Austria & Hungary—Dollarwise
Michelin: Austria
Nagel: Austria
U.S. Government: Austria: Area Handbook; Background Notes; Post
             Report

Background Books

Barker, Elizabeth   AUSTRIA, 1918-1972
A popular history that describes an Austria, grim in the 1930s, through the

period of Hitler and World War II, and finally independent of its lost empire mentality. U of Miami, 1973.

Brody, Elaine   MUSIC GUIDE TO AUSTRIA & GERMANY
One of a series of guides for individual European countries—a handbook of information for a range of travelers "from the music dilettante to the highly motivated specialist." Includes information on the country's musical history, concert halls, opera houses, festivals, etc. Dodd, 1975. (See also *Music Festivals in Europe and Britain* and *Music Lover's Europe* under "Europe/Background Reading.")

Clark, Ronald W.   THE ALPS
The past and future Alps in three parts—geography and history; expeditions, skiing and sports; people and animals; individual mountains. Knopf, 1973.

Comini, Allesandra   THE FANTASTIC ART OF VIENNA
Knopf, 1978.

Day, Ingeborg   GHOST WALTZ: A MEMOIR
A daughter (now a New Yorker) uncovers, and must come to terms with the activities of her father as an Austrian Nazi in World War II. Viking, 1980.

Feldkamp, Frederick   NOT EVERYBODY'S EUROPE
A grand tour of nine unique cities to think about adding to your itinerary—in Austria, it's Salzburg. Harper's Magazine Pr, 1976.

Gainham, Sarah   HABSBURG TWILIGHT
Eight essays by a novelist who knows Vienna well, describing life in late nineteenth-century Vienna. Atheneum, 1979. (See also her novels listed below.) Atheneum, 1979.

Gardiner, Muriel   CODE NAME "MARY"
Memoirs of an American woman in the Austrian underground in the years leading up to World War II. "An authentic heroine [who] does everything to convince you she is . . . ordinary"—she hid people, helped them escape, smuggled forged documents, and got out in June 1938 one step ahead of the Gestapo. (BRD) Yale U Pr, 1983.

Grunfeld, Frederic V.   VIENNA
Part of Wonders of Man series. Newsweek, 1981.

Gunther, John   TWELVE CITIES
The author of the highly popular "Inside" series of a couple of decades ago, here applied his unique zest and talent to cities, one of which is Vienna—mood, temper, problems, politics, government. Har-Row, 1969.

Handler, H.   THE SPANISH RIDING SCHOOL
Four centuries of classic horsemanship—the Spanish Riding School is, of course, located in Vienna, despite its name. McGraw, 1972.

Johnston, William M.   VIENNA, VIENNA: THE GOLDEN AGE
"A popular and richly illustrated social and intellectual history of Vienna" during its golden age. (BL) CN Potter, 1981.

Kallir, Jane   ARNOLD SCHOENBERG'S VIENNA
Fin-de-siècle Vienna of the early twentieth century—"describes the political, intellectual and artistic climate of the day [and a] discussion of Schoenberg's own creations." (PW) Rizzoli, 1985.

Maass, Walter B.   COUNTRY WITHOUT A NAME
The U.S. occupation in Europe after World War II—written basically for Americans, giving a description of events in Austria before and during World War II. Ungar, 1979.

Marek, George   THE EAGLES DIE
The drama of the Hapsburg Empire presented in terms of Emperor Franz Joseph and Empress Elizabeth—Vienna brought vividly to life, its cultural and intellectual life, and the personalities of the two rulers. Har-Row, 1974.

Morris, James   JOURNEYS
This collection of essays by a leading travel writer includes one on Vienna. Oxford U, 1984.

Morton, Frederic   A NERVOUS SPLENDOR
Centers around the suicides at Mayerling of Prince Rudolf and his mistress—"slices through the layers of Viennese society to look at them all concurrently within a specific time frame"—anecdotal portraits of individuals, gossip, daily life. See also Morton's *Forever Street* under "Novels," below. (BRD) Little, 1979.

Pick, Robert   THE LAST DAYS OF IMPERIAL VIENNA
Dial, 1976.

Pryce-Jones, David   VIENNA
One of Great Cities of the World series. Time-Life, 1978.

Wechsberg, Joseph   THE VIENNA I KNEW; MEMORIES OF A EUROPEAN CHILDHOOD
Reminiscences by a noted travel and food writer that make his family come alive for the reader, as well as the city and era. Doubleday, 1979.

GUIDEBOOKS

Jones, J. Sydney   VIENNAWALKS
Part of a series of chatty, anecdotal guides: four walking tours of the inner city. HR&W, 1985.

Kitfield, James and Walker, William WHOLE EUROPE ESCAPE MANUAL: GERMANY, AUSTRIA, SWITZERLAND
Part of a new series of guidebooks "designed to . . . put the fantasy and excitement back into travel." (Publisher) World Leis Corp, 1984.

HISTORY

Crankshaw, Edward THE FALL OF THE HOUSE OF HABSBURG
The monarchy from 1848 to 1918—"brings the past alive . . . with unusual force and clarity." (BRD) Penguin, 1983 (first published 1963).

May, Arthur J. THE HAPSBURG MONARCHY
Harvard U Pr, 1951; U of Pennsylvania, 1966.

Taylor, A.J.P THE HABSBURG MONARCHY, 1809-1918
U of Chicago, 1976.

Valiani, L. THE END OF AUSTRIA-HUNGARY
Knopf, 1973.

Novels

Albrand, Martha A CALL FROM AUSTRIA
Suspense and romance, set in an Austrian Alpine resort. Random, 1963.

Appelfeld, Aharon THE RETREAT
Set in 1937 in a hotel outside Vienna that promises to purge guests "of their Jewishness . . . to instill gentile attitudes and habits . . . . They all gradually backslide." (FC) Dutton, 1984.

Appelfeld, Aharon BADENHEIM 1939
A novel of self-delusion as Jewish guests at a pleasure resort near Vienna refuse to worry even though this is 1939, with Nazis in control of Austria—"the most shocking thing . . . is not its satirical humor but its charm . . . [an] appalling theme with grace." (FC) Godine, 1980. Also, *The Age of Wonders* (1981).

Behrman, S.N. THE BURNING GLASS
A novel about the world of the theatre, set in Salzburg (and New York and Hollywood) in 1937-40; the effect of the triumph of Nazism. Little, 1968.

Drucker, Peter F. THE LAST OF ALL POSSIBLE WORLDS
The financial and romantic intrigues of three wealthy partners in a fictional banking firm; Austria and London in 1906. Har-Row, 1982.

Fagyas, M.   THE DEVIL'S LIEUTENANT
"Unusual detective story [and] novel of psychological conflict"—set in pre-World War I Vienna in a declining Austro-Hungarian Empire. (FC) Putnam Pub Group, 1970.

Gainham, Sarah   NIGHT FALLS ON THE CITY
This is the first of a trilogy that tells of a prominent actress, and her world in Vienna, beginning with the war years 1938-45. HR&W, 1967. Following is *A Place in the Country* (1969), post World War II, and *Private Worlds* (1971), the final volume, which takes the plot to the 1950s.

Gainham, Sarah   TO THE OPERA BALL
An Austrian soldier accompanies a young woman to the Vienna Opera Ball as a favor to his friend and ends up eloping with the Austrian heiress. Doubleday, 1977.

Greene, Graham   THE THIRD MAN
The story *A Sense of Reality*, from this collection, was the basis for that marvelous movie *The Third Man*, about black marketeering, an amoral American (he's British in the book), and his longtime writer-friend in Vienna who tries to find out how he supposedly died. The story takes place during the period just following World War II, when Austria was still under the joint authority of the American, Russian, French and British military. Viking, 1950.

Haas, Ben   THE HOUSE OF CHRISTINA
The beautiful daughter of an Austrian general, married to an American, becomes romantically involved with both a Nazi officer and a Jewish resistance fighter during World War II. S&S, 1977.

Handke, Peter   THE GOALIE'S ANXIETY AT THE PENALTY KICK
Story of a former soccer player who is a psychopathic killer. FS&G, 1972.

Irving, John   SETTING FREE THE BEARS
In *3 by Irving*, a three-novel omnibus edition. The plot involves "a madcap scheme to liberate zoo animals, [a] balance between the humorous and the macabre." (FC) Random, 1969.

MacInnes, Helen   PRELUDE TO TERROR
A New York art consultant, sent to Vienna to purchase a painting, becomes involved in "a web of terrorism, laundered money, and intelligence agents." (FC) HarBraceJ, 1978.

MacInnes, Helen   THE SALZBURG CONNECTION
A chest, buried during World War II by the Nazis in an Austrian lake near Salzburg, is the focal point of the plot, with agents from Russia, Austria, Britain and America interested in its contents. HarBraceJ, 1968.

Meyer, Nicholas   THE SEVEN-PER-CENT SOLUTION
"Pastiche" is the term used to describe this detective story in which Sherlock Holmes and Sigmund Freud join forces to solve a criminal conspiracy—set in Vienna. Dutton, 1974.

Morton, Frederic   THE FOREVER STREET
Saga of a family dynasty, based on the author's memories of his family. It begins with the family's journey from Slovakia to Vienna in the nineteenth century and ends with their dispersal when the Nazis take over. The family (although "Jewish outsiders") prospers—"vividly realized, both in its . . . personal meanings and its social and cultural context." (FC) Doubleday, 1984.

Musil, Robert   THE MAN WITHOUT QUALITIES
Major Austrian fiction that was to be a four-volume novel but ended with the author's death in 1942 after only two. This first volume, complete in itself, is a panoramic study of upper class Viennese society on the eve of World War I. The second volume takes the plot to the point where the hero decides to leave Vienna. Coward, 1953-54.

Roth, Joseph   THE RADETSKY MARCH
A new translation of a novel written in 1932 traces the lives of three generations from 1859 to 1914. "Beautiful, elegiac novel [that] conveys the tenuousness with which the empire was held together: the many races, disparities . . . seemingly under the authority of a frail old man until World War I blows the illusion to shards." (PW) Overlook, 1984.

Schnitzler, Arthur   THE LITTLE COMEDY, AND OTHER STORIES
Stories set against the background of Vienna describing "with great charm the social and cultural atmosphere of Vienna before World War I." Several were made into a haunting series presented by PBS-TV, under the title "Tales of Love and Death." (FC) Ungar, 1977.

Solmssen, Arthur R.G.   ALEXANDER'S FEAST
An American lawyer returns to Salzburg (where he'd once been in the military government after World War II as an 18-year old)—colorful Salzburg background. Little, 1971.

Stewart, Mary   AIRS ABOVE THE GROUND
An English lady veterinarian helps her husband solve a mystery involving "Lipizzan horses, a medieval Austrian castle, a circus, a murder, and a narcotics ring." (FC) Morrow, 1965.

Stone, Irving   THE PASSIONS OF THE WIND
Fictionalized story of Sigmund Freud's life from his twenty-sixth year and on through half a century. Doubleday, 1971.

Thompson, Morton   THE CRY AND THE COVENANT
Based on the life and scientific discoveries of Dr. Ignaz Semmelweis who identified the cause of maternity deaths from puerperal fever. Doubleday, 1949.

TRAVEL ARTICLES

ARCHITECTURAL DIGEST
1985 Apr "Travel Notes: Vienna, Severe and Sensuous." Stanley Tigerman, p. 122

CONNOISSEUR

1985 Feb "Zurs: It All Begins At the Pass." Sporthotel Lorunser. Nancy Hoving, p. 96

1984 Oct "Vienna, the Ambivalent City." How the Viennese really see their capital. G.Y. Dryansky, p. 94

"A Sensual Education." Vienna's great art collections celebrate . . . all five senses. Thomas Hoving, p. 103

GLAMOUR

1985 Dec "Vienna and Budapest." p. 198

GOURMET

1984 Apr "Shopping in Vienna." Lillian Langseth-Christensen, p. 36

Aug "Austria's Narrow-Gauge Railways." Lillian Langseth-Christensen, p. 28

Sep "Viennese coffeehouses." Lillian Langseth-Christensen, p. 42

HOUSE & GARDEN

1985 Jan "Street Analysis." Probing the signs and symbols of Freud's Berggasse in Vienna. Alexander Cockburn, p. 36

HOUSE BEAUTIFUL

1985 Jun "Austrians Enjoy Their Pleasures Close-to-the-Earth." Heuriger wine-tasting taverns. p. 49

NATIONAL GEOGRAPHIC

1985 Apr "Those Eternal Austrians, and Traveler's Map of the Alps." John J. Putnam, p. 410

N.Y. TIMES SUNDAY TRAVEL SECTION (X)

1985 Mar 10 "St. Anton: Town of Skiers." Patricia A. Langan, p. 32

Aug 25 "The Capital from A to Z." Vienna is a place of coffeehouse culture, abundant music and an occasionally blue Danube. Paul Hofmann, p. 14

"Seeing Vienna in its Prime." Structures surviving from turn-of-century Vienna. Michael Ratcliffe, p. 15

"Where to stay, where to eat." The latest in dining . . . wining . . . and bastions of gemütlichkeit. Anne M. Zwack, p. 16

Dec 15 "Even Graz Can Cut Loose." The staid Austrian city now blends the avant-garde with its traditional wealth of music and art. Paul Hofmann, p. 10

1984 Aug 12 "Echoes of Vienna's Heritage." Plaques of music masters. Paul Hofmann, p. 31

Sep 2 "What's Doing in Vienna." Paul Hofmann, p. 19

Oct 7 (Part 2, "Sophisticated Traveler") "Vienna Past Tense." Anthony Burgess, p. 86; "The Viennese Baroque." Olivier Bernier, p. 114

Oct 21 "What's Doing in Salzburg." Paul Hofmann, p. 10

Dec 9 Shopper's World: "Shaping a Goblet to Suit a Wine." Kufstein. Anne M. Zwack, p. 13

Dec 16 Fare of the Country: "Vienna's Strudel—no substitution." Paul Hofmann, p. 20

SATURDAY REVIEW
1985 Aug "Follow the Lieder." Following in the footsteps of Mahler as a theme for an auto trip through Austria. Nino Lo Bello, p. 65

TOWN & COUNTRY
1984 Feb "The Little Season of Kitzbühel and Salzburg." Frederic Morton, p. 64

TRAVEL & LEISURE
1985 Jan "Holiday in Kitzbühel, Austria." Geoffrey Wolff, p. 46
Feb "A Morning at the Vienna Art Museum." Richard Covington, p. 149
Apr "Springtime in the Vienna Woods." Following the footsteps of Beethoven and Schubert. Richard Covington, p. 74
1984 May "In Vienna, Two Princely Hotels." Imperial and Schwarzenberg. Ian Keown, p. 130
Jun "Skimming Along the Danube from Vienna to Budapest." A scenic hydrofoil ride between two great capitals. Wallace White, p. 154
Jul "Old World Concert Cafes in Vienna." A little music, a little coffee, and a lot of atmosphere. Robert L. Sammons, p. 42
Dec "Vienna—Its Golden Days Are Right Now." Ila Stanger, p. 106

TRAVEL/HOLIDAY
1985 Aug "Vienna a La Carte." Medium to low price restaurants. Chef Louis Szathmary, p. 4
"The Vienna Woods—a Not-so-classic Tale." Denise Van Lear, p. 50
1984 Feb "Tales of the Vienna Opera." Robert L. Sammons, p. 110
Dec "Music and Mozart." Austria's winning combination. Helmut Koenig, p. 24

VOGUE
1985 Sep "This year at Badgastein: an intimate look at the good life . . . of a classic European spa." Despina Messinesi, p. 544

BELGIUM
and
LUXEMBOURG

Series Guidebooks (See Appendix 1)

Baedeker: Netherlands, Belgium, Luxembourg; Brussels
Berlitz: Brussels

Blue Guide: Belgium & Luxembourg
Country Orientation Update: Belgium
Fodor: Belgium & Luxembourg
U.S.Government: Belgium: Background Notes; Country Study; Post
                          Report
Luxembourg: Background Notes; Post Report
Low Countries: Pocket Guide—Belgium, Luxembourg, the
                          Netherlands

Background Reading

Aronson, Theo   DEFIANT DYNASTY: THE COBURGS OF BELGIUM
The kings of the House of Saxe-Coburg-Gotha from 1831 to 1950—"colorful,
gossipy, scandalous chapters . . . imbedded in a solid historical matrix." (BRD)
Bobbs, 1968.

Bailey, Anthony   REMBRANDT'S HOUSE
The artist's home (now a museum) is the takeoff point to tell the story of
Rembrandt's life as well as seventeenth-century life in general in and around
Amsterdam. Houghton, 1978.

**Brody, Elaine   THE MUSIC GUIDE TO BELGIUM, LUXEMBOURG,
                          HOLLAND AND SWITZERLAND**
One of a series of guides for individual European countries—a handbook of
information for a range of travelers "from the music dilettante to the highly
motivated specialist." Includes information on the country's musical history, concert halls, opera houses, festivals, etc. Dodd, 1977. (See also *Music Festivals in
Europe and Britain* and *Music Lover's Europe* under "Europe/Background Reading.")

Gunther, John   TWELVE CITIES
The author of the highly popular "Inside" series of a couple of decades ago
applies his unique zest and talent to a dozen cities, one of which is
Brussels—mood, temper, problems, politics, government. Har-Row, 1969.

GUIDEBOOKS

**Green, Kerry and Bythines, Peter   THE WHOLE EUROPE ESCAPE
                                                     MANUAL: FRANCE, HOLLAND,
                                                     BELGIUM WITH LUXEMBOURG**
One of a new series of guidebooks "designed to bring Europe to life and put the
fantasy and excitement back into travel." (Publisher) World Leis Corp, 1984.

Nelson, Nina   BELGIUM & LUXEMBOURG
Batsford, 1975.

Samson, Patricia M. and Dillon, Anne F.   BRUSSELS WALK GUIDE
Malvaux, 1974.

HISTORY
Kossman, E.H.   THE LOW COUNTRIES, 1780-1940
Oxford U, 1978.

Mallinson, Vernon   BELGIUM
Praeger, 1970.

Novels

Brontë, Charlotte   THE PROFESSOR
This and *Villette* are set in Brussels and were written out of the author's own experiences as a teacher in Belgium. Penguin, 1980 (first published 1857, 1853 respectively).

Darcy, Clare   ALLEGRA
Two sisters, left penniless, hatch a plot in Brussels for one of them to "move into society and attract beaux"—all is resolved when a distant cousin arrives. (FC) Walker & Co, 1975.

Johnson, Pamela H.   THE HOLIDAY FRIEND
Belgian seacoast background; an art history professor is followed on holiday by a student—"the climax is violent." (FC) Scribner, 1973.

Johnson, Pamela H.   TOO DEAR FOR MY POSSESSING
Bruges is the setting for this novel about the effects of a fascinating stepmother on a young man's loves—"bright with people and fine dialogue." (FC) Scribner, 1973 (first published 1940).

Johnson, Pamela H.   THE UNSPEAKABLE SKIPTON
A "swift-moving, witty, wicked comedy" of a self-exiled British novelist pursuing his writing in an attic in Bruges while also conniving to profit out of the British tourists. (FC) HarBraceJ, 1959.

Johnston, Jennifer   HOW MANY MILES TO BABYLON?
Two young men enlist in the British army in World War I with entirely different motives—"war . . . in all its desolation . . . love and friendship, set down with exactness and beauty." (FC) Doubleday, 1974.

McGivern, William P.   SOLDIERS OF '44
A World War II novel—an American gun section is cut off from their unit in the Ardennes forest. Arbor Hse, 1979.

Sarton, May   THE BRIDGE OF YEARS
Chronicle of a Belgian family, 1919-40—"rich family life which remains serene even under the shadow of the impending . . . war." (FC) Norton, 1971.

Stone, Irving   LUST FOR LIFE
A novelization of artist Van Gogh's tortured life, ending with his suicide at age 37. Doubleday, 1954 (first published 1934).

TRAVEL ARTICLES

ARCHITECTURAL DIGEST
1985 Mar "Architect's Travel Notes: Antwerp—Harbor of Tradition and Order." Hugh N. Jacobsen, p. 86

BON APPETIT
1985 Nov "The Best Restaurants of Belgium." Lynne Kasper, p. 104

GOURMET
1985 Jan "Luxembourg." Irene Corbally Kuhn, p. 50
1984 Nov "Brussels, an Epicurean Tour." Fred Ferretti, p. 54

MODERN MATURITY
1985 Jun/Jul "A Belgian Tapestry." Fred Ferretti, p. 54

N.Y. TIMES SUNDAY TRAVEL SECTION (X)
1985 Jan 13 "Patrician Quarters Where Rubens Painted." A gracious Antwerp house retains the artist's spirit. Theodore James, Jr. p. 9
Apr 21 Fare of the Country: "Endive, Queen of Vegetables." Theodore James, Jr., p. 24
May 12 Fare of the Country: "Sweet Taste of Pastry in Brussels." Barbara Bowers, p. 6
Jun 23 "Shopping Haunts Around the World." Includes Brussels. Amanda M. Stinchecum, p. 16
Jun 30 "A Guest Is Remembered in Brussels." The house that Erasmus loved. C.L. Sulzberger, p. 12
1984 Jan 22 "Brussels' Haven for Food Buffs." Agnes H. Gottlieb, p.12
Jun 17 "Facets of Antwerp." Michael Ruhlman, p. 12
Jul 22 "Except for the Windmills, the Belgian-Dutch Beach Is a Lot Like Home." James M. Markham, p. 35
Aug 19 "Near Bastogne, Distant Drums." The lush Belgian forest of Ardennes rekindles thoughts of a father's battle. James M. Markham, p. 31
Dec 9 "Relics of War in Bastogne." Fred Ferretti, p. 22
Dec 30 "What's Doing in Brussels." Paul Lewis, p. 10

TOWN & COUNTRY
1985 Apr "Vis-a-Vis the Low Countries." Jennifer Kramer, p. 206

TRAVEL & LEISURE
1984 May "Back Street Brussels." Just behind the Grand Place, a lively enclave of street life and fine restaurants. Fred Ferretti, p. 174

WORLD PRESS REVIEW
1984 Apr "The Contrasts of Brussels." James Holloway (*Irish Times*, Dublin), p. 62

BULGARIA

Series Guidebooks

Fodor: Eastern Europe
Nagel: Bulgaria
U.S. Government: Bulgaria: Area Handbook; Background Notes

Background Reading

Haskell, A.L.   HEROES AND ROSES: A VIEW OF BULGARIA
Written by an Englishman who went to Bulgaria to judge a ballet contest, stayed on and came to know and love the people—he shares this enthusiasm. Transatlantic, 1967.

HISTORY

**Spector, S.P. and Ristelhueber, Rene   A HISTORY OF THE
BALKAN PEOPLES**
General historical information for the many nationalities of the Balkan peninsula—Greeks, Rumanians, Bulgarians, Albanians, Serbs, Turks, others. Twayne, 1971.

Novels

Gilman, Dorothy   THE ELUSIVE MRS. POLLIFAX
An amusing spy adventure with Mrs. Pollifax, this time involved in smuggling forged passports into Bulgaria for the CIA. Doubleday, 1971.

Littell, Robert   THE OCTOBER CIRCLE
A group of Bulgarian performers resist the invasion of Czechoslovakia. Houghton, 1976.

Talev, Dimitur   THE IRON CANDLESTICK
First of a trilogy and family saga beginning in the early nineteenth century and continuing to the early twentieth century. The second and third titles in the trilogy are *St. Elijah's Day* (1953) and *The Bells of Prespa* (1954). Twayne, 1952.

TRAVEL ARTICLES
TRAVEL/HOLIDAY
1985 Feb "Sophisticated Sofia, Bulgaria's Special City." Charles E. Adelsen, p. 54

CZECHOSLOVAKIA

Series Guidebooks (See Appendix 1)

Fodor: Eastern Europe
Nagel: Czechoslovakia
U.S. Government: Czechoslovakia: Background Notes; Country
                    Study; Post Report

Background Reading

Chapman, Colin   THE RAPE OF CZECHOSLOVAKIA
On-the-spot accounts of the invasion of Czechoslovakia by the Russians in 1968 by two British journalists. Lippincott, 1968.

Hampl, Patricia   A ROMANTIC EDUCATION
"Begins as an extended essay on sensitivity to one's family and ends as a sort of travelogue describing the author's visits to Prague [by an author] born into a family [from St. Paul, Minnesota] that cultivated nostalgia for the past." (BL) Houghton, 1981.

**Kovaly, Hedy and Kohak, Erazim   THE VICTORS AND THE
                                    VANQUISHED**
This is a book written from two unique perspectives. Ms. Kovaly emerged from a German concentration camp at the end of World War II as a "victor" being a dedicated Communist married to a top party official; Mr. Kohak was the "vanquished" as an anti-Communist. Later, Ms. Kovaly's husband was executed and the book tells of her disillusionment, and the experiences of each from opposite sides of the barricades. Horizon, 1973.

Levy, Alan   ROWBOAT TO PRAGUE
A personal account by an American free-lance writer living in Prague during the spring of 1968, when Czechoslovakia appeared to have regained its freedom only to be invaded by Russia. Orion, 1972.

Mlynář, Zdeněk   NIGHTFROST IN PRAGUE
The disillusionment of a former Communist, once an absolute believer and a high official, and his realization of what Soviet Communism means. Karz, 1980.

Moorhouse, Geoffrey   PRAGUE
One of the Great Cities of the World series. Time-Life, 1981.

Pachman, Ludek   CHECKMATE IN PRAGUE
A footnote to history—the chess grandmaster comments on the Soviet occupation in 1968. Macmillan, 1975.

Parrott, Cecil   THE SERPENT AND THE NIGHTINGALE
Memoir with ambience of a diplomat who served in Czechoslovakia and of his last visit in 1967-68 following his retirement. Faber & Faber, 1978.

Paul, David W.   CZECHOSLOVAKIA: PROFILE OF A SOCIALIST
**   REPUBLIC AT THE CROSSROADS OF EUROPE**
"Excellent brief survey . . . for the general reader seeking a background knowledge of Czechoslovakia." (BRD) Westview, 1981.

Sterling, Clare   THE MASARYK CASE
Narrative of the events surrounding Masaryk's death in March 1948 when, as foreign minister, he supposedly committed suicide—"a fascinating, true, detective story" in which the author concludes that Masaryk was murdered by either the Czechoslovakian or Soviet secret police. (BRD) Har-Row, 1969.

Wechsberg, Joseph   PRAGUE: THE MYSTICAL CITY
The riches of the 1,000-year-old city, described beautifully by a leading travel writer, and one with a special empathy for the city—"like an unplanned stroll through the ancient quarters of the city letting imagination and impression have full play." (BRD) Macmillan, 1970.

Wechsberg, Joseph   THE VOICES
Wechsberg recorded the voices of clandestine radio stations that operated for many days following the Soviet invasion, from his hotel room in Vienna. His objective was "to preserve for posterity an act of enormous contribution made by the communications media, especially the radio, to the civilian opposition." (Publisher) Doubleday, 1969.

Zeman, Zbyněk   THE MASARYKS: THE MAKING OF CZECHOSLOVAKIA
A readable history and personal biography of Masaryk's life and the period. Har-Row, 1976. Also *Prague Spring* (1979.)

GUIDEBOOKS

Burke, J.F.   CZECHOSLOVAKIA
Batsford, 1976.

HISTORY

Hermann, A.H.   A HISTORY OF THE CZECHS
From earliest days (pre-Slav Bohemia) to 1968. Rowman, 1976.

Korbel, Josef   TWENTIETH-CENTURY CZECHOSLOVAKIA: THE MEANING OF ITS HISTORY
Columbia U Pr, 1977.

Seton-Watson, R.W.   A HISTORY OF THE CZECHS AND SLOVAKS
R. West, 1980 (first published 1943).

Wallace, William V.   CZECHOSLOVAKIA
Westview Pr, 1976.

Novels

Aleichem, Sholem   MARIENBAD
A "mischievous comedy of gossip, jealousy and deceit" as some bored women amuse themselves at a spa while their husbands remain at work in Warsaw. (BRD) Putnam Pub Group, 1982.

Bieler, M.   THE THREE DAUGHTERS
Chronicle of a Prague family in the 1930s. St. Martin, 1978.

Demetz, Hana   THE HOUSE ON PRAGUE STREET
The narrator is a young half-Jewish Czech girl as World War II starts—a story of the "indignities, hardships, and sorrows" of her life in two worlds while not really belonging to either. (FC) St. Martin, 1980.

Gruša, Jiři   THE QUESTIONNAIRE, OR PRAYER FOR A TOWN AND A FRIEND
This novel was originally published in an underground edition (nineteen typed copies) resulting in the arrest of its author. It has been translated into "crisp and vivid English." The plot is about a man who applies for a job which, in Czechoslovakia, means filling out a questionnaire on himself, family, neighbors, and on and on—"a satirical view of the past and an oblique criticism of the present." (BRD) FS&G, 1982.

Herlin, Hans   SOLO RUN
When the Eastern bloc countries plan an emergency summit in Prague, the West German Intelligence recalls a retired agent because he once had an affair with a woman in the East German secretariat. "More contemplative than action-propelled." (LJ) Doubleday, 1983.

Jacot, Michael   THE LAST BUTTERFLY
About the concentration camp at Terezin where Jews were held on their way to Auschwitz. Bobbs, 1974.

Kohout, Pavel   WHITE BOOK . . .
And the title continues: "Adam Juracek, professor of drawing and physical education at the Pedagogical Institute in K, vs Sir Isaac Newton, professor of physics at the University of Cambridge, reconstructed from contemporary records and supplemented by most interesting documents." The novel is a satire—the professor defies the law of gravity in K, a fictitious resort town. Braziller, 1977.

Kohout, Pavel   THE HANGWOMAN
Centers around a school for executioners—a "gallows humor" satire of how human life can be systematically devalued. (BRD) Putnam Pub Group, 1981.

Kundera, Milan   THE UNBEARABLE LIGHTNESS OF BEING
"Refreshingly readable and colloquial novel of ideas"—a successful surgeon, and "relentless womanizer" gets into conflict with the state, leaves for Switzerland and there sacrifices a promising career for his wife's sake. (FC) Har-Row, 1984.

Kundera, Milan   THE JOKE
A college student, and prankster, is stigmatized for life for having written an irreverent postcard as a joke; many years later he seeks vengeance with another "joke" by seducing the wife of the Communist leader who turned him in to the Party. Har-Row, 1982 (first published 1969).

Kundera, Milan   THE FAREWELL PARTY
Entertaining account of life in a Communist country, with an outrageous plot. Knopf, 1976.

Kundera, Milan   LIFE IS ELSEWHERE
The Communist takeover in 1948. Knopf, 1974. Also, *Laughable Loves* (1974), a collection of short stories.

Littell, Robert   THE AMATEUR
A shocking beginning, when a CIA cryptologist's fiancé is murdered, "moves towards a combination of satire and clever, fast action." The amateur "blackmails his superiors into training him and putting him into Czechoslovakia" where he is determined to find the terrorists who killed his fiancé. Doubleday, 1975. Also, *The October Circle* (1975) about a group of Bulgarian performers who resist the invasion of Czechoslovakia.

Peters, Ellis   THE PIPER ON THE MOUNTAIN
When her stepfather is mysteriously killed in the Tatra Mountains while mountain climbing, the heroine involves three friends from Oxford in solving the mystery. Morrow, 1966.

Rothberg, Abraham   THE SWORD OF THE GOLEM
Set in sixteenth-century Prague, the medieval legend of the Golem created by Rabbi Low to defend the Jewish community against the brutality of a fanatic village priest—"rich in paradox, in awareness of the mythic dimensions of the Golem idea." (BRD) McCall, 1971.

Škvorecký, Josef   **THE SWELL SEASON**
A trilogy published backwards, thus this novel is about Danny as a high school student in Czechoslovakia in 1967. He is 18 in *The Bass Saxophone* (1979); 20 in *The Cowards* (published in 1958)—"the fluctuating moods of adolescence" as they escape the political situation "in an underground cult of jazz." (BRD) L & O Dennys, 1982.

Škvorecký, Josef   **THE ENGINEER OF HUMAN SOULS**
"First of all the book is an entertainment . . . in humor ranging from slapstick to high wit in people from the utterly wicked to the virtually saintlike." An emigré writer's observations of his fellow emigrés in Toronto that also "amounts to a history of Czechoslovakia . . . from the Nazi occupation through the subsequent Sovietization . . . provides a bible of exile." (BRD) Knopf, 1984.

Škvorecký, Josef   **MISS SILVER'S PAST**
A satire on the publishing scene under communism. Grove, 1975.

TRAVEL ARTICLES

N.Y. TIMES SUNDAY TRAVEL SECTION (X)
1985 Mar 17 (Part 2, "Sophisticated Traveler") "The Triumph of Prague." James M. Markham, p. 129
     Oct 6 "A City of Illusions." In the cobbled streets of the ancient Czech capital. Andrew Sinclair, p. 14
     "Saints and Serendipity in Prague." Alternating castles and art with taverns and hot dogs helps put the city in focus. Jane Howard, p. 15
     "A Rich and Tragic Legacy." Jewish cemetery in Prague. Henry Kamm, p. 15

DENMARK (Including Scandinavia)

Note: All asterisked entries (*) are for Scandinavia as a whole. Books listed under "Denmark/Vikings," of course, are pertinent to the other Scandinavian countries, including Iceland.

Series Guidebooks (See Appendix 1)

Baedeker: Copenhagen; *Scandinavia
Berlitz: Copenhagen

Fodor: Budget Scandinavia; Scandinavia;
            Stockholm, Copenhagen, Oslo, Helsinki & Reykjavik
Frommer: Scandinavia: $-a-Day
Nagel: Denmark/Greenland
U.S. Government: Denmark: Background Notes; Post Report

Background Reading

*Connery, Donald S.   THE SCANDINAVIANS
Background reading that makes plain the clear differences among the various
Scandinavian peoples. S&S, 1966.

Hvidt, Kristian   FLIGHT TO AMERICA
The social background of 300,000 Danish emigrants. Acad Pr, 1975.

MacHaffie, Ingeborg and Nielsen, Margaret   OF DANISH WAYS
"A delightful panorama of the land and heritage" of Denmark—history, customs,
art, inventions, government, food, hospitality, more. (Publisher) Dillon, 1976.

**Michelsen, Peter   FRILANDS MUSEET: THE DANISH MUSEUM VILLAGE
AT SORGENFRI**
A history of the open-air museum and its buildings. Humanities, 1973.

Petrow, Richard   THE BITTER YEARS
The invasion and occupation of Denmark and Norway, from April 1940 to May
1945. Morrow, 1979.

*Sansom, William   THE ICICLE AND THE SUN
Four essays on Denmark, Sweden, Finland and Norway by an English visitor—"a
gem of a little book" offering truth and magic. (BRD) Greenwood, 1976 (first
published 1959).

*Shirer, William L.   THE CHALLENGE OF SCANDINAVIA
The economic and social achievements of the Scandinavian countries, written
at a time when Scandinavia was a role model for the world. Greenwood, 1977
(first published 1955).

*Streeter, Ed   SKOAL SCANDINAVIA
Perceptive, pleasant travelogue of a trip by car through Sweden, Norway and
Denmark. Har-Row, 1952.

Strode, Hudson   DENMARK IS A LOVELY LAND
An "almost-like-being-there" descriptive travelogue—history, customs. (BRD)
HarBraceJ, 1951.

Thomas, John O.   THE GIANT KILLERS
The story of the Danish resistance movement, 1940-45—the Danes' communal
and individual acts of resistance against their Nazi occupiers and the rescue of
nearly all Danish Jews. Taplinger, 1976.

*THE VIKINGS

Graham-Campbell, James   THE VIKING WORLD
"The best popular introduction to Viking culture yet compiled. One of the most beautiful . . . books on any archaeological subject"—chapters on Viking warriors, explorations, trade, arts, food, etc. (BRD) Ticknor & Fields, 1980.

Jones, Gwyn   A HISTORY OF THE VIKINGS
History based on surviving documents and archaeological finds—"a vivid and living picture of the Viking adventure." (BRD) Oxford U, 1969.

Magnusson, Magnus   VIKINGS!
Based on a ten-part public TV series—Viking culture, religion, mythology and literature and a reconstruction of origins in Denmark, Norway and Sweden. Dutton, 1980.

Simpson, Colin   THE VIKING CIRCLE
"Authentic and vivid picture of life in Viking times." (LJ) St. Martin, 1980.

GUIDEBOOKS

Munksgaardd, Elisabeth   DENMARK: AN ARCHAEOLOGICAL GUIDE
For travelers with an interest in archaeology. Divides Denmark into twenty-one areas and then gives a description, what can be seen, how to get there, towns to use as a base for day trips, museums to which remains have been removed, etc. Faber & Faber, 1974.

Nelson, Nina   DENMARK
Batsford guide. Hastings, 1974.

*Prag, Per   SCANDINAVIA BY CAR
Vanous, 1976.

HISTORY

*Derry, T.K.   A HISTORY OF SCANDINAVIA
U of Minnesota, 1979.

Lauring, Palle   A HISTORY OF THE KINGDOM OF DENMARK
Host, 1981.

Oakley, Stewart   A SHORT HISTORY OF DENMARK
Praeger, 1972.

Novels

Arnold, Elliott   A NIGHT OF WATCHING
The plot is about the smuggling of Danish Jews out of the country, in the fourth year of the German occupation (1943). Scribner, 1967.

Bjarnhof, Karl   THE STARS GROW PALE
A young, near-blind boy must leave the security of home for a special institute for the blind in Copenhagen. In a sequel, *The Good Light* (1960), the story is continued, following the boy into adolescence, manhood, discovery of the arts, his first love affair, and acceptance of the total blindness he knows must eventually come. The setting is pre-World War I Denmark—an "autobiographical memoir within the framework of a novel. . . . A haunting and evocative reminiscence." (FC) Knopf, 1958.

Bodelsen, Anders   THINK OF A NUMBER
Suspenseful police investigation mystery. Har-Row, 1968.

Canning, Victor   RAVEN'S WIND
Historical novel of the Danes' invasions of England; in this plot they capture an Englishman and take him back to Denmark as a slave. Morrow, 1983.

Dinesen, Isak   WINTER'S TALES
Seven gothic short stories, most of which are set in the Danish landscape. Random, 1942.

Eden, Dorothy   THE SHADOW WIFE
A contemporary gothic by a leading writer of such romances, set in Denmark. Coward, 1968.

Kelly, Michael   ASSAULT
A World War II episode in Copenhagen, involving the British and the Danish underground. HarBraceJ, 1969.

Lofts, Norah   THE LOST QUEEN
Historical novel of the eighteenth century; the sister of George III is married off to the crown prince of Denmark. Doubleday, 1969.

Orum, Poul   NOTHING BUT THE TRUTH
An introspective detective and his brash assistant solve a murder mystery with psychological insights. Pantheon, 1976. Also *Scapegoat* (1975), a murder mystery with a West Jutland setting.

Peters, Elizabeth   THE COPENHAGEN CONNECTION
A romantic suspense novel in which the heroine takes the place of secretary to her favorite author, following an accident at Copenhagen's airport. Congdon & Lattes, 1982. Also *Street of the Five Moons* (1978).

Stegner, Wallace   THE SPECTATOR BIRD
An aging man in twentieth-century California reflects on his past and an adventure in Denmark. Doubleday, 1976.

TRAVEL ARTICLES

N.Y. TIMES SUNDAY TRAVEL SECTION (X)
1985 Jan 13 Shopper's World: "Porcelain by Hand in Copenhagen." Ruth Robinson, p. 6

1985   Mar 17 (Part 2, "Sophisticated Traveler") "Copenhagen: Child's Play."
       Margaret Atwood, p. 39
       Jun 16 "What's Doing in Copenhagen." Ole Duus, p. 10
       Jun 16 "Seaside Village in Denmark." Dragor, eight miles from Copenhagen.
       Sara Evans, p. 16
1984   Jul 22 Fare of the Country: "Premier Pastries of Denmark." Sara Evans, p. 6
       Aug 12 "Danish by Design." An eighteenth century granary in Copenhagen
       transformed into a hotel. George O'Brien, p. 6
       Dec 9 Fare of the Country: "Aalborg Is the Toast of Aquavit Drinkers."
       Joshua Mills, p. 6

TRAVEL/HOLIDAY
1984   Apr "Summertime and All That Jazz." Take 5 on two continents (annual jazz
       festivals in Copenhagen, Montreux, Monterey, and New York). Steve
       Schneider, p. 68
       May "Bicycling in Denmark." Two-wheeled country tours, Helmut and Gea
       Koenig, p. 63

ENGLAND (Including Great Britain)

Note: All asterisked entries (*) indicate that "Britain" or "Great Britain" is stated or
implied and therefore may contain material on Ireland, Scotland, and/or Wales in
addition to England.

Series Guidebooks (See Appendix 1)

American Express: England & Wales; London
Baedeker: *Great Britain; London
Berlitz: Oxford & Stratford; London
Birnbaum: *Great Britain & Ireland
Blue Guide: England; Cathedrals and Abbeys of England and Wales;
                   Channel Islands; Oxford & Cambridge; London;
                   Museums & Galleries of London
Companion Guide: Shakespeare Country; London; Outer London
Fisher: *Britain; London

Fodor: *Great Britain; *Budget Travel Britain; London; Budget
          Travel London; Fun in London
Frommer: England & Scotland: Dollarwise; $-a-Day;
          London City Guide
Insight: *Great Britain
Let's Go: *Britain & Ireland (Scotland & Wales)
Michelin: England—the West Country; London City Guide;
          Southwest England
Nagel: *Great Britain
U.S.Government: *United Kingdom & Northern Ireland:
          Background Notes; Post Report; Pocket Guide

Background Reading

Ardagh, John   A TALE OF FIVE CITIES
See complete entry under "Europe"; includes Newcastle.

Blake, Robert, ed.   THE ENGLISH WORLD
Photographs and text—"irresistible for the Anglophile . . . essays by major
scholars who know how to write for the general reader." (TBS) Abrams, 1982.

Bradford, Ernie   THE STORY OF THE MARY ROSE
History and salvage story of this ship destined to be a prime tourist attraction
and a treasure of knowledge on Tudor life; the author "infuses his story with a
wonderful sense of excitement." (BL) Norton, 1982.

Bryant, Sir Arthur   SET IN A SILVER SEA
A social history of English life beginning with Pepys's London, to the end of
Queen Victoria's reign—touches on "sports, food, farming, kings . . . businessmen .
. . the pleasant English countryside in the 18th century and the teeming cities."
(BRD) Morrow, 1984 (first published 1968).

Burke, John   LOOK BACK ON ENGLAND
"Fascinating and informative journey into England's past . . . that lives visibly in
the architecture, countryside and villages. . . . rather than by studying dates,
battles, and cumbersome facts." (Publisher) Salem Hse, 1983.

*Crookston, Peter, ed.   THE AGES OF BRITAIN
Nine authors guide us through British history—Stone Age through the
Victorians, plus sections on daily life over the entire period by eight more experts.
Illustrated gazetteer arranged by periods and types of objects, relevant museums
and sights. St. Martin, 1983.

*Deighton, Len   BATTLE OF BRITAIN
Illustrated review of a pivotal battle of World War II; day-by-day account of the
summer of 1940. Coward, 1980. Also *Fighter: The True Story of the Battle of
Britain* (1978).

*Gelb, Norman   THE BRITISH: A PORTRAIT OF AN INDOMITABLE ISLAND PEOPLE
"Personal, informal definition of the British people . . . generally laudatory." Topics include the class society, sexuality and feminism, relations with America, royalty, how it is different from Scotland and Wales. (BL) Everett Hse, 1982.

*Hamilton, Ronald   NOW I REMEMBER: A HOLIDAY HISTORY OF BRITAIN
"All the English history you'll ever need." Chatto & Windus, 1983.

Jackson, Michael   THE ENGLISH PUB
Har-Row, 1976.

*Johnson, Paul   BRITISH CATHEDRALS
Construction methods, the role of the clergy, history and social history—"complicated history and ideas [rendered] into prose that is intelligible to general audiences." (BL) Morrow, 1980.

Jones, Christopher   THE GREAT PALACE: THE STORY OF PARLIAMENT
Companion book to a BBC TV series—setting and history of the U.K.'s legislative body, traditions and operations. Parkwest, 1985.

McClure, James   SPIKE ISLAND: PORTRAIT OF A POLICE DIVISION
"Acute depictions of police at work" in a rough Liverpool police district. (BL) Random, 1980.

*Marwick, Arthur   BRITAIN IN OUR CENTURY: IMAGES AND CONTROVERSIES
"The flavor of each decade from 1900 to the present . . . succinct commentary"—how Britain has changed yet remains in many ways unchanged. (PW) Thames Hudson, 1985.

*Morris, James   SPECTACLE OF EMPIRE
Overall title of a remarkable trilogy that is popular history, written by a renowned travel writer. Volume 1, *Heaven's Command: An Imperial Progress*, begins with Queen Victoria's accession to the throne in 1837 and ends with her Jubilee in 1897. Volume 2, *Pax Britannica, the Climax of an Empire*, is the British Empire in 1897, at its zenith. Volume 3, *Farewell the Trumpets: The Decline of an Empire*, takes the reader on to Churchill's funeral in 1965. (BRD) Doubleday, 1982.

*Muir, Richard   TRAVELLER'S HISTORY OF BRITAIN AND IRELAND
Photographs and text present "an intriguing guide to 54 prehistoric sites, medieval monuments, and stately mansions that epitomize a particular stage or facet of history. Arranged chronologically. . . . will enable the visitor to plan a fascinating itinerary." (Publisher) M Joseph, 1983.

*Norwich, John Julius, ed.   BRITAIN'S HERITAGE
Geology, geography, life-styles, cities, country houses, religion, arts, leisure and more—sumptuously illustrated. Continuum, 1983.

Pakenham, Valerie   OUT IN THE NOONDAY SUN: EDWARDIANS IN THE TROPICS
"Profiles those valiant, beleaguered, arrogant, dutiful soldiers, civil servants, adventurers" who sustained the British Empire at the turn of the century, and incidentally providing background for innumerable novels about India, Asia and Africa. (BL) Random, 1985.

Priestley, J.B.   THE ENGLISH
The author selected a highly personal choice of subjects to illustrate what he considers essentially English characteristics—biographical essays, chapters on the arts, England's future, etc. Viking, 1973. Also *English Journey* (1934), a travel memoir, which Beryl Bainbridge elected to follow fifty years later and record in *English Journey: On the Road to Milton Keynes* (see below).

*Richard, Ivor   WE, THE BRITISH
The author is a former MP, ambassador to the UN, and "familiar with what U.S. readers need to know if they are to understand the British"—engaging estimation of life in the United Kingdom. (BL) Doubleday, 1983.

*Sampson, Anthony   CHANGING ANATOMY OF BRITAIN
An update of Sampson's earlier work, *Anatomy of Britain*—a journalist's analysis of Britain. Random, 1984.

Smith, Godfrey   THE ENGLISH COMPANION
Subtitle: An idiosyncratic guide to England and Englishness from A to Z. A "charming, witty, and lively companion to English life, letters, and history" arranged alphabetically. (LJ) Potter, 1985.

Sutherland, Douglas   THE ENGLISH GENTLEMAN
And *The English Gentleman's Wife* (1979) and *The English Gentleman's Child* (1980)—the "system" of upper-class life in England, by an insider with wit. Penguin, 1980.

TRAVELOGUES, MEMOIRS, SPECIAL PERSPECTIVES

Bailey, Anthony   ENGLAND, FIRST AND LAST
A sequel to *America, Lost and Found*—the author's homecoming in 1944 and on through his West African military service in 1952—"details and insights of adolescence and awakening in fading postwar Britain." (LJ) Viking, 1985.

Bainbridge, Beryl   ENGLISH JOURNEY: ON THE ROAD TO MILTON KEYNES
The English novelist revisits many places visited fifty years earlier by J.B. Priestley in *English Journey* (above) and produces "a flat, banal description of an England . . . more dreary than the one that Paul Theroux described [see *The Kingdom by the Sea*, below]." Braziller, 1984.

Beadle, Muriel   THESE RUINS ARE INHABITED
An oldie, but still an enjoyable anecdotal account of the author's stay in England

while her husband was a visiting professor at Oxford. U of Chicago, 1977 (first published 1961).

*Blythe, Ronald, ed.   PLACES: AN ANTHOLOGY OF BRITAIN
A number of gifted authors share their memories and views of favorite residences or scenic spots. Contributors include the editor, Bawden, Sillitoe, Pym, etc. Oxford U, 1981.

*Brown, Hamish M.   HAMISH'S GROATS END WALK
Subtitle: One man and his dog on a hill route through Britain and Ireland. Diary of a 2,500-mile "walk" from John O'Groats to Land's End—historical anecdotes, observations on nature and environment, techniques. Gollancz, 1981.

Deindorfer, Robert G.   LIFE IN LOWER SLAUGHTER
A New York City writer's two-year stint in an English village. Dutton, 1971.

Dobie, J. Frank   A TEXAN IN ENGLAND
A year at Cambridge as professor of American history in 1943 is the basis for this chronicle, first published in 1945. U of Texas Press, 1980.

Entwistle, Frank   ABROAD IN ENGLAND
The author traveled by camper "doing much of his 'research' in pubs," pursuing his vocation as a student of the English race—"Anglophiles will love this." (BRD) Norton, 1983.

*Fellows, Arnold   A WAYFARER'S COMPANION
For leisurely and scholarly wayfarers who like a grasp of architecture, natural and historic backgrounds for sightseeing—England and Wales. Oxford U, 1937.

*Fowles, John and others   BRITAIN: A WORLD BY ITSELF
For Anglophiles, a "banquet" of writing by eleven authors describing "country nooks and vistas special to each"—for example, Jan Morris on the Black Mountains in Wales, R.S. Thomas on Lleyn, John Fowles on Dorset. (PW) Little, 1984. Also, by Mr. Fowles, *A Short History of Lyme Regis* (1983), providing a portrait of this "home of notables and eccentrics." See also *The French Lieutenant's Woman* under "England/Novels" (Devon).

*Frater, Alexander   STOPPING-TRAIN BRITAIN: A RAILWAY ODYSSEY
Originally a series of *Observer* articles—narrative of the author's "journeys on 10 small train lines [whose existence he says are in jeopardy] in rural England and Scotland . . . in crisp style they relate the landscapes and people the author encountered." (BL) Hodder & Stoughton, 1984.

Golding, William   A MOVING TARGET
A collection of the noted author's writings, including articles on Wiltshire and on cathedrals in England. FS&G, 1982.

Hillaby, John   JOURNEY HOME
The most recent of the author/naturalist's books on his walks about England.

This one starts in Cumbria and ends in London—"the rambling narrative is neatly paced with the path itself, providing a wonderful tour through the English countryside, its history, and Hillaby's own past." (BL) HR&W, 1984. His first book was *Walk Through Britain* (1969), an account of his journey from John O'Groats to Land's End in 1966 (recently reprinted). That was followed by *Journey Through Love* in 1977.

Jackson-Stops, Gervase, ed.   WRITERS AT HOME: NATIONAL TRUST STUDIES
A dozen British authors' homes that are now literary properties of the National Trust—buildings, landscapes, anecdotes, lives of Kipling, Lawrence, Shaw, Hardy, etc. Facts On File, 1985.

James, Henry   ENGLISH HOURS
Reissue of a classic; "collection of essays [that draw] one down into the English character as it illuminates the visitor's perspective." Oxford U, 1981 (first published 1905).

Llewellyn, Sam   THE WORST JOURNEY IN THE MIDLANDS
"One of the wittiest travel accounts in some time . . . an Englishman's three-week journey in an old rowboat from Wales to London, via river and canals, through locks and around weirs [told] as a misadventure. . . . fine writing style somewhat reminiscent of the Victorians but heavy with contemporary British slang." (LJ) Heinemann, 1984.

McKenney, Ruth and Branston, Richard   HERE'S ENGLAND
Another oldie, not quite a classic, first published in 1955, but still useful and entertaining in helping to get a focus, especially for a first trip to England. The authors feel you *must* have some understanding of English history and church architecture if the country is not to slide out from under you. And they offer interesting thoughts on itinerary-planning. Har-Row, 1971.

Morris, Jan   JOURNEYS; TRAVELS
In these collections of essays by one of the leading travel writers there are essays on Wells in *Journeys* and on Bath in *Travels*. Oxford U, 1980 and 1984.

*Morton, H.V.   MORTON'S BRITAIN
The "In Search of" series of travel guides, classics written in the 1920s and 1930s, have been culled for excerpts in this newer book, with updating editorial comments. Dodd, 1970. The originals from which the excerpts were taken—*In Search of England* (1927), *In Search of Ireland* (1931), *In Search of Scotland* (1930), *In Search of Wales* (1932)—have also been recently reissued (Dodd, 1984).

*National Geographic, eds.   DISCOVERING BRITAIN AND IRELAND
"One of the loveliest . . . books on the British Isles to appear in a long time. . . . animated but accurate text" plus photographs on the history, architecture, social customs, sights to see, etc. (BL) Natl Geog, 1985.

Simon, Kate   ENGLAND'S GREEN AND PLEASANT LAND
By a leading contemporary travel writer—"topographically arranged description of the aesthetic, historic, and legendary interest of numerous English towns and villages." (BRD) Knopf, 1974.

*Theroux, Paul   THE KINGDOM BY THE SEA: A JOURNEY AROUND THE COAST OF BRITAIN
The author, who has lived part-time in Britain for years, writes of a three-month tour around its coast via foot, bus and train, "observing the British public on holiday. . . . merciless in his portrayal of the tawdry seaside resorts . . . apathy of people." His aim was to write a book on the British themselves like the ones Britons have been writing for years about every place else—Anglophiles be forewarned! (PW) Houghton, 1983.

Tracy, Honor   THE HEART OF ENGLAND
A peevish book about rural areas and small towns chronicling the author's return trip to England from her home in Ireland, with reflections on people met, rude outsiders, the young, etc. Hamish Hamilton, 1983.

West, Jessamyn   DOUBLE DISCOVERY: A JOURNEY
Nostalgic memoir of the novelist's trip to England and France in the '20s, as a twenty-six-year old schoolteacher—letters, journal entries and "mature reflections . . . sightseeing . . . school days [Oxford]." (BL) HarBraceJ, 1980.

White, Theodore H.   ENGLAND HAVE MY BONES
New edition of an out-of-print classic first published in 1936—"mostly a paean to England's pastoral scenes of nearly 50 years ago." (PW) Putnam Pub Group, 1982.

THE ROYAL FAMILY

Aronson, Theo   ROYAL FAMILY: YEARS OF TRANSITION
A survey of the past five monarchs (Edward VII to Elizabeth II)—personalities, and how each generation "managed not only to succeed each other but also [to maintain] the monarchy's need to be . . . pertinent to changing times and enveloped in mystique." (BL) Salem Hse, 1984.

Coolican, Don   THE STORY OF THE ROYAL FAMILY
By a staff writer for the *London Daily Express*—begins with Edward VII at the start of the twentieth century to Elizabeth II—"informative and avoids tourist hype . . . a substantial treat for Anglophiles." (BL) Crown, 1982.

Edgar, Donald   PALACE
Subtitle: A fascinating behind-the-scenes look at how Buckingham Palace really works. "Relates the history of the structure and its grounds . . . the queen's average working day . . . roles of functionaries. . . . uses the recent state visit of Queen Beatrix of the Netherlands as an example of how lavishly important guests are treated." Photographs and watercolors done especially for the book. (BL) Salem Hse, 1984.

Hibbert, Christopher   THE COURT OF ST. JAMES
Subtitle: The monarch at work from Victoria to Elizabeth II. "Court traditions and working habits of five monarchs." (BRD) Morrow, 1983.

Lofts, Norah   QUEENS OF ENGLAND
By a contemporary British novelist—history through the lives of the women who have . . . ruled as sovereigns in their own right, or as royal consorts. Doubleday, 1977.

Packard, Jerrold M.   THE QUEEN AND HER COURT: A GUIDE TO THE BRITISH MONARCHY TODAY
"An excellent sorting out of the intricacies surrounding the functioning of the British crown." (BL) Scribner, 1981.

Ross, Josephine   THE MONARCHY OF BRITAIN
Monarchical history from 1066 to the present—"a clear impression of how the British monarchy evolved . . . engrossingly illustrated." (BL) Morrow, 1982.

Seymour, William   SOVEREIGN LEGACY: AN HISTORICAL GUIDE TO THE BRITISH MONARCHY
For the actual traveler or the armchair royalty enthusiast—covers the thousand years-plus of the British monarchy describing the manifestations (castles, churches, artwork, monuments) of each dynasty still on public view. Doubleday, 1980.

COUNTRY AND VILLAGE ENGLAND

Bailey, Brian   THE ENGLISH VILLAGE GREEN
"A lovely look at the center of English village life . . . anecdotes . . . charming illustrations. . . . 600 of the most important and attractive village greens in all parts of England." (Publisher) Salem Hse, 1985. Also *Villages of England* (1984).

Balderson, Eileen and Goodlad, Douglas   BACKSTAIRS LIFE IN A COUNTRY HOUSE
Life as a domestic servant in the 1930s. David, 1982.

Blythe, Ronald   AKENFIELD—PORTRAIT OF AN ENGLISH VILLAGE
Portrait of an East Anglia village through the words of its inhabitants—"provides an invaluable and horridly enjoyable corrective to the standard rose-pub-and-quaintness notion of bucolic England." (BRD) Pantheon, 1969.

Crookston, Peter   VILLAGE ENGLAND
Villages that have meaning in the context of English history that are not necessarily well-known to tourists. Hutchinson, 1980.

DuMaurier, Daphne   VANISHING CORNWALL
A new edition of a book first published in 1967, with new photos and an epilogue. "Celebrates the beauty and mourns lost elements of the Cornish countryside . . . stirring text that includes reminiscences, literary references, history and legends." (BL) Doubleday, 1981.

Gaster, Harold   A MORNING WITHOUT CLOUDS
A "wonderfully evocative portrait of rural England seventy years ago—its landscapes, lifestyles and people." (PW) St. Martin, 1982.

Girouard, Mark   LIFE IN THE ENGLISH COUNTRY HOUSE; A SOCIAL AND ARCHITECTURAL HISTORY
Houses as architectural digs. Yale U Pr, 1978. Also The *Victorian Country House* (1979).

Graham, Winston   POLDARK'S CORNWALL
General history, description of the country, plus sites used for filming the Poldark series—"thoroughly ingratiating tour of Cornwall." (BL) Bodley Head, 1985.

Herriott, James   THE BEST OF JAMES HERRIOT
Excerpts from *All Creatures Great and Small, All Things Wise and Wonderful, The Lord God Made Them All* by the veterinarian/author of Yorkshire whose books have been made into a widely popular TV series. St. Martin, 1983. Also *James Herriot's Yorkshire* (1979) with many photos.

Hill, Susan   THE MAGIC APPLE TREE: A COUNTRY YEAR
"Reflections on life in a country village" in Oxfordshire where the author, her husband and daughter moved into an eighteenth-century cottage—gardening, food, villagers, local church and festivals, and so on. (PW) HR&W, 1983.

Thompson, Flora   LARK RISE TO CANDLEFORD
An omnibus edition of the trilogy that includes *Lark Rise, Over to Candleford* and *Candleford Green*—life in a country hamlet and nearby market towns in the 1880s and 1890s. Penguin, 1983 (first published 1945).

LITERARY GUIDES FOR TRAVELERS

Adams, Robert M.   THE LAND AND THE LITERATURE OF ENGLAND: A HISTORICAL ACCOUNT
Retelling the "entire history of England (with side glances at Ireland, Scotland, and Wales) . . . to make clear . . . what was going on while all those plays, novels, essays and poems were being written." (BL) Norton, 1983.

Benningfield, Gordon   HARDY COUNTRY
Text and illustrations of the area indigenous to the Hardy classics—depicts England as it appeared to the novelist. (PW) Allen Lane, 1983.

Cooper, Robert M.   A LITERARY GUIDE AND COMPANION TO SOUTHERN ENGLAND
U of Ohio, 1985.

*Daiches, David and Flower, John   **LITERARY LANDSCAPES OF THE BRITISH ISLES**
Includes an atlas and gazetteer with information on 225 authors in 475 cities, towns and villages. Penguin, 1981.

*Drabble, Margaret   **A WRITER'S BRITAIN: LANDSCAPES IN LITERATURE**
By the novelist, combining literary quotations with relevant photographs—Shakespeare to Tolkien—"deserves to become a classic." (BRD) Knopf, 1979.

Eagle, Dorothy and Carnell, Hilary   **THE OXFORD ILLUSTRATED LITERARY GUIDE TO GREAT BRITAIN AND IRELAND**
"Identifies the many towns, homes, lakes and other places associated with British and Irish writers." (BRD) Oxford U, 1981

Fisher, Lois H.   **A LITERARY GAZETTEER OF ENGLAND**
Reference work of literary associations (settings of novels, authors' birthplaces, etc.) for 1,200 English localities with associations to some 500 authors—"an almost overwhelming mass of detail [presented] in a clear, precise, and engaging fashion." (BL) McGraw, 1980.

Graham, Winston   **POLDARK'S CORNWALL**
The author of the Poldark saga "describes how the novels came to be written and how the TV epic based on the saga came to be made . . . stunning array of photographs." (Publisher) Bodley Head, 1983; paper 1985.

Hardwick, Michael   **A LITERARY ATLAS AND GAZETTEER OF THE BRITISH ISLES**
Gale, 1973.

*Harting, Emilie C.   **LITERARY TOUR GUIDE TO ENGLAND AND SCOTLAND**
Homes and haunts of leading English authors and settings for some of their works. Morrow, 1976.

*Morley, Frank   **LITERARY BRITAIN: A READER'S GUIDE TO ITS WRITERS AND LANDMARKS**
"Journey through the literary highways and byways of England, Scotland and Wales in company with a remarkable and enthusiastic bibliophile." The book has a unique format in that it is organized around six ancient roads out of London and back again (now main "A" highways). (Publisher) Har-Row, 1980; paper, Moyer-Bell, 1985.

*Thomas, Edward   **A LITERARY PILGRIM: AN ILLUSTRATED GUIDE TO BRITAIN'S LITERARY HERITAGE**
A completely new edition (new photographs and contemporary portraits and

paintings) of a book first published in 1917. Edward Thomas was a poet of World War I, and goes in search of the homes and landscapes of some of Britain's most famous writers. Salem Hse, 1984.

STONEHENGE

Balfour, Michael D.   STONEHENGE AND ITS MYSTERIES
"A fascinating, imaginatively illustrated summary of the . . . lore, legends and theories" of the prehistoric stone circles at Stonehenge. (BL) Scribner, 1981.

Burl, Aubrey   RINGS OF STONE: THE PREHISTORIC STONE CIRCLES OF BRITAIN AND IRELAND
Goes beyond Stonehenge to include other similar antiquities in Britain and Ireland. Ticknor & Fields, 1980.

Fowles, John   THE ENIGMA OF STONEHENGE
The text by novelist Fowles covers the most credible of the myriad theories about Stonehenge. Summit, 1980.

OXFORD

Morris, Jan,   OXFORD
New revised edition of the book originally published in 1965—a comprehensive guide that is a "mixture of rhapsody and anecdote"—perfect preparatory reading for a visit. (BRD) Oxford U, 1978.

Morris, Jan, ed.   THE OXFORD BOOK OF OXFORD
An anthology—traces the history of the university from its foundation in the Middle Ages through to 1945, combining extracts from contemporary observers with Jan Morris's own linking commentary." (BRD) Oxford U, 1978.

Piper, David   THE TREASURES OF OXFORD
Oxford's art. Paddington Pr, 1977

Rowse, A.L.   OXFORD IN THE HISTORY OF ENGLAND
Oxford's contributions to the politics and culture of England. Putnam Pub Group, 1975.

THE ISLANDS OF BRITAIN

Gladwin, Mary Fane   CHANNEL ISLAND HOPPING: A GUIDE FOR THE INDEPENDENT TRAVELLER
Jersey, Guernsey, Alderney, Sark and Herm—history, accommodations, inter-island travel, etc. Hippocrene, 1984.

*ISLANDS OF THE WORLD SERIES
Individual books by various authors that emphasize history, culture, geography,

climate, geology and wildlife of the various islands. Available in the series are Aran Islands (1973), Guernsey (1977), Bute (1973), Arran (1985), Isle of Wight (1979), Jersey (1976), Kintyre (1974), Lundy (1984), Orkney (1985), Shetland (1984), the Uists and Barra (1974). David.

GUIDEBOOKS TO INSPIRE AN ITINERARY OR EXPLORE A THEME

*Ashe, Geoffrey   A GUIDE TO ARTHURIAN BRITAIN
Longman, 1983.

*Awdry, W. and Cook, Chris   A GUIDE TO THE STEAM RAILWAYS OF GREAT BRITAIN
Preserved and/or restored steam railway lines in Britain (a few in Ireland)—illustrated account for all train buffs—history, equipment in use, what the ride is like, etc. Michael Joseph, 1983.

Bacon, David & Maslov, Norman   THE BEATLES' ENGLAND: THERE ARE PLACES I'LL REMEMBER
For Beatles fans—birthplaces, childhood homes, "landmarks identified in their works (Penny Lane, Albert Hall, the Abbey Road crosswalk)"—then and now. (BL) 910 Press, 1982.

*Bence-Jones, Mark   THE NATIONAL TRUST GREAT ENGLISH HOMES OF ENGLAND AND WALES AND THE PEOPLE WHO LIVED IN THEM
"Anglophiles can explore the histories of 61 houses . . . all currently open to the public . . . profiled architecturally [and the] passage of lives under their roofs." (BL) Heritage, 1984.

*Bottomley, Frank   THE ABBEY EXPLORER'S GUIDE TO ENGLAND, SCOTLAND & WALES
Key & Ward, 1981. Also the *Castle Guide* (1979), *Church Guide* (1978), *Inn Guide* (1984) in this series.

Brereton, Peter   PETER BRERETON'S TOURING GUIDE TO ENGLISH VILLAGES
"A guide to the charming towns and villages of England . . . itineraries, historical details, information on where to eat and sleep." (BL) P-H, 1984.

*Brody, Elaine   MUSIC GUIDE TO GREAT BRITAIN: ENGLAND, SCOTLAND, WALES, IRELAND
One of a series of guides for individual European countries—a handbook of information for a range of travelers "from the music dilettante to the highly motivated specialist." Includes information on the country's musical history, concert halls, opera houses, festivals, etc. Dodd, 1975. (See also *Music Festivals in Europe and Britain* (1984) and *Music Lover's Europe* (1983) under "Europe/Art, Music, Literature.")

Burton, Neil   THE ENGLISH HISTORIC HOUSES HANDBOOK
"Information for the traveler with an interest in English architecture, history, or literature"—arranged by county. Includes information on over 500 houses open to the public and an additional 300 open by appointment for just a few days a year—covers the great country houses and literary shrines. (BRD) Facts On File, 1982.

*Butler, Lionel and Given-Wilson, Chris   MEDIEVAL MONASTERIES OF GREAT BRITAIN
A gazetteer and guide to "100 existing monasteries providing historic, architectural and tourist information." (BL) Michael Joseph, 1984.

Chamberlin, Russell   ENGLISH MARKET TOWNS
Architectural, historical and geographic background of fifty market towns where there are street markets (twenty-five more are briefly described). Harmony, 1985.

*Crowl, Philip A.   THE INTELLIGENT TRAVELER'S GUIDE TO HISTORIC BRITAIN
A "giant travel guide . . . geared toward the U.S. traveler." The first part provides historical background from prehistory to 1945 and highlights "visible and visitable" remains. The second part is a gazetteer of sites by region, with a star system for evaluating them. (BL) Congdon & Weed, 1983.

*Deal, W.   A GUIDE TO FOREST HOLIDAYS IN GREAT BRITAIN & IRELAND
"Pleasures and pastimes of several hundred forest parks"—tourist information as well as what you can expect in plant and animal life. (BRD) David, 1976.

*Fedden, Robin & Joekes, Rosemary   THE NATIONAL TRUST GUIDE TO ENGLAND, WALES AND NORTHERN IRELAND
"National Trust properties that help to preserve Britain's heritage and history"—arranged by category (houses, gardens, archaeological sites, etc.). (BL) Norton, 1984.

*Ferguson, George W.   BRITAIN BY BRITRAIL
How to tour Britain by train. B Franklin, 1982.

Foster, Richard   DISCOVERING ENGLISH CHURCHES
Subtitle: A beginner's guide to the story of the parish church from before the conquest to Gothic revival. This is the accompanying text to a BBC TV series for church-browsing tourists; also a source book on the history of English religious life. Oxford U, 1982.

*Fry, Plantaganet S.   THE DAVID & CHARLES BOOK OF CASTLES
Chapters on the construction, use, and everyday life in castles, plus a directory for England, Wales and Scotland. Included is access information for visitors, historic background, current condition, etc. (BL) David, 1980.

***Green, Kerry and Leocha, Charles   THE WHOLE EUROPE ESCAPE
MANUAL: U.K./IRELAND**
Part of a new series of guidebooks "designed to . . . put the fantasy and excitement back into travel." World Leis Corp, 1985.

**Hammer, David L.   THE GAME IS AFOOT: A TRAVEL GUIDE TO THE
ENGLAND OF SHERLOCK HOLMES**
Gaslight Pbns, 1983.

**Hill, David   IN TURNER'S FOOTSTEPS: THROUGH THE HILLS AND
DALES OF NORTHERN ENGLAND**
Retraces the English landscape painter's journey through Richmondshire, on the same days of the year and from the same vantage points that led to the artist's sketches and paintings. Salem Hse, 1985.

***Household, Joanna, ed.   DEBRETT'S GUIDE TO BRITAIN: WHERE TO
GO AND WHAT TO SEE**
A guide from the slant of the different social, sporting and cultural seasons. Putnam Pub Group, 1983.

***Jacobs, Michael   KNOPF TRAVELER'S GUIDE TO ART: GREAT BRITAIN
& IRELAND**
Suggested tours, routes, museums (including hours and fees and museum plans), guides to collections. The book is organized geographically by region, city and site, with an introduction to each. Knopf, 1984.

***Muir, Richard and Welfare, Humphrey   THE NATIONAL TRUST GUIDE
TO PREHISTORIC AND
ROMAN BRITAIN**
"For the more discerning visitor"—life in prehistoric and Roman Britain described, photographs of remains and places to visit. (LJ) Sheridan Hse, 1983.

Oakes, George W.   TURN LEFT AT THE PUB
Newly revised edition of a classic on "walks"—twenty-four tours through villages, university towns, ancient battlegrounds and ruins, including best place to stop for a bite. Congdon & Weed, 1985. Also *Turn Right at the Fountain* (1981), for Cambridge, Oxford and London.

***Palm, Charlene F.   DRIVING IN BRITAIN: WHAT THE GUIDE BOOKS
DON'T TELL YOU**
Bittersweet Pr, 1984.

*Peel, J.H.   ALONG THE GREEN ROADS OF BRITAIN
A country walking classic—nine road walks with maps, commentary, over relatively short distances. David, 1982.

PHAIDON CULTURAL GUIDE: GREAT BRITAIN AND IRELAND
P-H, 1985.

Pick, Christopher   OFF THE MOTORWAY
"Exploring the pretty, the interesting, and the unusual places which lie only a few miles from Britain's main motorway exits." (Publisher) Hippocrene, 1984.

Platt, Colin   THE TRAVELLER'S GUIDE TO MEDIEVAL ENGLAND: EIGHT TOURS FOR THE WEEKEND AND THE SHORT BREAK
By a university historian for the discriminating traveler—tours to countryside, castles, churches reflecting evidences of medieval life, what to see, recommended hotels, and so on. Salem Hse, 1985.

Ross, Anne and Cyprien, Michael   TRAVELLER'S GUIDE TO CELTIC BRITAIN
Routledge and Kegan, 1985.

*Smith, Roland   WILDEST BRITAIN: A VISITOR'S GUIDE TO THE NATIONAL PARKS
"Possible outdoor adventures in the country's 10 national parks in both England and Wales." (BL) Blandford, 1984.

Steves, Rick   GREAT BRITAIN IN 22 DAYS
John Muir, 1986.

Wilkinson, Gerald   WOODLAND WALKS IN BRITAIN
Four-hundred rambles, with maps and photographs for the walker (rather than the hiker.) HR&W, 1985.

Winks, Robin   AN AMERICAN'S GUIDE TO BRITAIN
One of the best books to read first; by a Yale professor of history—congenial, literate source for information on taking full advantage of all Britain has to offer; written with the American traveler in mind. Scribner, 1983.

HISTORY

Briggs, Asa   A SOCIAL HISTORY OF ENGLAND
"Traces the evolution of English society ... politics ... literature and the arts ... science and technology ... balances a depth of detail and interpretation with an ability [to] isolate" major events and influences. (BL) Viking, 1984.

*Churchill, W.S.   A HISTORY OF THE ENGLISH-SPEAKING PEOPLES
Abridged edition. Bantam, 1976.

*Derry, T.K. and others   GREAT BRITAIN: ITS HISTORY FROM EARLIEST TIMES TO THE PRESENT DAY
Standard, scholarly history. Oxford U, 1962.

Feiling, Keith G.   A HISTORY OF ENGLAND
From pre-Roman era to World War II—readable one-volume history by an Oxford professor. McGraw, 1966.

*Morgan, Kenneth O.   THE OXFORD ILLUSTRATED HISTORY
OF BRITAIN
Oxford U, 1984.

Trevelyan, G.M.   A SHORTENED HISTORY OF ENGLAND
Penguin, 1976.

LONDON

Background Reading (See Appendix 1)

Agutter, Jenny   SNAP: OBSERVATIONS OF LOS ANGELES AND LONDON
Text and photos "conveys the common exuberance . . . in the raffish and ungain-
ly street-side of both cities." (PW) Quartet, 1984.

Dale, Tim   HARROD'S—THE STORE AND THE LEGEND
Background history of the Knightsbridge landmark. Pan Bks, 1983.

Hibbert, Christopher   LONDON: THE BIOGRAPHY OF A CITY
"A delight to read or merely to peruse" with photos and maps showing London's
growth from a "walled city-port to the sprawl" of today—"a mine of information
and . . . nostalgic reminiscence." (BRD) Penguin, 1983.

Howard, P.   LONDON'S RIVER
Anecdotes and history of that section of the Thames that flows through Greater
London. St. Martin, 1977.

Jones, Christopher   NUMBER 10 DOWNING STREET
With a preface by Margaret Thatcher. Salem Hse, 1986.

Kiek, Jonathan   EVERYBODY'S HISTORIC LONDON
"Absorbing information . . . in very short space, it combines history of the British
capital with advice on what sights to see . . . which pertain to each epoch covered."
(BL) Salem Hse, 1985.

Kobayashi, Tsukasa and others   SHERLOCK HOLMES'S LONDON
Chronicle Bks, 1986.

Kramer, Jane   UNSETTLING EUROPE
Refugee families from Algeria, Uganda, Yugoslavia, living in France, London and
Sweden, respectively, and an Italian Communist family in Italy—their isolation
from traditions of those around them and the implications for Europe's future of
these rootless people. compelling reading. Random, 1981.

Miller, E.   THAT NOBLE CABINET: A HISTORY OF THE
BRITISH MUSEUM
Ohio U, 1974.

Montgomery-Massingberd, Hugh   THE LONDON RITZ
A social and architectural history of the hotel, and the role it has played in London's history. Salem Hse, 1983.

Morton, Brian N.   AMERICANS IN LONDON
Guide to residences and favorite haunts of illustrious Americans, from Abigail Adams and James Fenimore Cooper to Wallis Simpson and Joseph Kennedy. Morrow, 1986.

Rasmussen, Steen E.   LONDON, THE UNIQUE CITY
New edition of a book first published in 1934; written by a Danish architect and town planner—"the best general study of how London came to be as it is." (BRD) MIT Pr, 1982.

Roose-Evans, James   LONDON THEATER: FROM THE GLOBE TO THE NATIONAL
Dutton, 1977.

Rowse, A.L.   THE TOWER OF LONDON IN THE HISTORY OF ENGLAND
The Tower as a "mirror in which much of English history may be seen"—coronations, executions, processions, comic episodes. (BRD) Putnam Pub Group, 1973.

TRAVEL MEMOIRS AND SPECIAL PERSPECTIVES

Barich, Bill   TRAVELING LIGHT
London, California and Florence (Italy) are the chief subjects of this "masterful compilation of travel writing that may propel the reader out of her/his armchair into a plane to Florence or London." Based on an eighteen-month trip with "preoccupations en route with friends, family, fishing, horseracing, history, art." (BRD) Viking, 1984.

Borer, Mary C.   TWO VILLAGES: THE STORY OF CHELSEA AND KENSINGTON
"Traces a fascinating and enchanting story of two villages which . . . retain an atmosphere and beauty all their own." (BRD) Transatlantic, 1974.

Edel, Leon   BLOOMSBURY: A HOUSE OF LIONS
Intellectual life and biographies and critiques of the writers and artists of the "Bloomsbury" group in turn-of-the-century London to the 1920s. (BRD) Lippincott, 1979.

Hanff, Helen   84 CHARING CROSS ROAD; THE DUCHESS OF BLOOMSBURY STREET
These are almost classics—delightful armchair travel reading. The first is correspondence between the author, a New Yorker, and a bookstore in London. As a result of publication of the letters, the author became something of a celebrity and was invited to visit the London she so yearned to see over the years, and the second book is an account of that visit. Avon, 1978.

McGreevy, John, ed.   CITIES
Impressions of world cities as seen through the eyes of people intimately connected with them—for London it is Jonathan Miller's impressions. Outlet Bk, 1981.

Morris, Jan   DESTINATIONS
This collection of "impressionistic essays" originally printed in *Rolling Stone* includes an essay on London. Oxford U, 1980.

Partridge, Frances   LOVE IN BLOOMSBURY
A combination of remembrances and diary entries by a junior-league Bloomsbury-ite. Little, 1981.

Pritchett, V.S.   LONDON PERCEIVED
A photo book, but one with a superior text by a leading British critic and travel writer. HarBraceJ, 1966.

Shute, Nerina   LONDON VILLAGES
The history, anecdotes of famous figures, scenery, buildings, and more, of eleven London villages, including Chelsea, Hampstead, Greenwich. St. Martin, 1977.

Simon, Kate   LONDON PLACES AND PLEASURES
Out-of-date on practical information, but a classic, highly descriptive, "uncommon guidebook" by a leading travel writer. Putnam Pub Group, 1970.

Weintraub, Stanley   THE LONDON YANKEES
Subtitle: Portraits of American writers and artists in England, 1894-1914. "Literary and artistic expatriates in pre-World War I London. (BRD) HarBraceJ, 1979.

Woolf, Virginia   THE LONDON SCENE: FIVE ESSAYS
The subjects are Oxford Street, Westminster Abbey, the House of Commons, St. Paul's Cathedral, and great men's houses—leading to views on such less tangible subjects as commerce, the perishability of human structures, the nature of democracy. Random, 1982.

GUIDEBOOKS

Banks, F.R.   THE NEW PENGUIN GUIDE TO LONDON
Won a prize for Guide Book of the Year—36 sightseeing routes via foot and bus with maps and street plans. Penguin, 1984.

Dakers, Caroline   THE BLUE PLAQUE GUIDE TO LONDON
Blue plaques indicate places where the famous have dwelt. Norton, 1982.

Davies, Hunter   A WALK AROUND LONDON'S PARKS
Perambulations through London's major parks—history, what to see and do. Hamish Hamilton, 1983.

**Fischer, Mildred and Al   LONDON THEATRE TODAY: A GUIDE
FOR TRAVELERS**
Golden West, 1981.

Grunfeld, Nina   THE ROYAL SHOPPING GUIDE
Shops where the queen and royal family shop—"not just . . . jewels and china and gowns, but also soap . . . and dog food. . . . address, hours and mail-order possibilities" are included. (BL) Morrow, 1984.

**Jones, Edward and Woodward, Christopher   A GUIDE TO THE
ARCHITECTURE OF
LONDON**
Van Nostrand, 1983.

Lawson, Andrew   DISCOVER UNEXPECTED LONDON
Recommended highly by London afficionados (such as John Bainbridge who writes the "London Journal" for *Gourmet* magazine). This is a reissue, with an introduction by Hugh Trevor-Roper to assist tourists in discovering London for themselves. Salem Hse, 1986

Meiland, Jack   FIRST TIME IN LONDON
For the independent traveler—how to plan an itinerary for a one-, two- or three-week visit including less frequented places of exceptional interest and twenty original walks. Scribner, 1979.

**Oakes, George W.   TURN RIGHT AT THE FOUNTAIN: WALKING TOURS
OF LONDON, OXFORD, CAMBRIDGE**
See under "Oxford."

Pease, Martha R.   THE BOOKSHOPS OF LONDON
A guide for bibliophiles visiting London; "Shangri-la for bibliophiles." (BL) Salem Hse, 1985.

Powell, Anton   LONDONWALKS
One of a series of chatty, anecdotal city walking guides—enjoyable simply to read. HR&W, 1982.

**Saunders, Ann   ART AND ARCHITECTURE OF LONDON: AN
ILLUSTRATED GUIDE**
Salem Hse, 1984.

Scott, Kathie   LONDON FOR SINGLES
Hippocrene, 1983.

Steinbicker, Earl   DAYTRIPS FROM LONDON
Subtitle: Fifty one-day adventures by rail, bus or car. Especially useful for BritRail Pass holders, providing self-guided walking tours and maps once you get to locations reached easily by train. Hastings House, 1983.

Zeff, Linda   JEWISH LONDON
Salem Hse, 1986.

HISTORY

Borer, Mary C.   THE CITY OF LONDON: A HISTORY
Social and institutional history for the general reader and traveler. McKay, 1978.

Gray, Robert   A HISTORY OF LONDON
Architectural and social history intended for the layman. Taplinger, 1979.

Trease, Geoffrey   LONDON: A CONCISE HISTORY
The sweep of London history in readable style. Scribner, 1975.

Novels

NOTE: Please turn to Appendix 3 for further information on "England/Novels."

LONDON

Amis, Kingsley   THE RIVERSIDE VILLAS MURDER
The setting is a prosperous London suburb in the thirties. HarBraceJ, 1973.

Archer, Jeffrey   FIRST AMONG EQUALS
The careers of three people hoping to be prime minister, 1964-91—"manages the labyrinthine British Parliamentary system with an adroit hand and generates real suspense in the race." (FC) S&S, 1983.

Babson, Marian   THE TWELVE DEATHS OF CHRISTMAS
A demented killer, striking at random just before Christmas is the plot for this police mystery. G K & Co, 1981.

Bawden, Nina   FAMILIAR PASSIONS
Marriage and divorce and a search for the truth about real parents. Morrow, 1979. Also *The Ice House* (1983).

Bermant, Chaim   THE LAST SUPPER
Family chronicle of a Jewish family from pre-communist Petersburg to North London. HR&W, 1975. Also, *The Diary of an Old Man* (1966), about a group of old people in a rooming house.

Billington, Rachel   OCCASION OF SIN
"A journey of developing disintegration" of a barrister's wife involved in an infatuation. Summit Bks, 1983.

Binchy, Maeve   LIGHT A PENNY CANDLE
Two women's sustaining and lifelong friendship beginning when one was

evacuated, as a ten-year-old during the blitz, to the other's home in Ireland. Viking, 1983.

Bowen, Elizabeth   THE DEATH OF THE HEART
A "psychological study of a young girl . . . brought into conflict with the sophisticated futility of life in her half-brother's home in Regency Park." (FC) Knopf, 1939. Also *The Heat of the Day* (1949), set in wartime London.

Brookes, Owen   DEADLY COMMUNION
"Chillingly suspenseful novel [that] probes the frontiers of psychological research." (FC) HR&W, 1984.

Brookner, Anita   PROVIDENCE
An attractive professional woman craves a meaningful relationship—"prose in the tradition of Jane Austen, Barbara Pym, and Muriel Spark." (FC) Pantheon, 1984.

Brookner, Anita   THE DEBUT
A "buttoned-up, fortyish spinster professor of literature . . . finds role models in women of the classics." (FC) Linden Pr, 1981. Also *Look At Me* (1983).

Brown, Christy   A PROMISING CAREER
Novel of a publicly successful, privately unhappy pop music team. Secker & Warburg, 1982.

Bryher   BEOWULF
Wartime London through the experiences of two ladies who run a tea shop. Pantheon, 1956.

Buckley, William F., Jr.   SAVING THE QUEEN
One of a series of novels with an American CIA agent as protagonist—in this the plot concerns secrets leaked to the Soviet Union by the Queen. Doubleday, 1976.

Butler, Gwendoline   ALBION WALK
"The sophisticated ambiance of chancy show business life is captured" in this novel—the member of a theatrical family inherits a run-down theatre, restores it, and manages it for four decades. (FC) McCann, 1982.

Cadell, Elizabeth   THE ROUND DOZEN
Romantic suspense novel involving missing family treasure and set in London and its environs. Morrow, 1978.

Candy, Edward   BONES OF CONTENTION
"A wonderfully convoluted adventure [involving] cataclysmic happenings at London's Royal College of Pediatricians." (FC) Doubleday, 1983 (first published 1954).

Canning, Victor   MEMORY BOY
"A gentle father-son story in the guise of an adventure intrigue novel" in which

the British Intelligence Service recruits a thirteen-year-old boy with a super memory to uncover traitors operating in London. (FC) Morrow, 1981.

Clarke, Anna   SOON SHE MUST DIE
A series of shocking events ensue when a greedy nurse engineers a relationship between her boyfriend and a dying patient. Doubleday, 1983.

Cody, Liza   DUPE
A mystery novel (which won the Creasey Award for best first mystery of the year) has a new woman detective, Anna Lee, as the solver of crime. The plot concerns the making of illegal film copies for shipment to Third World countries. Scribner, 1981.

Cooke, Judy   NEW ROAD
Residents fight to save a Georgian terrace in south London. St. Martin, 1976.

Cooper, William   SCENES FROM PROVINCIAL LIFE AND SCENES FROM METROPOLITAN LIFE
One volume edition of two books first published separately in 1950 and 1982, respectively. (FC) Dutton, 1984. This is followed by *Scenes From Married Life and Scenes From Later Life* (1983), first published separately in 1961 and 1983, respectively. Collectively they recount the life of Joe Lunn, science teacher in a small town, beginning in 1939, his move to London in 1946, becoming a novelist and civil servant, and on through thirty years of marriage and later life. "The atmosphere of the era is caught perfectly . . . the peculiar tensions and idiosyncrasies of London civil servantdom are remarkably rendered."

Crane, Teresa   MOLLY
One woman's struggle for equal rights, beginning with her departure from a poor Irish home at 18 for London and on through becoming owner of an employment agency for women, marriage, widowhood, the Suffragist movement, ending with World War I. Coward, 1982.

Deighton, Len   SSS-GB—NAZI-OCCUPIED BRITAIN 1941
A fantasy in which the Germans have won the war, and King George is a prisoner. Knopf, 1979.

Delderfield, R.F.   THE AVENUE
Chronicle of twenty people, living in a south London suburb, from 1919 to 1947. S&S, 1969.

Dickinson, Peter   THE LIVELY DEAD
A rooming house in Kensington is the scene for a zany set of characters in this mystery. Pantheon, 1975.

Disch, T.M. and Naylor, Charles   NEIGHBORING LIVES
"An episodic, quasi-biographical novel about the artists and writers who lived in London's Chelsea between 1830 and 1870." (BRD) Scribner, 1981.

Donleavy, J.P. SCHULTZ
American expatriates in London—the West End musical comedy scene. Delacorte, 1979.

Donleavy, J.P. THE GINGER MAN
Picaresque novel of an ex-G.I. student at Trinity College in Dublin and in London. Delacorte Pr, 1965.

Drabble, Margaret THE MIDDLE GROUND
A journalist decides, in sorting out her life at 40, "to examine the paths taken by former schoolmates . . . London life in the 1970s, with traditional British values surviving amidst foreign immigration, terrorism and inflation." (FC) Knopf, 1980. Also, *The Needle's Eye* (1972), *Jerusalem the Golden* (1967) and *The Waterfall* (1969).

Duffy, Maureen CAPITAL: A FICTION
A history professor and an oddball student who audits his course give a composite picture of London from the earliest days to the present—"a celebration of London" told with irony and humor. (BRD) Braziller, 1976.

Eden, Dorothy MELBURY SQUARE
The lives, loves, the changing fortunes of a woman from girlhood to old age, in a mansion on Melbury Square in Kensington, "etching in the changing social picture of England over the years." (FC) Coward, 1970.

Emecheta, Buchi SECOND-CLASS CITIZEN
A Nigerian woman follows her emigrant husband to London and finds she is treated as second-class both in her marriage and in England—"completely engrossing melting-pot novel." (FC) Braziller, 1975.

Frankau, Pamela SING FOR YOUR SUPPER
First in a trilogy about an English theatrical family. This book is set in a seaside town in the summer of 1926. Random, 1964. *Slaves of the Lamp* (1965) and *Over the Mountains* (1967), which follow, are set in London and take the family on through World War II.

Gardner, John THE NOSTRADAMUS TRAITOR
A novel of treachery and deception switching between 1941 and 1978, which begins with a German tourist's unusual request at the Tower of London. Doubleday, 1979.

Gaskin, Catherine FAMILY AFFAIRS
"A long, well-done family saga . . . of two endowed families whose destinies are intertwined by pride of place"; set in London and on a sheep ranch. (FC) Doubleday, 1980.

Godden, Rumer THURSDAY'S CHILDREN
The sixth and last child of a London grocer and his starstruck wife survives the treacheries of his sister and the taunts of brothers to become a dancer—the be-

hind-the-scenes world of ballet. Viking, 1984. Also, a much earlier novel, *A Candle for St. Jude* (1948), about an old ballet mistress who plans a fifty-year anniversary gala.

Godwin, Gail   MR. BEDFORD
One of five stories set in a British boardinghouse; in *Mr. Bedford and the Muses*, of writers in various life stages. Viking, 1983.

Gordon, Richard   A QUESTION OF GUILT
Novelized version of an early-twentieth-century murder by a doctor of his wife. Atheneum, 1981.

Hardwick, Mollie   THE DUCHESS OF DUKE STREET
Adaptation of the public TV series about the woman who owned an exclusive residential hotel in Edwardian London where prominent people stayed and dined. HR&W, 1977.

Heath, Catherine   LADY ON THE BURNING DECK
A widow coping with life and her impossible children—"acute perception of social foibles. . . . [it is] hard to believe they aren't actually living somewhere in North London." (BRD) Taplinger, 1979.

Hoban, Russell   TURTLE DIARY
A funny book about two people with a bizarre plan to free all the sea turtles in the London Zoo. Random, 1976.

Household, Geoffrey   HOSTAGE LONDON: THE DIARY OF JULIAN DESPARD
High suspense as the heart of London becomes hostage to an anarchist plot. A member of the group defects, with a chase through London and the Cotswolds. Little, 1977.

Howard, Elizabeth J.   GETTING IT RIGHT
A London hairdresser, living in the suburbs with his parents but "waiting for life to change. . . . comic . . . compassionate [and] ends on a happy note." (FC) Viking, 1982.

Jones, Mervyn   NOBODY'S FAULT
The heroine is unable to choose between two men—"meticulously observed facets of modern English life." (BRD) Mason/Charter, 1977.

Kennedy, Lena   MAGGIE
Story of a survivor from the depression to post-World War II prosperity. Paddington Pr, 1979.

Le Carré, John   THE LOOKING GLASS WAR
"A bitter, cruel, dispassionate" story of a former military espionage unit in London. Coward, 1965. Also, *The Honorable Schoolboy* (1977); *Smiley's People* (1980); and *Tinker, Tailor, Soldier, Spy.* (1974).

Lurie, Alison   FOREIGN AFFAIRS
Two American professors on leave in London to do research, and their romantic entanglements and reactions—"a wry, wonderful book." Random, 1984.

Lyall, Gavin   THE CONDUCT OF MAJOR MAXIM
An intelligence aide at 10 Downing Street tries to follow the trail of an AWOL corporal from a German village to London's East End. Viking, 1983.

MacInnes, Colin   THE LONDON NOVELS OF COLIN MACINNES
Deals with various aspects of London life. FS&G, 1969.

Mankowitz, Wolf   A KID FOR TWO FARTHINGS
Enchanting story of Jewish life in London's East End. Dutton, 1954.

Miner, Valerie   BLOOD SISTERS
"Irish nationalism, political violence, feminism and sexuality underlie the moving story of two young women related by blood—and bloodshed." (BRD) St. Martin, 1982.

Moore, Brian   THE TEMPTATION OF EILEEN HUGHES
"Dissects the relationship between an innocent Irish shop girl and her employers." (FC) FS&G, 1981.

Murdoch, Iris   NUNS AND SOLDIERS
"Explores the tangled lives of recently widowed Gertrude; Tim, a painter; Anne a former nun; and 'Count' Peter who is in love with Gertrude." (FC) Viking, 1981.

Pearson, John   THE BELLAMY SAGA
The book version of that marvelous public TV series, "Upstairs, Downstairs." Praeger, 1976.

Pym, Barbara   AN UNSUITABLE ATTACHMENT
The "vanished world [of the] Anglican parish" and a cast of characters "no longer quite appropriate to the present day." (FC) Dutton, 1982. Also, about the "doings" of an Anglo-Catholic parish is *A Glass of Blessings* (1980). Other London novels include *No Fond Return of Love* (1982), *Excellent Women* (1978), *Less Than Angels* (1980), *The Sweet Dove Died* (1979). All Pym novels were originally published in the '50s and '60s.

Rubens, Bernice   FAVOURS
Cosily perverse novel of a spinster "who squanders her savings and her pension on a lout named Brian" who sells his "favours" to elderly women. (FC) Summit Bks, 1979.

Scholefield, Alan   VENOM
A boy from Eaton Square is taken hostage, but his captors must also deal with a pet snake. Morrow, 1978.

Sharp, Margery   BRITANNIA MEWS
Family chronicle from 1865 to 1940 as the Mews change from slum to

fashionable residential area. Little, 1946. Also *The Faithful Servants* (1975), vignettes of beneficiaries of a family trust, the trustees, and the family descendants.

Sillitoe, Alan   HER VICTORY
A complicated love story spanning two generation. Watts, 1982.

Snow, C.P.   A COAT OF VARNISH
The author's first mystery novel—set in upper-middle class London. Scribner, 1979.

Somers, Jane   THE DIARY OF A GOOD NEIGHBOR
Diary of Janna, a "modish Londoner" who befriends "an ancient bundle of smelly rags" and the love-hate relationship of two needy people. (FC) Knopf, 1983. Following is *If the Old Could . . .* (1984), in which Janna "stumbles upon her destined love . . . when it is impossible to take advantage of their mutual attraction."

Spark, Muriel   THE BALLAD OF PECKHAM RYE
Set in an industrial town near London. Lippincott, 1960. Also *The Girls of Slender Means* (1963), set in a London residence for women at the close of World War II, and *Loitering With Intent* (1981) in which an aspiring novelist takes a job as secretary to a group who are composing their memoirs in advance.

Taylor, Elizabeth   MRS. PALFREV AT THE CLAREMONT
A widow moves to a "shabbily respectable London hotel" and the lonely woman forms a beautiful friendship with a young, aspiring novelist. Viking, 1971.

Theroux, Paul   THE LONDON EMBASSY
An American diplomat's experiences at the London Embassy—"a sparkling portrait gallery of eccentric Brits and misplaced Americans." (Publisher) Houghton, 1984. Also *The Family Arsenal* (1976) in which an American ex-State Department employee becomes involved with the IRA.

Tine, Robert   UNEASY LIES THE HEAD
A Jack-the-Ripper-style series of murders is the basis for this mystery solved by an odd pair of detectives. Viking, 1982.

Van Slyke, Helen   NO LOVE LOST
Four generations of a family's women "embellished with a historical backdrop featuring New York City and London of the past forty years." (FC) Lippincott, 1980.

Weldon, Fay   THE PRESIDENT'S CHILD
A resemblance between the heroine's six-year-old son and an American presidential candidate and a conspiracy "that will stop at nothing . . . to get Our Man into the White House." (FC) Doubleday, 1983.

Winch, Arden   BLOOD ROYAL
An eleven-year-old prince is kidnapped by terrorists—the crisis-ridden conclusion [is] enough to raise almost anyone's blood pressure." (FC) Viking, 1982.

Woolf, Virginia   MRS. DALLOWAY
Stream-of-consciousness novel of a single day. HarBraceJ, 1949.

BEDFORDSHIRE

Veryan, Patricia   THE WAGERED WIDOW
The period is the Jacobite rebellions—an impecunious (wagered) widow is won by the right man. St. Martin, 1984.

BERKSHIRE

Eden, Dorothy   THE STORRINGTON PAPERS
The sorting out of her employer's family papers leads to mystery and romance for the heroine. Coward, 1978.

BUCKINGHAMSHIRE

Milne, A.A.   MR. PIM
Novel version of an English comedy of manners in which Mr. Pim (having died) briefly returns to the household where his widow lives with her second husband. Dutton, 1930.

CAMBRIDGESHIRE

Gloag, Julian   SLEEPING DOGS LIE
"Not an ordinary whodunit . . . an excellent psychological thriller." (FC) Dutton, 1980. Also *Our Mother's House* (1963), about a Cambridge psychiatrist and a student with an unusual phobia.

Johnson, Pamela Hansford   THE GOOD LISTENER
Three men begin their lives at Cambridge in 1950. Scribner, 1975. *The Good Husband* (1979) continues the saga of one of them in the 1960s.

CHANNEL ISLANDS & GUERNSEY

Edwards, G.B.   THE BOOK OF EBENEZER LEPAGE
A "fictionalized memoir of a simple but not simpleminded Guernsey-man . . . looking back from the 1960s on a life that began at the turn of the century." (FC) Knopf, 1981.

Marsh, Ngaio   LAST DITCH
A university don, vacationing on one of the Channel Islands, becomes involved in drug smuggling and a fatal accident. Little, 1977.

Robinson, Derek   KRAMER'S WAR
An American pilot bails out over the German-occupied Isle of Jersey in 1944. Viking, 1977.

CORNWALL

Brent, Madeleine   TREGARON'S DAUGHTER
A Gothic romance set in a Cornish fishing village in the early twentieth century.
Doubleday, 1971.

Christie, Agatha   THE ROSE AND THE YEW TREE
One of six novels in *The Westmacott Reader*—"a love story concerning a
Cornish plumber's son with social ambitions." (FC) Arbor Hse, 1983 (first
published 1948).

DuMaurier, Daphne   JAMAICA INN
One of several novels by DuMaurier, historic and contemporary, set in
Cornwall. Doubleday, 1960 (first published 1936). Other titles include: *The
King's General* (1946), *Frenchman's Creek* (1942), *The House on the Strand*
(1969), *Rule Britannia* (1973), *Rebecca* (1938), *My Cousin Rachel* (1952).

Godden, Rumer   CHINA COURT
Family chronicle of life in a house through five generations. Viking, 1961.

Graham, Winston   THE POLDARK NOVELS
The series on which the public TV series was based. Doubleday titles include:
The Black Moon (1974), *The Four Swans* (1977), *The Angry Tide* (1978), *The
Stranger from the Sea* (1982), *The Miller's Dance* (1983).

Graham, Winston   THE GROVE OF EAGLES
Historical novel of Elizabethan times and the Second Armada, and the hero's
service under Sir Walter Raleigh. Doubleday, 1964.

Heyer, Georgette   PENHALLOW
A novel of family life in the mid-1930s that is also "a murder story but not a
mystery story." Dutton, 1971 (first published 1942).

Holt, Victoria   BRIDE OF PENDORRIC
Suspense novel by the prolific master storyteller. Doubleday, 1963. Other
Cornwall novels by Holt include: *Curse of the Kings* (1973), *Legend of the Seventh
Virgin* (1965), *Manfreya in the Morning* (1966), *Mistress of Mellyn* (1960), *Lord
of the Far Island* (1975), *The Landower Legacy* (1984).

Howatch, Susan   PENMARRIC
The life and loves of a brutally selfish man, and his children, and their
children—legitimate and illegitimate. Historic parallel is made to Henry II and
Eleanor of Aquitaine, "adding piquancy and historical flavor to an interesting tale."
(FC) S&S, 1971.

Innes, Michael   THE AMPERSAND PAPERS
A retired Scotland Yard inspector gets back into harness to help solve a murder
mystery involving an Ampersand ancestor's correspondence with Percy Bysshe
Shelley. Dodd, 1979.

Marsh, Ngaio   DEAD WATER
Scotland Yard Superintendent Roderick Alleyn is unofficially involved in a mystery set on an island off the Cornwall coast; involving faith healing. Little, 1963.

Michaels, Barbara   WAIT FOR WHAT WILL COME
A young American schoolteacher inherits a mansion with a family curse—has a "nice spoofing tongue-in-cheek tone." (FC) Dodd, 1978.

Pearce, Mary E.   POLSINNEY HARBOUR
Following a family tragedy, a young woman flees her native village for a Cornish fishing village, to start over with her unborn child—"has all the stark simplicity of an enchanting ballad . . . a melodic commentary on the enduring powers of love and the sea." (FC) St. Martin, 1984.

Pilcher, Rosamunde   VOICES IN SUMMER
Feeling alienated from her husband's past and his family, Laura goes to visit with his aunt and uncle for a recuperative stay in their lovely home in Cornwall. St. Martin, 1984.

Quiller-Couch, Arthur and DuMaurier, Daphne   CASTLE D'OR
The story of a modern-day Tristan and Isuelt, started by Quiller-Couch and finished, at the request of his daughter, by Miss DuMaurier. Doubleday, 1962.

CUMBRIA

Forster, Margaret   THE BRIDE OF LOWTHER FELL
When her twin sister is killed, Alexandra is left responsible for their thirteen-year-old nephew and decides to move, with him, to an isolated cottage to "overcome her own restlessness and change the child . . . shrewd and peppery insight into the psychology of both young woman and boy who must work out their destinies together . . . even face possible death together." (FC) Atheneum, 1981.

DEVONSHIRE

Canning, Victor   THE KINGSFORD MARK
Murder plans of a guest and his host with some of the trappings of a Gothic novel—(the author's) "way with the Devonshire landscape heightens the drama of this well-told, suspenseful tale of love, betrayal and tangled heritage." (FC) Morrow, 1976. Also *Queen's Pawn* (1975), in which a man is blackmailed into stealing gold bullion from the *QE 2*, and *The Mask of Memory* (1975), an "absorbing study of adult civil servants who are in the messy business of intelligence."

Cary, Joyce   EXCEPT THE LORD
The Devonshire childhood and young manhood of Chester Nimmo, in the 1870s, revealing the "conditions and people that determined his life as preacher,

labor leader and politician." (FC) Har-Row, 1953. This is the middle volume of a trilogy, preceded by *Prisoner of Grace* (1952) and followed by *Not Honour More* (1955).

Crispin, Edmund   THE GLIMPSES OF THE MOON
An Oxford professor on sabbatical in Devonshire is called upon to help solve a triple murder case—"a gloriously funny book, witty and farcical by turns." (FC) Walker, 1978.

Delderfield, R.F.   A HORSEMAN RIDING BY
This and *Green Gauntlet* (1968) comprise a family saga beginning in 1902, as a young man returns from the Boer War to a run-down estate in Devonshire, and ending in the 1960s after following the family through World War II. S&S, 1966.

Delderfield, R.F.   TO SERVE THEM ALL MY DAYS
A schoolmaster's cavalcade of life at a West Country public school between World Wars I and II. S&S, 1972.

Gilbert, Michael   THE EMPTY HOUSE
An espionage novel involving genetics and a bio-warfare station—"narrative that is intriguing down to the last comma." (FC) Har-Row, 1979.

Goudge, Elizabeth   THE ROSEMARY TREE
About a writer who has been in jail, and his relationships in a Devon village. Coward, 1956.

Harris, Marilyn   THIS OTHER EDEN
Historical saga of eighteenth-century England peopled with the likes of Thomas Paine, Emma Hamilton and Lord Nelson. Putnam Pub Group, 1977. It is the first of four novels and is followed by *The Prince of Eden* (1978), *The Eden Passion* (1979) and *The Women of Eden* (1980).

Holt, Victoria   THE TIME OF THE HUNTER'S MOON
The heroine of this Gothic teaches at an exclusive academy in Devon and the story is set in the nineteenth century. Doubleday, 1984.

O'Donoghue, Maureen   JEDDER'S LAND
A historical novel that "is not only the gripping story of a determined girl's battle to fulfill the potential of her land, but a beautiful evocation of 18th-century country life." (FC) S&S, 1983.

Sharp, Margery   CLUNY BROWN
An amusing novel of a young girl who simply will not remember her social place as a plumber's niece and who ends up running off with a Polish emigré. Little, 1944.

Stevenson, D.E.   THE HOUSE ON THE CLIFF
An actress leaves London when she inherits a Devonshire estate, and also finds romance. HR&W, 1966.

DORSET

Fowles, John   THE FRENCH LIEUTENANT'S WOMAN
Lyme Regis is the setting for a love story told Victorian style but with contemporary insights. Little, 1969.

James, P.D.   THE BLACK TOWER
Scotland Yard commander Dalgliesh is involved in a mystery concerning deaths in a home for the disabled. Scribner, 1975.

Maybury, Anne   THE MINERVA STONE
A Gothic romance involving a TV personality, his wife, and the obligatory stately home—in Dorset. HR&W, 1968.

Murdoch, Iris   THE NICE AND THE GOOD
A love story as well as a mystery and a sexual comedy. Viking, 1968.

DURHAM

Cookson, Catherine   TILLY
A chronicle of a girl born into poverty and the hard life that meant in Victorian days, but who ends up as mistress of Sopwith Manor in Durham (with one part of her life spent in Texas). Morrow, 1980. First of a trilogy, followed by *Tilly Wed* (1981) and *Tilly Alone* (1982).

EAST ANGLIA

James, P.D.   DEATH OF AN EXPERT WITNESS
A forensic science lab in a small village is the scene for the murder of a biologist. Scribner, 1977.

Lofts, Norah   THE HOMECOMING
Chronicle of a house and its inhabitants, over 350 years. Doubleday, 1976.

Sharp, Margery   SUMMER VISITS
Events at a country estate from mid-nineteenth century to 1940. Little, 1978. Also *The Innocents* (1972), about a retarded child, her mother, and the foster mother who wishes to care for her.

GLOUCESTERSHIRE

Delving, Michael   NO SIGN OF LIFE
An American book buyer becomes involved in solving a murder; good descriptions of the countryside. Doubleday, 1979.

Huxley, Elspeth   THE PRINCE BUYS THE MANOR
A "comic extravaganza" set in a market town in the Cotswolds, occasioned by the decision of an African royal prince to buy a nearby manor house. (FC) Chatto & Windus, 1983.

HAMPSHIRE

Goudge, Elizabeth   THE BIRD IN THE TREE
A family chronicle that begins on the Hampshire coast in 1938 and ends following World War II, with an Austrian refugee and concert pianist sharing in the family's life—"exquisite portrayal of children, grownups, animals and the English countryside." Coward, 1940. First of a trilogy, followed by *Pilgrim's Inn* (1948) and *Heart of the Family* (1953).

HERTFORDSHIRE

Amis, Kingsley   THE GREEN MAN
The *Green Man* is a pub and also a "very nasty thing conjured up by the resident ghost." (FC) HarBraceJ, 1970.

ISLE OF MAN

Gash, Jonathan   GOLD BY GEMINI
A mystery involving buried Roman coins, and a search for lost treasure by an antique dealer. Har-Row, 1978.

KENT

DeBlasis, Celeste   WILD SWAN
An historical novel that moves from England to Maryland where the heroine and her brother-in-law's family emigrate during the period of pre-Civil War slavery. Bantam, 1984.

Godden, Jon   IN HER GARDEN
A 75-year-old widow in Kent "falls in love with her newly-hired [30-year-old] gardener, and tragedy results. . . . a genteel modern sketch of manners and morals." (FC) Knopf, 1981.

Holt, Victoria   THE SHIVERING SANDS
A gothic involving a piano teacher's search for her archaeologist sister. Doubleday, 1969.

Pearson, Diane   THE SUMMER OF THE BARSHINSKEYS
A three-part novel of the Willoughby family: the first part concerns the arrival in 1902 of an exotic Russian family with "odd gypsy ways" that has a profound effect on the 11-year-old Willoughby daughter; part two involves the love between the now-grown Willoughby son and the Barshinskey daughter; part three finds the oldest Willoughby daughter in love with Ivan Barshinskey—"a most entertaining and poignant novel." (FC) Crown, 1984.

LANCASHIRE

Bainbridge, Beryl   QUIET LIFE
The setting is a village near Southport—story of acute family strife told in flashback. Braziller, 1977.

Bainbridge, Beryl   YOUNG ADOLF
A novel growing out of a diary entry that, at age 23, young Adolf Hitler visited Liverpool. Braziller, 1979.

Bentley, Ursula   THE NATURAL ORDER
Three sisters working in a Catholic boys' school in Manchester and "trying to act out the genius of the Brontë myth" are each ensnared by the school's "most promising Sixth Former ever." (BRD) St. Martin, 1982.

Gillespie, Jane   LADYSMEAD
A "genteel tale of ordinary life in rural England," reminiscent of Jane Austen, and which, in fact, does borrow two characters from Austen's *Mansfield Park*. (FC) St. Martin, 1982.

Stubbs, Jean   BY OUR BEGINNINGS
The saga of the Howarth family in Lancashire—"social ferment and family history are vigorously blended" in this chronicle that begins in 1760 and ends following the Industrial Revolution, with the first railroad brought to the valley. St. Martin, 1979. First in a trilogy, followed by *An Imperfect Joy* (1981), *The Vivian Inheritance* (1982) and *The Northern Correspondent* (1984).

NORTHUMBERLAND

Cookson, Catherine   THE BLACK VELVET GOWN
A penniless widow's daughter rises from her lowly laundress position to that of lady's maid and becomes the center of a family scandal. Summit Bks, 1984. Also *Pure as a Lily* (1973), chronicle of a working class family, 1933-1973.

Cookson, Catherine   THE CINDER PATH
A young man finally liberates himself from his brutal childhood through reunion with a first love. The story is set in Northumberland from the Edwardian era through World War I. Morrow, 1978.

Cookson, Catherine   THE MALLEN STREAK
A family saga with unusual and complicated relationships, from mid-nineteenth century to World War I. Dutton, 1973. This book is followed by *The Mallen Girl* (1973) and *The Mallen Lot* (1974).

Cronin, A.J.   THE STARS LOOK DOWN
Life in a mining community during the first half of this century. Little, 1935.

Gilliatt, Penelope   MORTAL MATTERS
Lady Corfe recalls her life from suffragette days to the 1980s as she flees London for her Northumberland home—"gracefully combines past and present to . . . define [an] odd and interesting heroine." (FC) Coward, 1983.

Stewart, Mary   THE IVY TREE
A Canadian girl is mistaken for a dead heiress—vivid descriptions of the Northumberland countryside. Morrow, 1961.

NOTTINGHAMSHIRE

Sillitoe, Alan   SATURDAY NIGHT AND SUNDAY MORNING
An angry young man and his working-class life in industrial Britain, from which a memorable movie was made. Knopf, 1959.

Sillitoe, Alan   THE WIDOWER'S SON
A son becomes a highly successful military officer, but mismanages his private life. Har-Row, 1977.

Sillitoe, Alan   MEN, WOMEN AND CHILDREN
Short stories that explore some people's lives "through the emotion-stifled atmosphere of Nottingham." (FC) Scribner, 1974.

OXFORDSHIRE

Bowen, Elizabeth   THE LITTLE GIRLS
"Delineation of three aging but still personable English ladies and a look into a revealing incident of their childhood." (FC) Knopf, 1964.

Butler, Gwendoline   SARSEN PLACE
"Tale of ugly intrigue, whose elegantly phrased facade conceals both a solid social panorama [Oxford, the 1880s] and a witty employment of feminist sentiment that feminists may not like very much." (FC) Coward, 1974.

Colegate, Isabel   THE SHOOTING PARTY
The year 1913 in Oxfordshire; leading sportsmen and their wives are invited to a pheasant shoot—"deftly evokes the vanished confident world of the British aristocracy just before World War I. . . . vivid observations of . . . social snobbery are suffused with a brooding Chekhovian melancholy." (FC) Viking, 1981.

Dexter, Colin   THE SILENT WORLD OF NICHOLAS QUINN
St. Martin, 1977. This, *Last Bus to Woodstock* (1975) and *Last Seen Wearing* (1976) are Inspector Morse/Sergeant Lewis mysteries set in Oxfordshire.

Fowles, John   DANIEL MARTIN
Two friends at Oxford marry sisters and realize years later that each chose the wrong one. Little, 1977.

French, Marilyn   THE BLEEDING HEART
Two Americans, working temporarily in England, fall in love. Summit Bks, 1980.

Goudge, Elizabeth   THE SCENT OF WATER
At fifty, a woman inherits a house and the journals of an earlier resident, and gains from them spiritual regeneration and happiness. Coward, 1963.

Pym, Barbara   A FEW GREEN LEAVES
A woman anthropologist hopes to do an article on village life—"several people make a significant impact on her and eventually bring her to grips with reality."

(FC) Dutton, 1980. Also for Barbara Pym addicts, a newly discovered novel written and set at Oxford, with a plot revolving around "a pair of eminently unsuitable attachments": the title is *Crampton Hodnet.*

Stewart, J.I.M.   THE GAUDY
First of a series of novels on Oxford "attuned to the finer nuances of Oxford life," with the collective title *A Staircase in Surrey.* They were written by an Oxford don who writes mysteries under the name Michael Innes. A "gaudy" is an alumni gathering. (FC) Norton, 1975. Followed by *Young Patullo* (1976), *A Memorial Service* (1976), *Madonna of the Astrolabe* (1977).

Stewart, J.I.M.   ANDREW AND TOBIAS
The adopted heir to a large estate finds his double in the new gardener—"souffle of erudition and ingenuity, insubstantial but . . . delightful." (FC) Norton, 1980.

SHROPSHIRE

Webb, Mary   PRECIOUS BANE
A novel about farming life and country people and a plot in which a disfigured woman finds a husband who appreciates her. Dutton, 1926.

Wodehouse, P.G.   NO NUDES IS GOOD NUDES
The nude is a portrait who resembles various people, depending upon the eye of the beholder, "and practically everyone wants to pinch it." S&S, 1970.

SOMERSET

Heyer, Georgette   BATH TANGLE
A "saucy Regency novel" of mismatched, entangled lovers with the tangles skillfully unraveled by the author. Also, *Lady of Quality* another Regency novel by a writer noted for her authenticity of historical detail. Putnam Pub Group, 1972.

STAFFORDSHIRE

Heaven, Constance   THE WILDCLIFFE BIRD
"The backdrop of England during the period of incipient unionism provides added interest" to a historical romance with a heroine who discovers a "web of mysterious accidents and murder" in the family that offers her a position. (FC) Coward, 1983.

SUFFOLK

Lofts, Norah   THE OLD PRIORY
Elizabethan England is evoked in this novel about three generations of a family living in a cursed priory. Doubleday, 1982. Two other novels by Ms. Lofts that chronicle the lives of occupants of a house over the years are *Bless This House* (1954) and *The House at Old Vine* (1961).

Lofts, Norah   A WAYSIDE TAVERN
"In an engaging conceit" the novel chronicles English history from the late Roman period to the present in "the evolution of a wayside inn and its proprietors through the generations." (FC) Doubleday, 1980.

Lofts, Norah   THE CLAW
"Character study of a contemporary small town . . . shaken out of apathy into terror" by a rape-murder. (FC) Doubleday, 1982.

Rendell, Ruth   MAKE DEATH LOVE ME
A thriller with psychological insight involving two teenaged bank robbers and a bank manager who is a romantic at heart. Doubleday, 1979.

SURREY

Braddon, Russell   THE FINALISTS
Suspense story with a Wimbledon setting; a Russian defector must thwart a plan to assassinate the Queen during the singles finals. Atheneum, 1977.

Gardner, John   THE WEREWOLF TRACE
A furniture importer living in Surrey is discovered to have been present in the bunker where Hitler died, and is his spiritual heir. Doubleday, 1977.

SUSSEX

Gibbons, Stella   COLD COMFORT FARM
A parody of the earthy novel as an orphan intrudes upon her relatives' careless lives. Dial, 1964.

Godden, Rumer   THE DIDDAKOI
A poor little gypsy girl and her horse. Viking, 1972.

Heyer, Georgette   THE RELUCTANT WIDOW
A Regency-period mystery of a governess who is married off to a dying man. Putnam Pub Group, 1971.

Household, Geoffrey   WATCHER IN THE SHADOWS
A British agent believed to be a Nazi is hunted down by a former enemy. Little, 1960.

Howatch, Susan   THE SHROUDED WALLS
A turn-of-the-century gothic. Stein & Day, 1968.

Jordan, Lee   CAT'S EYES
Mysterious happenings to a novelist's wife left "almost alone in their gloomy house in England's Great Forest." (FC) NAL, 1982.

Laker, Rosalind   WARWYCK'S CHOICE
"Saga of the contentious, wealthy Warwycks . . . the England of 1884" set in the

seaside community of Easthampton. (FC) Doubleday, 1980. It is a sequel to *Warwyck's Woman* (1978) and *Claudine's Daughter* (1979).

WARWICKSHIRE

Lively, Penelope   NEXT TO NATURE, ART
The Framleigh Creative Study Centre in the Warwickshire countryside is an "artistic sanctuary," but really run by some con artists who entice "non-artists . . . fleeing their mundane lives [to] pay good money to spend a week there." (FC) Heinemann, 1983.

WILTSHIRE

Cutter, Leela   WHO STOLE STONEHENGE?
An aged mystery writer and a local newspaper reporter solve the mystery when Stonehenge is literally stolen from its site. St. Martin, 1983.

Golding, William   THE SPIRE
Building of the highest spire ever becomes an obsession of the dean of a medieval cathedral. HarBraceJ, 1964. Also *The Pyramid* (1967), about three separate incidents in a boy's life while growing up (1920-40).

Harrison, Harry and Stover, Leon   STONEHENGE
A fictionalized account of the origins of Stonehenge by a novelist and an anthropologist—"vivid, valid archaeological background and a psychology and ferocity of behavior appropriate to the age and peoples depicted." (FC) Scribner, 1972.

Shelby, Graham   THE CANNAWAY CONCERN
Part of a projected trilogy—this one begins in the year 1719. Doubleday, 1980. Sequel to *The Cannaways* (1978).

WORCESTERSHIRE

Pearce, Mary E.   CAST A LONG SHADOW
A blissful marriage in a "closed, watchful English village" is shattered by distortion of the husband's character through a horrifying experience—"people one cares about and low-key charm." (FC) St. Martin, 1983.

Pearce, Mary E.   THE LAND ENDURES
An old-fashioned family chronicle, with this volume commencing just after World War I. St. Martin, 1981. Sequel to *Apple Tree Lean Down* (1976).

YORKSHIRE

Braine, John   ROOM AT THE TOP
Story of a man with an "insatiable lust for wealth, social prestige and power. . . .

narrow but deadly accurate account of contemporary northern [England] small town life." (FC) Houghton, 1957. The sequel about what happens after the man has attained his ambition, is *Life at the Top* (1962). Also *The Queen of a Distant Country* (1973), about a successful novelist's reexamination of his life.

Carr, J.L.   A MONTH IN THE COUNTRY
Regeneration of a young veteran of World War I who arrives in a Yorkshire village to restore the wall painting in a local church—"the folk and landscape of Yorkshire play a crucial role . . . a small masterpiece." (FC) St. Martin, 1983.

Haines, Pamela   THE KISSING GATE
A three-generation family saga of two intertwined Yorkshire families. Doubleday, 1981.

Hill, Reginald   DEADHEADS
Inspectors Dalziel and Pascoe investigate a young rose-growing accountant when a series of "highly convenient accidental deaths" bring him good fortune. (BRD) Macmillan, 1983.

Jagger, Brenda   THE BARFORTH WOMEN
A family saga, following Verity's sons into the late 1800s. Doubleday, 1982. Sequel to *Verity* (1980).

Michaels, Barbara   GREYGALLOWS
A gothic set in the 1840s as a London girl is married off to the owner of Greygallows. Dodd, 1972.

Storey, David   A PRODIGAL CHILD
Pre-World War II is the setting—"concerns itself with class differences that are bridged by the budding artistic abilities of [the] son of a farm-worker father." (FC) Dutton, 1983.

Whitehead, Barbara   RAMILLIES
An unassuming village schoolmaster inherits an earldom and falls in love with a countess who wants to only marry a poor man. St. Martin, 1984.

Woods, Sara   THEY LOVE NOT POISON
A detective-barrister and his wife (the Maitlands) solve a murder mystery involving black marketing (just after World War II when England had food rationing). HR&W, 1972. Two other Maitland mysteries are *And Shame the Devil* (1967) and *Done to Death* (1974).

TRAVEL ARTICLES

ANTIQUES
1984 Jun "The Gardens at Sissinghurst Castle, Kent." Creation of Vita Sackville-West and Sir Harold Nicolson, with literary allusions. Deborah Nevins, p. 1332.

ARCHITECTURAL DIGEST

1985 Jun Special issue on the English country house; "Travel Notes: Mario Buatta." Castles, manors and halls. Louise Bernikow, p. 296
"The American Museum in Britain." Rediscovering the New World. Elizabeth Lambert, p. 244

1984 Jul "Historic Houses: Disraeli at Hughenden." The Buckinghamshire home of an English prime minister. Elizabeth Lambert, p. 122

ATLANTIC MONTHLY

1984 Sep "Stopping at the Savoy." Holly Brubach, p. 110

BON APPETIT

1985 Jun "A Taste of Oxford." Elegant restaurants, cheery pubs and echoes of history in a landmark city just one hour from London. Nao Hauser, p. 98

1984 Jun "A Taste of London." Nan and Ivan Lyons, p. 93

CONNOISSEUR

1984 May "The Staid and the 'Street' and Quintessential London." Lloyd Grossman and Judy Spours, pp. 94 and 110
Sep "Garden for Heroes." An American outpost in Liverpool (living memorial to the U.S. Eighth Air Force). C.Z. Guest, p. 106

ESQUIRE

1985 May "Checking into Cottages." Staying put in rental cottages. David Butwin, p. 36

1984 Mar "Taking Your Best Shot." The Holland & Holland Shooting School near London. Carl Navarre, p. 34
Apr "Why I Live Where I Live." Hampstead, London. Al Alvarez, p. 96

50 PLUS

1985 Oct "London: Welcome to a Timeless World of Genteel Manners." Alan Schwartz, p. 25

GLAMOUR

1985 Apr "The Best of Britain; an Opinionated Guide to America's Favorite Foreign Country." p. 217

1984 Apr "Survival Guide to Britain." p. 217

GOURMET

1985 Feb London Journal: "The Thames Flood Barrier." The Three Compasses (restaurant). John Bainbridge, p. 30
Mar "Her Majesty's Tradesmen." London shops with the Royal warrant of Appointment to the Crown for goods and services. C.P. Reynolds, p. 44
May London Journal: "Chez Nico." Restaurant. John Bainbridge, p. 12
Jul "Racing at Newmarket." Mollie E.C. Webster, p. 30
Aug London Journal: "Centenary of *The Lady*." Quintessential English magazine. John Bainbridge, p. 28
Nov London Journal: "The Old Bailey." John Bainbridge, p. 24
Dec Gourmet Holidays: "Christmas at an English Country Inn." Mimi Elder, p. 40

1984 Feb London Journal: "Culture Bus, Harrod's Sightseeing Bus Service"; "Coins Added to the Currency." John Bainbridge, p. 10

May London Journal: "Extension to Harrod's Food Hall." John Bainbridge, p. 14

Jun "A London Address Book." "Addresses of preferred purveyors of goods and services." C.P. Reynolds, p. 42

Jul "A Somerset Ramble." Elizabeth L. Ortiz, p. 34

Aug London Journal: "Churchill's Underground Cabinet War Rooms." John Bainbridge, p. 20

"The London Cocktail Scene." Henry McNulty, p. 40

Nov London Journal: *"The World of Waiters"* (book); "Vanity License Plates." John Bainbridge, p. 28

HARPER'S BAZAAR

1985 Apr "London's Prime Pubs." John Mariani, p. 34

May "Britain's Golden Ponds . . . the Fells, Valleys and Dales of England's Lake District." Nancy Ramsey, p. 46

Oct "Ransacking London." Treasure trove for antique hunters. George Whitmore, p. 40

1984 Jul "An Anglophile's London." Kati Marton, p. 8

HOUSE BEAUTIFUL

1985 Oct "Discovering the Best of English Style in London's Very Personal Decorating Shops." Claire Whitcomb, p. 45

NATIONAL GEOGRAPHIC

1985 Nov "The Great Good Places." English country houses. Mark Girouard, p. 658

N.Y. TIMES SUNDAY TRAVEL SECTION (X)

1985 Jan 6 "Correspondent's Choice: Finding First-Rate Steaks in Britain." R.W. Apple, Jr., p. 6

Jan 20 "Selective Guide to Posh London." Proper strolls through Mayfair, Belgravia and St. James' can combine history and elegance. Benedict Nightingale, p. 15

"A List of Lesser-Known London Stores That Sell the Best." Linens to hand knits to lacquer trays. Pamela Harlech, p. 16

"Speaking of Bespoke." The clubby ritual of acquiring a Turnbull & Asser shirt. Barbara Gelb, p. 17

"Classic Dining (London) Updated." R.W. Apple, Jr., p. 17

Feb 10 "Bittersweet Star of British Breakfasts." Marmalade has an industrious past. Paula Dietz, p. 55

Mar 3 Shopper's World: "London Trove for Bargains in Wool." Elaine Goodman, p. 12

Mar 17 "Cambridge Through Oxford Eyes." Viewing the colleges with affection. A.L. Rowse, p. 9

(Part 2, "Sophisticated Traveler") "Serendipity in Shropshire." Barnaby J. Feder, p. 133

Mar 24 "Trial by Afternoon Tea in London." Israel Shenker, p. 43

Mar 31 "House with a Lustrous Past: an Estate Near Oxford Traces the History and Taste of a Nation." Ditchley Park. Louisa Kennedy, p. 12

Apr 7 "A Bouquet of British Parks." Liverpool, London, Edinburgh. Paula Dietz, p. 14

Apr 14 Shopper's World: "London's Glittering Silver Vaults." Shops and booths that sell silver articles. Sara Evans, p. 12

Apr 28 "What's Doing in London." Jo Thomas, p. 10

May 12 "Folk Festival Time in Britain." Barnaby J. Feder, p. 12

May 19 "Britain's Haven for Wildfowl." Lailan Young, p. 24

May 26 "Footloose in Britain: Group Walks Gain Ground in London." Donald Goddard, p. 14; "The Long Way: Land's End to John O'Groats." John Hillaby, p. 15; "Along the Rugged Rim of Cornwall." Elizabeth Neuffer, p. 16

Jun 9 Shopper's World: "A Home of Guns Fit for a King." Purdey's in London. Drew Middleton, p. 6

Jun 23 "Beyond Portobello Road, for Serious Shoppers, Nothing Compares with Bermondsey." But don't forget Bath and Brighton. Donald Goddard, p. 14

"Behind the Scenes at the Savoy." Israel Shenker, p. 19

Jul 7 "Barristers on Their Own Ground." The Inns of Court Reward the Walker. Donald Goddard, p. 14

"More Than Law Books and Wigs: Old Bailey Is an Oddly Cheerful Venue." John Mortimer, p. 15

"Exploring the World of Rumpole." Visitors can answer a call to the bar. Sara Caudwell, p. 15

Jul 14 "Glimpses of Life Behind Eton's Walls." Museum traces school's history. Erica Brown, p. 22

Jul 28 "It's All in the Family at Muncaster." Lodging and heirlooms in England. Donald Goddard, p. 9

Aug 4 "Aplomb and Art Deco at Claridge's." p. 9

Aug 11 "Lilliputian Soldiers on Parade." Two little-known English collections. Theodore James, Jr., p. 19

Aug 18 "Country Jaunts." Hills, caves, stately homes, Alfred's tower to Wookey Hole (Bath area). p. 14

"Fabled Footprints in the Streets of Bath." Plots and fancies of a city's literary past. Benedict Nightingale, p. 15

"ABC's of shopping and staying in Bath." Pamela Harlech, p. 16

Sep 1 "Streetwise in London." Street names. Walter Goodman, p. 19

Sep 29 "Afoot on the Yorkshire Moors." A 100-mile hike, with stops for medieval ruins, a pint of ale, and darts. David Yeadon, p. 22

Oct 6 (Sophisticated Traveler) "England's Wildest West." Cornwall. A. Alvarez, p. 68

Oct 13 "Where Music Lives in London." Macdonald Harris, p. 14

Oct 27 "Scary Old England." Still wraiths and witches haunt West Sussex as of yore, dragons are reported on the wane. Sarah Caudwell, p. 9

Nov 3 "London's Global Village." Soho. Andrew Sinclair, p. 15

Nov 10 "A Castle Fit for Medieval Queens." England's Leeds was a royal gift. Louis Heren, p. 21

"Viewing London from the Inside Out." A journey along the Regent's Canal, by narrow boat or towpath, is rich in unexpected vistas. Leslie Mandel-Viney, p. 14

Dec 1 "What's Doing in London." Jo Thomas, p. 10
Dec 8 Shopper's World: "Sparkling Crystal from Dartington." Leslie Mandel-Viney, p. 12
"Yuletide in Britain." Elizabeth Neuffer, p. 22
1984 Jan 8 "A London Wonderland, the Museum of Childhood Overflows with Period Toys." Donald Goddard, p. 9
Jan 15 "A Tumultuous Corner of London." Smithfield meat market is a place of banter and barter, medieval and Hogarthian echoes. David Yeadon, p. 16
Jan 22 "On the Hunt for Antiques in London." Morton N. Cohen, p. 9
Jan 29 "Bedding Down Above the Pub." In Britain, the village bar wants families to stay over. Christine S. Cozzens, p. 12
Feb 5 "A Cockney Goes Home." In London's East End, life is clamorous and vital. Louis Heren, p. 15
Feb 19 Shopper's World: "In Britain, the Best by Design." British Design Centre. Michael Sterne, p. 6
Mar 11 "On England's Ancient Frontier (Northumbria)." R.W. Apple, Jr., p. 14
"Stops on a Northeast Tour." A guide to shrines, museums, castles, gardens and lodgings. Sheila Gruson, p. 15
Mar 18 (Part 2, "Sophisticated Traveler") "The Avon: a Journey in Time. . . . the River Runs Deep in literary and Historical Associations, Shakespeare is Only One . . ." A.L. Rowse, p. 40
Mar 25 "On the Trail of London's Sloane Rangers." Visitor's guide to a preppy province. Erica Brown, p. 12
"Where Caroline and Henry (the Preppies) Eat." Sheila Gruson, p. 12
"On the Streets Where They Lived." London's street plaques send a stroller back in time to the neighborhoods of literary lions. Herbert Mitgang, p. 45
Apr 1 "Britain's Restaurant Revolution." R.W. Apple, Jr., p. 14
Apr 15 Fare of the Country: "Wensleydale's Rich Cheese." David Yeadon, p. 6
"London Through Younger Eyes." The '60s swinging city now embraces fast food and punk. Joan Gage, p. 51
Apr 22 "Chic Comes to London's Pimlico." Douglas Sutherland, p. 12
Apr 29 "Rambling Through Yorkshire." R.W. Apple, Jr., p. 14
"Snickets Were Made for Walkers." Meandering in York along walls and ginnels. Ursula Wadey, p. 15
May 20 "An Old Oxonian's Oxford." A grand tapestry of spires and battlements, traceried windows and a splendid central dome. A.L. Rowse, p. 9
May 27 "Serendipity in the Cinque Ports." Hastings. Noela Whitton, p. 31
Jun 3 "Johnson's London Then and Now." Glimpses of the 1700s from Fleet Street to Greenwich. John Wain, p. 19
"Where He Labored, Where He Relaxed." Johnson. Kay Eldredge, p. 19
Jun 17 "Cross-Channel by Boat Train (Dover-Calais) or by Hovercraft." Joan Cook, p. 26
Jun 24 "The Little Train That Can." One-third size replica steam train on the Kent coast. p. 43
Jul 8 "Seeking the Soul of Derbyshire." A county of villages and glens lies in the ancient heart of English life. Alan Sillitoe, p. 14

"The Voice of England's Past." Upstairs, downstairs, in Eckington the language of Shakespeare lives. Paul West, p. 15
"300 Years of Treasures at Chatsworth." Layers of history come to life. Paula Dietz, p. 16
Jul 29 "Where Tennyson Shouted Stanzas to Queen Victoria." The Isle of Wight was a poetic haven, and today's sailors find it one, too. Tom Prideaux, p. 9
Aug 5 "Where Britannia Hails Her Seafaring Tradition." National Maritime Museum. C. Northcote Parkinson, p. 9
"A Century at Zero Longitude." The old royal observatory at Greenwich. Margot Slade, p. 9
Aug 12 "On Jersey, British Mood Just Off France." Relaxed pace, English weather. John Vinocur, p. 14
Aug 19 "London's Little Hill Town." Hampstead's fame embraces Constable, Le Carre, and a carefree heath. Louis Heren, p. 9
Aug 26 "Leys of the Land." Connections of prehistoric sites—Stonehenge, Salisbury Cathedral etc. MacDonald Harris, p. 29
Sep 9 "England: a Field Guide." Recognizing pecking orders in England. Margaret Atwood, p. 33
Oct 7 "Brighton's Antiques." The English seaside resort is a tonic for collectors. p. 12
(Part 2, "Sophisticated Traveler") "Bath's Fresh Sparkle." Maureen Howard, p. 8; "To London, with Paprika." R.W. Apple, Jr., p. 128
Oct 21 "A Somerset Ramble . . ." From Arthurian Glastonbury to Victorian resorts. A.L. Rowse, p. 15
Oct 28 "Afoot in London's Theaterland." From Shaftsbury Avenue to Drury Lane, playhouses evoke a rich tradition. Benedict Nightingale, p. 9
Nov 25 "A Slice of 17th-century Life." At Ham House, near London, a newly restored kitchen evokes cook and countess equally. Betty Fussell, p. 12
Dec 2 "Guide to a Victorian Lakeland." Exploring England's lakes, honored by poets, drivers and walkers. Donald Goddard, p. 14
"Homage to Cumbria." A resident's circuit over and around lake, dell, fell, tarn and beck. Norman Nicholson, p. 15
Dec 16 "In London, the Hot Rod on Parade." Vintage autos. Leslie Mandel-Viney, p. 39
Dec 23 "Christmas at London's Connaught." Lunch is stylish, formidable, merry. Herbert Mitgang, p. 19

SMITHSONIAN
1985 Apr "Once Upon a Time These Stones Marked the End of the Civilized World." Hadrian's Wall—Newcastle-on-Tyne to the Irish Sea. Timothy Foote, p. 70
1984 Aug "The Lords of Alnwick." A castle great with art and history. Israel Shenker, p. 72
Nov "Bumptious Bath, the Town That Beau Nash Built." Meryle Secrest, p. 122

SUNSET
1984 Feb "Steaming Around on Vintage Trains." p. 56
Apr "On Foot Through the Beckoning English Countryside." p. 42

TOWN & COUNTRY

1984 Apr "The English Experience." Inns, horseracing, club life, London, shopping, fishing. Catherine Calvert, ed., p. 147

TRAVEL & LEISURE

1985 Jan "The Green and Gentle Beauty of Yorkshire." Cobblestoned England, country squire England, Dickens's England. Anthony Weller, p. 58

Feb "Dining at London's Dorchester." George Lang, p. 126

Mar "The Design Centre, London." Purveying the best of British goods from flashlights to fabric. Robert L. Sammons, p. 201

"London's Lively Restaurant Scene." From the genial air of the Lamb and Flag Pub to the posh atmosphere of the Ritz Hotel. George Lang, p. 28

Apr "Chester—England's Timeless Walled City: Where the Past—from Roman ruins to Tudor Architecture—Has Been Preserved." Israel Shenker, p. 69

"London's Cabinet War Rooms." Exploring Churchill's secret underground chambers. Norman Zollinger, p. 154

May "Harrods—the British Museum of Shopping." Where the dazzling displays are all for sale. Susan H. Anderson, p. 60

"London's Anchor Pub." A cozy spot on the banks of the Thames. Durham Washburne, p. 184

Jun "The Tower of London." Scepters, glittering crowns, pomp and pageantry. Kate Simon, p. 124

"A Walk Through Hardy's England." The Dorset countryside. Bern Keating, p. 48

Aug "England's Idyllic Constable Country Just Two Hours from London." The spiritual home of a great landscape painter. Alan Littell, p. 26

Sep "Great Buys on Portobello Road." London's rollicking street market yields treasures and trash. John D. Wright, p. 30

Oct "A Morning at the Victoria and Albert." Strolling through London's celebrated museum of the decorative arts. John D. Wright, p. 206

Nov "London at its best (December)." Pamela Fiori, p. 8

"Simply Super Shopping from Harrods to Hyper Hyper." Susan H. Anderson, p. 78

"Marvelous Mayfair." London's Most Fashionable Neighborhood. Michael Jackson, p. 86

"Staying in Style." The big news is small hotels. Ian Keown, p. 94

"Terribly Trendy Restaurants." Drew Smith, p. 100

"Top Tours to London." Patricia Brooks, p. 110

"On the Prowl for Antiques in London." An expert's guide to markets, auction houses and galleries. Judith Friedberg, p. 118

"The Treasure Houses of Britain." Four stately homes near London. Susan Larkin, p. 130

"The Best Taxis in the World—and the Most Courteous Drivers." Fred Brack, p. 140

1984 Feb "A Cheese Taster's Tour of England." Sampling cheddar, Cheshire, Lancashire in some of Britain's loveliest countryside. Barbara Ensrud, p. 46

Apr "Stanfords: London's Great Map Store." Alan Littell, p. 206

May "Old England's Resurrected *Mary Rose*." Visiting the flagship of Henry VIII. Sherry Marker, p. 200

1984   "Latest from London." Wealth of new things for visitors to do. Doris Saatchi, p. 75

Jul "Sojourn in Salisbury." An English cathedral town that blends city and country. Henry Ehrlich, p. 19

Aug "Greenwich: A Delightful Day's Outing from London." Maritime history. Susan Larkin, p. 20

Sep "A Summer's Week in London." Pamela Fiori, p. 4

"The Isle of Scilly." Breakaway pleasures of England's southwest coast. Susan Larkin, p. 28

Oct "Getting Dressed on Savile Row." How to choose a London tailor. Alan Schwartz, p. 16

Nov "London Theater Restaurants." Where to have a great meal, before or after the show. Gareth Jones and Victoria Hine, p. 86

Dec "London's Burlington Arcade." A historic shopping promenade with everything from antique silver to hand-knit Shetlands. John D. Wright, p. 126

TRAVEL/HOLIDAY

1985   Apr "Europe's Unique Accommodations: England." Doing the country in style. Jack Heidenry, p. 68

Jul "An English Ancestral Guest . . . or Why Are There Yanks in the Rose Garden." Clair Robey, p. 40

Oct "London's Dining Delights." Chef Louis Szathmary, p. 18

Dec "Deck the Halls." An English yuletide celebration. Peter and Linda D'Aprix, p. 6

1984   Feb "Punting on the Cam." A different view from a famous English river." Steve Schneider, p. 6

Apr "Sherlock Holmes Pub." Ginny Turner, p. 114

VOGUE

1984   Jun "Grand Hotels." The Connaught. Barbara Kafka, p. 166

Jul "Isn't it Romantic!" Country house hotels. Jill Robinson-Shaw, p. 134

FINLAND

Note: See also asterisked entries (*) under "Denmark" for books on Scandinavia as a whole.

Series Guidebooks (See Appendix 1)

Baedeker: **Scandinavia; Helsinki**
Berlitz: **Helsinki**

Fodor: Scandinavia; Budget Scandinavia; Stockholm, Copenhagen,
           Oslo, Helsinki & Reykjavik
Frommer: Scandinavia: $-a-Day
Nagel: Finland
U.S. Government: Finland: Area Handbook; Post Report

Background Reading

Bradley, David   LION AMONG ROSES: A MEMOIR OF FINLAND
The author lived in Finland with his wife and five children and worked as a
teacher of English literature. The book is descriptive of daily life, family
adjustments, holidays, and so on. HR&W, 1965.

Lister, R.P.   THE HARD WAY TO HAPARANDA
An 1,800-mile adventurous trip through all of Lapland. HarBraceJ, 1966.

Rejanen, Aini   OF FINNISH WAYS
"A sometimes amusing, sometimes heartbreaking tale of what makes a Finn a
Finn. . . . of these people who fought 42 wars with Russia and lost every one."
(Publisher) Barnes & Noble, 1984.

Sykes, J.   DIRECTION NORTH: A VIEW OF FINLAND
The author served in the ambulance corps during the 1940 war with Russia; this
book describes his return visit twenty-five years later, and living with the families
of two old acquaintances. Chilton, 1967.

GUIDEBOOKS

Nickels, Sylvie   THE TRAVELLER'S GUIDE TO FINLAND
Chatto Bodley, 1979.

Nicol, Gladys   FINLAND
Batsford, 1975.

HISTORY

Jutikkala, E.   A HISTORY OF FINLAND
Praeger, 1974.

Kirby, D.G.   FINLAND IN THE 20TH CENTURY
U of Minnesota, 1980.

Wuorinen, John H.   A HISTORY OF FINLAND
Columbia U Pr, 1965. Also, *Finland and World War II, 1939-1944* (1983, first
published 1948).

Novels

Jansen, Tove   THE SUMMER BOOK
A summer idyll on a Finnish island shared by a girl and her grandmother.
Pantheon, 1975.

Sariola, Mauri   THE HELSINKI AFFAIR
A good detective story in which the lawyer is the hero; the courtroom scenes
and procedures are fascinatingly different from those in the United States. Walker,
1971.

Schoolfield, G.C., ed.   SWEDO-FINNISH SHORT STORIES
Regional and modern psychological stories by Finns whose native tongue is
Swedish. Twayne, 1975.

Sillanpaa, F.E.   THE MAID SILJA
A Finnish classic and a book that won a Nobel Prize for literature in 1939. The
story is about a well-to-do family brought to ruin by the father's ineptitude. N S
Berg, 1974 (first published 1939).

Thayer, Nancy   STEPPING
A young stepmother in Finland while her husband is on a Fulbright grant, struggling to resolve problems with her stepdaughters and the neurotic ex-wife who is
their mother. Doubleday, 1980.

Thomas, Craig   SNOW FALCON
Members of the anti-peace faction of the Red Army plan to sabotage Soviet/
Western arms limitation talks in Helsinki—for espionage addicts. HR&W, 1980.

TRAVEL ARTICLES

BON APPETIT
1984 Jul "Finland." Fred Gebhart, p. 28

CONNOISSEUR
1984 Nov "Aalto's Masterpiece." Villa Mairea open to the public Jul 1-Aug 14.
    Susan S. Szenasy, p. 130

GOURMET
1985 Aug Gourmet Holidays: "A Finnish Sojourn." Fred Ferretti, p. 34

N.Y. TIMES SUNDAY TRAVEL SECTION (X)
1984 Mar 11 "Searching for the Essence of Winter." Arctic silence at the top of the
    world. Adam Nicolson, p. 12
    Jun 17 "Turku, Where Finland's History was Wrought." Theodore James, Jr.,
    p. 24

TRAVEL HOLIDAY
1984 May "Behold Tampere." Finland's first-rate second city. Geraldine Merken,
    p. 34

FRANCE

Series Guidebooks (See Appendix 1)

American Express: The South of France; Paris
Baedeker: France; Paris; Loire; Provence
Berlitz: Paris, The French Riviera; The Loire Valley
Birnbaum: France
Blue Guide: France; Loire, Normandy, Brittany; Paris
Companion Guide: Normandy; Paris; South of France
Country Orientation Update: France
Fisher: France; Paris
Fodor: France; Budget Travel France; Paris
Frommer: France: Dollarwise; Paris: Arthur Frommer Guide
Let's Go: France
Michelin Green: Brittany; Chateaux of the Loire; Dordogne;
        Normandy; French Riviera; Provence; Paris
Nagel: France
U.S. Government: France: Background Notes; Post Report; Monaco:
        Background Notes

Background Reading

Adams, Henry   MONT SAINT MICHEL AND CHARTRES
A classic—"eloquent and profound . . . expression concerning the glory of medieval art and the elements that brought it into being." (BRD) Berg, 1978 (first published 1914).

Ardagh, John   FRANCE IN THE 1980s
By a former correspondent of the *London Times*—"complementing . . . *The French* [see Zeldin, below] . . . an absorbing model of timely, well-researched reportage." (BRD) Penguin, 1983. See also *A Tale of Five Cities*, under "Europe"; includes Toulouse.

Ardagh, John and others   RURAL FRANCE: THE PEOPLE, PLACES AND CHARACTER OF THE FRENCHMAN'S FRANCE
A "celebration of the French countryside and people . . . the special qualities of the provinces. . . . Designed with the tourist in mind." Includes specific information on waterway routes, châteaux, wine and cheese industries, festivals, etc. (BL) Salem Hse, 1985.

Collins, Larry   IS PARIS BURNING?
A suspenseful and exciting retelling of the liberation of Paris in 1944 and one German general's decision to save the city from being burned to the ground. S&S, 1965.

Dubois, Jacques   VERSAILLES: A GARDEN IN FOUR SEASONS
Essays introduce and expand upon various historical and artistic aspects of Versailles. The book is arranged according to the seasons. Vendome, 1983.

Feldkamp, Frederick   NOT EVERYBODY'S EUROPE
A grand tour of nine unique places to think about adding to your itinerary—for France, it's Lyon. Harper's Magazine Pr, 1976.

**Fielding, Xan   THE MONEY SPINNERS: MONTE CARLO AND ITS
                     FABLED CASINOS**
Little, 1977.

Glyn, Anthony   THE SEINE
A portrait of the river, its history, geography, people and legends. Putnam Pub Group, 1966.

Gramont, Sanche de   THE FRENCH, PORTRAIT OF A PEOPLE
The author seeks to explain why the French are admired, detested, misunderstood and unique. Putnam Pub Group, 1969.

Greene, Graham   J'ACCUSE: THE DARK SIDE OF NICE
The novelist recounts an episode on the French Riviera of gross injustice involving the daughter of a friend, the French government, and organized crime. Merrimack, 1982.

Jackson, Stanley   INSIDE MONTE CARLO
"A social history of Monaco's past one hundred years and of its resident and visiting celebrities and reigns of the Grimaldi princes." (BRD) Stein & Day, 1975.

**Jacobs, Michael and Stirton, Paul   THE KNOPF TRAVELER'S GUIDES TO
                                        ART: FRANCE**
Suggested tours and routes, museums (including hours and fees and museum plans), guides to collections. The book is organized geographically by region, city and site, with an introduction to each. Knopf, 1984.

Kramer, Jane   UNSETTLING EUROPE
Refugee families from Algeria, Uganda, Yugoslavia, living in France, London and Sweden, respectively, and an Italian Communist family in Italy, their isolation from traditions of those around them and the implications for Europe's future of these rootless people. Random, 1981.

**Lichine, Alexis and Perkins, Samuel   ALEXIS LICHINE'S GUIDE TO
                                         WINES AND VINEYARDS
                                         OF FRANCE**
"A fine series of tours, with maps, recommended hotels, and . . . suggested itineraries" have been added to the earlier edition, to help plan "wine and travel as a combined cultural experience." (TBS) Knopf, 1982.

Lofts, Norah   ETERNAL FRANCE
A history of France, 1789-1944, written by a novelist/historian. Doubleday, 1968.

Marnham, Patrick   LOURDES: A MODERN PILGRIMAGE
Description of the three sections of Lourdes—the old quarter on the hill, the new town on the river, and the ecclesiastical enclave—the focus of pilgrims. The author participated in an organized tour with a British group and gives an account of that experience, his conversations with tour members and local people. Vignettes, local color, and commentary on various themes from the conflicts between "high town and low, and between town and Domain—between God and Mammon" to an enthralling "description of the Blessed Sacrament procession that reaches its climax in the blessing of the sick." (NYT) Coward, 1981.

Raison, Laura   THE SOUTH OF FRANCE: AN ANTHOLOGY
Writings about southern France—Belloc on Arles, Evelyn Waugh on Marseilles, Sitwell on Monte Carlo, and so on. Beaufort, 1986.

Wheeler, Daniel and Réalités-Hachette, eds.   THE CHATEAUX OF FRANCE
Historical background, architectural description of more than seventy châteaux, along with photographs. Vendome, 1979.

Zeldin, Theodore   THE FRENCH
"The reader can finish the book with a sense of the dreams, fears, virtues, faults and contradictions of the people of France." (BL) Pantheon, 1983.

KINGS AND QUEENS

Castries, René de la Croix   THE LIVES OF THE KINGS AND QUEENS OF FRANCE
A survey of royalty from the Merovingian dynasty through Louis-Philippe (1848)—making obvious that the direction taken by the evolution of the French state was greatly the result of the personalities of its monarchs. Knopf, 1979.

Law, Joy   FLEUR DE LYS: THE KINGS AND QUEENS OF FRANCE
An entertaining anecdotal view of French monarchs from inside the palace, using contemporary accounts of ladies-in-waiting, priests, ambassadors, etc. McGraw, 1976.

Seward, Desmond   BOURBON KINGS OF FRANCE
"A series of light and heretofore scattered facts about the most colorful ruling family in European history." (BRD) Har-Row, 1976.

TRAVELOGUES, MEMOIRS

Durrell, Lawrence   THE SPIRIT OF PLACE
"Descriptive, frank . . . wonderful compilation of fact and fiction" that "includes

the Rhone River wine country and Southern France." (BRD) Leetes Isle, 1984 (first published 1969).

Fisher, M.F.K.   TWO TOWNS IN PROVENCE
Two books in one: *A Considerable Town*, about Marseilles—"its glory and wickedness, past and present; its life, its legends its mystery"; and *Map of Another Town, A Memoir of Provence*—two years lived in Aix-en-Provence and the daily adventures of living. Vintage, 1983.

Ford, Ford Madox   PROVENCE: FROM MINSTRELS TO THE MACHINE
"Delightful reminiscences . . . builds up a picture of the past and present of Provence." (BRD) Ecco Pr, 1979 (first published 1935).

James, Henry   A LITTLE TOUR IN FRANCE
"Lively, charming" series of essays about a trip taken in 1882 by the novelist, through Touraine, Languedoc and Provence. (BRD) Oxford U, 1984 (first published 1884).

Kimbrough, Emily   FLOATING ISLAND
Reminiscences of a barge trip, with friends, on the rivers and canals of France. Book & Tackle, 1984 (first published 1968).

More, Julian and Carey   VIEWS FROM A FRENCH FARMHOUSE
Text and photos by a father and daughter, of the four seasons in Provence. Holt, 1985.

Morris, James   PLACES
This collection of essays by a leading travel writer includes an essay on Trouville. HarBraceJ, 1973.

Pope-Hennessy, James   ASPECTS OF PROVENCE
The landscape and mood of Provence conveyed by a literary travel writer who is an artist as well. Little, 1967.

Streeter, Edward   ALONG THE RIDGE
Account of an unusually beautiful and diversified automobile trip from Paris south to Andorra, to Spain, across southern France through the Dolomites, and ending in Dubrovnik, Yugoslavia. Har-Row, 1964.

Wylie, Laurence W.   VILLAGE IN THE VAUCLUSE
Life in the French town where the author, his wife and two small sons lived for a year. Harvard U Pr, 1974 (first published 1957).

Zbigniew, Herbert   BARBARIANS IN THE GARDEN
Ten travel essays by a Polish poet, translated from French—"writes lyrically of French and Italian towns . . . intertwines his impressions with historical data, musings on art history [and] delightful anecdotes." (Arles, Lascaux, Valois, Siena and Orvieto.) (PW) Carcanet, 1985.

GUIDEBOOKS

Binns, Richard   FRANCE À LA CARTE
"Concentrates on sights and sites with heavy and delightful emphasis on thematic tours"—battlefields, Joan of Arc, William the Conqueror, etc. (BL) Ticknor & Fields, 1982. Also, *Hidden France* (1983) and *French Leave* (1982).

Cox, Thornton   THORNTON COX'S TRAVELER'S GUIDE TO SOUTH OF FRANCE
"Highly readable introduction to the area . . . getting there and getting about . . . suggested itineraries [designed for] economy of time and movement . . . historical and cultural background." (Publisher) Hippocrene, 1983.

Daniels, Dorothy and Sheppard, Stephen   MONTE CARLO
Dorchester Pub Co, 1981.

DUMONT GUIDE TO THE FRENCH RIVIERA
One of a new series of German travel guidebooks. Emphasis is on art, history, architecture—for the sophisticated tourist. Stewart, Tabori & Chang, 1984. Also *DuMont Guide to the Loire Valley* (1984).

Green, Kerry and Bythines, Peter   THE WHOLE EUROPE ESCAPE MANUAL: FRANCE, HOLLAND, BELGIUM, WITH LUXEMBOURG
One of a new series of guidebooks "designed to bring Europe to life and put the fantasy and excitement back into travel." (Publisher) World Leis Corp, 1984.

HACHETTE GUIDE TO FRANCE
First U.S. edition of a French guidebook. One reviewer termed it almost comical in its comprehensiveness: maps of roof styles, types of forests and cheeses, a history of France from prehistory to the present, drawings of the most common trees, and so on, in addition to an introduction to the country as a whole, hundreds of itineraries and maps, as well as hotel and restaurant evaluations. Divides the country into twenty-seven regions plus Paris. Pantheon, 1985.

MacDonald, Lyn   BORDEAUX AND AQUITAINE
Batsford, 1976. Other Batsford guides for France: *Dordogne* (1979, Patrick Turnbull) and *Burgundy* (1980, Anthony Turner).

Nicolson, Adam   LONG WALKS IN FRANCE
"Nine walks in country France. . . . The pace is leisurely and relaxed . . . informative, often witty. . . . A delight from start to finish." (LJ) Crown, 1983.

Sheppard, Stephen   MONTE CARLO
Zebra, 1985.

HISTORY

Guerard, Albert   FRANCE: A MODERN HISTORY
U of Michigan, 1969.

Maurois, André   A HISTORY OF FRANCE
FS&G, 1957.

PARIS

Background Reading

Buchwald, Ann and Art   SEEMS LIKE YESTERDAY
"A delightful, hilarious memoir" of the couple's meeting, living in Paris in the '50s—"name-dropping nonstop . . . glamour and mundane routes [a] wonderful nostalgia trip." (BL) Putnam Pub Group, 1980.

Clancy, Judith and Fisher, M.F.K.   NOT A STATION BUT A PLACE
Gare de Lyon, the train and its Train Bleu restaurant—drawings and text. Synergistic Press, 1979.

Cody, Morrill and Ford, Hugh   THE WOMEN OF MONTPARNASSE
A collective biography of English and American women on the Left Bank between World War I and II who, the authors claim, shaped and directed the life of the under-thirties of the Anglo-American art colony—profiles of Josephine Baker, Gertrude Stein, others. Cornwall Bks, 1984.

**Culbertson, Judi and Randall, Tom   PERMANENT PARISIANS: AN
                                     ILLUSTRATED GUIDE TO THE
                                     CEMETERIES OF PARIS**
Biographies, suggested walks, photographs and maps of such people as Colette, Gertrude Stein, Alexander Dumas, others. Chelsea Green, 1986.

Dill, Marshall   PARIS IN TIME
Historical guide to Paris in chatty style. Putnam Pub Group, 1975.

Evenson, Norma   PARIS: A CENTURY OF CHANGE
Focuses on the physical evolution of the city "with attention to social origins and consequences." Yale U Pr, 1979.

Frégnac C.   THE GREAT HOUSES OF PARIS
"Capsule history of social mores in the French haut monde," and photographs. (BRD) Vendome, 1979.

Gajdusek, Robert E.   HEMINGWAY'S PARIS
A "loving compilation of photographs of places mentioned by Hemingway and his friends, interspersed with passages from his writings." (TBL) Scribner, 1982.

Harriss, Joseph   TALLEST TOWER, EIFFEL AND BELLE EPOQUE
Social history of the Tower. Houghton, 1975.

Hemingway, Ernest   A MOVEABLE FEAST
Sketches of the years in Paris, 1921-26; published posthumously. Scribner, 1964.

Longstreet, Stephen WE ALL WENT TO PARIS: AMERICANS IN THE CITY OF LIGHT, 1776-1971
Americans from Benjamin Franklin to Henry Miller, Cole Porter to Richard Wright who went to Paris and were changed by the experience. Macmillan, 1972.

Morton, Brian N. AMERICANS IN PARIS
Fun for visitors or stay-at-homes—ancedotes relating to Americans who have visited Paris or lived there, from John Adams to Art Buchwald, why they went there and what they did. Morrow, 1986.

Paul, Elliott H. THE LAST TIME I SAW PARIS
Sketches of life in pre-World War II Paris, life on Rue de la Huchette before the Germans came. Random, 1942. *Springtime in Paris* (1950) is the same street ten years later.

Putnam, Samuel PARIS WAS OUR MISTRESS
Memoirs of a lost and found generation—Paris and Montparnasse in the 1920s and '30s. Southern Illinois U, 1970.

Simon, Kate KATE SIMON'S PARIS: PLACES AND PLEASURES
By the noted travel writer—comments on Paris and its sights, and suggestions for a ten-day visit with some alternatives. Putnam Pub Group, 1970.

Skinner, Cornelia Otis ELEGANT WITS AND GRAND HORIZONTALS
Paris during the 1890s—"sparkling panorama of 'la belle epoque,' its gilded society, irrepressible wits and splendid courtesans." (BRD) Houghton, 1962.

Stein, Gertrude PARIS, FRANCE
Impressions of the writer who had known Paris since 1900, a "love letter" published as Paris fell to the Germans in World War II. Liveright, 1970.

Temko, Allan NOTRE DAME OF PARIS
A biography of the cathedral. Viking, 1955.

White, Sam SAM WHITE'S PARIS
"Musings and reportage on Paris" originally published in the *Evening Standard* and *Spectator* over thirty-six years. (BL) New English Lib, 1984.

Wiser, William THE CRAZY YEARS: PARIS IN THE TWENTIES
Legends, scandals and the revolution in the arts during a decade when many Americans were lured to Paris. Atheneum, 1983.

GUIDEBOOKS

DUMONT GUIDE TO PARIS & THE ILE DE FRANCE
See DuMont Guide entry above, for "France."

Landes, Alison and Sonia PARISWALKS
Five two-and-one-half-hour walking tours with the objective of giving travelers

a familiarity with some of the fascinating neighborhoods and a feel for the city as a place of habitation, past and present. HR&W, 1982.

Wells, Patricia   THE FOOD LOVER'S GUIDE TO PARIS
"Irresistible to anyone interested in Paris, cooking, or good food." Arranged according to arrondissement, "the author's descriptions make delightful reading in themselves"—reviews of everything from wine bars and cafés to markets, pastry shops and tableware stores. (LJ) Workman, 1984.

Novels

Bogarde, Dirk   VOICES IN THE GARDEN (Southern France)
A villa in southern France is the setting for an "almost Noel Coward-ish" novel contrasting "youthful passion against a marriage gone stale." (FC) Knopf, 1981.

Boissard, Janine   CHRISTMAS LESSONS
Problems surface and threaten to disrupt the Christmas celebration of the Moreau clan—"warm, wonderful scenes . . . gentle 'slice-of-life.'" Little, 1984.

Durrell, Lawrence   LIVIA (Avignon)
Chronologically the first of the projected five-part sequence of novels. Following are *Monsieur* (1975) and *Constance* (1982). Viking, 1979.

Freeling, Nicolas   WOLFNIGHT
Just one of the many marvelous mysteries by this author. In this one the plot "reeks of Chappaquiddick" in its parallel events and the "tug of war . . . between police efforts to solve the mystery [of a young woman's death] and political efforts to cover it up." (FC) Pantheon, 1982. Other books by Freeling, set in France, include: *Arlette* (1981), *The Back of the North Wind* (1983), *The Bugles Blowing* (1976), *A Dressing of Diamond* (1974).

Hebden, Mark   DEATH SET TO MUSIC
Inspector Pel "unravels a cast that presents too many suspects, motives and alibis." (FC) Walker, 1982.

Holt, Victoria   THE QUEEN'S CONFESSION
A fictional memoir of Queen Marie Antoinette based on hardcore fact and taking the reader from her young womanhood in Austria to death on the guillotine—[the author] "embroiders the story delicately and makes the entire work believable." (FC) Doubleday, 1968.

Loraine, Philip   DEATH WISHES
A mixture of a gothic novel and one of Agatha Christie's housebound murder mysteries" in a chateau. (FC) St. Martin, 1983.

Meade, Marion   SYBILLE (Toulouse)
The history of the thirteenth-century religious wars in France "brought vividly to life." (FC) Morrow, 1983.

Sagan, Françoise   SALAD DAYS
"A lonely and timid young bookkeeper discovers a cache of jewels that changes his life." (FC) Dutton, 1984.

Salinger, Pierre   THE DOSSIER
"Insider's view of international double-dealing"—a tip from an Israeli informer that the French candidate for president was a Nazi collaborator in World War II becomes a matter of vital importance to Soviet, French and American espionage organizations. (FC) Doubleday, 1984.

Seton, Cynthia Propper   A PRIVATE LIFE (Languedoc)
Fanny Foote, member of an "upright and uptight" New England family is sent by a feminist magazine "to get the lowdown on her notorious Aunt Carrie" (who runs a sort of way stop for transient artists and visiting Americans in France). Norton, 1982.

Simenon, Georges   THE NIGHTCLUB (Nantes)
"Draws largely on autobiographical material"—a young reporter rebels by becoming involved in "a lengthy and sordid involvement" with a red light district club until his father's death "restore[s] him to grace in the provincial community." (FC) HarBraceJ, 1979. Also the many "Maigret" detective novels.

Stewart, Mary   THUNDER ON THE RIGHT (Pyrenees)
The heroine of this suspenseful romance arrives to visit her cousin only to find that she has died; a clue connected to the cousin's color-blindness leads to the solution of the apparent mystery. Morrow, 1958.

Thompson, Gene   NOBODY CARED FOR KATE
Seven passengers on board a luxury barge are suspects in the death of its owner; her San Francisco lawyer (Dade Cooley) unravels the case—"well-done concoction of atmosphere and character with delightfully detailed descriptions of old cathedrals and medieval towns." (FC) Random, 1983.

Wallace, Irving   THE MIRACLE (Lourdes)
The Catholic Church reveals the date that Bernadette predicted the Virgin Mary would appear in Lourdes and as the time approaches "an explosive mix of petitioners, journalists, and opportunists" descend upon Lourdes. Who is to be the one to whom Mary reveals herself, or to be blessed with a miraculous cure, or to "sniff out" fraud—these are questions around which the plot develops. (FC) Dutton, 1984.

THE ALPS (Haute Savoie)

Habe, Hans   THE MISSION
A story based on an actual conference held in Evian-les-Bains in 1938 to plan the purchase of Jews from Germany, as a method of saving them. Coward, 1966.

Stewart, Mary   NINE COACHES WAITING
Contemporary gothic—an English governess encounters murder and romance. Morrow, 1959.

BORDEAUX

Daley, Robert   STRONG WINE RED AS BLOOD
An American businessman sent to buy a wine chateau becomes enthralled with the life and the winemaking process—novel of the region and of winemaking. Harper's Magazine Pr, 1975.

Mauriac, François   MALTAVERNE
Autobiographical novel of conflict between a mother and son over his life's direction—Maltaverne is the family estate. FS&G, 1970.

Mauriac, François   QUESTIONS OF PRECEDENCE
Explores the moral implications of using another person for an unworthy purpose—in this case to enter Bordeaux society. FS&G, 1959. Also *Woman of the Pharisees* (1946) in which a woman interferes in other lives out of religious conviction.

Mauriac, François   A MAURIAC READER
Five novels set in Bordeaux and environs for which the author won the Nobel Prize for literature in 1952; includes *Woman of the Pharisees* (1946). FS&G, 1968 (first published 1952).

BRITTANY

Balzac, Honoré de   BEATRIX
Love story set in the early nineteenth century. P-H, 1970 (first published 1839).

Bates, H.E.   A BREATH OF FRENCH AIR
The happy-go-lucky, Rabelaisian Larkin family descends upon the Brittany coast for a month's holiday. Little, 1959.

Fowles, John   THE EBONY TOWER
Four ancient Celtic tales retold. Little, 1974.

Francis, Clare   NIGHT SKY
The heroine, unwed and pregnant, ends up with relatives in Brittany where she becomes part of a dangerous operation to evacuate Allied servicemen during World War II. Morrow, 1984.

Genet, Jean   QUERELLE
Story of a "murderous homosexual . . . masterful portrait of a man isolated from society and himself." (FC) Grove, 1974.

Loti, Pierre   AN ICELAND FISHERMAN
Breton fishermen and their lives of danger and hardship, by a nineteenth-century writer. Dutton, 1935 (first published 1896).

MacInnes, Helen   ASSIGNMENT IN BRITTANY
A British officer is sent on a mission to Brittany following the Dunkirk disaster in World War II. HarBraceJ, 1971.

Shute, Nevil   MOST SECRET
Exceptionally skillful adventure-and-espionage story of English and Free French officers sent to a Breton village to wreak havoc on German patrols. Morrow, 1945.

Stewart, Mary   MERLIN TRILOGY
Omnibus edition of a trilogy about Merlin and the Arthurian legend that includes *The Crystal Cave* (1970), *The Hollow Hills* (1973), *The Last Enchantment* (1979)—"high adventure, mystery and romantic intrigue . . . . produce an extremely entertaining tale." (FC) Morrow, 1980.

BURGUNDY

Colette   MY MOTHER'S HOUSE and SIDO
Autobiographical novels of the author's early years in the region. FS&G, 1975 (first published 1922 and 1929, respectively).

Hebden, Mark   PEL AND THE FACELESS CORPSE
World War II events are the basis for Pel solving the mystery of a corpse found in Burgundy near a resistance memorial. Walker, 1982.

CANNES, NICE, THE RIVIERA

Daley, Robert   THE DANGEROUS EDGE
Story about an egotistical expatriate American who plans a bank robbery—the author's "knowledge of [French] police procedure . . . insight into human nature . . . add up here to a gripping detective novel [and] romantic, moving love story." (FC) S&S, 1983.

Hopkins, Robert S.   RIVIERA
A novel about the Cannes Film Festival. Morrow, 1980.

Read, Piers Paul   THE VILLA GOLITSYN
The British foreign office assigns Simon Milson the task of finding out the truth about an incident in the 1960s during the conflict between Indonesia and Malaya, and involving the owner of Villa Golitsyn—"can be read once for fun and a second time for enlightenment." (FC) Har-Row, 1982.

Shaw, Irwin   EVENING IN BYZANTIUM
A has-been Hollywood producer at the Cannes film festival. Delacorte Pr, 1973.

NORMANDY

Holt, Victoria   DEMON LOVER
A typical Holt romance, set in Normandy during the Second Empire—"innocent heroine . . . roguishly incorrigible hero . . . happy ending." (FC) Doubleday, 1982.

Keyes, Frances   CAME A CAVALIER
Story of an American Red Cross girl during World War I who stays on in France until World War II. Messner, 1947.

Prescott, H.F.M. **SON OF DUST**
A historical romance set in eleventh-century Normandy—weaves "a rich tapestry, glowing with color and quick life." (FC) Macmillan, 1956 (first published 1932).

Shipway, George **THE PALADIN**
Historical novel, and a good suspense story, of eleventh-century England and Normandy—the plot revolves around the Norman knight Tirel. HarBraceJ, 1973.

PROVENCE

Boulle, Pierre **FACE OF A HERO**
"Study of a self-righteous man who preferred to sacrifice his career and the life of another man rather than acknowledge the fallacy of his idealized image of himself." (FC) Vanguard, 1956.

Conrad, Joseph **THE ROVER**
An old sea captain throws his life away in a scheme for outwitting Lord Nelson, and blockading Toulon. Doubleday, 1923.

Stewart, Mary **MADAM WILL YOU TALK?**
A young widow befriends a thirteen-year-old boy and discovers that his father is suspected of murder—a warm Provencal background. Morrow, 1956.

PARIS

Aiken, Joan **THE GIRL FROM PARIS**
Romantic suspense novel of a twenty-one-year old English girl faced with earning her own way as a governess in mid-nineteenth-century Paris. Doubleday, 1982.

Ajar, Emile **MOMO**
An old Parisian woman takes in the children of prostitutes. Doubleday, 1978.

Anthony, Evelyn **THE RETURN**
An American woman marries a White Russian involved with a group of half-crazed Russians, deranged by Allied treachery after World War II, in a scheme to kidnap a Soviet official in Chartres and overthrow the Soviet government. Coward, 1978.

Barber, Noel **A FAREWELL TO FRANCE**
A love story and a war story of the French occupation and resistance movement through the eyes of an American journalist. Macmillan, 1983.

Beauvoir, Simone de **THE MANDARINS**
"A group portrait of the Existentialist clique . . . the political role played . . . from the liberation to the late 1940s." (BRD) World, 1956. Also *Les Belles Images* (1968), which considers the heroine's involvements with people in her life.

Boissard, Janine   **A NEW WOMAN**
Portrait of "a woman starting at zero in mid-life" when her husband leaves her
for a younger woman. (FC) Little, 1982. Also *A Matter of Feeling* (1980), about a
"happy" family in a Paris suburb facing one daughter's first romance—with an
older man.

Brent, Madeleine   **A HERITAGE OF SHADOWS**
Novel of romantic intrigue set in Paris, then Mexico. Doubleday, 1984.

Cadell, Elizabeth   **THE MARRYING KIND**
"A pleasant story with lots of local color"—the plot involves a young
Englishwoman "not the marrying kind" who must deal with a problem father in
Paris, and finds herself in love. (FC) Morrow, 1980.

Colette   **THE COMPLETE CLAUDINE**
Omnibus edition of *Claudine at School, Claudine in Paris, Claudine Married,
Claudine and Annie*—semi-autobiographical novels written 1900-1903. Also, set
in Paris, are *Gigi, Julie De Carneilban, Chance Acquaintances, The Innocent
Libertine* (1909), and *The Vagabond* (1910). FS&G, 1976.

Deighton, Len   **AN EXPENSIVE PLACE TO DIE**
A clinic and its illegal experiments, concoctions, creations. Putnam Pub Group,
1967.

Delacorta (no first name)   **DIVA**
A thriller that features an unsuccessful classical pianist, a young kleptomaniac,
and a black American superdiva who refuses to have her voice recorded—"tale of
music and mayhem in Paris . . . playfully witty." (FC) Summit Bks, 1983.

Eberstadt, Isabel   **NATURAL VICTIMS**
"A singularly elegant horror story . . . about madness and money and the interac-
tion between them" set in Paris where the heroine has fled from her mother. (FC)
Knopf, 1983.

Forsyth, Frederick   **THE DAY OF THE JACKAL**
Meticulous plans for the assassination of de Gaulle, and the search when
authorities are alerted to the plan under way—almost seems like an actual event as
real people move in and out of the plot. Viking, 1971.

Freeling, Nicolas   **THE BUGLES BLOWING**
A government official is involved in a murder that reaches into the office of the
president of France. A Henri Castang police detective story. See also Freeling,
under "Novels" (general), above. Har-Row, 1976.

Gallico, Paul   **MRS 'ARRIS GOES TO PARIS**
A London charwoman is determined to own a Dior gown and invades his
salon—"improbable but amusing." (FC) Doubleday, 1958.

Gary, Romain   **KING SOLOMON**
A taxi driver narrates the plot; he is general helper in SOS, an organization in

Paris that is a "combination of Amnesty International and Meals on Wheels." (FC) Har-Row, 1983.

Giraudoux, Jean   LYING WOMAN
A woman is involved in simultaneous and parallel love affairs. Winter Hse, 1972.

Grayson, Richard   CRIME WITHOUT PASSION
"Clever plotting and the ambience of the glittering city during the last century ensure . . . a dandy entertainment"—Gautier of the Sureté investigates a crime-of-passion murder. (FC) St. Martin, 1984.

Harris, MacDonald   HERMA
"An extraordinary novel . . . turn-of-the-century California [earthquake included] is marvelously evoked, as is the Paris of Marcel Proust . . . one of the best novels about opera ever written." The plot involves a Southern California singer in a Baptist choir and her manager Fred, as she pursues her career in San Francisco and Paris. (FC) Atheneum, 1981.

Hemingway, Ernest   THE SUN ALSO RISES
Novel of the post-World War I lost generation, with scenes shifting between Paris and Spain. Scribner, 1926.

Hotchner, A.E.   THE MAN WHO LIVED AT THE RITZ
Set mostly at the Paris Ritz in the 1940s with "intimate glimpses of the famous and infamous" (Chanel, Goering, etc.) and "a lively, often vivid piece of chase-thriller narrative." (FC) Putnam Pub Group, 1981.

Jones, James   THE MERRY MONTH OF MAY
The student uprising in Paris, 1968. Delacorte Pr, 1971.

Krantz, Judith   MISTRAL'S DAUGHTER
Three generations of women in the life of France's supposed greatest artist. Crown, 1983.

Lyons, Nan and Ivan   CHAMPAGNE BLUES
A comedy about travel-guide authors in the grandest hotel in Paris. S&S, 1979. Also *Somebody's Killing the Great Chefs of Paris* (1976), a mystery.

MacInnes, Helen   THE VENETIAN AFFAIR
A suspense novel set in Paris and Venice with a plot that involves a Communist plan to assassinate de Gaulle and implicate the U.S. HarBraceJ, 1963.

Martin du Gard, Roger   SUMMER 1914
A family chronicle set in pre-World War I Paris. Viking, 1941. Sequel is *The Thibaults* (1939).

Miller, Henry   TROPIC OF CANCER
Autobiographical novel of an American in Paris in the early '30s. Modern Lib, 1983 (first published 1961).

Mitford, Nancy   THE BLESSING
The marriage of a beautiful English blonde to a French marquis provides an "analysis of the characteristic French and English virtues and faults . . . shrewd and just." (FC) Random, 1951.

Moore, Brian   THE DOCTOR'S WIFE
A love affair in Paris of an American and a London doctor's wife. FS&G, 1976.

Nin, Anaïs   LADDERS TO FIRE
Collected in *Cities of the Interior*—a largely American group of characters in Paris. Swallow, 1974.

Oldenbourg, Zoe   THE AWAKENED
A love story of the 1930s and the World War II years following. Pantheon, 1957.

Remarque, Erich Maria   ARCH OF TRIUMPH
Refugees from the Nazis in Paris just before World War II. This is another novel you can still catch in a movie version on late-night TV occasionally. Appleton, 1945.

Rhys, Jean   QUARTET
An English girl in Paris is victim of a rather sick couple. Har-Row, 1971 (first published 1928). Also *Good Morning, Midnight* (1939), in which the heroine—"beauty and youth dribbled away"—returns to Paris.

Romains, Jules   THE DEPTHS AND THE HEIGHTS
A political novel of Paris heading toward World War I. Knopf, 1937. Also *The Earth Trembles* (1936) and *Men of Good Will* (1932).

Sagan, Françoise   A CERTAIN SMILE
Love affair of a young student and an older married man. Dutton, 1956. Also, set in Paris, *La Chamade* (1966).

Sartre, Jean Paul   THE AGE OF REASON
Existentialism in Paris, 1938. Knopf, 1947.

Simenon, Georges   THE GRANDMOTHER
Novel of the clash between an 80-year-old woman and her granddaughter. HarBraceJ, 1980. Also with Paris settings: *The Old Man Dies* (1967), *The Glass Cage* (1973), *The Girl With a Squint* (1978).

Stead, Christina   HOUSE OF ALL NATIONS
Story of international finance, 1920-30, with a huge cast of characters and a banker as the central figure. HR&W, 1972 (first published 1938).

Steinbeck, John   THE SHORT REIGN OF PIPPIN IV
The monarchy is reinstated in the person of an amateur astronomer. Viking, 1957.

Uris, Leon   TOPAZ
Russian espionage penetrates the French government. McGraw, 1967.

Volkoff, Vladimir   THE TURN-AROUND
A plot to have a top Soviet spy in Paris come over to the French side works; he converts to Christianity as well, with "decidedly chilling" results. (FC) Doubleday, 1981.

Wiser, William   DISAPPEARANCES
A novel with two interlocking story frames—one is a crime documentary on a Bluebeard who murdered eleven people; the other is an American-in-Paris memoir of a reporter covering the trial. Atheneum, 1980.

TRAVEL ARTICLES

BLACK ENTERPRISE
1985 Sep "Paris Noirs: Black American." West Indian and African cultures make Paris sizzle. Charlotte Carter, p. 70
"A Film Buff's Guide to Paris." Theaters just off the Champs-Élysées. Patricia A. Singleton, p. 72

BON APPETIT
1985 Feb "Traveling with Taste: Around the Beauborg." National Center of Art and Culture, Paris. Nao Hauser, p. 34
1984 Oct "Alsace." Storybook France: charming towns, great wines, superb food. Jean Anderson, p. 118

CONNOISSEUR
1985 May "Along Rue Jacob." A stroll down one of Paris's fabled streets, J.-C. Suares, p. 73
Aug "Dordogne: Gastronome's Heaven." Paula Wolfert and William Bayer, p. 64
1984 Apr "A Letter from Paris" A long and luxurious weekend. Carol Borden, p. 140
Jun "The stars of Brantôme." A visit to a small French town with a huge gastronomic tradition. Leslie Rubinstein, p. 96

ESQUIRE
1984 "Revisiting Paris." Richard Z. Chesnoff, p. 47

ESSENCE
1984 Feb "Cannes, Heart of the Riviera." Dwight Brown, p. 44

GLAMOUR
1985 Sep "Paris: Where Everything's a Bargain This Year." p. 310

GOURMET
1985 Jan Paris Journal: "Au Quai Des Ormes." Restaurant with a water view. C.P. Reynolds, p. 34

1985 Feb "A Journey Through the Midi." Doone Beal, p. 40
Mar "Quimper." Southwestern Brittany. Terry Weeks, p. 50
Apr Paris Journal: "Malmaison and Le Camélia." Residence of Napoleon and Josephine, and a nearby restaurant. C.P. Reynolds, p. 12
Apr "Monet at Giverny." Marilyn Kluger, p. 52
May "Iles D'Hyeres." Idyllic islands off the coast of southern France. Doone Beal, p. 54
Jun "Chantilly." Kingdom of the Norse. Paul J. Wade, p. 54
Jul Paris Journal: "Going to the Dogs, Laurent, Renoir." C.P. Reynolds, p. 18
Oct Paris Journal: "The Grand Louvre, the New 8-digit Telephone Numbers." C.P. Reynolds, p. 24
1984 Jan Paris Journal: "Barthelmay's Cheese Shops, Coping with Traffic in Paris." C.P. Reynolds, p. 6
Feb Gourmet Holidays: "Two Hill Towns in Provence." Doone Beal, p. 28
Apr Paris Journal: "Hotel Crillon." C.P. Reynolds, p. 8
Jul Paris Journal: "Restaurants Newly Upgraded by Michelin." C.P. Reynolds, p. 22
Oct Paris Journal: "Walking the Seine Bridges." C.P. Reynolds, p. 20
Nov "Teatimes in Paris." Lillian Langseth-Christensen, p. 64
Dec "Playing the French Train Game." Peter Todd Mitchell, p. 42

HARPER'S BAZAAR
1985 Mar "The Vaucluse: a delicious discovery." Jacqueline Friedrich, p. 34
Apr "Paris: Aprés Nouvelle." What's happening in the gastronomic worlds. Jacqueline Friedrich, p. 36
Aug "There's a Small Hotel." Paradise found in the French provinces. Jacqueline Friedrich, p. 44
1984 Apr "Ballooning over Burgundy." Richard Z. Chesnoff, p. 22
Nov "Cap Ferrat." Peninsula pleasures. Doone Beal, p. 36

MODERN MATURITY
1985 Feb/Mar "Time Traveler to Paris." An author searches for the youth he left behind. Roy Bongartz, p. 104

N.Y. TIMES SUNDAY TRAVEL SECTION (X)
1985 Jan 6 Shopper's World: "A Louvre to Lure Collectors." Phyllis L. Levin, p. 12
Jan 27 Shopper's World: "Galerie Vivienne." Historic Paris mall. Vicky Elliott, p. 6
Feb 17 "A Lavish Castle That Talleyrand Called Home." Valençay. Olivier Bernier, p. 9
Mar 3 "French Resort with Trails for Many Tastes." Endless snowfields, 84 miles of runs (Courchevel). Bannon McHenry, p. 21
Mar 10 Shopper's World: "Nice's Flower Market Abloom." Robert Packard, p. 12
"Au Marché with Bocuse in Lyons." The city's open-air farmers' market provides a feast for both eye and palate. Ed Hotaling, p. 47
Mar 17 "An Inn Whose Setting Inspired Impressionists." At Ferme St.-Siméon haunting light, ever-shifting seas. Phyllis L. Levin, p. 12
Mar 24 Fare of the Country: "As French as Tarte Tatin." Patricia Wells, p. 12

1985   Apr 14 "Good Things in Small Packages." The fine little museums of Paris. Kathleen McNulty-Compagnon, p. 16
"For Parisians, It's Sweet in the 16th." A guide to a fashionable district. John Vinocur, p. 15
"How Taillevent Stays on Top." The goal is to do better through detail and discipline. Patricia Wells, p. 14
Apr 21 "Where Leaders Dined and Made History." Change comes to Lucas-Carton, a Paris landmark. C.L. Sulzberger, p. 43
Apr 28 Fare of the Country: "Pressing Walnut Oil in the Dordogne." Ann Barry, p. 6
May 5 Shopper's World: "A Paris Depot of Fine Design." Musée des Arts Décoratifs. Gloria Levitas, p. 6
May 19 "Chateau for a Royal Favorite." Maintenon still reflects the complex personality of its most famous owner. Olivier Bernier, p. 9
Jun 2 "A Traveller's Taste of Vintage France"; "Champagne: the Wine and the Country." An easy day's excursion from Paris. Frank J. Prial, p. 14
"A Little Town and its Big Red Wine." Vintage Chateauneuf-du-Pape. Florence Fabricant, p. 15
"The Essential Spirit of Paris." Sip by sip; wine bars: small, hectic, memorable. Frank J. Prial, p. 16
Jun 9 "Paris As a State of Mind." The City—by turns magnificent and infuriating—is encrusted with a magic that is nowhere else. Milton Mayer, p. 45
Jun 16 Shopper's World: "Cheap Parisian Chic." Maria Eder, p. 6
Jun 23 "Browsing the French Flea Markets, in Paris and Beyond . . ." Richard Bernstein, p. 15
"One Shopper's Choice: Paul-Bert." Hebe Dorsey, p. 15
Jul 7 "Grand Parisian Rooms on a Legendary Square." Hotel Crillon. Paul Goldberger, p. 9
Jul 21 Fare of the Country: "Goat's Milk Cheese from the Correze." Ann Barry, p. 12
Aug 4 "Nimes to Rousillon, a Weekend Journey." Provence can be sampled in a two-day trip from Paris. Paul Lewis, p. 14
"Enjoying the Bounty of Provence." Wine, goat cheese and chateaus. Patricia Wells, p. 15
Aug 11 "Grand Véfour: Grand Dining." Susan H. Anderson, p. 22
Fare of the Country: "Morbier—Cheese with a Dash of Ash." Patricia Wells, p. 12
Sep 8 "Season of Mists in Forests of Sologne." Autumn puts bloom on heather, game on table. Patricia Wells, p. 9
Sep 15 "The Garden Spot of Kings." Versailles. Guy Walton, p. 14
"Versailles: A Lively City on its Own." Markets, dining and leafy strolls. Patricia Wells, p. 14
"In the Palace of Versailles." Using history as a guidebook can help a visitor get the meaning behind the glittering surfaces. Richard Bernstein, p. 15
Sep 29 "Compiégne: Restrained, Extravagant." A sophisticated court in a forest. Phyllis Lee Levin, p. 16
Oct 6 "What's Doing in Paris." Paul Lewis, p. 10
(Sophisticated Traveler) "Treks for the Sophisticated Traveler." Learning the meaning of fear (mountain climbing). Jeremy Bernstein, p. 79

(Sophisticated Traveler) "Royal Meander Along the Loire." John Vinocur, p. 32

(Sophisticated Traveler) "Pleasures and Palaces." Patricia Wells, p. 104

Oct 13 Shopper's World: "Handmade Lace from Normandy." Ann Barry, p. 12

Oct 20 "On the Rue du Faubourg St. Honoré." Even the horse blankets have designer labels. Aline Mosby, p. 9

Nov 10 "Idling through the Midi." A cabin cruiser crawl from Castelnaudry to Marseilles proves to be a Francophile's delight. Hugh Leonard, p. 15

Nov 17 "British Pluck, Gallic Duck." A true tale from the Interieur Sauvage of Normandy and Brittany. Nick Yapp, p. 51

Nov 24 "Paris Has Plenty to Read (in English)." A long day's walk on both sides of the Seine to ten special bookstores. Jonathan Baumbach, p. 9

"Is That Miss Marple at the Next Table?" Phyllis Lee Levin, p. 9

Dec 8 "Napoleon's Last Quarters." Visiting St. Helena, where the only approach is still by sea and memories of Bonaparte abound. Robert Gordon, p. 9

Dec 22 "Chateaus in All Directions." France's Routes de Beaute lead to clusters of aristocratic homes. Hebe Dorsey, p. 9

Dec 29 "Parlay Voo Anything?" They don't speak college French in France. Ira Berkow, p. 19

1984 Jan 1 Fare of the Country: "A Visit to France's Capital of Foie Gras." Ann Barry, p. 6

Jan 8 (Alsace) "Colmar Enjoys a Good Bouquet." Center of Alsace's wine trade. Austin Hamel, p. 19

Feb 5 "Palais Royal: Serene Oasis in Central Paris." Frank J. Prial, p. 9

Mar 11 "Jefferson Abroad." Many of the sights the future president visited while assigned to Paris can still be seen. William H. Adams, p. 9

"Bicycle Tour of Normandy." Earl Ubell, p. 20

Mar 18 "Art Nouveau Adorns Nancy." Barbara L. Michaels, p. 26

(Part 2, "Sophisticated Traveler"): "Afloat in France."Along the Canal du Midi in a hotel barge. A. Alvarez, p. 36; "Light and Shadow in Brittany." A ramble along a rocky shore among blindingly white villages and ancient standing stones. John Russell, p. 42; "One Artist's Paris." Painting the Seine orange and other problems in capturing the essence of a grand and stately city. Red Grooms, p. 90

Mar 25 "A Bistro Lover's Choice: Fifteen Paris Favorites Offering Tradition and Quality." R.W. Apple, Jr., p. 9

Apr 1 Correspondent's Choice: "A Greek Treasure in France." Museum at Chatillon-sur-Seine. Paul Lewis, p. 6

"Ascending to the Stars in France." Michelin 2 and 3 star restaurants. Patricia Wells, p. 16

Apr 8 "Hills and Valleys of Provence." Bannon McHenry, p. 12

"The Concierge Then and Now." A Paris tradition yields to security systems and building guardians. Ellen Count, p. 45

Apr 29 "Cherchez la bouillabaisse." The soup in Marseilles. John Vinocur, p. 51

May 6 "Chablis: The Land Beyond the Label." Paul Lewis, p. 14

"Northern Burgundy's Earthy Local Fare." Patricia Wells, p. 15

May 13 "D-Day + 40 years." The invasion beaches are calm now, but reminders of the war abound. John Vinocur, p. 14

"On Hallowed Ground." The vast scale of the Normandy operation may come as a surprise. Jon Nordheimer, p. 15

May 20 "Touring France en Famille." Elizabeth F. Wallace, p. 22

Jun 10 "A Cheese Lover's Tour of France." In Paris scores of shops sell samples of the land's abundance (with some suggested "cheese" restaurants). Patricia Wells, p. 9

Jun 17 "Cross-Channel by Boat Train (Dover-Calais) or by Hovercraft." Joan Cook, p. 26

"The World of Père-Lachaise." Remembrances, tomb, etc., of Proust. Noela Whitton, p .51

Jun 24 Correspondent's Choice: "The Silent Realm of Chartreuse." In the French Alps. Paul Lewis, p. 6

Jul 15 "Hiking Alpine Trails." June P. Wilson, p. 19

Jul 29 "Stately Rivalry." Visiting Vaux-le-Vicomte, forerunner of Versailles. Phyllis L. Levin, p. 14

"Sorties in the Ile de France." Train trips in Paris region. Jack Beeching, p. 15

"Where to Go and What to See on the R.E.R. [railroad] Networks." p. 15

Aug 26 Fare of the Country: "Alsace's Eaux de Vie Pack a Fruity Punch." Susan H. Anderson, p. 6

Sep 2 "English Haven Prospers in Brittany." Dinard. Kay Eldredge, p. 13

Sep 9 "Old France Still Lives in Antiques." Paris antiques shops. Rita Reif, p. 9

Sep 23 "What's Doing in Paris." Richard Bernstein, p. 10

Sep 30 "Through the Valley of Chateaus: a Journey to the Loire's Lesser-Known Castles." Olivier Bernier, p. 14

"Tasting the Bounty of the Valley." Wines, cheese, sweets. Patricia Wells, p. 15

Oct 7 (Part 2, "Sophisticated Traveler") "The Way It Was." The fresh rewards of returning to a beloved place. M.F.K. Fisher, p. 26; "Timeless Deauville." Scott and Zelda would recognize it even today. John Vinocur, p. 85; "Old Normandy in Old Paris." Pierre Franey, p. 18; "Paris Is Always . . . Well, Paris." Margaret Atwood, p. 124

Oct 21 "Touring Toulouse." The southern charms of France's fourth largest city. Barbara Bell, p. 19

Nov 4 "The Watery Byways of Paris." City canals. Frank J. Prial, p. 9

Nov 25 "Normandy Out of Season." With the summer crowds gone, the region's solitude is inviting; Paths for weekenders. Two suggested itineraries for visitors from Paris to D-day beaches and to the Pays d'Auge. Richard Bernstein, pp. 14-15

"From Camembert to Seafood." Normandy. Patricia Wells, p. 14

SUNSET

1985 Jan "Renting an Old House in the French countryside." p. 42

Jun "The 21st Century Comes to Paris." La Villette complex. p. 32

Jul "Megaliths on Brittany's Coast." p. 66

Dec "The Santons of Provence." Clay figures on display or for sale. p. 36

1984 Jan "Cliff-Hanging Cactus Garden in Monaco." p. 29

Mar "Have You Been to a *Salon de l'Agriculture?*" Agricultural fair each March in Paris. p. 48

TRAVEL & LEISURE

1985 Jan "A Taste of Alsace." Reminiscences and recipes from the French countryside. Roy Andries de Groot, p. 84

Feb "The Arc de Triomphe." Historic centerpiece of the City of Light. Abby Rand, p. 58

Mar Travel & Architecture: "The Romance of the Romanesque." The exuberant style that emerged from the Dark Ages. Alexander Eliot, p. 76

May "The Seductive Pleasures of Provence." Van Gogh visits, earthy cuisine, and haunting ruins in the herb-scented air of Southern France; "Driving and Lingering in Provence." The author's route and where to stay and eat. Doone Beal, pp. 110, 123

Jun "Summer in Deauville, an Enclave by the Sea in France." Mollie E.C. Webster, p. 32

Jul "Summer Days in Paris." A jug of wine, a loaf of bread and the perfect spot of green. Richard Eder, p. 50

Aug "Renoir's 'Moulin de la Galette.'" John Canaday, p. 76

"Paris for Food Lovers." A fall feast for the senses. Patricia Wells, p. 88

Oct "Latest from Paris." Patricia Wells, p. 91

"The Wondrous Walled Towns of Europe." Carcassonne. Bern Keating, p. 100

Dec "The Liveliest Quarter in Paris." The Beaubourg, the Marais and beyond. Erica Kleine, p. 100

1984 Jan "On the Hair-Raising Roads of France." Christopher Hunt, p. 13

Feb "A Month in the Country." In France: hanging around Provence, *en famille*. Calvin Trillin, p. 90

Mar "Prehistoric Man's Sistine Chapel." Cave paintings at Lascaux II. Joan Scobey, p. 182

Apr "Learning to Love Paris." Pamela Fiori, p. 4

May "Paris, What's New and Notable." Pamela Fiori, p. 4

"The Loire Valley: Chateaus to Stay In." Baronial hotels along a fabled river. Elizabeth Venant, p. 100

"The Loire—Chateaus to See." Royal castles of a golden age. Christopher Hunt, p. 108

"The Hollywood Savoy in Paris." Wowing them with Noel Coward songs and Tex-Mex food. Julia Newman, p. 79

Jun "Normandy: D-Day Plus 40 Years, a Haunting Remembrance." Pierre Salinger, p. 129

"The Meaning of D-Day, Memories of a Moving Visit to the Normandy Coast." Pamela Fiori, p. 4

Jul "Touring a French Coppertown." For great buys in the kitchenware prized by chefs (Villedieu near Mont-Saint-Michel). Dan Carlinsky, p. 36

Sep "The Quiet Charm of the Alsace Wine Route." Scenic French villages, wonderful restaurants and wineries. Susan H. Anderson, p. 56

"Latest from Paris." Reigning restaurants, renovated hotels, fashion trends. Patricia Wells, p. 83

Nov "A Glorious Winery in Bordeaux." Visiting the gardens and vineyards of Chateau Bargaux. Charles Lockwood, p. 70

"The Pocket Museums of Paris." Superb little collections, from music boxes to Baccarat crystal. Richard Z. Chesnoff, p. 194

TRAVEL/HOLIDAY
1985 Jan "Skiing the French Way." Bill Wrenn, p. 56
    Apr "International Chef: A Sentimental Journey to Paris." Chef Louis
    Szathmary, p. 81
    Apr "Europe's Unique Accommodations: France." In search of perfection.
    Robert L. Sammons, p. 64
    Jul "Bartholdi's France." Creator of the Statue of Liberty. Gerard McTigue, p.
    84
    Nov "Dropping in on the Rhône Alps." A high-flying adventure. Gerard
    McTigue, p. 56
1984 Feb "Carnival on the French Riviera." Mardi Gras in Nice. Diane P. Marshall,
    p. 66
    May "Normandy, Four Decades Later." John Heidenry, p. 82
    Jun "Monaco." In the realm of luxury. John Coyne, p. 46

VOGUE
1985 Jun Grand Hotels: "Inside the Paris Ritz." The hotel that gave the world a
    new word for elegance. Barbara Kafka, p. 176
    Sep "A Country House." In Provence, the ultimate house in the country.
    Olga Carlisle, p. 558
1984 May "A Chateau of Your Own." The civilized joys of vacationing in a grand
    manor. Kathleen Beckett, p. 264
    Aug Grand Hotels: "Hôtel du Cap." Nice. Barbara Kafka, p. 272
    Oct Grand Hotels: "Hôtel Plaza-Athénée." The essence of Paris, mystery and
    luxury. Barbara Kafka, p. 540

GERMANY

Series Guidebooks

Baedeker: Germany; Rhine; Berlin; Frankfurt, Hamburg; Munich
Berlitz: Rhine Valley; Munich; Berlin
Country Orientation Update: Germany
Fisher: Germany
Fodor: Germany; Budget Travel Germany; Munich
Frommer: Germany: Dollarwise
Michelin: Germany
Nagel: German Federated Republic (West);
         German Democratic Republic (East)
U.S. Government: Germany: Pocket Guide
         German Federated Republic (West): Background
         Notes;

Country Study; Pocket Guide;
Post Report
German Democratic Republic (East): Background
Notes;
Country Study

Background Reading

Ardagh, John   A TALE OF FIVE CITIES
See complete entry under "Europe;" includes Stuttgart.

Bailey, George   MUNICH
One of the Great Cities of the World series, Time-Life, 1981.

Brody, Elaine   MUSIC GUIDE TO AUSTRIA AND GERMANY
One of a series of guides for individual European countries—a handbook of information for a range of travelers "from the music dilettante to the highly motivated specialist." Includes information on the country's musical history, concert halls, opera houses, festivals, etc. Dodd, 1975. See also *Music Festivals in Europe and Britain* and *Music Lover's Europe*, under "Europe/Art, Music, Literature."

Craig, Gordon A.   THE GERMANS
"A literate, eminently readable book . . . fundamental facets of German life and culture. . . . chapters on religion, money, women, romantics, soldiers, students, Germany and Jews, literature and society [trace] attitudes and experiences" over the last centuries. (NYTBR) Putnam Pub Group, 1982.

Feldkamp, Frederick A.   NOT EVERYBODY'S EUROPE
A grand tour of nine unique places to think about adding to your itinerary—in Germany it's Baden-Baden. Harper's Magazine Pr, 1976.

Gunther, John   TWELVE CITIES
The author of the highly popular "Inside" series of a couple of decades ago applies his unique zest and talent to a dozen cities, one of which is Hamburg—mood, temper, problems, politics, government. Har-Row, 1969.

Hanser, R.   A NOBLE TREASON
Story of the White Rose, a group of people in Munich who carried on a resistance movement against Hitler. Putnam Pub Group, 1979.

Hartrich, Edwin   THE FOURTH AND RICHEST REICH
An account of the "fortuitous circumstances, innovative thinking and daring leadership that transformed a pariah among nations into a stunning example of success." (PW) Macmillan, 1980.

Lang, Daniel   A BACKWARD LOOK—GERMANS REMEMBER
Recalling the Nazi era is a class assignment for high school students in a Rhineland town. McGraw, 1979.

Laqueur, Walter   GERMANY TODAY: A PERSONAL REPORT
"A blend of reportage and reminiscence, of impressions and erudition—served up lightly." (NYTBR) Little, 1985.

Morris, Jan   PLACES
Essays by a leading travel writer—this collection includes one on Baden-Baden. HarBraceJ, 1973.

Rippley, LaVern J.   OF GERMAN WAYS
"A bit of history, a bit of sports, art, music, literature, customs and food, and much of people." (Publisher) Barnes & Noble, 1979.

Schalk, Adolph   THE GERMANS
By an American journalist who lived in Germany for eight years—"he sets out to do for Germany what Barzini did for the Italians: to provide an informed portrait [of a] society living in the shadow of both a long romantic past and a recent terror-filled one." (BRD) P-H, 1972.

Senger, Valentin   NO. 12 KAISERHOFSTRASSE
A unique first-person chronicle of a Jewish family that survived the Nazis by pretending to be gentiles, though the entire block on which they lived knew of the charade. Dutton, 1980.

Shirer, William L.   THE RISE AND FALL OF THE THIRD REICH
A classic on the whole history of the Nazi movement through World War II. S&S, 1981 (first published 1960).

Spender, Stephen   EUROPEAN WITNESS
Impressions of post-World War II occupied Germany—German intellectuals, displaced persons, the British army, and so on. Greenwood, 1972 (first published 1946).

Switzer, E.E.   HOW DEMOCRACY FAILED
Interviews with many Germans about events preceding World War II and why Hitler succeeded in coming to power. Atheneum, 1975.

BERLIN

Agee, Joel   TWELVE YEARS; AN AMERICAN BOYHOOD IN EAST GERMANY
A unique view of life inside East Germany where the author (son of James Agee) lived with his American mother and German Communist stepfather from age eight until 1960 when his parents' marriage failed and he returned to America. "Catalogues his expatriate passage to manhood" and the adolescent rebellions of his age. "Recollections of a sensitive adolescent in East Germany . . . the memoir

fascinates with its rare view of the intimate and personal side of life in the other Germany." (PW) FS&G, 1981.

Collier, Richard   BRIDGE ACROSS THE SKY
The Berlin blockade and airlift, 1948-49—recreation of the period when the Russians attempted to drive the Allies out of Berlin by preventing food and medical supplies from reaching Berlin—"vivid and authentic." (BRD) McGraw, 1978.

Elon, Amos   JOURNEY THROUGH A HAUNTED LAND
Includes observations of East and West Berlin by this Israeli author, following a visit in 1965. HR&W, 1967.

Friedrich, Otto   BEFORE THE DELUGE
A portrait of Berlin in the 1920s. Har-Row, 1972.

Grunfeld, Frederic V.   BERLIN
One of the Great Cities of the World series. Time-Life, 1977.

McGreevy, John, ed.   CITIES
Impressions of world cities as seen through the eyes of people intimately connected with them—for Berlin it is Hildegarde Knef's impressions. Outlet Bk, 1981.

Ryan, Cornelius   THE LAST BATTLE
Story of the last three weeks of World War II in Europe, culminating in the fall of Berlin to the Soviets in 1945. PB, 1985 (first published 1966).

Stern, Herbert J.   JUDGMENT IN BERLIN
"True story of a couple's dramatic escape into West Berlin . . . proves as fascinating as the best espionage fiction." (BL) Universe, 1984.

Von Eckardt, Wolf   BERTOLT BRECHT'S BERLIN
"A scrapbook of the Twenties. . . . a very readable course in the civilization of a decade." (BRD) Doubleday, 1975.

GUIDEBOOKS

Bunting, James   BAVARIA
Batsford, 1972.

Kane, Robert S.   GERMANY
One of a new "World at Its Best" series of travel guidebooks by a noted travel authority, "oriented toward the discriminating traveler." Highlights the best each country has to offer, including hotels in a range of prices—"evaluates the entire itinerary. Big city wonders and . . . out-of-the-way adventure spots." Passport, 1985.

Kitfield, James and Walker, William   WHOLE EUROPE ESCAPE MANUAL: GERMANY, AUSTRIA, SWITZERLAND
Part of a new series of guidebooks "designed to . . . put the fantasy and excitement back into travel." (Publisher) World Leis Corp, 1984.

Marsden, Walter **WEST GERMANY**
A Batsford guide. David, 1978. Also *The Rhineland* (1973), armchair traveling
to castles, vineyards, special towns and villages from Neckar to Cologne.

Steinbicker, Earl **DAYTRIPS IN GERMANY**
"50 one-day adventures by rail or car"—using Hamburg, Frankfurt and Munich
as a base. "Extensive walking tours are outlined for each . . . tours to villages, towns
and areas within a short car or train ride . . . recommended eating and drinking
establishment[s]" along the way. (BL) Hastings, 1984.

HISTORY

Bendersky, Joseph W. **A HISTORY OF NAZI GERMANY**
Nelson-Hall, 1984.

Childs, David **GERMANY SINCE 1918**
St. Martin, 1980.

Detwiler, Donald S. **GERMANY: A SHORT HISTORY**
A very concise, one-volume history. Southern Illinois U, 1976.

Dill, Marshall Jr. **GERMANY: A MODERN HISTORY**
Succinct history for the general reader, emphasizing events of the twentieth
century. U of Michigan, 1970.

Ryder, A.J. **TWENTIETH-CENTURY GERMANY FROM BISMARCK
TO BRANDT**
Columbia U Pr, 1972.

Novels

Abish, Walter **HOW GERMAN IS IT**
Exploration of the psyche of modern Germany. New Directions, 1980.

Anthony, Evelyn **THE JANUS IMPERATIVE**
A political journalist investigates the coincidence of a German politician's
assassination in Paris, whose dying word is "Janus," having heard the same from a
dying man twenty-five years earlier. Coward, 1980.

Barrett, William E. **A WOMAN IN THE HOUSE (Munich)**
A young man, working in art restoration in Munich, befriends and falls in love
with a Czech girl and must "find solutions for which he has not been prepared by
his earlier life." (FC) Doubleday, 1971.

Berger, Thomas **CRAZY IN BERLIN**
An American G.I. of German background feels strong guilt about Nazi
Germany's treatment of the Jews—"a memorable gallery of German, Russian, and
American characters." Delacorte Pr, 1982 (first published 1958).

Böll, Heinrich   THE SAFETY NET
The experiences of the owner of a newspaper chain reflected in a series of monologues by members of his family, one of his police guards, etc. Knopf, 1982. Also *Lost Honor of Katharina Blum* (1975), which weighs the moral questions of the rights of the individual to privacy and the rights of a free press.

Böll, Heinrich   THE BREAD OF THOSE EARLY YEARS
Love transforms a cynic; a love story set in a Rhineland town in post-World War II Germany. McGraw, 1976. Also *And Never Said a Word* (1978) and *The Clown* (1965).

Boyle, Katherine   GENERATION WITHOUT FAREWELL
Complex story of relationships in an occupied German town after World War II. Knopf, 1960.

Brückner, Christine   FLIGHT OF CRANES
Document of a woman's survival from the end of World War II, fleeing the Russian troops, to middle-age in postwar Germany. Fromm, 1982. The companion book, about the woman's life up to the point of *Flight of Cranes*, is *Gillyflower Kid* (1982).

Buckley, William F.   STAINED GLASS
Adventure, unsavory aspects of international politics, in a "first-rate spy story" set in the early fifties. (FC) Doubleday, 1978.

Findley, Timothy   FAMOUS LAST WORDS
A serious novel in which the protagonist is Hugh Mauberley, from Ezra Pound's World War I poem of the same name. In World War II, he is horribly murdered fleeing the Allies and the Nazis, and on the walls of the room are his famous last words—the events he's witnessed in Europe between the wars. "This whole book is excessive, and mad, and marvelous, puzzling, disturbing, and utterly brilliant." (FC) Delacorte Pr, 1981.

Forsyth, Frederick   THE ODESSA FILE
A young reporter pentrates an organization that shields former Nazi SS officers, called ODESSA—"tough to put down" once started. (FC) Viking, 1972.

Freeling, Nicolas   NO PART IN YOUR DEATH (Munich)
Henri Castang attends a seminar in Munich and faces blackmail. He must also resolve the circumstances surrounding the suicide death of a friend's wife—"rich, dense, beautifully written and insightful." (FC) Viking, 1984.

Gary, Romain   THE DANCE OF GENGHIS COHN
A police official, and former Nazi, is possessed by the spirit of Genghis Cohn, a Jewish actor murdered in a German concentration camp. World, 1968.

Grass, Günter   THE MEETING AT TELGTE
Historical novel set in 1647 (at the end of the Thirty Years War) "brings together a fictional meeting of literati—theorists, poets, prose writers . . . for the purpose of strengthening the last bond within a divided nation: its language and

literature." It "mirrors a real meeting [of] Group 47, at the end of another ravaging war 300 years later." (FC)HarBraceJ, 1981. Also *Dog Years* (1965), *The Tin Drum* (1963), *Local Anesthetic* (1970).

Grass, Günter   HEADBIRTHS; OR, THE GERMANS ARE DYING OUT
"Collage of intellectual and ideological jabs at Germany . . . on the eve of the . . . 1980 elections." (FC) HarBraceJ, 1982.

Harrington, William   THE ENGLISH LADY
Espionage novel about a British aristocrat "married to a German cousin, friend of Hitler [and other] upper echelon Nazis" who becomes an agent for the British. (FC) Seaview, 1982.

Herlin, Hans   SOLO RUN
See under "Czechoslovakia/Novels."

Hochhuth, Rolf   A GERMAN LOVE STORY
A human tragedy in which a woman falls in love with a Polish PW while her husband is at the front. Little, 1980.

Kirst, Hans H.   REVOLT OF GUNNAR ASCH
Chronicle, in four novels, of the adventures of a German army sergeant beginning just before World War II—grim drama, suspense, high comedy, satire. Little, 1956. The titles that follow are *Forward Gunnar Asch* (1956), *Return of Gunnar Asch* (1957), *What Became of Gunnar Asch* (1964).

Kirst, Hans H.   THE AFFAIRS OF THE GENERALS
Fictionalized reconstruction of how Goering and Heydrich, with Hitler, destroyed two high-ranking army officers, making their way clear for a complete takeover of the Wehrmacht—"a vivid portrait of the Nazi organization." (FC) Coward, 1979.

Le Carré, John   A SMALL TOWN IN GERMANY (Bonn)
Britain must solve the mystery of a missing "green" file in Bonn. Coward, 1968.

Lenz, Siegfried   THE GERMAN LESSON (Schleswig-Holstein)
A son undermines his police chief father's attempts to censor the work of a controversial artist. Hill & Wang, 1972.

MacLean, Alistair   WHERE EAGLES DARE
Suspense story involving a mission to rescue an American general from a castle built by a mad Bavarian prince and now the headquarters of the German secret service and Gestapo. Doubleday, 1967.

McCormack, Russell   NIGHT THOUGHTS OF A CLASSICAL PHYSICIST
"Part history, part science lesson, part philosophical treatise . . . a profoundly moving portrait of a man and his time [Prussia, 1918]." (FC) Harvard U Pr, 1982.

Malraux, André   DAYS OF WRATH
Account of a communist's imprisonment by the Nazis, and his release and reunion with his wife when an unknown comrade takes his place. Random, 1936.

Schlee, Ann   RHINE JOURNEY
Set in the nineteenth century; a British woman at mid-life change is reunited with her brother and his family on a Rhine cruise—"commonsensical Jane Austen-like approach to ordinary people in ordinary situations . . . feeling for, and meticulous research into, period and place." (FC) HR&W, 1981.

Schmidt, Arno   SCENES FROM THE LIFE OF A FAUN
A German civil servant's notes "on the tedium, sycophancy and sexual daydreaming of a bureaucrat's life" in 1939; the plot then skips to 1944 with Germany near defeat. (FC) M Boyars, 1983.

Tennenbaum, Silvia   YESTERDAY'S STREETS
Saga of four generations of the wealthy Wertheim family, from 1903 to World War II. Random, 1981.

Thomas, Craig   JADE TIGER
A spy story involving an impending treaty that "threatens to remove the Berlin Wall [and] fears that the fragile balance of power will be destabilized . . . breathstopping tour through China, Australia and Spain as well as other places." (FC) Viking, 1982.

Uhlman, Fred   REUNION (Stuttgart)
Two young male friends, one Jewish, the other the son of a count whose family supports Hitler. Their friendship disintegrates, and one is forced to leave Germany. "The novella is simply, elegantly, and sweetly written . . . Arthur Koestler has said of the apparently autobiographical story, 'It is as though Mozart had re-written the Gotterdammerung.'" (FC) FS&G, 1977.

Uris, Leon   ARMAGEDDON: A NOVEL OF BERLIN
See below under "Berlin."

Walser, Martin   RUNAWAY HORSE (Lake Constance)
"A fascinating novella" in which a couple, on their annual visit to a lakeside resort, meet a friend from the husband's youth—"modern philosophical themes through the personae of fascinating characters and their intriguing dialogue." (FC) HR&W, 1980.

Walser, Martin   THE SWAN VILLA (Lake Constance)
A real estate agent's "public and private worth" is tested when a million-dollar villa on Lake Constance is listed for sale. (FC) HR&W, 1982.

Winward, Walter   THE MIDAS TOUCH
"For readers not bored with World War II espionage tales . . . a cliffhanger of a novel" with Allied agents assigned to rescuing Swedish hostages near a ball-bearing factory scheduled for bombing in Schweinfurt. (FC) S&S, 1982.

Wiseman, Thomas   THE DAY BEFORE SUNRISE
A suspense story and "first-rate look at the chaotic situation that existed in Nazi Germany during the last weeks of World War II" as a secret deal is hatched for the

surrender of German generals and to secure files on Germans of importance. (FC)
HR&W, 1976.

Wolf, Christa   NO PLACE ON EARTH
Fashioned from fragments of history, conjecture and imagination and set in a
Rhenish town in 1804. The plot describes an imaginary meeting between two
actual writers of the period at odds with their world. FS&G. 1982.

BERLIN & EAST GERMANY

Baum, Vicki   GRAND HOTEL
Two days in the lives of hotel guests and employees, in Berlin of the 1920s.
Doubleday, 1931.

Becker, Jurek   SLEEPLESS DAYS
A short novel that "evokes the daily grind of an authoritarian society, the
psychic drabness of it all." (BRD) HarBraceJ, 1979.

Buckley, William F.   THE STORY OF HENRI TOD
One of the super-spy Blackford Oakes series, this time concerning the exodus of
East Germans through West Berlin. Doubleday, 1984.

Carroll, James   FAMILY TRADE
A suspense/spy novel involving a rescue from East Berlin, "double and triple
crosses, two love themes, family anguish, patriotic ideals and a sensitive account
of transition from adolescence to adulthood." (FC) Little, 1982.

Clifford, Frances   THE NAKED RUNNER
"A grand, strong thriller" in which a British businessman, attending a trade fair in
Leipzig, agrees to perform an errand for the British secret service and is trapped by
the East Germans. (FC) Coward, 1966.

Deighton, Len   BERLIN GAME
A British agent assists an undercover agent to escape from East Berlin but a
security leak threatens the operation—"elaborately plotted [but] its best moments
derive from the setting [in Berlin] and from the force of this particular setting
upon behavior and psychology." Knopf, 1984. Also *Funeral in Berlin* (1965),
about a Russian scientist smuggled out of East Berlin.

Döblin, Alfred   A PEOPLE BETRAYED
This book and *Karl and Rosa* (1983), are the first two in a
trilogy—"Interweaves the lives of historical personages . . . and fictional
characters to portray the chaos of war and the failure of revolution." (FC) Fromm,
1983 (first published 1948-50).

Fagyas, Maria   COURT OF HONOR
The baroness wife of an army officer is involved in an affair that ends with her
husband's murder—"characters accurately reflect the mores of their milieu" in
pre-World War I Europe; "interesting and entertaining." (FC) S&S, 1978.

Gardner, John   THE GARDEN OF WEAPONS
A German-born British spy has to rescue his team in East Berlin when one of them becomes a double agent. McGraw, 1981.

Hall, Adam   THE QUILLER MEMORANDUM
A spy thriller set in West Berlin—"Englishmen and Germans are cooperating to flush out dangerous Nazis . . . still at large years after World War II." (FC) S&S, 1965.

Higgins, Jack   DAY OF JUDGMENT
Plot concerns the smuggling of people from East Berlin to the West, and a fictional account of Kennedy's visit to Berlin in 1963. R&W, 1979.

Isherwood, Christopher   THE BERLIN STORIES
Stories that reflect life in Berlin in the early 1930s and on which the play *I Am a Camera* and the musical *Cabaret* are based. New Directions, 1954.

Johnson, Uwe   THE THIRD BOOK ABOUT ACHIM
"A somewhat Joycean, somewhat Kafkaesque" story of the author's views on the split in Germany—"offers a dual perspective on life in East Germany." HarBraceJ, 1967. Also *Two Views* (1966), *Speculations About Jacob* (1962).

Kaufelt, David A.   SILVER ROSE
Suspenseful story of a young Jewish woman who assumes the identity of a gentile cabaret singer and succeeds in moving into Hitler's inner circle through marriage to a high-ranking Nazi—"period details and plenty of excitement" for melodrama fans. (FC) Delacorte Pr, 1982.

Kaye, M.M.   DEATH IN BERLIN
Murder mystery set in in West Berlin, 1953. St. Martin, 1984 (first published 1955).

Knebel, Fletcher   CROSSING IN BERLIN
"A tense, exciting, entertaining novel of supense" at the Berlin wall as a woman tries to get out of East Germany. "One should have a taste for unstressed satire and covert irony"—there are "weak, venal, stupid [characters], or the reverse" on each side of the Wall. (FC) Doubleday, 1981.

Kunze, Reiner   THE WONDERFUL YEARS
"49 small portraits and sketches of life behind the Iron Curtain . . . a latter-day Kafkaesque world." (BRD) Braziller, 1977.

Nabokov, Vladimir   THE GIFT
A Russian emigré in Berlin following World War I, his love affair, and literary endeavors. Putnam Pub Group, 1963 (first published 1935). Other novels set in Berlin between the wars are *Mary* (1926), *Laughter in the Dark* (1938), and *King, Queen, Knave* (1928).

Schneider, Peter   THE WALL JUMPER
A novel about the Berlin wall and its narrator's "relationship with and vision of

the divided city . . . and of his friendships with three East Berliners." Marvelous stories of wall-jumpers "balanced between the mythic, and the plausible, boundary-walking tales that create . . . the unreal reality of Berlin." (NYTBR) Pantheon, 1984.

Scholefield, Alan   BERLIN BLIND
The hero becomes involved in a terrorist assassination job in London through an acquaintance from World War II days in Berlin; his wife is killed and he returns to Berlin to find her killers when police fail to do so. Morrow, 1980.

Solmssen, Arthur R.   A PRINCESS IN BERLIN
"Set in inflation-ruined, ideologically seething Berlin during the early 1920s"—an American ex-soldier studying art in Berlin falls in love with a German-Jewish girl but her family is "deaf to his pleas that they leave Berlin or . . . let him marry Lilli and take her to America." (FC) Little, 1980.

Strindberg, August   THE CLOISTER
Incomplete autobiographical novel that covers a period in 1892 after the author's arrival in Berlin. Hill & Wang, 1969.

Trachtenberg, Inge   SO SLOW THE DAWNING
One Jewish family's slow realization of the true nature of Nazism, in the 1930s. Norton, 1973.

Uris, Leon   ARMAGEDDON: A NOVEL OF BERLIN
Saga of Berlin from the end of World War II to the Berlin airlift when the Allies and the Russians first came into conflict over Berlin and its access. There's a love story as well, between an American military government officer and a German girl. Doubleday, 1964.

Winward, Walter   SEVEN MINUTES PAST MIDNIGHT
"A fast-placed, exciting" novel of high-level political maneuvering in the last days of World War II, the author's premise being that Churchill was willing to deal with the Nazis to prevent Soviet postwar expansion in Europe. (FC) S&S, 1980.

TRAVEL ARTICLES

ANTIQUES
1985 Feb "Historic Houses: Epitomizing the Rococo." Prince Michael of Greece, p. 138

ATLANTIC
Aug "East Side, West Side." Berlin. Heidi Landecker, p. 82

ESQUIRE
1984 Jun "Special Places." Trekking lightly (Black Forest). David Butwin, p. 40

GOURMET
Nov "Trier: Germany's Oldest City." Lillian Langseth-Christensen, p. 66

HOUSE & GARDEN

1985 Feb "Bavarian pilgrimage." In search of the haunting masterpieces of Gothic sculptor Tilman Riemenschneider. A. Alvarez, p. 36

N.Y. TIMES SUNDAY TRAVEL SECTION (X)

1985 Jan 6 "What's Doing in Düsseldorf." Stephanie R. Markham, p. 10

Feb 3 "Munich: Lively Gateway to the Alps." Cosmopolitan Munich, Germany's "secret capital." James M. Markham, p. 14

"Wintering Around Munich." An array of Bavarian and Tyrolean ski resorts lies less than two hours away. Hans-Eckart Rubesamen, p. 15

"The City of Nine Seasons." John Dornberg, p. 15

Mar 3 Fare of the Country: "In Bavaria, Beer is Both Food and Drink." John Dornberg, p. 6

Mar 17 "Exploring the Museums of Berlin." Treasures on both sides of the Wall. Michael Ratcliffe, p. 19

(Part 2, "Sophisticated Traveler") "Braunschweig and Beyond." Tips of memorable discoveries. R.W. Apple, Jr., p. 18

Mar 31 (East Germany) "Weimar's Poets in Residence." The East German city celebrates Goethe and Schiller, and even William Shakespeare. Krista Weedman, p. 15

Jun 30 "Augsburg Marks 20 Centuries." Medieval alleys bustle as the city celebrates its heritage. John Dornberg, p. 9

Jul 14 Shopper's World: "Steiff's Lair for Bears." Stephanie R. Markham, p. 12

Jul 28 "Revisiting Ancient Trier." Echoes of Roman Empire linger in the city. James Salter, p. 14

"Meandering Along Germany's Moselle." The valley is rich in castles, half-timbered houses and inns at which to sip the local vintages. James M. Barkham, p. 15

"The Soil and the Vine." Slate and the Riesling grape combine in fine white wines. Frank J. Prial, p. 15

Aug 18 "Einbeck's Historic Bock." Beer. Fred Pieretti, p. 12

Sep 29 "Tracing Germany's Folklore Trail." Grimm brothers world of medieval towns and rustic inns. John Dornberg, p. 14

Nov 3 "A Small Town with a Footnote to History." Nazi A-bomb lab. Malcolm MacPherson, p. 10

Nov 24 "Historic Quarter of Augsburg." John Dornberg, p. 22

Dec 1 "City of Merchants and Mariners." Fiercely independent Bremen revels in being different. John Dornberg, p. 15

Dec 22 "In Germany, Halls Decked Royally." Christmas in a forest and castle hotel in Swabia. R.W. Apple, Jr., p. 15

1984 Mar 11 Fare of the Country: "Hamburg's Way with Eel Soup." Elizabeth Kolbert, p. 6

Apr 8 "Nuremberg Rebuilt: City at the Crossroads." Its 900 years encompasses the contradictions of Germany. John Dornberg, p. 19

Apr 22 Shopper's World: "The Salty Secret of German Pottery." (Hohr-Grenzhausen pottery.) Elizabeth Kolbert, p. 6

May 20 "What's Doing in Berlin." James M. Markham, p. 10

Aug 5 "What's Doing in Cologne." Stephanie R. Markham, p. 10

Sep 23 Fare of the Country: "In Swabia (Stuttgart Area), Mealtime Is Spätzle Time." Elizabeth Kolbert, p. 6

1984   Nov 11 "A Town Unlike Wagner." Bayreuth, home of his festival, is balanced and traditional. Henry Kamm, p. 9
Nov 18 Fare of the Country: "Sailor's Favorite Food (Labskaus) in Hamburg." Sally Hassan, p. 6
Dec 23 Fare of the Country: "Nuremberg's Christmas Cookie." John Dornberg, p. 6

SUNSET
1984   Mar "Wunderbiking or Wunderhiking in Southern Germany." p. 84

TOWN & COUNTRY
1984   Oct Vis-a-vis: "Rhine Wine Country." Peter Dragadze, p. 285

TRAVEL & LEISURE
1985   Feb "The Marvelous Motorcars of Germany: Celebrated in Style at Stuttgart's Daimler-Benz Museum." William Sertl, p. 194
Mar "A Romantic Hotel in Germany." The Eisenhut, nestled within the medieval city of Rothenburg. Michael Walsh, p. 42
May "The Magic of Southern Germany." From the worldly hotels of the Black Forest to the fantasy castles of Bavaria. Richard Covington, p. 104
"Driving and Lingering in Southern Germany." The author's route and where to stay and eat. Richard Covington, p. 112
1984   Feb "The Sumptuous Style of Baden-Baden." A fabled spa in Germany's Black Forest. Malachy Duffy, p. 64
Mar "Ancient Rome on the Banks of the Moselle." Exploring Trier, Germany's oldest city. William H. Marnell, p. 200
Apr "The Romance of Heidelberg." Germany's ageless university town still evokes *The Student Prince*. Helmut Koenig, p. 186
May "In Germany, Kronberg Castle." Fifteen kilometers and a world away from Frankfurt. Paul B. Finney, p. 143
Dec "Munich's Merry Christmas Market." Jean Anderson, p. 72

TRAVEL/HOLIDAY
1985   Apr "Europe's Unique Accommodations: The Aristocratic Domain." Helmut Koenig, p. 73
May "The Pied Piper of Hamelin." Hal Butler, p. 102
Oct "Munich's Lively Restaurant Scene." Great food reigns, from beer-hall casual to three-star elegant. George Lang, p. 36
1984   Feb "Full Spirits Ahead." Munich's festive Fasching. Bill Walker, p. 76
May "Cologne." Perfume, culture and history. Bryce Finley, p. 46

WORLD PRESS REVIEW
1984   May "Germany's Dutch Corner." Aldo Centis (*Tuttoturismo*, Milan), p. 76

GREECE
(Including Cyprus)

Series Guidebooks (See Appendix 1)

American Express: Greece
Baedeker: Greece; Athens
Berlitz: Athens; Corfu; Crete; Greek Islands; Rhodes; Salonica
Blue Guide: Athens & Environs; Greece; Crete; Cyprus
Companion Guide: Mainland Greece; Greek Islands
Fisher: Greece
Fodor: Greece
Frommer: Greece & Istanbul: $-a-Day
Athens City Guide
Let's Go: Greece (Cyprus & Turkish Coast)
Nagel: Greece; Cyprus
U.S. Government: Greece: Area Handbook; Background Notes;
Post Report
Cyprus: Background Notes; Country Study

Background Reading

Amos, H.D. and Lang, A.G.P.   THESE WERE THE GREEKS
"A general introduction to Greek culture . . . they convey much historical fact without losing either the reader's attention or the shape of the period treated." (BL) Dufour, 1982.

Biers, William R.   THE ARCHAEOLOGY OF GREECE
"An overview of Greek art and architecture from Minoan to Hellenistic times . . . functions well as an introduction for lay readers." (BL) Cornell, 1980.

Burn, A.R. and Mary   THE LIVING PAST OF GREECE
Subtitle: A time-traveller's tour of historic and pre-historic places. Visible historic remains described—a companion to Greek history. Little, 1980.

Ceram, C.W.   GODS, GRAVES AND SCHOLARS
The story of archaeology for the general reader/traveler and accounts of discoveries in Crete, Pompeii, Troy, the Middle East. Bantam, 1976.

Cotterell, Arthur   THE MINOAN WORLD
Scribner, 1980.

Crossland, John and Constance, Diana   MACEDONIAN GREECE
"A tantalizing, enthusiastic travelogue" to read in preparation for travel to northern Greece, with emphasis on newly excavated archaeological sites. (BL) Norton, 1982.

Crow, John A.   THE MAGIC SPRING
Cultural history of the main sources of Western civilization for the general reader. Har-Row, 1970.

Davenport, William   ATHENS
One of the Great Cities of the World series. Time-Life, 1978.

Douskou, Iris   ATHENS: THE CITY AND ITS MUSEUMS
Larousse, 1983.

DuBoulay, Juliet   PORTRAIT OF A GREEK MOUNTAIN VILLAGE
A tribute to the traditional culture on the island of Euboea. Oxford U, 1974.

Finley, M.I., ed.   THE LEGACY OF GREECE: A NEW APPRAISAL
A collection of essays on all aspects of Greek civilization, politics and philosophy to myth, arts and influences on Christianity. "Taken together [it] makes a coherent reappraisal of the enduring influence of Greek civilization—down to the present day." (BL) Oxford U, 1981.

**Grant, Michael   FROM ALEXANDER TO CLEOPATRA: THE
                    HELLENISTIC GREECE**
"A deceptively uncomplicated history of a very complicated era. . . . in Mr. Grant's experienced hands, history becomes a revelation." (NYTBR) Scribner, 1982.

Howarth, David A.   THE GREEK ADVENTURE
Subtitle: Lord Byron and other eccentrics in the war of independence. The Greek war of independence of the 1820s enlisted sympathies of well-to-do Western idealists and adventurers who hoped to help Greece revive its ancient glory. Atheneum, 1976.

Kubly, Herbert   GODS AND HEROES
A year spent touring Greece prior to the coup d'etat in 1967. Doubleday, 1969.

Levi, Peter   ATLAS OF THE GREEK WORLD
The text "traces the history and culture of Greece from Minoan times to the Roman conquest . . . augmented by a profuse assortment of maps, photographs, and drawings. . . . special inserts highlight different sites or aspects of Greek life." (BL) Facts On File, 1981.

Longford, Elizabeth   BYRON'S GREECE
Retraces Byron's two Greek journeys, evoking "the Greece that made Byron a poet, as he proclaimed. . . . a judicious balance between travelog and biography." (BRD) Har-Row, 1976.

McGreevy, John, ed.   CITIES
Impressions of world cities as seen through the eyes of people intimately connected with them—for Athens it's Melina Mercouri's impressions. Outlet Bk, 1981.

MacKendrick, Paul L.   THE GREEK STONES SPEAK
An introduction to archaeology and discoveries at Troy and Knossos, "cultural history based on a selection of archaeological evidence." (BL) Norton, 1982 (first published 1962).

Meinardus, Otto   ST. JOHN OF PATMOS AND THE SEVEN CHURCHES OF THE APOCALYPSE
See under "Turkey."

Miller, Helen D.   GREECE THROUGH THE AGES
Greece as seen by travelers from Herodotus to Byron. Funk & Wagnalls, 1972.

PHAIDON CULTURAL GUIDE: GREECE
P-H, 1985.

Roux, Jeanne and Georges   GREECE
How Greece's heritage is linked to Greek life today—"evocative description, scrupulous scholarship and historical and architectural knowledge." (BRD) Oxford U, 1965.

St. Clair, William   THAT GREECE MIGHT STILL BE FREE
Story of the Greek war of independence from the Turks and the nearly 1,000 foreigners (Panhellenes) who joined their fight, and the personalities of figures, such as, Byron associated "with the myth of the glorious fight for Greek freedom." Oxford U, 1972.

Woodford, Susan   THE ART OF GREECE AND ROME
First of a projected series of art histories for general readers and ideal background reading for travel. Cambridge U Pr, 1982.

TRAVEL MEMOIRS

Barret, André   GREECE OBSERVED
Athens and its environs; the history, atmosphere and people of each area. Oxford U, 1974.

Fermor, Patrick L.   ROUMELI: TRAVELS IN NORTHERN GREECE
"Long, probing examination" of the author's adopted homeland—"encyclopedic knowledge and grasp of the language, customs and history bring him into contact with . . . characters far out of reach of the ordinary traveler." Penguin, 1984 (first published 1933). Also *Mani: Travels in the Southern Peloponnese* (1984, first published 1960), of an extraordinary journey through the most remote and wildest region of Greece."

Golding, William   A MOVING TARGET
A collection of the noted author's writings, including a piece on Delphi. FS&G, 1982.

Levi, Peter   THE HILL OF KRONOS
Memoir of several sojourns in Greece "in the best tradition of travel writing . . . also instructive on all manner of things Greek." Dutton, 1981. Also, with photographer Eliot Porter, *The Greek World* (1980)—"joy-sprung and joy-giving book . . . personal survey of the Greek experience both modern and historical." See also *Atlas of the Greek World*, above.

Miller, Henry   THE COLOSSUS OF MAROUSSI
Travel memoir by the noted American writer. New Directions, 1973 (first published 1941).

GUIDEBOOKS

See also Guidebooks listed below under "Greek Islands."

Cox, Thornton   THORNTON COX'S TRAVELLER'S GUIDE TO GREECE
"Highly readable introduction to the area under consideration. . . . necessary data for getting there and getting about . . . suggested itineraries [designed for] economy of time and movement." (Publisher) Hippocrene, 1982.

**Dicks, Brian   GREECE: THE TRAVELLER'S GUIDE TO HISTORY
AND MYTHOLOGY**
David, 1980.

Haag, Michael and Lewis, Neville   TRAVELAID GUIDE TO GREECE
Practical handbook for the independent traveler, for all budgets. Hippocrene, 1984.

Laing, Jennifer   A POCKET GUIDE: THE GREEK AND ROMAN GODS
Handy take-along guide to keep all those statues and myths straight in your mind. David, 1982.

Nicol, Gladys   ATHENS
Batsford, 1978.

GREEK ISLANDS

Bowman, John   TRAVELLERS' GUIDE TO CRETE
One of a series of highly favored guidebooks that are both practical and pleasurable to read. Jonathan Cape, 1979. Also in the series are *Travellers' Guide Rhodes including Kos, Kalymnos, Leros, Patmos and Other Islands in the Dodecanese* (1981) by Jean Currie and *Travellers' Guide Corfu including Lefkas, Ithaca, Cefalenia & the Other Ionian Islands* (1979) by Martin Young.

Dicks, Brian   RHODES
Part of the Islands of the World Series. David, 1974.

DUMONT GUIDE TO THE GREEK ISLANDS
One of a new series of German travel guidebooks with an emphasis on art, history and architecture—for the sophisticated tourist. Stewart, Tabori, 1984.

Durrell, Lawrence   THE GREEK ISLANDS
"Description, history and myth . . . personal reminiscence" by a leading writer in the travel genre. Also, *Reflections on a Marine Venus* (1978), chronicles the author's sojourn on the island of Rhodes with a British occupation unit at the end of World War II. *Prospero's Cell* (1978) is about Corfu, and *Spirit of Place* is a compilation of (Durrell's) fact and fiction (1969) that includes a piece on Corfu. (BRD) Penguin, 1980.

Facaros, Dana   GREEK ISLAND HOPPING
For independent travelers—island descriptions, how to get there, background information on local customs and history, where to stay, and what to do. Hippocrene, 1982.

Mead, Robin   THE GREEK ISLANDS
Batsford, 1979. Also *Crete* (1980) and, by Adam Hopkins, *Corfu* (1980).

Rietveld, Gordon F. and Jane   GREECE: AEGEAN ISLAND GUIDE
Thirty-seven islands divided into five geographic regions, large and small—how to get there, hotels, history, sightseeing, travel tips. P-H, 1982.

CYPRUS

Crawshaw, Nancy   THE CYPRUS REVOLT
The political and military history of the Greek-Cypriot revolt during the 1950s. Allen Unwin, 1978.

Durrell, Lawrence   BITTER LEMONS
Experiences as a visitor, and as a resident teaching English; villages and ways of life in the 1950s. Dutton, 1959.

Hill, Sir G.F.   CYPRUS
A history of the island. Cambrige U Pr, 1972.

Hitchens, Christopher   CYPRUS
Explaining the Greek Cypriot side of the long Greek/Turkish struggles over Cyprus and blaming their plight on "careless and arrogant policies by the British, Greek, American and Turkish governments." (PW) Quartet, 1984.

Lee, Michael and Hanka   CYPRUS
David, 1974.

Thubron, Colin   JOURNEY INTO CYPRUS
Heinemann, 1975.

HISTORY

Clogg, R.   A SHORT HISTORY OF MODERN GREECE
Cambridge U Pr, 1979.

Woodhouse, Christopher M.   MODERN GREECE: A SHORT HISTORY
Faber & Faber, 1984.

Novels

Aiken, Joan   LAST MOVEMENT
An English girl visiting the island of Dendros becomes involved in romance and mystery. Doubleday, 1977. Also *A Cluster of Separate Sparks* (1972), set on Dendros.

Ambler, Eric   A COFFIN FOR DIMITRIOS
"An English writer traces the life history of a nondescript Greek fig-picker" to explain his criminal record and death—"social comment, authentic current history ... at the same time providing all the surprises ... that every thriller needs." (FC) Knopf, 1939.

Crane, Stephen   ACTIVE SERVICE
In *The Complete Novels of Stephen Crane*. Doubleday, 1967 (first published 1899).

Dickinson, Peter   THE LIZARD IN THE CUP
Suspense novel involving the drug traffic—"not only a travelogue about one of the Greek Islands [but] about people [who] talk as people really talk." (FC) Har-Row, 1972.

Durrell, Lawrence   TUNC
An inventor recounts his strange adventures in business, love, marriage. Set in Athens, Istanbul and London—"Athens . . . is vividly with us in this book." (FC) Dutton, 1968.

Fallaci, Oriana   A MAN
The tragedy of Allessandro Panagoulis, who tried to assassinate dictator George Papadopoulis, failed, and was imprisoned, tortured and finally murdered in 1976—told as fiction. The author selects "from the particulars of this one man's life to fashion clearsighted analyses into the nature of politics and power." (FC) S&S, 1980.

Fowles, John   THE MAGUS
The "harrowing misadventures" of a British schoolteacher who takes a teaching job on the island of Phraxos—"engrossing entertainment [blending] sensuous realism, suspenseful romanticism, hypertheatrical mystification . . . a gallery of unusual or exotic characters . . . vivid setting . . . of an isolated Greek island." (FC) Little, 1978 (first published 1966).

Haviaras, Stratis   THE HEROIC AGE
Tells how thousands of children became the army of a socialist faction in the civil war that followed World War II, ending up with the teenage-led guerillas in the stone caves of Mount Grammos. S&S, 1984. Also *When the Tree Sings* (1979), about the German occupation of Greece in World War II.

Hodge, Jane A.   STRANGERS IN COMPANY
Intrigue and romance as two women with a guided-tour bus group become unwilling participants in a plot to free a political prisoner because one of them is the prisoner's look-alike. Coward, 1973.

Kaye, M.M.   DEATH IN CYPRUS
"A romantic mystery cum travelogue. . . . Originally published in 1956 and revised. . . . The heroine is a hopelessly naive 20-year-old . . . who finds more than she bargained for when she embarks on a vacation to sunny Cyprus." (FC) St. Martin, 1984 (first published 1956).

Kazantzakis, Nikos   ZORBA THE GREEK (Crete)
The adventures and philosophy of Zorba ("hedonist raconteur and roué"), narrated by his employer ("a rich and cultivated dilettante"). "It is in every sense a minor classic. . . . among the significant and permanent characters in modern fiction." (FC) S&S, 1952. Also *The Fratricides* (1964), a "modern parable" of a priest's attempts to mediate between Communists and Loyalists in the Greek civil wars of the 1940s, and *Freedom or Death* (1956), about the Cretan Revolt of 1889.

MacInnes, Helen   DECISION AT DELPHI
Plot revolves about two friends sent to Greece on a magazine assignment; one, a Greek-American, disappears en route—"landscapes from Taormina to Sparta, all freshly observed" and the Acropolis, the streets of Athens are part of the plot's action, with a "panoramic finale on the noble heights of Delphi." (FC) HarBraceJ, 1960.

MacInnes, Helen   THE DOUBLE IMAGE (Mykonos)
The plot is about a supposedly-dead Nazi war criminal—"an intelligent amateur [becomes] part of the mixed crew of agents, double agents and bystanders involved in Operation Pear Tree" on Mykonos. HarBraceJ, 1966.

Read, Miss   FARTHER AFIELD (Crete)
The noted author of the "Miss Read" novels of English village life is also far afield in this story of two British ladies who vacation in Greece and return to England better able to cope with their respective single and married states. Houghton, 1975.

Rumanes, G.N.   THE MAN WITH THE BLACK WORRY BEADS (Piraeus)
"Masterful, fast moving" story of an underground leader during the German occupation who uses his relationship with the German commandant's mistress to sabotage shipments from Piraeus to Rommel's African campaign. (FC) Arthur Fields Bks, 1973.

Sarton, May   JOANNA & ULYSSES
A young woman on an idyllic holiday on a Greek island rescues a little donkey from ill-treatment and in the process recovers herself from a decade of family troubles. Norton, 1963.

Stewart, J.I.M.   VANDERLYN'S KINGDOM
Narrated by a "narrowly-educated Oxford don"—the plot is about a wealthy, art-loving American who buys an Aegean island as "prince of his own highly civilized court." For "Hardy enthusiasts and those who like a hypnotic sense of place." (FC) Norton, 1968.

Stewart, Mary   THIS ROUGH MAGIC (Corfu)
An English actress, vacationing on the isle reputed to be the setting of Shakespeare's *Tempest*, becomes involved in a smuggling plot. Morrow, 1964. Also by Miss Stewart, are mystery-romances set in Crete and Delphi, respectively, *The Moon Spinners* (1963) and *My Brother Michael* (1960).

Vassilikos, Vassilis   Z (Salonika)
The assassination of a left-wing deputy in 1963, based on the actual, brutal assassination of Deputy Lambrakis. FS&G, 1968.

Vrettos, Theodore   LORD ELGIN'S LADY
"A most intriguing" and fictionalized version of an event in art history when the Parthenon statues were moved from Athens to England in the early 1800s, and the event's effect on the marriage of Lord and Lady Elgin. (FC) Houghton, 1982.

ANCIENT GREECE

Caldwell, Taylor   GLORY AND THE LIGHTNING
The love story of Pericles and Aspasia—"Greek tragedy [reduced] to the level of soap opera . . . features torrid sex, violence, and an espousal of women's libera-tion." (FC) Doubleday, 1974.

Graves, Robert   HERCULES, MY SHIPMATE
Story of Jason and the Argonauts in quest of the golden fleece—"marked factual quality . . . painstakingness of the [voyage's] details . . . a lively story . . . of violent death, double-dealing, grand larceny and seduction. . . . A remarkable book." (FC) Creative Age, 1945.

Kazantzakis, Nikos   ALEXANDER THE GREAT
"An idealized and sentimental biography," first published in Greece in 1940 as a serial—"edifying and enjoyable reading" of Greek history. (FC) Ohio U, 1982.

Renault, Mary   FIRE FROM HEAVEN
This, *Persian Boy* (1972) and *Funeral Games* (1981), comprise a fictionalized version of the story of Alexander the Great—"an astounding grasp of the facts and the spirit of the ancient world . . . brings to life a great historical period." Pantheon, 1969.

Renault, Mary   THE KING MUST DIE
The story of Theseus, followed by its sequel *The Bull from the Sea* (1962). Others in the series of masterful novels by this author: *The Praise Singer* (1978), based on the story of Simonides; *The Mask of Apollo* (1966), about an actor's life in Syracuse and Athens in the fourth century B.C.; *The Last of the Wine* (1956), which recreates what it was like to be a well-to-do Athenian youth of that day as one of Socrates' pupils. Pantheon, 1958.

Vidal, Gore   CREATION
A rewarding historical novel that "dodges sensationalism"; a Persian diplomat in Periclean Athens dictates his memoirs "to correct the obfuscations of Herodotus . . . in recent years there has been no historical novel remotely like it." (FC) Random, 1981.

Wilder, Thornton   THE WOMAN OF ANDROS (Island of Byrnos)
The Woman of Andros, bound with Wilder's *The Cabala*, is based on a comedy by Terence. Har-Row, 1968 (first published 1930).

TRAVEL ARTICLES

ARCHITECTURAL DIGEST
1984 Jun "Glimpses of Global Treasures." Great museums in China, Greece and Russia, p. 218.

BLACK ENTERPRISE
1984 Aug "Sun and Antiquity in Athens." Lovett S. Gray, p. 75

CONNOISSEUR
1985 May "Briefing Paper." Letter from the Aegean (tips on cruising the Greek Islands). Carol Burden, p. 108

GOURMET
1984 Mar "Greece and the Olympic Games." Paul J. Wade, p. 28
     Oct "Northern Greece." Doone Beal, p. 60

HARPER'S BAZAAR
1985 Nov "Acropolis Now." Christopher Hitchens, p. 30

N.Y. TIMES SUNDAY TRAVEL SECTION (X)
1985 Feb 3 "On Skyros, an Ancient Rite." In spring, island shepherds pay homage to a wild Greek god. Fergus M. Bordewich, p. 21
     Apr 14 "Patmos: Isle of the Apocalypse." The treasures of St. John's shrine. Fergus M. Bordewich, p. 9
     Aug 4 "Ithaca: Odysseus' Isle." Sites from an epic enrich a visit. Edward Tick, p. 10
     Sep 1 Shopper's World: Mykonos Warmth Is More than Sun. Jan Shannon, p. 11

Nov 3 "Greece's Stubborn Island Fortress." Monemvasia. C.L. Sulzberger, p. 6

1984 Jan 15 "Rediscovering the Art of Iconography." Contemporary revival of a Byzantine art. David Plante, p. 19

Mar 18 "Socrates Spoke Here." The Agora evokes a lively tale of ancient Greece. Robert W. Stock, p. 41

Mar 25 "What's Doing in Athens." Paul Anastasi, p. 10

(Cyprus) "The Land of Aphrodite." Sara Caudwell, p. 27

Apr 8 "At Home in a Greek Village." A few remote places still offer the lure of belonging. Edmund Keeley, p. 14

"For Santorini Visitors, Restored Houses." A bit of tradition is for rent in little Oia. Robert W. Stock, p. 15

May 13 "Rite of Fire on a Greek Isle." Marvine Howe, p. 24

Jun 3 "Kastoria, City of Mink." Fur town on the Yugoslavia/Albania border of Greece. Margot Granitas, p. 24

Aug 12 "In Search of the Ultimate Island." Frederic Raphael, p. 14

Oct 7 (Part 2, "Sophisticated Traveler") "Possessed by Epirus." An ancient and much contested land revisited. Nicholas Gage, p. 33

Oct 14 "A Monument of Byzantium." Frescoes in Sparta and Mistra. Fergus M. Bordewich, p. 9

Nov 18 "A Deluxe Haven Outside Athens." Astis Palace. Janet Maslin, p. 22

Dec 2 "What's Doing in Athens." Henry Kamm, p. 10

SUNSET

1985 Apr "A Week of Cruising the Greek Islands by Motor Yacht." p. 108

TRAVEL & LEISURE

1985 Mar "A Morning at the Athens Archaeological Museum." Alexander and Jane Eliot, p. 140

Apr "Mykonos." A luscious Greek isle of crystalline beaches, dazzling white houses—and show-stopping people. Alexander and Jane Eliot, p. 106

Nov "A Greek Island Escape." Castellorizo, an idyllic retreat 80 miles and a world away from Rhodes. Jennifer Quale, p. 51

1984 Mar "A Revelation in Athens." Moment when time stood still above the Acropolis. John F. West, p. 172

Jul "A Pilgrimage to Mount Olympus." Seeking ancient gods in modern Greece, Abby Rand, p. 14

Oct Travel & Architecture: "The Brilliance of the Byzantine." In Istanbul, Venice and the Greek isles. Alexander Eliot, p. 26

TRAVEL/HOLIDAY

1984 Mar "Timeless Northern Greece. Celebrating an Age-Old Tradition." Robert S. Kane, p. 84

HUNGARY

Note: Books and novels on the Hapsburg monarchy and the Austro-Hungarian Empire, listed under "Austria," are also relevant.

Series Guidebooks (See Appendix 1)

Berlitz: Budapest; Hungary
Fodor: Eastern Europe
Frommer: Austria & Hungary: Dollarwise
Nagel: Hungary
U.S. Government: Hungary: Area Handbook; Background Notes;
             Post Report

Background Reading

Dobai, Peter   BUDAPEST
A photographic essay. Ungar, 1982.

Meray, Tibor   THAT DAY IN BUDAPEST—OCTOBER 23, 1956
Hour-by-hour description of the events of the uprising against the Soviets. Funk & Wagnalls, 1969.

Michener, James A.   THE BRIDGE AT ANDAU
A "first hand account of the revolt against the Soviets in Hungary in 1956" and refugees in Vienna. Fawcett, 1978 (first published 1957).

Porter, Monica   THE PAPER BRIDGE: A RETURN TO BUDAPEST
Affecting story of a woman's return to Budapest in search of her roots, twenty-five years after fleeing the 1956 revolution. Quartet, 1982.

Starkie, Walter   RAGGLE TAGGLE
An unconventional and adventurous travel memoir of pre-World War II Hungary. A professor-vagabond "fiddles" his way across Hungary living with peasants and gypsies—adventure, travel and music. Transatlantic, 1964 (first published 1933).

Völgyes, Ivan   HUNGARY: A NATION OF CONTRADICTIONS
"An excellent brief introduction to Hungary for students as well as tourists," by an expatriate professor. (BRD) Westview Pr, 1982.

GUIDEBOOKS

Halasz, Zoltan, ed.   HUNGARY: A GUIDE WITH A DIFFERENCE
History, many chapters on cultural life, and standard guide material. Ungar, 1982.

McNair-Wilson, Diana   HUNGARY
Batsford, 1976.

Rohonyi, K. and Marot, M.   BUDAPEST: WALKING AROUND
Vanous, 1976.

Wellner, Istvan   BUDAPEST: A COMPLETE GUIDE
Heinman, 1982.

HISTORY

Ignotus, Paul   HUNGARY
Praeger, 1972.

Sinor, Denis   HISTORY OF HUNGARY
Greenwood, 1976 (first published 1959).

Novels

Blackstock, Charity   THE KNOCK AT MIDNIGHT
The summer of 1938—a Scottish girl stays on in Hungary to rescue a Jewish friend. Coward, 1967.

Bridge, Ann   THE TIGHTENING STRING
The wife of a British diplomat devotes her time to POW relief—a "picture of a lovely, aristocratic old world [Hungary] giving way before the onslaught of World War II." (FC) McGraw, 1962.

Elman, Richard M.   THE 28TH DAY OF ELUL
This, *Lilo's Diary* (1968) and *The Reckoning* (1969), form a trilogy about the town of Clig, Hungary—a portrait of the town and its inhabitants. Scribner, 1967.

Holland, Cecelia   ROKÓSSY
Historical novel of sixteenth-century Hungary during a period of Turkish incursions. Atheneum, 1967.

Konrád, George   THE CASE WORKER
A case worker in Budapest struggles to find "philosophical equilibrium" to survive the daily horrors he faces in his job ministering to the lowest depths in Budapest society. (FC) HarBraceJ, 1974.

Pearson, Diane   CSARDAS
Saga of the Ferenc family "who are as enslaved to their [aristocratic] social class as are the peasants." Their fortunes crumble before two wars and communism and, symbolically, a peasant boy "rises well above his class and eventually marries into the Ferenc family." (FC) Lippincott, 1975.

Sjöwall, Maj   THE MAN WHO WENT UP IN SMOKE
By the noted Swedish writer of detective stories; this is about a missing Swedish journalist—"rich . . . sojourn in Budapest." (FC) Random, 1976.

Wiesel, Elie   THE TOWN BEYOND THE WALL
A survivor of concentration camps returns at great risk to his hometown in Hungary to find a man whose face has haunted him over the years, the man who stood impassively in the town square as Jews were carried off. He does locate the man, only to be arrested by the Russians as a spy. HR&W, 1967.

Zilahy, Lajos   CENTURY IN SCARLET
Saga of the Dukay family from 1815 to World War I. McGraw, 1965.

TRAVEL ARTICLES

CONNOISSEUR
1985 Mar "The Hungarian Experience . . . Offers Many Western Pleasures—With a Difference." Anthony Astrachan, p. 94
"Back to Budapest." A native son returns to review the pleasures of Hungary's lively capital. George Lang, p. 101
"Magnificent Esterháza." Life and music have returned to a great Hungarian palace. Robert Wernick, p. 110

50 PLUS
1984 May "If It's Mother's Day, This Must Be Budapest." Emoke de Papp Severo, p. 46

GLAMOUR
1985 Dec "Vienna and Budapest." p. 198

N.Y. TIMES SUNDAY TRAVEL SECTION (X)
1985 Oct 13 "Hungary's Versailles." Newly Restored, the Home of Prince Nikolaus Esterhazy. Paul Lewis, p. 9
1984 Feb 26 "By the Waters of Budapest." Dipping into a tradition at the baths. Andrew Marton, p. 12

TRAVEL & LEISURE
1985 Apr "An Artist's Colony on the Danube." Szentendre, a charming Hungarian village just upriver from Budapest. Robert L. Sammons, p. 33
1984 Jun "Skimming Along the Danube from Vienna to Budapest." A scenic hydrofoil ride between two great capitals. Wallace White, p. 154

TRAVEL/HOLIDAY
1985 Mar "Oh, So Romantic Budapest." The allure of Hungary's Danube City. Abby Rand, p. 64

WORLD PRESS REVIEW
1984 Jul "Hungary's Exuberant Charm." Gerit Overdijkink (*Het Parool*, Amsterdam), p. 62

ICELAND

Note: See also all asterisked (*) entries under "Denmark" for books on Scandinavia as a whole, as well as the books listed under "Denmark/Vikings."

Series Guidebooks (See Appendix 1)

Fodor: Scandinavia; Budget Scandinavia;
            Stockholm, Copenhagen, Oslo, Helsinki & Reykjavik
Nagel: Iceland
U.S. Government: Iceland: Background Notes

Background Reading

Auden, W.H. and MacNeice, L.   LETTERS FROM ICELAND
Two young poets on a trip to Iceland record their impressions in prose and
verse. Random, 1969 (first published 1937).

**Hannesson, Gunnar   REYKJAVIK: A PANORAMA IN FOUR
                         SEASONS**
Heinman, 1974.

Jones, Gwyn   NORSE ATLANTIC SAGA
A dramatic narrative history of the Norse voyages of discovery and settlement in
Iceland (and Greenland). Oxford U, 1964.

Linklater, Eric   THE ULTIMATE VIKING
An informal history of the Viking heroes of the Orkney Islands and Iceland—"a
fascinating epic . . . in heroic prose, peppered with dry witticisms." HarBraceJ,
1956.

Magnussen, S.   ICELAND: COUNTRY AND PEOPLE
Vanous, 1978.

Magnússon, Sigurdur   NORTHERN SPHINX
A general introduction to Iceland—settlement and history from A.D. 900 to
present, the Icelandic people, state of commerce, industry, literature, arts, music.
McGill-Queens U, 1977.

Magnússon, Sigurdur   STALLION OF THE NORTH
History and role of the distinctive breed of horse produced in Iceland. Longship
Pr, 1979.

Morris, Jan   PLACES
This collection of travel essays by a leading travel writer includes an essay on
Iceland. HarBraceJ, 1972.

Saunders, Pamela   ICELAND
Based on a series of trips with photographer Roloff Beny; tells of visits to
persons and places, including Halldór Laxness (the Nobel prize-winning novelist),
Thingvellir (birthplace of the country in 930), with generous quotes from
Icelandic sagas. "A striking informal introduction to Ultima Thule, and end of the
world." (BL) Salem Hse, 1985.

Scherman, Katharine   DAUGHTER OF FIRE
Leisurely, detailed, evocative travel book telling of a series of trips made by the
free-lance writer, with much description of nature and birds. Little, 1976.

HISTORY

Griffith, John C.   MODERN ICELAND
Praeger, 1969.

Stefansson, Vilhjalmur   ICELAND: THE FIRST AMERICAN REPUBLIC
A history and study of an island that was a republic by A.D. 900 and once had
peasants who spoke Latin—from settlement to contemporary times. Greenwood,
1971 (first published 1939).

Novels

Cooper, Dominic   MEN AT AXLIR
Story of a violent family feud in eighteenth-century Iceland—harsh passions in a
harsh land. St. Martin, 1980.

Gunnarsson, Gunnar   THE GOOD SHEPHERD
The life of a shepherd and his dog in the isolated and rugged mountains of
Iceland. Bobbs, 1940 (first published 1910).

Gunnarsson, Gunnar   THE BLACK CLIFFS
Story based on an actual nineteenth-century murder. U of Wisconsin, 1967 (first
published 1929).

Holland, Cecelia   TWO RAVENS
Historic novel set in twelfth-century Iceland involving family feuds and con-
flicts between those converted to Christianity and those who remained loyal to
Icelandic pagan beliefs. Knopf, 1977.

Laxness, Halldór   FISH CAN SING
Contrasts the simple life-style and unworldly values of fishermen in Iceland
with those who have come in contact with a more sophisticated world. Laxness is
a major Icelandic writer who has won a Nobel Prize for his literature. Also *Independent People* (1946), a story of sheep-raising and rural life in Iceland, and
World Light (1969), based on the life of Icelandic poet Magnusson. Crowell, 1967.

Laxness, Halldór   PARADISE RECLAIMED
Story of a man's pilgrimage, as a Mormon convert, from Iceland to Utah in the
nineteenth century. Crowell, 1962.

Seton, Anya   AVALON
A recreation, from early Anglo-Saxon and French manuscripts, of eleventh-
century England and the lands colonized by Norsemen (Iceland). Houghton,
1965.

ESQUIRE
1984 Oct "Fantasy Iceland." Welcome to the Great Gray North, where there are
    four sheep to every human, several excellent paved roads, and the best
    disco within driving distance of the Arctic Circle. Lewis Grossberger, p. 66

NATIONAL GEOGRAPHIC
1984 Sep "Running a Wild Glacier River in Iceland." Paul Vander-Molen, p. 306

VOGUE
1985 Jun "Icelandic Summer: An Encounter with the Wildest, Most Un-
    spoiled—and the Most Literate—Country on Earth." John J. Norwich, p. 179

IRELAND

Note: See also all asterisked entries (*) under "England" for additional Series
Guides, background books, and articles that may include Ireland.

Series Guidebooks

Berlitz: **Ireland**
Birnbaum: **Great Britain & Ireland**
Blue Guide: **Ireland**
Companion Guide: **Ireland**
Fodor: Ireland
Frommer: Ireland: **$-a-Day; Dublin & Ireland City Guide**
Let's Go: Britain & Ireland (Scotland & Wales)
Nagel: Ireland
U.S. Government: Ireland: Background Notes; Post Report

Background Reading

Connery, Donald S.   THE IRISH
    A look at Ireland—"a reasoned, objective study [in] lively journalistic style."
(BRD) S&S, 1968.

DeBreffny, Brian   IRELAND: A CULTURAL ENCYCLOPEDIA
    The most recent of three books that taken together, provide great background

for a trip to Ireland. The *Encyclopedia* "provides 600 entries on a wide range of cultural subjects extending from the Abbey Theatre to William Butler Yeats." (LJ) Facts On File, 1984. *The Irish World* (1977) is a "chronicle of Ireland . . . by eleven superb scholars of Irish history, art, archaeology, architecture and religion." (BRD) Finally there is *The Land of Ireland* (1979), a collection of photographs with some accompanying text on history, description and travel.

Dillon, Eilís   INSIDE IRELAND
"Splendidly evocative photographs" and text by an Irish novelist—"relates the prickly history of Ireland . . . in terms of her own family and personal life . . . remarkably intimate feel for the ways [of] the politics and culture of Ireland today." (BL) Hodder & Stoughton, 1984.

Feldkamp, Frederick   NOT EVERYBODY'S EUROPE
A grand tour of nine unique places to think about adding to your itinerary—in Ireland it's Tralee and the Dingle Peninsula. Harper's Magazine Pr, 1976.

FitzGibbon, Constantine   THE IRISH IN IRELAND
"Probes the meaning of the intrinsic qualities of the Irish people through an in-depth searching of the island's history." (BL) David, 1983.

Kee, Robert   IRELAND
A beginner's guide to the intricacies of Irish history, based on the BBC television series, identifying the themes, trends and individuals important in the sweep of national devlopment." Little, 1982. Also *The Green Flag* (1972), which is a history of the movement for the establishment of the Irish Free State in 1922.

Kimbrough, Emily   TIME ENOUGH
Reprint of a travelogue about a holiday cruise up the River Shannon. Book & Tackle, 1984 (first published 1974).

McHugh, Roger, ed.   IRELAND
Contemporary accounts of Easter Week 1916, about participants and eyewitnesses to the events of that historic week in Irish history. Hawthorn Bks, 1966.

Morris, Jan   PLACES
This collection of travel essays by the noted travel writer contains an essay on Ireland. HarBraceJ, 1973.

Morton, H.V.   IN SEARCH OF IRELAND
"To encourage the English to become acquainted" with the country and first published just eight years after Irish independence—"the book's observations are [still] completely up-to-date." Dodd, 1984 (first published 1930). See also *Morton's Britain* under "England."

Murphy, Dervla   IRELAND
"Ireland in terms of four modern revolutions: economic, journalistic, historigraphical and theological . . . freewheeling, whimsical, thoroughly engag-

ing. . . . probes the Irish psyche, culture, politics, English and Irish violence, the arts, economics and the sexual revolution." (BL) Salem Hse, 1985.

Murphy, Dervla   WHEELS WITHIN WHEELS
"Unraveling an Irish past" is the subtitle; by one of the leading contemporary travel writers who has traveled by bicycle (and written about it) in Europe, Asia and South America. Ticknor & Fields, 1980.

O'Brien, Edna   MOTHER IRELAND
The "mystique of Ireland"—history, mythology, the land, the people, books, plays, religion, Dublin. HarBraceJ, 1976.

O'Faolain, Sean   THE IRISH: A CHARACTER STUDY
The development of Ireland from its Celtic beginnings—"urban, shrewd, witty" and considered one of the best books on the Irish. (BRD) Devin, 1979 (first published 1949).

Olbricht, Klaus-Hartmut and Wegener, Helga M.   IRISH HOUSES:
HISTORY, ARCHITEC-
TURE, FURNISHING
An "impressive sampling" for the tourist of a range of architecture from Georgian town houses to castles with introductory history of each, ownership, workmanship, points of interest, location, hours. (BL) Salem Hse, 1985.

Plunkett, James   THE GEMS SHE WORE
"A personal journey [and] salute to Ireland's past . . . warm, charming, informative . . . a lovely piece of writing." (TL) Hutchinson, 1978. See also *Strumpet City* (1972) and *Farewell Companions* (1978), listed below under "Novels."

Ryan, Kathleen Jo and Share, Bernard, eds.   IRISH TRADITIONS
"17 short, bright essays by Irish specialists in fiction, poetry, archaeology, architecture, sports, art and other fields . . . from prehistoric people to neighborliness in rural areas." (BL) Abrams, 1985.

Shannon, Elizabeth   UP IN THE PARK
Diary of the wife of the American ambassador to Ireland, 1977-1981. Atheneum, 1983.

Smith, J.C.   THE CHILDREN OF MASTER O'ROURKE
Saga of one family as a microcosm of contemporary Ireland. (BRD) HR&W, 1977.

Somerville-Large, Peter   THE GRAND IRISH TOUR
Description and travel by a major writer about Ireland. See below for other titles by the author. Hamish Hamilton, 1983.

Tall, Deborah   THE ISLAND OF THE WHITE COW: MEMORIES OF AN
IRISH ISLAND
A record and "affectionate elegy for a way of life" of an American poet and an Irish professor, 1972-77. (PW) Atheneum, 1985.

Taylor, Sybil   IRELAND'S PUBS
Pubs of Dublin and the countryside. Penguin, 1983.

Thomson, David   WOODBROOK
The author spent ten summers (1932-42) as a tutor in an old Anglo-Irish family in West Ireland. This account of those years is at once a picture of country life then, personal observations and a love story. Penguin, 1981.

Uris, Jill   IRELAND REVISITED
A follow up to *Ireland: A Terrible Beauty* (1978), combined with relevant quotes from Irish writers. Doubleday, 1982.

Veber, May   IRELAND OBSERVED
Historical and cultural text and photographs provide a "sharp capsule of Ireland's appearance." Includes a brief history and information on pub life, drama, art, museums. (BL) Oxford U, 1980.

DUBLIN

See also books listed under "Literary Guides and Theater in Ireland," below.

Bowen, Elizabeth   SEVEN WINTERS
Memories of a Dublin childhood. Century, 1980 (first published 1962).

Lehane, B.   DUBLIN
One of the Great Cities of the World series. Time-Life, 1979.

McGreevy, John, ed.   CITIES
Impressions of world cities as seen through the eyes of people intimately connected with them—for Dublin it's John Huston's impressions. Outlet Bk, 1981.

Morris, Jan   TRAVELS
This collection of essays by the celebrated travel writer includes an essay on Dublin. HarBraceJ, 1976.

Pritchett, V.S.   DUBLIN, A PORTRAIT
"Delightful . . . perceptive" text, by the noted travel writer, and photographs. (BRD) Har-Row, 1967.

Somerville-Large, Peter   DUBLIN
History, people, artistic achievements, events, that have created this city and its past. Hamish Hamilton, 1979.

LITERARY GUIDES AND THEATER IN IRELAND

Bidwell, Bruce and Heffer, Linda   THE JOYCEAN WAY
A topographic guide to *Dubliners* and *A Portrait of the Artist as a Young Man*. Johns Hopkins U, 1982.

Byrne, Dawson   THE STORY OF IRELAND'S NATIONAL THEATRE
The Abbey Theatre, Dublin. Haskell, 1971 (first published 1929).

Cahill, Susan and Thomas   A LITERARY GUIDE TO IRELAND
Takes one through the literary landscape of Ireland's greatest writers—the
spires and towers of Swift, Yeats's lakes and mountains, Joyce's streets and strands,
Synge's glens, and Behan's pubs. Scribner, 1979.

**Carpenter, Andrew and Fallon, Peter   THE WRITERS: A SENSE
                                          OF IRELAND**
"Glimpses of recent work by 144 contemporary Irish writers." (PW) O'Brien Pr,
1982.

**Delaney, Frank   JAMES JOYCE'S ODYSSEY: A GUIDE TO THE
                    DUBLIN OF ULYSSES**
An "ingratiating guide [with photographs] to Joyce's *Ulysses*, to the actual city of
Dublin . . . on June 16, 1904, and to the city as it exists today." Its eighteen chapters
correspond to eighteen in the novel, and there are maps tracing movements of the
characters. (PW) HR&W, 1982.

Hunt, Hugh   THE ABBEY: IRELAND'S NATIONAL THEATRE
A history commissioned to celebrate the Theatre's seventy-fifth birthday.
Columbia, 1979.

Kenny, Herbert A.   LITERARY DUBLIN
"Survey and appreciation of Ireland's writers and writing from Celtic origins to
the present." (BRD) Taplinger, 1974.

O'Farrell, Padraic   SHANNON THROUGH HER LITERATURE
Mercier Pr, 1983.

O'Haodha, Michael   THEATRE IN IRELAND
Theater, dramatists, actors, etc. through history. Rowman, 1974.

Trevor, William   A WRITER'S IRELAND: LANDSCAPE IN LITERATURE
"A walk through [Ireland's] history with native writers (from Yeats to Seamus
Heaney), who have been inspired by the events and landscape of their homeland."
(BL) Viking, 1984.

SOME IRISH LIVES, ECCENTRIC AND OTHERWISE

**Court, Artelia   PUCK OF THE DROMS: THE LIVES AND LITERATURE OF
                    THE IRISH TINKERS**
Scholarly overview of a unique sub-culture—the life-style of "travelers" in
biographies of three of them in their own words and collected songs, folklore,
poems. U of California, 1985.

Gmelch, Susan   TINKERS AND TRAVELLERS: IRELAND'S NOMADS
O'Brien Pr, 1979.

Millman, Lawrence   OUR LIKE WILL NOT BE THERE AGAIN
Notes from the West of Ireland—recorded conversations with local folk. Little, 1977.

O'Hanlon, Thomas J.   IRISH . . .
"Sinners, saints, gamblers, gentry, priests, Maoists, rebels, Tories, Orangemen, dippers, heroes, villains, and other proud natives of the fabled isle." (BRD) Har-Row, 1975.

Scherman, Katherine   THE FLOWERING OF IRELAND: SAINTS, SCHOLARS AND KINGS
"Colorful figures" from the Ice Age through the Norman Period, written with "great flair." (PW) Little, 1981.

Somerville-Large, Peter   IRISH ECCENTRICS: A SELECTION
Fifteenth- to twentieth-century eccentric figures. Har-Row, 1975.

Wallace, Martin   100 IRISH LIVES
Biographies, historic sites. David, 1983.

Wiedel, Janine, ed.   IRISH TINKERS
Text, quotes of the tinkers, photos. St. Martin, 1979.

GUIDEBOOKS

Clarke, Desmond   DUBLIN
Batsford, 1977.

Cox, Thornton   THORNTON COX'S TRAVELLERS' GUIDE TO IRELAND
"Highly readable introduction to the area under consideration . . . necessary data for getting there and getting about . . . suggested itineraries [designed for] economy of time and movement." (Publisher) Hippocrene, 1982.

Day, Catharina   AROUND IRELAND
Part of the "Island Hopping" series of guides for independent travelers—island descriptions, how to get there, background information on local customs and history, where to stay and what to do. Hippocrene, 1982.

DUMONT GUIDE TO IRELAND
One of a new series of German travel guidebooks. Emphasis is on art, history, architecture—"for the sophisticated tourist." (BL) Stewart, Tabori, 1984.

Green, Kerry and Leocha, Charles   THE WHOLE EUROPE ESCAPE MANUAL: U.K./IRELAND
Part of a new series of guidebooks "designed to . . . put the fantasy and excitement back into travel." (Publisher) World Leis Corp, 1985.

McLellan, Robert   ISLE OF ARRAN
Part of Islands of the World Series. David, 1976. Also *Aran Islands* (1973) by Daphne Pochin-Mould.

HISTORY

Bottigheimer, Karl S.   IRELAND AND THE IRISH: A SHORT HISTORY
Columbia U Pr, 1982.

Inglis, Brian   THE STORY OF IRELAND
Considered to be a readable history with an unbiased viewpoint and one of the best introductory histories. Faber, 1958.

MacManus, Seumas   THE STORY OF THE IRISH RACE
Devin-Adair, rev. ed. 1968 (first published 1921).

Neill, Kenneth   AN ILLUSTRATED HISTORY OF THE IRISH PEOPLE
Mayflower, 1980.

Ranelagh, John O'B.   A SHORT HISTORY OF IRELAND
Cambridge U Pr, 1983. Also *Ireland: An Illustrated History* (1981).

Woodham-Smith, Cecil   THE GREAT HUNGER
Story of the famine of the 1840s that killed a million Irish peasants, sent hundreds of thousands to the New World, and influenced history down to the present day. Har-Row, 1962.

Novels

Bernen, Robert   TALES FROM THE BLUE STACKS (Donegal)
"Stories of the uncanny ways of sheep and sheep dogs, intransigence of the land . . . idiosyncrasies of the farmers" in a rugged, Gaelic-speaking area of Donegal. (FC) Scribner, 1978. And also *The Hills: More Tales from the Blue Stacks* (1984).

Binchy, Maeve   LIGHT A PENNY CANDLE
Chronicle of a friendship between two women beginning with Elizabeth's evacuation to Ireland during the blitz in World War II, to mutual widowhood. Viking, 1983.

Christopher, John   THE LITTLE PEOPLE
A young woman inherits a castle, turns it into a hotel and then the little people arrive—a chiller. S&S, 1967.

Clancy, Ambrose   BLIND PILOT
Terrorism in Ireland and smuggling of a huge arms shipment—"effectively evokes the political climate of modern-day Ireland and the factional disputes among the revolutionaries." (FC) Morrow, 1980.

Crane, Stephen   THE O'RUDDY
In *The Complete Novels of Stephen Crane*. Doubleday, 1967 (first published 1903).

DeMille, Nelson   CATHEDRAL
A siege by Irish extremists at St. Patrick's Cathedral during the annual St. Patrick's Day parade. Delacorte Pr, 1981.

Dillon, Ellis   BLOOD RELATIONS
Novel of a Catholic/Protestant couple during the period 1916-24. S&S, 1978.

Donleavy, J.P.   THE DESTINIES OF DARCY DANCER, GENTLEMAN
Tale of an Irish Tom Jones and squire of Andromeda Park. Delacorte Pr, 1977. There's a sequel, *Leila; Further in the Destinies of Darcy Dancer, Gentleman* (1983)—"riotous exuberance and invention. If Smollett were reborn today, it's tempting to think that he might write like this." (FC)

DuMaurier, Daphne   HUNGRY HILL
Saga of a family of mine owners through four generations, each with its own "tragedy of weak characters." (FC) Bentley, 1971 (first published 1943).

Edgeworth, Maria   CASTLE RACKRENT AND THE ABSENTEE
An Irish story of the evils of absentee landlords for the tenants. Originally published in the early 1800s. Dutton, 1960.

Flanagan, Thomas   THE YEAR OF THE FRENCH (Mayo)
Historical novel of 1798, when people of County Mayo revolted, aided by French revolutionists. HR&W, 1979.

Garrity, D.A., ed.   44 IRISH SHORT STORIES
An anthology of Irish short fiction from Yeats to Frank O'Connor. Devin-Adair, 1955.

Gash, Jonathan   THE SLEEPERS OF ERIN
Part of the Detective Lovejoy series; the plot moves from East Anglia to Ireland and involves antiques and a sinister couple looking for "sleepers" (antiques of great value that are deliberately concealed). Dutton, 1983.

Gaskin, Catherine   EDGE OF GLASS
Mystery and romance take a London model to a "moldering Irish manor" in search of her past. (FC) Doubleday, 1967.

Green, Henry   LOVING
A picture of the lives of the owners of a castle, during World War II, and their many servants—"light, witty social comedy." (FC) Viking, 1949.

Holden, Ursula   THE CLOUD CATCHERS
An Irish country girl flees a run-down farm and unloving, abusive parents for Dublin, but eventually returns with a new husband to make it "a place of light and welcome." (FC) Methuen, 1979.

Holland, Cecelia   THE KINGS IN WINTER
Historical novel of eleventh-century Ireland and attempts to unify the country. Atheneum, 1968.

Howatch, Susan   CASTLEMARA
Three generations of an Anglo-Irish family divided into six sections, each narrated by a different character. Provides a history also of the period 1859-91, of the plague, Parnell, and the troubles between starving Irish tenants and English landlords. S&S, 1974.

Johnston, Jennifer   THE CHRISTMAS TREE
"A warm and lovely novel about a quirky, courageous woman and the special legacy she leaves for those who survive her." (FC) Morrow, 1982. Also *How Many Miles to Babylon?* (1974), about two young men in World War I.

Keane, Molly   GOOD BEHAVIOR
Decline and fall of a genteel, Anglo-Irish family from Edwardian times through the twenties. Knopf, 1981. Also *Time After Time* (1984)—"decaying siblings in a decaying Irish country house."

Kiely, Benedict   THE STATE OF IRELAND
A novella and seventeen stories—"limns with acute sensitivity, traditional Irish ethics and contemporary sociopolitical living conditions." Godine, 1980.

Lavin, Mary   COLLECTED STORIES
"Cover almost every aspect of Irish life—the farmers, the fishermen, the well-off, the servant girls, lovers, husbands, wives, spinsters, bachelors and children. The dialogue is superb." (BRD) Houghton, 1971. Also *The Shrine and Other Stories* (1977).

Lockley, Ronald   SEAL WOMAN (Irish Coast)
A love story; time is the end of World War II. Bradbury Pr, 1974.

McGinley, Patrick   BOGMAIL
The "literate tender of the local pub" murders his young assistant setting off a "series of strange events. . . . yet nothing really disturbs [the] locals' chatter . . . wordy philosophizing . . . as interesting and central to the story as the murder investigation." (FC) Ticknor & Fields, 1981. Also *Foggage* (1983), about an incestuous relationship between twins (set in County Leix).

McMullen, Mary   MY COUSIN DEATH
A stranger tries to blackmail a widow about a business trip her husband had taken eight years earlier and the countryside is suddenly rocked by a series of murders. Doubleday, 1980.

Macken, Walter   RAIN ON THE WIND (Galway)
Story of a poor and disfigured fisherman who finds love. Macmillan, 1950.

Moore, Brian   THE MANGAN INHERITANCE
Clever contemporary plot about a poet's attempt to identify a family photo as the famous nineteenth-century poet, James Clarence Mangan. FS&G, 1979.

O'Brien, Kate   A GIFT HORSE, AND OTHER STORIES
Poignant vignettes of "an unfamiliar cultural viewpoint . . . the Anglo-Irish ascendancy, a small minority in republican Ireland." (FC) Braziller, 1980.

O'Connor, Frank   COLLECTED STORIES
One of several volumes of short stories by a leading Irish writer—"The Ireland he evokes . . . is the provincial life of his Cork boyhood. Loving but acute . . . reveals a humanity peculiarly Irish in its stubborn divisive ways." (FC) Knopf, 1981. Also, *The Stories of Frank O'Connor* (1952) and *More Stories* (1954).

O'Faolain, Sean   A NEST OF SIMPLE FOLK (Southwest Ireland)
Three generations of a family, through poverty and revolution, 1854-1916. Viking, 1934. Also, *The Finest Stories of Sean O'Faolain* (1957) and *Selected Stories of Sean O'Faolain* (1978).

O'Flaherty, Liam   FAMINE
Irish peasant life in the 1840s. Random, 1937.

Polland, Madeleine A.   THE HEART SPEAKS MANY WAYS
Spain and Ireland during the Spanish Civil War and World War II are the settings for a novel of a young Irish girl's search for "elusive love. . . . the flavor of Civil War Spain and hunt country Ireland comes across vividly." (FC) Delacorte Pr, 1982. Also *Sabrina* (1979) a poignant love story set in County Cork.

Stephens, James   THE CROCK OF GOLD
A "wise and aphoristic fairy tale for adults." (FC) Macmillan, 1960 (first published 1912).

Tracy, Honor   THE STRAIGHT AND NARROW PATH
An Irish village is the setting for various views of the straight and narrow path. (FC) Random, 1956. Other novels, set in Ireland, of her "humorous satire" classification are *The First Day of Friday* (1963), *In a Year of Grace* (1975) and *The Ballad of Castle Reef* (1980).

Trevor, William   FOOLS OF FORTUNE
An idyllic childhood is shattered by the Irish uprising and destruction of the family home. Viking, 1983.

Uris, Leon   TRINITY
The years 1840-1916 from the viewpoints of the trinity—British, Irish Catholics, and Ulster-Protestant families. Doubleday, 1976.

Woods, Stuart   RUN BEFORE THE WIND
Adventure novel in which a young man from Georgia is taken up by a wealthy couple and engaged to build a yacht for a tycoon; English and IRA hostilities collide on the project. Norton, 1983.

DUBLIN

Beckett, Samuel   MORE PRICKS THAN KICKS
Ten short stories that are episodes from an unfinished novel about Belacqua Shuah's "sometimes sad, sometimes thoroughly amusing life in the streets, hills, pubs and drawing rooms of Dublin." (FC) Grove, 1970 (first published 1934).

Brown, Christy   DOWN ALL THE DAYS
Semi-autobiographical story of a large Dublin working-class family, through the eyes of one member severely crippled with cerebral palsy—"brutally, bawdily, joyfully (and sadly) real." (FC) Stein & Day, 1970.

Cullinan, Elizabeth   A CHANGE OF SCENE
"The quintessential innocent abroad [a young woman from New York] who searches for legends that don't quite exist" in Dublin, and returns home "slightly sadder but wiser." (FC) Norton, 1982.

Donleavy, J.P.   THE GINGER MAN
Picaresque novel of an ex-G.I., begins in Dublin and moves on to London. Delacorte Pr, 1965. Also *The Beastly Beatitudes of Balthazar B.* (1968), about the lives and loves of the protagonist from youth in Paris, through adventures in an English prep school, to Trinity College, Dublin.

Gill, Bartholomew   McGARR AND THE P.M. OF BELGRAVE SQUARE
Peter McGarr, head of the Irish murder squad, must solve the death of an antiques dealer—"the Irish background is splendidly handled to give . . . the feel of the sights and smells of Dublin." (FC) Viking, 1983.

Herbert, Frank   THE WHITE PLAGUE
"A molecular biologist visiting Dublin, is driven to awful and brilliant insanity when he sees his wife and children killed by an IRA bomb." (FC) Putnam Pub Group, 1982.

Joyce, James   ULYSSES
The classic, first published in 1922, of thoughts and actions of a group of people in Dublin through a single day. Random, 1967 (first published 1922). Also *The Dubliners* (1914) (short stories), *Portrait of the Artist as a Young Man* (1914) and its earlier version *Stephen Hero* (1944), *Finnegan's Wake* (1939) and *A Shorter Finnegan's Wake* (1958). See also books listed under "Literary Guides and Theatre in Ireland," above, especially *James Joyce's Odyssey* by Frank Delaney.

McGahern, John   THE PORNOGRAPHER
Narration of a Dubliner "who, jilted in love, divides his time between writing formula porn . . . and visiting his favorite aunt dying of cancer." (FC) Har-Row, 1979.

Murdoch, Iris   THE RED AND THE GREEN
Stories of an Anglo-Irish family in Dublin during Easter Week, 1916. Viking, 1965.

O'Flaherty, Liam   THE INFORMER
The classic story of a former Irish revolutionary who betrays his comrades. Knopf, 1925.

Plunkett, James   STRUMPET CITY
Story of the Irish labor movement, to be read along with *Farewell Companions*

(1978), about the lives of three friends between the wars—in both novels the main character is the city of Dublin. Delacorte Pr, 1969.

Somerville-Large, Peter   A LIVING DOG
A schoolmaster in "drizzly Dublin . . . supplements his paltry pay by stealing antiques from . . . his bedridden aunt" and gets competition from a friend who has the same idea—"a wonderful read." (FC) Doubleday, 1982.

TRAVEL ARTICLES

ATLANTIC
1985 Apr "Between Two Economies." Life in the Irish village where *Moby Dick* was filmed is pleasant but poor. Alexander Cockburn, p. 28

HORIZON
1985 Mar "A Connoisseur's Dublin." A Dublin insider reveals the most interesting sites and the liveliest events. Desmond Guinness, p. 37

MODERN MATURITY
1984 Dec/83-Jan/84 "In Search of Ireland's Charm." Charles N. Barnard, p. 38

N.Y. TIMES SUNDAY TRAVEL SECTION (X)
1985 Feb 3 Fare of the Country: "The Irish Flair with Potatoes." Fred Ferretti, p. 6
Mar 24 "Genealogy by the Busload." Tours to their roots for people with the same Irish surname. Richard D. Lyons, p. 28
May 19 "What's Doing in Dublin." Sean O'Rourke, p. 10
Nov 17 "Here Lie the High Kings of Ireland." Graves of Clonmacnoise bridge fifteen centuries, from St. Kieran to Peter Daly. Thomas Mallon, p. 15
1984 Feb 22 "Irish Pubs Have Time for Tea." Arlene B. Isaacs, p. 39
Apr 8 "What's Doing in Dublin." Sean O'Rourke, p. 10
Aug 26 "What's Doing in Galway." Sean O'Rourke, p. 10
Oct 7 (Part 2, "Sophisticated Traveler") "Around Ireland and Its Own Little Islands." Where mystery is commonplace. Rachel Billington, p. 38; "Trout Fishing in Ireland." Hugh Leonard, p. 16
Dec 16 "Irish Comfort and Antiquity." Ashford Castle treats guests to a baronial setting amid links to a mystical past. Barbara Dubivsky, p. 6

TRAVEL & LEISURE
1985 Jun "Dublin's Lively Grafton Street." Fashionable shops, colorful street theater, and pubs for people-watching. Nancy Lyon, p. 58
1984 Mar "A Magical Irish Isle: Inishbofin." A place of grassy headlands, lonely bogs and heathery fields. Nancy Lyon, p. 54
Apr "The Spare Beauty of the Burren." Discovering a dramatic Land's End in Ireland. Charles N. Barnard, p. 194
May "In Ireland, Dromoland Castle." Relaxed elegance in Country Clare. Clem Taylor, p. 136
Jul "Ireland at Its Best (Tours)." From golfing to riding to tracing your roots. Abby Rand, p. 68

TRAVEL/HOLIDAY
1985 Feb "A Queen Among Cities." Ireland's endearing grand dame (Dublin).
Richard Roche, p. 63
Sep "Cork City—It's Not a City, It's a Frame of Mind." Lorcan Roche, p. 62

ITALY

Series Guidebooks (See Appendix 1)

American Express: Florence & Tuscany; Rome; Venice
Baedeker: Italy; Florence; Rome; Venice; Tuscany
Berlitz: Florence & Tuscany; Istria & the Croatian Coast; Italian
Adriatic; Italian Riviera; Malta; Rome & the Vatican;
Sicily; Venice
Blue Guide: Northern Italy; Southern Italy; Florence; Rome; Sicily;
Malta; Venice
Companion Guide: Florence; Rome; Venice
Fisher: Italy
Fodor: Italy; Budget Travel Italy; Rome
Frommer: Italy: Dollarwise
Rome: Arthur Frommer Guide
Insight: Italy
Let's Go: Italy (& Tunisia)
Michelin: Italy; Rome
Nagel: Italy; Malta
U.S. Government: Italy: Area Handbook; Background Notes;
Pocket Guide; Post Report
Vatican: Background Notes
Malta: Background Notes
San Marino: Background Notes

Background Reading

Amfitheatrof, Erik   THE ENCHANTED GROUND: AMERICANS IN ITALY,
1760-1980
The enchantment of Americans with Italy. Little, 1980.

Ardagh, John   A TALE OF FIVE CITIES
See under "Europe"; includes Bologna.

Baker, P.R.   THE FORTUNATE PILGRIMS
Americans in Italy from 1800-60 who first "discovered" it. Harvard U Pr, 1964.

Barzini, Luigi   THE ITALIANS
A full-length portrait that touches on many aspects of Italian life, its virtues and vices, achievements and failures—"enjoyable, indispensable introduction" to Italy. Penguin, 1984 (first published 1964). Also, *From Caesar to the Mafia, Sketches of Italian Life* (1971).

Brody, Elaine   MUSIC GUIDE TO ITALY
One of a series of guides for individual European countries—a handbook of information for a range of travelers "from the music dilettante to the highly motivated specialist." Includes information on the country's musical history, concert halls, opera houses, festivals, etc. Dodd, 1978. (See also *Music Festivals in Europe and Britain* and *Music Lover's Europe* under "Europe/Background Reading.")

Ceram, C.W.   GODS, GRAVES AND SCHOLARS
The story of archaeology for the general reader/traveler; discoveries in Crete, Pompeii, Troy, the Middle East and Central America. Bantam, 1976.

Clark, Ronald W.   THE ALPS
See under "Austria."

Cornell, Tim and Matthews, John   ATLAS OF THE ROMAN WORLD
"A superbly compact yet thorough, heavily illustrated and well-written history of the rise, zenith and decline of the Roman Empire." (Publisher) Facts On File, 1982.

Hauser, Ernest O.   ITALY, A CULTURAL GUIDE
"A quirky little reference book, compiled out of highly personal interests . . . 100 or so alphabetically arranged entries deal with such expected topics as Baroque architecture [but also] essays as odd as they are charming . . . biographical entries . . . an amusing and informative supplement to standard guides." (NYTBR) Atheneum, 1981.

James, Henry   ITALIAN HOURS
Travel essays by the nineteenth-century novelist. Grove, 1979 (first published 1909).

Kubly, Herbert   AMERICAN IN ITALY
A "chatty, anecdotal account of the author's fourteen-month sojourn in Italy and Sicily on a Fulbright grant." (BRD) S&S, 1955.

Langdon, Helen   THE KNOPF TRAVELER'S GUIDES TO ART: ITALY
Part of a series that "aims to cover major museums, art treasures, churches, important buildings that will appear on most travel itineraries." Includes essays on periods and artists, a star system to identify museums or works of particular note for the rushed tourist, practical travel information. (BL) Knopf, 1984.

Lawrence, D.H.   TWILIGHT IN ITALY
Travel sketches by the novelist, first published in 1916. Penguin, 1981.

MacKendrick, Paul   THE MUTE STONES SPEAK
A newly revised edition of an archaeological history of Italy, and how archaeological findings illuminate history. Norton, 1983 (first published 1961).

Morris, Jan   DESTINATIONS
This collection of travel essays by the noted travel writer includes an essay on Trieste. Oxford U, 1980.

Morton, H.V.   A TRAVELLER IN ITALY
Dodd, 1982 (first published 1964). Also *A Traveller in Southern Italy* (1984, first published 1969) and *A Traveller in Rome* (1984, first published 1957), travel classics by a leading writer in the genre—to be read whether or not you plan to go to Italy.

Murray, William   ITALY—THE FATAL GIFT
"Puts us in touch with the 'fatal gift' of beauty which is the special mark of that land"—a collection of essays on the author's sojourns in Rome and love affair with the country. (publisher) Dodd, 1981.

Norwich, John J., ed.   THE ITALIANS: HISTORY, ART AND THE GENIUS OF A PEOPLE
A cultural history of Italy from mythological origins to the twentieth century. Various experts contribute "highly individual and readable essays" of chronological periods—history, art, politics, music, literature, philosophy. Beautifully illustrated. (LJ) Abrams, 1983.

O'Faolain, Sean   A SUMMER IN ITALY; AN AUTUMN IN ITALY
Travel memoirs, by the Irish writer, of trips in 1948 to northern and southern Italy, respectively—"Amusing, wholly unpredictable, humorous, description of persons and places." (BRD) Devin, 1950, 1953.

Simon, Kate   ITALY, THE PLACES IN BETWEEN
Revised and expanded edition of the original published in 1970—"preserved are the author's superb qualifications as a travel companion, guide, and stylist [directing] the tourist . . . to a pleasant and fulfilling adventure. . . . travel outside the country's major cities." (BL) Har-Row, 1984.

Trease, Geoffrey   THE ITALIAN STORY: FROM THE ETRUSCANS TO MODERN TIMES
Readable "crisply compressed" history "to provide the traveler . . . with an outline of the significant events in the Peninsula's history." (BRD) Vanguard, 1984 (first published 1964).

Zbigniew, Herbert   BARBARIANS IN THE GARDEN
See under "France/Travelogues, Memoirs."

ROME AND THE VATICAN

Bowen, Elizabeth   A TIME IN ROME
Impressions of Rome, past and present by the novelist—"describing, reminiscing about, and explicating a city." (BRD) Knopf, 1960.

Bull, George   INSIDE THE VATICAN
The day-to-day life and work of the Pope and those who run the whole Vatican complex of museums, archives, radio station, etc. St. Martin, 1983.

Chamberlain, Russell   ROME
Part of Great Cities of the World series. Time-Life, 1976.

Clark, Eleanor   ROME AND A VILLA
"Evocative portrait of a city . . . teeming with life, memory, history, smells, and sights." (NYTBR) Atheneum, 1982 (first published in 1950; revised in 1974). Also *A Time in Rome* (1960), a reminiscence, description, explication, by a novelist.

Elling, Christian   ROME: THE BIOGRAPHY OF HER ARCHITECTURE FROM BERNINI TO THORVALDSEN
For people who love buildings. Westview Pr, 1976.

Fraser, Russell   THE THREE ROMES
The three Romes, in this author's concept, are Constantinople (now Istanbul), Moscow and Rome—cities that felt they had "received divine missions to amass and rule empires." The book is historical commentary and anecdotes, an "entertaining overview . . . encounters with modern inhabitants . . . the shadowy past [implanted in] the mind of citizens today." (BL) HarBraceJ, 1985.

Gunn, Peter and Beny, Roloff   THE CHURCHES OF ROME
Text and photographs reveal the wealth of art and architecture in Roman churches today. S&S, 1981.

Hibbert, Christopher   ROME: THE BIOGRAPHY OF A CITY
"Remarkable, gracefully written, humanizing chronicle . . . history unfolds as a pageant of patrons and parasites, saints and tyrants, poets and warriors." (PW) Norton, 1985.

Hofmann, Paul   O VATICAN! A SLIGHTLY WICKED VIEW OF THE HOLY SEE
"A lively discourse on personalities, motives, and morals" of the powers behind St. Peter's throne. (BL) Congdon & Weed, 1984.

Hofmann, Paul   ROME: THE SWEET TEMPESTUOUS LIFE
Charming essays on contemporary Rome—seminarians, terrorists, soccer fans, malingering office workers, grandmothers, waiters, prostitutes and much more. "Open[s] our eyes to a hundred Roman realities" guidebooks never mention. (BRD) Congdon & Lattés, 1982.

McGreevy, John, ed.   CITIES
Impressions of world cities as seen through the eyes of people intimately connected with them—for Rome it's Anthony Burgess's impressions. Outlet Bk, 1981.

Menen, Aubrey   UPON THIS ROCK
A study of St. Peter's Cathedral beginning with the burial of Peter—history, ceremonies and splendors of the basilica, the popes and the artists who worked on it. Saturday Rev Pr, 1973.

Mertz, Richard   TWO THOUSAND YEARS IN ROME
Subtitle: A chronological guide to the Eternal City—placing its works of art, its monuments, its turbulent history through the ages in lucid perspective for the modern traveler. Coward, 1968.

Packard, Jerrold M.   PETER'S KINGDOM: INSIDE THE PAPAL CITY
A guide to the history, operations and buildings, museums and art collections. Scribner, 1985.

Shetterly, Anya   ROMEWALKS
Organized in four walks: Papal Rome, the Jewish Ghetto, the Renaissance, the ancient and medieval city. "Vivid commentary, which is just as likely to point out a hidden art masterpiece as . . . where to stop for ice cream." Includes general information and advice and a selective list of restaurants and shops. (BL) HR&W, 1984.

Simon, Kate   ROME PLACES AND PLEASURES
Ideal companion to *The Places in Between*, above. Knopf, 1972.

FLORENCE & TUSCANY

Barich, Bill   TRAVELING LIGHT
See under "England/Travel Memoirs."

Barret, Andre   FLORENCE OBSERVED
"Arranged so that each chapter can form an itinerary for one day"—history, artists, description, photographs. (BRD) Oxford U, 1974.

Cole, Toby, ed.   FLORENCE: A TRAVELER'S ANTHOLOGY
Selections from writings about Florence. L. Hill, 1981.

Holler, Anne   FLORENCEWALKS
Four itineraries that intertwine history, art, architecture and contemporary Italian life-styles, plus general advice on housing, food, shopping, etc. HR&W, 1983.

King, F.H.   FLORENCE
Newsweek Bks, 1982.

McCarthy, Mary   STONES OF FLORENCE
A profile of Florence—history, architecture, art and people—"perceptive . . . interpretation of this heart of the Renaissance." HarBraceJ, 1976 (first published 1959).

Raison, Laura   TUSCANY: AN ANTHOLOGY
An illustrated anthology of prose excerpts, letters, poetry, stories, recipes—"a treasure trove of great writers sharing their delight in discovering some new and delightful facet of Tuscany." (NYT) Facts On File, 1984.

Romer, Elizabeth   THE TUSCAN YEAR
Details the cycle of her neighbors' year as farmers in a remote valley of Tuscany "in what is fundamentally a cookbook but one of particular interest to the traveler . . . in the Italian countryside." (NYT) Atheneum, 1985.

Serpell, Christopher and Jean   TRAVELLERS' GUIDE TO ELBA & THE TUSCAN ARCHIPELAGO
Jonathan Cape, 1979.

SOUTHERN ITALY & SICILY, MALTA, CAPRI

Brilliant, Richard   POMPEII AD 79: THE TREASURE OF REDISCOVERY
Crown, 1979.

Cornelisen, Ann   WOMEN OF THE SHADOWS
An American Protestant ran a day nursery for ten years in Lucania (south of Naples). She introduces the town, her neighbors and acquaintances, and their children in the "bare sepia world of Southern Italy." (BRD) Random, 1977. Also *Torregreca: Life, Death, Miracles* (1969).

Cox, Thornton   THORNTON COX'S TRAVELLERS' GUIDE TO MALTA
"Highly readable introduction to the area under consideration. . . . necessary data for getting there and getting about . . . suggested itineraries [designed for] economy of time and movement." (Publisher) Hippocrene, 1982.

Dennis, Nigel   AN ESSAY ON MALTA
Vanguard, 1974.

Dolci, Danilo   SICILIAN LIVES
Oral history of Sicilian life and society—peasants to nobility, street cleaners to Mafia bosses. Random, 1982.

Douglas, Norman   SIREN LAND
"'Sirenland' is Capri and the Peninsula of Sorrento . . . observations and reflections upon men, nature, and history of a gladly-tempted sojourner." Reprint of a classic. (BRD) David, 1983 (first published 1911).

Durrell, Lawrence   SICILIAN CAROUSEL
Lighthearted and humorous tour of Sicily on a carousel bus. Viking, 1977.

Feldkamp, Frederick   NOT EVERYBODY'S EUROPE
A grand tour of nine unique places to think about adding to your itinerary—for Italy, it's Sicily. Harper's Magazine Pr, 1976.

Kininmonth, Christopher   TRAVELLERS' GUIDE TO SICILY
Jonathan Cape, 1981. Also *Travellers' Guide to Malta & Gozo* (1979).

Kraus, Theodor   POMPEII AND HERCULANEUM: THE LIVING CITIES OF THE DEAD
History, life in the towns and how they fit into Roman history; surviving buildings and the contents. Abrams, 1975.

Kubly, Herbert   EASTER IN SICILY
Scenery and legends, ancient and modern—"a delightful reading experience." (BRD) S&S, 1956.

Levi, Carlo   CHRIST STOPPED AT EBOLI
Story of a year spent by the author (a doctor) among the people in Gagliano, a poverty-stricken area of Southern Italy. Time-Life, 1982 (first published 1947).

Lewis, Norman   NAPLES '44
The author's experiences in 1943-44 as a linguist and security officer during World War II—"remarkable [for its] awareness of the duality of wartime experience. . . . pain too great for relief but also . . . the latent greatness of a people." Humorous, sad, poignant, engrossing. (BRD) Pantheon, 1979.

Morris, Jan   PLACES
This collection of travel essays by a leading travel writer has essays on Capri and Malta. HarBraceJ, 1976.

Nelson, Nina   MALTA
Batsford, 1977.

Pereira, Anthony   POMPEII, NAPLES AND SOUTHERN ITALY
Batsford, 1977.

Simeti, Mary Taylor   ON PERSEPHONE'S ISLAND: A SICILIAN JOURNAL
Journal of a year in Sicily, in Palermo and the countryside, by the American wife of a Sicilian professor—"beautifully written," perceptive insights into the people and social customs. (PW) Knopf, 1986.

VENICE

Bull, George   VENICE: THE MOST TRIUMPHANT CITY
"Reflects the best of a . . . nineteenth-century style of journalistic travelogue"—cultural history, the author's travels. (LJ) St. Martin, 1982.

Cole, Toby, ed.   VENICE: A PORTABLE READER
An anthology of selections on the art, history and civilization of Venice—enjoyable introduction to a fabulous city. L Hill, 1980.

DeCombray, Richard   VENICE, FRAIL BARRIER
The art critic Kenneth Clark said: "In a class by itself among innumerable books on Venice. . . . the most accurate picture of Venetian life I have ever read." Doubleday, 1979.

**Lauritzen, Peter   VENICE, A THOUSAND YEARS OF CULTURE
AND CIVILIZATION**
History from settlement to Napoleon. Atheneum, 1981. Also, *Palaces of Venice* (1978) (who designed them, lived in them, changes) and *Islands and Lagoons and Venice* (1980).

McCarthy, Mary   VENICE OBSERVED
A books of photographs with superior text reflecting the author's "astonishing comprehension of the Venetian taste and character." (BRD) HarBraceJ, 1963.

Menen, Aubrey   VENICE
One of the Great Cities of the World series. Time-Life, 1976.

Morris, Jan   THE VENETIAN EMPIRE: A SEA VOYAGE
A travel guide to the Venetian empire of the twelfth to eighteenth centuries—a reconstruction of the period. HarBraceJ, 1980. Also *The World of Venice* (1961).

Morris, Jan   A VENETIAN BESTIARY
"She uses the factual and fantastic animals of Venice to tell again that magic city's story." (TBS) Thames Hudson, 1982.

Norwich, John J.   A HISTORY OF VENICE
The author "has managed to compress 1,000 years of . . . events [in] one book. . . a living book . . . full of blood, naval battles, sieges, adventures, conquests, strokes of luck, stupendous defeats, glorious victories, secret plots . . . sharp profiles of the protagonists [yet] found space to describe the incredible beauty of Venice and its Circean charm." (BRD) Knopf, 1982.

Ruskin, John   THE STONES OF VENICE (abridged)
A new "festive" edition of a "classic of art history and social criticism . . . enriched by splendid old and new photos, reproductions of Ruskin's diagrams, sketches, and watercolors, and a sensitive prefatory evaluation by editor Jan Morris—[a] selective abridgement [for] modern readers." (BL) Little, 1981.

Thubron, Colin   THE VENETIANS
Part of the Seafarer's Series. Time-Life, 1980.

Zorzi, Alvise   VENICE: THE GOLDEN AGE, 697-1797
Abbeville, 1983.

SARDINIA

Holme, T. and others   TRAVELLERS' GUIDE TO SARDINIA
Jonathan Cape, 1979.

Lawrence, D.H.   SEA AND SARDINIA
Travelogue describing a trip to Sardinia (from Sicily). Penguin, 1981 (first published 1921).

Waite, Virginia   SARDINIA
Batsford, 1977.

GUIDEBOOKS

Facaros, Dana   MEDITERRANEAN ISLAND HOPPING—THE ITALIAN ISLANDS
A handbook for the independent traveler that covers Corsica, Capri, Sicily, Malta and some less accessible islands. Island descriptions, how to get there, background information on local customs and history, where to stay and what to do. Hippocrene, 1982.

Kane, Robert S.   ITALY
One of a new "World at Its Best" series of travel guidebooks by a noted travel authority, "oriented toward the discriminating traveler." Highlights the best each country has to offer, including hotels in a range of prices—"evaluates the entire itinerary. Big city wonders and . . . out-of-the-way adventure spots." Passport, 1985.

Laing, Jennifer   GREEK & ROMAN GODS
Handy take-along guide to keep all those statues and myths straight in your mind. David, 1982.

HISTORY

Alexander, Sidney   LIONS AND FOXES: MEN AND IDEAS OF THE ITALIAN RENAISSANCE
Macmillan, 1974.

Bernard, Jack F.   UP FROM CAESAR
A survey of the history of Italy from the fall of the Roman Empire to the collapse of fascism. Doubleday, 1970.

Chamberlin, E. Russel   THE FALL OF THE HOUSE OF BORGIA
Pope Alexander VI and the Borgia family—"the embodiment of Renaissance evil." Dial, 1974.

Cronin, Vincent   THE FLOWERING OF THE RENAISSANCE
Dutton, 1969.

Gallo, Max   MUSSOLINI'S ITALY: TWENTY YEARS OF THE FASCIST ERA
Macmillan, 1973.

Giacosa, G.   WOMEN OF THE CAESARS
The history of ancient Rome with a unique point of departure—the women

whose portraits appear on early coins. "A brief and non-traditional introduction to Imperial history." Edizioni Arte E Moneta, 1977.

Gunn, Peter   A CONCISE HISTORY OF ITALY
Viking, 1972.

Hadas, M.   GIBBON'S THE DECLINE AND FALL OF THE ROMAN EMPIRE
A modern abridgement. Putnam Pub Group, 1962.

Smith, D.M.   MUSSOLINI'S ROMAN EMPIRE
Viking, 1976. Also *Italy: A Modern History* (1959).

Novels

Bassani, Giorgio   THE SMELL OF HAY (Ferrara)
Stories of Jews in Ferrara and their sufferings under the Fascists. HarBraceJ, 1975. Also *The Garden of the Finzi-Continis* (1965) and *The Heron* (1970).

Cornelisen, Ann   ANY FOUR WOMEN COULD ROB THE BANK OF ITALY (Tuscany)
Funny novel based on the premise that in chauvinist Italy women are invisible and therefore "any four women *could* rob the Bank of Italy," which premise six women decide to act upon. Set in a "deliciously detailed" Tuscan hilltop community. (FC) HR&W, 1984.

Crichton, Robert   THE SECRET OF SANTA VITTORIA
The townspeople conspire to hide all the wine in town before the Germans occupy it. S&S, 1966.

DeWohl, Louie   LAY SIEGE TO HEAVEN (Siena)
Story of St. Catherine of Siena. Lippincott, 1961.

Eco, Umberto   THE NAME OF THE ROSE
"An amalgam of the Avignon Papacy, secular intrigues, heresy . . . and a mysterious series of sophisticated murders" in fourteenth-century Italy. (FC) HarBraceJ, 1983.

Godden, Rumer   THE BATTLE OF THE VILLA FIORITA
Two English children, victims of a divorce, battle to force their mother to return home from the villa. Viking, 1963.

Godey, John   FATAL BEAUTY (Milan)
"Tense, complex story told with style, grace . . . humor" about a mother's attempts to see her son, kidnapped by Italian terrorists, with a trail of CIA, KGB and Italian agents on her trail. Atheneum, 1984.

Guareschi, Giovanni   THE LITTLE WORLD OF DON CAMILLO
The first in a series of humorous books about the ongoing war between Don

Camillo, local village priest, and the communist mayor. This and the titles that follow recount various contretemps involving local villagers, social activist younger priests, and flower children, and give a highly readable and insightful account of a country that can have a large Communist party and yet remain very Catholic. Pelligrini, FS&G, 1951. Also *Don Camillo and His Flock* (1952), *Don Camillo's Dilemma* (1954), *Don Camillo Takes the Devil By the Tail* (1957), *Comrade Don Camillo* (1964).

Heller, Joseph   CATCH-22
The contemporary classic about an American bombing squadron in World War II, stationed in Italy. S&S, 1961.

Hemingway, Ernest   A FAREWELL TO ARMS
A doomed love affair between an American and an English nurse during World War I. Scribner, 1983 (first published 1929).

Holland, Isabelle   THE LOST MADONNA
Blend of romance and suspense with a plot revolving around an art-collecting contessa. Rawson, 1981.

Johnston, Velda   THE ETRUSCAN SMILE (Tuscany)
A young woman travels to Tuscany to find her missing older sister—"mafioso connections . . . the smuggling of ancient art objects out of Italy." (FC) Dodd, 1977.

Klein, Norma   SEXTET IN A MINOR (Italian Alps)
A novella "contrasts the voices of two couples [one] whose marriage is disintegrating, and newlyweds who are just beginning [and] a bachelor" who are all guests at a pension in the Alps for a holiday—"amusing as it is moving." (FC) St. Martin, 1983.

Lem, Stanislaw   THE CHAIN OF CHANCE (Southern Italy)
Espionage and science fiction and the murders of middle-aged foreigners in southern Italy. HarBraceJ, 1978.

Malouf, David   CHILD'S PLAY
One of two novellas in *Child's Play and the Bread of Time to Come*; it is concerned with "an unnamed protagonist who is being groomed in Italy as a terrorist." (FC) Braziller, 1982.

Pavese, Cesare   THE SELECTED WORKS OF CESARE PAVESE (Turin)
Four novels of postwar Turin as a background for middle-class characters. FS&G, 1968.

Silone, Ignazio   FONTAMARA
Peasant life in Italy and disillusionment with communism. First published in 1934 then revised in 1949 to make it more universal in theme. Atheneum, 1960. Also about Italian peasant life, *Bread and Wine* (1962) and the sequel to it, *The Seed Beneath the Snow* (1965).

Spark, Muriel   THE TAKEOVER
"A duel between the effete Hubert and the earthy Maggie" over possession of a home in Nemi, Italy. (FC) Viking, 1976.

Stewart, Fred M.   CENTURY
Saga of two branches of an Italian family encompassing two world wars, Hollywood, the worlds of mansion and ghetto in New York, decadent aristocracy and beleaguered peasant in Italy. (FC) Morrow, 1981.

Styron, William   SET THIS HOUSE ON FIRE
Death and rape in an Italian village, encountered by a U.S. government employee. Random, 1960.

Svevo, Italo   A LIFE (Trieste)
Novel of a non-hero in turn-of-the-century Trieste. Knopf, 1963.

West, Morris L.   THE SALAMANDER (Tuscany)
Story of suspense and mystery that explores the tensions and contradictions between Left and Right. Morrow, 1973. Also *Daughter of Silence* (1961) about a revenge murder by a young woman and set in a small village in Tuscany.

FLORENCE

Anthony, Evelyn   MISSION TO MALASPIGA
An American woman, ostensibly a tourist and cousin of a leading Florentine family, is actually a government agent investigating the family's connection to a drug ring. Coward, 1974.

DuMaurier, Daphne   THE FLIGHT OF THE FALCON
A tour guide becomes involved when he finds his former nurse has been murdered. Doubleday, 1965. Also *My Cousin Rachel* (1952), which begins and ends in Cornwall, England, but much of the action takes place in Italy.

Forster, E.M.   A ROOM WITH A VIEW
The heroine is an upper-middle-class Englishwoman who exchanges rooms with lower-middle-class Mr. Emerson at her Florence hotel so that she can have a room with a view. The exchange leads to a profound change in her life and prejudices. Knopf, 1923 (first published 1908).

Howells, William D.   INDIAN SUMMER
Story of the American colony in nineteenth-century Florence, by one of America's leading writers of that period. Indiana U, 1972 (first published 1886).

Lawrence, D.H.   AARON'S ROD
A novel of "the chaos of impulses and incoherent aspirations in the break-up" of established moral standards . . . life in Florence is charmingly pictured. Seltzer, 1922.

Maugham, W. Somerset   THEN AND NOW
Novel about Machiavelli in 1502. Doubleday, 1948.

Michaels, Barbara   THE GREY BEGINNING
Mystery in which a young widow visits the ancestral home outside Florence, of her dead husband. Congdon & Weed, 1984.

Nabb, Magdalen   DEATH IN SPRINGTIME: A FLORENTINE MYSTERY
A race against the clock to find the young American who has been kidnapped, while she is still alive. Scribner, 1984. Two other mysteries by this author, with Florence settings, are *Death of a Dutchman* (1983) and *Death of an Englishman* (1982).

Stone, Irving   THE AGONY AND THE ECSTASY
A fictionalized life of Michelangelo, the renaissance artist, sculptor and poet. Doubleday, 1961.

CAPRI AND SICILY

Bryher   GATE TO THE SEA
Historical novel of the ancient Greek temples and the city of Paestum (south of Naples). Pantheon, 1958.

Douglas, Norman   SOUTH WIND
Capri is the fictional isle of Nepenthe in this classic. The novel is about the effect of the Capri life-style on visitors. Scholarly Pr, 1971 (first published 1917).

Griffin, Gwyn   A LAST LAMP BURNING
A story about postwar Neapolitan poor people, middle class, nouveaux riches, and degenerate nobility, with an Italian-Chinese slum boy as the book's hero. Putnam Pub Group, 1966.

Hazzard, Shirley   THE BAY OF NOON
An English girl grows up when she spends a year in Naples as a spectator to, and is influenced by, the life of a novelist to whom she's been given a letter of introduction. Little, 1970.

Hodge, Jane A.   SHADOW OF A LADY
Naples during the war between England and Napoleonic France. Coward, 1973.

Menen, Aubrey   FOUR DAYS OF NAPLES
Intriguing fragment of history in novelistic form about the uprising against the Germans and "filled with tongue-in-cheek comments on Italian mores." (BRD) Seaview, 1979.

Steegmuller, Francis   SILENCE AT SALERNO
An island in the Bay of Naples is the setting for this "comedy of intrigue." (FC) HR&W, 1978.

ROME AND THE VATICAN

Burgess, Anthony   BEARD'S ROMAN WOMEN
An "eerie farce" about a "middle-aged movie scriptwriter [who] buries his irascible wife . . . establishes himself in Rome . . . to work on a script about Byron, Shelley and Mary Shelley" [and with a "delectable" mistress] only to begin getting phone calls from his dead wife. McGraw, 1976.

Cleary, Jon   PETER'S PENCE
The IRA plots to steal Vatican treasures for ransom but ends up kidnapping the Pope himself—the author has "complete mastery over the setting. . . . a wholly possible and credible international incident." (FC) Morrow, 1974.

Gallico, Paul   THE SMALL MIRACLE
Set in Assisi and Rome—story of a war orphan and his donkey. Doubleday, 1952.

Gash, Jonathan   THE VATICAN RIP
A suspenseful caper in which an antiques dealer is forced to steal a piece of Chippendale from the Vatican. Ticknor & Fields, 1982.

MacInnes, Helen   NORTH FROM ROME
Suspense novel concerning the communist trafficking in narcotics, through Italy. HarBraceJ, 1958.

Marsh, Ngaio   WHEN IN ROME
"One of the most delightful" of the author's mysteries "with a wonderfully imaginative and romantic Roman setting"—a blackmailing tour entrepreneur meets a nasty demise and there are many suspects. (FC) Little, 1971.

Moravia, Alberto   THE WOMAN OF ROME
Story of a prostitute in Fascist Rome. FS&G, 1949. Also *Two Women* (1958)—the ordeal of a widow and her daughter in the closing days of World War II; *Roman Tales* (1957), *More Roman Tales* (1964), *Mistaken Ambitions* (1955).

Murphy, Walter F.   THE ROMAN ENIGMA
Nazi-occupied Rome just before the first shipment of Roman Jews to Birkenau—the plot concerns the German encoding machine, Enigma, and a plot to steal it so as to cover up the fact that the Allies had already broken the code. Macmillan, 1981.

Peters, Elizabeth   THE SEVENTH SINNER
An art history student becomes involved in a murder, which also involves a beautiful art historian. Dodd, 1972.

Spencer, Elizabeth   KNIGHTS AND DRAGONS
In *The Stories of Elizabeth Spencer*—novelette of an American divorcée living in Rome. Doubleday, 1981.

Stevenson, Anne   A COIL OF SERPENTS
In befriending an elderly fellow-passenger on the flight into Rome, a young

woman becomes involved in art fraud, murder, and romance with an enigmatic count. Putnam Pub Group, 1977.

Tucci, Niccoló   THE SUN AND THE MOON
A family saga. (BRD) Knopf, 1977. This is a sequel to *Before My Time* (1962), conveying the social levels and the spirit of Rome at the turn of the century.

West, Morris L.   THE SHOES OF THE FISHERMAN
A fictional new pope is from the Ukraine, and has spent many years as prisoner of the Russians in Siberia—"fantastic novel . . . a whopper, a spellbinder, a cliffhanger, an annoyance and a delight." (FC) Morrow, 1963.

Williams, Tennessee   THE ROMAN SPRING OF MRS. STONE
A fading beauty of fifty meets a gigolo in Rome. New Directions, 1950.

Yourcenar, Marguerite   A COIN IN NINE HANDS
"A fictional cross section of Italian society" in 1933; in the 1980s remains "an elegant but sharp slap at . . . political degeneracy." (FC) FS&G, 1982.

ANCIENT ROME

Asch, Sholem   THE NAZARENE
"A historical background against which the figure of Jesus [moves] authentically." The story is narrated by a scholar who, as a Roman official in an earlier incarnation, was involved in the persecution of Jesus. (FC) Putnam Pub Group, 1939.

Bryher   THE COIN OF CARTHAGE
See under "North Africa/Novels."

Bulwer-Lytton, Sir Edward G.   THE LAST DAYS OF POMPEII
Pompeii just before and during the Vesuvius eruption in A.D. 79—"full of learning and spirit . . . a charming novel." (FC) Dodd, 1946 (first published 1834).

Caldwell, Taylor   DEAR AND GLORIOUS PHYSICIAN
See under "Middle East/Novels." Also *The Pillar of Iron* (1965), a "massive fictional biography of Cicero . . . against a panoramic background of Imperial Rome."

Costain, Thomas B.   THE SILVER CHALICE
Based on legends of the years following Christ's crucifixion. The Silver Chalice was meant to hold the cup from which Christ drank at the Last Supper. Doubleday, 1964.

Douglas, Lloyd C.   THE ROBE
The story of Christ's robe and the influence it had on the soldier who won it in dice—Christianity during those first years after the crucifixion. Houghton, 1942.

Duggan, Alfred   CHILDREN OF THE WOLF
Fictionalized version of the founding of Rome. Coward, 1959.

Feuchtwanger, Lion   THE JEW OF ROME
And also *Josephus* (1932) and *Josephus and the Emperor* (1942)—a trilogy; fictionalized history of the Jewish historian from A.D. 64 to his return to Rome after the fall of Jerusalem. Viking, 1936.

Graves, Robert   I, CLAUDIUS
The fascinating story of Imperial Rome, and the basis for the public TV series. A "work of the imagination that has the effect of history." Random, 1977 (first published 1934). The sequel is *Claudius the God* (1977, first published 1934).

Hersey, John   THE CONSPIRACY
Depicts Nero's tyrannical regime through a "series of dispatches, intercepted letters, files and interrogations." Knopf, 1972.

Sienkiewicz, Henryk   QUO VADIS
Historical novel of Nero's Rome and the Christian martyrs—won a Nobel Prize for literature in 1905. Airmont, 1968 (first published 1896).

Vidal, Gore   JULIAN
"About Julian the Apostate . . . who tried to restore the old gods of Hellenism" when he became emperor in A.D. 361. Ballantine, 1986 (first published 1964).

Wallace, Lew   BEN HUR
Ben Hur is sentenced to be a Roman galleyslave as the result of a false accusation, and his family are also sentenced to dreadful punishments. He escapes, seeks revenge, and finds his family who are miraculously cured by Jesus. Buccaneer Bks, 1981 (first published 1880).

Waltari, Mika   THE ROMAN
Setting is first century A.D., and the reigns of Claudius and Nero—the decadence of Rome, the rise of Christianity and the existence of other religions. Putnam Pub Group, 1966.

Warner, Rex   THE YOUNG CAESAR
Biographical novel "with a poet's skill and style—and, most fortunately, with the caution of a sound historian." (BRD) Little, 1958. A sequel, *Imperial Caesar* (1960) covers his last fifteen years.

Wilder, Thornton   THE IDES OF MARCH
"Historical novel or fantasy . . . the life of Julius Caesar and some other Romans during the months preceding Caesar's assassination." (FC) Har-Row, 1948.

Yourcenar, Marguerite   MEMOIRS OF HADRIAN
Historical novel based on the life of Emperor Hadrian. FS&G, 1963.

SICILY

Hersey, John   A BELL FOR ADANO
Pulitzer Prize novel about Americans in World War II Italy. Knopf, 1944.

Higgins, Jack   LUCIANO'S LUCK
It is 1943 and General Eisenhower enlists Mafia support for the invasion of Sicily—"fast-paced, action-crammed plot . . . the romanticizing of the Mafia figures jars a little [but] the historical premises are acceptably plausible." (FC) Stein & Day, 1981.

Lampedusa, Giuseppe di   THE LEOPARD
A prince and his family (1860-1910) as a feudal era crumbles. Pantheon, 1960.

Puzo, Mario   THE SICILIAN
"A fine, fast-paced novel about Sicily in the mid-1940s," following the career of a renegade who incurs the enmity of the Mafia. (FC) S&S, 1984.

Seton, Cynthia Propper   A FINE ROMANCE
The lives of two American families are changed when they meet on a tour bus over Christmas in Italy. Norton, 1976.

VENICE

Anthony, Evelyn   THE COMPANY OF SAINTS
An American diplomat and his daughter are assassinated in this novel of international intrigue featuring British super-spy Davina Graham. Putnam Pub Group, 1984.

Brent, Madeleine   TREGARON'S DAUGHTER
A gothic romance that begins in Cornwall, England, but the Palazzo Chiavelli in Venice is integral to the plot. Doubleday, 1971.

Gash, Jonathan   THE GONDOLA SCAM
The narrator is an antiques dealer/detective; the story "takes him from an illegal auction in England to the canals of Venice . . . can almost serve as a travel guide. . . . conveys the feeling of all who first visit Venice." (FC) St. Martin, 1984.

Habe, Hans   PALAZZO
A woman struggles to save her palazzo from collapse and deals in fraudulent art to raise the needed money—"portrayal of Venetian life at every level, from that of the communist gondolier to the cheap chic . . . the bored, idle rich kids, the elderly eccentrics." (FC) Putnam Pub Group, 1977.

Hemingway, Ernest   ACROSS THE RIVER AND INTO THE TREES
An American colonel and his love affair in post-World War II Venice. Scribner, 1950.

Holme, Timothy   A FUNERAL OF GONDOLAS
"Re-creates the busy vibrance of Venice in a plot as delightfully tortuous as the streets and canals of this strange city." An "off-beat police procedural" involving a gondoliers' betting syndicate. (FC) Coward, 1982.

James, Henry   THE ASPERN PAPERS
Novelette set in Venice by the nineteenth-century writer, in *The Complete Tales of Henry James.* Lippincott, 1975.

MacInnes, Helen   THE VENETIAN AFFAIR
Venice and Paris in 1961 and a plot to assassinate de Gaulle; "MacInnes' usual skillful plotting . . . and happily authentic background." (FC) HarBraceJ, 1963.

Mann, Thomas   DEATH IN VENICE
A successful writer, on a visit to Venice becomes aware of decadent potentialities in himself. Knopf, 1965 (first published 1925).

Pasinetti, P.M.   VENETIAN RED
Fortunes and passions of two Italian families in the period 1938 to 1941. Random, 1960.

Shellabarger, Samuel   PRINCE OF FOXES
Historical novel of Renaissance Venice and the house of the Borgias. Little, 1947. Also, *Lord Vanity* (1953), historical novel of eighteenth-century Venice.

Spark, Muriel   TERRITORIAL NIGHTS
An international comedy of manners. Coward, 1979.

TRAVEL ARTICLES

AMERICAN HERITAGE
1984 Jun "Painted on Water." American artists in Venice. Jerome Tarshis, p. 36

ARCHITECTURAL DIGEST
1985 May Travel Notes: "The Golden Air of Rome." Robert Venturi, p. 90

ATLANTIC
1984 Jul "A Stop in Verona." Corby Kummer, p. 106

BON APPETIT
1985 May "Traveling with Taste: Siena." Shirley Slater, p. 34
       Oct "The Pleasures of Sicily." Exploring exotic sights and unique restaurants of this sensual Mediterranean island. Paula Wolfert and William Bayer, p. 130
1984 Feb "Traveling with Taste: Emilia-Romagna." North central Italy. Jan Weimer, p. 24

CONNOISSEUR
1984 Mar "Classical Revival." Cooking tours of classic Italian cuisine. Corby Kummer, p. 110
       Jun "The Palio: It Happens Twice a Summer in Siena." Part pageant, part horserace, part pandemonium. Marina Warner, p. 120

1984 Sep "The ideal Italy." It is Piemonte at its sumptuous best right now. Nancy
Jenkins, p. 94
Nov "Most serene Venice." Three fabulous tours for this quiet season.
Thomas Hoving, p. 102
"Where to Eat Well in Venice"; "Where to Stay Comfortably." Ariane and
Michael Batterberry, p. 112

ESQUIRE
1985 Apr "The Eyes of Corsica." Jan Morris, p. 140
Oct "Venice, My Love." p. 42 (following p. 124)
"My Venice, My Self." Lewis Grossberger, p. 48 (following p. 124)

GOURMET
1985 Feb Gourmet Holidays: "Naples." Anne M. Zwack, p. 34
Apr "Hill Towns in Umbria." Nadia Stancioff, p. 40
Jun "Sardinia." Doone Beal, p. 48
Jul Gourmet Holidays: "Lake Garda." Terry Weeks, p. 44
Aug "A Stellar Chef in Nice." Chantecler Restaurant. Henry McNulty, p. 42
Sep "The Florentine Restaurant Scene." Anne M. Zwack, p. 46
Oct "Lugano's Vintage Festival." Terry Weeks, p. 50
"Florence's Villa Stibbert." Gerri Grotta, p. 62
Nov "Rome's Campus Martius on Foot." p. 72
"Fountains of Rome." Nadia Stancioff, p. 90
1984 Mar "Ravenna and Imola." Peter Todd Mitchell, p. 42
Apr "Ferrara and Modena." p. 52
May "Venice for a Song." Doone Beal, p. 44
Jun Gourmet Holidays: "Montecatini." Tuscany. Lillian Langseth-
Christensen, p. 37
Oct "The Flavors of Abruzzi." Anna T. Callen, p. 78

HARPER'S BAZAAR
1985 Apr "Lover's Guide to Venice." Kirsten Grimstad, p. 28
Sep "Hemingway's Venice." A.E. Hotchner, p. 48
Dec "Pinnacles of Powder: Cortina." Pat Leri, p. 24
1984 Mar "Sardinian Paradise." Peter Andrews, p. 14
Aug "The Aeolian Islands." Doone Beal, p. 28

HOUSE & GARDEN
1985 Jun "A Choice of Cloisters . . . Rome's Cloisters Offer a Variety of Nourish-
ment for the Eye and Ear." Louis Inturrisi, p. 44
1984 Apr "Parma's Secrets Revealed." Unknown treasures of the city famous for
ham, cheese and violets. Olivier Bernier, p. 20
Jul "The Kingdom of the Thousand Sicilies." Jan Morris, p. 30
Dec "Serenissima in the Snow." Secret pleasures of Venice at Christmastime.
Jason Epstein, p. 52

MODERN MATURITY
1985 Oct "A Landscape to Soothe the Heart." Ann Cornelisen, p. 8
1984 Jun-Jul "Surprising Sojourn." A journey through the unexpected in Italy.
Charles N. Barnard, p. 50

NATIONAL GEOGRAPHIC

1985 Dec "Vatican City." James Fallows, p. 723
"Treasures of the Vatican." p. 764
1984 Feb "Surviving Italian Style." William S. Ellis, p. 185
May "The Dead Do Tell Tales at Vesuvius." Rick Gore, p. 557
"A Prayer for Pozzuoli." Rick Gore, p. 614

NATIONAL GEOGRAPHIC TRAVELER

1984 Autumn "Smiling Verona . . . Riches from Roman, Medieval, and Renaissance Times." Kate Simon, p. 64

N.Y. TIMES SUNDAY TRAVEL SECTION (X)

1985 Jan 6 "Palestrina." The town where the Italian composer was born and a Roman oracle once held sway. Louis Inturrisi, p. 19

Feb 10 "Venice's Fortuny Museum." The artist's palazzo, used as home and studio, reflects his range of interests. Barbara L. Michaels, p. 9

Feb 24 "Homey Ski Spa in the Italian Alps." Bormio has hot springs in Dantean caves, seven churches, and a 6,000 foot vertical drop. Barbara L. Ascher, p. 19

Mar 3 "Taormina's Stop for Sybarites." San Domenico Palace Hotel. Mary Simons, p. 24

Mar 10 "Narrow Slices of Italy's Past." On the small, crooked streets . . . it is easy to lose one's way—and like it. Louis Inturrisi, p. 16

Mar 17 Shopper's World: "Faenza's Grand Tradition." Ceramics. Anne M. Zwack, p. 6

(Part 2, "Sophisticated Traveler") "On the Street Where I Live." Via Margutta. E.J. Dionne, Jr., p. 24

Mar 31 "18th-century Gems in an Unlikely Setting." Tiepolo's frescoes bring glory to the little town of Udine. Olivier Bernier, p. 9

Apr 7 Shopper's World: "A Roman Retreat for Body and Soul." Mary Davis Suro, p. 6

"In Sulmona, Easter Drama in the Piazza." Italian pageant with life-size statues. Susan Lumsden, p. 27

Apr 14 "What's Doing in Florence." Anne M. Zwack, p. 10

Apr 28 "Hints of Past Grandeur Along the Appian Way." It's still possible to drive the highways of Imperial Rome. Paul Hofmann, p. 9

May 26 "Golf, Italian-Swiss Style." On Alpine courses, the scenery can make you forget your worst shot. Thomas L. Friedman, p. 6

Jun 9 "Many-Faced, Contradictory, Ancient Sicily." An island stamped by many cultures. E.J. Dionne, Jr., p. 14

"Baroque Spirit of a Place and Its People." Insights from a Sicilian novelist. Leonardo Sciascia, p. 15

Jun 16 "On Not Getting There from Here." On how Italians give directions. Louis Inturrisi, p. 45

Jun 23 "Italian Cooking Renaissance." Six country inns that offer seasonal, regional and innovative fare. R.W. Apple, Jr., p. 6

"Shopper's Haunts Around the World." Includes Rome. Amanda M. Stinchecum, p. 16

Jun 30 "In Florence, Rooms with a View, a Sampling of Pensions." E.M. Forster might have cherished one or two. Anne M. Zwack, p. 19

1985 Jul 7 Shopper's World: "In Praise of Paper." Little bits of Venice (hand-printed papers). Grace Hechinger, p. 12

Jul 14 "In a Region of Vineyards and Olive Groves." A cuisine drawn from land and sea (Apulia). Nika Hazelton, p. 14

"Apulia: an Ancient, Rugged Land." R.W. Apple, Jr., p. 15

Jul 21 "The Taste of Tuscany at a Hilltop Monastery." Memorable meals at the Convento San Francesco. Bryan Miller, p. 7

Jul 28 Fare of the Country: "Florence Summer—Ice Cream con Brio." Anne M. Zwack, p. 6

Aug 4 Fare of the Country: "Italian Radicchio—Toss it or Grill it." Louis Inturrisi, p. 12

Sep 1 "Exploring the Etruscan Mystery." Museum shows and archaeological sites in Tuscany plus guide to exhibits, dining and lodging. Nancy Jenkins, p. 13

Sep 8 "Descending into Naples." Two previously timid writers decide to brave all for art and pizza. Barbara Flanagan, p. 35

Oct 6 ("Sophisticated Traveler") "Treks for the Sophisticated Traveler—A Landscape to Soothe the Heart." Ann Cornelisen, p. 8

"A Walk in the Cinque Terre." In Italy's Riviera di Levante, 12 scenic miles and 5 medieval villages. Robert Packard, p. 9

"The City Beneath Rome." Excavations under the city. William Weaver, p. 36

Oct 20 "Tuscany's Timeless Landscape." Old frescoes reflect today's scene. Rachel Billington, p. 14

"Getting into the Heart of Italy." Tuscany, Umbria. John Wain, p. 15

"Living the Life of a Tuscan Village." Gargonza was once Dante's refuge. Constance Rosenblum, p. 16

Nov 3 Shopper's World: "Sparkle of Venice Glitters in Glass." Deborah Blumenthal, p. 12

"Val Gardena: a Chalet for Six." Mary Simons, p. 29

Nov 17 "Pleasures and Palaces in Ducal Mantua." Splendors of a Renaissance court. Beth Archer Brombert, p. 9

Nov 24 "Why Italians Think They Hate Romans." Paul Hofmann, p. 41

Dec 1 "A Showcase for Palladio." Vicenza is the setting for the Renaissance architect's grandest palaces and villas. Olivier Bernier, p. 9

Dec 8 Fare of the Country: "Italy's Truffled Boar." Betty Fussell, p. 6

Dec 15 Fare of the Country: "Saving the Fruits of Sicily's Past." Mary T. Simeti, p. 6

Dec 22 Fare of the Country: "Panettone is Milan's Yuletide Treat." Gloria Levitas, p. 6

Dec 29 "Turin's Elegant Piazzas and Palazzos." William Weaver, p. 9

1984 Jan 8 "Monsters and Other Marvels." A bizarre medley of mysterious stone figures heads a group of attractions north of Rome. Arthur Vivante, p. 43

Jan 29 "Traces of Mann: Dearth in Venice." Henry Kamm, p. 141

Feb 5 Shopper's World: "Cremona, the City of Violin Makers." Anne M. Zwack, p. 6

Feb 12 "The Italian Tradition." Even in provincial cities all roads lead to the opera house. William Weaver, p. 15

1984   Feb 19 "Rome: On Foot in the Past." Strolling through the ages as the Romans do (with dining suggestions, tips on four outings). William Weaver, p. 14

"Roads That Lead Away from the Eternal City." Outings into Etruscan, classical and Renaissance days. Henry Kamm, p. 15

Mar 4 "The Unsung Splendors of Florence." Small museums and special finds. Susan Lumsden, p. 9

Mar 11 "Dolce Skiing in the Dolomites." Adele Riepe, p. 24

Mar 18 Fare of the Country: "Sicily's Sweet Seafaring Wine." Kay Eldredge, p. 6

(Part 2, "Sophisticated Traveler") "Lookout on a Sunny Coastline." Ravello, beach holiday Italian style. R.W. Apple, Jr., p. 39

Apr 1 "Sicily's Ancient Aerie of Stone." Erice. Kay Eldredge, p. 12

"Tucked Away, Yet Another Sistine Chapel." Fra Angelico paintings in the Vatican. Louis Inturrisi, p. 37

Apr 15 "My Venice: A City Repays a Lifetime of Visits." Luigi Barzini, p. 9

Apr 22 "How to Win at Roman Roulette." Crossing streets in Rome. Louis Inturrisi, p. 31

Apr 29 Fare of the Country: "In Naples, What Else But Pizza?" Paul Hofmann, p. 45

May 6 "What's Doing in Rome." Henry Kamm, p. 10

May 13 "Counting Steps When Steps Count." A special person perspective on Rome (Rome with a wheelchair, or for anyone who dreads a lot of steps). Norman Kotker, p. 51

May 20 "In Sicily a Classic View, Ancient Temples, Modern Comforts." Kay Eldredge, p. 15

May 27 Shopper's World: "From Italy's Attics and the Orient." Arezzo antiques fair with a list of additional antique fairs in Italy. Anne M. Zwack, p. 12

Jun 24 "Gardena: Alpine Valley Fit for a President." Out of the way mountain valley where Italy's president vacations. Paul Hofmann, p. 14

"A Simple Cuisine Provides Prodigal Pleasures." Village and small-town restaurants in Northern Italy. R.W. Apple, Jr., p. 15

"Sojourn in a Tuscan Town." Margaret M. Gillette, p. 16

Jul 8 "Men of Bronze Defeat Time." Archaeology and art findings of Greek warriors in Italy. Louis Inturrisi, p. 12

Jul 15 Correspondent's Choice: "Favorita: a Wealth of Art in Lugano." R.W. Apple, Jr., p. 12

"Perspectives on the Eternal City." Savoring its charms "just sitting around." Henry Morgan, p. 41

Jul 22 "Roman August." Keeping cool. Louis Inturrisi, p. 12

Aug 5 Shopper's World: "Cameos—Gift from the Sea." Deborah Blumenthal, p. 6

Aug 12 "The Scoop on Rome's Sweet Snow." Flavors from apricot to zucchini draw crowds to gelaterias. Louis Inturrisi, p. 9

Sep 9 Fare of the Country: "A New Harry's and More, in Venice." R.W. Apple, Jr., p. 6

Sep 23 "Italian Isle for Fall Sun." Ponza. Karen Wolman, p. 12

1984   Oct 7 (Part 2, "Sophisticated Traveler") "Tuscan Side Roads." Beyond
Florence and into a Renaissance landscape. Muriel Spark, p. 28; "Encounter
with an Italian Faun." Arturo Vivante, p. 16
Oct 14 Correspondent's Choice: "Lake Como's Peerless Village." Bellagio.
Paul Lewis, p. 15
Oct 21 Fare of the Country: "In Modena, the Right Stuff." Florence Fabricant,
p. 6
Nov 4 "Orvieto: Marvel of the Middle Ages." A cathedral more like a jewel
than a church. Olivier Bernier, p. 19
Nov 11 "Hail Soccer! Game Is All to Roman Fans." With care, a visitor can
share fever. Paul Hofmann, p. 51
Nov 18 "Where Echoes of Verdi Are Only an Overture." A visit to Busseto,
the composer's hometown. Morton N. Cohen, p. 9
Nov 25 Shopper's World: "Milan's High Street of Fashion." Via Monte
Napoleone. Rosalind B. Resnick, p. 6
Dec 16 "Wintering in Tuscany." Exploring Arezzo, an Italian hill town, from
top to bottom. William Weaver, p. 14
"A Romantic in Italy." Reprint of a 1909 piece for Printer's Pie Annual. W.
Somerset Maugham, p. 14
"On Piero's Own Ground." Many of the master's works can be seen in a
three-day tour of his region (and an itinerary for art lovers). R.W. Apple, Jr.,
p. 15
Dec 23 "Creche Figures from Italy." In Lecce. Anne M. Zwack, p. 15

READER'S DIGEST
1984 Dec "A Tale of Two Italys." An antipasto of chronic calamities yet it thrives,
con brio. Jeff Davidson, p. 162

SATURDAY EVENING POST
1984 Oct "Italy's Generous Heart." The northern Italian region of Emilia-
Romagna treats visitors to the good life, Italian style. Robert H. Bradford, p.
90

SMITHSONIAN
1984 Sep "Mosaics of San Marco." Herbert L. Kessler, p. 43

TOWN & COUNTRY
1984 Mar Visa-vis: "Venice." Jennifer Kramer, p. 236
Apr "La Buona Cucina, a Guide to Cooking Schools." Janet Carlson, p. 100

TRAVEL & LEISURE
1985 Feb "Italy's Grand Hotel Villa d'Este." Living the lazy life on the shores of
Lake Como. Pamela Fiori, p. 104
"Bird's Eye View of Vesuvius." A pleasant hike to the crater of Italy's world-
famous volcano. Dan Carlinsky, p. 50
Apr "Venice's Musical Treasure." The most beautiful small opera house in
the world. John Gruen, p. 36
Apr "Latest from Rome." Dwight V. Gast, p. 85
May "The Glorious Hill Towns of Umbria." Golden echoes of the Italian
renaissance in Orvieto, Perugia, Assisi and Spoleto. Eric Newby, p. 84

1985 May "Driving and Lingering in Umbria." The author's route and where to stay and eat. p. 94 (See also article on European driving and tours, p. 134) Jun "The Splendors of Palladio Italy." Touring the exquisite villas from Venice to Vicenza and beyond. Pierre Schneider, p. 116
Sep "Italy's Land of 'Kiss Me Kate'." A lyrical quartet of cities—Cremona, Parma, Mantua and Padua. p. 69
Oct "Milan's Galleria." An elegant arcade of shops and restaurants strikes a gracious note in a fast-paced city. Roman Czajkowsky, p. 186
Nov "Venice's House of Gold, Cal D'Oro." A 15th-century palazzo full of artistic masterpieces. Paolo Lanapoppi, p. 48
"Discovering Italy in a Gas Station." Cultural lessons learned while getting a flat fixed. Lawrence Eisenberg, p. 210
Dec "The Pleasures of Parma." Renaissance art and architecture, plus the famous cheese and ham. Charles Monaghan, p. 36
1984 Jan "The ancient splendors of Sicily." Views of Syracuse, old and new. Stephen S. Hall, p. 88
Mar "Montecatini—Italy's Splendid Spa." Taking the waters in an elegant old-world retreat. Christopher Cox, p. 16
Apr "Savoring Spring in Portovenere." Harbor views and quiet cafes on the Mediterranean. Doris Saatchi, p. 34
Jun "A Shopper's Venice." From fashions to glass, prints to masks. Gregory Usher, p. 66
Aug "Fantasy Hotels of Venice." George Lang, p. 50
Sep Travel & Architecture: "The Harmony of the Renaissance." Classical purity, reborn and transformed in Italy. Carter Ratcliff, p. 68
"Ravenna: a Medieval Treasury." Pierre Schneider, p. 106
Oct Travel & Architecture: "The Brilliance of the Byzantine." In Istanbul, Venice and the Greek isles. Alexander Eliot, p. 26
Nov "A Sculptors' Mecca in Tuscany: Pietrasanta." Haven to artists, from Michelangelo to Henry Moore. Jennifer Quale, p. 176

TRAVEL/HOLIDAY
1985 Oct "Michelangelo's Rome: A City Built on Art." Daniel Bickley, p. 46
1984 Jan "Ischia, Italy." Lavish, lava and mud packs. John Heindenry, p. 48
Jul "Mysterious Malta." Unveiling the island's secrets. Michael Pauls, p. 24

VOGUE
1985 Apr "Sampling Rome Off Season." Restaurants. Mimi Sheraton, p. 275
May "Luxury on the Lake." Timeless lure and legendary splendors of Lake Como's Villa d'Este hotel. Andrea Chambers, p. 236
Jul "Exploring Sicily." Eric Newby, p. 110
Aug "Grand Hotels: Positano's Cliff-clutching Il San Pietro." Barbara Kafka, p. 253
Oct "A Night on Torcello." Venice's most romantic isle. Jan Morris, p. 431
1984 Feb "Great Escapes: Venice in Winter." The secret season of the world's dreamiest city. p. 138
Jun "Splendors of the Spa." On island of Ischia—a glorious stay at a great spa hotel. Despina Messinesi, p. 173

WORLD PRESS REVIEW
1985 Jul "Italy's Fortunate Land." Alto Adige in Northern Italy. (*Gente Viaggi,* Milan). Luca Villa, p. 62

THE NETHERLANDS

Series Guidebook (See Appendix 1)

Baedeker: Netherlands, Belgium, Luxembourg; Amsterdam
Berlitz: Amsterdam
Blue Guide: Holland
Fodor: Holland; Amsterdam
Frommer: Amsterdam & Holland City Guide
U.S. Government: Netherlands: Background Notes; Post Report
         Low Countries: Pocket Guide: Belgium,
         Luxembourg, the Netherlands

Background Reading

Bailey, Anthony   REMBRANDT'S HOUSE
Rembrandt's house, now a museum, is the point of departure for an account of both his life and life in the seventeenth century. Houghton, 1978.

Brody, Elaine   THE MUSIC GUIDE TO BELGIUM, LUXEMBOURG, HOLLAND, AND SWITZERLAND
One of a series of guides for individual European countries—a handbook of information for a range of travelers "from the music dilettante to the highly motivated specialist." Includes information on the country's musical history, concert halls, opera houses, festivals, etc. Dodd, 1977. (See also *Music Festivals in Europe and Britain* and *Music Lover's Europe* under "Europe/Background Reading.")

Colijn, Helen   OF DUTCH WAYS
By an author who was born and educated in the Netherlands and returns there annually—"written by an insider . . . will enhance any tourist's stay by providing a better understanding of the people." (Publisher) Barnes & Noble, 1984.

Cotterell, Geoffrey   AMSTERDAM, THE LIFE OF A CITY
A traveler's history of Amsterdam with special attention to the past 400 years,

emphasizing works of art, buildings and places still available for viewing by tourists. Little, 1972.

Feldkamp, Frederick   NOT EVERYBODY'S EUROPE
A grand tour of nine unique places to think about adding to your itinerary—in Holland, it's Maastricht. Harper's Magazine Pr, 1976.

Frank, Anne   DIARY OF A YOUNG GIRL
The experiences of a Jewish family, living in hiding in Amsterdam during the Nazi occupation. Doubleday, 1967 (first published 1952).

Golding, William   A MOVING TARGET
A collection of the noted author's writings, including an article on the Dutch waterways. FS&G, 1982.

Hoffman, William   QUEEN JULIANA: THE STORY OF THE RICHEST
WOMAN IN THE WORLD
HarBraceJ, 1979.

GUIDEBOOKS

Gelderman-Curtis, C.   HOLLAND—INSIDE INFORMATION: THE
COMPLETE GUIDE TO HOLLAND
Heinman, 1980.

Green, Kerry and Bythines, Peter   THE WHOLE EUROPE ESCAPE
MANUAL: FRANCE, HOLLAND,
BELGIUM WITH LUXEMBOURG
One of a new series of guidebooks "designed to bring Europe to life and put the fantasy and excitement back into travel." World Leis Corp, 1984.

Greenberg, M.   THE HAGUE
Newsweek Bks, 1983.

Koning, Hans, ed.   AMSTERDAM
One of the Great Cities of the World series. Time-Life, 1977.

Sitwell, Sacheverell   THE NETHERLANDS
A Batsford guide. David, 1974.

HISTORY

Huggett, Frank E.   THE MODERN NETHERLANDS
Praeger, 1971.

Kossman, E.H.   THE LOW COUNTRIES, 1780-1940
Oxford U, 1978.

Novels

Camus, Albert   THE FALL
A successful lawyer in Amsterdam bares his soul to a stranger. Knopf, 1957.

Dumas, Alexandre   THE BLACK TULIP
Historical romance associated with the Haarlem tulip craze and Dutch history 1672-75. Dutton, 1961 (first published 1850).

Freeling, Nicolas   THE LOVELY LADIES
A seemingly senseless murder in Amsterdam leads to Dublin for an answer. Harper, 1971. Other mysteries in the Inspector Van der Valk series set in the Netherlands are *Criminal Conversation* (1966), *Auprés de ma Blonde* (1972).

Hartog, Jan de   THE LITTLE ARK
This is about the 1953 hurricane and its aftermath in a country so vulnerable to the sea. Atheneum, 1970 (first published 1953). Also *The Lost Sea* (1966), the adventures of a Dutch orphan who is kidnapped by a fishing boat captain.

Hartog, Jan de   THE INSPECTOR
Story of a "heroic, middle-aged Dutch policeman" who undertakes to get a young Dutch-Jewish girl to Israel before she dies as a result of her experiences in a concentration camp; set in 1946. Atheneum, 1960. Also *The Captain* (1966), story of a Hollander who escapes from the Nazis and does convoy duty on the Iceland-Murmansk run.

Holland, Cecelia   THE SEA BEGGARS
Historical novel set in the sixteenth century; a brother and sister fight for freedom with William of Orange. Knopf, 1982.

Koning, Hans   DEWITT'S WAR
An "intelligent thriller" set in a small town in Holland during World War II—one of Europe's richest men is murdered and the Germans have removed critical documents. (FC) Pantheon, 1983.

MacLean, Alistair   FLOODGATE
A group of terrorists threaten to blow up the dikes and flood the Netherlands to force England to withdraw her troops from Northern Ireland—set in and around Amsterdam. Doubleday, 1984.

Mulisch, Harry   THE ASSAULT
The first novel by a prominent Dutch author to be translated and published in the United States. Set mostly in Amsterdam and Haarlem—"a political thriller. . . . communal secrets and cowardices and terrors" left over from the German occupation during World War II. (NYTBR) Pantheon, 1985.

Schmitt, Gladys   REMBRANDT
Fictionalization of the life of Rembrandt. Random, 1961.

Schoonover, Lawrence   KEY OF GOLD
Three novellas, linked by a golden key; one is about a Jewish physician in Amsterdam who treats Spinoza. Little, 1968.

Van de Wetering, Janwillem   THE STREETBIRD
A murder mystery set in the red light district of Amsterdam with a pimp as the murder victim—"night-watch tale of this bizarre, seamy city within a city is full of life, death, intrigue and a shadowy magic." Putnam, 1983. Others in the series of murder mysteries by this author, solved by the team of Grijpstra and deGier and set in Amsterdam, include: *The Mind-Murders* (1981), *The Corpse on the Dike* (1976), *Tumbleweed* (1976), *Outsider in Amsterdam* (1975), *The Japanese Corpse* (1977) (Japan and Amsterdam), *Death of a Hawker* (1977).

Williams John A.   THE MAN WHO CRIED I AM
A dying American black man in Amsterdam discovers a plot to wipe out black organizations in America. Little, 1967.

TRAVEL ARTICLES

CONNOISSEUR
1984 Dec "Glimpses of Holland's Golden Age." Seventeenth-century dollhouses in an Amsterdam museum. Shirley Glubok, p. 112

GOURMET
1984 May Gourmet Holidays: "Cruising Holland's Waters." Mimi Elder, p. 36

NATIONAL GEOGRAPHIC TRAVELER
1985 Spring "Dutch Treat: the Tulips of Holland." Dale M. Brown, p. 20

N.Y. TIMES SUNDAY TRAVEL SECTION (X)
1985 Mar 24 "2 Dutch Forts That Retired Gracefully." A museum and a literary shrine. Michael Kammen, p. 9
Sep 29 "Buying Bulbs on a Floral Dutch Tour." Theodore James, Jr., p. 12
Oct 27 Fare of the Country: "Traditional Dutch tasting houses (of distilled spirits)." Kathy P. Behan, p. 12
Nov 17 Fare of the Country: "Pancakes with a flourish." Theodore James, Jr., p. 12
1984 Apr 1 "Amsterdam Speaks for Itself." The best of four centuries in a relaxed, welcoming city of canals. Donald Goddard, p. 9
Jul 15 "Canalside Hospitality." Nineteen buildings make up Amsterdam's Pulitzer Hotel. Marylin Bender, p. 6
Jul 22 "Except for the Windmills, the Belgian-Dutch Beach is a Lot Like Home." James M. Markham, p. 35
Sep 30 "Haarlem for Art, Tulips and More." Michael Kammen, p. 19
Oct 7 "In Holland, a Royal House Tour." Just outside Amsterdam, a restored palace offers a rare glimpse of how Dutch rulers lived. Marylin Bender, p. 14
(Part 2, "Sophisticated Traveler") "Amsterdam's Sunday Bazaar." Donald E. Westlake, p. 123

SUNSET
1984 Oct "Holland's Quietest Resort?" Vlieland by ferry from the mainland. p. 66

TRAVEL & LEISURE
1984 Apr Special section—Netherlands: "Amsterdam." "A human-size place,
small and intimate." Donald E. Westlake, p. 104; "Elegant Country Inns." Ian
Keown, p. 114; "Sophisticated Country Restaurants." Jean Anderson, p. 116;
"Tours to Holland." Bunny Brower, p. 136

TRAVEL/HOLIDAY
1985 Jun "Life Along the Zuider Zee." Exploring the Holland of your mind. Bill
Walker, p. 58

NORWAY
(Including Lapland)

Note: See also all asterisked (*) entries under Denmark for books on Scandinavia
as a whole, as well as the books listed under "Denmark/Vikings."

Series Guidebooks (See Appendix 1)

Baedeker: Scandinavia
Berlitz: Oslo & Bergen
Fodor: Scandinavia; Budget Scandinavia;
              Stockholm, Copenhagen, Oslo, Helsinki & Reykjavik
Frommer: Scandinavia: $-a-Day
U.S. Government: Norway: Background Notes; Post Report

Background Reading

Baden-Powell, Dorothy   PIMPERNEL GOLD
An exciting, suspenseful, true story of the Norwegian race to save their gold
supply following the German invasion in 1940. St. Martin, 1978.

Caraman, Philip   NORWAY
Account of a three-year stay of a Jesuit priest in Norway, and a long journey from
Oslo to the Norwegian-Russian border in the Arctic during spring and summer of
1966. Paul S. Erikson, 1969.

Lister, R.P.   A JOURNEY IN LAPLAND
See under "Sweden."

Marsden, Walter   LAPLAND
One of the World's Wild Places series. Time-Life, 1976.

Maxwell, A.E.   THE YEAR-LONG DAY—ONE MAN'S ARCTIC
A young Norwegian's life on Spitzbergen Island. Lippincott, 1976.

**Semmingsen, Ingrid   NORWAY TO AMERICA: A HISTORY OF
THE MIGRATION**
U of Minnesota, 1978.

Taylor, Suzanne   YOUNG AND HUNGRY
"A charming culinary memoir" combining a child's memories of her summers in Norway visiting her grandparents in a town and in a mountain cabin. Houghton, 1970.

Vanberg, Bent   OF NORWEGIAN WAYS
"A humorous, quite irreverent, and highly interesting history and description of Norway, of the Norwegian people, and also of their cousins overseas." (Publisher) Har-Row, 1984.

GUIDEBOOKS

Lundevall, E.   NORWAY TOURIST
Vanous, 1983.

Welle-Strand, E.   NORWAY, MOUNTAIN TOURING HOLIDAYS
Vanous, 1981. Also *Tourist in Norway* (1980), *Motoring* (1983), *Two Thousand Five Hundred Miles of the Norwegian Coastal Steamer* (1982), and *Angling* (1981).

HISTORY

Derry, T.K.   A SHORT HISTORY OF NORWAY
Greenwood, 1979 (first published 1968).

Midgard, J.   NORWAY: A BRIEF HISTORY
Vanous, 1982.

Novels

Barnard, Robert   DEATH IN A COLD CLIMATE (Tromso)
The murder of a young oil company executive is discovered by a local university professor and solved by Inspector Fagermo. Scribner, 1980.

Bojer, Johan   THE GREAT HUNGER
Story of a man's "hunger for the divine on earth . . . [is achieved] through disaster, suffering and sacrifice" rather than through his success as an engineer or his happiness in love. (FC) Moffat, 1919.

Buchan, John   THE THREE HOSTAGES
In *Adventurers All*; the plot involves the disappearance of three people, hypnotism; pursuit leads to London and Norway. Houghton, 1942 (first published 1924).

Francis, Dick   SLAYRIDE
One of Francis's many mysteries involving horseracing. An investigator for the British Jockey Club is brought to Oslo to solve the disappearance of racing receipts—"more than a suspense story . . . [a] novel with humor and authenticity of setting and characters." (FC) Har-Row, 1974.

Frison-Roche, Roger   THE RAID (Lapland)
The plot "turns on a blood feud and on the love between a young Lapp girl and a half-Lapp, half-Finnish fur trader . . . harsh but starkly beautiful sub-Arctic [setting]. . . graphically described folkways." (FC) Har-Row, 1964.

Gulbranssen, Trygve   BEYOND SING THE WOODS
Set in eighteenth-century Norway, this is the saga of a family of woodsfolk who rise to power and wealth, and their conflict with villagers. Putnam Pub Group, 1936. Its sequel is *The Wind from the Mountains* (1937).

Hamsun, Knut   GROWTH OF THE SOIL
A novel of "rude peasant life in an out-of-the-way corner of Norway"—it won the Nobel Prize for literature in 1920. Knopf, 1968 (first published 1917). Other novels by Hamsun include: *Hunger* (1890), about a struggling writer; *Pan* (1894), a "game of love" ends in a ruined life for the man; also *Mysteries* (1892), *The Wanderer* (1909), *Victoria* (1898).

Reeman, Douglas   SURFACE WITH DARING
Story of the British fleet in World War II with the important action set in Norway—the author "writes with nothing less than love for the fjords and the ocean . . . at their shores." (FC) Putnam Pub Group, 1977.

Thomas, Craig   SEA LEOPARD
Two connected suspenseful plots—the Russian Navy captures a submarine testing an advanced technical device while the KGB pursues its inventor in northern England. Viking, 1981.

Undset, Sigrid   KRISTIN LAVRANSDATTER: A TRILOGY
Originally published singly as *The Bridal Wreath* (1923), *The Mistress of Husaby* (1925), and *The Cross* (1927)—it takes its heroine from "happy childhood and later romance as wife and mother on a great estate, to her old age

and loneliness . . . one of the most realistic stories of a woman's life ever written." The setting is medieval Norway and the book is considered a masterpiece; its author won the Nobel Prize for literature in 1928. (FC) Knopf, 1959. Also *The Master of Hestviken* (1952), a portrait of thirteenth- and fourteenth-century Norwegian life in four volumes: *The Axe* (1928), *The Snake Pit* (1929), *In the Wilderness* (1929), and *The Son Avenger* (1930), which ends in 1814.

TRAVEL ARTICLES

ARCHITECTURAL DIGEST
1985 May Historic Houses: "Edvard Grieg's Troldhaugen." The composer in harmony with a rugged homeland. Anthony Burgess, p. 248

HOUSE & GARDEN
1985 Apr "By the Light of the Midnight Sun." Leaving behind global concerns for the calming routine of the Norwegian coast. George Kennan, p. 178

HOUSE BEAUTIFUL
1984 Apr "Travel and Design: How to Uncover the Hidden Design Treasures of Norway." p. 60

N.Y. TIMES SUNDAY TRAVEL SECTION (X)
1985 Mar 17 (Part 2, "Sophisticated Traveler") "Oslo: Meet the Cafe." The theatercafeen. Joseph Heller, p. 38
Mar 24 "Reindeer Country Beckons." A ski trip to Norwegian Lapland. Ruth Robinson, p. 18
1984 Mar 11 "Searching for the Essence of Winter." Arctic silence at the top of the world. Adam Nicolson, p. 12
Mar 18 (Part 2, "Sophisticated Traveler") "Snug Little Bergen." The gateway to the fjords . . . you just have to get to know it. Jan Morris, p. 86; "A guide to Fjord Country." Barnaby J. Feder, p. 110
Jun 3 "What's Doing in Oslo." Barnaby J. Feder, p. 10
Jul 29 Shopper's World: "In the Arctic, Jewelry Inspired by the Lapps." Ruth Robinson, p. 6
Sep 9 Norway's Civilized Mountain Trails Where Vistas are Grand and Tourist Huts Only a Day Apart." p. 19

SUNSET
1985 Jul "Hut-to-hut Hiking in the Glacier-scoured Mountains of Norway." p. 38

TRAVEL & LEISURE
1984 Jan "Oslo's Munch Museum." Norway's most famous artist. Gordon Moyer, p. 78

WORLD PRESS REVIEW
1985 Feb (Lapland) "Touring Reindeer Country." Hans E. Rubesamen (*Neue Zuricher Zeitung*, Zurich), p. 62

POLAND

Series Guidebooks (See Appendix 1)

Fodor: Eastern Europe
Nagel: Poland
U.S. Government: Poland: Background Notes; Country Study;
                    Post Report

Background Reading

Ash, Timothy G.   THE POLISH REVOLUTION: SOLIDARITY
The events in 1980-81 and the impact of Solidarity on Poland. Scribner, 1984.

Bloch, Alfred, ed.   THE REAL POLAND: AN ANTHOLOGY OF NATIONAL SELF-PERCEPTION
Selections of Polish writing—fiction and nonfiction—with the intent to acquaint non-Poles "with the unique way in which Poles view the world." (LJ) Continuum, 1982.

Brandys, Kazimierz   A WARSAW DIARY: 1978-1981
By a Polish novelist, diary excerpts that convey the atmosphere and reality of life in Poland "just prior to imposition of martial law in 1982. "An extraordinary book." (BRD) Random, 1984.

Eisner, Jack   THE SURVIVOR
The remarkable story of survival by a thirteen-year-old, as Poland falls to the Nazis, from imprisonment in the ghetto, to a concentration camp, to liberation by the Americans six years later at age nineteen. Morrow, 1980.

Gunther, John   TWELVE CITIES
The author of the highly popular "Inside" series of a couple of decades ago applies his unique zest and talent to a dozen cities, one of which is Warsaw—mood, temper, problems, politics, government. Har-Row, 1969.

Jadzewski, K.   POLAND
Ancient Poland; antiquities and archaeology, cultural history. Praeger, 1965.

Korbonski, Stefan   POLISH UNDERGROUND STATE
Hippocrene, 1980. Also *Fighting Warsaw, the Story of the Polish Underground* (1956).

Kurzman, Dan   THE BRAVEST BATTLE
"This is an account of the armed uprising of the Warsaw ghetto Jews against their Nazi exterminators, from April 19 to May 16, 1943." (BRD) Pinnacle, 1980.

Nowak, Jan COURIER FOR WARSAW
Exciting memoir of the Polish underground in World War II. Wayne State U, 1982.

Sebastian, Tim NICE PROMISES
"Presenting a side of Poland rarely seen on the network news . . . an intimate, colorful and personal account of events in Poland from 1979 and the Pope's first visit through to the imposition of martial law." Written by a BBC reporter who had access to a diverse group of people "from the most privileged bastions of the state to the most downtrodden. . . . Lech Walesa and the Solidarity leadership . . . Party bureaucracy . . . the Church—all are portrayed with a racy immediacy." (Publisher) Chatto & Windus, 1985.

Stewart, Steven THE POLES
A book "rich in history and analysis" that describes the Polish people, their heritage, country and city life, politics, religion. By a British journalist with a Polish-born wife and access to people Westerners would not ordinarily meet. (BL) Macmillan, 1983.

Weschler, Lawrence THE PASSION OF POLAND: FROM SOLIDARITY TO THE STATE OF WAR
Previously published in *Rolling Stone* and the *New Yorker*, and based on three trips to Poland during 1981-82. "The first outbreak of optimism . . . the crushing opposition by the government . . . martial law . . . voices and opinions [of Solidarity representatives, workers, government officials] in vividly related conversations . . . the role of the Catholic church . . . in the Polish national character and in [now] muted resistance." (BL) Pantheon, 1984.

GUIDEBOOKS

Bajcar, A. POLAND: A TOURIST GUIDE
Heinman, 1977.

Heine, Marc E. POLAND
A guidebook written by an American-educated author and with the Anglo-American in mind. Emphasizes places tourists most wish to see and general information on history, food, etc. Hippocrene, 1980.

HISTORY

Davies, Norman HEART OF EUROPE: A SHORT HISTORY OF POLAND
The Solidarity movement serves as a frame for the nation's history. Oxford U, 1984. Also *God's Playground*, a two-volume history (NYTBR) (Columbia U Pr, 1981)—"superbly readable, rich in detail . . . recounts both fact and legends that [have] contributed to the Poles' perception of their own history . . . a biography of Poland and a work of art."

Leslie, R.F., ed., and others THE HISTORY OF POLAND SINCE 1863
Cambridge U Pr, 1980.

Watt, Richard M.   BITTER GLORY: POLAND AND ITS FATE, 1918 TO 1939
History of the struggles for independence from the two giants on either side—Germany and Russia—which lasted for one brief period, 1918-1939. S&S, 1979.

Wedel, Janine   THE PRIVATE POLAND: A CONTEMPORARY SOCIAL HISTORY
Facts On File, 1985.

Novels

Agnon, S.Y.   THE BRIDAL CANOPY
The setting is early nineteenth-century Galicia, and the story is about a Jew who must find dowries for three daughters. Schocken, 1967 (first published 1922). Also *A Guest for the Night* (1937).

Barash, Asher   PICTURES FROM A BREWERY
Family saga of Jewish life in a small Polish town in the early 1900s. Bobbs, 1974.

Brandys, Kazimierz   A QUESTION OF REALITY
Scribner, 1980.

Karmel-Wolfe, Henia   THE BADERS OF JACOB STREET (Krakow)
The impact of the German occupation on a Jewish family that has lived on Jacob Street for many generations. Lippincott, 1970.

Kosinski, Jerzy   THE PAINTED BIRD
Wanderings of a dark-haired child in Poland in World War II and the cruelties visited upon him because he is different-looking than the typical Polish child—an indictment of man's inhumanity to man. Houghton, 1976.

Kuniczak, W.S.   THE THOUSAND-HOUR DAY
The first thousand hours of World War II as Poland surrenders to the Germans. Dial, 1967.

Michener, James A.   POLAND
The author uses a fictional village on the Vistula River and vignettes from the 1200s to the 1980s to tell the saga of three families, and thereby the story of Poland—"historically accurate . . . highly vivid . . . an engrossing and fast moving novel by a superb storyteller." (FC) Random, 1983.

Milosz, Czeslaw   THE SEIZURE OF POWER
Begins in the summer of 1944; the author "catalogues the reactions of a broad swath of Poles to . . . first the splintered resistance to the Nazis and then the . . . compromises and killing that arrives with the Russians. . . . based on actual characters of the period." (FC) FS&G, 1982.

Morgulas, Jerrold   THE TWELFTH POWER OF EVIL
A labyrinthine plot involving a deal between I.G. Farben and the Criterion Oil
Company to share synthetic rubber patents, and a refugee organization
determined to stop their conspiracy and their efforts to keep U.S. bombing
missions away from Auschwitz and the nearby Farben rubber factory. Seaview,
1981.

Read, Piers Paul   POLONAISE
Saga of an aristocratic family from 1925 to 1958, set in Poland and later in
Paris—whirls through "sexual escapades, the Spanish Civil War, flight from the
Russians, and a jewel theft." (FC) Lippincott, 1976.

Singer, Isaac Bashevis   THE MANOR
Portrays the period between the Polish insurrection of 1863 and the end of the
nineteenth century. FS&G, 1967. Its sequel, *The Estate* (1969) covers the same
period. Other novels by this Nobel Prize-winning author, set in Poland, include:
Yoshe Kalb (1933), *The Brothers Ashkenazi* (1936), *The Magician of Lublin*
(1960), *The Slave* (1962), *Satan in Goray* (1955), *The Seance and other Stories*
(1968), and a recent novel, *Reaches of Heaven: A Story of the Baal Shem Tov*
(1980). See also under "Warsaw," below.

WARSAW

Asch, Sholem   MOTTKE, THE THIEF
Story of life in a Jewish village and in the underworld of Warsaw. Greenwood Pr,
1970 (first published 1917).

Hall, Adam   THE WARSAW DOCUMENT
Agent Quiller of the British secret service infiltrates the Polish underground.
Doubleday, 1971.

Hersey, John   THE WALL
The resistance of Polish Jews as they are systematically exterminated by the
Nazis. Knopf, 1962.

Hlasko, Marek   THE EIGHTH DAY OF THE WEEK
Set in Warsaw of 1956; story of a family's everyday life—"all waiting for that
eighth day of the week which will liberate them"—"illuminating insights into the
social and personal problems that beset the Poles." (FC) Dutton, 1958.

Konwicki, Tadeůsz   A MINOR APOCALYPSE
Chronicle of the Warsaw vagaries of a writer who has been asked to set himself
afire as a protest in front of Communist party headquarters—"combines the
surrealist detail of a dream with the repartee and reflection of a novel of ideas."
(FC) FS&G, 1983.

Orlev, Uri   THE LEAD SOLDIERS
A "semiautobiographical unreeling of a childhood mangled through the

German occupation of Poland, the Warsaw ghetto uprising . . . more telling for its sober inclusion of small normal joys in the picture of a life lived in flight and terror." (FC) Taplinger, 1980 (first published 1956).

Simpson, John   A FINE AND PRIVATE PLACE (Krakow)
An espionage thriller. A Polish defector, now at Cambridge University, is convinced to make a trip to Krakow to visit his dying father, but also to smuggle radio parts in for a Solidarity group. The inexperienced hero must deal with an informer and a double agent; this thriller by a BBC editor also provides "interesting bits of Polish history and glimpses of the beauty and austerity of present-day Cracow." (NYTBR) St. Martin, 1984.

Singer, Isaac Bashevis   SHOSHA
A young writer in Warsaw of the 1930s escapes political confrontations by involving himself with women, including his early love, Shosha. FS&G, 1978. Also *The Family Moskat* (1950), story of a Jewish family from the nineteenth century to the beginning of World War II.

Uris, Leon   MILA 18
Story of "the handful of men and women who, knowing they had to die, defied the whole German Army with their homemade weapons"—Mila 18 was their command post. (FC) Doubleday, 1961.

NO TRAVEL ARTICLES IN THIS SECTION

PORTUGAL

Series Guidebooks (See Appendix 1)

Baedeker: Portugal
Berlitz: Algarve; Lisbon; Madeira
Blue Guide: Portugal
Fisher: Spain & Portugal
Fodor: Portugal; Lisbon
Frommer: Lisbon, Madrid & Costa del Sol: $-a-Day
            Portugal, Madeira & the Azores: Dollarwise
Let's Go: Spain, Portugal & Morocco
Michelin: Portugal
Nagel: Portugal (Madeira, the Azores)
U.S. Government: Portugal: Area Handbook; Background Notes;
            Pocket Guide (includes the Azores); Post Report

Background Reading

Bridge, Ann and Lowndes, Susan **SELECTIVE TRAVELLER IN PORTUGAL**
Both authors lived in Portugal for many years—manners, customs, art, architecture, history, countryside. McGraw, 1968.

Dos Passos, John **THE PORTUGAL STORY**
"Three centuries of exploration and discovery" is the subtitle for this book by the American novelist, which tells of the extraordinary explorations of the Portuguese and establishment of the first extensive overseas empire of the period. Doubleday, 1969.

Gribble, F.A. **THE ROYAL HOUSE OF PORTUGAL**
Kennikat, 1970.

MacKendrick, Paul L. **THE IBERIAN STONES SPEAK**
Introduction to archaeology and cultural history through archaeological findings in Spain and Portugal. Funk & Wagnall, 1969.

Mailer, Phil **PORTUGAL: THE IMPOSSIBLE REVOLUTION?**
Recounts the events of April 1974, when the country moved from dictatorship to moderation. Free Life, 1977.

Read, Jan **MOORS IN SPAIN & PORTUGAL**
The aim is to help visitors and armchair travelers to appreciate and discern present-day effects of the Moorish presence (710-1614), and to see Spain and Portugal of today in historic perspective. Rowman, 1975.

Tuohy, Frank and Finlayson, Graham **PORTUGAL**
An introduction to the country in text and photos. Viking, 1970.

GUIDEBOOKS

Cox, Thornton **THORNTON COX'S TRAVELLERS' GUIDE TO PORTUGAL**
"Highly readable introduction to the area under consideration. . . . necessary data for getting there and getting about . . . suggested itineraries [designed for] economy of time and movement." (Publisher) Hippocrene, 1982.

Pink, Annette **MADEIRA & THE CANARIES**
Sidwick & Jackson, 1983.

Salter, Cedric **ALGARVE AND SOUTHERN PORTUGAL**
Hastings, 1974.

Steves, Rick **SPAIN AND PORTUGAL IN 22 DAYS**
John Muir, 1986.

Wuerpel, Charles E.   THE ALGARVE, PROVINCE OF PORTUGAL
David, 1974.

HISTORY

Figueiredo, Antonio de   PORTUGAL
Portrait of Portugal and its former colonies under Salazar, 1932-68. Holmes &
Meier, 1976.

Livermore, H.V.   A NEW HISTORY OF PORTUGAL
Cambridge U Pr, 1976.

O'Callaghan, J.F.   HISTORY OF MEDIEVAL SPAIN
The author's Spain "is the entire peninsula [and] Islamic, Jewish, Christian,
Portuguese, and Catalonian as well as Castilian" Spain and Portugal. (BRD) Cornell
U, 1983 (first published 1975).

Novels

Canning, Victor   BIRD CAGE
An ex-nun, and the man who saves her from intended suicide (and with whom
she falls in love), are "pawns in a dirty game . . . an intricate story . . . hard to put
down—or forget." (FC) Morrow, 1979.

Ferrars, E.X.   WITNESS BEFORE THE FACT (Madeira)
The murder of the director of a scientific institute is solved by Dr. Emma
Ritchie's "acute, scientific mind . . . bringing her into a taut showdown with the
killer." (FC) Doubleday, 1981.

Hodge, Jane A.   THE WINDING STAIR
A suspenseful Gothic romance set in early nineteenth-century Portugal with a
plot concerning a secret society determined to control Portugal. Doubleday,
1969. Also, set in Regency England and Portugal, *Marry in Haste* (1970).

Lambert, Derek   THE JUDAS CODE
A complicated plot in which a Russian in Lisbon (an illegitimate son of Stalin) is
recruited by British Intelligence to help Churchill's "plan to embroil Germany and
Russia in a mutually destructive war"; for "World War II buffs and espionage
devotees alike." (FC) Stein & Day, 1984.

L'Engle, Madeleine   THE LOVE LETTERS
A contemporary woman learns to deal with her own marriage after reading a
packet of old love letters. FS&G, 1966.

Patterson, Harry   TO CATCH A KING
Hitler sends an SS officer to Lisbon in 1940, to persuade the Duke and Duchess
of Windsor to join the Nazis, or to kidnap them, but the plot falls through when an
American singer intervenes. Stein & Day, 1979.

TRAVEL ARTICLES

BON APPETIT
1984 Nov "Inns and Vineyards of a Fascinating Country." Jean Anderson, p. 170

GLAMOUR
1984 Feb "Portugal is Europe Like It Used to Be (Pricewise) and It's Charmingly Old-Fashioned Too." p. 158

NATIONAL GEOGRAPHIC
1984 Oct "Iberia's Vintage River." With two names and a thousand dimensions (and a traveler's map of Spain). Marion Kaplan, p. 460

NATIONAL GEOGRAPHIC TRAVELER
1985 Winter "Sun, Sea, and History—Portugal's Algarve." Geoffrey Moorhouse, p. 124

N.Y. TIMES SUNDAY TRAVEL SECTION (X)
1985 Apr 21 Correspondent's Choice: "Jerónimos." The glory of Old Portugal. Paul Lewis, p. 6
Nov 17 Shopper's World: "In Portuguese rugs, a stitch out of time." Joan Chatfield-Taylor, p. 6
1984 Jan 22 "What's Doing in the Algarve." Marion Kaplan, p. 10
Feb 12 Fare of the Country: "Portugal's Savory Cataplana." Paul Lewis, p. 6
Feb 19 "One Man's Treasures." The Gulbenkian Museum in Lisbon. Olivier Bernier, p. 9
Jun 10 "What's Doing in Lisbon." Marion Kaplan, p. 10
Sep 2 "The Glittering Costa Smeralda Where Luxury and Rugged Landscape Coexist." Danielle Gardner, p. 8
Sep 9 "Sampling Portugal's Cities." Lisbon and beyond. Harold C. Schonberg, p. 14
"Buying Crafts Under the Trees of Barcelos." Lonnie Schlein, p. 14
"Recalling the Nation's Glory Days: Historic Towns of Braga and Coimbra." Sarah Caudwell, p. 15
Oct 21 "The Good Life, Portuguese Style." Manor houses taking in paying guests on Costa Verde. Marvine Howe, p. 9
Dec 2 "Portugal's Spas: Palaces from Another Era." David M. Alpern, p. 19

TRAVEL & LEISURE
1985 Jan "A Romantic Hill Town in Portugal." Immortalized by Byron, Sintra captures the heart with its uncommon beauty. Robert Packard, p. 120
Aug "Scenic Drive: Portugal's River of Gold." Jean Anderson, p. 129
Oct "Savoring the Algarve." Jean Anderson, p. 168
1984 Feb "Portugal's Center of Modern Art." Museum in Lisbon. Patricia Brooks, p. 40
Jun "Fine Dining in and Around Lisbon." Bunny Brower, p. 77
Sep "The Grace of Portuguese Bullfighting." A stirring (and bloodless) spectacle. Bern Keating, p. 92

VOGUE
1984 Oct (Madeira) "Island Out of Time." Amazing landscapes, sublime weather, the refined joys of a Victorian vacation. Alan Fraser, p. 544

RUMANIA

Series Guidebooks (See Appendix 1)

Fodor: Eastern Europe
Nagel: Rumania
U.S. Government: Rumania: Background Notes; Country Study;
               Post Report

Background Reading

MacKendrick, Paul   THE DACIAN STONES SPEAK
Archaeology and history based on archaeological sites in the Roman province of
Dacia, now roughly the country of Rumania. U of North Carolina Pr, 1975.

Pakula, Hannah   THE LAST ROMANTIC
Biography of the flamboyant Queen Marie of Rumania who reigned from 1914
to 1927. S&S, 1985.

Pilon, Juliana G.   NOTES FROM THE OTHER SIDE OF NIGHT
An account of the author's return to Rumania in 1975, having emigrated from
the country as a child. "Illuminates . . . the drabness, boredom and monotony" of
daily existence in a Communist country. (BRD) Regnery, 1979.

HISTORY

Fischer-Galati, Stephen A.   TWENTIETH CENTURY RUMANIA
Columbia U Pr, 1970.

Matley, I.M.   ROMANIA: A PROFILE
Overview and introduction for the foreign traveler. Praeger, 1970.

Novels

Bellow, Saul   THE DEAN'S DECEMBER
A Chicago newspaperman travels to Bucharest to help his wife care for her
mother who is dying, while back in Chicago his articles have embroiled him in
controversy. A "political, social and philosophical [novel] rather than personal.
The rapid switching back and forth between Bucharest and Chicago endows the
book with a nervous, flickering energy." (FC) Har-Row, 1982.

Dorian, Marguerite   RIDE ON THE MILKY WAY
An evocative story of childhood in Bucharest. Crown, 1967.

Dorian, Marguerite   THE YEAR OF THE WATER BEARER
Recreates a period in the life of the author's great grandmother in the 1860s in a
Rumanian village setting. Macmillan, 1976.

Eliade, Mircea   THE OLD MAN AND THE BUREAUCRATS
A retired schoolteacher is detained for questioning by the communist government and tells them tales of fantastic and miraculous adventures of his students
until the questioners begin to fall under the spell of the stories. U of Notre Dame,
1980.

Eliade, Mircea   THE FORBIDDEN FOREST
The changing worlds of Rumania and Europe from 1936 to 1948, with the rise of
fascism and the destruction of the bourgeoisie. U of Notre Dame, 1978.

Manning, Olivia   THE BALKAN TRILOGY
Three novels: *The Great Fortune* (1960), *The Spoilt City* (1962), *Friends and
Heroes* (1965). The first takes place in Rumania at the outbreak of World War II
and the plot revolves about an English lecturer at the local university in Bucharest
and his wife, as Poland falls to the Nazis and refugees begin flooding in. The second
is set in the 1940s and the last days of King Carol's reign. In the third, the couple
have fled from German-occupied Rumania to Greece. The trilogy is "full of intriguing minor characters . . . evocative of both place and mood . . . an amazingly full and
colorful canvas [that] hardly seems like fiction." Penguin, 1982 (first published
1960-65).

Stancu, Zaharia   BAREFOOT
Reprint of a novel about the peasant uprising in the early 1900s, which is a
Rumanian national classic. Twayne, 1972 (first published 1948).

TRAVEL ARTICLES

ARCHITECTURAL DIGEST
1984 Apr Historic Houses: "In the shadow of Dracula." The dark trail leading to
Bran Castle. Thomas O'Neil, p. 176

N.Y. TIMES SUNDAY TRAVEL SECTION (X)
1985 Jul 28 "Along an East European Border." One family of American tourists
finds entering and leaving Rumania an unsettling experience. Edward
Cowan, p. 37
1984 Oct 14 (Transylvania) "Pilgrimage to Sighet, a Haunted City." Elie Wiesel, p.
51

SCOTLAND

Note: See also all asterisked entries (*) under "England" for additional series
guides, background books, and articles that may include Scotland.

Series Guidebooks (See Appendix 1)

Berlitz: Scotland
Blue Guide: Scotland
Companion Guide: West Highlands of Scotland
Fodor: Scotland
Frommer: England & Scotland: $-a-Day; Dollarwise
Let's Go: Britain & Ireland (Scotland & Wales)

Background Reading

Anderson, Moira and Martin, Netta   SCOTLAND
Using Scottish songs as a takeoff point, the author (an international entertainer and recording artist) conducts "an elegant personal tour" of her country—"places that have a special Scottish significance." (Publisher) Salem Hse, 1983.

Begley, Eve   OF SCOTTISH WAYS
"A wealth of information on Scotland and the Scottish conveyed in a bright, spritely . . . style." (Publisher) Barnes & Noble, 1978.

Fraser, Amy   ROSES IN DECEMBER
Memoir of the Edwardian age in a country manse near Balmoral Castle. Routledge, 1981.

**Gordon, Sheila   A MODEST HARMONY: SEVERN SUMMERS IN A
                    SCOTTISH GLEN**
"A graceful, entertaining" account of the novelist's summers spent with her family in Perthshire—"characterizations of the people . . . regional lore and history." (BL) Seaview, 1982.

Hanley, Clifford   THE SCOTS
"Profiles noble and ignoble of Scots of the past . . . the difference between Highlands and Lowlands, [dips into] golf . . . haggis . . . Scotch whiskey . . . Scottish experiences and states of mind." (BL) Times Bks, 1980.

Hawken, Paul   THE MAGIC OF FINDHORN
An account of this unique international community in northeastern Scotland, from its beginnings to "spiritual greenhouse" for thousands of people who visit each year. Harper, 1975. Also *Findhorn Garden* (1976).

Little, G. Allen   SCOTLAND'S GARDENS
Salem Hse, 1984.

MacGregor, Geddes   SCOTLAND FOREVER HOME
An introduction to the homeland for American and other Scots—great introductory reading by a Scottish-American. Dodd, 1980.

Maxwell, Gavin   RING OF BRIGHT WATER
For anyone who loves nature and animals—description of a remote and lovely
area of coastal (Highland) Scotland, and the author's unique relationship with two
sea otters. Dutton, 1965.

Miller, Christian   A CHILDHOOD IN SCOTLAND
Amusing, nostalgic memories of life in the 1920s in a castle with friendly ghosts.
Doubleday, 1982.

Morton, H.V.   IN SEARCH OF SCOTLAND
Reprint of a travel classic. Dodd, 1984 (first published 1930). See also *Morton's
Britain* under "England."

**Orel, Harold and others   THE SCOTTISH WORLD: HISTORY AND
CULTURE OF SCOTLAND**
Ten essays seek to show that Scottish culture is distinctly different from
English—art, architecture, literature, music, history. Abrams, 1981.

Prebble, John   JOHN PREBBLE'S SCOTLAND
Survey of the land by a novelist and clan historian—"cordial prose intertwines
historical, literary, geographical, and autobiographical anecdotes delightfully."
(BL) Secker & Warburg, 1985.

Shenker, Israel   IN THE FOOTSTEPS OF JOHNSON & BOSWELL
The author follows the itinerary of Johnson and Boswell (taken and written
about some 200 years earlier) to tell what they saw and to talk to descendants of
those Johnson and Boswell talked to; visits to castles, churches, great homes, inns,
ruins—"often witty, always deft and engaging." (PW) Houghton, 1982.

Slavin, Ken and Julie   AROUND SCOTLAND: A TOURING GUIDE
A "pre-trip planning guide especially for travelers intending to tour by car, but
useful for anyone considering a visit to Scotland"—arranged by region. (PW)
Hippocrene, 1983.

Steel, Tom   SCOTLAND'S STORY
Scotland's love-hate relationship with England, its influence on Britain, the fate
of Scots who moved away—"brings history alive using the words of contemporary
people wherever possible." Salem Hse, 1986.

EDINBURGH, GLASGOW, ABERDEEN

Daiches, David   EDINBURGH and GLASGOW
Chronicles of the cities. Hamish Hamilton, 1979.

Gifford, John and others   EDINBURGH
"An architectural guide" for travelers and serious students. Provides an introduction to the city and indexes to buildings, streets and artists. (LJ) Viking, 1985.

Hamilton, Alan   ESSENTIAL EDINBURGH
A walking tour of the Scottish city by a staff writer of the *London Times*.
Deutsch, 1978.

McGreevy, John, ed.   CITIES
Impressions of world cities as seen through the eyes of people intimately connected with them—for Glasgow it's R.D. Laing's impressions. Outlet Bk, 1981.

Morris, Jan   JOURNEYS; TRAVELS
Two collections of travel essays by a leading travel writer; there's an essay on
Aberdeen in *Journeys* and one on Edinburgh in *Travels*. Oxford U, 1984.

**Royle, Trevor   PRECIPITOUS CITY: THE STORY OF
LITERARY EDINBURGH**
Literary history of the city "written in lively style . . . entertaining reading." (BL)
Taplinger, 1980.

ISLANDS

ISLANDS OF THE WORLD
A series of introductions to many islands including, for Scotland: the Shetlands
(1984), the Orkneys (1974), the Uists and Barra (1974), Kintyre (1974), Staffa
and Bute (1973). David.

MacLean, Charles   ISLAND ON THE EDGE OF THE WORLD
The story of St. Kilda, which, until 1930, was home for an isolated community
with commonly held property and an economy based on agriculture, sheep, birds,
feathers and oil. Nineteenth-century travelers brought disease and a decline in the
economy until remaining residents were evacuated in 1930. Taplinger, 1980.

McPhee, John   THE CROFTER AND THE LAIRD
Colonsay Island—its terrain, history, legends and gossip, by an American (a staff
writer for the *New Yorker*) whose ancestors once lived there. FS&G, 1970.

Schei, Liv and Moberg, Gunnie   THE ORKNEY STORY
Comprehensive guide to the Orkneys off Scotland's northeast coast—history,
folklore, language, culture, government, lives, occupations, photographs.
Hippocrene, 1985.

Shepherd, Stella   LIKE A MANTLE, THE SEA
Depicts a way of life on the Shetland Islands "both rare and refreshing" by a
woman who lived on them for eight years. Ohio U, 1971.

Tomkies, Mike   BETWEEN EARTH AND PARADISE
"A naturalist's outlook . . . on his lonely wilderness life on a beautiful coastal
island in the Scottish highlands . . . natural history laced with drama and humor."
(BL) Doubleday, 1982.

GUIDEBOOKS

Carter, Jenny   THE HIGHLANDS & ISLANDS OF SCOTLAND
Batsford, 1983.

**Crowl, Philip A.   THE INTELLIGENT TRAVELLER'S
GUIDE TO HISTORIC SCOTLAND**
Companion to the author's guide to historic Britain—narrative history and gazetteer. Congdon & Weed, 1985.

Hamilton, David   GOOD GOLF GUIDE TO SCOTLAND
A guided tour to championship courses, one-hole layouts, remote clubs, town clubs; maps, directions, nearby attractions. Pelican, 1984.

Tindall, Jemima   SCOTTISH ISLAND HOPPING
A handbook for the independent traveler—an uncommon travel ground, the remote (Hebrides, Orkneys, Shetlands) islands off the Scottish coast. Practical travel information, history and an introduction to the islands. Hippocrene, 1983.

HISTORY

Glover, Janet R.   THE STORY OF SCOTLAND
Faber & Faber, 1977.

Kellas, James G.   MODERN SCOTLAND
Allen Unwin, 1980.

Mackie, John D.   A HISTORY OF SCOTLAND
Penguin, 1978.

MacLean, Fitzroy   A CONCISE HISTORY OF SCOTLAND
Untangles the "incredibly complicated skein of Scottish history." (LJ) Thames Hudson, 1983 (first published 1970).

Somerset Fry, Plantaganet and Fiona   THE HISTORY OF SCOTLAND
The unique qualities that set Scotland apart from England. Routledge, 1982.

Novels

Aiken, Joan   CASTLE BAREBANE
A gothic set in a remote part of Scotland in the nineteenth century—after starting out at a "genteel [level] takes a turn to brutality, violence, terror and death." (FC) Viking, 1976.

Barrie, J.M.   LITTLE MINISTER
The classic romance—"skilful portrayal of the complexities of Scotch character." (FC) AMS, 1975 (first published 1891).

Black, Laura   STRATHGALLANT
St. Martin, 1981. This, and *Ravenburn* (1978), are romances set in nineteenth-century Scotland.

Crichton, Robert   THE CAMERONS
An "enslaving mining town" at the turn of the century is the setting for this novel about the impoverished miners of that day. (FC) Knopf, 1972.

Cronin, A.J.   THE GREEN YEARS
Story of a boy growing up in a small Scottish village. Little, 1944. The sequel is *Shannon's Way* (1948). Also *Hatter's Castle* (1931).

Dunnett, Dorothy   KING HEREAFTER
Historical novel of eleventh-century Scotland at a time when the Viking culture is challenged by the Christian influence. Knopf, 1982. Also *Disorderly Knights* (1966), *The Game of Kings* (1961) and *Queen's Play* (1964).

Gibbon, Lewis G.   A SCOTS QUAIR
Three novels—*Sunset Song*, *Cloud Howe*, and *Grey Granite*—tell of Christine Guthrie's life in a small Scottish village; subsequently made into a public TV series. Schocken, 1977 (first published 1932-34).

Herron, Shaun   ALADALE
Historical novel—fictionalized account of real events in 1817 when The Aladale was the best of the illegal whiskeys in Scotland. Summit Bks, 1979.

Hunter, Alan   THE SCOTTISH DECISION
One of a series of mysteries in which the sleuth is Chief Superintendent Gently—"the seemingly unrelated crash of a small aircraft and the kidnapping of [a] French industrialist" are the plot's basis. (FC) Walker, 1981.

Marshall, Bruce   THE WORLD, THE FLESH AND FATHER SMITH
"Endearing portrait study of a Catholic priest . . . his parishioners . . . his bishop" in a Scottish city that spurns their faith. (FC) Houghton, 1945.

Peters, Elizabeth   LEGEND IN GREEN VELVET
"Romantic suspense, steeped in Scottish history"—a young American student interested in archaeological sites meets a young Scot and they stumble on a murder. (FC) Dodd, 1976.

Plaidy, Jean   THE CAPTIVE QUEEN OF SCOTS
Historical novel of the last eighteen years of Queen Mary of Scots. Putnam Pub Group, 1970 (first published 1963). Also *Royal Road to Fotheringay* (1955) (story of Mary's childhood and early reign in France and Scotland).

Sayers, Dorothy L.   THE FIVE RED HERRINGS
A Peter Wimsey mystery set in a Scottish village. Har-Row, 1958.

Stevenson, D.E.   VITTORIA COTTAGE
First in a family trilogy. Holt, 1971 (first published 1949). *Music in the Hills*

(1950) and *Shoulder in the Sky* (1951), complete the series. Two other Scottish family sagas by Stevenson are *Mrs. Tim Christie* (1940), *Mrs. Tim Carries On* (1941), *Mrs. Tim Gets a Job* (1952), *Mrs. Tim Flies Home* (1952); and *Celia's House,* (1977) forty years of a family's life in the Scottish border country.

Tey, Josephine   THE SINGING SANDS
En route to Scotland by train, Inspector Grant finds a verse fragment on a dead man that leads to his identity—"a study in detection as a method of psychotherapy." (FC) Macmillan, 1953.

West, Pamela E.   MADELEINE
"Part courtroom drama and part detective story" based on an actual murder case in the nineteenth century. (FC) St. Martin, 1983.

PROVINCIAL & RURAL SETTINGS

Blackstock, Charity   A HOUSE POSSESSED (Loch Ness)
A novel about exorcism—"no exorcism will free you from its long term haunting." (FC) Lippincott, 1962.

Buchan, John   JOHN McNAB
In *Adventurers All. . . . ;* Sir Richard Hannay mystery set in the Highlands. Houghton, 1942 (first published 1925).

Caird, Janet   THE UMBRELLA-MAKER'S DAUGHTER
Into a "tight, Scottish village" moves the umbrella-maker and his daughter with a penchant for writing "trenchant verses"—amorous attentions and a clash with townspeople result from her sharp wit. St. Martin, 1980. Two other mysteries with rural settings are *Murder Remote* (1973) (a West Scotland fishing village) and *In a Glass Darkly* (1966) (a modern gothic that begins with murder in a museum).

Canning, Victor   FLIGHT OF THE GREY GOOSE
Set on a beautiful Scottish loch—story of a runaway boy with a wounded grey goose, and the old Laird who takes them in—"a marvelous tale for nature lovers and the young in heart." (FC) Morrow, 1973.

Fraser, Antonia   THE WILD ISLAND
A mystery that 'intermingles history with local folklore [and a] unique setting"—the plot concerns a TV personality on holiday in a Highlands cottage. (BRD) Norton, 1978.

MacLean, Alistair   WHEN EIGHT BELLS TOLL
A tense adventure story set in the western Scottish Highlands. Doubleday, 1966.

Ogilvie, Elisabeth   THE SILENT ONES
A specialist in folklore "falls in love with an enigmatic Highlander and finds herself enmeshed in a web of greed . . . murder." (FC) McGraw, 1981. Also *Jennie About to Be* (1984), set at the turn of the nineteenth century in the Highlands, and with a heroine who has a social conscience—"captivating start of a promised trilogy . . . a natural heroine."

Ostrow, Joanna   IN THE HIGHLANDS SINCE TIME IMMEMORIAL
"A beautiful novel about a man who returns to his dream of an uncomplicated life. . . . sensitivity, humor, wonderful characterization." (BRD) Knopf, 1970.

EDINBURGH

Brett, Simon   SO MUCH BLOOD
An actor/director becomes involved with a group of young drama students when he arrives in Edinburgh to put on a one-man play, and in the investigation of the murder of one of them. "Conveys the behind-the-scenes atmosphere . . . evokes the sights and malty smell of Edinburgh." (FC) Scribner, 1977.

Douglas, Colin   THE HOUSEMAN'S TALE
Serio-comic novel of backstairs and inside of the Royal Charitable Institute—a new intern (houseman, in Scottish parlance) is put in charge of a ward and has to deal with patients for the first time—infighting with peers and superiors, escapes into sex and alcohol. "Fresh and entertaining hospital drama with universal appeal." (FC) Taplinger, 1978. Continues with *The Greatest Breakthrough Since Lunchtime* (1979).

Spark, Muriel   THE PRIME OF MISS JEAN BRODIE
Set in Edinburgh of the 1930s—a character sketch of a schoolteacher at a girls' school. "A story that is funny, true, unpleasant . . . gloriously human—or ingloriously human—both, actually." (FC) Lippincott, 1962.

GLASGOW

Bermant, Chaim   THE PATRIARCH
Saga of a Jewish boy, sent at sixteen to Glasgow from Russia, who eventually brings over other members of his family—a family epic with the backdrop of the World Wars. St. Martin, 1981. Also *The Second Mrs. Whitberg* (1976), about the Pakistani influence on a Jewish neighborhood.

Buchan, John   HUNTINGTOWER
In *Adventurers All* . . . ; "a peaceful Glasgow grocer . . . assists in freeing an heiress from Bolshevik kidnappers" in one of the Sir Richard Hannay series of mysteries. Houghton, 1942 (first published separately, 1922).

Knox, Bill   THE HANGING TREE
A videotape piracy racket is the focus of this mystery—"interesting characters, a lively race and vivid descriptions of Glasgow's urban ills." (FC) Doubleday, 1984.

McIlvanney, William   THE PAPERS OF TONY FEITCH
"Glasgow, 'city of the stare,' is richly depicted" in a novel for mystery fans of the Police Detective Jack Laidlaw series. "Sure to be compared with Higgins's Boston and Wambaugh's Los Angeles." (FC) Pantheon, 1983. Also *Laidlaw* (1977).

Turnbull, Peter   DEAD KNOCK
A police procedural involving heroin—a woman predicts her own murder within twenty-four hours. St. Martin, 1983.

Webster, Jan   SATURDAY CITY
Family saga, 1880-1918, of the Kilgours after moving away from the mines to their "Saturday city"—Glasgow. St. Martin, 1979.

THE HEBRIDES AND OTHER ISLANDS

Beckwith, Lillian   A SHINE OF RAINBOWS
"A simple story, shot through with the cleansing air of the Hebrides" of an orphan adopted by a crofter and his wife—the life of "farming, fishing, peating . . . fortifies the frail, bespectacled, eight-year-old" to face loss and teaches his new father a "human lesson." St. Martin, 1984. Also *The Hills Is Lonely* (1959).

Brown, George M.   GREENVOE (Orkneys)
"Activities of [a] social mix" of Orkney types from a lord to a "thieving lobsterman" end when military-industrial progress destroys the 1,000-year-old village. (BRD) HarBraceJ, 1970. Also *A Time to Keep* (1969), memorable short stories.

Carothers, Annabel   KILCARAIG
Family saga set on the island of Mull in the Hebrides with "local color . . . loving-ly supplied in the detailed description of the landscape and people." (FC) St. Martin, 1982.

Dickinson, Peter   THE SINFUL STONES
Inspector Pibble is asked to rescue an elderly scientist reportedly held prisoner by a group of monks in a monastery on one of the Hebrides—"a kind of nostalgia for the Edwardian days which Pibble must re-live to make the present bearable." (FC) Har-Row, 1970.

Grindal, Richard   DEATH STALK
"Lots of wild scenery and misty atmosphere [and] information about the making of Scotch whiskey" plus a plot in which an American is suspected of rape and murder on a remote isle in the Hebrides. (FC) St. Martin, 1982.

Hardy, Robin   THE WICKER MAN
A missing twelve-year-old girl is the basis for this "horror-filled suspense" story set on an isolated island in the Hebrides where "mysterious fertility rites and pagan sacrifices are tellingly juxtaposed against straight-laced, introspective Christianity." (FC) Crown, 1978.

Howatch, Susan   THE WAITING SANDS
Set in an island home off the western coast of Scotland where a group of people have gathered to celebrate the hostess' twenty-first birthday—"opportunities and provocations for murder [are] abundant." (FC) Stein & Day, 1972.

Hubbard, P.M.   THE CAUSEWAY
The main character is forced ashore while sailing his boat on an island con-nected to the mainland by an intermittent causeway (depending on the tides)—he becomes dangerously involved in the affairs of two people who live in a lonely house on the island. Doubleday, 1978.

Innes, Hammond   ATLANTIC FURY
The story of moving a guided weapons unit from an island in the Outer Hebrides—"a tale of men battling the elemental forces of nature. Underlying the ordeal is the suspenseful mystery of the identity of Major Braddock," missing since World War II. (FC) Har-Row, 1970.

Knox, Bill   BLOODTIDE
One of the series of Webb Carrick mysteries—he's an officer in Her Majesty's Fishery Protective Service. This time he must solve the grotesque deaths of a Scottish fisherman and a Russian frogman as Soviet, British and American vessels "prowl their appointed circuits" in the North Sea. (FC) Doubleday, 1983. Also *Stormtide* (1973) (Isle of Skye), and *Whitewater* (1973).

Mackenzie, Compton   TIGHT LITTLE ISLAND
What happens on two little islands in the Outer Hebrides when whiskey runs short during World War II—"packed with chuckles"—made into a great and funny movie many years ago. Houghton, 1950.

Stewart, Mary   WILDFIRE AT MIDNIGHT
Romantic suspense story by one of the best authors in that genre; set on the Isle of Skye. Morrow, 1961.

West, Morris L.   SUMMER OF THE RED WOLF
"The wild and romantic outer isles of Scotland" are the setting for this novel—a writer, come to the island in search of spiritual renewal, is befriended by the "Red Wolf" but jealousy erupts because of the men's mutual interest in a woman doctor. (FC) Morrow, 1971.

TRAVEL ARTICLES

BON APPETIT
1984 Apr "A Visit to the Highlands, Celebrating the Pleasures of Scotland's Countryside, Castles and Cuisine." Jean Anderson, p. 93

ESQUIRE
1985 Apr "The Sound and the Fury." Playing the gentleman hunter on Scotland's misty moors. Alan Furst, p. 140

GOURMET
1985 May Gourmet Holidays: "Part 1—Castles of Scotland." Elisabeth L. Ortiz, p. 46
 Jun Gourmet Holidays: "Part 2—Castles of Scotland." Elisabeth L. Ortiz, p. 60

HARPER'S BAZAAR
1984 Jan "Edinburgh: the Heart of Scotland." Thoughtfully explored by one of America's foremost political writers. Garry Wills, p. 24

NATIONAL GEOGRAPHIC
1984 Jul "Scotland, Ghosts and Glory." Rowe Findley, p. 40

N.Y. TIMES SUNDAY TRAVEL SECTION (X)
1985 Mar 10 "Scottish Isle of Hills and Heather." Islay. Bernard MacLaverty, p. 15
Apr 7 "A Bouquet of British Parks." Edinburgh, Liverpool, London. Paula Deitz, p. 14
Jun 23 "The Highlands: A Royal Retreat." Mar Hunting Lodge in northern Scotland, open for guests. Joan Ryan, p. 28
Jul 21 "A Scottish Cruise by Rail." A private train with royal lineage offers courtly views of peak and loch. John Chancellor, p. 14
"Train Lover's Guide." Anthony J. Lambert, p. 14
"The View from Loch Fyne." Exploring the Highlands, from castles and gardens to harbors and islands. Fitzroy MacLean, p. 15
"What's Doing in Edinburgh." Anthony Troon, p. 16
"An Isle of Light and Lochs." Skye's appeal is its Gaelic warmth and a never-far-off sea. June P. Wilson, p. 19
"Living Off the Riches of the Land." Country restaurants and hotels offer local products and rural comforts. Anthony Troon, p. 20
"Storming the Ramparts." Inverlochy Castle, a luxury hotel, overcomes a determined foe. Israel Shenker, p. 21
Oct 6 ("Sophisticated Traveler") "The Munros: Dreams of Glory." Climbers of the Scottish hills. p. 130
Nov 24 Shopper's World: "Scottish Kilts and Tweeds." Joan Cook, p. 12
1984 Jan 1 "In Search of '1984.'" A visit to Jura, Orwell's windswept island retreat. Linda McK. Stewart, p. 89
Feb 26 "It's a Bonny Isle for Birders." Orkney Island. Joan Lee Faust, p. 33
Mar 18 (Part 2, "Sophisticated Traveler") "Scotland's Castles by the Sea." The Scotland of myth and legend brought slightly down to earth. Israel Shenker, p. 44
Jun 10 "A Culinary Highland Fling." Scottish inn offers worldwide flavors (Ledcreich). Israel Shenker, p. 12
"Paddles Churn Off Scotland." Paddle steamer trips. Karl Zimmermann, p. 20
Jun 17 Fare of the Country: "Arboath Smokies, Scotland's Pride." Smoked haddock. Lisa A. de Mauro, p. 6
Aug 12 "What's Doing in the Highlands." Joshua Mills, p. 10
Sep 2 Fare of the Country: "Off to a Good Start on a Scottish Morn." Breakfast in Scotland. Amanda M. Stinchecum, p.6
Nov 11 Shopper's World: "Scottish Agate Jewelry." Amanda M. Stinchecum, p. 6

SUNSET
1985 Apr "A Trip in the Scottish Highlands." p. 86

TRAVEL & LEISURE
1985 May "The Wild Beauty of the Scottish Highlands." Across an enchanted landscape from Loch Lomond to the sea. Susan Larkin, p. 94; "Driving and Lingering in the Highlands." Author's route, where to stay and eat, weather and wardrobe. Susan Larkin, p. 102
1984 Jan "Gentle Town on the Wild Scottish Coast." Oban, a place of flowers, stone houses, and sailing ships. Marilyn Green, p. 82
Feb "Home of Harris Tweed." Meadows, cottages and durable woolen cloth. Abby Rand, p. 116
Apr "Three Easy Walks in Edinburgh." Abby Rand, p.168
May "In Scotland." Inverlochy, a regal retreat deep in the Highlands. Ila Stranger, p. 110
Jun "St. Andrews: Not for Golfers Only." A beguiling university town on the Scottish coast. James W. Finegan, p. 48

TRAVEL/HOLIDAY
1985 Aug "Legendary Links: A Golfer's Half Dozen." Includes Scotland. p. 44
1984 Nov "A Rocky World Apart." Scotland's rustic and rugged Western islands. Ginny Turner, p. 36

VOGUE
1984 Sep Grand Hotels: "Inverlochy Castle . . . Scotland's Most Romantic Hotel." Marilyn Berger, p. 618

WORLD PRESS REVIEW
1985 Jun "A Highland Fling." Carlos Eduardo (*Folha de Sao Paulo*, Sao Paulo), p. 62

SOVIET UNION

Series Guidebooks

Berlitz: Moscow and Leningrad
Blue Guide: Moscow & Leningrad
Fodor: Soviet Union
Nagel: USSR; Leningrad and Its Environs
U.S. Government: USSR: Post Report
Soviet Union: Area Handbook; Post Report

Background Reading

Billington, James H.   THE ICON AND THE AXE
A readable survey of Russian cultural history through the post-Khrushchev era; the role played by organized religion. Random, 1970.

Binyon, Michael   LIFE IN RUSSIA
A thematic approach and filled with quotations and anecdotes as it comments on Soviet women, youth, workers, culture, health care system, life for the average citizen and social problems that parallel those in the West, from alcoholism and high divorce rates to "crazes" and status symbols. The author is a former Moscow correspondent for the *London Times* and sees the Soviet Union as being in "the midst of its [turbulent] adolescence as a nation." (BL) Pantheon, 1984.

Brokhin, Yuri   HUSTLING ON GORKY STREET
"Sex and crime in Russia. . . . entertaining rogues' gallery of the socialist underworld." (BRD) Dial, 1975.

Cross, Anthony   RUSSIA UNDER WESTERN EYES
An anthology of visitors' descriptions of Russia over three centuries, 1517-1825. St. Martin, 1971.

Fraser, Russell   THE THREE ROMES
The three Romes, in this author's concept, are Moscow, Constantinople (now Istanbul) and Rome—cities that felt they had "received divine missions to amass and rule empires." The book is historical commentary and anecdotes, an "entertaining overview . . . encounters with modern inhabitants . . . the shadowy past [implanted in] the mind of citizens today." (BL) HarBraceJ, 1985.

Hansson, Carola and Liden, Karin   MOSCOW WOMEN
In-depth interviews with thirteen predominantly young and educated Moscow women, discreetly obtained—the real lives of Soviet women in contrast with the official story. Pantheon, 1983.

Hingley, Ronald F.   THE RUSSIAN MIND
An analysis of what makes Russians tick—switching back and forth in Russian history and drawing on some of its most dramatic episodes and personalities. Scribner, 1977.

Jones, Proctor   CLASSIC RUSSIAN IDYLLS
A book that celebrates the natural beauty of the western part of the Soviet Union (Mother Russia)—photographs with epigrams from Russian writings, and a triple introduction by three American capitalists having long experience living and working in Russia. Proctor Jones, 1986.

Kaiser, Robert G. and Hannah   RUSSIA FROM THE INSIDE
Mr. Kaiser was *Washington Post* correspondent in the Soviet Union—photographs accompanied by expert comment, outwitting the Russian determination to present the carefully contrived impression it does for tourists. Dutton, 1980, WSP, 1984. Also *Russia: the People and the Power* (1976)—Soviet life and society.

Klose, Kevin   RUSSIA AND THE RUSSIANS
By a former Moscow correspondent for the *Washington Post* and "oriented more to the experience of individuals than to the examination of specific themes."

Interviews with recognizable figures as well as those with pseudonyms reveal the reporter's "uneasiness, and even terror, at the repression he found everywhere." (BL) Norton, 1984.

Kort, Michael　THE SOVIET COLOSSUS
A new "popular" history of Russia that presents a balanced view of their achievements and failures. The theme is "continuity of tradition and social structures from Tsarist Russia [and the] author's style is lively and holds the reader's attention." (LJ) Scribner, 1984.

MacLean, Fitzroy　HOLY RUSSIA: AN HISTORICAL COMPANION TO EUROPEAN RUSSIA
A history with the traveler in mind, including walking tours of cities. Atheneum, 1979.

Massie, Suzanne　LAND OF THE FIREBIRD, THE BEAUTY OF OLD RUSSIA
Dazzling cultural history of pre-revolutionary Russia, profusely illustrated. S&S, 1980.

Nagorski, Andrew　RELUCTANT FAREWELL
The memoir of a *Newsweek* correspondent. Nagorski felt his stint in Moscow had a moral imperative that made him look for stories rather than rely on hand-outs from the government—he was expelled after just 11 months. He is critical of the foreign press who remain in favor. Holt, 1985.

Onassis, Jacqueline K., ed.　IN THE RUSSIAN STYLE
A book about Russian art, prepared with the assistance of the Metropolitan Museum of Art. Viking, 1976.

Palmer, A.　RUSSIA IN WAR AND PEACE
Places the events in the novel *War and Peace* in historical context. Macmillan, 1972.

Pipes, Richard　RUSSIA UNDER THE OLD REGIME
The author's view is that the present Russian state under communism has its origins in the nature of the Russian state since its inception. Scribner, 1974.

Salisbury, Harrison E.　THE 900 DAYS
The siege of Leningrad. Avon, 1972 (first published 1969). Also, with Emil Schulthess, *Soviet Union* (1973), photographs with commentary.

Shipler, David K.　RUSSIA: BROKEN IDOLS, SOLEMN DREAMS
By a former *New York Times* correspondent—a "vivid account of his time in Moscow . . . a detailed portrayal of bleakness." (BL) Times Bks, 1983.

Silianoff, Eugene and Sichov, Vladimir　THE RUSSIANS
Photographs out of Russia by a photographer now working in Paris. "Sadly, patiently, and without undue emphasis shows us the limitations and hardships of

life in Russia . . . of the endurance, vitality and human warmth of so many of its people." (BL) Little, 1981.

Smith, Hedrick   THE RUSSIANS
By the then correspondent for the *New York Times* and now a regular participant in the TV program "Washington Week in Review"—a "compendium of his finest reporting . . . polished and amplified [with] some of the more reflective pieces he never had a chance to write while he was there." A 1976 best-seller that has been updated and expanded. (BRD) Times Bks, 1983.

Voslensky, Michael   NOMENKLATURA
The Soviet ruling class described by one who was a member of "this happy band." Gives "a vivid picture of a state where a few have very much and the mass has very little, with no prospect of reversing that equation." (LJ) Doubleday, 1984.

Wayne, K.P.   SHURIK; A STORY OF THE SIEGE OF LENINGRAD
A Russian actress who was there tells of her experience in caring for an orphaned boy during part of the three-year siege of Leningrad. Grosset, 1970.

Willis, David K.   KLASS: HOW RUSSIANS REALLY LIVE
How the rising class in Russia uses connections and money for everything from theater tickets to food, with the thesis that this cultivation of status and privilege will, in the end, undermine the Communist Party's power. Written by a Moscow bureau chief for the *Christian Science Monitor*. St. Martin, 1985.

TRAVELOGUES AND SOME UNIQUE PERSONAL PERSPECTIVES

See also "Moscow & Leningrad," and "Siberia & the Trans-Siberian Railroad," below.

Beloff, Nora   INSIDE THE SOVIET EMPIRE
A British journalist describes a car trip to many places closed to visitors—pre-1978. Times Bks, 1980.

Dumas, Alexandre   ADVENTURES IN CZARIST RUSSIA
A travelogue of 1858 by the French novelist—"pungent and vivid glimpses of a bygone era." Greenwood, 1975.

Gambino, Thomas   NYET
"An American rock musician encounters the Soviet Union." P-H, 1976.

MacLean, Sir F.H.   BACK TO BOKHARA
Written by a former British foreign officer, it is an account of his return after a twenty-year absence to Samarkand, Bokhara and Moscow. Har-Row, 1960.

**Pond, Elizabeth   FROM THE YAROSLAVSKY STATION: RUSSIA
                      PERCEIVED**
"Chronicle of her journey [through] the Russia of the early Dostoyevsky, the

late Tolstoy . . . the ripe and raging Solzhenitsyn" while traveling home from her assignment as chief of the Moscow bureau for the *Christian Science Monitor* via 5,800 miles across the Soviet Union and eastern Siberia. (NYTBR) Universe, 1982.

Schecter, Leona and Jerrold   AN AMERICAN FAMILY IN MOSCOW
Written by Leona, Jerrold and their children. Little, 1975.

Shostakovich, Dmitri   TESTIMONY
"Anecdotal, witty" memoirs dictated during the four years preceding the conductor's death, and smuggled abroad for publication. (BRD) Har-Row, 1979.

Steinbeck, John   RUSSIAN JOURNAL
With Robert Capa taking photographs, describes a journey by the prominent American writer through Moscow, Stalingrad, the Ukrainian countryside, and the Caucasus. Viking, 1948.

Thubron, Colin   WHERE NIGHTS ARE LONGEST: TRAVELS BY CAR THROUGH WESTERN RUSSIA
Account of a unique travel experience as the author manages to get permission to drive over hundreds of miles of the Soviet Union, camping and "chatting with whomever crossed his path." He sees and describes "marvelously varied scenery" and meets all kinds of people from loyal party members and dissidents to students and "repressed Methodists." (BL) Random, 1984.

Van der Post, Laurens   JOURNEY INTO RUSSIA
Reprint of a travelogue of a three-month trip, twenty years ago, alone and by plane, train and ship, from north to south and from west to east—the longest solitary journey made through Russia by a non-Communist. The trip, and the book, were commissioned by a travel magazine, and the sheer scope of the journey, and the level of the writing makes this a unique story. Island Pr, 1984 (first published 1964).

Vishnevskaya, Galina   GALINA: A RUSSIAN STORY
Autobiography of a Russian singer that provides an unusual perspective—"candid, often devastating, depiction of cultural life in postwar Russia . . . rare insights into the care and feeding of a Muscovite" prima donna. (NYTBR) HarBraceJ, 1984.

THE REVOLUTION AND SOME CONTEMPORARY DISSIDENTS

Aksyonov, Vasily and others, eds.   METROPOL: LITERARY ALMANAC
A collection of poems, essays and stories by some of Russia's most respected literary figures in a failed experiment to challenge Soviet censorship. Norton, 1983.

Cowles, Virginia   THE ROMANOVS
A popular history that reads "with the compelling excitement of a novel" and

more concerned with the personalities and daily routines than straight history—the ruling class that led to the revolution. (BRD) Har-Row, 1971.

Crankshaw, Edward   THE SHADOW OF THE WINTER PALACE
Russia's drift to Revolution, 1825-1917—a portrait of Russia through its last four czars. Penguin, 1978.

Kuznetsov, Edward   PRISON DIARIES
A "stunning addition to the most significant genre of contemporary Soviet letters." (BRD) Stein & Day, 1979.

Massie, Robert K.   NICHOLAS AND ALEXANDRA
"Intimate history at its magnificent best"—motivations and personal emotions of the royal family whose son's illness with hemophilia led to Alexandra's dependence on Rasputin for help, which in turn led to disastrous decisions that helped Kerensky and Lenin gain power. (BRD) Dell, 1978 (first published 1968).

Panin, Dimitri   NOTEBOOKS OF SOLOGDIN
Account of thirteen years in Russian prisons and labor camps. HarBraceJ, 1976.

Pearlstein, E.W., ed.   REVOLUTION IN RUSSIA!
The revolution as reported in contemporary accounts by the *New York Tribune* and the *New York Herald*, 1894-1921. Viking, 1967.

Pearson, Michael   SEALED TRAIN
Lenin's return to Russia from exile in Switzerland, in 1917, via a sealed train through Germany as events led to power seizure by the Bolsheviks—"generates excitement as though it were a contemporary account." (BRD) Putnam Pub Group, 1975.

Sakharov, Andre D.   MY COUNTRY AND THE WORLD
A book by a Russian emigré and dissident who believes that detente has only strengthened the Soviet Union and will eventually undermine American democracy. Random, 1975.

Salisbury, Harrison E.   BLACK NIGHT, WHITE SNOW
Russia's revolutions, 1905-1917. Da Capo Pr, 1981.

Shifrin, Avraham   THE FIRST GUIDEBOOK TO PRISONS AND
CONCENTRATION CAMPS OF THE SOVIET UNION
Written by a former inmate, using a new tactic to tell "the reality of these awful places in a fashion quite unlike . . . the fiction of Solzhenitsyn." He wants tourists to request admission to these facilities, even though the requests will be refused. To this end he provides maps and lists of the types of institutions (women's and children's camps, psychiatric prisons, etc.) for all known prisons and camps, arranged geographically. (BL) Bantam, 1982.

Solzhenitsyn, Aleksandr   THE GULAG ARCHIPELAGO
His own personal experiences and those of 227 other survivors. Har-Row, 1974.

MOSCOW & LENINGRAD

Berton, Kathleen   MOSCOW: AN ARCHITECTURAL HISTORY
Handy introduction and guidebook "to the architectural diversity and richness of Moscow." (BRD) St Martin, 1978.

Chernov, V.A.   MOSCOW (A SHORT GUIDE)
Typical tourist information as well as the key historical and cultural things to see. Imported Pubns, 1977.

Feldkamp, Frederick   NOT EVERYBODY'S EUROPE
A grand tour of nine unique places to think about adding to your itinerary—in Russia it's Leningrad. Harper's Magazine Pr, 1976.

Gruliow, Leo, ed.   MOSCOW
One of the Great Cities of the World series. Time-Life, 1977.

Gunther, John   TWELVE CITIES
The author of the highly popular "Inside" series of a couple of decades ago here applies his unique zest and talent to a dozen cities, one of which is Moscow—mood, temper, problems, politics, government. Har-Row, 1969.

Kelly, Laurence, ed.   MOSCOW/A TRAVELLERS' COMPANION; ST. PETERSBURG/A TRAVELLERS' COMPANION
A "You-are-there experience [for each city]. . . . excerpts from old novels, biographies, letters, poems, diaries, that describe or give impressions" of St. Petersburg (now Leningrad) and Moscow, with contemporary prints and photographs. They make ideal traveling companions. (BL) Atheneum, 1983.

Kennett, Audrey   THE PALACES OF LENINGRAD
Thames Hudson, 1984.

Lee, Andrea   RUSSIAN JOURNAL
Account of an eight-month residence in Moscow, and two in Leningrad, by a young woman from Harvard who "knows how to write . . . informative, ingratiating . . . moving." (TBS) Random, 1984.

McGreevy, John, ed.   CITIES
Impressions of world cities as seen through the eyes of people intimately connected with them—for Leningrad it's Peter Ustinov's impressions. Outlet Bk, 1981.

Pokrovskii, B.A.   THE BOLSHOI: OPERA AND BALLET
The greatest theater in Russia. Morrow, 1979.

Martin, Jay   WINTER DREAMS: AN AMERICAN IN MOSCOW
Good reporting, well-written, personal account of a five-month stint in Moscow as a visiting professor. Houghton, 1979.

Smith, Desmond   SMITH'S MOSCOW
For Western visitors—goes beyond a routine guidebook in offering background history and culture and bits of practical information—like where to get a tooth fixed. Random, 1980 (first published 1974).

Wechsberg, Joseph   IN LENINGRAD
Story of the fascinating city that was St. Petersburg. Doubleday, 1977.

SIBERIA & THE TRANS-SIBERIAN RAILROAD

Botting, Douglas   ONE CHILLY SIBERIAN MORNING
Travelogue of the remote places in Siberia—well-written, at times humorous, introduction to one of the unique and less known areas of the world. Macmillan, 1968.

Kuranov, V.   THE TRANS-SIBERIAN EXPRESS
Translation of a Russian book on the railroad line. Sphinx Pr, 1979.

Mowat, Farley   THE SIBERIANS
An account of two lengthy visits in 1966 and 1969 by a Canadian novelist. The author challenges "the myth of Siberia as . . . a desolate wilderness" and makes Siberia and the Siberians come alive for the reader as a "teeming and productive country." (BRD) Penguin, 1972.

Newby, Eric   THE BIG RED TRAIN RIDE
Newby's trip from Moscow to Vladivostok with his wife, a photographer, and their companion from the Soviet tourist agency. Observations of people and scenes along the way, with some background history thrown in. St. Martin, 1978.

Niven, Alexander C.   COMPANION GUIDE FOR TRAVELERS ON THE TRANS-SIBERIAN RAILROAD
Intl Inst Adv Stud, 1981.

Theroux, Paul   THE GREAT RAILWAY BAZAAR
A four-month lecture tour in 1973, via the Trans-Siberian Express (and the Orient Express and Khyber Mail), is the basis for these "conversations and impressions of people encountered." Houghton, 1975.

GUIDEBOOKS

Daglish, Robert   COPING WITH RUSSIA: A BEGINNER'S GUIDE TO THE USSR
A guide that touches on everything from getting ready to buying clothes and what to do on a cold winter's day. "Designed for tourists [but] includes enough general information about Russian manners and morals to make fascinating reading for all armchair travelers." (BL) Blackwell, 1985.

**Louis, Victor and Jennifer   THE COMPLETE GUIDE TO THE
SOVIET UNION**
Arranged alphabetically by city, and covers the fifteen republics of the USSR. St.
Martin, 1980.

Ward, Charles   NEXT TIME YOU GO TO RUSSIA
A guide to historical landmarks and art museums in fourteen cities. Scribner,
1980.

HISTORY

Dmytryshyn, Basil   USSR: A CONCISE HISTORY
"Brief, accurate, balanced survey." Scribner, 1984 (first published 1977).

Florinsky, Michael T.   RUSSIA: A SHORT HISTORY
Written "succinctly, concisely and interestingly [without] jargon." (BRD)
Macmillan, 1965.

Medish, Vadim   THE SOVIET UNION
"Brisk overview . . . using a tightly organized textbook type approach." (BL) P-H,
1981.

Riasanovsky, Nicholas V.   A HISTORY OF RUSSIA
Oxford U, 1984 (first published 1977).

Seton-Watson, Hugh   THE RUSSIAN EMPIRE, 1801-1917
The period as it was rather than in terms of what happened after the abdication
of Nicholas II—one of the best. Oxford U, 1967.

Treadgold, Donald W.   TWENTIETH CENTURY RUSSIA
Houghton, 1981.

Novels

Aksyonov, Vassily   THE BURN
A novel in three volumes, written in the 1960s and '70s (the author was forced
to emigrate to the U.S. in 1980). "Five gifted, sophisticated, cynical yet hopeful
young denizens of Moscow" each represent an aspect of Tolya Von Steinbock who
spent his childhood in Siberian work camps. Random, 1984.

Aksyonov, Vassily   THE ISLAND OF CRIMEA
"Political fantasy [in which] the Crimean peninsula has become an island . . .
masochistic attempt to rejoin the Soviet Union." (FC) Random, 1983.

Anatoli, A.   BABI YAR
The period 1941-43 when the Nazis systematically murdered two million
people at Babi Yar, outside of Kiev, including 50,000 Jews. FS&G, 1970.

Bainbridge, Beryl   WINTER GARDEN
The hero "truly an innocent abroad . . . embarks on a trip to Russia with his mistress" to correct his wife's impression that he is "incapable of straying beyond the confines of the winter garden." Despite a serious turn of events, the author's sense of humor makes the novel "thoroughly enjoyable." (FC) Braziller, 1981.

Buckley, William F.   MARCO POLO, IF YOU CAN
One of Buckley's Blackford Oakes spy novels—involves a covert operation to locate a leak to the Russians from within the National Security Council; "top notch spy thriller." (FC) Doubleday, 1982.

Butler, Gwendoline   THE RED STAIRCASE
See entry under "Leningrad."

Cleary, Jon   THE GOLDEN SABRE
An American oil agent meets an English governess, inadvertently kills her would-be rapist, and they all flee to southern Russia. "A series of exciting and comical escapades. . . . incredibly zany." (FC) Morrow, 1981.

Ehrenburg, Ilya   A CHANGE OF SEASON
Two sequential short novels—*The Thaw* and *The Spring*—the picture of a group of factory workers in a Russian town, by a leading Soviet writer. Knopf, 1962.

Forsyth, Frederick   THE DEVIL'S ALTERNATIVE
A series of events bring the world close to nuclear disaster—"a stupendous entertainment . . . the reader is swept into the counsels of the great, the intrigues of the loyal, and the plots of the lowly." (FC) Viking, 1980.

Fraser, George MacDonald   FLASHMAN AT THE CHARGE
More adventures of the legendary "Flashman"—this time he's part of the charge of the light brigade in the Crimea, 1854. Knopf, 1973.

Garfield, Brian   ROMANOV SUCCESSION
The setting is World War II, the plot concerns a plan by White Russians to assassinate Stalin, with U.S.-British backing. M. Evans, 1974.

Gray, Francine du Plessix   WORLD WITHOUT END
Three women, linked by a long friendship, "are pilgriming in Russia, seeking inspiration to give meaning to the last third of their lives." (FC) S&S, 1981.

Green, Gerald   KARPOV'S BRAIN
The anti-Semitic and most feared man in the KGB undergoes a transformation via surgery and Pavlovian therapy. Morrow, 1983.

Grekova, I.   RUSSIAN WOMEN
Consists of two stories, *The Hotel Manager* and *Ladies' Hairdresser*—"both stories depict contemporary Russian life as unending struggles with a rigid government, echoed in the male-female relationships." (FC) HarBraceJ, 1983.

Haskin, Gretchen   AN IMPERIAL AFFAIR
A novel of what might have happened if Prince Romanovsky had attempted to rescue the royal family from Ekaterinburg after the revolution—"builds authentic atmosphere and tension. . . . cleverly and suprisingly plotted." (FC) Dial, 1980.

High, Monique R.   THE FOUR WINDS OF HEAVEN
Based on diaries of the author's grandmother, living in St. Petersburg, the Crimea, Switzerland, Paris; "this superior saga recreates the lives of a family that in its heyday considered itself 'the First Jewish Family of Russia'. . . . destroyed at one blow by the Bolshevik Revolution . . . brims with social history, tragedy, romance." (FC) Delacorte Pr, 1980.

Iskander, Fazil   SANDRO OF CHEGEM
A comic epic of the adventures of Sandro, 1880 to 1960, which "touch on just about every conceivable subject: erotica, Joseph Stalin (known as 'Beloved Leader' and the 'Big Mustache'), ethnic antagonisms . . . Islam . . . collective agriculture." This irreverent book by an author who lives in Moscow was published in the Soviet Union ten years ago but "only about 10 percent of the present manuscript appeared in print. The real surprise is that the censors managed to leave one-tenth [of this] comedy of the blackest hue." (NYTBR) Vintage, 1985.

James, Donald   THE FALL OF THE RUSSIAN EMPIRE
In a "finely woven and intricate" plot, the author presents his vision of how the Russian empire collapses in the late 1980s, because of various crises and an internal battle for power—"The reader walks away . . . with a feeling that he understands . . . the sentiments of Russia." (FC) Putnam Pub Group, 1982.

Koestler, Arthur   DARKNESS AT NOON
First published in 1940, Koestler's disillusionment with the Communist party and the revolution—"a grimly fascinating interpretation of the logic of the Russian Revolution, indeed of all revolutionary dictatorships." It is based on Koestler's experiences and the plot concerns the imprisonment, torture, confession and execution of a composite old Bolshevik and one of the last survivors of the original Communist Party Central Committee. (BRD) Macmillan, 1941.

MacPherson, Malcolm   THE LUCIFER KEY
A computer genius, hired to find a fail-safe way to protect military secrets, is besieged by Russian agents, an anti-computer activitist, a corrupt general, and others. Dutton, 1981.

Malamud, Bernard   THE FIXER (Kiev)
A powerful story of injustice and endurance, based on a true incident in the anti-Semitic movement in czarist Russia—it won the Pulitzer Prize for literature in 1967. FS&G, 1966.

Moorcock, Michael   BYZANTIUM ENDURES
Kiev, Odessa, St. Petersburg in 1900-1917 is the setting for this novel—"slow, demanding reading, but in turn it offers a sensually detailed, historically rich portrait" of this period. (FC) Random, 1982.

Moss, Robert and DeBorchgrave, Arnaud   MOSCOW RULES
When a fifteen-year-old Saska learns that his father was killed by a fellow-soldier in World War II he embarks on a plan to bring him eventually into the inner workings of the highest levels of the government and to overthrow the politburo and central committee—"a portrait of a thoroughly corrupt . . . Soviet political and military hierarchy" for espionage fans. (FC) Villard, 1985.

Napier, Priscilla   IMPERIAL WINDS
Russia of 1914, an English governess is caught up in court life and the political happenings of the time—"teems with action." (FC) Coward, 1981.

Pasternak, Boris   DOCTOR ZHIVAGO
"Brilliant kaleidoscopic chronicle [that] illuminates the period of the Russian Revolution, the violent, proletarian upheaval and the Communist succession." (BRD) Pantheon, 1958.

Reeman, Douglas   TORPEDO RUN
A joint British-Russian sea sortie in World War II. Morrow, 1981.

Romains, Jules   THE WORLD IS YOUR ADVENTURE IN THE NEW DAY
An Englishman's experiences and observations on the Russian Revolution. Knopf, 1942.

Rubens, Bernice   BROTHERS
Saga of six generations of a Jewish family from the nineteenth century to Russia of today—"a window into the family life of each Blindel generation" and how they apply the lessons of survival taught by the family patriarch, through pogroms, the Nazis, the Soviet psychiatric hospitals. (FC) Delacorte Pr, 1983.

Salisbury, Harrison   GATES OF HELL
Fictionalized account of Solzhenitsyn's experiences. Random, 1975.

Scott, Justin   A PRIDE OF ROYALS
King George of England asks a U.S. Navy officer to rescue the czar from the revolution. In this imaginary version, he succeeds, and leaves a bunch of actors behind to take the royal family's place. "Absurd [but] a compulsive page-turner" with a remarkable, larger-than-life hero. (FC) Arbor Hse, 1983.

Sholokhov, Mikhail   AND QUIET FLOWS THE DON
First of a series of novels about the Cossacks and their region of Russia, the effects of the revolution and collectivization. Knopf, 1934. See also *Tales of the Don* (1962), *The Don Flows Home to the Sea* (1941), *Harvest on the Don* (1961), *Seeds of Tomorrow* (1959), *The Silent Don* (1961).

Solzhenitsyn, Aleksandr   AUGUST 1914
Russia at the outbreak of World War I. FS&G, 1972. Also *The Cancer Ward* (1969) and *For the Good of the Cause* (1970).

Sulzberger, C.L.   THE TOOTH MERCHANT
A parody of espionage, with such characters as Stalin, Nasser, Eisenhower, Ben-Gurion. Quadrangle Bks, 1973.

Thomas, Craig   FIREFOX
The CIA and British Intelligence join forces to steal an incredible new plane of the Soviets. Holt, 1977. In a sequel, *Firefox Down* (1983), the stolen MIG-3 has to make an emergency landing in a Finnish lake, with frantic British-American and Russian efforts to get to the plane first, hampered by the weather.

Trenhaile, John   A VIEW FROM THE SQUARE
The Russians steal an AWACS aircraft and an elite crew of Americans infiltrate before Red intelligence can uncover its secret. Congdon & Weed, 1983.

Viertel, Joseph   LIFELINES
"Encompasses 100 years of Jewish experience . . . set in Russia, America and Israel." (FC) S&S, 1982.

Vladimov, Georgi   FAITHFUL RUSLAN
"A compelling anthropomorphic tale" of a guard dog's bewilderment when turned loose from his duties at a concentration camp. (FC) S&S, 1979.

Voinovich, Vladimir   THE LIFE AND EXTRAORDINARY ADVENTURES OF PRIVATE IVAN CHONKIN
This and its sequel, *Pretender to the Throne* (1981), are a "burlesque of Soviet military life, bureaucracy and politics." Also *In Plain Russian* (1979), about "ordinary Soviet citizens going about the ordinary business of life." (FC) FS&G, 1981.

West, Rebecca   THE BIRDS FALL DOWN
Based on true events of Russian terrorists at the turn of the century. The plot is about a fantastic alliance between a double agent and a thirteen-year-old girl. Viking, 1966.

Wiesel, Elie   THE TESTAMENT
As he awaits his mother's arrival in Israel, with a planeload of Russian immigrants, Grisha rereads the memoirs of his father—"an idealist . . . an innocent victim of the machinations of the Soviet regime." European political history "revealed in brand-new dimensions when recalled from the perspective . . . of a Jew-turned-Communist." (FC) Summit, 1981.

LENINGRAD

Butler, Gwendoline   THE RED STAIRCASE
Set in St. Petersburg in 1912—a Scottish girl hired as companion to a young member of an aristocratic family finds that she's really been hired for her healing powers to help break Rasputin's hold on the czarina by helping the young crown prince who is ill with hemophilia. Coward, 1979.

Dostoevsky, Fyodor   CRIME AND PUNISHMENT
The classic story and psychological study of a criminal's mind, before during and after his murders. Norton, 1975 (first published 1866). Also *The Idiot* (1868).

Ilyin, Olga   THE ST. PETERSBURG AFFAIR
Based on notes left by a relative, this love story is set in the 1850s—"narration and dialogue capture a time when the political and philosophical changes delivered by the Industrial Revolution were just taking root in Europe." HR&W, 1982.

MOSCOW

Evans, Peter   THE ENGLISHMAN'S DAUGHTER
"Diverting look at English aristocracy and Soviet bourgeoisie on a clandestine collision course"—moves from Moscow to London to Venice. (FC) Random, 1983.

Francis, Dick   TRIAL RUN
The Olympic Games are scheduled for Moscow, and an Englishman is sent to Moscow to search out a man (knowing only the man's first name) who may prove to be an embarrassment to the British Crown. Har-Row, 1979.

Harcourt, Palma   A TURN OF TRAITORS
"Derring-do by dissident Soviet Jews, nice local color of London, Vienna and Moscow . . . are part of the brew" as an innocent becomes involved in a highly placed security leak. (FC) Scribner, 1982.

Littell, Robert   MOTHER RUSSIA
"Trivial satire of a modern-day Russian Don Quixote. . . . a miniscule tour of greater Moscow." (FC) HarBraceJ, 1978.

Olcott, Anthony   MURDER AT THE RED OCTOBER
A dead American is found in the Red October Hotel in this drug-related mystery—"description of the contemporary Moscow scene is the trademark of this work." (FC) Academy Chi, 1981.

Smith, Martin Cruz   GORKY PARK
"Believable, realistic and gripping portrayals of certain segments of Soviet society, and of one man's search for meaning." The plot involves three mutilated bodies found in Gorky Park and two police investigators—one Soviet, one American—determined to solve the mystery of their deaths. (FC) Random, 1981.

Solzhenitsyn, Aleksandr   THE FIRST CIRCLE
Five scientists working at the Technical Institute for favored treatment. Har-Row, 1968.

Topol, Edward and Neznansky, Fridrikh   RED SQUARE
Both authors are Russian emigrés and have been part of the bureaucracy. This is almost a novelized version of Brokhin's *Hustling on Gorky Street* listed above under Background Reading—"a veritable rogues' gallery of fictitious black marketeers, procurers, middlemen, officials on the take, and ladies of pleasure who are at times the strange bedfellows of the Kremlin elite." Fascinating characters and plot. (NYTBR) Quartet, 1985.

SIBERIA

Olcott, Anthony   MAY DAY IN MAGADAN
The hotel security officer of *Murder at the Red October* (see entry above), now exiled to Magadan in Siberia, stumbles on fur pelts connected to an airline disaster. "The dense atmosphere of squalor, coarseness, drunkenness, corruption, despair . . . is depressingly persuasive." (FC) Bantam, 1983.

Shalamov, Varlam   KOLYMA TALES
"Each [of the tales] vivify a particularly grim element of the forced labor camp while illuminating the spirit and humanity" of individuals incarcerated there. (FC) Norton, 1980.

Solzhenitsyn, Aleksandr   ONE DAY IN THE LIFE OF IVAN DENISOVICH
A modern classic by the Soviet dissident writer about prison life in a Siberian labor camp. Dutton, 1963.

Yevtushenko, Yevgeny   WILD BERRIES
Through a cosmonaut's look at the earth from space, and a group of geologists and those with whom they come in contact, the reader gets a panoramic view of modern Russia and its recent past. Morrow, 1984.

TRAVEL ARTICLES

ARCHITECTURAL DIGEST
1984 Jun "Glimpses of Global Treasures." Great museums in China, Greece and Russia. p. 218

CONNOISSEUR
1984 Mar "Paradox in Russia." Restoration of Pushkin, Catherine Palace. Dale Harris, p. 97

HOUSE & GARDEN
1984 Feb "To Azerbaijan and Back: an Old Russia Hand Travels the Southern Leg of the Ancient Silk Route to China." Sir Fitzroy MacLean, p. 30

MS
1985 Jun "How Not to Go to Russia: a Cautionary Tale for All Travelers." Carol Tavris, p. 10

N.Y. SUNDAY TIMES TRAVEL SECTION (X)
1985 Mar 17   (Part 2, "Sophisticated Traveler") "Turgenev Amid the Lindens." Former estate of the writer. Serge Schmemann, p. 128
Apr 28 "Siberia: the 'Wild East.'" Marion Kaplan, p. 21
1984 Feb 12   "Bolshoi: The Russian Classic." Serge Schmemann, p. 14
Jul 15 "Yalta: An Anomaly That Surprises in the Crimea." History and rare amenities. John F. Burns, p. 9
Oct 7 (Part 2, "Sophisticated Traveler") "Eat Your Nice Zakuski." Berlin Restaurant. Seth Mydans, p. 20

SPAIN

Series Guidebooks

American Express: Spain
Baedeker: Spain; Madrid
Berlitz: Barcelona & Costa Dorada; Canary Islands;
Costa Brava; Costa Blanca; Costa del Sol & Andalusia; Ibiza &
Formentera; Madrid; Majorca & Minorca
Blue Guide: Spain
Companion Guide: Madrid & Central Spain
Fisher: Spain & Portugal
Fodor: Spain; Budget Travel Spain; Madrid
Frommer: Spain & Morocco (plus Canary Islands): $-a-Day;
Lisbon, Madrid & Costa del Sol: City Guide
Let's Go: Spain, Portugal & Morocco
Michelin: Spain
Nagel: Spain
U.S. Government: Spain: Background Notes; Country Study;
Pocket Guide; Post Report
Andorra: Background Notes

Background Reading

Bendiner, Elmer   THE RISE AND FALL OF PARADISE
"Spirited and reliable history of the Moslem Caliphate of Cordoba" and the fall of this "seemingly idyllic state" in the eleventh century. Putnam Pub Group, 1983.

Brenan, Gerald   SOUTH FROM GRANADA
"A book of discovery and exploration . . . anatomy of village life [and] inquiry into character"—considered one of the most perceptive writers on Spain in the English language. Cambridge U Pr, 1980 (first published 1957). Also *The Face of Spain* (1951) (the author's return to his Andalusian house and village after many years of absence and travels in Madrid, Cordova, Toledo, Granada).

Crow, John A.   SPAIN: THE ROOT AND THE FLOWER
"The substance of Spanish culture—art, literature, architecture and music is emphasized [over] straight politics. . . . taps the very marrow of Spanish consciousness." This is the third edition and expands coverage of the post-Franco period. (BL) U of California, 1985.

Feldkamp, Frederick   NOT EVERYBODY'S EUROPE
A grand tour of nine unique places to think about adding to your itinerary—in Spain, it's Granada. Harper's Magazine Pr, 1976.

Graham, Robert   SPAIN: A NATION COMES OF AGE
A report by a non-Spanish correspondent on Spain's transition from Franco's authoritarianism to a democracy with king and parliament. St. Martin, 1985.

Hemingway, Ernest   DEATH IN THE AFTERNOON
His classic on bullfighting in Spain. Scribner, 1932.

Irving, Washington   ALHAMBRA
A travel classic of 1829. Washington Irving (who was the ambassador to Spain) rode from Seville to Granada on horseback and wrote this memoir about the experience and about the Alhambra where he lived for several months. Sleepy Hollow, 1982.

Lewis, Norman   VOICES OF THE OLD SEA
Intimate portrait of a remote Spanish fishing village where the author lived for several years and what happens when it becomes part of the tourism industry. "Not so much a travelogue as a rich biography of a town." (TL) Viking, 1985.

MacKendrick, Paul   THE IBERIAN STONES SPEAK
See under "Portugal."

Maugham, W. Somerset   DON FERNANDO
The author intended to write a novel on sixteenth-century life in Spain; instead he incorporated his notes with results of reading and observations into a series of informal chapters on a variety of topics from Spanish food and wines to El Greco and Cervantes. In his "intelligent and crafted style." (BRD) Ayer, 1977 (first published 1935).

Michener, James A.   IBERIA
A travelogue and interpretation of Spanish art, history, customs, politics, chapters on bullfighting, Las Marismas (wildlife preserve). Essential reading for Spain. Fawcett, 1978 (first published 1968).

Morris, Jan   SPAIN
One reviewer says: "One of the best descriptive essays on that country ever written." Originally written in 1965, the author revisited and retraced some of her travels. (BRD) Oxford U, 1979. Also in her collection of travel pieces, *Places*, there's an essay on the Basques.

Morton, H.V.   A STRANGER IN SPAIN
"Cities and their treasures of art and buildings . . . festivals, the wild remote hills and the warm plains"—by a leading travel writer. (BRD) Dodd, 1955.

Pritchett, V.S.   THE SPANISH TEMPER
A pocket analysis of the Spanish character—and an important addition to the literature on Spain by British writers (Brenan, Maugham, Morris, Morton). Greenwood, 1976 (first published 1954).

Read, Jan   MOORS IN SPAIN AND PORTUGAL
See under "Portugal."

Tracy, Honor   WINTER IN CASTILLE
Travels in Spain—cathedrals, monasteries, other places—by an "acerbic, compassionate satirist [with a] knack for conveying a sense of place." (BRD) Random, 1974. Other earlier travel books on Spain include *Silk Hats and No Breakfast* (1958) and *Spanish Leaves* (1965).

Walker, Bryce S.   THE ARMADA
Part of the Seafarers series. Time-Life, 1981.

Yglesias, José   THE GOODBYE LAND
Account of the author's pilgrimage in 1964 to Galicia, where he relates the events of his father's death thirty years earlier—a portrait of the peasants of that time and place. Pantheon, 1967.

THE SPANISH CIVIL WAR

Brenan, Gerald   THE SPANISH LABYRINTH
Macmillan, 1943.

Kazantzakis, Nikos   SPAIN
A journal of two trips to Spain before and during the war by one who admired Franco's Spain. S&S, 1963.

Kurzman, Dan   MIRACLE OF NOVEMBER: MADRID'S EPIC STAND
A reconstruction of the events in 1936 from interviews with participants. Putnam Pub Group, 1980.

Orwell, George   HOMAGE TO CATALONIA
A soldier-author's account of the Spanish Civil War. HarBraceJ, 1969 (first published 1952).

Thomas, Hugh   THE SPANISH CIVIL WAR
A history, from the origins of the war to Barcelona's fall in 1939. Har-Row, 1977 (first published 1961).

GUIDEBOOKS

Cox, Thornton   THORNTON COX'S TRAVELLERS' GUIDE TO MAJORCA

"Highly readable introduction to the area . . . getting there and getting about . . . suggested itineraries [designed for] economy of time and movement." (Publisher) Hippocrene, 1982.

Dennis, Philip   GIBRALTAR
David, 1977.

**Facaros, Dana   MEDITERRANEAN ISLAND HOPPING: THE
                          SPANISH ISLANDS**
A handbook for the independent traveler that covers Majorca, Minorca, Ibiza,

Formentera and Cabrera. Island descriptions, how to get there, background information on local customs and history, where to stay and what to do. Hippocrene, 1982.

Hayter, Judith   CANARY ISLAND HOPPING: THE AZORES/MADEIRA
Like Facaros, above, but for the Atlantic islands. Hippocrene, 1984.

Hoffman, Ann   MAJORCA
Part of Islands of the World series. David, 1978.

Kane, Robert S.   SPAIN
One of a new "World at Its Best" series of travel guidebooks by a noted travel authority, "oriented toward the discriminating traveler." Highlights the best each country has to offer, including hotels in a range of prices—"evaluates the entire itinerary. Big city wonders and . . . out-of-the-way adventure spots." Passport, 1985.

Launay, André and Pendered, Maureen   MADRID AND SOUTHERN
SPAIN
Batsford, 1976.

Pink, Annette   MADEIRA & THE CANARIES
Sidgwick & Jackson, 1983.

Steves, Rick   SPAIN AND PORTUGAL IN 22 DAYS
John Muir, 1986.

Thurston, Hazel   BALEARIC ISLANDS
Majorca, Minorca, Ibiza and Formentera; Batsford guide. Chatto Bodley, 1979.

Yeoward, Eileen   CANARY ISLANDS
Rogers Bk, 1981.

HISTORY

Bradford, Ernle D.   GIBRALTAR: THE HISTORY OF A FORTRESS
HarBraceJ, 1972.

Hills, George   SPAIN
Praeger, 1970.

Kamen, Henry A.   A CONCISE HISTORY OF SPAIN
From first settlements to Franco. Scribner, 1974.

O'Callaghan, J.F.   HISTORY OF MEDIEVAL SPAIN
The author's Spain "is the entire peninsula [and] Islamic, Jewish, Christian, Portuguese, and Catalonian as well as Castilian" Spain and Portugal. Cornell U, 1983 (first published 1975).

Vilar, Pierre   SPAIN: A BRIEF HISTORY
Pergamon, 1977.

Novels

Blasco-Ibanez, Vincente   BLOOD AND SAND
The novel of Spanish bullfighters—"no detail . . . is spared." (FC) Ungar, 1958 (first published 1908).

Cervantes, Miguel de   THE PORTABLE CERVANTES
An anthology that includes an abridged version of *Don Quixote de la Mancha*, and some of his novellas. Viking, 1951 (first published 1605).

Condon, Richard   THE OLDEST CONFESSION
In *The Two Headed Reader*—an American businessman lives by swindling and this is the "tale of an elaborate art robbery." (FC) Random, 1966 (first published 1958).

Conrad, Barnaby   MATADOR (Seville)
Story of a bullfighter about to retire who is challenged by a newcomer into making a comeback—"aims at a tragic denouement of classical proportions." (FC) Houghton, 1952.

Conrad, Joseph   THE ARROW OF GOLD
"Beautiful but transitory love idyll" of a gunrunning English sea captain and the Spanish woman who finances his operations. (FC) Doubleday, 1919.

Cornwell, Bernard   SHARPE'S SWORD
The adventures of a nineteenth-century British infantryman in the Salamanca campaign—realistic historic novel. Viking, 1983. Also *Sharpe's Honour* (1985), about the battle of Vitoria.

Del Castillo, Michel   CHILD OF OUR TIME
Story of a Spanish family forced into exile in France during the Spanish Civil War and a boy's great courage and strength. Knopf, 1958.

Fuentes, Carlos   TERRA NOSTRA
"An amalgam of the historical and religious consciousness and heritage of Spain; a biblical allegory; a sensuous, erotic, and fantastic journey through time." (FC) FS&G, 1976.

Gaskin, Catherine   THE SUMMER OF THE SPANISH WOMAN (Jerez)
"Lushly romantic tale" of an Irish girl who takes over her grandfather's vineyard in Spain—vivid story, especially rich in its evocation of Spain's sherry country. (FC) Doubleday, 1977.

Gironella, José Maria   THE CYPRESSES BELIEVE IN GOD (Catalonia)
First of a trilogy, by one of Spain's leading writers. The novel takes place in the

years prior to the Spanish Civil War, and is told through the experiences of a middle-class family. Knopf, 1955. Following is *One Million Dead* (1963) (during the War) and *Peace After War* (1969) (following the War).

Godden, Jon   IN THE SUN
A retired English spinster, living on the Spanish coast, is terrorized by her nephew. Knopf, 1965.

Goytisolo, Juan   MARKS OF IDENTITY
The narrator's memories of Spain (he is now living in France) and the revolution, told in soliloquies, free association, conventional narrative. Grove, 1969.

Greene, Graham   MONSIGNOR QUIXOTE
A retelling of the Don Quixote story in present-day Spain. S&S, 1982.

Hemingway, Ernest   FOR WHOM THE BELL TOLLS
Four days of an American working for the Loyalists in the Spanish Civil War—thought by many to be Hemingway's best novel. Scribner, 1940.

Hemingway, Ernest   THE SUN ALSO RISES (Pamplona)
A group of English and American expatriates in the 1920s drift between Paris and Spain. Scribner, 1983 (first published 1926). See also *Death in the Afternoon* (1932) for a nonfiction book on bullfighting.

Jeffries, Roderic   UNSEEMLY END
Inspector Alvarez of Palma de Mallorca investigates the murder of "wealthy, mean, middle-aged Dolly Lund" and he must tenaciously explore hidden corners of the town to get at the truth. (FC) St. Martin, 1982.

Lofts, Norah   KNIGHT'S ACRE
Europe of the 1450s—an English knight is made a slave following a battle with the Moors and escapes with a fugitive from Selim's harem. Doubleday, 1975.

MacInnes, Helen   MESSAGE FROM MALAGA (Granada/Málaga)
Intrigue and a plot that involves a Spanish dancer, the CIA and a Soviet defector. HarBraceJ, 1971.

Malraux, André   MAN'S HOPE
Story of the first eight months of the Civil War, based on the author's experiences. Random, 1938.

Plaidy, Jean   THE SPANISH BRIDEGROOM
Historical novel of Philip II of Spain, and the Inquisition. Putnam Pub Group, 1971 (first published 1954).

Plante, David   THE FOREIGNER (Barcelona)
A naive American's travels in 1959—"he finds himself embroiled in a world of violence, conspiracy and sexuality for which he is ill-prepared." (FC) Atheneum, 1984.

Polland, Madeleine A.   THE HEART SPEAKS MANY WAYS
See under "Ireland/Novels."

Schoonover, Lawrence   THE PRISONER OF TORDESILLAS
Historical novel of the reigns of Ferdinand and Isabella. Little, 1959. Also *The Queen's Cross* (1955), a fictionalized biography of Queen Isabella, and *The Key of Gold* (1968), in which the first novella is set in fifteenth-century Spain.

Unamuno, Miguel de   PEACE IN WAR (Bilbao)
Novel of the Carlist War in the 1870s—mingles fictional characters with the generals and politicians of Spain. Princeton U Pr, 1983 (first published 1897).

Viertel, Peter   AMERICAN SKIN (Costa del Sol)
An American in "Costa del Sol to find love and money among the rich expatriate exploiters of Spanish coastal real estate." (NYTBR) Houghton, 1984.

Wahloo, Per   A NECESSARY ACTION
A Norwegian couple traveling in Spain—"a graphic . . . depiction of secret police operations in Franco's Spain, the cruelty the tourist seldom sees." (FC) Pantheon, 1969.

MADRID

Del Castillo, Michel   THE DISINHERITED
The shattering effect of the Spanish Civil War on the Spanish. The plot is centered on a young man from the poorest section of Madrid. Knopf, 1960.

Perez Galdos, Benito   THE SPENDTHRIFTS
A comic novel of a wife who cannot resist spending more money than she has. FS&G, 1952.

Serafin, David   MADRID UNDERGROUND
A Superintendent Bernal police procedural, set in Madrid, where bloody corpses (first dummies, then the real thing) show up on the subway—"writes knowingly about life in contemporary Spain." (FC) St. Martin, 1984.

ANDALUSIA

Alarcón, Pedro A. de   THE THREE-CORNERED HAT
Classic based on a Spanish folktale of a miller and his perfect wife. Penguin, 1975 (first published 1874).

Feibleman, Peter S.   THE COLUMBUS TREE
"Event-packed novel of American tourists in Spain" in the 1950s and the inevitable tragic outcome of an encounter between an American girl and a Spanish count. Atheneum, 1973.

BALEARIC ISLANDS (Majorca)

Godwin, Gail   THE PERFECTIONISTS
Plot concerns a psychiatrist, his new American wife, his young illegitimate son, and a variety of resort habitués. Har-Row, 1970.

Jeffries, Roderic   THREE AND ONE MAKE FIVE
An Inspector Alvarez mystery provides interesting glimpses of Majorca, its native people and foreign visitors. St. Martin, 1984. Also *Unseemly End* (1982) about the murder of a middle-aged woman, with her young lover as the prime suspect.

CANARY ISLANDS

Cadell, Elizabeth   CANARY YELLOW
A London secretary wins a trip to the Canary Islands—adventures with her cabin mates and a former acquaintance on shipboard lead to danger in the idyllic setting of Las Palmas. Morrow, 1965.

Carr, Philippa   THE LION TRIUMPHANT
Historical romance; the period is the reign of Elizabeth I, the setting is England and the Canary Islands. Putnam Pub Group, 1974.

GIBRALTAR

Masters, John   THE ROCK
A two-track book that dramatizes Gibraltar's past. There are thirteen chapters arranged chronologically, each with its own historical essay and followed by a fictional section that traces one family in each of the eras, beginning with Gibraltar's earliest days and ending in contemporary times with questions about the future of the "rock." The author "crams a painless course in Western civilization into this novel [with] real live characters to keep history moving briskly along." (FC) Putnam Pub Group, 1970.

TRAVEL ARTICLES

BON APPETIT
1984 Apr "Traveling with Taste: Barcelona." Nan and Ivan Lyons, p. 38

ESSENCE
1985 Jul "Enchanted Isles—The Caribbean Islands." Elaine C. Ray, p. 35

GLAMOUR
1985 Mar "Spain." A sun-splashed country to fall in love with. p. 248

GOURMET
1985 Sep Gourmet Holidays: "Castles in Aragon." Peter Todd Mitchell, p. 38
1984 Sep Gourmet Holidays: "Golfing in Gerona." Paul J. Wade, p. 34

HORIZON

1984 Mar "Fiesta Spain!" A special section giving a guided tour of Spanish festivals. Milan Stitt, p. 21

NATIONAL GEOGRAPHIC

1984 Jan "Catalonia: Spain's Country Within a Country." Randall Peffer, p. 95
Oct "Iberia's Vintage River." With two names and a thousand dimensions (and a traveler's map of Spain). Marion Kaplan, p. 460

N.Y. TIMES SUNDAY TRAVEL SECTION (X)

1985 Jan 6 "Castilian Odyssey on Horseback." Arthur A. Cohen, p. 20
Mar 10 Fare of the Country: "Spanish Churros." A predawn snack. Penelope Casas, p. 6
Mar 17 (Part 2, "Sophisticated Traveler") "Tasty, Sí, Tidy, No." Tapas—bars—in Madrid. Edward Schumacher, p. 133
May 12 "In Barcelona, a Celebration of Singular Style." Its history, lore and food are its own. Edward Schumacher, p. 14
"Antonio Gaudi's Visions in Brick and Stone." Barbaralee Diamonstein, p. 15
"Guide to the Catalan Capital." Edward Schumacher, p. 15
Jun 23 "Shoppers' Haunts Around the World." Includes Madrid. Amanda M. Stinchecum, p. 16
Jul 14 "A Citadel that Bridges a Gorge and the Years." Visiting Spain's little altered Ronda. Jill Kearney, p. 9
"On Madrid's Strawberry Train." Isabel Soto, p. 26
Sep 1 "Almagro Still Lives in the Renaissance." Visiting a Spanish town that is a national monument. Robert Packard, p. 9
Sep 8 "What's Doing in Madrid." Edward Schumacher, p. 10
Oct 6 ("Sophisticated Traveler") "Highland of the Conquistadores." Estremadura. Frederic Raphael, p. 30
Nov 10 Fare of the Country: "Escudella, Catalonia's Meal in a Pot." Fred Ferretti, p. 12
Nov 24 "Hemingway's Spain." The fiesta he loved and wrote of, the restaurants he frequented. James M. Markham, p. 15
Dec 1 Fare of the Country: "Spanish Cider by the Inch." Penelope Casas, p. 12

1984 Jan 29 "Iberia: Good Weather for Golf." More than a dozen scenic courses dot the Algarve and the Costa del Sol. John Radosta, p. 18
Mar 11 "Crown Jewel of the Costa del Sol." Marbella. Walter Logan, p. 19
"Guide to Feasts and Forays in the Sun." Walter Logan, p. 19
Apr 29 "Pamplona in July." The running of the bulls is a singular fiesta (with tips on lodgings, restaurants, bullfight tickets). Penelope Casas, p. 19
Jun 17 "Madrid's Grand and Amiable Palacio Real, Fit for a King Who Knew Versailles." Olivier Bernier, p. 9
Jul 8 Fare of the Country: "Bubbles by the Glass in Barcelona's Bars." Penelope Casas, p. 6
Oct 7 Fare of the Country: "'Artisan' Blue Cheese: Cabrales from Spain." Penelope Casas, p. 6
(Part 2, "Sophisticated Traveler") "Sevillano Spirit." Notes from a theatrical city. V.S. Pritchett, p. 36

1984 Oct 14 Shopper's World: "In Madrid, One Store is Capital of Capes." Robert Packard, p. 6

Dec 16 "Ibiza: Its Blithe Spirit Carries On." One of Spain's less expensive havens. Jack Beeching, p. 9

SUNSET

1985 Mar "In Spain's Northwest Corner, Cool and Ancient Galicia." p. 92

TRAVEL & LEISURE

1985 Apr "A Pilgrimage in Spain." Visiting the holy city of Santiago de Capostela. Herbert B. Livesey, p. 98

Jun "Córdoba: The Heart of Moorish Spain." Richard Covington, p. 176

Jul "Catalonia." From the peaks of the Pyrenees to the beaches of the Med, it's Spain of unexpected pleasures. Peter Feibleman, p. 58

"Barcelona, the Worldly Exuberant Capital of Catalonia." Herbert B. Livesey. p. 64

Nov "The Mighty Rock of Gibraltar." Touring the citadel that guards the Mediterranean. Sybil Taylor, p. 68

1984 Feb "Barcelona: A Dream Fulfilled." A long-awaited visit to the home of Picasso, Miro, Antonio Gaudi. p. 15

Jun "The Secret Canary Island for Restful Resorts and Black Lava Beaches on the Blue Atlantic." Lanzarote. Robert Packard, p. 138

Jul "Madrid Lights Up! There's a New Spirit in Spain's Historic Capital." p. 96

"Madrid's Restaurant Awakening." From regional simplicity to international sophistication. Penelope Casas, p. 102

"Shopping in Madrid." Patricia Brooks, p. 104

"Tours to Madrid and to the Rest of Spain." Bunny Brower, p. 108

Aug "Spain." Leisurely rides across a romantic landscape (holidays on horseback). Paula Rodenas, p. 86

Nov "Spain's Paradise for Bird Watchers." The rich diversity of Doana National Park. Daniel Cameron, p. 168

TRAVEL/HOLIDAY

1985 Apr "Living Out the Fantasy." Unique accommodations. Judith Glynn, p. 71

Jul "Pageantry and Passion in Pollenca—a Spanish Encounter." Timothy McGlue, p. 26

1984 Jan "Gibraltar." Gateway to the Mediterranean. Mark Williams, p. 12

Apr "Don Quixote's Spain." Land of La Mancha. Charles Huckaba, p. 72

"Europe's Unique Accommodations: Spain." Living out the fantasy (paradores). Judith Glynn, p. 71

VOGUE

1984 Jan "The Spain Rush." Everybody's going to Spain for Picasso treasures, Moorish palaces, medieval splendors . . . and heady new freedom. Olivier Bernier, p. 132

Mar "Parador Pleasures." Kimberly Goad, p. 378

WORLD PRESS REVIEW

1984 Feb "The Legendary Canaries." Off the beaten path at a historic Spanish retreat. Jean Welle (*Porquois Pas?*, Brussels), p. 61

SWEDEN

Note: See also all asterisked (*) entries under "Denmark" for books on Scandinavia as a whole, as well as books listed under "Denmark/Vikings."

Series Guidebooks (See Appendix 1)

Baedeker: Scandinavia
Berlitz: Stockholm
Fodor: Scandinavia; Budget Scandinavia;
        Stockholm, Copenhagen, Oslo, Helsinki & Reykjavik
Frommer: Scandinavia: $-a-Day
Nagel: Sweden
U.S. Government: Sweden: Post Report

Background Reading

Huntford, Roland   THE NEW TOTALITARIANS
A polemic that presents Sweden as "totally controlled by a bureaucracy which . . .discourages all signs of individuality." Stein & Day, 1972.

Källberg, Sture   OFF THE MIDDLE WAY
Report from a Swedish village—the lives of twelve ordinary Swedes. "Middle Way" refers to Marquis Childs's book of the 1930s extolling the Swedish economic system. Pantheon, 1972.

Kramer, Jane   UNSETTLING EUROPE
Refugee families from Algeria, Uganda, Yugoslavia, living in France, London and Sweden respectively, and an Italian Communist family in Italy, their isolation from traditions of those around them and the implications for Europe's future of these rootless people. Random, 1981.

Lister, R.P.   A JOURNEY IN LAPLAND
Two walking tours beginning in Sweden and going through Swedish and Norwegian Lapland—"a first-rate guide . . . an intelligent observer . . . and a genuinely funny writer." HarBraceJ, 1966.

Ljungmark, Lars   SWEDISH EXODUS
Based on a Swedish radio series, it is an account of "why more than a million Swedes came to the U.S." (LJ) Southern Illinois U, 1979.

Lorénzen, Lilly   OF SWEDISH WAYS
"A lively account of the customs and traditions of that Northern Nation." (Publisher) Barnes & Noble, 1978.

McGreevy, John, ed.   CITIES
Impressions of world cities as seen through the eyes of people intimately connected with them—for Sweden it is Mai Zetterling's impressions of Stockholm. Outlet Bk, 1981.

Moberg, Vilhelm   A HISTORY OF THE SWEDISH PEOPLE FROM RENAISSANCE TO REVOLUTION
Popular history by a novelist (see below under "Novels")—an introduction to Sweden's history and its people. Pantheon, 1973.

Morris, Jan   JOURNEYS
This collection of travel essays by a leading travel writer includes an essay on Stockholm. Oxford U, 1984.

HISTORY

Elstob, Eric   SWEDEN, A POLITICAL AND CULTURAL HISTORY
Rowman, 1979.

Scobbie, Irene   SWEDEN
Praeger, 1972.

Scott, Franklin D.   SWEDEN: THE NATION'S HISTORY
U of Minnesota, 1979.

Novels

Barroll, Clare   SEASON OF THE HEART
Historical novel of fifteenth-century Sweden. Scribner, 1976.

Bjorn, Thyra F.   PAPA'S WIFE
An autobiographical novel beginning in Swedish Lapland and ending in New England, where the family emigrates after the author's father marries their housemaid. HR&W, 1955. *Papa's Daughter* (1958) is a sequel that continues with life in America.

Eden, Dorothy   WAITING FOR WILLA
An English writer goes to Stockholm after receiving a coded message from her cousin only to find that the cousin has disappeared; her search uncovers a spy ring. Coward, 1970.

Lagerkvist, Pär   THE ETERNAL SMILE
Short stories on many subjects by a Nobel Prize-winning author. Random, 1954.

Lagerlöf, Selma   THE GENERAL'S RING
A ring belonging to Charles XII brings disaster and death to three generations who come to possess it. Doubleday, 1928.

Lagerlöf, Selma   GÖSTA BERLING'S SAGA
The adventures of a young man with a gift for drawing people to him—particularly women—but who eventually marries and leads a life "that more nearly approximates his own ideals." (FC) American-Scandinavian Foundation, 1918 (first published 1891).

Moberg, Vilhelm   THE EMIGRANTS
Classic story of the Swedish migration to the American Midwest in the nineteenth century. S&S, 1951.

Moberg, Vilhelm   A TIME ON EARTH
A transplanted Swede in California reflects on his life and early days in Sweden. S&S, 1965.

Peters, Elizabeth   SILHOUETTE IN SCARLET
One of a series of romantic adventures involving art historian Vicky Bliss—in this one she is invited to Stockholm and finds herself, along with a former lover, held captive by a criminal organization. Congdon & Weed, 1983.

Sjöwall, Maj and Wahlöö, Per   THE TERRORISTS
The last of the Swedish husband-and-wife team's crime novels in which Martin Beck, head of the National Homicide Squad, is the sleuth. The series has been reviewed as being much more than simply stories of murders and police investigations—they present a picture of contemporary Sweden, "among the best—perhaps, they are the best—writers of detective fiction today."
Additional titles by this couple, set in Sweden, are *Roseanna* (1967), *The Man on the Balcony* (1968), *The Fire Engine That Disappeared* (1970), *The Laughing Policeman* (1970), *Murder at the Savoy* (1971), *The Abominable Man* (1972), *The Locked Room* (1973), *The Cop Killer* (1975), and *The Terrorists* (1976). Pantheon.

Wallace, Irving   THE PRIZE
Behind-the-scenes machinations and intrigues of the Nobel Prize ceremonies. S&S, 1962.

TRAVEL ARTICLES

BON APPETIT
1985 Dec "Traveling with Taste: Christmas in Old Stockholm." Lisa de Mauro, p. 40

N.Y. TIMES SUNDAY TRAVEL SECTION (X)
1985 Mar 3 "Baroque Stage in a Swedish Palace." Drottningholm, once reserved for royalty, now offers opera to the public. Jason Marks, p. 9
Jun 30 "What's Doing in Stockholm." Richard Soderlund, p. 10
1984 Feb 26 "A Small-Town Swedish Weekend." Mora ski resort. John Vinocur, p. 19
May 20 "For Fine Weaving, Try Stockholm." Betty Freudenheim, p. 6

Sep 23 "The Many Surprises of Stockholm." From Old Town to archipelago, Sweden's capital blends palaces, museums and a love of the sea. William H. Adams, p. 14
"An Elegant and Playful Architect." Architectural works of Eric Gunnar Asplund to see. William H. Adams, p. 14
"Getting a Taste of Northern Food." Restaurants and old market offer abundance. Edith Marks, p. 15

TRAVEL & LEISURE
1984 Jun Summer in Stockholm—Special Section: "Golden Days in Sweden's Sparkling Capital." Geoffrey Wolf; "Cruising the Gota Canal." Helmut Koenig; "Tours to Scandinavia." Patricia Brooks, pp. 104-114

TRAVEL/HOLIDAY
1984 May "Stockholm Naturally, the Essence of *hurtig* in Sweden." Diane P. Marshall, p. 58

WORLD PRESS REVIEW
1985 Aug "Sweden's serene interior." Jacques Bonnet, p. 62 (*Le Figaro*, Paris).
1984 Jun "Through Sweden's Canals." Henry Braunschweig (*Neue Zuricher Zeitung*, Zurich), p. 70

SWITZERLAND
(Including Liechtenstein)

Series Guidebooks (See Appendix 1)

Baedeker: Switzerland
Berlitz: Switzerland
Fodor: Switzerland
Frommer: Switzerland: Dollarwise
Michelin: Switzerland
U.S. Government: Switzerland: Background Notes; Post Report
                    Liechtenstein: Background Notes

Background Reading

Brody, Elaine   THE MUSIC GUIDE TO BELGIUM, LUXEMBOURG, HOLLAND AND SWITZERLAND
One of a series of guides for individual European countries—a handbook of

information for a range of travelers "from the music dilettante to the highly motivated specialist." Includes information on the country's musical history, concert halls, opera houses, festivals, etc. Dodd, 1977. (See also *Music Festivals in Europe and Britain* and *Music Lover's Europe* under "Europe/Background Reading.")

Clark, Ronald W.   THE ALPS
The past and future Alps in three parts: geography and history, expeditions, skiing and sports; people and animals; and various individual mountains. Knopf, 1973.

Kubly, Herbert   NATIVE'S RETURN
By an American academic of Swiss descent—"an observant, though quite subjective, set of vignettes, travel notes, and ruminations. . . . His characterizations of city and village life are entertaining, his analysis of the *malaise suisse* is provocative." (BL) Stein & Day, 1981.

Lunn, Sir A.H.M.   THE SWISS AND THEIR MOUNTAINS
A study of the influence of mountains on man. Rand, 1963.

McPhee, John   LA PLACE DE LA CONCORDE SUISSE
The paradox of a country that has not fought a war in nearly 500 years, yet has one of the world's biggest militia armies in proportion to its population—"puts his reader inside Switzerland with elegance and insight." (Publisher) FS&G, 1984.

Maeder, Herbert, ed.   THE MOUNTAINS OF SWITZERLAND: THE ADVENTURE OF THE HIGH ALPS
A book about "the mountain experience, what it is and what its satisfactions are"—of mountains and mountain climbing. (BRD) Allen Unwin, 1968.

Sauter, M.R.   ANTIQUITIES AND ARCHAEOLOGY
Switzerland from earliest times to the Roman conquest, written by the archaeologist for the canton and city of Geneva. Westview Pr, 1976.

Schwarz, Urs   THE EYE OF THE HURRICANE
Switzerland in World War II. A denial of the charge that Switzerland profitted from the war and the claim that "Swiss lives and money paid for neutrality." (LJ) Westview Pr, 1980.

Steinberg, Jonathan   WHY SWITZERLAND
"The Swiss success story through the ages" based on the author's premise that Switzerland is a unique country from which the world can learn much—"democracy rests ultimately on the community level." The author is a lecturer in history at Cambridge and is married to a Swiss-German woman. (BRD) Cambridge U Pr, 1976.

Ziegler, Jean   SWITZERLAND EXPOSED
Switzerland is the "fence" of world imperialism in this author's highly critical view of what seems to most of us to be a contemporary paradise. Schocken, 1981.

LIECHTENSTEIN

Kranz, Walter   LIECHTENSTEIN
Text and photographs. Hubert Gassner, 1977.

Raton, P.   LIECHTENSTEIN
A history of the principality. Liechtenstein-Verlag, 1970.

GUIDEBOOKS

Kitfield, James and Walker, William   WHOLE EUROPE ESCAPE MANUAL: GERMANY, AUSTRIA, SWITZERLAND
Part of a new series of guidebooks "designed to . . . put the fantasy and excitement back into travel." (Publisher) World Leis Corp, 1984.

HISTORY

Hughes, Christopher S.   SWITZERLAND
Praeger, 1975.

Novels

Ambler, Eric   THE INTERCOM CONSPIRACY (Geneva)
Two mellowing intelligence colonels at NATO plot to blackmail both the U.S. and Russia by publishing a newsletter with each side's military secrets. Atheneum, 1969.

Brookner, Anita   HOTEL DU LAC
A sedate Swiss hotel is the setting for an "oddly detached, very small-scale, faintly humorous" novel. Pantheon, 1985.

Bryher   ROMAN WALL
Historical novel of a third-century Roman outpost (now Switzerland)—the break-up of the outer reaches of Rome. Pantheon, 1954.

Cronin, A.J.   A POCKETFUL OF RYE
A British doctor is reunited in Switzerland with a former lover and the son he fathered. Little, 1969.

Daudet, Alphonse   TARTARIN ON THE ALPS
In *Tartarin of Tarascon*—as president of the local Alpine Club, in Provençal, France, Tartarin feels he must do something dramatic if he is to win the next election—like climbing in the Swiss Alps. Dutton, 1954 (first published 1885).

Davies, Robertson   THE MANTICORE (Zurich)
"Insightful, and a delightful psychological excursion" as a successful Canadian

lawyer submits himself to the Jung Institute in Zurich for analysis. (FC) Viking, 1972.

Duerrenmatt, Friedrich   THE PLEDGE
A genius detective seeks a killer of little girls to fulfill his pledge to a victim's mother—"an unusual and arresting level of crime and detection . . . some tantalizing moral questions." (FC) Knopf, 1959. Also *The Quarry* (1962), about the search for and execution of a former Nazi criminal—a doctor.

Durrell, Lawrence   SEBASTIAN (Geneva)
Part of the Avignon quartet series of novels, set in post-World War II Geneva. Viking, 1984.

Frisch, Max   MAN IN THE HOLOCENE (Ticino)
Profound novel of a man living alone in a mountain valley under threat from rockslides and avalanches. HarBraceJ, 1980.

Gilman, Dorothy   A PALM FOR MRS. POLLIFAX
This time Mrs. Gilman's free-lance assignment for the CIA is to study guests at a chic clinic to trace stolen plutonium. Doubleday, 1973.

Hesse, Herman   PETER CAMENZIND
A young man, born in a remote Alpine village, is taken under the wing of a monk who recognizes his superior potential, and given a fine education, continuing at a university in Zurich. FS&G, 1969.

James, Henry   DAISY MILLER (Vevey)
An international episode—will an English nobleman marry a "beautiful, dainty, innocent and very foolish" American girl? (FC) Har-Row, 1975 (first published 1878).

Kirst, Hellmut   THE NIGHTS OF THE LONG KNIVES (Lugano)
An unreconstructed Nazi is murdered—"expertly knits together the suspense of murder investigation with the brutal tone of the Nazi era." (FC) Coward, 1968.

Koestler, Arthur   THE CALL GIRLS
The "call girls" are what the author terms "intellectual prostitutes" in attendance at a symposium in Switzerland on Approaches to Survival—"overspecialized noncommunicators dourly patrol their own corners of thought, noisily collide, and produce no remedies." (FC) Random, 1973.

Solzhenitsyn, Aleksandr   LENIN IN ZURICH
Fictional account of Lenin's time in exile in Switzerland during World War I, until his departure in 1917 for Russia. FS&G, 1976.

Spark, Muriel   NOT TO DISTURB (Geneva)
A witty comedy about the aristocracy as seen through the eyes of servants. Viking, 1972.

Stead, Christina   THE LITTLE HOTEL (Montreux)
Time is the 1940s—"obscure, forgotten folk . . . within the genteel but thin walls of a cheap pension-hotel." (FC) HR&W, 1973.

Stewart, Fred Mustard   THE METHUSELAH ENZYME
"Urbane and breezy thriller" of three couples at a youth clinic, where the older member of each pair is to undergo rejuvenation treatment. (FC) Arbor Hse, 1970.

Ullman, James R.   THE WHITE TOWER
"Development and revelation of several characters" who attempt to climb "the White Tower," never before scaled from a particular side, and an adventure story as well. (FC) Lippincott, 1945.

Waller, Leslie   THE SWISS ACCOUNT (Basel)
Novel of high-level banking as an American is sent to Basel to take over the assets of the Staeli family—"crisply told with a splendid denouement." (FC) Doubleday, 1976.

Whiteman, John   GENEVA ACCORD
A thriller that also provides an armchair way to learn about arms control; it was written by a former CIA employee who was a member of the U.S. Salt II negotiating team. Crown, 1985.

TRAVEL ARTICLES

ARCHITECTURAL DIGEST
1984 Apr "Designer's Travel Notes: Once Around the Lake." Geneva's cottage crafts. Joseph Braswell, p. 260

BON APPETIT
1985 Apr "A Taste of Zurich." Nan and Ivan Lyons, p. 108

CONNOISSEUR
1984 Feb "The Spontaneous Chef, Fredy Girardet." Geoffrey Wheatcroft, p. 82
"Five Keys to Geneva." Dining, hotels, art, shopping, after hours. Mary Krienke, p. 86

ESQUIRE
1984 Jun Special Places: "Trekking Lightly." In the Alps. David Butwin, p. 40

GOURMET
1984 Jul "Summer in St. Moritz." Richard Condon, p. 40

N.Y. TIMES SUNDAY TRAVEL SECTION (X)
1985 Jan 13 "The Palace Clings to Its Swiss Legend." Elegance on parade in St. Moritz. Barbara Cansino, p. 12
Feb 10 Fare of the Country: "Fondue: a Swiss classic." Paul Hofmann, p. 6
Feb 24 Fare of the Country: "Beef with an Air of Switzerland." Fred Ferretti, p. 12

Mar 3 "What's Doing in Geneva." Paul Hofmann, p. 10

Mar 17 (Part 2, "Sophisticated Traveler") "Second Helpings at Chez Girardet." Conceivably the greatest restaurant in the world at Crissier. Barbara Gelb, p. 44

Mar 24 "What's Doing in Klosters." Paul Lewis, p. 10

May 12 (Liechtenstein) "Big Art in a Small Frame." Liechtenstein boasts a collection worth a prince's ransom. Olivier Bernier, p. 9

May 26 "Golf, Italian-Swiss Style." On Alpine courses the scenery can make you forget your worst shot. Thomas L. Friedman, p. 6

Aug 4 Shopper's World: "Traditional Crafts in the Swiss Style." Barbara Cansino, p. 6

Oct 6 ("Sophisticated Traveler") "Downhill on Europe's Longest Run." Parsenn in Klosters. James Salter, p. 92

Oct 13 Fare of the Country: "For the Swiss, What Else but Chocolate." Rose L. Beranbaum, p. 6

1984 Jan 1 "What's Doing in Zurich." Paul Hofmann, p. 13

Feb 19 "Riding the Glacier Express." Zermatt to St. Moritz train. Bannon McHenry, p. 20

Feb 26 "What's Doing in Davos." Paul Lewis, p. 10

Oct 14 "Switzerland's Little Italy: the Ticino Has a Style of Its Own." Paul Hofmann, p. 14

SUNSET

1985 Jun "It's Almost a Game with the Swiss: How Many Ways to Get Around on Public Transportation." p. 52

1984 Jul "Seeing One Corner of Switzerland by Way of Postal Coaches." p. 24B

TOWN & COUNTRY

1984 Jan Vis-a-vis: "St. Moritz." Jennifer Kramer, p. 132

TRAVEL & LEISURE

1985 Apr "Mountain Magic in Switzerland." The grand hotels of Bürgenstock. Ian Keown, p. 122

May "The Best Little Circus in Europe." Switzerland's enchanting Circus Knie. Leon Harris, p. 76

Jul "Switzerland's Richest Shopping Street." An acquisitive guide to that purchaser's paradise, Zurich's Bahnhofstrasse. William Cross, p. 26

Sep "Walking Tour: Geneva's Old Town." Dan Carlinsky, p. 189

Oct (Liechtenstein) "A Ramble Through Liechtenstein." Big on cultural attractions, fine dining and outdoor pleasures. Janice Brand, p. 44

Nov "Switzerland's Rigi." A William Cross wonderland of spas and ski resorts, forests and flowering fields. p. 152

1984 Mar "A Delicious Day in Zurich." Art at the Kuntzhaus; a meal at Agnes Amberg. Robert S. Kane, p. 28

Oct (Liechtenstein) "Great Find: the Hotel Restaurant Real." Curtiss Anderson, p. 86

Dec "Conquering St. Moritz's Cresta Run." World's fastest toboggan course. Ed Kerins, p. 54

TRAVEL/HOLIDAY
1985   Jan "Offbeat Ski Resorts." Includes Switzerland. Ken Castle, p. 46
          Aug "Geneva's Good Terms—Outings and Eating." Ann Byrd-Platt, p. 30
          Nov "Concerning Food and Wine—Swiss Chic in St. Moritz." Robert L.
          Balzer, p. 14
1984   Mar "Small Towns, Switzerland." Homegrown hospitality. W.D. Wetherell,
          p. 80

VOGUE
1984   Mar (Vevey) "Swiss Bliss, a Small Grand Hotel . . . a Lovely Lake . . . the
          Perfect Set-Up." Despina Messinesi, p. 367

WALES

Note: See also all asterisked entries (*) under "England" for additional series
guidebooks, background reading, and articles that may include Wales.

Series Guidebooks (See Appendix 1)

American Express: **England & Wales**
Blue Guide: **Wales; Cathedrals and Abbeys of England & Wales**
Let's Go: **Britain & Ireland (Scotland & Wales)**

Background Reading

Barber, Chris   **MYSTERIOUS WALES**
     "Folklore for armchair adventurers and real travelers. . . . thoroughly entertaining." (BL) David, 1982.

Barber, W.T.   **EXPLORING WALES**
     A lively guide to Welsh history, literature, architecture, archaeology, legend, fable and countryside, arranged in fourteen regions and organized into favorite tours by foot, car, train and boat. David, 1982.

Fishlock, Trevor   **TALKING OF WALES: A COMPANION TO WALES AND
THE WELSH**
     The *London Times* called this "a thinking person's guide to Wales." Academy Chi Ltd, 1978.

Hilling, John B.   **HISTORIC ARCHITECTURE OF WALES**
     A "sensitive architect's personal survey" of architecture in Wales from earliest times to the present. (BRD) Verry, 1977.

McMullen, Jeanine   MY SMALL COUNTRY LIVING
Life on a thirteen-acre farm, on a Welsh mountainside, owned by a BBC broadcaster who is star of a successful radio program on rural life—"a gem of the genre." (PW) Norton, 1984.

**Morris, Jan   THE MATTER OF WALES: EPIC VIEWS OF
A SMALL COUNTRY**
This noted travel writer's celebration of her native country: "what is special about it—from rocks and soil to history and religion to the prevailing national character." (BL) Oxford U, 1985.

Morton, H.V.   IN SEARCH OF WALES
Reprint of a travel classic. Dodd, 1984 (first published 1932). See also *Morton's Britain*, under "England."

Vaughan-Thomas, Wynford   WYNFORD VAUGHN-THOMAS'S WALES
St. Martin, 1981.

Wakefield, Paul and Morris, Jan   WALES: THE FIRST PLACE
Photographs that "reverberate with the spirit and essence of this . . . singular country" with parallel text by Jan Morris—natives, religion, legendry, language, and a selection also of Welsh poems. Crown, 1982.

**Waterson, Merlin   THE SERVANTS' HALL: THE "DOWNSTAIRS"
HISTORY OF A BRITISH COUNTRY HOUSE**
The 250-year history of the "deep and lasting relationship between owners and servants" in a Welsh country house—the Yorke family chronicle (the house is now under the British National Trust). Captures eccentricities and personalities of the family and individual servants. Pantheon, 1980.

Williams, G.   RELIGION, LANGUAGE AND NATIONALITY IN WALES
Historical essays by an outstanding authority—"provides the essential background to understanding modern Welsh nationalism." U of Wales, 1979.

GUIDEBOOKS

Hilling, John B.   SNOWDONIA AND NORTHERN WALES
Batsford, 1980.

HISTORY

Jones, Gareth Elwyn   MODERN WALES: A CONCISE HISTORY
History since the Tudors—"always striving to isolate what it is about the Welsh and their history that makes them special." Cambridge U Pr, 1985.

Novels

Aldridge, James   THE MARVELOUS MONGOLIAN
A child's book for adults—a Mongolian stallion captured and sent to Wales meets up with a Shetland mare and they try to escape. Little, 1974.

Bainbridge, Beryl   ANOTHER PART OF THE WOOD
Focuses on the relationships between people who are vacationing at a camp in Wales. This is a revised version of a novel previously published in 1968. Braziller, 1980.

Chatwin, Bruce   ON THE BLACK HILL
Identical twin brothers live out their lives on the Welsh-English border—"an odd, somber story." (FC) Viking, 1983.

Cordell, Alexander   THE RAPE OF THE FAIR COUNTRY
A family chronicle, and story of the ironworkers' attempts to unionize. Doubleday, 1975 (first published 1959). Its sequel is *Robe of Honour* (1960). Another novel of union struggles is *This Sweet and Bitter Earth* (1978).

Cronin, A.J.   THE CITADEL
The medical career of a young doctor in a Welsh mining town, his disillusionment and move to London. Little, 1937.

Davies, Rhys   THE BEST OF RHYS DAVIES
Selected by the author as his best—mostly with Welsh settings. David, 1979.

Delderfield, R.F.   CHARLIE, COME HOME
Suspenseful novel involving a bank clerk fretting in the strictures of his job, who is enticed into participating in a bank robbery. The time is 1929. S&S, 1976.

Fuller, John   FLYING TO NOWHERE
A "monastic horror tale" that is set on a Welsh island during the Middle Ages. (FC) Braziller, 1984.

Graham, Winston   WOMAN IN THE MIRROR
The heroine is hired as a secretary by a woman journalist/lecturer; the plot definitely thickens, and when she finds out that she bears a resemblance to nephew Simon's sister, she knows something is wrong and the plot becomes threatening. Doubleday, 1975.

Grumbach, Doris   THE LADIES
Based on the real and infamous "ladies of Llangollen" of the eighteenth century—two women who spurned convention and left Ireland to live together in a Welsh village. (FC) Dutton, 1984.

Hanley, James   A KINGDOM
Two sisters follow divergent paths—one leaves to marry, the other stays with their father on the family farm—and are reunited at the father's death. Horizon,

1978. Also *The Welsh Sonata* (1954), about a small-town tramp's disappearance and the "medley" of reactions, and *Another World* (1972).

Howatch, Susan   THE WHEEL OF FORTUNE
A family saga—five generations of a family beset by tragedy, "based loosely upon . . . Edward of Woodstock (the Black Prince) and his descendants." Stein & Day, 1972. Also *The Devil on Lammas Night* (1972), about satanic mystery in modern day South Wales.

Llewellyn, Richard   HOW GREEN WAS MY VALLEY
The story of Welsh mining country related by the youngest son of the family, and the gradual laying waste of the once-lovely countryside—"a remarkably beautiful novel of Wales." Macmillan, 1940. Its sequels are: *Up Into the Singing Mountain* (1960) and *Green, Green, My Valley Now* (1975), which takes the main character to Patagonia and back, to retire in Wales.

Martin, Gillian   PASSAGE OF TIME
A woman returns to Wales, to her childhood home, when she disintegrates emotionally following the breakup of her marriage. Scribner, 1978.

Melville, Jennie   NUN'S CASTLE
"No end of suspense . . . and the plot gets labyrinthine," in this modern gothic set in the Welsh countryside. (FC) McKay, 1974.

Roberts, Dorothy J.   KINSMEN OF THE GRAIL
Historical novel of the twelfth-century quest for the Holy Grail. Little, 1963.

Stewart, Mary   MERLIN TRILOGY
See under "France/Novels."

Stubbs, Jean   AN UNKNOWN WELSHMAN
The life of Henry VII from birth to marriage, in the fifteenth century. Stein & Day, 1972.

Thomas, Dylan   REBECCA'S DAUGHTERS
"Rebecca's Daughters" were a group of men who dressed as women in an uprising against the Turnpike Trusts when they set up road tollgates in the 1840s. New Directions, 1982.

Thomas, Gwyn   THE WORLD CANNOT HEAR YOU
Life in a Welsh valley—the plot concerns rivalries between a truck farmer and the heir to the leading family of the valley. "Every page of this village comedy is enlivened with the fantasy and fierce humor of the grubby, passionate people [with] the presence of tenderness in the midst of daftness and derision." (BRD) Little, 1952.

Wain, John   A WINTER IN THE HILLS
A university professor visiting in Wales (with hopes of picking up enough of the language to land a job in Sweden in Celtic studies), but suspense and surprises change his plans. Viking, 1970.

TRAVEL ARTICLES

AMERICAN HERITAGE
1985 Jun "Britain's Yankee Whaling Town." The curious story of Milford Haven (on the Welsh coast). Brian Dunning, p. 38

NATIONAL GEOGRAPHIC TRAVELER
1985 Summer "Broad Vistas on Narrow Gauge." Riding the little trains of Wales. Charlton Ogburn, p. 62

N.Y. TIMES SUNDAY TRAVEL SECTION (X)
1985 Jun 2 "In Wales, a Bookworm's Holiday." Room, board and 130,000 volumes (St. Deinioe's residential library in Hawarden). Israel Shenker, p. 9

YUGOSLAVIA

Series Guidebooks (See Appendix 1)

Baedeker: Yugoslavia
Berlitz: Dubrovnik; Split & Dalmatia
Companion Guide: Yugoslavia
Fodor: Yugoslavia
Nagel: Yugoslavia
U.S. Government: Background Notes; Country Study; Post Report

Background Reading

Ardagh, John   A TALE OF FIVE CITIES
See under "Europe"; includes Ljubljana.

Doder, Dusko   THE YUGOSLAVS
An emigrant from Yugoslavia returns twenty years later as Bureau Chief for the *Washington Post*—a panoramic, personal survey by a sympathetic and skilled observer. Description of the history, culture, ideology, profiles of Tito and Djilas. Random, 1978.

Durrell, Lawrence   SPIRIT OF PLACE
Letters and essays—"descriptive, frank . . . wonderful compilation of fact and fiction" that includes Yugoslavia. (BRD) Leetes Isle, 1984 (first published 1969).

Feldkamp, Frederick   NOT EVERYBODY'S EUROPE
A grand tour of nine unique places to think about adding to your itinerary—in Yugoslavia, it's Dubrovnik. Harper's Magazine Pr, 1976.

Kindersley, Anna   THE MOUNTAINS OF SERBIA: TRAVELS
THROUGH YUGOSLAVIA
A perceptive account of a series of journeys taken in 1964 and 1967 by the wife of a British diplomat. "Art and architecture of religious buildings . . . an account of succeeding waves of conquerors who tried to destroy them." (BRD) Transatlantic, 1977.

Lasić-Vasojević, Milija M.   ENEMIES ON ALL SIDES: THE FALL
OF YUGOSLAVIA
The author fought with the nationalist forces of the Serbs in World War II and feels that the partisans, under Tito, were as evil as the Nazis. North Am Intl, 1976.

Morris, Jan   JOURNEYS
This collection of essays by a leading travel writer includes an essay on Yugosalvia (Cetinji). Oxford U, 1984.

Robinson, G.J.   TITO'S MAVERICK MEDIA
The politics of mass communication—written for media people, but also for anyone interested in how the press, radio and television operate in Yugoslavia. U of Illinois, 1977.

Streeter, Edward   ALONG THE RIDGE
Account of an unusually beautiful and diversified automobile trip "from Paris south to Andorra, to Spain, across southern France, through the Dolomites, and ending in Dubrovnik. Har-Row, 1964.

West, Rebecca   BLACK LAMB AND GREY FALCON
A classic and important book. History, brilliant analysis of European culture and ideas, and a travel diary of a trip through Yugoslavia at Easter in 1937. Viking, 1943.

GUIDEBOOKS

Edwards, Lovitt F.   YUGOSLAV COAST
Hastings, 1974.

HISTORY

Dedijer, Vladimir and others   HISTORY OF YUGOSLAVIA
"A chronological outline of the social, economic, political and intellectual development of the various Yugoslav nationalities." (BRD) McGraw, 1974.

Wilson, Duncan   TITO'S YUGOSLAVIA
"Good account of the events of World War II, of the Yugoslav Revolution," and 1948 on as an independent state. (BRD) Cambridge U Pr, 1979.

Novels

Andric, Ivo   THE BRIDGE ON THE DRINA
First novel in the Bosnian trilogy. Chronicle of a bridge near Visograd over three and a half centuries. Allen Unwin, 1959 (first published 1945). The sequels are *Bosnian Chronicle* (1945), set in the capital of Bosnia in the years just before the fall of Napoleon; *The Woman from Sarajevo* (1945), set in the Balkans during the early twentieth century and including Sarajevo at the time of the assassination that started World War I (the "woman" is a girl, turned into an embittered miser by the bankruptcy and death of her father).

Bridge, Ann   ILLYRIAN SPRING
A woman runs off to Dalmatia (from Italy) because of the attitude of her children and husband—a "friendly psychologist and a young artist protégé . . . contribute to her understanding of herself." The story reflects the "loveliness of Dalmatian flowers, villages and mountains." (FC) Little, 1935.

Ćosić, Dobrica   A TIME OF DEATH
First in a trilogy. This is a story of Serbia during World War I and its fight for survival. HarBraceJ, 1978. It is followed by *Reach to Eternity* (1980), which tells of the aftermath of a decisive battle in 1914 when the Serbs defeated the Austrian forces. The third novel is *South to Destiny* (1981), which takes the story through 1916 when Serbia is defeated and abandoned by its allies.

Djilas, Milovan   UNDER THE COLORS
The "roots of nationalism" and the story of a peasant family in the 1870s engaged in the "seemingly hopeless task of rebelling against their Turkish overlords." (FC) HarBraceJ, 1971.

Durrell, Lawrence   WHITE EAGLES OVER SERBIA
Story of espionage to solve the murder of a British agent. Criterion, 1957.

Fagyas, Maria   DANCE OF THE ASSASSINS
The plot depicts the assassination of King Alexander and Queen Draga (and the twenty-four hours preceding it) in Serbia at the beginning of the twentieth century, thereby also illuminating the history of Yugoslavia and a view of some of the happenings that led to World War I. Putnam Pub Group 1973.

MacLean, Alistair   FORCE 10 FROM NAVARONE
Three men are assigned the mission in World War II of a drop into Yugoslavia to join the partisans, blow up a dam and divert German troops from Italy to Yugoslavia—"rapid-fire, thrill-on-every-page suspense story." (FC) Doubleday, 1968.

MacLean, Alistair   PARTISANS
A MacLean suspense story of World War II and the Nazi/partisan struggle—the vastness of the Balkan mountains is the setting. Doubleday, 1983.

Palmer, Lilli   NIGHT MUSIC
A professor of languages at the University of Munich reaches a crossroad in his life and decides to take the advice of his uncle to escape from his boxed-in life—"immobility, security, shelter"—and instead, "live, and stop dreaming." (FC) Har-Row, 1983.

Pekic, Borislav   THE HOUSES OF BELGRADE
A wealthy landlord's obsession with his buildings. HarBraceJ, 1978.

TRAVEL ARTICLES

BON APPETIT
1984 Jan "Traveling with Taste: Sarajevo." Patricia Brooks, p. 30

ESQUIRE
1984 May "A Trout for All Seasons." Fishing for trout in four seasons on different continents—Yugoslavia is summer. p. 33

GOURMET
1984 Feb "Glimpses of Yugoslavia." Geri Trotta, p. 18

HOUSE & GARDEN
1985 Oct "The Hvar Side of Paradise." A lavender-scented paradise off the Dalmation coast. Naomi Barry, p. 55
1984 Jan "Après Ski in Sarajevo." Vera Mijojlic, p. 50

N.Y. TIMES SUNDAY TRAVEL SECTION (X)
1985 Mar 17 (Part 2, "Sophisticated Traveler") "Adriatic Cliffhanger." Henry Kamm, p. 82
May 5 "Town of Bell Towers." On the Adriatic island of the same name, Rab offers medieval churches and lots of sun. Robert Packard, p. 18
Oct 13 "Montenegro's Legends, Coves and Mountains Remote but No Longer Inaccessible." David Binder, p. 23
1984 Jul 22 (Dubrovnik) "Brave Bastion of Adriatic Buccaneers." David Binder, p. 9
Aug 5 "Not Just Another Fish Story." Yugoslavia's rocky roads were a disaster, but what a lunch! Oscar Millard, p. 33

VI. LATIN AMERICA

Background Reading

Arciniegas, Germán   THE GREEN CONTINENT
An anthology of writings on Latin America by historians, essayists and novelists. 1944.

Fox-Lockert, Lucia   WOMEN NOVELISTS IN SPAIN AND SPANISH AMERICA
Novels reflecting women's issues with a "vanguard feminine perspective"—1639 to the present. Scarecrow, 1979.

Gunther, John   INSIDE LATIN AMERICA
Reprint of Gunther's immensely popular (in its day) journalistic surveys. Greenwood, 1975 (first published 1941).

Hanson, Earl P., ed.   SOUTH FROM THE SPANISH MAIN
The continent through the eyes of its discoverers—"significant and colorful selections culled from [contemporary] writings." (BRD) Delacorte Pr, 1967.

Hemming, John   THE SEARCH FOR EL DORADO
The search by European explorers for the legendary golden treasures of Latin America. Dutton, 1979.

Jackson, Richard L.   BLACK WRITERS IN LATIN AMERICA
An account of black Spanish language writing from the early 1800s to contemporary times. U of New Mexico, 1979.

Naipaul, V.S.   THE MIDDLE PASSAGE
The subtitle is: Impressions of five societies—British, French, and Dutch—in the West Indies and South America. The author is a Trinidadian of East Indian descent, and the five societies are Trinidad, British Guiana, Surinam, Martinique and Jamaica. An "armchair traveler's joy . . . a descriptive travel book [that] combines a novelist's sketches of character with an amateur historian-sociologist's speculation." (BRD) Vintage, 1981 (first published 1962).

Onis, Harriet de, ed.   THE GOLDEN LAND
An anthology of folklore themes in literature, from the Spanish conquests to the 1960s. Knopf, 1961 (first published 1948).

Parry, J.H.   THE DISCOVERY OF SOUTH AMERICA
Spanish explorations in Central America, Mexico, South America and the Antilles, based on contemporary chronicles and diaries. "Superbly written . . . the reader experiences with the conquistadores the wonder of the New World . . . conjures time, places [and] bedazzled Europeans' curiosity about exotic races, spectacular plans, unknown beasts." (BRD) Taplinger, 1979.

Prescott, W.H.   PRESCOTT'S HISTORIES—THE RISE AND DECLINE OF THE SPANISH EMPIRE
Selections from four of the author's historical classics: *Ferdinand and Isabella, The Conquest of Mexico, The Conquest of Peru, Philip II*. Viking, 1963 (first published 1837 through 1858).

Sitwell, Sacheverell   GOLDEN WALL AND MIRADOR
Musings on Latin American art, archaeology, social life and customs by the British poet and critic—Peru, Ecuador, Yucatan, Guatemala and other places in Latin America. World, 1961.

Theroux, Paul   THE OLD PATAGONIAN EXPRESS: BY TRAIN THROUGH THE AMERICAS
Theroux's insights and characterizations as he travels (mostly by train) through North and South America. Houghton, 1979.

Tschiffely, A.F.   SOUTHERN CROSS TO POLE STAR— TSCHIFFELY'S RIDE
Reprint of a travel classic. A Swiss schoolmaster and his two aging Criollo-bred ponies travelled 10,000 miles in a two-and-a-half-year journey from Buenos Aires to Washington, D.C.—"remarkable often terrifying exploits." Tarcher, 1982 (first published 1925).

Von Hagen, Victor   THE ANCIENT SUN KINGDOMS OF THE AMERICAS
"Exciting *magnum opus* on the life and times of the highly cultured peoples of the Sun Kingdoms"—Aztec, Maya and Inca. (BRD) Beekman, 1977 (first published 1960).

GUIDEBOOKS

Brooks, John, ed.   SOUTH AMERICAN HANDBOOK
Covers all of Latin America, despite its title, including lesser-known areas and islands. The "bible"—updated and reissued annually—gives not only an idea of the economics and politics of various countries but personal advice on getting there, traveling around, motoring trips, maps, etc. Trade & Travel, 1983.

Cohen, Marjorie A.   THE BUDGET TRAVELER'S LATIN AMERICA
Published under the auspices of Council on International Educational Exchange

and the Australian Union of Students. Includes orientation for planning a trip, information sources. Dutton, 1979.

Epstein, Jack   ALONG THE GRINGO TRAIL
Geared to independent and venturesome travelers; includes background reading on culture and the political and social realities of Mexico, Central and South America, and the West Indies. And/Or Press, 1979.

Jahn, Ernst A.   LATIN AMERICA TRAVEL GUIDE AND PAN AM HIGHWAY GUIDE
From Alaska and Canada to Mexico, Central and South America. Compsco, 1980.

Reaves, Verne   HEADING SOUTH: A GUIDE TO BUDGET TRAVEL IN LATIN AMERICA
Readable and informative—planning, packing, transportation, lodging and so on, both for those on package tours and those who travel independently. Second Thoughts Pr, 1982.

HISTORY

Burns, E. Bradford   LATIN AMERICA: A CONCISE INTERPRETIVE HISTORY
P-H, 1982.

Hennessy, Alistair   THE FRONTIER IN LATIN AMERICAN HISTORY
Comparative history of the frontier experience—missionaries, mining, cattle and cowboys, etc.—with that of the United States, Canada and Australia. U of New Mexico, 1978.

Herring, Hubert C.   HISTORY OF LATIN AMERICA
A standard one-volume survey. Knopf, 1968 (first published 1955).

Keen, Benjamin   A SHORT HISTORY OF LATIN AMERICA
Houghton, 1980.

THE CARIBBEAN

Series Guidebooks (See Appendix 1)

Baedeker: Caribbean
Berlitz: Southern Caribbean; Jamaica, Puerto Rico, Virgin Islands, French West Indies
Birnbaum: The Caribbean, Bermuda & the Bahamas

Fielding: Caribbean; Economy Caribbean
Fisher: Best of the Caribbean
Fodor: Caribbean; Caribbean & the Bahamas; Budget Travel
             Caribbean; Fun in St. Martin; Fun in Puerto Rico
Frommer: Caribbean: Dollarwise (incl. Bermuda & the Bahamas)
Insight: Jamaica
U.S. Government: Antigua and Barbuda: Background Notes
             Barbados: Background Notes; Post Report
             Caribbean: Pocket Guide
             Dominica: Background Notes
             Dominican Republic: Country Study
             Fr. Antilles & Guiana: Background Notes
             Grenada: Background Notes; Post Report
             Haiti: Background Notes; Country Study
             Jamaica: Area Handbook; Background Notes
             Martinique: Post Report
             Netherlands Antilles: Background Notes; Post
             Report
             Puerto Rico: Pocket Guide
             St. Lucia: Background Notes
             Trinidad & Tobago: Area Handbook;
             Background Notes; Post Report

Background Reading

Arciniegas, German   CARIBBEAN: SEA OF THE NEW WORLD
"Ties the tale of the Caribbean together" in a style that makes the history come alive, from Columbus's first sight of San Salvador on through the building of the Panama Canal. (BRD) Knopf, 1946.

Barry, Tom, and others   THE OTHER SIDE OF PARADISE: FOREIGN COUNTRIES IN THE CARIBBEAN
A study of the negative effect of foreign investment. Grove, 1985.

Davis, Gregson and Margo   ANTIGUA BLACK: PORTRAIT OF AN ISLAND PEOPLE
Text by an Antiguan with a special interest in Caribbean literature; photographs by his wife. Scrimshaw, 1973.

Eggleston, George T.   VIRGIN ISLANDS
A leisurely travelogue of American and British Virgins of particular interest to cruisers, but also with background reading on history and people. Krieger, 1973 (first published 1959).

Eggleston, Hazel   SAINT LUCIA DIARY: A CARIBBEAN MEMOIR
A chronicle of what it's like to live on St. Lucia plus historical background and a brief guide to the island. Devin, 1977.

Fermor, Patrick Leigh   TRAVELLER'S TREE: A JOURNEY THROUGH THE CARIBBEAN ISLANDS
"Island meanderings . . . in that literate, polished style [of the] British school of travel writers." (BRD) Har-Row, 1951.

Fillingham, Paul   PILOT'S GUIDE TO THE LESSER ANTILLES
Intended for pilots but valuable also to all travelers for the wealth of detail on islands from Puerto Rico to Tobago—history, politics, social characteristics, practical information on twenty-four islands and groups of islands including sightseeing, excursions and supplementary reading. McGraw, 1979.

Garreau, Joel   THE NINE NATIONS OF NORTH AMERICA
A *Washington Post* reporter's view of North America argues that arbitrary state and national boundaries mean nothing. His "nine nations" are based on economics, emotional allegiance, and attitudes, and each has its own capital and distinctive web of power and influence. Under this concept, the Caribbean is part of Miami. A highly readable and perceptive analysis. Houghton, 1981.

Gosner, Pamela   CARIBBEAN GEORGIAN
The great houses, and the small, of the Caribbean. Three Continents, 1982.

Harding, Bertita   THE LAND COLUMBUS LOVED: THE DOMINICAN REPUBLIC
Compact social and cultural history. Gordon Pr, 1978 (first published 1949).

Harman, Jeanne   THE VIRGINS: MAGIC ISLANDS
"Altogether delightful evocation"—legends, history, cultural past—by a longtime resident. (BRD) Appleton, 1961.

Howes, Barbara, ed.   FROM THE GREEN ANTILLES
Excerpts of writings from forty Caribbean authors representative of the four language groups—English, French, Spanish and Dutch. Macmillan, 1966.

Jinkins, Dana and Bobrow, Jill   ST. VINCENT AND THE GRENADINES: A PLURAL COUNTRY
A travelogue with "celebratory comments" by Margaret Atwood and Raquel Welch. (PW) Norton, 1985.

Morison, Samuel E.   CARIBBEAN AS COLUMBUS SAW IT
Photographs with text by the leading American historian. Little, 1964.

Naipaul, Shiva   THE LOSS OF EL DORADO
"The origin of modern Trinidad viewed in terms of the myth of El Dorado" told in stories of the search for the golden city of the Indian legend; and the British capture of Trinidad. (BRD) Knopf, 1970.

National Geographic Society   ISLES OF THE CARIBBEAN
Natl Geog, 1980.

Payne, Anthony   GRENADA: REVOLUTION AND INVASION
St. Martin, 1984.

Peterson, Mendel   THE FUNNEL OF GOLD
History of the straits of Florida, the main route for the Spanish shipments of New World gold—both "scholarly and filled with adventure . . . pirates, shipwrecks, storms, battles at sea." (BRD) Little, 1975.

Pope, Dudley   THE BUCCANEER KING
A biography of Sir Henry Morgan in the 1635-88 era of Spanish, Dutch, English and French Caribbean history. Dodd, 1978.

Radcliffe, Virginia   THE CARIBBEAN HERITAGE
An introduction to the region that provides a thumbnail historical sketch and suggestions for walking tours. Walker, 1976.

Rodman, Selden   THE CARIBBEAN
Travelogue of a visit to almost all of the West Indies, with a preference for Haiti, by an art critic/traveler. Hawthorn, 1968.

Seabury, Paul and McDougall, Walter A., eds.   THE GRENADA PAPERS
Edited, annotated documents seized during the Grenada invasion that illustrate the Communist threat. ICS Pr, 1984.

Severin, Timothy   THE GOLDEN ANTILLES
The El Dorado myth as reflected in the explorations of four English and Scottish explorers of the seventeenth century—"invaluable for understanding the minds of these explorers and adventurers . . . captivates the reader." (BRD) Knopf, 1970.

Sunshine, Catherine and Wheaton, Philip, eds.   GRENADA: THE PEACEFUL REVOLUTION
EPICA, 1982.

Toth, Charles W., ed.   THE AMERICAN REVOLUTION AND THE WEST INDIES
A collection of essays on the impact of the American Revolution on the West Indies. Kennikat, 1975.

Waugh, Alec   A FAMILY OF ISLANDS
Unique popular history—"a kind of novel with islands instead of individual characters as the protagonists." Covers the period from 1492 to 1898, with an epilogue sketching in events from the Spanish-American War up to the 1960s. "Packed with vivid portraits" of historical figures. (BRD) Doubleday, 1964.

Westlake, Donald E.   UNDER AN ENGLISH HEAVEN
Written by a novelist who "plays it with tongue in cheek as he recounts British embarrassment and frustration" in tiny Anguilla's successful fight to free itself from St. Kitts in 1969. (BRD) S&S, 1972.

Wood, Peter   THE CARIBBEAN ISLES
Part of the American Wilderness Series. Time-Life, 1975. Also *The Spanish Main* (1979), part of Time-Life's Seafarer Series.

HAITI

Cole, Hubert   CHRISTOPHE: KING OF HAITI
"The rise of Henri Christophe . . . from plantation scullion . . . to revolutionary colonel to self-proclaimed monarch" and Haiti's emergence as an independent nation. (BRD) Viking, 1967.

Deren, Maya   DIVINE HORSEMEN: VOODOO GODS OF HAITI
A personal account of the history of rituals from their African sources through mutations brought about by Indian and Catholic influences. Chelsea Hse, 1970 (first published 1953).

Dunham, Katherine   ISLAND POSSESSED
Memoir of the dancer, and her love for Haiti where she researched the dance and anthropology. Doubleday, 1969.

Heinl, Robert D., Jr. and Nancy J.,   WRITTEN IN BLOOD
"Personal experiences, anecdotes, feelings, as well as an historical treatise. . . . the style is chatty and informal . . . an excellent introduction to the country." (BRD) Houghton, 1978.

Hurston, Zora Neale   TELL MY HORSE
Story of a trip on a Guggenheim fellowship to Haiti (and Jamaica) and investigations into folklore and voodoo cults. "A curious mixture of remembrances, travelogue, sensationalism, anthropology." (BRD) Turtle Island Foundation, 1981 (first published 1938).

Parkinson, Wanda   THIS GILDED AFRICAN: TOUSSAINT L'OUVERTURE
Biography of the black general and diplomat who rose from slavery to lead his people against European colonialism. Quartet, 1982.

Rodman, Selden   HAITI: THE BLACK REPUBLIC
A revised version of a guide and background book for Haiti including history, customs and religion, travel information, and a basic Creole-French vocabulary supplement. Devin, 1984 (first published 1954).

Seabrook, William B.   THE MAGIC ISLAND
Adventures and emotional experiences of an American author, with drawings by Alexander King. Folecroft, 1977 (first published 1929).

Wilson, Edmund   RED, BLACK, BLOND AND OLIVE
Observations on four civilizations—Haiti is the "black." Oxford U, 1956.

JAMAICA

**Barrett, Leonard E.   THE RASTAFARIANS: SOUNDS OF
CULTURAL DISSONANCE**
The "belief system . . . rituals, art and music" of the Jamaican cult—"an enlightening book on that strange sect." (BRD) Beacon, 1977.

**Boot, Adrian and Thomas, Michael   JAMAICA: BABYLON ON A
THIN WIRE**
Photographs, song lyrics, text "vividly depict the intense spirit of the black Jamaican population." (BRD) Schocken, 1977.

Cargill, Morris   JAMAICA FAREWELL
By a man who was a widely read columnist in Jamaica, and is now a resident of the United States—writes sensitively of Jamaica and the people, amusing and sad story of a Jamaican preparing to leave the country forever. Lyle Stuart, 1978.

Cargill, Morris, ed.   IAN FLEMING INTRODUCES JAMAICA
Ian Fleming, Morris Cargill, and other writers—Jamaicans or long-term residents of Jamaica—contribute to a book that covers people, history, politics, relgions, dialects, birds, food, natural history, etc. Hawthorn, 1965.

Hurston, Zora Neale   TELL MY HORSE
See under "Haiti."

Nicholas, Tracy and Sparrow, Bill   RASTAFARI: A WAY OF LIFE
History and life-style of the Rastafarians. Doubleday, 1979.

White, Timothy   CATCH A FIRE: THE LIFE OF BOB MARLEY
About the recently deceased "King of Reggae" who made that music a social and political statement. HR&W, 1983.

PUERTO RICO

Hanberg, Clifford A.   PUERTO RICO AND THE PUERTO RICANS
The Puerto Rican experience, a survey from earliest island beginnings and conquest by Spain to the American takeover and migration to the mainland. Hippocrene, 1975.

LaBrucherie, Roger A.   IMAGES OF PUERTO RICO
"A compact overview of the true spirit of this Caribbean island." (LJ) C.E. Tuttle, 1985.

**Levine, Barry   BENJY LOPEZ: A PICARESQUE TALE OF EMIGRATION
AND RETURN**
Basic Bks, 1980.

Lewis, Oscar   LA VIDA
Chronicle of Puerto Rican life, a study of one thousand families from San Juan and their New York relatives. Irvington, 1982 (first published 1966).

Morales, Arturo, ed.   PUERTO RICO: A POLITICAL AND CULTURAL
ODYSSEY
By Puerto Rican scholars "but addressed to the general reader on the U.S.
mainland"—essays that function as a social, cultural and political history. (BL)
Norton, 1983.

Steiner, Stanley   THE ISLANDS: THE WORLDS OF PUERTO RICANS
"A sympathetic observer uses a personal journalistic approach to examine
thoughts and hopes of mainlanders and islanders." (Publisher) Har-Row, 1974.

GUIDEBOOKS

Babcock, Judy and Kennedy, Judy   THE SPA BOOK
A guided personal tour of health resorts and beauty spas in the United States,
Canada, Mexico and the West Indies. Crown, 1983.

Bellamy, Frank   CARIBBEAN ISLAND HOPPING
For independent and budget-minded travelers—history and culture along with
practical travel information on accommodations, food, sightseeing, and itineraries
for famous and less-famous areas. Hippocrene, 1982.

Bruning, Nancy   THE BEACH BOOK
Beaches in Mexico and the Caribbean, the United States and Canada—for those
in search of the perfect wave or a beach for surfing, skiing, singles, skinny dipping,
etc. Houghton, 1981.

Cox, Thornton   THORNTON COX'S TRAVELLER'S GUIDE TO
THE CARIBBEAN
"Highly readable introduction to the area under consideration. . . . necessary
data for getting there and getting about . . . suggested itineraries [designed for]
economy of time and movement." (Publisher) Hippocrene, 1982.

Garcia, Connie and Medina, Arthur   THE TRAVEL GUIDE TO
PUERTO RICO
Puerto Rico Almanacs, 1983.

Greenberg, Harriet and Arnold   U.S. VIRGIN ISLANDS ALIVE
The best the islands have to offer in all price ranges—St. Thomas, St. John and St.
Croix. Hippocrene, 1983.

Hildebrand, Volker   JAMAICA
Part of a new guidebook series originating in Germany. Hippocrene, 1985.

Hunte, George   JAMAICA
Batsford, 1976.

Moore, James E.   EVERYBODY'S VIRGIN ISLANDS
Lippincott, 1979.

Pariser, Harry   GUIDE TO PUERTO RICO AND THE VIRGIN ISLANDS
Moon Pbns Ca, 1986. Also *Guide to Jamaica* (and Haiti) (1985).

Robinson, Alan   VIRGIN ISLANDS NATIONAL PARK: THE STORY
BEHIND THE SCENERY
KC Pbns, 1974.

Villa, Antonio   TRAVEL GUIDE TO PUERTO RICO
Modern Guides, 1985.

HISTORY

Carrión, Arturo M.   PUERTO RICO: A POLITICAL AND
CULTURAL HISTORY
History with attention to problems related to the Puerto Rican's search for
identity. Norton, 1983.

Knight, Franklin W.   THE CARIBBEAN
Major themes of Caribbean history from a viewpoint hostile to European imperialism in the area. Oxford U, 1978.

Kuper, Adam   CHANGING JAMAICA
Routledge, 1976.

Logan, Rayford W.   HAITI AND THE DOMINICAN REPUBLIC
Oxford U, 1968.

Nicholls, David   FROM DESSALINES TO DUVALIER
History of Haiti and the role of race and color in Haitian independence.
Cambridge U Pr, 1979.

Rodman, Selden   QUISQUEYA: A HISTORY OF THE DOMINICAN
REPUBLIC
From Columbus to the overthrow of Bosch in 1963. U of Washington Pr, 1964.

Williams, Eric   FROM COLUMBUS TO CASTRO: THE HISTORY OF
THE CARIBBEAN
By a prime minister of Trinidad and Tobago—"interesting and well written
essay on slavery and sugar cane . . . the effects of their interaction on the peoples of
the Caribbean." (BRD) Random, 1983 (first published 1971).

Novels

Anderson, John L.   NIGHT OF THE SILENT DRUM (Virgin Islands)
A narrative of the slave rebellion when the Dutch West India Company
departed, leaving whites to run the plantations and the slaves who included
African noblemen, princes and a king. Scribner, 1975.

Anthony, Evelyn   THE TAMARIND SEED (Barbados)
Espionage and romance; a British widow meets a Russian agent. Coward, 1971.

Atwood, Margaret   BODILY HARM
An introspective, successful journalist takes a working holiday on a Caribbean island to restore normalcy to her life after a bout with cancer and loss of her lover. S&S, 1982.

Belasco, Lionel   STRANGE HAPPENINGS: TALES OF THE CARIBBEAN
Law Arts, 1973.

Benchley, Peter   THE ISLAND
A variation on *Jaws* but with "bloodthirsty buccaneers replacing the sharks" as the enemy. A writer for a newsmagazine and his son are kidnapped in the British West Indies and taken to a remote island in the Turks and Caicos. (BRD) Doubleday, 1979.

Brent, Madeleine   THE LONG MASQUERADE
Adventure novel—"twists, turns, surprises abound" as the heroine flees her husband's home disguised as a West Indian half-caste, earns entrée into English society. (FC) Doubleday, 1981.

Christie, Agatha   A CARIBBEAN MYSTERY
In *Five Complete Miss Marple Novels*. Avenal, 1980 ("Caribbean" first published 1965).

DeBoissiere, Ralph   CROWN JEWEL (Trinidad)
Story of a charismatic black activist and his attempts to unify blacks in Trinidad for social progress. Allison & Busby, 1981.

Fermor, Patrick L.   THE VIOLINS OF ST. JACQUES, A TALE OF THE ANTILLES (Martinique)
Nostalgic novel of a Creole island—"a lush, heady mixture." (BRD) Har-Row, 1953.

Forester, C.S.   THE CAPTAIN FROM CONNECTICUT
Adventure story of a frigate captain during the War of 1812—"naval battles, tropic skies and green West Indies islands." (FC) Little, 1941.

Forester, C.S.   ADMIRAL HORNBLOWER IN THE WEST INDIES
Classic Hornblower adventure set in the West Indies involving a Bonapartist uprising, piracy and the slave trade. Little, 1958.

Galvan, Manuel de Jesus   THE CROSS AND THE SWORD
Historical novel of the Columbus and post-Columbus period of Caribbean history, translated from the Spanish by Robert Graves. AMS, 1975 (first published 1954).

Gaskin, Catherine   FIONA
Mystery romance set on a small Caribbean island in 1833. Doubleday, 1970.

Holland, Isabelle   KILGAREN
A gothic—a girl returns to her ancestral home in the West Indies and finds mystery and romance. Weybright & Talley, 1974.

Kent, Alexander   SUCCESS TO THE BRAVE
Historical novel (1802)—Vice-Admiral Bolitho of the Royal Navy is sent on a diplomatic mission to the Caribbean to return an island to the French under the Treaty of Amiens. Putnam Pub Group, 1983. Another historical novel by Kent is *To Glory We Steer* (1968), set in 1782—a sea drama in which a British frigate is involved in battles with French, Spanish and American privateers in the Caribbean.

Kincaid, Jamaica   ANNIE JOHN
"A magical coming-of-age tale" of Annie John from 10 to 17, with "special ambiance of its tropical setting [Antigua] ... a poetic and intensely moving work." (FC) FS&G, 1985.

Lamming, George   IN THE CASTLE OF MY SKIN (Barbados)
An autobiographical novel of a boyhood in Barbados—"rarely has any island of the West Indies been presented so feelingly." (BRD) Schocken, 1983 (first published 1953).

Lehmann, Rosamond   A SEA-GRAPE TREE
"A short idyll on a lush, romantic Caribbean island [with a] supernatural aura." (BRD) HarBraceJ, 1980.

MacInnes, Colin   WESTWARD TO LAUGHTER
Picaresque historical novel of white and black slaves in the West Indies and the slave revolt in the 1750s. FS&G, 1970.

Marshall, Paule   THE CHOSEN PLACE, THE TIMELESS PEOPLE
Complex racial relationships as a group of Americans working on a research development project arrive on a West Indian island, and their interraction with an islander—"impressive, important—a parable of Western civilization and its relations with the undeveloped world." (BRD) Vintage, 1985 (first published 1969).

Marshall, Paule   PRAISESONG FOR THE WIDOW
A widow, on her annual Caribbean cruise, is troubled by strange dreams and symptoms. She gets off on a small island and is persuaded to join a ritual visit to a nearby island where she rediscovers her roots. Putnam Pub Group, 1983.

Matthiessen, Peter   FAR TORTUGA
A remote islet, south of Cuba, is the setting—men search for the last turtles of the season on Grand Cayman and the cays and reefs of Nicaragua. Random, 1975.

Morrison, Toni   TAR BABY
A novel of relationships between blacks and whites as a fugitive American is discovered in the retirement house of a wealthy Philadelphia couple. Knopf, 1981.

Moyes, Patricia   ANGEL DEATH
A Scotland Yard detective and his wife solve a mystery set in the Seaward Islands. HR&W, 1980.

Naipaul, Shiva   THE CHIP CHIP GATHERERS
Story of the futility that underlies West Indian life. Knopf, 1973. Also *Fireflies* (1971), about the Hindu community in Trinidad.

Naipaul, V.S.   THE MIMIC MEN
The memoirs of a politico in exile. Macmillan, 1967.

Naipaul, V.S.   GUERILLAS
The novel creates an island in the Caribbean complete with a history, geography, and population; it's a troubled island with a mixed population of British colonials, Africans, Americans and Asians. Knopf, 1975.

Naipaul, V.S.   THREE NOVELS: THE MYSTIC MASSEUR, THE SUFFRAGE OF ELVIRA, MIGUEL STREET (Trinidad)
The characters are mostly East Indians and the setting is Trinidad of the 1940s—"each . . . is a charming and delightful celebration of innocence, and readers will find the Calypso lilt of the dialogue quite wonderful." (FC) Knopf, 1982.

Naipaul, V.S.   A HOUSE FOR MR. BISWAS
Story of a poverty-stricken Indian journalist and a major novel of West Indian life in Trinidad. McGraw, 1961.

Plain, Belva   EDEN BURNING
"Eden" is an island in the Caribbean; half-brothers become enemies when the island explodes in a revolution—"interesting descriptions of the native habitat, culture, cuisine and history." (FC) Delacorte Pr, 1982.

Pope, Dudley   GOVERNOR RAMAGE, R.N.
S&S, 1980. This and an earlier novel published in 1969, *The Triton Brig*, are part of a series of adventure stories involving Lt. Lord Ramage of the British navy.

Pope, Dudley   BUCCANEER
The manager of his family's plantation, and the wife of a neighboring planter, flee by ship from Cromwellian forces who have confiscated their estates and threaten arrest as well. They take their indentured servants along and eventually link up with buccaneeers in the Caribbean. Walker, 1984.

Rhys, Jean   WIDE SARGASSO SEA
A Creole heiress (based on the mad Mrs. Rochester in *Jane Eyre*) is the main character—"this detailed and frightening study of the disintegration of a woman is played out in the lush and captivatingly sensuous environment of the tropics." Norton, 1967.

Schwarz-Bart, Simone   BETWEEN TWO WORLDS (Guadeloupe)
A "metaphoric fantasy [and] odyssey of Ti-Jean whose life is a parable of black people's existence in a white world." (FC) Har-Row, 1981.

Schwarz-Bart, Simone   THE BRIDGE OF BEYOND (Guadeloupe)
Chronicle of a girl's life on Guadeloupe—"memoir of tropical childhood . . . a West Indian Pastoral." (FC) Atheneum, 1974.

Schwarz-Bart, Simone   A WOMAN NAMED SOLITUDE (Guadeloupe)
The recreation of the life of a West African child, conceived on a slave ship en route to Guadeloupe, who refuses to return to slavery after the brief period of freedom that followed the French Revolution—based on an actual historical figure. Atheneum, 1973.

Selvon, Samuel   WAYS OF SUN LIGHT (Trinidad)
Short stories of life in Trinidad—half are about West Indians living in London. St. Martin, 1958.

Shacochis, Bob   EASY IN THE ISLANDS
A short-story collection of "the flip side of paradise, a world the tourist never sees." (TL) Crown, 1984.

Steinbeck, John   CUP OF GOLD
The subtitle is: a life of Sir Henry Morgan, buccaneer, with occasional reference to history. The novel begins in Wales, and tells of Morgan's life, first as a slave in Barbados, then as a buccaneer and on to his respectable death. R.M. McBride, 1980 (first published 1929).

Tattersall, Jill   DAMNATION REEF
A gothic set on Antilla, island in the West Indies. Morrow, 1979.

Waugh, Alec   LOVE AND THE CARIBBEAN
Excerpts from the author's writings (novels, magazine pieces, etc.) from 1928-55 selected to give the feel of the Caribbean, and divided into background, characters, snapshots, islands. Most is devoted to Guadeloupe, Martinique and Haiti, with vignettes of the Antilles, Leewards and Windwards. FS&G, 1959.

Whitney, Phyllis A.   COLUMBELLA (St. Thomas)
A mystery and romance set on St. Thomas; a governess becomes involved in a murder. Doubleday, 1966.

HAITI

Bourne, Peter   DRUMS OF DESTINY
Historical novel about the revolt of slaves in Haiti against their French masters. Putnam Pub Group, 1947.

Carpentier, Alejo   THE KINGDOM OF THIS WORLD
"Recreates the 18th-century era of foreign misrule in Haiti, the subsequent native uprising and . . . new conquerors" who turned out to be just as tyrannical. Historic figures are mixed with fictitious characters in a picaresque story. (FC) Knopf, 1957 (first published 1948).

Dickinson, Peter   WALKING DEAD
Elaborate experiment in intelligence, witchcraft, and experiments on humans. Pantheon, 1978.

Greene, Graham   THE COMEDIANS
Life in a run-down tourist hotel in Haiti with a group of diverse characters, "most of them in varying degrees comedians on the stage of life." (FC) Viking, 1966.

Heckert, Eleanor L.   THE LITTLE SAINT OF ST. DOMINGUE
The racial struggle of Creoles, mulattoes and blacks in the 1790s that produced Toussaint L'Ouverture—history and fiction woven together with ease. Doubleday, 1973.

Marlowe, Derek   NIGHTSHADE
Suspense novel with occult overtones—"the spell of Haiti is deadly in this valentine of horror." (BRD) Viking, 1976.

Roberts, Kenneth   LYDIA BAILEY
By the author of many historical novels about Maine; in this, a man from Maine finds love in Haiti and the period is 1791-1804. Doubleday, 1947.

Roumain, Jacques   MASTERS OF THE DEW
A novel of Haitian peasant life—"of the African heritage . . . impulsive, gravely formal folk, poetry of their speech [and] the love of a land and its people." (BRD) Heinemann, 1978 (first published 1947).

Thoby-Marcelin, Philippe   THE BEAST OF HAITIAN HILLS
"Fantastic voodoo tales . . . about paganized Christianity" in Haiti. (BRD) Rinehart, 1946.

Thoby-Marcelin, Philippe   ALL MEN ARE MAD
A comic novel of Catholicism in Haiti as a young French priest tries to eradicate ancestral religious influences in its practice there. FS&G, 1970.

JAMAICA

Banks, Russell   THE BOOK OF JAMAICA
An American novelist in Jamaica on a grant. "Provides armchair tourists with a rare . . . fictional view [of] history, landscape, language, religion and politics" of Jamaica. (BRD) Houghton, 1980.

Cliff, Michelle   ABENG
A young girl's rite of passage that explores Jamaican society's sensitive racial issues, and her "growing awareness of the gulf created by color and caste." (FC) Crossing Pr, 1984.

Eberhart, Mignon G.   ENEMY IN THE HOUSE
A murder mystery set against the unusual background of the American Revolution. Random, 1962.

Fleming, Ian   DOCTOR NO
One of several James Bond thrillers set partly in Jamaica. Macmillan, 1958. Also *Live and Let Die* (1955), *For Your Eyes Only* (1960), and *The Man With the Golden Gun* (1965).

Hughes, Richard   HIGH WIND IN JAMAICA
Plantation life in the 1860s. Har-Row, 1972.

McKay, Claude   BANANA BOTTOM
Novel of a Jamaica native who is adopted by English missionaries and sent to England for her education, and the conflict between this new life and her ancestry. Har-Row, 1933.

Reid, V.S.   NEW DAY
Jamaica from the rebellion in 1865 to 1944 when it became self-governing to a degree—"true to historical fact . . . a liquid, lyrical thing" by a Jamaican black. (BRD) Knopf, 1949.

Thelwell, Michael   THE HARDER THEY COME
Authentic, evocative portrait of the Jamaican poor. Grove, 1980.

Waugh, Alec   ISLAND IN THE SUN
The regime of a British governor confronts questions of colonialism, racial equality and self-government. FS&G, 1955.

PUERTO RICO

Babin, Maria Teresa   BORINQUEN: AN ANTHOLOGY OF PUERTO RICAN LITERATURE
Vintage, 1974.

Baldwin, James   IF BEALE STREET COULD TALK
New York City and Puerto Rico are the settings for a novel of a love between two young people that helps them to deal with racial oppression. Dial, 1974.

Sánchez, Luis R.   MACHO CAMACHO'S BEAT
"Macho Camacho's Beat" is a popular song that plays on the radio as a persistent background to a series of interrelated incidents. Pantheon, 1981.

TRAVEL ARTICLES

AMERICAS

1985 Jul-Aug (Trinidad & Tobago) "Calypso and Classics." Steelband music festival. Veronica G. Stoddart, p. 20

Oct "Grenada revisited." An unspoiled, uncluttered beauty welcomes visitors once again. Veronica G. Stoddart, p. 8

1984 Sep-Oct (St. Kitts & Nevis) "Profile: St. Christopher [Kitts] and Nevis." Barbara A. Currie, p. 64

Nov-Dec (Barbados) "The Island's East Coast is for Poets, Painters and Vagabonds." Michael Morgan, p. 14

(St. Lucia) "A Quiet Place in the Sun." St. Lucia is a verdant island with an intriguing past. Margaret Zellars, p. 6

BETTER HOMES & GARDENS

1985 Oct "The Best Caribbean Vacations." Barbara Humeston and Margaret Zellars, p. 162

BLACK ENTERPRISE

1985 May "The Lure of the Caribbean Islands." Special Section: Bahamas, Barbados, Bermuda, Jamaica, Puerto Rico, Trinidad & Tobago, U.S.V.I. p. 59

Jun (Guadeloupe and Martinique) "Vive la Difference." Frances E. Ruffin, p. 292

1984 May (Aruba, Bonaire, Curaçao) "Three Dots of Sunny Landscape and Dutch Charm." Marcia Wallace, p. 79

Special Section: "Caribbean Fun in the Sun." When you're hot you're hot; a guide to dining in the Caribbean. Jessica B. Harris, p. 83; "Jump up, Island Music." Where to hear it, dance to it. Jessica B. Harris, p. 84; "The Club Med Instead." Jane Abrams, p. 89; "More Sun for Less Money." Sylvia Rackow, p. 92; "Tropical Sabbatical: One Woman's Year Working in the Caribbean." Bonda E. Lee, p. 90

BON APPETIT

1985 Feb (Anguilla) "Welcome to Anguilla." The pleasures of an unspoiled Caribbean island. Jefferson Morgan, p. 100

1984 Sep (Martinique) "Traveling with Taste: Martinique." Jefferson Morgan, p. 32

EBONY

1984 May "South Southeast for Summer." Florida, Bahamas, U.S. Virgin Islands and Bermuda form a vacation fun triangle. p. 173

Nov (Trinidad & Tobago) "Caribbean Republic Features Two Islands." p. 102

ESQUIRE

1985 Feb (Antigua, Jamaica, Nevis, Puerto Rico) Special Places: "Six Great Ways to Get Out of the Sun." David Butwin, p. 26

1984 Jan (Caymans) "Where to Take a Dive." Edward D. Sheffe, p. 32

Oct (Virgin Islands) "The American Virgins." They're beautiful, they're warm, they're all ours. C.D.B. Bryan, p. 2 following p. 160

ESSENCE
1985 Jan "Trinidad, the People's Party." During Trinidad carnival, everybody jams. Elaine C. Ray, p. 32
      Apr "Cruise Alive '85." A cruise guide to the Caribbean and beyond. Sandra Jackson-Opoka, p. 34
      "The Secret Caribbean, St. Kitts and Nevis." The last of the *real* getaway islands. Barbara Brandon, p. 30
      Aug (Guadeloupe) "Great Guadeloupe." Joyce White, p. 30
      Oct (Virgin Islands) "Treasure Islands—the U.S. Virgin Islands Are a Triple Vacation Treat." Stephanie R. Hamilton, p. 18
1984 Apr "Martinique: Isle in the Sun." Stephanie R. Hamilton, p. 36
      May "The Best of the Fêtes." Island festivals. Sandra Jackson-Opoku, p. 52

50 PLUS
1985 Oct "The Caribbean: A Modern-day Robinson Crusoe Picks His Favorite Hideaways." Frank Greve, p. 42

GLAMOUR
1985 May "Summer Sale on Caribbean Hotels." p. 238
      Nov "Best Buys in the Caribbean." Beaches, condos, quiet, variety. p. 229
1984 May (Barbados, Trinidad/Tobago, Nassau, St. John, St. Vincent) "Best Buy for Summer." p. 254
      Nov (Puerto Rico, Aruba, Tortola, St. Kitts, Dominican Republic) "Six Good Reasons to Take a Winter Vacation in the Caribbean." p. 223

GOURMET
1984 Sep "Martinique." Doone Beal, p. 48
      Dec "The British Virgin Islands." Doone Beal, p. 54

HARPER'S BAZAAR
1984 May (Dominican Republic) "Dominican Hideaway." Punta Cana rates high as unspoiled (Club Med). Carla Engler, p. 18
      Jun "The Connoisseur's Caribbean." Philip Smith, p. 26

HOUSE BEAUTIFUL
1985 Nov Travel: "Your Guide to the Islands." Caribbean, Bermuda and Florida islands. Hazel Carr, p. 41

MADEMOISELLE
1985 Apr "Beaches, Bargains and Balmy Breezes." Unwinding in the Caribbean. Pamela Jablons, p. 252
1984 Apr "Warming Up Caribbean Style." Club Med and the Virgin Islands. Judith Thurman, p. 264

MODERN MATURITY
1985 Oct (St. Martin) "Clouds in the Living Room." Romare Bearden, p. 80

NATIONAL GEOGRAPHIC
1985 Jun (Cayman) "Fair Skies for the Cayman Islands . . ." Caribbean mecca for scuba divers, financiers and tourists. Peter Benchley, p. 798
1984 Nov (Grenada) "Marking Time in Grenada." Charles E. Cobb, Jr., p. 688

N.Y. TIMES SUNDAY TRAVEL SECTION (X)
1985 Jan 27 "The Caribbean: Small Universe for Sailors, Coral Reefs, Calm Seas and Pirates' Lairs." Lester Bernstein, p. 14
"Impromptu Island-Hopping." By air. Jane Rosen, p. 14   "Heading South in a Hurry." Spur-of-the-moment travels in the Caribbean, Mexico and Florida. Stanley Carr, p. 15
(Barbados) Fare of the Country: "From Sun and Sugar an Island Brew." Seeing rum made. Florence Fabricant, p. 16
Mar 31 (St. Barthelemy) "Castaways on a French Isle: St. Barthelemy's Admirers Find Respite Amid a Cote d'Azur in Miniature." Barbara Goldsmith, p. 16
"Housekeeping Havens—The Option of Fending for Oneself in the Islands and Stocking the Holiday Larder." Grocery shopping for your cottage. Florence Fabricant, p. 17
Oct 6 ("Sophisticated Traveler") (St. Martin) "Clouds in the Living Room." Romare Bearden, p. 80
Nov 17 "The Caribbean: In Shape for the Season." More hotel rooms and added flights. Joseph B. Treaster, p. 19
(St. Thomas) "In St. Thomas, Challenge is Par for the Course." No holes (golf) are dull at Mahogany Run. John Radosta, p. 20
(Grenada) "In Grenada, Life is Quiet, Hope is High, Mass Tourism Has Yet to Arrive." Jospeh B. Treaster, p. 21
Nov 24 (Mustique) "Unruffled Little Mustique." A Caribbean isle of villas and yachts. Sondra Gotlieb, p. 19
Dec 8 "1776 Came Early in the Caribbees." A journey back to another American Revolution and an era of sugar and plunder. Thomas Hoover, p. 41
Dec 15 "Barbados in Two Stages." From recuperation to exploration on an island that welcomes strangers with good humor. Robert W. Stock, p. 24
1984 Jan 8 "Dominica's Silver Lining." Luxuriant rain forest is Caribbean island's main attraction. Ronald Sullivan, p. 24
Jan 29 (Anguilla) "Austin Bay." The other Caribbean has no discos or casinos, very few people, and lots of empty beaches. p. 20
Feb 5 "Grenada: A Traveler's Briefing." Barbara Gelb, p. 19
(Grenada) "At Mama's the Diners are Part of the Family." The cuisine is Creole and the ambience is homey. Seth Mydans, p. 19
Feb 19 (Virgin Islands) Fare of the Country: "St. Croix Serves a Real Smorgasbord." Florence Fabricant, p. 12
Mar 18 (Part 2, "Sophisticated Traveler") "The First America."Legacies of time when the Caribbean was the center of wealth in the hemisphere. Garry Wills, p. 112
Mar 25 (Virgin Islands) "Caneel Bay and Its Allure." Charlotte Curtis, p. 16
"Around the Caribbean." Island advantages in off season. Barbara Crossette, p. 16
"Ports of Call: When the Ship Comes In." Cruise ship stops in the Caribbean. Stanley Carr, p. 17
Apr 8 (British Virgin Islands) "For Privacy, Peter Island." Deborah Blumenthal, p. 22
Oct 7 (Part 2, "Sophisticated Traveler") (Guadeloupe) "Caribbean Savoir-Faire." Frank J. Prial, p. 107

1984 Oct 28 (Anguilla) "On Anguilla, Afloat in Tranquillity." Barbaralee Diamonstein, p. 15
"The Beaches and Beyond." A 34-island guide to what's special and new in the Caribbean. p. 19
"A Choice of Tables." Seven food experts recall meals of note in the islands. p. 15
Dec 15 "Barbados in Two Stages." From recuperation to exploration on an island that welcomes strangers with good humor. Robert W. Stock, p. 24
Dec 30 (Virgin Islands) "Exploring a Trio of Islands."Attractions range from restored sugar plantations to rustic beaches (in St. Thomas, St. John, St. Croix). William Steif, p. 12
(Virgin Islands) "Variations on a Caribbean Theme . . ." The American Virgins reflect distinctive facets of island life. Jon Nordheimer, p. 13

SATURDAY EVENING POST
1985 May "Nevis: Queen of the Leewards." Maynard G. Stoddard, p. 82
Dec "Barbados—Civilized Paradise." L.S. Edward, p. 82
1984 Nov "Warming Up to the Caribbean." p. 90

SATURDAY REVIEW
1984 Feb (St. Kitts) "A Sweet Retreat." David Butwin, p. 34
Dec "Three escapes . . ." Romantic and secluded hideaways in the Caribbean. David Butwin, p. 98

SUNSET
1985 Oct "St. Lucia Is a Caribbean Discovery." p. 88

TRAVEL & LEISURE
1985 Feb (Montserrat) "The Quiet Caribbean." Montserrat, a lush little island off Antigua. Janice B. Brand, p. 158
Oct (St. Barts) "Sybaritic St. Barts—Caribbean Sand, Sun and Chic." Malachy Duffy, p. 108
1984 Feb (Barbados) "Andromeda Gardens." Six tropical acres of plants, pools and waterfalls. Michael Spring, p. 172
Apr "Aboard the S.S. *Norway*." Impressions of maiden voyage of the world's biggest cruise ship. Deborah Colussy, p. 31
Dec "Anguilla." A tiny Caribbean island is big news on the travel horizon. Malachy Duffy, p. 92

TRAVEL/HOLIDAY
1985 Feb (St. Kitts & Nevis) "Twin Sisters of the West Indies." Hal Butler, p. 72
May (St. Thomas) "The Charm of Charlotte Amalie." Something Danish in St. Thomas. José Fernandez, p. 62
Jun (Bonaire) "Of Coral Seas and Pink Flamingos." Joseph Wallace, p. 14
Aug (Grenada) "Spice of the Caribbean." Sam Alcorn, p. 54
Nov (Eustatius) "Saluting Saint Eustatius—An Old Caribbean Friend." Candyce Norvell, p. 34
"Saba's fanciful lace." Drawnwork. Alma E. Jelder, p. 84
Dec "Trinidad & Tobago—the Caribbean's Complementary Kin." Carolyn Males, p. 20

1984 Feb (Aruba) "Rapture in Aruba." Carnival Caribbean style. Arthur Solomone, p. 73

Mar "Economic Caribbean." Affordable island vacations. Margaret Zellars, p. 8

May (Caymans) "The Cayman Islands." More than just a money haven. Roger Cox, p. 72

Jul "Martinique." Susan Farlow, p. 8

Aug "Barbados: British Veneer, Caribbean Core." Roger Cox, p. 44

Oct (Montserrat) "The Caribbean's Emerald Isle." A wee bit o' Ireland in the Caribbean. Arthur Solomon, p. 44

Nov (Virgin Islands) "First Time Fishing in the British Virgin Islands." Jennifer Quale, p. 82

VOGUE

1985 Jan (Virgin Islands) "Discovering the Lush, Secret Pleasures of the U.S. Virgin Islands." Hillary Johnson, p. 149

Feb (Trinidad) "Carnival on Trinidad." Karen Anderegg, p. 272

Apr (Guadeloupe) "Iles des Saintes: These Tiny French Islands Are Everything the Caribbean Once Was—Lush, Secluded, Unpretentious." Susan Bolotin, p. 270

Dec "Special Report: the Caribbean." Despina Messinesi, p. 238

1984 Apr (St. Martin) "Why St. Martin: An Insider's Look." William P. Rayner, p. 261

Apr "Summer Escaping to the Caribbean—the Island Urge." Despina Messinesi, p. 250

Oct (Anguilla) "Ah, Anguilla." A sneak preview of the Caribbean's newest resort. William P. Rayner, p. 550

Nov (St. Barts) "Something Luscious Under the Sun." Lee Bailey, p. 340

(Peter Island) "Ecstasy and an Island: Peter Island." Deborah Mason, p. 47

WORLD PRESS REVIEW

1985 Jan "A Caribbean Melange." Annerose Lohberg-Goetz, p. 62

Dec "Tobago—A Castaway's Dream." (*Toronto Star*). Sid Fassler, p. 62

1984 Jan (Aruba, Bonaire, Curaçao) "The Caribbean ABCs." Three spots for sunning, snorkeling and shopping. Pam Hobbs, p. 62

HAITI

NATIONAL GEOGRAPHIC

1985 Mar "Of Spirits and Saints." Folk cult of Haiti, voodoo. Carole Devillers, p. 395

JAMAICA

AMERICAS

1984 Jan-Feb "Reggae, Roots and Razzmatazz." Jumping to Jamaica's sunsplash festival. Rebecca Read Medrano, p. 34

Jul-Aug "Jamaican Hospitality Brings Strangers Together." Meet-the-people program. Penny Rogers, p. 53

ESQUIRE
1984 Apr "Listen to the Music, It Sings Jamaica." Bobbie Mason, p.50

HARPER'S BAZAAR
1985 Jun "A Day in the Life of the Jamaica Inn." Jennifer Quale, p. 10

NATIONAL GEOGRAPHIC
1985 Jan "Jamaica: Hard Times, High Hopes." Charles E. Cobb, Jr., p. 114

N.Y. TIMES SUNDAY TRAVEL SECTION (X)
1985 Apr 7 "Port Antonio: Tranquillity and Luxury." Joseph B. Treaster, p. 12
"Carefree or Careful in Jamaica?" Major resort areas have been largely untouched by capital's disorders. Joseph B. Treaster, p. 12
1984 Jan 1 "Sampling the Varied Worlds of Jamaica." The third largest Caribbean isle has more than beaches. Barbara Crossette, p. 15

PUERTO RICO

AMERICAS
1985 Jul/Aug "Tropical Treasure." Ponci's art museum is the best in the Caribbean and worth a trip to Puerto Rico in and of itself. David Roberts, p. 24
"Country Roads." The roads that wind through the mountainous backbone linking the east and west coasts show off the island's real beauty. Kathryn Robinson, p. 30

N.Y. TIMES SUNDAY TRAVEL SECTION (X)
1985 Jan 20 "Where Ancient Indians Played." In Ponce, monkey statues and ball courts offer a vision of pre-Columbian life. Morton Cohen, p. 9
Mar 31 "Puerto Rico's Quiet Edge." The west and its old traditions remain largely isolated from tourism. Jorge Heine, p. 17
1984 Jan 15 "Vieques: Island of Slower Rhythms." Off the tourist track in Puerto Rico. David Binder, p. 37
Feb 12 "Resort Village in Puerto Rico." Palmas del Mar. Woody Klein, p. 22
Oct 28 "What's Doing in San Juan." Manuel Suarez, p. 16
Dec 16 "Lure of Fishing in San Juan." Roy S. Johnson, p. 26

SATURDAY EVENING POST
1984 Sep "Easygoing Puerto Rico." Jo and Rod Williams, p. 90

TRAVEL/HOLIDAY
1984 Nov "Perfection in Puerto Rico." An island that improves with age. Elaine Williams, p. 10

THE BAHAMAS

Series Guidebooks (See Appendix 1)

Berlitz: The Bahamas
Birnbaum: Caribbean, Bermuda & the Bahamas
Fielding: Bermuda & the Bahamas
Fisher: Bahamas
Fodor: Bahamas; Caribbean & the Bahamas; Fun in the Bahamas
Frommer: Caribbean (including Bermuda & the
                Bahamas): Dollarwise
U.S. Government: Background Notes; Post Report

Background Reading

Albury, Paul   THE STORY OF THE BAHAMAS
St. Martin, 1976.

Barratt, P.J.   THE GRAND BAHAMA
One of the Islands of the World series. David, 1973.

Bloch, Michael   THE DUKE OF WINDSOR'S WAR
The Windsors in the Bahamas, 1940-45, written by an attorney with access to the private correspondence of the couple. Coward, 1983.

**Ferro, Robert & Grumley, Michael   ATLANTIS: THE AUTOBIOGRAPHY
OF A SEARCH**
Account of a boat trip from New Jersey to Bimini to explore the Edgar Cayce prophecies of the lost continent of Atlantis. Doubleday, 1970.

Hannau, Hans W.   BAHAMA ISLANDS
E.E. Seemann, 1977.

Pye, Michael   THE KING OVER WATER
The Duke of Windsor's years as governor of the Bahamas—in the process it gives an admirable history of the country, its colorful characters, the money-laundering business, and "charts the Windsors' decline in the exotic, politically corrupt Bahamian society." (BRD) HR&W, 1981.

Wilson, Sloan   AWAY FROM IT ALL
Amusing account by the novelist (*The Man in the Gray Flannel Suit*) of taking off to a new life-style cruising in the Bahamas. Putnam, 1969.

Zink, David   THE STONES OF ATLANTIS
The author's theories of the legendary Atlantis being near Bimini. P-H, 1978.

GUIDEBOOKS

Cyman, Bina, ed.   THE AIRGUIDE TRAVELLER: BAHAMAS, FLORIDA, FLORIDA KEYS, SEA ISLANDS
Airguide Pub, 1980.

Moore, James F.   THE PELICAN GUIDE TO THE BAHAMAS
"By far the most comprehensive guide to the more than 700 diverse islands . . . people, customs, and colorful history" and including practical tourist information. (LJ) Pelican, 1984

HISTORY

Craton, Michael   A HISTORY OF THE BAHAMAS
Collins, 1963.

Novels

Hemingway, Ernest   ISLANDS IN THE STREAM
Posthumous novel of a man's reflections on his two marriages and his children. Bimini and Cuba. Scribner, 1970.

Mason, F. Van Wyck   STARS ON THE SEA
Part of a saga on the American Revolution; this part is about the involvement of privateers in the Bahamas. Lippincott, 1940.

Wilder, Robert   WIND FROM THE CAROLINAS
A family chronicle beginning with an American family's migration to the Bahamas following the American Revolution, and continuing to the Civil War when they become involved in the blockade and rumrunning. Putnam Pub Group, 1964.

Wilder, Robert   AN AFFAIR OF HONOR
The Bahamas as reflected in the parallel lives of a white Bahamian "with an insatiable greed for wealth and power" and a black Bahamian's ambition to establish a black government. Putnam Pub Group, 1969.

TRAVEL ARTICLES

BLACK ENTERPRISE
1984 May "Almost 700 Ways to Enjoy a Vacation." Rachel J. Christmas, p. 88

MADEMOISELLE
1985 Oct "Warming Up Bahamas Style." If barefoot on the beach is your speed, explore the far side of this tropical paradise. Meg Lukens, p. 226

TRAVEL & LEISURE
1985 Dec "The Bahamas by Mail Boat." Swept away on the lilting rhythms of island life. Anthony Weller, p. 60

TRAVEL/HOLIDAY
1985 Dec "On Intimate Terms, Up Close and Personal, Bahamas-style." Denise D. Meehan, p. 30

WORLD PRESS REVIEW
1985 Mar "The Bahamas—Relaxing, Remote Resorts." (*Frankfurter Allgemeine Zeitung*, Frankfurt), Sigrid Bauschinger, p. 62

BERMUDA

Series Guidebooks (See Appendix 1)

Berlitz: Bermuda
Birnbaum: Caribbean, Bermuda & the Bahamas
Fielding: Bermuda & the Bahamas
Fisher: Bermuda
Fodor: Bermuda
Frommer: Caribbean (including Bermuda & the Bahamas): Dollarwise
U.S. Government: Background Notes; Post Report

Background Reading

Berchen, William   BERMUDA IMPRESSIONS
Text and photographs that go beyond the usual tourist attractions. Hastings, 1976.

Berlitz, Charles F.   WITHOUT A TRACE
The mysterious area of the Atlantic called the Bermuda Triangle, and the vessels and airplanes that have disappeared in the area. Doubleday, 1977.

Kusche, Larry   THE DISAPPEARANCE OF FLIGHT 19
Solves the most famous Bermuda Triangle mystery—the disappearance of five bombers on a training flight out of Fort Lauderdale. Har-Row, 1980.

LaBrucherie, Roger A.   IMAGES OF BERMUDA
C.E. Tuttle, 1981.

Tucker, Ethel and Catherine   GLIMPSES OF BERMUDA: A FEW HIGHWAYS AND BYWAYS
Darby Books.

Tucker, Terry   BERMUDA: TODAY AND YESTERDAY
St. Martin, 1975.

GUIDEBOOKS

Hay, Nelson E.   GUIDE TO THE ALTERNATIVE BERMUDA: HOW TO HAVE A WONDERFUL TIME IN BERMUDA AT A PRICE YOU CAN AFFORD
Sea Pr, 1984.

HISTORY

Wilkinson, Henry C.   BERMUDA FROM SAIL TO STEAM
The history of the Island from 1784 to 1901. Oxford U, 1973.

Novels

Benchley, Peter   THE DEEP
Underwater diving explorations of a sunken World War II cargo ship lead to a heroin cache—"constant flow of information on history, sociology, climate of Bermuda . . . as well as the alarms and beauty" of underwater exploration. (BRD) Doubleday, 1976.

Kinsolving, William   BORN WITH THE CENTURY
Story of Magnus MacPherson's rise from Scottish poverty to corporate power. Putnam Pub Group, 1979.

Mason, F. Van Wyck   THE SEA VENTURE
Historical novel of Jamestown-bound pioneers who end up in Bermuda. Doubleday, 1961.

Mason, F. Van Wyck   THREE HARBOURS
Part of a series on the American Revolution. This part tells of Bermuda's assistance, 1774-78. Lippincott, 1938.

TRAVEL ARTICLES

GLAMOUR
1985 Aug "6 Great Getaways Where Early Fall is the Best Time of All." p. 234

GOURMET
1985 Oct "Winter Golf in Bermuda." Paul J. Wade, p. 56

HOUSE BEAUTIFUL
1985 Nov "Your Guide to the Islands." Caribbean, Bermuda and Florida islands. Hazel Carr, p. 41

NATIONAL GEOGRAPHIC TRAVELER
1984 Autumn "Sumptuous Civility." A fresh look at these Atlantic isles. Christopher Buckley, p. 18

N.Y. TIMES TRAVEL SECTION (X)
1985 Jul 28 "What's Doing in Bermuda." Sean Dill, p. 10

TRAVEL/HOLIDAY
1984 Dec "Moped Meanderings." Breezing along in Bermuda. Gerard McTigue, p. 10

CENTRAL AMERICA

Series Guidebooks (See Appendix 1)

Fodor: Central America
Nagel: Central America (Belize, Costa Rica, Guatemala, Honduras, Panama, El Salvador, Nicaragua)
U.S. Government: Belize: Background Notes
               Costa Rica: Country Study
               Guatemala: Country Study; Background Notes; Post Report
               Honduras: Background Notes; Country Study
               Panama: Background Notes; Country Study; Pocket Guide; Post Report (Caribbean Pocket Guide includes Panama also)

Background Reading

Barry, Tom and Wood, Beth   DOLLARS & DICTATORS: A GUIDE TO CENTRAL AMERICA

Grove, 1983.

Bunch, Roland and Roger   THE HIGHLAND MAYA: PATTERNS OF LIFE AND CLOTHING IN GUATEMALA

Indigenous Pbns, 1977.

Huxley, Aldous   BEYOND THE MEXIQUE BAY
   A travel diary by the noted writer with "digressions upon many matters suggested by the places visited" in Central America and Mexico. (BRD) Greenwood, 1975 (first published 1934).

Kelly, Joyce   THE COMPLETE VISITOR'S GUIDE TO MESO-AMERICAN RUINS
Background reading and guide to archaeological sites and museums in Central America (including Mexico)—history, and rating system for the sites and museums. U of Oklahoma Pr, 1981.

Kelsey, Vera and others   FOUR KEYS TO GUATEMALA
A serious travel book—Indian tribes, their customs and arts and crafts, along with history of the country. Crowell, 1978 (first published 1939).

Knapp, Herbert and Mary   RED, WHITE AND BLUE PARADISE: THE AMERICAN CANAL ZONE IN PANAMA
The authors spent sixteen years in the Zone as teachers, leaving when the treaty went into effect giving the Canal to Panama. "Notable for its elegantly ironic style . . . a lively examination of the political, sociological and cultural dynamics." (PW) HarBraceJ, 1984.

McCullough, David   THE PATH BETWEEN THE SEAS
Story of the creation of the Panama Canal, 1870-1914—"readable, informative, exciting. . . . steers readers through political, financial and engineering intricacies without fatigue or muddle." (BRD) S&S, 1978.

Marnham, Patrick   SO FAR FROM GOD: A JOURNEY TO CENTRAL AMERICA
"A book of travels—though not a travel book"—impressions and images of people encountered, incidents along the way in California, Mexico and Central America by a British reporter. (NYTBR) Viking, 1985.

Martinez, Orlando   PANAMA CANAL
"Fascinating chapters which bring the Canal out of the jungle and into reality [along with] a maze of names, dates and historical events"—necessary for the complete story. (BRD) Atheneum, 1978.

Morris, Jan   DESTINATIONS
A collection of essays by a leading travel writer; this one includes an essay on Panama. Oxford U, 1980.

Setzekorn, William D.   FORMERLY BRITISH HONDURAS: A PROFILE OF THE NEW NATION OF BELIZE
By an architect and travel writer—"provides a mini-encyclopedia on the subject of Belize . . . geographical, cultural and social features [and] tracing its history from its founding in 1638." (TA) Ohio U, 1981.

Tschiffely, A.F.   SOUTHERN CROSS TO POLE STAR
See under "South America."

Woodward, Ralph L.   CENTRAL AMERICA: A NATION DIVIDED
It is the author's premise that Guatemala, El Salvador, Honduras, Nicaragua and Costa Rica should be one national union; explains the history of major political, social and economic events in the region. Oxford U, 1976.

GUIDEBOOKS

Glassman, Paul   BELIZE GUIDE; COSTA RICA GUIDE; GUATEMALA GUIDE
Passport Pr, 1976-84. Also *Lake Atitlan and Chichicastenango: the Complete Guide* (1976).

Greenberg, Arnold & Harriet   GUATEMALA ALIVE and PANAMA ALIVE
Alive Pbns, 1979.

Searby, Ellen   THE COSTA RICA TRAVELER—GETTING AROUND IN COSTA RICA
Windham Bay, 1984.

Shawcross, Mike   ANTIGUA, GUATEMALA: CITY & AREA GUIDE
A guide to Guatemala's colonial capital and fascinating surrounding area. Bradt, 1979.

HISTORY

Helms, Mary W.   MIDDLE AMERICA: A CULTURE HISTORY OF HEARTLAND AND FRONTIERS
"Crisp, clear introduction" to Mexico and Central America, for the general reader—covers the cultural development from earliest aboriginal people to the twentieth century. (BRD) U. Pr of America, 1982.

Jorden, William J.   PANAMA ODYSSEY: FROM COLONIALISM TO PARTNERSHIP
U of Texas, 1984.

Parker, Franklin D.   THE CENTRAL AMERICAN REPUBLICS
Survey history of Guatemala, Nicaragua, Honduras, El Salvador and Costa Rica. Greenwood, 1981 (first published 1964).

Novels

Ambler, Eric   DOCTOR FRIGO
Mystery involving oil exploration and the French secret services—set in Central America and the French Antilles. Atheneum, 1974.

Asturias, Miguel A.   STRONG WIND
First of a trilogy on plantation life in a banana republic in Central America. In this, an enlightened American entrepreneur tries to influence the relationship of American companies and native growers. Delacorte Pr, 1968 (first published 1962). Following is *The Green Pope* (1954) in which a tramp steamer captain becomes representative ("green pope") for a banana company; he meets his downfall in *The Eyes of the Interred* (1960).

Asturias, Miguel Angel   MULATA
A chronicle of bizarre wanderings and adventures—"a witches' cauldron of poxes, curses, hexes, sex, underground worlds . . . all derived from Mayan legend." (FC) Delacorte Pr, 1967. Also *Men of Maize* (1949), a struggle between Indians and outsiders interwoven with the supernatural.

Asturias, Miguel Angel   EL SEÑOR PRESIDENTE
Written between 1923 and 1932 and based on the dictatorship of Guatemalan president Cabrera. Atheneum, 1964 (first published 1946).

Didion, Joan   A BOOK OF COMMON PRAYER
"The quintessential American innocent" involved in a political coup. (FC) S&S, 1977.

Forester, C.S.   BEAT TO QUARTERS
An early nineteenth-century sea story about the British navy. Little, 1937.

Peters, Daniel   TIKAL; A NOVEL ABOUT THE MAYA
Tikal was a Mayan city in southern Central America (Guatemala) more than 1,000 years ago, which was mysteriously evacuated. The novel creates a hypothesis of reasons for the exodus—"rich in texture [and] thorough knowledge of Mayan customs." (FC) Random, 1983.

Stone, Robert   A FLAG FOR SUNRISE
A political novel of ideas, and a thriller, set in a fictional Central American country. Knopf, 1981.

Theroux, Paul   THE MOSQUITO COAST
An American inventor, accompanied by his family, pursues his obsession to be totally self-sufficient on the wild coast of Honduras. Houghton, 1982.

Thomas, Ross   MISSIONARY STEW
"Intricately plotted, entertaining literary romp . . . witty dialogue . . . unconventional situations" in a novel set in twentieth-century Central America—an "examination of the abuse of power." (FC) S&S, 1983.

TRAVEL ARTICLES

AMERICAS
1985 Nov "A Wealth of Guatemalan Weaving." Textiles are the star of Chichicastenango's market. A.R. Williams, p. 22

BLACK ENTERPRISE
1985 Jan (Panama) "An Undiscovered Vacation Treasure—Panama." Connie Green, p. 78

CONNOISSEUR
1985 Jan (Belize) "The Great Escape." Tiny out-of-the-way Belize is just the ticket for travelers with a taste for adventure. Anthony Brandt, p. 49

ESSENCE
1985 Jun (Costa Rica) "Cooling Out in a Hotspot." San Jose and day-tripping. Constance Garcia-Barrio, p. 32

NATIONAL GEOGRAPHIC
1985 Oct "Usumacinta River: Troubles on a Wild Frontier." The authors trek the rain forest that shelters ancient Maya ruins and guerilla bases on the border that separates Mexico and Guatemala. Jeffrey K. Wilkerson and David Hiser, p. 514

N.Y. TIMES SUNDAY TRAVEL SECTION (X)
1985 Feb 3 (Belize) "Exploring Underwater Off Belize." A diver's report from reefs and atolls. Austin Bay, p. 9
Jul 28 "Costa Rica's Jungle Train." Rail line from San Jose to the Coast. Vicky Elliot, p. 20
Aug 25 "Cool Birds Fly South in July." Vermonter fleeing hayloft covets sloth in Costa Rica. Noel Perrin, p. 29
1984 Oct 28 (Belize) "Discovering Belize." The former British Honduras offers friendliness, beaches, mountains and Mayan ruins. Donald E. Westlake and Abby Adams, p. 14

TRAVEL & LEISURE
1984 Jun "The Romance of Pyramids." David L. Shirey, p. 32

TRAVEL/HOLIDAY
1985 May (Costa Rica) "A Jungle Adventure." Into the rain forest in Costa Rica. Jerry Ruhlow, p. 10

MEXICO

Series Guidebooks (See Appendix 1)

American Express: Mexico
Baedeker: Mexico
Berlitz: Mexico City
Birnbaum: Mexico
Country Orientation Update: Mexico
Fielding: Mexico
Fisher: Mexico
Fodor: Mexico; Budget Travel Mexico; Mexico City & Acapulco; Fun in Acapulco
Frommer: Mexico: $-a-Day; Mexico City & Acapulco: City Guide
Insight: Mexico
Let's Go: Mexico

Lonely Planet: Mexico
Nagel: Mexico
Sunset: Mexico
U.S. Government: Mexico: Background Notes; Country Study;
Post Report

Background Reading

Conrad, Jean-Baptiste   MEXICO: WHAT TO KNOW BEFORE YOU GO
A handbook of "preparatory information. . . . overview of Mexican history . . . the Mexican legal system relevant to the U.S. tourist" as well as tips on maintaining one's health, food, weather, language, transportation, etc. (BL) Learning Tree, 1982.

Cottrell, John   MEXICO CITY
One of Great Cities of the World series. Time-Life, 1979.

**Horgan, Paul   GREAT RIVER: THE RIO GRANDE IN NORTH
AMERICAN HISTORY**
"A joy to read"—history of the river and the entire border region of New Mexico and Texas from ancient days to modern times. Part 1 is about the Indians and Spain, Part 2 about Mexico and the United States. (BRD) Texas Monthly Pr, 1984 (first published 1954).

Lewis, Oscar   THE CHILDREN OF SANCHEZ
An in-depth study of one family in Mexico City. Random, 1966 (first published 1961). Also *Death in the Sanchez Family* (1969).

**Miller, Tom   ON THE BORDER: PORTRAITS OF AMERICA'S
SOUTHWESTERN FRONTIER**
The author's thesis is that the 2,000-mile Mexico/U.S. border is a third country—not Mexico, not America—with its own laws, customs, language and food. Combination of travelogue, history and sociology told in "a very entertaining manner." (BRD) Har-Row, 1981.

O'Gorman, Patricia W.   PATIOS AND GARDENS OF MEXICO
Architectural, 1979.

**Parmenter, Ross   LAWRENCE IN OAXACA: A QUEST FOR THE NOVELIST
IN MEXICO**
Scenes and sketches of Lawrence's life in Oaxaca that led to *Mornings in Mexico* (1927) and *The Plumed Serpent* (1926), and other writings during the period 1922-25—"fresh glimpses of [Lawrence's] extraordinarily changeable personality." (NYTBR) Peregrine Smith, 1985.

Paz, Octavio   THE LABYRINTH OF SÓLITUDE
An analysis of Mexican life and thought by a major poet. Grove, 1983 (first published 1962).

**Pettit, Florence H. & Ronald M.   MEXICAN FOLK TOYS, FESTIVAL
DECORATIONS AND RITUAL OBJECTS**
The history, significance and techniques involved as well as a calendar of festivals, fiestas, market days and museums and shops where items can be found. Hastings, 1978.

Reyes, Alfonso   MEXICO IN A NUTSHELL AND OTHER ESSAYS
Native themes by an author who is a leading man of letters in Mexico. U of California Pr, 1964.

**Riding, Alan   DISTANT NEIGHBORS: PORTRAIT OF
THE MEXICANS**
By a foreign correspondent for the *New York Times*—"short historical background. . . . the diverse heritage [and] economic situation and monumental problems" with profiles of major figures on the Mexican scene. "Assessments are pungent and provocative." (BL) Knopf, 1984.

Rodman, Selden   A SHORT HISTORY OF MEXICO
This is a newly revised edition of *The Mexico Traveler; a Concise History and Guide*, published in 1969, and is a summary of history, painting, architecture and literature by an art critic and travel writer. Stein & Day, 1982.

Smith, Bradley   MEXICO: A HISTORY IN ART
Mexico as reflected in its art—text and photographs. Doubleday, 1971.

**Walker, Ronald G.   INFERNAL PARADISE: MEXICO
AND THE MODERN ENGLISH NOVEL**
The book is an analysis of the fascination Mexico has The book is an analysis of the fascination Mexico has held for writers Lawrence, Huxley, Graham Greene and Malcolm Lowry, the journeys they made and an analysis of the fiction that emerged. U of California, 1978.

Waugh, Evelyn   MEXICO: AN OBJECT LESSON
"An analysis of life and politics . . . written from a conservative Catholic point of view." (BRD) Little, 1939.

Weismann, Elizabeth W.   ART AND TIME IN MEXICO
Comprehensive book on Mexico architecture. Har-Row, 1986.

TRAVELOGUES, MEMOIRS

**Bedford, Sybille   THE SUDDEN VIEW: A TRAVELLER'S TALE
FROM MEXICO**
"Stimulating, chatty travelogue" by the noted British writer, of her travels in Mexico. (BRD) Atheneum, 1963 (first published 1953).

**Bruccoli, Matthew J.   RECONQUEST OF MEXICO: AN AMIABLE
JOURNEY IN PURSUIT OF CORTES**
Retraces on foot the journey of Cortes from Vera Cruz to Mexico City. Vanguard, 1974.

Cadwallader, Sharon   SAVORING MEXICO: A TRAVEL COOKBOOK
A leisurely tour of Mexico with food as a theme. McGraw, 1980.

Dobie, J. Frank   TONGUES OF THE MONTE
Collected legends, stories and customs of northern Mexico "on the thread of his own adventures." (BRD) U of Texas, 1980 (first published 1935).

Foster, Harry LaTourette   A GRINGO IN MAÑANA LAND
Personal experiences of a free-lance newspaper correspondent in Mexico when "banditry was a profitable occupation." (BRD) Gordon Pr, 1976 (first published 1924).

Gangemi, Kenneth   THE VOLCANOES FROM PUEBLA
Images and experiences of the author's travel by motorcycle in the early 1960s. M Boyars, 1979.

Greene, Graham   ANOTHER MEXICO
"Impressionistic, personal account . . . with a jaundiced eye" of the author's visit in the spring of 1938. (BRD) Viking, 1981 (first published 1939). Also *The Lawless Roads* (1971), another memoir of Mexico which led to his novel *The Power and the Glory* (1940).

Lawrence, D.H.   MORNINGS IN MEXICO
"Pleasant, sun-baked essays . . . studies of the Mexican Indian in his life and at his rites." (BRD) Peregrine Smith, 1982 (first published 1927).

Lincoln, John   ONE MAN'S MEXICO
Based on this English writer's travel experiences (1958-64), about the "intrepid" school of travel. One reviewer comments: "best exposition of Mexico's past and present predicament" to have come to his attention—people watching, travels along the coast and in the mountains, experiences with LSD. (BRD) Hippocrene, 1983 (first published 1968).

Simon, Kate   MEXICO: PLACES AND PLEASURES
Essays, vignettes, sketches and a travel guide, by a noted travel writer. Har-Row, 1984.

Steinbeck, John   SEA OF CORTEZ
A leisurely journey of travel and research on marine animals by the novelist. Appel, 1971 (first published 1941).

ARCHAEOLOGY, THE MAYAS AND THE AZTECS

Bernal, Ignacio   A HISTORY OF MEXICAN ARCHAEOLOGY: THE VANISHED CIVILIZATIONS OF MIDDLE AMERICA
Traces prehistoric Mexican society through accounts by early travelers and conquerors, and modern archaeologists—read for pleasure or information. Thames Hudson, 1980.

**Brunhouse, Robert L.   IN SEARCH OF THE MAYA: THE FIRST
ARCHAEOLOGISTS**
Stories of eight amateur archaeologists who first reported on the Maya ruins,
their personalities and their contributions. U of New Mexico, 1973.

Caso, Alfonso   AZTECS: PEOPLE OF THE SUN
By a Mexican archaeologist and an expert in Aztec lore. U of Oklahoma Pr, 1978.

Diaz del Castillo, Bernal   DISCOVERY AND CONQUEST OF MEXICO
Eyewitness account by a soldier under Cortes who took part in the conquest of
Mexico—"historical source material and a thrilling yarn." (BRD) Octagon, 1970
(first published 1928).

Fagan, Brian M.   THE AZTECS
Introduction to the Aztec world—"a complete and accurate portrait of the
people and their culture." (BL) Freeman, 1984.

**Gallenkamp, Charles   MAYA: THE RIDDLE AND REDISCOVERY OF A
LOST CIVILIZATION**
Introduction for the general reader to Mayan civilization and archaeology—the
pageant of Middle America and synthesis of discoveries from 1517 on. Penguin,
1981 (first published 1959).

Gorenstein, Shirley   NOT FOREVER ON EARTH
An introduction for newcomers to archaeology—prehistory and methodology
of archaeology in Mexico. Scribner, 1975.

**Gyles, Anna & Sayer, Chloe   OF GODS AND MEN: THE HERITAGE OF
ANCIENT MEXICO**
Based on a BBC series—ideal introduction, for travelers who plan to visit
Mexico, to archaeology, society, crafts, rituals, pre-history. Har-Row, 1981.

Morley, Sylvanus G. and George W.   THE ANCIENT MAYA
Originally written twenty-five years ago, new discoveries and interpretations
have been added while retaining features that originally made this book the most
popular introduction to the Mayan world at the time it was first published.
Stanford U, 1981 (first published 1956).

Pearce, Kenneth   THE VIEW FROM THE TOP OF THE TEMPLE
Guides the reader "through ruins and resorts . . . rituals and customs the modern
Maya have steadfastly preserved. . . . mingles tales of archaeological shenanigans
with tips on what roads to take and where and what to expect when you arrive."
(TL) U of New Mexico, 1984.

**Portillo, Jose Lopez and others   QUETZALCOATL: IN MYTH,
ARCHEOLOGY AND ART**
A recreation of the Quetzalcoatl (feathered serpent) story and a historical,
psychological and literary survey of the civilizations that evolved from the cults.
(NYTBR) Continuum, 1982.

**Stuart, George E. and Gene S.   THE MYSTERIOUS MAYA;
THE MIGHTY AZTECS**
Two *National Geographic* books with text and photographs that give the reader a sense of sharing in the research and adventure. Natl Geog, 1977 and 1981.

Vaillant, George   THE AZTECS OF MEXICO
A "masterpiece of popularization" of Aztec life, art, religion, government, social customs, from ancient times to the Spanish conquest, by an outstanding authority on the subject. (BRD) Penguin, 1955 (first published 1941).

BAJA CALIFORNIA

Crosby, Harry   THE CAVE PAINTING OF BAJA CALIFORNIA
Copley Bks, 1984. Also *King's Highway in Baja California* (1979).

Gardner, Erle Stanley   OFF THE BEATEN TRACK IN BAJA
The mystery writer wrote a series of books about Baja. Morrow, 1967. Other titles include: *Mexico's Magic Square* (1968) and *Host with the Big Hat* (1968).

**Garrison, Chuck   OFFSHORE FISHING IN SOUTHERN CALIFORNIA
AND BAJA**
Comprehensive guide to sport fishing off the coast of Southern California and Baja. Chronicle Bk, 1980.

Hunter, Jim   OFFBEAT BAJA
A guide for travel by car (sometimes four-wheel-drive vehicles are recommended) to back country Baja. Darwin Pbns, 1985.

Johnson, William W.   BAJA CALIFORNIA
Part of the American Wilderness Series. Time-Life, 1972.

**Krutch, Joseph W.   THE FORGOTTEN PENINSULA: A NATURALIST IN
BAJA CALIFORNIA**
An informal portrait of Baja by a leading naturalist/writer. Sloane, 1961.

Miller, Tom   BAJA BOOK II
Baja Trail Pbns, 1983. Also *Angler's Guide to Baja California* (1979).

**Patchen, Marvin and Aletha   BAJA ADVENTURES BY LAND, AIR
AND SEA**
Baja Trail Pbns, 1981.

Robertson, Tomas A.   BAJA CALIFORNIA AND ITS MISSIONS
La Siesta Pr, 1978.

GUIDEBOOKS

Note also guidebooks listed under "Baja California," above.

Babcock, Judy and Kennedy, Judy   THE SPA BOOK
See under "Caribbean/Guidebooks."

**Barroso, Memo   YUCATAN, THE HIDDEN BEACHES:
A TRAVELER'S GUIDE**
Guide to off-the-beaten-track beaches and well-known resorts of the Yucatan peninsula; the best snorkeling, scuba diving, fishing, sailing, camping, bird-watching, hotels, restaurants, banks, gas stations and food stores. Harmony, 1983.

Baxter, Robert   BAXTER'S MEXICO
Rail-Europe-Baxter, 1984.

Bruning, Nancy   THE BEACH BOOK
See under "Caribbean/Guidebooks."

Carlson, Loraine   TRAVELEER GUIDE TO YUCATAN
Upland Pr, 1982.

Carlson, Loraine   TRAVELEER GUIDE TO MEXICO CITY
Upland Pr, 1981.

Fisher, John   THE ROUGH GUIDE TO MEXICO
For the more adventurous traveler; deals with such things as alcohol, bribes, drugs, sexual harassment, machismo, but also with traditional tourist information. Routledge & Kegan, 1985.

Franz, Carl   THE PEOPLE'S GUIDE TO MEXICO
Intended for tourists willing to rough it at times. John Muir Pbns, 1979.

Frost, Peter   EXPLORING CUZCO
History, background information and practical information. Bradt, 1981.

**Garrison, Chuck   OFFSHORE FISHING IN SOUTHERN CALIFORNIA
AND BAJA**
See under "Southern California."

Hunter, C. Bruce   A GUIDE TO ANCIENT MEXICAN RUINS
Background reading and guide to reaching various archaeological ruins. U. of Oklahoma Pr, 1977.

Hylton, Hilary   MEXICO: THE TEXAS MONTHLY GUIDEBOOK
Historical background, cities, hotels, restaurants, points of interest, fiestas, museums, etc. Texas Monthly Pr, 1983.

Jacobs, Charles and Babette   MEXICO TRAVEL DIGEST
A comprehensive guide that many travel agents use for itinerary planning. Travel Digest, 1983.

Mallan, Chicki   GUIDE TO THE YUCATAN PENINSULA
The Yucatan yesterday and today in a complete guidebook. Moon Pbns, 1986.

Schell, Rolfe F.   **SCHELL'S GUIDE TO YUCATAN &**
NEIGHBORING STATES
Island Pr, 1981.

Shawcross, Mike   **SAN CRISTOBAL DE LAS CASAS CHIAPAS: CITY AND**
AREA GUIDE
Bradt, 1980.

Wilhelm, John and others   **THE WILHELMS' GUIDE TO ALL MEXICO**
A family production—the sons did the Baja section, the parents the rest of
Mexico. McGraw, 1978.

Wood, Robert D.   **A TRAVEL GUIDE TO ARCHAEOLOGICAL MEXICO**
For travelers by car—itineraries by car, history and background information,
extensive coverage for each site. Hastings, 1979.

HISTORY

Cheetham, Sir Nicolas   **A SHORT HISTORY OF MEXICO**
Crowell, 1972.

Fehrenbach, T.R.   **FIRE AND BLOOD**
Macmillan, 1973.

Meyer, Michael C.   **THE COURSE OF MEXICAN HISTORY**
Oxford U, 1983.

Miller, Robert Ryal   **MEXICO: A HISTORY**
"A superb synthesis of Mexico's complex history." (LJ) U of Oklahoma Pr, 1985.

Novels

Azuela, Mariano   **TWO NOVELS OF THE MEXICAN REVOLUTION**
Principia Pr, 1963 (first published 1915 and 1918).

Bagley, Desmond   **THE VIVERO LETTER (Yucatan)**
An archaeological thriller—a London accountant solves his brother's murder.
Doubleday, 1968.

Benchley, Peter   **THE GIRL OF THE SEA OF CORTEZ**
Set on an island in the Gulf of California. A young girl's affinity for the sea and its
creatures conflicts with her brother's different attitude, as a fisherman, toward the
sea. Doubleday, 1982.

Brawley, Ernest   **THE ALAMO TREE**
A saga of two contrasting families set in Manzanillo and Acapulco and how the
political, economic and social conditions shape their lives. S&S, 1984.

Castellanos, Rosario   THE NINE GUARDIANS
Disintegration of a Mexican ranch family under the impact of land reforms—set in a remote province of southern Mexico. Vanguard, 1959.

Chandler, Raymond   THE LONG GOODBYE
Murder mystery involving a man who flees to Mexico thinking he has committed a murder. Houghton, 1953.

Doerr, Harriet   STONES FOR IBARRA
An American couple move to a small town in Mexico where they hope to revitalize a copper mine. Episodes of village life alternate with those of the couple's experiences. Viking, 1984.

Fuentes, Carlos   TERRA NOSTRA
"Fusion of history, myth and fiction on a grand scale. . . . the major work of the most important Mexican writer." (BRD) FS&G, 1976. Also, by Fuentes, *Where the Air is Clear* (1960), *A Change of Skin* (1968), *The Hydra Head* (1978), *The Death of Artemio Cruz* (1964).

Fuentes, Carlos   BURNT WATER
Short stories, the life of Mexico City "from street kids to aesthetes." (BRD) FS&G, 1980.

Gavin, Catherine   THE CACTUS AND THE CROWN
A love story set in the nineteenth century. Doubleday, 1962.

Gellhorn, Martha   THE LOWEST TREES HAVE TOPS
Expatriates living idle lives among the natives in a small Mexican town. Dodd, 1969.

Greene, Graham   THE POWER AND THE GLORY
A Catholic priest on the run is the central character—"the atmosphere and detail [of Mexico] are convincing." (FC) Viking, 1968 (first published 1940). See also *Another Mexico* under "Background Reading," above.

Hall, Oakley   THE CHILDREN OF THE SUN
"A strange, bloody, haunting historical novel" of a failed Spanish expedition to Florida and an historic 1,600-mile journey to Mexico to search for Cibola. (FC) Atheneum, 1983.

Herrin, Lamar   THE RIO LOJA RINGMASTER
An American baseball player returns to Mexico to find himself. Viking, 1977.

Highwater, Jamake   THE SUN HE DIES: A NOVEL ABOUT THE END OF THE AZTEC WORLD
Narrated by Montezuma's chamberlain, it tells how the 2000-year old Aztec civilization was destroyed by Cortez in six years. Lippincott, 1980.

Horgan, Paul   MEXICO BAY
A woman's relationships with various men in her life, including an artist and a historian researching the Bay for a book. FS&G, 1982.

Irving, Clifford   TOM MIX AND PANCHO VILLA
A "diverting entertainment" that is partly true and tells of Tom Mix's supposed service and adventures on Villa's staff. (FC) St. Martin, 1982.

Jennings, Gary   AZTEC
Reminiscences of an Aztec Indian before and after Cortez—accurate history blended with fictional drama. Atheneum, 1980.

Lawrence, D.H.   THE PLUMED SERPENT
"A powerful, vivid evocation of Mexico and its ancient Aztec religion." (FC) Random, 1955 (first published 1926).

Lea, Tom   THE BRAVE BULLS
A famous bullfighter recalls his past life. Little, 1949.

Lowry, Malcolm   UNDER THE VOLCANO
Remembrances of things past of a British ex-consul drinking himself to death. Har-Row, 1984 (first published 1947).

MacDonald John D.   DRESS HER IN INDIGO
Travis McGee murder mystery set in Oaxaca "among the gay, the depraved . . . drug addicted and the violent." (FC) Lippincott, 1971. Also, set in Mexico, *Cinnamon Skin* (1982), *A Deadly Shade of Gold* (1965).

Morris, Wright   THE FIELD OF VISION
Dissection of seven people attending a bullfight. U of Nebraska, 1974 (first published 1956). Also *Love Among the Cannibals* (1957), a love affair of a Hollywood songwriter.

Nin, Anais   SEDUCTION OF THE MINOTAUR
In *Cities of the Interior*—novelette about a woman seeking to escape her past. Swallow Pr, 1974.

Peters, Daniel   THE LUCK OF HUEMAC
Tenochtitlan (now Mexico City), 1428-1521, when the "god" Cortez conquers the city. Random, 1981.

Portillo, Jose Lopez   QUETZALCOATL
The ancient legend of the god Quetzalcoatl, the god of civilization represented by the plumed serpent. Seabury, 1976 (first published 1965).

Sharp, Marilyn   FALSEFACE
While an interim president is in charge in Washington following the supposed accidental death of his predecessor, a CIA agent deals with the kidnapping of a congressional delegation visiting Mayan ruins at Uxmal. St. Martin, 1984.

Shellabarger, Samuel   CAPTAIN FROM CASTILE
A young Spaniard joins Cortez in the capture of Mexico City in the sixteenth century. Little, 1945.

Steinbeck, John   THE PEARL
A parable based on a Mexican folk tale of a fishing family and the finding of a great pearl. Viking, 1947.

Stewart, Fred Mustard   A RAGE AGAINST HEAVEN
An outcast of the American Civil War becomes a bandit in Mexico and plots his revenge—"weaves together . . . diverse elements of late 19th-century America—slavery, civil rights, political corruption, women's rights." (FC) Viking, 1978.

Taylor, Robert L.   TWO ROADS TO GUADALUPE
War with Mexico in 1845, and two Missouri boys who fight in the war. Doubleday, 1964.

Traven, B.   THE TREASURE OF THE SIERRA MADRE
Basis for the classic movie of the search by three American "have-nots" for gold in the mountains of Mexico. Hill & Wang, 1967 (first published 1927). Also *The Carreta* (1931), about the poverty and naivete of the Mexican peasantry.

Westheimer, David   THE OLMEC HEAD
Action and suspense as an ex-Marine is involved in smuggling an artifact weighing tons (the Olmec head) out of Mexico. Little, 1974.

Wibberley, Leonard   THE ISLAND OF THE ANGELS
An island off the coast of Baja is the setting for this story of a fisherman's desperate attempts to save a young boy's life. Morrow, 1965.

Yanez, Agustín   THE LEAN LANDS
Rural Mexico in the 1920s—"tradition bound farmers . . . confronted with . . . change and progress." (FC) U of Texas, 1968. Also *The Edge of the Storm* (1947), set in pre-revolutionary Mexico—the essence of Mexican character and history reflected in the contrasting views of two parish priests.

TRAVEL ARTICLES

AMERICAS
1985 Jan-Feb "The Quiet Pleasures of Guadalajara." A.R. Williams, p. 38
     "Guadalajara with Gusto." Food markets, restaurants. Lorna J. Sass, p. 52
     Mar-Apr "Toluca's Glass-Covered Garden." A Mexican city turned an unused market into an urban paradise. Roderic A. Camp, p. 60
     Jul-Aug "The White City Shines Anew." Merida deserves a second look by travelers. A.R. Williams, p. 10
     Nov-Dec "Mexico's Religious Architecture Reinterprets a European Style." Elizabeth W. Weismann, p. 8
     "Taxco Offers Travelers Dramatic Scenery and Fine Silverwork." Susan M. Masuoka, p. 16
1984 Jul-Aug "From Colotypes to Cibachromes." Mexico City's Museum of Photography. Martha Davidson, p. 14
     Nov-Dec "Barranca Country—Trekking Mexico through Mexico's Spectacular Sierra Madres." Michael Rickie, p. 18

ATLANTIC
1984 Oct "The Pleasures of the Plaza." Wendy Lowe, p. 103

ESQUIRE
1984 Oct "The Mexican Baja." You have to see it to believe it, then see it again to believe what you saw. P.J. O'Rourke, p. 52

50 PLUS
1984 Sep "Cashing in on Mexico." Still a great travel bargain. Helen Cunningham, p. 40

GOOD HOUSEKEEPING
1984 Oct "Mexico's Best for Family Vacations: the Yucatan." Ancient treasures, modern pleasures. Barbara Humeston, p. 223

GOURMET
1985 Jan Gourmet Holidays: "San Miguel de Allende." Terry Weeks, p. 38

HORIZON
1985 May "Images of Mexico." Discover the arts and the best places to dine, lodge and shop in this land of contrasts. Florence Lemkowitz, p. 57

HOUSE & GARDEN
1984 May "In Tepozteco's Shadow." Summer haunt of Aztec princes still casts a fast spell. Luisa Valenzuela, p. 30

MADEMOISELLE
1985 Feb "Mexico: the Pleasure is Yours." In Mexico you can please your winter-weary body *and* your world-hungry soul. Lesley Dormen, p. 210

NATIONAL GEOGRAPHIC
1985 Jun "Life on the Line." U.S.-Mexican border. Mark Kramer, p. 720
1984 Aug "Mexico City: An Alarming Giant." Bart McDowell, p. 138
        Oct "Following Cortés." Retracing the 1519 path of the conquistador. S. Jeffrey, p. 420

NATIONAL GEOGRAPHIC TRAVELER
1985 Autumn "Mexican Pastimes: Exploring Yucatan." Joyce Diamanti, p. 72

N.Y. TIMES SUNDAY TRAVEL SECTION (X)
1985 Jan 6 "Where Mexico Plays: Acapulco, the Capital's Favorite Resort is Making a Comeback." Richard J. Meislin, p. 14
        "A Slow-Paced Weekend Retreat." Michoacan. Gordon Mott, p. 15
        Apr 14 "On the Road Through Baja California." Exploring a land of fine seafood, stark vistas and uncrowded white-sand beaches. William A. Orme, Jr., p. 19
        Apr 21 "On the Road from Sea to Sea." *Times* correspondents map their favorite routes. Various authors (includes Mexico), p. 15
        Jun 2 "Mexican Notebook." Impressions from a first visit: bold art, memorable food and not a few surprises. R.W. Apple, Jr., p. 19

1985 Sep 15 Fare of the Country: "Mexico's Rainy Season Delicacy." Richard J. Meislin, p. 6

Nov 10 "Valley of Ancient Gods." Oaxaca weaves unbroken threads of Mexico's pre-Columbian and Spanish histories. Olivier Bernier, p. 19

Nov 24 "On the Road to Mexico City." A journey through the Chihuahua Desert and the pastoral, higher plateaus of Mexico. William Stockton, p. 20

1984 Jan 8 "Mexico's Reverence for the Past." In and around the capital, the centuries thrive together (including some tips for amateur archaeologists). Richard J. Meislin, p. 14

"Legacy of the Conquistadores." Sampling five of Mexico's hacienda hotels. Gordon Mott, p. 15

"The Yucatan's Triple Appeal." Where Spanish charm, Mayan ruins and Caribbean sun join forces. Joseph Giovannini, p. 16

Feb 12 "Going, Going, Going, Gone." To Acapulco, a week in a beachside condominium. Susan Sheehan, p. 19

Feb 26 "Pacific Mexico: Puerto Vallarta." Nick Madigan, p. 20

Mar 18 (Part 2, "Sophisticated Traveler") "Mexico's Two Seas: The Old Caribbean Port of Veracruz, Looking Toward Europe, and the New Pacific Resort of Ixtapa-Zihuatanejo." Carlos Fuentes, p. 34

May 20 "Summer Abroad: the ABCs of Going with Children." 16 foreign correspondents and contributors to the *Times* offer tips on touring their corners of the world—includes Mexico. p. 21

Sep 30 "What's Doing in Mexico City." Richard J. Meislin, p. 10

Oct 7 (Part 2, "Sophisticated Traveler") "Mexico City's Touch of Paris." Richard J. Meislin, p. 127

Nov 25 "Rustic Refuge Off the Yucatan Coast." Cozumel. Richard Halloran, p. 21

Dec 9 "Mexico's Riviera-Style Resort." Designed for the super rich, Las Hadras strives to pamper the merely affluent. Eleanor Foa Dienstag, p. 19

SATURDAY EVENING POST

1984 Apr "Traveler's Advisory: Make it Mexico." Maynard G. Stoddard, p. 90

SUNSET

1985 Mar "Up from Cabo San Lucas, Almost 50 Newly Paved Miles." Opens up beaches, cuts out curves, saves time. p. 68

Oct "Dancing with Dolphins in Baja, California." And other close-up meetings with wildlife. p. 126

"Baja Wildlife Tours." Naturalists who will take you to meet Baja's wildlife. p. 58

Nov "Exploring Ancient Mexican Archaeological Sites." p. 98

1984 Mar "Acapulco's Market." Just blocks from the beach. p. 68

TRAVEL & LEISURE

1985 Mar "Mexico's Magnificent Monte Alban." The sun-scorched ruins of a splendid Zapotec city (near Oaxaca). Joseph McElroy, p. 58

Sep "Whale Watching in Baja." Geoffrey Wolff, p. 130

Oct "Oaxaca—Very Indian, Muy Spanish and Most Mexican." Lynn Ferrin, p. 135

1984 Jan "The Savage Beauty of Baja and the Sea of Cortez." Where to stay, resorts for the active and the contemplative. Richard J. Pietschmann, p. 60
Nov "A Spectacular Train Ride in Mexico." Splendid views and cliff-hanging thrills in the Sierra Madre. Robert Devine, p. 40
"Mexico Magnifico: From Acapulco to the Yucatan." Six festive trips. Janet Piorko, p. 84

TRAVEL/HOLIDAY
1985 Jan "Cancun: a Mexican Mix." An ancient civilization and a modern resort. Yolanda Mitisdale, p. 62
Apr "Mexico's Costa Bougainvillea." The good life in Las Hadas. Susan J. Vreeland, p. 8
Jul "Mexican Inn Spots Beyond High-rise Hotels." Toby Smith, p. 49
Nov "Puerto Vallarta—the Romance Survives in This Mexican Town." Michael Pennacchia, p. 52
1984 Jul Special Section: pp. 52-60 "Viva Mexico City, Ciudad of Shopping." The connoisseur's buying guide. Yolanda M. Tisdale; "Artful Indulgences." Exhibiting a flair for art. Ron Butler; "Affordable Fine Dining." Robert L. Balzer
Oct "Chiapas." A present-day glimpse of ancient Mexico. Denise Meehan, p. 40
Dec "Travel/Holiday's Annual Guide to Fine Dining." U.S., Canada, Mexico. p. 51

WORLD PRESS REVIEW
Oct "Baja's 'earthly paradise.'" (*Gente Viaggi*, Milan). Amalia Pellegrini, p. 62

SOUTH AMERICA

Series Guidebooks (See Appendix 1)

Birnbaum: **South America**
Fodor: **South America**
Frommer: **South America: $-a-Day**
Lonely Planet: **South America**

Note: Books on the Incas are entered under "Peru"; on Patagonia see under "Argentina."

Background Reading

Isherwood, Christopher   CONDOR AND THE COWS
"A South American travel diary . . . sharply witty, sometimes wicked . . . all times

fresh-eyed" impressions on a trip through the Andean countries and Argentina in 1947 and 1948. (BRD) Random, 1949

Kandell, Jonathan   PASSAGE THROUGH EL DORADO: THE CONQUEST OF THE WORLD'S LAST GREAT WILDERNESS
Account of a journey through the Amazon basin, an area that involves six nations, and the land rush going on in that part of the world today, with comparisons to our own westward migration in the nineteenth century. A "serious, probing and revealing book"—the author traveled the area and talked to many, from squatters and Indians to drug dealers and ranchers. (LJ) Morrow, 1984.

Matthiessen, Peter   THE CLOUD FOREST: A CHRONICLE OF THE SOUTH AMERICAN WILDERNESS
Chronicle of an eight-month journey by air, land and water to the Amazon, Macchu Picchu and other parts of the continent. Ballantine, 1973 (first published 1961).

Morris, Arthur S.   SOUTH AMERICA
A handbook that emphasizes the variety of geography, history, cultures and economies in South America. Barnes & Noble, 1980.

Rodman, Selden   SOUTH AMERICA OF THE POETS
Describes a journey through most of South America, meetings with the outstanding writers—a travel book with insights into the culture of each country. Southern Illinois U, 1972.

Topolski, Daniel and Feliks   TRAVELS WITH MY FATHER: A SOUTH AMERICAN JOURNEY
An itinerary covering most of the continent with emphasis on "pursuit of the erotic and dangerous." (BL) Hamish Hamilton, 1984.

Tschiffely, A.F.   SOUTHERN CROSS TO POLE STAR— TSCHIFFELY'S RIDE
Reprint of a travel classic which recounts the "remarkable, often terrifying exploits" of a Swiss schoolmaster and his two aging Criollo-bred ponies in a 10,000-mile, two-and-one-half year journey from Buenos Aires to Washington, D.C. (BRD) Tarcher, 1982 (first published 1933).

THE AMAZON AND THE ANDES

Andrews, Michael A.   FLIGHT OF THE CONDOR: A WILDLIFE EXPLORATION OF THE ANDES
Complementary book to a PBS series of experiences during the filming of a documentary. Little, 1982.

Benson, Elizabeth and Conklin, William   MUSEUMS OF THE ANDES
Newsweek, 1981.

Cousteau, Jacques and Richard   JACQUES COUSTEAU'S AMAZON
JOURNEY
Abrams, 1981.

Elder, Norman   THIS THING OF DARKNESS
"Interesting armchair excursion . . . a sad book about the shrinking Amazon jungle"—by a Canadian adventurer. (BRD) Everett Hse, 1980.

Fawcett, P.H.   LOST TRAILS, LOST CITIES
A classic in its field written by an explorer following his seventh trip into the Amazon area (he vanished on his eighth trip). Book Club, 1974 (first published 1953).

Kelly, Brian and London, Mark   AMAZON
Colorful, evocative account of the frontier being developed and exploited by entrepreneurs. The book is based on a trip sponsored by the *Chicago Sun-Times* and calls to mind parallels in the expansion of our own Wild West. HarBraceJ, 1983.

MacKinnon, Jack   ANDES
Part of the World's Wild Places series. Time-Life, 1976.

Shoumatoff, Alex   THE RIVERS AMAZON
A multi-faceted travelogue of jungle life, flora and fauna for the lay naturalist, a stay in a village, a cross-country trek, and a search for the source of the Amazon. Sierra Club, 1978.

Sterling, Tom   THE AMAZON
Part of the World's Wild Places series. Time-Life, 1973.

Stone, Roger D.   DREAMS OF AMAZONIA
History, personal experiences and interviews to support the author's thesis that human nature has an "inevitable need to pursue the dream of a conquered land." (BL) Viking, 1985.

Tomlinson, H.M.   THE SEA AND THE JUNGLE
Firsthand account of a trip made in the early 1900s from Swansea, Wales, across the ocean, and up the Amazon for 2,000 miles—observations and yarns about shipmates. Dutton 1961 (first published 1912).

Turolla, Pino   BEYOND THE ANDES
High adventure and archaeological discoveries pursuing an educated hunch that the Amazon is the cradle of the western hemisphere's civilization. Har-Row, 1980.

**Werner, Dennis   AMAZON JOURNEY: AN ANTHROPOLOGIST'S YEAR
AMONG BRAZIL'S MEKRANOTI INDIANS**
Research among one of the few tribes that still preserves its traditional way of life—"a fascinating and charming work." (BL) S&S, 1984.

THE FALKLANDS

Bishop, Patrick and Witherow   **THE WINTER WAR: THE FALKLANDS CONFLICT**
Quartet, 1983.

Hastings, Max and Jenkins, Simon   **THE BATTLE FOR THE FALKLANDS**
Norton, 1983.

Strange, Ian J.   FALKLAND ISLANDS
All aspects of the islands—history, geography, wildlife, the people and their daily lives in the countryside—and updated to include the recent conflict. David, 1983.

GUIDEBOOKS

Jacobs, Charles & Babette   SOUTH AMERICAN TRAVEL DIGEST
Designed for travel agents—the "bible" on South America. Travel Digest, 1983.

Shichor, Michael   MICHAEL'S GUIDE TO SOUTH AMERICA
Hippocrene, 1984.

Taylor, Maurice   SOUTH AMERICAN SURVIVAL: HANDBOOK FOR THE INDEPENDENT TRAVELER
Outlines a circle itinerary. Gentry, 1982.

TRAVEL ARTICLES

ESSENCE
1984 Oct "Trekking Through the Amazon." Stephanie R. Hamilton, p. 54

ANTARCTICA

Background Reading

Adams, Richard and Lockley, Ronald   VOYAGE THROUGH THE ANTARCTIC
An account of a tour to Antarctica (and Argentina and New Zealand) by a naturalist (author of *Watership Down*), as part of a Lindblad *Explorer* tour—"a delightful book . . . a birdwatcher's dream." (PW) Knopf, 1982.

Bond, Creina   ANTARCTICA: NO SINGLE COUNTRY, NO SINGLE SEA
History of the explorations and the political realities of the Southern ocean. Mayflower, 1979.

Brewster, Barney   ANTARCTICA: WILDERNESS AT RISK
A plea to defend the area's fragile environment from exploitation. Friends of the Earth, 1982.

Byrd, Richard E.   ALONE
Island Pr, 1984 (first published 1938).

Cameron, Ian   ANTARCTICA
History of Antarctica from the Greeks to the 1950s—both entertaining and informative. Little, 1974.

Carter, Paul A.   LITTLE AMERICA: TOWN AT THE END OF THE WORLD
Readable history of the American base from the Byrd expeditions through 1959. Columbia U Pr, 1979.

Gould, Laurence M.   ANTARCTIC GOLD
Richard Byrd called this account of the Byrd expedition in 1929-30 "a story without parallel in Antarctic literature." (BRD) Brewer, 1931.

Halle, Louis J.   THE SEA AND THE ICE: A NATURALIST IN ANTARCTICA
Emphasis is on the birds. Houghton, 1973.

Harrington, Richard   RICHARD HARRINGTON'S ANTARCTIC
Based on three voyages of the Lindblad *Explorer* to the Antarctic, Falklands, South Georgia, South Orkneys—impressions and background histories. Alaska Northwest, 1976.

Langone, John   LIFE AT THE BOTTOM: THE PEOPLE OF ANTARCTICA
A journalist with the National Science Foundation's research teams gives his observations of researchers and other people—"manages to catch the texture of life . . . the strange animals and unusual people that cling to its icy skirts." (BRD) Little, 1977.

Lansing, Alfred   ENDURANCE: SHACKLETON'S INCREDIBLE VOYAGE
"Epic adventure of endurance, survival and heroism"—the 1914-17 expedition of the *Endurance*. (BRD) Granada, 1984 (first published 1959).

Mountfield, David   A HISTORY OF POLAR EXPLORATION
Illustrated history of explorations to both poles, and the reasons. Dial, 1974.

Neider, Charles   BEYOND CAPE HORN
By an author fascinated by Antarctica who wishes to humanize it—a combination of journal, history and excerpts from other books. Sierra Club, 1980. Also *Edge of the World: Ross Island, Antarctica* (1974), which describes two visits the author made in conjunction with the National Science Foundation and the United States Navy.

Parfit, Michael   SOUTH LIGHT: A JOURNEY TO THE LAST CONTINENT
An account of the author's adventurous visit to Antarctica—"exceptionally well told story . . . filled with humor and awe." (BL) Macmillan, 1986.

Porter, Eliot   ANTARCTICA
A leading photographer, selected by the National Science Foundation to join its expedition to Antarctica, narrates his experiences along with photographs that match his prose descriptions of this sixth continent." Dutton, 1978.

Reader's Digest, eds.   ANTARCTICA: GREAT STORIES FROM THE FROZEN CONTINENT
"Wonderful illustrations . . . provide the centerpiece for this captivating history of Antarctica." Geography, a chronology of explorations, and many other peripheral topics are covered, such as sled dogs, etc. (BL) Readers Digest Pr, 1985.

Shackleton, Ernest   SOUTH: THE STORY OF SHACKLETON'S LAST EXPEDITION
Hippocrene, 1983 (first published 1920).

Novels

Barjavel, Rene   THE ICE PEOPLE
Science fiction—a 900,000-year-old city discovered beneath Antarctica. Morrow, 1971.

Batchelor, John C.   THE BIRTH OF THE PEOPLE'S REPUBLIC OF ANTARCTICA
A band of Swedish exiles, at the end of the twentieth century, after epic voyages from the Baltic to the South Atlantic, flee to Antarctica where the group leader becomes a "berserker warlord." (FC) Dial, 1983.

Cameron, Ian   THE WHITE SHIP
A "ten little indians"-type story with a plot that involves a British research group tracking down legendary gold seals on an island in the Antarctic archipelago—"topnotch adventure; an expert blend of the factual with the fictional." (PW) Scribner, 1975.

Herbert, Marie   WINTER OF THE WHITE SEAL
Diary epic of a hero marooned on an island and the seal pup he befriends who, in turn, gives him the heart to persevere. Morrow, 1982.

Holt, Kare   THE FACE: A NOVEL OF POLAR EXPLORATION
Documentary novel about the race between Scott and Amundsen to reach the South Pole. Delacorte Pr, 1976.

Keneally, Thomas   VICTIM OF THE AURORA
Murder on an Antarctic expedition in 1910. HarBraceJ, 1978.

Sillitoe, Alan   THE LOST FLYING BOAT
An RAF bomber crew at the close of World War II unknowingly becomes part of a treasure hunt for gold buried beneath Antarctic ice. Little, 1984.

TRAVEL ARTICLES

NATIONAL GEOGRAPHIC
1984 Nov "Icebound in Antarctica." David Lewin, p. 634

N.Y. TIMES SUNDAY TRAVEL SECTION (X)
1985 Jun 9 "Sailing South to the Land of the Penguin." Antarctica's rare denizens—up close. Arthur M. Panzer, p. 9

READER'S DIGEST
1985 Nov "Journey to the Bottom of the World." John Dyson, p. 189

SMITHSONIAN
1984 Oct "Antarctica, the Last Continent." Michael Parfit, p. 48

TRAVEL/HOLIDAY
1985 Nov "Antarctica —a Modern Polar Adventure." Robert L. Sammons, p. 10

ARGENTINA

Series Guidebooks (See Appendix 1)

U.S. Government: **Area Handbook; Background Notes; Post Report**

Background Reading

Alexander, Robert J. **JUAN DOMINGO PERON**
An introduction to Peron's Argentina for the general reader. Westview Pr, 1979.

Chatwin, Bruce **IN PATAGONIA**
A collection of "good stories" of the region's past—"a work of travel, observation . . . learning, reflection and art." The author is a descendant of a British sea captain who lost his ship in the Strait of Magellan when that was the only way to go from the Atlantic to the Pacific. (BRD) Summit Bks, 1977. Also *Patagonia Revisited* (1985), with Paul Theroux.

Durrell, Gerald **THE WHISPERING LAND**
Animal lore, landscapes, Argentinian characters, recorded as the result of an eight-month photography safari. Penguin, 1975 (first published 1961).

Fraser, Nicholas and Navarro, Marysa **EVA PERON**
"Thoroughly researched and historically accurate . . . fascinating story of her life, achievements and shrewdness." (LJ) Norton, 1981.

Hudson, W.H.   FAR AWAY AND LONG AGO
An autobiography of Hudson's early years on the pampas of which he wrote colorfully later in essays and stories—"like a mixture of a Conrad novel and Robinson Crusoe." (BRD) Biblio Dist, 1976 (first published 1918).

Hudson, W.H.   IDLE DAYS IN PATAGONIA
Classic book by the naturalist of a journey on the Rio Negro to Patagonia. Creative Arts Bk, 1979 (first published 1917).

Peron, Eva Duarte   EVITA
Her own story. Proteus, 1978.

Simpson, George   ATTENDING MARVELS: A PATAGONIAN JOURNAL
A "genial and discursive narrative adventure" intended to supplement the author's scientific pursuits on a trip for collecting fossils. (BRD) U of Chicago, 1982 (first published 1934).

Sofer, Eugene F.   FROM PALE TO PAMPA
A social history of the Jewish residents of Buenos Aires. Holmes & Meier, 1982.

Taylor, Julie M.   EVA PERON, THE MYTHS OF A WOMAN
A serious examination of legends that surrounded Eva Peron during her life and after her death and the different interpretations of similar facts that resulted in her being seen as evil, as a "lady," as a feminist, a revolutionary, a mystic. U of Chicago, 1981.

HISTORY

Ferns, Henry S.   ARGENTINA
General, readable history that unravels the complex Argentinian politics. Praeger, 1973.

Pendle, George   ARGENTINA
A compact history from the sixteenth century. Gordon Pr, 1976 (first published 1956).

Novels

Bioy, Casares A.   ASLEEP IN THE SUN
"A fussy horror story with a science-fiction twist." (BRD) Persea Bks, 1978.

Borges, Jorge L.   SIX PROBLEMS FOR DON ISIDRO PARODI
Six detective stories written "as a challenge to the frenetic action of American detective stories [and] cold intellectualism of the British school." The detective is a prisoner unjustly accused of murder. (FC) Dutton, 1981 (first published 1942).

Borges, Jorge L.   BORGES: A READER
Selections from his writings that offer a good survey of early and late writing, prose and poetry. Dutton, 1981. Also, *A Personal Anthology* (1967), those writings on which Borges would like his reputation to rest.

Costantini, Humberto   THE GODS, THE LITTLE GUYS, AND THE POLICE
Involves a police plot to massacre a "sadly deluded poetry circle." On one level the novel is "whimsical fantasy [but] beneath the quirky humor lies a frightening picture of political terror." (FC) Har-Row, 1984.

Gould, Lois   LA PRESIDENTA
A woman comes to power through marriage—a novel that evokes Eva and Isabella Peron in an imaginary South American country. S&S, 1981.

Greene, Graham   THE HONORARY CONSUL
Story of political kidnapping that combines violent action with religious speculation. S&S, 1973.

Guiraldes, Ricardo   DON SEGUNDO SOMBRA
"A series of swift and brilliant impressions" of a legendary gaucho of the Argentine pampas told by a boy who works on a ranch and rides with Don Segundo. (BRD) Farrar, 1935.

Higgins, Jack   EXOCET
A novel about the war in the Falklands and the struggle by the Argentinians to obtain Exocet missiles. Stein & Day, 1983.

Hudson, W.H.   TALES OF THE PAMPAS
Short stories—"marvelous and thrilling tales" by the English naturalist. (FC) Knopf, 1916.

Langley, Bob   FALKLANDS GAMBIT
The politics and people of the Falklands and Argentina's attempt to annex it—"portraits of Falklanders as 'more British than the British,' piercing glimpses of Antarctica's beauty and valid political points about Antarctic oil." (PW) Walker, 1985.

Llewellyn, Richard   UP INTO THE SINGING MOUNTAIN
Sequel to *How Green Was My Valley* (under "Wales")—a Welshman's new life in Patagonia. Doubleday, 1960.

Ludlum, Robert   THE RHINEMANN EXCHANGE
A novel that "has everything—espionage, professional killing, the Gestapo, the German High Command, Zionists. . . . romance too." (FC) Dial, 1974.

Onetti, Juan Carlos   THE SHIPYARD
Having been expelled five years earlier, the main character returns to manage a once prosperous shipyard—evokes futility and hopelessness. Scribner, 1968.

Puig, Manuel   KISS OF THE SPIDER WOMAN
Prison story of two men (one a homosexual; the other a revolutionary) whose "disparate dreams . . . are shared as they arrive at a strong—though dangerous—friendship." (FC) Knopf, 1979.

Puig, Manuel   HEARTBREAK TANGO
An unorthodox account of a woman's life revealing the character of the man she loved through newspaper clippings, picture albums, diary notes and her correspondence with a Lonely Hearts column. Dutton, 1973.

Puig, Manuel   BUENOS AIRES AFFAIR: A DETECTIVE NOVEL
Study of two people "disabled by indifferent or perverse parenting." (BRD) Dutton, 1976.

Puig, Manuel   BETRAYED BY RITA HAYWORTH
Toto—"born in 1932 in the bleakest flatland pampas of the Argentine"—and his friends are compulsive moviegoers who talk about their own lives through films. (FC) Dutton, 1971.

Sabato, Ernesto   ON HEROES AND TOMBS
A serious novel by an Argentinian physicist/writer, set in the early years of Peron. Godine, 1981 (first published 1961).

TRAVEL ARTICLES

ESQUIRE
1984 May "A Trout for All Seasons." Fishing for trout in four seasons on different continents. Argentina is spring. p. 33

N.Y. TIMES SUNDAY TRAVEL SECTION (X)
1985 Jun 23 Fare of the Country: "Teatime, a Bit of Britain in Argentina." Lydia Chavez, p. 12
Oct 20 "What's Doing in Buenos Aires." Lydia Chavez, p. 10
1984 Mar 4 "Journeying Through Patagonia." Touring the austere southern Argentine region of Tierra del Fuego. Edward Schumacher, p. 12
May 20 "Summer Abroad: the ABCs of Going with Children." Sixteen foreign correspondents and contributors to *The Times* offer tips on touring their corners of the world (includes Argentina). p. 21
Sep 9 "What's Doing in Buenos Aires." Edward Schumacher, p. 10.

TRAVEL/HOLIDAY
1985 Jan "Offbeat Ski Resorts." Includes Argentina. Ken Castle, p. 46

BOLIVIA

Series Guidebooks (See Appendix 1)

Nagel: **Bolivia**
U.S. Government: **Area Handbook; Background Notes**

Background Reading

Note: See also the several books on the Incas and archaeology under "Peru."

Anstee, Margaret J.   BOLIVIA: GATE OF THE SUN
The author served for six years as head of UN aid programs in Bolivia and fell in love with the country. "A fascinating travel-log by a very perceptive writer" that conveys the geographical diversity, the atmosphere of everyday life, and idiosyncrasies of people. Eriksson, 1971.

McEwen, William J.   CHANGING RURAL SOCIETY
A study of changes in six varied communities because of the revolution in 1952. Oxford U, 1975.

Nash, June   WE EAT THE MINES AND THE MINES EAT US
An anthropological study of a tin-mining town from its "mythological past to the . . . 1952 revolution"—family life, values, and religious and ritual beliefs. (BRD) Columbia U, 1979.

Nouwen, Henri J.M.   GRACIAS! A LATIN AMERICAN JOURNAL
Account of a six-month stay in Bolivia and Peru by a Dutch theologian who lived among the people. Har-Row, 1983.

GUIDEBOOKS

Meisch, Lynn   A TRAVELER'S GUIDE TO EL DORADO AND THE INCA EMPIRE
See under "Peru/Guidebooks."

HISTORY

Alexander, Robert J.   BOLIVIA: PAST, PRESENT AND FUTURE OF THE POLITICS
Praeger, 1982.

Novels

Pausewang, Gudrun   BOLIVIAN WEDDING
The events of a single All Soul's Day in a Bolivian mountain town. Knopf, 1972.

TRAVEL ARTICLES

N.Y. TIMES SUNDAY TRAVEL SECTION (X)
1985 Jan 27 "Touring La Paz: Up and Down Walking Guide." Mt. Illimanni is its
     21,000-foot landmark. Peter McFarren, p. 19
1984 Nov 11 Fare of the Country: "Bolivian Staple—Spicy Saltenas." p. 12

BRAZIL

Series Guidebooks (See Appendix 1)

Berlitz: Rio de Janeiro
Country Orientation Update: Brazil
Fodor: Brazil
Nagel: Brazil
U.S. Government: Background Notes; Country Study; Post Report

Background Reading

Botting, Douglas   RIO DE JANEIRO
Part of the Great Cities of the World series. Time-Life, 1978.

Cunha, Enclides da   REBELLION IN THE BACKLANDS
A study of the 1896 rebellion—"considered Brazil's literary classic . . . comes close to being the universal Latin American classic." (BRD) U of Chicago, 1944 (first published 1902).

Dos Passos, John   BRAZIL ON THE MOVE
The American novelist spoke Portuguese and visited Brazil in 1948, 1956 and 1962. This is his report on Brasilia at each stage—"gives the feel of Brazil's wondrously contrasting landscapes." (BRD) Greenwood, 1974 (first published 1963).

Draeger, Alain   BRAZIL
Candid discussion of the cultural diversity, stresses of a multiracial society, pagan cults and growth pains of this immense country. Overlook Pr, 1980.

Fleming, Peter   BRAZILIAN ADVENTURE
Class British travel book of the 1930s of an expedition to Brazil—"it became an adventure for which Rider Haggard might have written the plot, P.G. Wodehouse supplied the characters, and Joseph Conrad designed the scenery." (BRD) Tarcher, 1983 (first published 1933).

Freyre, Gilberto   THE MANSIONS AND THE SHANTIES
Social history—Freyre's writings are given credit for the creation of a national identity in Brazil. Greenwood, 1980 (first published 1963). Also *The Masters and the Slaves* (1964), *The Gilberto Freyre Reader* (1974).

Goldman, Albert   CARNIVAL IN RIO
Preparations for, proceedings, and the follow-up of the pre-Lenten carnival and extravaganza. Hawthorn Bks, 1978.

Parks, Gordon   FLAVIO
The prominent American photographer did a photographic essay on a young boy in Rio in the 1960s. This book picks up Flavio's story sixteen years later. Norton, 1978.

Rodman, Selden   THE BRAZIL TRAVELER
Background history for travelers, people and culture, with emphasis on the arts. Devin, 1975.

Shoumatoff, Alex   THE CAPITAL OF HOPE
The story of Brasilia, its people, politics, economic rigors, flora, fauna, climate and architecture. The author, who married into a Brazilian family in the course of doing this book, "wears his knowledge lightly [and] conveys his own sense of wonder" at the creation of the city. (BRD) Coward, 1980. Also *In Southern Light*, see under "Central Africa."

Waugh, Evelyn   NINETY-TWO DAYS
See under "Guianas."

GUIDEBOOKS

Greenberg, Arnold and Harriet   RIO ALIVE
Complete traveler's guide to the best in Rio and Brazil. Alive Pbns, 1979.

HISTORY

Burns, E. Bradford   A HISTORY OF BRAZIL
Updated version of a standard history. Columbia U, 1980.

Novels

Alegria, Ciro   THE GOLDEN SERPENT
Story of primitive Indian life on the Maranon River, and a white engineer who comes to make his fortune. FS&G, 1935.

Amado, Jorge   TEREZA BATISTA: HOME FROM THE WARS
One of many novels by this author that provide insights for the traveler into
Latin American culture—"the warmth, gaiety and romance of an Amado novel are
always a special treat." Knopf, 1975. Other titles set in Brazil are: *Tieta the Goat
Girl* (1979), *Tent of Miracles* (1971), *Dona Flor and Her Two Husbands* (1969),
Gabriela Clove and Cinnamon (1962), *Shepherds of the Night* (1967) and *Home
is the Sailor* (1964).

Castro, Josue de   OF MEN AND CRABS
The "miseries, poverty, disease and hunger of rural Brazil." (BRD) Vanguard,
1971.

Chatwin, Bruce   THE VICEROY OF OUIDAH
Slave traders in the nineteenth century. Summit Bks, 1980.

Courter, Gay   RIVER OF DREAMS
A young American from New Orleans sets off to join her parents—a saga that
captures the atmosphere and spirit of post-civil war Brazil and "large chunks of
Brazilian history." (FC) Houghton, 1984.

Dourado, Autran   THE VOICES OF THE DEAD
The state of Minas Gerais in the eighteenth century is the setting for this novel of
a recluse and the jack-of-all-trades who wanders into her life. Taplinger, 1981.

Doyle, Sir Arthur Conan   THE LOST WORLD
Four Englishmen come across a region in the Amazon Valley still in the
prehistoric period. Doran, 1912.

Geld, Ellen B.   THE GARLIC TREE
Life on a Brazilian *fazenda*—a New England girl in Mato Grosso with her
Brazilian husband. "What Edna Ferber did for Texas [*Giant*] Ellen Geld does here
for the Mato Grosso." (BRD) Doubleday, 1970.

Jaffe, Rona   AWAY FROM HOME
A novel about a colony of young American couples in Brazil in connection with
business careers and with too much time on their hands, problems, discon-
tent—"vivid description" of Rio. (BRD) S&S, 1960.

Levin, Ira   THE BOYS FROM BRAZIL
An organization of ex-Nazis tries to establish a Fourth Reich—"good, clean
horror." (FC) Random, 1976.

Lins Do Rego, Jose   PLANTATION BOY
Part of the sugar cane cycle of novels by this author, begun in the 1930s. Knopf,
1966.

Machado de Assis, Joachim Maria   ESAU AND JACOB
By a leading nineteenth-century Brazilian writer—a novel of social criticism
about the rivaly of twin brothers at the end of the Brazilian empire. Also *Epitaph of*

a Small Winner (1881) and *Helena* (1876). U of California, 1965 (first published in 1904).

MacLean, Alistair   RIVER OF DEATH
Set in the Mato Grosso area of Brazil—an "introspective hero guides a motley crew through awful perils to a 'lost city.'" (FC) Doubleday, 1982.

Matthiessen, Peter   AT PLAY IN THE FIELDS OF THE LORD
Four fundamentalist missionaries try to convert the primitive Indians in Oriente province—"the author shines as a naturalist and a storyteller." (BRD) Random, 1965.

Meyer, Nicholas   BLACK ORCHID
Suspenseful adventure novel of the late 1800s; a soldier of fortune seeks to break the monopoly two families have on rubber plantations. Dial, 1977.

Pryce-Jones, Alan   HOT PLACES
Three novelettes set in Brazil, Chile and Ecuador—"packed with local color." (BRD) Knopf, 1933.

Ribeiro, Joao Ubaldo   SERGEANT GETULIO
Psychological study of a killer and his assignnment to capture one of his employer's political enemies. Houghton, 1978.

Rosa, Joao Guimaraes   THE DEVIL TO PAY IN THE BACKLANDS
Lawless armed bands who fought each other, and the military, in the Brazilian northwest at the turn of the century. Knopf, 1963.

Souza, Marcio   THE EMPEROR OF THE AMAZON
Picaresque novel based on an 1899 revolution in northern Brazil in which a Spanish adventurer sets himself up as emperor. Avon, 1980.

Steiner, George   THE PORTAGE TO SAN CRISTOBAL OF A.H.
Hitler is not dead, in this novel, but alive in the Mato Grosso swamp, where he is tracked down by Nazi hunters. S&S, 1982.

Uys, Errol Lincoln   BRAZIL
Saga, over five centuries, of two remarkable families, and the history of Brazil. S&S, 1986.

Vargas Llosa, Mario   THE WAR OF THE END OF THE WORLD
Based on a bizarre, but true, uprising in northern Brazil at the turn of the century—"brilliant panorama of the forces great and small which fuel a revolution." (FC) FS&G, 1984.

Vasconcelos, Jose Mauro de   MY SWEET ORANGE TREE
The life and times of a five-year-old shoeshine boy and philosopher and his struggle for survival—a Brazilian best-seller in its day. Knopf, 1971.

TRAVEL ARTICLES

AMERICAS
1985 Oct "Jaugada Sails in the Sunset." Boats from Brazil's past work as fishing craft, delight tourists. Clodagh and Daniel Aubry, p. 42
1984 Jan-Feb "Saucy Salvador, a Brazilian Port Flaunts its History." Carrie Topliffe, p. 14
       Nov-Dec "Brazil's Past and Future Coexist Happily in Sao Luis." Jo Ann Hein, p. 10

GOURMET
1984 Oct Gourmet Holidays: "Bahia." Geri Trotta, p. 40

NATIONAL GEOGRAPHIC
1984 May "Indians Cursed by Gold." Vanessa Lea and Miguel R. Branco, p. 675

NATIONAL GEOGRAPHIC TRAVELER
1985 Spring "Rio—Carnival to a Samba Beat." Loren McIntyre, p. 86

N.Y. TIMES SUNDAY TRAVEL SECTION (X)
1985 Mar 17 (Part 2, "Sophisticated Traveler") "Lively Heart of Old Rio." Marlise Simons, p. 18
       Mar 24 "Golden Cities of Minas Gerais . . ." A treasury of baroque art and architecture. Fernando Sabino, p. 14
       "Brazilian City with African Echoes . . ." Bahia embodies her country's dramatic past. Marlise Simons, p. 15
       "Afloat in an Exotic Wilderness." Wildlife fanciers are discovering the Pantanal, a vast wetland in the continent's heart. Alan Riding, p. 16
       Nov 17 "What's Doing in Rio de Janeiro." Marlise Simons, p. 10
1984 May 29 "What's Doing in Rio de Janeiro." Alan Riding, p. 10
       Oct 7 (Part 2, "Sophisticated Traveler") "Brazilian Potpourri." Feijoada and Bahian treats. Craig Claiborne, p. 92; "Carioca Fin de Siecle." Marisa Simons, p. 18
       Nov 18 Shopper's World: "Handmade Lace in the Brazilian Style." Annette E. Dumbach, p. 6

TRAVEL & LEISURE
1985 Nov "Latest from Rio." Abby Rand, p. 59
       Dec "Buzios—the Sexiest Beach Resort in Brazil." Christopher Cox, p. 110
1984 May "Summer Festival in Brazil." An American priest looks at a stirring spectacle that is partly religious—mostly carnival. Andrew M. Greely, p. 182
       Dec "Brazil's Ouro Preto, an Extraordinary Enclave of Baroque Architecture." Teri Agins, p. 152

TRAVEL/HOLIDAY
1984 Feb "Rio de Janeiro—Carnival." Anton Angelick, p. 62
       Nov "Laidback in Bahia." Time out in Brazil. Patricia Brooks, p. 52

VOGUE
1985 Mar "Bahia: Brazil's Most Exotic City." Tracy Young, p. 418
       Nov "Paraty—Brazil's Best Kept Secret." Richard Alleman, p. 318
1984 Feb "The Rio thing!" In a world filled with beautiful beaches, there's still no
       place like Rio, p. 274

WORLD PRESS REVIEW
1984 Mar "Discovering Buenos Aires." The passions of Latin America's "European
       city." (*Jornal do Brasil*, Rio De Janeiro), Heliete Vaitsman, p. 62

CHILE

Series Guidebooks (See Appendix 1)

U.S. Government: **Background Notes; Country Study; Post Report**

Background Reading

Edwards, Agustin   MY NATIVE LAND
Chilean reminiscences, folklore, panorama, writers. Gordon Pr, 1976.

Putigny, Bob   EASTER ISLAND
Discovery by the Dutch of the mysterious statues of Easter Island, and current
life there. Two Continents, 1976.

Roxborough, Ian   CHILE: THE STATE AND REVOLUTION
Review of politics to 1970, formation of the Allende government, its end in
1973, and the aftermath. Holmes & Maier, 1977.

HISTORY

Loveman, Brian   CHILE
Oxford U, 1979.

Novels

Cameron, Ian   THE MOUNTAINS AT THE BOTTOM OF THE WORLD
Science fiction—the search for survivors of prehistoric man. Morrow, 1972.

Donoso, Jose   THE OBSCENE BIRD OF NIGHT
The "fading social order of a once-great Chilean estate." (FC) Knopf, 1973.

Pryce-Jones, Alan   HOT PLACES
Three novelettes set in Brazil, Chile and Ecuador—"packed with local color." (BRD) Knopf, 1933.

TRAVEL ARTICLES

GOURMET
1985 Dec "Santiago de Chili." Geri Trotta, p. 46

TRAVEL/HOLIDAY
1984 Aug "Ski Chile - Winter Sports South of the Equator." Thomas Traska, p. 18

COLOMBIA

Series Guidebooks (See (Appendix 1)

U.S. Government: Area Handbook; Background Notes; Post Report

See also the several books on Incas and archaeology under "Peru."

Background Reading

Moser, Brian   THE COCAINE EATERS
"Half way between serious ethnography and light travel literature"—customs, ceremonies of Colombian Indians, described by an anthropologist and geologist. (BRD) Taplinger, 1967.

Nicholl, Charles   THE FRUIT PALACE
A portrait of Colombia told by an author sent there to infiltrate and write about the drug traffic. St. Martin, 1986.

Niles, B.   COLOMBIA
History, legend, traditions—"impressionistic and successful in conveying the spirit and personality" of the country. (BRD) Gordon Pr, 1976 (first published 1924).

Rodman, Selden   THE COLOMBIA TRAVELER
History, people, culture, emphasis on the arts, in addition to the usual travel guide information. Devin, 1971.

Von Hagen, Victor   THE GOLDEN MAN: QUEST FOR EL DORADO
The legend that the treasure was in Colombia—saga of adventure. Book Club, 1974.

GUIDEBOOKS

Meisch, Lynn   A TRAVELER'S GUIDE TO EL DORADO AND THE INCA EMPIRE
See under "Peru/Guidebooks."

HISTORY

Galbraith, W.O.   COLOMBIA
Gordon Pr, 1976 (first published 1966).

Novels

Garcia Marquez, Gabriel   ONE HUNDRED YEARS OF SOLITUDE
Saga of an "exotic" clan over seven generations that "suggests the mythical development of civilization from Creation to the 20th century." This novel, which won the Nobel Prize for literature in 1982, is one of several set in the mythical town of Macondo (Aracataca, in the Magdalena state of Colombia). Har-Row, 1970. Also *In Evil Hour* (1979), and short story collections, *No One Writes to the Colonel* (1968), *Leaf Storm* (1972), *Collected Stories* (1984). For Marquez fans, Bradt Enterprises in Cambridge, Massachusetts, offers a map in color "with Aracataca precisely located."

Garcia Marquez, Gabriel   THE AUTUMN OF THE PATRIARCH
The last years of a dictator told with "hypnotic and brilliant . . . use of language." (PW) Har-Row, 1976.

Garcia Marquez, Gabriel   CHRONICLE OF A DEATH FORETOLD
A novella set in a Colombian town reconstructing an actual episode in which the entire town stood by and did nothing while two drunks planned, announced and carried out a murder. Knopf, 1983.

TRAVEL ARTICLES

AMERICAS
1984 Jan-Feb "Beyond the Gallery Wall." Billboard Art Museum in Roldanillo. Agueda Pizarro, p. 9
Mar-Apr "Triumphant Cartagena." Old charms, new energy and much, much more for tourists. Claire Walter, p. 6

BLACK ENTERPRISE
1985 Mar "Cartagena." Where African traditions thrive and Colombia's hottest night spots sizzle. p. 80

N.Y. TIMES SUNDAY TRAVEL SECTION (X)
1985 May 26 Shopper's World: "The Handicrafts of Colombia." Jan Shannon, p. 12

SMITHSONIAN
1985 Mar "How an Earthquake Brought to Light the Opulent Treasure of Popayan." One of the world's great ecclesiastical art collections. Neil Letson and Peter C. Keller, p. 139

ECUADOR

Series Guidebooks (See Appendix 1)

U.S. Government: **Area Handbook; Background Notes; Post Report**
Lonely Planet: **Ecuador & Galapagos**

Note: See also the several books on Incas and archaeology under "Peru."

Brooks, Rhoda and Earle   THE BARRIOS OF MANTA
Personal account of the Peace Corps in Ecuador and two people transplanted into a totally new environment. NAL, 1965.

Cousteau, Jacques-Yves   THREE ADVENTURES: GALAPAGOS, TITICACA, THE BLUE HOLES
Exploration of the Galapagos archipelago by the noted marine explorer. A&W, 1978 (first published 1973).

Harner, Michael J.   THE JIVARO: PEOPLE OF THE SACRED WATERFALLS
Study of unique, bizarre Indian people famous for witchcraft. U of California, 1983 (first published 1972).

Moore, Tui de Roy   GALAPAGOS: ISLANDS LOST IN TIME
"Evokes one of the most haunting landscapes on earth"—reminiscences of the author's childhood on the islands. (TL) Viking, 1983.

Wingate, Richard   LOST OUTPOST OF ATLANTIS
Everett Hse, 1980.

GUIDEBOOKS

Meisch, Lynn   A TRAVELER'S GUIDE TO EL DORADO AND THE INCA EMPIRE
See under "Peru/Guidebooks."

Novels

Icazu, J.   THE VILLAGERS: HUASIPUNGO
Peasant life in Ecuador. Arcturus, 1973.

Pryce-Jones, Alan   HOT PLACES
Three novelettes set in Chile, Brazil and Ecuador—"packed with excellent local color." (BRD) Knopf, 1933.

TRAVEL ARTICLES

AMERICAS
1985 Nov-Dec "A Tradition of Ecuadorian Textiles." Weavers near Otavio carry on the craft of their ancestors. Rob Rachowiecki, p. 34
1984 Nov-Dec "Preserving the Enchanted Isles." Super-guides in the Galapagos do more than herd tourists. Kim Heacox, p. 2

N.Y. TIMES SUNDAY TRAVEL SECTION (X)
1985 Mar 17 (Part 2, "Sophisticated Traveler") "Where Birds and Beasts Bewitch (Galapagos)." William F. Buckley, Jr., p. 90
1984 Jan 22 "City at the Middle of the World." Quito is just south of the equator and nearly two miles high. Tom Miller, p. 19

TRAVEL & LEISURE
1985 Mar "The Ancient Mysteries of Easter Island." Or why are those stone monoliths standing guard on a rock in the middle of the Pacific? Geri Trotta, p. 183
      Jul "Back to Nature in the Amazon Jungle." A riverboat trip through the watery wilds of Ecuador. Patti Hagan, p. 44
      Sep "Close Encounters in the Galapagos." David Attenborough, p. 108
      "Traveler's Guide to the Galapagos." Carla Hunt, p. 116

TRAVEL/HOLIDAY
1984 Mar "Darwin's Eden." Exploring the Galapagos Islands. Barbara Sleeper, p. 76

THE GUIANAS (French Guiana, Guyana, Surinam)

Series Guidebooks (See Appendix 1)

U.S. Goverment: French Antilles & Guiana: Background Notes
                   Guyana: Area Handbook; Background Notes; Post Report
                   Surinam: Background Notes

Background Reading

Attenborough, David   THE ZOO QUEST EXPEDITIONS: TRAVELS IN GUYANA, INDONESIA & PARAGUAY
An account of three animal-collecting expeditions. Penguin, 1983.

Naipaul, Shiva   JOURNEY TO NOWHERE: A NEW WORLD TRAGEDY
"Most thoughtfully wrought" of the Jim Jones/Jamestown books—the "profile of Guyana is a disturbing study of a fraudulent republic . . . the picture of the charismatic Jones [is] bone-chilling." (BL) S&S, 1981.

Naipaul, V.S.   THE MIDDLE PASSAGE
See under "Latin America."

Waugh, Evelyn   NINETY-TWO DAYS
Travelogue of a journey from Georgetown, British Guiana (now Surinam), to Brazil at a time when the area was little known to travelers—"lucid and fascinating picture of places and people." (BRD) FS&G, 1934.

HISTORY

Goslinga, Cornelis   A SHORT HISTORY OF THE NETHERLANDS ANTILLES & SURINAM
Kinwer, 1978.

Smith, Raymond   BRITISH GUIANA
Natural resources, history, social structure of the country that is now Surinam. Greenwood Pr, 1980 (first published 1962).

Novels

Coxe, George H.   DOUBLE IDENTITY
A pilot on his way to Surinam meets a fellow passenger on the plane who is his "double" and who is later found dead. Knopf, 1970.

Mittelholzer, Edgar   CHILDREN OF KAYWANA
"Sensuous and violent historical novel [of the van Groenwegel family]—a witches' brew of untamed sex and brutality." (BRD) Day, 1952.

Voorhoeve, Jan and Lichtveld, Ursy M., eds.   CREOLE DRUM
An anthology of Creole literature in Surinam. Yale U Pr, 1975.

PARAGUAY

Series Guidebooks (See Appendix 1)

U.S. Government: Background Notes; Post Report

Background Reading

Attenborough, David   THE ZOO QUEST EXPEDITIONS: TRAVELS IN GUYANA, INDONESIA & PARAGUAY
An account of three animal-collecting expeditions. Penguin, 1983.

Caraman, Philip   THE LOST PARADISE
Story of the Jesuits in Paraguay, 1607-1768, when they established a thriving utopian republic of thirty villages, 140,000 people, organized on a communal basis. It was finally destroyed by the Spaniards. The author "lovingly resurrects it and creates a surprising picture of South American life in the distant past." (BRD) Seabury, 1976.

Warren, Harris G.   PARAGUAY
An informal history and introduction to Paraguay that tells much "about a tragically unimportant country . . . memorable pages on wandering Spaniards, Portuguese, Americans [and] the curious diplomats from Washington." (BRD) Greenwood Pr, 1982 (first published 1949).

HISTORY

Harris, G.   PARAGUAY: AN INFORMAL HISTORY
Greenwood, 1982

Pendle, George   PARAGUAY: A RIVERSIDE NATION
Gordon Pr, 1976 (first published 1954).

Novels

Lieberman, Herbert   THE CLIMATE OF HELL
Suspense story with a chase through the "hell" of the Paraguayan jungle. The plot involves former Nazis who are being protected by the Paraguayan government. S&S, 1978.

TRAVEL ARTICLES

N.Y. TIMES SUNDAY TRAVEL SECTION (X)
1985 Nov 3 "Ten Hours from Asuncion." Filadelfia, a Mennonite settlement. Edwin McDowell, p. 18

PERU

Series Guidebooks (See Appendix 1)

Nagel: Peru
U.S. Government: Background Notes; Country Study; Post Report

Background Reading

Bingham, Hiram   LOST CITY OF THE INCAS: THE STORY OF MACHU PICCHU AND ITS BUILDERS
A summing up of archaeological labors of expeditions to Machu Picchu. Greenwood, 1981 (first published 1948). Also *Machu Picchu, A Citadel of the Incas* (1930), which gives an overall picture of archaeological procedures, historical significance, and the excitement of the search.

Clark, Leonard F.   RIVERS RAN EAST
The exploration into Grand Pajonal and the search for the seven cities of Cibola. Funk, 1953.

Engel, Frederic Andre   AN ANCIENT WORLD PRESERVED
"Highly readable, informative, archaeologically current" account of Andean prehistory; places the Incan achievements in perspective in comparison to other ancient cultures. (BRD) Crown, 1977.

Flornoy, Bertrand   THE WORLD OF THE INCA
Vivid picture of the Inca world until it was destroyed in 1532—"wonderful for the reader who heads for Peru." (BRD) Vanguard, 1956.

Hemming, John and Ranney, Edward   MONUMENTS OF THE INCAS
Introduction to a great lost nation through concise text and photographs of the towns and temples built 500 years ago. Little, 1982.

Hemming, John   MACHU PICCHU
The rediscovery of Machu Picchu by Hiram Bingham in 1911 is recreated. Newsweek Bks, 1981.

McIntyre, Loren   THE INCREDIBLE INCAS AND THEIR TIMELESS LAND
Natl Geog, 1975.

Morrison, Tony   PATHWAYS TO THE GODS
Written for a BBC documentary by a science reporter—a search for the meaning of the Andes lines on Peru's Nasca Plain. Har-Row, 1979.

Nouwen, Henri J.M.   GRACIAS! A LATIN AMERICAN JOURNAL
See under "Bolivia."

Poma de Ayala, Felipe   LETTER TO A KING
A Peruvian chief's account of life under the Incas and under Spanish rule.
Dutton, 1978.

Schneebaum, Tobias   KEEP THE RIVER ON YOUR RIGHT
An encounter by an American artist in Peru studying painting with the Indians
he wanted to paint—"introspective, wholly engaging adventure." (BRD) Grove,
1969.

Wachtel, Nathan   THE VISION OF THE VANQUISHED
The Spanish conquest of Peru through Indian eyes, 1530-1570—Indian sources
provide the Indian perspective. Barnes & Noble, 1977.

Wright, Ronald   CUT STONES AND CROSSROADS
"Enticing melange of archaeological fieldwork and exotic travel experiences . . .
in search of ancient Inca ruins. . . . fascinating personal chronicle of research and
travel." (BL) Viking, 1984.

GUIDEBOOKS

Frost, Peter   EXPLORING CUZCO
Includes surrounding area, Machu Picchu, Chinchero, Moray, Vilcabamba
Mountains—description and practical tourist information on accommodations,
food, shopping, etc. Bradt, 1984.

**Meisch, Lynn   A TRAVELER'S GUIDE TO EL DORADO AND THE INCA
EMPIRE**
"A superbly practical guide to the four Incan countries [Bolivia, Colombia,
Ecuador, Peru] . . . stupendously detailed and culturally informed." Chapters on
native handicrafts, fiestas, marketplaces, museums, food, etc. (NYTBR) Penguin,
1984.

HISTORY

Alba, Victor   PERU
Emphasis on the twentieth century and period since the 1968 revolution.
Westview Pr, 1977.

Dobyns, Henry F.   PERU: A CULTURAL HISTORY
Includes a selective guide to the literature of Peru. Oxford U, 1976.

Hemming, John   THE CONQUEST OF THE INCAS
History from Pizarro's first push down the west coast to the execution of the last
Incan ruler. HarBraceJ, 1973.

Martin, Luis   THE KINGDOM OF THE SUN: A SHORT HISTORY OF PERU
Scribner, 1974.

Werlich, David P.   PERU: A SHORT HISTORY
For both general reader and scholar. Southern Illinois U, 1978.

Novels

Alegria, Ciro   THE GOLDEN SERPENT
Incidents of Indian life on the Maranon River, and a classic novel. FS&G, 1943. Also *Broad and Alien is the World* (1941) about life in an Indian mountain village.

Arguedas, Jose Maria   DEEP RIVERS
A white boy's relationship with the Indians and how it helps him to cope with the realities of life. U of Texas, 1979.

Vargas Llosa, Mario   AUNT JULIA AND THE SCRIPTWRITER
A student who is a newswriter for a radio station in Lima falls in love with his older aunt (by marriage), which develops into a scandalous affair and marriage. FS&G, 1982.

Vargas Llosa, Mario   CONVERSATION IN THE CATHEDRAL
An experimental novel set in contemporary Peru and dealing with corruption, decay and terror. Har-Row, 1975.

Vargas Llosa, Mario   CAPTAIN PANTOJA AND THE SPECIAL SERVICE
A satire on the Peruvian army and its official prostitution corps. Har-Row, 1978. Other earlier novels by this author include: *The Green House* (1968), *The Time of the Hero* (1966).

Wilder, Thornton   THE BRIDGE OF SAN LUIS REY
The classic novel by a leading American novelist that won a Pulitzer Prize in 1928. It's set in Peru, 200 years ago; five travelers are killed when a bridge built by the Incas collapses. A Franciscan brother then retells their five individual life stories to prove that the accident "was the culmination of a finite pattern . . . according to God's plan" rather than an accident. (FC) Har-Row, 1967 (first published 1927).

TRAVEL ARTICLES

AMERICAS
1985 Nov "A Collection of Peruvian Crafts." Folk arts from all over Peru in the town of Cuzco. Peter Frost, p. 28

ESSENCE
1984 Jan "Cuzco: A South American Delight." Stephanie R. Hamilton, p. 30

N.Y. TIMES SUNDAY TRAVEL SECTION (X)
1985 Jun 9 "The Might of Machu Picchu." Getting to the Inca ruins is somewhat arduous, but it's worth the journey. Barbaralee Diamonstein, p. 19
1984 Apr 15 "Trek to Machu Picchu." Hardy hikers visit Incan ruins. Joan Ambrose-Newton, p. 26

TRAVEL & LEISURE
1984 Nov "The White City of Peru." Beautiful Arequipa, high in the Andes, where it's springtime year round. Marilyn Green, p. 52

URUGUAY

Series Guidebooks (See Appendix 1)

U.S. Government: Area Handbook; Background Notes; Post Report

Background Reading

Alisky, Marvin   URUGUAY
"A pleasant survey of Uruguayan society [in] light and readable style"—social structure, physical setting, culture, government of Latin America's "Switzerland." (BRD) Praeger, 1969.

Fitzgibbon, Russell H.   URUGUAY
General survey for the layman—history, politics, the arts. Allen Unwin, 1954.

Novels

Benedetti, Mario   TRUCE
A novel in the form of a journal written by a widowed accountant who falls in love with his young assistant. Har-Row, 1970.

Hudson, W.H.   THE PURPLE LAND
Pseudo-gothic mystery romance—"portrayal of the beauty of nature and the romance of native customs in a strange land." (FC) AMS, 1968 (first published 1885).

Onetti, Juan Carlos   A BRIEF LIFE
A major serious novel by one of Uruguay's leading writers and set in the imaginary town of Santa Maria. A man "begins retreating from reality . . . until he is living simultaneously in two fantasy worlds." (BRD) Grossman, 1976.

[NO ARTICLES]

VENEZUELA

Background Reading (See Appendix 1)

Country Orientation Series
Update: Venezuela
U.S. Government: Area Handbook; Background Notes; Post Report

Background Reading

Betancourt, Romulo   VENEZUELA: OIL AND POLITICS
By the ex-president of the country—the role of oil in making Venezuela a viable democracy. Houghton, 1979 (first published 1956).

Donner, Florinda   SHABONO
"Lush, florid" report on an anthropologist's study of Indian healers and shamans. (PW) Delacorte Pr, 1982.

Lieuwen, Edwin   VENEZUELA
"Brief, skilfull overview." (BRD) Oxford U, 1962.

Marsland, William   VENEZUELA THROUGH ITS HISTORY
A combination of general information and history—"full of action . . . studded with melodrama . . . peopled with authentic history." (BRD) Greenwood Pr, 1976 (first published 1954).

Wilcock, John   TRAVELING IN VENEZUELA
More akin to James Michener's *Iberia* than to an ordinary guidebook, a fascinating compendium of history, culture, politics with each area (including Caracas) described. Also the usual practical travel information on hotels, etc. Hippocrene, 1979.

GUIDEBOOKS

Greenberg, Arnold and Harriet   VENEZUELA ALIVE and CARACAS ALIVE
Alive Pbns, 1979.

HISTORY

Ewell, Judith   VENEZUELA: A CENTURY OF CHANGE
Stanford U., 1984.

Lombardi, John V.   VENEZUELA: THE SEARCH FOR ORDER, THE DREAM OF PROGRESS
Oxford U, 1982.

Moron, Guillermo   A HISTORY OF VENEZUELA
Narrative history for the general reader, from early history to the 1960s. Allen Unwin, 1964.

Novels

Hudson, W.H.   GREEN MANSIONS
Tale of the tropical forests of southern Venezuela where a political outcast, seeking solitude and the primitive life of the forest, falls in love with Rima, the Indian bird girl. AMS, 1968 (first published 1893).

L'Engle, Madeleine   DRAGONS IN THE WATERS
A mystery with a complicated plot involving the return of a portrait of Simon Bolivar (the national hero) to Venezuela. FS&G, 1976.

TRAVEL ARTICLES

N.Y. TIMES SUNDAY TRAVEL SECTION (X)
1984 Jun 17 "Venezuela Modern." Caracas offers cool breezes and city living in the equatorial sun. Tim Page, p. 18
"A Visitor's Guide to the City (of Caracas)." Joseph Mann, p. 40

SUNSET
1985 Sep "An Afternoon in Venezuela's Jungle." p. 44

TRAVEL/HOLIDAY
1985 Feb "Caracas, Venezuela." Enjoying the good life at 3,000 feet. Helmut Koenig, p. 58

VII.NORTH AMERICA

THE ARCTIC AND GREENLAND

Series Guidebooks (See Appendix 1)

Nagel: Denmark/Greenland

Note: See also books listed under "Yukon & the Northwest Territory."

Background Reading

Bruemmer, Fred   THE ARCTIC WORLD
Essays on history, people, animal and plant life of seven Arctic countries. Sierra Club, 1985. Also *The Artic* (1975).

DeLaguna, Frederica   VOYAGE TO GREENLAND
A young graduate student's introduction to anthropology and life in Greenland in a series of letters home. Written in 1925, with notes added in 1975. Norton, 1977.

Diubaldo, Richard J.   STEFANSSON AND THE CANADIAN ARCTIC
A study of character and relationships and the expeditions. McGill, 1978.

Dyson, John   THE HOT ARCTIC
Threats to Arctic life and ecology by mineral explorations. Little, 1980.

Freuchen, Peter   ARCTIC ADVENTURE: MY LIFE IN THE
FROZEN NORTH
Reproduction of the 1935 edition by the polar explorer. Darby Bks, 1982 (first published 1935). Also *The Peter Freuchen Reader* (1965), an anthology of his writings, edited by his wife.

Herbert, Marie   SNOW PEOPLE
Record of the vanishing Eskimo culture, with photos, of Ultima Thule in Greenland. Putnam Pub Group, 1973.

Jones, Tristan   ICE
"Lively, witty book" of a cruise around the high Arctic and Greenland, alone except for a dog, in a thirty-six-foot boat. Avon, 1980.

Kpomassie, Tete-Michel   AN AFRICAN IN GREENLAND
The author, born in Togoland, was fascinated as a boy with the idea of Greenland. Eventually, after travel in Europe, he reached his fantasy place and the book relates his adventures in Greenland, and about the people who found him equally astounding. HarBraceJ, 1983.

Lindbergh, Anne   NORTH TO THE ORIENT
Record of the trip made with her famous husband. HarBraceJ, 1966.

Lopez, Barry   ARCTIC DREAMS: IMAGINATION AND DESIRE IN A
NORTHERN LANDSCAPE
"Captures both the beauty and peril of this frozen land"—the northernmost region of North America. (BL) Scribner, 1986.

Mirsky, Jeanette   TO THE ARCTIC: THE STORY OF NORTHERN
EXPLORATION FROM EARLIEST TIMES
TO THE PRESENT
Explorations from the fourth century to flights over the pole by Admundsen and others, relates "with simplicity the complex and often overlapping stories of courageous men." Introduction by Vilhjalmur Stefansson. (BRD) U. of Chicago, 1970 (first published 1948).

Mowat, Farley, ed.   THE POLAR PASSION: THE QUEST FOR
THE NORTH POLE
With selections from the Arctic journals of various explorers. Little, 1968. Also *The Great Betrayal* (1977), about the environmental threat to Northern Canada and the Arctic by gas and oil interests.

Rasky, Frank   THE POLAR VOYAGERS: EXPLORERS OF THE NORTH
McGraw, 1976. And *North Pole or Bust* (1977)— a two-volume story of the explorations (the first, from the Vikings to the eighteenth century). Entertainment for readers unacquainted with the North and its history is the author's purpose, with emphasis on characterization of the many individual explorers.

Scherman, Katherine   ARCTIC SPRING
Expedition to the eastern Arctic—"elaboration of the post card everyone sends [written] with skill and vividness as an appreciative and cultivated person" rather than a professional explorer. (BRD) Little, 1956.

Novels

Beach, Edward L.   COLD IS THE SEA
Navy submarine drama as an American ship enters Russian waters. HR&W, 1978.

Buchan, John   MOUNTAIN MEADOW
See under "Yukon & the Northwest Territory," above.

Freuchen, Peter   ESKIMO
A novel about Eskimo life within the Arctic circle. Liveright, 1931.

Freuchen, Peter   WHITE MAN (Greenland)
Historical novel of the early eighteenth century that tells of Norwegian-Danish attempts to colonize Greenland; convicts were sent there to establish settlements. Rinehart, 1946.

Harris, Macdonald   THE BALLOONIST
Three people set off in a balloon in 1897 to discover the North Pole, a story inspired by a true incident in which a Swedish balloonist died in a similar attempt. FS&G, 1976.

Houston, James   THE SPIRIT WRESTLER (Baffin Island)
Eskimo life on Baffin Island and the deathbed story of a shaman who exploits his position for social advantage. HarBraceJ, 1980. Also *White Dawn* (1971).

Kyle, Duncan   WHITE OUT! (Greenland)
Adventure story and thriller of engineers and soldiers sent to test the winterability of new hovercraft in Greenland. St. Martin, 1976.

MacLean, Alistair   NIGHT WITHOUT END (Greenland)
Espionage and murder as an airliner crash-lands in Greenland. Doubleday, 1960.

MacLean, Alistair   ICE STATION ZEBRA
Russian-American cold-war adventure in the Arctic. Doubleday, 1956.

Mowat, Farley   THE SNOW WALKER
Short stories about life in the Arctic interwoven with myths, legends and mysteries. Little, 1975.

Ruesch, Hans   TOP OF THE WORLD
Life of an Eskimo family with a sequel, *Back to the Top of the World* (1973), that follows the wanderings of the family and collision with white civilization, their last

stand to keep a way of life and to survive—"background and customs of Arctic life are fascinating and characters . . . become believable." (BRD) Har-Row, 1950.

Scherman, Katherine   THE LONG WHITE NIGHT
A young writer travels to the Arctic on a twenty-four-hour assignment but decides to remain for the long white night of winter. Little, 1964.

Wilson, Sloan   ICE BROTHERS
Adventures of an American ice trawler patrolling the coast of Greenland during the early part of World War II. Arbor Hse, 1979.

TRAVEL ARTICLES

NATIONAL GEOGRAPHIC
1985 Feb "Mummies of Qilakitsoq." Startlingly well preserved . . . Inuit bodies offer new insights into the life of the early Greenlanders. Jens P.H. Hansen and Jorgen Nordqvist, p. 190.

CANADA

Series Guidebooks

Birnbaum: Canada
Fisher: Canada
Fodor: Canada; Budget Travel Canada
Frommer: Canada: Dollarwise
Lonely Planet: Canada
Michelin: Canada
Nagel: Canada
U.S. Government: Background Notes; Post Report

Note: Asterisked (*) titles of books and articles under "United States of America" (including the "East" and "West" sub-sections) apply to North America as a whole and therefore are relevant to Canada. Also some books on Alaska may have relevance to the west coast of Canada.

Background Reading

Boulton, Roger and others   CANADA COAST TO COAST
"Likable, rambling text" describes an east-west journey from Prince Edward Island to Vancouver Island, with spectacular photography. (LJ) Oxford U, 1982.

Broadfoot, Barry   MY OWN YEARS
By "a kind of Canadian Studs Terkel"—reflects the author's peripatetic life in Canada's west and the characters he's run across, from fishermen and frontiersmen to a dazzling call girl. (BL) Doubleday, 1984. Also his other chronicles of Canadian life: *10 Lost Years* (1974), *Pioneer Years* (1976), and *Years of Sorrow* (1978).

Callwood, June   PORTRAIT OF CANADA
An entertaining survey for Americans by a Toronto journalist. Doubleday, 1981.

Creighton, Donald   THE PASSIONATE OBSERVER
Collection of reviews, letters, and articles about a wide range of topics—history, friends and family, literature, the separatist movement, and so on. Written by "a great historian and major writer [with] style and spirit . . . great fun." (BRD) McClelland & Stewart, 1980.

Duggan, William R.   OUR NEIGHBORS UPSTAIRS: THE CANADIANS
"Contemporary Canada in historical, social, geographic, ethnic, economic, and political terms" especially intended to help Americans understand their neighbor. (BL) Nelson-Hall, 1979.

Farrow, Moira   NOBODY HERE BUT US
Pioneers of the north—twelve men talk about their lives on the Canadian frontier. J.J. Douglas, 1975.

Friedenberg, E.Z.   DEFERENCE TO AUTHORITY: THE CASE OF CANADA
An American exile's view of Canada; his thesis is that Canadians are too deferential and lacking in assertiveness. M.E. Sharpe, 1980.

Kettle, John   THE BIG GENERATION
A study of those Canadians born 1951-66, what they are doing to the system and what the system did to them. McClelland & Stewart, 1980.

Kilbourn, William   CANADA: A GUIDE TO THE PEACEABLE KINGDOM
The meaning of Canada and being Canadian, an anthology of Canada as Canadians see themselves and as others see them. St. Martin, 1970.

**Kostash, Myrna   LONG WAY FROM HOME: THE
STORY OF THE SIXTIES GENERATION IN CANADA**
Youth, politics and social change in the '60s written by a product of the era. Lorimer, 1980.

MacDonald, Ervin J.   THE RAINBOW CHASERS
Spans the period of mid-nineteenth to early twentieth century—"a vivid tale of a family's struggles and triumphs in the Canadian wilderness . . . [their] elusive dream . . . breathes life into the people and pioneering efforts of the western frontier." (BL) Salem Hse, 1984.

Malcolm, Andrew H.   THE CANADIANS
"Wide-ranging, perceptive view . . . exploring the awesome geography . . . interviews and personal recollections to describe its people, economy and close ties to the U.S." (PW) Times Bks, 1985.

Mills, Don   THE CANADIAN FAMILY TREE
The seventy-nine ethnic and cultural groups in Canada. Corpus, 1979.

Owram, Doug   PROMISE OF EDEN: THE CANADIAN EXPANSIONIST MOVEMENT AND THE IDEA OF THE WEST
U of Toronto, 1980.

Richler, Mordecai   HOME SWEET HOME: MY CANADIAN ALBUM
"Assorted essays on Canadian themes . . . light but tasty," by a Canadian novelist who returned to the country after twenty years in England. (PW) Knopf, 1984.

Soupcoff, Murray   CANADA 1984
A satirical look (with cartoons) at Canada, in the format of a legitimate yearbook told as if written from the perspective of 1985. Lester & Orpen, 1979.

Wilden, Tony   THE IMAGINARY CANADIAN
Anecdotal history with a thesis that there's a conspiracy preventing a genuine Canadian nationality from emerging, and fostering a morbid colonial dependence on Britain. Pulp Pr, 1980.

Woodcock, George   THE CANADIANS
Text enlivened with Canadian art, profiles of regional figures, and the "historical, geographic and artistic strands of the Canadian psyche." (BRD) Harvard U Pr, 1980.

NATURAL WONDERS & OUTDOOR CANADA

Crump, Donald J.   CANADA'S WILDERNESS LANDS
Natl Geog, 1982.

Marty, Sid   A GRAND AND FABULOUS NOTION
The first century of Canada's parks. NC Pr, 1984.

Mowat, Farley   THE WORLD OF FARLEY MOWAT
The best of serious and humorous writings by a leading Canadian nature writer, storyteller, humorist, prose poet. See also titles under "The Arctic & Greenland," above. Little, 1980.

Reader's Digest, eds.   THE CANADIAN BOOK OF THE ROAD
The forerunner of *America from the Road* and intended as a companion guide to take along for the enhancement of auto travel, both for planning and to identify things seen along the way. Arranged in road units from west to east with an introduction to each region, cities, major attractions. Norton, 1979.

Stephenson, Marylee   CANADA'S NATIONAL PARKS: A
VISITOR'S GUIDE
Covers Canada's twenty-nine national parks with trails, plants, animals, campsites, visitor facilities. P-H, 1984.

RAILWAYS & RAILWAY TRAVEL

Berton, Pierre   THE IMPOSSIBLE RAILWAY
Building the Canadian Pacific—"a marvelous story"—readable, anecdotal account and a history of the period. (BRD) Knopf, 1972.

Coo, Bill   SCENIC RAILGUIDE TO WESTERN CANADA
And also *Scenic Railguide to Central and Atlantic Canada* (1983). For anyone planning a trip by rail across Canada, these are traveler's companions to take along for enhancement of the journey. Written by the director of written communications for Via Rail Canada, they touch on everything from where to sit on the train, to background information on what you're seeing, and maps. Zoetrope, 1983.

Leggett, Robert F.   RAILWAYS OF CANADA
How the railways conquered Canada—the story of the Canadian railways from the 1830s to the present including the smaller companies. "Captures much of the romance of Canadian railroading as well as the facts." (Publisher) Salem Hse, 1983.

McKee, Bill and Klassen, Georgeen   TRAIL OF IRON: THE CPR AND THE
BIRTH OF THE WEST, 1880-1930
Another new history, this one is a centennial celebration history of the completion in 1885 of the Canadian Pacific Railroad that "bound the young divided nation together . . . shaping immigration and settlement patterns. . . . A significant volume on both Canadian and railroad history." (BL) Salem Hse, 1984.

Scheller, William G.   TRAIN TRIPS: EXPLORING AMERICA BY RAIL
A guide to American passenger service and complete Canadian Via Rail information as well—"mini guides to fifty-two major North American cities . . . how to get around, what to see, and where to dine." (BL) East Woods, 1984.

GUIDEBOOKS FOR CANADA

Note also guides listed under "Railways & Railway Travel," above.

Canadian Universities Travel Service   BUDGETTRAVEL IN CANADA
"Impressively thorough guide" to activities, hotels, places to eat . . . focus is not solely for student or youthful travelers." (BL) St. Martin, 1982.

Hall, Gerry and Brehl, John   ONE HUNDRED AND ONE UNUSUAL
VACATION ADVENTURES
NAL, 1981.

Hearn, John   COLLECTOR'S ITEMS
"A guide to antique hunting across Canada"—museums, antique shows, collectors' clubs—"opinionated introduction to antiques in Canada." (BL) Van Nostrand, 1981.

Moritz, Theresa and Albert   THE POCKET CANADA: A COMPLETE GUIDE TO THE WORLD'S SECOND LARGEST COUNTRY
Arco, 1984.

Nelson, Nina   CANADA
A Batsford Guide—"covers its subject remarkably well." (TBS)Batsford, 1980.

Patton, Brian   PARKWAYS OF THE CANADIAN ROCKIES: AN INTERPRETATION GUIDE
To Banff, Jasper, Kootenay and Yoho Parks. Summer Thought, 1982.

Stanley, David   ALASKA-YUKON HANDBOOK: A GYPSY GUIDE TO THE INSIDE PASSAGE AND BEYOND
See under "Yukon and the Northwest territory."

HISTORY

Bothwell, Robert and others   CANADA SINCE NINETEEN FORTY-FIVE: POWER, POLITICS AND PROVINCIALISM
An overview of the period since World War II; a partisan approach popularly written with good cultural sections—"breezy and cheery." (BRD) U of Toronto, 1981.

McNaught, Kenneth W.K.   THE PELICAN HISTORY OF CANADA
Penguin, 1982.

Novels

Buell, John   PLAYGROUND
A chartered plane crashes in the Canadian wilderness—a tale of survival. FS&G, 1976.

Costain, Thomas B.   HIGH TOWERS
Historical novel of early Canada. Two brothers who explored the Mississippi, one of whom founded New Orleans, and the Le Moyne family's efforts to establish a French empire in America. Doubleday, 1949.

Davies, Robertson   FIFTH BUSINESS
First of a trilogy that includes also *The Manticore* (1972) and *World of Wonders* (1976). Taken together they range over some sixty years, three continents and two wars. It begins with four friends in the Canadian midwest whose lives are

profoundly affected by a single badly aimed snowball—"a work of theological fiction that approaches Graham Greene . . . deceptively simple style that is also treacherously entertaining." (FC) Viking, 1970.

Hailey, Arthur   IN HIGH PLACES
About a futuristic plan to unify Canada and the United States against a possible nuclear war. Doubleday, 1962.

Innes, Hammond   CAMPBELL'S KINGDOM
Adventure novel about searching for oil in Canada. Knopf, 1952.

Kogawa, Joy   OBASAN
Autobiographical novel of a child and her brother, of Japanese descent, who are left with their aunt (Obasan) in Canada in 1941 when the Japanese bomb Pearl Harbor. Godine, 1982.

Laurence, Margaret   THE STONE ANGEL
A ninety-year-old's reminiscences of marriage and her life—"an unregenerate sinner declining into senility." (FC) Knopf, 1964.

Levine, Norman   THIN ICE
Short stories juxtaposing settings from Canada with scenes from England. Deneau & Greenberg, 1980.

Munro, Alice   THE MOONS OF JUPITER
Short stories set in rural and urban Canada. Knopf, 1983.

Van Herk, Aritha   JUDITH BROWN
A young woman returns to the family farm after an "ego-destroying" love affair. Little, 1978.

Whitaker, Muriel, ed.   GREAT CANADIAN ADVENTURE STORIES
An anthology of wilderness action stories by Canadian writers. Hurtig, 1979.

TRAVEL ARTICLES

BETTER HOMES & GARDENS
1985 Aug "Five Spectacular Close-to-home Vacations." Victoria, Vancouver, Waterton Lakes National Park in Alberta, Lake of the Woods, and the Southern Ontario Peninsula. p. 120
1984 Aug "Family Vacations in the Canadian Rockies." George S. Bush, p. 131

ESSENCE
1985 Sep "Another World Close to Home—Canada's Offerings East and West." Pamela K. Lyles, p. 34

50 PLUS
1984 Feb "Where Next." Secret destinations for the sophisticated traveler—includes Canada and the Alaska Highway. Robert S. Kane, p. 47

Aug "Falling for the Leaves." Autumn in various states of the U.S. plus Canada. Joseph Scott, p. 38

GLAMOUR
1984 Jun "Canada Celebrates." p. 172
Oct "New Ways to Get the Most from a Ski Vacation." Includes Canada. Abby Rand, p. 231

NATIONAL GEOGRAPHIC
1985 Nov (Canada's vacation lands, with special maps.) "Kluane: Canada's Icy Wilderness Park." Douglas Lee, p. 630

N.Y. TIMES SUNDAY TRAVEL SECTION (X)
1985 Jan 13 "Canada by Rail in a New Light." Joe La Rocca, p. 20
Nov 3 "Condominiums (for Skiing) from A to Z." Stanley Carr, p. 29
1984 May 20 "The ABCs of Going with Children." Sixteen foreign correspondents and contributors of the *Times* offer tips on touring their corners of the world—includes Canada. p. 21
Jun 3 "Polar Bear Express." Train to Moosonee on James Bay. Douglas Martin, p. 26
Jun 24 "Niagara Falls." Still awesome. Skip Rozin, p. 20
Sep 23 "The Rewards of Watching and Waiting." Birdwatching. Graeme Gibson, p. 9
"A Glimpse of the Birder's World." Best bird-watching sites in the east, from Canada to Florida. Richard J. Roberts, p. 9
Oct 28 "A True-Life Adventure Tale." Five urban males take on Canada's Moisie River. Bruce Porter, p. 45
Nov 11 (Skiing) "Making an Early Start in the West." Before the Christmas flurry, there's snow, room and discounts. Alex Ward, p. 27
"Choice Mountains, Great and Small." Guide to contrasting ski areas with notes on rooms and meals. Stanley Carr, p. 29

TRAVEL & LEISURE
1984 Jun "The Call of Canada." Classic trips by train, bus, car and boat. Joyce Kuh, p. 82

TRAVEL/HOLIDAY
1985 Dec "Travel/Holiday's Annual Guide to Fine Dining." U.S., Canada, Mexico. p. 50
1984 Dec "Travel/Holiday's Annual Guide to Fine Dining." U.S., Canada, Mexico. p. 51

VOGUE
1985 Mar "Special Report: Canada . . . up north." A great life; see also articles on British Columbia, Toronto, Montreal and Quebec below. p. 394

ALBERTA

Background Reading

Gibson, Morris   A VIEW OF THE MOUNTAINS
Account of the emigration of a British doctor and his physician wife from Yorkshire to a village in southwestern Alberta and their gradual adjustment to the people there and the landscape. Beaufort, 1984.

MacGregor, James C.   A HISTORY OF ALBERTA
Hurtig, 1981.

Mann, William E.   SECT, CULT AND CHURCH IN ALBERTA
U of Toronto, 1972.

Marty, Sid   MEN FOR THE MOUNTAINS
By a warden at Canada's Banff National Park, evoking "sights, sounds, smells of mountain life guaranteed to arouse nostalgia or anticipation." (BRD) Vanguard, 1979.

Patterson, Raymond M.   THE BUFFALO HEAD
Story of an English banker who fled England to live a "Lewis and Clark sort of life" in one of the most inaccessible areas of the Canadian Rockies. (BRD) Sloane, 1961. It is a sequel to *Dangerous River* (1954).

Russell, Andy   TRAILS OF A WILDERNESS WANDERER
The Canadian Rockies in the early days of this century and now, as seen through the eyes of a man born there and who runs a working ranch in Alberta. Knopf, 1971.

Simpkins, Bill   CHINOOK COUNTRY: ALBERTA SOUTH
Oxford U, 1979.

**Whyte, Jon and Harmon, Carole   LAKE LOUISE: A DIAMOND
                                     IN THE WILDERNESS**
Altitude, 1982.

Novels

Chalmers, John W. and others   DIAMOND JUBILEE
A set of three anthologies of writing by Alberta-born writers, or those who have lived there for a period of time—fiction, poetry and prose. The anthologies also attempt to include as many works of the fifty identifiable ethnic groups in Alberta as possible. Hurtig, 1979.

Freedman, Benedict   MRS. MIKE
Based on true experiences, told secondhand. A Boston girl moves to Canada,

marries a Canadian Mountie, and this is the story of their happiness, hardships and courage, with Indian and nature lore interwoven into the novel. Coward, 1947.

MacLean, Alistair   ATHABASCA
The inner workings of two kinds of oil companies as threats to disrupt the Alaska pipeline lead to hostage-taking, blackmail and murder. Doubleday, 1980.

TRAVEL ARTICLES

GOOD HOUSEKEEPING
1984 Apr "Ten Great Trips to Take with Your Kids." Calgary. Stephen Birnbaum, p. 228

NATIONAL GEOGRAPHIC
1984 Mar "Canada's Not-So-Wild West." Calgary. p. 378

NATIONAL GEOGRAPHIC TRAVELER
1985 Summer "Banff's Matchless Mountains." Michael Kernan, p. 76

TRAVEL/HOLIDAY
1985 Jan "Banff National Park." Beyond skiing in Canada's Rockies. Norman Sklarewitz, p. 52
       May "Stampede '85." Calgary's June jubilee. William Schemmel, p. 66
1984 Dec "Canada's World Class Whistle Stops." Chateaux (serving railroad lines) that parallel Europe's finest. Maxine Sevack, p. 26

ATLANTIC CANADA AND LABRADOR (New Brunswick, Newfoundland, Nova Scotia, Prince Edward Island)

Series Guidebooks (See Appendix 1)

Fodor: Canada's Maritime Provinces

Background Reading

Armstrong, Bruce   SABLE ISLAND
Highly readable account of the lore and lure of wild horses, seals, flora and fauna, and history of this island southeast of Halifax. Doubleday, 1981.

Chantraine, Pol   THE LIVING ICE
The story of the seals and the men who hunt them in the Gulf of St. Lawrence and the way of life in the Magdalen community of Acadians where seal hunting is not viewed as frivolous or wasteful but as "a fact of life, a way of life that provides much of the folklore . . . and is still dangerous." (BRD) McClelland & Stewart, 1981.

Christie, B.   THE HORSES OF SABLE ISLAND
Petheric Pr, 1980.

Furneaux, Rupert   THE MONEY PIT MYSTERY: THE COSTLIEST TREASURE HUNT EVER
This, and the book by O'Connor below, are about the area in Nova Scotia where rumors of Captain Kidd's treasure have resulted in costly searches from 1795 to the present. Woodhill, 1978.

Hiller, James and Neary, Peter, eds.   NEWFOUNDLAND IN THE NINETEENTH AND TWENTIETH CENTURIES
Ten essays about the history of Newfoundland and an overview of its literature. U of Toronto, 1980.

Mackay, Donald   SCOTLAND FAREWELL: THE PEOPLE OF HECTOR (Nova Scotia)
The author's ancestors on the sailing ship Hector and their emigration to Nova Scotia. McGraw, 1980.

MacLeish, William H.   OIL AND WATER: THE STRUGGLE FOR GEORGES BANK
"A lively account of people and their work" and the struggle for control involving oil companies, fishermen, and state and federal governments of the U.S. and Canada. (PW) Atl Monthly Pr, 1985.

Muskie, Stephen O.   CAMPOBELLO
Franklin D. Roosevelt's "beloved island." Down East, 1982.

O'Connor, D'Arcy   MONEY PIT: THE STORY OF OAK ISLAND AND THE WORLD'S GREATEST TREASURE (Nova Scotia)
Rumors of Captain Kidd's treasure and the searches for it from 1795 to the present. Coward, 1978.

Perkins, Robert F.   AGAINST STRAIGHT LINES: ALONE IN LABRADOR
Journal—and a journey into himself—of a Boston librarian who elects to spend a month on the Palmer River in Labrador: "A couple of leisure hours and this book are all you'll need to follow Robert Perkins to Labrador." (BRD) Atl Monthly Pr, 1983.

Pratson, Frederick   GUIDE TO EASTERN CANADA
Covers New Brunswick, Nova Scotia, Prince Edward Island, Newfoundland, Labrador, Ontario and Quebec. Comprehensive travel guide with all the useful information needed to discover the best of the eastern provinces. Restaurants, inns, castles, hotels, sightseeing, customs and background information, history, climate, outdoor recreation, fairs and festivals, the arts, and more. Pequot Globe, 1983.

Russell, Franklin   THE SECRET ISLANDS
An exploration of the inhabited and uninhabited islands off the coast of Canada and Newfoundland—"a treasure of fascinating observations and insights into nature." (BRD) Norton, 1966.

Stewart, Robert L.   LABRADOR
Part of the World's Wild Places series. Time-Life, 1977.

Street, David   THE CABOT TRAIL
Historical sketches, interviews with residents—a travelogue of the trail that loops around Cape Breton Island for 184 miles. Gage, 1979.

Thompson, Colleen   NEW BRUNSWICK IN AND OUT
Readable regional guide, formal and folk history, that includes towns, cities, walks, drives and festivals. Waxwing, 1979.

Trueman, Stuart   TALL TALES AND TRUE TALES FROM DOWN EAST
"Eerie experiences, heroic exploits, extraordinary personalities, ancient legends and folklore from New Brunswick and elsewhere in the Maritimes." (Publisher) McClelland & Stewart, 1979.

Vroom, Richard, ed.   OLD NEW BRUNSWICK: A VICTORIAN PORTRAIT
Oxford U, 1978.

Walden, Howard T., II   ANCHORAGE NORTHEAST (Nova Scotia)
One American family's discovery of their paradise—Jordan Bay in Nova Scotia, and the kind of life they'd thought was gone forever. Morrow, 1971.

Whiteley, George   NORTHERN SEAS, HARDY SAILORS (Nova Scotia, Newfoundland)
Account of a trip with friends by a retired marine biologist, from Friendship, Maine, to Newfoundland and back, and the places visited; stories of sealing, shipwrecks, some history, natural history, geology. Norton, 1982.

Novels

Currie, Sheldon   THE GLACE BAY MINER'S MUSEUM (Cape Breton)
Short stories with a Cape Breton setting. Deluge Pr, 1979.

Davis-Gardner, Angela   FELICE (Nova Scotia)
Life at a convent school in Nova Scotia during the 1920s.Random, 1982.

Gundy, Elizabeth   LOVE, INFIDELITY AND DRINKING TO FORGET
An artist who paints covers for romances and the owner of a New York antiques store decide to move to an abandoned farm in New Jerusalem in Atlantic Canada—the story of what they dreamed, the reality they find. The author "describe[s] a community so well that you . . . remember it as if you'd once stayed there." (FC) Dial, 1984.

Innes, Hammond   THE LAND GOD GAVE TO CAIN (Labrador)
Thrilling yarn about a search involving incredible hardships for the grandson of a prospector murdered in the wilds of Labrador. Knopf, 1958.

Mason, F. Van Wyck   THE YOUNG TITAN
Historical novel of the French and Indian Wars and the battle of Louisbourg. Doubleday, 1959.

Minot, Stephen   GHOST IMAGES (Nova Scotia)
A deserted area of the Nova Scotia coast is the setting—a radical writer gets caught up in reading his father's secret journal instead of working on the critical history he's supposed to be writing. Har-Row, 1979.

Ogilvie, Elisabeth   THE DEVIL IN TARTAN (Nova Scotia)
"What starts out as a glorified babysitting job with a little genealogical research thrown in becomes an adventure in ESP, Scottish history and Nova Scotia living." (FC) McGraw, 1980.

Walker, David   ASH (New Brunswick)
Suspenseful adventure story of a man being pursued in the north woods. Houghton, 1976.

Wynne-Jones, Tim   ODD'S END (Nova Scotia)
Suspenseful novel of a contest for ownership of an isolated Nova Scotia house. Little, 1980.

TRAVEL ARTICLES

AMERICANA
1984 Mar-Apr "Nova Scotia's Fortress of Louisbourg." Graham Schelling, p. 85

ARCHITECTURAL DIGEST
1985 Mar Historic Houses: "Campobello." Patrician simplicity at FDR's summer

cottage (between Eastport and New Brunswick—the island belongs to Canada). Arthur Schlesinger, Jr., p. 220

MODERN MATURITY
1985 Aug "Canada's Healing Place." Troubles melt away on Prince Edward Island. Charles N. Barnard, p. 78
1984 Dec-Jan "An Island in Time." Newfoundland is historic and a pleasant place to visit. Charles N. Barnard, p. 56

NATIONAL GEOGRAPHIC
1985 Jul "Discovery in Labrador." A 16th-century Basque whaling port and its sunken fleet. James A. Tuck and Robert Grenier, p. 40

NATIONAL GEOGRAPHIC TRAVELER
1985 Spring "From the Mists of History: the Fortress of Louisbourg." Step back in time to 1744 and join a sturdy band of French colonists in Nova Scotia. James Murfin, p. 130

N.Y. TIMES SUNDAY TRAVEL SECTION (X)
1985 Jul 28 Shopper's World: "In Nova Scotia, Mushrooms to Go." Joyce Barkhouse, p. 12
1984 Mar 18 (Part 2, "Sophisticated Traveler") "Landfall: Nova Scotia." The easternmost of Canada's Maritime Provinces and its gentle eccentricities. Margaret Atwood, p. 89
Jun 17 "Scotland on a Nearer Shore." Cape Breton. Douglas Martin, p. 14
"A Phoenix Rises in Louisbourg." Fortress of Louisbourg National Historic Park. Christopher Moore, p. 15
"Halifax Honors Its Roots." Joyce Barkhouse, p. 16

READER'S DIGEST
1985 Nov "The Way It Is in Lower East Pubnico." Condensed from *A New Kind of A Country*. Dorothy Gilman, p. 179

SATURDAY EVENING POST
1985 Oct "Newfoundland: A Real Find." Carolyn Crowley, p. 90

TRAVEL & LEISURE
1985 Apr "Canada's Cape Breton Island." A rugged beauty at the tip of Nova Scotia. Jay Sperling, p. 160

TRAVEL/HOLIDAY
1985 Mar "Picture Perfect in New Brunswick." Recalling Canada's British and French heritage. Diane Marshall, p. 84
1984 Apr "Prince Edward Island." Province of vivid colors. Pat Canova, p. 58

WORLD PRESS REVIEW
1985 Apr "Unspoiled Newfoundland." (*Frankfurter Allgemeine Zeitung*, Frankfurt), Dorothy S. Michelman, p. 62
1984 Jun "Canada's Cabot Trail." On Cape Breton Island. (*Toronto Globe and Mail*), Betty Zyvatkauskas, p. 69

BRITISH COLUMBIA

Background Reading

Arthur, Elizabeth   ISLAND SOJOURN
One couple's retreat to the wilderness—introspective observations on nature, wildlife and the wilderness. Har-Row, 1980.

Brook, Paula   VANCOUVER RAINY DAY GUIDE
Chronicle, 1984.

Carey, Neil G.   A GUIDE TO THE QUEEN CHARLOTTE ISLANDS
Intended for "untouristy" vacations by those who plan their travel around outdoor activities. Alaska Northwest, 1984.

Davis, Chuck, ed.   THE VANCOUVER BOOK
J.J. Douglas, 1976

Hoagland, Edward   NOTES FROM THE CENTURY BEFORE
Experiences on a trip in 1966 when the author followed the trails and talked to the old-timers . . . "about their heydays as trappers, prospectors, traders and explorers." (BRD) North Pt Pr, 1982 (first published 1969).

Jackman, S.W.   VANCOUVER ISLAND
History, description, wildlife, the economy, etc., supplementary reading lists—part of the Islands of the World series. David, 1974.

Johnston, Moira   RANCH: PORTRAIT OF A SURVIVING DREAM
Text and photos in a recreation of the past, the land and its people today—an absorbing evocation of ranch life and the author's journey, which includes the American high plains, California and British Columbia. Doubleday, 1983.

Kilian, Crawford   GO DO SOME GREAT THING
An account of the migration of blacks from San Francisco to Canada. U of Washington Pr, 1978.

Lawrence, R.P.   THE VOYAGE OF THE STELLA
A novelist's vivid account of six months spent exploring the coast of the Inland Passage in a twenty-four-foot boat. HR&W, 1982.

McKeever, Harry P.   BRITISH COLUMBIA
Outdoor recreation and activities are emphasized in this series of essays on British Columbia, along with history and background reading. Chronicle Bk, 1982.

Morton, James   IN THE SEA OF STERILE MOUNTAINS
The Chinese in British Columbia. U of Washington Pr, 1980.

Nicol, Eric   VANCOUVER
Doubleday Canada, 1978.

Obee, B.   THE GULF ISLANDS
Superior, 1981.

Ormsby, Margaret Anchoretta   BRITISH COLUMBIA: A HISTORY
Centennial history. Macmillan, 1971 (first published 1960).

Stanley, David   ALASKA-YUKON HANDBOOK: A GYPSY GUIDE TO THE INSIDE PASSAGE AND BEYOND
See under "Yukon & the Northwest Territory."

Tomkies, Mike   A WORLD OF MY OWN
An account of adventure and personal renewal in the wilderness—a columnist from England starts life over in the wilds of British Columbia and tells of his personal odyssey. Reader's Digest Pr, 1976.

Novels

Craven, Margaret   I HEARD THE OWL CALL MY NAME
A young and dying missionary is sent to a challenging post to work with Indians and to find fulfillment. Doubleday, 1973.

Deverell, William   NEEDLES
Suspenseful novel about the drug trade in Vancouver. Little, 1975.

Keeble, John   YELLOWFISH
Smuggling of Chinese into the United States via Canada—captures a "rootless, conscienceless segment of society . . . and the spirit of the Pacific northwest." (FC) Har-Row, 1980.

Laurence, Margaret   THE FIRE-DWELLERS
Middle-age crisis for a Vancouver woman. Knopf, 1969.

Lowry, Malcolm   OCTOBER FERRY TO GABRIOLA
A novel with autobiographical echoes published posthumously—"a journey within a journey . . . memories while traveling with his wife, by bus, in British Columbia." (FC) World, 1970.

St. Pierre, Paul   SMITH AND OTHER EVENTS; STORIES OF THE CHILCOTIN
Short story collection set in Chilcotin country in the 1940s and '50s—"features small-town farmer Smith . . . and characters from the author's CBC television series 'Cariboo Country.'" (FC) Beaufort, 1984.

TRAVEL ARTICLES

NATIONAL GEOGRAPHIC TRAVELER
1985 Winter "City Sophistication, Naturally—Vancouver." Including Expo '86. Pierre Berton, p. 90
1984 Autumn "Totems and Tudor: Victoria, B.C.." Heather Robertson, p. 124

N.Y. TIMES SUNDAY TRAVEL SECTION (X)
1985 Aug 4 "What's Doing in Vancouver." Moira Farrow, p. 18
"Canada's City of Flowers." An urban gardener visits Vancouver and confesses to a touch of envy. Linda Yang, p. 19
1984 Jul 29 "What's Doing in Victoria." Moira Farrow, p. 10

SUNSET
1985 Jun "New Hydrofoil Service: Seattle to Victoria to Vancouver, B.C." p. 33
Jul "Saturday Spectacles in Butchart Gardens." Summer fireworks displays that combine fire, light, water, poetry and music. p. 36
1984 Feb "Where the Snowcats Take You to High Powder." p. 34
Nov "Shopping for Cowichan Sweaters." p. 47

VOGUE
1985 "Vancouver: We're Talking Nature." Allan Fotheringham, p. 410
"Vancouver: Going to Heaven." Sally R. Warren, p. 412

MANITOBA

Background Reading

Davids, Richard C.   **LORDS OF THE ARCTIC: A JOURNEY AMONG POLAR BEARS**
"An enticing collection of legendary facts and eyewitness accounts" of the Arctic bears and interaction with Eskimos and population of Churchill, Manitoba. (BL) Macmillan, 1982.

Morton, William L.   **MANITOBA: A HISTORY**
U of Toronto, 1967.

Wells, Eric   **WINNIPEG: WHERE THE NEW WEST BEGINS**
An illustrated history of the city. Windsor, 1982.

Novels

Eckert, Allan W.   INCIDENT AT HAWK'S HILL
Based on a true story of a young, supposedly retarded, boy who goes to live with animals and returns as a normal child. Set in the 1870s. Little, 1971.

Laurence, Margaret   A JEST OF GOD
The self-liberation of a spinster schoolteacher from her trapped life in provincial Manitoba. Knopf, 1966. Also *A Bird in the House* (1970), short stories set in the 1930s and '40s.

TRAVEL ARTICLES

MODERN MATURITY
1984 Dec-Jan "Where the Bears Are." Churchill, Manitoba, is a mecca for tourists. Barbara Nielsen, p. 30

NATIONAL GEOGRAPHIC TRAVELER
1985 Autumn "Bearing North: An Uncommon Quest in Churchill, Manitoba (Bear Capital of the World)." William G. Scheller, p. 108

N.Y. TIMES SUNDAY TRAVEL SECTION (X)
1984 Nov 18 "Seeking the Perfect Pickerel Fillet." The flat expanse of Manitoba is home to ducks, Icelanders—and a renowned Canadian fish. Sondra Gotlieb, p. 47

TRAVEL/HOLIDAY
1985 Jun "The Secret Life of Winnipeg." Canada's unsung city. Gerard McTigue, p. 44

ONTARIO

Series Guidebooks (See Appendix 1)

Fodor: Toronto

Background Reading

Donaldson, Gordon   NIAGARA!
Historical narrative and stories from fact and legend—Ontario, Canada and New York State. Doubleday, 1979.

Galbraith, John K.   THE SCOTCH
A leading economist's boyhood impressions of the small Scottishcommunity where he grew up, on the north shore of Lake Erie. Houghton,1964.

Ladell, John   INHERITANCE: ONTARIO'S CENTURY FARMS PAST AND PRESENT
Ontario farms, and the families who own them. Macmillan, 1980.

Lehmberg, Paul   IN THE STRONG WOODS
A season alone in the north country—a young man spent three months alone in the Ontario Woods at Nym Lake, and writes about it. St. Martin, 1981.

McBurney, Margaret   HOMESTEADS: EARLY BUILDINGS AND FAMILIES FROM KINGSTON TO TORONTO
"Popular history in the best sense." (BRD) U of Toronto, 1979.

Martyn, Lucy B.   ARISTOCRATIC TORONTO
Fine homes and elegant people of nineteenth-century Toronto. Gage, 1980.

Pratson, Frederick   GUIDE TO EASTERN CANADA
See under "The Maritimes and Labrador," above - includes Ontario.

Scharfenberg, Doris   THE LONG BLUE EDGE OF ONTARIO
A vacation guide to Ontario's Great Lakes coast. Eerdmans Pub, 1984.

Novels

Atwood, Margaret   LIFE BEFORE MAN (Toronto)
A modern triangle and introspective view of modern marriage. S&S, 1980.

Beresford-Howe, Constance   THE MARRIAGE BED (Toronto)
A young pregnant housewife, abandoned by her husband, confronts her friends, parents, mother-in-law and spouse and finds that "they all have personal prisons as confining as hers." (FC) St. Martin, 1982.

Burnford, Sheila   THE INCREDIBLE JOURNEY
A book for animal lovers of all ages, about two dogs and a cat who set out to cross 300 miles of Ontario, and a picture of World War II life as well. Little, 1977.

Cobb, Jocelyn   BELMULLET
"An old-fashioned novel in concept and style" of a ten-year-old girl sent to the family farm in rural Ontario in 1933, ostensibly for a brief visit, but it becomes a permanent change for her. (FC) St. Martin, 1983.

Davies, Robertson   THE REBEL ANGELS (Toronto)
Involves a stolen Rabelaisian manuscript—"love and scholarship, and secret Gypsy lore" in a small college. (FC) Viking, 1982.

Davies, Robertson   MIXTURE OF FRAILTIES (Kingston)
This plus *Leaven of Malice* (1955) and *Tempest Tossed* (1952) are a trilogy (the Salterton trilogy) of "original, wry and amusing social comedy" set in a small Ontario city. Penguin, 1980 (first published 1958).

De La Roche, Mazo   THE JALNA SAGA
A sixteen-volume family saga of the Whiteoak family and Jalna, their family home on the shores of Lake Ontario. It begins in 1850, and goes on through to the mid-1950s and their centennial celebration. The books were not published chronologically, but are listed here in order of place in the story, to read in proper sequence: *The Building of Jalna* (1944), *Morning at Jalna* (1960), *Mary Wakefield* (1949), *Young Renny* (1935), *Whiteoak Heritage* (1940), *The Whiteoak Brothers: Jalna 1923* (1953), *Centenary at Jalna* (1958), *Whiteoaks of Jalna* (1929), *Finch's Fortune* (1931), *The Master of Jalna* (1933), *Whiteoak Harvest* (1936), *Wakefield's Course* (1941), *Return to Jalna* (1946), *Renny's Daughter* (1951), *Variable Winds at Jalna* (1954), and *Jalna* (1927). Little, 1927-1960.

Engel, Howard   THE SUICIDE MURDERS
Detective Benny Cooperman, working out of a small town near Niagara Falls, is hired to trail a woman's husband. St. Martin, 1984.

Engel, Marian   THE GRASSY SEA
The life of a woman, from growing up in a poor, strict, Canadian family on through her education, her time in an Anglican convent, marriage—"intricate, rich and sensuous." (FC) St. Martin, 1979. Also *Bear* (1976).

Faessler, Shirley   EVERYTHING IN THE WINDOW (Toronto)
A novel about the "psychology of failed love," set in the 1930s. (BRD) Little, 1980.

Laurence, Margaret   DIVINERS
About a middle-aged writer living on a backwoods farm with her daughter. Knopf, 1974.

Munro, Alice   THE BEGGAR MAID
Ten stories with one heroine, arranged chronologically from childhood in West Hanratty, Ontario, to success as an actress and TV interviewer. Knopf, 1979. Also *Lives of Girls and Women* (1971) and *Dance of the Happy Shades* (1973) (short stories).

Simpson, Leo   KOWALSKI'S LAST CHANCE
A farce—"picaresque escapades of a middle-aged policeman in a fictional small town in Ontario." (BRD) Clarke, 1980.

Skvorecky, Josef   THE ENGINEER OF HUMAN SOULS (Toronto)
"First of all the book is an entertainment . . . in humor ranging from slapstick to high wit and people from the utterly wicked to the virtually saintlike." An emigré from Czechoslovakia and his observations of fellow emigrés in Toronto—"provides a bible of exile." (FC) Knopf, 1984.

Wolfe, Morris L. and Douglas, Raymond, eds.   **TORONTO SHORT STORIES**
Stories that reflect "the character, texture, setting of Toronto in some way." (BRD) Doubleday, 1977.

Wood, Ted   DEAD IN THE WATER
Story set in Murphy's Harbor and Reid Bennett (ex-Toronto cop) is its one-man police force—"action-filled story . . . backdrop so real you can almost feel the mosquitoes biting. . . . satisfyingly tangled plot." (FC) Scribner, 1983. Another police procedural with the same protagonist and setting is *Murder on Ice* (1984)—the beauty queen is snatched during winter carnival and the plot thickens with multiple murders.

Wright, Richard B.   FINAL THINGS
A failed writer avenges his son's obscene death. Dutton, 1980.

TRAVEL ARTICLES

HORIZON
1984 May "Ontario: An Arts Buffet." p. 13

NATIONAL GEOGRAPHIC TRAVELER
1984 Winter "Please Touch! Exploring the Ontario Science Center." Toronto. Stephen S. Hall, p. 68

N.Y. TIMES SUNDAY TRAVEL SECTION (X)
1985 Aug 18 "What's Doing in Ottawa." Christopher S. Wren, p. 10
1984 Apr 15 "What's Doing in Toronto." Douglas Martin, p. 10
Jul 8 "Museum Hopping in Toronto." From science experiments to ceramics to Georgian architecture. Joanne Kates, p. 9

SATURDAY EVENING POST
1985 Oct "High-flying Toronto." Carolyn Crowley, p. 92

TRAVEL & LEISURE
1984 Jan "Follow the Voyageurs." A region where once only frontiersmen ventured to go. Bill Stoughton, p. 59
Apr "Latest from Toronto." Jennifer Fisher, p. 79

TRAVEL/HOLIDAY
1985 Apr "Canada's Fort William." Living portrait of the fur era. Robert and Marilyn Hrycenko, p. 14
1984 Dec "Canada's World Class Whistle Stops." Chateaux, serving railroad lines, that parallel Europe's finest. Maxine Sevack, p. 26

VOGUE
1985 Mar "Toronto: Canada's 'Big Apple'." Margaret Atwood, p. 406
"A Guide to the Glamour." Kathleen Madden, p. 396
"What's New in the City." L.A. Morse, p. 408

QUEBEC

Series Guidebooks (See Appendix 1)

Berlitz: Quebec
Fodor: Fun in Montreal
Frommer: Montreal & Quebec City: City Guide

Background Reading

Arnopoulos, Sheila M.   THE ENGLISH FACT IN QUEBEC
English, and other ethnic influences, in Quebec. McGill-Queens U, 1980.

**Jacobs, Jane   THE QUESTION OF SEPARATION: QUEBEC AND THE
STRUGGLE OVER SOVEREIGNTY**
Random, 1980.

Pratson, Frederick   GUIDE TO EASTERN CANADA
See under "The Maritimes and Labrador," above—includes Quebec.

Reid, Malcolm   THE SHOUTING SIGNPAINTERS
"Literary and political account of Quebec revolutionary nationalism"—the
literary group gathered around the *parti pris* movement for separation as well as
for political, social and sexual liberation. (BRD) Monthly Rev, 1972.

Richler, Mordecai   THE STREET
"A memoir of a place and of a time. . . stories, reminiscences and essays" of a
Montreal street. (NYTBR) New Republic, 1972.

Wilson, P. Roy   THE BEAUTIFUL OLD HOUSES OF QUEBEC
U of Toronto, 1975.

Novels

Atwood, Margaret   SURFACING
Two couples vacation together in a remote cabin and it puts a strain on their
relationship. S&S, 1973.

Blais, Marie Claire   ST. LAWRENCE BLUES (Quebec City)
"Picaresque journey through . . . contemporary Quebec society." (BRD) FS&G,
1974. Also *The Manuscripts of Pauline Archange* (1970), about a young girl's life
and Catholic upbringing.

Blicker, Seymour   THE LAST COLLECTION (Montreal)
A comic farce of big and small cons in Montreal. Morrow, 1977.

Brand, Max   THE STINGAREE
Suspenseful novel involving a half-Indian, half-civilized young boy and a man in search of revenge. Set on the French-Canadian frontier in the nineteenth century. Dodd, 1980 (first published 1930).

Carrier, Rock   THE HOCKEY SWEATER AND OTHER STORIES
Stories of a young boy growing up in a Quebec village of the 1940s. U of Toronto, 1979.

Cather, Willa   SHADOWS ON THE ROCK
Evocation of the French Quebec colony in the early eighteenth century through anecdotes and prose pictures of the homes, marketplace, missionary priests, the Ursuline convent—"characters historic and imagined . . . a charming idyll." (FC) Knopf, 1931.

Daymond, Douglas, ed.   STORIES OF QUEBEC
Ten short stories by English-Canadian authors set in Quebec. Oberon, 1980.

Hebert, Anne   IN THE SHADOW OF THE WIND
A limbless torso, washed up on the shore, is the center of the plot—"the story is told by six narrators [in a] claustrophobic village where anything and everyone are looked upon with . . . paranoia." (FC) Stoddart, 1983. Also *Children of the Black Sabbath* (1977) about exorcism and witchcraft as a nun is about to take final vows.

Henley, Gail   WHERE THE CHERRIES END UP
An Ontario farm girl has to bridge the gap between her squalid background and that of other students at the university. Little, 1979.

MacLennan, Hugh   TWO SOLITUDES
Story of old racial enmities—period is 1917-39. Duell, 1945.

Metcalf, John   GENERAL LUDD
A satire on contemporary values "as reflected in the role of the mass media and their pernicious influence on society." (BRD) ECW Pr, 1980.

Moore, Brian   THE LUCK OF GINGER COFFEY (Montreal)
An Irish family in Montreal survives near-disintegration. Little, 1960.

Popkin, Zelda   "DEAR ONCE"
Jewish immigrants in the early 1900s. The story is narrated by one of the family members who grows up in Montreal. Lippincott, 1975.

Richler, Mordecai   JOSHUA THEN AND NOW
A survey of Joshua's life from Montreal slum childhood to current fame. Knopf, 1980. Also *St. Urban's Horseman* (1971).

Trevanian   THE MAIN (Montreal)
A police lieutenant and a polyglot street in Montreal's seamy immigrant district. HarBraceJ, 1976.

TRAVEL ARTICLES

BON APPETIT
1985 Jul "A Taste of Quebec." Exploring the restaurants, cafes and hotels for the best in regional dining. Laurie G. Buckle, p. 92

ESSENCE
1984 Dec "More Than a Skiing Sensation." You can brave the slopes and hang out with Black Folks. Dari Giles, p. 38

GOURMET
1985 Nov "Cross-country Skiing in Quebec." Paul J. Wade, p. 78

HARPER'S BAZAAR
1984 Feb "Cold Comfort: Quebec, Head Off to One of the Most Charming Cities in North America." Alexander Cockburn, p. 32

NATIONAL GEOGRAPHIC TRAVELER
1984 Spring "Montreal Mosaic." Cultural potpourri. Mordecai Richler, p. 112
Summer "Gaspe." Quebec's wild peninsula. Kenneth Brower, p. 52

N.Y. TIMES SUNDAY TRAVEL SECTION (X)
1985 May 26 "What's Doing in Quebec City." Christopher S. Wren, p. 10
Jan 20 "What's Doing in Montreal." Rochelle L. Balfour, p. 10
Nov 3 "Quebec on Skis and on Foot." Mont Sainte-Anne overlooks the city. Christopher S. Wren, p. 28
Nov 24 "What's Doing in Montreal." Christopher S. Wren, p. 10
1984 Jan 15 Shopper's World: "Along Montreal's St. Denis Street." Rochelle L. Balfour, p. 12
Feb 12 "What's Doing in Montreal." Douglas Martin, p. 10
Feb 26 Shopper's World: "Quebec's Crafts Revival." David Yeadon, p. 6
Apr 22 "Table Talk in Montreal: Cafe Casual." Joanne Kates, p. 9
"Springtime in La Cité." Montreal. Douglas Martin, p. 9
Dec 9 "Quebec Abbey: Serene Retreat." Debra Weiner, p. 20

SUNSET
1985 Oct "Exploring Old and New Quebec." p. 34

TRAVEL & LEISURE
1985 Dec "Montreal's Basilica of Notre Dame." Nancy Lyon, p. 73

TRAVEL/HOLIDAY
1984 Dec "Canada's World Class Whistle Stops." Chateaux, serving railroad lines, that parallel Europe's finest. Maxine Sevack, p. 26

VOGUE
1985 Mar "Montreal: The Omens Are Good." Mordecai Richler, p. 394
      "Quebec City: A Love of a Place." Despina Messinesi, p. 398

SASKATCHEWAN

Background Reading

Binnie-Clark, G.   WHEAT AND WOMAN
An early book about Saskatchewan and farming, reissued because of revived interest in its woman author. U of Toronto, 1979 (first published 1914).

Bocking, D.H.   PAGES FROM THE PAST
Potpourri of subjects in essays that originally appeared in *Saskatchewan History*—history, early settlement and politics. Prairie Bks, 1978. Also *Saskatchewan: A Pictorial History* (1980).

Collins, Robert   BUTTER DOWN THE WELL
A personal memoir of a Saskatchewan childhood in the 1920s and 30s by an award-winning journalist. Prairie Bks, 1980.

Stegner, Wallace   WOLF WILLOW
Reminiscences and personalized history of the Saskatchewan southern plains where the author spent his boyhood, with a "wedge of fiction" in the middle recreating the winter of 1906. (BRD) U of Nebraska, 1980 (first published 1962).

Symons, R.D.   SILTON SEASONS
A year in Silton from "the diary of a country man." (BRD) Doubleday, 1975.

Novels

MacDonald, Malcolm   GOLDENEYE
Chronicles the life of a girl from Scotland, 1919 through the 1950s. Knopf, 1981.

Stegner, Wallace   THE BIG ROCK CANDY MOUNTAIN
Story of a footloose family constantly on the move in the west and Saskatchewan—"cruelty and often crushing poverty, alternating with occasional scenes of a simple family happiness which stand out beautifully and unforgettably." (FC) Duell, 1943.

[NO ARTICLES]

THE YUKON AND THE NORTHWEST TERRITORIES

See also books under "The Arctic & Greenland," above.

Background Reading

Berton, Pierre   DRIFTIN' HOME
"Fascinating weave of past and present"—facts and legends, family, history, in an account of a trip by raft on the Yukon. (BRD) Knopf, 1974.

Cole, Jean M.   EXILE IN THE WILDERNESS
Retelling of the author's great-grandfather's life as a clerk and chief representative of the British government in the Northwest Territory of the early nineteenth century. U of Washington Pr, 1980.

Iglauer, Edith   DENISON'S ICE ROAD
Suspense-filled, expert reporting of roadbuilding in the Territory, written by a woman who drove the trucks that opened an Arctic truck route. Portions of the book appeared in the *New Yorker*—"excitement, humor, the struggle of man against the elements." (BRD) U of Washington Pr, 1982 (first published 1975).

Lawrence, R.P.   THE VOYAGE OF THE STELLA
See under "British Columbia," above.

Mead, Robert D.   ULTIMATE NORTH: CANOEING MACKENZIE'S GREAT RIVER
Retracing a route taken by early explorers in 1789 from upper Alberta to northwest Canada. Doubleday, 1976.

Moore, Joanne R.   NAHANNI TRAILHEAD: A YEAR IN THE NORTHERN WILDERNESS
"An idyllic year spent in the fabled Nahanni River Valley" along with the couple's practical advice, stories, and photographs of wildlife encountered. (BRD) Mountaineers, 1984.

Olson, Sigurd   RUNES OF THE NORTH
The "face and facts" of nature as the author describes his experiences on a trip to Hudson Bay, the Northwest Territory, the Yukon and into Alaska. (BRD) Knopf, 1963.

Stanley, David   ALASKA-YUKON HANDBOOK: A GYPSY GUIDE TO THE INSIDE PASSAGE AND BEYOND
Comprehensive in serving all kinds of travelers from those who prefer regular passenger ferries, buses, and trains to those who hitchhike. Information on small hotels, hostels, campgrounds, local eating places, and thousands of specific tips. In addition to Alaska and the Yukon it provides detailed coverage for Washington State and British Columbia. Moon Pbns Ca, 1983.

Thomas, Lowell and others   ALASKA AND THE YUKON
"A splendid evocation of the continent's last frontier"—eight contributors write on history, recreation, sport, people past and present, animals, cities, and isolated settlements. Facts On File, 1983.

Novels

Buchan, John   MOUNTAIN MEADOW
The last adventure of a man given a year to live—he decides to die on his feet and joins an old comrade from World War I in a search for a man who has disappeared in Northern Canada. Houghton, 1941.

London, Jack   THE CALL OF THE WILD AND OTHER STORIES
Dodd, 1960 (first published 1903). Also *White Fang and Other Stories* (1906).

Pronzini, Bill   STARVATION CAMP
A corporal in the Mounted Police finds murder at Molly Malone's roadhouse and sets out on a hunt for vengeance. Doubleday, 1984.

Van Herk, Aritha   THE TENT PEG
Reactions of a nine-man uranium prospecting team to a woman in their midst when her disguise as a boy cook is found out. Seaview, 1982.

Whitaker, Muriel, ed.   STORIES FROM THE CANADIAN NORTH
Fourteen tales of Canada's last frontier that explore the land, nature and the people. Hurtig, 1980.

TRAVEL ARTICLES

TRAVEL/HOLIDAY
1985 Aug "Call of the Wild: A New Rush Along Canada's Klondike Trail." Harry Basch and Shirley Slater, p. 59

THE UNITED STATES (Including North America)

Series Guidebooks (See Appendix 1)

Baedeker: United States
Birnbaum: United States; U.S. for Business Travelers
Fodor: American Cities on a Budget; Budget Travel in America
Let's Go: U.S.A.
Nagel: U.S.A.

Note: Asterisked books (*) apply to North America as a whole (Canada and the U.S.).

Background Reading

Adams, Thomas Boylston   A NEW NATION
Essays based on *Boston Globe* editorials that "range throughout American history . . . direct, lucid and authoritative. . . . a fine work of popular history." (PW) Globe-Pequot, 1982.

Arnold, Eve   IN AMERICA
Looking at America "as an exotic country"—in the same way this photojournalist approached China in her book on that country—with an emphasis on people. "A stunning book [providing] a deep and revealing cross-section of American culture." (BL) Knopf, 1983.

Blair, Walter and Hill, Hamlin   AMERICA'S HUMOR: FROM POOR RICHARD TO DOONESBURY
Oxford U, 1978.

Boorstin, Daniel J.   THE EXPLORING SPIRIT
"Exploration . . . as a major theme of the American experience"—based on a series of lectures recorded for BBC in 1975. (BRD) Random, 1976. Also *The Americans* (1958), history intended for the general reader—"superb panorama of life in America."

Coe, Evan and others   IMAGES OF AMERICA
Selected readings based on Alistair Cooke's "America" broadcasts (see Alistair Cooke entry below). Knopf, 1977.

Conrad, Peter   IMAGINING AMERICA
An analysis of preconceived notions held by British writers who visited and wrote about America—includes Dickens, Wilde, Lawrence, Isherwood, others. Oxford U, 1980.

Cooke, Alistair   THE AMERICANS
Fifty talks on our life and times explains America to foreigners and represents a series of radio talks from 1969 to the 1970s. Knopf, 1979.

Cooper, Adrianne   LARA IN AMERICA
Travels by the author on horseback (Lara is the horse) from Wyoming to Nebraska—impressions and a "record of human contacts . . . an extended tribute to American hospitality." (BRD) McKay, 1977.

*De Voto, Bernard A.   COURSE OF EMPIRE
The exploration of the North American continent for the 300 years prior to 1805—considered one of the best books about the West, "consciously designed to engage the reader's imagination as well as his desire to be informed." (BRD) U of Nebraska, 1983 (first published 1952).

Dos Passos, John   STATE OF THE NATION
Reprint of the novelist's book on America in wartime. Greenwood Pr,1973 (first published 1944).

Dotson, Bob   . . . IN PURSUIT OF THE AMERICAN DREAM
"Offbeat and optimistic" sketches of Middle America from the "Today Show"—from Harlem to the Okefenokee Swamp. (PW) Atheneum, 1985.

Epstein, Joseph   FAMILIAR TERRITORY
Observations on American life from the "Life and Letters" column of an American scholar—"cultivated and humorous." (BRD) Oxford U, 1979.

Evans, J. Martin   AMERICA: THE VIEW FROM EUROPE
A Welsh immigrant-author reassesses his view of America after living here for twelve years, exploring themes in the works of European authors such as Dickens, Waugh, Nabokov, Greene, etc. Halsted Pr, 1979.

Fitzgerald, Frances   CITIES ON A HILL
"A Journey Through Contemporary American Cultures" from Jerry Falwell's church in Lynchburg, Virginia, and a gay neighborhood in San Francisco to a Florida retirement village and the now defunct commune of Rajneesh in Oregon—"triumph of detailed research and brilliant reportage." (Publisher Ad) S&S, 1986.

*Garreau, Joel   THE NINE NATIONS OF NORTH AMERICA
A *Washington Post* reporter's view of North America argues that arbitrary state and national boundaries mean nothing. His "nine nations" are based on economics, emotional allegiance, and attitudes, and each has its own capital and distinctive web of power and influence. Under this concept, for instance, the

Caribbean is part of Miami, Atlantic Canada part of New England, and so on. A highly readable and perceptive view of America. Houghton, 1981.

Heat Moon, William L.   BLUE HIGHWAYS: A JOURNEY INTO AMERICA
Traveling the back roads of America—those that rate a blue line on maps—vignettes of people and places with history and philosophy unobtrusively woven into the text. Little, 1983.

Hobson, Archie, ed.   REMEMBERING AMERICA: A SAMPLER OF THE WPA AMERICAN GUIDE SERIES
The editor has culled 500 entries from the auto tour guides written as part of the WPA writer's project from 1935-43, and organized them by theme rather than geographically. Columbia U Pr, 1985.

Honour, Hugh   THE NEW GOLDEN LAND
Images of America in the European imagination from discovery to the present. Flora, fauna, landscapes, people and customs as seen by European artists, with many illustrations plus literary background including Shakespeare, Montaigne, Byron, Goethe, Keats, etc. Pantheon, 1976.

Horwitz, Richard P.   THE STRIP: AN AMERICAN PLACE
A "fun to read" yet academic treatment of a unique aspect of America—the pop culture commercial strips of fast food places and neon on American highways. Focuses on one such strip in Iowa City, and the author conveys the humanness behind the strips and why they are useful. (BL) U of Nebraska, 1985.

Inge, M. Thomas, ed.   HANDBOOK OF AMERICAN POPULAR CULTURE
First of two volumes for nostalgia buffs, covering everything from literature and newspapers to TV, radio, film, sports, automobiles, etc. Greenwood, 1979.

Jenkins, Peter   A WALK ACROSS AMERICA
Literally a walk across America from Connecticut to New Orleans. The walk, and memoirs, were motivated by the author's desire to put his life back together—"vivid and thoughtful." (BRD) Fawcett, 1981. A sequel is *The Walk West* (1981), from New Orleans to the Pacific.

Kuralt, Charles   ON THE ROAD WITH CHARLES KURALT
A continuation of the TV commentator's earlier book, *Dateline America* (1979). More interviews of Americans with a special story to tell that emphasize themes of individuality and altruism—"different drummers." (BL) Putnam Pub Group, 1985.

L'Amour, Louis   FRONTIER
The popular author of many novels revisits the settings for them. A blend of history, personal experiences, travelogue—Maine Islands, the Outer Banks of North Carolina, to bayou country and canyons of the Southwest. Bantam, 1984.

Lanier, Alison R.   LIVING IN THE U.S.A.
"Fast-paced, readable survey" of how newcomers can deal with the culture and social realities of America. (publisher) Intercult Pr, 1981.

Malcolm, Andrew H.   UNKNOWN AMERICA
Vignettes on the mood of the nation, places and personalities, arranged according to the seasons and traversing the country from one corner to the other, by a roving reporter of the *New York Times*. Times Bks, 1975.

McFarland, Gerald   A SCATTERED PEOPLE: AN AMERICAN FAMILY MOVES WEST
History told through an extended family autobiography, atypical in its diversity of experiences . . . its participation in the events of the day as it drifts farther west as did the American people. Full of fascinating historical detail. Pantheon, 1985.

Michener, James   JAMES MICHENER'S USA
Based on a five-part TV series, with the country divided into five geographical regions. Crown, 1982. The popular novelist whose specialty is panoramic novels of particular places "here examines urban, suburban, and rural problems, all with optimistic and patriotic conclusions." (LJ)

Miller, Christian   DAISY, DAISY; A JOURNEY ACROSS AMERICA ON A BICYCLE
And by a British grandmother at that—but she cheated once in a while by taking the bike on a bus or taking a lift from a truck driver. Many adventures recounted "in a nice, chatty style. . . . A slightly daffy, endearing book." (NYT) Doubleday, 1981.

Moffitt, Donald   THE AMERICAN CHARACTER
Breezy, irresistible views of America from the *Wall Street Journal*. A collection of fifty articles offering telling glimpses of contemporary American life and work—everything from auto workers and stenographers to footballers and cowboys. Braziller, 1983.

Peirce, Neil R. and Hagstrom, Jerry   THE BOOK OF AMERICA: INSIDE FIFTY STATES TODAY
"Cogent, insightful" survey of the American states, region by region. There's an historical overview of each plus demography, state politics, local personalities, and much more. (BL) Norton, 1984.

Peirce, Neil R.   THE MEGASTATES OF AMERICA: PEOPLE, POLITICS AND POWER IN THE TEN GREAT STATES
See the Peirce entry under each of the four following regional sections. This book from that series provides additional insight and information regarding ten of the states covered also in the regional books—California, Florida, Illinois, Massachusetts, Michigan, New Jersey, New York, Ohio, Pennsylvania and Texas—the "megastates." Norton, 1972.

Reeves, Richard   AMERICAN JOURNEY: TRAVELING WITH TOCQUEVILLE IN SEARCH OF DEMOCRACY IN AMERICA
A recreation of Tocqueville's tour 150 years ago, from Newport, Rhode Island, through the south, to Wisconsin (then the frontier). A blend of interviews and reflections with passages from *Democracy in America* for a "splendid narrative."

He interviews everyone from Richard Nixon and New York's Mayor Koch to cab drivers and welfare recipients. (PW) S&S, 1982.

Roueche, Berton   SPECIAL PLACES: IN SEARCH OF SMALL TOWN AMERICA
Seven diverse towns described by an observant reporter, so that their unique qualities are revealed, ranging from a prairie town in Nebraska to a coal mining town in West Virginia. A portrayal of middle America that first appeared in the *New Yorker*—conversations with all sorts of people. Little, 1982.

Roueche, Berton   THE RIVER WORLD, AND OTHER EXPLORATIONS
Mini portraits of life-styles and manners—a towboat on the Mississippi River, with an Eskimo crew down the Alaskan waterways, in an Appalachian mining town, with a couple who run a winery on Long Island, and so on. These also first appeared in *The New Yorker*. Har-Row, 1978.

Sanford, John   A MORE GOODLY COUNTRY: A PERSONAL HISTORY OF AMERICA
The author "magnificently captures U.S. history [for] anyone looking for America. . . . Recreation of folk figures, pioneers, inventors, etc." in 200 vignettes. (BRD) Horizon, 1975.

*Savage, Henry   DISCOVERING AMERICA, 1700-1875
Chronicles both the explorations of North America and the interpretation of landscape, flora and fauna—text with art and photographs, intended for the general reader and students. Har-Row, 1979.

Shapiro, James E.   MEDITATIONS FROM THE BREAKDOWN LANE
Story of a marathon runner's solo run across America and impressions of loving and unloving people encountered along the way, with an "internal dialogue that touches on everything from Elks clubs . . . to massage parlors." (BL) Random, 1982.

Silk, Leonard S. and Mark   THE AMERICAN ESTABLISHMENT
What the Establishment is—Harvard, the *New York Times*, the Ford Foundation, Brookings Institute, and the Council on Foreign Relations are the most influential—how it operates and the role it plays in the U.S. today. Avon, 1981.

Stegner, Wallace and Page   AMERICAN PLACES
Evocative history, reminiscences of places the authors know well. Dutton, 1982.

Steinbeck, John   TRAVELS WITH CHARLEY IN SEARCH OF AMERICA
By a leading American novelist—"trenchant observations about life in general and about our country . . . penetrating insights into American mores." (BRD) Penguin, 1980 (first published 1962).

Tarshis, Barry   THE "AVERAGE AMERICAN" BOOK
A look at the traits, habits, tastes, life-styles and attitudes of Americans. Atheneum, 1979.

Terkel, Studs   AMERICAN DREAMS: LOST AND FOUND
A collection of statements by many Americans of their opinions, disappointments, fears and hopes for the nation. Pantheon, 1980.

*Theroux, Paul   THE OLD PATAGONIAN EXPRESS: BY TRAIN
THROUGH THE AMERICAS
Theroux's insights and characterizations as he travels (mostly by train) through North and South America—Boston to Patagonia. Houghton, 1979.

Trudgill, Peter   COPING WITH AMERICA: BEGINNER'S GUIDE
TO THE U.S.A.
Written for Europeans—"makes droll reading for Americans who forget how different we are from other folk." Blackwell, 1982.

Tschiffely, A.F.   SOUTHERN CROSS TO POLE STAR
J.P. Tarcher, 1983.

Wattenberg, Ben J.   THE GOOD NEWS IS THE BAD NEWS IS WRONG
A book of trends and progress to refute the doomsayers about America's future, which gloomy picture the author blames mostly on "media distortion of the quality of American life." He backs his thesis with statistics, other data, and polls "that show that U.S. disenchantment with and criticism of the naysaying press are facts of national life." (BL) S&S, 1984.

ETHNIC AND BLACK AMERICA

Brownstone, David M. and others   ISLAND OF HOPE, ISLAND OF TEARS
Ellis Island as millions of immigrants from Europe passed through—the essence of the immigrant experience. Rawson Assoc, 1979.

Harding, Vincent   THE OTHER AMERICAN REVOLUTION
"Interpretive survey of the black struggle in America from its African roots to the assassination of Martin Luther King . . . popularly written essays"—originally intended for a TV series. (BRD) Ctr Afro Am Stud, 1981.

Kessner, Thomas and Caroli, Betty B.   TODAY'S IMMIGRANTS, THEIR
STORIES: A NEW LOOK AT THE
NEWEST AMERICANS
Oxford U, 1981.

Morrison, Joan and Zabusky, Charlotte F.   AMERICAN MOSAIC
The immigrant experience in the words of those who lived it. Dutton, 1980.

Sowell, Thomas   ETHNIC AMERICA
Traces the historic experience of nine American ethnic groups, combining scholarship and readability in a compact form. Basic Bks, 1983.

THE NATIVE AMERICANS

Claiborne, Robert   **THE FIRST AMERICANS**
Time-Life, 1973.

Marquis, Arnold   **GUIDE TO AMERICA'S INDIANS, CEREMONIALS, RESERVATIONS AND MUSEUMS**
General history and information on the Indians, with an emphasis on the Southwest, but sections on all areas of the country. U of Oklahoma Pr, 1974.

Olson, James S.   **NATIVE AMERICANS IN THE TWENTIETH CENTURY**
Brigham Young U, 1984.

Spicer, Edward H.   **A SHORT HISTORY OF THE INDIANS OF THE U.S.**
Krieger, 1984 (first published 1969).

Vogel, Virgil J.   **THIS COUNTRY WAS OURS**
A documentary history related by Indians past and present. Har-Row, 1972.

RESTORATIONS & HISTORY TOURS, ARCHITECTURE, ARCHAEOLOGY

Note: See also multivolume and other guides listed under regions—East, South, Midwest and West.

*Boatner, Mark M.   **LANDMARKS OF THE AMERICAN REVOLUTION**
"A guide to locating and knowing what happened at the sites of independence . . . well-written, comprehensive and detailed. . .significance of the site in its local as well as national context." Includes both United States and Canada. (BRD) Stackpole, 1973.

Chamberlain, Holly and others   **VICTORIAN TRAVELER'S COMPANION**
A pocket guide to nineteenth-century houses, museums, inns, restaurants, tours, and historic sites, arranged alphabetically by state and town, practical tourist information—"beautifully written descriptions of each site." (LJ) Victorian Society in America, 1980.

*Cromie, Alice H.   **RESTORED AMERICA: A TOUR GUIDE**
Guide to preserved towns and historic city districts of the United States and Canada. Crown, 1984.

Cromie, Alice H.   **A TOUR GUIDE TO THE CIVIL WAR**
Museums, battlefields, and other special places connected with the Civil War. Dutton, 1975.

Eastman, John   **WHO LIVED WHERE: A BIOGRAPHICAL GUIDE TO HOMES AND MUSEUMS**
"A charming book" of travel/biography, giving some 600 homes and museums of persons (all deceased) whose careers affected U.S. cultural and political history, and ranging "from Abraham Lincoln to Gypsy Rose Lee." (BL) Facts On File, 1983.

Folson, Franklin and Mary E.   **AMERICA'S ANCIENT TREASURES:**
                                    GUIDE TO ARCHEOLOGICAL SITES
                                    AND MUSEUMS
U of New Mexico, 1983 (first published 1971).

Hart, Herbert M.   **TOUR GUIDE TO OLD FORTS**
Volume 1: Montana, North and South Dakota, Wyoming; Volume 2: Arizona,
Colorado, Nevada, New Mexico, Utah; Volume 3: California, Idaho, Oregon,
Washington; Volume 4: Kansas, Nebraska, Oklahoma, Texas. Pruett, 1980-81.

Kennedy, Roger   **AMERICAN CHURCHES**
"The way that tangible religious buildings represent intangible religious truths.
From Rhode Island's Touro Synagogue to California's Crystal Cathedral . . . the awe
and uplift that churches, temples, chapels and cathedrals produce in believers and
viewers." (BL) Stewart, Tabori & Chang, 1982.

Kern, Ellyn R.   **WHERE THE AMERICAN PRESIDENTS LIVED**
A chronological listing for each president of every place of residence, its
present status, and information on those presently open to the public. Cottontail
Pbns, 1982.

Kidder-Smith, G.E.   **THE ARCHITECTURE OF THE UNITED STATES:**
                         NEW ENGLAND AND THE MID-ATLANTIC STATES
Also the second and third volumes, *The South and Mid-West* (1981) and *The
Plains States and Far West* (1981). "A very special compendium" of architectural
sites which are mostly accessible to the public. The author's purpose is to engage
Americans in an active appreciation of their architecture. Doubleday, 1981.

McAlester, Virginia   **A FIELD GUIDE TO AMERICAN HOUSES**
Concentration is on the single-family house of pre-1940 vintage. Knopf, 1984.

National Trust for Historic Preservation   **AMERICAN LANDMARKS**
Historic buildings under the jurisdiction of the National Trust. Preservation Pr,
1980.

Rifkind, Carole   **A FIELD GUIDE TO AMERICAN ARCHITECTURE**
A "compendious guide to American architectural styles . . . traces the development of residential, church, civic, commercial and utilitarian structures in
separate sections. . . . includes examples of high style . . . vernacular style . . .
provincial adaptations." NAL, 1980.

Thum, Gladys and Marcella   **EXPLORING MILITARY AMERICA**
Battlefields, parks, museums, forts, and war memorials are listed, enabling
travelers to acquaint themselves with America's military heritage. Atheneum,
1982.

Wilson, Josleen   **THE PASSIONATE AMATEUR'S GUIDE TO**
                      ARCHAEOLOGY IN THE U.S.
Sites in progress, completed sites, related museums; including practical in-

formation for travelers as well as names of archaeological organizations. Macmillan, 1981.

NATURAL WONDERS & OUTDOOR AMERICA

Abbey, Edward   SLUMGULLION STEW: AN EDWARD ABBEY READER

An anthology of essays and novel excerpts covering "thirty years and thousands of miles of desert, canyon and river rapids" by one of America's "most articulate and engaging environmentalists . . . will delight his fans [while bedeviling his foes]." (PW) Dutton, 1984. See also *Beyond the Wall*, under "West/Background Reading."

*Durant, Mary and Harwood, Michael   ON THE ROAD WITH JOHN JAMES AUDUBON

Combining their talents of novelist, historian, journalist, and amateur ornithologist, the authors retrace Audubon's travels in Texas, Labrador, the Tortugas, using his journals, essays and letters as a guide. Dodd, 1980.

Frome, Michael   PROMISED LAND: ADVENTURES AND ENCOUNTERS IN WILD AMERICA

Based on thirty years of writing on conservation and travel—"an attempt to define wilderness through descriptions of the places and people he has known. . . . a mosaic of how wild places affect people." (LJ) Morrow, 1985. Also *National Park Guide* (1984).

*Huser, Verne   RIVER REFLECTIONS

"An eclectic collection of . . . writings about North American rivers, covering the past 350 years . . . excerpts from and stories about voyageurs, explorers, white water loggers, naturalists and historians, engineers, recreational boaters and many more." From famous authors such as Steinbeck, McPhee and Twain, to diaries of scientists, women pioneers and so on. (Publisher) East Woods, 1984.

Landi, Val   THE GREAT AMERICAN COUNTRYSIDE: A TRAVELLER'S COMPANION

"Superb" overview describing flora, fauna, natural and man-made sites of the United States. (BL) Macmillan, 1972.

Mohlenbrock, Robert H.   THE FIELD GUIDE TO U.S. NATIONAL FORESTS

Arranged by region—practical tourist information on accommodations, activities, information sources, plus evaluations as to the appeal of particular forests, favorite trails and special sights—alternatives to the more crowded national park system. Congdon & Weed, 1984.

*National Geographic Society   EXPLORING AMERICA'S VALLEYS: FROM THE SHENANDOAH TO THE RIO GRANDE

"Travel essays [and] photographs describe twenty North American Valleys. . . . focus is first on the history of the area and then on the present inhabitants' way of life. . . . personal stories of contemporary farmers and crafts people." Natl Geog, 1984. Typical of the many books on natural America published by The Society, some other titles include: *New America's Wonderlands: Our National Parks* (1980); *Exploring America's Scenic Highways* (1979); *Exploring America's Backcountry* (1979); *America's Majestic Canyons* (1979); *America's Hidden Corners—Places off the Beaten Path* (1983); *America's Magnificent Mountains* (1980); *Wild and Scenic Rivers* (1983); and *Wilderness USA* (1973).

**National Park Foundation   THE COMPLETE GUIDE TO AMERICA'S
                               NATIONAL PARKS**
The official visitor's guide of the National Park Foundation; comprehensive information on all of America's national parks. Viking, 1982.

**Reader's Digest eds.   OUR NATIONAL PARKS: AMERICA'S
                          SPECTACULAR WILDERNESS HERITAGE**
Our parks from Acadia, Maine, to Zion, Utah, in alphabetical order, with a final chapter on the new Alaskan parks. Random, 1985.

Reader's Digest eds.   AMERICA FROM THE ROAD
"A motorist's guide to our country's natural wonders and most interesting places. . . . one-volume tour guide for auto-trippers." Planned tours, avoiding for the most part major metropolises, with notes on distinctive regional characteristics plus all kinds of information to enhance trips by car—photographs and drawings of flora, fauna and farm equipment one might see en route, previews of scenery along the way, etc. (BL) Random, 1982.

Riley, Laura   GUIDE TO THE NATIONAL WILDLIFE REFUGES
Most are open to the public—where located, how to get there, what to see and do, where to camp and stay, best time for visiting, etc. Anchor Pr, 1979.

Sifford, Darrell   THE LOVE OF THE LAND
Farming in America—"by turns amusing, enlightening, sobering and touching"—intended for cityfolks as well as those with an interest in farming. (BL) Farm Journal, 1980.

GUIDES TO ARTS AND LITERARY LANDMARKS

Note: See also multi-volume and other guides listed under the four regions—East, South, Midwest and West.

Benedict, Stewart, ed.   A LITERARY GUIDE TO THE UNITED STATES
Six regions, organized chronologically and geographically—"more than a road map . . . chronicles the genesis, growth and maturation of American literature in light of social, geographic, and cultural influences." (BRD) Facts On File, 1981.

**Ehrlich, Eugene and Carruth, Gorton   THE OXFORD ILLUSTRATED
                                          LITERARY GUIDE TO THE
                                          UNITED STATES**
Cities and other places associated with particular authors and books, cross-

indexed—"delightful and informative production—a pleasure to behold and to browse in." (BL) Oxford U, 1982.

Freundenheim, Tom L., ed.   AMERICAN MUSEUM GUIDES: FINE ARTS
A handbook for the general public arranged by category (American, ancient, European, etc.)—collection holdings are surveyed. Also provides tourist information on hours, admissions, etc. Macmillan, 1983.

Gusikoff, Lynne   GUIDE TO MUSICAL AMERICA
Guide to all kinds of musical activities organized by region and by genre within each region—"specific references to many of the backwater and less publicized festivals, clubs and discos, arts centers, dance halls . . . where one finds live music today." (Choice) Facts On File, 1984.

Jacobs, Ben, ed.   FESTA! THE FIRST GUIDE TO PERFORMING ARTS IN THE U.S.A.
Symphony concerts, jazz, theatre, opera, historic pageants, year-round festivals and events. Musica, 1980.

Kraft, Stephanie   NO CASTLES ON MAIN STREET: AMERICAN AUTHORS AND THEIR HOMES
Thirty of the most original regional authors in U.S. literary history. Rand, 1979.

Lord, Suzanne   AMERICAN TRAVELER'S TREASURY: A GUIDE TO THE NATION'S HEIRLOOMS
Where to find the fine arts, folk arts and other displays of our national heritage. Morrow, 1977.

*McLanathan, Richard   WORLD ART IN AMERICAN MUSEUMS
A guide to museums in the United States and Canada, organized by periods and special collections (modern, primitive, Far East, decorative arts, etc.). Doubleday, 1983.

Rabin, Carol Price   MUSIC FESTIVALS IN AMERICA
A unique planning guide—gives the history of each festival, location, performance dates, ambience, accommodations and more, for all kinds of musical festivals from classical and opera to bluegrass and jazz. Berkshire Traveller, 1983.

*Sherman, Lila   ART MUSEUMS OF AMERICA: A GUIDE TO COLLECTIONS IN THE U.S. AND CANADA
"A Baedeker-thorough guidebook to 550 museums and galleries . . . that have permanent fine arts collections." (BL) Morrow, 1980.

GUIDEBOOKS TO INSPIRE AN ITINERARY OR EXPLORE A THEME

Arbeiter, Jean and Cirino, Linda D.   PERMANENT ADDRESSES: A GUIDE TO THE RESTING PLACES OF FAMOUS AMERICANS
Grouped by occupation and alphabetically by state. Dutton, 1983.

*Babcock, Judy and Kennedy, Judy   THE SPA BOOK: A GUIDED
PERSONAL TOUR OF HEALTH
RESORTS AND BEAUTY SPAS
FOR MEN AND WOMEN
Organized by region, with entries for the United States, Mexico, West Indies and
Canada. Crown, 1983.

Baxter, Robert   BAXTER'S U.S.A. BY CAR, BUS, TRAIN AND PLANE
Rail-Europe-Baxter, 1984.

Bayer, Patricia and Goldman, Michael   ANTIQUES WORLD TRAVEL
GUIDE TO AMERICA
A bonanza of information for antiques collectors—shops with specialties,
addresses and hours, fairs, museums, restorations, flea markets, auctioneers.
Dolphin, 1982.

*Berger, Terry and Gardner, Roberta   McCLANE'S GREAT HUNTING
AND FISHING LODGES OF
NORTH AMERICA
A sampler of twenty of the top-notch lodges in the United States, Canada and
Mexico and a cross-section—remote or just off the highway, expensive and inex-
pensive, family or to go alone, etc. HR&W, 1984.

Brandon, Jim   WEIRD AMERICA: A GUIDE TO PLACES OF MYSTERY
IN THE U.S.
For those interested in unusual phenomena from UFO sightings to ghosts and
monsters. Dutton, 1978.

British Tourist Authority   DISCOVER AMERICA
Traveling America with a British travel guide might just add a different touch to
the experience. BTA, 1982. Also *Destination USA:The East* (1983) and *Destination USA: The West* (1983).

Brooklyn Botanical Gardens eds.   AMERICAN GARDENS: A TRAVELER'S
GUIDE
Botanical gardens, estate gardens, nature preserves and commercial gardens.
Booklyn Botanical Gardens, 1977.

Chambers, Andrea   DREAM RESORTS: 25 EXCLUSIVE AND UNIQUE
AMERICAN HOTELS, INNS, LODGES AND SPAS
Potter, 1983.

Daniel, Joseph   THE GREAT AMERICAN ADVENTURE BOOK
100 unusual vacation opportunities, some requiring physical venturesomeness,
others simply unusual (covered-wagon holidays, etc.). Dolphin, 1985.

Dickerman, Pat   FARM, RANCH AND COUNTRY VACATIONS
Berkshire Traveller, 1983.

Fegan, Patrick W.   VINEYARDS AND WINERIES OF AMERICA: A TRAVELER'S GUIDE
930 wineries arranged by region. Stephen Greene, 1982.

*Fensom, Rod   AMERICA'S GRAND HOTELS: EIGHTY CLASSIC RESORTS IN THE UNITED STATES AND CANADA
"Working, historic resorts. . .built between 1847 and 1929. . . .a wonderful book for armchair travelers" or to use as a practical guide. The author provides anecdotes of famous guests, history, architecture, decor. (Publisher) East Woods, 1985.

Fistell, Ira   AMERICA BY TRAIN
A guidebook by a rail buff who also happens to be among the most literate of the radio talk-show hosts. Combines rail information with history and "sights along the way . . . story of AMTRAK's 23,000-mile national network [with] highlights of 49 main streets . . . thumbnail sketches of hundreds of small towns and way-stations." (NYT) B Franklin, 1983.

*Goldenson, Suzanne   VINTAGE PLACES: A CONNOISSEUR'S GUIDE TO NORTH AMERICAN WINERIES AND VINEYARDS
Histories, practical data, tour information, directions, suggested readings, from the little-known to the major vineyards, in the U.S.A., British Columbis, Nova Scotia and Ontario. Main Street Pr, 1985.

*Haag, Michael and others   THE MONEYWISE GUIDE TO NORTH AMERICA
Thousands of budget places to eat and stay, public transit information, special discounts, travel bargains, descriptions of cities, towns, parks, information on what to wear, visas, currency, health and welfare, etc. Includes Canada and Mexico. Presidio Pr, 1983.

Hayes, Bob   THE BLACK AMERICAN TRAVEL GUIDE
Black history and background of fourteen U.S. cities; travel information. Straight Arrow, 1973.

Hoffmann, Paul, ed.   AMERICAN MUSEUM GUIDE: SCIENCE
A handbook of science museums for the general public arranged by category (air and space, natural history, science, etc.). Macmillan, 1983.

Interstate Guides eds.   TRAVELERS GUIDE TO INTERSTATE 80, COAST TO COAST
Interstate Guides, 1984.

*Kaufman, William   THE TRAVELER'S GUIDE TO THE VINEYARDS OF NORTH AMERICA
Mostly covers California and New York, but unexpected places are also included (Emmett, Idaho, for instance). Includes history, address, hours, types of grape, etc. Penguin, 1980.

Kenny, Maurice   GREYHOUNDING THIS AMERICA
Heidelberg, 1984.

Kirby-Smith, Henry T.   U.S. OBSERVATORIES: A DIRECTORY AND TRAVEL GUIDE
Three hundred observatories, museums and planetariums—compiled by an amateur astronomer. Van Nostrand, 1976.

Ludwig, Jack   GREAT AMERICAN SPECTACULARS: THE KENTUCKY DERBY, MARDI GRAS, AND OTHER DAYS OF CELEBRATION
Chosen because of who participates and each event's mystique. Doubleday, 1976.

Marx, Robert F.   BURIED TREASURE OF THE U.S.
How and where to locate hidden wealth, with a reading list on specific treasure hunting goals. McKay, 1978.

*Scheller, William G.   TRAIN TRIPS: EXPLORING AMERICA BY RAIL
"Guide to American passenger service . . . complete Canadian Via Rail information." (Publisher) East Woods, 1984.

Shemanski, Frances   GUIDE TO FAIRS AND FESTIVALS IN THE U.S.
Greenwood, 1984.

*Spivack, Carol and Weinstock, Richard A.   BEST FESTIVALS OF NORTH AMERICA
"A practical guide to festival/vacations"—arranged by topic (dance, opera, jazz, etc.). "The authors have been very selective . . . criteria such as duration of at least one week, a variety of events or performers, availability of other vacation attractions in the area . . . caliber of talent." Much additional useful information such as nearby festivals and things to do, nearby activities and attractions for children, and so on. (BL) Printwheel Pr, 1984.

*Spivack, Carol and Weinstock, Richard A.   GOURMET FOOD AND WINE FESTIVALS OF NORTH AMERICA
Written for those who like to eat well, drink fine wine, when on vacation; provides information about major annual food and wine festivals in the U.S. and Canada, covering everything from lobster to chocolate and strawberries. Also gives addresses, lodgings available, and other practical information. Printwheel Pr, 1986.

Thompson, Toby   SALOON: A GUIDE TO AMERICA'S GREAT BARS, SALOONS, TAVERNS, DRINKING PLACES AND WATERING HOLES
"Where the weary traveler can find quiet comfort, cheap drinks, reasonably good food and occasionally a congenial bar stool buddy." (BRD) Viking, 1976.

Thum, Marcella   EXPLORING BLACK AMERICA: A HISTORY AND GUIDE
"Many of the passages missing from America's history books are found in this entertainingly written, informative guide"—monuments, historic sites, museums. (BRD) Atheneum, 1975.

Ulmer, Jeff   AMUSEMENT PARKS OF AMERICA: A COMPREHENSIVE GUIDE
Theme parks, boardwalks, game farms, amusement parks, restored villages, etc. Dial, 1980.

Van Meer, Mary and Pasquarelli, Michael A., eds   FREE ATTRACTIONS U.S.A.
Notable monuments, parks, zoos, museums, landmarks, churches, shrines, historic houses, farms, gardens, cultural centers, wineries, galleries, etc., etc.—"all sorts of sights to intrigue all sorts of travelers." Arranged alphabetically by state and then by city with description, hours and directions. (BL) East Woods, 1984.

*Vokac, David   THE GREAT TOWNS OF THE WEST: A GUIDE TO THEIR SPECIAL PLEASURES
A guide to fifty locales in the Western United States, Alberta and British Columbia that are desirable for sightseeing, aside from cities and the well-known parks. West Pr, 1985.

Wasserstein, Susan   COLLECTOR'S GUIDE TO U.S. AUCTIONS AND FLEA MARKETS
Three hundred country auction firms, 500 established flea markets are described—frequency, size, specialty, on-site facilities, nearby travelers' amenities, terms of sale, forms of payment, name of a contact. Penguin, 1981.

Weinreb, Risa and Alpine, Lisa C.   THE ADVENTURE VACATION CATALOG
"An encyclopaedic resource covering all sorts of exotic and exciting travel opportunities" from covered-wagon vacations and opera tours to windjamming and dogsledding. It is arranged topically and explains activity and skills or other requirements needed to participate, organizations to contact, relevant clubs and associations, rates. (BL) S&S, 1984.

Young, Judith   CELEBRATIONS: AMERICA'S BEST FESTIVALS, CARNIVALS, JAMBOREES AND PARADES
Capra Pr, 1986.

HISTORY

Burns, James MacGregor   THE VINEYARD OF LIBERTY
First in a projected series of three volumes with the overall title of *The American Experiment*. This covers that period between the Constitution and the Emancipation Proclamation. Random, 1983.

Commager, Henry Steele, ed.   THE AMERICAN DESTINY
An illustrated bicentennial history of the United States from discovery and settlement by Europeans to the 1970s. Danbury Pr, 1975.

Morison, Samuel Eliot   THE GROWTH OF THE AMERICAN REPUBLIC
Revised 7th edition—"thorough, objective treatment . . . plus lucid writing." Oxford U, 1980. Also *The Great Explorers* (1978), story of the voyages to America from A.D. 500 to 1616.

Nevins, Allan and Commager, Henry S.   A POCKET HISTORY OF THE
                                        UNITED STATES
Pocket Books, 1981.

Tindall, George B.   AMERICA: A NARRATIVE HISTORY
Two volumes, history from pre-Columbian times to the Reagan administration—"the author's engrossing style makes it possible for readers to dip comfortably here and there . . . and be absorbed in any section that might be of interest." (BL) Norton, 1984.

Zinn, Howard   THE TWENTIETH CENTURY, A PEOPLE'S HISTORY
An antidote to establishment history of "those whose plight has been largely omitted from most histories." (LJ) Har-Row, 1984.

TRAVEL ARTICLES

AMERICANA
1985 May-Jun "Steam Trains, There Are Still Steam Trains Aplenty." For tourists and rail buffs. Susan Vreeland, p. 34
1984 Jul-Aug "The Merry-Go-Round Rides Again." Where to find restored carousels. Jay Fromkin, p. 33
      Oct-Nov "Old-Time Farms." Living-history farms to visit in many states. Quinith Janssen, p. 110

BETTER HOMES & GARDENS
1985 Apr "Destination U.S.A." Great family vacations: a planning guide. Barbara Humeston and George S. Bush, p. 155
      Jul "Discovering the Delights of Train Travel." Barbara Humeston, p. 132
      Nov "America's 18 Best Ski Resorts, Downhill and Cross-country, for Families." George S. Bush, p. 198
1984 May "A Family Guide to Outfitted Wilderness Vacations." George S. Bush, p. 173
      Nov "Winter Wonderland Vacations in Our National Parklands." p. 223
      Dec "The Six Best Big-City Holiday Vacations for Families." Barbara Humeston, p. 38

BLACK ENTERPRISE
1984 Feb "Romantic Getaways for Two." In NYC, Chicago, Atlanta, D.C., Houston, San Francisco, New Orleans, New England. p. 110

Sep "Fall Foliage Tours." Jessica Harris, p. 71
Dec "Christmas Festivals U.S.A." A round-up of holiday events from the Rockefeller Center Christmas tree to the fiesta of lights in San Antonio. Jessica Harris, p. 102

CHANGING TIMES
1985 Jun "Vacation Ideas." You don't have to go to Europe to find good travel values. p. 38

EARLY AMERICAN LIFE
1985 Jun "Discover Historic America." Living history museums. Sarah Cupps, p. 32
1984 Jun "Discovering Historic America with Children." Special section. Loretta and William Marshall, p. 57

ESQUIRE
1984 Apr "Summer Traveler: Special Section." p. 114
"On the Town, On the Job." A guide to surviving big-city blues while on business trips in N.Y.C., Dallas, Atlanta, Los Angeles, D.C., Chicago, San Francisco. p. 114
Oct "31 Winter Escapes for the Active Traveler Via Trains, Planes, Boats and Feet to Sun, Slopes, Surf and Sand." (Includes the U.S.) Wendy Love and Mark Ingebretsen, p. 160

50 PLUS
1984 *Aug "Falling for the Leaves." Autumn in New York, New England, North Carolina, Virginia, Canada. Joseph Scott, p. 38

GLAMOUR
1985 Apr "What's Hot: What's Happening in the U.S. of A." p. 246
Aug "6 Great Getaways Where Early Fall Is the Best Time of All." Cape Cod, Santa Fe, Santa Barbara. p. 234
1984 Apr "Travel U.S.A." What's special for summer '84. p. 234
Sep "Great Country Inns for Fall Weekend Getaways." In Connecticut, Vermont, North Carolina, Mississippi, Minnesota, Arizona, California. p. 286
*Oct "New Ways to Get the Most from a Ski Vacation." U.S. and Canada. Abby Rand, p. 231

GOOD HOUSEKEEPING
1985 Dec "Christmas Getaways." Inns and Museums. Stephen Birnbaum, p. 76
1984 Apr "Ten Great Trips to Take with Your Kids." Stephen Birnbaum, p. 228
Jun "A Guide to National Parks." Stephen Birnbaum, p. 192
Aug "The Ten Best Beaches in the U.S." Stephen Birnbaum, p. 172
Dec "Super Celebrations." Cities with spectacular Christmas displays. Vera F. Bradshaw, p. 218

HARPER'S BAZAAR
1985 Jul "America's best beaches." Parke Puterbaugh, p. 30

HOUSE BEAUTIFUL
1985 May "Great American Gardens." To include in your itinerary planning. Ken Druse, p. 47
Dec "Inns to Visit at Christmas—from Vermont to Hawaii." Brenda B. Chapin, p. 31
1984 May "Inn-Keeping with Our Times: Styles of Hospitality." In Connecticut, Vermont, Florida, South Carolina, New Mexico. p. 40

MADEMOISELLE
1985 Nov "Ski Sprees: Hot Places to Cool Your Heels." p. 198

MODERN MATURITY
1985 Apr-May "Ships to Stir Our Souls." They tell the battle history of America. Charles N. Barnard, p. 78
"They Also Served: America's Peacetime Fleet." Maureen Doe, p. 82
(Note: both articles are on ships travelers can visit.)

NATIONAL GEOGRAPHIC
1985 Dec "Daniel Boone's America—Sorting Fact from Fiction." Elizabeth A. Moise, p. 812
1984 Jul "The Underground Railroad." Network of paths and safe houses used by slaves seeking freedom are traced. Charles L. Blockson, p. 3
Sep "Beyond the Dust Bowl." Follows the trail of the Okies during the depression from the High Plains to California. William Howarth, p. 322

NATIONAL GEOGRAPHIC TRAVELER
1985 Winter "'Tis the season." Museum displays, special festivities for Christmas. Maria M. Mudd, p. 139

N.Y. TIMES SUNDAY TRAVEL SECTION (X)
1985 Apr 14 "Seeking the Lost Amusement Park." Traditional carousels and roller coasters survive on the outskirts of a few American towns. Richard Snow, p. 41
Apr 21 "On the Road from Sea to Sea." *Times* correspondents map their favorite routes (New England, District of Columbia, Florida, South Carolina, Michigan, Missouri, the Rockies, California, Arizona, Texas). Various authors, p. 15
Sep 8 "A Selection of Fall Events Around the United States." Reports from Maine to California. Various authors, p. 15
Sep 29 "Getting the Lay of the Land." From the air, reading the continent's long history (how to look at the land below from a window seat). Walter Sullivan, p. 21
Oct 6 ("Sophisticated Traveler") "Treks for the Sophisticated Traveler." New Mexico's Sangre De Cristos. Elizabeth Tallent, p. 80;
"House of the Hawaiian Sun." Fletcher Knebel, p. 14
"Closing In on the Rockies." Ivan Doig, p. 12
Nov 3 "Condominiums (for Skiing) from A to Z." Stanley Carr, p. 29
1984 Apr 15 "Seasonal Excursions Coast to Coast." Springtime highlights in many states by sixteen national correspondents and contributors to the *Times*. p. 14

1984 May 13 "Around America by Rail." 8,000 miles, 5 AMTRAK trains, 1 case of
champagne—all in two weeks. Dorothy J. Gaiter, p. 18
Aug 5 "Sampling Shaker Life from Maine to Ohio." See also the *Times* article
under "Kentucky." Carol Plum, p. 16
Sep 23 "The Rewards of Watching and Waiting." Birdwatching. Graeme
Gibson, p. 9
Oct 28 "The View from Behind the Handlebars." Cycling across America.
Gwyn Ballard, p. 10
Dec 2 "Reserving Top Tables." Advice and a list of top restaurants in the
United States and Europe, and how to reserve a table. Florence Fabricant, p.
20

READER'S DIGEST
1985 Oct "Land of Plenty." America's back roads. Charles Kuralt, p. 119

SMITHSONIAN
1985 Aug "The Lincoln Highway, First Across the Country." Drake Hokanson, p.
58

TOWN & COUNTRY
1984 Jan "The Spas That Refresh." The *Town & Country* select guide to America's
health and beauty havens. Jane Wilkens Michael, p. 46
"The Wild White Yonder." *Town & Country's* guide to the newest high
adventure in the snow. Abby Rand, p. 62

TRAVEL & LEISURE
1985 Jan Travel & Architecture: "The Flamboyance of Art Deco." Wolf von
Eckardt, p. 54
Mar "Latest from the National Parks." George S. Bush, p. 67
Jul "Thomas Cole's 'The Oxbow.'" The romance and harmony of the
American landscape. James Thomas, p. 80
Oct "You Are Where You Eat." N.Y.C. (21 Club), Beverly Hills (Simpson's
Polo Lounge), Miami Beach (Joe's Stone Crab). George Lang, p. 118
1984 Apr "Six Special Restaurants, from Courtly Elegance in New York to
Waterside Informality in Seattle." New York, Pennsylvania, Texas,
Washington, Alaska. p. 64
May Travel & Architecture: "The Glory of the Gothic, from Middle Ages to
the Mid-20th Century." Carter Ratcliff, p. 62
Jul Travel & Architecture: "The Clarity of the Classical." From the Acropolis
to Monticello. Alexander Eliot, p. 54
Aug Travel & Architecture: "The Grandeur of the Baroque in Rome,
Versailles, Munich and San Francisco." Carol H. Krinsky, p. 32
Oct "Great U.S. Skiing, East to West." Tours. Abby Rand, p. 90
Nov Travel & Architecture: "The Skyscraper." An American original that
altered the urban skyline. Rosemarie H. Bletter, p. 32

TRAVEL/HOLIDAY
1985 Jan "One-of-a-Kind Museums." Eclectic collections in the U.S.A. Kim and
Victor Schlich, p. 40

1985 Jul "America's Wild Kingdoms—From Zoo to Shining Zoo." Jeffrey P. Cohn, p. 44

Aug "Legendary Links: A Golfer's Half Dozen." Includes North Carolina, California, Florida. Brian McCallen, p. 44

Dec "*Travel/Holiday* Guide to Fine Dining." Robert L. Balzer, p. 50

1984 Aug "Overnights in Native America." Sampling Indian-owned accommodations. Grace Ertel, p. 4

Dec "*Travel/Holiday's* Annual Guide to Fine Dining." U.S., Canada, Mexico. p. 51

VOGUE
1985 Oct "Discovering America by Train." Michael Sorkin, p. 440

WORKING WOMAN
1984 Jan "Fitness for the Business Traveler." Hotels in business centers with on-site health clubs in many cities. p. 86

THE EAST

Series Guidebooks (See Appendix 1)

Fisher: New England
Fodor: New England
Frommer: New England: Dollarwise
Insight: New England
Michelin: New England

Note: Asterisked entries (*) indicate a book or article pertaining to the Eastern U.S. or the coast, or Atlantic coast, and thus also including material on the South.

Background Reading

Bragin, Joan   THE WEEKEND CONNOISSEUR
Antiquing between Maine and Maryland—critiques shops and offers tips on museums, restaurants and lovely things to enjoy along the way. Doubleday, 1979.

Deedy, John   LITERARY PLACES: A GUIDED PILGRIMAGE TO NEW YORK AND NEW ENGLAND
"Places . . . where persons might commune with the spirits of those who helped create an American literature [with] emphasis on the 19th century." (BRD) Sheed, 1978.

Edey, Maitland A.   NORTHEAST COAST
Part of the American Wilderness series. Time-Life, 1972.

Farlow, Susan   MADE IN AMERICA (Northeast Edition)
A guide to tours of workshops, farms, mines and industries. Hastings, 1979.

Frazier, Nancy   SPECIAL MUSEUMS OF THE NORTHEAST: A GUIDE TO UNCOMMON COLLECTIONS FROM MAINE TO WASHINGTON, D.C.
"Fascinating worlds . . . in 144 small but outstanding museums. Discover everything from aircraft to holography, hummingbirds to witches." Factual information on hours, directions, plus evaluative information on whether children will like it, length of a typical visit, atmosphere and scope of each museum. (Publisher) Globe Pequot, 1985.

*Gosner, Kenneth L.   A FIELD GUIDE TO THE ATLANTIC SEASHORE
A field guide for amateurs—invertebrates and seaweeds of the Atlantic coast from the Bay of Fundy to Cape Hatteras. Houghton, 1982.

Harting, Emilie C.   A LITERARY TOUR GUIDE TO THE UNITED STATES: NORTHEAST
Authors' homes, inns and hotels frequented, museums, special libraries, and places associated with their writing. Morrow, 1978.

Hill, Kathleen   FESTIVALS USA
Volume II of this series covers festivals in the Eastern States. Hilltop, 1984.

*Kopper, Philip   THE WILD EDGE: LIFE AND LORE OF THE GREAT ATLANTIC BEACHES
Potpourri of information on beaches from the Bay of Fundy to the Carolinas—wildlife, geology, the "art" of beaching from having a clambake to how to avoid drowning. Penguin, 1981.

*Leonard, Jonathan N.   ATLANTIC BEACHES
Part of the American Wilderness Series. Time-Life, 1972.

Miller, Stephen and Merwin, Janet   THE COUNTRY AUCTION WEEKEND BOOK
Twenty-one country auction houses from Maine to Maryland with maps, directions, places to stay and to eat, things to see and do. Includes a directory of one hundred additional galleries, barns and houses that hold auctions in the Northeast. St. Martin, 1982.

*Morrison, H. Robert and Lee, Christine E.   AMERICA'S ATLANTIC ISLES
Natl Geog, 1981.

*Perry, Jane and John   THE RANDOM HOUSE GUIDE TO THE NATURAL AREAS OF THE EAST COAST
A directory of "quiet places, where plants grow, birds sing, and artifacts are

few"—covers the Atlantic coastal states, from Maine to Florida, plus West Virginia and Vermont. (LJ) Random, 1980.

Postal, Bernard and Koppman, Lionel   AMERICAN JEWISH LANDMARKS: A TRAVEL GUIDE AND HISTORY
Volume I covers the Northeast. Fleet, 1977.

*Ricciuti, Edward R.   THE BEACHWALKER'S GUIDE: THE SEASHORE FROM MAINE TO FLORIDA
Animal, plant and sea life found along the Atlantic coast. Doubleday, 1982.

*Scott, David L. and Kay W.   TRAVELING AND CAMPING IN THE NATIONAL PARK AREAS—EASTERN STATES
Includes the areas administered by the National Park Service, national seashores, historic sites, monuments, historic parks—descriptions and information on facilities, activities, camping, fishing and more. Globe Pequot, 1979.

*Spring, Michael   THE GREAT WEEKEND ESCAPE BOOK FROM WILLIAMSBURG TO CUTTYHUNK ISLAND
A planning tool for weekend and longer trips, to some nineteen regions from the popular to the less well-known. Dutton, 1985.

*Stone, Doris M.   THE GREAT PUBLIC GARDENS OF THE EASTERN UNITED STATES: A GUIDE TO THEIR BEAUTY AND BOTANY
Thorough, candid guide to thirty-four gardens. Pantheon, 1982.

Warner, William W.   DISTANT WATER
"Superb first-hand accounts of the fishing life" as it is lived in the North Atlantic on factory-equipped freezer trawlers. (BL) Little, 1983.

*Yeadon, David   SECLUDED ISLANDS OF THE ATLANTIC COAST
A report on twenty-one inhabited islands from Newfoundland to the Dry Tortugas—"information on inhabitants, local industry, island lore . . . enticing scenic descriptions . . . specifics (ferry schedules, shops, inns and dining facilities) are blended neatly into the narrative." (BL) Crown, 1984.

*Zinn, Donald J.   THE HANDBOOK FOR BEACH STROLLERS FROM MAINE TO CAPE HATTERAS
"Substantive essays about every sea organism or animal you might find on the coast, from sponges and lobster, to sand dollars and coral. Anyone who revels in . . . beachcombing . . . will surely enjoy this book." (BL) Globe Pequot, 1975.

NEW ENGLAND

Bachman, Ben   UPSTREAM: A VOYAGE ON THE CONNECTICUT RIVER
"Leisurely exploration of the river [by tugboat and canoe] with a finely tuned

sense of the region's history and ecology. . . mountains and valleys, old mill towns and dams, dairy farms." Plus there are encounters with animals—beaver, otter and moose. The Connecticut River has its source near the Canadian border and flows through the heart of New England to the Long Island Sound. (PW) Houghton, 1985.

Borland, Hal   A PLACE TO BEGIN—THE NEW ENGLAND EXPERIENCE
A "love song to New England" combining text and photographs. (Publisher) Sierra Club, 1976.

Brooks, Van Wyck   THE FLOWERING OF NEW ENGLAND, 1815-65
Classic literary history interpreted as a reflection of the social, political and religious life of the period. Houghton, 1981 (first published 1936). *New England: Indian Summer 1865-1915* (1940), brings this literary history to 1915.

Chambers, S. Allen, ed.   DISCOVERING HISTORIC AMERICA
Volume I covers New England. A guide to historic buildings, parks, museums, villages, historic inns, hotels and restaurants. Dutton, 1982.

Clayton, Barbara & Whitley, Kathleen   EXPLORING COASTAL NEW ENGLAND
From Gloucester to Kennebunkport—twenty-one mini tours of the historic homes, museums, recreational sites and beautiful natural views along the seaboard between Gloucester and Kennebunkport for motorists, bicyclists and hikers. Dodd, 1979.

Delaney, Edmund   THE CONNECTICUT RIVER: NEW ENGLAND'S HISTORIC WATERWAY
"Panoramic story of life along New England's 410-mile river. . . . A detailed appendix features a town-by-town guide to the major historic sites and museums along the river." (Publisher) Globe Pequot, 1983.

Demos, John Putnam   ENTERTAINING SATAN: WITCHCRAFT AND THE CULTURE OF EARLY NEW ENGLAND
New England society in the seventeenth century—"fascinating portraits of non-literate people through court and probate records." (LJ) Oxford U, 1982.

Facaros, Dana and Pauls, Michael   NEW ENGLAND
One of a new series of handbooks for the independent traveler.
Regnery-Gateway, 1982.

Faison, S. Lane, Jr.   THE ART MUSEUMS OF NEW ENGLAND
In three volumes: Volume 1: Connecticut and Rhode Island; Volume 2: Massachusetts; Volume 3: New Hampshire, Vermont, Maine. "Critical and art-historical exposition on more than five-hundred works of art [over one hundred museums]. . . a sense of the museums' character . . . like taking a personal tour with this noted art historian." Also includes practical information on hours, admissions, etc. (LJ) Godine, 1982.

**Foulke, Patricia   DAYTRIPS AND BUDGET VACATIONS IN
NEW ENGLAND**
Six itineraries of the best of New England, with the travel budget kept in mind.
Globe Pequot, 1983.

**Griffin, Arthur   ARTHUR GRIFFIN'S NEW ENGLAND, THE
FOUR SEASONS**
Original essays by fifty-one famous authors, and photographs. Houghton, 1980.

Hale, Judson   INSIDE NEW ENGLAND
By the editor of *Yankee*—"components of the New England image, from food
and humor to family connections and language" for each of its six states. (BL)
Har-Row, 1982.

**Hechtlinger, Adelaide   THE PELICAN GUIDE TO HISTORIC HOMES
AND SITES OF REVOLUTIONARY AMERICA**
Volume 1 covers New England. State landmarks dating from the American
Revolution era. Pelican, 1976.

**Hitchcock, Anthony and Lindgren, Jean   COUNTRY NEW ENGLAND
HISTORICAL AND
SIGHTSEEING GUIDE**
Historic sites as well as folk festivals and such activities as barn dances, bathtub
races, etc. B Franklin, 1979.

Hubka, Thomas C.   BIG HOUSE, LITTLE HOUSE, BACK HOUSE, BARN
The title is a nineteenth-century children's sing-song describing the connected
farm buildings of New England—the book addresses the question of why this
unusual style of farmstead was adopted. "A humanistic architectural history . . . an
engaging tribute to our nineteenth-century forbears." (LJ) U Pr of New England,
1984.

Jorgensen, Neil   A GUIDE TO NEW ENGLAND'S LANDSCAPE
"Guide to the quirks and shapes of the New England landscape leads you
through a spectrum of breathtaking land and water formations from the Green
Mountains to Cape Cod. . . . Significant places to visit and books to read."
(Publisher) Globe Pequot, 1981.

Kull, Andrew   NEW ENGLAND CEMETERIES: A COLLECTOR'S GUIDE
For whatever reason, graveyards avoided at home are quite intriguing as a part
of travels—especially in New England. Stephen Greene Pr, 1975.

Levine, Miriam   A GUIDE TO WRITERS' HOMES IN NEW ENGLAND
Relates the authors' lives to the homes—"chatty, even gossipy biographical
piece" for each, plus practical information of schedules, addresses, phone
numbers. (BL) Apple-Wood Bks, 1984.

**Matthews, Diane L.   NEW ENGLAND VISITOR'S GUIDE TO BOTANICAL
GARDENS AND NATURE CENTERS**
D.L. Matthews, 1984.

Moorhouse, Geoffrey   THE BOAT AND THE TOWN
Through the seasons of a coastal New England town, by a British journalist—trawling, weather, ethnic mix, foreign competition, and summer tourists. Little, 1979.

Mutrux, Robert   GREAT NEW ENGLAND CHURCHES: 65 HOUSES OF WORSHIP THAT CHANGED OUR LIVES
A guide to New England's architecturally distinguished churches by a designer of churches. Anecdotes on history and construction of both traditional and modern buildings. Globe Pequot, 1982.

Nearing, Helen and Scott   THE MAPLE SUGAR BOOK
The history and lore of maple sugaring by the pioneers in the back to the land movement, sugaring as a way of life. Schocken, 1971 (first published 1950).

Newhall, Nancy and Strand, Paul   TIME IN NEW ENGLAND
Excerpts from three centuries of writings about New England, with photographs, in a historical look at the area. Aperture, 1980.

Parks, Roger, ed.   THE NEW ENGLAND GALAXY
"The best of twenty years from Old Sturbridge Village." Globe Pequot, 1980.

Payne, Rolce R.   NEW ENGLAND GARDENS OPEN TO THE PUBLIC
Godine, 1979.

Peirce, Neal R.   NEW ENGLAND STATES: PEOPLE, POLITICS AND POWER IN THE SIX NEW ENGLAND STATES
Patterned after the late John Gunther's series of "inside" books—"part history, part politics, part travel guide" describing the essential character and power structure of each state and the region in which it is located. See also Peirce's books under "U.S.A." Norton, 1976.

Primack, Phil   NEW ENGLAND COUNTRY FAIR! TRAVELS TO FAIRS BIG AND SMALL
"Captures the true feel of small-town Yankee America gently showing off," says Studs Terkel. Globe Pequot, 1982.

Robinson, William F.   ABANDONED NEW ENGLAND
Its hidden ruins and where to find them, history of abandoned houses, railways, schools and where to find relics of them. New Graphic Soc, 1978.

Robinson, William F.   COASTAL NEW ENGLAND: ITS LIFE AND PAST
The focus is on specific places at critical periods—Salem and the China trade, the mills of Fall River, etc.—taking the reader in time from historical periods to the present day. N.Y. Graphic Society, 1983.

Ross, Corinne M. and Woodward, Ralph   NEW ENGLAND: OFF THE BEATEN PATH
East Woods, 1981.

**Schuman, Michael A.   NEW ENGLAND SPECIAL PLACES: A
DAYTRIPPER'S GUIDE.**
Countryman Pr, 1986.

**Smith, Sharon, ed.   YANKEE MAGAZINE'S TRAVEL GUIDE TO NEW
ENGLAND**
Updates issued each year. Yankee Bks, 1984.

Smith, Sharon, ed.   HANDCRAFT CENTERS OF NEW ENGLAND
Yankee Bks, 1981.

Tanner, Ogden   NEW ENGLAND WILD
One of the American Wilderness series. Time-Life, 1974.

Thollander, Earl   BACK ROADS OF NEW ENGLAND
Potter, 1982.

Thoreau, Henry D.   THOREAU COUNTRY
Text selections from the words of Thoreau, with photographs. Sierra Club,
1975.

**Tree, Christina   HOW NEW ENGLAND HAPPENED: A GUIDE TO NEW
ENGLAND THROUGH ITS HISTORY**
Little, 1976.

Webster, Harriet   COASTAL DAYTRIPS IN NEW ENGLAND
Yankee Bks, 1984.

**Wikoff, Jerold   THE UPPER VALLEY: AN ILLUSTRATED TOUR ALONG
THE CONNECTICUT RIVER BEFORE THE TWENTIETH
CENTURY**
Chronicle of local history and the evolution of the area, enhanced by rare prints
and photos. Chelsea Green, 1985.

**Witteman, Betsy and Webster, Nancy   DAYTRIPPING AND DINING 2 IN
NEW ENGLAND**
"An eclectic guide to 50 special places and restaurants"—introduction to each
destination with a "light and personal" touch, sightseeing, lodgings, shopping and
restaurants. (LJ) Wood Pond, 1982. Also *Weekending in New England: A Selective
Guide to the Most Appealing Destinations for all Seasons* (1980).

Wood, William   NEW ENGLAND'S PROSPECT
Reprint of the first book to provide reliable firsthand information on British
America for prospective colonists. U of Massachusetts, 1977 (first published
1634).

THE MIDDLE ATLANTIC STATES

**Benton, Christine M.   COUNTRY ROADS AND SCENIC DRIVES IN THE
MIDDLE ATLANTIC STATES**
Back roads and nonmajor routes in New York, New Jersey, Pennsylvania,
Delaware and Maryland. Contemporary Bks, 1979.

Chambers, S. Allen, ed.   DISCOVERING HISTORIC AMERICA
Volume III covers the mid-Atlantic states. A guide to historic buildings, parks, museums, villages, historic inns, hotels and restaurants. Dutton, 1983.

Facaros, Dana and Pauls, Michael   NEW YORK AND THE MID-ATLANTIC STATES
One of a new series of handbooks for the independent traveler. Regnery-Gateway, 1982.

Foulke, Patricia and Robert   DAY TRIPS AND BUDGET VACATIONS IN THE MID-ATLANTIC STATES
Eight suggested itineraries covering major tourist attractions and lesser-known spots in New York, New Jersey, Pennsylvania, Delaware, Maryland and Washington, D.C. Globe-Pequot, 1986.

Hechtlinger, Adelaide   THE PELICAN GUIDE TO HISTORIC HOMES AND SITES OF REVOLUTIONARY AMERICA, VOLUME 2, MIDDLE ATLANTIC STATES
See under "The East/New England."

Peirce, Neal R.   MID-ATLANTIC STATES OF AMERICA: PEOPLE, POLITICS AND POWER IN THE FIVE MID-ATLANTIC STATES
Patterned after the late John Gunther's series of "inside" books—"part history, part politics, part travel guide" describing the essential character and power structure of each state and the region in which it is located. The five mid-Atlantic states are New York, New Jersey, Pennsylvania, Maryland, Delaware and the District of Columbia. Norton, 1976. See also Peirce's books under "U.S.A."

Willis, Gwyn   SHIFRA STEIN'S DAY TRIPS FROM GREATER BALTIMORE
One of a series of guides to daytrips less than two hours' driving time from a base city. This one uses Baltimore as a base and reaches Pennsylvania, Delaware, Virginia and West Virginia. Includes hundreds of money-saving things to do and see, quaint villages, farming and agricultural areas, restaurants, inns, festivals and celebrations, parks, campgrounds, etc. There are also suggestions for combining trips into a longer journey and a "worth-a-little-more time" section of places beyond the two-hour limit. East Woods, 1985.

TRAVEL ARTICLES

AMERICANA
1985 Mar-Apr (New England and N.Y.S.) "Roundup When the Sap Runs." Maple sugar festivals and celebrations. Greer Underwood, p. 74

BETTER HOMES & GARDENS
1984 *Sep "Extra Special Island Vacations for Your Family." Along the Atlantic coast. G.S. Bush, p. 183

CONNOISSEUR
1985 Jun "Collectors' Houses." Three old New England beauties in Gloucester, Massachusetts, New Ipswich, N.H. and South Berwick, Maine. Plus a list of

houses under jurisdiction of the Society for Preservation of New England Antiquities. Diane Carasik Dion, p. 102

ESSENCE
1984 Oct (New England) "Bicycling New England Style." Stephanie R. Hamilton, p. 54

MADEMOISELLE
1984 Nov "Ski Report." New England and the West. Brie P. Quinby and Catherine Ettinger, p. 213

NATIONAL GEOGRAPHIC
1985 Mar "Susquehanna: America's Small-Town River." Central New York State to Chesapeake Bay. Peter Miller, p. 352
1984 *Dec "A Journey Down U.S. 1." First highway from Maine to Florida. Bruce Dale, p. 790

N.Y. TIMES SUNDAY TRAVEL SECTION (X)
1985 May 19 (New England) "Preserving Old New England." A tour of the twenty-four houses and farms of the Society for the Preservation of New England Antiquities, from Branford, Ct., to Wiscasset, Me. John Deedy, p. 15
1984 May 6 (New England) Fare of the Country: "Lobster Unadorned." David Shribman, p. 6
     Aug 12 "The Sailing Life Aboard Tall Ships." An account of a total escape (sailing ships out of Connecticut and Maine). Terence Smith, p. 12
     *Sep 23 "A Glimpse of the Birder's World." Best bird-watching sites in the East from Canada to Florida. Richard J. Roberts, p. 9

READER'S DIGEST
1985 *Feb "The Potomac—Mainstream of American History." Maryland, District of Columbia, Virginia, West Virginia. Ernest B. Furgurson, p. 137

TOWN & COUNTRY
1985 Jul "A Berkshire Sampler." Elizabeth Heilman, p. 30

TRAVEL & LEISURE
1984 Sep (New England) "Classic, Cozy New England Inns." Joseph P. Kahn, p. 114
     (New England) "A Guide to New England Bed and Breakfast." Joyce Kuh, p. 128

TRAVEL/HOLIDAY
1985 Jul "Aboard the *Olad* and *Hindu*." Sailing out of Provincetown. G. Gordon Long, p. 4
     Nov "A Compendium of Northeastern Winter Resorts." Denise Van Lear, p. 44
1984 Feb (New England) "In the Wake of Yankee Seafarers." New England's maritime museums. Jay F. Butera, p. 10

YANKEE
1985 Jan "Skiing Under the Stars." Shaw McCutcheon, Jr., p. 46
    May (New England) "In Search of the Top Dog." Where to find the best hot
    dogs in New England. Rollin Riggs, p. 30
    Jun (New England) "Guardians of New England's Noble Houses." Houses
    under supervision of the Society for the Preservation of New England
    Antiquities. Marilyn M. Slade, p. 36
    Jul "Rhapsody in Raspberries." Where you can pick your own. John Pierce,
    p. 32
    Sep "Voices of the Valley." The Connecticut River Valley, Part 1. Edie Clark,
    p. 120
    Oct "The Colors of the River." The Connecticut River Valley, Part 2. Edie
    Clark, p. 102
    "October on the River." Narraganset. Susan H. Shetterly, p. 240
    Dec "On New Wings of Art." Additions to New England art museums in New
    Haven, Manchester (NH), Boston, Portland, Hanover. Simon Flagg, p. 32
1984 Mar (New England) "Shopping Around Historic Structures."Historic
    buildings converted into shopping malls. Lynda Morgenroth, p. 46
    May (New England) "Our Farming Heritage on Display." Farm museums. p.
    46
    Jul (New England) "Vaudeville Reprise." Annual vaudeville festival. E.
    Doyle, p. 30
    Aug (New England) "Where Indian Ways Are Preserved in Southern New
    England." A calendar of Indian Cultural Events, museums, exhibits. L.F.
    Willard, p. 118
    Oct (New England) "Where's the Best Indian Pudding in the World?" A
    baker's dozen honor roll. p. 106
    Nov (New England) "Where to Look for Little Things." Miniatures—shows,
    shops, museums. Nora Kerr, p. 54

THE SOUTH

Series Guidebooks (See Appendix 1)

Fisher: **Florida & the Southeast**
Fodor: **The South**
Frommer: **Southeast and New Orleans: Dollarwise**

Note: See also asterisked (*) books and articles listed under "The East" for titles
about the east coast, and under "The Midwest" for titles about the Mississippi
River.

Background Reading

Binding, Paul   A SEPARATE COUNTRY: A LITERARY JOURNEY THROUGH THE AMERICAN SOUTH
The South and its writers, a literary travelogue. Paddington Pr, 1979.

Blount, Roy   CRACKERS
About Southern "crackers" (like himself)—specifically Jimmy Carter and his relatives are the springboard for observations about the South. Portions of the book appeared as articles in *Esquire, New Yorker, Sports Illustrated,* and *Playboy.* Knopf, 1980.

Carter, Hodding   LOWER MISSISSIPPI
Story of the Indians, explorers—Spanish, French, English—settlers, engineers and builders "and the river that nourished and tempted and troubled them." (BRD) FS&G, 1942.

Cash, Wilbur J.   THE MIND OF THE SOUTH
Observations of a loyal son and a discerning critic. Random, 1960 (first published 1941).

Catton, Bruce   AMERICAN HERITAGE PICTURE HISTORY OF THE CIVIL WAR
American Heritage, 1961. Also Catton's whole series of books on the Civil War: *Mr. Lincoln's Army* (1951), *Glory Road* (1952), *A Stillness at Appomattox* (1953), and *Terrible Swift Sword* (1963).

Chambers, S. Allen, ed.   DISCOVERING HISTORIC AMERICA
Volume IV covers the southeast. A guide to historic buildings, parks, museums, villages, historic inns, hotels and restaurants. Dutton, 1982.

Cronkite, Walter   SOUTH BY SOUTHEAST
Watercolors and Cronkite's sensitively written text on the Intracoastal waterway from Norfolk, Virginia, to Key West, Florida, and adjacent bays, rivers and areas. Oxmoor, 1983.

Davis, Burke   SHERMAN'S MARCH
"With as much dramatic flair as *Gone with the Wind* and with . . . factual accuracy [it] reconstructs Sherman's infamous, but vastly consequential, march." (BL) Random, 1980.

Doolittle, Jerry   SOUTHERN APPALACHIANS
Part of the American Wilderness series. Time-Life, 1976.

Frady, Marshall   SOUTHERNERS: A JOURNALIST'S ODYSSEY
Essays on personalities, particularly those in politics, of the past fifty years. NAL, 1981.

Fuller, Chet   I HEAR THEM CALLING MY NAME
A journey through the new South—this is an account by a black *Atlanta Journal* reporter who, in 1978, posed as a poor, unemployed man; the people he met. Houghton, 1981.

Gleasner, Diane C. and Bill   SEA ISLANDS OF THE SOUTH
A guide to the barrier islands from North Carolina to Florida. East Woods, 1980.

Hechtlinger, Adelaide   THE PELICAN GUIDE TO HISTORIC HOMES AND SITES OF REVOLUTIONARY AMERICA, VOLUME 3, THE SOUTH
See under "The East/New England."

Kilpatrick, James and Bake, William A.   THE AMERICAN SOUTH: TOWNS AND CITIES; THE AMERICAN SOUTH: FOUR SEASONS OF THE LAND
Perceptive overview of the south, and its growth over the last twenty-five years. The text, by the newspaper columnist and TV commentator is folksy, vibrant, and rich with historical nuance." The book on towns and cities provides a city-by-city tour from Baltimore to Tulsa. (BL) Har-Row, 1982.

Lockwood, C.C.   THE GULF COAST: WHERE LAND MEETS SEA
Exploration of this coast from the Florida Keys to southwest Texas—"a splendid excursion for nature lovers. . . . Wildlife refuges, island rookeries, fishing grounds" and the teeming animal life. (PW) Louisiana State U Pr, 1984.

McGill, Ralph   THE SOUTH AND THE SOUTHERNER
A portrait of the south in the 1960s, by the publisher of the *Atlanta Constitution*. Little, 1963.

Mayfield, Chris, ed.   GROWING UP SOUTHERN
"*Southern Exposure* [a liberal quarterly] looks at childhood, then and now. . . . Black and white perspectives and experiences are related in various degrees of eloquence." (BL) Pantheon, 1981.

Nicholson, Diana and McDonald, Maureen   I-GUIDE TO THE SOUTHEAST
Florida, Georgia, and Tennessee. Marmac, 1982.

Peirce, Neal R.   THE BORDER SOUTH STATES OF AMERICA: PEOPLE, POLITICS, AND POWER IN THE FIVE STATES OF THE BORDER SOUTH
Patterned after the late John Gunther's series of "inside" books—"part history, part politics, part travel guide," describing the essential character and power structure of each state and the region in which it is located. The five border states are Virginia, West Virginia, North Carolina, Kentucky and Tennessee. Norton, 1975. In the same series, *The Deep South States of America* (1974), the states

covered are Arkansas, Alabama, Florida, Georgia, Louisiana, Mississippi and South Carolina. See also Peirce's books under "U.S.A."

Postal, Bernard   AMERICAN JEWISH LANDMARKS: A TRAVEL GUIDE AND HISTORY
Volume II covers the South and the Southwest. Fleet, 1979.

Powledge, Fred   JOURNEYS THROUGH THE SOUTH, A REDISCOVERY
Written by a native North Carolinian living in Brooklyn who traveled the South in 1977 and concludes that the South is a positive place these days. Vanguard, 1979.

Price, Steve   WILD PLACES OF THE SOUTH
Twenty-three places in twelve states where wilderness can be experienced by nature lovers and outdoor sports enthusiasts.
East Woods, 1980.

Rubin, Louis D., ed.   THE AMERICAN SOUTH: PORTRAIT OF A CULTURE
The South as a distinctive cultural and literary phenomenon—twenty-one essays and two transcribed Voice of America broadcasts—"literate but highly in-dividual opinions." (LJ) Louisiana State U Pr, 1980.

Stein, Rita   A LITERARY TOUR GUIDE TO THE U.S.: SOUTH AND SOUTHWEST
This is a continuation of the series begun by Emilie C. Harting (see "East"), and covers sixteen states from the District of Columbia to Texas and landmarks of Faulkner, Hemingway, Thomas Wolfe, Will Rogers, Poe and others. Morrow, 1979.

Willis, Gwyn   SHIFRA STEIN'S DAY TRIPS FROM GREATER BALTIMORE
Includes Virginia and West Virginia—see under "The Northeast" for full description. East Woods, 1985.

APPALACHIA, THE BLUE RIDGE, THE GREAT SMOKIES

Blake, William A.   THE BLUE RIDGE
A history of the Blue Ridge region, spanning Georgia to the reaches of the Potomac, and a sympathetic account of the people of that area. Oxmoor, 1984.

Bradley, Jeff   A TRAVELER'S GUIDE TO THE SMOKY MOUNTAINS REGION
Embraces the hill country of eastern Tennessee, western North Carolina, southwestern Virginia and northern Georgia—"an idiosyncratic collection of historical facts, anecdotes and descriptive details that will add to the delight of any journey in the area and any encounter with its people." Also has practical tourist information on getting there, sightseeing, seasonal events, facilities for eating and sleeping. (NYT) Harvard Common Pr, 1985.

Caraman, Guy   VOICES FROM THE MOUNTAINS
Prose, song and photos of what it means to be a mountaineer in Appalachia in today's world. U of Illinois, 1983 (first published 1975).

Dagneaux, Christine   A SEPARATE PLACE, A UNIQUE PEOPLE
People of Appalachia. McClain, 1981.

Doolittle, Jerry   SOUTHERN APPALACHIANS
Part of the American Wilderness series. Time-Life, 1976.

Frome, Michael   STRANGERS IN HIGH PLACES: THE STORY OF THE GREAT SMOKY MOUNTAINS
History, geology, anthropology, biographical sketches, local mores. U of Tennessee, 1979 (first published 1966).

Higgs, R.J.   VOICES FROM THE HILLS
Selected readings of southern Appalachia, an anthology of 300 years of fact and fiction. Ungar, 1975.

Ogburn, Charlton   THE SOUTHERN APPALACHIANS, A WILDERNESS QUEST
A visit to the southern Appalachians with an eloquent writer—"an immensely satisfying experience for any nature lover." (PW) Morrow, 1975.

Wenberg, Donald C.   BLUE RIDGE MOUNTAIN PLEASURES
"An A-Z guide to North Georgia, Western North Carolina and the upcountry of South Carolina"—arts, crafts, festivals, factory outlets, country inns, outdoor recreation, and sports. (Publisher) East Woods, 1985.

Wigginton, Eliot and Bennett, Margie   FOXFIRE
A multivolume series of books begun by a teacher in Georgia (see under "Georgia"). Volume 7 of the series is an examination of Appalachian Christianity. Doubleday, 1984.

TRAVEL ARTICLES

EBONY
1984 Jan "Winter Vacation." You can go home again; blacks who left the South will find a warm welcome at hotels, resorts, parks." p. 107

HOUSE & GARDEN
1985 May "In Search of the South." An English novelist's journey to small-town America. William Boyd, p. 82

HOUSE BEAUTIFUL
1984 Mar "Travel South: Up the Lazy Rivers on Some of America's Greatest Surviving Riverboats." p. 41

NATIONAL GEOGRAPHIC
1984 Dec "A Journey Down U.S. 1." First highway from Maine to Florida. Bruce
      Dale, p. 790

NATIONAL GEOGRAPHIC TRAVELER
1985 Summer "Mississippi River Boats." They just keep rolling along. Joyce
      Diamanti, p. 20

N.Y. TIMES SUNDAY TRAVEL SECTION (X)
1985 Apr 21 "On the Crest of the Blue Ridge." The 469-mile parkway meanders
      through dramatic woodland rich in vistas, blossoms and lore. Wilma
      Dykeman, p. 14
1984 May 27 "At Home in the Old South." A visitor's guide to plantation homes
      and grounds in nine states. Carol Plum, p. 15

READER'S DIGEST
1985 Feb "The Potomac." Mainstream of American history (Maryland, District of
      Columbia, Virginia, West Virginia). Ernest B. Furgurson, p. 137
      Nov "The Blue Ridge: Mountains, Mists and Memories." (condensation).
      William A. Bake, p. 121

TRAVEL/HOLIDAY
1984 Jul "Celebrated Southern Resorts." A quartet of grande dames. William
      Schemmel, p. 44

THE MIDWEST

Background Reading

**Adams, Alexander B.   SUNLIGHT AND STORM: THE GREAT
                        AMERICAN PLAINS**
  The American great plains—comprised of portions of Colorado, Kansas,
Montana, Nebraska, New Mexico, North Dakota, Oklahoma, South Dakota, Texas
and Wyoming—from the appearance of the first Europeans to the opening of the
twentieth century. Putnam Pub Group, 1977.

Andrews, Clarence, ed.   GROWING UP IN THE MIDWEST
  The "spirit and reality of the Midwest are captured" in selections from poetry,
prose and fiction—"a rich patchwork of midwestern memories." (BL) Iowa State
U, 1981.

Banta, Richard E.   THE OHIO
  A history of the river and the valley from prehistory to the Civil War. Rinehart,
1949.

Beatty, Michael and Nolte, James   GUIDE TO ART MUSEUMS:
MIDWEST EDITION
And Bks, 1984.

Bissell, Richard   MY LIFE ON THE MISSISSIPPI, OR WHY I AM NOT
MARK TWAIN
Reminiscences of the author's years as a boatman and pilot on the river using
Twain's writings to "manage several good laughs at himself." (BRD) Little, 1973.

Bogue, Margaret B.   AROUND THE SHORES OF LAKE MICHIGAN: A
GUIDE TO HISTORIC SITES
Points of historic, cultural, religious, ethnic, architectural, natural interest in a
journey around Lake Michigan's perimeter. An overview also of the areas of
Michigan, Wisconsin, Illinois, that are the lake's shore. U of Wisconsin, 1985.

Bonnifield, Paul   THE DUST BOWL
Men, dirt and depression—the drought and depression of 1932-38. U of New
Mexico, 1979.

Burman, Ben Lucien   LOOK DOWN THAT WINDING RIVER: AN
INFORMAL PROFILE OF THE MISSISSIPPI
Anecdotes of steamboating days. Taplinger, 1973.

Cantor, George   THE GREAT LAKES GUIDEBOOK
"Terrific guidebooks by a Detroit journalist . . . comments on the lakeside and
island towns and sights combine historical information and evocative scenic
description. . . . A very useful section on sidetrips." In three volumes: Lake Huron
and Eastern Lake Michigan; Lake Superior and Western Lake Michigan; Lake
Ontario and Erie. (BL) U of Michigan, 1980-84.

Caplow, Theodore and others   MIDDLETOWN FAMILIES
Muncie, Indiana fifty years after the Lynd sociological study of "Middletown"
families. U of Minnesota, 1982.

Childs, Marquis   MIGHTY MISSISSIPPI: BIOGRAPHY OF A RIVER
Reminiscences and "a superb history" by a Pulitzer Prize-winning journalist.
(BRD) Ticknor & Fields, 1982.

Cochrane, Hugh F.   GATEWAY TO OBLIVION: THE GREAT LAKES'
BERMUDA TRIANGLE
A section of Lake Ontario with the same type of mysterious happenings as the
Bermuda Triangle. Doubleday, 1980.

Curry, Jane, ed.   THE RIVER'S IN MY BLOOD: RIVERBOAT PILOTS TELL
THEIR STORY
"A wonderfully evocative book about the river pilots on the Mississippi and
Ohio Rivers"; reminiscences, history, technology. (BRD) U of Nebraska, 1983.

Dary, David   TRUE TALES OF THE OLD-TIME PLAINS
"Reads like a collection of short stories, but it is not fiction." (BRD) Crown,
1979.

Davis, Norah Deakin   THE FATHER OF WATERS: A MISSISSIPPI RIVER CHRONICLE
"Articulate and informative" account of a writer/photographer's expedition from source to delta in 1979. Text and photos describe flora, fauna, history and economic activity along the river's banks down to the present day. (BL) Sierra Club, 1982.

Davis, Peter   HOMETOWN: A CONTEMPORARY AMERICAN CHRONICLE
Unforgettable portrait of middle America—the Middletown series on public TV came out of the research. S&S, 1983.

Eckert, Allan W.   GATEWAY TO EMPIRE
Epic struggle of whites and Indians for control of the Great Lakes wilderness area, the beginnings of Chicago and Detroit. Captures with "novelistic techniques . . . the living texture of the . . . human and political motives fueling that struggle." (PW) Little, 1982.

Havighurst, Walter   RIVER TO THE WEST: THREE CENTURIES OF THE OHIO
Vignettes of events and individuals with the unifying theme of the river. Putnam, 1970.

Hill, Kathleen   FESTIVALS USA
Volume III of this series covers festivals in the central states. Hilltop, 1984.

Keating, Bern   THE MIGHTY MISSISSIPPI
Natl Geog, 1971.

Kern, Ben   100 TRIPS
"Whimsical, entertaining guide" to Minnesota as well as parts of Wisconsin and Iowa. "For those who want to . . . discover the best of what lies beyond the byways." (Publisher) Dillon, 1979.

Kohler, Jack and Schuchard, Oliver   TWO OZARK RIVERS: THE CURRENT AND THE JACKS FORK
"Graceful, limpid . . . gently humorous" text, with photographs, of the natural and human history of the two rivers. (BL) U of Missouri, 1984.

Komaiko, Jean R. and others   AROUND LAKE MICHIGAN
This guide gives a history of over one hundred localities directly on the lake, starting with Chicago and going clockwise around the lake, plus what to see and do and a selective list of places to eat and shop. (LJ) Houghton, 1980.

Laycock, George and Ellen   THE OHIO VALLEY: YOUR GUIDE TO AMERICA'S HEARTLAND
Follows the course of the river from the beginning to the Mississippi, emphasizing local attractions—fishing holes and hiking trails to performing arts and historical sites—festivals, seasonal celebrations, local lore, hotels and restaurants.

Covers parts of Illinois, Indiana, Kentucky, Ohio, Pennsylvania and West Virginia. Doubleday, 1983.

Madson, John   UP ON THE RIVER
The author views the Upper Mississippi (St. Louis north) as "reflecting the soul of America. . . . Lovingly shares a lifetime's interest, experiences and pleasure [and] moves easily from literary, historical, and bureaucratic accounts to those of his river acquaintances." (LJ) Nick Lyons, 1985.

Madson, John   WHERE THE SKY BEGAN: LAND OF THE TALL GRASS PRAIRIE
Profile of a unique geographical area, the eastern portion of the great grasslands of the United States. Describes the incredulous reactions of those discoverers who first came upon the vast area, pioneer life, geography, weather, natural history, flora and fauna. Houghton, 1982.

Myrick, Burny   THE TIMELESS RIVER: A PORTRAIT OF LIFE ON THE MISSISSIPPI 1850-1900
"A magnificent series of paintings and studies . . . accompanied by excerpts from Mark Twain's exuberant *Life on the Mississippi*." (BL) Oxmoor, 1981.

Nelson, Jerry L.   THE MIDWEST FAMILY VACATION BOOK
Nelson, 1983.

Olson, Sigurd F.   OF TIME AND PLACE
Reminiscences of a lifetime of experiences in the wilderness area around Lake Superior, and north of it. Knopf, 1982.

O'Neil, Paul   THE RIVER MEN
Time-Life, 1975.

Peirce, Neal R.   THE GREAT PLAINS STATES OF AMERICA: PEOPLE, POLITICS AND POWER
Norton, 1974. This and *The Great Lakes States* (1980), in the same series, together cover the Midwest. Patterned after the late John Gunther's series of "inside" books—"part history, part politics, part travel guide" describing the essential character and power structure of each state and the region in which it is located. See also Peirce's books under "U.S.A."

Postal, Bernard   AMERICAN JEWISH LANDMARKS
Volume III covers the Midwest and West. Fleet, 1977.

Raban, Jonathan   OLD GLORY: AN AMERICAN VOYAGE
A British journalist's odyssey down the Mississippi River in a sixteen-foot boat inspired by longtime dreams of emulating Huck Finn. One reviewer describes the author's style as "a sort of English Capote: vivid, funny, accurate [combined with] the ability to make an instant connection with virtually any human being whomsoever." (NYTBR) S&S, 1981.

Scharfenberg, Doris   **THE LONG BLUE EDGE OF SUMMER**
A vacation guide to the shoreline of Michigan. Eerdmans, 1982.

Scott, David L. and Kay W.   **TRAVELING AND CAMPING IN THE NA-
TIONAL PARK AREAS—MID-AMERICA**
Includes the areas administered by the National Park Service, national
seashores, historic sites, monuments, historic parks—descriptions and information on facilities, activities, camping, fishing and more. Globe Pequot, 1979.

Severin, Timothy   **EXPLORERS OF THE MISSISSIPPI**
The river from the viewpoint of those who explored it—"magic itself . . .the
fickle politicians . . . heroism of the clerics . . . the Indians more friendly than
malevolent" and explorers from conquistadores to gentlemen-explorers. (BRD)
Knopf, 1968.

Stein, Rita   **A LITERARY TOUR GUIDE TO THE U.S.: WEST AND
MIDWEST**
This is a continuation of the series begun by Emilie C. Harting (see "Northeast"),
and covers twenty-three states from Ohio to Alaska and Hawaii, highlighting Mark
Twain, Willa Cather, Jack London, other authors. Morrow, 1979.

TRAVEL ARTICLES

AMERICANA
1985 Mar-Apr "Roundups When the Sap Runs." Maple sugar festivals and
celebrations—includes Ohio, Pennsylvania, Indiana. Greer Underwood p.
74

GOOD HOUSEKEEPING
1984 May "A Great Lakes Holiday." Stephen Birnbaum, p. 192

HOUSE BEAUTIFUL
1985 Mar "Along the Midwest's Scandinavian Trail . . ." The Nordic traditions of
fine, honest craftsmanship are still visible today (museums, restorations,
etc.). Patricia Brooks, p. 38

NATIONAL GEOGRAPHIC TRAVELER
1985 Summer "Mississippi River Boats." They just keep rolling along. Joyce
Diamanti, p. 20.

N.Y. TIMES SUNDAY TRAVEL SECTION (X)
1984 Nov 25 "Riding High in the Middle West." From the top of Amtrak's
doubledecker train, the country's heartland is seen in vivid detail. Noel
Perrin, p. 37

READER'S DIGEST
1985 Sep "Bound for the Wild Missouri (River)." A ride on the "Gateway to the
West." Richard Dunlop, p. 148
1984 Jan "Mississippi: Father of Waters." Norah Deakin Davis, p. 135

SATURDAY EVENING POST
1984 Jul-Aug "Cruising Up the River." A Mississippi steamboat ride from New Orleans to Memphis is a journey back in history. Rafe Gibbs, p. 90

SUNSET
1985 Jun "Rendezvousing with the Mountain Men." Join in as the buckskinners, muzzle-loaders and friends recreate the West's fur trade. Almost everyone's in costume, what about you? Includes Nebraska and North Dakota. p. 98; "More Mountain Man Rendezvous and Other Old West Celebrations." p. 92
1984 Mar "Sternwheeling on the Mississippi." To and from the world's fair at New Orleans. p. 70

TRAVEL/HOLIDAY
1984 Aug "Harvesting the Best of the Midwest." A cornucopia of state fairs. Rebecca Christian, p. 39

THE WEST

Series Guidebooks (See Appendix 1)

Fisher: **California and the West**
Fodor: **Far West; Pacific Northwest**
Frommer: **Northwest: Dollarwise; Southwest: Dollarwise**
Insight: **American Southwest**
Let's Go: **California & the Pacific Northwest**
Lonely Planet: **U.S.A. West**

Note: Asterisked entries (*) indicate a book or article pertaining also to Canada.

Background Reading

Abbey, Edward   BEYOND THE WALL
A collection of previously published essays by a conservationist, transporting readers into "western deserts and exploration of diverse wilderness areas. . . . For aficionados of nature, backpacking, and good writing." (BL) HR&W, 1984. Also *Down the River* (1982), reflections while on river trips, campouts, mountain climbs in the West—"lively, filled with irony, with wonder, and a vivid sense of place."

*Batman, Richard   THE OUTER COAST
Biographical vignettes of people involved in the history of the Pacific coast, to the 1840s. HarBraceJ, 1985.

Brown, Dee   THE WESTERNERS
A popular history using selected individuals as examples of the larger story.
HR&W, 1974. Also *Bury My Heart at Wounded Knee: An Indian History of the
American West* (1971).

**Butler, Ron   BEST OF THE OLD WEST: THE TEXAS MONTHLY
                  GUIDEBOOK**
A travel planner book intended "to prove that the legend of the Wild West still
lives"—ghost towns, border towns, museums, grand resorts, dude ranches,
historic hotels and saloons, panning for gold, and more. (LJ) Texas Monthly Pr,
1983.

Calder, Jenni   THERE MUST BE A LONE RANGER
Comparison of the American West, as seen in film and literature, with reality.
Taplinger, 1975.

Chambers, S. Allen, ed.   DISCOVERING HISTORIC AMERICA
Volume II covers California and the West. A guide to historic buildings, parks,
museums, villages, historic inns, hotels and restaurants. Dutton, 1982.

Cromie, Alice H.   TOUR GUIDE TO THE OLD WEST
Settlements, forts, museums, battlegrounds, landmarks, relics, cowboys and
characters. Times Bks, 1982.

DeVoto, Bernard   ACROSS THE WIDE MISSOURI
Story of the mountain men and fur trade of the 1830s described vividly and with
"splendid reproductions of sketches made on the trail in 1837-38." (BRD) Crown,
1985 (first published 1947). Also DeVoto's one-volume edition of *Journals of
Lewis & Clark* (1953)—"the quintessential American journey."

Ellis, W.S.   THE MAJESTIC ROCKY MOUNTAINS
Natl Geog, 1976.

Erdoes, Richard   SALOONS OF THE OLD WEST
History of saloons and the human and social needs they filled. Knopf, 1979.

Fradkin, Philip L.   A RIVER NO MORE
Historical and political account of the Colorado River and the seven states
through which it flows to Mexico. U of Arizona, 1984.

Grey, Loren   LANE GREY: A PHOTOGRAPHIC ODYSSEY
By the author's son—a photographic essay of the American frontier about
which Grey wrote, with the sites and excerpts from his novels correlated (includes Grey's travels to Tahiti, Fiji, New Zealand and Australia). Taylor Pub, 1986.

Hawke, David F.   THOSE TREMENDOUS MOUNTAINS
Story of the Lewis and Clark expedition, interweaving selections from their
journals and other interesting resource material. Norton, 1980.

Hill, Kathleen   FESTIVALS USA
Volume I of this series covers festivals in the Western states. Hilltop, 1984.

Hoffman, Wilbur   SAGAS OF OLD WESTERN TRAVEL AND TRANSPORT
Interestingly told story of the many forms of transport in the old West—pack trains, wagon trains, mail and freight express, stagecoaches, steamships and boats, railroads. "Checkered histories of some of the men and companies . . . first-hand accounts of episodes, adventures, and tragedies along the trail." (LJ) Howell-North, 1980.

Horan, James D.   THE AUTHENTIC WILD WEST: THE LAWMEN
Crown, 1980. Also, *The Gunfighters* (1977) and *The Outlaws* (1977)—a trilogy of books based on primary sources, contemporary accounts and personal testimonies of the period.

Jeffrey, Julie Roy   FRONTIER WOMEN
"Women's experience during the westward migration" with extensive use of original letters and diaries. Hill & Wang, 1979.

Katz, William L.   THE BLACK WEST
Authentication of the black man's presence in the history of the West. Doubleday, 1971.

Kaysing, Bill   GREAT HOT SPRINGS OF THE WEST
Capra Pr, 1984.

Lavender, David S.   THE ROCKIES
U of Nebraska, 1981 (first published 1968).

May, Robin   HISTORY OF THE AMERICAN WEST
By a British author—"well researched yet entertaining record of the U.S. frontier era . . . a comprehensive and insightful view of the entire epic." (BL) Exeter, 1984.

Mondy, Robert W.   PIONEERS AND PREACHERS: STORIES OF THE OLD FRONTIER
Anecdotes that dispel all myths about the "romantic" frontier. Nelson, 1980.

Moser, Don   SNAKE RIVER COUNTRY
One of the American Wilderness series. Time-Life, 1974.

National Geographic eds.   ALONG THE CONTINENTAL DIVIDE
Natl Geog, 1981. Also *Rocky Mountains* (1976); *America's Sunset Coast* (1978).

Patterson, Richard   HISTORICAL ATLAS OF THE OUTLAW WEST
Vintage (1880) maps plus directions for landmarks—"an indispensable aid to anyone interested in the 'good guys-bad guys' aspect of the American West." (BL) Johnson, 1985.

Peirce, Neal R.   THE PACIFIC STATES OF AMERICA: PEOPLE, POLITICS AND POWER IN THE FIVE PACIFIC STATES
Patterned after the late John Gunther's series of "inside" books—"part history, part politics, part travel guide," describing the essential character and power structure of each state and the region in which it is located. The five Pacific states are California, Oregon, Washington, Alaska and Hawaii. Norton, 1972. In the same series *The Mountain States of America* (1972) covers Arizona, Colorado, Idaho, Montana, Nevada, New Mexico, Utah and Wyoming. See also Peirce's books on America as a whole under "U.S.A."

Postal, Bernard   AMERICAN JEWISH LANDMARKS
Volume II, South and Southwest, and Volume III, Midwest and West, cover the area. Fleet, 1979.

Rochlin, Harriet and Fred   PIONEER JEWS: A NEW LIFE IN THE

An account of Jewish migration to the West beginning with their movement from Spain to the Mexican territory in the sixteenth century and on through the Gold Rush to the 1920s—"a dramatic story and a mind-broadening journey into the past." (PW) Houghton, 1984.

Ross, Nancy W.   WESTWARD THE WOMEN
Account of the roles of various women in the taming of the American West, through diaries and other contemporary writings. North Point Pr, 1985.

Schultheis, Rob   THE HIDDEN WEST
"Profound, haunting travelogue that evokes the magic" of the Western landscape and its ecological precariousness. (BL) Random, 1982.

Snyder, G.S.   IN THE FOOTSTEPS OF LEWIS AND CLARK
Natl Geog, 1970.

*Stegner, Page   ISLANDS OF THE WEST: FROM BAJA TO VANCOUVER
Sierra Club, 1986.

Stein, Rita   A LITERARY TOUR-GUIDE TO THE UNITED STATES: WEST & MID-WEST
Morrow, 1979. Continuation of the series begun by Emilie C. Harting (see "East"), highlighting authors such as Mark Twain, Willa Cather, Jack London, others.

Stone, Irving   MEN TO MATCH MY MOUNTAINS: THE STORY OF THE OPENING OF THE FAR WEST
The story of the West told with the special talents of a novelist dedicated to imparting information with enjoyment and zest. Berkley, 1982 (first published 1956).

*Vokac, David   THE GREAT TOWNS OF THE WEST: A GUIDE TO THEIR SPECIAL PLEASURES
A guide to 50 locales in the western United States, Alberta and British Columbia

that are desirable for sightseeing and away from cities and the well-known parks. West Pr, 1985.

Wallace, Robert   THE GAMBLERS
Part of a series of books on the Old West. Time-Life, 1979.

Watkins, T.H. and others   THE GRAND COLORADO
The story of the river and its canyons—portrays 4,000 years of human history from Indian days through the period of Coronado, priests to twentieth-century engineers. American West, 1970.

**West, Elliott   THE SALOON ON THE ROCKY MOUNTAIN
MINING FRONTIER**
A valuable contribution to social history. U of Nebraska, 1979.

Western Writers of America eds.   THE WOMEN WHO MADE THE WEST
Compiled vignettes of eighteen women, ranging from horse traders and quilters to ranchers and healers. Doubleday, 1980.

**Wiley, Peter and Gottlieb, Robert   EMPIRES IN THE SUN: THE RISE OF
THE NEW AMERICAN WEST**
"From Brigham Young . . . to Ronald Reagan"—with a thesis that government subsidies and military bases provided "the impetus to the phenomenal growth" now reaching a breaking point. (BRD) Putnam Pub Group, 1982.

Williams, Brad   LOST TREASURES OF THE WEST
Tales of lost treasures and where to find them—but entertaining reading for the stay-at-home as well. HR&W, 1975.

COWBOYS AND COWGIRLS

**Ackerman, Diane   TWILIGHT OF THE TENDERFOOT: A
WESTERN MEMOIR**
The author visited a New Mexico cattle ranch in March, June and September for a full cycle of ranch work and cowboy life as basis for this account of its social life and customs. Morrow, 1980.

**Davis, Tom   BE TOUGH OR BE GONE! THE ADVENTURES OF A MODERN
DAY COWBOY**
"Uplifting, true-adventure tale in which Tom Davis set a world record by taking a pack train of horses and mules from El Paso, Texas to Fairbanks, Alaska in less than six months." (BL) Northern Trails Pr, 1984.

Durham, Philip and Jones, Everett L.   THE NEGRO COWBOYS
U of Nebraska, 1983 (first published 1965).

*Johnston, Moira   RANCH: PORTRAIT OF A SURVIVING DREAM
Text and photos in a recreation of the past, the land and its people today. An absorbing evocation of ranch life and the author's journey which includes the American high plains, California and British Columbia. Doubleday, 1983.

Jordan, Teresa   COWGIRLS: WOMEN OF THE AMERICAN WEST
Stories of the counterparts to the cowboy based on interviews and excerpts from nineteenth- and early twentieth-century newspaper articles, songs, poetry and diaries. Doubleday, 1982.

Martin, Russell   COWBOY: THE ENDURING MYTH OF THE WILD WEST
Updating of the status of the cowboy myth in a large format, heavily illustrated book. Stewart, Tabori & Chang, 1983.

**Savage, William W., Ed.   COWBOY LIFE: RECONSTRUCTING AN
                             AMERICAN MYTH**
Selections from thirteen accounts written by nineteenth- and early twentieth-century observers. U of Oklahoma Pr, 1975.

Steiner, Stan   THE RANCHERS: A BOOK OF GENERATIONS
Vignettes of twenty ranching families from Montana, New Mexico and Oregon and why they hold on to "a way of life and a way of thinking that the rest of the country long ago abandoned and forgot." (BRD) Knopf, 1980.

PACIFIC NORTHWEST

Bancroft, Hunt N.   PEOPLE OF THE TOTEM
The Indians of the Pacific Northwest, whose art and culture have fascinated Europeans since the eighteenth and nineteenth centuries, before their civilization was changed by the white man—from Alaska to Upper Washington and through British Columbia. Putnam Pub Group, 1979.

**Brown, Bruce   MOUNTAIN IN THE CLOUDS: A SEARCH FOR THE
                 WILD SALMON**
"Part lyrical nature writing, part sportsman's adventure story, part . . . political exposé with history and ecology information. (LJ) S&S, 1982.

Franzwa, Gregory M.   THE OREGON TRAIL REVISITED
For those who would like to retrace this historic trail from Missouri to Oregon. Patrice Pr, 1983.

**Hitchcock, Anthony and Lindgren, Jean   CALIFORNIA AND THE
                                         PACIFIC NORTHWEST
                                         HISTORICAL AND
                                         SIGHTSEEING GUIDE**
B Franklin, 1981.

National Geographic eds.   AMERICA'S SPECTACULAR NORTHWEST
Natl Geog, 1982.

Olmsted, Gerald   LEWIS & CLARK TRAIL
With this book (part of the Fielding series) you can follow in the footsteps of the explorers, from your armchair or for real; excerpts from their journals, practical travel tips, a wealth of historical detail. Morrow, 1987.

Rankin, Marni and Jake   THE GETAWAY GUIDE: SHORT VACATIONS IN
THE PACIFIC NORTHWEST
Pacific Search Pr, 1982.

Reece, Daphne   HISTORIC HOUSES OF THE PACIFIC NORTHWEST
Chronicle, 1984.

Strickland, Ron, ed.   RIVER PIGS AND CAYUSES: ORAL HISTORIES
FROM THE PACIFIC NORTHWEST
"Regional history told in vivid style—a collection of thirty personal histories,
primarily gathered 1978-79, of recognizable western characters . . . cowboys,
moonshiners, and frontier brides." (BL) Lexikos, 1984.

Williams, Richard L.   THE CASCADES; THE NORTHWEST COAST
Two books, part of the American Wilderness series. Time-Life, 1974.

THE SOUTHWEST

Abbey, Edward   CACTUS COUNTRY
Part of the American Wilderness series. Time-Life, 1973.

Casey, Robert L.   JOURNEY TO THE HIGH SOUTHWEST: A TRAVELER'S
GUIDE
"Very personal and engaging guide to the region where Arizona, New Mexico,
Colorado, and Utah meet. . . . Natural wonders, archaeological ruins, Indian
reservations, parks . . . historic sites" with practical information on housing,
restaurants, shopping, and tourist tips. (BL) Pacific Search Pr, 1985.

Dobie, James Frank   CORONADO'S CHILDREN: TALES OF LOST MINES
AND BURIED TREASURE IN THE SOUTHWEST
"Packed full of treasure tales"—the myths and legends of buried gold in the old
Southwest beginning with the seven cities of Cibola sought by Coronado, with
map and charts. (BRD) Southwest Pr, 1930. *Apache Gold and Yaqui Silver* (1939)
is its sequel.

Doolittle, Jerry   CANYONS AND MESAS
Part of the American Wilderness series. Time-Life, 1974.

Faulk, Odie B.   DESTINY ROAD: THE GILA TRAIL AND THE OPENING
OF THE SOUTHWEST
Oxford U, 1973.

Foster, Lynn V. and Lawrence   SPANISH TRAILS IN THE SOUTHWEST
With this book (part of the Fielding series) you can follow in the footsteps of the
Spanish conquistadores in New Mexico and Arizona, from your armchair or for
real. Includes travel tips for contemporary explorers. Morrow, 1987.

Hitchcock, Anthony and Lindgren, Jean   TEXAS AND THE SOUTH WEST
HISTORICAL AND
SIGHTSEEING GUIDE
B Franklin, 1981.

Horgan, Paul   GREAT RIVER: THE RIO GRANDE IN NORTH AMERICAN HISTORY
Reprint of a book that won a Pulitzer Prize. Texas Monthly Pr, 1984 (first published 1954).

Jenkinson, Michael   LAND OF CLEAR LIGHT
The wilder regions of the American Southwest and northwest Mexico and how to reach them—for those who appreciate less-traveled routes. Dutton, 1977.

Lavender, David   THE SOUTHWEST
Exploration of the land, the history and the peoples of the Southwest, with emphasis on Arizona and New Mexico, from Spanish and Indian days to the present. U of New Mexico, 1984.

Miller, Tom   ON THE BORDER: PORTRAITS OF AMERICA'S SOUTHWESTERN FRONTIER
Documents the lifestyles, competition, cooperation, tensions and conflicts on the "friendship" frontier. Har-Row, 1981.

National Geographic eds.   THE GREAT SOUTHWEST
Natl Geog, 1980.

Page, Susanne and Jake   HOPI
"The physical world and spiritual universe" of the Hopi Indian in text and photographs. (BL) Abrams, 1982.

Sierra Club Guides eds.   NATIONAL PARKS OF THE DESERT SOUTHWEST; NATIONAL PARKS OF THE PACIFIC SOUTHWEST AND HAWAII
Random, 1984.

Simmons, Marc   FOLLOWING THE SANTA FE TRAIL
A guide for modern travelers. Ancient City Pr, 1984.

Stein, Rita   A LITERARY TOUR-GUIDE TO THE UNITED STATES: SOUTH AND SOUTH-WEST
Continuation of the series begun by Emilie C. Harting (see "East"). Morrow, 1979.

Zwinger, Ann   WIND IN THE ROCK
A naturalist explores the canyon country in the four corners area where Arizona, New Mexico, Utah and Colorado meet—"lively, readable nature writing," with sketches. (BRD) Har-Row, 1978.

TRAVEL ARTICLES

AMERICANA
1985 Dec "Trail into Timelessness." Santa Fe Trail. Malinda Elliott, p. 52

1984 Jan-Feb "Four Corners of History." Where the fascinating prehistoric civilization of Anasazi blends with the culture of native Americans living there today (Arizona, Colorado, New Mexico, Utah). Roy Bongartz, p. 53

ESQUIRE
1985 Jan "Special Places: Peak Lodgings." At Steamboat Springs, Busterback Ranch, Love Mountain Ranch, Old Faithful Snow Lodge, Togwotee Mountain Lodge. George Rush, p. 20

50 PLUS
1984 Feb "Where Next." Secret destinations for the sophisticated traveler (Alaska Highway). Robert S. Kane, p. 47
Aug "Finding the Swell Small Town." In Western states—see also the article under "California". Paula Patyk, p. 52

HOUSE & GARDEN
1984 Mar "Under the Big Sky." Camping out in the western wing of America's vast museum of landscapes. Alexander Cockburn, p. 30

MADEMOISELLE
1984 Nov "Ski Report." New England and the West. Brie P. Quinby and Catherine Ettlinger, p. 213

N.Y. TIMES SUNDAY TRAVEL SECTION (X)
1985 Sep 1 "Anasazi times in old America." "Ancient ones" in four corners area of the southwest. Jim Robbins, p. 15
1984 Jun 10 "A Tale of Four Corners." Natural monuments and Indian cultures are signposts of this southwest region (Arizona, Colorado, New Mexico, Utah). Iver Peterson, p. 14
Nov 11 (Skiing) "Making an Early Start in the West Before the Christmas Flurry." There's snow, room and discounts. Alex Ward, p. 27
"Choice Mountains, Great and Small." Guide to contrasting ski areas, with notes on rooms and meals. Stanley Carr, p. 29

READER'S DIGEST
1985 Sep "Bound for the Wild Missouri (River)." A ride on the "Gateway to the West." Richard Dunlop, p. 148
1984 Mar "Roll On, Columbia." River. Larry Van Goethem, p. 155

SUNSET
1985 Jun "Rendezvousing with the Mountain Men." Join in as the buckskinners, muzzle-loaders, and friends recreate the West's fur trade. Almost everyone's in costume, what about you? p. 98; "More Mountain Man Rendezvous and Other Old West Celebrations." p. 92
Aug "Two-mile-high Detouring Near Four Corners." State Highway 145 scenic route in Colorado, Arizona, Utah, New Mexico. p. 50
Dec "Christmas Theater in the West's Small Towns." Dickens, Dylan Thomas, Menotti and more. p. 44
"Rediscovering the Small-town Christmas." Tips on 46 towns in the west and Hawaii. p. 68

1984 Jan "Magnificent Sand Seas of the West." From California to Colorado, sand dune systems await discovery. p. 46

Apr "You're the Wrangler Vacations." Working ranches welcome guests. p. 105

May "Wilderness in the West." A report on the wilderness, plus trips and outings you can join. p. 94

Aug "Here Come the Northwest Wines." Guides to wines and back road wineries in Washington, Oregon and Idaho. p. 61

Nov "Old English Feasts for the Yule Season." Restaurants in the West. p. 38

TRAVEL & LEISURE

1985 Apr Travel & Architecture: "The Grace of the Mission Style." A rich architectural tradition in California and the Southwest. David Gebhard, p. 26

1984 Nov "Latest from the Rockies." What's doing on the ski slopes, Montana to New Mexico. Abby Rand, p. 77

ALABAMA

Agee, James   LET US NOW PRAISE FAMOUS MEN
A study in words and pictures of a sharecropper's family in 1936. Houghton, 1960 (first published 1941).

Carmer, Carl   STARS FELL ON ALABAMA
Tales, sketches and impressions of life in Alabama. FS&G, 1934.

Gray, Daniel S.   ALABAMA: A PLACE, A PEOPLE, A POINT OF VIEW
Kendall-Hunt, 1977.

Haagen, Victor B.   ALABAMA: PORTRAIT OF A STATE
Southern U, 1963.

Hamilton, Virginia   ALABAMA
One of a series of popular histories for each state, published as part of the Bicentennial observance in 1976. Norton, 1984 (first published 1977).

Hamilton, Virginia   SEEING HISTORIC ALABAMA
Fifteen guided tours of historic sights and museums. U of Alabama, 1982.

Higginbotham, Jay   OLD MOBILE
Personalities and events surrounding the establishment and life of Old Mobile. Museum of the City of Mobile, 1977.

Kirk, Mary W.   LOCUST HILL
Life of an antebellum mansion. U of Alabama, 1975.

Murari, Timeri   GOIN' HOME
A black family moves back to Alabama from Boston. The book is written by a British-raised, India-born writer who followed the family in its experience. Putnam Pub Group, 1980.

Sangster, Tom   ALABAMA'S COVERED BRIDGES
For anyone who thinks New England has a monopoly on covered bridges. Coffeetable Pbns, 1981.

Scott, Carolynne   COUNTRY ROADS: A JOURNEY THROUGH RUSTIC ALABAMA
Portals Pr, 1979.

Sulzby, James F., Jr.   HISTORIC ALABAMA HOTELS AND RESORTS
U of Alabama, 1960.

Windham, Kathryn T.   ALABAMA: ONE BIG FRONT PORCH
Strode, 1981 (first published 1975).

Novels

Brown, Rita Mae   SOUTHERN DISCOMFORT
Novel of the rigid class and racial lines of Montgomery society during the early decades of this century. Har-Row, 1982.

Calisher, Hortense   FALSE ENTRY
An unconventional telling of the life of a young man who effects false entry into other lives. His boyhood years are set in Tuscaloosa. Little, 1961.

Capote, Truman   A CHRISTMAS MEMORY
Autobiographical story of a boy's Christmas with elderly relatives. Random, 1966. Also *The Thanksgiving Visitor* (1968).

Coleman, Lonnie   ORPHAN JIM
Orphans find security with a black prostitute. Doubleday, 1975.

Hannah, Barry   RAY
Soliloquy of a young doctor, set in Tuscaloosa. Knopf, 1980.

Lee, Harper   TO KILL A MOCKINGBIRD
Adult injustice and violence are brought into the lives of two children when their father courageously defends a black accused of rape—set in a small southern town. Lippincott, 1960.

McCammon, Robert   MYSTERY WALK
Two young brothers (one a tent revival faith healer, the other with the gift to help spirits of those who die violently to "pass over") in a novel of horror and the supernatural—"delivers a good scare with style." (FC) Holt, 1983.

Raines, Howell   WHISKEY MAN
An evocation of small-town life in 1932. Viking, 1977.

Stribling, T.S.   THE VAIDAN TRILOGY
Northern Alabama from 1860 to 1920. The three individual titles are *The Forge* (1931), *The Store* (1932), and *The Unfinished Cathedral* (1934).

Warren, Robert Penn   A PLACE TO COME TO
A dissatisfied youth tries to find happiness in Chicago, grows up and returns home to Alabama. Random, 1977.

Weidman, Jerome   COUNSELORS-AT-LAW
An involved tale of love, politics, power struggles and revenge among the legal set. Doubleday, 1980.

TRAVEL ARTICLES

HORIZON
1985 Dec "Montgomery: Alabama's Capital City Mixes a Rich Cultural Heritage with a Graceful Southern Lifestyle." Susan Y. Richard, p. 36

TRAVEL/HOLIDAY
1985 Apr "Huntsville's Heyday." Jonathan Siskin, p. 6

ALASKA

Series Guidebooks

Fodor: Alaska
Insight: Alaska
Lonely Planet: Alaska

Background Reading

Alaska Geographic Soc., eds.   ADVENTURE ROADS NORTH
The story of the Alaska Highway and other roads in the Milepost. Alaska Geo Svc, 1983.

Alaska Geo Staff eds.   ISLAND OF THE SEALS: THE PRIBILOFFS
History, description, travel and sealing—this is the area of confrontation between conservationists and those who hunt seals for a livelihood each year. Alaska Northwest, 1982.

Balcolm, Mary   KETCHIKAN, ALASKA'S TOTEMLAND
Balcolm, 1980. Also *Ghost Towns of Alaska* (1980).

Baxter, Robert   BAXTER'S ALASKA
Rail-Europe-Baxter, 1984.

Brower, Charles D.   FIFTY YEARS BELOW ZERO
The author's life in Alaska from 1883 to the 1940s, and reminiscences of explorers, Eskimos, adventurers, family and friends. Dodd, 1942.

Brown, Dale   WILD ALASKA
Part of the American Wilderness series. Time-Life, 1972.

Christy, Jim   ROUGH ROAD TO THE NORTH: TRAVELS ALONG THE ALASKA HIGHWAY
Personal experiences, history, and the contrasts that exist; use of the highway and the folklore that has grown up about the region. Doubleday, 1980.

Crump, Donald J., ed.   ALASKA'S MAGNIFICENT PARKLANDS
Natl Geog, 1984.

Dixon, Mim   WHAT HAPPENED TO FAIRBANKS?
The effects of the trans-Alaska oil pipeline on the community. Westview Pr, 1980.

Eppenbach, Sarah   ALASKA'S SOUTHEAST: TOURING THE INSIDE PASSAGE
A book for traveling in the southern panhandle area of Alaska from Ketchikan to Skagway, by ferry, cruise ship or private yacht—an area it is claimed is undiscovered, hospitable, and temperate in climate. Pacific Search Pr, 1983.

Gruening, Ernest, ed.   AN ALASKA READER, 1867-1967
Anthology of descriptive nature pieces, poetry, Klondike tales, the struggle for statehood, and more. The editor was both a senator and a governor of the state. Meredith Pr, 1966.

Hunt, William R.   ALASKA
One of a series of popular histories for each state, published as part of the Bicentennial in 1976. Norton, 1976.

Hunt, William R.   NORTH OF 53
The wild days of the Alaska-Yukon mining frontier, 1870-1914—a social history of the early Alaska frontier days. Macmillan, 1975.

Johnson, Beth   YUKON WILD
The adventures of four Texas women who paddled through America's last frontier. Their journal includes preparations for and the canoe trip itself—people they met along the way, cafes along the river, weather, bugs, "all add up to a saga that will entertain prospective river travelers and armchair adventurers alike." (PW) Berkshire Traveller Pr, 1984.

Landru, H.C.   THE BLUE PARKA MAN, ALASKAN GOLD RUSH BANDIT
The story of a "gold stealing highwayman" in gold rush days. (BRD) Dodd, 1980.

McGinnis, Joe   GOING TO EXTREMES
"A wanderer's chronicle" of vignettes about bar friends, rural entrepreneurs, company officials and all the various types drawn to the Alaska life-style. (BRD) Knopf, 1980.

McPhee, Joe   COMING INTO THE COUNTRY
Story of America's last frontier and of its colorful people, wild animals and magnificent land through all its moods—the next thing to being there. FS&G, 1977. Also *Alaska: Images of the Country* (1981), color photographs to complement excerpts from the text of *Coming Into the Country*, published by the Sierra Club.

Milepost eds.   ALL-THE-NORTH TRAVEL GUIDE
Updated every spring, a comprehensive guide for travelers who are planning a trip by train, boat, plane or car. Alaska Northwest, 1985.

Morgan, Lael, ed. and others   THE ALEUTIANS
History, description and travel. Alaska Geo Soc, 1980.

Morgan, Lael   AND THE LAND PROVIDES
Cultural changes and problems faced by people in six native Alaskan villages. Doubleday, 1974.

Nelson, Richard K.   SHADOW OF THE HUNTER
Stories of the Inuit Indian by an anthropologist—a descriptive account of a living culture. U of Chicago, 1980.

Olson, Sigurd   RUNES OF THE NORTH
The "face and facts" of nature as reflected in the author's experiences on a trip to Saskatchewan, Hudson Bay, the Yukon and into Alaska. (BRD) Knopf, 1963.

Roscow, James P.   800 MILES TO VALDEZ
The building of the Alaska pipeline. P-H, 1977.

Searby, Ellen   THE INSIDE PASSAGE TRAVELER
The eighth edition of this guidebook by an author who has worked for many years on the ferries. Complete information needed to plan a trip as comfortable or

adventurous as you choose. Transportation; the advantage of traveling from Prince Rupert, B.C.; minor ports and native villages served by smaller ferries; things to do in each town; where to stay (hotels, campgrounds, hostels, and more). Windham Bay Pr, 1985.

Simmerman, Nancy L.   ALASKA'S PARKLANDS: THE COMPLETE GUIDE
Guide, with ratings, to wild rivers, refuges, forests, historic sites and major parks. Mountaineers, 1983.

Specht, Robert   TISHA
The time is 1927—autobiographical account of a year in the life of Anne Hobbs who falls in love with a half-Indian. St. Martin, 1976.

Spring, Norma   ALASKA: THE COMPLETE TRAVEL BOOK
Macmillan, 1979.

Stanley, David   ALASKA-YUKON HANDBOOK: A GYPSY GUIDE TO THE INSIDE PASSAGE AND BEYOND
Comprehensive in serving all kinds of travelers from those who prefer regular passenger ferries, buses and trains to those who hitchhike. Information on small hotels, hostels, campgrounds and local eating places, with thousands of specific tips. In addition to Alaska and the Yukon it provides detailed coverage for Washington State and British Columbia. Moon Pbns, 1984.

Thomas, Lowell Jr. and others   ALASKA AND THE YUKON
Splendid evocation of the continent's last frontier—eight contributors write on people past and present, animals, recreation, sports, history, cities and isolated settlements. Facts On File, 1983.

Vick, Ann   THE CAMA-I BOOK
A Foxfire-like project (see "Georgia") of students in the most isolated southwestern region of the state—"kayaks, dogsleds, salmonberry jelly, ivory carving, smoked fish, mukluks" and other crafts, customs and lore. (BL) Doubleday, 1983.

Washburn, Bradford   A TOURIST GUIDE TO MOUNT MCKINLEY
"The story of Denali—'the great one': mile-by-mile through the Park over Mount McKinley Park Highway, the record of McKinley climbs." (Publisher) Alaska Northwest, 1980.

Wayburn, Peggy   ADVENTURING IN ALASKA
A treasure-trove for modern-day adventurers—background information, practical tips, specifics on travel in major cities and wilderness areas. Sierra Club, 1982.

Wright, Billie   FOUR SEASON NORTH: A JOURNAL OF LIFE IN THE ALASKAN WILDERNESS
A year spent recreating the traditional Eskimo life-style. Har-Row, 1973.

Novels

Boyer, G.G.   MORGETTE IN THE YUKON
"Old-fashioned, action-packed tale" of gunfighters, claim-jumpers and a long-lost gold mine. (FC) Walker, 1983.

Dailey, Janet   THE GREAT ALONE
Historic, epic novel of Alaska, beginning with arrival of Russian fur traders in the Aleutians in the 17th century. Poseidon Pr, 1986.

Doig, Ivan   THE SEA RUNNERS
Adventure novel of Alaska's Russian period when Scandinavians worked as indentured servants in the tsar's service. A story of the escape of four of them from Sitka to Astoria, Oregon. Atheneum, 1982.

Ferber, Edna   ICE PALACE
A public and private tug-of-war over the years between two onetime partners over the issues of statehood for Alaska and affection and loyalty of their granddaughter—"eye-opening glimpses of . . . Alaska." (FC) Doubleday, 1958.

Jones, Robert F.   SLADE'S GLACIER
Two newcomers arrive in Alaska to work as bush pilots following World War II—one a man with integrity, the other greedy and typical of those who came to exploit Alaska's resources. The novel tells how they, and the state, fare over the following thirty years. S&S, 1981.

London, Jack   CALL OF THE WILD
Classic adventure story of a man and his dog in the Klondike. Dodd, 1960 (first published 1903).

MacLean, Alistair   ATHABASCA
Threats to disrupt the Alaska pipeline lead to blackmail, hostages and murder. Doubleday, 1980.

Marshall, James V.   A RIVER RAN OUT OF EDEN
A family drama about the slaughter of seals in the Aleutians. Morrow, 1963.

White, Stewart E.   WILD GEESE CALLING
A young couple in Oregon meet, marry and pursue their pioneering spirit first to Seattle, finally to the Alaskan wilderness. Doubleday, 1940.

TRAVEL ARTICLES

AMERICANA
1985 May-Jun "Boomtown in the Klondike." Restoration in Skagway. Dwight Holing, p. 54

BON APPETIT
1985 Aug "Traveling with Taste: the Klondike." Shirley Slater, p. 30

CONNOISSEUR
1984 Jul "Angler's Paradise." Lake Clark. Ogden Tanner, p. 92

ESQUIRE
1985 Apr "Stalking Alaska." Michael Kinsley, p. 140
1984 Mar "Alaska: Big, Bold and 25 Years Old." John Zinsser, p. 40
      "In love with Alaska." Lowell Thomas, Jr., p. 45

50 PLUS
1985 Oct "Our Northernmost State Is a Wonderland of Unspoiled Nature." Edwin
      Kiester, Jr. p. 31

HOUSE & GARDEN
1984 Jun "Out from Fort Yukon." A trip with a trapper on the Porcupine River.
      Edward Hoagland, p. 52

NATIONAL GEOGRAPHIC
1984 Jan "A Place Apart: Alaska's Southeast." Bill Richards, p. 50

NATIONAL GEOGRAPHIC TRAVELER
1984 Summer "Denali—a Peaceable Kingdom." Spectacular scenery, wildlife and
      majestic Mount McKinley. Dale M. Brown, p. 102

N.Y. TIMES SUNDAY TRAVEL SECTION (X)
1985 Jul 7 Fare of the Country: "Feasting on Salmon in Alaska's Wilds." Craig
      Claiborne, p. 6
1984 Jan 3 "Refuge for the Travel-Weary." Village roadhouse in the Alaska wilder-
      ness. David Eames, p. 55
      Jan 24 Shopper's World: "Eskimo Visions in Ivory." Alberta Eiseman, p. 12
      Jul 8 "New Museum for Alaska." The state's cultural and natural history
      museum in Fairbanks. Alberta Eisenman, p. 20
      Oct 21 "Along the Gold Rush Trail." A nostalgic trip to Alaska by ferry recalls
      a gritty, gallant era. Michael T. Kaufman, p. 33

SUNSET
1985 Jul "Tours Above Alaska's Arctic Circle." p. 62
      Dec "Planning an Alaska Cruise." p. 50
1984 May "On a Few Hours' Walk, You See Tlingit and Russian Sitka." p. 48
      Jun "40 Minutes Out of Anchorage." One-day fishing adventures. p. 88

TRAVEL/HOLIDAY
1985 Feb "Getting to Know Juneau." Gateway to Alaska's frozen frontier. Andrew
      Yarrow, p. 50
      Jun "Alone with Alaska." Exploring Kenai Peninsula. Carolyn Males and Judy
      Raskin, p. 48

1984 Feb "Cruising the Inland Passage." Linda and Peter D'Aprix, p. 56
"The Southwest Frontier." Savoring the scenic panhandle. Margaret Zellars,
p. 56

ARIZONA

Background Reading

Babbitt, Bruce   GRAND CANYON: AN ANTHOLOGY
Northland, 1978.

Baxter, Robert   BAXTER'S NATIONAL PARKS: VOLUME 1
A guide to the Grand Canyon National Park. Rail-Europe-Baxter,1984.

Coffer, William E.   PHOENIX: THE DECLINE AND REBIRTH OF THE
INDIAN PEOPLE
As told by Koi Hosh, an American Cherokee/Choctaw Indian—"a thorough and
eminently readable history and analysis of an amazing people's struggle to
survive." (BL) Van Nostrand, 1979.

Cook, James E.   ARIZONA ONE HUNDRED ONE
"An irreverent short course for new arrivals." (Publisher) Cocinero Pr, 1981.

DeMente, Boye   GUIDE TO ARIZONA'S INDIAN RESERVATIONS
Phoenix, 1985.

Dyk, Walter and Ruth, eds.   LEFT HANDED: A NAVAJO
AUTOBIOGRAPHY
Everyday Navajo life in the early 1880s from childhood to maturity. Columbia U
Pr, 1980.

Everhart, Ronald E.   GLEN CANYON-LAKE POWELL
Guide to the Glen Canyon and Lake Powell Recreation Areas in Arizona and
Utah. KC Pbns, 1983.

Faulk, Odie B.   TOMBSTONE: MYTH AND REALITY
Recreation of life in Tombstone and the Wyatt Earp story. Oxford U, 1972.

Fletcher, Colin   THE MAN WHO WALKED THROUGH TIME
A two-month solitary hike through the Grand Canyon from one end to the
other. Random, 1972.

Goldwater, Barry   DELIGHTFUL JOURNEY: DOWN THE GREEN AND
COLORADO RIVERS
AZ Hist Found, 1970.

Heatwole, Thelma   ARIZONA—OFF THE BEATEN PATH
Golden West, 1981. Also *Ghost Towns and Historical Haunts in Arizona* (1981).

Kant, Candace C.   ZANE GREY'S ARIZONA
"Describes Grey's life in Arizona . . . how his firsthand observations inspired some of his most memorable tales" in their Arizona setting. (BL) Northland, 1984.

Krutch, Joseph W.   GRAND CANYON
Unhurried view of "one of nature's most impressive phenomena . . . nature writing at its best." (BRD) Morrow, 1968. Also *Desert Year* (1952), a literary work on the natural setting of the Southwest, desert life, and the author's personal philosophy.

Lavender, David   RIVER RUNNERS OF THE GRAND CANYON
Early-day river runners and their "breathtaking experiences"—explorers, surveyors, miners, thrill-seekers. (PW) U of Arizona, 1985.

Leon, Vicki   THE MONEYWISE GUIDE TO CALIFORNIA WITH EXCURSIONS TO RENO, LAS VEGAS, THE GRAND CANYON AND BAJA CALIFORNIA
See full annotation under "California/Guidebooks."

Lesure, Thomas B.   ALL ABOUT ARIZONA
"The healthful state where it's great to live and vacation" is the book's subtitle. Harian, 1983.

Loving, Nancy J.   ALONG THE RIM: A ROAD GUIDE TO THE SOUTH RIM OF GRAND CANYON
GCNHA, 1981.

McAdams, Cliff   GRAND CANYON
Guide and reference book. Pruett, 1981.

Miller, Donald C.   GHOST TOWNS OF THE SOUTHWEST: ARIZONA, UTAH, NEW MEXICO
Pruett, 1980.

Morgan, Anne H. and Strickland, Rennard, eds.   ARIZONA MEMORIES
A collection of reminiscences of diverse people, in their own words—an Apache scout, a frontier doctor, a soldier's wife, a cowboy—and about ranching, mining, Christmas, July 4th and more. U of Arizona, 1984.

Powell, Lawrence C.   ARIZONA
One of a series of popular histories for each state published as part of the Bicentennial observance in 1976. Norton, 1976.

Reed, Allen C.   GRAND CIRCLE ADVENTURE
Traveling to national parks and reserves in Arizona, Colorado and Utah. KC Pbns, 1983.

Schullery, Paul, ed.   THE GRAND CANYON: EARLY IMPRESSIONS
Reactions of writers from 1869 to 1941 (Zane Grey, John Muir, etc.), pioneers, scholars, on first seeing the Canyon, and ranging from "scholarly or pioneering reports to enthusiastic travelogues or satiric jabs." (BL) Colorado Association U Pr, 1981.

Sikorsky, Robert   FOOLS' GOLD
"The facts, myths and legends of the Lost Dutchman Mine and the Superstition Mountains." The author's experiences as a geologist provide history of this fabled treasure "separating fact from fantasy." (BL) Golden West, 1983.

**Sonnichsen, C.L.   TUCSON: THE LIFE AND TIMES OF AN
                       AMERICAN CITY**
"Robust story that traces Tucson's 200-year growth. . . its unique southwestern character." (BRD) U of Oklahoma Pr, 1982.

Stocker, Joseph and Holden, Wesley   TRAVEL ARIZONA
Arizona Hwy, 1981.

Sunset Magazine and Book, eds.   ARIZONA
Sunset-Lane, 1985.

Thollander, Earl and Abbey, Edward   BACKROADS OF ARIZONA
Northland, 1978.

Trimble, Marshall   ROADSIDE HISTORY OF ARIZONA
A history for the traveling public, organized by sections of highway. Golden West Pbns, 1986.

Varney, Philip   ARIZONA'S BEST GHOST TOWNS: A PRACTIAL GUIDE
Northland, 1980.

Wallace, Robert   THE GRAND CANYON
Part of the American Wilderness series. Time-Life, 1972.

**Warren, Colin   VELVET WATERS, CANYON WALLS: A LAKE POWELL
                   ADVENTURE**
Travel in the Lake Powell and Glen Canyon National Recreation Areas in Arizona and Utah. Northland, 1983.

Weir, Bill   ARIZONA HANDBOOK
Moon Pbns Ca, 1986.

Whitney, Stephen   A FIELD GUIDE TO THE GRAND CANYON
History, formation, human inhabitants, and explorations of the canyon combined with travel information, whether one is seeing the canyon by foot, river, or mule train. Additional sections describe the geology, plants and animals. Morrow, 1982.

Woodin, Ann   HOME IS THE DESERT
"Delightful reading for those who know the desert or hope to at some time."
The book explores aspects of the desert environment and its effect on the mental
and spiritual development of her family (the author's husband was curator of the
Arizona-Sonora Museum outside of Tucscon). (BRD) U of Arizona, 1984 (first
published 1965). See also the author's book *In the Circle of the Sun*, listed under
"Northern Africa."

Novels

Abbey, Edward   THE MONKEY WRENCH GANG
A group of improbable conservationists sabotage bulldozers, power lines and
bridges, in their private war against those who would destroy the
landscape—"terrific chase sequences . . . eloquent landscapes." (FC) Lippincott,
1975.

Arnold, Elliott   BLOOD BROTHER
A fictionalized version of the story of Cochise and peacemaker
Tom Jeffords. U of Nebraska, 1979.

Ballard, Todhunter   THE SHERIFF OF TOMBSTONE
Western saga of a cattleman who tames that Arizona town. Doubleday, 1977.

Garfield, Brian   THE THREEPERSONS HUNT
Mystery and a chase involving an Indian, who has escaped the penitentiary
where he is serving time for murder, and the man who is tracking him
down—"gives a fine picture of reservation Indians and the white men surrounding
them." (FC) M. Evans, 1974. Also *Relentless* (1972)—five men rob a bank on
payroll day at the copper company, with a chase, by car and plane, headed by a
Navajo Indian in the Arizona Highway Patrol.

Green, Gerald   AN AMERICAN PROPHET
The story of a retired professor living in the Arizona desert and his efforts to
preserve it from destruction by developers and ranchers. Doubleday, 1977.

Grey, Zane   THE ARIZONA CLAN
Feuding clans in the Tonto Basin. Har-Row, 1958. Also *To the Last Man.* (1922)

Henry, Will   MACKENNA'S GOLD
A mystery/melodrama set in 1897—"based on a first-rate Southwestern lost
mine tale and a . . . little-read personal narrative." (FC) Random, 1963.

Hogan, William   THE QUARTZITE TRIP
"Provocative funny/serious story" of a group of adolescents who accompany
their teacher on a trip to Arizona in 1962. (BRD) Atheneum, 1980.

Horgan, Paul   A DISTANT TRUMPET
The action surrounds a U.S. Army outpost in the 1870s, during the Apache Indian Wars. FS&G, 1960.

Houston, Robert   BISBEE '17
A novel based on the strike at the copper mines in 1917. Pantheon, 1979.

LaFarge, Oliver   LAUGHING BOY
An idyll of the Navajo country—it won a Pulitzer Prize. Buccaneer Bks, 1981 (first published 1929).

Lawrence, D.H.   ST. MAWR, AND OTHER STORIES
St. Mawr is a "psychological novella" set in Arizona. (FC) Cambridge U Pr, 1983 (first published 1925).

Peters, Elizabeth   SUMMER OF THE DRAGON
A suspenseful romance involving a woman archaeologist and a gullible millionaire interested in pseudo-science. Dodd, 1979.

Seton, Anya   FOXFIRE
Story of the problems and conflicts to be resolved when a cultured Eastern girl marries a mining engineer who is one-quarter Apache. Houghton, 1950.

Smith, Martin C.   NIGHTWING
"Downright terrifying" novel of killer vampire bats conjured up by a Hopi medicine man. (FC) Norton, 1977.

Whitney, Phyllis A.   VERMILION
A mystery romance of a New York designer who returns to Arizona when she receives a letter that offers to explain her father's mysterious death—"evocation of . . . the Southwest is superb and integral to the plot." (FC) Doubleday, 1981.

TRAVEL ARTICLES

AMERICANA
1985 May-Jun "Native Peoples." New permanent exhibit at Heard Museum in Phoenix lets viewers experience other cultures. Bruce Berger, p. 22

BLACK ENTERPRISE
1984 Jun "The Long Hike." One couple's determined trek through the Grand Canyon. Lester Sloan, p. 266

NATIONAL GEOGRAPHIC TRAVELER
1985 Winter "Secrets of the Dry Lands." Arizona-Sonora Desert Museum. Michael Collier, p. 46
1984 Spring "My 40 Years as a Grand Canyoneer." An appreciation. Edward Abbey, p. 19
       "Unconquerable Chasm." Exploring the Grand Canyon (a mule trip down to Phantom Ranch). Robert Laxalt, p. 22
       Winter "Welcome to Wickenburg." Guest ranches. Merrill Windsor, p. 40

N.Y. TIMES SUNDAY TRAVEL SECTION (X)

1985 Feb 24 "At 2,400 Feet, the 'Left Bank' of Tucson." The desert city boasts a student oasis. Paul West, p. 37

1984 Feb 5 "What's Doing in Tucson." Carol Ann Bassett, p. 10

SUNSET

1985 Feb "More Indian Doings at Museums in California, Arizona, N.M." p. 62
"Splendid New Showcases for Southwest Indian Art." Heard and Southwest Museums in Phoenix and Los Angeles. p. 78
Mar "Biking to Tucson's Cactus Country." p. 58
Apr "A 500-Mile Arizona Bike Adventure." Grand Canyon to the border. p. 92
Oct "The Beautiful Baskets of Arizona's Paiutes." p. 76

1984 Jan "Havasu by Jeep, Para-Sail, Ferry." p. 24
Mar "Trolleys on Tires in Five Arizona Cities." p. 76
Jul "Quick Trips Down Or Above the Colorado River." Page, Arizona. p. 48
Dec "Bike, Skate, Jog on Scottsdale's Path Through the Cactus." p. 34

TRAVEL & LEISURE

1985 Jan "Dining Out in Phoenix and Scottsdale." Charles Monaghan, p. 128
Oct "Scenic Drive: Arizona's Red Rocks Country." Ian Keown, p. 87

1984 Feb "Arizona, Land of Ancient Civilizations." Doug Emerson, p. 53

TRAVEL/HOLIDAY

1984 Mar "Aglow with the Good Life—Phoenix." Carole Harshman, p. 68

ARKANSAS

Background Reading

Ashmore, Harry S.   ARKANSAS
Revised edition of one of a series of popular histories for each state published as part of the Bicentennial observance in 1976. The Association, 1984 (first published 1978).

Brown, Dee   THE AMERICAN SPA: HOT SPRINGS, ARKANSAS
Anecdotal history of what has been a "hot spot" from DeSoto's discovery in 1541 to the present. Rose, 1982.

Fletcher, John G.   ARKANSAS AS A STATE AND A STATE OF MIND
Combines factual material with the fascination of folk tales, comic interludes, personalities—written by a native son who is a Pulitzer Prize-winning poet. U of North Carolina Pr, 1947.

Hampel, Bet   THE PELICAN GUIDE TO THE OZARKS
Divided into eleven area tours, what to see, getting there, fairs and events, where to sample authentic Ozark food and culture, historic sites. Pelican, 1982.

Rafferty, Milton D.   THE OZARKS OUTDOORS
For sportsmen (fishermen, hunters) and tourists, and comprehensive background source on history, folkways, vacationing, tourism. U of Oklahoma Pr, 1985. Also *The Ozarks* (1980), on cultural patterns and development of the area.

**Randolph, Vance   WE ALWAYS LIE TO STRANGERS: TALL TALES FROM
                            THE OZARKS**
Americana, both scholarly and entertaining—wild and absurd anecdotes and jokes . . . a hearty skimming of regional humor." (BRD) Greenwood, 1974 (first published 1951).

Reed, Roy   LOOKING FOR HOGEYE
Essays by a professor of journalism at the University of Arkansas—"engaging prose" about the people of the Ozarks, families, cities, back roads, weather, making do. (NYTBR) U of Arkansas Pr, 1986.

Rhodes, Richard   OZARKS
Part of the American Wilderness series. Time-Life, 1974.

Williams, Miller, ed.   OZARK, OZARK: A HILLSIDE READER
"A rich anthology of works by writers from the Ozark Mountain region of Missouri and Arkansas . . . all from the twentieth
century . . . imbued with a marvelous combination of naivete and sophistication."
(BL) U of Missouri, 1981.

Novels

Burchardt, Bill   BLACK MARSHALL
A tale of the Oklahoma Territory and a black marshal with an "uncanny knowledge of people and nature." (FC) Doubleday, 1981.

DiDonato, Georgia   WOMAN OF JUSTICE
Historical novel of a woman judge assigned to work with "hanging Judge Parker" in the late 1800s. Doubleday, 1980.

Harrington, Donald   ARCHITECTURE OF THE ARKANSAS OZARKS
"Lives, homes and adventures of six generations . . . of an Ozark mountain family." Little, 1975.

Jones, Douglas C.   ELKHORN TAVERN
The Civil War as experienced by a farming family in Arkansas. HR&W, 1980.

Jones, Douglas C.   WEEDY ROUGH
"Coming of age of a boy in the small Arkansas town Weedy Rough" during the period of World War I to the 1930s—"amusing and tender narrative . . . is actually background to the novel's climactic event: a bank robbery in Weedy Rough." (FC) HR&W, 1981.

Pharr, Robert D.   THE BOOK OF NUMBERS
Two black waiters in the 1930s become wealthy through running a numbers racket in the ghetto—all of the characters are finally destroyed one way or another. Doubleday, 1969.

Portis, Charles   THE DOG OF THE SOUTH
A man trails his runaway wife. Knopf, 1979. Also by Portis is *True Grit* (1968), on which the movie was based—the heroine begins her adventures in Yell County, Arkansas.

TRAVEL ARTICLES

READER'S DIGEST
1984 Sep "Arkansas Odyssey." Paul Hemphill, p. 154

SATURDAY EVENING POST
1985 Jul "Arkansas Springs Eternal." G. Maynard Stoddard, p. 91

TRAVEL/HOLIDAY
1984 Feb "An Arkansas Rite of Spring." Pleasures of the country and city. Denise Meehan, p. 52

CALIFORNIA

Series Guidebooks (See Appendix 1)

American Express: California
Baedeker: San Francisco
Berlitz: California
Birnbaum: Disneyland
Fisher: California & the West
Fodor: California; Los Angeles; San Franciso; San Diego
Fun in San Francisco
Frommer: Los Angeles: City Guide; San Francisco: City Guide
California & Las Vegas: Dollarwise
Insight: Northern California; Southern California
Let's Go: California & the Pacific Northwest

Background Reading

Barich, Bill   TRAVELING LIGHT
California, London and Florence (Italy) are the chief subjects of this "masterful compilation of travel writing that may propel the reader out of her/his armchair into a plane to Florence or London [or California]." Based on an eighteen-month trip and preoccupations en route with friends, family, fishing, horseracing, history, art. (LJ)Viking, 1984.

Berger, Bennett M.   HIPPIE COUNTRY
Ideology and everyday life in rural communes in California. U of California, 1981.

Birmingham, Stephen   CALIFORNIA RICH
Anecdotal stories of the Stanfords, Hearsts, Huntingtons and other powerful California families—"their ventures, shenanigans, and offspring." (BRD) S&S, 1981.

Bowen, Ezra   HIGH SIERRA
Part of the American Wilderness series. Time-Life, 1972.

Dallas, Sandra   GASLIGHTS AND GINGERBREAD: CALIFORNIA'S HISTORIC HOMES
Ohio U, 1984.

Eisen, Jonathan and Fine, David, eds.   UNKNOWN CALIFORNIA
A collection of essays, letters and stories spanning California's history from the gold rush to the present. Selections include writings of people such as Steinbeck, Mailer, Stegner, Carey McWilliams, a woman's letter from a mining outpost in 1852, and more. (PW) Collier, 1985.

Feimling, Jean   GREAT PIERS OF CALIFORNIA
History, description of life on and near California's piers—for ocean watchers, fishermen, anyone who enjoys the coast. Mostly Southern California, but also piers from Santa Cruz heading north. Capra Pr, 1984.

Fletcher, Colin   THE THOUSAND-MILE SUMMER IN DESERT AND HIGH SIERRA
Howell-North, 1982 (first published 1964).

Gold, Herbert   A WALK ON THE WEST SIDE: CALIFORNIA ON THE BRINK
"Novelist Gold takes the trendy pulse of his adopted state in this bemused travelogue. . . experiences among people and in places that have helped give California its reputation as the melting pot of the American dream." (BL) Arbor Hse, 1981.

Harlow, Neal   CALIFORNIA CONQUERED, 1846-50
"Good reading and good history" of the end of the Mexican era in California. (BRD) U of California, 1982.

Hart, James D.   A COMPANION TO CALIFORNIA
Two-thousand brief entries on people, incidents, places, and longer pieces on issues and aspects of California, including literature. Oxford U, 1978.

Houston, James D.   CALIFORNIANS: SEARCHING FOR THE GOLDEN STATE
"A remarkable blend of travel writing, interpretive profiles, and reflective essay" to define California—movies, freeway, travel, Chicanos, computer industry, vineyards and more. Knopf, 1982.

Lavender, David   CALIFORNIA
One of a series of popular histories for each state published as part of the Bicentennial observance in 1976. Norton, 1976.

Lee, Hector   HEROES, VILLAINS AND GHOSTS: FOLKLORE OF OLD CALIFORNIA
An anthology of tales based on California history or pure folklore. Capra Pr, 1984.

Lennon, Nigey   MARK TWAIN IN CALIFORNIA
"The turbulent California years of Samuel Clemens . . . humorous and well-researched diversion" of Twain's years in the state. (BL) Chronicle, 1982.

Reece, Daphne   HISTORIC HOUSES OF CALIFORNIA
A directory of restored historic structures you can visit in California. Chronicle Bk, 1983.

Sanborn, Margaret   YOSEMITE: ITS DISCOVERY, ITS WONDER AND ITS PEOPLE
Random, 1981.

Teale, Edwin Way, ed.   THE WILDERNESS WORLD OF JOHN MUIR
Anthology of Muir's writings chronologically arranged to provide a cohesive portrait of the naturalist/writer's view of life—"reading that is often magnificent . . . awe-inspiring." (BRD) Houghton, 1954.

Tunstall, Jeremy   MEDIA MADE IN CALIFORNIA
By two English authors who spent a year in the film capital—"the structure, struggles, power and influence" of the media world in California. History of the major studios, today's independents, creative accounting, and package deals. (BRD) Oxford U, 1981.

Wallace, David R.   THE WILDER SHORE
"A stunning book"—an examination of some literature about California: Dana, London, Frank Norris, Steinbeck, Robinson Jeffers, Gary Snyder, Joan Didion, Henry Miller and others—"we see the land as an earthly paradise . . . to be exploited . . . a threat to life." (PW) Sierra Club, 1984.

Watkins, T.H.   CALIFORNIA: AN ILLUSTRATED HISTORY UPDATED
American Legacy Pr, 1983.

Wilson, William   THE LOS ANGELES TIMES BOOK OF
                   CALIFORNIA MUSEUMS
The story of California's museums—"tastes, idiosyncracies,
egos . . . of enormously wealthy collectors . . . the style of the book is casual and
beautiful." (TL) Written by the art editor of the *Los Angeles Times*. Abrams, 1984.

THE GOLD RUSH

Bristow, Gwen   GOLDEN DREAMS
Story of the gold rush, with a "novelist's flair" for bringing events alive. (BRD)
Crowell, 1980.

Buck, Marcia C. and Smith, Patricia C.   GOLD RUSH NUGGETS
"A gold mine of information about ten counties in California's Mother Lode area
. . . offers comprehensive descriptions of each community [and] brief histories of
past days and glories." Also tourist information on hotels, lodges, restaurants, side
trips to Yosemite, Tahoe and Squaw Valley. (Publisher) Castle Ventures, 1984.

Holliday, J.S.   THE WORLD RUSHED IN
"An authentic vicarious experience" of the gold rush based on the diary of one
William Swain, who left his family and farm in New York in 1849 to find gold in
California. (BRD) S&S, 1981.

Jackson, Donald D.   GOLD DUST
"A ripe, utterly engrossing version of the California gold rush of 1848. . . .
suspenseful delivery of masses of contemporary information" from diaries,
journals, letters and travelogues. (BL) Knopf, 1980.

Moore, Charles K.   THE MOTHER LODE
A pictorial guide to California's gold rush country. Chronicle Bk,1983.

Seidman, Laurence I.   THE FOOLS OF '49, THE CALIFORNIA GOLD
                        RUSH 1848-1856
"Skillful use of original documents, including songs"—traces the history and
impact of the gold rush on the state's development. (BRD) Knopf, 1976.

GUIDEBOOKS

Chester, Carole   CALIFORNIA
A Batsford guide. Hippocrene, 1982.

Coleberd, Frances   HIDDEN COUNTRY VILLAGES OF CALIFORNIA
Chronicle Bk, 1982.

Delehanty, Randolph   CALIFORNIA: A GUIDEBOOK
Describes what the author feels are the *best* areas, "the most intriguing or
enjoyable aspects" of these areas—"his knowledgeable exuberance is infectious."
(BL) HarBraceJ, 1984.

Dirksen, D. J.   RECREATION LAKES OF CALIFORNIA
Sail Sales Pub, 1984.

Gleason, Bill   BACKROAD WINERIES OF CALIFORNIA
Small country wineries throughout the state. Chronicle Bk, 1985.

**Leon, Vicki   THE MONEYWISE GUIDE TO CALIFORNIA WITH
EXCURSIONS TO RENO, LAS VEGAS, THE GRAND
CANYON AND BAJA CALIFORNIA**
Aims to "help the California-bound traveler have the widest range of experiences for the least cost"—background on culture and life-style, facts on lodging, food, sightseeing, low-cost alternatives. Descriptive material on 180 cities and
towns, discounts and resources for over-55 travelers, students, families, women
traveling alone. The *Los Angeles Herald Examiner* praised it as "simply the best
one-volume guide to the Golden State ever written." (LJ) Presidio Pr, 1982.

**McDermott, John W.   HOW TO GET LOST AND FOUND IN CALIFORNIA
AND OTHER LOVELY PLACES**
One of a new series of guidebooks with a personal approach—"delightful read-
ing. . . solid information on where to go and what to see." Orafa Pub, 1984.

Old California Series eds.   OLD CALIFORNIA: VISITOR'S GUIDE
One of a series of guides to historic California. Camaro, 1983. Other titles in the
series are *Gold Mines and Gold Mining Towns* (1985), *Historical Landmarks &
Scenic Backroads* (1984), *The Missions, Ranchos & Romantic Adobes* (1983) and
Art, Theatre & Museums (1983).

**Perry, John and Greverus, Jane   THE SIERRA CLUB GUIDE TO THE
NATURAL AREAS OF CALIFORNIA**
Sierra Club, 1983.

LOS ANGELES & SOUTHERN CALIFORNIA

Agutter, Jenny   SNAP OBSERVATIONS OF LOS ANGELES AND LONDON
See under "London."

Cartnal, Alan   CALIFORNIA CRAZY
"Mind-blowing gazetteer" of Los Angeles—"the flashy stylization and the knowing tone make the report memorable, if not high-minded." (BL) Houghton, 1981.

Finch, Christopher   GONE HOLLYWOOD
Informative, amusing account of the pre-World War II movie industry.
Doubleday, 1975.

**Gebhard, David and Winter, Robert   ARCHITECTURE IN LOS ANGELES:
A COMPLETE GUIDE**
Reworking of the author's earlier guide to architecture into two volumes. This
is the first, and concentrates on buildings, parks, and other physical features in Los

Angeles County and City. The arrangement is by neighborhood and region from Malibu to the Sierra Madre Mountains. Peregrine Pr, 1984.

Gill, Brendan   THE DREAM COME TRUE
Great houses of Los Angeles, "real" architecture as well as homes of the stars, and eccentric, out-of-the-way houses. HR&W, 1980.

Henstell, Bruce   LOS ANGELES: AN ILLUSTRATED HISTORY
Knopf, 1980.

Hutchinson, Tom   NIVEN'S HOLLYWOOD
"Stars and starlets, tycoons and fleshpeddlers, moviemakers and moneymakers, hopefuls and has-beens, great lovers and sex symbols."
(Publisher) Limelight Edns, 1984.

Kotkin, Joel and Grabowicz, Paul   CALIFORNIA, INC.
The thesis is that Los Angeles sets the pattern for what sooner or later is adopted elsewhere in the U.S. and that California also has ever-increasing corporate power and influence. Avon, 1983.

Lamparski, Richard   LAMPARSKI'S HIDDEN HOLLYWOOD: WHERE THE STARS LIVED, LOVED AND DIED
S&S, 1981.

Lockwood, Charles   DREAM PALACES: HOLLYWOOD "AT HOME"
Reconstructs the domestic life led by Hollywood "royalty" in its prime. Viking, 1981.

Moore, Charles and others   THE CITY OBSERVED: LOS ANGELES, A GUIDE TO ITS ARCHITECTURE AND LANDSCAPES
The authors are the "perfect guides to a city whose chief vernacular icon is Disneyland . . . travels from Spanish missions to arts-and-crafts bungalow to art deco to international style [and] post-modern homes." Also includes theme parks, museums. "A surprising and fascinating handbook." (BL) Random, 1984.

Morley, Sheridan   TALES FROM THE HOLLYWOOD RAJ: THE BRITISH, THE MOVIES AND TINSELTOWN
The cultural invasion of Hollywood, over several decades, by the British, which the author terms "India all over again." An "anecdotally rich but perfectly serious account [of] who these individuals were . . . what they came for, what they accomplished personally . . . their combined influence." (BL) Viking, 1984.

Morris, Jan   DESTINATIONS
This book of travel essays by a leading travel writer includes an essay on Los Angeles. Oxford U, 1980.

Nelson, Howard J.   THE LOS ANGELES METROPOLIS
Description and travel, social conditions, economics, etc., of the Los Angeles region. Kendall/Hunt, 1983.

Niven, David   BRING ON THE EMPTY HORSES
One of the best of the genre of actor memoirs. Putnam Pub Group, 1975.

Patton, Annie and Campbell, Pamela   MOVING TO LOS ANGELES
"The inside scoop on starting out, settling in and making it in the big city. . . It's hard to think of anything the authors have left out [and] all this information is handed out in a sensible yet wry manner." (BL) Putnam Pub Group, 1984.

Seidenbaum, Art   LOS ANGELES 200
A bicentennial celebration arranged like an annotated family album, from the city's "Hispanic roots to its heterogeneous present." (BRD) Abrams, 1980.

Stuart, Sandra Lee   THE PINK PALACE
Behind closed doors at the Beverly Hills Hotel. Stuart, 1978.

Thorpe, Edward   CHANDLERTOWN: THE LOS ANGELES OF PHILIP MARLOWE
This is both a biography and a photo-essay of the neighborhoods of Los Angeles where Chandler's classic stories were set, 1939-58, in which Philip Marlowe was the hard-boiled but sensitive private eye. "Surviving sites appear in the text . . . graced by liberal quotations from *The Big Sleep* and other tales." (PW) St. Martin, 1984.

Wagner, Walter   BEVERLY HILLS: INSIDE THE GOLDEN GHETTO
History of the community—"entertaining and colorful . . . anecdotes and scandals." (BRD) Grosset, 1976.

Wilkerson, Tichi and Borie, Marcia   THE HOLLYWOOD REPORTER: THE GOLDEN YEARS
History of Hollywood 1930-50, based on material originally appearing in the *Hollywood Reporter*—"a treasure trove of juicy talk . . . features of old Hollywood that made those three decades the glamour years" and including some articles by actors. (BL) Coward, 1984.

GUIDEBOOKS FOR LOS ANGELES & SOUTHERN CALIFORNIA

Alleman, Richard   THE MOVIE LOVER'S GUIDE TO HOLLYWOOD
"Sites that are (or were) important to the film industry . . . lesser known places and buildings that tourists would have trouble finding on their own"—for instance, the apartment at the beginning of *Sunset Boulevard* where Holden sits typing—with maps arranged by locales. Har-Row, 1985.

Appleberg, Marilyn   I LOVE LOS ANGELES
Part of a series—see annotation for "Boston." Macmillan, 1982.

Baxter, Robert   BAXTER'S CALIFORNIA
Volume 1 covers Southern California. Rail-Europe-Baxter, 1984.

Crain, Mary Beth   THE BEST OF LOS ANGELES
"A comprehensive look at all the best in a city known for its extremes"—by the editors of *Los Angeles Weekly*—where to "acquire or view just about anything one would want," from food and restaurants to a funeral monument. (BL) Chronicle, 1984.

Grimm, Michele and Tom   AWAY FOR THE WEEKEND
Great getaways less than 250 miles from Los Angeles—compilation of fifty-two "Trip of the Week" columns from the *Los Angeles Times*. Gives driving instructions, sights, lodgings and restaurants from San Simeon to San Diego and the Baja Peninsula, as well as east to the mountains. Crown, 1984.

Kirk, Ruth   EXPLORING DEATH VALLEY
A guide to the Death Valley National Monument area—natural and social history, weather and desert survival, sights on the main roads and in the back country, trips by truck and jeep, plus practical travel information on lodgings, where to eat, other services. Stanford U, 1981.

Lockwood, Charles   THE GUIDE TO HOLLYWOOD AND BEVERLY HILLS
"The best driving tours, walks, restaurants, homes, shopping, sights and architecture" with anecdotal commentaries and travel tips. (BL) Crown, 1984.

McAdams, Cliff   DEATH VALLEY PAST AND PRESENT: COMPLETE
GUIDE AND REFERENCE BOOK
Pruett, 1981.

Mallan, Chicki   GUIDE TO CATALINA ISLAND
Includes history, natural history, travel, recreation tips and maps. Moon Pbns, 1984.

Marinacci, Barbara   TAKE SUNSET BOULEVARD: THE FABULOUS NEW
WAY TO SEE L.A.
"Covers more than just a street. . . . A readable potpourri of history." The Boulevard is divided into seven sections suitable for walking trips, with subsections detailing places to visit. (LA Times) Presidio Pr, 1981.

Pashdag, John   HOLLYWOODLAND U.S.A.
The sub-title is: "The moviegoer's guide to Southern California." Chronicle, 1984.

Schwartz, Ronni   LA INSIDE OUT: THE PRACTICAL GUIDE TO
LOS ANGELES
A comprehensive sourcebook to LA with over 1,300 listings. APCO Pbns, 1983.

Sunset eds.   SOUTHERN CALIFORNIA
Sunset-Lane, 1979.

SAN FRANCISCO & NORTHERN CALIFORNIA

Aidala, Thomas   THE GREAT HOUSES OF SAN FRANCISCO
Knopf, 1981.

Beebe, Morton   SAN FRANCISCO
Essays by Herb Caen, Herbert Gold, Barnaby Conrad, and others, that reflect the history of the town, its nightlife and ambiance. Abrams, 1985.

Cole, Tom   A SHORT HISTORY OF SAN FRANCISCO
"Wonderful . . . authoritative . . . a comprehensive story told with literary grace." (SF Chronicle) Lexikos, 1981.

Dillon, Richard   NORTH BEACH: THE ITALIAN HEART OF SAN FRANCISCO
History and historic photos of North Beach, the way it was. Presidio Pr, 1985.

Ferlinghetti, Lawrence   LITERARY SAN FRANCISCO
Text and photos trace significant literary events and writers in the city's history. Har-Row, 1981.

Futcher, June and Conover, Robert   MARIN
Profile of the California county just across Golden Gate Bridge—the place and the people. HR&W, 1981.

Gentry, Curt   THE MADAMS OF SAN FRANCISCO: AN IRREVERENT HISTORY OF THE CITY BY THE GOLDEN GATE.
Comstock Edns, 1977 (first published 1964).

Horton, Tom   SUPERSPAN: THE GOLDEN GATE BRIDGE
"A dramatic account of the bridge from its creation to the present day," along with spectacular color photographs. (BL) Chronicle Bk, 1983.

Loewenstein, Louis K.   STREETS OF SAN FRANCISCO: THE ORIGINS OF STREET AND PLACE NAMES
Lexikos, 1984.

Moffat, Frances   DANCING ON THE BRINK OF THE WORLD: THE RISE AND FALL OF SAN FRANCISCO SOCIETY
"History of the social life of the upper class in San Francisco." (BRD) Putnam Pub Group, 1977.

Moorhouse, Geoffrey   SAN FRANCISCO
Part of Great Cities of the World series. Time-Life, 1979.

Odier, Pierre   THE ROCK: A HISTORY OF ALCATRAZ, THE FORT/THE PRISON
"Comprehensive and fascinating history" from the discovery of Alcatraz in 1769 through the years it was used as a fort and then a prison, to today's status as a tourist attraction. (BL) L'Image Odier, 1983.

Saul, Eric   THE GREAT SAN FRANCISCO EARTHQUAKE AND FIRE, 1906
An outline of the disaster, eyewitness accounts, and a pictorial record using resources of the San Francisco Public Library collections. Celestial Arts, 1981.

Siefkin, David   CITY AT THE END OF THE RAINBOW: SAN FRANCISCO AND ITS GRAND HOTELS
History of the Palace, the Fairmont, the St. Francis, and the Mark Hopkins from 1876-1976. Putnam Pub Group, 1976.

Taper, B., ed.   MARK TWAIN'S SAN FRANCISCO
Compilation of eighty-three pieces that the author wrote for newspapers and magazines during his years in California and Nevada. (BRD) McGraw, 1963.

Thomas, Gordon   THE SAN FRANCISCO EARTHQUAKE
Graphic history of the 1906 quake—the courage, compassion and ingenuity, along with the political corruption and deception. Stein & Day, 1971.

Wollenberg, Charles   GOLDEN GATE METROPOLIS: PERSPECTIVES ON BAY AREA HISTORY
"Short, readable essays" by a social historian, mostly about San Francisco, but also about the Oakland area and Silicon (Santa Clara) Valley—"Geography, history, and political and social influence." (LJ) U of California Inst of Govt Studies, 1985.

Woodbridge, Sally   ARCHITECTURE—SAN FRANCISCO: THE GUIDE
By the Architectural Institute of America, San Francisco chapter. 101 Prodns, 1982. Also *Bay Area Houses* (1976)—6 essays cover periods from the turn of the century to the present day of a distinctive local tradition in housing.

Zachreson, Nick   THE SAN JOAQUIN VALLEY
"Pastiche" of text and photos—"sensitive yarns, anecdotes, history" and a ribute to the San Joaquin heritage. (BL) Hammond, 1979.

GUIDEBOOKS FOR SAN FRANCISCO & NORTHERN CALIFORNIA

Arrigoni, Patricia   MAKING THE MOST OF MARIN: A CALIFORNIA GUIDE
Sausalito, Muir Woods, Mt. Tamalpais, Stinson Beach, Angel Island, China Camp, the earthquake trail, old military forts and bunkers, Indian burial mounds—and more. Presidio Pr, 1981.

Bailey, John   SAN FRANCISCO INSIDER'S GUIDE
"A unique guide to Bay Area restaurants, bars, best bets, bargains, sex and sensuality, the outdoors, and much more." (BL) Non-Stop Bks, 1984.

Bakalinsky, Adah   STAIRWALKS IN SAN FRANCISCO
The author has connected dozens of stairways into twenty-six guided walks—Bernal Heights, "Dogs, Cats, Children," and so on, each graded for difficulty and access, and mapped. There's an appendix listing the stairways by neighborhood and they are rated for beauty, safety and difficulty. "A unique

encounter with the fascinating past and present of San Francisco." (Publisher) Lexikos, 1984.

Baxter, Robert   BAXTER'S CALIFORNIA
Volume 2 covers Northern California. Rail-Europe-Baxter, 1984.

Brant, Michelle   TIMELESS WALKS IN SAN FRANCISCO: A HISTORIC GUIDE TO THE CITY
MJB CA, 1982.

Delehanty, Randolph   SAN FRANCISCO: WALKS AND TOURS IN THE GOLDEN GATE CITY
Twelve tours "realistically accomplished on foot . . . combines a deeply informed background with lively and very readable writing." Rewarding to take along or to use for pre-travel reading. (BL) Dial, 1980.

Doss, Margot Patterson   A WALKER'S YEARBOOK: FIFTY-TWO WALKS IN THE SAN FRANCISCO BAY AREA
"Each season has a special show—by the sea, in the parks, at the waterfront, on the trail in city and country . . . The most fascinating places to go and things to see . . . A favorite walk for each week of the year . . . the next best thing to a personally guided jaunt." A pleasure just to read, if you would rather not walk. (Publisher) Presidio Pr, 1983.
Other walking guidebooks by Ms. Doss for the area are: *Golden Gate Park at Your Feet* (1978), *The Bay Area at Your Feet* (1981), and *There, There East San Francisco Bay at Your Feet* (1978).

Edwards, Don   MAKING THE MOST OF SONOMA: A CALIFORNIA GUIDE
An insider's guide to the land and people of Sonoma County—Russian River, seaside village, country towns, the coast, the wine country and Farm Trail. Presidio Pr, 1982.

Hayden, Mike   EXPLORING THE NORTH COAST
Chronicle Bk, 1982.

Herron, Don   THE LITERARY WORLD OF SAN FRANCISCO & ITS ENVIRONS
"Neighborhood-by-neighborhood literary walks over Nob Hill, Russian Hill, and Telegraph Hill, through the Mission, the Haight-Fillmore," plus major sites outside the city. Also *Dashiell Hammett Tour: A Guidebook*, which is the well-known tour conducted by the author, in book form for a self-guided walk through the San Francisco of Hammett and Sam Spade, and including a biography, photos and bibliography. (Publisher) City Lights, 1984.

Liberatore, Karen   THE COMPLETE GUIDE TO GOLDEN GATE NATIONAL RECREATION AREA
The area encompasses historic sites from the Cliff House on the Pacific to Alcatraz Island in the Bay, to Marin County's redwood trees. History and complete guide to facilities within the National Recreation Area. Chronicle Bk, 1982.

Magary, Alan and Kerstin F.   ACROSS THE GOLDEN GATE:
CALIFORNIA'S NORTH COAST,
WINE COUNTRY AND REDWOODS
"Combination travel guide and wine reference book [written] so well that even ordinary information sounds graceful." Star system for rating where to stay and eat and the authors' favorites. Lists of main sights and sources of information. (BL) Har-Row, 1980.

Meyers, Carole T.   WEEKEND ADVENTURES FOR CITY-WEARY PEOPLE:
OVERNIGHT TRIPS IN NORTHERN CALIFORNIA
Covers a 300-mile radius. "Caters to families, especially those traveling out of the city by car . . . . Theme destinations [antique-hunting, wildlife areas, etc.] . . . activities, events . . . lodgings, restaurants, routes, background information." (BL) Carousel, 1984.

Olmsted, John & Huggins, Eleanor   ADVENTURES ALONG
INTERSTATE 80
A guide to nature and history along the pioneer and gold rush corridor from San Francisco to Nevada. Tioga, 1984.

Riegert, Ray   HIDDEN SAN FRANCISCO AND NORTHERN CALIFORNIA:
THE ADVENTURER'S GUIDE
"Detailed suggestions for experiences beyond . . . standard travel guides [that will] challenge even jaded visitors to the area." (BL) Ulysses Pr, 1984.

Shelton, Jack   HOW TO ENJOY 1 TO 10 PERFECT DAYS IN
SAN FRANCISCO
Shelton Pbns, 1983.

Shepard, Susan   IN THE NEIGHBORHOODS
Chronicle Bk, 1981.

Sunset eds.   NORTHERN CALIFORNIA
Sunset-Lane, 1980.

Thollander, Earl   BACK ROADS OF CALIFORNIA
Back roads and little-known places in northern California. Potter, 1983.

Weaver, Harriet E.   REDWOOD COUNTRY
Chronicle Bk, 1983.

Whitnah, Dorothy L.   POINT REYES
A guide to the trails, roads, beaches, campgrounds, lakes, trees, flowers and rocks of Point Reyes National Seashore. Wilderness Pr, 1981.

Young, George and others   SAN FRANCISCO BY CABLE CAR
By a former cable car conductor—"chatty, personal tour guide takes the traveler to all the neighborhoods the three cable car lines serve, giving their history . . . special sights, and recommending shops and restaurants." (LJ) Wingbow, 1984.

CALIFORNIA CENTRAL COAST

Aidala, Thomas   HEARST CASTLE: SAN SIMEON
The building and history of William Randolph Hearst's dream
castle—illustrated. S&S, 1981.

California Coastal Commission   CALIFORNIA COASTAL ACCESS GUIDE
Combination reference guide and travel book with detailed maps of access
areas for each coastal county. U of California, 1983.

Carr, Pat and Tracy, Steve   MONTEREY PENINSULA WALKING TOURS
Hampton-Brown, 1984.

**Conrad, Rebecca and Nelson, Christopher H.   SANTA BARBARA: A
                                                 GUIDE TO EL
                                                 PUEBLO VIEJO**
A guide to the city's historic districts. Capra Pr, 1986.

**Foster, Lee   MAKING THE MOST OF THE PENINSULA: A CALIFORNIA
                GUIDE TO SAN MATEO, SANTA CLARA & SANTA CRUZ
                COUNTIES**
"The only complete guide to this diverse and exciting region . . . . A mix of
history, natural history and detailed information on where to go and what to see."
(Publisher) Presidio Pr, 1983.

Gaasch, Irene   WALK THIS WAY PLEASE
On foot on the Monterey Peninsula and Carmel Valley, Big Sur. Hummingbird
Pr, 1984.

**Jackson, Ruth A.   COMBING THE COAST: SAN FRANCISCO TO SAN
                      LUIS OBISPO**
Chronicle Bk, 1982. And *Combing the Coast II: Santa Cruz to Carmel*
(1982)—guides to beaches, back roads, parks and communities, and historic sites.

**Knox, Maxine and Rodriguez, Mary   STEINBECK'S STREET:
                                       CANNERY ROW**
Guide to Cannery Row's shops, restaurants and historical sites, including "tales
of Steinbeck, his friends, and local characters who made their way into his books
and stories." (Publisher) Presidio Pr, 1984.

**Knox, Maxine and Rodriguez, Mary   MAKING THE MOST OF THE
                                       MONTEREY PENINSULA AND
                                       BIG SUR**
"Delightfully descriptive . . . practical guide"—Monterey, Cannery Row, Carmel
and historic trails. (Publisher) Presidio Pr, 1979.

Magary, Alan and Kerstin F.   SOUTH OF SAN FRANCISCO
"California's central coast—San Mateo, Santa Cruz, Monterey, Carmel, Big Sur,
Hearst Castle. . . . Interesting, accurate historical information, special events,
references to other sources . . . Steinbeck country." (LJ) Har-Row, 1983.

Temple, David   SANTA BARBARA
Skyline Pr, 1984.

**Thompson, Pauline J.   SANTA BARBARA: HOW TO DISCOVER
AMERICA'S EDEN**
Kricket Pbns, 1984.

SAN DIEGO & BAJA CALIFORNIA

Note: See also travel articles on Baja Peninsula under "Mexico," and books under
"Mexico/Background Reading/Baja California."

**Abbott, Helen and others   THE BEST OF SAN DIEGO: A
DISCRIMINATING GUIDE**
"Essential companion for residents and visitors alike [by] thirteen of San Diego's
finest journalists. . . . Includes Tia Juana and Ensenada." (Publisher) Rosebud Bks,
1982.

**Bruns, Bill   A WORLD OF ANIMALS: THE SAN DIEGO ZOO AND THE
WILD ANIMAL PARK**
History of the zoo and an introduction to some of its animal inhabitants—"both
narrative and pictures do justice to this great zoo." (PW) Abrams, 1983.

McClure, James   COP WORLD: POLICING THE STREETS OF SAN DIEGO
This is the American counterpart of the author's earlier *Spike Island* (see
"England"), about Liverpool's police. Pantheon, 1985.

McKeever, Michael   A SHORT HISTORY OF SAN DIEGO
"Describes the city's growth from the first California mission to one of the
world's most refreshing cities"—one of a series of "sprightly, authoritative" city
histories. (Publisher) Lexikos, 1985.

Pryde, Philip R., ed.   SAN DIEGO: AN INTRODUCTION TO THE REGION
Kendall-Hunt, 1983.

Wambaugh, Joseph   LINES AND SHADOWS
True story of Lt. Snider of San Diego who organized the Border Crime Task
Force, using Mexican-Americans on the Los Angeles police force to stop the
banditry against illegal aliens at the border—"no one writes better about cops than
Mr. Wambaugh. . . . An off-trail, action-packed true account of police work and the
intimate lives of policemen." (NYTBR) Morrow, 1985.

Novels

Banis, V.J.   THIS SPLENDID EARTH
A post-Revolution French family escapes to America with cuttings from their
vineyard to build a wine dynasty in California. St. Martin, 1978.

Boyle, T. Coraghessan   BUDDING PROSPECTS; A PASTORAL
A "quitter" takes on a nine-month stint in northern California, growing marijuana and resolved not to quit this time. Viking, 1984.

Brautigan, Richard   THE ABORTION: AN HISTORICAL ROMANCE, 1966
A novel of contemporary California hedonism. S&S, 1971.

Bristow, Gwen   THE JUBILEE TRAIL
Historical novel of the Spanish trail that led in the 1840s from Santa Fe to Los Angeles, and one family's trek. Crowell, 1950.

DeBlassis, Celeste   THIS PROUD BREED
Three-generation family saga of nineteenth-century California. Coward, 1978.

Didion, Joan (Sacramento Valley)   RUN RIVER
Story of the despair and gradual self-destruction of Lily Knight McClellan. Washington Square Pr, 1978 (First published 1961).

Galloway, David   TAMSEN
A novel about the Donner party's tragic journey. HarBraceJ, 1983.

Gavin, Catherine   THE SUNSET DREAM
A family saga (1846-1941) of California's "rapid, often violent, transition from a pastoral paradise to a thriving, open-ended society. Tumultuous historical events [gold rush, earthquake, war with Mexico] provide a colorful backdrop." (FC) St. Martin, 1984.

Gold, Herbert   TRUE LOVE
"A twice-divorced law professor who tames onrushing age with running" and loneliness with the wife of a dentist—"one of the most reliable correspondents we have in California. . . . Forever uncovering the latest totems and odd social byways of the Pacific shore." Arbor Hse, 1982.

Hailey, Arthur   OVERLOAD
The myriad behind-the-scenes functions of a power and light utility company, with executives in the company as leading characters. Doubleday, 1979.

Harris, MacDonald   TENTH
A music teacher is asked to do a radio program on the unfinished "tenth" of an obscure composer and is "beset by romantic intentions" of the composer's daughter. (FC) Atheneum, 1984.

Johnson, Diane   LYING LOW
Two women on the run find safety in northern California. Knopf, 1978. Also *The Shadow Knows* (1974), set in Sacramento.

L'Amour, Louis   THE CALIFORNIOS
California in the 1840s and the story of a woman who is led to a gold cache while being pursued by murderers. Saturday Rev Pr, 1974.

L'Amour, Louis   THE LONESOME GODS
The early years of California—"filled with splendid descriptions of the desert country, historical facts, and nature lore." (FC) Bantam, 1982.

McDonald, Gregory   FLETCH
Suspense story with a "riveting plot [and] background of beach bums, incompetent newspaper editors and the idle rich." (FC) Bobbs, 1974.

MacDonald, John D.   THE GREEN RIPPER
Travis McGee mystery—in this he poses as a cult convert in a remote part of California to spy on the cult's activities and solve the murder of his fiancée. Lippincott, 1979.

Matheson, Richard   BID TIME RETURN
The Hotel Del Coronado (San Diego) is the setting for a romance of the narrator, who travels back in time to meet his true love in 1896. Viking, 1975.

Meschery, Joanne   IN A HIGH PLACE (High Sierras)
Set in a shabby High Sierra town—a woman brings her children to Tullease and finds it is due to be a Disney recreation area—"satirizes the Disney invasion . . . Los Angeles and San Francisco [as] capitals of pollution and perversion." (FC) S&S, 1981.

Morris, Wright   FIRE SERMON
The generational clash and "inevitability of youth taking over" in contemporary California. (FC) U of Nebraska, 1979.

Pronzini, Bill   SNOWBOUND (Sierras)
A snowbound Sierra town is taken over by gunmen. Putnam Pub Group, 1974.

Rhodes, Richard   THE UNGODLY
Story of the doomed Donner party and their attempt to cross the Sierras in 1846. Charterhouse, 1973.

Roper, Robert   ON SPIDER CREEK
Saga of a family on the decline, set in a Northern California valley. S&S, 1978.

Ross, Dana F.   CALIFORNIA
Part of a series of novels with the overall title of *Wagons West* that chronicles the conquest and settlement of the American West. Bantam, 1981.

Saroyan, William   THE HUMAN COMEDY
"Thoroughly good characters" in a series of episodes as observed by a fourteen-year-old boy during World War II. (FC) HarBraceJ, 1944.

Searls, Hank   BLOOD SONG
A retired admiral and his 12-year-old granddaughter set out from Manhattan for Nevada City using his ancestor's diaries and letters to duplicate their emigrant trip in 1849. Dangers jeopardize the trip at the same location as the earlier trip was endangered 130 years earlier. "The respective travelogues appear . . . in alternating chapters, eerily paralleling one another." (FC) Villard Bks, 1984.

Setlowe, Richard   THE HAUNTING OF SUZANNA BLACKWELL
A young woman is haunted by her dead mother, her mother's beau, and deaths near a moth-balled warship on which hundreds died during World War II—"a gem of a spooky thriller . . . the impossible story becomes believable . . . because of the inclusion of so many persons, places, and events during and after World War II." (FC) HR&W, 1984.

Silva, Julian   THE GUNNYSACK CASTLE (San Joaquin Valley)
A family saga of the rise of an Americanized Portuguese immigrant in the Valley's fruit-growing region. Ohio U, 1983.

Skimin, Robert   CHIKARA!
"A sweeping novel of Japan and America from 1907 to 1983" is the subtitle of this saga of three generations of a Japanese immigrant family. St. Martin, 1984.

Steinbeck, John   CANNERY ROW (Monterey)
Viking, 1945. This and its sequel, *Sweet Thursday* (1954) revolve around a bunch of diverse characters and "Doc" and his laboratory. *Tortilla Flat* (1935) is another funny, bawdy Steinbeck novel set in Monterey.

Steinbeck, John   EAST OF EDEN (Salinas)
Saga of a half-century in the lives of two families. Viking, 1952. *Of Mice and Men* (1937), is also set in Salinas.

Steinbeck, John   THE GRAPES OF WRATH
The Pulitzer Prize-winning novel about Okies during the depression who fled the Oklahoma dust bowl for a new future in California as migrant workers. Viking, 1939. *In Dubious Battle* (1936) is about a strike of migrant workers.

Steinbeck, John   THE WAYWARD BUS
A group of bus passengers and the people who run a gas station and lunchroom where the bus is stranded and the effects of each of them on the others. Viking, 1947.

Thomas, Ross   CHINAMAN'S CHANCE
A complicated plot of a mob's plans to take over a California town—"a page-turner . . . in a literate, entertaining style." (FC) S&S, 1978.

Whitney, Phyllis A.   EMERALD (Palm Springs)
The heroine, seeking refuge with her great aunt (a former movie star), finds a mystery that leads to murder—"solving the mystery [she] solves her own personal problems." (FC) Doubleday, 1983.

HOLLYWOOD, LOS ANGELES AND ENVIRONS

Ball, John   THE EYES OF THE BUDDHA (Pasadena)
Virgil Tibbs, a black detective on the Pasadena police force, is the crime-solver in Ball's series of police procedurals. Delacorte Pr, 1977. Also *Five Pieces of Jade* (1972).

Barnes, Joanna   SILVERWOOD
Family saga beginning in the early part of this century about the lives of rich, privileged people and of those of the movie colony who infiltrate their set. S&S, 1985.

Bogarde, Dirk   WEST OF SUNSET (Hollywood)
A "strikingly well-observed portrait" of Hollywood as seen through the eyes of a British novelist who is "repelled by the fakery . . . smog, showbiz . . . displaced people." He visits an ex-mistress and becomes involved in the mysterious circumstances of her husband's death. (FC) Viking, 1984.

Briskin, Jacqueline   EVERYTHING AND MORE (Beverly Hills, Los Angeles)
"Love, hate, murder, suicide, rape, incest" in a tri-generational novel based in Beverly Hills. (FC) Putnam Pub Group, 1983. Also *Paloverde* (1978), a family saga set in Los Angeles, beginning in the nineteenth century.

Chandler, Raymond   THE RAYMOND CHANDLER OMNIBUS
Includes *The Big Sleep* (1939), *Farewell My Lovely* (1940), *The High Window* (1942), *The Lady in the Lake* (1944)—mystery classics set in "the big, sordid, dirty city" (as Chandler characterized it) of Los Angeles. Modern Library, 1975. Also *The Little Sister* (1949) and *Playback* (1958).

Note also the book *Chandlertown* under "Background Reading/Los Angeles & Southern California." Also, Aaron Blake Publishers offers the "Raymond Chandler Mystery Map of Los Angeles" which covers Downtown L.A., Hollywood, Santa Monica, Lake Arrowhead and Mexico.

Cunningham, E.V.   THE CASE OF THE POISONED ECLAIRS (Beverly Hills)
HR&W, 1979. A Nisei detective solves this mystery, and also *The Case of the Russian Diplomat* (1978).

Deighton, Len   CLOSE-UP (Hollywood)
Behind the scenes in the movie industry during the 1940s and '50s. Atheneum, 1972.

Didion, Joan   PLAY IT AS IT LAYS (Hollywood)
"Using a frenetic milieu of drugs, pills, sexual aberrancy, Didion elliptically etches the self-destruct life of Maria Wyeth." (FC) FS&G, 1970.

Dunne, John G.   TRUE CONFESSIONS (Los Angeles)
The story of two brothers—a cop and a priest—in "corruption-ridden LA in the late 1940s." (FC) Dutton, 1977.

Egan, Lesley   CRIME FOR CHRISTMAS (Glendale-Hollywood)
One of several mysteries by Egan set in the Glendale-Hollywood area. Doubleday, 1983. Other titles include: *Random Death* (1982), *A Choice of Crimes* (1980), *The Blind Search* (1977) and *Malicious Mischief* (1971).

Fast, Howard   MAX
An engrossing novel that is also a history of the motion-picture industry from nickelodeons to talkies as Max moves from bagel-peddler on the Lower East Side in New York to movie mogul. Houghton, 1982.

Fitzgerald, F. Scott   THE LAST TYCOON
Unfinished novel about a Hollywood producer, with an outline by Edmund Wilson of how Fitzgerald intended to develop the plot. Scribner, 1969 (first published 1941).

Goldman, William   TINSEL (Hollywood)
The plot is about the casting of someone to play Marilyn Monroe in a movie to be based on her life. Delacorte Pr, 1979.

Gordons, The   NIGHT BEFORE THE WEDDING (Los Angeles)
A woman is forced to be the go-between in an extortion plot—"gripping, edge-of-the-chair mystery." (FC) Doubleday, 1969. Also *Night After the Wedding* (1979), another mystery.

Greenleaf, Stephen   THE DITTO LIST
Three unusual women clients come into a lawyer's office. The "ditto list" is a roster he maintains of mostly routine, non-paying divorce cases. Villard Bks, 1985.

Grumbach, Doris   THE MISSING PERSON (Hollywood)
Travails of a Hollywood movie queen of the 1930s. Putnam Pub Group, 1981.

Hansen, Joseph   THE MAN EVERYBODY WAS AFRAID OF (Los Angeles)
A murder mystery investigated by a death-claims investigator for an insurance company. HR&W, 1978.

Highland, Monica   LOTUS LAND (Los Angeles)
Los Angeles from the 1880s to World War II through the lives of a Chinese man, a woman fleeing poverty in Mexico, and a member of Baltimore society who just wants to go West—"the reader is caught up in the era. . . . Interesting notes at the back of the book explaining some events and authenticating historical details." (FC) Coward, 1980.

Kohan, Rhea   HAND ME DOWNS
"Warm, wise, witty and often wickedly funny" novel of a daughter who assumes the role of a sterotypical Jewish mother by following in the footsteps of her infamous grandmother, thus bringing her own mother to the point of plotting revenge. Random, 1980.

Linington, Elizabeth   SKELETONS IN THE CLOSET (Los Angeles-Hollywood)
One of several police procedurals—in this one some old bodies are found inside a demolished house. Doubleday, 1982. Other titles include: *Crime by Chance* (1973), *Greenmask* (1967), *No Villain Need Be* (1979), *Perchance of Death* (1977), *Policeman's Lot* (1968), and *Practice to Deceive* (1971).

Lovesey, Peter   KEYSTONE (Hollywood)
"Takes us back to the era of silent films . . . the hysterical staccato comedy world of Mack Sennett and the Keystone Cops." The plot combines real people from that era with a fictional British vaudevillian who gets mixed up in burglary and homicide. (FC) Pantheon, 1983.

Lurie, Alison   THE NOWHERE CITY
Comic novel of a Harvard historian and his wife in Los Angeles. Coward, 1966.

Macdonald, Ross   THE UNDERGROUND MAN
One of many mysteries that have been described as "the finest series of detective novels ever written by an American . . . nobody writes Southern California like Macdonald." (FC) Knopf, 1971. Other titles include: *Archer at Large* (1970), *Archer in Hollywood* (1967), and *Archer in Jeopardy* (1979) (all of which are omnibus books containing several mysteries each); also *The Blue Hammer* (1976), *The Goodbye Look* (1969), and *Sleeping Beauty* (1973).

MacLean, Alistair   GOODBYE CALIFORNIA
Thriller about a mad terrorist who has the ultimate weapon—the ability to trigger an earthquake by nuclear power. Doubleday, 1978.

McMurtry, Larry   SOMEBODY'S DARLING (Hollywood)
The involvement of a movie actress with two men. S&S, 1978.

Mailer, Norman   DEER PARK
Life and sexual habits of a group living in a desert town controlled by the movie industry. Putnam Pub Group, 1955.

Pentecost, Hugh   THE CHAMPAGNE KILLER (Hollywood)
"Hits the high spots of Hollywood and New York" and involves a singer/trumpeter, blackmail and murder. (FC) Dodd, 1972.

Perry, Thomas   METZGER'S DOG (Los Angeles)
"Smoothly-styled and humorous" novel with an incredible plot—four friends steal a million dollars worth of cocaine. (FC) Scribner, 1983.

Rebeta-Burditt, Joyce   TRIPLETS
One of the mid-life change category of novels—its heroine is one of a set of father-dominated triplets, now 35, with a TV career, who must cope "with a succession of disillusioning but cathartic traumas." (FC) Delacorte Pr, 1981.

Robinson, Jill   PERDIDO (Hollywood)
Hollywood in the 1950s. The granddaughter of a studio head tries to reconcile life with reality as she goes through adolescence. Knopf, 1978.

Sanchez, Thomas   ZOOT-SUIT MURDERS (Los Angeles)
Plot with drugs, spies, counterspies, naive sailors, set in the Los Angeles barrio during World War II. Dutton, 1978.

Santiago, Danny   FAMOUS ALL OVER TOWN
Coming of age in a Mexican-American barrio in Los Angeles. S&S, 1983.

Saroyan, William   PAPA, YOU'RE CRAZY
A 10-year-old boy and his father at Malibu and a Saroyanesque plot—the two talk at the beach of writing and other things, ride bicycles, take a trip up the coast in an old car. Little, 1957.

Schulberg, Budd   THE DISENCHANTED (Hollywood)
Based on the life of F. Scott Fitzgerald—a has-been writer gets one more chance in Hollywood. Random 1950. Also *What Makes Sammy Run?* (1941).

See, Carolyn   RHINE MAIDENS (Brentwood)
A mother and her Brentwood-matron daughter, and their respective responses to infidelity—"immensely appealing and amusing observations made about the two women and life in general." (FC) Coward, 1981.

Shannon, Dell   DESTINY OF DEATH
One of the several police procedurals in which Lt. Luis Mendoza of the Los Angeles Police Department is the key character. Other titles include: *The Motive on Record* (1982), *Exploit of Death* (1983), *Felony File* (1980), *Murder Most Strange* (1981), *Appearance of Death* (1977), *Cold Trail* (1978), *Crime File* (1974), *Felony at Random* (1979), *Kill With Kindness* (1968), and *Streets of Death* (1976). Morrow.

Steel, Danielle   FAMILY ALBUM
Traces the fortunes of an actress and director, and her family, from World War II—"characteristic milieu of the beautiful, talented and privileged . . . characters have a bit more depth." (FC) Delacorte Pr, 1985.

Streshinsky, Shirley   HERS THE KINGDOM (Malibu)
Family saga of two sisters, with one seemingly destined to live in the shadow of the other "feisty and adventuresome" sister. Putnam Pub Group, 1982.

Tryon, Thomas   CROWNED HEADS
"Interlocking destinies of four fictionalized movie stars' lives." (FC) Knopf, 1976.

Wambaugh, Joseph   THE GLITTER DOME
Hollywood—"dope, sex and crime-ridden" is the backdrop for the story. (BRD) Morrow, 1981.

Wambaugh, Joseph   THE NEW CENTURIONS (Los Angeles)
Little, 1971. This and *The Blue Knight* (1972), *The Delta Star* (1983), *The Black Marble* (1978), are highly regarded novels about policemen in general, and the Los Angeles Police Department in particular. "No one writes better about cops than Mr. Wambaugh" seems to reflect the opinion of both reviewers and cops.

West, Nathanael   THE DAY OF THE LOCUST
"A bitter tale of Hollywood and its hangers-on" in *The Complete Works of Nathanael West*. (FC) Farrar, Straus, 1957 (first published 1939).

Westheimer, David   THE AVILA GOLD (Los Angeles)
A UCLA professor discovers the location of buried treasure in some old Spanish documents. Putnam Pub Group, 1974.

Wharton, William   DAD
A son returns to Los Angeles from Paris and attempts to restore his ill father to emotional health. Knopf, 1981.

Wolitzer, Hilma   IN THE PALOMAR ARMS
The setting is a Southern California nursing home where its chief character works as a kitchen aide—"a tough novel, rough on feelings." (FC) FS&G, 1983.

SAN FRANCISCO

Adams, Alice   LISTENING TO BILLIE
A woman's story of youth to grandmotherhood. Knopf, 1978.

Berriault, Gina   THE LIGHTS OF EARTH
"An evocation of her time of despair" at the end of the heroine's love affair—"permeated by a sense of the hills, mists and nearby beaches" of San Francisco. (NYTBR) North Pr, 1985.

Brautigan, Richard   DREAMING OF BABYLON: A PRIVATE EYE NOVEL 1942
A perverse mystery about the most unsuccessful private eye in San Francisco who is offered money to steal a body from the morgue by an unexpected client. Delacorte Pr, 1977.

Bristow, Gwen   CALICO PALACE
Historical romance about the gold rush and the late 1800s. Crowell, 1970.

Busch, Niven   THE SAN FRANCISCANS
About a family-owned bank involved in a lawsuit "that could besmirch its reputation [and] deplete its treasury." (FC) S&S, 1962.

Fast, Howard   THE IMMIGRANTS
A family saga in three volumes beginning with the early twentieth century and on through post-World War II. Houghton, 1977. *Second Generation* (1978) and *The Establishment* (1979) are the second and third books.

Freeman, Catherine   FAIRY TALES
When her husband decides he wants to be a senator, his wife plots to embarrass her ambitious spouse. Arbor Hse, 1977. Also *A World Full of Strangers* (1975) saga of a Jewish San Francisco family.

Hammett, Dashiell   THE MALTESE FALCON
The classic Sam Spade mystery (see guides by Herron listed under Guidebooks for San Francisco above). North Pr, 1984 (first published 1930). See also Don Herron's *Dashiell Hammett Tour: A Guidebook* under "Background Reading/San Francisco & Northern California," above.

Harris, MacDonald   HERMA
See under "Paris/Novels."

Longstreet, Stephen   PEDLOCK AND SONS
Story of a wealthy, slightly decadent family and the department store empire they own. McKay, 1972. *The Pedlock Inheritance* (1972) is the sequel.

McFadden, Cyra   THE SERIAL (Marin County)
A year in the life of Marin County in fifty-two fictional episodes—a very funny book that captures a way of life and manner of speaking. Knopf, 1977.

MacLean, Alistair   THE GOLDEN GATE
Kidnapping of the president as his motorcade crosses Golden Gate Bridge. Doubleday, 1976.

Michael, Judith   POSSESSIONS
A believable modern odyssey of a woman creating a new life for herself in San Francisco when her husband deserts her. (FC) Poseidon, 1984.

Michaels, Leonard   THE MEN'S CLUB
Expanded from a prize-winning story of the same name—"men trying to make sense of their lives with women." FS&G, 1984.

Norris, Frank   McTEAGUE
A "naturalistic novel" first published in 1899 of life in San Francisco of that time—"heredity and environment unleash a series of disasters." Penguin, 1982 (first published 1899).

Stegner, Wallace   ALL THE LITTLE LIVE THINGS
A couple's idyllic retirement is changed by a troubled young man who camps on their property. U of Nebraska, 1979 (first published 1967).

Thompson, Gene   MURDER MYSTERY
A San Francisco attorney investigates the death of an art dealer client. Random, 1980.

Whitney, Phyllis   TREMBLING HILLS
Skeleton-in-the-closet mystery set in San Francisco during the earthquake. Appleton, 1956.

Wilcox, Collin   DOCTOR, LAWYER . . .
A "rich, swinging doctor" is murdered, with a threat that murders will continue through lawyer, merchant and chief if ransom is not paid. (FC) Random, 1977. Also set in San Francisco are *Stalking Horse* (1982) and *Aftershock* (1975).

Wilhelm, Kate   FAULT LINES
An old woman relives her life when she's trapped by an earthquake in an isolated cottage—"her grandfather's first adventures in San Francisco . . . historic events her family experienced in California." (FC) Har-Row, 1977

TRAVEL ARTICLES

ATLANTIC
1984 Jun "Comfortable on the Coast." Coastal highway from Los Angeles to San Francisco. Wendy Lowe, p. 104

BETTER HOMES & GARDENS
1985 Sep "San Francisco: A Guide to America's Favorite Family-vacation City." p. 76
1984 Jun "Family Vacations in Southern California." p. 161

BON APPETIT
1985 Jul "Traveling with Taste: San Diego." Shirley Slater, p. 28
1984 Apr "The Pleasures of Cabernet Sauvignon." Wine tour of Napa, Sonoma, Monterey. Anthony Dias Blue, p. 130
    Aug "Traveling with Taste: Los Angeles." June R. Galer, p. 24

CONNOISSEUR
1985 Mar "Museum of the Sea." Monterey's new aquarium may be the world's best. Thomas Hoving, p. 83
1984 Mar "The Sun Queen." La Villade Soleil—French country-look shop in San Francisco. Steven Winn, p. 116

ESQUIRE
1984 Apr "Los Angeles Beach Towns." Charlie Haas, p. 114

ESSENCE
1984 Jul "Black Los Angeles." Bebe Moore Campbell, p. 39

50 PLUS
1984 Jul "Finding the Swell Small Town." California is loaded with perfect retirement spots. Paula Patyk, p. 48
    "Going for the Golden State." Helene Brooks, p. 60

GOOD HOUSEKEEPING
1984 Sep "California Wine Country." Stephen Birnbaum, p. 210

GOURMET
Note: "Specialités de la Maison" by Caroline Bates is an article each month in *Gourmet* that reviews California restaurants.

HARPER'S BAZAAR
1985 Feb "A Traveling Woman's Guide to the World's Great Hotels." Hotel del Coronado in California. Kit Snedaker, p. 48

HORIZON
1985 Sep "Santa Clara: Arts in the Silicon Valley." Museums, galleries, lodgings, restaurants. Chuck Myer, p. 33

HOUSE & GARDEN
1984 Sep "Gone with the Prunes: a Napa Valley Native Returns to Find His Roots Have Been Becoming Newly Chic." William Hamilton, p. 30
Oct "Escape from Esalen." Big Sur. Jonathan Lieberson, p. 30

HOUSE BEAUTIFUL
1985 Aug "Searching Out the Romantic Spanish Style in California." Jim Powell, p. 40
1984 Feb "A Walking Tour of San Francisco's Shopping and Design Delights." p. 41

MODERN MATURITY
1984 Apr-May "Renaissance of a City." Long Beach. Charles N. Barnard, p. 50

NATIONAL GEOGRAPHIC
1985 Jan "Yosemite—Forever?" The hazards of "being loved too much." David S. Boyer, p. 52
1984 Apr "East of Eden: California's Mid-Coast." Harvey Arden, p. 424

NATIONAL GEOGRAPHIC TRAVELER
1985 Spring "Wild and Windswept: Channel Islands National Park." Rick Ridgeway, p. 32
Summer "Day-Tripping in San Francisco: Golden Days in Golden Gate Park." James Armstrong, p. 92
"Escape to Alcatraz." Stephen S. Hall, p. 108
Winter "Follow Your Star to Hollywood." Guided tours, etc. Jerry C. Dunn, Jr., p. 66
1984 Autumn "Napa—Valley of Vin Extraordinaire." Jerry C. Dunn, Jr., p. 152

N.Y. TIMES SUNDAY TRAVEL SECTION (X)
1985 Jan 6 "The 24-Hour-a-Day Hotelkeeper." Stanford court. Marian Burros, p. 16
Jan 27 "Menus of Note at a Coast Hotel." Campton Place in San Francisco. Marian Burros, p. 12
Feb 3 "What's Doing in Palm Springs." Lynn Rosellini, p. 10
Mar 3 "In the Redwood Empire." 60 miles of the great trees. Sedgefield Thomson, p. 14
"The Vinification of the North Coast." New wineries are making their mark in Mendocino. Frank J. Prial, p. 14
"Heading North in California." Beyond San Francisco lies a land of rocky shores, forests and vineyards. Robert Lindsey, p. 15
Mar 17 "Table-Hopping in Hollywood." A selection of the movie business's favorite restaurants for deal-making and scene-stealing. Bryan Miller, p. 15
"Stars and Moguls—and Food, Too." Robert Lindsey, p. 15
"What's New in Los Angeles Hotels." Building boom provides wide choice. Robert Lindsey, p. 16

1985 Apr 14 "On the Road Through Baja California." Exploring a land of fine seafood, stark vistas and uncrowded white-sand beaches. William A. Orme, Jr., p. 19

Jun 9 "What's Doing in San Francisco." Robert Lindsey, p. 10

Jun 30 "Southern California's Ubiquitous Malls." Grand tours and shopping safaris in Los Angeles and environs. Vanessa W. Page, p. 16

Jul 7 "An Inland Empire Built on Oranges." Southern California groves preserve an older way of life. Joseph Giovannini, p. 19

Aug 18 "California Grows Her Own Cuisine." Sampling menus in restaurants from La Jolla to Boonville. p. 9

Sep 1 "Correspondent's Choice: Elegant Lodgings in Redwood Country." Robert Lindsey, p. 7

Sep 15 "What's Doing in San Diego." Robert Lindsey, p. 10

Oct 6 ("Sophisticated Traveler") "Beyond Reality: Death Valley." Macdonald Harris, p. 38

Nov 3 "Los Angeles Exuberant." Architecture in downtown area. Charles Lockwood, p. 20

Nov 10 "An Enclave in Big Sur." Castro Canyon. Joseph Giovannini, p. 28

"Survival Tips for Women in Los Angeles Where 'Young at Heart' Doesn't Count." Jane Adams, p. 47

Nov 17 "California's Other Wine Country." Santa Cruz. James D. Houston, p. 16

Dec 15 "A 1920's Architectural Tour." Sampling the city's collection of craftsmen and Spanish-style buildings (in Pasadena). Charles Lockwood, p. 14

"Roses in January." Pasadena is an old-fashioned city that enjoys palms and peace—364 days a year. Macdonald Harris, p. 15

1984 Jan 29 "To (and in) Big Sur, the Way is Clear." Road reopened. Herbert Gold, p. 15

"An Inn on the Pacific's Edge." The Ventana provides a luxurious window on the ocean. p. 16

Feb 19 "Insider's Guide to Pacific Palisades." Movieland's coveted community is so exclusive it's not even on the map. Oscar Millard, p. 37

Apr 8 "Hollywood Boulevard: a Movie Fan's Tour." Tarnished relics of filmdom's golden age. Charles Lockwood, p. 20

Jun 24 "What's Doing in San Francisco." Robert Lindsey, p. 10

Jul 8 "What's Doing in Los Angeles." Robert Lindsey, p. 10

Jul 15 "A taste of San Francisco." Each neighborhood shows a facet of the city's special character. David Harris, p. 15

"Four Walks in the City." Downtown, Russian Hill, Pacific Heights, Castro-Noe. Paul Goldberger, p. 16

Aug 5 "California's Chinoise Cuisine." David Yeadon, p. 12

Oct 7 "Easy living in Marin." The California dream thrives north of the Golden Gate. Herbert Gold, p. 9

(Part 2, "Sophisticated Traveler") "A Pink Hotel." The Beverly Hills Hotel around the clock. Garson Kanin, p. 40

Nov 25 "Discovering the Other Yosemite." High Sierra camps offer tranquillity and an escape from the crowds of the valley floor. Lynn Rosellini, p. 9

1984   Dec 2 "Searching Out [Frank Lloyd] Wright's Imprint in Los Angeles."
       Charles Lockwood, p. 9
       Dec 9 "What's Doing in San Diego." At Christmastime. Sarah Ferrell, p. 10

READER'S DIGEST
1984   Dec "Los Angeles, City of Superlatives." Gregory Jaynes, p. 10

SATURDAY EVENING POST
1985   Dec "San Francisco: Weather or Not." Ted Kreiter, p. 84

SMITHSONIAN
1985   Jun "A Stunning New Aquarium for Cannery Row." In the heart of Steinbeck
       country, a marine complex takes visitors into the depths of Monterey Bay.
       Marquis Childs, p. 94

SUNSET
1985   Jan "Cross-country Skiing without the Crowds in Northeastern California."
       p. 10
       "Half-Day Fishing Out of San Diego or Mission Bay." p. 36
       "More Cross-Country in Yosemite." p. 46
       Feb "Downtown L.A. Is Coming Alive After 5." New restaurants, theatre,
       shuttle, etc. p. 12
       "West of Santa Maria, Beach Hiking and Fishing." Guadalupe Dunes National
       Park. p. 42
       "Touring La Jolla's Masterpiece." Salk Institute. p. 44
       "Lodging in Northern California." Information sources. p. 46
       "More Indian Doings at Museums in California, Arizona, New Mexico." p. 62
       "Splendid New Showcases for Southwest Indian Art." Heard and Southwest
       Museums in Phoenix and Los Angeles. p. 78
       Mar "In Search of the 'Inland Orange Empire.'" Riverside and Redlands
       areas. p. 14
       "Photography As Art . . ." Museums and galleries from Santa Barbara to San
       Diego that feature photography. p. 64
       Apr "Ranch Life in the Santa Clara Valley." At three big county parks, you'll
       find cattle, barns, ruins, memories and open space. p. 14
       "Salmon Fleet Parades in Bodega Bay." Blessing of the salmon-fishing fleet
       and annual festival. p. 52
       "A Blue Whale in Santa Barbara." p. 54
       "Maritime Past at Fort Mason." Museum in San Francisco. p. 70
       "Looking in on Altamont's Wind Farms . . . by Car on Tour." Windmill energy
       development farm. p. 75
       "San Francisco's Architects' Enclave." Jackson Square district. p. 104
       "An I-5 Detour Through Coalinga." p. 114
       "Diablo—the 'Island Mountain.'" Mt. Diablo State Park. p. 118
       May "Primate See, Primate Do." Primate center at the San Francisco Zoo. p.
       10
       "A Gallery of Gems." New gemstones and their origins exhibit at the Natural
       History Museum of Los Angeles County. p. 53
       "The Winding Wine Roads of the Santa Cruz Mountains." Twenty-seven
       wineries open for tasting, touring. p. 62

1985 "Inns of the Redwood Coast." Arcata, Eureka, Ferndale. p. 73
      "Spectacular, Rugged, and Beginning to Open Up . . ." Feather Falls country.
      p. 77
      "Riding the Rails on the San Francisco Peninsula." p. 94
      "Yosemite . . . Still Magnificent." Extensive article including a Yosemite
      planning guide. p. 108
      Jun "Mellow Living Among Majestic Mountains." It's Alpine County . . . only
      an hour from Tahoe but ever so different. p. 11
      "So Many Ways to Get Out on Santa Barbara Harbor." Sailing, boating, fish-
      ing, diving, cruises, etc. p. 60
      "Crayfish to Chateaubriand . . . Dining in the Delta (Area of Sacramento-San
      Joaquin)." Nineteen choices accessible by boat or car. p. 72
      Jul "Tiburon—New Ferry, Panoramic Views." p. 78
      "Much Is Going On in Old Monterey." Walking tour. p. 10
      "Discovering L.A.'s Film Archives." p. 30
      "Salinas to Carmel to Cannery Row . . . Steinbeck Country." p. 46
      "I-5 Detour—Castle Crags Near Shasta." p. 60
      Aug "Military History on Angel Island." p. 36
      "When the Wooden Boats Come Out on Tahoe." p. 42
      "Shipwreck Walk Along San Francisco's Land's End." p. 52
      "Malakoff Diggins . . . Miners Dug It." Park and museum of mining in the
      Gold Rush Days. p. 38
      Sep "Small Farm Detours in San Luis Obispo County." p. 10
      "Crush Time in the Livermore Valley." Tasting, touring, boating, picknick-
      ing almost any time. p. 38
      "Looking In on Peregrine Falcons at UC, Santa Cruz." p. 35
      "Mission San Jose Now Looks Just As It Did 150 Years Ago." p. 48
      "A 35-mile Loop Through Watsonville Apple Country." Its festival, fair and
      harvest time. p. 54
      "Italian Museum in San Francisco." Museo Italo Americano. p. 58
      Oct "On the San Mateo Coast, It's the Best and Busiest Season." p. 12
      "'Rain Forest' Walk Near San Diego." p. 32
      "Back Roads of Santa Barbara." p. 63
      "Mansions to Rent in the Bay Area for a Wedding, Reunion, Party." p. 64
      "A New East Bay Park." Nineteenth-century farm of George Patterson. p. 70
      "Into the Heart of Point Reyes." Via re-opened road. p. 84
      "San Francisco Plaza Walk." Green and granite gardens of San Francisco's
      financial district. p. 93
      Nov "Fresh-from-the-grower Citrus in the Central Valley." Where to shop,
      taste, tour. p. 10
      "Old Dumbarton Takes You Out to Where Fish Are." Fishing piers on San
      Francisco Bay. p. 38
      "Biking Up Mount Tam on the Old Railroad Grade." p. 26
      "Lake Sonoma Is Filling Up and Ready for Fishing, Boating, Hiking." p. 50
      "How to Find the Ojai Artists." p. 74
      "Koalas at Home in San Francisco Zoo." p. 96
      Dec "Palm Springs Biking: Six Trails." p. 66
      "A Farm-town Christmas in Arroyo Grande." Near San Luis Obispo. p. 38

1984 Jan "Cruising Close to the Bald Eagle." Lake San Antonio. p. 32
  "Ski Trails, Guided Tours, Snow Camping." Ten miles south of Tahoe City. p. 44
  Feb "You Can Egret-Watch, Canoe, Picnic in Marin's McInnis Park." p. 30
  "Mine Touring at Black Diamond." Near Oakland. p. 32
  "Shuttling from San Diego to Tia Juana Airport." p. 40
  "Livelier Than Ever, San Diego's Balboa Park." p. 78
  Mar "Almost a Ghost." China Camp State Park on San Pablo Bay. p. 34
  "Winter Beaching, Marin to Monterey." p. 54
  "Architectural Rubbernecking in San Francisco." p. 88
  Apr "Tuolumne River." Camping, fishing, rafting. p. 58
  "Around and About Los Angeles. . . . Tours by Bus or Van, by Day or Night." Hunt wildflowers, see *Ramona*, rediscover downtown. p. 96
  "For a Performance or Just a Look . . . San Francisco's Herbst Theatre." p. 102
  May "On and Off Campus, Architectural Doings in Berkeley." p. 46
  "Now That You Can Drive the Length of Big Sur Again." p. 62
  "Wooden Boats and Sea Chanteys on San Francisco Bay." p. 68
  "New Warm-Up Park and an Old Adobe on the San Mateo Coast." p. 88
  Jun "Riverside County's New Nature and Ranch Preserve." p. 34
  "New Architecture and Much Else at Santa Barbara's Old Museum." p. 42
  "Sunday Art Fun at Los Angeles' Barnsdall Park." p. 44
  "One-Day Tours and Hikes to Los Angeles' Wild Places." p. 48
  "Thirteen State Parks." p. 52
  "Tours and Trails Through the Astonishing Landscape of Mono Lake." p. 66
  "Mountain Mansions at Tahoe Invite You in for a Visit." p. 80
  Jul "30 Horse-Drawn Vehicles in Santa Ynez's New Carriage House." p. 24
  "19th-century Los Gatos." Walking tour. p. 34
  "Environmental Cabins in Marin." Steep ravine campground. p. 41
  "Defenders of San Francisco Bay." Tours, demonstrations, museums, at various forts. p. 42
  "There's News at Golden Gate Park." New additions. p. 50
  "Cafes, Cantinas, Delis Near the Moscone Center." p. 58
  "11 Paved Miles Out of Bridgeport, Two Placid High-Mountain Lakes." p. 76
  "Orange County's Theme Parks." p. 64
  "San José's New Park." Lake Cunningham Regional Park. p. 70
  "Political Wit and Walking Tours of San Francisco's City Hall." p. 75
  "Surprises in and Around Los Angeles." p. 108
  "Take Your Imagination to Old La Porte." p. 28
  Aug "I-5 Detour to 'Real' Rocks." Picnic, fish or camp at Castle Crags. p. 36
  "Valley History." Chinese jade in Fresno's new museum. p. 50
  "Getting Out on Tahoe." By motor, sail, paddle wheel. p. 52
  "Where the Southern California Coast Bends North." Wild and wide beaches. p. 34
  "An Old-Fashioned Slow-Down-and-Look Road." Through redwoods north of San Francisco. p. 28
  Sep "Conversations Across the Footlights." All part of Berkeley's innovative theater scene. p. 25
  "Boating and Birding on New Shoreline Park." San Francisco. p. 31

1984 "Indoor-Outdoor Art Strolling in Sacramento's Capitol District." p. 32
"Watching Salmon Head Up the Sacramento." p. 36
"To the Top of Half Dome, Fifty People Do It Every Summer Day." Yosemite. p. 42
"Getting to Catalina." Many choices. p. 46
"High Seas Birding." Boat trips to deep sea birds. p. 52
"Over Mountains to the Candy Dance and Nevada's Oldest Settlement." p. 58
"Quiet Catalina." After Labor Day. p. 60
Oct "The Country Roads of Apple Hill." Just off U.S. 50. p. 30
"Restoring Mexican Murals in San Francisco." p. 46
"Napa and Sonoma Valleys by Horse, Balloon, Glider, Plane, Van, Bike, Foot, Boat." p. 42
"Ocean Kayaking." Mendocino. p. 46B
"The Bass are Bigger at Lake Isabella." p. 54
"Woodland's Opera House Is Back After 71 Years." p. 56
"Antique Hunting in San Francisco." p. 58
"Autumn Angling at Pyramid Lake." p. 62
Nov "Bike-BART Adventures." Biking trails, San Francisco Bay area. p. 12
"San Francisco's Cable Car Barn is Open Again." p. 48
"Santa Monica's Carousel Spins Again." p. 53
"Russian Hill (San Francisco)." Exploring on foot. p. 72
"Downtown L.A. Bed-and-Breakfast." p. 88
"Monterey Bay and Its Astonishing New Aquarium." p. 92
Dec "San Diego Harbor Has News Ashore and Afloat." Cruises and excursions. p. 12
"San José's Trolleys." You can watch, even help. p. 14
"On the Spectacular Mendocino Coast, It Was a Logging Truck Road." Cycling, hiking, jogging. p. 28
"Earthquake Ride and Other New Science Adventures in Golden Gate Park." p. 32
"Hollywood Dreams at Three Museums." p. 36
"Inside and Up the Stanford Tower." p. 44
"The Small Inns of Tahoe." p. 58
"Yosemite's Back-Country Camps, Reserve Now for Summer." p. 62
"Face to Face with Desert Creatures Near Palm Springs." p. 68
"Berkeley's Fabric Artist Country." Specialty shops. p. 70

TOWN & COUNTRY
1985 Aug "Visa-Vis: Hotel Bel-Air." Jennifer Kramer, p. 175

TRAVEL & LEISURE
1985 Jan "Romantic Hideaways." L.A.'s Hotel Bel-Air—lush, seductive and secluded. Dena Kaye, p. 86
Feb "Relaxation and Renewal at Florida's Palm-Aire." And other soothing places (spas). Judith B. Wylie, p. 114
Mar "The Rugged Grandeur of California's Highway 1." A spectacular coastal drive between Los Angeles and San Francisco. Brian Moore, p. 96
"Highlights of Highway 1." Where to eat and stay along the way. Daniel Bickley, p. 120

1985 May "Latest from San Francisco." Marty Olmstead, p. 67
Jul "Savoring the Napa Valley, Its Inns, Its Restaurants and Its Wines." Robert Finigan, p. 82
Dec "Scenic Drive: East from San Diego's Classic Coast." Judith B. Morgan, p. 45
1984 Apr "What's Happening in Los Angeles." New restaurants and hotels, arts festival (includes L.A. environs, Orange County, Palm Springs, San Diego, Santa Barbara, Ventura, Marina del Rey). Richard J. Pietschmann, p. 88
May "A Sentimental Journey on the California Coast." North from San Francisco through wine country to the sea. Adrian Taylor, p. 68
Jun "Latest from San Francisco." Cable cars, Ghirardelli Square, new hotels, etc. Marty Olmstead, p. 75
Aug "The Low-Key Luxury of Pebble Beach." Adrian Taylor, p. 69
Oct "A Morning at the J. Paul Getty Museum." California's formidable art collection (Malibu). Laurence Shames, p. 32
Nov "Redwoods." Silent majesty in California. G.S. Bush, p. 125
Dec "San Francisco's Small, Sumptuous Hotels." Daniel Bickley, p. 100

TRAVEL/HOLIDAY
1985 Jan "California's Rush." Tales from the Mother Lode. Charles E. Adelsen, p. 20
Feb "Brother, What a Lighthouse." East Brother Light Station (San Francisco Bay). Nancy H. Belcher, p. 96
May "Laguna Beach." California's city of art. Sean P. Reily, p. 22
Aug "The Getty Legacy: California's Art-ful Experience." Museum in Malibu. Barbara and William Kraus, p. 64
Sep "Calistoga: the Saratoga of California." Indulging in mud, minerals and wine. Carol Canter, p. 4
Dec "More stately Mansions—California's Filoli and Montalvo." Near San Francisco. Barbara Karoff, p. 10
1984 Jan "California Dreamin'." Santa Monica and Venice. Andrew Yarrow, p. 22
Mar "San Francisco." Ambling by the bay. Daniel Bickley, p. 72
Jul "Ahhh, Garlic." Festival in Gilroy in July, garlic capital of the world. Ana Marcelo, p. 82
Nov "Catching Fish, Not Cold, in San Diego." An angler's winter destination. Diane P. Marshall, p. 42

VOGUE
1985 Sep "Hollywood as History." Richard Alleman, p. 552
1984 May "Great Hotels: Los Angeles' Dreamy Hotel Bel-Air." Richard Alleman, p. 256

COLORADO

Series Guidebooks (See Appendix 1)

Fodor: **Colorado**

Background Reading

Athearn, Robert G.   THE COLORADANS
Personalities and people, forces that have shaped Colorado. U of New Mexico, 1982.

Borland, Hal G.   HIGH, WIDE AND LONESOME
The naturalist's boyhood on the eastern Colorado plains where his family homesteaded in 1909. G.K. Hall, 1984 (first published 1956).

Clifford, Peggy   TO ASPEN AND BACK: AN AMERICAN JOURNEY
Aspen as a smaller version of America, ever-growing from mining town to ski resort. St. Martin, 1980.

Cochran, Alice C.   MINERS, MERCHANTS AND MISSIONARIES
A history of the missionaries' role in creating a society in the wilderness. Scarecrow, 1980.

Dorsett, Lyle W.   THE QUEEN CITY: A HISTORY OF DENVER
Informative, interesting description of people, events anddevelopment in a chronological format. Pruett, 1980.

Eberhart, Philip   GUIDE TO COLORADO GHOST TOWNS &
                    MINING CAMPS
Swallow, 1969.

Griffiths, Thomas   SAN JUAN COUNTRY
Description and travel in the San Juan Mountains region. Pruett, 1983.

Kane, Kay   DISCOVER DENVER
Gold Kane Enter, 1983.

Koch, Don   AN ENDLESS VISTA: A GUIDE TO COLORADO'S
                RECREATIONAL LANDS
Pruett, 1982.

LeCompte, Janet   PUEBLO, HARDSCRABBLE, GREENHORN
History of three walled towns as they were in frontier days—today they are Pueblo, Walsenburg and Canon City. U of Oklahoma Pr, 1981.

Love, Frank   A GUIDE TO GHOST TOWNS AND MINING CAMPS OF THE
                YUMA AND LOWER COLORADO REGION
Little London Pr, 1980.

Moody, Ralph   HOME RANCH
Reminiscences of a ranch boyhood through the eyes of a twelve-year-old. Norton, 1956.

Norton, Boyd and Barbara   BACKROADS OF COLORADO
Mini-tours around which to plan itineraries. Rand, 1979.

Pearson, Jeff   NO TIME BUT PLACE: A PRAIRIE PASTORAL
Combination of journal and oral history of some hundred people interviewed.
McGraw, 1980.

Reed, Allen C.   GRAND CIRCLE ADVENTURE
Traveling to national parks and reserves in Arizona, Colorado and Utah. KC
Pbns, 1983.

Robinson, Linda   MILE HIGH DENVER: A GUIDE TO THE QUEEN CITY
Pruett, 1981.

Sprague, Marshall   NEWPORT IN THE ROCKIES
The life and good times of Colorado Springs. Swallow, 1981.

Sprague, Marshall   COLORADO
One of a series of popular histories for each state published as part of the
Bicentennial observance in 1976. Norton, 1984 (first published 1976).

Whitney, Gleaves   COLORADO FRONT RANGE: A LANDSCAPE DIVIDED
The effect of population growth on the quality of life in north central Colorado.
Johnson, 1983.

Novels

Blume, Judy   SMART WOMEN (Boulder)
About three families from the east, re-settled into suburban Boulder after
broken marriages—"moving, often witty story." (FC) Putnam Pub Group, 1984.

Borland, Hal   WHEN THE LEGENDS DIE
Story of an Indian boy brought up in the wilderness who is later forced to
become "civilized"—he becomes a bronc-buster with a reputation for a
murderous riding style. The period is 1910-20. Lippincott, 1963.

Burns, Rex   THE ALVAREZ JOURNAL (Denver)
Denver and its environs are the setting for this police procedural story with a
part-Chicano detective. Har-Row, 1975. Another title in the series is *Speak for the
Dead* (1978) about murder in Denver's botanic gardens.

Cather, Willa   THE SONG OF THE LARK
A young woman from Moonstone, Colorado, becomes a great American singer.
Houghton, 1915.

Greenberg, Joanne   THE FAR SIDE OF VICTORY
A "frivolous bachelor" is responsible for the death of a man and his three
children, then succeeds in marrying the widow. "His attempt to understand her
turns the novel . . . into a thoughtful character study." (FC) HR&W, 1983.

Greenberg, Joanne   FOUNDER'S PRAISE
Three generations of a farming family in eastern Colorado. HR&W, 1976.

Grey, Zane   THE VANISHING AMERICAN
An Indian boy is sent to an Eastern university and returns, with an Eastern girl, to help his people—"tragedy of the Indian people, despoiled by government agent and missionary." (FC) Har-Row, 1925.

King, Stephen   THE SHINING
One of King's scary novels, set in the Overlook Hotel in the Colorado mountains and involving spirits of the dead who have stayed at the hotel and a precognitive, telepathic caretaker's son—"relentless heightening of horror." (FC) Doubleday, 1977.

L'Amour, Louis   OVER ON THE DRY SIDE
A Western action/adventure story. The hero—"a literate quick-draw artist . . . who can fight or talk"—solves the murder of his brother. (FC) Saturday Rev Pr, 1975.

Macdonald, Elisabeth   THE HOUSE AT GRAY EAGLE
A traditional gothic with an unusual setting—an isolated Colorado ranch in 1904 complete with cowboys, Indians and half-breeds. Scribner, 1976.

Michener, James A.   CENTENNIAL
One of Michener's panoramic novels that combine comprehensive history and background with an engrossing plot. This one covers Colorado's history from prehistoric times to the present day. Random, 1974.

Millhiser, Marlys   THE MIRROR (Boulder)
A modern-day bride is zapped back to her grandmother's time, and grandmother simultaneously becomes the present-day bride. Putnam Pub Group, 1978. Another romantic mystery by this author, set in Colorado, is *Willing Hostage* (1976).

Patten, Lewis B.   MAN OUTGUNNED
Six escaped convicts invade a Fourth of July picnic, gun down four of the people and murder a sixteen-year-old girl. Sheriff Morgan McGuire and a posse vow to track the killers "all the way to hell"—"a first-rate western chase." (FC) Doubleday, 1976.

Ross, Dana F.   COLORADO
Part of a series of novels, with the overall title of *Wagons West*, that chronicles the conquest and settlement of the American West. Bantam, 1981.

Sinclair, Upton   THE COAL WAR
Documentary novel of the coal strike in 1913-14 by the writer of social protest novels. Colorado Associated U Pr, 1976 (first published 1917).

Van Slyke, Helen   SISTERS AND STRANGERS (Denver)
Three sisters are reunited and their complicated pasts unfold. Doubleday, 1978.

Whitney, Phyllis A.   DOMINO
One of Ms. Whitney's romantic suspense novels; this one is set in an abandoned silver mine camp in the Colorado Rockies. Doubleday, 1979.

TRAVEL ARTICLES

AMERICANA
1985 Mar-Apr "Bridge to Nowhere." The restoration of the Devil's Gate high bridge brings back mining and railroad history. Karl Zimmermann, p. 66

ESSENCE
1985 Mar "Rocky Mountain High! Rafting and Horseback Riding in Colorado." Cheryl Everette, p. 42

HARPER'S BAZAAR
1985 Dec "Steamboat Springs." J.A. Beer, p. 24

HOUSE BEAUTIFUL
1984 Nov "Skiers and History Buffs Are at Home in Three Victorian Towns That Reflect the Old West." p. 56

NATIONAL GEOGRAPHIC
1984 Aug "Colorado Dreaming." Mike Edwards, p. 186

NATIONAL GEOGRAPHIC TRAVELER
1984 Spring "Floating Through Dinosaur." Explore the wonders of Dinosaur National Monument in Colorado and Utah. Jennifer C. Urquhart, p. 104
Autumn "Mesa Verde, Land of the Cliff Dwellers." Michael W. Robbins, p. 140

N.Y. TIMES SUNDAY TRAVEL SECTION (X)
1985 Dec 8 "High Noon at Steamboat." "A Coloradeo ski resort emphasizes balloons, saloons and Stetsons." Bernard Kirsch, p. 14
"A Resort for Athlete and Esthete." Aspen offers an abundance of diversions for body and mind. Peter Tauber, p. 15
"Aspen: Staying and Playing." Dyan Zaslowsky, p. 16
1984 Jun 10 "Climbing to a Palace in the Desert." Mesa Verde's cliffs hold secrets of the Anasazi. David R. Jones, p. 15
Jun 17 "The High Rails of Old Colorado." Traveling along railbeds, by car, and mountain trains. p. 20
Nov 11 "What's Doing in Denver." Iver Peterson, p. 10

TOWN & COUNTRY
1985 Oct "The Lodge at Vail." Jennifer Kramer, p. 273

TRAVEL & LEISURE
1985 Jun "Scenic Drive: Colorado's Trail Ridge Road." Robert Devine, p. 193

TRAVEL/HOLIDAY
1985 Mar "The Delights of Durango." Colorado's colorful little corner. Ruth W. Armstrong, p. 4
Nov "Colorado's Finest: Resorts for Winter Retreats." Diane P. Marshall, p. 48
1984 Jan "Grand Old Hotels of Colorado." Gary Ferguson, p. 18

CONNECTICUT

Background Reading

Bailey, Anthony   IN THE VILLAGE
"An intimate look at life in a small American town"—Stonington. (BRD) Knopf, 1971.

Beaubelle, Marcy   COASTAL CONNECTICUT
Western Region and Eastern Region, two volumes. Peregrine Pr, 1979.

Gannett, L.S.   CREAM HILL
"A book for all who love country ways and country things to savor"—reminiscences of years on a summer vacation farm in Cornwall that gradually became the family's year-round home. (BRD) Viking, 1949.

Harwood, Michael   A COUNTRY JOURNAL
A couple from New York leave their publishing world life for a village in northwestern Connecticut. Dodd, 1974.

Henning, Alyson and MacColl, Gwynne   A GUIDE TO HARTFORD
Cultural highlights, sports and outdoor activities, dining and lodging, parking and public transit. Globe Pequot, 1978.

Jones, Stephen   BACKWATERS
A charming book about the Long Island Sound and its backwaters in Connecticut and Long Island. Norton, 1979.

Keyarts, Eugene   SIXTY SHORT WALKS IN CONNECTICUT
"60 walks through the most stimulating scenery in every county, with footnotes on flora, fauna, and history." (Publisher) Globe Pequot, 1979.

Roth, David M.   CONNECTICUT
One of a series of popular histories for each state published as part of the Bicentennial observance in 1976. Norton, 1979.

Taber, Gladys   BEST OF STILLMEADOW
Philosophizing and description of life on a Connecticut farm around the seasons—"quiet charm." Har-Row, 1976 (first published 1948). Also *Stillmeadow Sampler* (1981), *Illustrated Book of Stillmeadow* (1984).

Tarrant, John J.   END OF EXURBIA
The assault by outsiders on affluent enclaves in Connecticut. Stein & Day, 1976.

Teale, Edward W.   A WALK THROUGH THE YEAR
A naturalist's observations of animals and plant life and the seasons on a Connecticut farm. Dodd, 1978.

Novels

Beach, Edward L.   RUN SILENT, RUN DEEP (New London)
A submarine patrol, from training in New London to World War II duty in the Pacific, seen through the eyes of an Annapolis graduate with his first command. HR&W, 1955.

Beattie, Ann   FALLING IN PLACE
Summer of 1979—witty depiction of the broken American dream in suburban Connecticut. Random, 1980.

DeVries, Peter   MADDER MUSIC
"Copiously funny book about a man unfitted either for marriage or adultery." (FC) Little, 1977. Other funny, satirical novels by DeVries, set in Connecticut, include: *The Tunnel of Love* (1954), *The Mackerel Plaza* (1958), *The Tents of Wickedness* (1959), and *Reuben, Reuben* (1964).

Dolson, Hildegarde   BEAUTY SLEEP
The murder of an artist's employer leads her to use her amateur detective skills to solve it. Lippincott, 1977. Another murder mystery, *Please Omit Funeral* (1975), set in a prosperous Connecticut village, concerns book-banning at the high school library and the death of one of the authors who has been banned.

Eberhart, Mignon G.   MURDER IN WAITING
A retired judge, working on his memoirs, is murdered—with many people in the Connecticut village having reason to fear what he'd planned to reveal in the memoirs. Random, 1973.

Fast, Howard   THE OUTSIDER
A New Yorker becomes a rabbi in a small Connecticut town. The novel chronicles the growth of "this rural Jewish society [and] historical events [Rosenberg trial, civil rights marches, etc.] in which minor characters embody major conflicts." (FC) Houghton, 1984.

Fast, Howard   THE HESSIAN
The trial of a Hessian drummer boy for a war crime during the Revolutionary War. Morrow, 1972.

Florey, Kitty B.   CHEZ CORDELIA
An upper-class girl marries the son of a middle-class Italian grocery store owner. Seaview, 1980.

Hersey, John   THE WALNUT DOOR
A novel of young people struggling with the collapse of their idealism. Knopf, 1977.

Hodgins, Eric   MR. BLANDING BUILDS HIS DREAM HOUSE
Comedy of the trials and tribulations of building a new house just after World War II. S&S, 1946.

Kluger, Phyllis   GOOD GOODS
Vicissitudes of a Connecticut woman juggling home, children, and a career, an affair that leads to her divorce—a heroine with "freshness, wit, and intelligence." (FC) Macmillan, 1982.

Knowles, John   INDIAN SUMMER
Novel of a lifelong friendship destroyed when one realizes the other seeks to turn him into a hanger-on—"theme of individualism is explored . . . commentaries on the rich, the poor, success, failure, and politics." (FC) Random, 1966.

Malone, Michael   DINGLEY FALLS
Old-fashioned novel set in a Connecticut town in which a devoted wife shocks everybody by running off with a poet. HarBraceJ, 1980.

Millhauser, Steven   PORTRAIT OF A ROMANTIC
Knopf, 1977. This, and the book that precedes it, *Edwin Mullhouse* (1972) is the account of the life of a genius who dies at age 11.

Queen, Ellery   INSPECTOR QUEEN'S OWN CASE: NOVEMBER SONG
The father of Ellery Queen, and a retired police inspector himself, is the sleuth in a murder while vacationing in Connecticut. S&S, 1956.

Shulman, Max   RALLY ROUND THE FLAG, BOYS
A new Nike base in a Connecticut town "leads to no end of hilarious complications" involving the struggle for dominance of the three groups in the village—commuters, Yankee natives and Italian-Americans. (FC) Doubleday, 1957.

Straub, Peter   FLOATING DRAGON
"Examines the consequences of an industrial accident coupled with supernatural evil." (FC) Putnam Pub Group, 1983.

Streeter, Edward   CHAIRMAN OF THE BORED
Comedy of a man forced into retirement and life in the country. Har-Row, 1961.

Tryon, Thomas   LADY
Growing up in Connecticut during the depression narrated by an eight-year-old boy "hopelessly in love with the grande dame of his little hometown." (FC) Knopf, 1974.

Tryon, Thomas   THE OTHER
A series of horrendous mishaps affects the family of twin boys; the period is the 1930s in the country. Knopf, 1971.

Updike, John   MARRY ME
Affairs of four people in two unsatisfactory marriages—"the world of well-to-do [Connecticut] adultery in the 1960s." (FC) Knopf, 1976.

Yates, Richard   A GOOD SCHOOL
Life at a less-than-great prep school in Connecticut for a boy on half-tuition who feels inferior to his affluent classmates, with shifting viewpoints to the lives of the faculty and problems other students are having. The time is just prior to World War II. Delacorte Pr, 1978.

TRAVEL ARTICLES

AMERICAN HERITAGE
1985 Feb-Mar "Our Neighbor Mark Twain." His home in Redding. Coley Taylor, p. 102

BON APPETIT
1985 Jan "The Charming Inns of Connecticut." Patricia Brooks, p. 70

EARLY AMERICAN LIFE
1985 Dec "Holiday Breakfast in Connecticut." Golden Lamb Buttery in Brooklyn. Mimi Handler, p. 29

GOURMET
1984 Dec "Mark Twain's Hartford House." Geoffrey C. Ward, p. 60

NATIONAL GEOGRAPHIC TRAVELER
1985 Winter "Under a Seasonal Spell at Caprilands Herb Farm." Eliot Tozer, p. 20
1984 Spring "Mystic." Connecticut's historic Seaport Museum . . . a 17-acre riverfront museum complete with artisans' shops, a full-rigged sailing ship, and a 19th-century wooden whaler. William P. Beaman, p. 132

N.Y. TIMES SUNDAY TRAVEL SECTION (X)
1985 May 19 "Browsing on Connecticut's Antique Trail." Frances Phipps, p. 16
Sep 29 "Along the Connecticut Shore, Yankee Traditions Survive in Mystic and Its Environs." Nancy Jenkins, p. 9
Oct 6 "Retracing History at 10 MPH." Housatonic railroad, West Cornwall to Canaan. James Brooke, p. 19
Oct 27 "Along the Connecticut River—a Leisurely Trip by Car from Long Island Sound to the Canadian Border." p. 21

VOGUE
1985 Jul "The Cotswold Inn." Jill Robertson-Shaw, p. 108

YANKEE
1985 Apr "This New England: Hartford." Lary Bloom, p. 60
1984 Jan "This New England: Stony Creek." Karen Bussolini, p. 70
Jul "This New England: The Seven Faces of Cornwall." Laurie A. O'Neill, p. 54

DELAWARE

Background Reading

Canby, Henry Seidel   THE BRANDYWINE
"Intimately charming"—part history, part reminiscences, part taken from private journals—story of the river area where the author's family settled in the 1700s. Illustrations by Andrew Wyeth. (BRD) Schiffler, 1977 (first published 1941).

Gates, John D.   THE DU PONT FAMILY
Family history from the first American Du Pont, 1739-1817, to date, and the sheer concentration of economic power. Doubleday, 1979.

Hoffecker, Carol E.   DELAWARE
One of a series of popular histories for each state published as part of the Bicentennial observance in 1976. Norton, 1977.

Mosley, Leonard   BLOOD RELATIONS
The rise and fall of the Du Ponts of Delaware—a family biography, family intrigue, jealousy, infidelities, etc. Atheneum, 1980.

Phelan, James   THE COMPANY STATE
Ralph Nader's study of the Du Ponts in Delaware. Grossman, 1978.

Vessels, Jane and Fleming, Kevin   DELAWARE: A SMALL WONDER
Text and photographs describe "a uniquely serene yet diverse strip of land on the East coast . . . explicates the nuances of Delaware's high-tech, agricultural, and seaside-resort characteristics, offering tidbits of history and latter-day facts and lore." (BL) Abrams, 1984.

[No Fiction]

TRAVEL ARTICLES

EARLY AMERICAN LIFE
1984 Dec "Touring Christmas Houses: Odessa, Delaware." Carol McCabe, p. 56

NATIONAL GEOGRAPHIC TRAVELER
1985 Spring "Winterthur: American Elegance." Most glorious of all testaments to American taste—the Du Pont mansion-turned-museum of the best in decorative arts. Craig Claiborne, p. 98

THE DISTRICT
OF COLUMBIA

Series Guidebooks (See Appendix 1)

Fisher: Washington, D.C. and Vicinity
Fodor: Washington D.C.
Frommer: Washington, D.C.: City Guide; $-a-Day

Background Reading

Aikman, Lonnelle   WE, THE PEOPLE
The story of the U.S. capital, its past and its promise; produced by the National Geographic Society. U.S. Capitol Hist Soc, 1978.

Daniels, Jonathan   WASHINGTON QUADRILLE
"The dance beside the documents. . . . Women who were leaders of Washington society from Abraham Lincoln to FDR" and their influence on the men who ran the nation. (BRD) Doubleday, 1968.

Gutheim, Frederick   WORTHY OF THE NATION: THE HISTORY OF
                     PLANNING FOR THE NATIONAL CAPITAL
Smithsonian, 1977.

Harrington, Ty   THE LAST CATHEDRAL
Provides a wealth of information on the nation's last cathedral and one of Washington's most famous tourist attractions. P-H, 1979.

Jensen, Amy   THE WHITE HOUSE AND ITS THIRTY-FIVE FAMILIES
First published in 1958, revised to include presidential families through Carter. McGraw, 1979.

Junior League of Washington eds.   THE CITY OF WASHINGTON
An illustrated history of the city. Knopf, 1977.

Kilian, Michael and Sawisiak, Arnold   WHO RUNS WASHINGTON?
"Antic but informed guidebook to life in the nation's capital . . . The roles, influence, and foibles of the current ruling class." (BL) St. Martin, 1982.

Lewis, David L.   DISTRICT OF COLUMBIA
One of a series of popular histories for each state published as part of the Bicentennial observance in 1976. Norton, 1976.

Menendez, Albert J.   CHRISTMAS IN THE WHITE HOUSE
Westminster, 1983.

**Meyer, A., ed.   A ZOO FOR ALL SEASONS: THE SMITHSONIAN
ANIMAL WORLD**
Norton, 1979.

**Moore, Derry and Mitchell, Henry   WASHINGTON HOUSES OF
THE CAPITAL**
"Lively accounts of Washington's beautiful people [past and present] and the
houses they inhabit," in text and pictures. (LJ) Viking, 1982.

Morris, Jan   DESTINATIONS; TRAVELS
Two of this leading travel writer's collections of travel writings that include
essays on Washington, D.C. Oxford U, 1980.

Rash, Bryson B.   FOOTNOTE WASHINGTON
"Tracking the engaging, humorous and surprising bypaths of Capital history."
(Publisher) EPM, 1983.

**Ryan, William and Guinness, Desmond   THE WHITE HOUSE: AN
ARCHITECTURAL HISTORY**
The evolution of the White House from early plans through restorations—"peppered with fascinating accounts of the sometimes makeshift living
conditions and grandiose schemes" of several presidents. (LJ) McGraw, 1980.

White House Historical Assn.   THE WHITE HOUSE
Historical guide prepared with the cooperation of the National Geographic
Society. The Association, 1979.

GUIDEBOOKS FOR WASHINGTON, D.C.

Appleberg, Marilyn J.   I LOVE WASHINGTON GUIDE
Part of a series—see annotation for "Boston." Macmillan, 1982.

**Applewhite, E.J.   WASHINGTON ITSELF: AN INFORMAL GUIDE TO THE
CAPITAL OF THE UNITED STATES**
Provides architectural and historical notes, and an education on the capital for
residents and for those who lack the opportunity to see these sights in
person—designed for compatability with a walking tour. Knopf, 1981.

Cox, Brian   500 THINGS TO DO IN WASHINGTON, D.C. FOR FREE
Plus a hundred more for less than a dollar. New Century, 1983.

Duffield, Judy and others   WASHINGTON, D.C.
History, description, basic information, as well as information on metro stops,
bus lines, parking, special treats for children, etc. Organized to systematically
move through each neighborhood. Random, 1982.

Gershkoff, Ira and Trachtman, Richard   THE WASHINGTON DRIVER'S
HANDBOOK: A GUIDE TO
CAPITAL CRUISING
How to cope with crosstown expressways, downtown traffic, the Beltway, driving in winter, even how to tell if a cabbie is "taking you for a ride." "A good job of explicating the navigational difficulties of this beautiful metropolis . . . humorous . . . . informative . . . a big help to potential tourists." (BL) Addison-Wesley, 1984.

Gilbert, Elizabeth R.   FAIRS AND FESTIVALS: A SMITHSONIAN GUIDE
TO CELEBRATIONS IN MARYLAND, VIRGINIA
AND D.C.
"Everything from national holidays and flower festivals to ethnic and religious events." (BL) Smithsonian, 1982.

Hart, Robert S.   EXACT DIRECTIONS: HOW TO SEE YOUR NATION'S
CAPITAL WITHOUT AN EXPENSIVE TOUR OR A TOUR
GUIDE
R.S. Hart, 1981.

Hodge, Allan and Carola   WASHINGTON ON FOOT
Twenty-three walking tours of Washington D.C., Alexandria and Annapolis. Smithsonian, 1980.

Kramer, William and others   WASHINGTON, D.C., THE COMPLETE
GUIDE
Random, 1982.

Lee, Richard M.   MR. LINCOLN'S CITY
Illustrated guide to Civil War sites of Washington. EPM, 1981.

Smith, Jane O.   ONE-DAY TRIPS THROUGH HISTORY
Two hundred excursions within 150 miles of Washington, D.C. EPM, 1983. Also *Washington One-Day Trip Book: 101 Offbeat Excursions in and Around the Nation's Capital* (1982).

Thomas, Bill and Phyllis   NATURAL WASHINGTON
Parks, trails, museums and wildlife sanctuaries within a fifty-mile radius of the capital. HR&W, 1980.

Novels

Adams, Henry   DEMOCRACY
By the nineteenth-century American novelist and published anonymously in 1879—portrays the political society of Washington during President Ulysses S. Grant's second administration (1873-77). HR&W, 1980.

Agnew, Spiro T.   THE CANFIELD DECISION
Downfall of an ambitious vice president, written by an ambitious vice president who had his own downfall. Playboy Pr, 1976.

Anderson, Patrick   THE PRESIDENT'S MISTRESS
A man tries to solve the death of a girl he loved who left him to have an affair with the president. S&S, 1976.

Banks, Carolyn   THE GIRLS ON THE ROW
Thriller involving the murders of beautiful yuppies. Crown, 1983.

Bar-Zohar, Michael   THE DEADLY DOCUMENT
"Polished, professional" spy thriller as the imminent uncovering of a CIA agent within the KGB leads to "murders, defections, ploys, ruses, blackmail." (FC) Delacorte Pr, 1980.

Blatty, William P.   THE EXORCIST (Georgetown)
A young girl is possessed by the devil. Har-Row, 1971. *Legion* (1983) is a "sequel of sorts" to *The Exorcist*. This time the possessing is of senior citizens.

Carroll, James   MADONNA RED
Suspense story of a group of Catholic clergy and an IRA terrorist plot against a British embassy official. Little, 1976. See also *Family Trade* (1982) under "Germany," which takes place in Berlin and Washington.

Clark, Mary Higgins   STILLWATCH
A young woman moves into a house in D.C. in which she lived as a child, despite being warned not to. She's in town to produce a TV documentary on a senator, and his background is part of the plot of this chiller. S&S, 1984.

DeBorchgrave, Arnaud   THE SPIKE
A spy thriller about the Soviet infiltration of the media and government—by an expert on international intrigue and politics. Crown, 1980.

Dos Passos, John   DISTRICT OF COLUMBIA
Three political novels, from the Spanish Civil War to the New Deal. Houghton, 1952. Also *The Grand Design* (1949), about the New Deal's "merry-go-round."

Drury, Allen   DECISION
Two Supreme Court justices are faced with a moral dilemma when they must judge a case involving the deaths of their two daughters. [The reviewer added that in the real world they'd just disqualify themselves.] Doubleday, 1983. Other novels by Drury about the inner workings of Washington are: *Advise and Consent* (1959), *Anna Hastings* (1977), *Preserve and Protect* (1968), and *Come Ninevah, Come Tyre* (1973).

Duggan, Ervin S. and Wattenberg, Ben   AGAINST ALL ENEMIES
Written by two veteran professionals and observers of the Washington scene. The story is about a national crisis as the vice president challenges the president and encourages demonstrations against him. Doubleday, 1977.

Ehrlichman, John   THE WHOLE TRUTH
Cover-up of a CIA plot to kill a Marxist leader; by one of the Watergate figures. S&S, 1979.

Erdman, Paul E.   THE BILLION DOLLAR SURE THING
An American with Mafia connections plots to manipulate the international money market. Scribner, 1973.

Goodrum, Charles A.   DEWEY DECIMATED
Murder mystery set in a private Washington library. Crown, 1977.

Grady, James   SIX DAYS OF THE CONDOR
"Fast-paced spy-counterspy tale"—the only survivor of the wholesale murder of an entire CIA branch is the object of a massive and varied chase. (FC) Norton, 1974.

Heller, Joseph   GOOD AS GOLD
"Stinging satire etched in acid" of a Jewish professor of English who is recruited to come to Washington with the potential of becoming the nation's first Jewish Secretary of State. (FC) S&S, 1979.

Howar, Barbara   MAKING ENDS MEET
A 45-year-old TV personality takes stock of her life. Random, 1976.

Just, Ward   IN THE CITY OF FEAR
A political novel focused around a Georgetown dinner party during the Vietnam War—"captures the movement of the Washington scene . . . a high comedy of manners and of acid-etched vignettes." (FC) Viking, 1982. Another novel of the Washington political scene is *Nicholson at Large* (1975), about a journalist who joins the federal government to work as spokesman for the Secretary of State. Also *The Congressman Who Loved Flaubert* (1973) (short stories).

Kosinski, Jerzy   BEING THERE
A former gardener is propelled into national politics when his simplistic solutions to world problems attract attention. HarBraceJ, 1980.

Ludlum, Robert   THE CHANCELLOR MANUSCRIPT
J. Edgar Hoover is assassinated because he knows too much about you and me. Dial, 1977.

McCarthy, Abigail   CIRCLES: A WASHINGTON STORY
The ex-wife of Senator Eugene McCarthy is the author of this novel about presidential politics; based on an actual incident in 1972. Doubleday, 1977.

MacLeish, Roderick   A CITY ON THE RIVER
Fictional and nonfictional passages describe what happens when a new president from New York State takes office. Dutton, 1973.

McMurtry, Larry   CADILLAC JACK
A former rodeo man who now scouts for antiques in his Cadillac undergoes a mid-life crisis "in the amiable venality and lechery of Washington, D.C." (FC) S&S, 1982.

Morice, Anne   MURDER IN MIMICRY
Washington from the British point of view—murder and blackmail behind the scenes of a British acting company making its U.S. debut. St. Martin, 1977.

Oates, Joyce Carol   ANGEL OF LIGHT
A philosophical novel of revenge and justice told in flashback. Dutton, 1981.

O'Hehir, Diana   I WISH THIS WAR WERE OVER
A woman comes to D.C. in 1944 to rescue her mother from alcoholism. Atheneum, 1984.

Patterson, Richard N.   THE LASKO TANGENT
Fast-moving novel of a lawyer's investigations of financial manipulation by a close friend of the president. Ballantine, 1979.

Pearson, William   "CHESSPLAYER"
A taxi passenger falls ill and an innocent cabbie finds the briefcase he leaves behind, which contains top-secret plans for a takeover of the Middle East by the United States. When the cabbie mails the material to Washington to get rid of it, an intense investigation is launched into how it got out and just as mysteriously returned. Viking, 1984.

Safire, William   FULL DISCLOSURE
A suspense thriller in which the Soviet premier is assassinated and the president of the United States blinded in a coordinated attack upon the two. Doubleday, 1977.

Sheed, Wilfrid   PEOPLE WILL ALWAYS BE KIND
Story of a 1960s president who overcame childhood polio to become a brilliant, cynical politician. FS&G, 1973.

Stein, Benjamin   ON THE BRINK
"Can a novel about runaway inflation be exciting, suspenseful and totally absorbing?" It evidently has been done in this novel—"economic theories in zingy dialogue . . . socially diverse characters, varied locales and government high jinks in a fast-paced plot." (FC) S&S, 1977.

Thomas, Ross   YELLOW DOG CONTRACT
A mystery involving labor and government leaders. Morrow, 1977.

Truman, Margaret   MURDER AT THE FBI
The latest of a series of mysteries by the former president's daughter that also give readers a view of inside workings of various parts of the government in Washington. Arbor Hse, 1985. Other titles by Ms. Truman are: *Murder in the Smithsonian* (1983), *Murder on Embassy Row* (1984), *Murder in the Supreme Court* (1982), *Murder on Capitol Hill* (1981), *Murder in the White House* (1980), and *Murder in Georgetown* (1986).

Vidal, Gore   WASHINGTON, D.C.
Third in a series depicting Washington political life since the Revolutionary War. Random, 1976. Preceding this are *Burr* (1973) and *1876* (1976).

Wicker, Tom   FACING THE LIONS
A cynical reporter and his senator friend who wants to be president—"the clash of power and principle." (FC) Viking, 1973.

TRAVEL ARTICLES

BON APPETIT
1985 Sep "A Taste of Washington." Constance Stapleton, p. 102

CONNOISSEUR
1984 May "Hillwood, a Gloriously Eccentric American Museum." Most satisfying "real home" museum in the U.S. Thomas Hoving, p. 90
Jun "Monument City." The best, the worst, the funniest . . . of public monuments. Peter Blake and Thomas Walton, p.86

NATIONAL GEOGRAPHIC
1985 May "Vietnam Memorial." America remembers. Timothy S. Kolly, p. 552
"To Heal a Nation." Joel J. Swerdlow, p. 554

NATIONAL GEOGRAPHIC TRAVELER
1985 Autumn "Travels Along the Canal—Goin' Slow on the C&O." Travels along the Canal on the Chesapeake & Ohio. Eugene L. Mayer, p. 84
Winter "Capital's Children's Museum: Close Encounters of the Imaginative Kind." Brigitte Weeks, p. 114
1984 Spring "A Capital Visit." A springtime pilgrimage lets you explore the city behind the marble facades. Howard Means, p. 76

N.Y. TIMES SUNDAY TRAVEL SECTION (X)
1985 Dec 1 "A Wordless, Anonymous Memorial—the Story Behind the Masterpiece." St. Gaudens' statue in Rock Creek cemetery. Joseph Gallagher, p. 31
1984 Jan 15 "The Nation's Book Trove." Library of Congress. Seth S. King, p. 20
Nov 18 "Sleeper Services to the Capital." Amtrak N.Y. to D.C. Betsy Wade, p. 28

TRAVEL & LEISURE
1985 Oct "Washington's Hotel Renaissance." Charles Monaghan, p. 128
1984 Mar "Latest from Washington D.C.." New hotels, distinctive restaurants, cherry blossoms. Jean Lawrence, p. 33
Dec "Christmas at the White House." Jeanne Howard, p. 67

TRAVEL/HOLIDAY
1985 Feb "Country Walks." Washington D.C.'s unsung byways. Penelope Lemov, p. 14
"The Next Giant Step." Exploring D.C.'s space museum. Joseph Wallace, p. 20
1984 Mar "D.C.'s Dining Renaissance." Robert L. Balzer, p. 18
"Washington, D.C." Politics aside, a capital idea. Robert Hoffman, p. 63

FLORIDA

Series Guidebooks (See Appendix 1)

Berlitz: Florida
Birnbaum: Disney World
Fisher: Florida & the Southeast
Fodor: Florida; Greater Miami & the Gold Coast
Frommer: Orlando, Disney World & EPCOT
Florida: Dollarwise
Insight: Florida

Background Reading

Burnett, Gene M.   FLORIDA'S PAST
A collection of readable essays that appeared in *Florida Trend* magazine—people and events that shaped the state. Pineapple Pr, 1986.

Carr, Archie   THE EVERGLADES
Part of the American Wilderness series. Time-Life, 1973.

Committee of the Junior League eds.   PALM BEACH ENTERTAINS
The lavish life of a prestigious resort town. Coward, 1976.

Cortes, Carlos E.   THE CUBAN EXPERIENCE IN THE U.S.
Arno, 1980.

Cox, Christopher   A KEY WEST COMPANION
"The Island's naval, economic, social, and architectural past and present" and how it evolved—for both natives and tourists. (BL) St. Martin, 1983.

Douglas, Marjory S.   THE EVERGLADES: RIVER OF GRASS
Mockingbird, 1981.

**Green, Ben   FINEST KIND: A CELEBRATION OF A FLORIDA
               FISHING VILLAGE**
Intelligent, down-home treatment of one of the few remaining fishing villages in Florida. Oral history of Cortez, and its people, and a plea to save it from real estate development and drug smuggling. Mercer U, 1985.

Harper, Francis and Presley, Delma   OKEFENOKEE ALBUM
Folklore, language, customs, songs, wildlife of the swamp. U of Georgia, 1981.

Jahoda, Gloria   FLORIDA
One of a series of popular histories for each state published as part of the

Bicentennial observance in 1976. Norton, 1984 (first published 1976). Also *The Other Florida* (1984), about the Pensacola-Tallahassee area.

Kaufelt, Lynn   KEY WEST WRITERS AND THEIR HOUSES
Writers who make up the legend of the Keys—Hemingway, Wallace Stevens, Tennessee Williams, others. Pineapple Pr, 1986.

Langley, Joan and Wright   KEY WEST, IMAGES OF THE PAST
Images, 1982.

Morris, Jan   JOURNEYS
This collection of essays by a leading travel writer includes an essay on Miami. Oxford U, 1984.

Nolan, David   FIFTY FEET IN PARADISE: THE BOOMING OF FLORIDA
Florida's flamboyant story from its first boom in the 1830s to the 1920s. HarBraceJ, 1984.

Rawlings, Marjorie K.   CROSS CREEK
Recreates vividly the memorable people the author knew from thirteen years of living at Cross Creek—a classic. Scribner, 1984 (first published 1942).

Redford, Polly   BILLION DOLLAR SANDBAR
A biography of Miami Beach—a "shrewdly knowing chronicle" and chatty history from coconut plantation to Jackie Gleason and the Republican National Convention. (BRD) Dutton, 1970.

Rothchild, John   UP FOR GRABS: A TRIP THROUGH TIME AND SPACE IN THE SUNSHINE STATE
"Personal memoir [and] history of Florida . . . grand
reading. . . . deliciously underscores the bizarre quality of Florida life." (PW) Viking, 1985.

Rudloe, Jack   THE LIVING DOCK AT PANACEA
The author started a business for providing marine life specimens to colleges—writes beautifully of the teeming life of his dock. Knopf, 1977.

Russell, Franklin   THE OKEFENOKEE SWAMP
Part of the American Wilderness series. Time-Life, 1973.

Sherrill, Chris and Aiello, Roger   KEY WEST: THE LAST RESORT
Banyan, 1980.

Shoumatoff, Alex   FLORIDA RAMBLE
An offbeat travelogue of a sixty-two day sojourn—subjects range from "indigenous birds and mushrooms to the proliferating retiree communities." (BRD) Har-Row, 1974.

Tebeau, Charlton W.   A HISTORY OF FLORIDA
The story of Florida's singular growth. U of Miami, 1981.

FLORIDA GUIDEBOOKS

Baxter, Robert   BAXTER'S FLORIDA
Rail-Europe-Baxter, 1984.

Blum, Ethel   MIAMI ALIVE
By an experienced travel writer and a resident of Miami, and intended for foreign and U.S. visitors to the area. Includes tips on Disney World, Kennedy Space Center, the Keys, and other special places in Florida. Hippocrene, 1982.

Delaney, Jack   PALM SPRINGS A LA CARTE
ETC, 1978.

Firestone, Linda and Morse, White   FLORIDA'S ENCHANTING
                                       ISLANDS— SANIBEL & CAPTIVA
Good Life, 1980.

Ford, Norman D.   NORMAN FORD'S FLORIDA
Harian, 1983.

Hayes, Edward   THE FLORIDA ONE-DAY TRIP BOOK
Orlando is the base for fifty-two offbeat excursions. EPM, 1981.

Rabkin, Richard and Jacob   NATURE GUIDE TO FLORIDA
Banyan, 1978.

Riggs, Rollin   THE RITES OF SPRING: A STUDENT'S GUIDE TO
                  SPRING BREAK IN FLORIDA
Arbor Hse, 1982.

Sehlinger, Bob   CENTRAL FLORIDA ATTRACTIONS
Menasha Ridge Pr, 1983.

University Press of Florida, ed.   FLORIDA'S SANDY BEACHES
How to get to beaches on both coasts, facilities for each, history, flora and fauna. U Pr of Florida, 1985.

Novels

Banks, Russell   CONTINENTAL DRIFT
The intersecting paths of two people told in alternating chapters: one is a New Hampshire native who takes off for Florida with his family, seeking a better life; the other a poverty-stricken Haitian who leaves Haiti for "the bright promise of America." (FC) Har-Row, 1985.

Cozzens, James G.   GUARD OF HONOR
The plot encompasses three days at a Florida air base in 1943—the conflict of

personalities, problems of authority; but in the end loyalty to one another prevails. The book won a Pulitzer Prize in 1949. HarBraceJ, 1948.

Hemingway, Ernest   TO HAVE AND HAVE NOT (Key West; Cuba)
The locale is Key West (and Cuba)—an American gets involved in smuggling when he loses his charter boat in a swindle. Scribner, 1937.

Holleran, Andrew   NIGHTS IN ARUBA
A novel about the relationship of a homosexual with his retired parents in Florida. Morrow, 1983.

Hunter, Evan   FAR FROM THE SEA
A five-day vigil at the bedside of his dying father results in spiritual rebirth for a New York lawyer. Atheneum, 1983.

Hurston, Zora Neale   SERAPH ON THE SUWANEE
By a leading black writer and a best-seller when published—about poor white "crackers" in west Florida at the beginning of the century. AMS (first published 1948). Also the recent reprint *Zora Neale Hurston Reader* (1979).

Leonard, Elmore   LA BRAVA
A former movie star now living in the South Beach area of Florida, who played a predatory spider woman, is now herself the victim of extortion. Arbor Hse, 1983.

Leonard, Elmore   STICK
An ex-convict pulls a scam on drug dealers in Miami, leaving a trail "across yachts, through mansions, and to a country club gate." (FC) Arbor Hse, 1983.

McBain, Ed   GOLDILOCKS
A gory triple murder is the basis of this police procedural. Arbor Hse, 1977.

MacDonald, John D.   THE EMPTY COPPER SEA
Set on the Florida Gulf coast and one of many Travis McGee mysteries set in Florida. Lippincott, 1978. Other titles include: *A Deadly Shade of Gold* (1974), *The Deep Blue Good-by* (1975), *The Dreadful Lemon Sky* (1975), and *The Turquoise Lament* (1973). Also *The Condominium* (1977), about life in a badly-built condo as Hurricane Ella arrives.

McGuane, Thomas   PANAMA (Key West)
Set in Key West, an ex-punk rock star tries to get his lost girlfriend back. FS&G, 1978.

McIlvain, John   WORTH AVENUE (Palm Beach)
Thirty years in the life of a heroine who is widowed by the Korean War, invited to live with her husband's dowager aunt and ends up as administrator of the family's foundation. Seaview, 1983.

Mayerson, Evelyn W.   NO ENEMY BUT TIME
A hotel in Miami Beach during World War II is the backdrop for a story that

includes two children, their parents who manage the kitchen, and assorted fascinating humans whose experiences move the reader to laughter and tears. Doubleday, 1983.

Merkin, Robert   THE SOUTH FLORIDA BOOK OF THE DEAD
A "counter-culture adventure—drugs, guns, violence and craziness" as three friends decide to try a cocaine run but quickly learn the difference between "playing for kicks and playing for keeps." (FC) Morrow, 1982.

Merle, Robert   THE DAY OF THE DOLPHIN
Political and social satire with a fantasy plot of mankind on the brink of World War III and only the "humanity" of two trained dolphins can save the world. S&S, 1969.

Moss, Robert and De Borchgrave, Arnaud   MONIMBO
"Miami [presented] with almost devastating accuracy" in a novel of international intrigue and Castro's plan for eventual destruction of the United States (based on a meeting of revolutionary leaders in Monimbo, Nicaragua). The plot takes us to many locales in telling the story, including Miami. (FC) S&S, 1983.

Palmer, Thomas   THE TRANSFER
"A first-rate thriller" about a man blackmailed by his brother into drug smuggling. Ultimately he is forced to make a decision that will allow him to go back to his former peaceful existence. (FC) Ticknor & Fields, 1983.

Price, Eugenia   MARGARET'S STORY
Third volume in a trilogy based on a nineteenth-century real life heroine; set on the St. Johns River in northern Florida. Lippincott, 1980. *Don Juan McQueen* (1974) and *Maria* (1977) are the first two books in the trilogy.

Rawlings, Marjorie K.   THE MARJORIE RAWLINGS READER
Includes *South Moon Under* and selections from novels and short stories by a leading Florida writer whose home has become a state historic site. Scribner, 1956.

Richards, Judith   SUMMER LIGHTNING
Local color and regional flavor with a plot about a young boy who prefers visiting an 80-year-old man, whose swamp shack has snakes and crocodile skins and other fascinating things, to attending first grade. St. Martin, 1978.

Smith, Patrick   A LAND REMEMBERED
Saga of the MacIvey family beginning in 1858. Pineapple Pr, 1985.

Whitney, Phyllis A.   POINCIANA
Atmospherically authentic Palm Beach background and a mildly suspenseful plot. Doubleday, 1980. Also *Dream of Orchids*, "played against a colorful backdrop of libertines and literati, gold-seekers and sun-worshipers" in Key West. (FC) (1985).

Wilder, Robert   BRIGHT FEATHER
Historical novel of Florida in the 1830s. The heir to a large plantation is involved in the plot to cheat Indians out of their lands in northern Florida. Putnam Pub Group, 1948.

Williford, Charles   MIAMI BLUES
A police procedural involving a criminal psychopath who gives a police sergeant a personal stake in locating the enemy. St. Martin, 1984.

Yglesias, Jose   THE TRUTH ABOUT THEM
Story of a "multifarious Cuban clan" beginning in Tampa in 1890. World, 1971.

TRAVEL ARTICLES

AMERICAS
1984 Jan "The World's Largest Jigsaw Puzzle." Transplanted Spanish monastery—San Bernardo de Clairvaux in Miami. Omar G. Amador, p. 23

EARLY AMERICAN LIFE
1985 Oct "Early American Destinations: Pensacola, Florida." Carol McCabe, p. 60

EBONY
1984 May "South Southeast for Summer." Florida, Bahamas, U.S. Virgin Islands and Bermuda form a vacation fun triangle. p. 173

ESQUIRE
1985 Mar "Special Places: Islands in the Stream." South Seas Plantation, Amelia Island Plantation, Cheeca Lodge, Useppa Island Club, Cabbage Key. Steven Raichlen, p. 28

ESSENCE
1984 Jun "The Wonders of Disney World." It's more than an amusement park. Sandra Jackson-Opoku, p. 34
Oct "Discovering Wildlife in Florida." Stephanie R. Hamilton, p. 58

50 PLUS
1985 Feb "It's a Small World After All." For millions of kids and their doting grandparents, Disney World remains a mecca of magic. John Zinsser, p. 42

HORIZON
1985 Jan-Feb "Dade County: A New Cultural Vision." Arts renaissance in Miami—experiencing the best it offers. Rick Eyerdam, p. 33
1984 Oct "Palm Beach: Arts Adventures in Paradise." Thriving arts community in a beautiful locale. Carolyn Jack and Gary Schwen, p. 27

HOUSE BEAUTIFUL
1985 Nov "Travel: Your Guide to the Islands." Caribbean, Bermuda and Florida islands. Hazel Carr, p. 41

NATIONAL GEOGRAPHIC TRAVELER

1985 Winter "Florida's Underwater Wilderness." Jerry Greenberg, p. 80
1984 Spring "EPCOT—the Ultimate World's Fair." Here's how to minimize waits
and maximize enjoyment. Catherine O'Neill, p. 42

N.Y. TIMES SUNDAY TRAVEL SECTION (X)

1985 Jan 27 "Heading South in a Hurry." Spur-of-the-moment travels in the
Caribbean, Mexico and Florida. Stanley Carr, p. 15
Feb 3 "From English Pub to Chinese Pagoda." EPCOT's eerie but endearing
sameness. Paul Goldberger, p. 19
Feb 24 "What's Doing in Palm Beach." Jon Nordheimer, p. 10
Mar 3 "The Spa Life in Florida." Tia S. Denenberg, p. 22
Mar 31 "What's Doing in Fort Lauderdale." Jon Nordheimer, p. 10
Aug 18 Shopper's World: "Prints to Cherish in Paris." Museum shops. Selma
Rattner, p. 6
Dec 29 "What's Doing in Key West." Walter Logan, p. 10
1984 Jan 8 "Japanese Idyll in Florida." Morikani Museum. Lewis Funke, p. 20
Jan 15 "What's Doing in Tampa." Reginald Stuart, p. 10
Jan 22 "Birdwatchers' Florida Retreat." Ira H. Freeman, p. 20
Jan 29 "What's Doing in Sarasota." Fred Ferretti, p. 10
Mar 11 "Swamp Life of Okefenokee." National Wildlife Refuge on the
Florida-Georgia border. D.W. Bennett, p. 22
Mar 18 "What's Doing in Orlando." Cheryl Blackerby, p. 10
Mar 18 (Part 2, "Sophisticated Traveler") "Key West Dialogues." Two
writers compare notes on views of the resort from Conchtown to
celebritytown, with many detours. Mary Lee Settle and Ann Beattie, p. 92
Apr 8 "Boca Raton: Florida Luxury." Cheryl Blackerby, p. 24
1984 Nov 25 "What's Doing in Miami." Jon Nordheimer, p. 10

SATURDAY EVENING POST

1985 Oct "Renaissance in Miami—New Moon Over Miami." John McCollister, p.
62

SUNSET

1985 Oct "Pogo's Swampy Home: Okefenokee." p. 29

TRAVEL & LEISURE

1985 Feb "Relaxation and Renewal at Florida's Palm-Aire." And other soothing
places (spas in Florida and California). Judith B. Wylie, p. 114
Aug "Dining Out in Sarasota." Charles Monaghan, p. 42
Oct "Florida: Where the Bargains Are." David Martindale, p. 30
1984 Feb "Latest From Walt Disney World." Sandra Hinson, p. 37
"A Special Place in the Sun." Daytona Beach, year-round playground right at
the surf's edge. Richard Carroll, p. 66
May "Restaurants of Walt Disney World." Charles Monaghan, p. 84
Nov "At Ease in the Florida Keys." A soft swing south to Key West.
Christopher Cox, p. 100

TRAVEL/HOLIDAY

1985 Jan "Captiva Castaways." Hiding away in Florida. Lorcan Roche, p. 14
Jun "Miami—on the Crest of a New Wave." Scott Shane, p. 52

1984 Mar "Shuttle Gazing." James Piper, p. 144
    Oct "Sarasota's Ringling Museums—Legacy of a Ringmaster." Tom and
    Joanne O'Toole, p. 4
    Dec "Port of Call: Pensacola." R&R on Florida's west coast. Paul Cook, p. 20

WORKING WOMAN
1984 Feb "A Businesswoman's Guide to Miami." Molly A. Staub, p. 124

GEORGIA

Background Reading

**Bessonette, Colin   BACK ROADS AND CITY STREETS: WEEKEND
                    GETAWAYS IN AND AROUND GEORGIA**
Peachtree Pbns, 1984.

Fancher, Betsy   THE LOST LEGACY OF GEORGIA'S GOLDEN ISLES
A combination of history, anecdote, folklore and local customs of islands from
Beaufort to Brunswick. Larlin, 1979.

**Givin, Yolande   YOLANDE'S ATLANTA: FROM THE HISTORICAL TO
                   THE HYSTERICAL**
Peachtree Pbns, 1983.

Harper, Francis and Presley, Delma   OKEFENOKEE ALBUM
Folklore, language, customs, songs, wildlife of the swamp in southeastern
Georgia and northern Florida. U of Georgia, 1981.

Kahn, E.J. Jr.   GEORGIA FROM RABUN GAP TO TYBEE LIGHT
Cherokee, 1978.

Klenbort, Daniel and Marcia   THE ROAD TO PLAINS
Guide to Plains and nearby places of interest in southwest Georgia. Avery, 1977.

Maister, Philippa   THE INSIDER'S ATLANTA
Good Hope, 1982.

Martin, Harold H.   GEORGIA
One of a series of popular histories for each state published as part of the
Bicentennial observance in 1976. Norton, 1977.

Price, Eugenia   AT HOME ON ST. SIMONS
The story of finding the island and writing the St. Simons trilogy of novels (see
under "Novels," below). Peachtree Pbns, 1981.

Rauers, Betty   SOJOURN IN SAVANNAH
The official guidebook and map of Savannah and the surrounding countryside.
Sojourn in Savannah, 1980.

Russell, Franklin   THE OKEFENOKEE SWAMP
Part of the American Wilderness series. Time-Life, 1973.

Smith, Susan H.   MARMAC GUIDE TO ATLANTA
Marmac, 1983.

Steed, Hal   GEORGIA: THE UNFINISHED STATE
Story of a still-evolving dynamic state. Cherokee, 1976.

Stokes, Thomas L.   SAVANNAH
U of Georgia, 1982.

Trillin, Calvin   AN EDUCATION IN GEORGIA
The integration of Charlayne Hunter and Hamilton Holmes into the Georgia
university system; began a new era for black students. Viking, 1964.

Van Story, Burnette L.   GEORGIA'S LAND OF GOLDEN ISLES
Georgia's offshore islands, with an introduction by novelist Eugenia Price (see
"Novels," below). U of Georgia, 1980.

Watters, Pat   COCA COLA: AN ILLUSTRATED HISTORY
The born-in-Georgia American pop culture symbol. Doubleday, 1978.

Wigginton, Eliot   FOXFIRE
A landmark series of books that has since been emulated by other high schools
in other states. It was begun by a schoolteacher in north Georgia as a classroom
writing project that would help to preserve local culture while providing students
with an educational experience in research and writing. The series (there are
eight books at this time) covers all aspects of "plain living" from log-cabin building
to midwifery to musical instruments and gardening, toys and games—every imaginable subject. *Foxfire* 7 is about the single subject of mountain religion.
Doubleday/Anchor, 1970.

Williford, William B.   PEACHTREE STREET
Originally published by the University of Georgia Press. Mockingbird, 1975.

Novels

Andrews, Raymond   BABY SWEET'S
One of several novels about black life in a small southern town in Muskhogean
County. Baby Sweet's is an eatery turned sporting house. Dial, 1983. In
Appalachee Red (1978) a mulatto son of an influential white man and a black maid
returns to the south to face his father. *Rosiebelle Lee Wildcat* (1980) is a novel of a

half-Indian, half-black woman in 1906 who becomes the mistress of the richest man in town.

Bambara, Toni C.   THE SALTEATERS
Two black women of different generations—an old-timer and a young revolutionary. Random, 1980.

Battle, Lois   SOUTHERN WOMEN
Saga of a prominent Savannah family. St. Martin, 1984.

Burns, Olive Ann   COLD SASSY TREE
"Humorously poignant coming-of-age story set in turn-of-the-century Georgia . . . . Authentic period piece brimming with charm, sentiment and local color." (BL) Ticknor & Fields, 1984.

Caldwell, Erskine   TOBACCO ROAD
Degeneration of a poor-white Georgia family, living on the once-prosperous farm of Jeeter Lester's grandfather—told with humor and irreverence "that verges upon the . . . ribaldry of a burlesque show." (FC) Bentley, 1978 (first published 1932). Also *God's Little Acre* (1932)—"one of the finest studies of the Southern poor white."

Coleman, Lonnie   BEULAH LAND
This, followed by *Look Away Beulah Land* (1977) and *The Legacy of Beulah Land* (1980), begins a trilogy about nineteenth-century, antebellum plantation life. Doubleday, 1973.

Feegel, John R.   MALPRACTICE
Set in a small Georgia town—a young lawyer takes a poor black's malpractice suit involving the death of her son; his inquiries uncover gross negligence at the local hospital. NAL, 1981.

Fields, Jeff   A CRY OF ANGELS
An orphan, with his great-aunt, runs a boarding house in Quarrytown. Atheneum, 1974.

Hodge, Jane A.   SAVANNAH PURCHASE
Historical novel, set in Savannah, involving a plan to free Napoleon. Doubleday, 1971.

Hood, Mary   HOW FAR SHE WENT
"Wonderful, and often heartbreaking" short stories of the rural South. (FC) U of Georgia, 1984.

Kay, Terry   THE YEAR THE LIGHTS CAME ON
Story of youth in rural Georgia in 1947. Houghton, 1975.

Kluger, Richard   MEMBERS OF THE TRIBE
A young Jewish man from New York City in post-Civil War Savannah. Doubleday, 1977.

McCammon, Robert   MYSTERY WALK
Two young brothers (one a tent revival faith healer, the other with the gift to help spirits of those who die violently to "pass over") in a novel of horror and the supernatural—"delivers a good scare with style." (FC) Holt, 1983.

McCullers, Carson   MEMBER OF THE WEDDING
A fictional study in child psychology—the wedding of her older brother seen through the eyes of a twelve-year-old girl "with her six-year-old cousin, and the black cook as chorus." (FC) Houghton, 1946.

Mitchell, Margaret   GONE WITH THE WIND
Winston Churchill called it America's *War and Peace*. The Civil War, and Atlanta and plantation life, just before, during and following the war. Macmillan, 1936.

O'Connor, Flannery   FLANNERY O'CONNOR'S GEORGIA
Stories by a leading American writer. FS&G, 1980. Also *The Complete Stories of Flannery O'Connor* (1971).

Price, Eugenia   SAVANNAH
A leisurely "excursion through 13 years of the city's history" told through the story of an orphan who immigrates to Savannah and is befriended by both imagined and actual historical characters. The story begins in 1812. (Publisher) Doubleday, 1983. *To See Your Face Again* (1984) is a sequel, beginning in 1838—"scrupulously researched . . . fascinating history."

Price, Eugenia   THE BELOVED INVADER (St. Simons Island)
Based on an actual event and the person who rebuilt a Civil War church. Lippincott, 1965. It is the first published of a trilogy that includes *Lighthouse* (1971) and *New Moon Rising* (1969), but chronologically takes place last.

Siddons, Anne R.   FOX'S EARTH
A girl rescued from poverty succeeds in taking over the mansion of her rescuer and establishing her own succession to the mansion. S&S, 1981.

Siddons, Anne R.   HEARTBREAK HOTEL
A Southern sorority girl grows up. S&S, 1967.

Vonnegut, Kurt   JAILBIRD
"Superb, zany satire" of a victim of Watergate, released from jail, who retreats into flashbacks of his past. (FC) Delacorte Pr, 1979.

Walker, Margaret   JUBILEE
A novel of the pre- and post-Civil War south—"fidelity of fact and detail . . . presents little-known every day life of slaves" as well as landowners and poor whites. (FC) Houghton, 1966.

Whitney, Phyllis A.   LOST ISLAND
A romance set on an island off the coast of Georgia—the heroine returns after many years' absence to confront the truths of the past. Doubleday, 1970.

Woods, Stuart   CHIEFS
Three police chiefs—a farmer, a racist, a black—must deal with the same case in a small Georgia town involving the disappearance of a series of white, teenaged boys. Norton, 1981.

TRAVEL ARTICLES

GOURMET
1984 Dec "Atlanta's High Museum." Of art. Irene Corbally Kuhn, p. 48

HOUSE BEAUTIFUL
1984 Dec "Christmas in Savannah." Mervyn Kaufman, p. 43

NATIONAL GEOGRAPHIC TRAVELER
1985 Spring "Okefenokee." Georgia's watery wilderness: on a canoe expedition, paddle past a basking alligator. Edward Hoagland, p. 120

N.Y. TIMES SUNDAY TRAVEL SECTION (X)
1985 Mar 17 "What's Doing in Savannah." Fay S. Joyce, p. 10
        Apr 7 "What's Doing in Atlanta." William E. Schmidt, p. 10
1984 Mar 11 "What's Doing in Atlanta." William E. Schmidt, p. 10
        "Swamp Life of Okefenokee." National Wildlife Refuge on the Florida-Georgia border. D. W. Bennett, p. 22
        Oct 7 (Part 2, "Sophisticated Traveler") "Atlanta: Beer and the Bard." Manuel's Tavern. William E. Schmidt, p. 126

SATURDAY EVENING POST
1985 Apr "Georgia's Answer to Eden." Callaway Gardens. Maynard G. Stoddard, p. 90

TRAVEL & LEISURE
1984 Jan "The Flowering of Savannah." Maria Shaw, p. 44

TRAVEL/HOLIDAY
1985 May "Georgia at Its Finest." Making time for Macon. Frank Bianco, p. 70
        Dec "Marching Onward, Atlanta's Historical Rebirth." Joseph Wallace, p. 12

VOGUE
1985 Apr "Seductive Savannah: a Powerful Port Town with Gutsy Charm." Jan Morris, p. 266

HAWAII

Series Guidebooks (See Appendix 1)

Berlitz: Hawaii
Birnbaum: Hawaii
Fisher: Hawaii
Fodor: Hawaii; Budget Travel Hawaii;
        Fun in Waikiki;
        Good Time Guide to Oahu
Frommer: Hawaii: $-a-Day; Hawaii: City Guide
Insight: Hawaii

Background Reading

Bailey, Paul   THOSE KINGS AND QUEENS OF OLD HAWAII
Hawaii's early native royalty makes for fascinating history. Western Lore, 1975.

Bisignani, J.D.   MAUI HANDBOOK
Moon Pbns Ca, 1986.

Bone, Robert W.   MAVERICK GUIDE TO HAWAII
A comprehensive guide to all six islands including background material and a review of tourist services for the prospective traveler—literate, accurate, comprehensive. (BP) Pelican, 1984.

Brennan, Joseph   THE PARKER RANCH OF HAWAII
"Saga of a ranch and a dynasty" chronicling the varying fortunes and history of an influential family whose founder jumped ship in 1809 and married the king's granddaughter. (BRD) Barnes & Noble, 1974.

Chester, Carol   HAWAIIAN ISLANDS
Hippocrene, 1984.

Clark, John R.   THE BEACHES OF MAUI COUNTY
History and anecdotes along with practical information on every beach of Maui, Molokai, Lanai, Kahoolawe and Molokini. U. Pr of Hawaii, 1980. Also *The Beaches of O'ahu* (1977).

Daws, Gavan   SHOAL OF TIME
A history of the Hawaiian Islands "told with style and, at times, a nice wit." (PW) U. Pr of Hawaii, 1974.

Day, Arthur G. and Stroven, Carl, eds.   A HAWAIIAN ISLAND READER
Literary writings of Mark Twain, James Michener, Jack London and others, arranged chronologically. Appleton, 1959.

Gleasner, Bill and Diana   MAUI TRAVELER'S GUIDE
Oriental, 1985. Part of a series that also includes: *Kauai* (1978), *Oahu* (1978), *Big Island* (1978)—all the basic information plus material on adventures, car and camper rentals, tours, etc.

Gray, Francine du Plessix   HAWAII: THE SUGAR-COATED FORTRESS
"A compelling and fascinating account" of Hawaii just as it became our fiftieth state, with a focus on its problems. (BRD) Random, 1972.

Joesting, Edward   HAWAII: AN UNCOMMON HISTORY
"A very readable work on snippets of Hawaiian history" and emphasizing personalities and colorful events of its past. (BRD) Norton, 1978.

Kane, Robert S.   ALL THE BEST IN HAWAII
One of a new "World at Its Best" series of travel guidebooks by a noted travel authority, "oriented toward the discriminating traveler." Highlights the best a place has to offer, including hotels in a range of prices—"evaluates the entire itinerary. Big city wonders and . . . out-of-the-way adventure spots." Passport, 1985.

Lawliss, Chuck   HAWAII FOR THE SOPHISTICATED TRAVELER
Island by island impressions with specific advice on where to "stay and play . . . touring ideas . . . odd scraps of information." (LJ) McGraw, 1984.

Loomis, Albertine   FOR WHOM ARE THE STARS?
Three years starting from 1893, when the last queen of Hawaii surrendered the throne, the beginning of Hawaii as a republic, and the attempt of the queen's supporters to restore the monarchy. U. Pr of Hawaii, 1976.

Rapson, Richard L.   FAIRLY LUCKY YOU LIVE HAWAII
Hawaii's cultural pluralism. U. Pr of America, 1980.

Riegert, Ray   HIDDEN HAWAII: THE ADVENTURER'S GUIDE
"For those who like to get away from the tourist lanes and follow a fresh track. . . . Inexpensive lodgings and restaurants, groceries and gift shops . . . beaches and parks . . . how to live off the land, etc. (LJ) Ulysses, 1983.

Smith, Bradford   YANKEES IN PARADISE—THE NEW ENGLAND IMPACT ON HAWAII
Based on diaries and journals, the story of three decades of missionaries. Lippincott, 1956.

Stephan, John   HAWAII UNDER THE RISING SUN
Japan's plans for conquest of Hawaii after Pearl Harbor and the role that Japanese-Americans in Hawaii were expected to play. U. Pr of Hawaii Pr, 1984.

Stevenson, Robert L.   TRAVELS IN HAWAII
The author's experiences and reactions to Hawaii in the nineteenth century. U. Pr of Hawaii, 1973.

Sunset eds.   HAWAII: A GUIDE TO ALL THE ISLANDS
Sunset-Lane, 1984.

Tabrah, Ruth   HAWAII
One of a series of popular histories for each state published as part of the
Bicentennial observance in 1976. Norton, 1980 (first published 1976).

Twain, Mark   LETTERS FROM HAWAII
Edited by A. Grove Day (see *Hawaiian Reader*, above). U. Pr of Hawaii, 1975.

Van Campen, Shirley   HAWAII: A WOMAN'S GUIDE
Chicago Review, 1979.

Wallace, Robert   HAWAII
Part of the American Wilderness series. Time-Life, 1973.

Novels

Bushnell, Oswald A.   THE WATER OF KANE
The Japanese in Hawaii. U. Press of Hawaii, 1980.

Jones, James   FROM HERE TO ETERNITY
The best-seller, in its day, of army life in pre-Pearl Harbor Hawaii and a love
affair between an enlisted man and an officer's wife. Delacorte Pr, 1980.

Katkov, Norman   BLOOD AND ORCHIDS
Set in Hawaii in the 1930s and based on an actual case of a group of Hawaiian
beach boys accused of raping an American officer's wife; vigilante justice. The
ultimate truth revealed is "even more sordid and scandalous than originally
supposed." (FC) St. Martin, 1983.

London, Jack   STORIES OF HAWAII
Stories written while London was living in Hawaii, with a wide range of
themes—"captures the flavor of life there at the turn of the century." (FC)
Appleton, 1965.

Michener, James A.   HAWAII
A "monumental account of the islands from geologic birth to emergence as a
state," explored through its racial origins and several narrative strands. (FC)
Random, 1959.

Moore, Susanna   MY OLD SWEETHEART
The narrator, Lily, is the daughter of an "elegant, erratic mother" who becomes
dependent on her when on drugs or suffering from delusions. Lily finds, years
later, that she herself must deal with a similar dependency developing with her
own daughter. "The lush atmosphere of Hawaii hangs over the reader's armchair."
(FC) Houghton, 1982.

Nash, N. Richard   **EAST WIND, RAIN**
Illicit love, revenge and espionage at Pearl Harbor in 1941. Atheneum, 1977.

TRAVEL ARTICLES

BLACK ENTERPRISE
1985 Nov "Great Wheels of Fire." The fun and excitement of bicycling down a
volcano (Haleakala). Robert Steyer, p. 103

BON APPETIT
1985 Nov "Traveling with Taste: Waikiki." Richard J. Pietschmann, p. 40

ESQUIRE
1985 Oct "Blue Hawaii." Michael Leonard, p. 16 (following p. 124)
1984 Apr "Seven Trips to Work in Around Work." Includes Hawaii. p. 114

50 PLUS
1985 Oct "The Necklace of Lush Tropical Islands Will Stir Your Soul." Edwin
Kiester, Jr., p. 35

GLAMOUR
1984 Aug "Hawaii: There's an Island in Paradise for You." p. 216

GOOD HOUSEKEEPING
1984 Feb "The Best of Hawaii." Stephen Birnbaum, p. 180

GOURMET
1984 Apr Gourmet Holidays: "Hawaii, the Big Island." Caroline Bates, p. 44

HARPER'S BAZAAR
1984 Oct "Unknown Oahu." Digby Diehl, p. 28

MODERN MATURITY
1985 Dec-Jan "Waikiki Wanderings." The heart of a small town beats strongly
among big hotels and shops. Charles Barnard, p. 42
1984 Aug-Sep "An Island Affair: Why I'm in Love with Hawaii." Charles N. Barnard,
p. 48

NATIONAL GEOGRAPHIC TRAVELER
1985 Autumn "The Big Island: Hawaii in Essence." Kenneth Brower, p. 30
1984 Spring "Maui." Hawaii's valley isle. Robert W. Bone, p. 148

N.Y. TIMES SUNDAY TRAVEL SECTION (X)
1985 Jan 13 "Hawaii's Lunar Land." Volcanic eruptions shaped the Big Island's
northwest. Marcia Seligson, p. 14
"In the Crater of Haleakala." Fletcher Knebel, p. 14
"Along the Kona Coast." Sites and structures form a link with Hawaii's rich
history. James D. Houston, p. 15
"What's Doing in Honolulu." Robert Trumbull, p. 16

Feb 24 "Maui's Sleepy Hamlet." Lush little Hana has 400 permanent residents and about 1,000 visitors a day. Fletcher Knebel, p. 9

Jun 2 "Riding [Horseback] Holiday in Hawaii." Tia S. Denenberg, p. 25

Sep 22 "Path of the Fire-eyed Goddess." Volcanoes. James D. Houston, p. 15

Dec 15 "My Little Grass Condo." A visitor has seen dramatic changes over more than fifty years—not all for the best—in Hawaii. Robert Trumbull, p. 37

1984 Mar 18 (Part 2, "Sophisticated Traveler") "My Good Green Place." A Hawaiian landscape so verdant that the occasional gray day has the value of a pearl. Leon Edel, p. 85

Oct 7 (Part 2, "Sophisticated Traveler") "Surprises Great and Small: New England in Honolulu." Fletcher Knebel, p. 8

SATURDAY EVENING POST

1984 Mar "Hawaii: Outlook on Paradise." Ted Kreiter, p. 90

SUNSET

1985 Jan "Where Children Can Discover Hawaii." Bishop Museum. p. 56

Mar "Blame It on the Road . . . Maui's Hana . . ." A glorious piece of old Hawaii (Hana Highway and how to explore the Hana coast). p. 100

May "Just North of Hilo, a Tropical Garden Invites Strolling." p. 48

Jun "Hawaii's Japanese Are Celebrating Their Centennial." p. 78

"Video Art in San Francisco . . ." Screenings, classes at museums. p. 82

Jul "Off-the-beaten-track Lodging." p. 54

Dec "Holiday Doings in Hawaii's Churches, Temples, Shrines." p. 30b

1984 Jan "Old, Exotic Market in Honolulu." Oahu. p. 36

Feb "Tropical Discovery on Kauai." Plan ahead to see the Pacific Tropical Botanical Garden. p. 86

Mar "Honolulu's New Maritime Museum." p. 39

Apr "Lonesome Lighthouse at Kauai's Tip." p. 72

Aug "Where to Run in Hawaii." p. 46

Oct "Hawaii's Plate Lunch, Generous, Never Gourmet, 2 to 5 Dollar Bargain." p. 70

Dec "Snorkeling Hawaii's West Coast." p. 52

TRAVEL & LEISURE

1985 Oct "Hawaii: America the Exotic." Pamela Fiori, p. 4

1984 Jan "Where to Eat in Honolulu." From homegrown Hawaiian to haute French. Charles Monaghan, p. 62

Sep "Hawaii Beckons with a Sunny Assortment of Trips." Tours. Richard J. Pietschmann, p. 90

Dec "Latest from Hawaii." The scoop on what's new and different in the islands. Darian Dixon, p. 33

TRAVEL/HOLIDAY

1985 Mar "Five Island Adventures." Taking advantage of Hawaii's great outdoors. Carol Canter, p. 80

Oct "Paradise: the Way It Should Be." A guide to low-cost attractions in Hawaii. Dr. Sarkis A. Takesian, p. 32

Nov "The Rising Sun Sets in Hawaii— Tale of Two Cultures." Rita Ariyoshi, p. 60

1984 May "Captain Cook Never Had It So Good." Dining in paradise, a cruise around the Hawaiian Islands. Robert L. Balzer, p. 80

"Diamond Head." A high point of Hawaii. Hal Butler, p. 32

VOGUE

1984 May "Hawaiian High! An Adventure in Paradise." At Mauna Kea. Dena Kaye, p. 259

IDAHO

Background Reading

Conley, Cort   IDAHO FOR THE CURIOUS: A GUIDE
Backeddy Bks, 1982.

Jensen, Dwight W.   VISITING BOISE: A PERSONAL GUIDE
Caxton, 1981.

Oppenheimer, Doug and Poore, Jim   SUN VALLEY
A biography of the town and resort. Beatty, 1976.

Peterson, F. Ross   IDAHO
One of a series of popular histories for each state published as part of the Bicentennial observance in 1976. Norton, 1976.

Sparling, Wayne   SOUTHERN IDAHO GHOST TOWNS
Caxton, 1974.

Novels

Brink, Carol   STRANGERS IN THE RIVER
Story about the efforts of a group of U.S. foresters in the panhandle section of Idaho to conserve the forests there in the early years of the century, and the secret mission of one of them to try to figure out which homesteaders would actually farm the land and which would sell out to the lumber industry. Macmillan, 1960. Other novels with an Idaho background by this author are: *Buffalo Coat* (1944) and *Snow in the River* (1964).

Fisher, Vardis   IN TRAGIC LIFE
One of Fisher's highly realistic novels—"crudities and hardships of life on a western farm a generation ago." (BRD) Caxton, 1932. Other novels by Fisher with an Idaho setting are: *Dark Bridwell* (1931) and *Toilers of the Hill* (1928).

Ross, Dana F.   IDAHO!
Part of a series of novels with the overall title of *Wagons West* that chronicles the conquest and settlement of the American West. Bantam, 1984.

TRAVEL ARTICLES

NATIONAL GEOGRAPHIC TRAVELER
1984 Winter "Sun Valley's a Peak Experience." Sandra Lee Crow, p. 140

N.Y. TIMES SUNDAY TRAVEL SECTION (X)
1985 Jun 23 "The Power of Hell's Canyon." Snake River. Skip K. Rosin, p. 20

SUNSET
1985 Feb "Above and Beyond the Slopes at Sun Valley." Soaring, sledding, snowshoeing, and much more to do. p. 50

VOGUE
1985 Dec "Sun Valley: the Glamour Goes On." Jeanne McCulloch, p. 232

ILLINOIS

Series Guidebooks (See Appendix 1)

Fodor: Chicago

Background Reading

Algren, Nelson   CITY ON THE MAKE
New edition of the novelist's hymn to Chicago, with an introduction by Studs Terkel. McGraw, 1983 (first published 1951).

Appleberg, Marilyn J.   I LOVE CHICAGO GUIDE
Part of a series—see annotation for "Boston." Macmillan, 1982.

Bach, Ira J. and Wolfson, Susan   A GUIDE TO CHICAGO'S HISTORIC SUBURBS ON WHEELS AND ON FOOT
Walking guides to Lake, McHenry, Kane, DuPage, Will and Cook Counties and to neighborhoods and architectural landmarks. Swallow, 1981.

Bach, Ira J.   A GUIDE TO CHICAGO'S PUBLIC SCULPTURES
U of Chicago, 1983.

Berger, Philip   HIGHLAND PARK: AMERICAN SUBURB AT ITS BEST
Chicago Review Pr, 1983.

Berkow, Ira   MAXWELL STREET: SURVIVAL IN A BAZAAR
Focuses on Eastern European Jews and the open-air markets on Chicago's west side, 1880-1924. Doubleday, 1977.

Black, Harry G.   TRAILS TO ILLINOIS HERITAGE
Guidebook for historic sites of Illinois. HMB Pbns, 1982.

Cromie, Robert   CHICAGO
"A tribute to a city" by a noted Chicago journalist and broadcaster. "Text and photographs emphasize the geographical features and architectural treasures that set Chicago apart." (BL) Rand, 1980.

Cromie, Robert   A SHORT HISTORY OF CHICAGO
"Anecdotal . . . entertaining, history of Chicago from Marquette's icebound explorations in 1674 [to] Harold Washington." (BL) Lexikos, 1984.

Cutler, Irving   CHICAGO: METROPOLIS OF THE MID-CONTINENT
Third edition of a history. Kendall-Hunt, 1982.

Dedmon, Emmett   FABULOUS CHICAGO
"A respected Chicago journalist takes a lively, long view of his home town's feats and foibles." (TL) Atheneum, 1983.

DeMuth, James   SMALL TOWN CHICAGO
"The comic perspective of Finley Peter Dunne, George Ade and Ring Lardner . . . ordinary life that surrounds the creation of literature." Kennikat, 1980.

Drury, John   OLD ILLINOIS HOUSES
U of Chicago, 1977.

**Eberle, Nancy   RETURN TO MAIN STREET: A JOURNEY TO
                      ANOTHER AMERICA**
Evokes the dream of many—moving from the city to a farm and small river town in Illinois. Norton, 1982.

Fleming, Thomas   LIVING LAND OF LINCOLN
Readers' Digest Pr, 1980.

Jensen, Richard J.   ILLINOIS
One of a series of popular histories for each state published as part of the Bicentennial observance in 1976. Norton, 1978.

**Kelson, Allen H. and others   CHICAGO MAGAZINE'S GUIDE
                                    TO CHICAGO**
"Potpourri of notable sights and activities throughout Chicago's neighborhoods"—lists of shops, useful phone numbers, chapters on museums,

libraries, sports, etc., restaurants, and it has a foreword by Studs Terkel. (TL) Contemporary Bks, 1983.

Longstreet, Stephen   CHICAGO, AN INTIMATE PORTRAIT OF PEOPLE, PLEASURES, AND POWER: 1860-1919
The book draws upon firsthand memories and commentary of Dreiser, Upton Sinclair, Sandburg, Sinclair Lewis and others. McKay, 1973.

McGreevy, John, ed.   CITIES
Impressions of world cities as seen through the eyes of people intimately connected with them—for Chicago, it's Studs Terkel's impressions. Potter, 1981.

Madden, Betty I.   ARTS, CRAFTS AND ARCHITECTURE IN EARLY ILLINOIS
American artifacts as "mirroring regional history." (BRD) U of Illinois, 1974.

Mark, Norman   CHICAGO: WALK, BICYCLING AND DRIVING TOURS OF THE CITY
"The city itself is the star of the tours.... The descriptions and histories ... are so entertaining [that] some may consider it unnecessary to take the walks [and rides] at all. But that would be a shame." Fourteen walking tours, a bicycle tour along the lakefront, three driving tours, and six "pub crawls." (Heise) Chicago Rev Pr, 1980.

Michaelson, Mikle   WEEKEND GETAWAY GUIDE, CHICAGO
Rand, 1984.

Morris, Jan   PLACES
This collection of a leading travel writer's essays includes one on Chicago. HarBraceJ, 1973.

Royko, Mike   LIKE I WAS SAYIN'
Columns from Chicago newspapers over two decades—"observes the passing parade with inimitable wit and intelligence." (PW) Dutton, 1984.

Stein, Shifra   GAS-SAVING GETAWAY LESS THAN TWO HOURS FROM GREATER MINNEAPOLIS-ST. PAUL
The day trips described spill over into Illinois, as do the excursions included in Stein's similar guide to Greater St. Louis. Har-Row, 1982.

Struever, Stuart and Holton, Felicia A.   KOSTER: AMERICANS IN SEARCH OF THEIR PREHISTORIC PAST
Excavations of a 9500-year-old site in Illinois. NAL, 1980.

Terkel, Studs   DIVISION STREET: AMERICA
Interviews by a master interviewer with seventy people living in or near Chicago and of diverse ages, ethnic backgrounds and general circumstances—"a remarkable book" evoking city life through the eyes of these people. (BRD) Pantheon, 1982 (first published 1966).

Williams, Kenny J.   IN THE CITY OF MEN: ANOTHER STORY OF CHICAGO
Chiefly concerned with writers and architects. Townsend Pr, 1974.

Novels

Bradbury, Ray   DANDELION WINE
A summer in the life of a twelve-year-old boy and his brother in Green Town, Illinois, in 1928—"a rare reading experience." (FC) Knopf, 1975.

Ferber, Edna   SO BIG
A young woman's never-ending drudgery as wife of a farmer and her "gay, indomitable spirit" and disappointment in being unable to transmit her view of life to her son. (FC) Doubleday, 1951 (first published 1924).

Greenberg, Marilyn   THE RABBI'S LIFE
Set in a Chicago suburb—a rabbi returns from his sabbatical in Israel only to be asked for his resignation. "A depiction of the tangled motives of a diverse community . . . a saintly man trying to cope with his rejection." (FC) Doubleday, 1983.

Maxwell, William   SO LONG, SEE YOU TOMORROW
A retrospective search for understanding of boyhood events fifty years earlier—the death of his mother, the trial of a friend's father for murder, his own sin against that friend. Knopf, 1980.

Smiley, Jane   BARN BLIND
The story of a controlling woman who breeds and shows horses, and applies some of the same disciplines to managing her family. Har-Row, 1980.

Wakefield, Dan   UNDER THE APPLE TREE
A pleasant stroll down Memory Lane of the homefront in Illinois during World War II. Delacorte Pr, 1982.

Wilder, Thornton   THE EIGHTH DAY
Saga of two Coaltown, Illinois, families whose lives intertwine over the period of three generations. Har-Row, 1967.

Woiwode, Larry   BEYOND THE BEDROOM WALL
A family chronicle beginning in Illinois in the 1930s, ending in contemporary North Dakota. FS&G, 1975.

CHICAGO

Algren, Nelson   THE MAN WITH THE GOLDEN ARM
Chicago slum life that leads to suicide. Bentley, 1978 (first published 1949).

Bellow, Saul   THE ADVENTURES OF AUGIE MARCH
Life of the son of Russian-Jewish immigrants; Bellow won a Nobel Prize in 1976.

Viking, 1953. Also set in Chicago, *Humboldt's Gift* (1975) and *Dangling Man* (1944). *The Dean's December* (1982) is set in both Chicago and Bucharest (see "Rumania/Novels").

Birmingham, Stephen   THE AUERBACH WILL
"Saga of a mail-order house family dynasty. . . . [Sears & Roebuck come to mind . . . though without substantiation]." (FC) Little, 1983.

Brooks, Gwendolyn   MAUD MARTHA
Life of a poor black girl on Chicago's south side. AMS, 1974 (first published 1953).

Dreiser, Theodore   SISTER CARRIE
Realistic novel of lower middle class life in Chicago (later New York) and the particular life of a woman's career in vice and a man's moral disintegration. Penguin, 1981 (first published 1900). *Jennie Gerhardt* (1911) is another turn-of-the-century novel of the "realism" genre, set in Chicago.

Elkin, Stanley   THE CONDOMINIUM
In *Searches and Seizures*—a novella of life in a Chicago apartment complex that's "a nightmare of materialism." (FC) Random, 1973.

Elward, James   ASK FOR NOTHING MORE
The plot involves a realtor, his ill wife, and the nurse brought in to care for her, who becomes the husband's "back street" mistress. Har-Row, 1984.

Farrell, James T.   STUDS LONIGAN
A trilogy that includes the titles *Young Lonigan*, *The Young Manhood of Studs Lonigan* and *Judgment Day*, about Irish-Americans in Chicago. Vanguard, 1978 (first published 1932-35). Also *The Dunne Family* (1976) and its sequel *The Death of Nora Ryan* (1978), and *A World I Never Made* (1936) set in Chicago and about Irish-Americans.

Gash, Joe   PRIESTLY MURDERS
A police procedural involving the Chicago police department—"terse, gritty and exciting." The plot concerns a priest who is shot during mass; several eyewitnesses identify a cop as his murderer. (FC) HR&W, 1984.

Greeley, Andrew M.   LORD OF THE DANCE
Third in a trilogy about the misdeeds of a powerful Irish Catholic family, called "The Passover Trilogy." Warner Bks, 1984. *Thy Brother's Wife* (1982) is first, followed by *Ascent Into Hell* (1983). Also, by Greeley, is *The Cardinal Sins* (1981).

Griffith, Bill   TIME FOR FRANK COOLIN
"An engaging portrait of a tough guy under pressure"—a Chicago hustler in the building trades is implicated in a theft ring. (FC) Random, 1982.

Hailey, Arthur   AIRPORT
Behind-the-scenes at a major airport during one day when "every imaginable man, machine or function goes wrong." (FC) Doubleday, 1968.

Howland, Bette   BLUE IN CHICAGO
"Short stories centering on people and events drawn from the author's working class Jewish background." (BRD) HR&W, 1978.

Levin, Meyer   THE OLD BUNCH
Follows the lives of a group of Jewish young people from high school in the 1920s to the Chicago World's Fair in 1934—"a remarkable piece of mosaic work in social history." (FC) Viking, 1937.

Motley, Willard   KNOCK ON ANY DOOR
Stark story of the dregs of society in Chicago. Random, 1947. The sequel is *Let No Man Write My Epitaph* (1958).

Norris, Frank   THE PIT
Muckraker novel of manipulation in the Chicago grain market. Bentley, 1971 (first published 1903).

Powers, John R.   THE LAST CATHOLIC IN AMERICA
A man's return to the old neighborhood sparks boyhood memories of the 1950s. Saturday Rev Pr, 1973.

Roth, Philip   LETTING GO
Novel of the Jewish academic community at the University of Chicago in the 1950s. Random, 1962.

Sinclair, Upton   THE JUNGLE
Another of the muckraking novels at the turn-of-the-century. This is about the life of immigrants and the Chicago stockyards. Bentley, 1971 (first published 1906).

Smith, Charles M.   REVEREND RANDOLPH AND THE FALL FROM GRACE, INC.
"Suavely written and amusing" novel of a pastor who acts as sleuth in an investigation of the application for membership in his church of a TV evangelist whose associates are murdered. "A tantalizing glimpse of the working of the church from the inside." Putnam Pub Group, 1978. Another mystery, set in Chicago, in which Reverend Randolph plays detective is *Reverend Randolph and the Wages of Sin* (1974).

Wright, Richard   NATIVE SON
"An extraordinary story movingly told" of a young black on Chicago's south side in the 1940s who is taken up by a wealthy family, leading to tragedy. Har-Row, 1969 (first published 1940). Also set in Chicago are *Lawd Today* (1963) and *The Outsider* (1953).

TRAVEL ARTICLES

BON APPETIT
1984 Sep "Chicago Style." Discover the unexpected pleasures of this spirited city.
     Nao Hauser, p. 112

CONNOISSEUR
1984 Apr "Welcome to Peruvian Cuisine." How the best food in Lima came to Chicago. Jo Durden-Smith and Diane Desimone, p. 128

GOURMET
1985 Oct "City Dining: Chicago." Mimi Elder, p. 38

NATIONAL GEOGRAPHIC TRAVELER
1985 Spring "The Many Lives of Chicago." Five writers reflect on the best of Windy City (architecture, museums, sports, entertainment, neighborhood life). William Brashler and others, p. 46

N.Y. TIMES SUNDAY TRAVEL SECTION (X)
1985 Mar 17 (Part 2, "Sophisticated Traveler") "Huck Finn's Two Rivers." The merging of the Ohio and Mississippi near Cairo. Andrew H. Malcolm, p. 128
    May 15 "The Midwest's Brawny Capital." Chicago: an intense mixture of ethnicity, innovative architecture and even baseball in the sun. p. 14
    "A Metropolis of No Little Plans." From Picasso to Ella Fitzgerald, the arts thrive. Pat Collander, p. 15
    "The Art of Politics, Chicago Style." A visitor can trace the scenes of the best game in town. Eugene Kennedy, p. 16
1984 Sep 30 "Time is Essence in One Museum." The Time Museum in Rockford. Andrew H. Malcolm, p. 21

TRAVEL & LEISURE
1985 Jul "Latest from Chicago." Summer fun in the city on the lake. Kitty Mackey, p. 33
1984 Mar "Hopper's 'Nighthawks.'" A haunting vision of America (at the Art Institute in Chicago). Alexander Eliot, p. 21

INDIANA

Background Reading

Black, Harry G.   TRAILS AND TALES OF NORTHWEST INDIANA
HMB Pbns, 1984. Also *Trails to Hoosier Heritage* (1981). Guidebooks for historical sites in Indiana.

Daniel, Glenda   DUNE COUNTRY
Background reading for a unique natural feature of the state—the dunes near Gary—both for hikers and for those interested as naturalists. Swallow, 1977.

Dreiser, Theodore   A HOOSIER HOLIDAY
Literary memorabilia—travel narrative of an auto trip taken by Dreiser back around 1916, with Franklin Booth, from New York to Indiana. There is much comment on America's mores and future by Dreiser, who was one of the most controversial writers of the day. Greenwood, 1974 (first published 1916).

Hoover, Dwight W.   A PICTORIAL HISTORY OF INDIANA
The text can stand alone as a short history of the state. Indiana U, 1981.

Kleinfeld, Sonny   A MONTH AT THE BRICKYARD: THE INCREDIBLE INDY 500
Annual auto races at the Indianapolis Speedway. HR&W, 1977.

Lane, James B.   CITY OF THE CENTURY
A history of Gary, which was founded by U.S. Steel as an experiment in industrial planning. Indiana U, 1978.

Osler, Jack   FIFTY GREAT MINI TRIPS FOR INDIANA
Media Ventures, 1978.

Peckham, Howard H.   INDIANA
One of a series of popular histories for each state published as part of the Bicentennial observance. Norton, 1978.

Peden, R.   SPEAK TO THE EARTH
"Pages from a farm wife's journal, a book of rural virtues and a naturalist's philosophy." Knopf, 1974.

Schaeffer, Norma and Franklin, Kay   'ROUND AND ABOUT THE DUNES
Geology and history of a midwestern natural wonder, but also explores the surrounding area "to uncover the most interesting shops, dining spots, recreational facilities and natural sights for visitors." (BL) Dunes Enterprises, 1984.

Thomas, Bill and Phyllis   INDIANA: OFF THE BEATEN PATH
The back roads of the Hoosier state "lead to many special and unusual places, some virtually undiscovered"—not a state to go through on the way to someplace else. Includes places to eat and stay. (Publisher) East Woods, 1985.

Novels

Clauser, Suzanne   A GIRL NAMED SOONER
Set in southern Indiana in the 1930s—the story of a backwoods girl who is taken in by the local veterinarian and his wife. Doubleday, 1972.

Hayes, Joseph   THE DESPERATE HOURS
Suspenseful tale of a family held hostage in Indianapolis by escaped convicts. Random, 1954.

Lockridge, Ross   RAINTREE COUNTY
An epic novel of the period from the Civil War to 1892, in Raintree County, and the lives of the local schoolteacher and his friends. Houghton, 1948.

Stone, Irving   ADVERSARY IN THE HOUSE
Biographical novel of Eugene Debs, the socialist idealist. Doubleday, 1947.

Tarkington, Booth   ALICE ADAMS
Classic story of small-town life in the 1920s as a young girl must overcome her lack of money and background—it won the Pulitzer Prize in 1922. Doubleday, 1921. Also *The Gentleman from Indiana* (1899), about the editor of a country newspaper, and *The Magnificent Ambersons* (1918), a saga of a wealthy family in the 1870s.

Tesich, Steve   SUMMER CROSSING
An introspective novel of a young man going through a series of traumatic events, just out of high school, "in the industrial hell-hole of East Chicago, Indiana [from which] he emerges a better person and a budding writer." (FC) Random, 1982.

Vonnegut, Kurt   GOD BLESS YOU, MR. ROSEWATER
A wacky story of the administration of the Rosewater Foundation by the last direct descendant of its founder—a "black" satire of Norbert Wiener's book *The Human Use of Human Beings.* HR&W, 1965.

Wakefield, Dan   GOING ALL THE WAY
"Amiable . . . often wonderfully funny" novel of two young men who return to Indianapolis in 1954 following their army service; their questioning of society and chasing after booze and sex. (FC) Delacorte Pr, 1970.

West, Jessamyn   THE FRIENDLY PERSUASION
Quakers in Indiana during the period following the Civil War. HarBraceJ, 1945. *Except for Me and Thee* (1969) is a companion novel that rounds out the story of the Birdwell family. Also *The Massacre at Fall Creek* (1975), fictional treatment of the Indian slaughter at Fall Creek in 1824, and *The Witch Diggers* (1951).

TRAVEL ARTICLES

AMERICANA
1984 May-Jun "River Town on the Rise." Revival and preservation of Madison. Joan Mellon, p. 46

ARCHITECTURAL DIGEST
1984 May Historic Houses: "James Whitcomb Riley, the Hoosier Poet on Lockerbie Street." Indianapolis. David Block, p. 193

EARLY AMERICAN LIFE
1985 Apr "Indiana's New Harmony." John H. Williams, p. 53

HOUSE BEAUTIFUL
1984 Jun "For the Intrepid Antiquer, Indiana Is 'Still One of This Country's Better Kept Secrets.'" Claire Whitcomb, p. 54

N.Y. TIMES SUNDAY TRAVEL SECTION (X)
1985 Jun 9 "Back Home in Indiana." Brown County's multicolored vistas are the scene of struggle between charm and progress. Pat Colander, p. 16

TRAVEL & LEISURE
1985 Apr "America's Own Notre Dame." Touring the campus of a historic Indiana university. Eugene Kennedy, p. 94

TRAVEL/HOLIDAY
1985 Apr "An Insider's Indianapolis." The real Speed City. Rebecca Christian, p. 76

IOWA

Background Reading

Andrews, Clarence A.   CHRISTMAS IN IOWA
Iowa State U, 1978. Also *Growing Up in Iowa* (1979).

Bauer, Douglas   PRAIRIE CITY, IOWA
Iowa State U, 1982.

Childs, Marquis and Engel, Paul   THIS IS IOWA
Midwest Heritage, 1982.

Engel, Paul and Zielinski, John M.   PORTRAIT OF IOWA TRAVEL GUIDE
Wallace-Homestead, 1975.

Harnack, Curtis   GENTLEMEN ON THE PRAIRIE
Story of an unusual British colony and prairie community near Le Mars, of upper-class Britons, begun in the 1880s. Iowa State U, 1985.

Hofsommer, Don   PRAIRIE OASIS
The railroads, steamboats and resorts of Iowa's Spirit Lake Country. W&M Pr, 1975.

Pelton, Beulah   WE BELONG TO THE LAND
Memories of a midwesterner. Iowa State U, 1984.

Toth, Susan   BLOOMING: A SMALL-TOWN GIRLHOOD
"A gracefully nostalgic return to a midwestern childhood in Ames, Iowa"—growing up in the '50s. (BRD) Little, 1981.

Wall, Joseph F.   IOWA
One of a series of popular histories for each state published as part of the Bicentennial observance in 1976. Norton, 1978.

Woolston, Bill   IOWA'S FAIR
The classic state fair. Thorn Creek Pr, 1975.

Novels

Aldrich, Bess   MISS BISHOP
Fifty years in a country teacher's life in the late nineteenth and early twentieth centuries. Aeonian, 1975 (first published 1933).

Casey, John   AN AMERICAN ROMANCE
A theatrical commune in Iowa in the early 1960s. Atheneum, 1977.

DeVries, Peter   I HEAR AMERICA SWINGING
"Sly boots commentary on present-day mores" narrated by an Iowa marriage counselor. (FC) Little, 1976.

Harnack, Curtis   LIMITS OF THE LAND
Life on a small Iowa farm in the 1940s and the "love-hate relationship between men and the soil." (BRD) Doubleday, 1979.

Kantor, MacKinlay   SPIRIT LAKE
The story of the Spirit Lake massacre, when some thirty settlers were slaughtered by a band of renegade Indians. World, 1961.

Kinsella, W.P.   SHOELESS JOE
Fantasies of a fanatical baseball fan come true when a ballpark gets built and long-dead Chicago Black Sox players play on it. Houghton, 1982.

Manfred, Frederick   GREEN EARTH
"Lyrical saga of family life in rural Iowa in the early part of this century." (FC) Crown, 1977.

Millhiser, Marlys   NELLA WAITS
Horror tale set in a small Iowa town. The malevolent spirit of a dead woman haunts the home to which a young widow returns for her father's funeral. Putnam Pub Group, 1974.

TRAVEL ARTICLES

NATIONAL GEOGRAPHIC TRAVELER
1984 Summer "Come to the Fair—Des Moines, Iowa." A wry guide to the Iowa State Fair. Michael Cartner, p. 32

TRAVEL/HOLIDAY
1985 Jul "What's Doing in Des Moines." Iowa's history and culture. Hal Butler, p. 6

KANSAS

Background Reading

Athearn, Robert G.   IN SEARCH OF CANAAN
The black migration to Kansas following the Civil War. U. Pr of Kansas, 1978.

Davis, Kenneth S.   KANSAS
One of a series of popular histories for each state published as part of the Bicentennial observance in 1976. Norton, 1984 (first published 1976).

Dykstra, Robert R.   THE CATTLE TOWNS
"A social history of the Kansas cattle trading centers—Abilene, Ellsworth, Wichita, Dodge City, and Caldwell, 1867-1885," with a conclusion that their "romantic past was no more romantic than Lima, Ohio." (BRD) Knopf, 1968.

Faulk, Odie B.   DODGE CITY: THE MOST WESTERN TOWN OF ALL
How Dodge City developed, from the arrival of the first white settler to its emergence as a farming center. Oxford U, 1977.

**Shortridge, James R.   KAW VALLEY LANDSCAPES: A GUIDE TO
EASTERN KANSAS**
Coronado Pr, 1977.

**Stein, Shifra   GAS SAVINGS GETAWAYS LESS THAN TWO HOURS FROM
GREATER KANSAS CITY**
"Arranged geographically by the direction from the central city . . . areas worth visiting along the route . . . short descriptions of noteworthy historic sites, quaint locales, galleries and museums, festivals, sporting events and outdoor activities, and shops and restaurants." A directory of motels, hotels, useful addresses and phone numbers is added as an appendix. (BL) Rainy Day Bks, 1980.

**Stratton, Joanna L.   PIONEER WOMEN: VOICES FROM THE
KANSAS FRONTIER**
A remarkable book that evolved from memoirs of hundreds of pioneer women, the memoirs collected by the author's grandmother with the intention of editing into book form. They tell of shoot-outs, Indians, grasshopper plagues, and fear. S&S, 1981.

Weathers, Ginny, ed.   DISCOVER KANSAS
Unicorn Pbns, 1983.

Yost, Nellie S.   MEDICINE LODGE
The story of a Kansas frontier town. Swallow, 1970.

Novels

Braun, Matthew   THE KINCAIDS
An action-filled western of a frontier family whose saga begins when Jake Kincaid wins a saloon in a poker game; he parlays it into a business empire, and his two sons take the divergent paths of lawman and outlaw. Putnam Pub Group, 1976.

Day, Robert   THE LAST CATTLE DRIVE
A "new-to-the-saddle schoolteacher" narrates a modern-day cattle drive along the highways to Kansas City—adventures with the law, in bars, and romance along the way. (FC) U. Pr of Kansas, 1983 (first published 1977).

Ehrlich, Leonard   GOD'S ANGRY MAN
The story of John Brown and his fight against slavery in the nineteenth century. S&S, 1932.

Hayden, Torey   THE SUNFLOWER FOREST
The reason for a Hungarian-born mother's periods of depression are explained when her World War II experiences are revealed. Putnam Pub Group, 1984.

Hughes, Langston   NOT WITHOUT LAUGHTER
Novel about growing up in a small Kansas town by the noted black poet. Knopf, 1930.

Inge, William   GOOD LUCK, MISS WYCKOFF
A schoolteacher in a town in Kansas is driven out when she becomes sexually involved with a high school football player. Little, 1970.

Inge, William   MY SON IS A SPLENDID DRIVER
"The textures of midwestern American family life" in the form of the memoir of an English teacher in a Kansas town who is doomed to failure by the memory of his dead older brother. (FC) Little, 1971.

Parks, Gordon   THE LEARNING TREE
Story of a black boy growing up in the 1920s in Kansas, by the noted photographer. Har-Row, 1963.

Rhodes, Richard   SONS OF EARTH
An ex-astronaut settles down on a Kansas farm, and his son is kidnapped by a psychopath. Coward, 1981.

Roderus, Frank   LEAVING KANSAS
A "young misfit" at the turn of the century makes a series of blunders that lead to his leaving his Kansas town and heading west. (FC) Doubleday, 1983.

TRAVEL ARTICLES

AMERICANA
1984 Jan-Feb "Requiem for a Tourist Trap." A changed Boot Hill Museum that will document Dodge City's true role in the development of the West. Teresa Byrne-Dodge, p. 62

NATIONAL GEOGRAPHIC
1985 Sep "Home to Kansas." Cliff Tarpy, p. 352

NATIONAL GEOGRAPHIC TRAVELER
1985 Autumn "Merrie Olde . . . Kansas?" Kansas City renaissance festival, David Arnold, p. 20

TRAVEL/HOLIDAY
1984 Jun "Kansas City." A destination mushrooms. John Garrity, p. 58
        "Dining in Kansas City." Chef Louis Szathmary, p. 60
     Aug "A Plains Perspective." Indian imprints. Edward Renno, p. 30

KENTUCKY

Background Reading

Caudill, Harry M.   WATCHES OF THE NIGHT
The effects of Vista Volunteers on a coal mining community in Appalachia. Little, 1976.

Channing, Steven A.   KENTUCKY
One of a series of popular histories for each state published as part of the Bicentennial observance in 1976. Norton, 1977.

Chew, Peter   THE KENTUCKY DERBY
The first hundred years of this annual event. Houghton, 1974.

Courier Journal eds.   TRAVELS THROUGH KENTUCKY HISTORY
Historical background information for the traveler. Data Courier, 1976.

Egerton, John   GENERATIONS: AN AMERICAN FAMILY
Social history of a middle-class family viewed as a paradigm of the changes in the American family. U of Kentucky, 1983.

Gazaway, Rena   THE LONGEST MILE
This is a book that will delight the hearts of all conservatives. It "employs the technique of the novelist" to show that the rural poor in eastern Kentucky are more trapped than they were fifty years earlier and blames it on "fruitless govern-

ment projects, rabble-rousing do-gooders and a welfare system that perpetuates indigence." Read also Caudill's book above on Vista Volunteers for another view. (BRD) Doubleday, 1969.

Osler, Jack   FIFTY BEST MINI-TRIPS FOR KENTUCKY
Media Ventures, 1977.

Slone, Verna Mae   WHAT MY HEART WANTS TO SEE
The author is the tenth generation of a family to live in Pippa Passes, within two miles of the place they settled in 1790. Reminiscences that are "beyond the cliches of mountain life" as the author seeks to preserve the culture and traditions of a soon to be forgotten way of life. Har-Row, 1980.

**Strode, William   THE COMPLETE GUIDE TO KENTUCKY
HORSE COUNTRY**
Where to go, what to see, how to enjoy it. Classic Pbns, 1981.

Novels

Anderson, V.S.   KING OF THE ROSES
Suspense story of bribery at the Kentucky Derby—an intricate plot with "vivid descriptions of . . . Derby Week buffoonery . . . magnificently exciting description of the race itself." (FC) St. Martin, 1983.

**Arnow, Harriette   THE KENTUCKY TRACE: A NOVEL OF THE
AMERICAN REVOLUTION**
Frontier life in the Cumberland region, descriptive of daily life and customs. Knopf, 1974.

Arnow, Harriette   THE DOLLMAKER
A country woman with a passion for whittling objects out of wood is forced by World War II to leave her home for Detroit's mean streets so that her husband can work in a factory. (FC) Macmillan, 1954. Also *Hunter's Horn* (1949), "unforgettable many-sided picture of family life and community life in the Kentucky hills."

Giles, Janice H.   THE KENTUCKIANS
Historical novel of the period 1769-77 when Kentucky was still part of Virginia. G.K. Hall, 1980 (first published 1953). *Hannah Fowler* (1956) is another novel of frontier life.

Giles, Janice H.   THE ENDURING HILLS
Twentieth-century rural life in Kentucky. Houghton, 1971 (first published 1950). Also *The Believers* (1957), about the Shaker colony in Kentucky.

Gordon, Caroline   THE COLLECTED STORIES OF CAROLINE GORDON
Four decades of stories of Southern landscapes and inbred counties. FS&G, 1981. Also an early saga of a Kentucky plantation family, *Penhally* (1931).

McClanahan, Ed   THE NATURAL MAN
A "seriocomical" story of growing up in Kentucky in the 1940s—"the characters' overblown reactions to the town's trivial doings." (FC) FS&G, 1983.

Marshall, Catherine   CHRISTY
A schoolteacher in 1912 goes from a comfortable home to join a mission in Cutter Gap—based on the life of the author's mother. McGraw, 1967.

Sherburne, James   HACEY MILLER
Historical and fictional persons in a Civil War novel that "vividly evokes the passions of the day." Houghton, 1971.

Stuart, Jesse   TAPS FOR PRIVATE TUSSIE
"Comical, regional tale" of what sudden wealth does to an improvident family happily living on welfare. Dutton, 1943. Also *The Best-Loved Short Stories of Jesse Stuart* (1982) and *A Jesse Stuart Harvest* (1965) (anthology).

Warren, Robert Penn   BAND OF ANGELS
A girl discovers she's part black, and is sold as a slave. Random, 1955. Also *World Enough and Time* (1950), based on a true 1820 murder trial, and *Night Rider* (1939).

Yount, John   HARDCASTLE
Strikes and labor organizers in the Kentucky coal mines in 1931. Marek, 1980.

TRAVEL ARTICLES

AMERICANA
1985 Sep-Oct "Hoofbeats of History." Kentucky Horse Park and Museum in Lexington. Jessica Tanno, p. 92

EARLY AMERICAN LIFE
1984 Apr "Inns and Taverns of Kentucky." Marty Godbey, p. 65

NATIONAL GEOGRAPHIC TRAVELER
1984 Autumn "Mammoth Cave." Kentucky's buried treasure. Laura W. Anderson, p. 104

N.Y. TIMES SUNDAY TRAVEL SECTION (X)
1985 Apr 21 "What's Doing in Louisville." James Barron, p. 10
     Aug 18 "Kentucky's Living Fiction." Jesse Stuart country. Dee Wedemeyer, p. 26
     Oct 20 "Oasis in Appalachia." Boone Tavern. Alan Cheuse, p. 12
1984 Aug 5 "Where Shaker Simplicity Endures." Pleasant Hill restored village. Wilma Dykeman, p. 15

SMITHSONIAN
1984 Dec "Bluegrass Exhibit Corrals Tiny Models of Famous Horses." The Kentucky Horse Park near Lexington. Grayce P. Northcross, p. 146

TRAVEL & LEISURE
1985 Apr "Racy Doings at the Kentucky Derby." Galloping thoroughbreds and nonstop celebration. Christopher Hunt, p. 128

TRAVEL/HOLIDAY
1984 Aug "Kentucky Drives Off the Beaten Path." Branley Allan and Mary Louise Branson, p. 58

LOUISIANA

Series Guidebooks (See Appendix 1)

Fodor: New Orleans
Frommer: The Southeast & New Orleans: Dollarwise;
           New Orleans: City Guide

Background Reading

Arrigo, Joseph A. and Batt, Cara M.   PLANTATIONS: FORTY-FOUR OF LOUISIANA'S MOST BEAUTIFUL ANTEBELLUM HOUSES
Drawings, architectural descriptions, history and travel directions for each of the plantations of Old Louisiana. Lexikos, 1983.

Broven, John   RHYTHM AND BLUES IN NEW ORLEANS
History of a unique music form—"overview of the remarkable music scene inside the borders of this one town." (Publisher) Pelican, 1983.

Bruce, Curt   THE GREAT HOUSES OF NEW ORLEANS
Knopf, 1977.

Calhoun, Nancy H. and James   THE PELICAN GUIDE TO PLANTATION HOMES OF LOUISIANA
Handbook of over 200 homes of architectural and historic significance, both those that are open to the public and some that are not. Suggested tours for the traveler. Pelican, 1982.

Chase, John C.   FRENCHMEN, DESIRE, GOOD CHILDREN
Just some of the intriguing New Orleans street names—the book provides history, anecdotes and background reading that reflect the mood of the city and explain the street names. Macmillan, 1979.

Cowan, Walter G. and others   NEW ORLEANS YESTERDAY AND TODAY: A GUIDE TO THE CITY
History, culture, inhabitants, background and atmospheric detail. Lousiana State U Pr, 1983.

Faulkner, William   NEW ORLEANS SKETCHES
Stories and articles written early in his writing career when working for the *New Orleans Times-Picayune* and *Double Dealer*, with an introduction about the prominent author's years in New Orleans. Random, 1968.

Feibleman, Peter S.   THE BAYOUS
Part of the American Wilderness series. Time-Life, 1973.

Griffin, Thomas K.   THE PELICAN GUIDE TO NEW ORLEANS
Useful as a guidebook and for pre-travel background reading on New Orleans. Pelican, 1983.

Hallowell, Christopher   PEOPLE OF THE BAYOU: CAJUN LIFE IN LOST AMERICA
"Living at the edge of the marshland that skirts the Gulf of Mexico"—trapping, oystering and trawling for shrimp. (BRD) Dutton, 1979.

Henstell, Bruce   LOUISIANA: AN ILLUSTRATED HISTORY
"A fascinating group portrait of the people, topography, landmarks and events." (BRD) Knopf, 1980.

Hoover, Edwin C.   CITY GUIDE, 1984: GREATER NEW ORLEANS
Area Echos Pbns, 1984.

Joynes, St. Leger and DuArte, Jack   INSIDERS' GUIDE TO NEW ORLEANS
Insiders Pub Group, 1984.

Kane, Harnett   LOUISIANA HAYRIDE
"Records accurately the wild political hayride [Huey] Long engineered and the scandals that followed his death." (Publisher) Pelican, 1971 (first published 1941).

Kolb, Carolyn   DOLPHIN GUIDE TO NEW ORLEANS
Doubleday, 1984.

Leavitt, Mel   A SHORT HISTORY OF NEW ORLEANS
"It reads like a first-rate historical novel." (Publisher) Lexikos, 1982.

Leavitt, Mel   GREAT CHARACTERS OF NEW ORLEANS
An assemblage of forty-three fascinating characters—"geniuses, madams, and charlatans from every era of the city's tumultuous history." (Publisher) Lexikos, 1984.

LeBlanc, Joyce Y.   THE PELICAN GUIDE TO GARDENS OF LOUISIANA
Louisiana's climate makes it perfect "for some of America's most enchanting

garden spots"—complete information and descriptions for travelers who wish to discover the gardens of Louisiana. (Publisher) Pelican, 1974.

McCarthy, Liz and Cary, Beth   MARMAC GUIDE TO NEW ORLEANS
Marmac, 1984.

Rose, Al   STORYVILLE, NEW ORLEANS
"Being an authentic, illustrated account of the notorious redlight district" (an area excluded from a ban on prostitution from 1898-1917). (BRD) U of Alabama, 1974.

Rose, Al and Souchon, Edmond   NEW ORLEANS JAZZ: A FAMILY ALBUM
Louisiana State U Pr, 1984.

Rushton, William F.   THE CAJUN FROM ACADIA TO LOUISIANA
Traces the roots of the Cajuns whose Acadian ancestors settled in Canada in 1604, then migrated to the bayou country of Louisiana in the mid-1700s when they were expelled from Canada by the British. FS&G, 1979.

Tallant, Robert   MARDI GRAS
"The best general introduction—a sane contemplation of a hopelessly insane subject"—parades, floats, the balls, the crowds. (Publisher) Pelican, 1976.

Taylor, James and Graham, Alan   NEW ORLEANS ON THE HALF SHELL
"A 'survival manual' for those going for Mardi Gras or just for vacation... staying in either a hostel or a Hilton." (TA) Pelican, 1982.

Taylor, Joe G.   LOUISIANA
One of a series of popular histories for each state published as part of the Bicentennial observance in 1976. Norton, 1984 (first published 1976).

Turner, Frederick   REMEMBERING SONG: ENCOUNTERS WITH THE NEW ORLEANS JAZZ TRADITION
The New Orleans musical story with emphasis on the author's encounters with people and the city and the life histories of several of its musicians. Viking, 1982.

Novels

Basso, Hamilton   SUN IN CAPRICORN
One of several novels based on the life of Huey Long. He's Gilgo Slade in this one—a power-mad politician who wrecks the lives of two lovers who stand in his way. Scribner, 1942.

Bristow, Gwen   DEEP SUMMER
First in a trilogy of plantation life from the eighteenth to the twentieth centuries. Crowell, 1964. *The Handsome Road* (1968) and *This Side of Glory* (1940) complete the trilogy.

Capote, Truman   OTHER VOICES, OTHER ROOMS
"Abnormal maturing of a loveless thirteen-year-old boy." (FC) Random, 1968 (first published 1948).

Corrington, John W.   SO SMALL A CARNIVAL
Thriller, set in New Orleans. Viking, 1986.

Dos Passos, John   NUMBER ONE
"Fictional portrait of an American demagogue, obviously based on the life and career of Huey Long." (BRD) Houghton, 1943.

Dubus, Elizabeth N.   CAJUN
"Multigenerational family saga of French Canadians in Acadia and New Orleans." (FC) Seaview, 1983.

Gaines, Ernest J.   A GATHERING OF OLD MEN
When a white man is found dead on a black man's farm, the aging black population defies the traditional outcome of white revenge. (FC) Knopf, 1983. Also *In My Father's House* (1978), in which an illegitimate son returns to confront his father, a civil rights activist, and *The Autobiography of Miss Jane Pittman* (1971), a centenarian's life from slavery to the civil rights movement.

Grau, Shirley Ann   THE HARD BLUE SKY
Cajun life on Isle aux Chiens and the "nature and character . . . of the island itself." (FC) Knopf, 1958. Also *Keepers of the House* (1964), saga of a Delta family that won a Pulitzer Prize, and *The Black Prince, and Other Stories* (1955), short stories of black life in Louisiana.

Groom, Winston   AS SUMMERS DIE
Oil is discovered in a port town on the Gulf of Mexico. Summit Bks, 1980.

Hitchens, Dolores   IN A HOUSE UNKNOWN
A gothic involving two sisters in an antebellum mansion. Doubleday, 1973.

Keyes, Frances P.   STEAMBOAT GOTHIC
Family saga of plantation life on the Mississippi, 1865-1930. Messner, 1952. A second family saga, *River Road* (1945), covers the period 1918-1945.

Keyes, Frances P.   BLUE CAMELLIA
Pioneer life of the 1880s in Cajun country. Messner, 1957.

L'Enfant, Julie   THE DANCERS OF SYCAMORE STREET
A New York choreographer arrives in a small town in Louisiana to direct a gala for its local ballet school. The story is told through the eyes of "a precocious, likeable girl . . . reminiscent of Carson McCullers . . . nothing less than enchanting." (FC) St. Martin, 1983.

Martin, Valerie   ALEXANDRA
An eerie novel set on a secluded bayou estate. FS&G, 1979.

Warren, Robert Penn   ALL THE KING'S MEN
Huey Long is embodied in Willie Stark in this fictionalization of the rise of a political leader, with a lust for power, from farm to law and politics. HarBraceJ, 1946.

Wilcox, James   MODERN BAPTISTS
Life in Tula Springs vividly depicted as a man's life is generally fouled up when his half-brother moves in with him. Dial, 1983.

NEW ORLEANS

Algren, Nelson   A WALK ON THE WILD SIDE
Vivid novel of slum life in New Orleans during the depression. FS&G, 1956.

Chopin, Kate   THE AWAKENING
Novel of an early feminist whose books were considered too racy for her time, in the early 1900s, but now as a result of the women's movement are enjoying a revival of interest. Avon, 1972.

Costain, Thomas B.   HIGH TOWERS
See under "Canada/Novels."

Fairbairn, Ann   FIVE SMOOTH STONES
Chronicles a black man's life from poverty in New Orleans through a distinguished career and the civil rights movement. Crown, 1966.

Ferber, Edna   SARATOGA TRUNK
An adventuress in New Orleans of the 1880s who returns to blackmail her father's aristocratic family. Doubleday, 1951 (first published 1941).

Grau, Shirley Ann   THE CONDOR PASSES
Rags-to-riches rise of a multimillionaire, told in flashback, and the story of the generation that followed "inevitably weakened and corrupted by ... the Old Man's personality and need to dominate." (FC) Knopf, 1971.

Hailey, Arthur   HOTEL
One week behind the scenes of one of New Orleans' great hotels. Doubleday, 1956.

Harris, Thomas   BLACK SUNDAY
An Arab terrorist group plots to blow up the Super Bowl. Putnam Pub Group, 1975.

Keyes, Frances Parkinson   DINNER AT ANTOINE'S
A murder mystery and study of the interplay of emotions and desires beginning with a dinner at the famous New Orleans restaurant. S&S, 1948.

Plain, Belva   CRESCENT CITY
A European Jewish heroine and her brother in New Orleans during the Civil

War adjusting to "a bright, promising new land . . . as well as its grimmer aspects." (FC) Delacorte Pr, 1984.

Rice, Anne   THE FEAST OF ALL SAINTS
   Historical novel of the Free People of Color in antebellum New Orleans—"a fascinating glimpse into a little known and intriguing segment of American history." (FC) S&S, 1979.

Toole, John Kennedy   A CONFEDERACY OF DUNCES
   "Farcical, ribald" story of Ignatius Reilly—captures the flavor of New Orleans. (BRD) Louisiana State U Pr, 1980.

Warren, Robert Penn   BAND OF ANGELS
   See under "Kentucky/Novels."

Yerby, Frank   THE FOXES OF HARROW
   Historical saga that begins in 1825 and chronicles its hero's rise to wealth, ending with the Civil War and the mansion at Harrow in ruins. Dial, 1946.

TRAVEL ARTICLES

BETTER HOMES & GARDENS
1984 May "New Orleans Bound!" Vacations and food. p. 114

BON APPETIT
1985 Mar "River to the Past." Fascinating towns, historic homes and great cuisine along the lower Mississippi (Louisiana and Mississippi). Shirley Slater, p. 102

CONNOISSEUR
1984 Jun "A Taste of New Orleans." If you avoid its tacky tourist beat, New Orleans can be a warm bath of pleasures. Siste Viator, p. 54

GOURMET
1984 May "New Orleans at Table." Geri Trotta, p. 50

HORIZON
1984 Apr "A Special Travel Section on New Orleans." Arts, highways, plantations, New Orleans, jazz, architecture, galleries, restaurants, hotels, shopping and the long-gone Fair. pp. 21-42

NATIONAL GEOGRAPHIC TRAVELER
1985 Autumn "Bayou Bienvenue: Welcome to Louisiana's Cajun Country." Carol L. McCabe, p. 60

N.Y. TIMES SUNDAY TRAVEL SECTION (X)
1985 Feb 17 "What's Doing in New Orleans." Frances F. Marcus, p. 11
        Oct 27 "What's Doing in New Orleans," Frances F. Marcus, p. 10
1984 Feb 26 "The Allure of New Orleans." Roy Reed, p. 14

1984 "Traditions at the Table." A selection of New Orleans restaurants where Creole and Cajun creations are savored. Fred Ferretti, p. 15
"A New Orleans Sampler of Hotels, Restaurants, Museums, Day Trips, Events, Miscellany." p. 15
Apr 29 "High Ceilings and Cozy Cottages." Small hotels in New Orleans. Frances F. Markus, p. 12

TRAVEL & LEISURE
1984 Feb "A Gracious Antebellum Plantation." Nottoway near Baton Rouge). Michael Kimmitt, p. 124
Mar "New Orleans: City to Celebrate." Peter Feibleman, p. 62
"The French Quarter." With map and walking tour. Jennifer Quale, p. 68
"Beyond Bourbon Street." City sights and country sites in and around New Orleans. Michael Kimmitt, p. 76
"The Inns and Hotels of New Orleans." Fred Ferretti, p. 81
"The Exuberant Restaurants of New Orleans." Charles Monaghan, p. 87
"New Orleans' Jazzy Nightlife." From dusk to dawn, from bourbon to beignets. Dorothy G. Weiss, p. 97
"Life on the Mississippi." Riverboat gambols out of New Orleans. Bern Keating, pp. 104-5
"Tours to New Orleans." For Expo and for any time. Bunny Brower, p. 124

TRAVEL/HOLIDAY
1985 Jul "Having Fun on the Bayou." Lafayette, Louisiana. Carol Reed, p. 16
1984 Feb "A New Orleans Retrospective." An eyewitness account of a bygone Carnival. George A. Sala, p. 70
Apr "Dining Options in New Orleans' Outskirts." Louis Szathmary, p. 6
"Beyond New Orleans." Out of town day trips. Mark Thompson, p. 46
"New Orleans." Exploring Expo city. John Kemp, p. 62

VOGUE
1984 Jul "Coming Home to the Great American Kitchen: New Orleans." Lee Bailey, p. 143

MAINE

Barrette, Roy A COUNTRYMAN'S JOURNAL; VIEWS OF LIFE AND NATURE FROM A MAINE COASTAL FARM
"Short sketches [that give] the rich flavor of Maine." (BRD) Rand, 1981.

Brown, Allen D. THE GREAT LOBSTER CHASE
The real story of Maine lobsters and the men who catch them. Intl Marine, 1985.

Caldwell, Bill   ISLANDS OF MAINE
Colorful history of early explorers and settlers on Maine coastal islands. G. Gannett, 1981. Also by Caldwell, *Enjoying Maine* (1978) and *Maine Magic* (1981), yarns and stories about Maine people, places and activities.

Clark, Charles E.   MAINE
One of a series of popular histories for each state published as part of the Bicentennial observance. Norton, 1977.

Coffin, Robert P. Tristram   YANKEE COAST
Essays on coastal Maine by a native poet. Macmillan, 1947. Also *Lost Paradise* (1934), an autobiographical account of boyhood in Maine, and *Kennebec* (1975), an impressionistic biography of the river.

Conkling, Philip W.   ISLANDS IN TIME
"A natural and human history of the islands of Maine"—history, ecology. (Publisher) Down East, 1981.

D'Amato, Albert C. and Miriam F.   DISCOVERING ACADIA NATIONAL PARK AND MOUNT DESERT ISLAND, MAINE
Acadia, 1985

Dibner, Martin   SEACOAST MAINE: THE PEOPLE AND PLACES
The mystique and beauty of an individualistic region and the natives and outsiders who make it their home—including some surprising celebrities. Down East, 1982 (first published 1973).

Dietz, Lew   NIGHT TRAIN AT WISCASSET STATION
A Maine retrospect. Doubleday, 1977.

Dodge, Ernest   MORNING WAS STARLIGHT: MY MAINE BOYHOOD
"First-hand portrait of turn-of-the-century life in coastal Maine. . . . just inland from Mount Desert Island" by the former director of the Peabody Museum, "recalls the final days of the coasting schooner and self-sufficient family." (Publisher) Globe Pequot, 1981.

Gilpatrick, Gil   ALLAGASH, THE STORY OF MAINE'S LEGENDARY WILDERNESS WATERWAY
DeLorme Pub, 1983.

Gould, John   STITCH IN TIME
"Observations of the Maine difference . . . both nostalgia-rich and scholarly-inquisitive." (PW) Norton, 1985. Also *This Trifling Distinction: Reminiscences from Down East* (1978)—"some of the fun it has been to live and write . . . in the Pine Tree State."

Hillaby, John   JOURNEY THROUGH LOVE
Observations of the British "walking" naturalist (see also his walk books listed

under Europe and Great Britain) that interweave heritage and culture. Houghton, 1977.

Huber J. Parker   THE WILDEST COUNTRY: A GUIDE TO
THOREAU'S MAINE
Appalachian Mtn, 1982.

Jack, Susan   MAINE ADVENTURE GUIDE: GREATER PORTLAND
G. Gannett, 1981.

McClane, Charles B.   ISLANDS OF THE MID-MAINE COAST:
BLUE HILL BAY
Kennebec River Pr, 1984.

Melnicove, Mark   THE UNCENSORED GUIDE TO MAINE
L. Tapley, 1984.

Miller, Dorcas S.   THE MAINE COAST: A NATURE LOVER'S GUIDE
East Woods, 1978.

Nearing, Helen   CONTINUING THE GOOD LIFE:
HALF A CENTURY OF HOMESTEADING
Sequel to *Living the Good Life* (Vermont); this covers the period since 1952. An account of living a Thoreau-like life by the author and her husband who were pioneers in this twentieth-century movement of living simply and resourcefully. Schocken Bks, 1979.

Pohl, William L.   THE VOICE OF MAINE
Oral history approach—the 'voices' range from the grandson of L.L. Bean and bush pilots to crafts people and an ex-sea captain. Thorndike Pr, 1983.

Pratt, Charles   HERE ON THE ISLAND
Being an account of a way of life several miles off the coast of Maine. Har-Row, 1974.

Rich, Louise Dickinson   MY NECK OF THE WOODS
Just one of several of this author's books on Maine. Down East, 1976 (first published 1950). Other titles include: *Coast of Maine* (1956), a combination of history and contemporary attractions of the Maine coastline, *State o'Maine* (1964), *The Forest Years* (1963), and *Peninsula* (1958).

Roberts, Kenneth   TRENDING INTO MAINE
A lovely mishmash of history, memorable "little" people in Maine's history, his grandmother's recipes, lobstering and so on. Down East, 1975 (first published 1938). Also *We Took to the Woods* (1942) and *Don't Say That About Maine* (1950).

Smith, Robert   MY LIFE IN THE NORTH WOODS
Nostalgic Americana of the rough male life of a lumber camp in the Maine Woods. Atlantic Monthly, 1986.

Smith, Susan H.   MARMAC GUIDE TO MAINE
Marmac, 1983.

Stinnett, Caskie   ONE MAN'S ISLAND
Reflections on Maine life from slightly offshore. Down East, 1984.

Tree, Christina   MAINE: AN EXPLORER'S GUIDE
One of a series of books by this author intended both for residents and travelers, with a focus on inexpensive pleasures suitable for the entire family. Countryman Pr, 1984.

Whitely, George   NORTHERN SEAS, HARDY SAILORS
See under "Atlantic Canada & Labrador."

Wood, Pamela   THE SALT BOOK
This is a book inspired by the Foxfire series (see under "Georgia"); in this case the books are the work of English classes of Kennebunk High School. "Lobstering, sea moss pudding, stone walls, rum running, maple syrup, snow shoes, and other Yankee doings" recorded in this and its sequel *Salt Book 2* (Swan's Island). (BRD) Doubleday, 1977 and 1980.

Novels

Bosworth, David   THE DEATH OF DESCARTES
A title novella in a collection of short stories portrays an aging detective on his last case and coming to grips with personal traumas. (FC) U of Pittsburgh, 1981.

Busch, Frederick   TAKE THIS MAN
A story told in flashback of a man, his common-law wife, and their son, reunited and living in Maine after a twelve-year separation—"a tour de force of comedy and pathos." (FC) FS&G, 1981.

Carroll, Gladys Hasty   AS THE EARTH TURNS
Chronicle of a year's events in the life of a farmer in the 1930s. Norton, 1978 (first published 1933). Also *Next of Kin* (1974), a family chronicle retold to a contemporary family member.

Carroll, James   FAULT LINES
A novel about a draft-dodging radical and the widow of his dead brother, a Vietnam veteran—"smashing climax" in a house in Maine. (FC) Little, 1980.

Chase, Mary Ellen   THE LOVELY AMBITION
About a Methodist minister and his family who emigrate from England to Maine around 1900. Norton, 1960. Other books set in Maine by Chase include: *Mary Peters* (1934), *Silas Crockett* (1935), and *Windswept* (1941).

Chute, Carolyn   THE BEANS OF EGYPT, MAINE
A poverty-stricken Maine family—the Beans "are on the very bottom" of the

social scale, "devoid of the desire or will to rise above their sordid legacy." (PW) Ticknor & Fields, 1984.

Gilman, Dorothy   THE TIGHT ROPE WALKER
An antique shop owner is involved in the search for a potential murder victim. Doubleday, 1979.

Gould, John A.   THE GREENLEAF FIRE
Backwoods Maine in the 1940s is the setting for a novel about northern "poor white trash." "Beautifully rendered accounts of the geography/history of the local countryside." (BRD) Scribner, 1978.

Jewett, Sarah Orne   THE COUNTRY OF THE POINTED FIRS
Local color sketches of a Maine seaport town, written by a Maine writer whose home is now a literary landmark. Arden Lib (first published 1896).

Johnston, Velda   A PRESENCE IN AN EMPTY ROOM
Spooky story of a newly married New York City heroine transported to a remote town in Maine. Dodd, 1980.

King, Stephen   PET SEMATARY
Their new home in Maine is perfection for the Creed family, except for an old pet burial ground with a terrifying secret. Doubleday, 1983. Other horror stories by Stephen King with a Maine setting include: *Cujo* (1981), *Salem's Lot* (1975), *Carrie* (1974).

King, Tabitha   CARETAKERS
"A curious relationship between a member of the Maine gentry and a handyman ten years her senior . . . moving tale, sensitively written." (LJ) Macmillan, 1983.

Koontz, Dean R.   NIGHT CHILLS
A Maine town is the scene for the shakedown exercise of an experiment in mind control and mass manipulation. Atheneum, 1976.

Michaels, Barbara   THE CRYING CHILD
A gothic complete with a haunted house, set on an island in Casco Bay. Dodd, 1971.

Mojtabai, A.G.   AUTUMN
A widower's first winter in the retirement home he had planned to live in with his wife—"humorous, achingly real without mawkish sentimentality." (FC) Houghton, 1982.

Moore, Ruth   SARAH WALKED OVER THE MOUNTAIN
The heroine follows her husband from Wales to Maine in 1784 only to find later (after having her children) that her husband has a second, rich wife in Gloucester, Massachusetts. She burns her bridges and crosses over the mountain to Machias to find a better life. The second half of the story is about her twentieth-century descendants. "The author's love of Maine land, Maine talk, and Maine people

makes this [a] lovely tale." (FC) Morrow, 1979. Also *Candlemas Bay* (1950) and *Spoonhandle* (1946), family dramas set in coastal Maine villages.

Ogilvie, Elisabeth   THE ROAD TO NOWHERE
Mystery and romance with a surprise conclusion—two women, raised as sisters, meet years later and open "a Pandora's box of sinister events." (FC) McGraw, 1983.

Ogilvie, Elisabeth   AN ANSWER IN THE TIDE
"Lobstermen and their ladies, living and working on an island off the coast of Maine." McGraw, 1978. Also *Strawberries in the Sea* (1973), set on a Penobscot Bay island, about a woman working out a personal crisis, and a family drama also with an island setting, *Waters on a Starry Night* (1968).

Raucher, Herman   MAYNARD'S HOUSE
A tale of "love, death and bewitchment" in the Maine woods when the hero is left a house by a Vietnam buddy. (FC) Putnam Pub Group, 1980.

Roberts, Kenneth   ARUNDEL
The beginning of a series of historical novels—*Arundel* is about a secret expedition led by Benedict Arnold against Quebec. Doubleday, 1930. Following, in order, to form a complete chronicle from the Revolutionary War to the War of 1812, are *Rabble in Arms* (1933), *The Lively Lady* (1931), and *Captain Caution* (1934).

Spencer, Scott   PRESERVATION HALL
Two New Yorkers buy a farm in Maine that becomes a "psychological prison." (FC) Knopf, 1976.

Trillin, Calvin   RUNESTRUCK
Lighthearted novel of the pandemonium that ensues when two young clammers believe they've come across a Viking artifact. Little, 1977.

Van de Wetering, Janwillem   THE MAINE MASSACRE
The prolific writer of mysteries with European settings (see "France," "Netherlands") has now happily moved to Maine and written a story in which Grijpstra and deGier of the Amsterdam police become embroiled in a series of suspicious accidents in Cape Orca, Maine. Houghton, 1979.

TRAVEL ARTICLES

AMERICANA
1985 Jan-Feb "Baked Beans for Supper . . ." Consider a trip to Orff's Corner, Maine. Nancy Naglin, p. 54

ARCHITECTURAL DIGEST
1985 Mar Historic Houses: "Campobello—Patrician Simplicity at FDR's Summer Cottage." Between Eastport and New Brunswick—the island belongs to Canada. Arthur Schlesinger, Jr., p. 220

1984 Jul Historic Houses: "Winslow Homer at Prout's Neck." Avis Berman, p. 136

BON APPETIT
1985 May "Along the Coast of Maine." E.C.K. Read, p. 90

50 PLUS
1985 Aug "Island Paradise in New England." Casco Bay islands. Mark McCain, p. 45

GOURMET
1984 Jan "The American Scene." Mussels, recipes, lore, etc. Evan Jones, p. 74
      Aug "Lobster in the Rough." Caroline Bates, p. 34

NATIONAL GEOGRAPHIC
1985 Feb "Maine's Working Coast . . . Meet the Lobstermen, Boatbuilders, and Entrepreneurs Who Carve a Living from This Granite Shore." p. 208

N.Y. TIMES SUNDAY TRAVEL SECTION (X)
1985 May 19 "Edna St. Vincent Millay's Maine." Whitehall Inn, Camden. Emilie C. Harting, p. 20
      Jun 9 "Maine Recalls a Yankee Diva." Nordica's home in Farmington. Tim Page, p. 20
      Jul 14 Fare of the Country: "In Maine, lobster on a roll." Nancy Jenkins, p. 6
      Aug 25 "What's Doing in Ogunquit." Laurie O'Neill, p. 10
      Oct 6 Fare of the Country: "Fresh Sauerkraut from Maine." Leslie Land, p. 12
      ("Sophisticated Traveler") "Down East Almanac." Jose Yglesias, p. 90
1984 Feb 26 "Skiing and Then Some in Bethel, Maine." Fred Hill, p. 22
      Aug 12 "Maine Woods Holiday." Morgan McGinley, p. 20
      Aug 19 Correspondent's Choice: "Sunsets Gleam on a Maine Retreat." Isleboro Inn. Fox Butterfield, p. 6
      Aug 26 "Maine's Misty Kingdoms." Offshore islands. David Yeadon, p. 9

TOWN & COUNTRY
1985 Jul "Northeast Harbor." Lorna Livingston, p. 124

TRAVEL/HOLIDAY
1984 Jan "Maine Sail." Annual great schooner race in July. H. Shaw McCutcheon, Jr., p. 51
      Jul "Augusta, a Capital Exploration." Tom Bross, p. 18
      Aug "The Goods on L.L. Bean." Freeport, Maine's claim to fame. Janet Holman, p. 20

YANKEE
1985 Feb "This New England: Wilson's Mills, Maine." Ernest Hebert, p. 62
      Mar "A Place of Fishermen's Dreams." Grand Lake Stream. Mel Allen, p. 32
      Dec This New England: "Christmas Cove, Maine." S.F. Tomajczyck, p. 58
1984 Feb This New England: "Winter Camping in the Allagash Wilderness." Stephen O. Muskie, p. 54
      Sep This New England: "Rangely, Maine." Jack Oley, p. 76
      "Off-season Bargains on the South Coast of Maine." Mel Allen, p. 28

MARYLAND

Background Reading

Anderson, Elizabeth B.   ANNAPOLIS, A WALK THROUGH HISTORY
A guide to its historic buildings and architecture. Tidewater, 1984.

Beirne, Francis F.   THE AMIABLE BALTIMOREANS
Part of the same series that includes *The Proper Bostonians* (see "Massachusetts")—intended to "portray individual characteristics, underscore the idiosyncrasies . . . local traditions." (PW) Johns Hopkins U, 1984.

Bode, Carl   MARYLAND
One of a series of popular histories for each state published as part of the Bicentennial observance in 1976. Norton, 1978.

Dorsey, John R.   A GUIDE TO BALTIMORE ARCHITECTURE
Tidewater, 1981.

Footner, Hulbert   RIVERS OF THE EASTERN SHORE: SEVENTEEN MARYLAND RIVERS
"The seventeen sweet aftons of the Eastern shore" flowing into the Chesapeake—"a mellow nostalgic book." (BRD) Tidewater, 1979 (first published 1944).

Gilbert, Elizabeth R.   FAIRS AND FESTIVALS: A SMITHSONIAN GUIDE TO CELEBRATIONS IN MARYLAND, VIRGINIA AND D.C.
"Everything from national holidays and flower festivals to ethnic and religious events." (BL) Smithsonian, 1982.

Greene, Suzanne E.   BALTIMORE: AN ILLUSTRATED HISTORY
Published under the auspices of the Baltimore City Commission on Historical and Architectural Presentation and the Greater Baltimore Committee. Windsor, 1980.

Hardie, Dee   HOLLYHOCKS, LAMBS AND OTHER PASSIONS: A MEMOIR OF THORNHILL FARM
Reminiscences and anecdotes about a family and a Maryland farm. Atheneum, 1985.

Hodge, Allan and Carola   WASHINGTON ON FOOT
Twenty-three walking tours of Washington, D.C., Alexandria and Annapolis. Smithsonian, 1980.

Joynes, St. Leger M. and others   INSIDERS' GUIDE TO OCEAN CITY, MARYLAND
Insiders Pub Group, 1981.

Kytle, Elizabeth   HOME ON THE CANAL
"Informal history of the Chesapeake and Ohio Canal . . . oral history interviews that chronicle working life on the canal." (BRD) Seven Locks, 1983.

Nast, Lenora H. and others   BALTIMORE: A LIVING RENAISSANCE
Hist Balt Soc, 1982.

Peffer, Randall S.   WATERMEN
The author moved to Tilghman Island and worked as a waterman, crabbing and oystering—"it is a better evocation of life today on the Eastern Shore than Michener" (reference is to *Chesapeake*, listed under "Novels," below). (BRD) Johns Hopkins U, 1979.

Smith, Daniel B.   INSIDE THE GREAT HOUSE: PLANTER FAMILY LIFE IN 18TH-CENTURY CHESAPEAKE SOCIETY
Explores the character of family experience in the pre-industrial South in Maryland and Virginia. Cornell U, 1980.

Stevens, Elisabeth   ELISABETH STEVENS' GUIDE TO BALTIMORE'S INNER HARBOR
A tour of the exciting new downtown area. Stemmer Hse, 1981.

Sussman, Vic S.   NEVER KISS A GOAT ON THE LIPS: THE ADVENTURES OF A SUBURBAN HOMESTEADER
Anecdotes from ten years of homesteading in suburban Maryland, raising goats, saving turtles, baking bread, having a baby at home. Rodale Pr, 1981.

Swann, Don   COLONIAL AND HISTORIC HOMES OF MARYLAND
Etchings and text describing dwellings and historic buildings. Liberty, 1983.

Warner, William W.   BEAUTIFUL SWIMMERS: WATERMEN, CRABS, AND THE CHESAPEAKE BAY
Lore of the blue crab, history and cycle of the Chesapeake Bay and the watermen who work it, written with "love and flair." Suggestions for additional reading, and places and events in the area for travelers to visit. (BRD) Atl Monthly Pr, 1976.

Willis, Gwyn   SHIFRA STEIN'S DAY TRIPS FROM GREATER BALTIMORE
One of a series of guides to day trips less than two hours' driving time from a base city. This one uses Baltimore as a base and reaches Pennsylvania, Delaware, Virginia and West Virginia. Includes hundreds of money-saving things to do and see, quaint villages, farming and agricultural areas, restaurants, inns, festivals and celebrations, parks, campgrounds, etc. There are also suggestions for combining trips into a longer journey and a worth-a-little-more-time section of places beyond the two-hour limit. East Woods, 1985.

Novels

Barth, John   SABBATICAL: A ROMANCE
Story of a sailboat trip from Chesapeake Bay to the Caribbean using the voyage to explore "the difficulties of both midlife and artistic passages." (FC) Putnam Pub Group, 1982.

Barth, John   THE END OF THE ROAD
Set in a small college—"comic, tragic and satirical frontal attack on the excesses of Sartrean existentialism" of the 1950s. (FC) Doubleday, 1967. Also, a novel on academic politics, *Letters* (1979).

Barth, John   THE SOT-WEED FACTOR
Historical novel of the seventeenth century and a satire of historical novels as well. Doubleday, 1967.

DeBlasis, Celeste   WILD SWAN
Historical novel that moves from England to Maryland where the heroine and her brother-in-law's family emigrate during the period of pre-Civil War slavery. Bantam, 1984.

Greene, Annie   BRIGHT RIVER TRILOGY
Stories of three women in a Maryland town whose lives intersect in one man—as son, friend, lover, respectively. S&S, 1984.

Michaels, Barbara   PRINCE OF DARKNESS
In *Dark Duet*, the story of an "orphan turned governess, who marries her charge's guardian"—a gothic with an unexpected ending. Congdon & Weed, 1982.

Michener, James A.   CHESAPEAKE
Four centuries of life on Maryland's eastern shore. Random, 1978.

Noble, Hollister   WOMAN WITH A SWORD
A biographical novel of a Civil War heroine—Anna Ella Carroll—who planned Lincoln's Tennessee campaign. Doubleday, 1948.

Peters, Elizabeth   THE LOVE TALKER
"A mix of comedy, frights and the supernatural." (FC) Dodd, 1980.

Richter, Conrad   THE GRANDFATHERS
The setting is western Maryland—story of a young girl growing up in an isolated farmhouse with grandparents, mother, aunt and younger children. Knopf, 1964.

Robertson, Don   BY ANTIETAM CREEK
Historical novel of the Civil War battles where thousands of lives were lost, weaving together personal stories of soldiers. P-H, 1960.

Salamanca, J.R.   LILITH
Lilith is a rich and beautiful patient in a private mental hospital who corrupts a young man working there. S&S, 1961.

Tyler, Anne   DINNER AT THE HOMESICK RESTAURANT
Thirty-five troubled years of a working-class family in Baltimore and how the matriarch's bitterness at having been deserted scars the children. Knopf, 1982.

Tyler, Anne   CELESTIAL NAVIGATION
A bachelor lives in and runs a run-down boarding house in Baltimore. Knopf, 1977. Other novels by Anne Tyler with a Baltimore setting are: *Accidental Tourist* (1985), *Earthly Possessions* (1977), *Searching for Caleb* (1976), and *The Clock Winder* (1972).

TRAVEL ARTICLES

CONNOISSEUR
1984 Jul "A Day at the Teeming, Joyful Lexington Market, in Baltimore." Colette Rossant, p. 50

EARLY AMERICAN LIFE
1984 Aug "Annapolis." Carol McCabe, p. 24

ESQUIRE
1984 Oct "Can the Best Mayor Win?" Mayor Schaefer's Baltimore. Richard Ben Cramer, p. 57

HORIZON
1984 Jul-Aug "Baltimore—Star-Spangled Arts." Museums, galleries, lively arts, festival, dining, shopping, lodging, tours, etc. Mary Lou Baker, p. 25

HOUSE BEAUTIFUL
1984 Sep "Maryland's Eastern Shore." Jim Powell, p. 51

NATIONAL GEOGRAPHIC TRAVELER
1985 Autumn "Travels Along the Canal—Goin' Slow on the C&O." Travels along the Canal on the Chesapeake & Ohio. Eugene L. Mayer, p. 84

N.Y. TIMES SUNDAY TRAVEL SECTION (X)
1984 Apr 1 "What's Doing in Baltimore." Peter J. Kumpa, p. 10
Jun 24 "Ponies of Childhood's Wonder." On Assateague Island, home of Misty, the roundup and swim highlight the season. Diane Ackerman, p. 19

SUNSET
1985 "America's Finest Topiary Garden?" p. 58

TRAVEL/HOLIDAY
1985 Jun "Baltimore's Shining Cuisine." Chef Louis Szathmary, p. 6
1984 Jan "Historic Annapolis." Coming about in Maryland. Carolyn Males, p. 38

MASSACHUSETTS

Series Guidebooks (See Appendix 1)

Blue Guide: Boston & Cambridge
Fodor: Boston; Cape Cod
      Cape Cod & Islands of Martha's Vineyard & Nantucket
Frommer: Boston: City Guide

Background Reading

Brown, Richard D.   MASSACHUSETTS
One of a series of popular histories for each state published as part of the
Bicentennial observance in 1976. Norton, 1978.

Caffrey, Kate   THE MAYFLOWER
"For the reader who enjoys a light touch of historical fact mixed into a number
of stories well told." (BRD) Stein & Day, 1975.

Clayton, Barbara and Whitley, Kathleen   GUIDE TO NEW BEDFORD
Walking tours, festivals and a concise history of a once-prominent whaling city.
Globe Pequot, 1979. See also Geoffrey Moorhouse's book *The Boat and the Town*,
listed under "New England."

Clayton, Barbara and Whitley, Kathleen   EXPLORING COASTAL
**   MASSACHUSETTS**
Mini-tours of historic homes, museums, recreational sites, natural views for
motorists, bicyclists and hikers. Dodd, 1983. There's a companion volume for the
coast from Gloucester north to Kennebunkport in Maine, *Exploring Coastal
Maine*.

Cummings, A.L.   THE FRAMED HOUSES OF MASSACHUSETTS BAY
Architecture and social history, 1625-1725. Harvard U Pr, 1982.

Frost, A.N.   THE SALEM WITCHCRAFT PAPERS
The actual documents surrounding the events. Da Capo Pr, 1977.

Heaton, Vernon   THE MAYFLOWER
A lively retelling of the Pilgrims' voyage and the settlement of Plymouth that
highlights personalities. Mayflower, 1980.

O'Connell, James C.   INSIDE GUIDE TO SPRINGFIELD AND THE
**   PIONEER VALLEY**
Western Mass Pub, 1986

Osborn, Beverly H.   IN AND ABOUT WORCESTER: A GUIDEBOOK
A guide for a central Massachusetts city that is experiencing growth and revival. Commonwealth Pr, 1983.

Owens, Carole   THE BERKSHIRE COTTAGES
"A social history of America's Inland Newport . . . the fabulous mansions built in the Berkshire hills and the fairy tale lives of the families who built them." (Publisher) Cottage Pr, 1985.

Randall, Peter   SALEM AND MARBLEHEAD
Guidebooks to dwellings and architecture of two historic towns. Down East, 1983.

Starkey, Marion L.   THE DEVIL IN MASSACHUSETTS
A modern inquiry into the Salem witch trials. Time-Life, 1982 (first published 1949).

Sternfield, Joshua   THE BERKSHIRE BOOK: A COMPLETE GUIDE
Guide to western Massachusetts and the Berkshires, including history, things to do, shopping, hotels, restaurants. Berkshire Hse, 1986.

**Tolles, Bryant F., Jr.   ARCHITECTURE IN SALEM: AN
ILLUSTRATED GUIDE**
Essex Institute, 1983.

**Tree, Christina M.   THE OTHER MASSACHUSETTS: AN EXPLORER'S
GUIDE**
A guidebook for the Bay state other than Boston and Cape Cod, intended both for residents and visitors with a focus on inexpensive pleasures suitable for the entire family. Countryman Pr, 1987.

**Young, Allen   NORTH OF QUABBIN: A GUIDE TO NINE
MASSACHUSETTS TOWNS**
A guide to the Quabbin Reservoir region of Massachusetts. Millers River Pub Co, 1983.

BOSTON & CAMBRIDGE

Amory, Cleveland   THE PROPER BOSTONIANS
Witty social history of Boston's first families based on family writings, conversations, anecdotes and Boston stories, by an author who is, himself, a proper Bostonian. Parnassus Imprint, 1984 (first published 1947).

Appleberg, Marilyn   I LOVE BOSTON GUIDE
"Information vital to making the best choices as to what to see and do according to one's personal needs and interests. . . . a first-rate traveler's helper." Macmillan, 1983.

Boston Society of Architects   ARCHITECTURE BOSTON
Boston's buildings "related to local history and the cityscape"—"downtown, the North End, Beacon Hill, Back Bay, Fenway, Southie, Charlestown, Roxbury and Cambridge." (BRD) Crown, 1976.

Chesler, Bernice   IN AND OUT OF BOSTON WITH
                                           (AND WITHOUT) CHILDREN
Globe Pequot, 1982.

Dickson, Harry E.   ARTHUR FIEDLER AND THE BOSTON POPS
Houghton, 1981.

Falls, Joe   BOSTON MARATHON
"Vividly captures the Walter Mitty atmosphere that envelops the marathon" held each year on Patriot's Day. (BRD) Macmillan, 1977.

Freely, John   BOSTON AND CAMBRIDGE
"Neighborhood-by-neighborhood survey of the city's historical sites, buildings, museums and attractions" with background information, history, public transportation routes, etc. (BL) Norton, 1984.

Frost, Jack   BOSTON'S FREEDOM TRAIL
Globe Pequot, 1981.

Harris, John   THE BOSTON GLOBE HISTORIC WALKS IN OLD BOSTON
Globe Pequot, 1982.

Lee, Mary P.   THE STUDENT TRAVELER IN BOSTON-CAMBRIDGE
Rosen Group, 1984.

Lukas, J. Anthony   COMMON GROUND: A TURBULENT DECADE IN THE
                                            LIVES OF THREE AMERICAN FAMILIES
A working-class Irish Catholic family, a black Roxbury family, and an upper-middle-class suburban family speak to the school busing controversy that tore Boston apart. A fascinating addition to this readable social history are biographies of key figures in the controversy: Louise Day of the School Committee, Judge Garrity, the editor of the *Boston Globe*, a Catholic cardinal, the mayor, and so on. Knopf, 1985.

Lyndon, Donlyn   THE CITY OBSERVED: BOSTON
Walking tours of Boston's architectural sites with history and critical commentary—suitable for tourists or architecture buffs. Random, 1982.

Maynard, Mary and Dow, Mary-Lou   HASSLE-FREE BOSTON: A MANUAL
                                                                FOR WOMEN
"A unique and comprehensive guide . . . geared toward the [single woman] visitor and relocator with a minimum of time. . . . marvelous biographical tidbits on the indomitable, intelligent [women] who lived in and influenced the history of Boston. Thoroughly delightful." (LJ) Lewis, 1984.

**Primack, Mark L.   THE GREATER BOSTON PARK AND
                      RECREATION GUIDE**
Globe Pequot, 1983.

Snow, Edward R.   THE ISLANDS OF BOSTON HARBOR
Dodd, 1971.

Southworth, Michael and Susan   THE A.I.A. GUIDE TO BOSTON
Traditional architecture guide in neighborhood-by-neighborhood format—"illustrated [with] many anecdotes and stories . . . maps and suggested tours are included." (BL) Globe Pequot, 1984.

Warner, Sam Bass, Jr.   PROVINCE OF REASON
Based on the premise that the past can be better understood through the lives of individuals rather than through statistics and stock phrases (industrial obsolescence, etc.). "Offers incisive sketches [of Bostonians] that reveal much about the region and U.S. urban life generally." Individual subjects range from old-time radio comedian Fred Allen and former president of Harvard James Conant to housewives and businessmen. (PW) Harvard U Pr, 1984.

CAPE COD

Beston, Henry   THE OUTERMOST HOUSE
"A year of life on the great beach of Cape Cod"—a classic. (BRD) Ballantine, 1976 (first published 1928).

Chesler, Bernice   THE FAMILY GUIDE TO CAPE COD
Barre, 1976.

Finch, Robert   COMMON GROUND: A NATURALIST'S CAPE COD
Thirty-two essays from Cape Cod newspaper columns. Godine, 1981. Also *The Primal Place* (1983), about the area around Brewster.

**Hutchins, Francis G.   MASHPEE: THE STORY OF CAPE COD'S
                         INDIAN TOWN**
Account of Mashpee's Indians from the 1600s to the 1970s, who became "Americanized," did not leave, accepted Christianity, and sued for the return of their lands. Amarta Pr, 1981.

**Koehler, Margaret   A VISITOR'S GUIDE TO CAPE COD
                       NATIONAL SEASHORE**
Chatham Pr, 1973.

Robinson, William F.   CAPE COD
Henry David Thoreau's complete text, with the journey recreated in pictures. Includes watercolors, botanical illustrations, period maps, early photos and contemporary photographs "of a Cape Cod Thoreau would recognize today." Little, 1985.

**Sadlier, Hugh and Heather   SHORT WALKS ON CAPE COD AND
THE VINEYARD**
"Twenty-six tantalizing walks through the Cape area's special beauty."
(Publisher) Globe Pequot, 1983.

**Sargent, William   SHALLOW WATERS: A YEAR ON CAPE COD'S
PLEASANT BAY**
"A seasonal chronicle of Cape Cod's cycle of nature . . . brings to vivid life the
plants and creatures whose existence depends upon this fragile . . . environment."
(BL) Houghton, 1981.

Taber, Gladys   STILL COVE JOURNAL
A journal completed shortly before the author's death of "random thoughts,
recipes, neighborhood news and nature reports" written for a local Cape Cod
newspaper. (See also this writer's books under "Connecticut.") Har-Row, 1981.
Also *My Own Cape Cod* (1971), about her love for the Cape and its seasons,
written in 1970 and recently issued in a reprint.

Teller, Walter   CAPE COD AND THE OFFSHORE ISLANDS
The offshore islands being Martha's Vineyard and Nantucket. "Following in
Thoreau's footsteps" in a changed world. (BRD) P-H, 1970.

Wilkinson, Alec   MIDNIGHTS: A YEAR WITH THE WELLFLEET POLICE
The author spent a year as a rookie policeman on the nine-man Wellfleet police
force. Reminiscences of fellow officers, the job, mundane events—the author "has
that rare ability to extract universal significance from commonplace events. . . .
fairly enchants the reader into caring about the subject and wanting to read on."
(BL) Random, 1982.

MARTHA'S VINEYARD & NANTUCKET

Allen, Everett S.   MARTHA'S VINEYARD: AN ELEGY
"Leisurely essays explore the mystique of island existence . . . memorable
anecdotes . . . felicitous reading" about a place irrevocably changed by the influx of
new residents and tourists. (PW) Little, 1982.

Ames, Evelyn and others   ON THE VINEYARD
Photographs laced with comments, stories, poems and memory pieces by
prominent Vineyarders. Anchor Pr, 1980.

**Burroughs, Polly   GUIDE TO MARTHA'S VINEYARD; GUIDE
TO NANTUCKET**
"A sensitive introduction to the history, traditions, and geography of Martha's
Vineyard . . . an amazingly thorough and accurate guide to the special places and
events found on the Island." (Publisher) Globe Pequot, 1985.

Grossfeld, Stan   NANTUCKET, THE OTHER SEASON
What Nantucket is like after the tourists leave—photographs and anecdotes and
an introduction by Nantucket resident, David Halberstam. Globe Pequot, 1982.

**Hough, Henry Beatle   REMEMBRANCE AND LIGHT: IMAGES OF
                          MARTHA'S VINEYARD**
Impressions of each season on the island by the editor of *Vineyard
Gazette*—some of the pieces appeared there first—and photographs. Harvard
Common Pr, 1984. Also *Soundings at Sea Level* (1980) and *Martha's
Vineyard—Summer Resort After One Hundred Years* (1966).

Hoyt, Ed Palmer   NANTUCKET: THE LIFE OF AN ISLAND
The island from Indian days to 1977 when the island sued for secession from the
state of Massachusetts. Stephen Greene Pr, 1978.

**Mackay, Dick   NANTUCKET! NANTUCKET! NANTUCKET!: AN
                   INSIDER'S GUIDE**
Sakaty Head, 1981.

Stackpole, E.A.   NANTUCKET DOORWAYS: THRESHOLD TO THE PAST
History and architecture of the island as reflected in its homes. Hastings, 1974.

Teller, Walter   CAPE COD AND THE OFFSHORE ISLANDS
See above under "Cape Cod."

Whipple, Addison B.C.   VINTAGE NANTUCKET
Uses walks along the island streets to begin each chapter, tying past to present,
and imparting much about Indians, Quakers, whaling wives, eccentrics, old
families, etc. Dodd, 1978.

Novels

Benchley, Nathaniel   THE OFF-ISLANDERS (Nantucket)
The book on which the movie *The Russians Are Coming* was based. McGraw,
1961.

Carlisle, Henry   THE JONAH MAN (Nantucket)
Grim tale of a nineteenth-century whaling ship master whose past "taints all his
dealings with his neighbors." (FC) Knopf, 1984.

Chute, Patricia   EVA'S MUSIC (Martha's Vineyard)
The heroine finds herself pregnant and with a dying mother; she decides to
move to Martha's Vineyard with the baby after her mother's death. Doubleday,
1983.

Clark, Mary Higgins   WHERE ARE THE CHILDREN? (Cape Cod)
Suspenseful, scary story of an unsolved murder years earlier, which seems
about to be repeated in the heroine's new life on the Cape. S&S, 1975.

**Coleman, Terry   THANKSGIVING: A NOVEL IN CELEBRATION
                    OF AMERICA**
Written by an Australian; a historical novel of Puritan Massachusetts and

cosmopolitan Nieuw Amsterdam—"full of fascinating historical detail" and combining real and fictional characters. (FC) S&S, 1981.

Cooney, Ellen   ALL THE WAY HOME
A former athlete's attempt to rebuild her life through establishing Curry Crossing's first female softball team. Putnam Pub Group, 1984.

Fast, Howard   APRIL MORNING
Fictionalized version of the shot heard round the world. Crown, 1961.

Ford, Elaine   MISSED CONNECTIONS
The "frayed circuits of domestic life" are the missed connections in this novel of family life in a blue-collar suburb of Boston. (FC) Random, 1983.

Heidish, Marcy M.   WITNESSES
Biographical novel of Anne Hutchinson, who was banished to Rhode Island for her views on religious freedom in seventeenth-century Massachusetts. Houghton, 1980.

Hospital, Janette T.   THE TIGER IN THE TIGER PIT
Reunion of a New England family gathered for their parents' fiftieth wedding celebration. Dutton, 1984.

Hunter, Evan   LIZZIE
The author uses actual trial and inquest records along with fictional invention for a fascinating portrait of Lizzie Borden. Arbor Hse, 1984.

Lovecraft, H.P.   THE DUNWICH HORROR, AND OTHER COLLECTED LOVECRAFT STORIES
First of three volumes of collected Gothic horror stories many of which are set in both a real and an imaginary Massachusetts (Salem, the area around the Quabbin Reservoir, Pioneer Valley). (Dunwich is supposedly based on the villages of Wilbraham, Hampden and Monson.) See also guidebooks on the area under "Background Reading" above, and *Abandoned New England* under "U.S.A., The East/New England." Arkham, 1985. Also Volume 2, *At the Mountains of Madness* (1985) and Volume 3, *Dagon and Other Macabre Tales* (1986).

Mailer, Norman   TOUGH GUYS DON'T DANCE (Provincetown)
A writer comes to after a night of drinking to find a strange tattoo on his arm, blood all over his car and two decapitated heads buried with his marijuana supply—he's a prime suspect for the murders. Random, 1984.

Marquand, John P.   WICKFORD POINT
The "vagaries of [an] ingrown New England family" set in the family home at Wickford Point (Newburyport). (FC) Little, 1939.

Parker, Robert B.   PROMISED LAND (Cape Cod)
"Excellently tangled" plot of a runaway wife located by a detective on Cape Cod. (FC) Houghton, 1976.

Pentecost, Hugh   DEADLY TRAP (Berkshires)
A PR man on vacation becomes involved in the mystery surrounding the kidnapping of an Arab oil magnate's daughter. Dodd, 1978.

Rich, Virginia   THE NANTUCKET DIET MURDERS
One of a series of mysteries by a chef-turned-sleuth. In this, people on Nantucket are seemingly "starving themselves to death under the influence of a spellbinding guru." (Publisher) Delacorte Pr, 1985.

Rushing, Jane G.   COVENANT OF GRACE
Another novel (see Heidish, above) of the Anne Hutchinson story. Doubleday, 1982.

Saul, John   THE GOD PROJECT
Medical horror genre—suspense story of a "megalomaniacal scientist experimenting with children to 'improve' the race for dubious ends." (FC) Bantam, 1982.

Seton, Anya   THE HEARTH AND EAGLE (Marblehead)
History of Marblehead interwoven with a family's history. Houghton, 1948.

Theroux, Paul   PICTURE PALACE (Cape Cod)
A photojournalist reflects on her life—an "elaborate, visual conceit." (FC) Houghton, 1978.

Zaroulis, Nancy   CALL THE DARKNESS LIGHT (Lowell)
The sad life of an orphan who must go to work first as a household servant and then in a cotton mill—"comprehensive account of industrialization and immigration in the early nineteenth century." (FC) Doubleday, 1979.

BOSTON & CAMBRIDGE

Banks, Oliver   THE REMBRANDT PANEL
A murder mystery that takes us behind the scenes in the world of art dealers, museum directors and art fakery. Little, 1980.

Bernays, Anne   THE ADDRESS BOOK
A Boston woman is "catapulted into a crisis" when offered a New York job that will make her a commuting wife and mother. She finds five strange names in an old address book, phones each of them, and finds they were part of her life and have definite ideas about the choice she should make. (FC) Little, 1983. Also *The School Book* (1980), a feminist novel set in a private school in Cambridge.

Carroll, James   MORTAL FRIENDS
Story of an Irish immigrant, and Boston itself, from the 1920s to just before Kennedy's assassination. Little, 1978.

Cook, Robin   GODPLAYER
The latest of Cook's medical mysteries set in a Boston hospital. In this, the

subject is SSDs—sudden surgical deaths. Putnam, 1983. *Fever* (1982) is about a medical researcher whose daughter has leukemia as a result of toxic wastes, and *Coma* (1977) concerns a medical student's attempts to discover the reason for a rash of comas following surgery.

Fried, Albert   THE PRESCOTT CHRONICLES
Chronicle of a Boston political family from 1630 to 1973. Putnam Pub Group, 1976.

Gifford, Thomas   THE GLENDOWER LEGACY
"Masterful, irony-filled espionage thriller" involving a document owned by a Harvard professor that seems to prove George Washington was a traitor. (FC) Putnam Pub Group, 1978.

Greenan, Russell H.   THE SECRET OF ALGERNON PENDLETON
"An excursion into the macabre" with the chief character living in a town house in Boston and listening to inner voices. (FC) Random, 1973.

Gurney, A.R.   ENTERTAINING STRANGERS
Ironic comedy of academia set in an unnamed institute of technology in Cambridge. Doubleday, 1977.

Higgins, George V.   A CHOICE OF ENEMIES
"Mordantly witty and dismayingly believable" novel of Boston-style politics. (PW) Knopf, 1984. Other novels by Higgins on various aspects of the Boston scene include: *The Patriot Game* (1982), *Kennedy for the Defense* (1980), *The Digger's Game* (1973), *The Friends of Eddie Coyle* (1972), and *The Rat on Fire* (1980).

Jaffe, Rona   CLASS REUNION
The twentieth reunion of four Radcliffe classmates and what's happened to them in the interim. Delacorte Pr, 1979.

Kaufman, Myron S.   THE LOVE OF ELSPETH BAKER
Odyssey of a Jewish-American princess in Boston of the 1970s from Mount Holyoke to an orthodox synagogue. Arbor Hse, 1982.

Marquand, John P.   THE LATE GEORGE APLEY
Story of a Boston Brahmin, which won a Pulitzer Prize in 1938. Little, 1937. Also about the socially elite in Boston is *H.M. Pulham, Esquire* (1941).

Mason, F. Van Wyck   GUNS FOR REBELLION
The Battle of Bunker Hill from the point of view of a Boston resident who is forced to fight on the side of the British. Doubleday, 1953.

Myrer, Anton   A GREEN DESIRE
Two brothers—one rescued from poverty by a wealthy aunt, the other remaining to support their mother—vie for the same woman. The love triangle "serves as the focal point [for] practically all the major historical events of the present

century" through World War II. (FC) Putnam Pub Group, 1982. Also *The Last Convertible* (1978), which takes a group of Harvard students from 1938 through World War II and the years that follow.

O'Connor, Edwin   ALL IN THE FAMILY
Story of a rich Irish family's entry into politics. Little, 1966. Also *Edge of Sadness* (1961), the saga of another Irish-Catholic family in Boston.

Parker, Robert B.   MORTAL STAKES
The world of baseball and the Red Sox is background for this mystery. Houghton, 1975. Also *God Save the Child* (1974), about the kidnapping of an emotionally disturbed child from a Boston suburb.

Piercy, Marge   FLY AWAY HOME
A woman's successful life as wife, mother, cookbook writer and daughter falls apart when her mother dies and she has to face disillusionment with both her husband and daughter. Summit Bks, 1984. Also *Small Changes* (1973), about two women in Cambridge whose lives are radically changed over a decade.

Read, Piers Paul   THE PROFESSOR'S DAUGHTER
Father and daughter become involved with campus radicals. Lippincott, 1971.

Reed, Barry   THE VERDICT
"Superb courtroom drama" of medical malpractice in which the two lawyers are "Boston's most upright lawyer [and] a hard-drinking . . . ambulance chasing lawyer who will cheat anyone." (FC) S&S, 1980.

Sarton, May   ANGER
"Romantic, yet realistic portrait" of the marriage of an unlikely couple, one a successful Boston banker, the other a "determined-to-be-famous" soprano. (FC) Norton, 1982.

Savage, Elizabeth   THE LAST NIGHT AT THE RITZ
A meeting at the Ritz intended to be a riotous reunion of three longtime friends somehow goes wrong. Little, 1973.

Sexton, Linda G.   RITUALS
A young woman fills the family power vacuum when her mother dies, with disastrous effects on her personal life. Doubleday, 1982.

Wakefield, Dan   STARTING OVER
A divorced New Yorker tries to fashion a new life in Boston. Delacorte Pr, 1973.

Wolfe, Thomas   OF TIME AND THE RIVER
A young man's three years at Harvard. (See also the author's autobiographical novels under "North Carolina.") Scribner, 1935.

TRAVEL ARTICLES

AMERICANA
1985 Mar-Apr "A New Saw Mill for Old Sturbridge." Peter V. Fossel, p. 82

ANTIQUES
1985 Mar "Historic Deerfield." The entire issue is devoted to this destination for New England travelers. pp. 520-691
1984 Feb "The Paul Revere and Moses Pierce-Hichborn Houses in Boston." Paul B. Jenison, p. 454
Mar "House of Seven Gables: Hawthorne's Memorial." Edward M. Stevenson, p. 666
Aug "The Mayflower Society Museum, Plymouth." Ruth B. Hall, p. 294

CONNOISSEUR
1984 Jul "Art Town U.S.A." Williamstown has "more fine art per capita than anywhere else." Jo Durden-Smith and Diane de Simone, p. 86

EARLY AMERICAN LIFE
1984 Aug "The Fourth of July at Old Sturbridge Village." p. 28

GOURMET
1985 Dec "City Dining—Boston." Andy Birsh, p. 28
1984 Mar "Provincetown's Yankee-Portuguese Flavor." Molly O'Neill, p. 46
Nov "Old Deerfield." Terry Weeks, p. 48

HARPER'S
1985 Jun "Walking the Cape." In Thoreau's footsteps. David Black, p. 49

HORIZON
1985 Jun "Lowell: Mill Town Renaissance." Dorothy A. Schecter, p. 25
"U.S. Arts: Strategies for the 80s." The "Lowell Plan" and the Arts. p. 33

HOUSE & GARDEN
1984 Jul "Boston—I Recommend: Sunrise Walk Through Boston When Its Buildings Are Bathed in Soft Light." Jim Powell, p. 41

NATIONAL GEOGRAPHIC TRAVELER
1985 Autumn "Lowell Weaves a Spell." Restoration of a textile mill city. Jack Beatty, p. 118
1984 Summer "The Outermost Land." A Cape Cod panorama. p. 76

N.Y. TIMES SUNDAY TRAVEL SECTION (X)
1985 Mar 17 (Part 2, "Sophisticated Traveler") "A Salem sampler." A visual education in the history and architecture of New England . . . unsurpassed on the Eastern seaboard. P.D. James, p. 85
May 12 "What's Doing in the Berkshires." Linda Charlton, p. 10
May 19 "Learning to Love Springfield, Mass. and a Guide for Sojourning in Springfield." Norman Kotker, p. 15

1985 Jun 16 "Mountain Greenery." The Berkshires at their summer peak. Constance Rosenblum, p. 21

Jun 23 "What's Doing in Cape Cod." Milton Moore, p. 10

Jun 30 "Critics' Choices, Personal Favorites When They're Not Dining at Taillevant." Various authors (includes Massachusetts), p. 14

Jul 7 "What's Doing in Martha's Vineyard." Harvey Ewing, p. 10

Jul 14 "Brahmin Boston Preserved." The Athenaeum in Beacon Hill is a repository of more than books. Mark C. Hansen, p. 19

Sep 8 "In the Country: Three Inns Celebrate Gifted Elegance." Marian Burros, p. 15

"Where to Buy Unusual Gifts on Cape Cod—Suncooked Fruit ($4), Ruanas ($475)." Pamela Harlech, p. 18

Oct 20 Shopper's World: "Providing for Cape Cod's Birds." Birdwatcher's General Store on 6A. Corinne K. Hoexter, p. 6

Nov 10 "What's Doing in Boston." Fox Butterfield, p. 10

Dec 8 "Dining Out in Old Boston." Patrons favor the classic restaurants for oysters, lobster and even the din. Alexander Theroux, p. 20

1984 Feb 5 Fare of the Country: "In Search of Real Boston Baked Beans." Lisa Hamel, p. 12

Apr 15 "Fenway Court." Shortcut to Italian riches—visiting Boston's Gardiner Museum. Phyllis Lee Levin, p. 12

Jun 3 "Tradition by the Sea." Cape Ann. John Deedy, p. 9

Jun 17 "What's Doing on Cape Cod." Susan Daar, p. 10

Jun 24 "Comparing Luxury in Boston Hotels." A guest's report on three in the top class. Marian Burros, p. 9

Jul 8 "Sailing Days and Peaceful Anchorages." A journey among the Elizabeth Islands, off the coast of Massachusetts. Barbar L. Ascher, p. 19

Jul 22 "Returning to a Beloved Island." Martha's Vineyard. Ruth Gordon, p. 14

"What's Doing on Martha's Vineyard. Ira H. Freeman, p. 15

Sep 9 "Chugging Through the Berkshires." 1920s scenic train ride. James Brooke, p. 12

Oct 14 "What's Doing in Boston." Fox Butterfield, p. 10

Oct 21 "As the Days Dwindle, a Quiet Cape Beckons. Betsy Wade, p. 16

Oct 28 Fare of the Country: "America's Berry Stages Annual Show." Cape Cod's cranberry country. Regina Schrambling, p. 6

Nov 4 "Pilgrimage to Plymouth." James Carroll, p. 12

Nov 11 "Beacon Hill: Where the Past Is Present." Notes for a history-filled stroll. Phyllis Lee Levin, p. 16

Dec 2 Shopper's World: "A Street with a Dickens Air." Charles Street shops, etc. Phyllis L. Levin, p. 6

Dec 16 Shopper's World: "Quilts for Collectors." Keepsake Quilts in Lenox. Sara Evans, p. 19

TOWN & COUNTRY

1985 Jul "Classic New England Hideaway." Marion, Massachusetts. G.Y. Dryansky, p. 136

"A Berkshire Sampler." Elizabeth Heilman, p. 30

TRAVEL & LEISURE
1985 Jul "A Nantucket Summer." Images of the sweet season and a visitor's guide to Nantucket. Joseph P. Kahn, p. 70

"Walking Tour: Boston's Beacon Hill." Janice Brand, p. 133

Oct "Cape Cod Thanksgiving," Charles N. Barnard, p. 181

1984 Jan "Boston's Great Hotel Restaurants." George Lang, p. 24

TRAVEL/HOLIDAY
1985 Mar "Institutional Boston." Cultivating culture in New England. Janice Brand, p. 70

"Concerning Food and Wine: Edible Boston." Robert L. Balzer, p. 74

Oct "Lowell Offerings: From Factories to Trolleys in Massachusetts." Raymond Nathan, p. 12

1984 Dec "Faneuil Hall Marketplace." Boston's premier emporium. Helen Boursier, p. 38

VOGUE
1985 Oct "Autumn on Nantucket." Alan Fraser, p. 434

YANKEE
1985 Feb "The Gardens of Winter." Isabelle Gardner Museum in Boston and other "winter gardens" in the Boston area. Lynda Morgenroth, p. 44

Apr "Finding the Japanese Face of Boston." Lynda Morgenroth, p. 30

May This New England: "Rowe, Massachusetts." Michael E. C. Gery, p. 54

Jun This New England: "Thacher Island, Mass." Tim Clark, p. 60

"The Bridge of Flowers." Joining Buckland and Shelburne. Edie Clark, p. 78

Aug This New England: "Revere Beach." Tim Clark, p. 52

"History and Hospitality in New Bedford." Jared Mayfield, p. 28

Sep "Boston unchanging—Learning How to Appreciate . . . This 'Most Civilized of Cities.'" Robert E. Ginna, Jr., p. 164

Oct "Still the Ritz (Hotel in Boston)." Gene Autry rode his horse in once, but Joe Kennedy wasn't allowed. James Dodson, p. 94

Nov "Big Bargains in Old Mills." Factory outlets in Blackstone Valley. Larry Willard, Sr., p. 38

1984 Jan "Winter Days at Sturbridge." Workshops include everything from hearth-cooking . . . learning essentials of making rabbet, mortise and tenon, and dado joints—all done as it was many years ago. Julie Welch, p. 134

Apr "Renaissance in Worcester." Garrett Newman, p. 46

Jun This New England: "Whately, Massachusetts." Shelley Rotner, p. 62

Dec This New England: "Cuttyhunk, Massachusetts." Gunnar Hansen, p. 60

MICHIGAN

Background Reading

Brough, James   THE FORD DYNASTY: AN AMERICAN STORY
Lives, trials and fortunes of Henry, Edsel and Henry II. Doubleday, 1977.

Catton, Bruce   MICHIGAN
One of a series of popular histories for each state published as part of the
Bicentennial observance in 1976. Norton, 1977.

Conot, Robert E.   AMERICAN ODYSSEY
Life story of America from the perspective of the history and growth of Detroit.
Morrow, 1974.

Fischoff, Martin   DETROIT GUIDE
"First rate coverage . . . trenchant, witty, and
knowledgeable . . as useful to the resident as to the tourist [with] value as a commentary on popular culture and as social history." Food and drink, shops, sports
and recreation, sightseeing and arts and letters. (LJ) Glastonbury, 1983.

Inglis, James G.   HANDBOOK FOR TRAVELERS: NORTHERN MICHIGAN
Black Letter, 1973.

Lacey, Robert   FORD—THE MEN AND THE MACHINE
"Two books in one"—first the Horatio Alger story of Henry Ford; second, a
Dynasty-like story of Grosse Pointe—"rich in incident and character as the prime-
time soaps and requires no suspension of disbelief, being true." (NYTBR) Little,
1986.

Meyer, Katherine M., ed.   DETROIT ARCHITECTURE: A.I.A. GUIDE
Neighborhood-by-neighborhood guide by the American Institute of Architects.
Wayne State U, 1980.

Osler, Jack   FIFTY GREAT MINI-TRIPS FOR MICHIGAN
Media Ventures, 1977.

**Wamsley, James S.   AMERICAN INGENUITY: HENRY FORD MUSEUM
                       AND GREENFIELD VILLAGE**
Story of the Ford indoor-outdoor museum of American industry and cultural
history and its contents—everything from the chair on which Lincoln was sitting
when shot to a replica of the Menlo Park lab where Edison worked to an entire
nineteenth-century jewelry store transplanted to the museum. (PW) Abrams,
1985.

Wrobel, Paul   OUR WAY
"Family, parish, and neighborhood in a Polish-American community" in Detroit.
An anthropologist analyzes his family's life. (BRD) U of Notre Dame, 1979.

Novels

Arnow, Harriette   THE WEEDKILLER'S DAUGHTER (Detroit)
A fifteen-year-old sees through the hypocrisy and shallowness of her parents'
life-style. Knopf, 1970. Also *The Dollmaker* (see under "Kentucky").

Briskin, Jacqueline   THE ONYX
A chronicle of the early days of the automobile industry, with a lead character who bears a striking resemblance to Henry Ford. Delacorte Pr, 1982.

Dickinson, Charles   WALTZ IN MARATHON
Life in Marathon, Michigan, a small town, as seen through the life of a gentleman-ly loan shark. His life is greatly changed when he meets a fortyish woman lawyer. Knopf, 1983.

Estleman, Loren D.   KILL ZONE
Terrorists take over a passenger-carrying steamboat on Lake Erie—"enough action and colorful characters for three ordinary thrillers." (FC) Mysterious Pr, 1984.

Fuller, Iola   THE LOON FEATHER (Mackinac Island)
Historical novel of the 1880s—fur trading and Indian life. HarBraceJ, 1940.

Guest, Judith   SECOND HEAVEN (Detroit)
A depressed woman whose husband has left her, and a lawyer still suffering from his own divorce unhappiness, join forces to expose a child abuse case—"in the process . . . find they can join together as a new family." (FC) Viking, 1982.

Hailey, Arthur   WHEELS
"An expose of and salute to the auto industry." (FC) Doubleday, 1971.

Harrison, Jim   SUNDOG (Upper Peninsula)
A writer tape-records a dying man's life story as foreman on dam construction projects. Dutton, 1984. Also *Farmer* (1976), about a Swedish-American teacher and farmer and midwest Americana of a generation ago.

Hemingway, Ernest   THE TORRENTS OF SPRING (Petosky)
A working-class comedy by the noted writer. Scribner, 1972 (first published 1926).

Kienzle, William X.   THE ROSARY MURDERS (Detroit)
Murder mystery about a series of Lenten murders in Detroit's Catholic community, solved when a priest breaks the madman's code. Andrews, 1979.

Lancaster, Bruce   THE BIG KNIVES (Detroit)
Historical novel of the American Revolutionary War and a raid on British supply headquarters. Little, 1964.

McGuane, Thomas   THE SPORTING CLUB (Upper Peninsula)
"High-toned sportsmen and their wives" at the centennial celebration of the Centennial Club—"this tight, funny, elusive and aristocratic novel reminds one of *The Great Gatsby*." (FC) FS&G, 1974.

Oates, Joyce Carol   DO WITH ME WHAT YOU WILL (Detroit)
Examination of personalities and motives, back to their childhoods, of two

people involved in an extramarital affair. (FC) Vanguard, 1973. Also *Them* (1969), "violence and poverty in the lives of . . . a blue-collar white family" from 1930-67; and a book of short stories, *The Wheel of Love* (1970).

Piercy, Marge   BRAIDED LIVES
Lives of two women from the 1950s, as adolescents in working-class Detroit, to college in Ann Arbor, to New York—a feminist, political novel. Summit Bks, 1982.

Price, Nancy   AN ACCOMPLISHED WOMAN (Detroit)
Relationship of an orphaned girl with her guardian. Coward, 1979.

Rogers, Thomas   AT THE SHORES (Lake Michigan)
Set in a post-World War II Michigan and about the adolescent hero's marvelous fantasies—combinations of movie stars, fictional characters, strangers in the neighborhood—and his real involvement with a girl from the East. S&S, 1980.

Traver, Robert   PEOPLE VS. KIRK
A murder mystery that uses hypnotism to probe the chief suspect's guilt or innocence and provides readers with knowledge of hypnosis' legal status. St. Martin, 1981. Also *Anatomy of a Murder* (1958), the story of an Army officer who murders his wife's rapist, that was made into a popular movie.

TRAVEL ARTICLES

GOURMET
1985 Apr Gourmet Holidays: "Inns of the Midwest, Part II." Michigan and Wisconsin. Mimi Elder, p. 48

NATIONAL GEOGRAPHIIC
1985 Apr "A North Woods Park Primeval: Isle Royale." National Park in Lake Superior. John L. Eliot, p. 534

NATIONAL GEOGRAPHIC TRAVELER
1985 Autumn "Yesterday in America—the Henry Ford Museum and Greenfield Village." James S. Walmsley, p. 50
1984 Autumn "Salmon Run, Michigan Style." Tom Opre, p. 80

N.Y. TIMES SUNDAY TRAVEL SECTION (X)
1985 May 26 "A Serenade to Leelanau, Michigan's Little Enclave [of] Vineyards As Well As Dunes and Lakes." Mary A. Rodgers, p. 9
    Nov 24 "Up in Michigan." The area where Ernest Hemingway spent his summers is still a quiet and sylvan place. James Barron, p. 14
1984 Sep 2 "Durable Mackinac." Michigan resort retains the ability to transport visitors back to the turn of the century. Robert D. Hersey, Jr., p. 12

TOWN & COUNTRY
1985 Jul "Happiness Is Harbor Springs." Wendy L. Moonan, p. 139

TRAVEL/HOLIDAY
1985 Feb "Ann Arbor, Michigan." Rooting out the past. Diane Marshall and Denise
    Meehan, p. 68
1984 Aug "Dune Slide!" Dunes National Lakeshore. Norman Lobsenz, p. 82

MINNESOTA

Background Reading

Blacklock, Les   MINNESOTA WILD
Description and travel, natural history, and photographs. Voyageur Pr, 1983.

Bly, Carol   LETTERS FROM THE COUNTRY
Essays "to raise rural consciousness" by a fiction writer about the "essence of small
town life." (BRD) Har-Row, 1981.

Cheeseborough, G.R.   WHERE TO GO IN MINNEAPOLIS AND ST. PAUL
Where to Go, 1984.

Ervin, Jean   THE TWIN CITIES PERCEIVED
A study in words and drawings. Adams Minn, 1979.

Hampl, Patricia   A ROMANTIC EDUCATION
"Begins as an extended essay on sensitivity to one's family and ends as a sort of
travelogue describing the author's visits to Prague." The author was born into a St.
Paul, Minnesota, family that "cultivated nostalgia for the past." (BRD) Houghton,
1981.

Lass, William E.   MINNESOTA
One of a series of popular histories for each state published as part of the
Bicentennial observance in 1976. Norton, 1977.

Olsenius, Richard   MINNESOTA TRAVEL COMPANION
A guide to the history along Minnesota's highways. Bluestem, 1983.

**Stein, Shifra   GAS-SAVING GETAWAYS LESS THAN TWO HOURS FROM
    GREATER MINNEAPOLIS-ST. PAUL**
The trips within a two-hour range spill over into Wisconsin. Har-Row, 1982.

**Umhoefer, Jim   GUIDE TO MINNESOTA'S PARKS, CANOE ROUTES
    AND TRAILS**
Outdoor recreation in Minnesota. Northword, 1984.

Whitman, Lawrence   TRAVEL GUIDE TO MINNESOTA
Nodin Pr, 1977.

Novels

Christgau, John   SPOON
Historical novel of the Sioux-Santee uprising in 1862. Spoon is an Indian interpreter. Viking, 1978.

Gernes, Sonia   THE WAY TO ST. IVES
Story of a 41-year old spinster told with compassion and humor. Scribner, 1982.

Gifford, Thomas   THE CAVANAUGH QUEST
A murder mystery with Minneapolis "recreated in meticulous local detail." (FC) Putnam Pub Group, 1976.

Hassler, Jon   STAGGERFORD
A week in the life of a mild-mannered Minneapolis high school teacher, involving a romance and the town's Indians. Atheneum, 1977.

Keillor, Garrison   LAKE WOBEGONE DAYS
The mythical Minnesota town began as a series of radio monologues, expanded into a novel. Viking, 1985.

Lewis, Sinclair   MAIN STREET
The classic novel of Sauk Center and middle America in the 1920s. S&S, 1950 (first published 1920). Also *Cass Timberlane* (1945), the story of a second marriage.

Moberg, Vilhelm   UNTO A GOOD LAND
S&S, 1954. Originally written in Swedish, it follows *The Emigrants* (see "Sweden"). This tells of the emigration experience of a farmer and his group of peasants from a parish in Smaland, who left in 1850 for America. They arrive in New York and reach Minnesota by riverboat, steam wagon, foot, ox-drawn cart, to create a new home. S&S, 1954. Also *The Last Letter Home* (1961), final volume in the epic story.

O'Brien, Tim   NORTHERN LIGHTS
Two brothers decide to ski all the way home from a weekend lodge in northern Minnesota. Delacorte Pr, 1975.

Powers, J.F.   MORTE D'URBAN
A satire on clericals—the rise and fall of a priest who "just can't help being quite an operator" on behalf of his impoverished order. (FC) Doubleday, 1962.

TRAVEL ARTICLES

ESQUIRE
1985 Apr "Taming the Moose River." Peter N. Nelson, p. 140

GOURMET
1985 Mar Gourmet Holidays: "Inns of the Midwest, Part I." Mimi Elder, p. 38

HOUSE & GARDEN
1984 Feb "Mount Curve." Turn-of-the-century street near downtown Minneapolis. Christopher Gray, p. 192

NATIONAL GEOGRAPHIC TRAVELER
1984 Winter "Winter Carnival." St. Paul's annual snowfest. K.M. Kostyal, p. 52

N.Y. TIMES SUNDAY TRAVEL SECTION (X)
1985 Oct 27 "A Minnesota from a Gentler Era." At the Lowell, some things haven't changed in 50 years. Pat Colander, p. 6
1984 Aug 26 "Escaping the Amenities." Mountain wilderness area is for the hardy. William Serrin, p. 12

SMITHSONIAN
1985 Dec "Sauk Center Today, 65 Years After *Main Street*." Red Lewis' town is kinder to him than he was to it. Vance Bourjaily, p. 46

MISSISSIPPI

Background Reading

Bell, Jimmy   GULF COAST GUIDE
Insight and information on the Mississippi coast. Guide Living, 1984.

Cornwell, Ilene J.   TRAVEL GUIDE TO THE NATCHEZ TRACE PARKWAY
A guide to the parkway between Natchez, Mississippi and Nashville, Tennessee. Southern Resources, 1984.

Ferris, William   LOCAL COLOR: A SENSE OF PLACE IN FOLK ART
Self-portraits of twentieth-century folk artists through reflections on their lives, their art, and photographs of their work. McGraw, 1983.

**Kempe, Helen K.   THE PELICAN GUIDE TO OLD HOMES
OF MISSISSIPPI**
Volume 1: Natchez; Volume 2: Columbus and northern Mississippi. Pelican, 1977.

Skates, John R.   MISSISSIPPI
One of a series of popular histories for each state published as part of the Bicentennial observance in 1976. Norton, 1979.

Novels

Brown, Rosella   CIVIL WARS
A couple brought together by the civil rights movement two decades earlier find a growing distance between them that is further complicated when, as the result of an auto accident, they are bequeathed two additional children who have been raised in a racist atmosphere. Knopf, 1984.

Faulkner, William   SARTORIS
Family saga of the Sartoris family. *Flags in the Dust* (1929) is the uncut version, extending from the Sartoris clan "to the full range of Faulkner's Yoknapatawpha social structure." *The Unvanquished* (1938) is a series of stories of the Sartoris family during the Civil War. NAL, 1983 (first published 1929).

Faulkner, William   THE HAMLET
First in the trilogy of the Snopes saga. Following is *The Town* (1957) and *The Mansion* (1959). Random, 1964 (first published 1940).

Faulkner, William   SANCTUARY
Random, 1962 (first published 1931). This, and its sequel, *Requiem for a Nun* (1951), tell the story of Temple Drake from college coed to eight years later.

Faulkner, William   THE SOUND AND THE FURY
The disintegration of "a southern family of gentle blood." Random, 1966 (first published 1929). Other tales set in Mississippi by Faulkner, in order of publication, are: *Light in August* (1932),*Absalom, Absalom!* (1936),*Go Down Moses* (1942) (short stories), *Intruder in the Dust* (1948) and *The Portable Faulkner* (1948) (short stories).

Flagg, Fannie   COMING ATTRACTIONS
"Zany spoof of southern culture." (FC) Morrow, 1981.

Hill, Rebecca   BLUE RISE
"A delightful story of small-town life in the South with its long-established rituals and codes of behavior." (FC) Morrow, 1983.

Kane, Harnett   BRIDE OF FORTUNE
Biographical novel of Mrs. Jefferson Davis, first lady of the Confederacy. Doubleday, 1948.

Lowry, Beverly   COME BACK, LOLLY RAY
Lolly is a baton twirler and the novel is about life in a class-conscious town. Doubleday, 1977.

Mitchell, Paige   THE COVENANT
A Jewish lawyer in a small Southern town confronts the Klan. Atheneum, 1973.

Morgan, Berry   THE MYSTIC ADVENTURES OF ROXIE STONER
Stories that originally appeared in the *New Yorker*—"companion and guide to
the intricacies of King County through the eyes of a naive black woman." (BRD)
Houghton, 1974.

Spencer, Elizabeth   THE SALT LINE
Set in a Mississippi Gulf Coast town—"one man's efforts to halt rampant
commercialization" following a hurricane that levels the town, and rivalry with a
former colleague over both his cause and the colleague's wife. (FC) Doubleday,
1984. Also *The Face at the Back Door* (1956), about a new county sheriff and the
changing pattern of race relations.

Street, James   TAP ROOTS
Family saga of the Civil War era (1858-65). Dial, 1942. Also *Oh, Promised Land*
(1940), historical novel of Natchez during the period 1794-1817, and *Good-Bye
My Lady* (1954) a contemporary story of a boy and his dog.

Welty, Eudora   DELTA WEDDING
Story of a large southern family—"presents the essence of the deep south."
HarBraceJ, 1946. Also by this distinguished writer, with a Mississippi background,
are: *The Ponder Heart* (1954), *Losing Battles* (1970), *The Optimist's Daughter*
(1972), *The Golden Apples* (1949).

Williams, Joan   COUNTY WOMAN
A middle-aged farm housewife in a conservative Southern town in 1962, a time
when the South is at the edge of great change, is impelled to try to find out the true
circumstances surrounding her mother's death when her killer (a black) escapes
from prison. "In doing so [she] shakes up the whole community, her marriage and
her sense of self." (FC) Little, 1982. Also *Pariah, and Other Stories* (1983)—"the
social fabric of the rural South."

Young, Stark   SO RED THE ROSE
Story of two plantation families of Natchez, during the Civil War. Brief episodes
make clear the whole panorama of the War with a special sense of time and place.
Scribner, 1934.

TRAVEL ARTICLES

BON APPETIT
1985 Mar "Rivers to the Past." Fascinating towns, historic homes and great cuis-
    ine along the lower Mississippi (in Louisiana and Mississippi). p. 102

EARLY AMERICAN LIFE
1985 Apr "Bed and Breakfast in Old Natchez." Jerry de Laughter, p. 46

N.Y. TIMES SUNDAY TRAVEL SECTION (X)
1984 Nov 25 "An Old World the Mississippi Left Behind." Lost towns along the
    Natchez Trace. Barbara L. Archer, p. 19

TRAVEL/HOLIDAY
1985 Jun "The Gray Ghosts of Mississippi." Champion Hill battlefield near Jackson/Vicksburg. Herb Phillips, p. 90
1984 Feb "The Natchez Trace." Sampling the history of the South. Henry N. Ferguson, p. 21

MISSOURI

Background Reading

Brown, A. Theodore   KANSAS CITY
A history of the city that has emerged as a civic-minded business-oriented community and claims to be "one of the few livable cities left." (BRD) Pruett, 1978.

Dillon, Anne F. and others   THE COMPLETE ST. LOUIS GUIDE
Background information, suggestions for excursions, and the unexpected pleasures of the city. Gateway Pub Co, 1984.

Hampel, Bet   THE PELICAN GUIDE TO THE OZARKS
See under "Arkansas."

Kantor, MacKinlay   MISSOURI BITTERSWEET
A portrait of Missouri today [1969] and as he knew it years ago by a prominent novelist. Doubleday, 1969.

Kinney-Hanson, Sharon, ed.   ART MUSEUMS AND GALLERIES IN MISSOURI
Sheba Rev, 1983.

Knittel, Robert   WALKING IN TOWER GROVE PARK: A VICTORIAN STROLLING PARK
Grass-Hooper, 1985.

Nagel, Paul C.   MISSOURI
One of a series of popular histories for each state published as part of the Bicentennial observance in 1976. Norton, 1977.

Rafferty, Milton D.   THE OZARKS OUTDOORS
See under "Arkansas."

Rhodes, Richard   OZARKS
Part of the American Wilderness series. Time-Life, 1974.

Stein, Shifra   **GAS-SAVING GETAWAYS LESS THAN TWO HOURS FROM GREATER ST. LOUIS**
One of a series of day-trip books from a base city. (The two-hour range in this case spills over into Illinois.) Har-Row, 1982.

Thomas, Tracy   **RIGHT HERE IN RIVER CITY: A PORTRAIT OF KANSAS CITY**
Intended to correct the impression that it is a cultureless cowtown stranded in the middle of nowhere. Doubleday, 1976.

Williams, Miller, ed.   **OZARK, OZARK: A HILLSIDE READER**
"A rich anthology of works by writers from the Ozark Mountain region of Missouri and Arkansas . . . all from the twentieth century . . . imbued with a marvelous combination of naivete and sophistication." (BL) U of Missouri, 1981.

Novels

Bellamann, Henry   **KING'S ROW**
The underside of small-town life in a midwestern town in the 1890s (said to be based on Fulton, Missouri). S&S, 1940.

Blum, Carol O'Brien   **ANNE'S HEAD**
A novel inspired by a tragedy in the author's family history during the early 1900s—"the theme is distressing but brightened by the author's natural humor and magnetic evocations of the times, especially the great St. Louis Fair." (FC) Dial, 1982.

Borland, Hal   **THE AMULET**
A young man's coming of age as a soldier on the Confederate side of the Civil War. Lippincott, 1957.

Cleary, Jon   **VORTEX**
Mystery and suspense and a complicated plot that includes a tornado. Morrow, 1978.

Connell, Evan S.   **MRS. BRIDGE; MR. BRIDGE**
Set in Kansas City. Companion volumes of the marriage of a suburban couple, its everyday incidents, loneliness, and boredom of middle age—"the cumulative effect of these episodic snapshots is a discerning full-length portrait." Viking, 1959, 1969.

Dew, Robb F.   **THE TIME OF HER LIFE**
Set in a provincial university town in Missouri—story of an unhappy marriage and the struggle for psychological survival visited upon the children when parents split up. Morrow, 1984.

Finley, Joseph E.   **MISSOURI BLUE**
A man who would prefer to work for the railroad casts his lot with his wife's

large extended family working a cotton field. They survive to prosper, but the novel gives a vivid picture of what it took for farmers to survive the depression. Putnam Pub Group, 1976.

Fraser, George M.   FLASH FOR FREEDOM!
St. Louis at mid-nineteenth century figures in Flashman's adventure—this time he's involved with "all manner of Americans connected with the slave trade." (FC) Knopf, 1972.

Hotchner, A.E.   KING OF THE HILL
The depression era in St. Louis through the eyes of a twelve-year-old boy. Har-Row, 1972.

Kantor, MacKinlay   THE VOICE OF BUGLE ANN
Bugle Ann is a very special fox hunting dog; the plot is set in rural Missouri—"a story of primitive passions." (FC) Coward, 1935. Also *The Romance of Rosy Ridge* (1937).

Ross, Dana F.   INDEPENDENCE
Part of a series of novels with the overall title of *Wagons West* that chronicles the conquest and settlement of the American West. Bantam, 1982.

Roueche, Berton   THE LAST ENEMY
The story is set in and near Kansas City, prior to World War II. There is the murder of a young woman, and the story depicts the psychological consequences to a man who is wrongfully accused of the murder. Har-Row, 1975 (first published 1956).

Twain, Mark   THE ADVENTURES OF TOM SAWYER
Classic story of boyhood adventures. U of California, 1982 (first published 1876). Also *The Adventures of Huckleberry Finn* (1883) and *Pudd'nhead Wilson* (1894).

TRAVEL ARTICLES

BON APPETIT
1985 Apr "Traveling with Taste: St. Louis," Patricia Brooks, p. 34

EARLY AMERICAN LIFE
1984 Oct "Sainte Genevieve, Missouri." A Mississippi river town with unique architecture. p. 44

N.Y. TIMES SUNDAY TRAVEL SECTION (X)
1984 May 22 "Memories of a Cherished Home." The Truman home in Independence. Margaret Truman , p. 14

WORKING WOMAN
1984 Sep "A Businesswoman's Guide to St. Louis." Katherine Rodeghier, p. 230

MONTANA

Background Reading

Ambrose, Stephen E.   CRAZY HORSE AND CUSTER
"The parallel lives of two American warriors . . . curious and suggestive social history." (BRD) Doubleday, 1975.

Doig, Ivan T.   THIS HOUSE OF SKY: LANDSCAPES OF A WESTERN MIND
"Extraordinary, eloquent memoir" that recreates the hardscrabble lives of the last generation of aging cowboys and ranch hands in rural Montana. (BRD) HarBraceJ, 1978.

Howard, Joseph K.   MONTANA HIGH WIDE AND HANDSOME
"Colorful, amusing, and quick-moving. . . . A history and a description of that great and beautiful and various state." (BRD) U of Nebraska, 1983 (first published 1943).

Johnson, Dorothy M.   THE BLOODY BOZEMAN: THE PERILOUS TRAIL TO MONTANA'S GOLD
Mountain Pr, 1983 (first published 1971).

Johnson, Dorothy M.   WHEN YOU AND I WERE YOUNG WHITEFISH
Collection of stories of the author's childhood at the turn of the century—"delightful . . . social and personal history" of Whitefish, a western Montana town. (BL) Mountain Pr, 1982.

Lang, William L.   MONTANA, OUR LAND AND PEOPLE
Pruett, 1981.

Spence, Clark C.   MONTANA
One-third mountains, two-thirds plains—one of a series of popular histories for each state published as part of the Bicentennial observance in 1976. Norton, 1978.

Turbak, Gary   THE TRAVELER'S GUIDE TO MONTANA
Falcon Pr, 1983.

Novels

Brautigan, Richard   THE TOKYO-MONTANA EXPRESS
Brief, anecdotal sketches of people in the American West and Japan. Delacorte Pr, 1980.

Brown, Dee   CREEK MARY'S BLOOD
Fictional account by her grandson of Creek Mary and her sons—one the son of a

Cherokee warrior, the other of a Scottish trader. "In microcosm, a history of the despoliation and destruction of American Indians." (FC) HR&W, 1980.

Doig, Ivan   ENGLISH CREEK
"A portrait of a place and family . . . about a single summer, one after which nothing would ever be quite the same." (Publisher) Atheneum, 1985. See also *This House of Sky*, listed under Background Reading, above.

Farris, Jack   ME AND GALLAGHER
Setting is Virginia City, Montana, in 1863. The story of a frontier man with "golden-rule righteousness" who helps form a vigilance committee to deal with a county sheriff who is victimizing Montana territory citizens. (FC) S&S, 1982.

Grady, James   CATCH THE WIND
The conflict between local people and greedy power companies and railroads; set in Montana ranch country in the late 1870s. Coward, 1980.

Guthrie, A.B.   ARFIVE
Set in a small Montana town at the beginning of the twentieth century without the stock all-conquering hero type of characters. The people—new principal of the high school from the East with his family, a rancher, a non-hero deputy sheriff, a prostitute and so on—"taken together with the townsfolk [are] the type that really built the West." (FC) Houghton, 1971. A sequel with some of the same characters is *The Last Valley* (1975) which covers the period 1920-40, when the town is becoming beset with some of the common contemporary problems such as freedom of the press, the power of corporations, and progress vs. ecology.

Guthrie, A.B.   NO SECOND WIND
Winter in a Montana town—a Western suspense story of strip miners vs. townspeople and ranchers. Houghton, 1980.

Huffaker, Clair   THE COWBOY AND THE COSSACK
Western with an offbeat theme. In the 1880s, a group of Montana cowboys, escorted by a bunch of anti-Tsarist cossacks, take a longhorn herd to Vladivostok and then across Siberia to the starving town of Bakaskaya—"hostility turns to respect and then to something deeper in the face of shared hardships." (FC) Trident Pr, 1973.

Hugo, Richard   DEATH AND THE GOOD LIFE
A mystery by a Pulitzer Prize-winning poet—about a Montana deputy and a series of ax murders. St. Martin, 1981.

Jennings, William D.   THE COWBOYS
A group of schoolboys are reluctantly taken on as hands for a 400-mile cattle drive—"countless details of ranch and cowboy work, life, and language" and the maturing of the boys. (FC) Stein & Day, 1971.

McCaig, Donald   THE BUTTE POLKA
A suspense novel about unions and a coppermining town with portraits of place and of an uneasy way of life in 1946. Wade, 1980.

McGuane, Thomas   NOBODY'S ANGEL

At 36, the main character—"ex-juvenile delinquent, ex-prep-school student, ex-Army captain"—decides it's time he grew up and returns to the family ranch. Action involves his work in keeping family and ranch shipshape and wooing Claire, "beautiful, oil-rich and married." (FC) Random, 1981.

MacLean, Norman   A RIVER RUNS THROUGH IT

A novella, first published in *A River Runs Through It, and Other Stories* in 1976. The author and his brother ("one of the West's greatest fly fishermen") go fishing on the Big Blackfoot River—"unique and marvelous: a story that is at once an evocation of nature's miracles and realities and a probing of human mysteries." Text and photographs in this edition. (In the 1976 edition, the "other stories" touched on work in the Forest Service, logging, trail-cutting and so on.) (FC) U of Chicago, 1983.

Ross, Dana F.   MONTANA!

Part of a series of novels with the overall title of *Wagons West* that chronicles the conquest and settlement of the American West. Bantam, 1983.

Savage, Elizabeth   HAPPY ENDING

Set on a Montana ranch during the depression. "Four people who need each other for survival"—the aging couple hoping to stay on the ranch as long as possible, a hired girl, and a hired hand. "From their mutual dependence comes trust, understanding, and love." (FC) Little, 1972.

Stout, Rex   DEATH OF A DUDE

Nero Wolfe mystery set on a Montana dude ranch. Viking, 1969.

Stuart, Colin   SHOOT AN ARROW TO STOP THE WIND

In 1926, a young boy looks back on his Indian heritage. Dial, 1970. Another novel of Indian life by Stuart is *Walks Far Woman* (1976).

Taylor, Robert L.   A ROARING IN THE WIND

"Being a history of Alder Gulch, Montana, in its great and its shameful days." (FC) Putnam Pub Group, 1978.

Vogan, Sara   IN SHELLEY'S LEG

Shelley's Leg is a bar that sponsors a woman's softball team. The story is about various people "trying to make fresh starts." Knopf, 1981.

Walker, Mildred   WINTER WHEAT

"A novel of character and place rather than plot"—for Ellen the yearly round of the seasons on a wheat farm is beautiful and full of drama; to the young man she loves the ranch is drab and lonely and Ellen's parents are "beyond his comprehension." HarBraceJ, 1944.

Welch, James   THE DEATH OF JIM LONEY

A half-Indian, half-white man tries to deal with his unhappy childhood and its effects on his life. (FC) Har-Row, 1979. An earlier novel by Welch (who is himself an Indian) was *Winter in the Blood* (1974), the story of an Indian in contemporary Montana and his return to his roots.

TRAVEL ARTICLES

NATIONAL GEOGRAPHIC TRAVELER
1985 Summer "Down a Lazy River." Canoeing the upper Missouri. Bill Richards, p. 130

N.Y. TIMES SUNDAY TRAVEL SECTION (X)
1985 Apr 28 "Exploring Custer's Land." Jim Robbins, p. 24
1984 Apr 29 "Way Stations in the Wild." For hikers' comfort in the back country. Jeff Grath, p. 24
Sep 23 "Stars over Montana." Renting a firetower in Kootenai National Forest. Andrew H. Malcolm, p. 33

SUNSET
1984 May "Antique Fords, Old Montana Prison on a Detour to Deer Lodge." p. 76

TRAVEL & LEISURE
1984 Jun "Fishing the Bighorn River." Montana's mecca for trout anglers is now open to all. Barnaby Conrad, p. 40

TRAVEL/HOLIDAY
1985 Aug "A Tale of Two Cities." Butte and Helena. Mary Natali, p. 16
Sep "Backdoor Country—Entering the Real Outdoors." Targhee National Forest. C.J. Burkhart, p. 58
1984 May "Montana's Bison Range." In search of the American buffalo. Gary Turbak, p. 12

NEBRASKA

Background Reading

Creigh, Dorothy W.   NEBRASKA
One of a series of popular histories for each state published as part of the Bicentennial observance in 1976. Norton, 1977.

Faulkner, Virginia, ed.   ROUNDUP: A NEBRASKA READER
U of Nebraska, 1975.

Janovy, John R.   KEITH COUNTRY JOURNAL
"A very different look at the wonders of nature, fascinating, well written, and enlightening"—west central Nebraska, including the sand hills, the Platte rivers, lakes, bluffs, canyons, marshes and creeks. St. Martin, 1978. Also *Back in Keith County* (1983).

Novels

Aldrich, Bess S.   A WHITE BIRD FLYING
Pioneer family saga. Aeonian Pr, 1975 (first published 1931). Other novels of frontier life in Nebraska by the same author include: *A Lantern in Her Hand* (1928), *Spring Came on Forever* (1935), and *The Lieutenant's Lady* (1942).

Cather, Willa   O PIONEERS!
A classic novel of Swedish immigrants in Nebraska in the 1880s, by one of America's leading writers, and winner of a Pulitzer Prize. Houghton, 1929 (first published 1913). Other novels by Cather with a Nebraska setting are: *My Antonia* (1918), *One of Ours* (1922), and *A Lost Lady* (1923).

Morris, Wright   PLAINS SONG
Saga of farm life from 1900 to the 1970s—"the textures of farm life on the plains are beautifully rendered. Animals . . . contribute to the novel's quiet humor." (FC) Har-Row, 1980. Also *Ceremony in Lone Tree* (1960), about the Scanlon family's reunion in a Nebraska ghost town where a 90-year-old Scanlon is the only resident.

Ross, Dana   NEBRASKA!
Part of a series of novels with the overall title of *Wagons West* that chronicles the conquest and settlement of the American West. Bantam, 1979.

Sandoz, Mari   MISS MORISSA, DOCTOR OF THE GOLD TRAIL
Story of a woman doctor on the Nebraska frontier in the 1870s. Hastings, 1975 (first published 1955).

TRAVEL ARTICLES

AMERICANA
1985 Aug "Riding the Covered Wagons." Hard beds, long hours, friendly indians—in all, a fine way to spend a weekend. Gary D. Ford, p. 46

ARCHITECTURAL DIGEST
1985 Nov Historic Houses: "Willa Cather, the House at Red Cloud." Yehudi Menuhin and Phyllis C. Robinson, p. 228

N.Y. TIMES SUNDAY TRAVEL SECTION (X)
1985 Apr 21 "Tracing Willa Cather's Nebraska" Red Cloud preserves her memory. A.L. Rowse, p. 9

SMITHSONIAN
1985 Oct "One-room Schools." Nebraska parents and teachers cherish and support their last 350 one-roomers for solid reasons. Mark M. Kindley, p. 118

TRAVEL/HOLIDAY
1985 Aug "Willa Cather's Nebraska—Home on the Plains." Richard Sassaman, p. 28
1984 Aug "A Plains Perspective." Indian imprints. Edward Renno, p. 30

NEVADA

Series Guidebooks

Frommer: Las Vegas: City Guide
              California & Las Vegas: Dollarwise

Background Reading

Alvarez, A.   THE BIGGEST GAME IN TOWN
Sketches of professional poker players at the World Series of Poker held annually at the Horsehoe Casino in Las Vegas; some sketches originally appeared in the *New Yorker*—"this field guide is the equivalent of an inside straight." (BRD) Houghton, 1983.

**Fried, Elliott and Enriquez, Helen   THE WEEKEND GAMBLER'S GUIDE
                                        TO LAS VEGAS**
Deep River Pr, 1980.

Glass, Mary Ellen   TOURING NEVADA: A HISTORIC AND SCENIC GUIDE
U of Nevada, 1983.

Kovell, Hank   POOR MAN'S GUIDE TO LAS VEGAS
Comprehensive, insider's guidebook to everything from where to stay and how to save money on rooms and food to "words to the wise" on escort services and massage parlors. Owl Pr, 1981.

Laxalt, Robert   NEVADA
One of a series of popular histories for each state published as part of the Bicentennial observance in 1976. Norton, 1977.

Leon, Vicki   THE MONEYWISE GUIDE TO CALIFORNIA WITH EXCURSIONS TO RENO, LAS VEGAS, THE GRAND CANYON AND BAJA CALIFORNIA
See full annotation under "California/Guidebooks."

McDonald, Douglas   NEVADA: LOST MINES AND BURIED TREASURE
Nevada Pbns, 1981.

Marshall, Howard W. and Ahlborn, Richard E.   BUCKAROOS IN PARADISE
The workings of a modern ranch in Paradise, Nevada—people, tools and artifacts. U of Nebraska, 1981.

Miller, Donald C.   GHOST TOWNS OF NEVADA
Pruett, 1979.

Morris, Jan   JOURNEYS
This collection of essays by a leading travel writer includes an essay on Las Vegas. Oxford U, 1984.

Olmsted, John and Huggins, Eleanor   ADVENTURES ALONG INTERSTATE 80
A guide to nature and history along the pioneer and gold rush corridor from San Francisco to Nevada. Tioga, 1984.

Puzo, Mario   INSIDE LAS VEGAS
Preparation for the "shock of a city that never sleeps"—anecdotes about gamblers, employees, customers and photographs. (BRD) Grosset, 1977.

Toll, David W.   THE COMPLEAT NEVADA TRAVELER
Historical background, perceptive observations beyond the purely practical travel guide. Practical information on points of interest for the entire state with emphasis on the countryside rather than on Las Vegas. Gold Hill, 1981.

Novels

Brown, J.P.S.   THE OUTFIT
The lives of some modern-day cowboys who run a ranch owned by a TV star for its tax-loss benefits. They are underpaid and unrewarded except for belief in themselves as skilled husbandmen. Dial, 1971.

Clark, Walter Van Tilburg   THE OXBOW INCIDENT
Nevada in 1885 is the setting and this is a story, based on a true incident, of a group of citizens who form an illegal posse that lynches some cattle rustlers for the murder of one of their members. Random, 1940.

Clark, Walter Van Tilburg   THE TRACK OF THE CAT
A novel of symbolism depicting the struggle between good and evil in terms of a

hunt for the panther that has been killing cattle on an isolated Nevada ranch. Random, 1949.

Demaris, Ovid   THE VEGAS LEGACY
Plot traces the life of a potential vice-presidential nominee with Las Vegas background and atmosphere, and a Nevada-style Republican convention. Delacorte Pr, 1983.

Kirsch, Robert   CASINO
The story of "what happens one August evening when an unusual group of individuals . . . a sort of microcosm of the city . . . vie for their goal of happiness and riches at a Las Vegas casino ruled by a power-drunk millionaire." (Publisher) Lyle Stuart, 1979.

McMurtry, Larry   THE DESERT ROSE
The decline of a topless dancer approaching thirty-nine as her teenage daughter becomes her contender for the title of 'the best legs in Las Vegas'—"touching, low-key, convincing novel." (FC) S&S, 1983.

Puzo, Mario   FOOLS DIE
"A tale of power, brutality and tawdry glamor" set in the 1950s and 1960s. (FC) Putnam Pub Group, 1978.

Ross, Dana F.   NEVADA!
Part of a series of novels with the overall title of *Wagons West* that chronicles the conquest and settlement of the American West. Bantam, 1982.

TRAVEL ARTICLES

MADEMOISELLE
1984 Sep "Winner's Guide to Las Vegas." Close your eyes to the glitter, open them to spectacular vistas. Linda Hubbard, p. 41

NATIONAL GEOGRAPHIC TRAVELER
1984 Autumn "Queen of the Comstock Lode." Virginia City. Joyce Diamanti, p. 90

N.Y. TIMES SUNDAY TRAVEL SECTION (X)
1984 Sep 30 Shopper's World: "The Real Thing for Cowboys." Capriola's emporium of clothes, saddles, etc., in Elko. p. 6

SUNSET
1985 Apr "Mine Touring in Nevada." Eight mines you can visit. p. 100
Jun "Reasons to Slow Down in Eastern Nevada." Las Vegas to Ely scenic route and parks. p. 44
Sep "Hoover at 50." The great dam and Lake Mead. p. 68

TRAVEL/HOLIDAY
1984 Jul "Basque country USA." Old ways to thrive in the New West (Basque festival in Elko in July). Harry Basch, p. 48

NEW HAMPSHIRE

Background Reading

Barracliffe, Ron   NEW HAMPSHIRE INSIDER'S GUIDE
New Impression, 1983.

Blaisdell, Paul H.   25 WALKS IN THE LAKES REGION OF NEW HAMPSHIRE
One of a series that includes *25 Walks in the Dartmouth-Lake Sunapee Region* (1979). Footpaths, leisurely strolls on level ground. Backcountry Pbns, 1977.

Chase, Heman   MORE THAN LAND: STORIES OF NEW ENGLAND COUNTRY LIFE AND SURVEYING
"Nostalgic accumulation of a lifetime of surveying lands, people and events in New Hampshire and Vermont." (BDR) Bauhan, 1978.

Gilmore, Robert C.   NEW HAMPSHIRE LITERATURE: A SAMPLER
U Pr of New England, 1981.

Hall, Donald   STRING TOO SHORT TO BE SAVED
"Recollections of summers on a New England farm" by a poet—incidents and people made memorable. (BRD) Godine, 1979 (first published 1962).

Hill, Evan   THE PRIMARY STATE
An historical guide to New Hampshire. Countryman Pr, 1976.

Jager, Ronald and Grace   NEW HAMPSHIRE
An illustrated history of the Granite State published in cooperation with the New Hampshire Historical Society. Windsor, 1983.

Morison, E.F.   NEW HAMPSHIRE
One of a series of popular histories for each state published as part of the Bicentennial observance in 1976. Norton, 1976.

Randall, Peter   NEW HAMPSHIRE: FOUR SEASONS
Also by Randall, *All Creation and the Isle of Shoals* (1980), *Mount Washington: A Guide and Short History* (1982) and *Portsmouth & the Piscataqua* (1982). Down East, 1979.

Tolman, Newton F.   NORTH OF MONADNOCK
A single year in Nelson, New Hampshire—pieces that originally appeared in *Atlantic Monthly* and local journals—"written in sophisticated crackerbarrel style." (BRD) Little, 1962. Also *Our Loons Are Always Laughing* (1963).

Novels

Banks, Russell   TRAILERPARK
A collection of interrelated stories set in a trailer park and the nearby town—"moral castaways and solitaries on the periphery of society." (FC) Houghton, 1981.

Benet, Stephen Vincent   THE DEVIL AND DANIEL WEBSTER
A twentieth-century version of the Faust legend—"a poor New Hampshire farmer, the devil in a new guise, and New Hampshire's famous native son, Daniel Webster." (FC) Rinehart, 1937.

Cannon, Le Grand   LOOK TO THE MOUNTAIN
Novel of a young bride and groom who left the settlements to pioneer in the New Hampshire Grants, 1769-77—"simple, vivid and beautiful. . .partly idyl. . . partly realistic adventure story." (BRD) Holt, 1942.

Hebert, Ernest   A LITTLE MORE THAN KIN
New Hampshire version of Yoknapatawpha County—the Jordan clan in Darby, New Hampshire, and a continuation of characters and setting begun in *The Dogs of March* (1979). Viking, 1982.

Houston, James   GHOST FOX
"Stunning frontier novel" of the French and Indian Wars in the eighteenth century. (FC) HarBraceJ, 1977.

Johnson, Pamela H.   NIGHT AND SILENCE, WHO IS HERE
"Humorous novel about some visiting scholars cast adrift in the glacial regions of a New Hampshire liberal arts college . . . cold in both climate and welcome." (FC) Scribner, 1963.

Knowles, John   PEACE BREAKS OUT
Set in a boys' school in New Hampshire in 1945. A group of boys viciously turn on a classmate. HR&W, 1981. Also *A Separate Peace* (1960).

MacDougall, Ruth D.   THE FLOWERS OF THE FOREST
Stark rural life in turn-of-the-century New Hampshire. Atheneum, 1981. Also *Aunt Pleasantine* (1978).

Maynard, Joyce   BABY LOVE
"Several days in the lives of . . . girls living in a New Hampshire town . . . three are new mothers, one is pregnant." (BRD) Knopf, 1981.

Samson, Joan   THE AUCTIONEER
Allegorical novel of a "pied piper in the guise of an auctioneer . . . a demagogue's misuse of traditional New England values" in a remote New Hampshire township. (FC) S&S, 1976.

Sarton, May   KINDS OF LOVE
"The touching friendship of two elderly women" who decide to stay the winter for the first time, after having been summer people for many years, and "the love/ hate relationship of the permanent residents and the summer people." (FC) Norton, 1970. Also *The Poet and the Donkey* (1969).

Smith, Mark   THE DELPHINIUM GIRL
"Tale about a coterie of intellectual New Hampshire suburbanites." (BRD) HR&W, 1980. Also *The Moon Lamp* (1976), in which a ghostly first husband returns to make a shambles of the heroine's life.

Whitney, Phyllis A.   SILVERHILL
One of Ms. Whitney's romantic mysteries—in this a young woman accompanies her mother's body to New Hampshire for burial and "uncovers old hatreds and fears when she begins probing into family secrets." (FC) Doubleday, 1967.

Williams, Thomas   THE FOLLOWED MAN
Penetrating study of life in a small town in northern New Hampshire—the plot is about a writer, living in Paris after World War II, called back home because of his brother's illness. Marek, 1978. Also *Whipple's Castle* (1969), chronicle of a Dartmouth student, crippled in an auto accident, from the 1930s to the Korean War.

Williams, Thomas   THE MOON PINNACE
Coming of age of a returning 21-year-old veteran just after WWII. Doubleday, 1986.

TRAVEL ARTICLES

AMERICANA
1985 Aug "Art at Apset." Saint-Gaudens's summer home in Cornish. Patrick T. Reynolds, p. 50

ANTIQUES
1985 Nov "The Saint-Gaudens National Historic Site." Cornish. John H. Dryfhout, p. 982

BON APPETIT
1984 May "A Sophisticated New England Sampler." Bernerhof Inn and Cooking School. Zack Hanle, p. 54

ESQUIRE
1984 Aug "Special Places: Rooms at the Inns." Steven Raichlen, p. 26

GOURMET
1984 Jul "Summertime on Laurel Lake." (Near Fitzwilliam). Dixie L. Clifford, p. 48

HOUSE & GARDEN
1985 Dec "The Gardens of August Saint-Gaudens—the Illustrious Sculptor . . . Is Having a Renaissance of His Own." John Dryfhout, p. 142

N.Y. TIMES SUNDAY TRAVEL SECTION (X)

1985 Feb 3 "56 Ways to Tour Jackson, N.Y." The town is a center of Nordic skiing. Mark C. Hansen, p. 12

May 19 "Poking Along New Hampshire Roads." Joyce Maynard, p. 15

Jun 2 "Way Up North: Whitefield, N.H." A season's worth of quiet pleasures. Edward Cowan, p. 12

1984 Jan 15 "Skiing in New England's North Country." In New Hampshire the sport is still a simple pleasure. David Shribman, p. 9

Aug 19 "What's Doing in the Connecticut River Valley." Marilyn Stout, p. 10

Sep 30 "Uncommon Village Greens." In fifteen New Hampshire villages. Thomas A. Gaines, p. 12

TRAVEL/HOLIDAY

1985 May "Portsmouth, N.H." Of Strawberry Banke and Puddle Dock. Tom Bross, p. 7

YANKEE

1985 Mar This New England: "Kancamangus Highway." One of the five most scenic in America. Tim Clark. p. 54

Sep This New England: "Nelson, N.H." Susan Mahnke, p. 104

Nov "This New England: Lake Winnipesaukee, New Hampshire." Judson D. Hale, Sr., p. 98

"It's Not Boasting If You Can Do It!" Madeleine Kammen's restaurant and cooking school in Glen, New Hampshire. p. 142

1984 Mar This New England: "Berlin, N.H.," p. 62

Jun "Good Swapping and Time for Talking." Annual rock swap in Gilsum. E. Doyle, p. 46

Oct "Beauty with Bargains Besides." North Conway, renowned for scenery, is rapidly becoming a mecca for factory-outlet shopping. Rollin Riggs, p. 46

Nov "This New England: Squam Lakes." Golden Pond. Edie Clark, p. 82

NEW JERSEY

Series Guidebooks

Frommer: **Atlantic City & Cape May: City Guide**

Background Reading

Beck, Henry C. **FORGOTTEN TOWNS OF SOUTHERN NEW JERSEY**
Reprint of a book written in 1936. Rutgers U., 1984. Also *The Roads of Home:*

Lanes and Legends of New Jersey (1983), *Tales and Towns of Northern New Jersey* (1983) and *Forgotten Towns of Central New Jersey* (1984).

Cunningham, John T.   THIS IS NEW JERSEY
County by county guide, including the shore area—history, description, and travel. Rutgers U Pr, 1983.

Fleming, Thomas J.   NEW JERSEY
One of a series of popular histories for each state published as part of the Bicentennial observance in 1976. The Association, 1984 (first published 1977).

Funnell, Charles E.   BY THE BEAUTIFUL SEA
"The rise and high times of that great American resort, Atlantic City. . . . Atlantic City in its prime [1890s] . . . depicted in all of its variety and vitality." (BRD) Rutgers U Pr, 1983 (first published 1975).

Hudgins, Barbara   TRIPS AND TREKS: A GUIDE TO FAMILY OUTINGS IN THE NEW JERSEY AREA
Woodmont Pr, 1983.

McPhee, John   THE PINE BARRENS
"The special atmosphere of the Barrens," a unique wilderness area in the center of New Jersey; a new edition with photographs. (BRD) FS&G, 1981 (first published 1968).

Sternlieb, George and Hughes, James   THE ATLANTIC CITY GAMBLE
Two Rutgers professors examine the results and consequences of legalized casino gambling in Atlantic City. Harvard U Pr, 1983.

Novels

Algren, Nelson   THE DEVIL'S STOCKING
"The story is built up around a black boxer from New Jersey . . . convicted of murder . . . released and convicted again." (FC) Arbor Hse, 1983.

Clark, Mary Higgins   THE CRADLE WILL FALL
A can't-put-it-down spine tingler involving a young woman assistant prosecutor who believes she's seen a body loaded into a car, while she was in the hospital recovering from a car accident. S&S, 1980.

Fleming, Thomas   LIBERTY TAVERN
Historical novel of the Revolutionary War. Doubleday, 1976.

Ford, Paul   JANICE MEREDITH: A STORY OF THE AMERICAN REVOLUTION
The daughter of a Tory falls in love with a general in the American revolutionary army. Dodd, 1980 (first published 1899).

Markus, Julia   AMERICAN ROSE
Narrative of a Jewish novelist's family from his great grandmother on. Houghton, 1981.

Pentecost, Hugh   THE STEEL PALACE
An adventure story and mystery of a public relations genius hired to promote an Atlantic City luxury hotel owned by a Howard Hughes-like figure. Dodd, 1977.

Rothberg, Abraham   THE STALKING HORSE
Espionage plot that begins in Moscow and ends on a New Jersey farm where a Russian defector is housed. Saturday Review Pr, 1972.

Sheed, Wilfrid   THE HACK
Satiric view of Catholicism. FS&G, 1968. Also *Square's Progress* (1965), a satire on modern marriage.

Sorrentino, Gilbert   ABERRATION OF STARLIGHT
New Jersey during the depression and four views of a single evening. Random, 1980.

Updike, John   THE POORHOUSE FAIR
A "handful of marvelously eccentric people" in a New Jersey poorhouse. (FC) Knopf, 1977 (first published 1959).

TRAVEL ARTICLES

AMERICANA
1985 Nov-Dec "Christmas at Cape May." Donna Freeman, p. 38

ESQUIRE
1984 Aug "Special Places: Rooms at the Inns." Steven Raichlen, p. 26

TRAVEL & LEISURE
1985 Mar "The Glitz and Glitter of Atlantic City." Proof positive that, in America, nothing succeeds like excess. Fred Ferretti, p. 104
1984 Jan "Latest from Atlantic City." Big-name entertainment, casino-hotels. p. 33

TRAVEL/HOLIDAY
1984 Jul "The Pine Barrens." Getting away from it all in New Jersey. Brett Shapiro, p. 30

NEW MEXICO

Series Guidebooks (See Appendix 1)

Fodor: New Mexico

Background Reading

Ackerman, Diane   TWILIGHT OF THE TENDERFOOT
The author visited a New Mexico cattle ranch in March, June and September for a full cyle of ranch work and cowboy life, as a basis for this account of its social life and customs. Morrow, 1980.

Bodine, John J.   TAOS PUEBLO: A WALK THROUGH TIME
A visitor's guide to the Pueblo, its people, their customs and their long history. Lightning Tree, 1977.

Bullock, Alice   MOUNTAIN VILLAGES
Sunstone, 1981.

Chilton, Lance   NEW MEXICO: A NEW GUIDE TO THE COLORFUL STATE
U of New Mexico, 1984.

Coe, Wilbur   RANCH ON THE RUIDOSO
The story of a pioneer family in New Mexico, 1871-1968. The book traces the fortunes of a cattle family that were among the early settlers to come over the Santa Fe Trail and knew Billy the Kid and other colorful characters of the era. As it traces the family's fortunes it also traces the evolution of the cattle business and the special experience of music on the ranch. Knopf, 1968.

Gibson, Arrel Morgan   THE SANTA FE AND TAOS COLONIES
History of the cultural renaissance of these two interesting places before and after the "artistic invasion," which included (among many others) D.H. Lawrence and Georgia O'Keeffe. (BL) U of Oklahoma Pr, 1983.

Historic Santa Fe Foundation   OLD SANTA FE TODAY
Guide to architecture and historical buildings in Santa Fe. U of New Mexico, 1982.

Johnson, Kathryn   THE TAOS GUIDE
Sunstone, 1983.

Looney, Ralph   HAUNTED HIGHWAYS: THE GHOST TOWNS OF NEW MEXICO
U of New Mexico, 1979.

Miller, Donald C.   GHOST TOWNS OF THE SOUTHWEST: ARIZONA, UTAH, NEW MEXICO
Pruett, 1980.

Morris, Jan   JOURNEYS
This collection of a leading travel writer's essays includes an essay on Santa Fe. Oxford U, 1984.

Muth, Marcia   IS IT SAFE TO DRINK THE WATER?
A GUIDE TO SANTA FE
Sunstone, 1983.

Nichols, John   THE LAST BEAUTIFUL DAYS OF AUTUMN
A "paean to Taos and the surrounding country" by a novelist. "An extraordinary personal essay about one of the most stunning sections of the country." (LJ) HR&W, 1982. Also *If Mountains Die: A New Mexico Memoir* (1979).

Simmons, Marc   NEW MEXICO
One of a series of popular histories for each state published as part of the Bicentennial observance in 1976. Norton, 1977.

Sinclair, John   COWBOY RIDING COUNTRY
Reminiscences of years as a young cowpoke in the early 1900s in the El Capitan Mountains. U of New Mexico, 1982. Also *New Mexico: The Shining Land* (1983).

Thompson, Waite   THE SANTA FE GUIDE
Sunstone, 1984.

Varney, Philip   NEW MEXICO'S BEST GHOST TOWNS: A PRACTICAL
GUIDE
Northland, 1981.

Young, John V.   THE STATE PARKS OF NEW MEXICO
U of New Mexico, 1984.

Novels

Arnold, Elliott   BLOOD BROTHER
Historical novel about the period 1856-70. U of Nebraska, 1979 (first published 1947).

Benchley, Nathaniel   WELCOME TO XANADU
A girl is kidnapped by a mental patient and taken to a hideout in New Mexico. Atheneum, 1968.

Bradford, Richard   SO FAR FROM HEAVEN
A group of Mexicans in the United States attempt to claim federal land. Lippincott, 1973. Also *Red Sky at Morning* (1968), about life in the Southwest during World War II.

Butler, Robert O.   COUNTRYMEN OF BONES
Set in 1945, a time-is-running-out story involving an archaeologist and a member of Oppenheimer's team working on the atomic bomb. Horizon, 1983.

Cather, Willa   DEATH COMES FOR THE ARCHBISHOP
A classic by one of America's leading writers—based on the lives of two French

clerics who won the Southwest for the Catholic Church in the period of the mid-1800s. Modern Lib, 1984 (first published 1927).

Clarke, Richard   THE COPPER DUST HILLS
"Vivid depiction of animal life and the beauty of the west enhance this engrossing tale" of a cowhand's determination to avenge his brother's hanging. (FC) Walker, 1983.

Culp, John H.   THE TREASURE OF THE CHISOS
A young man's courageous journey from St. Louis to New Mexico to reclaim his family's land. HR&W, 1971.

Durham, Marilyn   DUTCH UNCLE
A roving gunslinger becomes saddled with two orphans, and then with the job of temporary town marshal of Arredondo. HarBraceJ, 1973.

Eastlake, William   PORTRAIT OF AN ARTIST WITH TWENTY-SIX HORSES
Reflects on the relationship of Indians and whites. S&S, 1963. Also *Dancers in the Scalp House* (1975), in which the Navajos and their teacher fight the construction of a new dam.

Hillerman, Tony   PEOPLE OF DARKNESS
Police procedural in which the detective is a Navajo. The plot concerns a mysterious Navajo cult. Har-Row, 1980. Also *Dance Hall of the Dead* (1973).

Horgan, Paul   THE THIN MOUNTAIN AIR
Setting is the early 1920s as a young man leaves college to accompany his father to Albuquerque to a tuberculosis ranch—"sense of place is palpable and magical." FS&G, 1977. Also *Far from Cibola* (1938) and *The Common Heart* in *Mountain Standard Time* (1942).

Nichols, John   THE MILAGRO BEANFIELD WAR
"A bawdy, slangy, modern proletarian novel" of Chicanos vs. land developers. HR&W, 1974. Also *The Magic Journey* (1978).

Richter, Conrad   THE LADY
Story of violence and revenge set in New Mexico of the 1880s—"bathed in the light and legends of territorial New Mexico." (FC) Knopf, 1957.

Schaefer, Jack   MONTE WALSH
A cowboy's life parallels the "rise, peak, and eventual collapse of the open range." (FC) Houghton, 1963.

Silko, Leslie M.   CEREMONY
A Navajo reservation in New Mexico, post-World War II is the setting—"geographical and emotional landscapes of the American Indian." (BRD) Viking, 1977.

Swarthout, Glendon   SKELETONS
A complex mystery involving a writer's investigation of the disappearance of his ex-wife's boyfriend. Doubleday, 1979.

Whitney, Phyllis A.   THE TURQUOISE MASK
A New England girl visits her grandfather in Santa Fe and becomes involved in a mystery—"beautifully appreciative of the New Mexico scene." (FC) Doubleday, 1974.

TRAVEL ARTICLES

AMERICANA
1985 Aug "Restoration: Las Vegas, NM—Small Town with Big Ideas." Sandra Dallas, p. 58
1984 Jul-Aug "Pueblo Deco." Restored movie theatre. Nancy C. Benson, p. 36

AMERICAS
1985 Jan-Feb "A Feast of Folk Art." Museum of International Folk Art, Santa Fe. Charlene Cerny, p. 31

BON APPETIT
1985 Dec "Yuletide in New Mexico." Taos and Santa Fe offer super skiing, beautiful scenery, cozy inns. Shirley Slater, p. 130

NATIONAL GEOGRAPHIC TRAVELER
1985 Summer "A Ballooning Interest: Albuquerque's Hot-Air Fiesta." Tony Hillerman, p. 142
1984 Summer "A Town to Restore the Spirit." Taos in summer. Tony Hillerman, p. 18

N.Y. TIMES SUNDAY TRAVEL SECTION (X)
1985 Jan 27 "The Hidden Snow of Taos." A dozen miles from the Rio Grande, the ski slopes are modest, steep, and Oh my gosh! Norman Zollinger, p. 9
Feb 10 "What's Doing in Santa Fe." William Hart, p. 10
Feb 24 "New Mexico's Sky-High Inn." Inn of the Mountain Gods, built by the Mescalero Apaches. William Hart, p. 23
Mar 17 (Part 2, "Sophisticated Traveler") "Discovering the Land of Light." N. Scott Momaday, p. 40
Jun 23 "Venturing into a Black Hole of New Mexico." Cave exploring in Slaughter Canyon. p. 47
Jul 14 "The Taming of the Old Wild West." Today's cowboys and Indians in Santa Fe sell beads and drive VW's. Arnold Benson, p. 39
1984 May 13 "What's Doing in Santa Fe." William Hart, p. 10
Jun 3 "Santa Fe Folk Art, Funny and Ferocious." Didi Moore, p. 6
Jul 15 "Santa Fe's Indian market." Didi Moore, p. 22
Jul 22 "A Timeless Pueblo Ritual." New Mexico's corn dance celebrates ancient tribal bonds. Betty Fussell, p. 10
Oct 6 "House of the Hawaiian Sun." Fletcher Knebel, p. 14

1984   "Closing In on the Rockies." Ivan Doig, p. 12
        ("Sophisticated Traveler") "Treks for the Sophisticated Traveler—New
        Mexico's Sangre De Cristos." Elizabeth Tallent, p. 80

SUNSET
1985   Feb "More Indian Doings at Museums in California, Arizona, New Mexico."
        p. 62
1984   Jul "Uncommon Glimpses of the Taos Reservation." p. 32

TRAVEL/HOLIDAY
1985   Oct "New Mexico's North Pole from Raton to Shiprock." In far northern
        New Mexico. Susan Hazen-Hammond, p. 52
1984   Jan "Albuquerque, a City for All Seasons." Buddy Mays, p. 62
        Jun "The Annual Escape of Billy the Kid." August in Lincoln, N.M. Justin F.
        Gleichauf, p. 82

VOGUE
1985   Aug "Santa Fe: The Battle between the True and the Trumped Up and Who's
        Winning." Jan Morris, p. 248
        "The Best of Santa Fe: Insider's Guide." Sheila Gruson, p. 251

NEW YORK

Series Guidebooks (See Appendix 1)

American Express: **New York City**
Baedeker: **New York City**
Berlitz: **New York**
Blue Guide: **New York City**
Companion Guide: **New York City**
Fodor: **New York City**
Frommer: **New York: $-a-Day; New York: City Guide**
Insight: **New York State**
Michelin: **New York City**
Nagel: **New York City**

Background Reading

Aber, Ted   ADIRONDACK FOLKS
Anecdotes and history of this remarkable area of the state. Prospect Bks, 1980.

Adams, Arthur Gray   THE HUDSON: A GUIDEBOOK TO THE RIVER
State U of NY, 1981. Also *The Hudson River in Literature: An Anthology* (1980), edited by Adams.

**Adams, Arthur Gray   GUIDE TO THE CATSKILLS AND THE
                         REGION AROUND**
History, geography and sightseeing for the area in "lively and evocative" prose. Sun, 1977.

Barnett, Lincoln   ANCIENT ADIRONDACKS
Part of the American Wilderness series. Time-Life, 1974.

Bliven, Bruce   NEW YORK
One of a series of popular histories for each state published as part of the Bicentennial observance in 1976, with the author's personal analysis of the qualities he believes make New York both significant and different from the other states. Norton, 1981.

**Boyle, Robert H.   THE HUDSON RIVER, A NATURAL AND
                      UNNATURAL HISTORY**
"Highly entertaining and informative book . . . frequent quotes from original manuscripts." (BRD) Norton, 1969.

Carmer, Carl   THE TAVERN LAMPS ARE BURNING
A literary journey through six regions and four centuries of New York State. McKay, 1964. Also *Listen For a Lonesome Drum* (1936)—historical sketches, folklore and tall stories—and *The Hudson* (1939).

Davidson, Marshall B.   NEW YORK
A pictorial history of the state. Scribner, 1981.

Donaldson, Gordon   NIAGARA!
Historical narrative and stories from fact and legend—Ontario (Canada) and New York State. Doubleday, 1979.

Dumbleton, Susanne and Older, Anne   IN AND AROUND ALBANY
Guidebook for the capital of the state and its environs. Washington Park Pr, 1980.

Ellis, David M.   NEW YORK: STATE AND CITY
Explores the growth, literature, regional conflicts, and politics of the State. Cornell U, 1979.

Evers, Alf   THE CATSKILLS FROM WILDERNESS TO WOODSTOCK
Lore, legend, flora and fauna, natural and unnatural wonders, history and present of the region. Overlook Pr, 1984 (first published 1972).

Hope, Jack   A RIVER FOR THE LIVING: THE HUDSON AND ITS PEOPLE
Encounters with people who live, work and play on the river. Barre, 1975.

Jamieson, Paul ADIRONDACKS: A READER
Anthology. Adirondack Mountain Club, 1983.

Kennedy, William O ALBANY! AN URBAN TAPESTRY
"Improbable city of political wizards, fearless ethnics, spectacular aristocrats, splendid nobodies, and underrated scoundrels. . . . fascinating view of the American experience." (Publisher) Viking, 1983.

Mulligan, Tim THE HUDSON RIVER VALLEY: A HISTORY GUIDE
First of a new travel series to be enjoyed "before, during, and after a trip. . . . literate guide that will inspire travelers to visit the Hudson River (with a) personal view"—what to see, avoid, and limited recommendations for accommodations and dining. Random, 1985.

O'Brien, Raymond J. AMERICAN SUBLIME: LANDSCAPE AND SCENERY OF THE LOWER HUDSON VALLEY
Description, travel and history from pre-Revolutionary period to the present with much on efforts toward preservation from industrial development. Columbia U Pr, 1981.

O'Connor, Lois A FINGER LAKES ODYSSEY
North Country, 1975.

Roseberry, Cecil R. FROM NIAGARA TO MONTAUK: THE SCENIC PLEASURES OF NEW YORK STATE
"Extensive, delightful view" of the natural wonders and why they are of interest to scientists and tourists; directions for finding and exploring them. (BL) State U of NY, 1981.

Shoumatoff, Alex WESTCHESTER: PORTRAIT OF A COUNTY
"Gets at the heart and truth of an American county . . . the portrait is distinctly Westchester" but with application to all suburban counties. Coward, 1979.

Thomas, Bill and Phyllis NATURAL NEW YORK
HR&W, 1983.

Van der Zee, Henri and Barbara A SWEET AND ALIEN LAND: THE STORY OF DUTCH NEW YORK
Viking, 1978.

Wilson, Edmund UPSTATE: RECORDS AND RECOLLECTIONS
"Anecdotal combination of family reminiscences, explorations . . . visits with literary figures . . . sketches of local characters"—much of the material appeared originally in the *New Yorker*. (BRD) FS&G, 1971.

LONG ISLAND - FIRE ISLAND - SHELTER ISLAND

Albright, Rodney and Priscilla SHORT WALKS ON LONG ISLAND
Walks on beaches, bogs, woodlands, towns, former estates, and more, from the

Jamaica Bay Wildlife Refuge to Montauk State Park and intended to be "relaxing and leisurely, educational and enlightening . . . fun." (Publisher) Globe Pequot, 1983.

Bookbinder, Bernie   LONG ISLAND
People and places, past and present. Abrams, 1983.

Capon, Robert F.   THE YOUNGEST DAY
"Shelter Island's seasons in the light of grace." Har-Row, 1983.

Garfield, Bee   FIRE ISLAND GUIDE
Trigar, 1980.

Johnson, Madeleine C.   FIRE ISLAND: 1650'S TO 1980'S
Shoreland Pr, 1983.

Jones, Stephen   BACKWATERS
All about the Long Island Sound, both its Connecticut and Long Island backwaters—"a charming book." (BRD) Norton, 1979.

McCarthy, Mary   SAPPHO BY THE SEA
An illustrated guide to the Hamptons. Chelsea Hse, 1980.

Mannello, George   OUR LONG ISLAND
R.E. Krieger, 1980.

**Masters, James I.   THE HAMPTONS GUIDEBOOK AND NORTH FORK &
SHELTER ISLAND GUIDEBOOK**
Blue Claw Pr, 1981.

Nichols, Jack   WELCOME TO FIRE ISLAND
Cherry Grove and the Pines. St. Martin, 1976.

Randall, Monica   MANSIONS OF LONG ISLAND'S GOLD COAST
Hastings, 1979.

Rattray, Everett T.   THE SOUTH FORK
The land and the people of Eastern Long Island—natural and social history by the publisher of the local newspaper and a lifelong resident of the Hamptons. Random, 1979.

Rattray, Jeanette   SHIP ASHORE
History of the maritime disasters off eastern Long Island, 1640-1955, by a member of an old Suffolk County family. Coward, 1955.

**Sclare, Lisa and Donald   BEAUX-ARTS ESTATES: A GUIDE TO THE
ARCHITECTURE OF LONG ISLAND**
The houses built by the wealthy from the late nineteenth century to the depression "live on—as museums, schools, and conference centers. Thirty-two are in-

cluded in this elegant guidebook." There is also background on the houses' architecture and on their famous owners, as well as practical information on entry fees, hours, etc. (LJ) Viking, 1980.

NEW YORK CITY

Anderson, Jervis   THIS WAS HARLEM: A CULTURAL PORTRAIT
"We see the elegant, stylish, and literary Harlem of the 1920s decline to poverty and despair by 1950." (BRD) FS&G, 1982.

Barlow, Elizabeth   THE CENTRAL PARK BOOK
Material on the English design influence, social history, statuary, geology, birds, etc. Random, 1978.

Batterberg, Michael and Ariane   ON THE TOWN IN NEW YORK FROM 1776 TO THE PRESENT
History of social life and customs, hotels, taverns, restaurants, and amusements. Scribner, 1973.

Bell, James B. and Abrams, Richard I.   IN SEARCH OF LIBERTY: THE STORY OF THE STATUE OF LIBERTY AND ELLIS ISLAND
"A centennial keepsake, heavy on sentiment and unabashed patriotism, celebrating France's gift to the U.S." of the Statue of Liberty. (PW) Doubleday, 1984.

Birmingham, Stephen   LIFE AT THE DAKOTA
Inside view of one of New York's most famous addresses. Random, 1979.

Blanchet, Christian and Dard, Bertrand   STATUE OF LIBERTY: THE FIRST HUNDRED YEARS
Illustrated history of the Statue, translated from the French for American readers—from idea for the Statue to its unveiling in 1886, and its subsequent history as an international symbol and American shrine. American Heritage, 1985.

Botkin, Benjamin A., ed.   NEW YORK CITY FOLKLORE
"Legends, tall tales, anecdotes, stories, sagas, heroes and characters, customs, traditions and sayings." (Publisher) Greenwood, 1976.

Brown, Claude   CHILDREN OF HAM
Twelve young Harlemites in an urban commune in an abandoned apartment and their survival over drugs and inhumanity. Stein & Day, 1976.

Brownstone, David M. and others   THROUGH ELLIS ISLAND TO THE NEW WORLD
Vanguard, 1984. Also *Island of Hope, Island of Tears* (1979)—"travelog epoch" that recaptures experiences of the millions who moved through Ellis Island from 1892-1930. (LJ)

Burgess, Anthony   NEW YORK
Part of Great Cities of the World series. Time-Life, 1977.

Daley, Robert   WORLD BENEATH THE CITY
New York's subterranean lifelines—subways, telephone, electricity, sewer lines, water and gas mains. A story of politics, geniuses, crackpots, crooks, bizarre accidents, spectacular engineering. Lippincott, 1959.

Durso, Joseph   MADISON SQUARE GARDEN: 100 YEARS OF HISTORY
The various arenas that have been Madison Square Garden up to its present location at 33rd Street. S&S, 1979.

**Edmiston, Susan and Cirino, Linda   LITERARY NEW YORK: A HISTORY
                                        AND GUIDE**
Houghton, 1976.

**Fischler, Stan   UPTOWN, DOWNTOWN: A TRIP THROUGH TIME ON
                     NEW YORK'S SUBWAYS**
A potpourri on subways—history, subway buffs, and disasters. Hawthorne, 1976.

Fox, Ted   SHOWTIME AT THE APOLLO
Chronicle of the Apollo Theatre in Harlem which was a showcase for black performers from 1934 to the 1980s—famous personalities from Bessie Smith to Aretha Franklin. HR&W, 1983.

**Goldberger, Paul   THE CITY OBSERVED: NEW YORK, A GUIDE TO THE
                       ARCHITECTURE OF MANHATTAN**
Intended as background reading at home, as well as a functional guide to carry along. Random, 1979.

James, Theodore   EMPIRE STATE BUILDING
Entertaining and informative history, and all about the famous landmark. Har-Row, 1975.

**Karp, Walter   THE CENTER: A HISTORY AND GUIDE TO
                  ROCKEFELLER CENTER**
History, planning, construction, expansion, the Music Hall, photos and maps of the complex. Van Nostrand, 1983.

Kasson, John F.   AMUSING THE MILLIONS
Coney Island at the turn of the century. Hill & Wang, 1978.

**Koolhaas, Rem   DELIRIOUS NEW YORK: A RETROACTIVE MANIFESTO
                   FOR MANHATTAN**
"Both pop polemic and serious architectural history." (BRD) Oxford U, 1978.

Krinsky, Carol H.   ROCKEFELLER CENTER
From concept to execution and expansion. Oxford U, 1978.

Lewis, David L.   WHEN HARLEM WAS IN VOGUE
The Harlem renaissance of the 1920s when "almost everything seemed possible"—achievements in writing, music, and art. (PW) Vintage, 1982.

Lockwood, Charles   MANHATTAN MOVES UPTOWN
An illustrated history of Manhattan. Houghton 1976.

McCullough, David W.   BROOKLYN AND HOW IT GOT THAT WAY
Extensively illustrated history of the borough by a Brooklyn aficionado—"the varied, colorful stream of residents who have passed through. . . its indomitable though sorely tried spirit." (BL) Doubleday, 1983.

McDarrah, Fred W.   MUSEUMS IN NEW YORK
Newly revised descriptive reference guide to fine arts, local history, and specialized museums such as museums of science, natural history, botanical parks, etc. Frommer-Pasmantier, 1983.

Marqusee, Mike and Harris, Bill, eds.   NEW YORK: AN ANTHOLOGY
"The complexity and wonder, the naughtiness and niceties, the silliness and splendor, or life in the world's first city." Includes writings of Dorothy Parker, Henry James, E.B. White, Gorky, Chesterton, others. Little, 1985.

Miller, Saul   NEW YORK CITY STREET SMARTS
Information on day-to-day life in the boroughs and in the Manhattan neighborhoods not generally found in conventional guidebooks. Part 1: Politics, ethnics, general conditions; Part 2: sights, shops, restaurants in lesser-known neighborhoods. HR&W, 1983.

Morris, Charles R.   THE COST OF GOOD INTENTIONS
"New York City and the liberal experiment 1960-1975," which led to the near-bankruptcy of the city. (BRD) McGraw, 1980.

Nevins, Deborah   GRAND CENTRAL TERMINAL: CITY WITHIN A CITY
"Celebrates Grand Central in picture, prose . . . perceptive essays by historians, architects, attorneys," with an introduction by Jacqueline Onassis. (LJ) Municipal Art Soc, 1982.

Novotny, Ann   STRANGERS AT THE DOOR: ELLIS ISLAND, CASTLE GARDEN & THE GREAT MIGRATION TO AMERICA
Devin, 1984.

Patterson, Jerry E.   THE CITY OF NEW YORK: A HISTORY
A thorough, informative city history illustrated from the collections of the Museum of the City of New York. Abrams, 1978.

Phillips, McCandlish   CITY NOTEBOOK
"A reporter's portrait of a vanishing New York. . . . easily read collection for those who like the city whether they live here, visit here or know it only as a

setting in American fiction," by a feature writer of *The New York Times*. (BRD) Liveright, 1974.

Reed, Henry H.   CENTRAL PARK
A history and general guide to the first example of an urban park in America. Potter, 1967.

Reynolds, Donald M.   THE ARCHITECTURE OF NEW YORK CITY
"Weaves little-known stories of eighty buildings and landmarks into a colorful tapestry of New York's whirlwind history. . . . can be read from beginning to end with great pleasure." (PW) Macmillan, 1984.

Robinson, Francis   CELEBRATION: THE METROPOLITAN OPERA
A guided tour to the Met, past and present. Doubleday, 1979.

St. George, Judith   BROOKLYN BRIDGE: THEY SAID IT COULDN'T BE BUILT
Putnam Pub Group, 1982.

Schiffman, Jack   HARLEM HEYDAY
A pictorial history of modern black show business and the Apollo Theatre. Prometheus, 1984.

Shaw, Arnold   THE STREET THAT NEVER SLEPT
"New York's fabled 52nd Street—and the bootleggers, comics, characters, strippers, club owners and jazzmen that made it swing." (Publisher) Coward, 1971.

Simon, Kate   FIFTH AVENUE: A VERY SOCIAL HISTORY
The avenue from its beginnings and the lives of illustrious inhabitants. HarBraceJ, 1978.

Sutton, Horace   CONFESSIONS OF A GRAND HOTEL: THE WALDORF-ASTORIA
History of the hotel, beginning with 1893. HR&W, 1953.

Tauranac, John   ESSENTIAL NEW YORK
A guide to the history and architecture of Manhattan's important buildings, parks and bridges. HR&W, 1979.

Trachtenberg, M.   THE STATUE OF LIBERTY
By an art historian—"informative and fascinating reading" with an emphasis on political origins of the idea to give America a statue, construction and design, site, etc. (BRD) Viking, 1976.

Ultan, Lloyd   THE BEAUTIFUL BRONX
The Bronx from 1920-50, with assistance from the Bronx County Historical Society. Crown, 1979.

Wagenvoord, James   CITY LIVES
"The kinds and qualities of life in a city's myriad neighborhoods" in photos and narrative. (BRD) HR&W, 1976.

TRAVELOGUES, MEMOIRS, SPECIAL PERSPECTIVES FOR NEW YORK CITY

Brook, Stephen   NEW YORK DAYS, NEW YORK NIGHTS
By a British writer—"goes well beyond the usual traveler's haunts . . . offers lively, highly personal observations" on aspects of the city, from bathhouses and subways to restaurants and museums. "Deft portraits of politicians, intellectuals, developers and others now shaping the city's life." (PW) Atheneum, 1985.

Cline, Francis X.   ABOUT NEW YORK: SKETCHES OF THE CITY
Eighty-five sketches originally published in the *New York Times*"give a vivid, humorous and touching portrait of the place and its people." McGraw, 1980.

Colby, Constance T.   THE VIEW FROM MORNINGSIDE: ONE FAMILY'S NEW YORK
Raising a family on the upper West Side of New York from first city apartment to graduation from high school. Lippincott, 1978.

Hanff, Helen   APPLE OF MY EYE
Humorous anecdotes and little-known facts about some of the author's favorite places. See also her near-classics listed under "London/Background Reading." Doubleday, 1978.

Jastrow, Marie   A TIME TO REMEMBER: GROWING UP IN NEW YORK BEFORE THE GREAT WAR
Memoir of an Austrian Jew who immigrated in the early 1900s—"the unbelievable efforts and teamwork required of a typical immigrant family to make it . . . description of their life during this period—the apartments, the shopping, the traditions, the people—are absolutely wonderful." (BRD) Norton, 1979.

Klein, Alexander, ed.   THE EMPIRE CITY: ALL THE BEST EVER WRITTEN ABOUT NEW YORK
Reprint of a thirty-year-old book—anthology of essays and articles by such as Truman Capote, Tallulah Bankhead, Lewis Mumford, Stephen Crane, Mark Twain, Walter Winchell, and so on. Ayer Co. (1975) (first published 1955).

McGreevy, John ed.   CITIES
Impressions of world cities as seen through the eyes of people intimately connected with them—for New York it's George Plimpton.
Potter, 1981.

Morris, James   THE GREAT PORT: A PASSAGE THROUGH NEW YORK
A book commissioned by the New York Port Authority and written by one of the leading contemporary travel writers and observers of places, cities and people.

HarBraceJ, 1969. Also *Destinations* (1980), a collection of travel essays that includes a piece on New York.

Orkin, Ruth   A WORLD THROUGH MY WINDOW
Very interesting concept—photographs taken through the same window on Central Park West over a period of twenty-three years. Har-Row, 1978.

Pritchett, V. S.   NEW YORK PROCLAIMED
Impressionistic essays by the leading British travel writer and "word painter of cities." (BRD) HarBraceJ, 1965.

Ross, Lillian   TALES: STORIES FROM THE "TALK OF THE TOWN"
An anthology of reactions to New York City, from Ed Koch and Abe Beame to visiting celebrities—"alternate between warmth and cynicism." (BL) Congdon & Weed, 1983.

Simon, Kate   NEW YORK: PLACES AND PLEASURES: AN UNCOMMON GUIDE BOOK
Classic travel writing combined with uncommon advice for the traveler. Har-Row, 1980 (first published 1971).

Stevenson, James   UPTOWN LOCAL, DOWNTOWN EXPRESS
"Appealing . . . vignettes by a *New Yorker* writer who turns his acutely observant eye and whimsical curiosity to some little known aspects of the urban scene." (PW) Viking, 1983.

Talese, Gay   FAME AND OBSCURITY, PORTRAITS
Reprint of articles and short stories about New York. Dell, 1984 (first published 1970).

White, E.B.   HERE IS NEW YORK
Reprint of a magazine article and an essay, about the author's love affair with New York—"one man's private vision of the city." (BRD) Har-Row, 1949.

GUIDEBOOKS FOR NEW YORK CITY

Appleberg, Marilyn J.   I LOVE NEW YORK
Part of a series—see annotation for "Boston." Macmillan, 1981.

Barrett, John G.   NEW YORK IN TWELVE EASY WALKS
Twelve walks, twelve neighborhoods. Barret Pr, 1984.

Berman, Eleanor   AWAY FOR THE WEEKEND: NEW YORK
Fifty-two ideas for getaways within 200 miles of New York City, arranged by season "to take advantage of special events and seasonal activities . . . historic restorations and museums, seaports, gardens, beaches, summer theater," etc. (LJ) Potter, 1982.

Cartoun, Susan   THE COMPLETE NEW YORK GUIDE FOR SINGLES
"An insider's handbook to entertainment, establishments, activities and services." The emphasis is on Manhattan but there are listings also for other boroughs, Long Island and Westchester. (BL)Macmillan, 1983.

Chester, Carole   NEW YORK
A Batsford guide. David, 1977.

Cultural Assistance Center Staff, eds.   NEW YORK CITY MUSEUMS
Dover, 1983.

Fein, Cheri   NEW YORK—OPEN TO THE PUBLIC
"A comprehensive guide to museums, collections, exhibition spaces, historic houses, botanical gardens and zoos." (BL) Stewart, Tabori & Chang, 1982.

Ford, Clebert and McPherson, Cynthia   A GUIDE TO THE BLACK APPLE
L.J. Martin, 1977.

Glickman, Toby   THE NEW YORK RED PAGES: A RADICAL TOURIST GUIDE
Praeger, 1984.

Gourse, Leslie   STUDENT GUIDE TO NEW YORK
Hippocrene, 1984.

Hamilton, Marion   THE BEST THINGS IN NEW YORK ARE FREE
Over a thousand free events and activities and institutions in all five boroughs, are described as well as categorized with a star rating system, along with a calendar of regularly scheduled events, special activities for senior citizens and children. Harvard Common Pr, 1985.

Latham, Caroline   THE BEST BARS OF NEW YORK
Three hundred and fifty of the most exciting watering holes in Manhattan. Putnam Pub Group, 1984.

Lorillard, Didi   N.Y.C. SLICKER: A COUNTER CHIC GUIDE TO MANHATTAN
Untouristy itineraries for travelers who want to avoid the typical tourist activities and are not worried about money. Viking, 1979.

Newberry, Lida   ONE-DAY ADVENTURES BY CAR
With full road directions for drives out of New York City. Hastings, 1980.

Page, Tim and others   THE HIP POCKET GUIDE TO NEW YORK CITY
"Opinionated . . . survival manual and sourcebook . . . guide to inexpensive living in Manhattan and the New York underground" for both residents and visitors. Har-Row, 1982.

Patton, Annie and Campbell, Pamela   MOVING TO NEW YORK
"The inside scoop on starting out, settling in and making it in the big city. . . . it's hard to think of anything the authors have left out [and] all this information is handed out in a sensible yet wry manner." (BL) Putnam Pub Group, 1984.

Postal, Bernard   JEWISH LANDMARKS OF NEW YORK: A TRAVEL GUIDE AND HISTORY
Fleet Pr, 1978.

Rosenthal, A.M. and Gelb, Arthur, eds.   WORLD OF NEW YORK: AN UNCOMMON GUIDE TO THE CITY OF FANTASIES
"A delight for jaded New Yorkers as well as for out-of-towners"—sections contributed by notable writers (Nora Ephron, Bernard Kalb, Craig Claiborne, etc.) on art, music, books, food, nightlife, walks. (LJ) Times Bks, 1986.

Schnurnberger, Lynn   KIDS LOVE NEW YORK!
"Topical, alphabetical arrangement . . . plentiful cross-references" for all kinds of ideas for entertaining or occupying pre-teen travelers (or residents). Includes a range from sightseeing and library activities, to park programs, boating, fishing, gymnastics—and more. (BL) Congdon & Weed, 1984.

Scull, Theodore W.   THE CAREFREE GETAWAY GUIDE FOR NEW YORKERS: DAY AND WEEKEND TRIPS WITHOUT A CAR
For the city, Long Island, the Hudson Valley and four adjacent states; using public transportation, nearby restaurants and lodgings to the destinations, detailed instructions for reaching them easily. Harvard Common Pr, 1985.

Shapiro, Mary J.   THE DOVER NEW YORK WALKING GUIDE, FROM THE BATTERY TO WALL STREET
Dover, 1982.

Siegfried, Alanna and Seeman, Helen Z.   SOHO: A GUIDE
Neal-Schuman, 1978.

Stern, Zelda   THE COMPLETE GUIDE TO ETHNIC NEW YORK
St. Martin, 1980.

Thomas, Bill and Phyllis   NATURAL NEW YORK
Within 50 miles of New York, 250 places where the city-bound may walk, fish, birdwatch, ice skate, etc. HR&W, 1983.

Wolfe, Gerard R.   NEW YORK: A GUIDE TO THE METROPOLIS
Walking tours with an architectural and history theme. McGraw, 1982.

Yeadon, Ann   FREE NEW YORK: 1500 FREE PLEASURES & ENTERTAINMENTS AND MUCH, MUCH MORE
Free City Bks, 1982.

Yeadon, David   NOOKS AND CRANNIES: AN UNUSUAL WALKING TOUR
GUIDE TO NEW YORK CITY
Scribner, 1979.

Novels

UPSTATE NEW YORK

Adams, Samuel H.   CANAL TOWN
The building of the Erie Canal in the 1820s and attendant social and economic conflicts. Random, 1944.

Broughton, T. Allen   THE HORSEMASTER
A small Adirondacks community is the setting for this novel about a loner who must learn to take responsibility for another human being. Dutton, 1982.

Busch, Frederick   ROUNDS
A pediatrician arranges an adoption and things turn out badly. FS&G, 1979.

Carmer, Carl   GENESEE FEVER
The story of English settlers in the Genesee region "written with high ardor" for this section of the state, which the author knows well. (FC) McKay, 1980 (first published 1941).

Cheever, John   BULLET PARK
Contemporary issues and problems reflected in interplay between suburbanites. Knopf, 1969.

Conners, Bernard F.   DANCEHALL (Lake Placid)
A compelling suspense novel that also brings up the question of capital punishment. Setting is Lake Placid and Tarrytown—a woman's body is discovered twenty years after her death and a man's seemingly ideal life begins to crumble. Bobbs, 1983.

Doctorow, E.L.   RAGTIME
An anti-nostalgic novel of the fictions and realities of the era of ragtime as lives of an upper-middle-class New Rochelle family, a Jewish immigrant family, and a black musician are intertwined. Random, 1975.

Dreiser, Theodore   AN AMERICAN TRAGEDY
The classic of an impoverished young man, corrupted by promise of wealth and social position, leading to the murder of the young woman who stands in his way. Bentley, 1978 (first published 1925).

Edmonds, Walter D.   DRUMS ALONG THE MOHAWK
The Revolutionary War and frontier life in the Mohawk Valley. Little, 1936. Also three novels of Erie Canal life in the early 1800s: *Erie Water* (1933), *Rome Haul* (1929), and *The Wedding Journey* (1947).

Elfman, Blossom   THE STRAWBERRY FIELDS OF HEAVEN
Story of a family's sojourn in the Oneida Community of the 1870s—"how a cult develops and maintains its hold on its members." (FC) Crown, 1983.

Ferber, Edna   SARATOGA TRUNK
An adventuress from New Orleans takes on society and big business in Saratoga, when it was a prominent resort for the very wealthy. Doubleday, 1951 (first published 1941).

Gardner, John   NICKEL MOUNTAIN (Catskills)
A plain, good-hearted man marries a pregnant girl. Knopf, 1973. Also *The Sunlight Dialogues* (1972), a mystery set in Batavia.

Gilman, Dorothy   NUN IN THE CLOSET
A group of nuns get caught up with Mafia hit men—"a thriller with charm." (FC) Doubleday, 1975.

Holland, Isabelle   COUNTERPOINT (Westchester)
"A Gothic for readers who ordinarily turn up their noses at the genre." (FC) Rawson, Wade, 1980.

Kennedy, William   IRONWEED
Third volume in "the Albany cycle," about the Albany underworld from the 1920s and on. (FC) Viking, 1983. The first two are *Legs* (1975) and *Billy Phelan's Greatest Game* (1978)—"rich in plot and dramatic tension."

Lockridge, Richard   NOT I, SAID THE SPARROW
Putnam County is the setting for this story of a policeman who becomes involved when his neighbor is shot with an arrow. Lippincott, 1973.

Lurie, Alison   ONLY CHILDREN
The time is 1935, the plot is about domestic problems that besiege a Fourth of July weekend in the Catskills. Random, 1979. Also with a New York State setting are *The War Between the Tates* (1974), about 1960s campus life, and *Imaginary Friends* (1967), about some local people in touch with outer space.

Lyons, Nan and Ivan   SOLD!
"Comedy, romance and a touch of mystery" concerning an antiques auctioneer in a small town who finds a treasure of Faberge eggs among the rather sparse possessions of an elderly spinster. Coward, 1982.

Malamud, Bernard   DUBIN'S LIVES
A triangle set in an upstate town on the Vermont border. FS&G, 1979.

Oates, Joyce Carol   MYSTERIES OF WINTERTHURN
Set in upstate New York—three cases of a detective that are failures, not successes—"takes a satirical look at 19th-century society as well as the beginnings of criminology." (FC) Dutton, 1984. *Unholy Loves* (1979), also set in upstate New

York, is a contemporary novel about faculty life, focusing on a novelist "struggling with fears of failure as an artist."

Perry, Richard N.   MONTGOMERY'S CHILDREN
The construction in 1948 of a racetrack in a central New York village destroys part of the adjacent woodland of a small black community, signaling many changes in the years to come. HarBraceJ, 1984.

Rawlings, Marjorie Kinnan   THE SOJOURNER
The satsifactions and rewards of farm life, "conflict between good and evil and final triumph of the good man." (FC) Larlin, 1977 (first published 1953).

Rikhoff, Jean   BUTTES LANDING
Dial, 1973. This and its sequel, *One of the Raymonds* (1974), tell of a pioneer and his wife in the Adirondacks in the early 1800s and father-son conflicts, followed by the grandson's post-Civil War life in the Adirondacks and in Reconstruction North Carolina.

Sanders, Lawrence   THE SIXTH COMMANDMENT
Shocking secrets about a small town's most famous citizen (a former Nobel laureate) are unearthed by a private investigator for a philanthropic group hired to investigate a grant application. Putnam Pub Group, 1979.

Shaw, Irwin   RICH MAN, POOR MAN
Success-to-failure, poor-to-rich spectrum is experienced in this saga of the Jordache family from 1940s to 1970s. Delacorte Pr. 1970. *Beggarman, Thief* (1977) continues the chronicle of the second generation of the family.

Taylor, Robert L.   NIAGARA
Niagara Falls when it was a fashionable resort in the early 1800s—a reporter is sent to the town to investigate scandals and ends up going into the wine business. "Rich in historical details . . . rife with comic wit. . . . the story is outrageous and delicious." (FC) Putnam Pub Group, 1980.

Truscott, Lucian K.   DRESS GRAY
An upperclassman at West Point questions the ruling of accidental death when a cadet is found drowned—"corruption and collusion among the powers that be . . . of the Academy is found out." (FC) Doubleday, 1979.

Weingarten, Violet   MRS. BENEKER (Westchester)
A middle-aged woman enrolls in a comparative religion class to find the meaning of life while actually "life is running wild" all about her in terms of what her son, daughter, husband and parents are feeling and doing—"a veritable bouquet of middle-class hangups." (FC) S&S, 1968.

Whitney, Phyllis A.   THE STONE BULL
A woman must solve the murder for which her dead sister was blamed—the plot involves a stone bull, a dark tower, and a murky vault in the Catskills. Doubleday, 1977.

Wilson, Sloan   SMALL TOWN (Adirondacks)
A divorced man returns to help his teenage son, and finds both romance and a challenging job as editor of a newspaper— "memorable . . . for its lovingly detailed descriptions of the Adirondack countryside." Arbor Hse, 1978. Also *All the Best People* (1970), a chronicle of upper-middle-class Wasps who own a resort at Lake George.

LONG ISLAND & FIRE ISLAND

Ball, John   THE KILLING IN THE MARKET
The murder of a stockbroker in his Long Island home is solved by a local policeman. Doubleday, 1978.

Benchley, Peter   JAWS
A shark terrorizes a summer resort on Long Island's east end. Doubleday, 1974.

DeMille, Nelson   THE TALBOT ODYSSEY
Novel of espionage that begins as a prank when a Glen Cove student breaks into the mansion that houses the Soviet Union's UN delegation. It escalates into a full-scale confrontation between the United States and Russia, and a Russian plan to defuse U.S. computers. Delacorte Pr, 1984.

Fitzgerald, F. Scott   THE GREAT GATSBY
Long Island society in the 1920s—"its false glamor and cultural barrenness." (FC) Scribner, 1953 (first published 1925).

Green, Gerald   THE HEALERS
Twenty-five years in the lives of a Long Island pharmacist and his three children, each of whom reaches various heights in the medical world. Putnam Pub Group, 1979.

Harris, Leonard   THE HAMPTONS
A threatened expose of Hampton society is the focus of the plot. Wyndam, 1980.

Hirschfield, Burt   RETURN TO FIRE ISLAND
A sequel to *Fire Island* (1970), which introduced readers to "the sizzling summer scene" on the island. In this are the same characters, years later, with most of them bitter and cynical, their earlier bright futures unfulfilled. (PW) Avon, 1984.

Hobson, Laura Z.   FIRST PAPERS
"Dramatizes the socialist liberal movement in the U.S.A. 1911-1920 [through] the lives of two families"—one, Russian-Jewish emigres, the other, New England Unitarians. (FC) Random, 1964.

Hoffman, Alice   ANGEL LANDING
"Affecting love story, laced with humor" of a therapist in a no-longer fashionable Long Island town and a welder at the nearby nuclear power plant. (FC) Putnam

Pub Group, 1980. Also *The Drowning Season* (1979), about a clannish family in a secluded compound on Long Island ruled over by the grandmother.

Isaacs, Susan   CLOSE RELATIONS
A "romantic, feminist, political" novel of a political speechwriter who finds a seemingly perfect new man with only one strike against him—her family approves. (FC) Lippincott, 1980. Also *Compromising Positions* (1978), social comedy and a murdered dentist-Lothario.

Johnston, Velda   THE FATEFUL SUMMER
Set in East Hampton and New York City in 1910—"turn-of-the-century romantic suspense with elements of love, treachery, blackmail, murder." (FC) Dodd, 1981. *I Came to the Highlands* (1974) is a pre-Revolutionary historical romance set in Southampton.

Koenig, Laird   THE LITTLE GIRL WHO LIVES DOWN THE LANE
Thriller about a British girl who is not what she appears to be. Coward, 1974.

Lancaster, Bruce   THE SECRET ROAD
Historical novel of the Revolutionary War and George Washington's secret service on Long Island. Little, 1952.

Leonard, George   THE ICE CATHEDRAL
A thriller about a Long Island Bay man turned mass murderer. The setting is the Great South Bay, Whole Neck (Merrick) and Crab Meadow (Freeport), with an aging south shore detective as the main protagonist. S&S, 1983.

Mitgang, Herbert   THE MONTAUK FAULT
The director of the U.S. Air Force security service has to figure out a way to let Moscow know that if they use their new discovery (how to set off an earthquake) the U.S. will retaliate with *its* new discovery (how to boil away lakes). Arbor Hse, 1981.

Seton, Cynthia Propper   THE HALF-SISTERS
Covers the period 1937-70 as the half-sisters first spend summers together on Long Island as children, go their separate ways, and resume the relationship some thirty years later. Norton, 1974.

Skelton, Alison Scott   DIFFERENT FAMILIES
A pulp mystery writer's ex-wife comes to Fire Island from her home in England where she's remarried, to pick up her teenaged son who has spent the summer with his American father—"abounds with potential conflicts between generations and cultures." (FC) Seaview, 1980.

Tennenbaum, Silvia   RACHEL, THE RABBI'S WIFE
The rabbi's wife's feminism and artistic ambitions conflict with what the congregation expects of her—a behind-the-scenes look at family problems in a rabbi's life. Morrow, 1978.

Watson, Clarissa   THE BISHOP IN THE BACK SEAT
"A fun, furious chase through the varied worlds of socialites, politicians, and would-be artists"—a part-time detective on the board of a Long Island museum is faced with the theft of a newlyacquired Rembrandt by a group dressed as nuns. (FC) Atheneum, 1980.

Westlake, Donald E.   BANK SHOT
Mastermind Dortmunder wants to rob a Long Island bank by literally stealing the whole bank. S&S, 1972.

Whitney, Phyllis A.   THE GOLDEN UNICORN (East Hampton)
An adopted girl searches for her biological parents and uncovers a family scandal. Doubleday, 1976.

Whitney, Phyllis A.   RAINSONG (Cold Spring Harbor)
An estate, on the north shore of Long Island, and the pop music field are the background for this mystery/romance of a heroine trying to put her life back in order following the suicide of her husband. Doubleday, 1984.

NEW YORK CITY

Adams, Jane   TRADEOFFS
The tradeoffs women make in choosing between career and home—authentic background in journalism, advertising and government. Morrow, 1983.

Albrand, Martha   MANHATTAN NORTH
The crux of the plot for this political murder mystery is the murder of a justice of the Supreme Court in Central Park. Coward, 1971.

Asch, Sholem   THE MOTHER
An immigrant family from Poland on the Lower East Side and the universal theme of the heroic role of the mother in the struggles they face. AMS, 1970 (first published 1930).

Auchincloss, Louis   THE BOOK CLASS
Seemingly a Manhattan upper-crust version of . . . *and Ladies of the Club* (see "Ohio/Novels")—the son of one of the members of the Book Class narrates the story of a collection of Park Avenue debutantes who meet for book discussions beginning in 1908 and lasting 64 years—individual participants' lives, their disappointments, tragedies and passions over the years. "No one excels his [Auchincloss] finely etched portraits of sophisticates of good breeding and inherited wealth." Houghton, 1984. Other novels set in this milieu of wealthy, socially elite, and powerful New Yorkers of various time periods are (in order of publication date): *The House of Five Talents* (1960), *Portrait in Brownstone* (1962), *The Embezzler* (1966), *A World of Profit* (1968), *The Dark Lady* (1977), *The Country Cousin* (1978), and *Watchfires* (1982). Also two collections of short stories with a Manhattan setting: *Tales of Manhattan* (1967) and *Second Chance* (1970).

Baehr, Consuelo   NOTHING TO LOSE
A Cinderella plot—overweight April not only loses sixty pounds but "wins the heart of the company president" of a Newark department store. (FC) Putnam Pub Group, 1982.

Baldwin, James   IF BEALE STREET COULD TALK
New York City and Puerto Rico are the settings for a novel of a love between two young people that helps them to deal with racial oppression. Dial, 1974. Other books by this author about black life and New York are *Go Tell It on The Mountain* (1963), *Another Country* (1962), and *Tell Me How Long the Train's Been Gone* (1968).

Bayer, William   SWITCH
An introspective police officer with a psychological approach to crime is assigned to a gruesome double murder. S&S, 1984.

Bell, Madison S.   THE WASHINGTON SQUARE ENSEMBLE
Drug dealers in Washington Square on a summer weekend narrate their individual pasts—"brilliantly evokes a world of violence, depravity and despair without inducing lowering of the spirits." (FC)Viking, 1983.

Berger, Thomas   WHO IS TEDDY VILLANOVA?
A former English literature teacher, turned private investigator, has to prove he is *not* Teddy Villanova. Delacorte Pr, 1977.

Burgess, Anthony   THE CLOCKWORK TESTAMENT
Satiric look at New York City of a visiting professor from England. Knopf, 1975.

Bush, Lawrence   BESSIE
Bessie, the American-Jewish radical heroine, is part of major events in the various movements of the century—the Triangle fire, the Sacco-Vanzetti trial, and so on. The novel is based on experiences of the author's grandmother. Putnam Pub Group, 1983.

Calisher, Hortense   THE NEW YORKERS
Chronicle of the wealthy Mannix family from 1934-55. Little, 1969. Also *Textures of Life* (1963), an account of a struggling married couple played against the solid marriage of their parents.

Caunitz, William J.   ONE POLICE PLAZA
Lt. Dan Malone solves a murder involving international terrorism and espionage as well as internal vigilante activities. Crown, 1984.

Charyn, Jerome   PANNA MARIA
Recreation of Hell's Kitchen (midtown West side) at the beginning of the century. Arbor Hse, 1982.

Childress, Alice   A SHORT WALK
A mulatto girl makes the physical and psychological journey from South Carolina to Harlem. Coward, 1979.

Clark, Mary Higgins   A STRANGER IS WATCHING
Murder-horror story with "precise and evocative sense of place . . . particularly Grand Central Station." (FC) S&S, 1978.

**Coleman, Terry   THANKSGIVING; A NOVEL IN CELEBRATION
OF AMERICA**
Written by an Australian; a historical novel of Puritan Massachusetts and cosmopolitan Nieuw Amsterdam—full of fascinating historical detail and combining real and fictional characters. S&S, 1981.

Collins, Larry   THE FIFTH HORSEMAN
An international thriller—"Qaddafi gives a Carter-like president an ultimatum . . . or a hydrogen bomb hidden in Manhattan will be detonated." (FC) S&S, 1980.

Colwin, Laurie   FAMILY HAPPINESS
"The mainstay of an attractive, well-to-do New York Jewish family . . . falls headlong in love with a painter." (FC) Knopf, 1982. Also *Happy All the Time* (1978)—engaging, funny dual courtships.

Cook, Robin   BRAIN
One of the author's medical mystery novels—this one involves the stealing of a dead patient's brain, and is set at Hobson University Medical Center in New York. Putnam, 1981.

Corman, Avery   KRAMER VERSUS KRAMER
When a woman leaves her husband and son the husband thrives and learns to cope and the wife returns to try to regain custody of her child. Random, 1977.

Courter, Gay   THE MIDWIFE
The Lower East Side and Jewish immigrants is the background for this story about a threat to the honorable profession of midwifery by male-dominated obstetrics. Houghton, 1981.

Cravens, Gwyneth   LOVE AND WORK
The singles scene in Manhattan. Knopf, 1982.

Crosby, John   PARTY OF THE YEAR
"Unutterably chic . . . hifalutin gothic"—an ex-CIA agent is hired to protect a twelve-year-old Italian contessa in a maximum-security high-rise for the "frightened filthy rich." (FC) Stein & Day, 1979. A kind of sequel is *Men in Arms* (1983), with the agent involved in a "crackerjack, fast-moving spy tale with a wildly complicated plot."

Daley, Robert   YEAR OF THE DRAGON
Crime in today's Chinatown—"convincing picture of how the powers that be, American and Chinese . . . make sure nothing will really change." (FC) S&S, 1981.

Davenport, Marcia   MY BROTHER'S KEEPER
Based on the famous case of the Collier brothers, who seemingly died in poverty in a Harlem house but were then found to have amassed wealth they did not use. There's "pathos and horror" in the life stories that emerge. (FC) Bentley, 1979 (first published 1954).

Davies, Valentine   MIRACLE ON 34TH STREET
The classic movie about Santa Claus coming true in Macy's department store is based on this happy novel. HarBraceJ, 1947.

DeFelitta, Frank   AUDREY ROSE
A chiller set in the Central Park West section of Manhattan—reincarnation of one little girl in another. Putnam Pub Group, 1975.

DeMille, Nelson   CATHEDRAL
Irish extremists seize the cathedral on St. Patrick's Day. Delacorte, 1981.

Denker, Henry   THE HEALERS
Historical novel of an Austrian Jew and his convert wife who together fight poverty and disease in nineteenth-century Manhattan, in a clinic that eventually becomes Mount Sinai Hospital. Morrow, 1983.

Dennis, Patrick   AUNTIE MAME
A nephew reminisces about his unconventional aunt who played each of the roles life handed her—shopgirl, showgirl, authoress, etc.—to the hilt. Vanguard, 1955.

DiDonato, Pietro   CHRIST IN CONCRETE
Italian-American bricklayers in New York, and the specific story of a young boy who takes over financial responsibility for his family when his father is killed working on a construction job. Bobbs, 1980 (first published 1939).

Dos Passos, John   MANHATTAN TRANSFER
A "brilliant composite" of vivid vignettes and the author's conception of New York through many characters—"as impressive as it is depressing." (FC) Har-Row, 1980 (first published 1925).

Ellin, Stanley   THE DARK FANTASTIC
"Expertly horrifying tale" of stolen art and a racist landlord's plan to blow up his building, with an "incredibly ingenious" finale. (FC)Mysterious Press, 1983.

Ellison, Ralph   INVISIBLE MAN
A black's loss of identity—final invisibility—in a world of rejection that has been compared to Dostoevski's Notes from the Underground. Modern Lib (first published 1952).

Feldman, Ellen   A.K.A., KATHERINE WALDEN
"Delightful, humorous, wry novel" of Katherine and her four friends from college days and her attempts "to sort out her own best interests from the good intentions of her friends." (FC) Morrow, 1982.

Fitzgerald, F. Scott   THE BEAUTIFUL AND THE DAMNED
A story of the roaring twenties set in Manhattan. Scribner, 1950 (first published 1922).

Garfield, Brian   DEATH WISH
A man avenges the brutal death of his wife and destruction of his daughter's sanity by becoming a one-man vigilante against criminals in New York. McKay, 1972.

Goldman, James   THE MAN FROM GREEK AND ROMAN
A curator at the Metropolitan Museum absconds with a valuable chalice—"marvelously funny, intellectually satisfying tale." (FC) Random, 1974.

Goldman, William   CONTROL
Psychological thriller; "disparate vignettes [a woman goes berserk in Bloomingdale's, a young man rejects a career in psychiatry to be a cop, etc.] converge to reveal an ominous conspiracy involving psychic research, time travel and mind control." (FC) Delacorte Pr, 1982. Also *Marathon Man* (1974).

Goldreich, Gloria   FOUR DAYS
Whether or not to seek an abortion is the moral dilemma of a successful businesswoman that expands to include coming to terms with the whole Jewish experience and the Holocaust. HarBraceJ, 1980. Also *Leah's Journey* (1978), saga of a Jewish immigrant family.

Goldstein, Arthur D.   A PERSON SHOULDN'T DIE LIKE THAT
A retired clothing cutter on the Lower East Side investigates the disappearance of an acquaintance, with whom he plays checkers, and enters a whole new world of crime, terror and danger. Random, 1972.

Gordon, Noah   THE JERUSALEM DIAMOND
Enthralling novel that, in the process, gives the reader an education in diamond cutting and polishing, set in the 47th Street diamond district of Manhattan. The plot concerns a diamond that has significance for the Christian, Jewish and Muslim religions. Random, 1979.

Gordon, R.L.   THE LADY WHO LOVED NEW YORK
Nostalgic novel, told in flashback, of life among the rich at the turn of the century. Crowell, 1977.

Greenburg, Dan   LOVE KILLS
Police mystery involving a homicidal killer of young women. HarBraceJ, 1978.

Greenfield, Robert   TEMPLE
Each member of a Jewish family experiences a major trauma during the period between the Jewish and secular New Years and each "emerges changed and with a new understanding of friends and family." (FC) Summit Bks, 1983.

Guy, Rosa   A MEASURE OF TIME
Picaresque novel of a woman from Montgomery, Alabama, who seeks her fortune in Harlem of 1926—"an evocative tour of 20th-century black America from the rural South to streets of New York City." (BRD) HR&W, 1983. Also *Ruby* (1976) about a young woman from the West Indies adjusting to a lonely and frustrating life in Harlem in the 1970s.

Hauser, Thomas   ASWORTH AND PALMER
Life inside a Wall Street law firm. Morrow, 1981.

Hearon, Shelby   GROUP THERAPY
"A charming comedy of manners and morals" about a Texas woman who becomes a visiting professor at SUNY in Purchase, New York, and "swings between the fading gentility of the Southern family to whom she has promised to return and the caffeinated-vitality of her new Northern friends." (FC) Atheneum, 1984.

Hentoff, Nat   BLUES FOR CHARLES DARWIN
Police Detective Noah Green solves the murder of a Greenwich Village freelance editor married to a professor at NYU—"the criminal underbelly of the city [but] enough flashes of . . . love and good sense and jazz . . . to relieve the gloom." (FC) Morrow, 1982.

Herlihy, James Leo   MIDNIGHT COWBOY
"An appalling story, told with great skill" of three misfits living in an abandoned building. (FC) S&S, 1965.

Hobson, Laura Z.   UNTOLD MILLIONS
Manhattan in 1923. A talented newcomer falls in love with an agency copywriter and supports him in his ambition to write a novel. Har-Row, 1982. Also *Gentleman's Agreement* (1947), about a journalist who pretends to be a Jew to research anti-Semitism.

Holland, Isabelle   THE MARCHINGTON INHERITANCE
A woman moves to an East Side brownstone and becomes involved with children in a school next door. Rawson, 1979.

Horan, James D.   THE BLUE MESSIAH
Saga of two boys from Hell's Kitchen, from World War I to the 1950s, and their rise from petty hooliganism to the inner councils of organized crime. Crown, 1971.

Horwitz, Julius   THE DIARY OF A.N.
A welfare caseworker's account of a hopeless, fatherless black family. Coward, 1970. Also *Natural Enemies* (1974).

Hughes, Langston   SIMPLE SPEAKS HIS MIND
First of three novels in which a Harlem black speaks his mind in a sardonic spoof of race relations, followed by *Simple Takes a Wife* (1953) and *Simple Stakes a Claim* (1957). Also, a collection of short stories, *Simple's Uncle Sam* (1965). S&S, 1950.

Hunter, Evan   STREETS OF GOLD
Story of his Italian immigrant family in New York told from the viewpoint of a middle-aged, blind jazz pianist. Har-Row, 1974. Also *The Blackboard Jungle* (1954), about violence in an inner city vocational high school.

Isaacs, Susan   CLOSE RELATIONS
Set in New York, Queens, and Long Island—"simultaneously romantic, feminist, and political" and a satire of many contemporary cliches—latearrying Irishmen, Jewish mothers, WASP mores and American political campaigns (FC). Lippincott, 1980.

Jhabvala, Ruth Prawer   IN SEARCH OF LOVE AND BEAUTY
An emigre from Austria in the 1930s is the focus around which the story of three generations of an emigre family is told. Morrow, 1983.

Johnston, Velda   THE FACE IN THE SHADOWS
Suspense novel that begins when the heroine finds a drugged child on the doorstep at the Cloisters (New York's museum of medieval art). Dodd, 1971. Also *The People on the Hill* (1971), about a murder in Central Park.

Kaufman, Sue   DIARY OF A MAD HOUSEWIFE
Story of a contemporary marriage—a wife who thinks she's going mad decides to write out the things that frighten her and reveals much about her husband, children, and life-style in a Central Park West apartment. Random, 1967.

Kazan, Elia   THE ANATOLIAN
A sequel to *America, America* (see "Turkey/Novels"), it begins in 1909 when the hero's family of seven brothers and sisters arrive in New York and he is expected to "take up the patriarchal mantle [and of the] struggle for wealth, influence and an illusive Americanization." (FC) Knopf, 1982.

Kluger, Phyllis and Richard   GOOD GOODS
See "Connecticut/Novels."

Koenig, Laird   ROCKABYE
"Slick thriller" about child theft, with much action and an evocative atmosphere. (FC) St. Martin, 1981.

Kotzwinkle, William   CHRISTMAS AT FONTAINE'S
"Bounces between rowdy satire and tearjerking sentiment" as a disparate group of employees of a NYC department store experience Christmas when a young boy is found hiding there. (FC) Putnam Pub Group, 1982.

Krantz, Judith   I'LL TAKE MANHATTAN
Saga of a beautiful heroine's career in the New York publishing world. Crown, 1986.

L'Engle, Madeleine   A SEVERED WASP
"A New York novel, filled with big-city tensions." (FC) FS&G, 1982. The plot includes a character from one of her other novels, *The Small Rain* (1984), a

retired concert pianist, who becomes involved in the lives of Episcopal clergy, their wives and children. FS&G, 1982.

Leuci, Bob   DOYLE'S DISCIPLES
A newly promoted detective has to deal with conflicts between friendship and personal integrity when a murder investigation points to police corruption. Freundlich, 1984.

Levin, Ira   ROSEMARY'S BABY
A story of the supernatural as a young couple's apartment is taken over by an evil neighbor. Random, 1967.

Lieberman, Herbert   NIGHTBLOOM
Detective story involving an over-the-hill detective obsessed with finding the man who, each spring, has killed someone in the theatre district by pushing a cinderblock off a roof. Putnam Pub Group, 1984.

McBain, Ed   FUZZ
The first of the 87th Precinct series of police procedurals. Other titles, in order of publication, are: *Jigsaw* (1970), *Sadie When She Died* (1972), *Hail to the Chief* (1973), *Let's Hear It For the Deaf Man* (1973), *Bread* (1974), *Blood Relatives* (1975), *So Long As You Both Shall Live* (1976), and *Long Time No See* (1977). Doubleday, 1968.

McInerney, Jay   BRIGHT LIGHTS, BIG CITY
"Very funny, oddly touching" novel of a would-be writer—"elements of a roman a clef about life at *The New Yorker*," the protagonist's employer. (BRD) Vintage, 1984.

McMullen, Mary   BUT NELLIE WAS SO NICE
Greenwich Village is the setting for this murder mystery of a woman who knows too much. Doubleday, 1979.

Mukherjee, Bharati   WIFE
About a young wife from a submissive Bengali background in Calcutta living in and coping with a hostile New York. Houghton, 1975.

Neely, Richard   AN ACCIDENTAL
"A servile, sexually repressed" copy editor is transmuted by the slip of a surgeon's knife into the opposite. (FC) HR&W, 1981.

O'Donnell, Lillian   THE CHILDREN'S ZOO
Detective Norah Mulcahaney solves a mystery involving the death of animals in the Central Park Zoo and the evidence points to some students at a private school. Also *No Business Being a Cop* (1979), another Detective Mulcahaney mystery in which someone is killing off policewomen. Putnam Pub Group, 1981.

O'Hara, John   BUTTERFIELD 8
Novelization of an actual murder case in New York when party girl Starr Faithfull is drowned on a Long Island beach. HarBraceJ, 1935.

Piercy, Marge   BRAIDED LIVES
"Hefty feminist novel" that follows the lives of two women friends from Detroit to New York City. (FC) Summit Bks, 1982.

Prose, Francine   HOUSEHOLD SAINTS
"Captures the domestic scenes and smells of Little Italy" with a plot about an Italian sausage maker who wins a new wife in a pinochle game. (FC) St. Martin, 1981.

Puzo, Mario   THE GODFATHER
The blockbuster novel of an Italian-American crime family. Putnam Pub Group, 1969. Also *The Fortunate Pilgrim* (1965) about a close-knit Italian family and community life in 1928.

Rhodes, Evan H.   THE PRINCE OF CENTRAL PARK
A boy leaves his abusive foster mother to live in Central Park—"unabashedly sentimental treat" as Jay-Jay befriends an old lady, acquires a dog for himself, and deals with a vicious mugger. (FC) Coward, 1975.

Roiphe, Anne R.   UP THE SANDBOX
"Minutiae of matrimony and maternity" related in a combination of inner musings of a young mother and outrageous fantasies. (FC) S&S, 1970.

Rosten, Leo   SILKY! A DETECTIVE STORY
"Super-ethnic, very funny" thriller. (FC) Har-Row, 1979.

Runyon, Damon   GUYS AND DOLLS
Short stories, some of which were the basis for the musical. Lippincott, 1950. Also *Best of Runyon* (1938).

Sanders, Lawrence   THE SECOND DEADLY SIN
A disparate trio take on the murder of a painter who was a "thoroughly unlikable genius" in this police procedural. Putnam Pub Group, 1977. Also *The First Deadly Sin* (1973) and *The Anderson Tapes* (1970).

Schickel, Richard   ANOTHER I, ANOTHER YEAR
A love affair between two newly divorced people and told against a "palpably felt" Manhattan background. (BRD) Har-Row, 1978.

Schulberg, Budd   WATERFRONT
An indictment of racketeering and labor unions on the waterfront. Bentley, 1979 (first published 1955).

Schwartz, Lynne S.   DISTURBANCES IN THE FIELD
"Journey from resignation to a grudging reaffirmation of living" as a Manhattan chamber musician and her artist husband face profound tragedy and marital problems. (FC) Har-Row, 1983.

Scott, Justin   NORMANDIE TRIANGLE
"Tantalizingly plausible . . . World War II yarn" of a plot to sink the Queen Mary in New York harbor. (FC) Arbor Hse, 1981.

Shaw, Irwin   ACCEPTABLE LOSSES
Suspenseful novel in which threatening phone calls to a New York literary agent end in a "nightmarish netherland he experiences in ICU of a leading New York hospital." (FC) Delacorte Pr, 1981. Also *Bread Upon Waters* (1981)—"the effects of misdirected philanthropy on a middle-class New York family."

Smiley, Jane   DUPLICATE KEYS
A librarian finds two rock musicians dead in her best friend's apartment, to which too many people have duplicate keys. Knopf, 1984.

Smith, Dennis   GLITTER AND ASH
Arson investigation of a fire in a new and chic disco that, in the process, addresses the rivalry between the police and fire departments, corrupt politicians, the jet set, and gay subculture. Dutton, 1980.

Spark, Muriel   THE HOTHOUSE BY THE EAST RIVER
"Tense, fetid" relationships between a couple, and between them and their "odd, uncaring children" in their East River apartment. (FC) Viking, 1973.

Stewart, Edward   BALLERINA
A couple of talented teenagers and the world of professional ballet in New York City. Doubleday, 1979.

Stone, Alma   NOW FOR THE TURBULENCE
"Sardonic wit, poignancy and suspense . . . unforgettable story" of an aging woman in a West Side apartment, warned of an imminent attack. (FC) Doubleday, 1983.

Tax, Meredith   RIVINGTON STREET
Family chronicle of a woman-dominated Lower East Side family as well as the garment industry and suffragist movement of the early 1900s. Morrow, 1982.

Thomas, Michael M.   SOMEONE ELSE'S MONEY
"About financial intrigue, Wall Street and the international art market. . . . The setting is Manhattan with excursions to Europe and Texas." (FC) S&S, 1982.

Uhnak, Dorothy   FALSE WITNESS
"The investigative process prevails" in the story of an ambitious female in the D.A.'s office involved in a political bombshell case that presents conflicts both for her career ambitions and her personal life. (FC) S&S, 1981. Other novels by Uhnak with a New York City setting are *Law and Order* (1973), saga of an Irish family, and two police mysteries, *The Ledger* (1970) and *The Witness* (1969).

Van Slyke, Helen   PUBLIC SMILES, PRIVATE TEARS
Story of a woman who chose in the 1940s and 50s to have a career in retailing in a large department store, at a time when most women were opting for homemaking. Har-Row, 1982. Also set in New York are *Always Is Not Forever* (1977) about modern married life, and *The Mixed Blessing* (1975), in which a mulatto's background is exposed.

Wallach, Anne   WOMEN'S WORK
The advertising industry seen as sexist, cynical, and degrading for an ambitious executive. NAL, 1981.

Wallant, Edward L.   THE PAWNBROKER
A bitter Harlem pawnbroker, haunted by memories of the concentration camp, and self-hating, rejoins the "emotionally living." HarBraceJ, 1961. Also *The Tenants of Moonbloom* (1963), about a humanistic hero working as rental agent for his slumlord brother.

Weidman, Jerome   FOURTH STREET EAST
"An episodic, fictionalized, autobiographical evocation of New York's lower east side." Random, 1970. *Last Respects* (1972) and *Tiffany Street* (1974) continue the family chronicle. Also with a New York setting are *I Can Get It for You Wholesale* (1937), *The Enemy Camp* (1958) and *The Sound of Bow Bells* (1962).

Westlake, Donald E.   WHY ME
An unlucky burglar robs a small jewelry store and unwittingly takes in his haul a ruby ring hidden out there that everybody from the FBI and terrorist groups to NYC police and top criminals are after—"screwball characters, hilarious dialogue." (FC) Viking, 1983. Also *Dancing Aztecs* (1976), *The Fugitive Pigeon* (1965), *Cops and Robbers* (1972)—crime capers set in New York. In *Brother's Keeper* (1975), a monastery's lease is up and the brothers work to save their Park Avenue address.

Williams, John A.   CLICK SONG
Set in and around New York since World War II with a plot about a black novelist's experience in establishing himself as a "novelist of distinction." Houghton, 1982.

Wouk, Herman   MARJORIE MORNINGSTAR
Story of a Jewish girl growing into womanhood. Doubleday, 1955. Also *Youngblood Hawke* (1962), an aspiring novelist from Kentucky who makes it big in the city.

BROOKLYN, THE BRONX AND QUEENS

Bonanno, Margaret W.   EMBER DAYS (Brooklyn)
Saga of the women in an Irish-Catholic family in a close, rigid culture in the first generation, that culture virtually gone by the fourth. Seaview, 1980. Also *A Certain Slant of Light* (1979), in which one of the earlier novel's main characters is a secondary character.

Breslin, Jimmy   FORSAKING ALL OTHERS (Bronx)
"A tough, unflinching look at the lower depths"—the plot involves a Harvard-educated Puerto Rican lawyer, the daughter of a Mafia don, and the murder of a dope seller. (FC) S&S, 1982.

Breslin, Jimmy   THE GANG THAT COULDN'T SHOOT STRAIGHT (Brooklyn and Queens)
Story of a disorganized crime family, and Kid Sally Palumbo's attempt to take over from the big boss. Viking, 1969. Also *Table Money* (1985).

Brown, Wesley   TRAGIC MAGIC (Queens)
A literate college-educated black, just released on parole from prison for draft resistance, returns to his Queens neighborhood. Random, 1979.

Corman, Avery   THE OLD NEIGHBORHOOD (Bronx)
The author "writes deliciously" of the life-turn-around of an ad executive who takes a summer off and spends it traveling daily from his Long Island home to the Bronx neighborhood where he grew up. (FC) Linden Pr, 1980.

Dintenfass, Mark   OLD WORLD, NEW WORLD (Brooklyn)
Family chronicle of Jewish immigrants—"spins the multi-colored, multi-faceted threads of the family into a huge . . . tapestry." Morrow, 1982. Also with a Brooklyn setting, *Montgomery Street* (1978), about a filmmaker producing a movie about the Brooklyn neighborhood where he grew up.

Flaherty, Joe   TIN WIFE (Brooklyn)
A "tin wife" [cop's wife] reviews her life on the day she's due to receive her husband's posthumous award from the mayor. S&S, 1984.

Green, Gerald   THE CHAINS (Brooklyn)
Family chronicle of a "brawling, semi-criminal" Jewish family—"passionate, violent story, streetwise and rich in authentic detail." Also set in Brooklyn are *The Last Angry Man* (1957), about a doctor's life in the Brooklyn slums, and *To Brooklyn With Love* (1967), Brooklyn youth during the depression. Seaview, 1980.

Holland, Isabelle   MONCRIEFF (Brooklyn)
Mysterious happenings and "gothic thrills" in an old Brooklyn Heights house. Weybright & Talley, 1975.

Konecky, Edith   ALLEGRA MAUD GOLDMAN (Brooklyn)
Growing up in Brooklyn in the 1930s. Har-Row, 1976.

Malamud, Bernard   THE ASSISTANT (Brooklyn)
A Jewish grocer and his family—"simple people struggling to make their lives better in a world of bad luck." (FC) FS&G, 1957.

Morley, Christopher   THE HAUNTED BOOK SHOP (Brooklyn)
A secondhand book shop in Brooklyn of an earlier day is the setting for a mystery and "much good discussion of books and reading sandwiched with the plot." (FC) Avon, 1983 (first published 1919).

Potok, Chaim   THE CHOSEN (Brooklyn, Bronx)
Friendship between two boys in the Williamsburg section of Brooklyn. S&S,

1967. *The Promise* (1969) continues the story as the boys grow up. Also *In the Beginning* (1975), about growing up in the Bronx in the early 1900s, and *My Name is Asher Lev* (1972), about a boy who wants a career as an artist in a family of intense religious beliefs.

Price, Richard   BLOODBROTHERS (Bronx)
"Unsparingly savage picture of life among the New York proletariat" in Coop City. (FC) Also *The Wanderers* (1974). Houghton, 1976.

Smith, Betty   A TREE GROWS IN BROOKLYN
Life in an impoverished family for an exceptional young girl in the early 1900s. Har-Row, 1947. Also *Maggie-Now* (1958), a girl grows into responsible womanhood.

Smith, Robert K.   SADIE SHAPIRO'S KNITTING BOOK (Queens)
An elderly Jewish lady sends some of her knitting patterns off to a publishing house and ends up with a best-seller. S&S, 1973.

Styron, William   SOPHIE'S CHOICE
A Southern writer, a Polish Catholic survivor of the Holocaust, and her Jewish lover, living in a Brooklyn boardinghouse—the novel traces the writer's "intense involvement with the lovers . . . and his growing fascination with the horror of Sophie's past." (FC) Random, 1979.

Uhnak, Dorothy   THE INVESTIGATION (Queens)
A Queens mother is suspected of murdering her two children. S&S, 1977.

Wolitzer, Hilma   IN THE FLESH (Queens)
"Saga of an endearing heroine-narrator [who] has to get married in pre-abortion 1957" and leads a blissful life in Queens becoming "everybody's Jewish mother" until another woman enters the picture. (FC) Morrow, 1977.

Wouk, Herman   CITYBOY: THE ADVENTURES OF HERBIE BOOKBINDER (Bronx)
"Adventures in public school, at home, and at summer camp . . . sharp, light-hearted picture of public school life in the Bronx twenty years ago." (FC) Doubleday, 1969 (first published 1948).

TRAVEL ARTICLES

AMERICANA
1985 Nov-Dec "Museum of the Airways." The Museum of Broadcasting. Jean Rosenbluth, p. 69

ANTIQUES
1985 Jul History in Towns: "Saratoga Springs, the Queen of American Resorts." Mosette G. Broderick, p. 96
Dec "Winter Holidays at Sleepy Hollow Restoration." Joseph T. Butler, p. 1190

BON APPETIT

1985 Jun Traveling with Taste: "Saratoga Springs." Patricia Brooks, p. 30

1984 Oct Traveling with Taste: "New York's Finger Lakes." Charles Monaghan, p. 36

CONNOISSEUR

1985 Sep "Upscale at the Beaverkill." A Rockefeller inn revives a beautiful valley (a revived old fishing inn). David W. McCullough, p. 120

EARLY AMERICAN LIFE

1985 Feb "Historic Cherry Hill: Textbook House." Margaret Kent, p. 54

Apr "The Monroe Bank: A Restoration Story." Pittsford, p. 28

GOURMET

Each month there's an article on restaurants in New York City, "Specialites de la Maison," by Jay Jacobs, which reviews three individual restaurants.

1985 Jul "South Street Seaport." Alice R. Gochman, p. 36

Sep Along the Avenues: "The Rainbow Room and the Rainbow Grill." Hudson Bridges, p.12

1984 Jan "Little Italy." Fred Ferretti, p. 14

Jun Along the Avenues: "Chelsea Hotel, Kitchen Arts & Letters Bookstore, the Anna Held Museum." Hudson Bridges, p. 30

Sep Along the Avenues: "Museum of American Folk Art." Hudson Bridges, p. 28

Oct "A Wall Street Journal." Alice R. Gochman, p. 52

Dec Along the Avenues: "FAO Schwartz, the cookbook collection at the N.Y. Academy of Medicine." Hudson Bridges, p. 24

HORIZON

1985 Mar "Springtime in New York." Special section covering art galleries, auctions, museums, dance, specialty bookstores, music, theatre, stores and dining. Various authors, begins p. 21

Jul-Aug "Brooklyn." Across the Brooklyn Bridge to enter a world of the arts; strategies for the 80s (Brooklyn Museum of Art and Academy of Music). Michael McEvoy and Mila Bare, p. 33

Nov "Corning." Glassworks, crafts, arts, historic Market Street area. pp. 25, 32

HOUSE & GARDEN

1985 Aug "All the Best Places: Sag Harbor, Long Island's Historic Whaling Port." Jason Epstein, p. 32

HOUSE BEAUTIFUL

1985 Sep "Uptown and Downtown, New York's Shops and Galleries Provide Insight—and Access—to the Best in Decorative Arts." Sandra Hart, p. 45

1984 Aug "At Chautauqua a New Definition of Relaxation Was Coined: Don't Stop Doing—Do Something Else." Paula Rice Jackson, p. 36

NATIONAL GEOGRAPHIC TRAVELER

1985 Spring "Baseball Scrapbook: Cooperstown's Hall of Fame and Museum." Stephen S. Hall, p. 74

1985 Summer "Saratoga Chic." Queen of the Spas. Betty Ross, p. 34
1984 Winter "A Taste of the Orient." New York's Chinatown. Van Wall, p. 156

N.Y. TIMES SUNDAY TRAVEL SECTION (X)
1985 Jan 27 "A Passionate New York Skiier." Skiing the Catskills. John Bowers, p. 43
      Mar 24 "Travel Notes on New York," pp. 20, 21
      "Touring the City on Foot, in Depth." Hope Cooke, p. 20
      "Sampling the Atriums." Andrea Israel, p. 20
      "The Sidewalks of New York—Indoors." Paul Goldberger, p. 21
      "Sipping and Snacking." Bryan Miller, p. 21
      May 19 "The Finger Lakes: 25 Miles by Bike." Dorothy Pasternak, p. 19
      Jun 16 "Mountain Greenery." Exploring the wild Adirondacks. William Howarth, p. 19
      "The Catskills Cast Their Quiet Spell, Streams Full of Brown Trout Draw Fly Fishermen." J.I. Merritt, p. 20
      Jun 23 "Rebirth of Fort Stanwix." Restoratiaon of the Fort and an Erie Canal village. R.V. Denenberg, p. 24
      Jul 14 "What's Doing in Saratoga." Peter T. Leach, p. 10
      Aug 11 "What's Doing in the Finger Lakes." Dorothy Pasternak, p. 10
      Sep 15 "Finger Lakes Vintage Time." Wineries, p. 22
      Nov 3 "Exploring Soho on Foot." Walking and eating tour. Annasue M. Wilson, p. 14
      [Also in November 3rd issue is "The World of New York," a special supplement to the magazine section, entirely about New York City—ethnic groups and food, neighborhoods, etc.]
      Dec 15 "New York Dining By Design . . . the (NYC) Architect Shares Honors with the Chefs." Paul Goldberger, p. 20
      "Upstate Inns in the Grand Manner." Former mansions with vintage appointments have opened their doors to guests. Jane Perlez, p. 21
1984 May 13 "A Younger Chautauqua." A resort whose name suggests Victorian rusticity is appealing increasingly to youth. James Feron, p. 9
      Jun 3 "Roughing It In Style." The Point, former Rockefeller camp on Saranac Lake. Irene M.K. Rawlings, p. 12
      Jun 17 "Making Music with Machines." Play-it-yourself collection of mechanical music instruments in Deansboro. James Feron, p. 22
      Jun 24 "Niagara Falls: Still Awesome." Skip Rozin, p. 20
      Aug 5 "Rooms with a View." NYC hotels. Paul Goldberger, p. 18
      "Getting to the Plane on Time." Traveling to Kennedy, LaGuardia and Newark airports. Paul Grimes, p. 19
      Nov 18 "Sleeper Service to the Capital." AMTRAK to D.C. Betsy Wade, p. 28

TOWN & COUNTRY
1984 Sep "New York Newsletter." Where to eat, meet, have tea, shops, galleries, boites; everything to make going out great in Gotham. p. 173

TRAVEL & LEISURE
1985 Jan "The Dazzling New Museum of Modern Art." Carter Ratcliff, p. 74

1985 May "The Wonder of Niagara Falls." An appreciative look at America's favorite cascade. Elaine D. Goldstein, p. 49

Jun "The Adirondacks, New York's Civilized Wilderness." Richard Covington, p. 108

"The Fabulous Frick Collection." A jewel of a Manhattan art museum. Herbert B. Livesey, p. 88

Aug "Mad for Madison Avenue." New York's most glamorous mile. Erica Kleine, p. 61

"The Whitney—a Lively Landmark for American Art on Madison." Richard Covington, p. 70.

Nov Walking Tour: "Christmas in New York." Marion Gough, p. 215

1984 Jan "The South Street Seaport, New York's Newest Place to Be." An ongoing festival of eating, shopping and maritime history. Janice B. Brand, p. 67

Feb "America's Greatest Museum." The Met. Carter Ratcliff, p. 52

"Shopping and Eating at the Met." Deborah Colussy, p. 74

Apr "The Welcome Return of Manhattan's Museum of Modern Art." Avis Berman, p. 81

Jun "The New York Public Library." Much to see as well as read on Fifth Avenue. Charles Monaghan, p. 148

Jul "The Statue of Liberty and Ellis Island." Pamela Fiori, p. 4

"Saluting the Statue of Liberty, and Remembering Ellis Island." Kate Simon, p. 78

"A Splendid Restoration Begins." Fred Ferretti, p. 86

"Van Gogh's 'Starry Night' at the Museum of Modern Art." Laurence Shames, p. 110

Sep "Happy Birthday Lincoln Center." America's cultural capital turns 25. Fred Ferretti, p. 96

"Wining and Dining Around Lincoln Center," p. 102

Oct "The Four Seasons Restaurant at 25." George Lang, p. 70

"Latest from New York." Rockefeller Center to South Street Seaport, p. 83

TRAVEL/HOLIDAY

1985 Jan "A Bit of Bordeaux in New York State." Long Island vineyards. Robert L. Balzer, p. 70

Mar "Chautauqua." New York's summer place. Linda Kundell, p. 16

Jul "Ellis Island—Threshold to Liberty." Rick Moran, p. 34

"Manhattan's Menus—N.Y.'s Melting Pot of Fine Food." Robert L. Balzer, p. 58

Oct. "Saugerties, N.Y., Mum's the Word." Annual chrysanthemum festival. Raymond Steiner, p. 4

1984 Apr "Summertime and All That Jazz." Take five on two continents (annual jazz festivals in Copenhagen, Montreux, Monterey and New York). Steve Schneider, p. 68

Aug "Adventure in the Adirondacks." New York's outdoor experience. Jim Powell, p. 49

Dec "Christmas on the Avenue." Fifth. Scott Shane, p. 84

VOGUE

1984 Aug "Great Days at the Races." August in Saratoga. Nick Vanderbilt, p. 276

NORTH CAROLINA

Background Reading

Bledsoe, Jerry   CAROLINA CURIOSITIES
"Jerry Bledsoe's outlandish guide to the dadblamedest things to see and do in North Carolina." A combination of tour guide and "believe it or not" book of North Carolina oddities. (BL) East Woods, 1984. Also *Just Folks: Visitin's with Carolina People* (1980).

Cambios, Ruth and Winger, Virginia   NORTH CAROLINA ROUND THE MOUNTAINS GUIDE BOOK
Cambios-Winger, 1981.

Conway, Martin   THE OUTER BANKS: AN HISTORICAL ADVENTURE FROM KITTY HAWK TO OCRACOKE
Carabelle, 1984.

Durant, David N.   RALEIGH'S LOST COLONY
The story of the ill-fated Lost Colony told in a historical narrative that explores the mystery of what happened to the Roanoke settlement. Atheneum, 1981.

Joynes, Leger M. and others   THE INSIDER'S GUIDE TO THE OUTER BANKS OF NORTH CAROLINA
Storie McOwen, 1984.

Kupperman, Karen O.   ROANOKE: THE ABANDONED COLONY
"Cogent and vivacious account of the twice-failed settlement. . . . also interprets Roanoke's significance in both British imperial history and the development of the U.S." (BL) Rowman & Allanheld, 1984.

Lord, William G.   THE COMPLETE GUIDE TO THE BLUE RIDGE PARKWAY
Covers the Parkway from Rockfish Gap in Virginia to Oconaluftee River Bridge in North Carolina. Eastern Acorn Pr, 1981.

Parramore, Thomas C.   EXPRESS LANES AND COUNTRY ROADS
Life in North Carolina, 1920-70. U of North Carolina Pr, 1983.

Powell, William S.   NORTH CAROLINA
One of a series of popular histories for each state published as part of the Bicentennial observance in 1976. Norton, 1977.

Robert, Bruce and Nancy   THE GOODLIEST LAND: NORTH CAROLINA
Doubleday, 1973.

Schumann, Marguerite   TAR HEEL SIGHTS: GUIDE TO NORTH CAROLINA'S HERITAGE
More than 1,000 historical cultural sites statewide. East Woods, 1983. Also *Grand Old Ladies: Victorian Architecture in North Carolina* (1984).

Stick, David   ROANOKE ISLAND: THE BEGINNINGS OF ENGLISH AMERICA
U. of North Carolina Pr. 1983. Also *The Outer Banks of North Carolina* (1958).

Wolcott, Read   ROSE HILL
Tape recorded conversations of residents in a small North Carolina farming town that contradict many of our fantasies and fictions about small town life. Putnam Pub. Group, 1976.

Novels

Boyd, James   DRUMS
Scottish settlers in North Carolina. Scribner, 1928. A family chronicle beginning in 1771 and continuing to the Civil War in its sequel, *Marching On* (1927).

Dykeman, Wilma   THE TALL WOMAN
A mountain woman's life during the Civil War. HR&W, 1962.

Ehle, John   LAST ONE HOME
A family leaves the farm to try the insurance business in the growing little city of Asheville at the turn of the century—"strong place description [of city and country] . . . regional writing at its best." (FC) Har-Row, 1984.

Ehle, John   THE WINTER PEOPLE
Set during the depression, and part of a series of novels about two North Carolina mountain families over several generations. Har-Row, 1982. Preceding it are: *The Land Breakers* (1964), *The Journey of August King* (1971), and *The Road* (1967).

Fletcher, Inglis   RALEIGH'S EDEN
Fletcher's first historical novel (1940) set in Albemarle County. Other titles in the series include: *Men of Albemarle* (1942), *Lusty Wind for Carolina* (1944), *Toil of the Brave* (1946), *Roanoke Hundred* (1948), *The Scotswoman* (1954),and *The Wind in the Forest* (1957). Queens Hse, 1976-78.

Flynt, Candace   CHASING DAD
The effect of a son's suicide on his father. Dial, 1980.

Godwin, Gail   A MOTHER AND TWO DAUGHTERS
What happens to the three women when the mother's husband suddenly dies—"an expansive and imaginative celebration of American life." (FC) Viking, 1982.

Lockridge, Richard   DEATH IN A SUNNY PLACE
A young woman is invited by an aunt to visit her at Hilltop Club and becomes involved in a murder. Lippincott, 1980.

McCammon, Robert R.   USHER'S PASSING
"Spine-tingling, atmospheric" suspense story of the descendants of Poe's Usher family as they gather to see who will inherit the ill-gotten Usher fortune. One of the descendants is a horror novelist intent on discovering the family's secrets. (FC) HR&W, 1984.

McCorkle, Jill   JULY 7TH
Two thugs, a drunk, a teenaged waitress, an 80-year-old, a hitchhiker with literary ambitions, are just some of the varied characters who figure in the story of a brutal murder at the Quik Pik on July 7th—"comedy and poignancy, romance, suspense . . . surprise." (FC) Algonquin Bks, 1984.

Malone, Michael   UNCIVIL SEASONS
The wife of a state senator is murdered during a snowstorm that reveals family secrets as her nephew, a homicide detective, solves the crime—"suspense . . . a range of memorably realized characters. The North Carolina Piedmont town fleshed out to the last detail [with] a rich seasoning of humor." (FC) Delacorte Pr, 1983.

Marshall, Edison   THE LOST COLONY
Fictional version of the vanished Ralegh Colony. Doubleday, 1964.

Price, Reynolds   MUSTIAN
Omnibus edition of two novels about the Mustian family: *A Generous Man* (1966), about an adolescent's three-day quest after life and love, and *A Long and Happy Life* (1962), about the young man's sister. Atheneum, 1983 (first published in 1962).

Seeman, Ernest   AMERICAN GOLD
The rise and evolution of a North Carolina tobacco town. Dial, 1978.

Shivers, Louise   HERE TO GET MY BABY OUT OF JAIL
"Two men in love with one woman, and the consequences of such a triangle. . . . Sights, sounds, smells, textures" of the North Carolina tobacco country in 1937. (FC) Random, 1983.

Tyler, Anne   A SLIPPING-DOWN LIFE
Lives of quiet desperation and a "tragi-comic" marriage. (FC) Knopf, 1970. Also *The Tin Can Tree* (1965).

Wolfe, Thomas   LOOK HOMEWARD ANGEL
Autobiographical novel of a native son of Asheville (Altamont in the book). Scribner, 1957 (first published 1929). Also *The Web and the Rock* (1939). A Thomas Wolfe memorial has been established in Asheville.

TRAVEL ARTICLES

ARCHITECTURAL DIGEST
1985 Apr Historic Houses: "Carl Sandburg's Mountain Years." A million acres of sky. Paula Steichen, p. 226
1984 Sep Historic Houses: "Thomas Wolfe Remembered." Looking homeward to Asheville, N.C. David Gebhard, p. 194

ESQUIRE
1984 Feb "Getting the Hang of Hang Gliding." In Nag's Head. Randall Rothenberg, p. 32

GOURMET
1984 Apr "Southern Hospitality at the Fearrington House." Evan Jones, p. 58

MODERN MATURITY
1985 Aug-Sep "Road That Rides the Fog." A golden anniversary look at the Blue Ridge Parkway. Diane K. Gentry, p. 48

N.Y. TIMES SUNDAY TRAVEL SECTION (X)
1985 Jan 13 "A Walk Through Wilmington's Past." John B. Albright, p. 10
Jan 20 "Working on the Railroad." North Carolina Transportation Museum. J. Barlow Herget, p. 20
Apr 28 Correspondent's Choice: "A Highly Private Little Guesthouse." Greystone in Wilmington. William E. Schmidt, p. 12
Dec 15 Shopper's World: "Carolina Pottery, Shaped by Tradition." Michael Ruhlman, p. 12
1984 Jul 15 "What's Doing in Asheville." Cecily D. McMillan, p. 10
Aug 12 "Where Civilization Is an Echo." Ocracoke, on a barrier reef off North Carolina. Joan Gould, p. 15
Sep 30 "In the Land of the Cherokee." Indian reservation in western North Carolina. Andrew L. Yarrow, p. 22

SATURDAY EVENING POST
1984 May-Jun "North Carolina: Inside the Outer Banks." David Barudin, p. 90

TOWN & COUNTRY
1985 Jul "Highland Fling." Linville, N.C. Hugh Best, p. 124

TRAVEL/HOLIDAY
1984 May "Great Smoky Mountains National Park." Yvette Cardozo. p. 68

NORTH DAKOTA

Background Reading

Berg, Francie M.   NORTH DAKOTA: LAND OF CHANGING SEASONS
Flying Diamond, 1977.

Schneider, Bill   THE DAKOTA IMAGE: A PHOTOGRAPHIC
CELEBRATION
Falcon Pr, 1980.

Wilkins, Robert P. and Wynona, H.   NORTH DAKOTA
One of a series of popular histories for each state published as part of the
Bicentennial observance in 1976. Norton, 1977.

Novels

Bojer, Johan   THE EMIGRANTS
Story of a group of land-hungry, impoverished Norwegian immigrants who
settled in the Red River Valley area of North Dakota, and their battle against the
elements. Greenwood, 1974 (first published in Norway in 1924).

Jones, Douglas C.   ARREST SITTING BULL
The story of what happened when the order 'arrest Sitting Bull' went out—"the
torment of a minority of decent white men and women who really cared about the
Indians and of the Indians, trapped between a fight to the death and a willingness
to try to assimilate." (FC) Scribner, 1977.

Lane, Rose Wilder   YOUNG PIONEERS
A graphic picture of early pioneer days in Dakota of a young couple. McGraw,
1976 (first published 1933).

Rolvaag, O.E.   PEDER VICTORIOUS
Realistic portrayal of pioneer life on the plains—"penetrating study of pioneer
psychology." (FC) Har-Row, 1929.

Ross, Dana F.   DAKOTA!
Part of a series of novels with the overall title of *Wagons West* that chronicles
the conquest and settlement of the American West. Bantam, 1983.

Sinclair, Harold   THE CAVALRYMAN
Beginning of the Sioux Indian Wars. Har-Row, 1958.

Unger, Douglas   LEAVING THE LAND
"Set in the west Dakotas dramatizes the destruction of the American family farm

. . . a whole way of life"—compared to Willa Cather's *O Pioneers!* (Publisher) Har-Row, 1984.

Woiwode, Larry   BEYOND THE BEDROOM WALL
Family chronicle beginning in the 1930s (in Illinois), to present-day North Dakota—the "real theme [is] about the love between parents and children." (FC) FS&G, 1975.

TRAVEL ARTICLES

TRAVEL/HOLIDAY
1985 Jul "High Plains Driftin'—Footloose in North Dakota." Gary Ferguson, p. 54

OHIO

Background Reading

Bailey, Anthony   AMERICA, LOST AND FOUND
The author recalls a near perfect four years when, as a child of seven, he was evacuated from England during World War II, and came to live with a remarkable family in Ohio. Random, 1981.

Baskin, John   NEW BURLINGTON: THE LIFE AND DEATH OF AN AMERICAN VILLAGE
A "prose elegy" about rural life in America, and a town in southwestern Ohio destroyed by the U.S. Corps of Engineers. (BRD) Norton, 1976.

Carr, Carolyn K.   OHIO: A PHOTOGRAPHIC PORTRAIT
Unusual photographic essay of the depression in Ohio, 1935-41—the photographs were taken by the Farm Security Administration. Kent State U, 1980.

Davis, Peter   HOMETOWN
The author selected Hamilton, Ohio, with the assistance of the Bureau of Census, as a typical town of 50,000 to 100,000 population. His chapters focus on various events—a basketball game, a wedding, a policeman's routine day, a day in court, a fundamentalist church, and so on. Several of the chapters were produced as a PBS TV series. S&S, 1982.

Gerrick, David J.   BACK ROADS OF OHIO
A travel guide to back roads and wilderness areas in Ohio. Dayton Labs, 1974.

Havighurst, Walter   OHIO
One of a series of popular histories for each state published as part of the Bicentennial observance in 1976. Norton, 1976.

Hunter, David   SHIFRA STEIN'S DAY TRIPS FROM CINCINNATI: GETAWAYS LESS THAN TWO HOURS AWAY
More than 200 interesting and unique places within approximately 100 miles of Cincinnati including places in the neighboring states of Indiana and Kentucky. East Woods, 1984.

Osler, Jack M.   FIFTY FAVORITE MINI TRIPS FOR OHIO
Media Ventures, 1983.

Williams, Philip G.   FREE CLEVELAND: A GUIDE TO LEISURE FUN IN THE CLEVELAND AREA
P Gaines, 1982.

Zimmerman, George   OHIO: OFF THE BEATEN PATH
"Nostalgia, tranquility and charm are predominant characteristics of the sites—an antidote to fast-paced city life." (Publisher) East Woods, 1983.

Novels

Anderson, Sherwood   WINESBURG, OHIO
The classic autobiographical novel of small-town life (Clyde is Winesburg)—"trials of adolescence [and] barren narrowness of small town life." Viking, 1960 (first published 1919). Also *Tar: A Midwest Childhood* (1926).

Anderson, Sherwood   POOR WHITE
Industrialism replaces the agrarian, craft-centered society of a nineteenth-century Midwestern town. Huebsch, 1980 (first published 1920).

Dew, Robb F.   DALE LOVES SOPHIE TO DEATH
A wife's summer spent in Ohio with her three children while her husband remains back east. FS&G, 1981.

Eckert, Allan W.   JOHNNY LOGAN, SHAWNEE SPY
A novel based on fact of a captured Shawnee Indian youth who spies for the Americans—"the only Indian in Ohio history to be buried with military honors." (FC) Little, 1983.

Gold, Herbert   FAMILY
A "first-generation Jewish mother trying to impose her Old World standards" on her son. Arbor Hse, 1981. Also *Fathers* (1967), early novel in this Russian-Jewish immigrant saga..

Green, Hannah   THE DEAD OF THE HOUSE
Coming of age in Ohio the 1940s and '50s. Doubleday, 1972.

Hintze, Naomi A.   YOU'LL LIKE MY MOTHER
A gothic novel with a sinister mother-in-law as the villain. Putnam Pub Group, 1969.

McInerny, Ralph   GATE OF HEAVEN
About the current state of the Catholic church. Har-Row, 1975. Also *Rogerson at Bay* (1976), about the identity crisis of a middle-aged academic.

Morrison, Toni   SULA
The friendship of two young black women in Medallion, Ohio. Knopf, 1974. Also *The Bluest Eye* (1970), depicting the life of a poor black girl.

O'Connor, Philip F.   STEALING HOME
Funny, sad story of a father managing his son's Pee Wee League baseball team, which leads to far more complicated effects on the family than intended. Knopf, 1979.

Richter, Conrad   THE AWAKENING LAND
Comprised of three separate novels: *The Trees* (1940), *The Fields* (1946), and *The Town* (1950). "Fictional Americana"—depicting the settlement of Ohio, beginning with primitive pioneering in the American wilderness north of the Ohio River, and on through making a farm out of the cleared land and the establishment of the town. (FC) Knopf, 1966.

Robertson, Don   THE GREATEST THING SINCE SLICED BREAD
The life of Morris Bird III beginning at age nine and continuing to age seventeen when Morris is playing basketball on a Cleveland high school team. Set in the 1940s. "Very funny character whose life has tragi-comic overtones." Putnam Pub Group, 1965. Succeeding novels in the series are: *The Sum and Total of Now* (1966) and *The Greatest Thing That Almost Happened* (1970).

Santmyer, Helen Hoover   ". . . AND LADIES OF THE CLUB"
A small Ohio town from the perspective of a women's literary club, the lives of its members and their descendants. Putnam Pub Group, 1984.

Stewart, Fred Mustard   THE MANNINGS
Chronicle set in Elkins, of a man's business success at the expense of all else. Arbor Hse, 1973.

Vreuls, Diane   ARE WE THERE YET?
Funny, poignant episodes and adventures as a mother and daughter move from an Ohio city to a farm in the southern part of the state. S&S, 1975.

West, Jessamyn   LEAFY RIVERS
What life was like in the early days of the nineteenth century in the Ohio Territory and the effect of homesteading on a young woman. HarBraceJ, 1967.

TRAVEL ARTICLES

CONNOISSEUR
1984 Jun "Cincinnati's Netherland Plaza Hotel, an Art Deco Masterpiece Is Now Restored." Jayne Merkel, p. 67

GOURMET
1985 Aug "Cleveland's Farmers' Markets." Evan Jones, p. 66

HOUSE BEAUTIFUL
1985 Feb "Granville, Ohio." Its architecture is "a microcosm of this country's history." Jim Powell, p. 37

N.Y. TIMES SUNDAY TRAVEL SECTION (X)
1984 Dec 16 "A Bit of Yankee Flavor in Ohio." Cuyahoga Valley. Abe Zadan, p. 22

TRAVEL/HOLIDAY
1985 Aug "Cleveland Better Than Ever." Denise D. Meehan, p. 8
1984 Jan "Ohio's Football Shrine." The Pro Football and College Football Halls of Fame. Hal Butler, p. 84

WORKING WOMAN
1984 Oct "A Businesswoman's Guide to Cincinnati." Ira S. Jones. p. 158

OKLAHOMA

Background Reading

Debo, Augie   PRAIRIE CITY
Reprint of a book about the American frontier in the Oklahoma Territory—"splendid social history, the quintessential American story of people and community" through the eyes of the author who came to the Territory in the 1890s as a child, and on up to World War II. (PW) Council Oak, 1985.

Fischer, John   FROM THE HIGH PLAINS
"Part history, part memoir, part elegy" about the panhandle section of Oklahoma and Texas. (FC) Har-Row, 1978.

Hunt, David C.   GUIDE TO OKLAHOMA MUSEUMS
U of Oklahoma Pr, 1981.

Keegan, Marcia   OKLAHOMA
Photographic essay with an introduction by Will Rogers, Jr. Abbeville Pr, 1979.

Morgan, Anne H. and Strickland, Rennard   OKLAHOMA MEMORIES
A collection of reminiscences of diverse people in their own words. U of Oklahoma Pr, 1981.

Morgan, H. Wayne   OKLAHOMA
One of a series of popular histories for each state published as part of the Bicentennial observance in 1976. American Assn for State and Local History, 1984 (first published 1977).

Morris, John   GHOST TOWNS OF OKLAHOMA
U of Oklahoma Pr, 1978.

Ruth, Kent   OKLAHOMA TRAVEL HANDBOOK
U of Oklahoma Pr, 1979.

Wilson, Steve TREASURES AND TREASURE TALES
U of Oklahoma Pr, 1976.

Novels

Braun, Matthew   THE KINCAIDS
A western, and a family saga, spanning several generations in which the first Kincaid "parlays a saloon won in a poker game into a business empire." (FC) Putnam Pub Group, 1976.

Capps, Benjamin   THE WHITE MAN'S ROAD
A Comanche son of a white father and an Indian mother, and his quest for manhood in a society where Indian lands have been taken over. Set in the 1890s. Har-Row, 1969.

Ferber, Edna   CIMARRON
Life in the land rush days of the 1880s as seen through the eyes of Sabra, the wife of a pioneering newspaper editor. It continues through the years of the oil boom, her husband's disappearance and her eventual election to Congress. Doubleday, 1930.

Giles, Janice H.   JOHNNY OSAGE
A young man whose friendship with the Indians earns him the nickname of Johnny Osage finds an adversary in a white woman teacher who is dedicated to educating the Indian children in white ways. Houghton, 1960.

Hunt, John   THE GREY HORSE LEGACY
"Absorbing, unpredictable" thriller set in Grey Horse in the 1920s and then in the 1950s. (FC) Knopf, 1968.

Morgan, Speer   BELLE STARR
Novelization of the notorious woman outlaw's life and death. Little, 1979.

TRAVEL ARTICLES

AMERICANA
1984 Oct "Guthrie's Revenge." Restoration of the only intact territorial capital in the U.S. Sandra Dallas, p. 76

HORIZON
1984 Sep "Oklahoma: Crossroads of the Arts." Eric Minton, p. 53

TRAVEL/HOLIDAY
1985 Mar "Tulsa, O.K." Of oil, art and Indians. Carolyn S. Thornton, p. 8

OREGON

Background Reading

Bell, Mimi   OFFBEAT OREGON
Chronicle Bk, 1983.

Bleything, Dennis and Hawkins, Susan   GETTING OFF ON NINETY-SIX
Getting off the main highways for less-traveled roads. Touchstone Pr, 1975.

Blood, Marje   EXPLORING THE OREGON COAST BY CAR
Writing Works, 1980.

Dodds, Gordon B.   OREGON
One of a series of popular histories for each state published as part of the Bicentennial observance in 1976. Norton, 1977.

Holden, Glenda and Ronald   TOURING THE WINE COUNTRY OF OREGON
Holden, 1984.

Lampman, Linda   OREGON FOR ALL SEASONS
A month by month guide to activities, happenings and events. Writing Works, 1979.

Mainwaring, William L.   EXPLORING THE OREGON COAST
Westridge, 1981.

Perry, John and Greverus, James   THE SIERRA CLUB GUIDE TO THE NATURAL AREAS OF OREGON AND WASHINGTON
Sierra Club, 1983.

Smith, Kathy   A RAINY DAY GUIDE TO PORTLAND
The "Rose City"—history, tourist activities, performing arts, etc. Chronicle Bk, 1983.

Sunset eds.   OREGON
Sunset-Lane, 1981.

Thollander, Earl   BACK ROADS OF OREGON
Maps, illustrations, combined with evocative prose, for those who like to wander the rural back roads. Crown, 1979.

Thompson, Philip   STRANGER IN TOWN
A guide to taverns in Oregon and southwest Washington. Breitenbush Pbns, 1983.

Novels

Berry, Don   TRASK
The book is based on the life of an actual person—Eldridge Trask—who pioneered in the Oregon Territory in the 1840s. "One of the few [books] that attempt to deal with the quality, character, and motives of the Indian." Viking, 1960.

Brautigan, Richard   THE HAWKLINE MONSTER
A hilarious spoof of both classic horror tales and the traditional western. The setting is Oregon in 1902 as men meet a rather strange pair of sisters. S&S, 1974.

Chowder, Ken   DELICATE GEOMETRY
"A menage-a-trois in Portland . . . three books, each one written by one of the characters about another." (FC) Har-Row, 1982.

Davis, H.L.   HONEY IN THE HORN
A novel about homesteading in the early 1900s that won a Pulitzer Prize in 1936. Larlin, 1975 (first published 1935).

Duncan, David J.   THE RIVER WHY
"Relates the reclusive backwoods exploits" of a man in pursuit of his true love—fly fishing." (FC) Sierra Club, 1983.

Kesey, Ken   SOMETIMES A GREAT NOTION
"Oedipal-like enmity" of a weak and a strong brother in logging country setting. (FC) Viking, 1964.

Lesley, Craig   WINTERKILL
A modern-day Nez Perce Indian rodeo performer drives from Oregon to Nebraska to find the son he's not seen for years and to teach him Indian tribal ways. Houghton, 1984.

Ross, Dana F.   OREGON!
Part of a series of novels with the overall title of *Wagons West* that chronicles the conquest and settlement of the American West. Bantam, 1980.

TRAVEL ARTICLES

BON APPETIT
1984 Mar "Traveling with Taste: The Oregon Coast." Jerome Richard, p. 28

N.Y. SUNDAY TIMES TRAVEL SECTION (X)
1984 May 27 "What's Doing in Portland." Scotta Callister, p. 10

SUNSET
1985 Jun "An Important 50th Birthday in Ashland." Oregon Shakespearian Festival. p. 40
Jul "On the Mend near Grants Pass." p. 50
1984 Feb "Viewing Oregon's Crater Lake on Skis and Snowshoes." p. 66
"Kyoto in Portland . . ." Five and one-half acre Japanese garden. p. 42
Apr "Skiing Above Treeline Late into the Season at Mt. Bachelor." p. 65
"A Good Look at the Oregon Dunes Just off U.S. 101." p. 76
Aug "Assaulting Mount Hood." You don't need to be an experienced climber. Joel W. Rogers, p. 54

TRAVEL/HOLIDAY
1984 Aug "Cape Arago, A Place Worth Remembering." Robert Harrington, p. 14

PENNSYLVANIA

Series Guidebooks

Fodor: Philadelphia
Frommer: Philadelphia - City Guide

Background Reading

Busch, Noel F.   WINTER QUARTERS
George Washington and the Continental Army at Valley Forge. NAL, 1975.

Cochran, Thomas C.   PENNSYLVANIA
One of a series of popular histories for each state published as part of the Bicentennial observance in 1976. Norton, 1978.

Curson, Julie P.   A GUIDE'S GUIDE TO PHILADELPHIA
A guide to the history, culture, transportation, museums, sightseeing and sports of the city—for "the young and the young in heart." (Post) Curson Hse, 1982.

**Fairmont Park Art Assn.   SCULPTURE OF A CITY: PHILADELPHIA'
TREASURES IN BRONZE AND STONE**
A guide to public sculpture in Philadelphia covering some 200 years of history. Walker, 1974.

Frassanito, William A.   GETTYSBURG: A JOURNEY IN TIME
A pictorial book reflecting Gettysburg right after the battle, with a good text. Scribner, 1976.

Gallery, John A.   PHILADELPHIA ARCHITECTURE
MIT, 1984.

Good, Merle   WHO ARE THE AMISH?
Many of the general questions raised by outsiders about activities of the Amish are answered. Good Bks, 1985.

**Keehn, Sally M. & David C.   HEXCURSIONS: DAYTRIPPING IN AND
AROUND PENNSYLVANIA'S DUTCH
COUNTRY**
Hastings, 1982.

**Lukacs, John   PHILADELPHIA: PATRICIANS AND PHILISTINES, 1900-
1950**
The unique spirit of Philadelphia life, 1900-1950, with biographical sketches of seven people who flourished. FS&G, 1980.

Marion, John F.   WALKING TOURS OF HISTORIC PHILADELPHIA
Inst for Study of Human Issues, 1984.

Milgrim, Shirley   PATHWAYS TO INDEPENDENCE
The buildings in Philadelphia's National Historic Park. Chatham Pr, 1975.

Miller, Dorothy A.   POOR MAN'S GUIDE TO PITTSBURGH
New Pittsburgh, 1981.

Osler, Jack   FIFTY GREAT MINI TRIPS FOR PENNSYLVANIA
Media Ventures, 1978.

Romberg, Gary and Chris   MARMAC GUIDE TO PHILADELPHIA
Marmac, 1984.

Swetnam, George and Smith, Helene   A GUIDEBOOK TO HISTORIC
WESTERN PENNSYLVANIA
An insightful, well-organized guide to a historically rich area of the country. U of Pittsburgh, 1976.

Novels

Allen, Hervey   THE CITY IN THE DAWN
An abridgement of the Colonial saga of a backwoodsman's progress from the forest primeval (as a Shawnee captive) to the civilization of a provincial Philadelphia. Rinehart,1950. Titles in the original series are: *The Forest and the Fort* (1943), *Bedford Village* (1944), and *Toward the Morning* (1948).

Bradley, David   SOUTH STREET
"A long bitter look at Black Philadelphia." (BRD) Grossman, 1975.

Bradley, David   THE CHANEYSVILLE INCIDENT
Reconstruction, by a black university professor, of an incident during slave days in a town on the Pennsylvania/Maryland border, and the professor's reunion with his origins. Har-Row, 1981.

Brown, Rita   SIX OF ONE
Rivalries and a variety of women's lives in a town split by the Pennsylvania/Maryland border as well as the Mason-Dixon line. Har-Row, 1978.

Caldwell, Taylor   ANSWER AS A MAN
Saga of an Irish immigrant's rise to wealth and power. Putnam Pub Group, 1981. Another family saga set in Pennsylvania is *Dynasty of Death* (1938), about the armaments industry and three generations of a family involved in it. Also with a Pennsylvania setting are *Testimony of Two Men* (1968) and *Ceremony of the Innocent* (1976).

Constantine, K.C.   ALWAYS A BODY TO TRADE
A western Pennsylvania town, Rocksburg, with Mario Balzic as police chief and main protagonist—"sense of character and place is superb." (FC) Godine, 1983. Another Balzic mystery is *The Man Who Liked Slow Tomatoes 1982).*

Coover, Robert   THE ORIGIN OF BRUNISTS
Story of a religious cult in a Western Pennsylvania mining town. Viking, 1978 (first published 1966).

Davenport, Marcia   THE VALLEY OF DECISION
Saga of an Irish family in Pittsburgh, from 1873 to World War II. Bentley, 1979 (first published 1942).

Dexter, Pete   GOD'S POCKET
"A tough, funny articulate book about violent, sad, tragically inarticulate people" in a Philadelphia blue-collar neighborhood. The plot centers around a man who is killed for taunting a fellow worker. (FC) Random, 1983.

Dreiser, Theodore   THE BULWARK
"The shattering effects of twentieth-century materialism on the life of . . . a devout Pennsylvania Quaker." (FC) Doubleday, 1980 (first published 1946).

Fast, Howard   CITIZEN TOM PAINE
Fictionalized biography of the Revolutionary figure. Duell, 1943.

Gardner, John   MICKELSSON'S GHOSTS
A professor of philosophy "retreats from the world into an old Pennsylvania farmhouse" despite a rumor that it is haunted. "Contrasts Mickelson's two milieus—rigid academia and Susquehanna County." (FC) Knopf, 1982.

Hartog, Jan de   THE PEACEABLE KINGDOM
Recreation of Quaker life in Pennsylvania beginning in England in the seventeenth century, from which they were forced to flee to America. Atheneum, 1972.

Jakes, John   NORTH AND SOUTH
First in a projected series of three books that will chronicle the parallel lives of the Main and Hazard families from South Carolina and Pennsylvania, respectively, beginning in 1842, who are tied through their sons' attendance at West Point. Their lives also parallel America's struggles. "The characters, both fictional and real, make this era seem almost current." (FC) HarBraceJ, 1982. The second book, *In Love and War* (1984).

Kantor, MacKinlay   VALLEY FORGE
A recreation of the battle. Coward, 1934. Also *Long Remember* (1934), which depicts daily life on a day in July 1863.

King, Stephen   CHRISTINE
For horror fans—a car named Christine with "mysterious regenerative powers" is bought by a teenager who becomes both "obsessed by the car and possessed by its previous owner." (FC) Viking, 1983.

McCarthy, Mary   THE GROVES OF ACADEME
"Intelligent and sophisticated dissection of faculty life at a small, progressive college." (FC) HarBraceJ, 1952.

McHale, Tom   PRINCIPATO
Two families in Philadelphia, one Italian-American, whose son marries into an

"arch-conservative, hypocritical type of Irish-Catholic" family—aspects of Catholicism "are satirized mercilessly." (FC) Viking, 1970.

Marshall, Catherine   JULIE
Julie's father, a minister, gives up his post as an Alabama minister to purchase a smalltown newspaper—"a family's triumph . . . during a critical time in America's history." (FC) McGraw, 1984.

Mayerson, Evelyn W.   IF BIRDS ARE FREE
The picaresque life of a "feisty independent bag lady" on the streets of Philadelphia. (BRD) Lippincott, 1980.

Michaels, Barbara   SOMEONE IN THE HOUSE
"Supernatural occurrences" in Grayhaven Manor, moved from England to Pennsylvania, "provide ample chills." (FC) Dodd, 1981. Also *House of Many Shadows* (1974), a mystery with psychic phenomena as part of the plot, set in a Bucks County mansion.

Oates, Joyce Carol   SOLSTICE
The "parasitical relationship" of a recently divorced woman working as a teacher in a boys' school, and a locally famous woman artist. (FC) Dutton, 1985.

O'Hara, John   TEN NORTH FREDERICK
Character study of Joe Chapin, "first citizen of Gibbsville," and the woman he marries. Random, 1955. Also about people in the author's fictional hometown of Gibbsville, Pennsylvania (Pottsville), are: *The Cape Cod Lighter* (1962), *And Other Stories* (1968) and *Sermons and Soda Water* (1960).
Other novels by O'Hara with a Pennsylvania setting include: *A Rage to Live* (1949), *From the Terrace* (1958), *Ourselves to Know* (1960), *Elizabeth Appleton* (1963) and *The Lockwood Concern* (1965).

Richter, Conrad   A COUNTRY OF STRANGERS
Daughter of Pennsylvania pioneers is kidnapped by Indians, later returned to her family, but in the end chooses the Indian way of life. Knopf, 1966.

Richter, Conrad   THE WATERS OF KRONOS
A man returns to scenes of his boyhood in a Pennsylvania-Dutch mining town. Knopf, 1960. *A Simple Honorable Man* (1962) is a companion story, about the man's father's life as a Lutheran preacher in the early twentieth century.

Shreve, Susan R.   MIRACLE PLAY
An "engaging Quaker family saga" set in Bucks County. (FC) Morrow, 1981.

Updike, John   RABBIT, RUN
"Grotesque allegory of American life with its myth of happiness and success." Knopf, 1960. Also *Rabbit Redux* (1971) (10 years later) and *Rabbit is Rich* (1981).

Updike, John   OF THE FARM
A visit to his mother's farm reveals the complicated interrelationships of four characters. Knopf, 1965.

Whitney, Phyllis A.   SNOWFIRE
A skiing resort in the Poconos is setting for a mystery-romance. Doubleday, 1973.

Wideman, John E.   SENT FOR YOU YESTERDAY
A young black writer returns to Pittsburgh to assume the roles of son and father. The setting, "Homewood," is an imaginary place, a black ghetto, based on an actual district in Pittsburgh. Schocken, 1984. Also *Hiding Place* (1981) and *Damballah* (1981), a collection of short stories.

TRAVEL ARTICLES

ANTIQUES
1984 Mar "Bartram's Garden in Philadelphia." America's oldest botanical garden. D. Roger Mower, Jr., p. 630

BON APPETIT
1985 Nov "A Taste of Philadelphia." Hotels and restaurants. Zack Hanle and E.C.K. Read, p. 162

GOURMET
1985 May "A Philadelphia Story." Fred Ferretti, p. 38

MODERN MATURITY
1984 Aug-Sep "Treasures on the Brandywine." Brandywine River Museum. Jane Tulik Jones, p. 70

NATIONAL GEOGRAPHIC
1984 Apr "The Plain People of Pennsylvania." Douglas Lee, p. 492

NATIONAL GEOGRAPHIC TRAVELER
1984 Summer "Life in the Slow Lane." A visit to Pennsylvania's Amish country. Shirley Elder, p. 88
Winter "Mummers on Parade." Philadelphia's New Year's Day extravaganza. Clark De Leon, p. 130

N.Y. TIMES SUNDAY TRAVEL SECTION (X)
1985 Jun 16 "Mountain Greenery." The Poconos beyond the billboards. Robert M. Peck, p. 22
Jun 30 "Critics' Choices, Personal Favorites When They're Not Dining at Taillevant." Includes Pennsylvania. Various authors, p. 14
Aug 4 "Steamtown in the Poconos." Karl Zimmermann, p. 20
Sep 8 Fare of the Country: "Where Scrapple Meets Mesquite." Amanda M. Stinchecum, p. 6
Sep 15 "A Historic Inn in Pennsylvania." Cameron Estate Inn. Joan Mellen, p. 18
"Antique Hunting in Bucks County." Lita Solis-Cohen, p. 23
1984 Apr 29 "Pennsylvania's Horse Country." Jan Benzel, p. 20

TRAVEL & LEISURE
1985 Sep "Latest from Philadelphia." A restaurant boom, luxurious new hotels and a disco or two. Nao Hauser, p. 77

TRAVEL/HOLIDAY
1985 May "Most Livable Pittsburgh." They're number one! Jim Powell, p. 52
      "A Sensory Experience in Pittsburgh." Restaurants. Robert L. Balzer, p. 56
      Aug "Rabbit's Realm—Finding Inspiration in Pennsylvania." John Updike country south of Reading. William Ecenbarger, p. 20
1984 Dec "Vintage Brandywine." Recapturing Christmas past. Claire Walter, p. 4

RHODE ISLAND

Background Reading

Dow, Richard A. and Mowbray, E. Andrew   NEWPORT
Mowbray, 1976.

Formwalt, Elizabeth and John   A VISITOR'S GUIDE TO AQUIDNECK ISLAND
This is the island on which Newport is located. Aquidneck Pr, 1976.

Hitchcock, Henry-Russell   RHODE ISLAND ARCHITECTURE
Da Capo Pr, 1968.

Lippincott, Bertram   INDIANS, PRIVATEERS AND HIGH SOCIETY
"A collection of historical sketches about Rhode Island from earliest days through to the 1960s Jazz Festival riots." Lippincott, 1961.

McLoughlin, William J.   RHODE ISLAND
One of a series of popular histories for each state published as part of the Bicentennial observance in 1976. Norton, 1978.

O'Connor, R.   THE GOLDEN SUMMERS
"An antic history of Newport during its years of glory." Putnam Pub Group, 1974.

Randall, Anne   NEWPORT: A TOUR GUIDE
Peregrine Pr, 1983.

Whitman, Herbert   EXPLORING OLD BLOCK ISLAND
Chatham, 1980.

Williamson, Chilton   SALTBOUND: A BLOCK ISLAND WINTER
Fall through spring on the island—town meetings, a blizzard, church services, the impact of summer people, and local history. Methuen, 1980.

Novels

Auchincloss, Louis   THE HOUSE OF FIVE TALENTS
"The effects of great wealth upon . . . numerous members of the family and those who marry into it"—with a Newport setting. (FC) Houghton, 1960.

Barker, Shirley   STRANGE WIVES
The fight for religious freedom in Newport during the American Revolution. Crown, 1963.

Herzog, Arthur   EARTHSOUND
Complicated, suspenseful novel combining geology and events in a Rhode Island town. S&S, 1975.

LaFarge, Christopher   THE SUDDEN GUEST
A 1944 hurricane prompts memories of the earlier hurricane in 1938. Coward, 1946.

Paul, Raymond   THE TRAGEDY AT TIVERTON: AN HISTORICAL NOVEL OF MURDER
When a 29-year-old unmarried, pregnant woman is found hanged, suicide is presumed, but evidence in her belongings results in the first trial for murder in America in which the accused is a minister. Based on historical fact—"a riveting tale . . . all the more tragic and lurid in its puritanical New England setting. . . . sure to please readers of both historical fiction and mysteries." (FC) Viking, 1984.

Plante, David   THE FAMILY
First of a trilogy about a French-Canadian family in Providence, beginning in the 1950s—"takes on the dimensions of O'Neill's *Long Day's Journey into Night*," in its exploration of relationships between parents and sons. Atheneum, 1978. Following are *The Country* (1981) and *The Woods* (1982).

Ravin, Neil   INFORMED CONSENT
A medical novel set in Newport, in which a young researcher in endocrinology makes a remarkable diagnosis of adrenal cancer—"good local color of the College Hill section of Providence [and] real insight into medicine and medical ethics." (FC) Putnam Pub Group, 1983.

Sapir, Richard B.   SPIES
The co-owner of a hardware store has a World War II past of being leader of a German spy ring; his pleasant life since then is endangered when the FBI reopens investigation of the ring. Doubleday, 1984.

Updike, John   WITCHES OF EASTWICK
Three women with failed marriages are the witches, empowered by their new independence and "the very air of Eastwick." (FC) Knopf, 1984.

Whitney, Phyllis A.   SPINDRIFT
Murder mystery and romance on a Newport estate. Doubleday, 1975.

Wilder, Thornton   THEOPHILUS NORTH
A schoolteacher defines nine social classes in Newport—nine "separate cities" within the city—and the novel tells of his encounters with each. The period is the 1920s. (FC) Har-Row, 1973.

TRAVEL ARTICLES

ARCHITECTURAL DIGEST
1985 Oct "Mr. & Mrs. William K. Vanderbilt's House in Newport." John A. Cherol, p. 130

BON APPETIT
1984 Jun "Traveling with Taste: Providence and Newport." Patricia Brooks, p. 26

N.Y. TIMES SUNDAY TRAVEL SECTION (X)
1985 Jul 21 "Time Warp off Rhode Island's Coast." With its gingerbread hotels and chugging ferries, Block Island retains its quiet Victorian aura. Ralph Blumenthal, p. 8
Sep 1 "What's Doing in Newport." Cory Dean, p. 10
1984 Apr 15 "Rhode Island's May Breakfasts Keep Sizzling." Hearty eye-opening; then sightseeing. Betsy Wade, p. 21

TRAVEL & LEISURE
1984 Jun "Newport—the Good Life Goes On: Marble Halls, Breezy Beaches, Old Money, and New Faces." William Wright, p. 116

TRAVEL/HOLIDAY
1984 Apr "Architectural Bliss." Festival of historic homes in Providence. Denise D. Meehan, p. 37
Aug This New England: "Warren, Rhode Island." Bob Wyss, p. 54

YANKEE
1985 Jul This New England: "Charlestown, R.I." James Dodson, p. 54
Nov "Big Bargains in Old Mills." Factory outlets in Blackstone Valley. Larry Willard, Sr., p. 38

SOUTH CAROLINA

Background Reading

Bethel, Elizabeth R.   PROMISELAND, SOUTH CAROLINA
A century of life in a Negro community. Temple U, 1981.

Fields, Mamie G. and Karen   LEMON SWAMP AND OTHER PLACES: A CAROLINA MEMOIR
Memoir of a black grandmother (born in 1888) written for her granddaughters—"her youth, teaching school on John's Island, of parties and courtship . . . of the easy relation between the races before Jim Crow rules . . . a simple life but an engrossing one." (BL) Free Pr, 1983.

Johnson, Elmer D. and Sloan, Kathleen L.   SOUTH CAROLINA: A DOCUMENTARY PROFILE OF THE PALMETTO STATE
The South Carolina story in the words of the people who lived it. U of South Carolina, 1971.

Ravenal, St. Julien   CHARLESTON: THE PLACE AND THE PEOPLE
Southern History, 1981.

Rhyne, Nancy   THE GRAND STRAND: AN UNCOMMON GUIDE TO MYRTLE BEACH AND ITS SURROUNDINGS
"A lively and informative tour of an area steeped in history and tradition. . . . there is much more to do in Myrtle Beach, SC, than lie in the sun." (Publisher) East Woods, 1985.

Roberts, Nancy and Bruce   SOUTH CAROLINA GHOSTS: FROM THE MOUNTAINS TO THE COAST
U of South Carolina, 1983.

Rosen, Robert N.   A SHORT HISTORY OF CHARLESTON
"Sprightly and entertaining . . . has captured the flavor and flair of Charleston as few writers have been able to do." (Publisher) Lexikos, 1982.

Verner, Elizabeth O.   MELLOWED BY TIME, A CHARLESTON NOTEBOOK
Tradd Street Pr, 1978.

Wright, Louis B.   BAREFOOT IN ARCADIA
Recollections of boyhood in the Piedmont area of South Carolina—memories of a more innocent era in the early decades of this century. U of South Carolina, 1981 (first published 1974).

Wright, Louis B.   SOUTH CAROLINA
One of a series of popular histories for each state published as part of the Bicentennial observance in 1976. Norton, 1977.

Novels

Basso, Hamilton   THE LIGHT INFANTRY BALL
A Carolina planter's experiences during the Civil War is the plot for this romantic historical novel. Doubleday, 1959.

Boyd, Blanch M.   MOURNING THE DEATH OF MAGIC
Three family members assemble in South Carolina after a long period of going their separate ways into radical politics, drugs, nervous breakdowns and other vicissitudes. Macmillan, 1977.

Bristow, Gwen   CELIA GARTH
Historical novel of South Carolina during the Revolutionary War—spies, the siege of Charleston, etc. Crowell, 1959.

Buechner, Frederick   TREASURE HUNT
A couple drives to South Carolina to find out about the family homestead they have inherited and a stipulation concerning the Church of Holy Love. Atheneum, 1977.

Childress, Alice   A SHORT WALK
A mulatto girl makes the physical and psychological journey from South Carolina to Harlem. Coward, 1979.

Conroy, Pat   THE LORDS OF DISCIPLINE
A Carolina military school in the 1960s. Houghton, 1980.

Heyward, Du Bose   MAMBA'S DAUGHTERS
A black woman ingratiates herself with a white Charleston family as protection for her own family should they need it. Larlin, 1974 (first published 1929).

Heyward, DuBose   PORGY
Classic story, and plot for the opera, of a crippled black and his love for Bess. Larlin, 1970 (first published 1925).

Holland, Isabelle   DARCOURT
The mystery of a dead mother's past is explored by her reporter-daughter on an island off the coast of South Carolina. Weybright & Talley, 1976.

Humphreys, Josephine   DREAMS OF SLEEP
A first novel that "provides a fresh, new perspective" of alienation and parent/child, black/white, male/female relationships. (FC) Viking, 1984.

Jakes, John   NORTH AND SOUTH
First in a projected series of three novels that will chronicle the parallel lives of the Main and Hazard families in South Carolina and Pennsylvania, respectively, beginning in 1842, who are tied through their sons' attendance at West Point. Their lives also parallel America's struggles. "The characters both fictional and real, make this era seem almost current." (FC) HarBraceJ, 1982. The second book, *In Love and War* (1984).

Mason, F. Van Wyck   OUR VALIANT FEW
The South's efforts during the Civil War to break the northern blockade of their ports, and a courageous newspaperman's expose of war profiteering. Little, 1956.

Peterkin, Julia   SCARLET SISTER MARY
Won the Pulitzer Prize in 1929—"sympathetic, colorful tale, with mingled humor and pathos . . . of the Gullah Negro of South Carolina." (FC) Larlin, 1970 (first published 1928).

Powell, Padgett   EDISTO
Set in a coastal town—the adolescent education of a "Holden Caulfield for the 1980s." (FC) FS&G, 1984.

Ripley, Alexandra N.   ON LEAVING CHARLESTON
Sequel to *Charleston* (1982)—saga of a decadent southern plantation family. Doubleday, 1984.

TRAVEL ARTICLES

CONNOISSEUR
1985 Feb "Magic Garden." Magnolia Plantation has been getting more beautiful during the past 350 years. Henry Mitchell, p. 62

ESSENCE
1985 May "Black Charleston." Sandra Jackson-Opoku, p. 20

50 PLUS
1985 Oct "South Carolina: Discover the Old South in Full Flower." Helene M. Brooks, p. 47

HOUSE BEAUTIFUL
1985 Jan "Charleston." Once the center of the South's plantation aristocracy, Charleston is beautifully and intimately preserved. Elaine Edelman, p. 40

NATIONAL GEOGRAPHIC TRAVELER
1985 Winter "Hilton Head—tennis heaven." Jennifer C. Urquhart, p. 56

N.Y. TIMES SUNDAY TRAVEL SECTION (X)
1985 Oct 13 "Welcome to Parris Island." Visiting the Marine camp. George McMillan, p. 20
1984 Dec 2 "An Unadorned Survivor." The strength of South Carolina's Drayton Hall is its lack of "improvements." Betsy Wade, p. 22

TRAVEL/HOLIDAY
1985 Sep "Revisiting a First Love—Enjoying South Carolina's Coast." Bill Walker, p. 50
1984 Jan "Kiawah Island, The Harboring of Wildlife and Resort Life." Roy Attaway, p. 54

VOGUE
1984 Sep "The Seductive South—Charleston." Rita Mae Brown, p. 624

SOUTH DAKOTA

Background Reading

Berg, Francie M.   SOUTH DAKOTA: LAND OF SHINING GOLD
One of the Old West regional series—"an enticement to
tourists . . . a source book for the researcher [includes] business and industry,
agriculture, the arts, early ranching, the fur trade, vacation spots." (BL) Flying
Diamond, 1982.

Fielder, Mildred   A GUIDE TO BLACK HILLS GHOST MINES
North Plains, 1972.

Jackson, Donald D.   CUSTER'S GOLD
The U.S. Cavalry expedition of 1874. U of Nebraska, 1972.

Milton, John   SOUTH DAKOTA
One of a series of popular histories for each state published as part of the
Bicentennial observance in 1976. Norton, 1977. Also *The Literature of South
Dakota* (1975) an anthology of prose and poetry about South Dakota.

Parker, Watson   DEADWOOD: THE GOLDEN YEARS
"Lively, colorful . . . amusing" account of the gold-mining boom in South
Dakota's Black Hills and in Deadwood—"boss city of the Hills." (PW) U of
Nebraska, 1981.

Rezatto, Helen   MOUNT MORIAH
"Kill a man—start a cemetery"—history and life in Deadwood. (Publisher)
North Plains, 1980.

**Schneider, Bill   THE DAKOTA IMAGE: A PHOTOGRAPHIC CELEBRA-
TION**
Falcon Pr, 1980.

Novels

Hall, Oakley   THE BAD LANDS
Set in the 1880s, a western with the main protagonist a "monied
Easterner . . . modeled loosely on the young Theodore Roosevelt" and a plot about
the Johnson County cattle war. Atheneum, 1978.

Jones, Douglas C.   A CREEK CALLED WOUNDED KNEE
Last book in a trilogy about the tragedy of Wounded Knee from three
perspectives—Indians, the press, the Federal troops. Scribner, 1978. Previous

titles are: *The Court-Martial of George Armstrong Custer* (1976) and *Arrest Sitting Bull* (1977) (listed under "North Dakota").

Olsen, Tillie   YONNONDIO: FROM THE THIRTIES
A family in the 1920s trying to make a living as tenant farmers. Delacorte Pr, 1974 (first published 1937).

Rolvaag, O.E.   GIANTS IN THE EARTH
Prairie saga of Norwegian immigrants and life on the frontier. Har-Row, 1965 (first published 1927). Also with similar themes, *The Third Life of Per Smevik* (1912) and *Peder Victorious* (1929).

Ross, Dana F.   DAKOTA!
Part of a series of novels with the overall title of *Wagons West* that chronicles the conquest and settlement of the American West. Bantam, 1983.

Unger, Douglas   LEAVING THE LAND
"Set in the west Dakotas. Dramatizes the destruction of the American family farm . . . a whole way of life"—compared to Willa Cather's *O Pioneers!* (Publisher) Har-Row, 1984.

TRAVEL ARTICLES

NATIONAL GEOGRAPHIC TRAVELER
1985 Spring "The Black Hills: Where the Buffalo Roam." Custer's legend and Plains Indian lore, Deadwood and Mount Rushmore are all part of a visit to the forested hills of South Dakota. Tom Rogers, p. 108

N.Y. TIMES SUNDAY TRAVEL SECTION (X)
1984 Oct 14 "Another World Beneath the Surface." Wind Cave National Park. Andrew H. Malcolm, p. 16

TRAVEL/HOLIDAY
1984 Jul "Of Men and Mountains, Where History Is Carved in Stone." Susan Vreeland, p. 38

TENNESSEE

Background Reading

Acuff, Roy and Neely, William   ROY ACUFF'S NASHVILLE
The life and good times of country music. Putnam Pub Group, 1983.

Callahan, North   TVA: BRIDGE OVER TROUBLED WATERS
History of the TVA by an early participant and a lifetime resident of the
area—intended for the general reader. Cornwall Bks, 1980.

Cornwell, Ilene J.   TRAVEL GUIDE TO THE NATCHEZ TRACE PARKWAY
A guide to the parkway between Natchez, Mississippi, and Nashville, Tennessee.
Southern Resources, 1984.

Creekmore, Betsey   KNOXVILLE
U of Tennessee, 1976.

Dykeman, Wilma   TENNESSEE
One of a series of popular histories for each state published as part of the
Bicentennial observance in 1976. Norton, 1984 (first published 1977).

Dykeman, Wilma   THE FRENCH BROAD
An account of the river and people who have lived and thrived in this area. U of
Tennessee, 1965 (first published 1955).

Jenkins, Peter, and others   THE TENNESSEE SAMPLER
Definitive guide to the author's adopted state following his two Walk Across
America books (see under "United States"). He tells about the state's music, wit
and wisdom, where to eat and sleep, the outdoors, in homespun prose along with
local expert commentary. Nelson, 1985.

Lomax, John, III   NASHVILLE: MUSIC CITY USA
Celebration of Nashville offers a fine overview of country music and enjoyable
tour of Music City USA. Abrams, 1985.

McLean, Virginia O.   THE MEMPHIS GUIDE
Redbird, 1982.

**Matthews, Elmora M.   NEIGHBOR AND KIN: LIFE IN A TENNESSEE
RIDGE COMMUNITY**
The hill folk of middle Tennessee—"sociology written as though it were fic-
tion." (BRD) Vanderbilt U, 1966.

Ornelas-Struve, Carole M.   MEMPHIS
History of the city. Nancy Powers, 1982.

Schemmel, William   HOW, WHEN AND WHERE IN TENNESSEE
A guide to Knoxville, Nashville, Memphis, Chattanooga, Gatlinburg and the
Smokies. Marmac, 1982.

Schemmel, William   MARMAC GUIDE TO NASHVILLE
Marmac, 1984.

Smith, Reed   MAJESTIC MIDDLE TENNESSEE
Pelican, 1983.

Wolfe, Charles K.   TENNESSEE STRINGS: THE STORY OF COUNTRY
MUSIC IN TENNESSEE
U of Tennessee, 1977.

Novels

Agee, James   A DEATH IN THE FAMILY
A few days in the lives of a Knoxville family at the turn of the century, from just
before a man dies until the day of his funeral—poses "a universal human situation
most affectingly." (FC) McDowell, 1957.

Alther, Lisa   KINFLICKS
Story of a woman's life told in flashback, as she moves from cheerleader, to
collegian, anti-war lesbian, organic farmer, and finally to her present predicament.
Knopf, 1981. Also *Original Sins* (1981), growing up of a mill owner's daughter,
the mill foreman's sons, and the black maid's son.

Faulkner, William   THE REIVERS
Reminiscence of a youthful escapade—"smuggling a horse across country, planning a bizarre race, and ending in jail." (FC) Random, 1962.

Ford, Jesse Hill   THE LIBERATION OF LORD BYRON JONES
A black man files a divorce suit charging his wife with having an affair with a
white policeman. "The involvements and responses of each major and minor
character ... revealed from his particular personal point of view." (FC) Little, 1980
(first published 1965). Also *Fishes, Birds and Sons of Men* (1967), short stories
set in the same town of Summerton.

Ford, Jesse Hill   THE RAIDER
Historical novel, based on stories passed down in his own family, of a
frontiersman in west Tennessee who carves a plantation out of the wilderness
only to lose it, his slaves, his wife and son, in the Civil War. Atlantic Monthly Pr,
1975.

Gerson, Noel B.   OLD HICKORY
Fictionalized biography of Andrew Jackson. Doubleday, 1964. Also, a biographical novel about Andrew Johnson, *The Yankee from Tennessee* (1980).

Harris, Charlaine   A SECRET RAGE
Following a successful career as a New York model, the heroine returns to
Tennessee to finish college and finds "mannered dignity . . . distrust . . . overt
racism" and becomes victim to violence—"extraordinary novel [that] offers more
than a saga of victimization and recovery." (FC) Houghton, 1984.

Jones, James   WHISTLE
The author's unfinished novel about post-World War II life for four soldiers.
Delacorte Pr, 1978.

Lancaster, Bruce   NO BUGLES TONIGHT
A Northern officer becomes involved with a Southern widow who aids the Union Army during the Civil War. Little, 1948.

McCarthy, Cormac   SUTTREE
Life among Knoxville's subculture in the early 1950s. Random, 1979.

Mason, F. Van Wyck   WILD HORIZON
Historical novel of frontier life during the Revolutionary War. Little, 1966.

O'Connor, Flannery   WISE BLOOD
"An important addition to the grotesque literature of Southern decadence" and religious fanaticism. FS&G, 1962 (first published 1952). Also *The Violent Bear It Away* (1960).

Taylor, Peter   IN THE MIRO DISTRICT, AND OTHER STORIES
Short stories about the generation gap between a pioneering grandfather and his grandson born to a "genteel, contented life" in the Nashville basin. (FC) Knopf, 1977. Also *Collected Stories of Peter Taylor* (1969).

Warren, Robert Penn   THE CAVE
A young hillbilly becomes trapped in a cave and the effects of this event on many people in a small town. Random, 1959. *Flood* (1964) is another novel about the reactions of a town in western Tennessee—the building of a dam is the event around which the plot develops. Also *At Heaven's Gate* (1943) and *Circus in the Attic and Other Stories* (1948) have Tennessee settings.

Whitney, Phyllis A.   THE GLASS FLAME
A young widow is involved in an arson case—a romance and mystery set in the Great Smoky Mountains. Doubleday, 1978.

TRAVEL ARTICLES

AMERICANA
1984 Jul-Aug "Wild about Appalachia." Museum of mountain life and crafts, near Knoxville, p. 27

HOUSE & GARDEN
1984 Jul "Elvis Presley's Graceland, an American Shrine." Martin Filler, p. 140

NATIONAL GEOGRAPHIC TRAVELER
1984 Summer "Saying It with Music." Gather round for an old-fashioned fiddlers' jamboree in friendly Smithville, Tennessee. Michael Kernan, p. 130

N.Y. TIMES SUNDAY TRAVEL SECTION (X)
1985 Jun 30 "Critics' Choices, Personal Favorites When They're Not Dining at Taillevent." In Pennsylvania, Tennessee, Massachusetts. Various authors, p. 14

Sep 15 "The Storytelling Capital of Tennessee." Yarn spinners at Jonesborough festival. Wilma Dykeman, p. 12

1984 Apr 8 "Appalachia's Pioneer Past." Tennessee museum and store. Wilma Dykeman, p. 9

Apr 15 "Chickamauga: Green Place." Civil War memorial. Jerry Klein, p. 24

May 6 "Sewanee: A Bit of Oxford in Tennessee." English towers and Southern blooms. Alan Cheuse, p. 9

TRAVEL/HOLIDAY

1985 Apr "Greeneville, Tennessee: Southern Hospitality Served with Pride." Tom and Joanne O'Toole, p. 22

1984 May "Great Smoky Mountains National Park." Yvette Cardozo, p. 69

TEXAS

Series Guidebooks (See Appendix 1)

Fodor: Texas; Dallas-Fort Worth; Houston and Galveston
Fisher: Texas & the South West
Insight: Texas

Background Reading

Bones, Jim   TEXAS WEST OF THE PECOS
Photographs, text, description and natural history. Texas A&M U, 1981.

Brook, Stephen   HONEYTONK GELATO: TRAVEL THROUGH TEXAS
A British author's "whirlwind romp around Texas. . . . a fresh, informative look at the larger-than-life state." (PW) Atheneum, 1985.

Davenport, John C.   HOUSTON
A guidebook to Texas' international city, as well as for current and potential residents—the personality of the malls and freeways, hotels, museums, restaurants, schools, libraries, layout of the city and the unique neighborhoods. Texas Monthly Pr, 1985.

Davidson, John   THE LONG ROAD NORTH
"Investigative journalism . . . and a novelist's style . . . document the plight of Mexican aliens coming into and working in the U.S. illegally." Texas Monthly Pr, 1981.

Erickson, John R.   THE MODERN COWBOY
By a Texas rancher who knows the subject firsthand—"the modern Texas cowboy, who really differs from his counterparts in other western states due to climate, terrain, history, and tradition. . . . his work, family, philosophy, recreation, horses." (BL) U of Nebraska, 1981.

Fischer, John   FROM THE HIGH PLAINS
"Part history, part memoir, part elegy" about the panhandle section of Oklahoma and Texas. (BRD) Har-Row, 1978.

Frantz, Joe B.   TEXAS
One of a series of popular histories for each state published as part of the Centennial observance in 1976. Norton, 1984 (first published 1976).

Graves, John   FROM A LIMESTONE LEDGE: SOME ESSAYS AND OTHER RUMINATIONS ABOUT COUNTRY LIFE IN TEXAS
Essays on septic tanks, patching a leaky trough for heifers, vain hunts for legendary riches of Spanish silver, beekeeping, etc.—"delightfully fresh figures of speech and literary allusions." (BRD) Knopf, 1980. Also *Hard Scrabble* (1974)—"folklore, people and natural history of north central Texas."

Greene, A.C.   DALLAS USA
"Past, present, and future of Big D . . . treasure trove of worthwhile information . . invaluable [for in-depth visit or relocation]." (BL) Texas Monthly Pr, 1984.

Greene, A.C.   TEXAS SKETCHES
Essays that cut through the tall tales, by a Texas historian—"succinctly rendered prose . . . fascinating reading." (BL) Taylor Pub, 1985.

Haley, James L.   TEXAS: AN ALBUM OF HISTORY
Key events, quotes from primary sources, provide a vivid history of the state. Doubleday, 1985.

Hoffman, William   TEXAS: A YEAR WITH THE BOYS
"Odyssey of a displaced New Yorker who spent a year with some of Texas' richest native sons. . . . An outrageous glimpse into a megabuck society." (BL) Taylor, 1983.

Holmes, Jon   TEXAS: A SELF-PORTRAIT
"The essence of the Lone Star State. . . . how Texans view themselves and how they are seen by the rest of the world." A chronology of dates and people, history, contemporary "Texas talk, clothing, food and drink." (BL) Abrams, 1983.

Hurt, Harry   TEXAS RICH
"A composite biography of the Hunt family from the early oil days through the silver crash." (BRD) Norton, 1982.

Johnson, Lady Bird   TEXAS: A ROADSIDE VIEW
The First Lady made a special project of beautifying roadside America. Trinity U, 1980.

Kent, Rosemary   THE GENUINE TEXAS HANDBOOK
"Playful/serious" guide for urban cowboys and cowgirls—"how to dress, dance, drink, cook, look, inflect, and behave like a Texan, plus what to know and where to go if one actually gets to the Lone Star State." (BL) Workman, 1981.

Kramer, Jane   THE LAST COWBOY
"The plight of the cowboy in the age of computer ranching." (BRD) Har-Row, 1978.

Lea, Tom   THE KING RANCH
Two-volume story by a Texas writer-artist of the making of a man, a ranch and a way of life. Little, 1957.

Morris, Jan   JOURNEYS
This collection of travel essays by a leading travel writer includes an essay on Houston. Oxford U, 1984.

Nackman, Mark E.   NATION WITHIN A NATION
The rise of Texas nationalism—why Texas is "a nation irrepressible under the larger canopy of the United States." (BRD) Assoc Faculty Pr, 1975.

Porterfield, Bill   THE GREATEST HONKY-TONKS IN TEXAS
History and lore of honky-tonks on the outskirts of Texas towns and a guide to the best—"entertaining anecdotes and background details for each [with a] concluding primer on country-and-western dance steps." (BL) Taylor Pub, 1983. Also *Texas Rhapsody: Memories of a Native Son* (1981).

Presley, James   A SAGA OF WEALTH: THE RISE OF THE TEXAS OILMEN
Anecdotal and popular history of Texas oil. Texas Monthly Pr, 1983.

Samora, Julian   GUNPOWDER JUSTICE: A REASSESSMENT OF THE TEXAS RANGERS
Thesis is that the image of the Texas Ranger as a heroic figure does not bear examination, especially regarding Mexican-Americans. U of Notre Dame, 1979.

Sharpe, Patricia and Weddle, Robert   TEXAS: THE NEWEST, THE BIGGEST, THE MOST COMPLETE GUIDE TO ALL TEXAS
A "fun paperback . . . a browser's delight." State history, sketches of the famous and infamous Texans, what is the right boot, the right hat and how to crease it. As a guidebook it provides region by region traversal of the land, where to go, what to see, where to stay and eat, and covers small towns as well as big cities, parks and recreation areas. (Publisher) Texas Monthly Pr, 1983.

Thompson, Thomas   BLOOD AND MONEY
A true account of a murder set against the background of "the rich, arrogant and venal" society of Houston. (BRD) Doubleday, 1976.

**Webb, Walter P.   THE TEXAS RANGERS: A CENTURY OF
                     FRONTIER DEFENSE**
A comprehensive history of the Rangers. U of Texas, 1965 (first published 1935).

West, Richard   RICHARD WEST'S TEXAS
A collection of essays, each on a distinct part of the state highlighted by a town in that section—vignettes, history, each area seen through local eyes—"delightful reading." (LJ) Texas Monthly Pr, 1982.

GUIDEBOOKS

Bailes, Carlton and Hudson, Danny L.   A GUIDE TO TEXAS LAKES
Gulf Pub, 1983.

**Barrington, Carol   SHIFRA STEIN'S DAY TRIPS FROM HOUSTON:
                       GETAWAYS LESS THAN TWO HOURS AWAY**
Part of a series that provides maps and detailed information on day-tripping from a particular city. "Twenty-two day trips with information on museums, shops, restaurants, farms, campgrounds, trails, canoe routes, sporting events, celebrations, historic sites, and much more." (BL) East Woods, 1984.

**Bloom, Joel A.   500 THINGS TO DO IN HOUSTON FOR FREE
                    INCLUDING GALVESTON**
New Century, 1981.

Coates, Felicia   THE TEXAS MONTHLY GUIDEBOOKS: HOUSTON
Texas Monthly Pr, 1980.

**Driskill, Frank and Grisham, Noel   A TOUR GUIDE TO HISTORIC SAN
                                       ANTONIO AND THE BORDER
                                       COUNTRY**
Eakin, 1982.

Foster, Nancy H.   SAN ANTONIO: TEXAS MONTHLY GUIDEBOOK
Texas Monthly Pr, 1983. Also *The Alamo and other Texas Missions to Remember* (1984).

Gonzalez, Catherine T.   TOUR GUIDE TO NORTH TEXAS
Eakin, 1982.

Kirkley, Gene   GUIDE TO TEXAS RIVERS AND STREAMS
Gulf Pub, 1983.

McIlvain, Myra H.   TEXAS AUTO TRAILS
Three separate books: *The Northeast* (1984), *The Southeast* (1982), *6 Central Texas Auto Tours* (1981). U of Texas.

Miller, Ray   EYES OF TEXAS TRAVEL GUIDE SERIES
Includes: Dallas-Gulf Coast (1978), Fort Worth-Brazos Valley (1981), Hill Country-Permian Basin (1980), Panhandle-Plains (1982), San Antonio-Border (1979). Also *Ray Miller's Galveston* (1983) and *Ray Miller's Houston* (1983). Cordovan Pr.

Ramsdell, Charles   SAN ANTONIO: A HISTORICAL AND PICTORIAL GUIDE
Includes much history of the city. U of Texas, 1976.

Rodriguez, Barbara   THE HILL COUNTRY: TEXAS MONTHLY GUIDE BOOK
Texas Monthly Pr, 1983.

Rodriguez, Barbara   FIFTY-TWO GREAT TEXAS GETAWAY WEEKENDS
Texas Geograph, 1985.

Ruff, Ann and Burke, Michael   TRAVELING TEXAS BORDERS
Lone Star Bks, 1983.

Ruff, Ann   AMAZING TEXAS MONUMENTS AND MUSEUMS
Lone Star Bks, 1984.

Tyler, Paula E. and Ron   TEXAS MUSEUMS: A GUIDEBOOK
U of Texas, 1983.

Young, Dale   MARMAC GUIDE TO HOUSTON
Marmac, 1983.

Zelade, Richard   THE HILL COUNTRY: THE TEXAS MONTHLY GUIDEBOOK
"Pleasures and surprises in central Texas" via back road itineraries, restaurants and "water holes." (Publisher) Texas Monthly Pr, 1983. Also *Austin: Texas Monthly Guidebook* (1984).

Novels

Brinkley, William   PEEPER: A COMEDY
An "insouciant romp" about a gift-giving peeping Tom. Viking, 1981.

Erdman, Loula Grace   THE EDGE OF TIME
Frontier life in the panhandle in 1885—"honest, literate telling of one of the lesser-known chapters" in the American saga. Dodd, 1950. Also *The Far Journey* (1955), about a pioneer woman heading west.

Estes, William M.   A SIMPLE ACT OF KINDNESS
A simple act of kindness results in an accusation of murder. Lippincott, 1973.

Ferber, Edna   GIANT
Epic of Texas and Texans through the eyes of the Virginia-born wife of the owner of the huge Benedict Ranch. Doubleday, 1952.

Gipson, Fred   SAVAGE SAM
Frontier life in the 1870s and a very special dog. Har-Row, 1962. Two other novels in which special dogs are important to the plot are *Old Yeller* (1956) and *Hound-Dog Man* (1949).

Hailey, Elizabeth Forsythe   A WOMAN OF INDEPENDENT MEANS
A woman's life from 1899 to the 1970s told through letters, cables and newspaper clippings. Viking, 1978.

Harrigan, Stephen   ARANSAS
Set in Port Aransas, Corpus Christi, and about the capture and training of dolphins for a sea circus. Knopf, 1980.

Hearon, Shelby   GROUP THERAPY
"A charming comedy of manners and morals" about a Texas woman who becomes a visiting professor at SUNY (in Purchase, New York) and "swings between the fading gentility of the Southern family to whom she has promised to return and the caffeinated vitality of her new Northern friends." (FC) Atheneum, 1984. Also *A Prince of a Fellow* (1978), about a radio disc jockey in a small Texas town seeking true love.

Hines, Alan   SQUARE DANCE
An eleven-year-old girl is needed by her "isolated, cranky, half-blind" grandfather on their chicken farm outside Twilight, Texas. She runs away briefly to see her mother in Fort Worth, but returns. (FC) Har-Row, 1984.

Horgan, Paul   WHITEWATER
A man looks back at tragic happenings to his friends in high school with the changed perceptions of a mature person. FS&G, 1970.

Humphrey, William   PROUD FLESH
A matriarch's final illness causes a gathering of the clan and a search for her favorite son who has deserted Texas. Knopf, 1973. Also *The Ordways* (1965), about another Texas family, and *Home from the Hill* (1957).

Jenkins, Dan   BAJA OKLAHOMA
"A novel of middle-class Texas low-life set mostly in a Fort Worth cafe." (FC) Atheneum, 1981.

Kelton, Elmer   STAND PROUD: A TEXAS SAGA
A combination mystery novel and western set in West Central Texas at the turn of the century—a Texas pioneer on trial for his life. Doubleday, 1984. Other Texas frontier novels by Kelton include *The Good Old Boys* (1978), *The Day the Cowboys Quit* (1971) and *The Wolf and the Buffalo* (1980).

Lindsey, David L.   A COLD MIND
Three of Houston's most beautiful call girls die and the detective's investigation takes him from "shadowy wharves and warehouses of the city's back streets to the exotic world of Houston's wealthy Brazilian expatriate community." (FC) Har-Row, 1983.

Lowry, Beverly   DADDY'S GIRL
A widow and country Western composer ("daddy's girl") and her offspring live in suburban Houston—she comes to realize she must begin to live her own life without Big Daddy. Viking, 1981.

McElroy, Lee   EYES OF THE HAWK
"All the Western cliches [woven] into a stirring novel." (FC) Doubleday, 1981.

McMurtry, Larry   TERMS OF ENDEARMENT
The story of a Texas widow who tries to dominate those around her, and the basis for the recent movie of the same name—"some of the funniest dialogue in a long, long time" and a complete change of pace when her daughter dies of cancer. (FC) S&S, 1975.

Mewshaw, Michael   EARTHLY BREAD
Set in Austin—a Catholic priest is embroiled in the deprogramming of a Jesus freak. Random, 1976.

Michener, James   TEXAS
The latest of Michener's fictionalized histories, following several generations of the prototype characters in the novel—Mexicans, Scotch-Irish, German and Spanish. A modern-day governor appoints a task force to come up with an outline of what students should be taught of Texas history—and this provides a framework for the book. Random, 1985.

Ross, Dana F.   TEXAS
Part of a series of novels with the overall title of *Wagons West* that chronicles the conquest and settlement of the American West. Bantam, 1980.

Smith, C.W.   COUNTRY MUSIC
Highly accurate descriptions of the people, towns and countryside of West Texas. FS&G, 1975.

Swarthout, Glendon   THE SHOOTIST
More than a western—story of the last of the gunfighters, in 1901, who is dying of cancer in El Paso. Doubleday, 1975.

Swift, Edward   PRINCIPIA MARTINDALE
"About a naively religious young woman who becomes a faith healer. . . . she is taken up by hucksters, with disastrous results." Har-Row, 1983. Also *Splendora* (1978), about a young man who returns to his east Texas town in a rather unusual way.

Thompson, Thomas   BLOOD AND MONEY
"High society of Houston's ultra rich is the setting . . . spellbinding account of mysterious death" based on a true story. Doubleday, 1976.

Thompson, Thomas   CELEBRITY
Three friends from high school "whose lives, in complex sort, bear out their roles in a high school play" are haunted by an adolescent crime they committed. (FC) Doubleday, 1982.

Wellman, Paul I.   THE COMANCHEROS
A gentleman gambler from New Orleans joins the Texas Rangers and his first job is to destroy a band of Comancheros who are attacking white settlers on the Texas border. Doubleday, 1952.

Wier, Allen   BLANCO
Four unhappy lives in a small Texas town. Louisiana State U Pr, 1978.

TRAVEL ARTICLES

BON APPETIT
1985 Oct "Traveling with Taste: Texas Hill Country." Shirley Slater, p. 30

EARLY AMERICAN LIVING
1985 Jun "Where the Rhine Meets the Medina: Castroville, Texas." Mimi Handler, p. 60

50 PLUS
1985 Oct"The Texas Gulf—the Newest American Winter Resort Is a Dream Come True." Anne C. Heller, p. 50

GOURMET
1984 Mar Gourmet Holidays: "Dallas." Richard Condon, p. 34

HOUSE BEAUTIFUL
1985 Jul "Texas's German Heritage." Following Texas's blue hill country highways in pursuit of frontier decorative arts. Richard Zelade, p. 47

NATIONAL GEOGRAPHIC
1984 Feb "Texas West of the Pecos." Griffin Smith, Jr., p. 210
      Sep "Dallas—Telling a Tale of Two Cities in One." Griffin Smith, Jr., p. 272

NATIONAL GEOGRAPHIC TRAVELER
1985 Spring "Texas Wildflower Trails . . . " A springtime jaunt through the Lone Star State's blossoming glory. Jerry C. Dunn, Jr., p. 145
      Autumn "Big Bend: Desert Rough and Tumble." Big Bend National Park. Edward Abbey, p. 94
1984 Autumn "San Antonio's Paseo del Rio (River Walk)." History with flair. Christine E. Lee, p. 56

N.Y. SUNDAY TIMES TRAVEL SECTION (X)
1985 May 5 "What's Doing in Austin." Robert Reinhold, p. 10
      Jul 7 "Lodes of art in Texas." Michael Kammen, p. 20
      Nov 10 Shopper's World: "Western Gear Sold in a Big Texan Way." Joan
      Ryan, p. 6
1984 Feb 12 "Abloom in the Heart of Texas." In April the hill country west of
      Austin blossoms. Charlotte Curtis, p. 9
      Feb 19 "What's Doing in Dallas." Peter Appleborne, p. 10
      Mar 4 "Miss Ima's Legacy of Americana." Antiques collection in a Houston
      mansion. Michael Kammen, p. 14
      May 6 "A Festival Nearly as Big as Texas." San Antonio Festival of the Arts.
      Wayne King, p. 51
      Aug 19 "Out Where the East Begins." Dallas. Wayne King, p. 14
      "Four Excursions in the Metroplex." Freeway landscape, downtown Dallas,
      Wilson block on Swiss Avenue, and Fort Worth. Paul Goldberger, p. 15
      "Monuments to Comfort." Dallas hotels. Marian Burros, p. 16
      Dec 9 "Big Bend Adventure." An autumn account of three days in an ex-
      traordinary wilderness. Robert Reinhold, p. 9

SMITHSONIAN
1985 Dec "In Old San Antonio, a New American Way." Melding of Anglos and
      Hispanics. p. 114

TRAVEL & LEISURE
1984 May "The Great Museums of Texas." Five treasuries of painting, sculpture
      and architecture. Leon A. Harris, Jr., p. 22

TRAVEL/HOLIDAY
1985 Jun "The Coast with the Most." Life on the Riviera, Texas-style. Carol M.
      Reed, p. 62
      Dec "Christmas in San Antonio." Candace Leslie, p. 36
1984 Feb "Fort Worth." "Foat Wuth, ah luv ya." Hal Butler, p. 32
      Oct "Big Bend." A Texas-style national park. John F. Whisler, p. 30

WORKING WOMAN
1985 Mar "A Businesswoman's Guide to San Antonio." Carole Martin, p. 10

UTAH

Background Reading

Abbey, Edward   DESERT SOLITAIRE
The author worked as a park ranger at Arches National Monument in

southeastern Utah and this is his account of "day-to-day desert" with information about the desert—"literature, not just a guidebook." (BRD) Peregrine Smith, 1981 (first published 1968).

Arrington, Leonard J.   THE MORMON EXPERIENCE
An interpretive history of the Mormon Church aimed at the general reader. Knopf, 1979.

Brown, Joseph E.   THE MORMON TREK WEST
Retraces the journey from Nauvoo, Illinois, to Great Salt Lake Valley in search of religious freedom, one of the key events in Mormon history. Doubleday, 1980.

Carr, Stephen L.   THE HISTORICAL GUIDE TO UTAH GHOST TOWNS
Western Epics, 1972.

Fox, Theron   UTAH TREASURE HUNTER'S GHOST TOWN GUIDE
Nevada Pbns, 1983.

Gottlieb, Robert and Wiley, Peter   AMERICA'S SAINTS: THE RISE OF MORMON POWER
"The church's role in conservative politics . . . the lives of Mormon women. . . . an excellent portrait of a major but often overlooked power in contemporary America." (LJ) Putnam Pub Group, 1984.

Madsen, Brigham and Betty M.   NORTH TO MONTANA!
The freight and passenger road that starts in Salt Lake City and ends in Fort Benton, the experiences of those who traveled it. U of Utah, 1980.

Peterson, Charles S.   UTAH
One of a series of popular histories for each state published as part of the Bicentennial observance in 1976. Norton, 1977.

Reed, Allen C.   GRAND CIRCLE ADVENTURE
Traveling to national parks and reserves in Arizona, Colorado and Utah. KC Pbns, 1983.

Roylance, Ward J.   UTAH: A GUIDE TO THE STATE
Western Epics, 1982.

Stegner, Wallace E.   THE GATHERING OF ZION: THE STORY OF THE MORMON TRAIL
The epic migration of the Mormons—"interweaving diarists' accounts with historical data . . . with freshness and perspective." (BRD) Howe Bros, 1982 (first published 1964).

Taylor, Samuel W.   ROCKY MOUNTAIN EMPIRE: THE LATTER-DAY SAINTS TODAY
"Largely anecdotal, interesting account of the transformation of strict pioneer

Mormonism . . . into a part of mainstream American culture." (BRD) Macmillan, 1978.

Thompson, George A.   SOME DREAMS DIE
Utah's ghost towns and lost treasures. Dream Garden Pr, 1982.

Warren, Colin   VELVET WATERS, CANYON WALLS: A LAKE POWELL ADVENTURE
See under "Arizona."

Novels

Abbey, Edward   THE MONKEY WRENCH GANG
About a band of conservationists trying to preserve the wilds. Lippincott, 1975.

Bart, Peter   THY KINGDOM COME
People, power and corruption in Mormon life. Linden Pr, 1981.

Cook, Thomas H.   TABERNACLE
A series of Mormons are murdered and by approaching the murders from a new perspective a former New York City cop figures out who the next victim will be. Houghton, 1983.

Doyle, Sir Arthur Conan   A STUDY IN SCARLET
The story within the story—"deals with adventures in Utah and the wrong committed by two brutal Mormons on a girl and her lover." It is surrounded by a more typical Sherlock Holmes setting in London. Doubleday, 1977 (first published 1887).

Fisher, Vardis   CHILDREN OF GOD
Novelization of the Mormon epic by an author of Mormon descent. "Glosses over neither misdeeds of the Mormons nor the brutality of their enemies as he depicts . . . the trek west, or minutely envisages domestic conflicts resulting from plural marriage." (FC) Holmes, 1977 (first published 1939).

Grey, Zane   RIDERS OF THE PURPLE SAGE
Mormon vengeance in southwestern Utah in 1871. Har-Row, 1980 (first published 1912).

Henry, Will   ALIAS BUTCH CASSIDY
The saga of Butch Cassidy and Robbers' Roost, a notorious Utah hideout for outlaws. Random, 1968.

Kennelly, Ardyth   THE PEACEABLE KINGDOM
Mormon life before plural marriages were outlawed. Houghton, 1949.

Laxness, Halldor   PARADISE RECLAIMED
Mormon Icelanders in the United States. Crowell, 1962.

Mailer, Norman   THE EXECUTIONER'S SONG
A documentary narrative of Gary Gilmore from April 1976, when he was released from prison, until early 1977 when he was executed for the murder of two people. The second half is about the "marketing of Gilmore as he awaits—and demands—death in the Utah state prison." (FC) The novel won a Pulitzer Prize. Little, 1979.

Ross, Dana F.   UTAH
Part of a series of novels with the overall title of *Wagons West* that chronicles the conquest and settlement of the American West. Bantam, 1984.

Stegner, Wallace   RECAPITULATION
A man returns to Salt Lake City fifty years after having left to attend law school and faces what he's spent his whole life trying to live down —by an author with an often praised gift for the recreation of place. Doubleday, 1979.

TRAVEL ARTICLES

BON APPETIT
1984 Nov "Traveling with Taste: Skiing in Utah." Richard J. Pietschmann, p. 34

GOURMET
1984 Jan Gourmet Holidays: "Skiing Utah's Deer Valley." Gerald Asher, p. 22

HOUSE BEAUTIFUL
1984 Nov "Skiers and History Buffs Are at Home in Three Victorian Towns That Reflect the Old West." p. 56

NATIONAL GEOGRAPHIC TRAVELER
1984 Spring "Floating Through Dinosaur." Wonders of Dinosaur National Monument in Colorado and Utah. p. 104
Winter "Palaces in Wonderland." Bryce Canyon National Park. John Boslough, p. 78

N.Y. TIMES SUNDAY TRAVEL SECTION (X)
1984 Feb 12 "Soaring on Snowbird Powder." A mountain's mountain. Tobi Sanders, p. 12
Oct 3 (Part 2, "Sophisticated Traveler") "On Lake Powell." Houseboating in the heart of Utah's red rock country. Edward Abbey, p. 89
Dec 9 "Salt Lake City's Special Season." William E. Schmidt, p. 24

SATURDAY EVENING POST
1985 Sep "The Rainbow That Never Fades." Bryce Canyon. C.J. Burkhart, p. 92

SUNSET
1985 Nov "Science Museum in Salt Lake City." p. 80
1984 Jun "Cliff and Cranny Crawling in Southwest Utah." p. 96
      Aug "Flood Control and Fun . . ." Utah's Jordan River Parkway provides both.
      p. 22

TRAVEL & LEISURE
1985 Mar "The Primeval Beauty of Utah's Bryce Canyon." G.S. Bush, p. 112
      Dec "Deer Valley: A Sophisticated New Ski Area in the Legendary White
      Powder of Utah." Dena Kaye, p. 94

TRAVEL/HOLIDAY
1984 Apr "Utah's Promised Land." Salt Lake City, city of surprises. Jerry and Merry
      Dunn, p. 76
      Jul "Dinosaurland, Utah." A prehistoric resting place. Richard Sassaman, p.
      22

VERMONT

Background Reading

Bixby, William   MANCHESTER: THE VISITOR'S GUIDE
Profile of Manchester using the restoration of the Equinox House, Vermont's
grand nineteenth-century hotel, as a focus. What to see and do, where to stay, eat
and shop. Countryman Pr, 1985.

Chase, Heman   MORE THAN LAND
"Nostalgic accumulation of a lifetime of surveying lands, people and events in
New Hampshire and Vermont." (BRD) Bauhan, 1978.

**Fisher, Dorothy Canfield   VERMONT TRADITION: THE BIOGRAPHY OF
AN OUTLOOK ON LIFE**
How Vermont developed its unique qualities, by a prominent Vermont writer
whose family roots go back to the state's earliest days. Little, 1953.

Hoyt, Edwin P.   DAMNDEST YANKEES: ETHAN ALLEN AND HIS CLAN
The importance of the Allen family in the history of Vermont—they are more
than staid New Englanders! Stephen Greene Pr, 1976.

Ketchum, Richard   SECOND CUTTING
By the editor of *Country Journal*—"delightful volume of short essays. . . .
neighborly, terse, cheerful" on his farm in Vermont, the town, the world away.
(PW) Viking, 1981.

Meeks, Harold A.   TIME AND CHANGE IN VERMONT
The author calls this "human geography"—Vermont over four centuries "from the arrival of Samuel de Champlain to the recent advent of General Electric and IBM. . . . the many changes . . .in the use of the land and the changing population." (Publisher) Globe Pequot, 1984.

Mitchell, Don   MOVING UP COUNTRY: A YANKEE WAY OF KNOWLEDGE
In the city-person-turned-country-settler genre—originally published in the "R.F.D." column of *Boston* magazine. The author's "bright style and good humor make his rural adventures . . . vivid and appealing." (PW) Yankee Bks, 1984.

Morrissey, Charles T.   VERMONT
One of a series of popular histories for each state published as part of the Bicentennial observance in 1976—"will tell you truly what it is like there." (BRD) Norton, 1981.

Nearing, Helen   LIVING THE GOOD LIFE
Account of self-sufficient homesteading long before its vogue in the 1960s. Published privately in 1954. See also the Nearing book under "Maine" in which Mrs. Nearing and her husband continued their self-sufficient life-style. Schocken, 1970.

Perrin, Noel   FIRST PERSON RURAL: ESSAYS OF A SOMETIME FARMER
This and its sequel, *Second Person Rural* (1980), are a transplanted urbanite's observations on the realities of country life. Godine, 1978. *Third Person Rural* (1983), essays and linked pieces entitled *A Country Calendar* [provide] a fitting finale to the series.

Redfield, Melissa   SCENES FROM COUNTRY LIFE
"Account of a middle-aged New York couple who bought an old farmhouse in Vermont, had it renovated, and went to live there." (BRD) P-H, 1979.

Schwenke, Karl   IN A PIG'S EYE
This is by a Californian, city-bred, who launched his Vermont farming venture with a single pig. "Manages to capture the lifestyle, the personalities, even the dialect of rural Vermont. . . . anecdotes, farming stories . . . lore and 'shaggy pig' tales . . . some first-rate writing." (PW) Chelsea Green, 1985.

Tinney, Donald L.   VERMONTERS
Oral history interviews with farmers, craftspeople, shopkeepers, loggers, mechanics, artists, writers and professional men and women, both native and "from away," combined with photographs. Countryman Pr, 1985.

Tree, Christina and Jennison, Peter S.   VERMONT: AN EXPLORER'S GUIDE
"A helpful source book"—alphabetical list of activities, calendar of events, descriptions of major cities, special small towns, things to do, lodgings and restaurants. (BL) Countryman Pr, 1983.

Novels

Brown, Reeve Lindbergh   MOVING TO THE COUNTRY
Problems of transition when a family moves from suburban Massachusetts to rural Vermont—honest and believable portrait of marriage changes and putting down roots. Doubleday, 1983.

Cardiff, Sara   THE SEVERING LINE
Escape fiction set in rural Vermont in the 1970s. Random, 1974.

Clark, Eleanor   GLORIA MUNDI
Old and new values, natives and outsiders conflict, with a plot involving an unscrupulous land developer and the murder of a hiking couple. Pantheon, 1979.

Connolly, Edward   DEER RUN
Two Vietnam War veterans set up the commune of Heartwell in a remote area of Vermont. A local farmer befriends them, but they meet with much hostility from the village and eventually the commune collapses. Scribner, 1971.

Delbanco, Nicholas   POSSESSION
"One day in the life of . . . a rich, eccentric, seventy-six year old Vermont farmer" and recollections of his life. (BRD) Morrow, 1977. *Sherbrookes* (1979) continues the family chronicle—"a Greek-revival sort of story, in the manner of Eugene O'Neill."

Gardner, John   OCTOBER LIGHT
Liberal vs. conservative on a family farm, an exploration of a people and place uniquely American. Knopf, 1976.

Mather, Melissa   ONE SUMMER IN BETWEEN
"The experiences of a very black Southern girl in a very white Northern community"—a student from a South Carolina teacher's college is hired by an East Barnstead couple to spend the summer helping out with their house and children. (FC) Har-Row, 1967.

Peck, Robert N.   A DAY NO PIGS WOULD DIE
An autobiographical novel "effectively evoking Shaker life in all its austerity and gentle lovingness" on a Shaker farm of the 1920s. Knopf, 1973.

Schaeffer, Susan F.   TIME IN ITS FLIGHT
Family saga "delineative of small-town America's manners and morals" in the nineteenth century. (FC) Doubleday, 1978.

Shaw, Irwin   THE TOP OF THE HILL
A sports daredevil becomes a ski instructor in Vermont and comes to term with his attraction to life-threatening impulses. Delacorte Pr, 1979.

TRAVEL ARTICLES

GOURMET
1984 Dec "Reveillon in Vermont." Evan Jones, p. 72

HOUSE BEAUTIFUL
1985 Dec "West Dover Inn at Sawmill farm." p. 318

NATIONAL GEOGRAPHIC TRAVELER
1984 Autumn "Leaves of Autumn: A Vermont Sampler." Excursions combining fall foliage and history. Ethel A. Starbird, p. 42

N.Y. TIMES SUNDAY TRAVEL SECTION (X)
1985 Feb 10 "Woodstock in Winter—Low-Key Elegance in a Serene Setting." And church bells by Revere. Alberta Eiseman, p. 12
       Feb 17 "A Touch of the Tyrol in Stowe, Vt." Skiing at the Trapp family lodge. Laurie O'Neill, p. 12
       May 19 "In Pursuit of Music in Vermont." David Duncan, p. 23
       Jun 2 Shopper's World: "Reaping a Harvest of Wildflowers." Vermont Wildflower Farm. Debra Weiner, p. 6
       Aug 25 Fare of the Country: "Foods Help Spice Vermont Image." Marilyn Stout, p. 12
       Dec 22 "What's Doing in Vermont." Neil E. Callahan, p. 10
1984 Mar 18 "Fresh Air and Fresh Eggs." How to serve up an old-fashioned farm vacation in Vermont. Noel Perrin, p. 9
       Aug 19 "What's Doing in the Connecticut River Valley." Marilyn Stout, p. 10
       Aug 26 "Summer Stroll in Middlebury." Barbara L. Michaels, p. 19
       Sep 23 "Vermont in Autumn's Dazzle." Scenic drives and chicken pie suppers. Linda Charlton, p. 19
       Nov 4 Shopper's World: "Timeless Vermont Toys." Debra Weiner, p. 6

SATURDAY EVENING POST
1984 Dec "The Trapp Family Lodge: Room at the Inn." Stowe. William T. Anderson, p. 84

TRAVEL & LEISURE
1985 Aug "Vermont's Golden Days." Celebrating in Newfane, the perfect New England village. Joseph P. Kahn, p. 51
1984 Nov "Vermont's Snowy Stowe." Winter pleasures of a New England town. Andrew Nemethy, p. 112

TRAVEL/HOLIDAY
1984 Jun "The Shelburne Museum, an American Treasury in Vermont." Helmut Koenig, p. 26
       Aug "Savoring Vermont." Chef Louis Szathmary, p. 12

YANKEE
1985 Jan This New England: "Newport, Vt." Stephen O. Muskie, p. 62
       Oct "This New England: Strafford, Vermont." Edie Clark, p. 82

1984 Jan "The Vermont Experience . . . and Exactly How to Tell If You're Ready
for It." p. 152

Feb "Finding Your Own Winter Fun." Unique list of wintertime activities.
Geoffrey Norman, p. 118

Apr This New England: "Danville, Vt.." Stephen O. Muskie, p. 62

Oct This New England: "Middletown Springs." p. 76

Dec "Going with the Dogs." Dogsledding tours. Ross Connolly, p. 46

VIRGINIA

Background Reading

Adams, William H.   JEFFERSON'S MONTICELLO
Text "perfectly suited to . . . 'the quintessential example of the autobiographical
house,'" with photographs and illustrations. (Publisher) Abbeville Pr, 1983.

Barbour, Philip L.   POCAHONTAS AND HER WORLD
Recreation of a fascinating legend—Pocahontas and the three Englishmen
whose lives affected hers, along with much early Virginia history. Houghton,
1970.

Dowdey, Clifford   THE VIRGINIA DYNASTIES
"The emergence of 'king' Carter and the golden age"—political greats produced
in the first century-and-a-half of Virginia history. (Publisher) Little, 1969. Also *The
Golden Age: A Climate for Greatness, 1732-1775* (1970).

**Firestone, Linda   VIRGINIA'S FAVORITE ISLANDS: CHINCOTEAGUE
AND ASSATEAGUE**
Good Life, 1982.

**Gilbert, Elizabeth R.   FAIRS AND FESTIVALS: A SMITHSONIAN GUIDE
TO CELEBRATIONS IN MARYLAND, VIRGINIA
AND D.C.**
"Everything from national holidays and flower festivals to ethnic and religious
events." (BL) Smithsonian, 1982.

Grosvenor, Donna K.   THE WILD PONIES OF ASSATEAGUE ISLAND
Natl Geog, 1975.

Hodge, Allan and Carola   WASHINGTON ON FOOT
Twenty-three walking tours of Washington, D.C., Alexandria and Annapolis.
Smithsonian, 1980.

Jordan, James M.   VIRGINIA BEACH
A pictorial history. Jordan Assoc, 1984.

Kocher, Alfred L. and Dearstyne, Howard   COLONIAL WILLIAMSBURG
Its buildings and gardens—a descriptive tour of the restored capital of the British Colony of Virginia. Har-Row, 1976.

Lord, William G.   THE COMPLETE GUIDE TO THE BLUE
                     RIDGE PARKWAY
Covers the Parkway from Rockfish Gap in Virginia to Oconaluftee River Bridge in North Carolina. Eastern Acorn Pr, 1981.

Morris, Shirley   THE PELICAN GUIDE TO VIRGINIA
Alphabetical listing of three hundred attractions—historic homes and estates, battlefields, recreational areas, from the blue ridge to the eastern shore. Pelican, 1981.

Robertson, James I.   CIVIL WAR SITES IN VIRGINIA: A TOUR GUIDE
U Pr of Virginia, 1982.

Rouse, Parke Jr.   VIRGINIA: THE ENGLISH HERITAGE IN AMERICA
Hastings, 1976.

Rubin, Louis D. Jr.   VIRGINIA
One of a series of popular histories for each state published as part of the Bicentennial observance. Norton, 1977.

Sherry, John   MAGGIE'S FARM
Memoir by an author who decided to buy a dairy farm in southwest Virginia to provide income and the time to write—"an entertaining account [of dairy farming] and getting along with the natives." (PW) Permanent Pr, 1984.

Smith, Daniel B.   INSIDE THE GREAT HOUSE: PLANTER FAMILY LIFE
                     IN 18TH-CENTURY CHESAPEAKE SOCIETY
Explores the character of family experience in the pre-industrial South in Maryland and Virginia. Cornell U, 1980.

Voges, Nettie Allen   OLD ALEXANDRIA
History of the city combined with walking tours and information on restorations being done. EPM, 1985.

Woodlief, Ann   IN RIVER TIME: THE WAY OF THE JAMES
The James River, a chronology from prehistoric times to the present—"novels, poems, art work, and exploration accounts . . . emphasize a predominantly human river relationship." History, biology, and ecology lessons become part of the reading. (IJ) Algonquin, 1985.

Novels

Canby, Vincent   UNNATURAL SCENERY
A wealthy New Yorker looks back to his youth in Virginia. Knopf, 1979.

Disney, Doris M.   DO NOT FOLD, SPINDLE OR MUTILATE
A murder mystery involving a computerized dating service and an Alexandria spinster. Doubleday, 1970.

Epps, Garrett   THE SHAD TREATMENT
Contemporary political scene in Virginia as a young man comes of age. Putnam Pub Group, 1977.

Gerson, Noel B.   GIVE ME LIBERTY
A fictionalized biography of Patrick Henry that humanizes his legend and provides a picture of the political and other pressures of the period. Doubleday, 1966.

Glasgow, Ellen   IN THIS OUR LIFE
Story of "decayed aristocrats" in Virginia that won a Pulitzer Prize in 1942. HarBraceJ, 1941. Also set in Virginia are *Vein of Iron* (1935), a family saga set in the Virginia mountains, and *Barren Ground* (1925), about a poor farm family.

Goodwin, Stephen   THE BLOOD OF PARADISE
A couple from the city attempt a simple life in the mountains of Virginia and react differently to the experience. Dutton, 1979.

Hamner, Earl   SPENCER'S MOUNTAIN
A boy's account of life in the Blue Ridge Mountains and his struggle for an education. Dial, 1961. Also *The Homecoming* (1970), story of a 1930s Christmas Eve.

Kane, Harnett T.   THE LADY OF ARLINGTON
Historical novel based on the life of Mrs. Robert E. Lee. Doubleday, 1953.

L'Amour, Louis   TO THE FAR BLUE MOUNTAINS
Begins in England and is a sequel to *Sackett's Land* (1974). In this, Sackett decides to leave England for Virginia, assembles a band of "brave settlers and strong women" and they follow the James River to rich farmland to establish a community. Saturday Review Pr, 1976.

Lancaster, Bruce   ROLL SHENANDOAH
The Shenandoah Valley campaign in the Civil War. Little, 1958.

McCaig, Donald N.   NOP'S TRIALS
About stock dogs and stock dog trials, set in rural Virginia—"refreshing, heartwarming, wellcrafted." (FC) Crown, 1984.

Mason, F. Van Wyck   TRUMPETS SOUND NO MORE
Picking up the pieces after the Civil War, for a Confederate officer. Little, 1975.

Mason, F. Van Wyck   THE SEA VENTURE
The early years of Jamestown (and the Bermuda settlement) are the basis for the plot. Doubleday, 1961.

Michaels, Barbara   WITCH
The heroine's beautiful house is haunted by a witch and a cat—suspenseful gothic novel. Dodd, 1973.

Page, Elizabeth   THE TREE OF LIBERTY
The making of the nation told through a Tidewater family whose members' various political views epitomize "the political history of the country, the conflicting loyalties to different leaders, the economic differences, and the regional partisanships." HR&W, 1939.

Ponicsan, Darryl   CINDERELLA LIBERTY
A Navy seaman's service records are lost and his ambiguous status is the basis for this comic novel—"rowdy assault on the workings of military bureaucracy" set in Portsmouth, Virginia. (FC) Har-Row, 1973.

Reed, Ishmael   FLIGHT TO CANADA
A slave flees his Virginia master for Canada and the scenes alternate between back at the plantation and the slave's precarious freedom—"brilliant, outrageous spoof . . . mixes fact and fiction, hilarious anachronisms, folklore and personal mythology, caricature and idiom." (FC) Random, 1976.

Settle, Mary Lee   O BEULAH LAND
"Excellently written chronological novel with a fascinating story told in the idiom of the day and place." The plot centers on a Virginia gentleman and the group of early Americans he takes west with him to "Beulah," beyond the king's proclamation line. Period is 1754-75. See "Novels/West Virginia." Viking, 1956.

Styron, William   THE CONFESSIONS OF NAT TURNER
A Pulitzer Prize-winning novel of the 1831 slave rebellion. Random, 1967.

Thane, Elswyth   DAWN'S EARLY LIGHT
An orphaned English boy in colonial Williamsburg of 1774. Hawthorn, 1943. Also set in Williamsburg during and following the Civil War, are *Yankee Stranger* (1944) and *Ever After* (1945).

Theroux, Alexander   DARCONVILLE'S CAT
An instructor in a small woman's college in Virginia is spurned by one of his students, moves on to teach at Harvard but plots his revenge. Doubleday, 1981.

Wicker, Tom   UNTO THIS HOUR
Civil War novel by the *New York Times* columnist—defeat of the North at Manassas is the focus of the plot. Major historical figures—Lee, Longstreet, others—combined with many and varied ordinary characters. Viking, 1984.

Williams, Ben Ames   HOUSE DIVIDED
Novel about the Civil War and its effect on an old Virginia family. Houghton, 1947.

TRAVEL ARTICLES

AMERICAN HERITAGE
1984 Jun "The Lawn: America's Greatest Architectural Achievement." Design of the University of Virginia. James M. Fitch, p. 49

BON APPETIT
1984 May "Around the Alleghenies." Crafts, food, inns. Shirley Slater, p. 28

EARLY AMERICAN LIFE
1984 Aug "Virginia Country Inns." Roon Frost, p. 46

GOURMET
1985 Dec "Christmas in Colonial Williamsburg." Marilyn Kluger, p. 54

MODERN MATURITY
1985 Aug-Sep "Road That Rides the Fog." A golden anniversary look at the Blue Ridge Parkway. Diane K. Gentry, p. 48

NATIONAL GEOGRAPHIC
1985 Jul "Hampton Roads, Where the Rivers End." William S. Ellis, p. 72

NATIONAL GEOGRAPHIC TRAVELER
1984 Summer "Thomas Jefferson's Country." Monticello and University of Virginia, p. 66
Winter "Christmas in Williamsburg." Philip Kopper, p. 21

N.Y. TIMES SUNDAY TRAVEL SCTION (X)
1985 Jan 27 "Virginia's Homes and Grounds." Garden week offers a chance to view formal settings, Presidential sites, beach cottages. Sarah B. Wright, p. 21
Jun 16 "From Williamsburg's Attic." New museum displays 8,000 colonial antiques, including a famous clock. Rita Reif, p. 15
1984 May 13 "A Brighter Mount Vernon." Restoration of Washington's plantation home. Seth S. King, p. 22
May 27 "Carried Back to Old Virginia." The great houses along the James River bear witness to 400 years of social history. Mary Lee Settle, p. 14

READERS DIGEST
1985 Jul "Williamsburg's Enduring Grace." Judith B. Morgan, p. 148

SMITHSONIAN
1984 Jul "Jefferson: The Most Ardent Farmer in the State." Restoration of Monticello gardens to the way they looked when Jefferson cultivated them. p. 68

TRAVEL & LEISURE

1985 Mar "The Enduring Grace of Colonial Williamsburg." 18th-century America, brilliantly alive. Judith B. Morgan, p. 86

1984 Apr "Mount Vernon Revisited." A fresh look at George Washington's revealing retreat. James T. Flexner, p. 138

TRAVEL/HOLIDAY

1985 Jul "At Home with George and Martha." Virginia's Mount Vernon. Janet W. Connor, p. 10

WASHINGTON

Series Guidebooks (See Appendix 1)

Sunset: Washington

Background Reading

Burke, Clifford   A RAINY DAY GUIDE TO SEATTLE
Walks along the waterfront, art galleries, restaurants, nightlife, etc. Chronicle Bk, 1983.

Clark, Norman H.   MILLTOWN
A social history of Everett, Washington, from its earliest beginnings on the shores of Puget Sound to the tragic and infamous event known as the Everett massacre. U of Washington Pr, 1970

Clark, Norman H.   WASHINGTON
One of a series of popular histories for each state published as part of the Bicentennial observance in 1976. Norton, 1976.

Combs, Ann   HELTER SHELTER
An Air Force retiree renovates a house on Bainbridge Island—"delightful story in *The Egg and I* genre." (BRD) Har-Row, 1979.

Doig, Ivan   WINTER BROTHERS: A SEASON AT THE EDGE OF AMERICA
A diary within a diary—the discovery of the diaries of James G. Swan, an obscure nineteenth-century artist and observer of Indian life, leads the author to interweave his own contemporary diary of a winter with that of Swan for a unique reading experience. HarBraceJ, 1980.

Espy, Willard R.   OYSTERVILLE: ROADS TO GRANDPA'S VILLAGE
Family chronicle and that of a small coastal village. Crown, 1977.

Gidley, M.   WITH ONE SKY ABOVE US
Life on an Indian reservation at the turn of the century. Putnam Pub Group, 1979.

Hershman, Marc J. and others   SEATTLE'S HISTORIC WATERFRONT: THE WALKER'S GUIDE
U of Washington Pr, 1981.

Kirk, Ruth   EXPLORING THE OLYMPIC PENINSULA
Culture, history, people, nature and facts for enjoying all of them. U of Washington Pr, 1980.

Morgan, Murray   PUGET'S SOUND: A NARRATIVE OF EARLY TACOMA AND THE SOUTHERN SOUND
History of the region in terms of selected historical personalities, from the arrival of Vancouver until the establishment of Fort Lewis—lively history and fascinating characters. (BRD) U of Washington Pr, 1981.

Nelson, Gerald B.   SEATTLE: THE LIFE AND TIMES OF AN AMERICAN CITY
Knopf, 1977.

Nisbet, Jack   SKY PEOPLE
Colville Valley—"collage of impressions . . . a cast of vivid and unforgettable characters, human and otherwise . . . nature, legends and people." (BL) Quartzite Bks, 1984.

Perry, John and Greverus, Jane   THE SIERRA CLUB GUIDE TO THE NATURAL AREAS OF WASHINGTON
Sierra Club, 1983.

Satterfield, Archie and others   THE SEATTLE GUIDEBOOK
Writing Works, 1981.

Shane, Scott   DISCOVERING MOUNT ST. HELENS: A GUIDE TO THE NATIONAL VOLCANIC MONUMENT
To aid tourists visiting the monument. An account of volcanism in general and the Mt. St. Helens eruption in 1980, in particular; the plant and human culture of the area. U of Washington Pr, 1985.

Stanley, David   ALASKA-YUKON HANDBOOK: A GYPSY GUIDE TO THE INSIDE PASSAGE AND BEYOND
See under "Alaska/Background Reading."

Thollander, Earl   BACKROADS OF WASHINGTON
Potter, 1981.

Novels

Ball, John   POLICE CHIEF
The police chief of Whitewater finds his job far more complicated than his former job on Pasadena homicide. Doubleday, 1977.

McKay, Allis   THE WOMEN AT PINE CREEK
Two young women inherit a tract of land and decide to live there. Macmillan, 1966.

Roberts, Willo Davis   THE SNIPER
Inheritance from a distant relative of a Victorian house leads to murders—the heroine must solve them or be next. Doubleday, 1984.

Ross, Dana F.   WASHINGTON
Part of a series of novels with the overall title of *Wagons West* that chronicles the conquest and settlement of the American West. Bantam, 1982.

Shiner, R.H.   THE CRICKET CAGE
A gothic set in Seattle of 1886 and the struggle for statehood. Har-Row, 1975.

White, Stewart E.   WILD GEESE CALLING
A young couple's adventure, meeting in Oregon, living in Seattle, then to Alaska as the "call of the wild geese" lures them farther. (FC) Doubleday, 1940.

TRAVEL ARTICLES

ARCHITECTURAL DIGEST
1984 Jun "Gardens: Nature in Gentle Custody." The Bloedel Reserve in Puget Sound. Heather Lockman, p. 122

BON APPETIT
1985 Jan "Traveling with Taste: Seattle." Shirley Slater, p. 24

GOOD HOUSEKEEPING
1985 Mar "Seattle: Rain or Shine." Stephen Birnbaum, p. 190

MODERN MATURITY
1985 Mar-Apr "Retirement in the San Juans." A tropical oasis in the northwest. Janis Miglaos, p. 42

NATIONAL GEOGRAPHIC
1984 May "The Olympic Peninsula." Bill Richards and Sam Abell, p. 644

NATIONAL GEOGRAPHIC TRAVELER
1984 Summer "Washington's San Juan Islands." Mark Miller, p. 118

N.Y. TIMES SUNDAY TRAVEL SECTION (X)
1985 Feb 17 Fare of the Country: "Geoduck." Seattle's tasty big clam. Susan H. Loomis, p. 6
"Taking a Cure on the Coast." Carson Hot Mineral Springs Resort. Amanda M. Stinchecum, p. 20
Mar 24 Shopper's World: "Indian Art from the Northwest." Susan H. Loomis, p. 6
Jun 2 "What's Doing in Seattle." Susan H. Loomis. p. 10
Sep 1 Fare of the Country: "In the Northwest, Sturgeon Is King." Susan H. Loomis, p. 6
Dec 29 Fare of the Country: "Feasting on Dungeness Crab." Susan H. Loomis, p. 6
1984 Jan 15 "Comeback for a Seattle Landmark." Olympic Hotel. Wallace Turner, p. 38
Jul 29 Fare of the Country: "Savoring Seattle's Salmon." Susan H. Loomis, p. 12

SUNSET
1985 May "From Icarus to Space Shuttle, the Saga of Flight in Seattle." Seattle's Museum of Flight. p. 54
Jun "New Hydrofoil Service: Seattle to Victoria to Vancouver B.C." p. 33
Jul "Snowfields and Meadows on a Classic Olympic Park Hike." Wildlife Images Rehab & Educational Center. p. 52
1984 Jun "The Olympic Peninsula." p. 98

TRAVEL/HOLIDAY
1984 Apr "Spokane—the all-American City." H. Shaw McCutcheon, p. 54
May "Mount St. Helens." From the ashes, a park. Earl Clark, p. 6

WEST VIRGINIA

Background Reading

Cohen, Stan B.   HISTORIC SITES OF WEST VIRGINIA
Pictorial Hist, 1979.

Williams, John A.   WEST VIRGINIA
One of a series of popular histories for each state published as part of the Bicentennial observance in 1976. Norton, 1976. Also *West Virginia and the Captains of Industry* (1976), which covers the period 1880-1913, the era of coal, oil, timber, and railroad barons.

Novels

Eberhart, Mignon G.   FAMILY FORTUNE
"Story of intricate relationships and loyalties split by the Civil War" and a struggle to gain control of the family plantation. (FC) Random, 1976.

Ehrlich, Leonard   GOD'S ANGRY MAN
Fictionalized story of John Brown, the fanatical foe of slavery, and the raid on Harper's Ferry. S&S, 1932.

Grubb, Davis   THE NIGHT OF THE HUNTER
Suspense novel of a young boy pitted against an evil man masquerading as "the preacher," who wants the boy to reveal information about hidden money. This was made into a great movie with Robert Mitchum as the menace. Har-Row, 1953.

Knowles, John   A VEIN OF RICHES
West Virginia in 1909, and the boom time for the coal industry. Little, 1978.

Pancake, Breece D'J.   THE STORIES OF BREECE D'J. PANCAKE
Short stories—"a dark Faulknerian view of contemporary West Virginia hill life
. . .with a naturalist's sensitivity." (FC) Little, 1983.

Phillips, Jayne Anne   MACHINE DREAMS
"The transformations [of] individuals and . . . society as a whole" from years of the depression to the Vietnam War—a "postmodernist" family saga. (FC) Dutton, 1984.

Settle, Mary Lee   THE KILLING GROUND
FS&G, 1982. Final novel of a five-book saga by a leading contemporary writer. *The Beulah Quintet* traces a family and the land for 300 years. Prior titles are *Prisons* (1973), *O Beulah Land* (1956) (see "Virginia"), *Know Nothing* (1960) and *The Scapegoat* (1980).

TRAVEL ARTICLES

BON APPETIT
1984 May "Around the Alleghenies." Crafts, food, inns. Shirley Slater, p. 28

EARLY AMERICAN LIFE
1985 Aug "Early American Destinations: Blennerhassett." Caroline Auvergne, p. 49

ESQUIRE
1984 Jun "The Enlightened Traveler." Plying the old-time arts (Appalachian crafts). Ronni Lundy, p. 34

N.Y. TIMES SUNDAY TRAVEL SECTION (X)
1985 Mar 31 Fare of the Country: "Ramp Feasting in West Virginia." Lind Jeffries, p. 6

1984 Mar 25 "Life's Comforts Carry the Day at Greenbrier." West Virginia's pala-
tial resort. Phyllis Lee Levin, p. 14

TRAVEL/HOLIDAY
1985 Oct "West Virginia: A State of Extremes—Country Roads That Take Us
Home." Brenda Chapin, p. 56

WISCONSIN

Background Reading

Abrams, Lawrence and Kathleen   **EXPLORING WISCONSIN**
Rand, 1983.

Current, Richard N.   WISCONSIN
One of a series of popular histories for each state published as part of the
Bicentennial observance in 1976. Norton, 1977.

Derleth, August W.   WALDEN WEST; RETURN TO WALDEN WEST
"Remembered scenes and remembered village people . . . sights and sounds and
smells" of the river town Sac Prairie. See also books by Derleth under "Novels,"
below. (BRD) Duell, 1962, 1970.

Engelmann, Ruth   LEAF HOUSE: DAYS OF REMEMBERING
Memoir of a Finnish immigrant family in Rivier during the 1920s and '30s—the
author leaves at eighteen for Milwaukee to work as a domestic and later to attend
university. Har-Row, 1982.

Leopold, Aldo   SAND COUNTRY ALMANAC
Essays for each month of the year about the author's Wisconsin farm—a classic
of nature/ecology writing. Oxford U, 1949.

**Logan, Ben   LAND REMEMBERS: THE STORY OF A FARM AND
ITS PEOPLE**
Remembrance of growing up on a Wisconsin farm in the 1920s and '30s, and the
farm itself as it changes through the seasons. Viking, 1975.

Olsenius, Richard and Zerby, Judy   WISCONSIN TRAVEL COMPANION
A unique guide to the history along Wisconsin highways. Bluestem, 1983.

Olson, Sigurd F.   OPEN HORIZONS
Youth on a Wisconsin farm in the far northern part of the state, by a leading
nature writer/philosopher. Knopf, 1969. Also *Wilderness Days* (1972).

Stein, Shifra   GAS-SAVING GETAWAYS LESS THAN TWO HOURS FROM GREATER MINNEAPOLIS-ST. PAUL
The trips within a two-hour range spill over into Wisconsin. Har-Row, 1982.

Umhoefer, Jim   GUIDE TO WISCONSIN'S PARKS, FORESTS, RECREATION AREAS AND TRAILS
Northword, 1982.

Novels

Derleth, August W.   THE HILLS STAND WATCH
Marriage of an easterner to a Wisconsin tradesman and life in a mining village in the 1840s. Duell, 1960. Also *Wind Over Wisconsin* (1938) and *Still Is the Summer* (1937). *Sac Prairie People* (1948) and *Wisconsin Earth: Sac Prairie Sampler* (1948) are, respectively, a collection of the author's short stories and an anthology of selections from his novels.

Ellis, Mel   THE WILD RUNNERS
Story of an Indian half-breed who fits in neither with the white nor Indian societies, and the half-dog/half-coyote he befriends. HR&W, 1970.

McPherson, William   TESTING THE CURRENT
A story seen through the eyes of a seven-year-old boy at his family's island summer home in 1939, and his gradual awareness that family members and friends are not what they seem to be. S&S, 1984.

Wescott, Glenway   THE GRANDMOTHERS
Cosmopolite grandson recreates his pioneer background from keepsakes of his family—"a series of fragmentary narratives welded . . . into a moving chronicle." (FC) Har-Row, 1927. Also *Good-bye Wisconsin* (1928), short stories.

TRAVEL ARTICLES

EARLY AMERICAN LIFE
1984 Feb "Kilbournton House: a Modest Marvel." Greek revival house in Milwaukee. Alex Thien, p. 74

GOURMET
1985 Apr Gourmet Holidays: "Inns of the Midwest, Part II." Mimi Elder, p. 48

NATIONAL GEOGRAPHIC TRAVELER
1985 Summer "Wingding at Oshkosh." The annual aircraft fly-in. Tom D. Crouch, p. 50
Winter "Wisconsin's Birkebeiner: Cross-country Ski Racing at Its Best." Thomas B. Allen, p. 108
1984 Spring "Wisconsin: Say "Cheese." Visit a cheese factory and rediscover a picturesque rural America. Rebecca Kirtland, p. 6

N.Y. TIMES SUNDAY TRAVEL SECTION (X)
1985 Aug 25 "Wright's (Frank Lloyd) Legacy in Wisconsin." An excursion to Taliesin and beyond. John Welchman, p. 9
Sep 29 Fare of the Country: "Finding Wisconsin's Old-style Cheeses." Betty Fussell, p. 6

TRAVEL/HOLIDAY
1985 Oct "Sights and Sounds of Southwestern Wisconsin." More than just a pasture land. Patricia Brooks, p. 60

WYOMING

Background Reading

Baxter, Robert   NATIONAL PARKS, VOLUME 2
Guide to Yellowstone Park. Rail-Europe-Baxter, 1984.

Burt, Nathaniel   JACKSON HOLE JOURNAL
Memoir of a poet-novelist-composer of life in Jackson Hole in the 1920s and 30s when his writer parents managed a dude ranch. U of Oklahoma Pr, 1983.

Calkins, Frank   JACKSON HOLE
History, reminiscences, yarns and observations that "read like racy talk around the campfire." Knopf, 1973.

Craighead, Frank C.   TRACK OF THE GRIZZLY
A study of the grizzly bear at Yellowstone. Sierra Club, 1982.

Haines, Aubrey L.   THE YELLOWSTONE STORY
A history of America's first national park by a retired park historian and touching on major themes in American history as well. Colorado Association U Pr, 1977.

Larson, Taft A.   WYOMING
One of a series of popular histories for each state published as part of the Bicentennial observance in 1976. Norton, 1984 (first published 1977).

MacAdams, Cliff   GRAND TETON NATIONAL PARK
Guide and reference book. Caxton, 1983.

Miller, Don   GHOST TOWNS OF WYOMING
Pruett, 1979.

Morris, Jan   PLACES
This collection of travel essays by a leading travel writer includes an essay on Wyoming. HarBraceJ, 1973.

**Sanborn, Margaret   THE GRAND TETONS: THE STORY OF THE MEN
WHO TAMED THE WESTERN WILDERNESS**
Informative and exciting history of the area—Lewis and Clark, Indians, fur trade, cattle raising and rustling, outlaws, the Grand Tetons in fiction, and so on. Putnam Pub Group, 1978.

Schullery, Paul   MOUNTAIN TIME
"A splendid private tour of [Yellowstone Park]" by an author who worked there as a ranger-naturalist—reminisces about his experiences as a ranger and casts a "jaded eye at the American tourist." (PW) Schocken, 1984.

Williamson, Chilton   LIFE IN THE OVERTHRUST
The author of *Saltbound* (see entry under "Rhode Island") ventures to the "overthrust belt" of Wyoming—"colorful and trenchant observations on American types and lifestyles . . . ranchers, oil-field roughnecks, law-and-order politicians." (BRD) S&S, 1982.

Novels

Baird, Thomas   POOR MILLIE
A handsome drifter and his rich new wife on a backpack trip in Wyoming—"vivid description of a rough terrain." (BRD) HR&W, 1978.

Durham, Marilyn   THE MAN WHO LOVED CAT DANCING
The hero is an ex-Army officer, just released from prison for the murder of those who killed his Indian wife (Cat Dancing), and is now intent upon robbing a train. The heroine is fleeing her husband and plans to take that train but is kidnapped by the robbers instead. Set in the Wyoming territory in the 1880s. HarBraceJ, 1972.

Hogan, Ray   THE DOOMSDAY TRAIL
A United States marshal is on the trail of killers—one a beautiful woman—and walks into an ambush. Doubleday, 1979.

James, Will   SAND
The regeneration of a young man parallels that of the "capture and gentling of a black stallion"—written in cowboy vernacular and by an author familiar with that way of life. (FC) Scribner, 1929.

L'Amour, Louis   BENDIGO SHAFTER
"Marvelous mural of post-Civil War Wyoming and the people who settled it." (FC) Dutton, 1979.

Lutz, Giles   THE FEUD
A greedy banker connives to resurrect from Old West days the conflict between cattlemen and sheep ranchers. Doubleday, 1982.

MacInnes, Helen   REST AND BE THANKFUL
A wealthy widow is stranded in Wyoming because of a rainstorm, falls in love with the country and way of life, and stays. Little, 1949.

Ross, Dana F.   WYOMING!
Part of a series of novels with the overall title of *Wagons West* that chronicles the conquest and settlement of the American West. Bantam, 1982.

Schaefer, Jack   SHANE
Story of the stranger who comes into the life of a homesteading family, affects them all profoundly, and moves on. Houghton, 1954. Also *Collected Short Novels* (1967).

TRAVEL ARTICLES

GOURMET
1985 Aug "A Dude Ranch in Wyoming." Moose Head in Jackson Hole. Paul J. Wade, p. 46

NATIONAL GEOGRAPHIC TRAVELER
1985 Winter "Yellowstone—Wonderland at Zero Degrees." Visiting in winter. Rob Schultheis, p. 28
1984 Summer "Homage to Buffalo Bill." Historical center and museums devoted to Plains Indians, Western art, firearms, Buffalo Bill. Dee Brown, p. 46

N.Y. TIMES SUNDAY TRAVEL SECTION (X)
1985 Jan 13 "Going to School in Yellowstone." Jim Robbins, p. 19
Feb 17 "A Cattle Drive for Amateurs." Joan Chatfield-Taylor, p. 22
1984 May 6 "Floating on the Waters of Wyoming." A scenic raft trip on the Snake River. Curt Leviant, p. 26

SUNSET
1985 Jan "Yellowstone Winter . . . Magic." Uncrowded for skiing, wildlife, or geyser watching. p. 56
"Planning a Visit to Yellowstone." p. 54
Jul "Sinks Canyon State Park in Wyoming." p. 58
1984 May "Stamps and Envelope Art in Cheyenne." First Day Cover Museum. p. 34

TRAVEL & LEISURE
1984 Apr "The Grand and Glorious Tetons." A practical guide to a poetic place. G.S. Bush, p. 142

TRAVEL/HOLIDAY
1985 Sep "Backdoor Country—Entering the Real Outdoors." Targhee National Forest. C.J. Burkhart, p. 58

APPENDIX 1
Key to Source Codes
and Series Guides

AS   Asia Society
ARBA   American Review Book Annual
BL   Booklist
BP   Catalog from Book Passages (a travel book store)
CSM   Christian Science Monitor
JAS   Japanese-American Society
LJ   Library Journal
NYT   New York Times
NYTBR   New York Times Book Review Section
Publisher Publisher's catalog, ad, or cover copy
PW   Publisher's Weekly
SD   San Diego Magazine
TBS   Traveler's Book Society (a newsletter of reviews and commentary on travel books, now defunct)
TA   The Travel Agent (trade magazine)
TL   Travel & Leisure

American Express   American Express Pocket Guides (Simon & Schuster)
Baedeker   Baedeker Guides and Baedeker City Guides (Prentice-Hall and Auto Assn/British Tourist Assn)
Berlitz   Berlitz Pocket Guides (Macmillan)
Birnbaum   Birnbaum Guides, edited by Stephen Birnbaum (Houghton Mifflin)
Blue Guide   Blue Guides (Norton)
Companion Guide   Companion Guides (Prentice-Hall)
Country Orientation   By Alison Lanier, Intercultural Press, Inc. Series (intended for people planning to move to or live in a country)
Fielding   Fielding Guide Series (Morrow)
Fisher   Fisher Annotated Guides (New American Library)
Fodor   Fodor Guides (McKay)
Frommer   Frommer Guides (Simon & Schuster)
Insight   Insight Guides (Prentice-Hall)
Let's Go   Harvard Student Agency Guides (St. Martin)
Lonely Planet   Lonely Planet and "On-A-Shoestring" Guides
Michelin   Michelin Green Guides only (Michelin)
Nagel   Nagel's Encyclopedia Guides (Nagel Switzerland/Hippocrene)

U.S. Government

Available from U.S. Government Printing Office, using Catalog SB-166, 302 and 093, 1986 edition. ("Area Handbooks" are available in many libraries, and are redesignated "Country Studies" as they are revised; "Background Notes" are short, factual pamphlets written by the State Department; "Pocket Guides" are produced by the Department of Defense for military personnel; "Post Reports" are a State Department series for orientation of diplomatic personnel)

APPENDIX 2
EDITORIAL AND
RESEARCH NOTES

Traveler's Reading Guide is an informal, "derivative" bibliography, consisting largely of data collected from standard bibliographic sources and rearranged and edited for a specific audience.

The editorial perspective is that of a compulsive travel reader and library user, compiling information for armchair travelers who do not have the patience, library skills or eyesight to do it for themselves.

It is intended to provide a time-saving tool for librarians who recommend reading to travelers, armchair travelers, travel professionals. It can also be simply handed to the general reader/traveler to do his own browsing, much as one browses in a library for a title or subject that is intriguing. Adult services librarians have used the original paperback edition in connection with travel film programs and for counseling the. many retirees who travel extensively.

The *Reading Guide* provides a unique reference and idea source for writers and travel writers, as well as a supplementary resource for the growing number of ' travel management degree programs and courses in junior and senior colleges. Travel agents and tour operators can use the *Reading Guide* to provide suggested reading lists for their clientele. Elementary and high school librarians can use it to assist teachers and students in country study projects.

This book was previously published by Freelance Publications as a three-volume paperback, under the same title: *Traveler's Reading Guide—Volume 1 (Europe), Volume 2 (North America), Volume 3 (Rest of the World)*. This hardcover edition has been considerably revised and expanded.

Each reading list is arranged in several sub-sections:

Background Reading Primary sources for books listed under "Background Reading" are the standard library review media (*Booklist, Publisher's Weekly, Library Journal*) and the compilation of reviews in *Book Review Digest*, plus the various volumes of *Books in Print*. Occasionally the source is a travel book or article, the *New York Times*, or the publisher's catalog or ad copy. In addition to these primary sources, titles were culled from some selective bibliographies (such as *Good Reading, Good Books*, etc.) as well as from just plain browsing around in the bookstacks.

Some categories of travel reading were excluded entirely, or with only an occasional exception. Excluded are: guides that are purely guidebooks for hotels and/or restaurants, bed and breakfast guides, the vast literature of guides for outdoor travel (hikers, backpacking, trail guides, etc.), those specifically geared to children, "how-to-travel" guidebooks, maps, cruising guides.

Obviously, however, many of the books listed include information from these excluded subject areas.

Most of the purely photographic travel books are excluded, with exceptions made when material for the area is skimpy, or when the text is of particular interest because of its author or the particular approach.

Excluded also, with a few exceptions, is the whole body of contemporary writings by eighteenth- and nineteenth-century travelers and explorers. But I do list books *about* such people.

Series Guidebooks The series included are those that are well-known among travelers and/or cover many geographic areas. Newer or less comprehensive, less well-known series (Robert Kane, Barbie Engstrom, etc.) are listed under Background Reading or Background Reading-Guidebooks.

Novels Sources for books are the 10th edition (plus supplements) and 11th edition of *Fiction Catalog, Book Review Digest*, selective bibliographies, suggestions from travel writers and readers. Some of the lengthier lists for novels have been shortened to include primarily books with twentieth-century settings.

To solve the dilemma of the inordinate quantity of books with settings in England, the book lists only novels that are designated as having a specific setting within England (London, Cornwall, etc.). Appendix 3 provides additional information to assist readers in locating additional England-set novels and mysteries in their libraries.

Travel Articles The major travel magazines (*National Geographic, National Geographic Traveler, Travel/Holiday, Travel & Leisure*) plus the *New York Times Sunday Travel Section* are included, along with a selected list of general interest magazines widely held by public libraries, such as *Gourmet, Americana, Essence, Vogue, Yankee*. The articles listed cover 1984 and 1985. Article titles are generally explicit. In cases where they are not I've added parenthetical clarification. Articles were selected by scanning the medium itself, rather than using either *Reader's Guide* or *Magazine Index*.

General The book is divided into five main sections. Some decisions as to where a particular country should be listed were arbitrary; I tried to make these decisions with the typical traveler in mind rather than the geography student. Thus Hawaii is listed under the U.S. (rather than the Pacific), Mexico under Latin America (even though a part of North America), and Turkey and Egypt under the Middle East (instead of Europe and Northern Africa).

A professor of African history suggested the division of Africa into northern, southern etc., as a way to deal with the myriad countries and name changes over the past few decades. (However, I did not take her advice on Egypt. It is listed under the Middle East because my feeling is that's how travelers perceive it; the overlapping literature also made this decision seem logical.)

Appendices provide additional useful information both for librarians and for the general reader who wishes to explore further some aspect of travel reading.

The Author Index was added to Volume 3 of the original paperback series (because it was the single, most often mentioned suggestion I received from readers) and is continued in this new, revised edition.

APPENDIX 3
ENGLAND

Background Reading and Guidebooks

Those with a particular interest in England should be sure to check the catalogs of Salem House Publishers and the Merrimack Publishers' Circle in Topsfield, Massachusetts. They represent many British publishers, and their catalogs reveal a constant stream of intriguing titles for Great Britain, as well as series guides (such as the AA series, Nicholson Tourist Guides, etc.) not included in this book.

Novels and Mysteries

Because of the inordinate number of novels and mysteries with an English setting, only a limited number are listed herein—those for specific places within England (London, Cornwall, etc.)

Fortunately for Anglophiles, there are many fine literary guides for travelers, with which they can explore the works and lives of suchclassic and standard British authors as Dickens, Austen, Trollope, Hardy and Lawrence. These are listed under "England—Literary Guides."

Then you can use the following list of authors who have written mysteries, novels, and short stories, with an English setting, compiled from the 20th Century-England, Family Chronicles, and Mystery and Detective Stories categories of *Fiction Catalog*. It provides a convenient, alphabetized checklist for locating additional novels and mysteries, which may have English settings, at your library. Some of the authors listed below may also be included in one or more of the literary guides as well, thus providing additional information about place settings of plots or places relevant to the authors' lives. In parentheses are alternate names under which the author has written books.

*This indicates that the author is designated as having written in the mystery and detective story genre, in case your library separates this genre from the general fiction.

**Miss Read is the pseudonym for Dora Jessie Saint, author of a series of truly addictive novels about life in an English village. I do not know the actual county where her fictional Caxley, Fairacre, Thrush Green are; they've been referred to as "West Country" or "Cotswold" villages.

Aiken, Joan
*Aird, Catherine
*Allingham, Margery
*Amis, Kingsley
*Anderson, James
*Anderson, John R.L.
Anthony, Evelyn
Archer, Jeffrey
*Babson, Marian
Bagnold, Enid
Bainbridge, Beryl
Banks, Lynne Reid
*Bannister, Jo
Barker, Pat
*Barnard, Robert
Bates, H.E.
Bawden, Nina
Beckett, Samuel
*Bell, Josephine
Benson, E.F.
*Bentley, E.C.
Bentley, Ursula
Berckman, Evelyn
Bermant, Chaim
Billington, Rachel
Binchy, Maeve
Blackstock, Charity
Bottome, Phyllis
Bowen, Elizabeth
Braddon, Russell
Bradford, Barbara T.
Braine, John
*Brand, Christianna
Brent, Madeleine
*Brett, Simon
Brookes, Owen
Brookner, Anita
Brown, Christy
Bruce, Leo
Buchan, John
*Burley, W.J.
Butler, Gwendoline
*Cadell, Elizabeth
Campbell, Ramsey
*Candy, Edward
*Cannell, Dorothy
*Canning, Victor
Carr, J.L.

*Carter, Youngman
*Carvic, Heron
Cary, Joyce
*Charteris, Leslie
*Chesterton, G.K.
*Christie, Agatha
Clarke, Anna
Clarkson, Ewan
*Cleary, Jon
Clifford, Francis
*Cody, Liza
Colegate, Isabel
Compton-Burnett, Ivy
Cooke, Judy
Cookson, Catherine (Catherine Marchant)
Cooper, William
Crane, Teresa
*Creasey, John (J.J. Marric)
Crichton, Michael
Crisp, N.J.
*Crispin, Edmund
Cronin, A.J.
*Cutter, Leela
*Davies, L.P.
*Dean, S.F.X.
Deighton, Len
Delderfield, R.F.
*Delving, Michael
*Derleth, August
Dewhurst, Eileen
*Dexter, Colin
*Dickinson, Peter
Disch, T.M.
Donleavy, J.P.
Drabble, Margaret
DuMaurier, Daphne
Durrell, Gerald
Eden, Dorothy
Edwards, G.B.
*Egleton, Clive
*Ferrars, E.X.
*Fleming, Joan
Follett, Ken
Forster, E.M.
Forster, Margaret
Fowles, John
*Fox, Peter
*Francis, Dick

Frankau, Pamela
*Fraser, Antonia
Freeman, Cynthia
*Fremlin, Celia
Galsworthy, John
Gardner, John
*Garfield, Leon
*Garve, Andrew
*Gash, Jonathan
Gaskin, Catherine
Gee, Maggie
Gibbons, Stella
Gilbert, Anna
*Gilbert, Michael
Gilliatt, Penelope
*Giroux, E.X.
Gloag, Julian
Godden, Jon
Godden, Rumer
Godwin, Gail
Golding, William
Goudge, Elizabeth
Graham, Winston
Greene, Graham
*Grimes, Martha
Haines, Pamela
Hanley, James
Hardwick, Mollie
Harris, Marilyn
Harrison, Harry
*Harrison, Ray
Harrison, Sarah
*Haymon, S.T.
*Heald, Tim
Heath, Catherine
*Heyer, Georgette
*Hill, Reginald
*Hilton, James
*Hilton, John B.
Hoban, Russell
Holland, Isabelle
Holt, Victoria
Horwood, William
Hough, Richard
*Household, Geoffrey
Howard, Elizabeth Jane
Howatch, Susan
*Hunter, Alan

Huxley, Aldous
Huxley, Elspeth
*Innes, Michael (J.I.M. Stewart)
Jagger, Brenda
*James, P.D. (Phyllis D. White)
*Jeffreys, J.G.
Johnson, Pamela Hansford
Jolley, Elizabeth
Jones, Mervyn
Jordan, Lee
*Keating, H.R.F.
Kennedy, Lena
*Kenney, Susan
Kyle, Duncan
Laker, Rosalind
LeCarre, John
*LeMarchand, Elizabeth
Lessing, Doris (Jane Somers)
Lively, Penelope
Llewellyn, Richard
Lodge, David
Lofts, Norah
*Lovesey, Peter
Lyall, Gavin
Macdonald, Malcolm
*MacDonald, Phillip
MacInnes, Colin
MacKenzie, Donald
MacKintosh, Elizabeth (Josephine Tey)
McMullen, Mary
Mankowitz, Wolf
Marchant, Catherine (Catherine Cookson)
*Marric, J.J. (John Creasey)
*Marsh, Ngaio
Masters, John
Maybury, Anne
Melville, Anne
*Meyer, Nicholas
*Michaels, Barbara (Elizabeth Peters)
*Milne, A.A.
*Mitchell, Gladys
Moore, Brian
*Morice, Anne
Mortimer, John
Mortimer, Penelope
*Moyes, Patricia
Murdoch, Iris
Naylor, Charles

*Oliver, Anthony
Orwell, George
*Parrish, Frank
Pearce, Mary E.
Pearson, Diane
Pearson, John
*Perowne, Barry
*Perry, Anne
*Peters, Elizabeth (Barbara Michaels)
Phillips, Dee
Pilcher, Rosamunde
Powell, Anthony
*Priestley, J.B.
Pritchett, V.S.
Pym, Barbara
Pynchon, Thomas
*Quest, Erica
*Radley, Sheila
Raymond, Ernest
Rayner, Claire
**Read, Miss
Read, Piers Paul
*Rendell, Ruth
Rhys, Jean
Rock, Phillip
*Ross, Jonathan
Ross, Malcolm
Rubens, Bernice
Sackville-West, Victoria
*Sayers, Dorothy L.
Scholefield, Alan
*Selwyn, Francis
Sharp, Margery
*Shaw, Howard
Shelby, Graham
Sillitoe, Alan
*Simpson, Dorothy
*Snow, C.P.
Somers, Jane (Doris Lessing)
Spark, Muriel
Stevenson, D.E.

Stewart, J.I.M. (Michael Innes)
Stewart, Mary
Stirling, Jessica
Storey, David
Struther, Jan
*Stubbs, Jean
*Symons, Julian
*Taylor, Andrew
Taylor, Elizabeth
*Tey, Josephine (Elizabeth MacKintosh)
Thane, Elswyth
Theroux, Paul
Thirkell, Angela
*Thomas, June
*Tine, Robert
*Tourney, Leonard
Trapido, Barbara
*Underwood, Michael
Van Slyke, Helen
Veryan, Patricia
Wain, John
Walpole, Hugh
*Watson, Colin
Waugh, Evelyn
Waugh, Hilary
Way, Peter
Weldon, Fay
Wells, H.G.
Wesley, Mary
White, Patrick
White, Phyllis D. (P.D. James)
Whitney, Phyllis A.
Williams, Emlyn
Wilson, A.N.
Wilson, Angus
Winch, Arden
Wodehouse, P.G.
*Woods, Sara
Woolf, Virginia
*Yorke, Margaret
Zilinsky, Ursula

INDEX

bbey, Edward 155, 509, 539, 545, 558, 559, 773, 775
bbott, Helen 576
be, Kobo 120
ber, Ted 703
bish, Walter 270
brahams, Peter 25, 29
brams, Kathleen 791
brams, Lawrence 791
brams, Richard I. 707
chebe, Chinua 35, 36
ckerley, J. R. 96
ckerman, Diane 543, 699
cuff, Roy 761
dams, Alexander B. 534
dams, Alice 584
dams, Arthur Gray 704
dams, Edward B. 134
dams, Henry 245, 605
dams, Jane 720
dams, Richard 446
dams, Robert M. 206
dams, Samuel H. 715
dams, Thomas Boylston 501
dams, William H. 781
damson, Joy 10
gee, James 548, 763
gee, Joel 268
gnew, Spiro T. 605
gnon, S. Y. 340
gutter, Jenny 213, 567
hlborn, Richard E. 691
idala, Thomas 570, 575
iello, Roger 611
iken, Joan 256, 284, 351
ikman, Lonnelle 603
jar, Emile 256
jayi, J.F. 35
ksyonov, Vasily 362, 366
kutagawa, Ryunosuke 120
larcon, Pedro A. de 379
laska Geographic Soc 550
laska Geo Staff 551
lba, Victor 467

Albery, Nibuko 120
Albrand, Martha 181, 720
Albright, Priscilla 705
Albright, Rodney 705
Albury, Paul 422
Aldred, Cyril 48
Aldrich, Bess S. 638, 689
Aldridge, James 158, 394
Alegria, Ciro 455, 468
Aleichem, Sholem 192
Alexander, Robert J. 449, 453
Alexander, Sidney 314
Algren, Nelson 628, 631, 648, 697
Alisky, Marvin 469
Alland, Alexander, Jr. 34
Alleman, Richard 569
Allen, Charles 1, 96
Allen, Everett S. 665
Allen, Hervey 750
Allen, Philip M. 5
Allen, Steve 82
Alpine, Lisa C. 515
Alter, Stephen 104
Alther, Lisa 763
Alvarez, A. 690
Amado, Jorge 456
Ambler, Eric 69, 113, 284, 388, 428
Ambrose, Stephen E. 685
Ames, Evelyn 665
Amfitheatrof, Erik 306
Amin, Mohamed 130
Amis, Kingsley 217, 229
Amory, Cleveland 662
Amos, H. D. 279
Anand, Valerie 105
Anatoli, A. 366
Andayn, Barbara 128
Andayn, Leonard 128
Anderson, Elizabeth B. 657
Anderson, Jervis 707
Anderson, Jessica 158

Anderson, John L. 409
Anderson, Moira 348
Anderson, Patrick 606
Anderson, Sherwood 742
Anderson, V. S. 642
Andrews, Clarence A. 534, 637
Andrews, Michael A. 444
Andrews, Raymond 618
Andric, Ivo 398
Anstee, Margaret J. 453
Anthony, Evelyn 256, 270, 317, 322, 410
Antunes, Antonio L. 29
Appelfeld, Aharon 181
Apple, R. W., Jr. 168
Appleberg, Marilyn 569, 604, 628, 662, 712
Applewhite, E. J. 604
Arbeiter, Jean 511
Archer, Jeffrey 217
Arciniegas, German 400, 403
Ardagh, John 168, 199, 245, 267, 306, 396
Arguedas, Jose Maria 468
Armah, A. K. 36
Armstrong, Bruce 484
Arnold, Elliott 196, 559, 700
Arnold, Eve 501
Arnold, William 138
Arnopoulos, Sheila M. 495
Arnow, Harriette 642, 674
Aronson, Theo 186, 204
Arrigo, Joseph A. 644
Arrigoni, Patricia 572
Arrington, Leonard J. 774
Arthur, Elizabeth 105, 488
Asch, Sholem 48, 58, 320, 341, 720
Ash, Timothy G. 338
Ashe, Geoffrey 209
Ashford, Bob 102
Ashmore, Harry S. 561

Ashton-Warner, Sylvia 165
Asturias, Miguel A. 428, 429
Athearn, Robert G. 594, 639
Attenborough, David 17, 72, 112, 149, 155, 464, 465
Attenborough, Richard 101
Atwood, Margaret 410, 492, 495
Auchincloss, Louis 720, 755
Auden, W. H. 80, 292
Austin, Clifford 155
Austin, R. W. J. 39
Avedon, John F. 141
Awdry, W. 209
Awoonor, Kifi 36
Azuela, Mariano 437

Babbitt, Bruce 556
Babcock, Judy 408, 436, 512
Babin, Maria Teresa 415
Babson, Marian 217
Bach, Ira J. 628
Bachman, Ben 522
Bacon, David 209
Baden-Powell, Dorothy 334
Baehr, Consuelo 721
Bagley, Desmond 13, 20, 165, 437
Bailes, Carlton 768
Bailey, Anthony 169, 186, 201, 330, 598, 741
Bailey, Brian 205
Bailey, George 267
Bailey, John 572
Bailey, Paul 622
Bain, David H. 132
Bainbridge, Beryl 201, 229, 230, 367, 394
Baines, John 46
Baird, Thomas 794
Bajcar. A. 339
Bakalinsky, Adah 572
Bake, William A. 531
Baker, Carroll 1
Baker, P. R. 306
Balcolm, Mary 551
Balderson, Eileen 205
Baldwin, James 415, 721
Balfour, Michael D. 208
Ball, John 105, 579, 718, 788
Ballard, J. G. 86
Ballard, Todhunter 559
Ballinger, William Sanborn 145
Balzac, Honoré de 254
Bambara, Toni C. 619
Bancroft, Hunt N. 544

Banerji, Bibhutibhushan 105
Banis, V. J. 576
Banks, Carolyn 606
Banks, F. R. 215
Banks, Oliver 668
Banks, Russell 414, 612, 694
Banta, Richard E. 534
Barash, Asher 340
Barber, Chris 392
Barber, Noel 49, 85, 104, 256
Barber, Richard 169
Barber, W. T. 392
Barbour, Philip L. 781
Barclay, Glen St. John 151
Barich, Bill 214, 310, 564
Barjavel, Rene 448
Barker, Elizabeth 178
Barker, Shirley 755
Barlow, Elizabeth 707
Barnard, Christiaan N. 26, 29
Barnard, Robert 335
Barnes, Joanna 580
Barnett, Lincoln 704
Barr, Pat 86, 97, 118
Barracliffe, Ron 693
Barratt, P. J. 422
Barret, Andre 281, 310
Barrett, John G. 712
Barrett, Leonard E. 407
Barrett, Norman 39
Barrett, William E. 86, 105, 270
Barrette, Roy 650
Barrie, J. M. 351
Barrington, Carol 768
Barroll, Clare 384
Barroso, Memo 436
Barry, Tom 403, 426
Bart, Peter 775
Barth, John 659
Barzini, Luigi 72, 169, 307
Bar-Zohar, Michael 606
Basche, James 138
Baskin, John 741
Bassani, Giorgio 315
Basso, Hamilton 646, 757
Batchelor, John C. 448
Bates, Daniel G. 39
Bates, H. E. 77, 254
Batman, Richard 539
Batt, Cara M. 644
Batterberg, Ariane 707
Batterberg, Michael 707
Battle, Lois 619
Bauer, Douglas 637
Baum, Vicki 274
Bawden, Nina 23, 69, 217
Baxter, Robert 436, 512, 551, 556, 569, 573, 612, 793

Bayer, Patricia 512
Bayer, William 23, 721
Bazak Guide to Israel 57
Beach, Edward L. 474, 599
Beadle, Muriel 201
Bean, George E. 68
Beardsley, R. K. 119
Beasley, W. G. 119
Beattie, Ann 599
Beatty, Michael 535
Beaubelle, Marcy 598
Beauvoir, Simone de 256
Bebey, Francis 3, 36
Beck, Henry C. 696
Becker, Jurek 274
Becker, Peter 26
Becker, Stephen 77, 87
Beckett, Samuel 303
Beckwith, Lillian 355
Bedford, Sybille 432
Bedi, R. 101
Beebe, Morton 571
Begley, Eve 348
Behrman, S. N. 181
Beirne, Francis F. 657
Belasco, Lionel 410
Belfrage, Sally 97
Bell, James B. 707
Bell, Jimmy 679
Bell, Madison S. 721
Bell, Mimi 746
Bellamann, Henry 683
Bellamy, Frank 408
Bellonci, Maria 74
Bellow, Paul 52, 346, 631
Bellwood, Peter S. 151
Beloff, Nora 361
Bence-Jones, Mark 209
Benchley, Nathaniel 666, 70
Benchley, Peter 410, 425, 437, 718
Bendersky, Joseph W. 270
Bendiner, Elmer 373
Benedetti, Mario 469
Benedict, Ruth 115
Benedict, Stewart 510
Benet, Stephen Vincent 694
Bennett, Isobel 156
Bennett, Margie 533
Benningfield, Gordon 206
Benson, Elizabeth 444
Bentley, Ursula 230
Benton, Christine M. 526
Benvenisti, Meron 52
Beny, Roloff 171, 309
Berchen, William 424
Beresford-Howe, Constance 492
Berg, Francie M. 740, 760
Berger, Bennett M. 564
Berger, Philip 629
Berger, Terry 512

ger, Thomas 270, 721
kow, Ira 629
litz, Charles F. 424
man, Eleanor 712
mant, Chaim 217, 354
mont, John 171
nal, Ignacio 433
nard, Jack F. 314
nays, Anne 668
nen, Robert 300
nstein, Burton 45
nstein, Ken 174
nstein, Richard 79
riault, Gina 584
ry, Don 747
ton, Kathleen 364, 478
ton, Pierre 499
sonette, Colin 617
ton, Henry 664
ancourt, Romulo 470
hel, Elizabeth R. 756
hell, Nicholas 52
rati, Mukherjee 97
well, Bruce 297
ler, M. 192
rs, William R. 279
ington, James H. 358
ington, Rachel 217
chy, Maeve 217, 300
ding, Paul 530
gham, Hiram 466
ney, Marcus 169
nie-Clark, G. 498
ns, Richard 249
yon, Michael 359
y, Casares A. 450
d, Isabella L. 127, 133
ningham, Stephen 564, 32, 707
hop, John M. 102
hop, Patrick 446
hop, Witherow 446
gnani, J. D. 118, 622
sell, Richard 535
by, William 777
ler, Norma 76
rnhof, Karl 197
rn, Thyra F. 384
ck, Gavin 93, 128
ck, Harry G. 629, 634
ck, Laura 352
cklock, Les 677
ckstock, Charity 290, 353
ckwood, Sir Robert 139
ir, Leona 58
ir, Walter 501
is, Marie Claire 495
isdell, Paul H. 693
ise, Clark 97
ke, Robert 199
ke William A. 532
nchet, Christian 707

Blandford, Linda 63
Blasco-Ibanez, Vincente 377
Blatty, William P. 606
Bledsoe, Jerry 736
Bleything, Dennis 746
Blicker, Seymour 496
Bliven, Bruce 704
Bloch, Alfred 338
Bloch, Michael 422
Blofield, John 139
Blood, Marje 746
Bloodworth, Dennis 79
Bloom, Harry 29
Bloom, Joel A. 768
Blount, Roy 530
Blum, Carol O'Brien 683
Blum, Ethel 612
Blume, Judy 595
Blumenthal, Susan 5
Blunden, Caroline 79
Bly, Carol 677
Blythe, Ronald 202, 205
Boatner, Mark M. 507
Bobrow, Jill 404
Bocking, D. H. 498
Bode, Carl 657
Bodelsen, Anders 197
Bodine, John J. 699
Bogarde, Dirk 113, 252, 580
Bogue, Margaret B. 535
Bohm, Robert 97
Boissard, Janine 252, 257
Bojer, Johan 336, 740
Böll, Heinrich 271
Bonanno, Margaret W. 730
Bonavia, David 79
Bond, Creina 446
Bone, Robert W. 157, 164, 622
Bones, Jim 765
Bonnifield, Paul 535
Bookbinder, Bernie 706
Boone, Sylvia A. 35
Boorstin, Daniel J. 501
Boot, Adrian 407
Borer, Mary C. 214, 217
Borges, Jorge L. 450, 451
Borie, Marcia 569
Borland, Hal G. 523, 594, 595, 683
Bosse, Malcolm 87
Boston Society of Architects 663
Bosworth, David 653
Bothwell, Robert 479
Botkin, Benjamin A. 707
Bottigheimer, Karl S. 300
Botting, Douglas 169, 365, 454
Bottomley, Frank 209
Boulle, Pierre 87, 140, 256
Boulnois, Luce 86

Boulton, Roger 475
Bourne, Marjorie 172
Bourne, Peter 172, 413
Bowen, Elenore S. 36
Bowen, Elizabeth 218, 231, 297, 309
Bowen, Ezra 564
Bowles, Paul 23
Bowman, John 282
Boyd, Blanch M. 758
Boyd, James 737
Boyd, William 13, 36
Boyer, G. G. 554
Boyle, Katherine 271
Boyle, Robert H. 704
Boyle, T. Coraghessan 36, 577
Brackman, Arnold C. 47
Bradbury, Ray 631
Braddon, Russell 233
Bradford, Ernie D. 199, 376
Bradford, Richard, 700
Bradley, David 243, 750
Bradley, Jeff 532
Braganti, Nancy L. 171
Bragin, Joan 520
Brain, Robert 8
Braine, John 234
Brand, Max 496
Brandon, James R. 74
Brandon, Jim 512
Brandys, Kazimierz 338, 340
Branston, Richard 203
Brant, Michelle 573
Brata, Sasthi 97
Braudel, Fernand 169
Braun, Matthew 640, 745
Brautigan, Richard 577, 584, 685, 747
Brawley, Ernest 437
Bredsdorff, Jan 82
Brehl, John 478
Brenan, Gerald 373, 375
Brennan, Joseph 622
Brent, Madeleine 87, 144, 225, 257, 322, 410
Brereton, Peter 209
Breslin, Jimmy 730, 731
Brett, Simon 354
Brewster, Barney 447
Breytenbach, Breyten 26
Bridge, Ann 290, 343, 398
Bridgeman, Harriet 172
Briggs, Asa 212
Brilliant, Richard 311
Brink, Andre 29, 29
Brink, Carol 627
Brinkley, William 769
Briskin, Jacqueline 580, 675
Bristow, Gwen 566, 577, 584, 646, 758

British Tourist Authority 512
Britton, Dorothy 118
Broadfoot, Barry 476
Brodrick, Alan 18
Brody, Elaine 179, 186, 209, 267, 307, 330, 386
Brokhin, Yuri 359
Bromfield, Louis 105
Broner, E. M. 58
Bronte, Charlotte 187
Brook, Paula 488
Brook, Stephen 711, 765
Brookes, Owen 218
Brooklyn Botanical Gardens 512
Brookner, Anita 218, 388
Brooks, Earle 462
Brooks, Gwendolyn 632
Brooks, John 401
Brooks, Rhoda 462
Brooks, Van Wyck 523
Brough, James 673
Broughton, T. Allen 715
Broven, John 644
Brower, Charles D. 551
Brower, Kenneth 145, 146
Brown, Allen D. 650
Brown, A. Theodore 682
Brown, Bruce 544
Brown, Christy 218, 304
Brown, Claude 707
Brown, Dale 551
Brown, Dee 540, 561, 685
Brown, George M. 355
Brown, Hamish M. 202
Brown, Jan 118
Brown, Joseph E. 774
Brown, J. P. S. 691
Brown, Reeve Lindbergh 779
Brown, Reginald A. 169
Brown, Richard D. 661
Brown, Rita Mae 549, 750
Brown, Rosella 680
Brown, Wesley 731
Browning, Robert 68
Brownstone, David M. 506, 707
Bruccoli, Matthew J. 432
Bruce, Curt 644
Bruckner, Christine 271
Bruemmer, Fred 472
Brunhouse, Robert L. 434
Bruning, Nancy 408, 436
Bruns, Bill 576
Bryan, C. D. B. 134
Bryant, Sir Arthur 199
Bryher 20, 218, 318, 320, 388
Bryson, William 172
Buchan, John 69, 336, 353, 354, 474, 500

Buchanan, Keith M. 79
Buchwald, Ann 250
Buchwald, Art 250
Buck, Marcia C. 566
Buck, Pearl S. 87, 134
Buck, Peter H. 147
Buckland, Gail 19, 41
Buckley, William F., Jr. 218, 271, 274, 367
Buechner, Frederick 758
Buell, John 479
Bull, George 309, 312
Bulliet, Richard 66
Bullock, Alice 699
Bullock, John 63
Bulwer-Lytton, Sir Edward G. 320
Bunch, Roger 426
Bunch, Roland 426
Bunting, James 269
Burchardt, Bill 562
Burgess, Anthony 128, 319, 708, 721
Burke, Clifford 786
Burke, J. F. 191
Burke, John 199
Burke, Michael 769
Burl, Aubrey 208
Burman, Ben Lucien 535
Burn, A. R. 279
Burn, Mary 279
Burnett, Gene M. 610
Burnford, Sheila 492
Burns, E. Bradford 402, 455
Burns, James MacGregor 515
Burns, Olive Ann 619
Burns, Rex 595
Burroughs, Polly 665
Burrows, Millar 53
Burt, Nathaniel 793
Burton, Neil 210
Buruma, Ian 115
Busch, Frederick 653,715
Busch, Niven 584
Busch, Noel F. 749
Buschow, Rosemarie 64
Bush, Lawrence 721
Bushnell, Oswald A. 624
Butler, Gwendoline 218, 231, 367, 370
Butler, Lionel 210
Butler, Robert O. 700
Butler, Ron 540
Butterfield, Fox 79
Byrd, Richard E. 447
Byrne, Dawson 298
Byrne, Donn 87
Byrne, Peter 22, 186, 249, 331

Cadell, Elizabeth 105, 218, 257, 380

Cadet, J. M. 139
Cadwallader, Sharon 433
Caffrey, Kate 661
Cahill, Susan 298
Cahill, Thomas 298
Caird, Janet 353
Calder, Jenni 540
Caldwell, Bill 651
Caldwell, Erskine 619
Caldwell, Taylor 43, 286, 320, 754
Calhoun, James 644
Calhoun, Nancy H. 644
California Coastal Commiss 575
Calisher, Hortense 549, 72
Calkins, Frank 793
Callahan, North 762
Callwood, June 476
Cambios, Ruth 736
Cameron, Ian 447, 448, 459
Cameron, Nigel 93
Cameron, Roderick 158
Campbell, Pamela 569, 714
Camus, Albert 20, 21, 332
Canadian Universities Trav Service 478
Canby, Henry Seidel 602
Canby, Vincent 783
Candy, Edward 218
Canetti, Elias 22
Canning, Victor 197, 218, 226, 344, 353
Cannon, Le Grand 694
Cantor, George 535
Caplow, Theodore 535
Capon, Robert F. 706
Capote, Truman 549, 647
Capps, Benjamin 745
Capstick, Peter H. 5
Caputo, Philip 14
Caraman, Guy 334, 533
Caraman, Philip 465
Cardiff, Sara 779
Carey, Neil G. 488
Cargill, Morris 407
Carim, Enver 5
Carlisle, Henry 666
Carlson, Loraine 436
Carmer, Carl 548, 704, 715
Carnell, Hilary 207
Caroli, Betty B. 506
Carothers, Annabel 355
Carpenter, Andrew 298
Carpentier, Alejo 414
Carr, Archie 610
Carr, Carolyn K. 741
Carr, J. L. 235
Carr, Pat 575
Carr, Philippa 380
Carr, Stephen L. 774
Carrier, Rock 496

rion, Arturo M. 409
roll Gladys Hasy 653
roll, James 274, 606,
·53, 668
·ruth, Gorton 510
·ter, Hodding 530
·ter, Jenny 351
·ter, John 150
·ter, Lillian 97
·ter, Paul A. 447
·tnal, Alan 567
·toun, Susan 713
·y, Beth 646
·y, Joyce 36, 36, 226
·ey, John 638
·ey, Robert L. 545
·h, Wilbur J. 530
·imati, Nina 8, 12, 17,
·03
·o, Alfonso 434
·tellanos, Rosario 438
·tries, René de la Croix
·47
·stro, Josue de 456
·ther, Willa 496, 595, 689,
·00
·to, Nancy 159
·tton, Bruce 530,674
·dill, Harry M. 641
·unitz, William J. 721
·ute, David 26
·vers, Mark 77, 127, 139
·am, C. W. 39, 279, 307
·vantes, Miguel de 377
·almers, John W. 482
·amberlain, Holly 507
·amberlain, Russell 309
·amberlin, E. Russel 314
·amberlin, Russell 210
·ambers, Andrea 512
·ambers, S. Allen 523, 527,
·530, 540
·and, Meira 120
·andler, David 172
·andler, Raymond 438, 580
·anning, Steven A. 641
·antraine, Pol 484
·apman, Alexandra 173
·apman, Colin 190
·arters, Samuel 34
·aryn, Jerome 721
·ase, Heman 693, 777
·ase, John C. 644
·ase, Mary Ellen 55, 653
·atwin, Bruce 36, 394, 449,
·456
·eeseborough, G. R. 677
·eetham, Sir Nicolas 437
·eever, John 715
·en, Jack 83
·en, Jo-Hsi 87
·en, Yuan-Tsung 87

Chernov, V. A. 364
Chesanow, Neil 172
Chesler, Bernice 663, 664
Chesnoff, Richard Z. 132
Chester, Carole 566, 713
Chester, Carol 622
Chew, Peter 641
Chiang, Yee 115
Ch'ien, Shung-Shu 87
Childress, Alice 722, 758
Childs, David 270
Childs, Marquis 535, 637
Chiles, Webb 147
Chilton, Lance 699
Chinweizu 1
Chopin, Kate 648
Chowder, Ken 747
Choy, Bon-Youn 134
Christgau, John 678
Christian, Glynn 148
Christie, Agatha 49, 225,
410
Christie, B. 484
Christopher, John 300
Christopher Robert C. 115
Christy, Jim 551
Churchill, W. S. 212
Chute, Carolyn 653
Chute, Patricia 666
Cirino, Linda D. 511, 708
Claiborne, Robert 507
Clancy, Ambrose 300
Clancy, Judith 250
Clark, Charles E. 651
Clark, Eleanor 18, 309, 779
Clark, James 26
Clark, John R. 622
Clark, Leonard F. 466
Clark, Mary Higgins 606, 666,
697, 722
Clark, Norman H. 786
Clark, Ronald W. 179, 307,
387
Clark, Walter Van Tilburg
691
Clarke, Anna 219
Clarke, Desmond 299
Clarke, Richard 701
Clauser, Suzanne 635
Clavell, James 93, 94,
121, 128
Clayre, Alasdair 79
Clayton, Barbara 523, 661
Clayton, Peter A. 47
Cleary, Jon 105, 151, 159,
319, 367, 683
Cliff, Michelle 415
Clifford, Frances 274
Clifford, Peggy 594
Cline, Francis X. 711
Cloete, Stuart 29
Clogg, R. 284

Coates, Austin 93
Coates, Felicia 768
Cobb, Jocelyn 492
Coburn, Broughton 102
Cochran, Alice C. 594
Cochran, Thomas C. 749
Cochrane, Hugh F. 535
Cody, Liza 219
Cody, Morrill 250
Coe, Evan 501
Coe, Wilbur 699
Coetzee, J. M. 30
Coffer, William E. 556
Coffin, Robert P. Tristram
651
Cohan, Tony 94
Cohen, Marjorie A. 401
Cohen, Stan B. 789
Colby, Constance T. 711
Cole, Hubert 406
Cole, Jean M. 499
Cole, Toby 310, 312
Cole, Tom 571
Coleberd, Frances 566
Colegate, Isabel 231
Coleman, Lonnie 549, 619
Coleman, Terry 159, 666, 722
Colette 255, 257
Colijn, Helen 330
Collier, Richard 269
Collins, Larry 53, 97, 245,
722
Collins, Robert 498
Collis, Maurice 76
Colwin, Laurie 722
Combs, Ann 786
Comini, Allesandra 179
Commager, Henry Steele 516
Committee of the Junior
League 610
Condon, Richard 377
Conklin, William 444
Conkling, Philip W. 651
Conley, Cort 627
Connell, Evan S. 683
Conners, Bernard F. 715
Connery, Donald S. 195, 294
Connolly, Edward 779
Connor, Judith 118
Conot, Robert E. 674
Conover, Robert 571
Conrad, Barnaby 377
Conrad, Jean-Baptiste 431
Conrad, Joseph 8, 128, 151,
256, 377
Conrad, Peter 502
Conrad, Rebecca 575
Conroy, Pat 758
Constance, Diana 280
Constantine, K. C. 750
Converse, Gordon 55
Conway, Martin 736

Coo, Bill 478
Cook, Chris 209
Cook, James E. 556
Cook, Robin 668, 722
Cook, Thomas H. 775
Cooke, Alistair 502
Cooke, Hope 102
Cooke, Judy 219
Cookridge, E. H. 67, 169
Cookson, Catherine 228, 230
Coolican, Don 204
Coon, Carleton 18, 39, 41
Cooney, Ellen 667
Cooper, Adrianne 502
Cooper, Dominic 293
Cooper, Michael 115, 119
Cooper, Nanthapa 139
Cooper, Robert M. 139, 206
Cooper, William 219
Coover, Robert 750
Coppel, Alfred 66, 121
Cordell, Alexander 87, 394
Corman, Avery 722, 731
Cornelisen, Ann 311, 315
Cornell, Tim 39, 307
Cornwell, Bernard 377
Cornwell, Ilene J. 679, 762
Corrington, John W. 647
Corser, Frank 150
Corser, Rose 150
Cortazzi, Hugh 116
Cortes, Carlos E. 610
Cosic, Dobric 398
Costain, Thomas B. 320, 479, 648
Costantini, Humberto 451
Cotterell, Arthur 279
Cotterell, Geoffrey 330
Cottrell, Alvin J. 64
Cottrell, John 431
Coulson, David 26
Courdy, Jean C. 115
Courier Journal 641
Court, Artelia 298
Courtauld, Caroline 77
Courter, Gay 456, 722
Cousteau, Jacques 445, 462
Cousteau, Richard 445
Covarrubias, Miguel 112
Cowan, Walter G. 645
Coward, Noel 152
Cowles, Virginia 362
Cowley, Joy 165
Cox, Brian 604
Cox, Christopher 610
Cox, Thornton 13, 28, 57, 249, 282, 299, 311, 343, 375, 408
Coxe, George H. 464
Cozzens, James G. 612
Craig, Gordon A. 267
Craig, Jo Ann 127

Craighead, Frank C. 793
Crain, Mary Beth 570
Crane, Stephen 284, 300
Crane, Teresa 219
Crankshaw, Edward 181, 363
Crapanzano, Vincent 26
Craton, Michael 423
Craven, Margaret 489
Cravens, Gwyneth 722
Crawshaw, Nancy 283
Creekmore, Betsey 762
Creigh, Dorothy W. 688
Creighton, Donald 476
Crewe, Quentin 19
Crichton, Michael 8
Crichton, Robert 315, 352
Crispin, Edmund 227
Criswell, Colin 137
Critchfield, Richard 49
Cromie, Alice H. 507, 540
Cromie, Robert 629
Cronin, A. J. 88, 230, 352, 388, 394
Cronin, Vincent 314
Cronkite, Walter 530
Crookston, Peter 199, 205
Crosby, Harry 435
Crosby, John 722
Crosland, Margaret 174
Cross, Anthony 359
Crossland, John 280
Crow, John A. 280, 373
Crowe, Sylvia 97
Crowl, Philip A. 210, 351
Crump, Donald J. 477, 551
Culbertson, Judi 250
Cullinan, Elizabeth 304
Culp, John H. 701
Cultural Assistance Center Staff 713
Cummings, A. L. 661
Cunha, Enclides da 454
Cunningham, E. V. 580
Cunningham, John T. 697
Current, Richard N. 791
Currie, Sheldon 486
Curry, Jane 535
Curson, Julie P. 749
Cutler, Irving 629
Cutter, Leela 234
Cyman, Bina 423
Cyprien, Michael 212

Daglish, Robert 365
Dagneaux, Christine 533
Dahm, Bernard 113
Daiches, David 207, 349
Dailey, Janet 554
Dakers, Caroline 215

Dale, Tim 213
Daley, Robert 254, 255, 70 722
Dallas, Sandra 564
D'Alpuget, Blanche 128
Dalton, Bill 112, 127
D'Amato, Albert C. 651
D'Amato, Miriam F. 651
Danforth, Kenneth C. 79
Daniel, Glenda 634
Daniel, Joseph 512
Daniell, Jo 156
Daniels, Dorothy 249
Daniels, Jonathan 603
Daniken, Erich von 146
Darcy, Clare 187
Dard, Bertrand 707
Dark, Eleanor 159
Dary, David 535
Daudet, Alphonse 21, 388
Davenport, John C. 765
Davenport, Marcia 723, 75
Davenport, T. R. H. 28
Davenport, William 280
David-Neel, Alexandra 14
Davids, Richard C. 490
Davidson, Basil 1, 3, 5
Davidson, J. W. 146
Davidson, John 765
Davidson, Lionel 58
Davidson, Marshall B. 704
Davidson, Robyn 156
Davies, Hunter 215
Davies, Norman 339
Davies, Rhys 394
Davies, Robertson 388, 47* 492, 493
Davies, Valentine 723
Davis, Burke 530
Davis, Chuck 488
Davis, Gregson 403
Davis, H. L. 747
Davis, John G. 94
Davis, Kenneth S. 639
Davis, Maggie 24
Davis, Margo 403
Davis, Norah Deakin 536
Davis, Peter 536, 741
Davis, Tom 543
Davis-Gardner, Angela 48
Daws, Gavan 148, 622
Day, Arthur Grove 147, 1! 153, 622
Day, Catharina 299
Day, Ingeborg 179
Day, Robert 640
Dayan, Moshe 55
Dayan, Yael 58
Daymond, Douglas 496
Dazai, Osamu 115
Deal, W. 210
Dearstine, Howard 782

eBlassis, Celeste 577, 659
ebo, Augie 744
eBoissiere, Ralph 410
eBorchgrave, Arnaud 369, 606, 614
eBreffny, Brian 294
eCombray, Richard 19, 41, 313
edijer, Vladimir 397
edmon, Emmett 629
eedy, John 520
eFelitta, Frank 723
eGaury, Gerald 72
eighton, Len 199, 219, 257, 274, 580
eindorfer, Robert G. 202
eKeijzer, Arne J. 85
elacorta 257
eLaguna, Frederica 472
elaney, Edmund 523
elaney, Frank 298
elaney, Jack 612
e La Roche, Mazo 493
elbanco, Nicholas 779
el Castillo, Michel 377, 379
elderfield, R. F. 219, 227, 394
elehanty, Randolph 566, 573
eLisle, Gordon 156
elving, Michael 228
emaris, Ovid 692
eMente, Boye 119, 556
emery, Leroy W., Jr. 119
emetz, Hana 192
eMille, Nelson 301, 718, 723
emos, John Putnam 523
empsey, Michael 39
eMuth, James 629
enker, Henry 723
ennis, Nigel 311
ennis, Patrick 723
ennis, Philip 375
enton, Kit 30, 159
eren, Maya 406
erleth, August W. 791, 792
ermout, Maria 113
erry, T. K. 196, 212, 335
esai, Anita 105, 105
eSilva, Colin 136
e Silva, K. M. 136
etwiler, Donald S. 270
eVere, John 34
everell, William 489
evine, Elizabeth 171
evine, Laurie 49
e Voto, Bernard A. 502, 540
eVries, Peter 599, 638
ew, Robb F. 683, 742
eWohl, Louie 315
exter, Colin 231

Dexter, Pete 751
Diaz del Castillo, Bernal 434
Dibner, Martin 651
Dickerman, Pat 512
Dickinson, Charles 675
Dickinson, Mary B. 79
Dickinson, Peter 36, 66, 152, 153, 219, 284, 355, 414
Dicks, Brian 282, 283
Dickson, Harry E. 663
Didion, Joan 429, 577, 580
DiDonato, Georgia 562
DiDonato, Pietro 723
Diehl, Charles 68
Dietz, Lew 651
Dill, Marshall, Jr. 250, 270
Dillon, Anne F. 187, 682
Dillon, Eilis 295, 301
Dillon, Richard 571
Dimbleby, Jonathan 53
Dimond, E. Grey, M.D. 83
Dinesen, Isak 2, 10, 197
Dintenfass, Mark 731
Diop, Cheikh Anta 48
Diqs, Isaak 53
Dirksen, D. J. 567
Disch, T. M. 219
Disney, Doris M. 783
Diubaldo, Richard J. 472
Dixon, Mim 551
Djilas, Milovan 398
Dmytryshyn, Basil 366
Dobai, Peter 289
Dobie, J. Frank 202, 433, 545
Doblin, Alfred 274
Dobyns, Henry F. 467
Doctorow, E. L. 715
Dodd, Edward 151
Dodds, Gordon B. 746
Doder, Dusko 396
Dodge, Ernest S. 146, 651
Doerr, Harriet 438
Doig, Ivan 554, 685, 686, 786
Dolci, Danilo 311
Doll, John 74
Dolson, Hildegarde 599
Donaldson, Gordon 491, 704
Donleavy, J. P. 220, 301, 304
Donner, Florinda 470
Donoso, Jose 460
Doolittle, Jerry 530, 533, 545
Dore, Ronald P. 116
Dorian, Marguerite 346, 347
Dorsett, Lyle W. 594
Dorsey, John R. 657

Dos Passos, John 343, 454, 502, 606, 647, 723
Doss, Margot Patterson 573
Dostoevsky, Fyodor 370
Dotson, Bob 502
Douglas, Colin 354
Douglas, Lloyd C. 59, 320
Douglas, Marjory S. 610
Douglas, Norman 24, 311, 318
Douglas, Raymond 494
Dourado, Autran 456
Douskou, Iris 280
Dow, Mary-Lou 663
Dow, Richard A. 754
Dowdey, Clifford 781
Downs, Hugh R. 102
Doyle, Sir Arthur Conan 456, 775
Drabble, Margaret 207, 220
Draeger, Alain 454
Dreiser, Theodore 632, 635, 715, 751
Drewe, Robert 159
Driscoll, Peter 21, 94
Driskill, Frank 768
Drucker, Peter F. 181
Drummond, Emma 106
Drury, Allen 45, 49, 606
Drury, John 629
Du' Arte, Jack 645
DuBois, David G. 49
DuBois, Jacques 246
DuBois, W. E. B. 5
DuBoulay, Juliet 280
Dubus, Elizabeth N. 647
Dudman, Helga 53
Duerrenmatt, Friedrich 389
Duffield, Judy 604
Duffy, Maureen 220
Duggan, Alfred 320
Duggan, Ervin S. 606
Duggan, William R. 476
Dumas, Alexandre 332, 361
DuMaurier, Daphne 205, 225, 226, 301, 317
Dumbleton, Susanne 704
Dumont Guide to Ireland 299
Dumont Guide to Paris & the Isle De France 251
Dumont Guide to the French Riviera 249
Dumont Guide to the Greek Islands 283
Duncan, Andrew 40
Duncan, David J. 747
Duncan, Robert L. 121
Duncan, William 139
Duncan, W. R. 140
Dunham, Katherine 406
Dunne, John G. 580
Dunnett, Dorothy 352
Durant, David N. 736

Durant, Mary 509
Durham, Marilyn 701, 794
Durham, Philip 543
Durrell, Gerald 17, 449
Durrell, Lawrence 45, 49, 247, 252, 283, 284, 311, 389, 396, 398
Durso, Joseph 708
Dyk, Ruth 556
Dyk, Walter 556
Dykeman, Wilma 737, 762, 762
Dykstra, Robert R. 639
Dyson, John 148, 473

Eagle, Dorothy 207
Eastlake, William 701
Eastman, John 172, 507
Eban, Abba 53
Eberhard, Wolfram 86
Eberhardt, Isabelle 21
Eberhart, Mignon G. 415, 599, 790
Eberhart, Philip 594
Eberle, Nancy 629
Ebersohn, Wessel 30
Eberstadt, Isabel 257
Echewa, T. O. 37
Eckert, Allan W. 491, 536, 742
Eco, Umberto 315
Edberg, Rolf 10
Edel, Leon 214
Eden, Dorothy 88, 159, 166, 197, 220, 224, 384
Edey, Maitland A. 521
Edgar, Donald 204
Edgeworth, Maria 301
Edmiston, Susan 708
Edmonds, I. G. 137
Edmonds, Paul 77
Edmonds, Walter D. 715
Edwards, Agustin 459
Edwards, Amelia B. 45
Edwards, Don 573
Edward, G. B. 224
Edwards, Lovitt F. 397
Egan, Lesley 580
Egerton, John 641
Eggleston, George T. 403
Eggleston, Hazel 403
Ehle, John 737, 737
Ehrenburg, Ilya 367
Ehrlich, Eugene 510
Ehrlich, Leonard 641, 790
Ehrlichman, John 606
Eisen, Jonathan 564
Eisner, Jack 338
Ekert-Rotholz, Alice 140, 159
Elder, Norman 445

Elegant, Robert 88, 92, 94
Elfman, Blossom 716
Eliade, Mircea 347
Eliovson, Sima 26
Elkin, Stanley 632, 723
Elling, Christian 309
Elling, David M. 704
Elling, Mel 792
Ellis, W. S. 540
Ellison, Joseph W. 146
Ellison, Ralph 723
Elman, Richard M. 290
Elon, Amos 45, 269
Elstob, Eric 384
Elvin, Mark 79
Elward, James 632
Emecheta, Buchi 37, 220
Encyclopaedia Brittanica 66
Endo, Shusaku 121
Engel, Frederic Andre 466
Engel, Howard 493
Engel, Marian 493
Engel, Paul 637
Engelmann, Ruth 791
Engstrom, Barbie 13, 47, 103, 136, 144
Enriquez, Helen 690
Entwistle, Frank 202
Eppenbach, Sarah 551
Epps, Garrett 783
Epstein, Jack 402
Epstein, Joseph 502
Erdman, Loula Grace 769
Erdman, Paul E. 43, 66, 607
Erdoes, Richard 540
Erickson, John R. 766
Ervin, Jean 677
Espy, Willard R. 787
Estes, William M. 769
Estleman, Loren D. 675
Evans, Humphrey 47
Evans, J. Martin 502
Evans, Peter 371
Evenson, Norma 250
Everhart, Ronald E. 556
Evers, Alf 704
Ewell, Judith 470

Facaros, Dana 283, 314, 375, 523, 527
Faessler, Shirley 493
Fagan, Brian M. 434
Fage, J. D. 6, 35
Fagyas, Maria 182, 274, 398
Fairbairn, Ann 648
Fairbanks, John K. 75, 79
Fairmont Park Art Assn. 749
Faison, S. Lane, Jr. 523
Fallaci, Oriana 284

Fallon, Peter 298
Falls, Joe 663
Fancher, Betsy 617
Far East Economic Review Staff 74
Farlow, Susan 521
Farrant, Leda 10
Farrell, James T. 632
Farrell, J. G. 106, 128
Farris, Jack 686
Farrow, Moira 476
Farwell, Byron 102
Fast, Howard 49, 581, 584, 599, 667, 751
Fatesinghrao, Gaekwad 97
Faulk, Odie B. 545, 556, 639
Faulkner, Virginia 688
Faulkner, William 645, 680, 763
Fawcett, P. H. 445
Feban, Patrick W. 513
Fedden, Robin 210
Feegel, John R. 619
Fegan, Patrick W. 513
Fehrenbach, T. R. 437
Feibleman, Peter S. 379, 645
Feiling, Keith G. 212
Feimling, Jean 564
Fein, Cheri 713
Feldkamp, Frederick A. 179, 246, 267, 295, 312, 331, 364, 373, 397
Feldman, Ellen 723
Fellows, Arnold 202
Fensom, Rod 513
Ferber, Edna 554, 631, 648, 716, 745, 770
Ferdon, Edwin N. 149
Ferguson, George W. 172, 21?
Ferlinghetti, Lawrence 571
Fermor, Patrick Leigh 169, 281, 404, 410
Fernea, Elizabeth W. 22, 40
Fernea, Robert A. 40
Ferns, Henry S. 450
Ferrars, E. X. 344
Ferris, William 679
Ferro, Robert 422
Feuchtwanger, Lion 321
Fielder, Mildred 760
Fielding, Xan 246
Fields, George 116
Fields, Jeff 619
Fields, Karen 757
Fields, Mamie G. 757
Figueiredo, Antonio de 344
Fillingham, Paul 404
Finch, Christopher 567
Finch, Robert 664
Findley, Timothy 271
Fine, David 564
Finegan, Jack 57

lay, Iain 148
layson, Graham 343
ley, Joseph E. 683
ley, M. I. 280
ney, Ben R. 148
estone, Linda 612, 781
cher, Al 216
cher, John 744, 766
cher, Louis 101
cher, Mildred 216
cher-Galati, Stephen A. 346
chler, Stan 708
choff, Martin 674
h, Robert L. 59
her, Dorothy Canfield 777
her, John 436
her, Lois H. 83, 207
her, M. F. K. 248, 250
her, Sidney 40
her, Vardis 627, 775
hlock, Trevor 97, 392
tell, Ira 513
zgerald, F. Scott 581, 718, 724
zgerald, Frances 502
zgerald, Valerie 106
zGibbon, Constantine 295
zgibbon, Russell H. 469
gg, Fannie 680
herty, Joe 731
anagan, Thomas 301
aubert, Gustave 25
eming, Ian 415
eming, Kevin 602
eming, Peter 72, 142, 455
eming, Thomas J. 629, 697
etcher, Colin 556, 564
etcher, John G. 561
etcher, Inglis 737
ood, Josephine 156
orey, Kitty B. 599
orinsky, Michael T. 366
ornoy, Bertrand 466
ower, John 207
ynt, Candace 737
llett, Ken 49
lson, Franklin 508
lson, Mary E. 508
otner, Hulbert 657
rbath, Peter 7
rd, Clebert 713
rd, Elaine 667
rd, Ford Madox 248
rd, Jesse Hill 763
rd, Hugh 250
rd, Norman D. 612
rd, Paul 697
rester, C. S. 9, 410, 429
rmwalt, Elizabeth 754
rmwalt, John 754

Forster, E. M. 45, 98, 106, 317
Forster, Margaret 226
Forsyth, Frederick 37, 257, 271, 367
Foster, Harry Latourette 433
Foster, Lawrence 545
Foster, Lee 575
Foster, Lynn V. 545
Foster, Nancy H. 768
Foster, Richard 210
Foulke, Patricia 524, 527
Foulke, Robert 527
Fowles, John 202, 208, 228, 231, 254, 284
Fox, Ted 708
Fox, Theron 774
Fox-Lockert, Lucia 400
Fradkin, Philip L. 540
Frady, Marshall 530
France, Anatole 49
Francis, Clare 254
Francis, Dick 30, 159, 336, 371
Frank, Anne 331
Frankau, Pamela 220
Franklin, Kay 635
Franklin, Miles 159
Frantz, Joe B. 766
Franz, Carl 436
Franz, Michael 142
Franzwa, Gregory M. 544
Fraser, Amy 348
Fraser, Antonia 353
Fraser, George M. 17, 106, 367, 684
Fraser, John 83
Fraser, Mary 116
Fraser, Nicholas 449
Fraser, Russell 67, 309, 359
Frassanito, William A. 749
Frater, Alexander 202
Frazier, Nancy 521
Freedman, Benedict 482
Freeling, Nicolas 252, 257, 271, 332
Freely, John 663
Freely, Maureen 69
Freeman, Catherine 584
Freeman, Cynthia 59
Freeman, Derek 146
Freeth, Zahrra 64
Fregnac, C. 250
French, Marilyn 231
Freuchen, Peter 474, 475
Freundenheim, Tom L. 511
Freyre, Gilberto 455
Fried, Albert 669
Fried, Elliott 690
Friedenberg, E. Z. 476
Friedrich, Otto 269
Frisch, Max 389

Frison-Roche, Roger 336
Frolic, B. Michael 80
Frome, Michael 509, 533
Frost, A. N. 661
Frost, Jack 663
Frost, Peter 436, 467
Fry, Helen 1
Fry, Plantaganet S. 210, 351
Fuentes, Carlos 377, 438, 438
Fugard, Athol 30
Fuller, Chet 531
Fuller, Hoyt W. 34
Fuller, Iola 675
Fuller, John 394
Funnell, Charles E. 697
Furneaux, Rupert 484
Futcher, June 571

Gaan, Margaret 83, 88
Gaasch, Irene 575
Gafni, Shlomo S. 57
Gaines, Ernest J. 647
Gainham, Sarah 179, 182
Gajudsek, R. E. 250
Galbraith, John K. 492
Galbraith, W. O. 461
Gale, John 34
Gallenkamp, Charles 434
Gallery, John A. 749
Gallico, Paul 257, 319
Gallo, Max 314
Galloway, David 577
Galvan, Manuel de Jesus 410
Gambino, Thomas 361
Gandhi, Indira N. 98
Gangemi, Kenneth 433
Gannett, L. S. 598
Garcia, Connie 408
Garcia Marquez, Gabriel 461
Gardiner, Muriel 179
Gardner, Erle Stanley 435
Gardner, John 220, 233, 275, 716, 751, 779
Gardner, Mona 121
Gardner, Roberta 512
Garfield, Bee 706
Garfield, Brian 367, 559, 724
Garreau, Joel 404, 502
Garrison, Chuck 435, 436
Garrity, D. A. 301
Garside, Evelyn 85
Garside, Roger 80
Garve, Andrew 69
Gary, Romain 9, 257, 271
Gash, Joe 632
Gash, Jonathan 229, 301, 319, 322

Gaskin, Catherine 220, 301, 377, 410
Gaster, Harold 206
Gates, John D. 602
Gauguin, Paul 149
Gavin, Catherine 160, 438, 577
Gavron, Daniel 53
Gazaway, Rena 641
Gebhard, David 567
Gedge, Pauline 50
Gelb, Arthur 171, 714
Gelb, Norman 200
Geld, Ellen B. 456
Gelderman-Curtis, C. 331
Gellhorn, Martha 14, 438
Genet, Jean 254
Gentry, Curt 571
Gernes, Sonia 678
Gerrick, David J. 741
Gershkoff, Ira 605
Gerson, Noel B. 763, 783
Giacosa, G. 314
Gibbon, Lewis G. 352
Gibbons, Robert 102
Gibbons, Stella 233
Gibney, Frank 116
Gibson, Arrel Morgan 699
Gibson, Morris 482
Gide, Andre 7
Gidley, M. 787
Gifford, John 349
Gifford, Thomas 669, 678
Gilbert, Elizabeth R. 605, 657, 781
Gilbert, Martin 56
Gilbert, Michael 227
Gilead, Zerubavel 53
Giles, Janice H. 642, 745
Gill, Bartholomew 304
Gill, Brendan 568
Gillesplie, Jane 230
Gilliatt, Penelope 230
Gilman, Dorothy 30, 69, 88, 94, 189, 389, 655, 716
Gilmore, Robert C. 693
Gilpatrick, Gil 651
Gipson, Fred 770
Giraudoux, Jean 258
Gironella, José Maria 377
Girouard, Mark 206
Given-Wilson, Chris 210
Givin, Yolande 617
Gladwin, Mary Jane 208
Glasgow, Ellen 783
Glass, Mary Ellen 690
Glassman, Paul 428
Glazebrook, Philip 67, 69, 170
Gleasner, Bill 531, 629
Gleasner, Diane C. 531, 629
Gleason, Bill 567

Glen, Jan 20
Glen, Simon 20
Glickman, Toby 713
Gloag, Julian 224
Glover, Janet R. 351
Glyn, Anthony 246
Gmelch, Susan 298
Godden, Jon 98, 106, 229, 378
Godden, Rumer 98, 106, 106, 152, 153, 220, 225, 233, 315
Godey, John 315
Godwin, Gail 221, 380, 737
Gold, Herbert 564, 577, 742
Goldberger, Paul 708
Goldenson, Suzanne 513
Golding, William 45, 202, 234, 282, 331
Goldman, Albert 455
Goldman, James 724
Goldman, Michael 512
Goldman, William 581, 724
Goldreich, Gloria 724
Goldstein, Arthur D. 724
Goldwater, Barry 556
Gonzalez, Catherine T. 768
Good, Merle 749
Goodlad, Douglas 205
Goodrum, Charles A. 607
Goodwin, June 26
Goodwin, Stephen 783
Gordimer, Nadine 30, 66
Gordon, Caroline 642
Gordon, Noah 59, 724
Gordon, R. L. 724
Gordon, Rene 3
Gordon, Richard 221
Gordon, Sheila 30, 348
Gordons, The 581
Gorenstein, Shirley 434
Gornick, Vivian 46
Goslinga, Cornelis 464
Gosner, Kenneth L. 521
Gosner, Pamela 404
Gottlieb, Robert 543, 774
Goudge, Elizabeth 166, 227, 229, 231
Gougaud, Henri 46
Gould, John 651, 654
Gould, John A. 655
Gould, Laurence M. 447
Gould, Lois 451
Goulden, Joseph C. 134
Gourguechon, Charlene 146
Gourse, Leslie 713
Gouvion, Colette 46
Goytisolo, Juan 378
Grabowicz, Paul 568
Grady, James 607, 686
Graham, Alan 646
Graham, Peter 172

Graham, Robert 374
Graham, Winston 206, 207, 225, 225, 394
Graham-Campbell, James 1
Gramont, Sanche de 34, 246
Grant, Maxwell 160
Grant, Michael 280
Grass, Gunter 271, 272
Grau, Shirley Ann 647, 648
Graves, John 766
Graves, Robert 286, 321
Gray, Basil 98
Gray, Daniel S. 548
Gray, Francine du Plessix 367, 629
Gray, Robert 217
Gray, Seymour, M.D. 64
Gray, William R. 148
Grayson, Richard 258
Greeley, Andrew M. 632
Green, Ben 610
Green, Gerald 367, 559, 718, 731
Green, Hannah 742
Green, Henry 301
Green, Kerry 186, 211, 249, 299, 331
Greenan, Russell H. 669
Greenberg, Arnold 408, 428, 455, 470
Greenberg, Harriet 408, 424, 455, 470
Greenberg, Joanne 595, 595
Greenberg, M. 331
Greenberg, Marilyn 331, 632
Greenburg, Dan 724
Greene, A. C. 766
Greene, Annie 659
Greene, Graham 34, 37, 182, 246, 378, 414, 433, 438, 451
Greene, Suzanne E. 657
Greenfield, Darby 113
Greenfield, Robert 724
Greenleaf, Stephen 581
Grekova, I. 367
Greverus, James 747
Greverus, Jane 567, 787
Grey, Loren 540
Grey, Zane 559, 596, 775
Gribble, F. A. 343
Griffin, Arthur 524
Griffin, Gwyn 318
Griffin, James 149
Griffin, Thomas K. 645
Griffith, Bill 632
Griffith, John C. 293
Griffith, Susan 68, 74
Griffiths, Thomas 594
Grimm, Michele 570
Grimm, Tom 570
Grindal, Richard 355

Grisham, Noel 768
Groom, Winston 647
Grose, Peter 53
Grossfeld, Stan 665
Grosvenor, Donna K. 781
Grubb, Davis 790
Gruening, Ernest 551
Gruliow, Leo 364
Grumbach, Doris 394, 581
Grumley, Michael 422
Grunfeld, Frederic V. 179, 269
Grunfeld, Nina 216
Grusa, Jiri 192
Guareschi, Giovanni 315
Guerard, Albert 249
Guest, Judith 675
Guinness, Desmond 604
Guiraldes, Ricardo 451
Gulbranssen, Trygve 336
Gulik, Robert van 88
Gundy, Elizabeth 486
Gunn, Peter 309, 315
Gunnarsson, Gunnar 293
Gunther, John 179, 186, 267, 338, 364, 400
Gurney, A. R. 669
Gurung, K. K. 102
Gusikoff, Lynne 511
Gutheim, Frederick 603
Guthrie, A. B. 686
Guy, Rosa 725
Gyles, Anna 434

Haag, Michael 48, 282, 513
Haagen, Victor B. 548
Haas, Ben 182
Habe, Hans 253, 322
Hachette Guide to France 249
Hadas, M. 315
Haggard, H. Rider 9
Hagstrom, Jerry 504
Hahn, Emily 132
Hailey, Arthur 480, 577, 632, 648, 675
Hailey, Elizabeth Forsythe 770
Haines, Aubrey L. 793
Haines, Pamela 235
Halabi, Rafile 53
Halasz, Zoltan 289
Hale, Judson 524
Haley, James L. 766
Halkin, John 14
Hall, Adam 88, 94, 135, 140, 275, 341
Hall, D. G. E. 75, 77
Hall, Donald 693
Hall, Gerry 478
Hall, James N. 152, 153, 161

Hall, John W. 119
Hall, Oakley 438, 760
Hall, Richard 4
Halle, Louis J. 447
Hallowell, Christopher 645
Halsell, Grace 54
Hamilton, Alan 350
Hamilton, David 351
Hamilton, Marion 713
Hamilton, Virginia 548
Hamilton, Ronald 200
Hammer, David L. 211
Hammett, Dashiell 585
Hammond, Dorothy 4
Hamner, Earl 783
Hampel, Bet 562, 682
Hampl, Patricia 190, 677
Hamsun, Knut 336
Han, Suyin 80, 88, 89, 92, 106, 140, 142
Hanberg, Clifford A. 407
Handke, Peter 182
Handler, H. 179
Hane, Mikiso 116
Hanff, Helen 214, 711
Hanley, Clifford 348
Hanley, Gerald 10, 14, 106
Hanley, James 394
Hannah, Barry 549
Hannau, Hans W. 422
Hannesson, Gunnar 292
Hansen, Joseph 581
Hanser, R. 267
Hanson, Earl P. 400
Hansson, Carola 359
Harcourt, Palma 371
Hardie, Dee 657
Harding, Bertita 404
Harding, Vincent 506
Hardwick, Michael 207
Hardwick, Mollie 221
Hardy, Robin 355
Hardy, Ronald 30
Hareven, Shulamith 59
Harkabi, Y. 54
Harlow, Neal 564
Harman, Jeanne 404
Harmon, Carole 482
Harnack, Curtis 637, 638
Harner, Michael J. 462
Harper, Francis 610, 617
Harper, Peter 132
Harrer, Heinrich 142, 149
Harrigan, Stephen 770
Harrington, Donald 562
Harrington, Richard 447
Harrington, Ty 603
Harrington, William 272
Harris, Bill 709
Harris, Charlaine 763
Harris, G. 465
Harris, John 663

Harris, Joseph E. 3
Harris, Leonard 718
Harris, MacDonald 258, 474, 577, 585
Harris, Marilyn 227
Harris, Thomas 648
Harrison, David 26
Harrison, Harry 234
Harrison, Jim 675
Harrison, William 6
Harriss, Joseph 250
Har-Shefi, Yoella 54
Hart, Henry H. 74
Hart, Herbert M. 508
Hart, James D. 565
Hart, Robert S. 605
Harting, Emilie C. 207, 521
Hartog, Jan de 113, 128, 332, 751
Hartrich, Edwin 267
Harvester, Simon 66
Harvey, Andrew 142
Harwood, Michael 509, 598
Haskell, A. L. 189
Haskin, Gretchen 368
Hasluck, N. 160
Hassler, Jon 678
Hastings, Adrian 3
Hastings, Max 446
Hatada, Takashi 134
Hauser, Ernest O. 307
Hauser, Thomas 725
Haviaras, Stratis 285
Havighurst, Walter 536, 741
Hawes, Naomi 102
Hawke, David F. 540
Hawken, Paul 348
Hawkes, Jacquetta 50
Hawkins, Susan 746
Hay, Nelson E. 425
Hayden, Mike 573
Hayden, Torey 640
Hayes, Bob 513
Hayes, Edward 612
Hayes, Joseph 635
Hayter, Judith 376
Hazleton, Lesley 40
Hazzard, Shirley 318
Head, Bessie 30
Hearn, John 479
Hearn, Lafcadio 116
Hearon, Shelby 725, 770
Heat Moon, William L. 503
Heath, Catherine 221
Heaton, Vernon 661
Heatwole, Thelma 557
Heaven, Constance 232
Hebden, Mark 252, 255
Hebert, Anne 496
Hebert, Ernest 694
Hechtlinger, Adelaide 524, 527, 531

Heckert, Eleanor L. 414
Hedin, Sven 142
Heffer, Linda 297
Heidish, Marcy M. 667
Heine, Marc E. 339
Heine, Nancy J. 406
Heinl, Robert D., Jr. 406
Heller, Joseph 316, 607
Helms, Mary W. 428
Hemingway, Ernest 10, 14,
  250, 258, 316, 322, 374,
  378, 423, 613, 675
Heminway, John 2
Hemming, John 400, 466, 467
Henley, Gail 496
Henning, Alyson 598
Hennessy, Alistair 402
Henry, Will 559, 775
Henstell, Bruce 568, 645
Hentoff, Nat 725
Herbert, Frank 304
Herbert, Marie 448, 473
Herbert, Xavier 160
Herbstein, Denis 28
Herlihy, James Leo 725
Herlin, Hans 192, 272
Hermann, A. H. 192
Herrin, Lamar 438
Herring, Hubert C. 402
Herriott, James 206
Herron, Don 573
Herron, Shaun 352
Hersey, John 89, 321, 341,
  599
Hershman, Marc J. 787
Herzog, Arthur 755
Herzog, Chaim 58
Hesse, Herman 389
Hetherington, Paul 67
Heyer, Georgette 225, 232,
  233
Heyerdahl, Thor 17, 40, 148
Heym, Stefan 59
Heyward, DuBose 758
Hibbert, Christopher 4, 205,
  213, 309
Higginbotham, Jay 548
Higgins, George V. 669
Higgins, Jack 275, 322, 451
Higgins, Paul L. 174
Higgs, R. J. 533
High, Monique R. 368
Highland, Monica 581
Highwater, Jamake 438
Hildebrand, Volker 17, 28,
  77, 85, 103, 113, 119,
  136, 139, 157, 164, 408
Hill, David 211
Hill, Evan 693
Hill, Hamlin 501
Hill, Kathleen 521, 536, 541
Hill, Rebecca 680

Hill, Reginald 235
Hill, Sir G. F. 283
Hill, Susan 206
Hillaby, John 11, 170, 202,
  651
Hillary, Sir Edmund 98
Hiller, James 484
Hillerman, Tony 701
Hilling, John B. 392, 393
Hills, George 376
Hilton, James 144
Hines, Alan 770
Hingley, Ronald F. 359
Hinton, A. 93
Hinton, William 80
Hintze, Naomi A. 742
Hirschfield, Burt 718
Historic Santa Fe Foundation
  699
Hitchcock, Anthony 524, 544,
  545
Hitchcock, Henry-Russell 754
Hitchcock, John 102
Hitchens, Christopher 283
Hitchens, Dolores 647
Hitti, Philip K. 41
Hlasko, Marek 341
Hoagland, Edward 7, 488
Hoban, Russell 221
Hobson, Archie 503
Hobson, Laura Z. 718, 725
Hobson, Sarah 98
Hochhuth, Rolf 272
Hockney, David 84
Hodge, Allan 605, 657, 781
Hodge, Carola 605, 657, 781
Hodge, Jane A. 285, 318,
  344, 619
Hodgins, Eric 599
Hoffecker, Carol E. 602
Hoffman, Alice 718
Hoffman, Ann 376
Hoffman, Wilbur 541
Hoffman, William 331, 766
Hofmann, Paul 309, 513
Hofsommer, Don 637
Hogan, Ray 794
Hogan, William 559
Holden, David 64
Holden, Glenda 746
Holden, Ronald 746
Holden, Ursula 301
Holland, Wesley 558
Holland, Cecelia 290, 293,
  301, 332
Holland, Isabelle 316, 411,
  716, 725, 731, 758
Holler, Anne 310
Holleran, Andrew 613
Holliday, J. S. 566
Holme, Timothy 313, 322
Holmes, Jon 766

Holmes, Richard 170
Holt, Kare 448
Holt, Victoria 50, 137, 152,
  153, 160, 225, 227, 229,
  252, 255
Holton, Felicia A. 630
Hone, Joseph 2
Honour, Hugh 503
Hood, Mary 619
Hooker, Richard 135
Hookham, Hilda 86
Hoover, Dwight W. 635
Hoover, Edwin C. 645
Hoover, Thomas 107, 116
Hope, Christopher 31
Hope, Jack 704
Hopkins, Robert S. 255
Hopkirk, Peter 80, 142
Hopwood, Derek 46
Horan, James D. 541, 725
Horgan, Paul 431, 438, 546,
  560, 701, 770
Horton, Tom 571
Horwitz, Julius 725
Horwitz, Richard P. 503
Hospital, Janette T. 107,
  667
Hotchner, A. E. 258, 684
Hough, Henry Beatle 666
Household, Geoffrey 221, 233
Household, Joanna 211
Houston, James D. 474, 565,
  694
Houston, Robert 560
Hoving, Thomas P. 47
Howar, Barbara 607
Howard, Elizabeth J. 221
Howard, Joseph K. 685
Howard, P. 213
Howarth, David A. 149, 280
Howatch, Susan 225, 233,
  302, 355, 395
Howells, William D. 317
Howes, Barbara 404
Howland, Bette 633
Hoyt, Ed Palmer 666
Hoyt, Edwin P. 134, 777
Hsia, Chin-yen 89
Hsiao, Hung 89
Hsu, Immanuel C.Y. 86
Hubbard, P. M. 356
Huber, J. Parker 652
Hubka, Thomas C. 524
Hudgins, Barbara 697
Hudson, Danny L. 768
Hudson, W. H. 450, 451, 469,
  470
Huffaker, Clair 686
Huggett, Frank E. 331
Huggins, Eleanor 574, 691
Hughart, Brian 89
Hughes, Christopher S. 388

ughes, James 697
ughes, Langston 640, 725
ughes, Richard 93, 415
ugo, Richard 686
ull, Richard W. 26
umphrey, William 770
umphreys, Josephine 758
unt, David C. 744
unt, Hugh 298
unt, John 745
unt, William R. 551
unte, George 408
Hunter, Alan 352
Hunter, C. Bruce 436
Hunter, David 742
Hunter, Evan 613, 667, 726
Hunter, Jim 435
Huntford, Roland 383
Hurston, Zora Neale 406, 407, 613
Hurt, Harry 766
Huser, Verne 509
Hutchins, Francis G. 664
Hutchinson, Tom 568
Huxley, Aldous 426
Huxley, Elspeth 11, 34, 228
Hvidt, Kristian 195
Hyde-Chambers, Frederick R. 144
Hylton, Hilary 436
Hylton, Sara 50

Ibuse, Masuji 121
Icazu, J. 462
Iglauer, Edith 499
Ignotus, Paul 290
Ilyin, Olga 371
Inder, Stuart 150
Inge, M. Thomas 503
Inge, William 640, 640
Ingersoll, Joshena M. 132
Ingham, Kenneth 13
Inglis, Brian 300
Inglis, James G. 674
Innes, Hammond 14, 66, 137, 153, 356, 480, 486
Innes, Michael 225
Interstate Guides 513
Irish, Lola 160
Irvine, Lucy 156
Irving, Clifford 439
Irving, Clive 43
Irving, John 182
Irving, Robert 98
Irving, Washington 374
Isaacs, Jennifer 158
Isaacs, Marty 57
Isaacs, Susan 719, 726
Isherwood, Christopher 80, 275, 443

Iskander, Fazil 368
Islands of the World 17, 208, 350

Jablow, Alta 4
Jack, Susan 652
Jackman, Brian 11
Jackman, S.W. 488
Jackson, Donald D. 566, 760
Jackson, Keith 165
Jackson, Michael 200
Jackson, Richard L. 400
Jackson, Ruth A. 575
Jackson, Stanley 246
Jackson-Stops, Gervase 203
Jacobs, Babette 74, 150, 436, 446
Jacobs, Ben 511
Jacobs, Charles 74, 150, 436, 446
Jacobs, Jane 495
Jacobs, Michael 211, 246
Jacobsen, Bruce 172
Jacobson, Dan 31
Jacoby, Annalee 82
Jacot, Michael 192
Jadzewski, K. 338
Jaffe, Rona 456, 669
Jager, Grace 693
Jager, Ronald 693
Jagger, Brenda 235
Jahn, Ernst A. 402
Jahoda, Gloria 610
Jakes, John 751, 758
James, Donald 368
James, Henry 203, 248, 307, 323, 389
James, P. D. 228
James, Theodore 708
James, Will 794
Jamieson, Paul 705
Janovy, John R. 689
Jansen, Godfrey H. 42
Jansen, Tove 244
Jastrow, Marie 711
Jay, G. Charlotte 153
Jefferson, Louise E. 3
Jeffrey, Julie Roy 541
Jeffries, Roderic 378, 380
Jenkins, Dan 770
Jenkins, Nancy 47
Jenkins, Peter 83, 143, 503, 762
Jenkins, Simon 446
Jenkinson, Michael 546
Jennings, Gary 439
Jennings, Penny 85
Jennings, Russell 85
Jennings, William D. 686
Jennison, Peter S. 778

Jensen, Amy 603
Jensen, Dwight W. 627
Jensen, Richard J. 629
Jewett, Sarah Orne 654
Jhabvala, Ruth Prawer 107, 726
Jigmei-Ngapo, Ngawang 143
Jinkins, Dana 404
Joekes, Rosemary 210
Joesting, Edward 623
Johnson, Beth 552
Johnson, Diane 577
Johnson, Dorothy M. 685
Johnson, Elmer D. 757
Johnson, Emilie 83
Johnson, Kathryn 699
Johnson, Lady Bird 766
Johnson, Madeleine C. 706
Johnson, Pamela Hansford 187, 224, 694
Johnson, Paul 47, 58, 200
Johnson, Uwe 275
Johnson, William W. 435
Johnston, Jennifer 187, 302
Johnston, Moira 488, 543
Johnston, William M. 180
Johnston, Velda 316, 654, 719, 726
Jones, Christopher 200, 213
Jones, Douglas C. 562, 563, 740, 760
Jones, Edward 216
Jones, Everett L. 543
Jones, Gareth Elwyn 393
Jones, Gwyn 196, 292
Jones, James 258, 624, 763
Jones, J. Sydney 180
Jones, Mervyn 221
Jones, Proctor 359
Jones, Robert F. 554
Jones, Stephen 598, 706
Jones, Tristan 473
Jordan, James M. 782
Jordan, Lee 233
Jordan, Teresa 544
Jorden, William J. 428
Jorgensen, Neil 524
Joyce, James 304
Joyce, Roy 163
Joynes, St. Leger M. 645, 657, 736
Juliano, Annette 80
July, Robert W. 6
Jumsai, M. L. 140
Junior League of Washington 603
Just, Ward 607
Jutikkala, E. 243

Kahn, E. J., Jr. 617
Kaiser, Hannah 359

Kaiser, Robert G. 359
Kalb, Marvin 43
Källberg, Sture 383
Kallir, Jane 180
Kamata, Satoshi 116
Kamen, Henry A. 376
Kaminker, Sarah Fox 57
Kandell, Jonathan 444
Kane, Harnett T. 645, 680, 783
Kane, Kay 594
Kane, Robert S. 269, 314, 376, 623
Kaniuk, Yaram 59
Kant, Candace C. 557
Kantor, MacKinlay 638, 682, 684, 751
Kaplan, Frederic M. 85
Kaplan, Marion 2
Kapuscinski, Ryszard 11
Karmel-Wolfe, Henia 340
Karp, Walter 708
Kasson, John F. 708
Kates, George 83
Katkov, Norman 624
Katz, William L. 541
Kaufelt, David A. 275
Kaufelt, Lynn 611
Kaufman, Myron S. 669
Kaufman, William 513
Kaufman, Sue 726
Kaul, H. K. 98
Kawabata, Yasunari 121
Kawasaki, Ichiro 116
Kay, Shirley 23
Kay, Terry 619
Kayam, Umar 112
Kaye, M. M. 14, 18, 98, 107, 275, 285
Kaysing, Bill 541
Kazan, Elia 67, 726
Kazantzakis, Nikos 46, 70, 285, 286, 375
Keane, Molly 302
Keating, Bern 536
Keating, H.R.F. 107
Kee, Robert 295
Keeble, John 489
Keegan, Marcia 744
Keehn, David C. 749
Keehn, Sally M. 749
Keen, Benjamin 402
Keillor, Garrison 678
Kellas, James G. 351
Kelly, Brian 445
Kelly, Joyce 427
Kelly, Laurence 364
Kelly, Michael 197
Kelsey, Vera 427
Kelson, Allen H. 629
Kelton, Elmer 770
Kemal, Yashar 70, 70

Kemelman, Harry 59
Kempe, Helen K. 679
Keneally, Thomas 156, 160, 448
Kennedy, Judy 408, 436, 512
Kennedy, Lena 221
Kennedy, Roger 508
Kennedy, William 705, 716
Kennelly, Ardyth 775
Kennett, Audrey 364
Kenny, Herbert A. 298
Kenny, Lona B. 8
Kenny, Maurice 514
Kent, Alexander 411
Kent, Rosemary 767
Kern, Ben 536
Kern, Ellyn R. 508
Kesey, Ken 747
Kessel, Joseph 14
Kessner, Thomas 506
Ketchum, Richard 777
Kettle, John 476
Keyarts, Eugene 598
Keyes, Frances Parkinson 255, 647, 648
Kidder-Smith, G. E. 508
Kiek, Jonathan 213
Kiely, Benedict 302
Kienzle, William X. 675
Kilbourn, William 476
Kilian, Crawford 488
Kilian, Michael 603
Kilner, Peter 65
Kilpatrick, James 531
Kim, H. Edward 133
Kimbrough, Emily 248, 295
Kincaid, Jamaica 411
Kindersley, Anna 397
King, Francis 107
King, F. H. 310
King, Michael 163
King, Richard E. 135
King, Stephen 596, 654, 751
King, Tabitha 654
Kingery, Alan 173
Kingery, Phyllis 173
Kingsnorth, G. W. 13
Kininmonth, Christopher 23, 312
Kinney-Hanson, Sharon 682
Kinross, Lord 69
Kinsella, W. P. 638
Kinsolving, William 425
Kipling, Rudyard 107
Kirby, D. G. 243
Kirby-Smith, Henry T. 514
Kirk, Mary W. 549
Kirk, Ruth 570, 787
Kirkley, Gene 768
Kirsch, Robert 692
Kirst, Hans H. 272
Kirst, Hellmut 389

Kita, Mario 121
Kitfield, James 181, 269, 388
Klassen, Georgeen 478
Klein, Alexander 711
Klein, Norma 316
Kleinfeld, Sonny 635
Klenbort, Daniel 617
Klenbort, Marcia 617
Kling, Kevin 143
Klose, Kevin 359
Kluger, Phyllis 600, 726
Kluger, Richard 619, 726
Knapp, Herbert 427
Knapp, Mary 427
Knebel, Fletcher 275
Knight, Franklin W. 409
Knight, Kathryn L. 170
Knittel, Robert 682
Knowles, John 600, 694, 79(
Knox, Bill 354, 356
Knox, Maxine 575, 575
Kobayshi, Tsukasa 213
Koch, Don 594
Kocher, Alfred L. 782
Koehler, Margaret 664
Koenig, Laird 719, 726
Koestler, Arthur 368, 389
Kogawa, Joy 480
Kohak, Erazim 190
Kohan, Rhea 581
Kohler, Jack 536
Kohout, Pavel 193
Kolb, Carolyn 645
Komaiko, Jean R. 536
Konecky, Edith 731
Koning, Hans 46, 331, 332
Konràd, George 290
Konwicki, Tadeusz 341
Koolhaas, Rem 708
Koontz, Dean R. 654
Koppel, Ted 43
Kopper, Philip 521
Koppman, Lionel 522
Korbel, Josef 192
Korbonski, Stefan 338
Kort, Michael 360
Kosinski, Jerzy 340, 670
Kossman, E. H. 187, 331
Kostash, Myrna 476
Kotkin, Joel 568
Kotzwinkle, William 726
Kovaly, Hedy 190
Kovell, Hank 690
Kowalczyk, Robert 134
Kpomassie, Tete-Michel 473
Kraft, Stephanie 511
Kramer, Jane 23, 213, 246, 383, 767
Kramer, William 605
Krantz, Judith 258, 726
Kranz, Walter 388

raus, Theodor 312
rich, John 40
rinsky, Carol H. 174, 708
rook, Dorothy 53
rutch, Joseph W. 435, 557
ubly, Herbert 280, 307, 312, 387
ull, Andrew 524
Kundera, Milan 193
Kuniczak, W. S. 340
Kunze, Reiner 275
Kuper, Adam 409
Kupperman, Karen O. 736
Kuralt, Charles 503
Kuranov, V. 365
Kurzman, Dan 338, 375
Kusche, Larry 424
Kuznetsov, Edward 363
Kyle, Duncan 474
Kytle, Elizabeth 658

LaBrucherie, Roger A. 407, 424
Lacey, Robert 674
Ladell, John 492
LaFarge, Christopher 755
LaFarge, Oliver 560
Lagerkvist, Pär 384
Lagerlöf, Selma 384, 385
Lai, T. C. 80
Laing, Jennifer 282, 314
Laker, Rosalind 233
Lamb, David 2
Lambert, Derek 344
Lamming, George 411
L'Amour, Louis 503, 577, 578, 596, 783, 794
Lamparski, Richard 568
Lampedusa, Giuseppe di 322
Lampman, Linda 746
Lancaster, Bruce 675, 719, 764, 783
Landay, Jerry M. 56
Landes, Alison 251
Landes, Sonia 251
Landi, Val 509
Landon, Margaret D. 139
Landru, H. C. 552
Lane, James B. 635
Lane, Rose Wilder 740
Lang, A. G. P. 279
Lang, Daniel 268
Lang, William L. 685
Langdon, Helen 307
Langley, Bob 451
Langley, Joan 611
Langley, Wright 611
Langone, John 447
Lanier, Alison R. 503
Lannoy, Richard 104

Lansing, Alfred 447
Lao, She 89
Lapierre, Dominique 53, 97
Laqueur, Walter 268
Laracy, Hugh 146
Larson, Taft A. 793
Lasic-Vasojevic, Milija M. 397
Lass, William E. 677
Latham, Caroline 713
Lattimore, Owen 73
Launay, André 376
Laurence, Margaret 11, 37, 480, 489, 491, 493
Lauring, Palle 196
Lauritzen, Peter 313
Lavender, David S. 541, 546, 557, 565
Lavin, Mary 302
Law, Joy 247
Lawless, Richard 43
Lawliss, Chuck 623
Lawrence, D. H. 308, 314, 317, 433, 439, 560
Lawrence, R. P. 488, 499
Lawrence, T. E. 64
Lawson, Andrew 216
Law-Yone, Wendy 78
Laxalt, Robert 690
Laxness, Halldór 293, 776
Laycock, Ellen 536
Laycock, George 536
Lea, Tom 439, 767
Leak, J. 103
Leavitt, Mel 645
LeBlanc, Joyce Y. 645
LeCarre, John 59, 221, 272
LeCompte, Janet 594
Lee, Andrea 364
Lee, Christine E. 521
Lee, Hanka 283
Lee, Harper 549
Lee, Hector 565
Lee, Mary P. 663
Lee, Michael 283
Lee, Peter H. 135
Lee, Sherman E. 73
Lee, Richard M. 605
Leggett, Robert F. 478
Lehane, B. 297
Lehmann, Rosamond 411
Lehmberg, Paul 492
Leland, Louis S., Jr. 164
Lelyveld, Joseph 27
Lem, Stanislaw 316
L'Enfant, Julie 647
L'Engle, Madeleine 344, 471, 726
Lennon, Nigey 565
Lenz, Siegfried 272
Leocha, Charles 22, 211, 299
Leon, Vicki 557, 567, 691

Leonard, Elmore 613
Leonard, George 719
Leonard, Jonathan N. 521
Leopold, Aldo 791
Lesley, Craig 748
Leslie, R. F. 339
Leslie-Melville, Betty 11
Leslie-Melville, Jock 11
Lessing, Doris 6
Lesure, Thomas B. 557
Letson, Barbara 85
Leuci, Bob 727
Levi, Carlo 312
Levi, Peter 280, 282
Levin, Ira 456, 727
Levin, Meyer 59, 60, 633
Levine, Barry 407
Levine, Miriam 524
Levine, Norman 480
Levy, Alan 190
Lewis, Bernard 42
Lewis, David L. 603, 709
Lewis, Elaine 139
Lewis, Neville 282
Lewis, Norman 77, 140, 312, 374
Lewis, Oscar 407, 431
Lewis, Paul 139
Lewis, Robin Jared 98
Lewis, Sinclair 678
Lewis, Wyndham 22
Leys, Simon 80
Li, Dun J. 86
Liberatore, Karen 573
Lichine, Alexis 246
Lichtveld, Ursy M. 464
Liden, Karin 359
Lieberman, Herbert 465, 727
Lieuwen, Edwin 470
Lin, Robert H. 138
Lin, Yutang 89
Lincoln, John 433
Lindbergh, Anne 473
Lindgren, Jean 524, 544, 545
Lindsey, David L. 771
Linington, Elizabeth 581
Linklater, Eric 292
Lins do Rego, Rose 456
Lippincott, Bertram 754
Lippmann, Thomas W. 42
Lister, R. P. 68, 243, 335, 383
Littell, Franklin H. 57
Littell, Robert 189, 193, 371
Little, G. Allen 348
Little, Tom 48
Lively, Penelope 234
Livermore, H. V. 344
Ljungmark, Lars 383
Llewellyn, Richard 395, 451
Llewellyn, Sam 203

Lloyd, Sarah 99
Lo Bello, Nino 173
Locke, Elliott S. 160
Lockley, Ronald 164, 302, 446
Lockridge, Richard 716, 738
Lockridge, Ross 636
Lockwood, C. C. 531
Lockwood, Charles 568, 570, 709
Loewenstein, Louis K. 571
Lofts, Norah 114, 197, 205, 228, 232, 233, 247, 378
Logan, Ben 791
Logan, Rayford W. 409
Lomax, John, III 762
Lombardi, John V. 470
London, Jack 153, 500, 554, 624
London, Mark 445
Longford, Elizabeth 280
Longstreet, Stephen 251, 585, 630
Loomis, Albertine 623
Looney, Ralph 699
Lopez, Barry 473
Loraine, Philip 252
Lord, Bette Bao 89
Lord, John 99
Lord, Suzanne 511
Lord, William G. 736, 782
Lorénzen, Lilly 387
Lorillard, Did 713
Loti, Pierre 254
Louis, Jennifer 366
Louis, Victor 366
Love, Frank 594
Lovecraft, H. P. 667
Loveman, Brian 459
Lovesey, Peter 582
Loving, Nancy J. 557
Lowndes, Susan 343
Lowry, Beverly 680, 771
Lowry, Malcolm 439, 489
Luard, Nicholas 27
Lucas, Christopher 112
Lucey, Robert 64
Luck, Peter 156
Ludlum, Robert 451, 607
Ludwig, Jack 514
Lukacs, John 749
Lukas, J. Anthony 663
Lundevall, E. 335
Lunn, Sir A. H. M. 387
Lurie, Alison 222, 582, 716
Lutz, Giles 794
Lyall, Gavin 222
Lyndon, Donlyn 633
Lynton, Harriet R. 112
Lyons, Ivan 258, 716
Lyons, Nan 258, 716

Maas, Walter B. 180
MacAdams, Cliff 557, 570, 793
Macdonald, Elisabeth 596
MacDonald, Ervin J. 476
McDonald, Gregory 578
Macdonald, John D. 439, 578, 613
MacDonald, Lyn 249
MacDonald, Malcolm 498
MacDonald, Ross 582
MacDougall, Ruth D. 694
MacGregor, Geddes 348
MacGregor, James C. 482
MacHaffie, Ingeborg 195
MacInnes, Colin 222, 411
MacInnes, Helen 182, 182, 254, 258, 285, 318, 323, 378, 795
MacIntyre, Michael 117
Mackay, Dick 666
Mackay, Donald 484
MacKay, Roy 149
MacKen, Walter 302
Mackenzie, Compton 356
Mackie, John D. 351
MacKinnon, Jack 445
Mack-Smith, D. 351
MacLean, Alistair 272, 332, 353, 398, 398, 457, 474, 474, 483, 554, 582, 585
MacLean, Charles 350
MacLean, Fitzroy 73, 351, 360
MacLean, Norman 687
MacLean, Sir F. H. 361
MacLeish, Roderick 607
MacLeish, William H. 484
MacLennan, Hugh 496
MacManus, Seumas 300
MacNeice, L. 292
MacPherson, Cynthia 713
MacPherson, Malcolm 368
McAlester, Virginia 508
McBain, Ed 613, 727
McBurney, Margaret 492
McCaig, Donald N. 686, 783
McCammon, Robert R. 550, 620, 738
McCarthy, Abigail 607
McCarthy, Cormac 764
McCarthy, Liz 646
McCarthy, Maryl 311, 706, 751
McCawley, James D. 85
McClanahan, Ed 643
McClane, Charles B. 652
McClure, James 31, 200, 576
MacColl, Gwynne 598
McCorkle, Jill 738
McCormack, Russell 272
McCullers, Carson 620

McCullough, Colleen 153, 1
McCullough, David W. 427, 709
McCurry, Steve 100, 130
McCutchan, Philip 70, 153
McDarrah, Fred W. 709
McDermott, John W. 113, 1: 157, 164, 567
McDonald, Douglas 691
McDonald, Maureen 531
McDougall, Walter A. 405
McElroy, Lee 771
McEwen, William J. 453
McFadden, Cyra 585
McFarland, Gerald 504
McGahern, John 304
McGill, Ralph 531
McGinley, Patrick 302
McGinnis, Joe 552
McGivern, William P. 187
McGreevy, John 54, 156, 21! 269, 281, 297, 310, 350, 364, 384, 630, 711
McGuane, Thomas 613, 675, 687
McHale, Tom 751
McHugh, Roger 295
McIlvain, John 613
McIlvain, Myra H. 768
McIlvanney, William 354
McInerney, Jay 727
McInerny, Ralph 743
McIntyre, Loren 466
McKay, Allis 788
McKay, Claude 415
McKee, Bill 478
McKeever, Harry P. 488
McKeever, Michael 576
MacKendrick, Paul L. 19, 281, 308, 343, 346, 374
McKenna, Richard 89
McKenney, Ruth 203
McLachlan, Ian 94
McLanathan, Richard 511
McLean, Virginia O. 762
McLellan, Robert 299
McLoughlin, William J. 754
McMullen, Jeanine 393
McMullen, Mary 302, 727
McMurtry, Larry 582, 607, 692, 771
McNair-Wilson, Diana 289
McNaspy, C. J. 174
McNaught, Kenneth W. K. 479
McNeish, James 54
McPhee, Colin 112
McPhee, Joe 552
McPhee, John 350, 387, 697
McPherson, William 792
Macready, Daphne L. 73
Madden, Betty I. 630
Madden, Daniel M. 174

Madsen, Betty M. 774
Madsen, Brigham 774
Madson, John 537
Maeder, Herbert 387
Magary, Alan 13, 574, 575
Magary, Kerstin F. 13, 574, 575
Magnússen, S. 292
Magnússon, Magnus 56, 196
Magnússon, Sigurdur 292
Magubane, Peter 27
Maharajah of Baroda 99
Mailer, Norman 50, 582, 667, 776
Mailer, Phil 343
Maillaret, Ella 73
Mainwaring, William L. 746
Maister, Philippa 617
Malamud, Bernard 368, 716, 731
Malcolm, Andrew H. 477, 504
Malek, Jaromir 46
Malka, Victor 54
Mallan, Chicki 436, 570
Mallinson, Vernon 187
Mallows, Wilfrid 27
Malone, Michael 600, 738
Malouf, David 160, 316
Malraux, André 89, 272, 378
Manfred, Frederick 638
Mango, Cyril 68
Mankowitz, Wolf 222
Mann, Thomas 50, 323
Mann, William E. 482
Mannello, George 706
Manning, Olivia 50, 347
Mansfield, Peter 64, 66
Marechaux, Pascal 64
Marek, George 180
Mares, William J. 65
Marinacci, Barbara 570
Marion, John F. 749
Mark, Norman 630
Markandaya, Kamala 108
Markham, Beryl 11
Markus, Julia 698
Marlowe, Derek 414
Marnham, Patrick 2, 247, 427
Marot, M. 289
Marquand, John P. 667, 669
Marquis, Arnold 507
Marqusee, Mike 709
Marsden, Walter 270, 335
Marsh, Ngaio 164, 166, 224, 226, 319
Marsh, Zoe 13
Marshall, Bruce 352
Marshall, Catherine 156, 643, 752
Marshall, Edison 738
Marshall, Howard W. 691
Marshall, James V. 161, 554

Marshall, Paule 411
Marshall, William 94
Marsland, William 470
Martin, Gillian 395
Martin, Harold H. 617
Martin, Jay 364
Martin, Luis 467
Martin, Malachi 60
Martin, Russell 544
Martin, Valerie 647
Martin du Gard, Roger 258
Martinez, Orlando 427
Martini, Frederic 146
Marty, Sid 477, 482
Martyn, Lucy B. 492
Marwick, Arthur 200
Marx, Robert F. 514
Maslov, Norman 209
Mason, F. Van Wyck 423, 425, 486, 669, 758, 764, 784
Mason, Richard 94
Massie, Robert K. 363
Massie, Suzanne 360
Masters, James I. 706
Masters, John 108, 380
Masterton, Graham 31
Mather, Melissa 779
Matheson, Richard 578
Mathews, Jay 80
Mathews, Linda 80
Matley, I. M. 346
Matsubara, Hisako 122
Matthews, Diane L. 524
Matthews, Elmora M. 762
Matthews, John 39, 307
Matthiessen, Peter 11, 102, 149, 411, 444, 457
Maugham, W. Somerset 78, 128, 153, 318, 374
Mauriac, François 254
Maurois, André 250
Maxwell, A. E. 335
Maxwell, Gavin 22, 349
Maxwell, William 631
May, Arthur J. 181
May, Robin 541
Maybury, Anne 20, 94, 228
Mayerson, Evelyn W. 613, 752
Mayfield, Chris 531
Maynard, Joyce 694
Maynard, Mary 663
Mead, Margaret 147
Mead, Robert D. 499
Mead, Robin 157, 283
Meade, Marion 252
Medina, Arthur 408
Medish, Vadim 366
Meeks, Harold A. 778
Mehta, Gita 99
Mehta, Ved 99, 99
Meiland, Jack 216
Meinardus, Otto 68, 281

Meisch, Lynn 453, 461, 462, 467
Melnicove, Mark 652
Melville, Herman 152 or 153
Melville, James 122
Melville, Jennie 395
Menen, Aubrey 108, 310, 313, 318
Menendez, Albert J. 604
Méras, Phyllis 170
Meray, Tibor 289
Merkin, Robert 614
Merle, Robert 614
Mertz, Richard 310
Merwin, Janet 521
Meschery, Joanne 578
Metcalf, John 496
Metge, Joan 164
Mewshaw, Michael 20, 771
Meyer, A. 604
Meyer, Charles 81
Meyer, Katherine M. 674
Meyer, Lawrence 54
Meyer, Michael C. 437
Meyer, Nicholas 182, 457
Meyers, Carole T. 574
Michael, Judith 585
Michael, Prince of Greece 70
Michaels, Barbara 226, 235, 318, 654, 659, 752, 784
Michaels, Leonard 585
Michaelson, Mikle 630
Michaud, Roland 134
Michelsen, Peter 195
Michener, James A. 31, 60, 122, 147, 147, 153, 289, 340, 374, 504, 596, 624, 659, 771
Midgard, J. 335
Mikes, George 157
Milepost 552
Milgrim, Shirley 749
Miller, Arthur 83
Miller, Christian 349, 504
Miller, Don 793
Miller, Donald C. 557, 691, 699
Miller, Dorcas 652
Millder, Dorothy A. 749
Miller, E. 213
Miller, Harold G. 164
Miller, Helen D. 281
Miller, Henry 258, 282
Miller, J. Maxwell 57
Miller, Ray 769
Miller, Robert Ryal 437
Miller, Saul 709
Miller, Stephen 521
Miller, Tom 431, 435, 546
Millhauser, Steven 600
Millhiser, Marlys 596, 638
Millman, Lawrence 299

Millon, Kim 173
Millon, Marc 173
Mills, Don 477
Mills, James 140
Milne, A. A. 224
Milosz, Czeslaw 340
Milton, John 760
Milton, Nancy D. 89
Minai, Naila 42
Miner, Valerie 222
Minot, Stephen 486
Mirsky, Jeanette 473
Mishima, Yukio 122
Mitchell, Don 778
Mitchell, Henry 604
Mitchell, Margaret 620
Mitchell, Paige 680
Mitford, Nancy 259
Mitgang, Herbert 719
Mittelholzer, Edgar 464
Mlynar, Zdenek 191
Moberg, Gunnie 350
Moberg, Vilhelm 384, 385, 678
Moffat, Frances 571
Moffitt, Donald 504
Mohanti, Prafulla 99
Mohlenbrock, Robert H. 509
Mojtabai, A. G. 131, 654
Mondy, Robert W. 541
Montalbano, William D. 90
Montgomery-Massingberd, Hugh 214
Montserrat, Nicholas 6
Moody, Ralph 594
Moorcock, Michael 368
Moore, Brian 222, 259, 302, 496
Moore, Charles K. 566, 568
Moore, Derry 604
Moore, James E. 408
Moore, James F. 423
Moore, Joanne R. 499
Moore, Ruth 654
Moore, Susanna 624
Moore, Tui de Roy 462
Moorehead, Alan 2, 46, 147, 157, 157
Moorhouse, Geoffrey 19, 99, 130, 191, 525, 571
Moraes, Don 99
Morales, Arturo 408
Moravia, Alberto 319
More, Carey 248
More, Jasper 48
More, Julian 248
Morgan, Anne H. 557, 744
Morgan, Berry 681
Morgan, H. Wayne 745
Morgan, Kenneth O. 213
Morgan, Lael 552, 552
Morgan, Murray 787

Morgan, Speer 745
Morgulas, Jerrold 341
Morice, Anne 608
Morison, E. F. 693
Morison, Samuel Eliot 404, 516
Moritz, Albert 479
Moritz, Theresa 479
Morley, Christopher 731
Morley, Frank 207
Morley, George W. 434
Morley, John D. 117
Morley, Sheridan 568
Morley, Sylvanus G. 434
Moron, Guillermo 470
Morris, Arthur S. 444
Morris, Charles R. 709
Morris, Donald R. 28
Morris, Edita 122
Morris, Edwin T. 81
Morris, Ivan 117
Morris, James 27, 68, 136, 147, 180, 200, 248, 711
Morris, Jan 46, 81, 99, 99, 127, 157, 203, 208, 208, 215, 268, 292, 295, 297, 308, 312, 313, 350, 374, 384, 393, 397, 427, 568, 604, 611, 630, 691, 699, 767, 793
Morris, John 745
Morris, Shirley 782
Morris, Wright 170, 439, 578, 689
Morrison, H. Robert 521
Morrison, Joan 506
Morrison, Toni 411, 743
Morrison, Tony 466
Morrissey, Charles T. 778
Morse, White 612
Mortimer, Edward 42
Morton, Brian N. 214, 251
Morton, Frederic 180, 182
Morton, H. V. 203, 295, 308, 349, 374, 393
Morton, Henry C. 56
Morton, James 488
Morton, William L. 490
Morton, W. Scott 81, 120
Moser, Brian 460
Moser, Don 541
Mosher, Stephen 84
Moskin, J. Robert 54
Mosley, Leonard 602
Moss, Cynthia 12
Moss, Robert 369, 614
Motley, Willard 633
Mountfield, David 447
Mowat, Farley 365, 473, 474, 477
Mowbray, E. Andrew 754
Moyes, Patricia 412

Mphahlele, Ezekiel 3
Mrabet, Mohammed 23
Muir, Richard 200, 211
Mukherjee, Bharati 108, 727
Mulisch, Harry 332
Mulligan, Tim 705
Munksgaardd, Elisabeth 196
Munro, Alice 480, 493
Murari, Timeri 549
Murasaki, Shikibu 122
Murdoch, Iris 222, 228, 304
Murnane, William J. 48
Murphy, Dervla 11, 100, 102, 295, 296
Murphy, Walter F. 319
Murphy-O'Connor, Jerome 5
Murray, Jocelyn 3
Murray, William 308
Musallam, Basim 64
Musil, Robert 182
Muskie, Stephen O. 484
Muth, Marcia 700
Mutrux, Robert 525
Mydans, Shelley 122
Myrer, Anton 669
Myrick, Burny 537

Nabb, Magdalen 318
Nabokov, Vladimir 275
Nackman, Mark E. 767
Nagel, Paul C. 682
Nagorski, Andrew 360
Nauipaul, Shiva 2, 404, 412, 464
Naipaul, V. S. 14, 42, 100, 112, 127, 130, 400, 412, 464
Namioka, Lensey 81, 119
Nance, John 132
Napier, Priscilla 369
Narayan, R. K. 108
Nash, June 453
Nash, N. Richard 625
Nast, Lenora H. 658
National Geographic Society 203, 404, 509, 541, 544, 546
National Park Foundation 51
National Trust for Historic Preservation 508
Navarro, Marysa 449
Naylor, Charles 219
Nearing, Helen 525, 652, 778
Nearing, Scott 525
Neary, Peter 484
Needham, D. E. 8
Neely, Richard 727
Neely, William 761
Negev, Avraham 56
Neider, Charles 447

ill, Kenneth 300
ill, Wilfred T. 113
lson, Christopher H. 575
lson, Gerald B. 787
lson, Howard J. 568
lson, Jerry L. 537
lson, Nina 24, 93, 186, 196, 312, 479
lson, Richard K. 552
erbonne, J. J. 138
esbitt, Ludovico M. 12
evins, Allan 516
evins, Deborah 709
ewberry, Lida 713
ewby, Eric 2, 19, 40, 68, 100, 170, 365
ewby, P. H. 50
ewhall, Nancy 525
eznansky, Fridrikh 371
gugi Wa Thiong'o 14
Nicholas, Tracy 407
Nicholl, Charles 460
Nicholls, David 409
Nichols, Jack 706
Nichols, John 700, 701
Nicholson, Diana 531
Nicholson, Louise 103
Nickels, Sylvie 243
Nicol, Eric 489
Nicol Gladys 127, 139, 243, 282
Nicolson, Adam 249
Nielsen, Margaret 195
Niles, B. 460
Nin, Anais 259, 439
Nisbet, Jack 787
Niven, Alexander C. 365
Niven, David 569
Nketia, Joseph 4
Noble, Hollister 659
Nolan, David 611
Nolledo, Wilfrido D. 133
Nolte, James 535
Noonan, Michael 161
Norbu, T. J. 143
Norbury, Paul 117
Norden, Hermann 12
Nordhoff, Charles 153, 161
Norris, Frank 585, 633
North, James 27
Norton, Barbara 594
Norton, Boyd 594
Norwich, John Julius 200, 308, 313
Nouwen, Henri J. M. 453, 466
Novotny, Ann 709
Nowak, Jan 339

Oakes, George W. 173, 211, 216

Oakley, Stewart 196
Oates, Joyce Carol 608, 675, 716, 752
Obee, B. 489
O'Brien, Edna 296
O'Brien, Kate 302
O'Brien, Raymond J. 705
O'Brien, Tim 678
O'Callaghan, J. F. 344, 376
O'Connell, James C. 661
O'Connor, D'Arcy 484
O'Connor, Edwin 670
O'Connor, Flannery 620, 764
O'Connor, Frank 303
O'Connor, Lois 705
O'Connor, Philip F. 743
O'Connor, R. 754
Odier, Pierre 571
O'Donnell, Lillian 727
O'Donoghue, Maureen 227
O'Faolain, Sean 296, 303, 308
O'Farrell, Padraic 298
O'Flaherty, Liam 303, 304
Ogburn, Charlton 533
Ogilvie, Elisabeth 353, 486, 655
O'Gorman, Patricia W. 431
O'Hanlon, Redmond 127
O'Hanlon, Thomas J. 298
O'Haodha, Michael 298
O'Hara, John 727, 752
O'Hehir, Diana 608
Olbricht, Klaus-Hartmut 296
Olcott, Anthony 371, 372
Old California Series 567
Oldenbourg, Zoe 70, 259
Older, Anne 704
Oldhiambo, E. S. 13
Oliver, Roland 6
Oliver, W. H. 165
Olmstead, Gerald 173, 544
Olmsted, John 574, 691
Olsen, Tillie 761
Olsenius, Richard 677, 791
Olson, James S. 507
Olson, Sigurd F. 499, 537, 552, 791
Onassis, Jacqueline K. 360
Ondaatje, Michael 137
O'Neil, Currey 158
O'Neil, Paul 537
Onetti, Juan Carlos 451, 469
Onis, Harriet de 401
Openshaw, Gene 174
Oppenheimer, Doug 627
Orel, Harold 349
Orkin, Ruth 712
Orlev, Uri 341
Ormsby, Margaret Anchoretta 489

Ornelas-Struve, Carole M. 762
Orum, Poul 197
Orwell, George 78, 375
Osae, T. A. 35
Osborn, Beverly H. 662
Osler, Jack M. 635, 642, 674, 742, 750
Ostrogorsky, George 69
Ostrow, Joanna 354
Ousmane, Sembene 37
Owens, Carole 662
Owens, Delia 28
Owens, Mark 28
Owram, Doug 477
Oz, Amos 54, 60

Pachman, Ludek 191
Packard, Jerrold M. 205, 310
Paffrath, James D. 117
Page, Elizabeth 784
Page, Jake 546
Page, Susanne 546
Page, Tim 136, 713
Pakenham, Valerie 201
Pakula, Hannah 346
Pallis, Marco 143
Palm, Charlene F. 211
Palmer, A. 360
Palmer, Lilli 399
Palmer, Nigel 136
Palmer, Paige 104
Palmer, Thomas 614
Paludan, Ann 81
Pancake, Breece D'J. 790
Panin, Dimitri 363
Panter-Downes, Mollie 100
Pape, Gordon 50
Pardey, Larry 73, 171
Pardeny, Lin 73, 171
Parfit, Micjhael 447
Pariser, Harry 409
Parker, Franklin D. 428
Parker, Robert B. 667, 670
Parker, Watson 760
Parkinson, Wanda 406
Parks, Gordon 455, 640
Parks, Roger 525
Parmenter, Ross 431
Parramore, Thomas C. 736
Parrott, Cecil 191
Parry, J. H. 401
Partington, Norman 109
Partridge, Frances 215
Pashdag, John 570
Pasinetti, P. M. 323
Pasquarelli, Michael A. 515
Passin, Herbert 117
Pasternak, Boris 369
Patchen, Aletha 435

Patchen, Marvin 435
Paton, Alan 31
Patten, Lewis B. 596
Patterson, Harry 344
Patterson, Jerry E. 709
Patterson, Raymond M. 482
Patterson, Richard 541
Patterson, Richard N. 608
Patton, Annie 569, 714
Patton, Brian 479
Paul, David W. 191
Paul, Elliott H. 251
Paul, Raymond 755
Pauls, Michael 523, 527
Pausewang, Gudrun 454
Pavese, Cesare 316
Payne, Anthony 405
Payne, Roīce R. 525
Paz, Octavio 431
Pearce, Jean 119
Pearce, Kenneth 434
Pearce, Mary E. 226, 234
Pearlman, Moshe 56
Pearlstein, E. W. 363
Pearson, Diane 229, 290
Pearson, Jeff 595
Pearson, John 222
Pearson, Michael 363
Pearson, William 608
Pease, Martha R. 216
Peck, Robert N. 779
Peck, Stacey 81
Peckham, Howard H. 635
Peden, R. 635
Peel, J. H. 211
Peffer, Randall S. 658
Peirce, Neil R. 504, 504,
  525, 527, 531, 537, 542
Peissel, Michel 103
Pekic, Borislav 399
Pelton, Beulah 637
Pelzer, Dorothy W. 112
Pendered, Maureen 376
Pendle, George 450, 465
Pentecost, Hugh 582, 668,
  698
Pepper, Elizabeth 174
Pereira, Anthony 312
Perez Galdos, Benito 379
Perkins, Robert F. 485
Perkins, Samuel 246
Pern, Stephen 35
Peron, Eva Duarte 450
Perrin, Noel 778
Perry, Jane 521
Perry, John 521, 567, 747,
  787
Perry, Richard N. 717
Perry, Thomas 582
Peterkin, Julia 759
Peters, Daniel 429, 439

Peters, Elizabeth 50, 197,
  319, 352, 385, 560, 659
Peters, Ellis 109, 193
Peters, F. E. 56
Peterson, Charles S. 774
Peterson, F. Ross 627
Peterson, Mendel 405
Petrow, Richard 195
Pettit, Florence H. 432
Pettit, Ronald M. 432
Phaidon Cultural Guide: Great
Britain and Ireland 211
Phaidon Cultural Guide:
  Greece 281
Pharr, Robert D. 563
Phelan, James 602
Phillips, John 54
Phillips, Jayne Ann 790
Phillips, McCandlish 709
Phillips, Wendell 65
Pick, Christopher 212
Pick, Robert 180
Piercy, Marge 670, 676, 728
Pilcher, Rosamunde 226
Pilon, Juliana G. 346
Pink, Annette 343, 376
Piper, David 208
Pipes, Daniel 42
Pipes, Richard 360
Plaidy, Jean 352, 378
Plain, Belva 412, 648
Plante, David 378, 755
Platt, Colin 212
Plunkett, James 296, 304
Plutschow, Herbert E. 119
Pohl, William L. 652
Pokrovskii, B. A. 364
Polk, William R. 65
Polland, Madeleine A. 303,
  379
Poma de Ayala, Felipe 467
Pommaret-Imaeda, Françoise
  103
Pond, Elizabeth 361
Ponicsan, Darryl 784
Poore, Jim 627
Pope, Diana 165
Pope, Dudley 405, 412, 412
Pope, Jeremy 165
Pope-Hennessy, James 93, 248
Popham, Peter 117, 119
Popkin, Zelda 496
Porch, Douglas 19, 22
Porter, Eliot 81, 448
Porter, Jonathan 81
Porter, Monica 289
Porter, Peter 157
Porterfield, Bill 767
Portillo, Jose Lopez 434,
  439
Portis, Charles 563

Postal, Bernard 174, 522,
  532, 537, 542, 714
Potok, Chaim 731
Powell, Anton 216
Powell, Lawrence C. 557
Powell, Padgett 759
Powell, William S. 736
Power, Brian 84
Powers, J. F. 678
Powers, John R. 633
Powledge, Fred 532
Pownall, Glen 164
Prag, Per 196
Pratson, Frederick 485, 492
  495
Pratt, Charles 652
Prebble, John 349
Prescott, H. F. M. 256
Prescott, W. H. 401
Presley, Delma 610, 617
Presley, James 767
Price, Eugenia 614, 617,
  620
Price, Nancy 676
Price, Polly S. 48
Price, Reynolds 738
Price, Richard 732
Price, Steve 532
Price, Willard 147
Priestley, J. B. 201
Primack, Mark L. 664
Primack, Phil 525
Prising, Robin 132
Pritchett, V. S. 215, 297,
  374, 712
Pronzini, Bill 500, 578
Prose, Francine 728
Pruitt, Ida 84
Pryce-Jones, Alan 457, 460,
  463
Pryce-Jones, David 180
Pryde, Philip R. 576
Puig, Manuel 452, 452, 452,
  452
Putigny, Bob 459
Putnam, Samuel 251
Puzo, Mario 322, 691, 692,
  728
Pye, Michael 422
Pym, Barbara 222, 231

Queen, Ellery 600
Quiller-Couch, Arthur 226
Quinnell, A. J. 43, 60

Raban, Jonathan 65, 537
Rabin, Carol Price 174, 511
Rabkin, Jacob 612

abkin, Richard 612
achleff, Owen S. 56
adcliffe, Virginia 405
afferty, Milton D. 562, 682
agghianti, C. L. 47
aines, Howell 550
aison, Laura 247, 311
ajan, Mohmi 112
ama Rau, Santa 109
amsdell, Charles 769
and, Christopher 93
andall, Anne 754
andall, Monica 706
andall, Peter 662, 693
andall, Tom 250
andolph, Vance 562
anelagh, John O'B. 300
Rankin, Jake 545
Rankin, Marni 545
Ransford, Oliver 27
Rapson, Richard L. 623
Rash, Bryson B. 604
Rasky, Frank 473
Rasmussen, Steen E. 214
Rassam, Amal 39
Raton, P. 388
Rattray, Everett T. 706
Rattray, Jeanette 706
Raucat, Thomas 122
Raucher, Herman 655
Rauers, Betty 618
Ravenal, St. Julien 757
Ravin, Neil 755
Rawlings, Marjorie Kinnan
  611, 614, 717
Rawson, Philip 73
Read, Jan 343, 374
Read, Kenneth E. 149
Read, Miss 285
Read, Piers Paul 255, 341,
  670
Reader, John 12
Reader's Digest 56, 448,
  477, 510, 510
Realites-hachette 247
Reaves, Verne 402
Rebeta-Burditt, Joyce 582
Redfield, Melissa 778
Redford, Polly 611
Reece, Daphne 545, 565
Reed, Allen C. 557, 595, 774
Reed, Barry 670
Reed, Henry H. 710
Reed, Ishmael 784
Reed, Roy 562
Reeman, Douglas 37, 129,
  336, 369
Reeves, Richard 130, 504
Reid, Malcolm 495
Reid, V. S. 415
Reinhardt, Richard 70
Reischauer, Edwin O. 117

Rejanen, Aini 243
Remarque, Erich Maria 259
Renault, Mary 43, 286, 287
Rendell, Ruth 233
Rennert, Maggie 55
Reyes, Alfonso 432
Reynolds, Donald M. 710
Rezatto, Helen 760
Rhodes, Evan H. 728
Rhodes, Richard 15, 562,
  578, 640, 682
Rhyne, Nancy 757
Rhys, Jean 259, 412
Riasanovsky, Nicholas V. 366
Ribeiro, Joao Ubaldo 457
Ricciardi, Lorenzo 17, 40
Ricciuti, Edward R. 522
Rice, Anne 649
Rice, Edward 100
Rich, Louise Dickinson 652
Rich, Virginia 668
Richards, Ivor 201
Richards, Glyn 101
Richards, Judith 614
Richards, Sir J. M. 104
Richardson, Henry H. 161
Richardson, Hugh E. 143, 144
Richler, Mordecai 477, 495,
  496
Richter, Conrad 659, 701,
  743, 752
Riding, Alan 432
Riefenstahl, Leni 4
Riegert, Ray 574, 623
Rietveld, Gordon F. 283
Rietveld, Jane 283
Rifkind, Carole 508
Riggs, Rollin 172, 612
Rikhoff, Jean 717
Riley, Laura 510
Ripley, Alexandra N. 759
Rippley, LaVern J. 268
Ristelhueber, Rene 189
Rizal y Alonso, José 133
Robbins, Harold 43
Roberts, Bruce 736, 757
Roberts, Dorothy J. 395
Roberts, James 122
Roberts, Kenneth 414, 652,
  655
Roberts, Nancy 736, 757
Roberts, Sheila 31
Roberts, Willo Davis 788
Robertson, Don 659, 743
Robertson, James I. 782
Robertson, Tomas I. 435
Robeson, Eslanda C. 27
Robinson, Alan 409
Robinson, Derek 224
Robinson, Francis 42, 710
Robinson, G. J. 397
Robinson, Jill 582

Robinson, Linda 595
Robinson, William F. 525,
  525, 664
Rochlin, Fred 542
Rochlin, Harriet 542
Roderus, Frank 640
Roditi, Edouard 70
Rodman, Selden 405, 406,
  409, 432, 444, 455, 460
Rodriguez, Barbara 769
Rodriguez, Mary 575, 575
Rogers, Thomas 676
Rogerson, John 56
Rohonyi, K. 289
Roiphe, Anne R. 728
Rolvaag, O. E. 740, 761
Romains, Jules 259, 369
Romberg, Chris 750
Romberg, Gary 750
Romer, Elizabeth 311
Romer, John 47
Roper, Robert 578
Roose-Evans, James 214
Rosa, Joao Guimaraes 457
Roscow, James P. 552
Rose, Al 646
Roseberry, Cecil R. 705
Rosen, Robert N. 757
Rosenthal, A. M. 171, 714
Rosovsky, Nitza 57
Ross, Anne 212
Ross, Corinne M. 525
Ross, Dana F. 578, 596, 628,
  684, 687, 689, 692, 740,
  748, 761, 771, 776, 788,
  795
Ross, Josephine 205
Ross, Lillian 712
Ross, Michael 19
Ross, Nancy Wilson 73, 542
Rosten, Leo 728
Roth, David M. 598
Roth, Philip 633
Roth, Joseph 183
Rothberg, Abraham 193, 698
Rothchild, John 611
Rothermund, Dietmar 100
Roueche, Berton 505, 684
Roumain, Jacques 414
Rouse, Parke Jr. 782
Roux, Georges 281
Roux, Jeanne 281
Rowell, Galen 81, 143
Rowland, Benjamin 100
Rowse, A. L. 208, 214
Roxborough, Ian 459
Royko, Mike 630
Roylance, Ward J. 774
Royle, Trevor 350
Ruark, Robert 15
Ruben, Olaf 147

Rubens, Bernice 114, 222, 369
Rubin, Louis D., Jr. 532, 782
Rudloe, Jack 611
Ruesch, Hans 474
Ruff, Ann 769
Rumanes, G. N. 285
Runyon, Damon 728
Rush, Norman 31
Rushdie, Salman 109, 131
Rushing, Jane G. 668
Rushton, William F. 646
Ruskin, John 313
Russell, Andy 482
Russell, Franklin 485, 611, 618
Ruth, Kent 745
Ruthven, Malise 46
Ryan, Cornelius 269
Ryan, Kathleen Jo 296
Ryan, William 604
Ryder, A. J. 270
Ryga, George 84

Sabato, Ernesto 452
Sachar, Howard M. 40, 58, 60
Sadlier, Heather 665
Sadlier, Hugh 665
Safire, William 608
Sagan, Francoise 253, 259
Said, Edward W. 55
St. Albans, Suzanne 65
St. Clair, William 281
St. George, Judith 710
St. Pierre, Paul 489
Saitoti, Tepilit Ole 12
Sakharov, Andre D. 363
Salamanca, J. R. 660
Salinger, Pierre 253
Salisbury, Carola 50
Salisbury, Charlotte Y. 143
Salisbury, Harrison E. 86, 360, 363, 369
Salter, Cedric 343
Samora, Julian 767
Sampson, Anthony 201
Samson, Joan 694
Samson, Patricia M. 187
Sanborn, Margaret 565, 794
Sanchez, Luis R. 415
Sanchez, Thomas 582
Sanders, Lawrence 37, 717, 728
Sandoz, Mari 689
Sanford, John 505
Sangster, Tom 549
Santiago, Danny 583
Sansom, William 195
Santmyer, Helen Hoover 743

Sapir, Richard B. 60, 755
Sargent, William 665
Sariola, Mauri 244
Saroyan, William 573, 583
Sarton, May 188, 286, 670, 695
Sartre, Jean Paul 259
Satterfield, Archie 787
Saudray, Nicolas 43
Saul, Eric 571
Saul, John 571, 668
Saunders, Ann 216
Saunders, Pamela 292
Sauter, M. R. 387
Savage, Elizabeth 670, 687
Savage, Henry 505
Savage, William W. 544
Savory, R. M. 42
Sawisiak, Arnold 603
Saxton, Mark 152 or 153
Sayer, Chloe 434
Sayers, Dorothy L. 352
Schaefer, Jack 701, 795
Schaeffer, Norma 635
Schaeffer, Susan F. 779
Schalk, Adolph 268
Schaller, George B. 5, 103
Scharfenberg, Doris 492, 538
Schecter, Jerrold 362
Schecter, Leona 362
Schei, Liv 350
Schell, Orville 81
Schell, Rolfe F. 437
Scheller, William G. 478, 514
Schemmel, William 762, 762
Scherman, Katherine 293, 299, 474, 475
Schickel, Richard 728
Schiffer, Michael 41, 73, 100
Schiffman, Jack 710
Schlee, Ann 273
Schmidt, Arno 273
Schmitt, Gladys 60, 332
Schneebaum, Tobias 467
Schneider, Bill 740, 760
Schneider, Dux 68
Schneider, Peter 275
Schnitzler, Arthur 183
Schnurnberger, Lynn 714
Schoeman, Karel 31
Scholefield, Alan 2, 32, 222, 276
Schoolfield, G. C. 244
Schoonover, Lawrence 333, 379
Schuchard, Oliver 536
Schulberg, Budd 583, 728
Schullery, Paul 558, 794
Schultheis, Rob 542
Schuman, Michael A. 526

Schumann, Marguerite 737
Schwarcz, Vera 84
Schwartz, Brian 85, 144
Schwartz, Lynne S. 728
Schwartz, Ronni 570
Schwarz, Urs 387
Schwarz-Bart, Simone 413, 413, 413
Schwenke, Karl 778
Sclare, Donald 706
Sclare, Lisa 706
Scobbie, Irene 384
Scott, A. C. 84
Scott, Carolynne 549
Scott, David L. 522, 538
Scott, Franklin D. 384
Scott, Justin 369, 728
Scott, Kathie 216
Scott, Kay W. 522, 538
Scott, Paul 109
Scull, Theodore W. 714
Seabrook, William B. 406
Seabury, Paul 405
Searby, Ellen 428, 552
Searls, Hank 578
Sebastian, Tim 339
See, Carolyn 583
Seeman, Ernest 738
Seeman, Helen Z. 714
Segal, Aaron 5
Segal, Brenda L. 60
Segev, Tom 55
Sehlinger, Bob 612
Seidenbaum, Art 569
Seidman, Laurence I. 566
Selvon, Samuel 413
Semmingsen, Ingrid 335
Senger, Valentin 268
Serafin, David 379
Serpell, Christopher 311
Serpell, Jean 311
Seth, Vikram 82
Setlowe, Richard 579
Seton, Anya 293, 560, 668
Seton, Cynthia Propper 253, 322, 719
Seton-Watson, Hugh 366
Seton-Watson, R. W. 192
Settle, Mary Lee 70, 784, 790
Setzekorn, William D. 427
Severin, Tim 4, 17, 41, 73, 405, 538
Seward, Desmond 247
Sexton, Linda G. 670
Seymour, William 205
Shackleton, Ernest 448
Shacochis, Bob 413
Shadbolt, Maurice 147, 166
Shagan, Steve 44, 135
Shahar, David 60
Shalamov, Varlam 372

Shane, Scott 787
Shannon, Dell 583
Shannon, Elizabeth 296
Shannon, John 32
Shapiro, Harry Lionel 148
Shapiro, James E. 505
Shapiro, Mary J. 714
Share, Bernard 296
Sharma, B. N. 100
Sharp, Lauriston 140
Sharp, Margery 222, 228
Sharp, Marilyn 439
Sharpe, Patricia 767
Shaw, Arnold 710
Shaw, Irwin 255, 717, 729, 779
Shaw, Robert 60
Shawcross, Mike 428, 437
Shearer, Alistair 104
Sheed, Wilfrid 608, 698
Shelby, Graham 234
Shellabarger, Samuel 323, 439
Shelton, Jack 574
Shemanski, Frances 514
Shenker, Israel 349
Shepard, Susan 574
Shepherd, Stella 350
Sheppard, Stephen 249
Sheppard, Trish 148
Sherburne, James 643
Sherman, D. R. 109
Sherman, Lila 511
Sherrill, Chris 611
Sherry, John 782
Sherwood, Shirley 171
Shetterly, Anya 310
Shichor, Michael 446
Shick, Tom W. 35
Shifrin, Avraham 363
Shiner, R. H. 788
Shipler, David K. 360
Shipway, George 256
Shirer, William L. 101, 195, 268
Shivers, Louise 738
Sholokhov, Mikhail 369
Shortridge, James R. 639
Shostak, Marjorie 4
Shostakovich, Dmitri 362
Shoumatoff, Alex 8, 445, 611, 705
Shreve, Susan R. 752
Shulman, Max 600
Shute, Nerina 215
Shute, Nevil 129, 255
Sichov, Vladimir 360
Siddons, Anne R. 620
Sidhwa, Bapsi 131
Siefkin, David 572
Siegfried, Alanna 714
Sienkiewicz, Henryk 321

Sierra Club Guides 546
Siers, James 147, 149, 150
Sifford, Darrell 510
Sikorsky, Robert 558
Silberman, Neil A. 57
Silianoff, Eugene 360
Silk, Leonard S. 505
Silk, Mark 505
Silko, Leslie M. 701
Sillanpaa, F. E. 244
Sillitoe, Alan 223, 231, 448
Silone, Ignazio 316
Silva, Julian 579
Simenon, George 253, 259
Simeti, Mary Taylor 312
Simmerman, Nancy L. 553
Simmons, Marc 546, 700
Simon, Kate 204, 215, 251, 308, 310, 433, 710, 712
Simon, Roger L. 90
Simpkins, Bill 482
Simpson, Colin 196
Simpson, George 450
Simpson, John 342
Simpson, Leo 493
Sinclair, Harold 740
Sinclair, John 700
Sinclair, Upton 596, 633
Singer, André 130
Singer, Isaac Bashevis 60, 341, 342
Sing, Khushwant 109
Singhal, Damodar P. 131
Sinor, Denis 290
Sithole, Ndabaningi 32
Sitwell, Sacheverell 42, 331, 401
Sivasankara, Pillai 109
Sjowall, Maj 290, 385
Skates, John R. 679
Skelton, Alison Scott 719
Skimin, Robert 123, 579
Skinner, Cornelia Otis 251
Skvorecky, Josef 194, 493
Slater, Mariam 12
Slaughter, Frank G. 51
Slavin, Julie 349
Slavin, Ken 349
Sloan, Ethel B. 157
Sloan, Kathleen L. 757
Slone, Verna Mae 642
Smiley, Jane 631, 729
Smith, Betty 732
Smith, Bradford 623
Smith, Bradley 86, 120, 432
Smith, C. W. 771
Smith, Charles M. 633
Smith, D. M. 315
Smith, Daniel B. 658, 782
Smith, Desmond 365
Smith, Dennis 729
Smith, Godfrey 201

Smith, Hedrick 361
Smith, Helene 750
Smith, Henry D. 120
Smith, J. C. 296
Smith, Jane O. 605
Smith, Kathy 747
Smith, Mark 695
Smith, Martin Cruz 371, 560
Smith, Patricia C. 566
Smith, Patrick 614
Smith, R. J. 118
Smith, Raymond 464
Smith, Reed 762
Smith, Robert 652
Smith, Robert K. 732
Smith, Roland 212
Smith, Sharon 526, 526
Smith, Susan H. 618, 653
Smith, Wilbur 15, 32, 32
Snellgrove, David L. 143
Snow, C. P. 223
Snow, Edward R. 664
Snyder, G. S. 542
Snyder, Louis L. 171
Sofer, Eugene F. 450
Solmssen, Arthur R. G. 183, 276
Solzhenitsyn, Aleksandr 363, 369, 371, 372, 389
Somers, Jane 223
Somerset Fry, Fiona 210, 351
Somerset Fry, Plantaganet 210, 351
Somerville-Large, Peter 296, 297, 299, 305
Sonnichsen, C. L. 558
Sorrentino, Gilbert 698
Souchon, Edmond 646
Soupcoff, Murray 477
Southworth, Michael 664
Southworth, Susan 664
Souza, Marcio 457
Sowell, Thomas 506
Spark, Muriel 60, 223, 317, 323, 354, 389, 729
Sparling, Wayne 627
Sparrow, Bill 407
Spate, O. H. K. 151
Specht, Robert 553
Spector, S. P. 189
Spence, Clark C. 685
Spence, Jonathan D. 82
Spencer, Elizabeth 319, 681
Spencer, Scott 655
Spencer, William 21
Spender, Stephen 84, 268
Spicer, Edward H. 507
Spivack, Carol 514
Sprague, Marshall 595
Spring, Michael 522
Spring, Norma 553
Stackpole, E. A. 666

Stancu, Zaharia 347
Stanley, David 150, 151, 158, 165, 479, 489, 500, 553, 787
Stark, Freya 41, 65, 68
Starkey, Marion L. 662
Starkie, Walter 289
Statler, Oliver 118
Stead, Christina 259, 390
Steed, Hal 618
Steegmuller, Francis 46, 318
Steel, Danielle 583
Steel, Tom 349
Stefansson, Vilhjalmur 293
Stegner, Page 505, 542
Stegner, Wallace 197, 498, 498, 505, 585, 774, 776
Stein, Benjamin 608
Stein, Gertrude 251
Stein, Rita 532, 538, 542, 546
Stein, Shifra 630, 639, 677, 683, 792
Steinbeck, John 259, 362, 413, 433, 440, 505, 579, 579, 579
Steinberg, David 132
Steinberg, Jonathan 387
Steinbicker, Earl 216, 270
Steiner, George 457
Steiner, Stan 544
Steiner, Stanley 408
Stephan, John 623
Stephens, James 303
Stephenson, Marylee 478
Sterling, Clare 191
Sterling, Tom 445
Stern, Herbert J. 269
Stern, Zelda 714
Sternfield, Joshua 662
Sternlieb, George 697
Stevens, Elisabeth 658
Stevenson, Anne 319
Stevenson, D. E. 227, 352
Stevenson, James 712
Stevenson, Robert Louis 623
Stevenson, William 15
Steves, Rick 173, 174, 212, 343, 376
Stewart, Desmond 46
Stewart, Edward 729
Stewart, Fred Mustard 317, 390, 440, 743
Stewart, J. I. M. 232, 232, 286
Stewart, Mary 183, 230, 253, 253, 255, 256, 286, 356, 395
Stewart, Robert L. 485
Stewart, Steven 339
Stick, David 737

Stier, Wayne 75, 77, 127, 139
Stinnett, Caskie 653
Stirton, Paul 246
Stocker, Joseph 558
Stokes, Thomas L. 618
Stone, Alma 729
Stone, Doris M. 522
Stone, Irving 183, 188, 318, 542, 636
Stone, Robert 429
Stone, Roger D. 445
Storey, David 235
Stout, Rex 687
Stover, Leon 234
Strand, Paul 525
Strange, Ian J. 446
Strather, Andrew 149
Stratton, Joanna L. 639
Straub, Peter 600
Street, David 485
Street, James 681
Streeter, Edward 195, 248, 397, 600
Streshinsky, Shirley 583
Stribling, T. S. 550
Strickland, Rennard 557, 744
Strickland, Ron 545
Strindberg, August 276
Strode, Hudson 195
Strode, William 642
Stroven, Carl 622
Struever, Stuart 630
Stuart, Colin 687
Stuart, Gene S. 435
Stuart, George E. 435
Stuart, Jesse 643
Stuart, Sandra Lee 569
Stubbs, Jean 230, 395
Styron, William 317, 732, 784
Sulzberger, C. L. 369
Sulzby, James F., Jr. 549
Sunset 75, 158, 165, 173, 570, 574, 624
Sunset Magazine 558, 747
Sunshine, Catherine 405
Sussman, Vic S. 658
Sutherland, Douglas 201
Sutherland, Mary 118
Sutton, Horace 710
Svevo, Italo 317
Swann, Don 658
Swarthout, Glendon 702, 771
Swetnam, George 750
Swift, Edward 771
Swift, Jeremy 19
Swindells, Madge 32
Switzer, E. E. 268
Sykes, J. 243
Symons, R. D. 498

Taber, Gladys 598, 665
Tabrah, Ruth 624
Talbott, John E. 21
Talese, Gay 712
Talev, Dimitur 189
Tall, Deborah 296
Tallant, Robert 646
Tanizaki, Junichiro 123
Tanner, Ogden 526
Taper, B. 572
Tarkington, Booth 636
Tarrant, John J. 598
Tarshis, Barry 505
Taschdjian, Claire 90
Tattersall, Jill 413
Tauranac, John 710
Tawil, Raymonda H. 55
Tax, Meredith 729
Taylor, A. J. P. 181
Taylor, Elizabeth 223
Taylor, James 646
Taylor, Jane 5, 27
Taylor, Jared 118
Taylor, Joe G. 646
Taylor, Julie M. 450
Taylor, Leah 5
Taylor, Maurice 446
Taylor, Peter 764
Taylor, Robert L. 440, 687, 717
Taylor, Samuel W. 774
Taylor, Suzanne 335
Taylor, Sybil 297
Teale, Edwin Way 565, 598
Tebeau, Charlton W. 611
Teller, Walter 665, 666
Temko, Allan 251
Temple, David 576
Temple, Philip 164
Tennenbaum, Silvia 273, 719
Terkel, Studs 506, 630
Terrill, Ross 82
Tesich, Steve 636
Tetley, Brian 12
Tey, Josephine 353
Thane, Elswyth 784
Thayer, Nancy 244
Thelwell, Michael 415
Theroux, Alexander 784
Theroux, Joseph 153
Theroux, Paul 9, 15, 74, 82, 100, 129, 130, 204, 223, 365, 401, 429, 506, 668
Thesiger, Wilfred 65
Thoby-Marcelin, Philippe 414
Thollander, Earl 526, 558, 574, 747, 787
Thomas, Audrey 37
Thomas, Bill 605, 635, 705, 714
Thomas, Craig 244, 273, 336, 370

Thomas, Dylan 395
Thomas, Edward 207
Thomas, Gordon 572
Thomas, Gwyn 395
Thomas, Hugh 375
Thomas, John O. 195
Thomas, Lowell 500, 553
Thomas, Michael 407
Thomas, Michael M. 66, 729
Thomas, Phyllis 605, 635,
  705, 714
Thomas, Ross 429, 579, 608
Thomas, Tracy 683
Thompson, Colleen 485
Thompson, Flora 206
Thompson, Gene 253, 585
Thompson, George A. 775
Thompson, Morton 183
Thompson, Pauline J. 576
Thompson, Philip 747
Thompson, Thomas 767, 772
Thompson, Toby 514
Thompson, Waite 700
Thomson, David 297
Thoreau, Henry D. 526
Thorpe, Edward 569
Thubron, Colin 55, 68, 283,
  313, 362
Thum, Gladys 508
Thum, Marcella 508, 515
Thurston, Hazel 24, 376
Thwaite, Anthony 171
Tidrick, Kathryn 65
Tindall, George B. 516
Tindall, Jemima 351
Tine, Robert 223
Tinney, Donald L. 778
Toland, John 120
Toll, David W. 691
Tolles, Bryant F., Jr. 662
Tolman, Newton F. 693
Tomikel, John 137
Tomkies, Mike 350, 489
Tomkinson, Michael 13
Tomlinson, H. M. 445
Tonaha, Sen'o 118
Toole, John Kennedy 649
Topol, Edward 371
Topolski, Daniel 444
Topolski, Feliks 444
Topping, Audrey 143
Toth, Charles W. 405
Toth, Marian Davies 139
Toth, Susan 638
Trachtenberg, Inge 276
Trachtenberg, M. 710
Trachtman, Richard 605
Tracy, Honor 204, 303, 375
Tracy, Steve 575
Traveler's Guide to Central
  and South Africa 8
Traveler's Guide to East

Africa and the Indian
  Ocean 13, 17
Traveler's Guide to the
  Middle East 43
Traveler's Guide to North
  Africa 20
Traveler's Guide to Southern
  Africa 28
Traveler's Guide to West
  Africa 35
Traven, B. 440
Traver, Robert 676
Treadgold, Donald W. 366
Trease, Geoffrey 308
Tree, Christina 526, 653,
  662, 778
Trench, Richard 19, 41
Trenhaile, John 370
Trevanian 497
Trevelyan, G. M. 213
Trevor, William 298, 303
Trillin, Calvin 618, 655
Trimble, Marshall 558
Trollope, Joanna 109
Trudgill, Peter 506
Trueman, Stuart 485
Truman, Margaret 608
Trumbull, Robert 147
Truscott, Lucian K. 717
Tryon, Thomas 583, 600
Ts'ao, Chan 90
Tschiffely, A. F. 401, 427,
  444, 506
Tucci, Niccolo 320
Tucker, Catherine 424
Tucker, Ethel 424
Tucker, Terry 425
Tunstall, Jeremy 565
Tuohy, Frank 343
Turbak, Gary 685
Turnbull, Colin M. 4, 8, 128
Turnbull, Michael 165
Turnbull, Peter 355
Turner, Frederick 646
Turolla, Pino 445
Tutuola, Amos 38
Twain, Mark 624, 684
Tyler, Anne 660, 738
Tyler, Paula E. 769
Tyler, Ron 769
Tyler, W. T. 9, 9

Uhlman, Fred 273
Uhnak, Dorothy 729, 732
Ullman, James R. 103, 390
Ulmer, Jeff 515
Ultan, Lloyd 710
Umba, Benjamin 153
Umhoefer, Jim 677, 792
Unamuno, Miguel de 379

Undset, Sigrid 336
Ungar, Sanford J. 3
Unger, Douglas 740, 761
University Press of Florida
  612
Unsworth, Walt 103
Updike, John 6, 600, 698,
  752, 755
Upfield, Arthur W. 161
Uris, Jill 55
Uris, Leon 44, 55, 60, 260,
  273, 276, 297, 303, 342
Uys, Errol Lincoln 457

Vaczek, Louis 19, 41
Vaidon, Lawdon 22
Vaillant, George 435
Valiani, L. 181
Vanberg, Bent 335
Van Campen, Shirley 624
Van Der Post, Laurens 3, 27,
  28, 32, 33, 362
Van der Zee, Barbara 705
Van der Zee, Henri 705
Van de Wetering, Janwillem
  123, 333, 655
Van Herk, Aritha 123, 480,
  500
Van Lustbader, Eric 123
Van Meer, Mary 515
Van Slyke, Helen 223, 586,
  729
Van Story, Burnette L. 618
Vargas Llosa, Mario 457, 468
Varney, Philip 558, 700
Vasconcelos, José Mauro de
  457
Vassilikos, Vassilis 286
Vaughan-Thomas, Wynford 393
Veber, May 297
Verner, Elizabeth O. 757
Veryan, Patricia 224
Vessels, Jane 602
Vick, Ann 553
Vidal, Gore 287, 321, 608
Viertel, Joseph 370
Viertel, Peter 379
Vilar, Pierre 377
Villa, Antonio 409
Villet, Barbara 28
Vilnay, Zev 58
Vishnevskaya, Galina 362
Vishniac, Roman 171
Vladimov, Georgi 370
Vogan, Sara 687
Vogel, Virgil J. 507
Voges, Nettie Allen 782
Voinovich, Vladimir 370
Vokac, David 515, 542
Volgyes, Ivan 289

Volkoff, Vladimir 260
Von Eckardt, Wolf 269
Von Hagen, Victor 401, 461
Vonnegut, Jurt 620, 636
Voorhoeve, Jan 464
Vorster, Gordon 33
Voslensky, Michael 361
Vrettos, Theodore 286
Vreuls, Diane 743
Vroom, Richard 485

Wachtel, Nathan 467
Wagenvoord, James 711
Wagner, Walter 569
Wahid, Siddiq 143
Wahloo, Per 379, 385
Wain, John 395
Waite, Virginia 314
Wakefield, Dan 631, 636, 670
Wakefield, Paul 393
Walden, Howard T. 485
Waley, Paul 119
Walker, Bryce S. 375
Walker, David 486
Walker, Margaret 620
Walker, Mildred 687
Walker, Murray 157
Walker, Ronald G. 432
Walker, William 181, 269, 388
Wall, Joseph F. 638
Wallace, David R. 565
Wallace, Irving 253, 385
Wallace, Lew 321
Wallace, Martin 299
Wallace, Robert 543, 558, 624
Wallace, William V. 192
Wallach, Anne 730
Wallade, Jonathan 65
Wallant, Edward L. 730
Waller, Leslie 390
Wallis, Kathleen 134
Walser, Martin 273
Waltari, Mika 51, 321
Walther, Wiebke 42
Wambaugh, Joseph 576, 583
Wamsley, James S. 674
Ward, Charles 366
Ward, Philip 139
Ward, Russel B. 158
Warner, Rex 321
Warner, Sam Bass, Jr. 664
Warner, William W. 522, 658
Warren, Colin 558, 775
Warren, Harris G. 465
Warren, Robert Penn 550, 643, 648, 649, 764
Warshaw, Steven 120
Washburn, Bradford 553

Wasserstein, Susan 515
Waterson, Merlin 393
Watkins, T. H. 543, 565
Watson, Clarissa 720
Watson, Francis 104
Watson, Lyall 4
Watt, Richard M. 340
Wattenberg, Ben J. 506, 606
Watters, Pat 618
Waugh, Alec 405, 413, 415
Waugh, Evelyn 6, 12, 18, 171, 432, 455, 464
Wayburn, Peggy 553
Wayne, K. P. 361
Weathers, Ginny 639
Weaver, Harriet E. 574
Webb, Forrest 38
Webb, Mary 232
Webb, Walter P. 768
Webster, Harriet 526
Webster, Jan 355
Webster, Nancy 526
Wechsberg, Joseph 180, 191, 365
Weddle, Robert 767
Wedel, Janine 340
Wegener, Helga M. 296
Weidman, Jerome 550, 730
Weingarten, Violet 717
Weinreb, Risa 515
Weinstock, Richard A. 514
Weintraub, Stanley 215
Weir, Bill 558
Weismann, Elizabeth W. 432
Welch, James 687
Weldon, Fay 223
Welfare, Humphrey 211
Welle-Strand, E. 335
Wellman, Paul I 772
Wellner, Istvan 290
Wells, Eric 490
Wells, Patricia 252
Welty, Eudora 681
Welty, Thomas 74
Wenberg, Donald C. 533
Werchik, Arne 158
Werchik, Ruth 158
Were, Gideon S. 29
Werlich, David P. 467
Werner, Dennis 445
Weschler, Lawrence 339
Wescott, Glenway 792
West, Elliott 543
West, Jessamyn 204, 636, 743
West, John A. 48
West, Morris L. 60, 153, 154, 161, 317, 320, 356
West, Nathaniel 584
West, Pamela E. 353
West, Rebecca 370, 397
West, Richard 768

Western Writers of America 543
Westheimer, David 440, 584
Westlake, Donald E. 405, 720, 730
Weston, Christine 109
Wharton, Edith 22
Wharton, William 584
Wheaton, Philip 405
Wheeler, Daniel 247
Whipple, Addison B. C. 666
Whitaker, Muriel 480, 500
White, E. B. 712
White, Patrick 161
White, Sam 251
White, Stewart E. 554, 788
White, Theodore H. 82, 90, 204
White, Timothy 407
White, Walter G. 127
Whitehead, Barbara 235
White House Historical Assn. 604
Whitely, George 485, 653
Whiteman, John 390
Whitley, Kathleen 523, 661
Whitman, Herbert 754
Whitman, Lawrence 677
Whitnah, Dorothy L. 574
Whitney, Gleaves 595
Whitney, Phyllis A. 70, 413, 560, 579, 596, 614, 621, 695, 702, 717, 720, 753, 755, 764
Whitney, Stephen 558
Whittemore, Edward 44, 60
Whyte, Jon 482
Wibberley, Leonard 15, 440
Wicker, Tom 609, 784
Wideman, John E. 753
Wiedel, Janine 299
Wier, Allen 772
Wiesel, Elie 60, 290, 370
Wigginton, Eliot 533, 618
Wikoff, Jerold 526
Wilcock, John 470
Wilcox, Collin 585
Wilcox, James 646
Wilden, Tony 477
Wilder, Robert 423, 615
Wilder, Thornton 287, 321, 468, 631, 756
Wiley, Peter 543, 774
Wilhelm, John 437
Wilhelm, Kate 586
Wilkerson, Tichi 569
Wilkins, Robert P. 740
Wilkinson, Alec 665
Wilkinson, Gerald 212
Wilkinson, Henry C. 425
Willets, Duncan 130
Williams, Ben Ames 785

Williams, B. R. 165
Williams, Brad 543
Williams, Eric 409
Williams, G. 393
Williams, Joan 681
Williams, John A. 333, 730, 789
Williams, Kenny J. 631
Williams, Lea E. 75, 77
Williams, L. F. Rushbrook 104, 130, 136
Williams, Maslyn 150
Williams, Miller 562, 683
Williams, Philip G. 742
Williams, Richard L. 545
Williams, Tennessee 320
Williams, Thomas 695
Williamson, Chilton 754, 794
Williford, Charles 615
Williford, William B. 618
Willis, David K. 361
Willis, Gwyn 527, 532, 658
Wilson, Derek 8, 29
Wilson, Duncan 397
Wilson, Edmund 55, 406, 705
Wilson, Ellen 35
Wilson, Forbes 150
Wilson, Josleen 508
Wilson, P. Roy 495
Wilson, Robert 158
Wilson, Sloan 133, 422, 475, 718
Wilson, Steve 745
Wilson, William 566
Winch, Arden 223
Winchester, Simon 99
Windham, Kathryn T. 549
Wingate, Richard 462
Winger, Virginia 736
Winks, Robin 212
Winstedt, Richard O. 128
Winstone, H. V. F. 72
Winstone, Victor 64
Winter, Robert 567
Winward, Walter 273, 276
Wiseman, Thomas 273
Wiser, Charlotte V. 100
Wiser, William 251, 260
Witteman, Betsy 526
Wodehouse, P. G. 232

Woiwode, Larry 631, 741
Wolcott, Read 737
Wolf, Christa 274
Wolfe, Charles K. 763
Wolfe, Gerard R. 714
Wolfe, Morris L. 494
Wolfe, Thomas 670, 738
Wolfson, Susan 628
Wolitzer, Hilma 584, 732
Wollenberg, Charles 572
Wolpert, Stanley 104, 109
Wongar, B. 162
Wood, Christopher 137
Wood, Pamela 653
Wood, Peter 406
Wood, Robert D. 437
Wood, Ted 494
Wood, William 526
Woodbridge, Sally 572
Woodcock, George 477
Woodford, Susan 281
Woodham-Smith, Cecil 300
Woodhouse, Christopher M. 284
Woodin, Ann 19, 41, 130
Woodlief, Ann 782
Woods, Donald 28
Woods, Sara 235
Woods, Stuart 303, 621
Woodward, Christopher 216
Woodward, Ralph L. 427, 525
Woolf, Virginia 215, 224
Woolfson, Marion 65
Woolston, Bill 638
Worrall, Nick 8
Wouk, Herman 730, 732
Wren, Percival C. 20
Wright, Austin 154
Wright, Billie 553
Wright, Louis B. 757
Wright, Richard 35, 633
Wright, Richard B. 494
Wright, Ronald 467
Wrobel, Paul 674
Wuerpal, Charles E. 344
Wuorinen, John H. 243
Wyatt, David K. 140
Wylie, Laurence W. 248
Wyllie, John 38
Wynd, Oswald 129

Wynne-Jones, Tim 486
Wynona, H. 740

Yanez, Agustín 440
Yanni, Yaacov 56
Yates, Richard 601
Yeadon, Ann 714
Yeadon, David 173, 522, 715
Yehoshua, A. B. 60
Yeoward, Eileen 376
Yerby, Frank 649
Yevtushenko, Yevgeny 372
Yglesias, José 375, 615
Yi, Ki-baek 134
Yogerst, Joe 13
Yoshida, Mayumi 118
Yost, Nellie S. 640
Young, Allen 662
Young, Dale 769
Young, George 574
Young, John V. 700
Young, Judith 515
Young, Stark 681
Yount, John 643
Yourcenar, Marguerite 320, 321

Zabusky, Charlotte F. 506
Zachreson, Nick 572
Zaroulis, Nancy 668
Zbigniew, Herbert 248, 308
Zeff, Linda 217
Zelade, Richard 769
Zelazny, Roger 110
Zeldin, Theodore 247
Zeman, Zbynek 191
Zerby, Judy 791
Zewen, Luo 82
Zhuoyan, Yu 82
Ziegler, Jean 387
Zielinsky, John M. 637
Ziesler, Gunter 12
Zilahy, Lajos 291
Zimmerman, George 742
Zink, David 422
Zinn, Donald J. 522
Zinn, Howard 516
Zorzi, Alvise 313
Zwinger, Ann 546